D0920556

Scandinavian Europe

Paul Harding, Carolyn Bain, Katharina Lobeck, Fran Parnell,
John Spelman, Andrew Stone

Contents

ICELAND
p211

FAROE ISLANDS
p103

FINLAND
p127

NORWAY
p265

ST PETERSBURG
p204

SWEDEN
p355

TALLINN
p199

DENMARK
p24

Destination Scandinavia

Imagine standing on the bow of a ship, cruising through a narrow fjord with waterfalls cascading from sheer walls rising 1000m on all sides. Imagine another ship and a blue whale surfacing from the depths just metres away. Picture cycling through medieval villages and farmland on a lazy summer's afternoon, or sitting in a crowded beer terrace sipping a beer in bright sunshine – at midnight. You could be standing in the darkness on a still winter's night, swathed in layers of woolly clothes and staring up mesmerised by nature's greatest light show, the aurora borealis.

It's all possible in Scandinavia. While it's natural to imagine snow, ice and freezing temperatures when you think of this part of the world, that's only part of the picture. In summer southern Scandinavia can be as warm as southern Europe.

Scandinavians live for those summer months when the days are long and there's a buzz of excitement and energy everywhere you go from June to August. Summer festivals explode throughout the region, you can hike and cycle in pristine forests, fells or across lava fields, and cruise through stunning island archipelagos.

The cities brim with history, architectural highlights, active harbour scenes and culture. There's nothing better than getting lost in the tangled back streets of Stockholm's Gamla Stan, picnicking on Suomenlinna island in Helsinki or soaking up the atmosphere serenaded by buskers at an outdoor café in Copenhagen. Taking the stunning rail trip from Oslo to Bergen, getting sprayed by Europe's biggest waterfall, Dettifoss, in Iceland, or meeting Santa at his official residence in Finland are all part of the package.

ANDERS BLOMQVIST

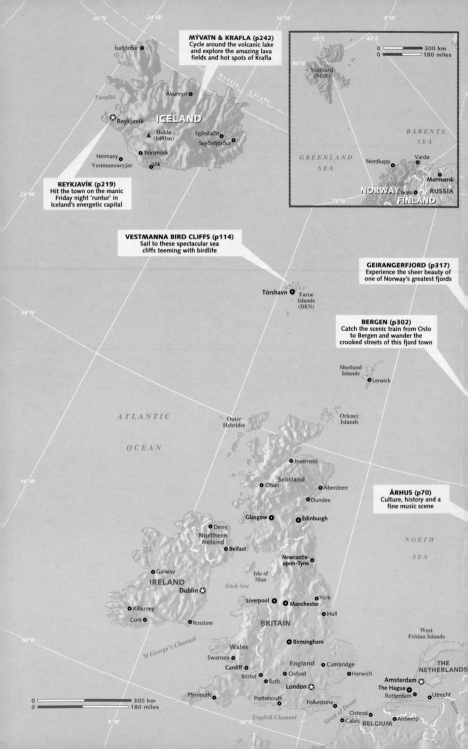

MÝVATN & KRAFLA (p242)
Cycle around the volcanic lake and explore the amazing lava fields and hot spots of Krafla

Ísafjörður

Faxaflói

Akureyri

◯ Reykjavík

ICELAND

▲ Hekla (1491m)

Egilsstaðir
Seyðisfjörður

Heimaey
Vestmannaeyjar

Þórsmörk

Vík

REYKJAVÍK (p219)
Hit the town on the manic Friday night 'runtur' in Iceland's energetic capital

0 ___ 300 km
0 ___ 180 miles

Svalbard (NOR)

BARENTS SEA

GREENLAND SEA

Nordkapp

Vardø

Murmansk

NORWAY Ivalo **RUSSIA**

FINLAND

VESTMANNA BIRD CLIFFS (p114)
Sail to these spectacular sea cliffs teeming with birdlife

GEIRANGERFJORD (p317)
Experience the sheer beauty of one of Norway's greatest fjords

Tórshavn ◯ Faroe Islands (DEN)

BERGEN (p302)
Catch the scenic train from Oslo to Bergen and wander the crooked streets of this fjord town

Shetland Islands

Lerwick

ATLANTIC

OCEAN

Outer Hebrides

Orkney Islands

Inverness

Scotland

Oban

Aberdeen

Dundee

Glasgow

Edinburgh

ÅRHUS (p70)
Culture, history and a fine music scene

Derry

Northern Ireland

Belfast

NORTH

SEA

Galway

IRELAND

Dublin ◯

Isle of Man

Irish Sea

Newcastle-upon-Tyne

Killarney

Cork

Rosslare

Liverpool

Manchester

York

Hull

BRITAIN

West Frisian Islands

Birmingham

Wales

Swansea

England

Cambridge

THE NETHERLANDS

Cardiff

Oxford

Harwich

Amsterdam ◯

Bristol

Bath

The Hague ◯

St George's Channel

London ◯

Rotterdam

Utrecht

Plymouth

Portsmouth

Folkestone

0 ___ 300 km
0 ___ 180 miles

Ostend

Calais

BELGIUM

Antwerp

English Channel

Strait of Dover

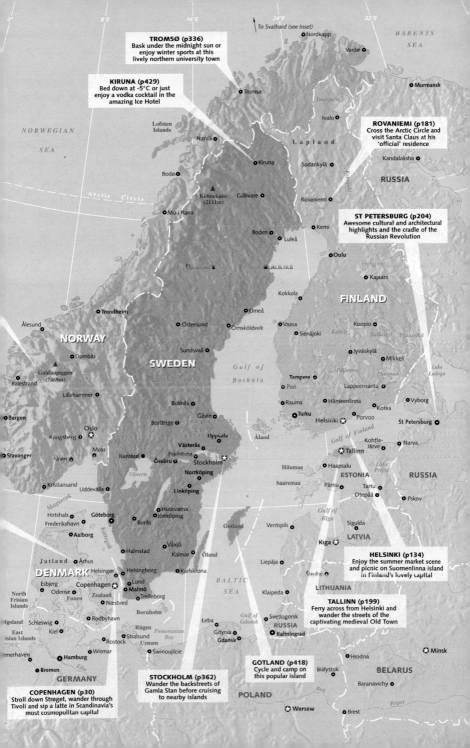

TROMSØ (p336)
Bask under the midnight sun or enjoy winter sports at this lively northern university town

KIRUNA (p429)
Bed down at -5°C or just enjoy a vodka cocktail in the amazing Ice Hotel

ROVANIEMI (p181)
Cross the Arctic Circle and visit Santa Claus at his 'official' residence

ST PETERSBURG (p204)
Awesome cultural and architectural highlights and the cradle of the Russian Revolution

HELSINKI (p134)
Enjoy the summer market scene and picnic on Suomenlinna island in Finland's lovely capital

TALLINN (p199)
Ferry across from Helsinki and wander the streets of the captivating medieval Old Town

GOTLAND (p418)
Cycle and camp on this popular island

STOCKHOLM (p362)
Wander the backstreets of Gamla Stan before cruising to nearby islands

COPENHAGEN (p30)
Stroll down Strøget, wander through Tivoli and sip a latte in Scandinavia's most cosmopolitan capital

To Svalbard (see inset)

BARENTS SEA

NORWEGIAN SEA

Nordkapp
Vardø
Murmansk
Tromsø
Inarijärvi
Lofoten Islands
Narvik
Ivalo
Kandalaksha
Lapland
Kiruna
Sodankylä
RUSSIA
Bodø
Kebnekaise (2111m)
Gällivare
Rovaniemi
Mo i Rana
Boden
Kemi
Luleå
Oulu
Kajaani
Trondheim
Kokkola
FINLAND
Ålesund
Östersund
Umeå
Vaasa
Kuopio
Örnsköldsvik
Si13näjoki
Jyväskylä
Mikkeli
NORWAY
SWEDEN
Sundsvall
Gulf of Bothnia
Tampere
Lappeenranta
Dombås
Pori
Rauma
Hämeenlinna
Kotka
Vyborg
Galdhøpiggen (2469m)
Bollnäs
Turku
Porvoo
St Petersburg
Balestrand
Lillehammer
Borlänge
Gävle
Helsinki
Gulf of Finland
Bergen
Kongsberg
Oslo
Uppsala
Åland
Tallinn
Narva
Skien
Moss
Västerås
Hiiumaa
Stavanger
Karlstad
Eskilstuna
Stockholm
Haapsalu
ESTONIA
RUSSIA
Örebro
Norrköping
Pskov
Kristiansand
Uddevalla
Vänern
Linköping
Saaremaa
Pärnu
Tartu
Otepää
Hirtshals
Göteborg
Huskvarna
Jönköping
Gulf of Riga
Frederikshavn
Borås
Gotland
Sigulda
Aalborg
Växjö
Ventspils
Riga
LATVIA
Halmstad
Kalmar
Öland
Jutland
Århus
Helsingør
Helsingborg
Karlskrona
Liepāja
Esbjerg
Odense
Lund
BALTIC SEA
Šiauliai
LITHUANIA
DENMARK
Copenhagen
Malmö
Trelleborg
North Frisian Islands
Funen
Zealand
Næstved
Klaipėda
East Frisian Islands
Schleswig
Kiel
Bornholm
Rødbyhavn
Gulf of Gdańsk
Świnoujście
Svetlogorsk
RUSSIA
Rügen
Usedom
Łeba
Kaliningrad
Hamburg
Wismar
Stralsund
Pomeranian Bay
Gdynia
Gdańsk
Hrodna
Bremen
Rostock
Białystok
BELARUS
GERMANY
Minsk
Baranavichy
POLAND
Warsaw
Brest

Nature reigns supreme in Scandinavia. Cruise down Norway's fjords, watch puffins hatch and whales breach in Iceland, or see the saturation of seabirds in the Faroes.

Getting around Scandinavia can be half the fun. Hop a ferry between Helsinki and Stockholm or Tallin, or sail from Bergen in Norway to Seyðisfjörður in Iceland. The mountainous Oslo–Bergen train trip is one of the world's most scenic.

Things not to miss? A **sauna** (p171) in Finland; the **Ice Hotel** (p431) in Kiruna, Sweden; **Bergen** (p302) in Norway; a **summer festival** (p97, p436) anywhere.

Peer at the puffins amid the volcanoes of
Vestmannaeyjar (p249), Iceland

STEVE HUTTON

Wander the captivating old town in Tallinn (p199),
Estonia

STEVE KOKKER

ANDERS BLOMQ

Cruise down Norway's glorious
Geirangerfjord (p317)

Immerse yourself in the café culture of cosmopolitan Copenhagen (p40)

Explore the cultural and
architectural delights of
St Petersburg (p205)

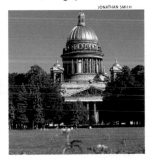

Witness the spectacular Gullfoss waterfall (p232) in
Iceland

Enjoy winter sports under the midnight sun in Tromsø (p336), Norway

NED FRIARY

Catch the Norwegian coastal steamer through the stunning Lofoten islands (p331), Norway

Visit Santa in his very own village on the Arctic Circle (p185) in Lapland, Finland

JOHN BORTHWICK

MARTIN MOOS

Bar-hop your way through Copenhagen's active nightlife scene (p41)

Stroll through the convoluted back streets of Gamla Stan (p367) in Stockholm

JONATHAN SMITH

Getting Started

Scandinavia is a big place. Although only six countries, there's a lot of diversity from the Arctic north to the forest and farmland of the south, and midsummer has little in common with midwinter. Depending on where and when you go, you'll probably need to pack winter and summer clothes. No matter how long you plan to travel here, and whatever your budget, a little forward planning will help you squeeze the most out of your trip. There's no point turning up at Bergen to catch the ferry to Iceland in April or planning to see the aurora borealis in September.

The following tips can help ensure you don't miss that music festival you've been wanting to see for years, and make the most of your kronur or euro in Scandinavia.

WHEN TO GO

Scandinavia has very distinct summer and winter seasons and extreme climates, especially when comparing the north and the south. For most travellers, the best time to visit is undoubtedly summer – the brief window from late June to August – when you can usually be guaranteed some fine weather and long hours of daylight, and when camping grounds and hostels are all open, summer festivals are in full swing, there's a buzz of excitement on the streets and lots of shiny, happy Scandinavians. The Scandinavian holiday season begins after Midsummer's Day (usually the last week in June). This is when locals take their holidays and vacate the cities for the countryside, but Scandinavia rarely feels overcrowded (unlike other parts of Europe) and hotels actually drop their rates in summer. The exceptions are camping grounds and family attractions, which are often packed.

See Climate Charts (p451) for more information.

DON'T LEAVE HOME WITHOUT...

- **Sleeping bag** or **sleeping sheet** – even if you're not camping you'll sleep cheaper in hostels with your own sheets, and a sleeping bag is a must in Iceland
- **Insect repellent** – for keeping mosquitoes and biting insects at bay in summer, especially in Finland and Iceland
- **Swiss army knife** – essential multipurpose tool
- **Watch** – everything in Scandinavia runs on time!
- **Mobile phone** – it's easy and inexpensive to get hooked up to local prepaid networks in Scandinavia and handy for making bookings or keeping in touch with other travellers
- **Padlock** – useful for locking your pack, or lockers at hostels
- **Swimsuit and towel** – for soaking in 'hot pots' or thermal springs in Iceland, postsauna swims and spas in Finland, or for the beaches of southern Sweden and Denmark
- **Credit card** – Scandinavians love to pay with the plastic so it's handy to have a credit card for general use or emergencies; essential for car hire
- **Eye mask, earplugs and torch** – useful for sleeping on long summer nights; rowdy hostels; and finding your way in the dark
- **Sense of adventure and humour** – vital for when those fjords and glaciers are lost in fog, when you just missed the last bus by 30 seconds, when you get the bill for that fancy restaurant 'splurge', and for making new discoveries away from the beaten track

The best place in
Finland for a legendary
Finnish sauna. Check
the website www
.kuopioinfo.fi

In Denmark, southern Sweden and Finland and even Iceland, temperatures can be surprisingly warm in summer. Spring and autumn – May, June and early September – are also good times to visit. You can still expect fine, sunny days and fewer tourists, and most things are open. Temperature changes can be swift at this latitude – above the Arctic Circle you might find yourself wrapped in layers one day, but wearing only a T-shirt the next. Iceland and the western coast of Norway remain mild thanks to the Gulf Stream, but this also brings rain – hikers and campers should always carry sufficient waterproof gear.

Winter (and early spring in the far north) brings its own tourist season, where winter activities such as skiing and snowboarding, dogsledding, ice-fishing and snowmobiling are popular. Peak ski season in Lapland and the north is generally February to April, when the snow is deep but the gloomy depths of winter are over. Unless you're here to see the northern lights, travel in Scandinavia from November to January is a pretty cold, dark and miserable option, and much of the tourist infrastructure outside the main cities shuts down completely. Autumn (late August to September) is a fine time for hiking and cycling, thanks to the beautiful forest colours.

See the Climate & When to Go section of the country chapters for more information.

COSTS & MONEY

By any standards Scandinavia can be expensive, especially for accommodation, eating out and nightlife, but overall costs are comparable to northern Europe and in some cases cheaper than London or Paris. And there are plenty of free things for travellers to do: hiking, visiting churches, parks and gardens, national parks, fjords, glaciers and beaches can all be enjoyed *gratis*. Travel costs vary slightly from country to country – Denmark is probably cheapest (and being a small country, transport costs are lower), followed by Finland, Sweden, Norway and Iceland. Tallinn and St Petersburg are much cheaper than anywhere in Scandinavia.

Once you're in the region, your biggest unavoidable expense is finding a bed, but camping (you can pitch a tent in many places for free) and Scandinavia's excellent network of hostels will keep costs down, and hotels discount their rates on weekends and in summer. A night on the town in Stockholm, Oslo or Helsinki – say dinner, a few drinks (alcohol is highly taxed in bars) and a nightclub or music bar (or the manic *runtur* in Reykjavík) – can easily require a small bank loan, but shopping at markets, filling up on lunch buffets and buying alcohol from supermarkets or state-run liquor stores is relatively cheap. Little things like a cup of coffee, doing your laundry or storing your bag in a locker cost about US$2.50 to $3.

Sightseeing costs can add up (museum admissions range from US$2 to $8) but most capital cities offer good-value discount cards that give free admission to sights for a limited period. An ISIC student card or youth card can cut costs in half.

On a rock-bottom budget – camping or staying in hostels, self-catering, using a rail pass or bus transport – you can squeak by on US$40 to $60 a day, which is pretty tight and doesn't allow for much amusement. Staying in private hostel rooms, guesthouses or two people sharing in a cheap hotel, eating at least one sit-down meal a day and seeing a few sights, expect to budget US$60 to $80 per person per day. Add to that the 'nonessentials' – shopping, drinking, activities such as cruises, tours and skiing – to come up with your own budget. Travel is a personal thing and everyone spends differently. With US$100 a day and some common sense you can travel pretty comfortably.

Norway, Sweden, Denmark, the Faroes and Iceland each have their own kronur, while Finland uses the euro. The euro is often accepted as currency in Denmark (and in Tallinn), and you can usually use Norwegian and Swedish kronur interchangeably at border areas.

Forget the bank queues and the blank looks when you hand over a travellers cheque – the easiest way to carry or obtain money in Scandinavia is with debit and credit cards. Nothing beats seeing a crisp wad of kronur electronically spat out at you whenever you need it. ATMs (24-hour) linked to international networks (Cirrus, Maestro, Eurcard, Plus, Visa and Master-Card) are common. Cash and travellers cheques can, of course, be exchanged at banks and foreign exchange bureaux in most towns for a fee.

READING UP

There are lots of ways to pique your interest, pick up ideas and fuel the dream before your trip. Reading travel books, studying maps and surfing the Net will all help drive that wanderlust.

Books

Last Places: A Journey in the North by Lawrence Millman. This is an entertaining travelogue, with Millman following the Viking trail from Scotland to Newfoundland via Iceland, the Faroes and Greenland.

Frost on My Moustache: The Arctic Exploits of a Lord and a Loafer by Tim Moore. In this contemporary account following 19th-century traveller Lord Dufferin, British writer Moore hauls himself across the North Atlantic, enduring chronic seasickness, cycling through Iceland's interior, taking a Viking longboat to Norway via the Faroes and finally landing in Spitzbergen. A great read.

Pole to Pole by Michael Palin. The former Monty Python star and his BBC crew travel from the North to South Pole along the 30° line of longitude. The early part of the trip conveniently includes the far north of Norway, Finnish Lapland, Helsinki, Tallinn and St Petersburg (Leningrad). Palin's casual journal-style narrative is typically funny and engaging.

Neither Here Nor There by Bill Bryson. Bryson's hilarious account of his travels in Europe – 20 years after his first backpacking trip – starts in Hammerfest, Norway, with a quest to see the northern lights. Chapters on Copenhagen, Göteborg and Stockholm, and Bryson's dry, bumbling wit, make it well worth a read.

A unique and super-cool experience in Kiruna Sweden. See www.icehotel.com

To the Top of the World: Norway's Coastal Voyage by PE Johnson. The author takes the stunning coastal route from Bergen to Kirkenes, stopping in villages along the way. This is a must-read if you're planning this awesome sea journey.

A Year in Lapland: Guest of the Reindeer Herders by Hugh Beach. This is a unique peek into the lives of the Sami reindeer herders, written by an anthropologist who spent a year living among the Sami in the Jokkmokk district of Swedish Lapland.

In Forkbeard's Wake: Coasting Around Scandinavia by Ben Nimmo. With his sailing boat and a quest to retrace the steps of a Norse warrior, British writer Nimmo comes up with a quirky and funny collection of experiences that reveal a lot about Scandinavia and its people.

Websites

Go Scandinavia (www.goscandinavia.com) Site of the Scandinavian Tourist Board in North America; links to country sites, tour ideas

Lonely Planet (www.lonelyplanet.com) This site has destination summaries on all Scandinavian countries, plus the Thorn Tree bulletin board for travellers

Scandinavia News (www.scandinavianews.com) World News network site with English-language news and views from Scandinavia
Scandinavia Travel (www.budgettravel.com/scandinavia.htm) Comprehensive site of links and budget travel info for all of Scandinavia
Scandinavica (www.scandinavica.com) Site devoted to Nordic culture and tourism with links to country sites

TOP 10 MOVIES

- *The Man Without a Past* (2002; director Aki Kaurismäki)
- *101 Reykjavík* (2000; director Baltasar Kormákur)
- *ABBA the Movie* (1977; director Lasse Hallström)
- *My Life as a Dog* (1987; director Lasse Hallström)
- *Fanny & Alexander* (1982; director Ingmar Bergman)
- *Buddy* (2003; director Morten Tyldum)
- *Pelle the Conqueror* (1988; director Bille August)
- *Children of Nature* (1991; director Friðrik Thór Friðriksson)
- *Babette's Feast* (1988; director Gabriel Axel)
- *Leningrad Cowboys Go America* (1989; director Aki Kaurismäki)

TOP 10 FESTIVALS

- **Midsummer** (around 23 June) – celebrated throughout Scandinavia in late June, this a national holiday; Midsummer Eve is usually a big party with bonfires and dancing
- **May Day & Eve** – 1 May is the Labour Day holiday everywhere except Denmark; 30 April is Valborgsmässoafton in Sweden (p436) and Vappu in Finland (p191), with some of the biggest liquid-fuelled student celebrations imaginable
- **Copenhagen Jazz Festival** (Denmark, July) – 10-day jazz fest (p37)
- **Þjóðhátíð** (Iceland, early August) – this crazy festival celebrating Iceland's independence is held on Vestmannaeyjar island a month after the rest of the country (p259)
- **Roskilde Rock Festival** (Denmark, late June/early July) – one of Europe's biggest rock music festivals (p51)
- **World Wife-Carrying Championships** (Finland, July) – one of Finland's many whacky events (p173)
- **Stockholm Pride** (Sweden, late July/early August) – Scandinavia's biggest gay and lesbian festival (p437)
- **Savonlinna Opera Festival** (Finland, July) – a month of high culture in the stunning Olavinlinna Castle (p166)
- **Jokkmokk Winter Fair** (Sweden, February) – Sami celebration in Swedish Lapland (p428)
- **Tromsø International Film Festival** (Norway, mid-January) – one of Norway's most exciting cultural festivals (p337)

If you're visiting in summer, get to a summer festival. Details at www.euro-festival.net/

RESPONSIBLE TRAVEL

Scandinavia is largely a clean, green environment. Air and water pollution from pulp factories and power plants, deforestation and acid rain are certainly environmental issues facing the Nordic countries, but on the whole travellers will breathe in clean air, see virtually no litter and drink pristine water.

Travellers can have a potentially negative impact particularly when hiking in forests or national parks. The Right of Common Access (Everyman's Right) is a code that applies in Norway, Sweden, Finland and Iceland, meaning you can walk virtually anywhere, provided you respect private land and behave responsibly. Stick to marked trails, leave flora and fauna alone, and always carry rubbish out with you – don't leave it on trails, at camp sites or around huts. Don't use soap or detergent when washing in streams (use a bucket).

If you're using wilderness huts that require paying a fee on an honesty system (as in Iceland), make sure you pay, and leave the huts as you found them. Don't make campfires on private land, and check local regulations before making a fire anywhere. Never cut down wood for a fire, use only dead wood.

In many cities and towns, recycling bins are provided for plastics and paper etc, so use them. In Sweden and Finland there are collection points (at Alko stores in Finland, for instance) for glass and plastic bottles.

If you're driving, particularly in the far north, keep your speed down. Domesticated reindeer herds frequently wander onto the road, and quite apart from your own safety, a dead reindeer is a financial loss to its owner.

Finally, be sensible. Don't exploit the land and its people, and respect local culture.

Itineraries
CLASSIC ROUTES

SCANDI IN A NUTSHELL
Ten Days to Three Weeks

The best place to start any tour of Scandinavia is **Copenhagen** (p30). Spend a couple of days in this cosmopolitan city before catching a train to **Stockholm** (p362) for two days. Take the overnight ferry to **Helsinki** (p134). If you're in a hurry you could spend just the day in Helsinki and catch the ferry back to Stockholm, especially if you book a cabin and get some sleep. With two days in Helsinki you can enjoy some nightlife and take a day trip to **Porvoo** (p147) or even **Tallinn** (p199). From Stockholm take the overnight train to **Oslo** (p272) for the day, then the scenic rail trip to **Flåm** (p314) and the combination boat/bus trip along the Sognefjord to **Bergen** (p302). From here, travel to **Kristiansand** (p292) and take the ferry to **Hirtshals** (p88) in Denmark then return to Copenhagen via **Århus** (p70).

With the full three weeks or longer you could spend more time in Sweden, stopping at **Malmö** (p392), **Göteborg** (p399) or **Kalmar** (p414), more time in Norway, adding three days in the western fjords, including **Fjærland** (p315) and **Geiranger** (p317), or more time in Denmark, stopping at **Odense** (p60) and **Ærø** (p68) on the way back to Copenhagen.

A quick city-hop using the train or bus and ferries. If time is very short, you'll be limited to the capitals or you may have to skip Helsinki. Iceland is out of the question!

BALTICS & THE EAST   Three Weeks

Finland, sharing a border and a fair slice of history with Russia, is quite unlike the Scandinavian ideal presented by Sweden, Norway and Denmark. This itinerary combines a brief tour of the Baltics with southern Finland.

Start in Stockholm so you can take advantage of the fantastic overnight **ferries** (p442) to **Helsinki** (p134), with their smorgasbord meals and all-night partying. After a couple of days in the Finnish capital take the ferry (1½ to three hours) to medieval **Tallinn** (p199) in Estonia. From here you can tour the Baltics (Latvia and Lithuania) but you'll need another guidebook! Return to Helsinki (Tallinn can be seen as a day trip if time is short) and take the overnight sleeper train to **St Petersburg** (p204). You must have a visa, which can be obtained in Helsinki through specialist agents or at the Russian embassy (allow at least a week). After a few days in this enchanting, Imperial city, return to Helsinki.

If you have time and want to explore some of Finland, take the train to the Lakeland towns of **Savonlinna** (p166), with its awesome medieval castle and opera festival, or **Kuopio** (p169), home of the world's biggest smoke sauna, or northwest to the dynamic, cultural city of **Tampere** (p158). You could also take the overnight train to **Rovaniemi** (p181), cross the Arctic Circle and visit Santa.

Finally, you can return to Sweden by taking the train to **Turku** (p148) then the ferry to Stockholm through the southern archipelago via the **Åland islands** (p154) – stop off at the islands for as long as you wish.

The Finnish capital Helsinki offers easy access to the charming and splendidly preserved old town of Tallinn as well as the cultural treasures of St Petersburg. Finland's own attractions include Father Christmas himself.

ROADS LESS TRAVELLED

THE VIKING TRAIL
Four to Six Weeks

Start in **Copenhagen** (p30), then head to **Roskilde** (p49) for the **Viking Ship Museum** (p50) and to **Trelleborg** (p52) for the Viking fortress. Cross from Zealand to Funen – with a side trip to **Ladbyskibet** (p65) to see the Viking ship – then to **Århus** (p70) before taking the ferry from Hirtshals to **Kristiansand** (p292) in Norway. Spend a couple of days in **Bergen** (p302) before taking the train to **Flåm** (p314) and the boat/bus trip along the **Sognefjord** (p312) – there are Viking ruins at **Balestrand** (p315). From Bergen, there is one ferry a week in summer to Iceland, via the Faroes (or fly direct from Oslo or Copenhagen).

You can get off at the **Faroes** (p103) and wait for the following week's ferry, or alternatively catch the same ferry from **Hanstholm** in Denmark, instead of Bergen, which gives you two days in the Faroes (see p100).

The ferry continues to Iceland, arriving at **Seyðisfjörður** (p246). From here the best route to Reykjavík is along the south coast past the **Vatnajökull icecap** (p247). In **Reykjavík** (p219), visit the Saga Museum and the Viking village of **Hafnarfjörður** (p233), take a trip to the **Blue Lagoon** (p233), then fly out. If you plan to return by ferry, take a bus trip through the interior to **Akureyri** (p238) then bus back to Seyðisfjörður on the Ring Road. Remember there's only one ferry a week, so plan for either one or two weeks in Iceland.

The Viking Age had its beginnings in Denmark, Norway and Sweden in the 9th century AD, and it's still possible to see the remains of Viking fortresses, burial grounds, longboats and churches.

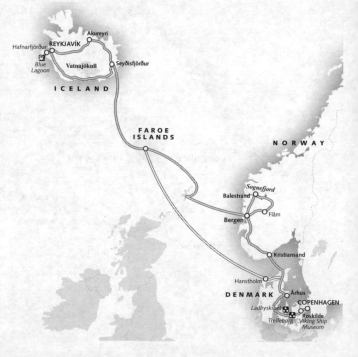

BEYOND THE ARCTIC CIRCLE

Three to Five Weeks

There's something magical and foreboding about the Arctic Circle, the imaginary line at 66°33´N latitude where the sun never truly sets in midsummer and never peeps above the horizon in winter. The remarkable clarity of light, eerie remoteness, Sami culture and reindeer herds add to the mystique. A trip to the North Cape (Nordkapp), the most northerly point in Europe, is something of a spiritual pilgrimage for many travellers. This trip is best tackled in summer (July–August), when the midnight sun shines and all public transport is running. You may be surprised to find there's little or no snow around after July.

A good starting point is **Helsinki** (p134). Take the overnight train to **Rovaniemi** (p181), visit the **Santa Claus Village** (p185) then take a bus up to the Sami village of **Inari** (p186). From here there are direct buses all the way to **Nordkapp** (p342) via Karasjok in Norway. After standing at the top of Europe with a glass of champagne, catch the coastal steamer **Hurtigruten** (p352) to the stunning **Lofoten Islands** (p331) with a possible stop in **Tromsø** (p336). From here you can continue on the steamer all the way to **Bergen** (p302), or get back to the mainland at **Narvik** (p329) and take the train to **Kiruna** (p429) in Sweden. Unfortunately, the famous **Ice Hotel** (p431) will have melted away by summer (it's open from December to late April) but you can still visit the Ice Hotel Art Centre in a giant freezer!

From Kiruna head south to Haparanda where you can cross back into Finland at the border town of **Tornio** (p180) – and have a round of midnight golf before returning to Helsinki. Or go to Boden, perhaps via the Sami village of **Jokkmokk** (p428), and catch the train to Stockholm.

Go to the top of Europe, visit a Sami village, play a round of golf through two countries – all possible above 66°33´N.

TAILORED TRIPS

THE GREAT OUTDOORS
Two Weeks to Three Months

Scandinavia's pristine environment begs to be explored at close range – on foot, a bicycle, canoe, skis, skates or dogsled! This itinerary is not a point-to-point tour, but suggestions on where you can enjoy some of Scandinavia's best activities.

Spring/Summer

Flat, rural and not too big, Denmark is a haven for cycling. Popular areas include **Bornholm** (p55), **Funen** (p60), **Langeland** (p68) and the Lake District of **Jutland** (p77). The Finns are also avid cyclists. The best region for pedalling is the **Åland islands** (p154), but rides anywhere in the eastern Lakeland area and around **Turku** (p148) or **Oulu** (p177) are rewarding. In Sweden head for **Skåne** (p392) or **Gotland** (p418).

Hiking in national parks and forests is sensational in Scandinavia – Iceland and Lapland in particular have some of Europe's last great wilderness areas, and trails, huts and camping grounds are set up for walkers. In Iceland, the **Landmannalaugar-Þorsmörk trek** (p253) is brilliant. In Finland, try **Oulanka National Park** (p133) and treks in **Karelia** (p174). In Sweden, the 450km **Kungsleden** (King's Trail, p431) is a major marked hiking route.

Other summer activities include canoeing, white-water rafting and fishing; see the Activities section of each chapter for information.

Winter/Spring

Skiing – both downhill and cross-country – is a national obsession in Finland, Sweden and Norway, and December to April is the time to go. The best resorts include **Lillehammer** (p300) in Norway, **Åre** (p425) in Sweden, and **Levi** (p188) and **Ruka** (p190) in Finland.

Think of Arctic Lapland and it's not hard to imagine mushing through the snow behind a team of huskies or a reindeer-sleigh. While you'll have to budget big for these activities, Scandinavia is one of the best places in the world to do it. In Norway, try **Tromsø** (p336) or **Karasjok** (p343) and in Sweden head to **Kiruna** (p429) or **Abisko** (p431). In Finland, **Rovaniemi** (p181) is a magnet for winter activities and there are husky farms organising safaris at **Muonio** (p188) and **Ivalo** (p186).

Other winter highlights to add to your itinerary should include the **Ice Hotel** (p431) at Kiruna in Sweden, and the **Arctic Icebreaker cruise** (p181) at Kemi in Finland.

ON THE RAILS

Three to Six Weeks

With a **ScanRail Pass** (p477) you can take to the rails and cover a lot of ground in Scandinavia economically, including discounts on ferries. To get the most out of your pass, long (possibly overnight) trips work well, but you can always pay for shorter trips to reach more places. Consider this megacircuit.

Start in **Copenhagen** (p30) and take the train via **Malmö** (p392) to **Stockholm** (p362). Cruise on the overnight ferry (50% discount) to **Helsinki** (p134), then the overnight train to **Oulu** (p177) or **Rovaniemi** (p181), almost at the Arctic Circle – if you have time, consider stops in **Kuopio** (p169) or **Tampere** (p158). Rail down the Gulf of Bothnia coast to **Vaasa** (p163), where you can catch a ferry across to **Umeå** (p426) in Sweden. From here catch a train south to lakeside **Östersund** (p424), then west to **Trondheim** (p323) in Norway. You're now heading toward the spectacular fjords of Norway, where you'll have to combine bus and boat travel with the train. The rail line heads south to **Dombås** (p301) and on to Oslo: detour on the spectacular journey to **Åndalsnes** (p318). Take the bus to **Geiranger** (p317) for the unmissable cruise on **Geirangerfjorden** (p317).

From here you can return to the main train line and Oslo, or make your way through the western fjords to **Bergen** (p302) and take the spectacularly scenic train to **Oslo** (p272) from there. Finally, board the train for **Göteborg** (p399), Sweden, and back to Copenhagen.

The Authors

PAUL HARDING
Coordinating Author, Front Chapters & Finland

Paul first left his comfy job as a newspaper reporter and strapped on a backpack to explore Europe 10 years ago. Mesmerised by the midnight sun, stunned by Scandinavia's pristine environment and wooed by Helsinki's summer energy and nightlife, he has made several trips to Scandinavia, particularly Finland. This time he snowmobiled on frozen lakes in Lapland, cycled in Åland, sweated in a sauna whenever possible and managed to survive Vappu (but only just). Fortunate enough to travel and work as a writer and photographer for the past six years, Paul has contributed to Lonely Planet's Finland and Iceland guides.

Life on the Road

I love ferry travel and the Baltic Sea gives you plenty of opportunities to sail on some pretty luxurious boats without breaking your budget. You can start with the short ferry ride from Germany to Denmark (p100) and spend some time in Copenhagen (p30) before heading up to Stockholm (p362). Book on the overnight ferry to Helsinki (p134), which passes through a beautiful archipelago of forested islands. On board you can gorge on the smorgasbord and listen to bands or melancholy Finnish karaoke. From Helsinki take another ferry for the short hop across to Tallinn (p199) in Estonia and spend the day exploring the medieval Old Town. From Helsinki it's worth taking the train to Turku (p148) and returning to Stockholm on the day ferry via the Åland islands (p154).

CAROLYN BAIN
Sweden

Melbourne-born Carolyn was raised on a steady diet of Abba and first travelled around Scandinavia as a teenager, while living and studying in Denmark. That experience left her with a love of all the best that Scandinavia has to offer – open, egalitarian societies populated by unfairly attractive people, long summer nights and cosy winters, wonderful art and design, unpronounceable vowels – and she jumped at the chance to return to Sweden for this project. She is also the author of Lonely Planet's Sweden guide.

KATHARINA LOBECK
Faroe Islands

Katharina's penchant for off-the-beaten-track destinations, where nature still makes her humbling power felt, has taken her from the equatorial regions of Guinea right through to Arctic climates. Travels through northern Norway prepared her for nature and culture on the Faroes, and extensive tours around Africa in the wet season equipped her with a stoic indifference towards rain and storms. The vibrant folk music scene of the Faroes had long yielded an irresistible attraction for the music researcher, who has developed a curious liking for chain dancing on windy beaches. Both London and Schwarzenberg (Germany) are home to her and her well-travelled daughter.

FRAN PARNELL   Iceland, Directory & Transport

After a childhood spent in Singapore and other humid hot spots, Fran developed a passion for cold and empty places. This fact, combined with an ever-handy masters degree in Anglo-Saxon, Norse and Celtic, meant that Iceland was the perfect choice for her first Lonely Planet assignment. The outstanding Vestmannaeyjar, history-steeped saga sites, deserted Westfjords and barren southern lava fields left the deepest impressions. Memorable incidents included being harried into hymn-singing at a small museum, falling down a volcano and having her head set on fire on the *runtur*. Still pining for glaciers, Fran is desperate to return to Iceland soon, if only to get a balanced haircut.

JOHN SPELMAN   Norway

Making a career out of the generosity of others, John Spelman has spent too much time sleeping on his friends' floors in Oslo and beyond. When he's not busy interrupting otherwise happy marriages with his prostrate, slumbering body, John is usually drunk or hanging out with Norwegian architects. Upon learning of these qualifications, Lonely Planet immediately put John on a plane, with his full duty-free allotment, en route to his favourite European destination.

In his second life, John is a PhD student studying cultural landscapes and urbanism, some of them Norwegian. He currently resides in Charlottesville, Virginia.

ANDREW STONE   Denmark

Andrew first visited Denmark in the 1990s to see a friend who had the good sense to marry a Dane. He has been back regularly since then to visit them, to enjoy the country's fantastic café culture, pretty countryside and charming natives, and to feed his interest in its rich Iron Age, Viking and Renaissance history.

CONTRIBUTING AUTHORS

Steve Kokker Steve is a die-hard Eastern European lover, having spent most of his time since 1996 living away from his native Montreal, basing himself in his father's homeland of Tallinn, Estonia, and trekking through the Baltic region, Russia and beyond. He's been writing and photographing for Lonely Planet since 1998, and was responsible for the Tallinn chapter of this book.

Tom Masters Aged 15 Tom travelled around Eastern Europe by train with his intrepid mother, and at 18 finally got to see Russia, his true passion. Since graduating from the University of London with a degree in Russian, Tom has returned more times than he can remember, living in St Petersburg and working throughout the region. Now living in London, he finds himself back in Russia all the time. He wrote the St Petersburg chapter for this book.

Snapshot

Scandinavians aren't renowned for being outspoken and opinionated. You're unlikely to get into a debate over politics or economics at a bar in Stockholm or Helsinki; however, there are plenty of hot topics to get you started.

WHALES & THE ENVIRONMENT

Whaling is an issue guaranteed to start some finger-pointing and divided opinion in Iceland and Norway. While most of the world opposes whale-hunting, Iceland ended its own 14-year ban on whaling in 2003, allowing a quota of 500 whales to be hunted over two years 'for scientific purposes'. Icelanders on the whole support the decision, or at least their government's right to make it. One view is that an overpopulation of whales affects fish stocks, a major issue in Iceland and Norway since it's the backbone of their economy. Others say it's damaging the nation's international standing and, more tangibly, its multimillion-dollar whale-watching industry. Whether tourists are actually boycotting whale-watching is another matter. It's easy to turn down the blubber on the supermarket shelf, but not so easy to miss the opportunity to see these magnificent creatures up close.

Norway has been quietly culling minke whales since 1993 so the issue is no longer such a hot topic, but you'll find the average Norwegian fisherman willing to argue strongly in favour of it. At present, all whale meat is used for the domestic market, not export.

The other divisive environmental issue in Iceland is the Kárahnjúkar hydroelectric project which will flood a large area of eastern Iceland in order to power a massive new aluminium smelter. Björk's mother, Hildur Hauksdóttir, famously staged a hunger strike in protest.

In Finland, there's controversy over the expansion of nuclear energy and the disposal of nuclear waste. In 2002 the government gave approval in principal to the construction of a fifth nuclear power plant. The four existing plants currently supply 27% of Finland's electricity supply.

Learn more about whaling at www .iwcoffice.org, website of the International Whaling Commission.

THE EUROPEAN UNION

Sweden, Denmark and Finland are members of the European Union (EU), but Norway and Iceland are holding out. Both countries are extremely protective of their fishing rights and fear they may lose some of their territorial waters and quotas under EU rules. Iceland spent many years during the so-called 'Cod Wars' with Britain fighting for its 200-mile exclusion zone and doesn't want to lose it now. Norwegians rejected EU membership in a referendum in 1994 but the issue is back on the political agenda and many predict a future referendum will see Norway join the Union. Many Icelanders also believe membership is necessary for future economic stability.

Denmark has been in the EU/EC since 1973, and Finland and Sweden joined in 1995. However, Finland is the only Nordic country to adopt the euro – Denmark and Sweden have both rejected it at referendums

DID YOU KNOW?

In Denmark, there are twice as many pigs as people.

IMMIGRATION

One of the big issues of debate in Denmark's government continues to be immigration. Denmark has not caught the extremist bug like other European nations and the Danes remain remarkably generous hosts to new migrants who enter the country each year. But while the media talks of integration, many Danes are uneasy about the rapid changes taking place in the country's ethnic mix, and fear having to support dependent incomers. The government's increasingly hard-line attitude to immigration (such as limiting the right of asylum seekers to migrate to Denmark with their families) led to a censure from the likes of the Council of Europe and the Danish Red Cross over the country's role in upholding international human rights.

In Iceland there are similar fears, mainly focusing on the belief that foreign immigration will create unemployment among Icelanders, though only 6% of the population is of foreign origin. In Finland, only 2% of residents are foreigners – the lowest number in Europe.

ROYAL FEVER

Everyone loves a good royal wedding and the flag-waving Danes were united in joy when one of their own tied the knot. Since Crown Prince Frederik of Denmark married popular Tasmanian Mary Donaldson in the 2004 wedding of the year, the Danish royal family has rarely been out of the papers or the trashy mags.

The royals of Sweden and Norway are equally loved by the populace – despite the odd scandal, they're rarely hyped and hounded like Britain's royals!

SPORT

Sport certainly raises some interest and makes for a good bar-stool topic. In Finland and Sweden ice hockey really stirs the emotions, especially when the two countries are playing against each other. Sweden made it to the final of the world championships in 2004 but lost to Canada. In Finland, the entire city of Oulu was on a high after its team won the national championships in 2003–04.

Football (soccer) has a following throughout the region, but it doesn't even come close to the single-minded passion you'll see elsewhere in Europe. The Danes do reasonably well in European leagues (they won the Euro championships in 1992 and made the quarter-finals in 2004) and most Scandinavians have a couple of pin-up players flying the flag in the English premiership or European league teams.

REMEMBER ABBA...?

Lycra suited ABBA won the Eurovision Song Contest for Sweden in 1974, and neither the group nor the competition has waned in popularity in Scandinavia since that time. Eurovision parties are held each May and fans sit glued to television screens to see if one of the Nordic countries can pull it off again. Finns, Norwegians and Icelanders will tell you blithely that they always come last (and in the case of the Finns and Norwegians it's half true!), while attempting to give the impression that they couldn't care less. Swedes (1999 winners) and Danes (2000) are much more optimistic about their chances. The contest is also big in Tallinn, since Estonia won it in 2001.

Music in general is a great conversation-starter – young Scandinavians take considerable interest if you know a bit about their local music scene. Iceland is a great example. In Reykjavík, just about everyone under 30 seems to be in a band or producing their own CD of 'experimental music'. Everyone has heard of Björk, but does anyone know the legendary Megas? Or the avant-garde rockers Sigur Ros? Tune in to some Reykjavík pub goss – you'll probably find the band under discussion is playing in Damon Albarn's bar next door. Finland is another country where you could bump into famous musicians at a bar or club in Helsinki. The Flaming Sideburns and the Rasmus are names to look out for.

DID YOU KNOW?

The Alþing, established in 930, makes Iceland the oldest continuous parliamentary democracy in the world.

DID YOU KNOW?

'Ski' is a Norwegian word and Norway lays claim to having invented the sport.

DID YOU KNOW?

During the past 40 years, more than 300 million children have played with Lego bricks, a Danish invention.

DENMARK

Denmark

CONTENTS

Denmark (Danmark), Scandinavia's smallest country, may lack the natural grandeur of its neighbours but within its modest borders it boasts a compelling mix of lively modern cities, historic towns, rolling farmland, graceful beech woods and sleepy islands full of medieval churches, Renaissance castles and pretty harbours. Copenhagen, Scandinavia's largest and most cosmopolitan capital, is a compact but world-class destination with superb museums, a vibrant cultural life and a burgeoning bar, café and restaurant scene.

You'd be well advised to make some time for the regional capitals too: Århus and Odense are sophisticated and friendly university cities, brimming with art, music and lively nightlife. Beyond the cities lies much of the country's extraordinarily rich historic and natural wealth. Its treasures include haunting Neolithic burial chambers; the bodies of well-preserved Iron-Age people exhumed from their slumber in peat bogs; and atmospheric Viking ruins that reflect the country's dramatic history and sea-centred character.

Denmark's wealth and power have stemmed from its mastery of the sea from Viking days and the sea remains a central part of Denmark's allure. Coastal attractions for the visitor are numerous, with kilometres of white-sand beaches and a wealth of archipelagos and islands, including magical Bornholm, stuck out in the middle of the Baltic.

Getting around in Denmark is easy. Public transport is generally excellent and the Danish road system straightforward and efficient. The country is mainly flat, with only occasional areas of gentle hills, making it an ideal place to explore by bike, particularly on its extensive network of cycle routes.

FAST FACTS

- **Area** 43,075 sq km
- **Capital** Copenhagen
- **Currency** Danish krone; US$1 = Dkr6.01; £1 = Dkr10.00; €1 = Dkr7.44; A$1 = Dkr4.41; C$1 = Dkr4.79; NZ$1 = Dkr4.10; ¥100 = Dkr5.50
- **Famous for** Hans Christian Andersen, the Little Mermaid, bacon, Carlsberg beer, marauding Vikings
- **Official Language** Danish
- **Phrases** *jah/nie* (yes/no), *tak* (thanks), *farvel* (goodbye), *skål* (cheers)
- **Telephone Code** country code ☎ 45; international access code ☎ 00
- **Visa** None needed for citizens of the EU, USA, Canada, Australia and New Zealand

HIGHLIGHTS

- Exploring **Copenhagen** (p30), with its history-packed centre, taking plenty of stops to enjoy the café scene by day, then bar hopping and clubbing by night
- Meandering around the unique fortress churches, escaping to empty beaches and extensive forests, and relaxing beside some picture-postcard ports on the idyllic island of **Bornholm** (p55)
- Sampling the cultural, artistic and historical treasures as well as the lively nightlife of fashionable **Århus** (p70)
- Canoeing, cycling and generally taking it easy in Jutland's low-key but delightful **Lake District** (p77)
- Standing on Denmark's slender northern tip above luminous **Skagen** (p86), where two angry seas collide

ITINERARIES

- **One week** Get a 72-hour Copenhagen Card and explore the capital. If there's time, use it to visit North Zealand's castles, Roskilde or Køge. Then choose between a few days on Funen, to see Odense and the island's pretty southern towns, or a three-day break on Bornholm.
- **Two weeks** As above but extend your stay around Funen to take in the idyllic island of Ærø before hopping over to Århus, Ribe, Skagen and other Jutland sights of interest.

HOW MUCH?

- **Danish pastry** Dkr8
- **Loaf of bread** Dkr11
- **Bottle of wine (takeaway)** Dkr50
- **Royal Copenhagen Porcelain souvenir mug** Dkr580
- **Cappuccino** Dkr25

LONELY PLANET INDEX

- **Litre of petrol** Dkr8
- **Litre of bottled water** Dkr12
- **Beer – pint of pilsner** Dkr25
- **Souvenir T-shirts** Dkr100
- **Street snack – smørrebrød open sandwich** Dkr30-70

CLIMATE & WHEN TO GO

Despite its northerly position Denmark has a relatively mild climate. May and June can be a delightful time to visit: the countryside is a rich green and you'll beat the rush of summer tourists. There's usually a good summer but expect to see rain and grey skies in Denmark at any time of year.

July to August is peak tourist season with many open-air concerts, lots of street activity and beach basking. Other advantages to visiting in midsummer include longer opening hours at sightseeing attractions and potential savings on accommodation, as some business hotels drop their rates. Autumn is pleasant and can be a visual feast of golden colours in wooded areas. Winter is cold, dark and wet.

HISTORY

Denmark was the ancient heart of Scandinavia: prehistoric hunter-gatherers from central and southern Europe moved north to what are now Jutland and Funen as the ice sheets retreated. Neolithic people settled on this new landscape in 4000 BC and by 500 BC Iron-Age farms and trading centres were well established.

Only the haunting remnants of burial chambers and vestigial fortifications survive from prehistory. Some of the best are on the island of Møn (see p53). Present-day Denmark traces its linguistic and cultural roots to the arrival of the Danes, a tribe thought to have migrated south from Sweden around AD 500. In the late 9th century, warriors led by the Viking chieftain, Hardegon, conquered the Jutland Peninsula. The Danish monarchy, Europe's oldest, dates back to Hardegon's son, Gorm the Old, who reigned in the early 10th century. Centuries worth of Danish kings and queens are laid to rest in sarcophagi on dramatic display at Roskilde Cathedral (p49). Gorm's son, Harald Bluetooth, completed the conquest of Denmark and spearheaded the conversion of the Danes to Christianity. Successive Danish kings sent their subjects to invade England and conquer most of the Baltic region. They were accomplished fighters, swordsmiths, shipbuilders and sailors, qualities well-illustrated at the excellent Viking Ship Museum in Roskilde (p50).

In 1397 Margrethe I of Denmark established a union between Denmark, Norway and Sweden to counter the influence of the

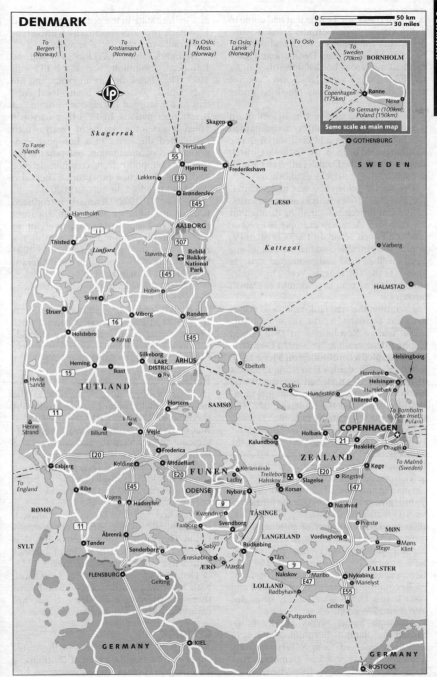

powerful Hanseatic League that had come to dominate the region's trade. Sweden withdrew from the union in 1523, and over the next few hundred years Denmark and Sweden had numerous border skirmishes and a few fully fledged wars, largely over control of the Baltic Sea. Norway remained under Danish rule until 1814.

In the 16th century the Reformation swept through the country, accompanied by church burnings and civil warfare. The fighting ended in 1536, the Catholic Church was ousted and the Danish Lutheran Church headed by the monarchy established.

Denmark's golden age was under Christian IV (1588–1648), with Renaissance cities, castles and fortresses flourishing throughout his kingdom. A superb example is Egeskov (p66) on Funen Island. In 1625 Christian IV, hoping to neutralise Swedish expansion, entered an ill-advised and protracted struggle known as the Thirty Years' War. The Swedes triumphed and won large chunks of Danish territory.

Literature, the arts, philosophy and populist ideas flourished in the 1830s, and Europe's 'Year of Revolutions' in 1848 helped inspire a democratic movement in Denmark, which adopted a constitution on 5 June 1849, forcing King Frederik VII to relinquish most of his power to an elected parliament and become Denmark's first constitutional monarch. Denmark lost the Schleswig and Holstein regions to Germany in 1864.

Denmark remained neutral throughout WWI and also declared its neutrality at the outbreak of WWII. Nevertheless, on 9 April 1940, an unfortified Denmark faced either a quick surrender or a full-scale invasion by German troops massed along its border. The Danish government settled for the former, in return for an assurance that the Nazis would allow the Danes a degree of autonomy. For three years the Danes managed to walk a thin line, running their own internal affairs under Nazi supervision, until in August 1943 the Germans took outright control. The Danish Resistance movement mushroomed and 7000 Jewish Danes were quickly smuggled into neutral Sweden.

Although Soviet forces heavily bombarded the island of Bornholm, the rest of Denmark emerged from WWII relatively unscathed. Postwar Social Democrat governments introduced a comprehensive so-cial welfare state in the postwar period, and Denmark provides its citizens with extensive cradle-to-grave social security.

Denmark joined NATO in 1949 and the European Community – now the EU – in 1973. The Danes support an expanding EU only tepidly. Many fear losing local control to a European bureaucracy dominated by stronger nations. In 1993 they narrowly voted to accept the Maastricht Treaty, which established the terms of a European economic and political union, only after being granted exemptions from common-defence and single-currency provisions. They also voted not to adopt the euro in 2000.

In May of 2002 Denmark introduced tougher immigration laws in an apparent response to Europe-wide anxiety about an increase in illegal immigration, earning it a rebuke from the European council in 2004 for tarnishing its reputation as a tolerant upholder of human rights.

In 2004 the already popular and much-loved royal family gave Danes a reason to celebrate its enduring appeal when the country's most eligible bachelor Crown Prince Frederik married Australian Mary Donaldson in a hugely popular and exhaustively covered fairy-tale wedding.

PEOPLE

Denmark's often difficult history at the heart of a volatile part of Europe has taught the modern Dane to avoid too much conflict or rivalry. Danes are refreshingly self-effacing and reserved about themselves and their achievements. It springs from a long-standing belief among Danes that no-one should think of themselves as being better than the average and that you should always keep your feet firmly on the ground.

Travellers will find Danes to be relaxed, casual and not given to extremes or to ostentation. They are tolerant of different lifestyles: in 1989 Denmark became the first European nation to legalise same-sex marriages.

Denmark's population is about 5.3 million, with 70% living in urban areas, 1.5 million of them in Copenhagen. Foreign nationals account for 7.8% of Denmark's population.

RELIGION

About 90% of Danes belong to the state-supported National Church of Denmark – an Evangelical Lutheran denomination, but less than 5% of the population are regular churchgoers.

ARTS

Literature

Hans Christian Andersen has long loomed large over Denmark's literary landscape, particularly so now, around the bicentenary of his birth in 1805 (see the boxed text, p62). His fairy tales are the second most translated work worldwide, surpassed only by the Bible. Other notable literary Danes include religious philosopher Søren Kierkegaard, whose writings were a forerunner of existentialism, and Karen Blixen, who penned *Out of Africa* and *Babette's Feast*. One of Denmark's foremost contemporary authors is Peter Høeg, who had international success with his suspense mystery, *Miss Smilla's Feeling for Snow*.

Architecture & Design

Denmark is a leader in industrial design, with a style marked by cool, clean lines applied to everything from architecture to silverware and furniture (during your stay you'll more than likely park yourself on a chair designed by Arne Jacobsen, the godfather of Danish design). Café Stelling (p42) in Copenhagen has a Jacobsen interior and lamps. Denmark has produced a number of leading 20th-century architects, including Jørn Utzon who designed Australia's Sydney Opera House.

Cinema & TV

Babette's Feast, a movie adaptation of Blixen's novel by Danish film director Gabriel Axel, won the Academy Award for Best Foreign Film in 1988. The following year, director Bille August won an Academy Award and the Cannes Film Festival's Palme d'Or for *Pelle the Conqueror*, adapted from the novel by Danish author Martin Andersen Nexø. Gudhjem harbour (p58) in Bornholm was used as a location for the film. In 1997 Bille August directed the film *Smilla's Sense of Snow*, an adaptation of Peter Høeg's novel. In 2000, Danish director and maverick Lars von Trier won the Cannes Film Festival's Palme d'Or for his film *Dancer in the Dark*.

Visual Arts

Before the 19th century Danish art was mainly formal portraiture, exemplified by the works of Jens Juel (1745–1802). A 'Golden Age' ushered in the 19th century with such fine painters as Wilhelm Eckersberg (1783–1853) and major sculptors such as Bertel Thorvaldsen (1770–1844).

Later in the century the 'Skagen School' evolved from the movement towards outdoor painting of scenes from working life, especially of fishing communities on the northern coasts of Jutland and Zealand. Much of it is exhibited at the Skagens Museum (p86). Leading exponents were PS Krøyer and Michael Ancher and Anna Ancher. In the mid-20th century, a vigorous modernist school of Danish painting emerged, of which Asger Jorn (1914–73) was a leading exponent. Much of his work is on display at the art museum in Silkeborg (p77).

Denmark's towns and cities contain a vibrant selection of home-grown and international contemporary art; even the smallest towns can surprise. Two of the best art museums and galleries outside the capital are the sprawling Brandts Klædefabrik (p62) in Odense and ARoS (p72), the shiny new gallery in Århus.

Theatre & Dance

The Royal Danish Ballet, which performs in Copenhagen's Royal Theatre from autumn to spring, is regarded as northern Europe's finest. The Royal Theatre is also the venue for the Royal Orchestra, Royal Opera and various theatrical performances.

ENVIRONMENT

The eco-conscious Danes are keen recyclers and users of alternative energy (such as wind turbines or their own pedal power) and they are increasingly interested in sourcing sustainable, organic and fair-trade food and goods, so it's an easy country in which to be environmentally responsible.

The Land

The Danish landmass has been heavily exploited by agriculture and 70% of its land is farmed mainly for barley and root crops, which are used to feed livestock. With almost 20% of farmland near sea level, many environmentally sensitive wetlands were made arable by draining. EU quotas now make farming such land less viable, and the Danish government has initiated an ambitious plan to restore these wetlands and re-establish marshes and streams throughout the country.

DENMARK

Wildlife

Still commonly seen in Denmark are wild hare, deer and many species of birds, including magpies, coots, swans and ducks. Returning the wetlands should help endangered species such as the freshwater otter make a comeback.

FOOD & DRINK
Staples & Specialities

You could live happily and inexpensively for days on the twin Danish delights of *smørrebrød* and *wienerbrød*. Nothing epitomises Danish food more than *smørrebrød* (literally 'buttered bread'), an open-faced sandwich that ranges from very basic fare to some elaborate sculpture-like creations. Typically, it's a slice of rye bread topped by roast beef, tiny shrimps, roast pork or fish fillet and various garnishes. It's served in many restaurants at lunch time but is cheapest at bakeries and butcher shops.

The rich pastry known worldwide as a 'Danish' is called *wienerbrød* in Denmark, and nearly every second street corner has a bakery with mouthwatering varieties that go exceptionally well with a cup of coffee.

Typical Danish dishes include *frikadeller* (minced pork meatballs), *kogt torsk* (poached cod in mustard sauce), *flæskesteg* (roast pork with crackling), *hvid labskovs* (beef and potato stew) and *hakkebøf* (beefburger with fried onions). Then there's the *koldt bord*, a buffet-style spread of cold foods, including herring dishes, salads, cold cuts, smoked fish and cheeses. Smoked fish (particularly abundant and tasty on Bornholm), pickled herring and fried beef patties (served with a raw egg yolk, pickles and horseradish) are other common specialities.

Where to Eat & Drink

To enjoy a day sipping coffee, having a light lunch, devouring an evening meal or indulging in a night out on the tiles you may not have to stir from your seat in many of Denmark's excellent multipurpose bar/café/restaurant hybrids which can buzz all day and night (in the main cities and towns at least).

Gourmets will be happy in Denmark, where there's an increasingly good choice of fine dining places. Copenhagen remains the culinary jewel in Denmark's crown though.

If you're on a tighter budget but still want the best, consider splashing out at the pricier places for lunch, when menus and courses are markedly cheaper than in the evening.

The cheapest restaurant food is generally pizza and pasta; you can eat your fill for about Dkr55 at lunch, Dkr75 at dinner.

Dagens ret, which means daily special, is usually the best deal on the menu, while the *børn* menu is for children.

Breakfast is usually a light continental buffet with white bread or bagels and a selection of meats or cheeses.

Drinks

Denmark's Carlsberg and Tuborg breweries both produce good lagers and pilsners. The most popular spirit in Denmark is caraway-spiced Aalborg aquavit; it's drunk straight down as a shot, followed by a chaser of beer. *Øl* (beer), *vin* (wine) and spirits are reasonably cheap compared to those in other Scandinavian countries. There are a few good microbreweries and pubs selling real ale in Denmark.

COPENHAGEN

pop 1.5 million

Copenhagen (København) is Scandinavia's largest and liveliest city and is one of Europe's most seductive destinations. It has the cultural and social attractions of a major European capital, yet is as compact as they come.

Its allure lies in the irresistible buzz of its central streets and squares and the throngs that gather at the countless bars, cafés, restaurants and music venues that line them. Central Copenhagen (and increasingly many of the adjoining neighbourhoods) has an active nightlife that rolls on well into the early hours of the morning.

There's a treasure trove of museums, castles and old churches to explore too, including the Nationalmuseet (national museum) and the Statens Museum for Kunst (national art gallery).

It's a simple city to navigate by foot, by bike, or by the excellent and improving transport system. Much of the central area is pedestrianised and the main roads have cycle lanes that are as flat as a Dutch pancake.

HISTORY

Copenhagen began life as a fishing village and developed within the shelter of Slotsholm,

DENMARK

COPENHAGEN IN TWO DAYS

Spending a day taking in some or all of the sights in the city centre is a good way to get a feel for the city, but with ample time for a leisurely *smørrebrød* lunch and some breaks for drinks in the city-square cafés (Café Stelling is a stylish bet). In summer **Tivoli** is a good evening destination, especially during the Friday evening concerts.

On the second day choose between the **National Museum** and **Gallery** and from the many sights around **Slotsholm**. Perhaps round off the day with a relaxing **canal tour**. In the evening, dine in the centre or strike out for the cafés, restaurants and bars of Vesterbro.

the island that is now dominated by the monumental Christiansborg Palace. Slotsholm was fortified during the 12th century by Bishop Absalon of Roskilde as a stronghold to defend the area against marauding groups of Wends from Germany and a base for offensives against them. You can still see this kernel of the old city underneath the new one at Slotsholmen (see p34). The settlement that developed around it was named Kømanshavn, later amended to København, meaning the 'port of the merchants'. The much-expanded settlement became the capital of Denmark during the early 15th century and flourished during the reign of Christian IV (1588–1648), under whom so many of the city's most impressive buildings were constructed. The occasional fire during the 18th century and a devastating bombardment in 1807 by British naval hero Horatio Nelson (who then made off with the entire Danish fleet) did not stop the city's growth for long. By the 1830s the city was the centre for a revolutionary time in art, philosophy and literature.

ORIENTATION

The always bustling train station, Central Station (Hovedbanegården or København H), is flanked on its west by the main hotel zone, where modernised hotels rub shoulders with sex shops. To the east of the station's main entrance, across the broad and busy Bernstorffsgade, is the Tivoli amusement park. Beyond traffic-bound HC Andersens Boulevard lies the spacious Rådhuspladsen:

the central city square, main bus transit point and gateway to Copenhagen's heart.

From Rådhuspladsen, the narrow opening of Frederiksberggade is the unassuming introduction to Strøget, a linked sequence of lively, crowded streets (made up of Frederiksberggade, Nygade, Vimmelskaftet, Amagertorv and Østergade) running through the city linking Rådhuspladsen and the other great square of Kongens Nytorv and, beyond it, Nyhavn canal.

INFORMATION
Bookshops

Nordisk Korthandel (Studie-stræde 26-30) Offers a superb collection of travel guides and maps. Foreign newspapers are available at Central Station and a few newsstands.

Discount Cards

Copenhagen Card (24hr card adult/child Dkr199/129, 72hr card Dkr399/229, adult card covers 2 children under 10) secures unlimited travel on buses and trains around Copenhagen and North Zealand, and on the city's waterbuses. It also gives free or discounted admission to most of the region's museums and attractions. Cards are sold at the Wonderful Copenhagen tourist office (p33), Central Station, major DSB stations, and at many hotels, camping grounds and hostels. If you want to tick off a lot of sights in a few days this card can be a real bargain. Grab the Copenhagen Card guide from the tourist office, which lists the free travel, admission and discounts available.

Internet Access

Boomtown (☎ 33 32 10 32; Axeltorv 1-3; per hr Dkr30; ☺ 10am-11pm) There's WiFi access.
Hovedbiblioteket (☎ 33 73 60 60; 15 Krystalgade; ☺ 10am-7pm Mon-Fri, 10am-2pm Sat) A public library offering free Internet access but you must book a slot.
Use It (Rådhusstræde 13) Information centre that offers free Internet access, within reasonable time constraints.

Laundry

Istedgades Møntvask (Istedgade 45; wash/dry 10kg load Dkr30; ☺ 7am-9pm)

Left Luggage

Central Station (per 24hr small/large locker Dkr25/35, maximum 72hr) Lockers are in the lower level near the Reventlowsgade exit.

Medical Services

Frederiksberg Hospital (☎ 38 16 38 16; Nordre Fasanvej 57) West of the city centre, has a 24-hour emergency ward.
Private doctor visits (☎ 33 93 63 00 for referrals) Usually cost around Dkr350.

COPENHAGEN (KØBENHAVN)

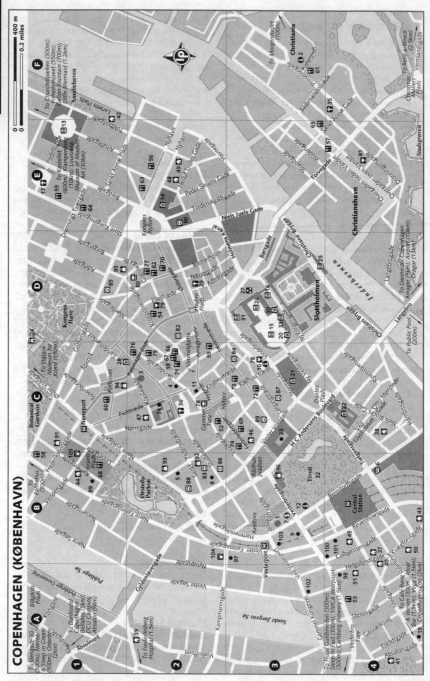

Steno Apotek (Vesterbrogade 6c; ☼ 24hr) Pharmacy opposite Central Station.

Money

Banks, all of which charge transaction fees, are found throughout the city centre. Banks in the airport arrival and transit halls are open 6am to 10pm daily.

The **Forex exchange booth** (Central Station; ☼ 8am-9pm) has the lowest fees.

You'll find 24-hour, cash-exchange ATMs that exchange major foreign currencies for Danish kroner, minus a hefty Dkr25 to Dkr30 fee, at **Den Danske Bank** (Central Station) and **Nordea** (Axeltorv).

Post

Main Post Office (Tietgensgade 35-39; ☼ 11am-6pm Mon-Fri, 10am-1pm Sat) Offers poste-restante services.

Central Station Post Office (☼ 8am-9pm Mon-Fri, 9am-4pm Sat, 10am-5pm Sun)

Tourist Information

Wonderful Copenhagen (☎ 70 22 24 42; www.visit copenhagen.dk; Vesterbrogade 4a; ☼ 9am-8pm Mon-Sat, 10am-8pm Sun May-Aug, 9am-4.30pm Mon-Fri, 9am-1.30pm

Sat Sep-Apr) Distributes the informative *Tourist in Copenhagen* and *Copenhagen This Week*, a free city map, and brochures for all regions of Denmark. In summer especially, queues can be long and fretful.

Use It (☎ 33 73 06 20, www.useit.dk; Rådhusstræde 13; ☼ 9am-7pm mid-Jun–mid-Sep; 11am-4pm Mon-Wed, 11am-6pm Thu, 11am-2pm Fri mid-Sep–mid-Jun) First class information centre aimed at young budget travellers, but open to all. It books rooms for free, stores luggage (by day only), holds mail, offers free Internet use and provides lots of useful information. *Playtime* is Use It's free annual guide to the city and around.

Travel Agencies

Kilroy Travels (☎ 33 11 00 44; www.kilroytravels.com; Skindergade 28)

Wasteels (☎ 33 14 46 33; Skoubogade 6; ☼ 9am-5pm Mon-Fri, 10am-noon Sat)

SIGHTS

It could take weeks to explore all of Copenhagen's museums and attractions. They cover almost every special interest, including Danish design, architecture, Jewish history, decorative art, erotica, medical sciences, geology, working-class cultural history, tobacco and

DENMARK

pipes, Copenhagen city history, shipbuilding, Danish naval history, European musical instruments, drawings of humorist Storm P, and the silver designs of Georg Jensen. *Copenhagen This Week* has a list of the full range of options with addresses, admission fees and hours.

Statens Museum for Kunst

Denmark's national **gallery** (☎ 33 74 84 94; www.smk.dk; Sølvgade 48-50; adult/child Dkr50/free, Wed free; 🕑 10am-5pm Tue & Thu-Sun, 10am-8pm Wed) contains an enormous collection of superb paintings. Taking everything in at one go can be exhausting. The main collection is on the 2nd floor and includes works by 19th-century Danish masters such as Jens Juel, Wilhelm Eckersberg, Constantin Hansen, PS Krøyer and Kristian Zahrtmann, as well as the 17th-century Dutch and Flemish masters, Rembrandt and Rubens. Leading European artists including Matisse, Picasso, Braque, Utrillo and Munch are well represented. There are contemporary, and often engagingly provocative, installations by Danish artists. The ground floor stages temporary exhibitions of major international paintings for which there is a separate admission fee.

Slotsholmen

On an island separated from the city centre by a moat-like canal, Slotsholmen is the site of **Christiansborg Palace** (☎ 33 92 64 92) and the seat of Denmark's national government. Of the many sites, the grandest is the **Royal Reception Chambers** (adult/child Dkr40/10 🕑 guided tours 11am, 1pm & 3pm May-Sep, 11am & 3pm Tue, Thu, Sat & Sun Oct-Apr), the ornate Renaissance hall where the queen entertains heads of state. The tours have commentary in English.

The **Ruins of Absalon's Fortress** (adult/child Dkr25/10; 🕑 9.30am-3.30pm May-Sep, 9.30am-3.30pm Tue, Thu, Sat & Sun Oct-Apr) are the excavated foundations of Bishop Absalon's original castle of 1167 and of its successor, Copenhagen Slot. They can be visited in the atmospheric basement of the present palace tower.

Tøjhusmuseet (☎ 33 11 60 37; adult/child Dkr50/free, Wed free; 🕑 noon-4pm Tue-Sun), the royal arsenal built in 1600, has an impressive collection of hand weapons and old armour and a huge hall filled with historic cannons and more modern killing machines, including a WWII V-1 'Doodlebug' rocket.

At the **Museum of Royal Coaches** (☎ 33 40 10 10; adult/child Dkr20/10; 🕑 2-4pm Fri, Sat & Sun May-Sep, 2-4pm Sat & Sun Oct-Apr), the horse-drawn carriages used for regal events are housed among the rich, horsey scent of the royal stables (next door but not open to the public).

Teatermuseet (adult/child Dkr30/5; 🕑 2-4pm Wed, noon-4pm Sat & Sun), which houses the royal stage, dates from 1766 and has many exhibits on Danish theatre history.

Thorvaldsens Museum (☎ 33 32 15 32; Bertel Thorvaldsens Plads; adult/child Dkr20/free; Wed free; 🕑 10am-5pm Tue-Sun) features grand statues by the famed Danish sculptor Bertel Thorvaldsen, who was heavily influenced by Greek and Roman mythology. Enter from the direction of Vindebrogade.

The **Royal Library** (☎ 33 47 47 47; Søren Kierkegaards Plads; 🕑 10am-7pm Mon-Sat) dates from the 17th century, but the focal point these days is its ultramodern walkway-connected extension dubbed the 'Black Diamond' for its shiny black granite facade. The sleek, seven-storey building houses 21 million books and other literary items such as Hans Christian Andersen's original manuscripts. The building itself is open for **visits and guided tours** (adult/child Dkr25/10; 🕑 10am-11pm).

Nationalmuseet

The **National Museum** (☎ 33 13 44 11; Ny Vestergade 10; www.natmus.dk; adult/child Dkr25/free, Wed free; 🕑 10am-5pm Tue-Sun) holds the world's most extensive collection of Danish artefacts from the Palaeolithic period to the 19th century. Highlights include Bronze-Age burial remains in oak coffins and *lurs* (musical horns) that were used for ceremony and communication, ancient rune stones, a golden sun chariot, the silver Gundestrip cauldron and Viking weaponry. The prehistory and Viking displays are the main reason for coming, although there are worthwhile collections covering the Middle Ages and Renaissance period, Egyptian and classical antiquities. There's even a small **Children's Museum**.

Rosenborg Slot

This 17th-century **castle** (☎ 33 15 32 86; adult/child Dkr60/10; 🕑 10am-4pm May & Sep, 10am-5pm Jun-Aug, 11am-3pm Oct, 11am-2pm Tue-Sun Nov-Apr), built by Christian IV in Dutch Renaissance style, stands at the edge of the peaceful Kongens Have (King's Gardens). There are glorious marbled and painted ceilings, gilded mirrors,

Dutch tapestries, silver lions, and gold- and enamel-ware. The Royal Treasury is in the castle basement where the Danish crown jewels – including Christian IV's crown, the sword of Christian III and Queen Margrethe II's pearls – glow in the subdued lighting of soundless rooms.

Tivoli
Right in the heart of the city, Copenhagen's century-old **amusement park** (☎ 33 15 10 01; www .tivoli.dk; adult/child Dkr65/35; ☺ 11am-11pm Sat-Thu, 11am-1am Fri mid-Apr–mid-Jun & mid-Aug–mid-Sep, 11am-midnight Sun-Thu, 11-1am Fri & Sat mid-Jun–mid-Aug) is something of a mishmash of gardens, food pavilions, amusement rides, carnival games and various stage shows. The Demon, a cork-screwing, feet-in-space roller coaster, and the 'dead drop' tower are two of the most high-adrenaline and stomach-lurching rides. It's well worth checking out the free programme of Friday concerts (included in admission prices), with mostly Danish bands and occasionally more widely known bands like the Cardigans. Fireworks light up the skies at 11.45pm on Saturday.

Rundetårn
The **Round Tower** (☎ 33 73 03 73; Købmagergade 52; adult/child Dkr20/5; ☺ 10am-8pm Mon-Sat & noon-8pm Sun Jun-Aug, 10am-5pm Mon-Sat & noon-5pm Sun Sep-May) provides a fine vantage point for viewing the old city's red-tiled rooftops and abundant church spires. It was built by Christian IV in 1642 as an astronomical observatory. Halfway up the 209m spiral walkway is a hall with changing exhibits. Peter the Great of Russia is said to have ridden his horse up the ramp followed by the czarina in a horse-drawn carriage; everyone else walks. The observatory offers winter **astronomy programmes** (☺ 7-10pm Tue & Wed Oct-May) and by day you may also be lucky enough to see a dramatic, live projection of the sun too.

Ny Carlsberg Glyptotek
This splendid **museum** (☎ 33 41 81 41; Dantes Plad 7, HC Andersens Blvd; adult/child Dkr30/free, Wed & Sun free; ☺ 10am-4pm Tue-Sun), occupying a grand period building near Tivoli, would usually be well worth a visit. Unfortunately it probably won't contain many of the exceptional Greek, Egyptian, Etruscan and Roman sculptures, Gauguin, Monet and Van Gogh paintings and Degas bronzes for which it's famous

when you read this. Major renovation works are underway until 2006 and all but 25% of its works have gone on an extended world tour to other galleries.

Latin Quarter
The university district north of Strøget, all narrow streets lined with cafés, bars and an eclectic mix of shops, has a fun and lively atmosphere.

Climb the stairs of the **University Library** (enter from Fiolstræde) to see one quirky remnant of the 1807 British bombardment of Copenhagen – a cannonball in five fragments and the object it hit, a book titled *Defensor Pacis* (Defender of Peace).

Opposite the university is **Vor Frue Kirke** (☺ 8am-5pm, closed to viewing during services and concerts), Copenhagen's neoclassical cathedral. The building dates from 1829, but stands on the site of earlier churches. It has a strong classical design with a high, vaulted ceiling and a rather stark interior containing powerful statues of Christ and the 12 apostles, the most acclaimed works of the Golden Age sculptor, Bertel Thorvaldsen. A couple of blocks east of the cathedral is the pretty square of **Gråbrdre Torv** and its flanking restaurants. On the northern side of the Latin

---

WHAT'S FREE?

Want to spend a day sightseeing and amusing yourself in Copenhagen for free? Make it a Wednesday as many of the museums and galleries in town are free. Take in an impromptu street show by random performers along Strøget on your way to the daily noontime changing of the guard at the Royal Palace. To rest those aching feet, pop into the plush 'Black Diamond' at the Royal Library to peruse the international papers or surf the Internet *gratis*. Alternatively avoid walking altogether by finding a Citybike. Parked at various points around town, they are free to use (you'll need a Dkr20 coin as deposit). Build up a thirst at the free Carlsberg Brewery tour, or if it's hot consider heading to the free outdoor (saltwater) swimming pool in the heart of the city on Islands Brygge. On all but the warmest weeks you may want to grease up, cross-channel swimmer style, with some insulating lard before braving those waters.

Quarter is **Kultorvet**, a lively square where you'll almost certainly find impromptu street entertainment on sunny days, as well as beer gardens, flower stalls and produce stands.

Gardens

The green stretch of gardens along Øster Voldgade offers a refuge from the city traffic. **Kongens Have**, the large public park behind Rosenborg Slot, is a popular picnic spot.

The extensive **Botanical Gardens** (8.30am-6pm May-Sep, 8.30am-4pm Tue-Sun Oct-Apr) on the western side of Rosenborg Slot has fragrant trails. The **Palmehus** (10am-3pm Mon, Tue, Thu & Fri; 1-3pm Wed, Sat, Sun & public holidays) is a large, walk-through glasshouse growing a variety of tropical plants.

Christianshavn

Christianshavn was established by King Christian IV in the early 1600s as a commercial centre and military buffer for the expanding city of Copenhagen. Still surrounded by ramparts and cut by canals, Christianshavn today is a mix of residential development and cultural enclave with some good cafés and bars. There's a distinctly relaxed lifestyle along the canalsides, and the area is attracting an increasing number of artists and craftspeople.

To get to Christianshavn, walk over the bridge from the northeastern side of Slotsholmen or you can take bus No 8 from Rådhuspladsen.

VOR FRELSERS KIRKE

Close to Christiania is the 17th-century **Vor Frelsers Kirke** (☎ 31 57 27 98; Sankt Annæ Gade 29; admission free, tower adult/child Dkr20/10; 11am-4.30pm Apr-Aug, 11am-3.30pm Sep-Mar, closed during services, tower closed Nov-Mar), which has a huge and impressive baroque altar and an elaborately carved pipe organ, propped up by two unhappy looking decorative elephants. For a panoramic city view, climb the 400 steps of the church's 95m spiral tower. The last 160 steps run spectacularly and dizzyingly along the outside rim, narrowing to the point where they disappear at the top.

THE 'FREETOWN' OF CHRISTIANIA

Things are changing in Christiania, a self-declared 'independent state' in the very heart of Denmark. It's a social experiment on the edge of Christianshavn, a haven from conventional living or an anarchic den of iniquity that should be bulldozed to release a valuable piece of real estate, depending on who you talk to.

The story started in the early 1970s when hippies, artists, political activists and other urban escapees, fired with the dream of an alternative 'New Society' run by and for the community (not to mention the lure of no rent or local taxes), broke into an abandoned barracks here and refused to leave despite violent confrontations with the state.

A hard drugs problem resulted in police raids, a moral backlash and much soul-searching within Christiania's community, which banned the use of hard drugs in the early 1980s.

The government eventually agreed to let Christiania be as a 'social experiment' and it has emerged as a 1000-strong alternative ghetto with its own commercial life, political structure, education system, radio station and a thriving music, theatre and social scene.

It is famous (or notorious) to most visitors, however, for its hash culture and was, until recently, the place where every type of weed, resin and perception-altering fungus was openly, though illegally, sold from Pusherstreet's stalls.

But no more. The uneasy truce between state and dealers ended with a massive police raid in 2004, which netted dozens of suspected drug dealers and smashed a hash trade worth an estimated Dkr80 million. Christianians no longer sell hash openly and fear politicians and developers could use its druggy reputation against Christiania in the ongoing debate about the area's future and as a pretext to reclaim the site, ending this long social experiment, and perhaps the last vestige of the 1960s hippy, 'peace and love' dream.

Pusherstreet may be an emptier, rather deflated place these days but Christiania has many other attractions (inexpensive cafés and restaurants, eccentric shops, clubs and galleries) that make it well worth a visit. The **information office** (☎ 32 95 65 07; www.christiania.org; Nyt Forum, Pusherstreet; noon-6pm Mon-Thu, noon-4pm Fri) organises guided tours most days in summer.

Carlsberg Brewery

At the **Carlsberg Brewery visitor centre** (☎ 33 27 13 14; Gamle Carlsberg Vej 11; ☯ 10am-4pm Tue-Sun), free self-guided tours provide the lowdown on the history of Danish beer, capped off with a sampling of the present-day product. Take bus No 26 westbound.

Waterfront

Amalienborg Palace (adult/child Dkr40/5; ☯ 10am-4pm May-Oct, 11am-4pm Nov-Apr) has been the home of the royal family since 1794. The palace's four, nearly identical, rococo mansions surround the central square and are guarded by sentries, who are relieved at noon by a ceremonial changing of the guard. You can view the interior of the northwestern mansion, with its royal memorabilia and the study rooms of three kings.

Inland along Frederiksgade is the splendid **Frederikskirken** (admission free, guided tour adult/child Dkr20/10; ☯ 10am-5pm Mon-Thu, noon-5pm Fri-Sun, tower tour 1pm & 3pm mid-Jun—Aug). It's known universally as Marmorkirken (Marble Church) because of its magnificent marble dome. The panelled and gilded frescoes inside have breathtaking colours.

Back on Amalienborg Plads, and 500m north along Amaliegade, is Churchillparken, where you'll find **Frihedsmuseet** (admission Dkr25, Wed free; ☯ 10am-4pm Tue-Sat, 10am-5pm Sun May—mid-Sep, 11am-3pm Tue-Sat, 11am-4pm Sun mid-Sep—Apr), which depicts the history of Danish Resistance against Nazi occupation.

About 150m straight on from the Frihedsmuseet you pass the spectacular **Gefion Fountain** that features the goddess Gefion, ploughing the island of Zealand with her four sons yoked as oxen. Another 400m north along the waterfront is the statue of the famed **Little Mermaid** (Den Lille Havfrue), a rather forlorn little bronze statue that tends to disappoint all but the most steadfast Hans Christian Andersen fans.

ACTIVITIES
Swimming & Sunbathing

Weather permitting, there are reasonably good opportunities to swim and sunbathe on stretches of beach around 5km from the city centre at Amager Strand; take the Metro to Lergravsparken and then walk east for about a kilometre. But for central swimming (apart from the indoor pool at the DGI-byen centre near the station) you could brave the cold, salty but clean waters of the free public pool at Islands Brygge, right in the heart of the city.

TOURS
Quickshaw Tours

Copenhagen's 'quickshaws' are two-seater, open carriages powered from behind by fit young pedal-pushers. They operate daily and can be found at most main squares. Tours start at Dkr190 for an hour. They can also be used as taxis with payment by zone system. Rådhuspladsen to Nyhavn costs Dkr65.

Canal Tours

For a different angle on the city, hop onto one of the hour-long boat tours that wind through Copenhagen's canals from April to mid-October. Multilingual guides give a lively commentary in English. The largest company, **DFDS Canal Tours** (www.canaltours.dk; adult/child Dkr50/20), leaves from the head of Nyhavn. Tours pass by the Little Mermaid, Christianshavn and Christiansborg Slot, and leave a few times an hour between 10am and 5pm. **Netto-Boats** (☎ 32 54 41 02; adult/child Dkr25/10) are cheaper, run the same times and depart from Holmens Church and from Nyhavn.

Canal boats also make an excellent, traffic-free alternative for getting to some of Copenhagen's waterfront sites. DFDS Canal Tours charges Dkr45 for a one-day 'waterbus' pass (Dkr 20 for children) from mid-May to mid-September. The boats leave Nyhavn every 30 minutes between 10.15am and 4.45pm (to 5.45pm mid-June to mid-August) and make a dozen stops, including at the Little Mermaid, Nationalmuseet and Vor Frelsers Kirke, allowing you to get on and off as you like. In addition, the **HUR public transport system** (www.hur.dk) has a new boat service linking the Royal Library, Nyhavn and Nordre Toldbod, near the Little Mermaid, every 20 minutes until 7pm.

FESTIVALS

The **Copenhagen Jazz Festival** (☎ 33 93 20 13; www.cjf.dk) is the biggest event of the year, with 10 days of music in early July. The festival presents a wide range of Danish and international jazz, blues and fusion music. It's a positive cornucopia of some 500 indoor and outdoor concerts, with music wafting out of practically every public square, park, pub and café from Strøget to Tivoli.

DENMARK

SLEEPING

Copenhagen's main hotel area lies in Vesterbro on the western side of Central Station, where rows of six-storey, century-old buildings house one hotel after the other. Many of them are members of chains and reflect a rather bland business and conference ambience.

This is also Copenhagen's red-light district, though the only visible sign by day is a scattering of porn shops and strip clubs. There is no overt sense of menace though and Vesterbro has a fairly cheerful atmosphere overall.

The tourist office can book rooms in private homes (Dkr300/500 for singles/doubles). It also books unfilled hotel rooms, often at discounted rates, for a Dkr60 booking fee. The airport information booth outside customs offers a similar service.

Use It (Rådhusstræde 13) books private rooms (singles/doubles from Dkr200/300), free of booking fees, and keeps tabs on which hostel beds are available.

Budget

Camping Absalon (☎ 36 41 06 00; www.camping -absalon.dk, Danish only; Korsdalsvej 132; adult/child/tent Dkr64/32/20) About 9km west of the city centre near Brøndbyøster Station on the S-train's line B.

City Public Hostel (☎ 33 31 20 70; www.city-public -hostel.dk; Absalonsgade 8; dm Dkr130; ⊙ early May– mid-Aug, 24hr reception) This central, well-run hostel sleeps 200. There's one 72-bed dorm but most range from six to 23 beds each. Breakfast costs Dkr25, or Dkr20 if included with the bed price. From Central Station, walk west for 10 minutes along Vesterbrogade, then bear off left at Vesterbro Torv.

Mick & Blodwyn's Backpackers Inn (☎ 33 93 23 00; http://mickandblodwyns.homepage.dk; Herluf Trolles Gade 9; dm Dkr180; 🖳) This brand new hostel in a tiny old inn promises 'cheap accommodation, great location' and that sums it up. A stumble from the bars of Nyhavn, it's small, friendly, has a small bar with cheap beer, and includes breakfast, bedding and free Internet access in its rates. Bathroom facilities and accommodation in the four- or six-bed dorms are a tad cramped.

Copenhagen has two HI hostels, each about 5km from the city centre. Both have laundry facilities and guest kitchens. They often fill early in summer so book ahead.

Danhostel Copenhagen Bellahøj (☎ 38 28 97 15; www.danhostel.dk/bellahoej; Herbergvejen 8; dm/d Dkr95/ 300; ⊙ Feb-early Jan, 24hr reception; ℗ 🖳) Bellahøj is in a quiet suburban neighbourhood with 250 dorm beds and a limited number of family rooms (doubles). You can take bus No 2-Brønshøj from Rådhuspladsen and get off at Fuglsangs Allé. The night bus is 82N.

Danhostel Copenhagen Amager (☎ 32 52 29 08; www.danhostel.dk/copenhagen; Vejlands Allé 200, Amager; dm/d Dkr95/300; ⊙ early Jan–mid-Dec; ℗ 🖳) In an isolated part of Amager just off the E20 is one of the largest hostels in Europe, with 528 beds in two-bed and five-bed rooms. Take the S-train to Sjælør Station, then change to bus No 100S, which stops in front of the hostel. Until 5pm Monday to Friday, bus No 46 runs from Central Station directly to the hostel.

Even when the HI hostels are full you can nearly always find a bed at one of the city-sponsored hostels (just a few are in the following list). The larger ones tend to be a crash-pad scene but are more central than the HI hostels, and sleeping bags are allowed.

Sleep-In Green (☎ 35 37 77 77; www.sleep-in-green .dk; Ravnsborggade 18; dm Dkr85; ⊙ mid-May–mid-Oct; ℗ 🖳) In the Nørrebro area, close to its buzzing cafés and bars, Sleep-in Green has 68 dorm beds. Take bus No 5a, night bus 81N or 84N or the S-train to Nørreport Station, then walk northwest on Frederiksborggade over the canal. The organic breakfast costs Dkr30.

YMCA Interpoint (☎ 33 31 15 74; Valdemarsgade 15; dm Dkr85; ⊙ end Jun-early Aug; reception 8.30-11.30am, 3.30-5.30pm & 8pm-12.30am) The small 28-bed YMCA is in the heart of the increasingly lively Vesterbro area. Bed sheets (Dkr15), breakfast (Dkr25) and a kitchen are available. It's a 15-minute walk from Central Station (take Vesterbrogade west to Valdemarsgade), or you can take bus No 6a or 26.

Sleep-In Fact (☎ 33 79 67 79; Valdemarsgade 14; www .sleep-in-fact.dk; dm Dkr120; ⊙ mid-Jun–end-Aug, reception 7am-noon & 3pm-3am; 🖳 🛒) In a refurbished factory building close to YMCA Interpoint, this is another reasonably central place with 10-bed to 30-bed dorms and plenty of activities offered, including bike rental, a gym, pool and table football. Breakfast is included.

Belægningen Avedørelejren (☎ 36 77 90 84; www .belaegningen.dk; Avedøre Tværvej 10, Hvidovre; dm Dkr100, s/d from Dkr350/450) An enjoyable alternative southwest of the city limits is in the renovated barracks of a former military camp.

Sleeping bags are not allowed, but bed linen and towels are included in the price. Dorms are small (two-, three- or four-bed). Breakfast (Dkr45) is available and there's free Internet access, cheap bicycle rental and a group kitchen. Take bus No 650S from Central Station to Avedøre School.

Hotel Jørgensen (☎ 33 13 81 86; hotel@post12.tele .dk; Rømersgade 11; dm/s/d Dkr135/475/575, s/d with private bathroom Dkr575/700) A great budget hotel near Nørreport Station and the area's lively cafés and bars. The simpler rooms have shared bathroom. Dorms are either six or 12-beds.

Mid-Range

Bed & Breakfast Bonvie (☎ 33 93 63 73; www.bb bonvie.dk; Fredericksberggade 25 C, 2; d with/without bathroom Dkr500/600; 🖳) The floor below the Hotel Rainbow is tiny but worth mentioning for its central location and friendly hosts.

Cab Inn City (☎ 33 46 16 16; www.cabinn.com; Mitchellsgade 14; s/d/tr/q Dkr510/630/750/870; Ⓟ ✕ ✕ 🖳) The promise that you'll 'sleep cheap in luxury' is bold (the rooms are small, uniform and rather clinical, most with sleeper-train–style folding bunk beds) but rooms are also very good value. They're modern, spotless and boast good facilities (including kettle and TV) and a good location. There's free lobby Internet access.

Cab Inn Scandinavia (☎ 35 36 11 11; www.cabinn .com; Vodroffsvej 57; s/d Dkr510/630; Ⓟ) Cab Inn has 201 compact rooms in this chain's familiar clinical style. The rooms are comfortable and have TV and private bathroom.

Cab Inn Express (☎ 33 21 04 00; www.cabinn.com; Danasvej 32-34; s/d Dkr510/630; Ⓟ) A few blocks away from the Scandinavia is the third sister hotel.

Sømandshjemmet Bethel (☎ 33 13 03 70; http: //hotel-bethel.dk; Nyhavn 22; s/d Dkr595/745) Inside the tall, steepled, period building in a great location on Nyhavn are bright, pleasant rooms, some with views of Nyhavn's quays, although you pay more for these.

Hotel Rainbow (☎ 33 14 10 20; www.copenhagen -rainbow.dk; Fredericksbergadde 25; r Dkr720-890, r with private bathroom Dkr890; ✕ 🖳) Hotel Rainbow is a small, friendly and exclusively gay hotel in an excellent location right near the Rådhus end of Strøget so the city's shopping, drinking and clubbing are at your feet. The hotel is on the top floor and has just a few bright and airy rooms. Use the street-level intercom. Book ahead.

Top Hebron Hotel (☎ 33 31 69 06; www.hebron.dk; Helgolandsgade 4; s/d Dkr750/975; 🖳) One of the best choices in town for location and general appeal, this hotel has large modern, well-equipped rooms, good facilities and a quiet ambience.

Missionshotellet Nebo (☎ 33 21 12 17; www.nebo .dk; Istedgade 6; s/d from Dkr360/690, s/d with private bathroom Dkr760/860; Ⓟ 🖳) Only a few metres from Central Station, the rooms here are small but comfy, and the shared showers are large and clean.

Absalon Hotel (☎ 33 24 22 11; www.absalon-hotel.dk; Helgolandsgade 15; s/d Dkr495/650, s/d with private bathroom Dkr875/1095; 🖳) Though central, the Absalon's decor is rather dreary '80s style. There's free Internet access, and you may find cheaper room deals on its website.

Tiffany Hotel (☎ 33 21 80 50; www.hoteltiffany.dk; Colbjørnsensgade 28; s/d Dkr895/1095) At a quiet location is this smart, modern, upmarket hotel. Spacious rooms have fridge, microwave and water-heating facilities. The breakfast, delivered to your room, is rather basic.

Centrum Hotel (☎ 33 31 31 11; www.hotelcentrum .dk; Helgolandsgade 14; s/d Dkr975/1175) Centrum is a modern, contemporary place with simple, well-renovated rooms. Free entry to the excellent nearby DGI-byen spa and swimming pool complex is included in the rates.

Copenhagen Admiral Hotel (☎ 33 74 14 14; www .admiralhotel.dk; Toldbodgade 24-28; s/d Dkr775/1105, with harbour view Dkr1225/1470; Ⓟ ✕ 🖳) This grand place on the waterfront near Nyhavn occupies a renovated, 18th-century granary. Its 366 rooms are criss-crossed with thick wooden beams, and blend period charm and modern conveniences. Breakfast is an extra Dkr105.

Top End

Hotel Guldsmeden (☎ 33 22 15 00; www.hotelgulds meden.dk, Danish only; Vesterbrogade 66; s/d Dkr1025/1325; Ⓟ ✕ 🖳) It's over 1km from the city centre, but Guldsmeden is an exceptionally stylish and welcoming place with lovely rooms and comfy beds.

DGI Byens Hotel (☎ 33 29 80 50; www.dgi-byen .dk; Tietgensgade 65; s/d Dkr1295/1495; Ⓟ ✕ 🖳 🐾) One of the more upmarket places in the area, DGI Byens has large rooms furnished in simple but swish Scandinavian style with lots of light and bare wood. Guests get free use of the spa and swimming pool complex. Rates are about 25% cheaper at weekends.

Hotel Skt Petri (☎ 33 45 91 00; www.hotelsktpetri .com; Krystalgade 22; r from Dkr1200; P ⊠ ☒ ▣) Copenhagen's new luxury place, occupying a former department store, is a contender for most stylish and best-located hotel in town. The rooms are cosseting, and some have balconies and/or enchanting city views. There's a gym and a magnificent, bright, high lobby just made for sipping cocktails and feeling fabulous in.

EATING
Around Central Station

Ankara (☎ 33 31 14 99; Vesterbrogade 35; lunch/dinner buffet Dkr49/79; ☻ noon-midnight) The extensive Middle Eastern buffet at Ankara includes dishes such as calamari, chicken, lamb and salads.

Central Station has a **DSB café** (☻ 5.30-12.45am Sun-Thu, 5.30-1.45am Fri-Sat), a **supermarket** (☻ 8am-midnight), the Kringlen bakery with good breads and pastries, a fruit shop and fast-food outlets.

Rådhusarkaden (Vesterbrogade), a shopping centre near Rådhus, has the Irma grocery store and Conditori Hans Christian Andersen, offering sandwiches, pastries and coffee.

Around Strøget

Café Zirup (☎ 33 13 50 60; Læderstræde 32; mains Dkr70-99, brunch Dkr89) Usually packed inside and out, Zirup serves fresh, light food such as tasty wraps (like marinated chicken with guacamole and salsa), burgers and great sandwiches (parma ham, manchego cheese, olives, cornichons and Dijon mayo on focaccia for instance) in generous portions, accompanied by large, peppery-leafed and tastily-dressed salads. It does a mean brunch too.

Sushi Time (☎ 33 11 88 99; Grønnegade 28; mains Dkr100-170, menus Dkr80-170; ☻ noon-3pm & 4-8.30pm Mon-Wed, noon-3pm & 4-9pm Thu & Fri, noon-6pm Sat) It's tiny and rather cramped but we know of no better place in Copenhagen to come for an authentic and reasonably priced sushi fix.

Peder Oxe (☎ 33 11 00 77; Gråbrødre Torv; mains Dkr79-179) An old favourite with visitors and locals alike in a historic building in the cobbled square just north of Strøget, Peder Oxe serves tasty fish and organic meat dishes with a fine salad buffet. There's a good cocktail bar downstairs.

Restaurant Gråbrødre Torv 21 (☎ 33 11 47 07; mains around Dkr150, 3-course meal Dkr298) A top venue near Peder Oxe with good atmosphere both

inside and on its outside terrace. Imaginatively prepared lamb and fish dishes are a good choice.

Pasta Basta (☎ 33 11 21 31; Valkendorfsgade 22; lunch Dkr59-69, mains Dkr79-169; ☻ 11.30am-3am Sun-Thu, 11am-5am Fri & Sat) Stylish and friendly, this is probably the best, and best-value, pasta/buffet-style place in town. There's a superb selection of hot pasta dishes served with fish and meat mains. Eat as much as you like of cold pasta dishes and salads for Dkr30 to Dkr69, with or without other courses. Book ahead. Downstairs is the Coconut Beach Bar, open the same late hours and with good drink deals.

Riz Raz (☎ 33 15 05 75; Kompagnistræde 20; day/evening buffet Dkr59/69; ☻ 11.30am-11pm) Another excellent-value, high-quality buffet-style place, just south of Strøget, offering a fresh, tasty Mediterranean-style vegetarian buffet including salads, pasta and felafels. There are good meat mains too (Dkr89 to Dkr169).

Restaurant Puk (☎ 33 11 14 17; Vandkunsten 8; lunch platter Dkr79-128; ☻ 11am-late) Puk serves up a tempting range of inexpensive Danish food inside and out. Smørrebrød, such as the house special pickled herring or smoked eel with scrambled egg, costs Dkr38 to Dkr79, while a generous platter of traditional hot and cold comfort food (Danish ribs with red cabbage, herring fillet with curry mayonnaise, poultry-salad with bacon) costs Dkr128.

At the snackier end of the dining spectrum, Strøget has an abundance of cheap fast food joints including hole-in-the-wall kebab joints selling falafels and kebabs for under Dkr30.

Shawarma Grill House (16 Frederiksbeggade; sandwiches Dkr30-40, kebabs Dkr44; ☻ 11am-10pm) The best kebab joint is a bustling spot a two-minute walk from Rådhuspladsen at the western end of Strøget.

There's a **7-Eleven** (cnr Gameltorv; ☻ 24hr) mini-market. Several bakeries occupy the Strøget area including **Reinh van Hauen** (east end of Strøget), which uses organic ingredients. **Netto super-market** (near east end of Strøget) has relatively cheap prices. Next to Use It is a **bakery** (sandwiches Dkr28-Dkr35) that does delicious sandwiches, including a vegetarian option.

The Latin Quarter

Studenterhusets (☎ 35 32 38 61; Købmagergade 52; ☻ noon-midnight Mon-Fri) A relaxed student hang-out with drinks and light eats, including vegetarian or meat sandwiches for Dkr20.

Klaptræet (Kultorvet 13; dishes under Dkr70) Another popular student hang-out overlooking Kultorvet square, Klaptræet serves burgers, chilli con carne and salads. Continental breakfast costs Dkr28. Kultorvet itself becomes a popular beer garden in summer.

Café Sommersko (Kronprinsensgade 6; dishes Dkr90-110; ☽ 10am-midnight Mon-Fri, 10am-2am Sat) This café has a big selection of beers and a menu that includes salads (Dkr75) and lasagne (Dkr85).

Elsewhere in Central Copenhagen

Nyhavns Færgekro (☎ 33 15 15 88; Nyhavn 5; herring buffet Dkr89; ☽ 11.30am-late) For a thoroughly Danish experience, try the herring buffet here, one of the more atmospheric restaurants on the canalside where model sailing ships hang above diners' heads. There are 10 different kinds of prepared herring including baked, marinated and rollmops, with condiments to sprinkle on top and boiled potatoes to pad it all out.

Cap Horn (☎ 33 12 85 04; Nyhavn 21; mains Dkr95-185; ☽ 9am-11pm) Amid many a middling canalside restaurant, Cap Horn stands out, serving excellent, fresh Danish organic food including a three-item *smørrebrød* plate for Dkr69 or a herring, steak and potato plate for Dkr105. If it's in season try the superb rhubarb soup with vanilla ice cream to finish.

Govindas (☎ 33 33 74 44; Nørre Farimagsgade 82; buffet Dkr59; ☽ noon-8.30pm Mon-Sat) You can get good vegetarian food at this spot south of the Botanical Gardens, where the Hare Krishna members offer an all-you-can-eat buffet and vegan meals. Students and senior citizens pay Dkr45 for the standard buffet.

Ida Davidsen (☎ 33 91 36 55; Store Kongensgade 70; smørrebrød Dkr55-165) Considered the top *smørrebrød* restaurant in Denmark, Ida Davidsen has a dark, hugely atmospheric interior and offers an extensive menu of *smørrebrød* options with some exotic toppings, such as beef tartare topped with raw egg.

Produce market (Israels Plads; ☽ 9am-5pm Mon-Fri, 9am-2pm Sat) This is the main city produce market, just a few minutes' walk west of Nørreport Station. On Saturday it doubles as a flea market.

Ostehjørnet (☎ 33 15 50 11; Store Kongensgade 56) Good speciality shops include this delicatessen just along from Ida Davidsen restau-

---

THE AUTHOR'S CHOICE

Spisebilletten (☎ 33 12 58 03; Skindergade 3; mains Dkr85-135; ☽ 4-10pm Tue-Sat, closed most of Jul) Simple, clean flavours, often from seasonal organic ingredients, are blended to good effect at Spisebilletten, an unpretentious place that cares about good food and doesn't charge too much for it. Sample dishes include an incredibly fresh green-pea soup accompanied by a pea and pancetta salad; risotto with spinach, mushrooms and ricotta cheese; and rhubarb cake with a rhubarb granité.

---

rant, with terrific cheese, meat and wine selections.

Christianhavn & Christiania

Christianshavns Bådudlejning (☎ 32 96 53 53; Overgaden neden Vandet 29; fish & meat mains Dkr115-125) This deservedly popular place on a canalside deck does a tasty lunch menu, including sandwiches (Dkr45) and salads (Dkr60 to Dkr70). You can hire rowing boats as well.

Oven Vande Café (☎ 32 95 96 02; Overgaden oven Vandet 44; mains Dkr150-190) Oven Vande boasts a sunny, corner location. As well as an evening menu it offers lunch dishes, including sandwiches and salads (Dkr60 to Dkr70).

Morgenstedet (Langgaden; mains Dkr35; ☽ noon-9pm; ☒) This long-established vegetarian and vegan place has a pretty garden in the heart of Christiania.

Spiseloppen (☎ 32 57 95 58; Loppebygningen; fish & meat mains Dkr165-195) Another Christiania institution and a general favourite in Copenhagen. Prices are not entirely budget, but it has excellent food, wildly varying in style of cuisine depending on the nationality of the chef that day (well this is Christiania after all). Vegetarian main dishes cost around Dkr140. Spiseloppen is in the big Loppe building that also houses the Loppen dance club (see p42).

DRINKING

Visitors are utterly spoilt for choice as far as cafés and bars go in Copenhagen. Many are jack-of-all trade places, as good for food as they are for a lively evening spent drinking pilsner or an afternoon sipping coffee. There are countless excellent bars to choose from too; this is just a small selection of some of the better central places but the further flung districts such as Nørrebro and Vesterbro (especially along Istedgade, east of the red light district, and Halmtorvet, closer to the station) are well worth exploring too.

Café Stelling (☎ 33 32 93 00; Gammeltorv 6) Showy and very smartly decked out by celebrated Danish designer Arne Jacobsen, this is a great new place to mingle with well-heeled Danes, gaze at the square through the huge glass windows, peruse one of the dozens of magazines from the racks and enjoy a coffee or light lunch.

Joe & the Juice (Ny Østergade 11; ◷ 9am-7pm Mon-Sat) One of the few fresh fruit juice bars in town also serves coffee, sandwiches, cake and light snacks.

Charlie's Bar (☎ 33 32 22 89; Pilestræde 33) Charlie's is tiny, cosy, scruffy and hugely popular with pilsner-sated Danes who worship enthusiastically at this temple to the gods of real British cask ale. There's a small but very well chosen selection of bitters and stouts and some wonderful and pricey rare single-malt whiskies.

Café Bang & Jensen (130 Istedgade) Small and a fair trek from the centre, this is just one of many hip little bars springing up all over Vesterbro. We choose this bar-cum-café for its reliably relaxed but buzzing atmosphere.

Ideal Bar (☎ 33 25 70 11; Enghavevej 40) A young, painfully hip crowd hangs out here, often for preclubbing drinks before heading next door to Vega Nightclub (see right). The music at Ideal is pumping, danceable and mostly excellent, ranging from hip-hop to more ragga-based and African-style sounds.

Sofie Kælderen (☎ 32 57 27 87; Sofiegade 1) An engaging local bar tucked away in Christianshavn that opens at noon. There's often live jazz and rock until late.

ENTERTAINMENT

Copenhagen is a 24-hour party city. For free entertainment simply stroll along Strøget, especially between Nytorv and Højbro Plads, which is a bit like an impromptu three-ring circus of musicians, magicians, jugglers and other street performers. In addition, numerous free concerts are held throughout the summer in city parks and squares.

Copenhagen has scores of backstreet cafés with live music. Entry is often free on weeknights, while there's usually a cover charge averaging Dkr60 at weekends.

Available from Wonderful Copenhagen, the free publications *Nat & Dag, Musik Kalenderen, Film Kalenderen* and *Teater Kalenderen* list concerts and entertainment schedules in detail.

Live Music

Rust (☎ 35 24 52 00; Guldbergsgade 8; Dkr30-50) Just one of several good entertainment spots on the western side of the Nørrebro area, Rust has a multilevel dance venue attracting a college-age crowd; it can get busy and there are queues at weekends.

Studenterhuset (☎ 35 32 38 61; Købmagergade 52; admission Dkr60-80) Another popular student venue with live music (jazz on Thursdays and rock on Fridays) and DJ nights on the other weeknights. There's a very cheap beer happy hour from noon to 7pm.

Stengade 30 (☎ 35 36 09 38; Stengade 18; admission price varies) A spirited alternative live music and dance scene.

Vega (Enghavevej 40) Far out at the western end of the Vesterbro district, this place remains one of the city's cooler venues staging hugely popular Friday and Saturday night sessions. Big-name rock bands and underground acts play the 'Big Vega' 1500-capacity venue.

Copenhagen Jazz House (☎ 33 15 26 00; Niels Hemmingsensgade 10) The city's leading jazz spot with a terrific ambience. Danish musicians and occasional international names feature, and after concerts on Thursday, Friday and Saturday nights, the place becomes a lively **disco** (admission Dkr65; ◷ 1-5am).

Mojo (☎ 33 11 64 53; Løngangstræde 21; Dkr50; ◷ 8-3am) Small, scruffy and friendly, this is a prime spot for blues. Bands play most nights of the week.

Huset (☎ 33 15 20 02; Rådhusstræde 13) In the same courtyard as Use It you'll find the Huset complex with a cinema, theatre, café and restaurant. There's often music, including good jazz. Many music events are free, but it costs about Dkr50 for special events.

Loppen (☎ 32 57 84 22; Loppebygningen, Christiania; Dkr50-70; ◷ nightclub 2-5am Fri-Sat) A celebrated and much-loved veteran on the Copenhagen live music scene that hosts bands playing everything from soul to punk rock on various nights and runs a late disco.

Gay & Lesbian Venues

Copenhagen has a good number of gay and lesbian bars and clubs and there's a great ease and confidence about gay life in this most civilised and tolerant of cities. For more information and listings check *Out and About*, a guide to Copenhagen gay life, or the annual *Gay and Lesbian Guide to Copenhagen*, both available in gay cafés and clubs. Alternatively, go to www.panbladet .dk (in Danish).

PAN Club (☎ 33 11 37 84; Knabrostræde 3; cover Dkr50; ☺ 11–6am Thu-Sat) The largest gay club in town with five levels, two dance floors, seven bars and entertaining cross-dressing and karaoke nights (Thursday to Saturday).

Oscar (☎ 33 12 09 99; Rådhuspladsen 77; ☺ noon-2am, kitchen noon-10pm) A popular meeting place for gay men near the Rådhus.

Never Mind (Nørre Voldgade 2; ☺ 10–6am) A long-established, late-night dance bar for mainly gay men, but with a few lesbians and trans-gendered clientele enjoying its kitsch decor.

Kvindehuset (The Women's House; Gothersgade 37) Kvindehuset stages various dance nights for lesbians and has a café and bar.

Masken (Studiestræde 33) Small, smoky and popular with students at weekends, not least because of its special drinks prices, Masken is friendly and puts on no airs or claims to being hip (and neither does the music in the jukebox). There's a lesbians-only night in the basement section on Thursdays.

Cosy Bar (Studiestræde 24) Near Masken, this is a recently brightened up, late-night place for gay men, with a cruisy ambience.

Cinemas

There are numerous cinemas showing first-release movies along Vesterbrogade between Central Station and Rådhuspladsen.

SHOPPING

Copenhagen's main shopping street is Strøget where you can find speciality shops selling top-quality amber and Danish silver, china and glass. Denmark is famous for its design and designers; many of their products are found in the upmarket department stores, Magasin and Illum, and the stylish Illums Bolighus, noted for its designer furniture, all in the Strøget area.

Outlets for clothing from young Danish and Scandinavian designers include **Mensch** (☎ 33 11 57 55; Peder Hvitfeldts Str), **København K** (☎ 33 16 15 19; Teglgårdstræde) and **Munthe Plus Simondsen** (☎ 33 32 03 12; 10 Grønnegade), a celebrated Danish women's fashion label. The Latin

Quarter is a good hunting ground for funky little clothes shops and record stores, plus the large **Guf** (Larsbjørnsstræde 21), an excellent music shop with a big selection. There are several outdoor suppliers along the north side of Frederiksborggade. **Fjeld & Fritid** (☎ 33 11 35 36; Frederiksborggade 28) is one of the best.

GETTING THERE & AWAY
Air

Copenhagen's modern international airport is in Kastrup, 10km southeast of the city centre. Flights connect frequently with most major Danish and Scandinavian destinations. Many airline offices are north of Central Station near the intersection of Vester Farimagsgade and Vesterbrogade.

Boat

The ferry to Oslo, operated by **DFDS Seaways** (☎ 33 42 30 00; Dampfærgevej 30), departs from the Nordhavn area just north of Kastellet.

Bus

International buses leave from Central Station; advance reservations on most routes can be made at **Eurolines** (☎ 33 88 70 00; Reventlowsgade 8).

Car & Motorcycle

The main highways into Copenhagen are the E20, which goes west to Funen and east to Malmö, Sweden; and the E47, which connects to Helsingør. If you're coming into Copenhagen from the north on the E47, exit onto Lyngbyvej (Rte 19) and continue south to get into the heart of the city.

As well as airport booths, the following rental agencies have city branches:

Avis (☎ 33 15 22 99; Kampmannsgade 1)
Budget (☎ 33 55 05 00; Helgolandsgade 2)
Europcar (☎ 33 55 99 00; Gammel Kongevej 13)
Hertz (☎ 33 17 90 20; Ved Vesterport 3)

A fair trek from the centre at Amager Strand, **Rent A Wreck** (☎ 70 25 26 70; Amagerstrandvej 100) hires out battered but usually reliable old wagons from as little as Dkr239 per day. Rates are even more competitive on longer hires. The downside is having to drive around with the company name emblazoned on the doors.

Train

Long-distance trains arrive and depart from Central Station, a huge complex with eateries

DENMARK

and numerous services. There are public showers (Dkr15) at the underground toilets opposite the police office.

There are three ways of buying a ticket, and the choice can be important depending on how much time you have before your train leaves. *Billetautomats* are coin-operated machines and are the quickest, if you've mastered the zone-system prices. They are best for S-train tickets. If you're not rushed, then **DSB Billetsalg** (🕒 8am-7pm Mon-Fri, 9.30am-4pm Sat) is best for reservations. There's a numbered-ticket queuing system. **DSB Kviksalg** (🕒 5.45am-11.30pm) is for quick ticket buying, although queues can build at busy times.

GETTING AROUND
To/From the Airport
A train links the airport with Central Station (Dkr19.50, 12 minutes, three times hourly). The airport is 15 minutes and about Dkr170 from the city centre by taxi.

Bicycle
At Central Station, **Københavns Cykler** rents out bicycles for Dkr75 a day. For cheaper prices (Dkr40 a day) walk a few blocks northwest to **Danwheel** (Colbjørnsensgade 3).

If you just want to ride in the city centre, look for a free-use City Bike – they've got solid spokeless wheels painted with sponsors' logos. There are about 125 City Bike racks scattered throughout central Copenhagen, although available bikes are often few and far between. If you're lucky enough to find one with a bike, deposit a Dkr20 coin in the stand to release the bike. You can return the bicycle into any rack to get your money back.

Except during weekday rush hours, you can carry bikes on S-trains for Dkr12.

Bus & Train
Copenhagen has an extensive public-transport system consisting of a small but excellent new underground and overground driverless Metro system (trains run a minimum of every three minutes); an extensive metropolitan rail network called S-train, whose 10 lines pass through Central Station (København H); and a vast bus system, whose main terminus is nearby at Rådhuspladsen.

Buses, Metro and trains use a common fare system based on the number of zones you pass through. The basic fare of Dkr17 for up to two zones covers most city runs and allows

transfers between buses and trains on a single ticket as long as they're made within an hour. Third and subsequent zones cost Dkr8 more with a maximum fare of Dkr59.50 for travel throughout North Zealand. Alternatively get a 24-hour pass allowing unlimited travel in all zones for Dk100/50 per adult/child. Children under 12 travel free when accompanied by an adult.

On buses, fares are paid to the driver when you board, while on S-trains tickets are purchased at the station and then punched in the yellow timeclock on the platform.

Trains and buses run from about 5am to 12.30am, though buses continue to run through the night (charging double fare) on a few main routes. For schedule information about buses, call ☎ 36 13 14 15; for trains call ☎ 33 14 17 01.

Car & Motorcycle
With the exception of the weekday-morning rush hour, when traffic can bottleneck coming into the city (and going out around 5pm), traffic is usually manageable. Getting around by car is not problematic other than for the usual challenges of finding parking spaces. Still, it's best to explore sights within the city centre on foot or by using public transport.

For kerbside parking, buy a ticket from a streetside 'parkomat' and place it inside the windscreen. Search out a blue or green zone where parking costs Dkr7 to Dkr12 an hour; in red zones it's a steep Dkr20. Parking fees must be paid 8am to 6pm in blue and green zones, 8am to 8pm in red zones Monday to Friday, and 8am to 2pm in red and green zones on Saturday. Overnight kerbside parking is generally free and finding a space is not usually too much of a problem.

Taxi
Taxis with signs saying *'fri'* can be flagged down or you can phone ☎ 35 35 35 35. The basic fare is Dkr23 plus Dkr10 per kilometre between 6am and 4pm, Dkr11 between 4pm and 6am, and Dkr13 from 11pm to 7am Friday to Saturday. Fares include a service charge, so tipping is not expected. Most taxis accept credit cards.

AROUND COPENHAGEN
Dragør
If Copenhagen begins to feel crowded, consider an afternoon excursion to Dragør, a

quiet maritime town on the island of Amager a few kilometres south of the airport.

During the early 1550s King Christian II allowed Dutch farmers to settle in Amager to provide his court with flowers and produce, and Dragør still retains a hint of Dutch flavour.

The waterfront is dotted with fishing boats, smokehouses and the **Dragør Museum** (☎ 32 53 41 06; Havnepladsen; adult/child Dkr20/10; ☺ noon-4pm Tue-Sun May-Sep), a half-timbered house holding ship paraphernalia, period furnishings and locally produced needlework. The winding cobblestone streets leading up from the harbour are lined with the thatch-roofed, mustard-coloured houses that comprise the old town.

It is a 35-minute ride on bus No 30 or 33 (Dkr25.50) from Rådhuspladsen.

Klampenborg

Klampenborg is a favourite spot for people taking family outings from Copenhagen. It is only 20 minutes from Central Station on the S-train's line C (Dkr34). **Bellevue Beach**, 400m east of Klampenborg Station, is a sandy strand that gets packed with sunbathers in summer. A large grassy area behind the beach absorbs some of the overflow. A 10-minute walk west from the station is **Bakken** (☎ 39 63 73 00; Dyrehavevej 62; ☺ noon-midnight Apr-late Aug), the world's oldest amusement park. A blue collar version of Tivoli, it's a honky-tonk carnival of bumper cars, slot machines and beer halls.

Bakken is on the southern edge of **Dyrehaven**, an extensive expanse of beech woods and meadows crossed with peaceful walking and cycling trails. Dyrehaven was established in 1669 as a royal hunting ground and is the capital's most popular picnic area. At its centre, 2km north of Bakken, is the old manor house **Eremitagen**, a good vantage point for spotting herds of deer.

Louisiana Museum of Modern Art

Denmark's foremost modern **art museum** (☎ 49 19 07 19; Gl Strandvej 13; adult/child Dkr74/23; ☺ 10am-5pm Thu-Tue, 10am-10pm Wed) is on a seaside knoll in a striking modernistic complex. It is surrounded by delightful grounds full of sculptures by the likes of Henry Moore and Alexander Calder. The permanent collection features works by Giacometti, Picasso, Warhol, Rauschenberg and many more, and

there are outstanding changing exhibitions. It's a terrific spot even if you're not passionate about modern art. There's a diverting **Children's Wing** and a lakeside **garden**, café and restaurant with views across the water to Sweden.

The museum is a 10-minute walk north on Strandvej from Humlebæk Station, which is 35 minutes on the S-train's line C from Copenhagen (Dkr59.50).

ZEALAND

Zealand (Sjælland) offers a tempting range of places for day trips or longer breaks if you want a brief respite from the capital's relentless charm. Northern Zealand has wonderful beaches, likeable fishing villages and some breathtaking castles, most of them easily accessible and just an hour or so's journey thanks to the excellent rail network. A trip to the more remote and less well-connected southern islands of Møn and Falster reveals rural Denmark at its most serene and absorbing, with a number of interesting churches and some small but haunting prehistoric burial chambers to discover.

NORTH ZEALAND

The northern part of Zealand is a compact region of wheat fields and beech woodlands interspersed with small towns and tiny hamlets and with a surprisingly remote northern coastline.

One of the most popular day trips from Copenhagen is a loop tour taking in Frederiksborg Slot in Hillerød and Kronborg Slot in Helsingør. With an early start you might even have time to reach one of the north-shore beaches before making your way back to the city, although it is more rewarding to allow an extra day for wandering between shoreline towns.

If you're driving between Helsingør and Copenhagen, ignore the motorway and take the coastal road, Strandvej (Rte 152), which is far more scenic.

Frederiksborg Slot

Hillerød, 30km northwest of Copenhagen, is the site of **Frederiksborg Slot** (☎ 48 26 04 39; adult/child Dkr60/15; ☺ 10am-5pm Apr-Oct, 11am-3pm Nov-Mar), an impressive Dutch Renaissance castle that's spread across three islands. The

DENMARK

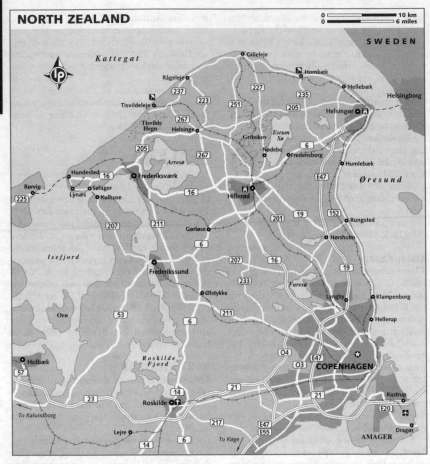

NORTH ZEALAND

oldest part of the castle dates from Frederik II's time, though most of the present structure was built by his son Christian IV in the early 1600s. After parts of the castle were ravaged by fire in 1859, Carlsberg beer baron JC Jacobsen spearheaded a drive to restore the castle and make it a national museum.

The sprawling castle has a magnificent interior with gilded ceilings, full wall-sized tapestries, royal paintings and antiques. The richly embellished **Riddershalen** (Knights' Hall) and the **coronation chapel**, where Danish monarchs were crowned between 1671 and 1840, are well worth the admission fee.

The S-train (A and E lines) runs every 10 minutes between Copenhagen and Hillerød (Dkr59.50), a 40-minute ride. From Hillerød Station follow the signs to Torvet, then continue along Slotsgade to the castle, a 15-minute walk in all. Alternatively, take bus No 701 or 702, which can drop you at the gate.

Helsingør (Elsinore)
pop 35,000

Helsingør is a busy, attractive port town, with ferries continuously shuttling across the Øresund Strait to and from Sweden to disgorge thirsty Swedes who stock up on booze here. The **tourist office** (☎ 49 21 13 33; www .visithelsingor.dk; Havnepladsen 3; 🕐 9am-5pm Mon-Thu, 9am-6pm Fri, 10am-3pm Sat mid-Jun–Jul, 9am-4pm Mon-Fri, 10am-1pm Sat Aug–mid-Jun) is opposite the train station.

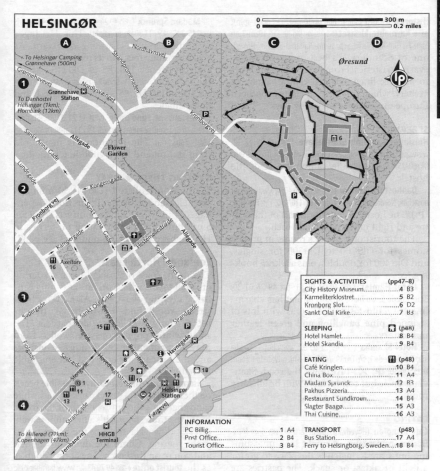

HELSINGØR

0 — 300 m
0 — 0.2 miles

Øresund

PC Billig (☎ 49 21 52 93; Stengade 28D; per hr Dkr20; ☾ 10am-5.30pm Mon-Sat) is an Internet centre.

SIGHTS

Helsingør's top sight is **Kronborg Slot** (☎ 33 92 65 33; adult/child Dkr50/15; ☾ 10.30am-5pm Jul-Sep, 11am-4pm Oct & Apr, 11am-3pm Tue-Sun Nov-Mar, May & Jun), made famous as the Elsinore Castle of Shakespeare's *Hamlet* (it has been and remains the venue for summer performances of the play in recent decades during the annual Hamlet festival). Kronborg's primary function was not as a royal residence, but rather as a grandiose tollhouse, wresting taxes (the infamous and lucrative 'Sound Dues') for more than 400 years from ships passing through the narrow Øresund. Stand by the cannons fac-

ing Sweden and you immediately see what a key strategic military and naval choke point this was. You can cross the moat and walk around the courtyard for free. A **guided tour** of the magnificent chapel, dungeons (where you'll find a statue of mythical hero Holger the Dane) and royal quarters costs Dkr40/15 per adult/child; or get a combined ticket that includes the **Danish Maritime Museum**, a paradise for model ship fans, for Dkr70/25 per adult/child. The castle is on the northern side of the harbour.

From the tourist office head up Brostræde and along Sankt Anna Gade. This will take you through the **medieval quarter** and past the old cathedral, **Sankt Olai Kirke** (☾ 10am-4pm Mon-Sat Apr-Oct, 10am-2pm Mon-Sat Nov-Mar); the **City**

History Museum (adult/child Dkr10/free; ☷ noon-4pm); and **Karmeliterklostret** (admission Dkr10; ☷ 10am-3pm Mon-Fri mid-May–mid-Sep, 10am-2pm mid-Sep–mid-May), one of Scandinavia's best-preserved medieval monasteries. From here Sudergade leads to the tree-lined, cobbled central square of **Axeltorv**, which can have an almost southern European ambience on sunny days.

SLEEPING
Helsingør Camping Grønnehave (☎ 49 28 12 12; www.helsingorcamping.dk; Strandalléen 2; adult/child/tent Dkr60/25/35) Beachside camping east of the hostel.

Danhostel Helsingør (☎ 49 21 16 40; www.helsingor hostel.dk; Nordre Strandvej 24; dm/r Dkr110/450; ☷ Feb-Nov; Ⓟ). The hostel is 2km northwest of the centre and right on the Øresund beach.

The tourist office books rooms in private homes for Dkr200 to Dkr300 for singles, and Dkr400 for doubles, plus a Dkr25 booking fee.

Hotel Hamlet (☎ 49 21 05 91; fax 49 26 01 30; Bramstræde 5; s/d Dkr685/895) Hamlet has charming, cosy, old-fashioned rooms with lots of stripped pine panelling and green leather upholstery.

Hotel Skandia (☎ 49 21 09 02; www.hotel-skandia .dk; Bramstræde 1; s/d Dkr395/495, s/d with private bathroom Dkr550/650; Ⓟ ⌧) Just down the road, Skandia is basic but comfortable with bright, airy rooms.

EATING
Café Kringlen (Hovedvagtsstræde 2; ☷ 7am-6pm Mon-Fri, 7am-5pm Sat & Sun) It might look unassuming but Café Kringlen is the place to go for a light breakfast or snack. The pastries are mouthwateringly good and it serves bottomless cups of coffee.

Thai Cuisine (☎ 49 25 15 11; Torvegade 5; mains Dkr85-95) A moderately priced eatery on Axeltorv square, four blocks northwest of the train station. The square is otherwise a good, leafy place for outside dining and drinking.

Slagter Baagø (☎ 49 21 11 84; Bjergegade 3) An excellent *smørrebrød* outlet where you can get a mixed lunch plate of fish and meat for Dkr95.

China Box (Stengade 28; ☷ noon-9pm Mon-Sat, 2-9pm Sun) Food box takeaways for Dkr28.

Pakhus Pizzeria (☎ 49 21 10 50; Stengade 26C; pizza & pasta Dkr49-60) Pakhus, set back from the street in an attractive courtyard, serves decent Italian fare.

Madam Sprunck (☎ 49 26 48 49; Stengade 48; mains Dkr145-205; ☷ 11.30am-midnight) This Helsingør institution is in a charming courtyard. As well as evening meals in its restaurant, it does a lavish brunch (Dkr88 to Dkr115), salads (Dkr65) and sandwiches, pizzas and burgers (Dkr40 to Dkr85). The food is fresh and home-made.

Restaurant Sundkroen (☎ 49 21 37 36; Stationspladsen 3; 3-course menu Dkr176; ☷ 11am-9pm Mon-Sat, 11am-7pm Sun) The restaurant is in the old train station and has a good lunch menu.

GETTING THERE & AWAY
Trains from Hillerød (Dkr51, 30 minutes) run at least once hourly. Trains from Copenhagen run a few times hourly (Dkr59.50, 55 minutes). For information on ferries to Helsingborg (Dkr18, 20 minutes) see p467.

Zealand's North Coast
The north coast of Zealand has a scattering of small towns whose origins as fishing centres date from the 1500s. Along their back streets you'll find half-timbered, thatch-roofed houses and flower-filled gardens. The small winter populations are swollen from May to September by throngs of visitors and the beaches are crowded but enjoyable nonetheless.

Hornbæk has the best easily accessible beach on the north coast, a vast expanse of silky white sand that runs the entire length of the town. From the train station, it's a five-minute walk directly down Havnevej to the harbour and yacht marina. Climb the dunes to the left and you're on the beach. The library doubles as the **tourist office** (☎ 49 70 47 47; www.hornbaek.dk; Vester Stejlebakke 2A; ☷ 2-5pm Mon, Tue & Thu, 10am-5pm Wed & Fri, 10am-2pm Sat); when closed its window displays a useful map that shows the local accommodation.

Zealand's northernmost town, **Gilleleje**, has the island's largest fishing port. Around the harbour and yacht marina there's always something interesting to watch, while the thatched houses of the town add to its character. The **tourist office** (☎ 48 30 01 74; www.gilleleje.info; Hovedgade 6; ☷ 10am-6pm Mon-Sat mid-Jun–Aug, 10am-4pm Mon-Fri & 10am-3pm Sat Aug–mid-Jun) is in the centre. There are **beaches** either side of the town and others along the coast to the west, especially at Rågeleje and at Smidstrup Strand, where conditions are often good for **windsurfing**.

Tisvildeleje is a pleasant seaside village with a long, straggling main street that leads to an even longer beach. The **tourist office** (☎ 48 70 74 51; www.helsinge.com; Banevej 8; ☻ noon-5pm Mon-Fri, 10am-3pm Sat mid-Jun–Aug) is in the train station. Behind the beach is **Tisvilde Hegn**, a windswept forest of twisted trees and heather-covered hills laced with good paths.

SLEEPING & EATING

Camping Hornbæk (☎ 49 70 02 23; www.camping -hornbaek.dk, Danish only; Planetvej 4; adult/child/tent Dkr62/31/20) This very presentable camping ground is in a pleasant-enough spot behind a small plantation, although it's set a fair way back from the beach

Hotel Villa Strand (☎ 49700088; www.villastrand.dk; Kystvej 2; s/d from Dkr850/1150; P ☐) Villa Strand is a pleasant, quiet place to the west of Hornbæk centre and close to the beach. There are cheaper doubles in garden bungalows and plusher rooms with balconies in the main building.

You can get cheap food at the bars and fast-food places at the harbourside and at the western end of Øresundsvej, the road that runs parallel to the beach.

Bella Italia (Nordre Strandvej; pizzas Dkr30) On the main road.

Fiskehuset (☎ 49 70 04 37; ☻ 9.30-5pm) Sit out in the appealing outdoor seating area by the harbour where you can devour its excellent fishcake and chips (around Dkr50) or buy fresh fish.

Camping Rågeleje (☎ 48 71 56 40; www.camping -raageleje.dk, Danish only; Heatherhill, Hostrupvej 2; adult/ child/tent Dkr62/31/20) This camping ground is at Rågeleje, about 10km southwest of Gilleleje, on a sweeping stretch of coast.

The tourist office in Gilleleje books rooms in private homes at around Dkr275/350 for singles/doubles, plus a Dkr25 booking fee.

Hotel Strand (☎ 48 30 05 12; http://hotel-strand.dht .dk; Vesterbrogade 4; s/d Dkr510/760; P ✗) Gilleleje's Strand is a small hotel with reasonable rooms, although some singles are rather small. It's just west of the harbour.

Hos Karen & Marie (☎ 48 30 21 30; Nordre Havnevej 3; fish & meat mains Dkr130-170) Gilleleje has several dockside smokehouses where you can buy cheap takeaway fish, but for a real treat try this charming place where you can get deliciously prepared hake and trout dishes among others. A terrific lunch platter of fish and meat costs Dkr149.

Danhostel Tisvildeleje (☎ 48 70 98 50; www.helene .dk, Danish only; Bygmarken 30; dm/s/d Dkr118/425/445; P ☐) In Tisvildeleje, this modern 272-bed hostel is a 10-minute walk from the beach. The most appealing rooms are in the small huts, well spaced out on the grounds.

GETTING THERE & AWAY

Trains from Hillerød run to Gilleleje and to Tisvildeleje (Dkr42.50), but there's no rail link between the two. Trains from Helsingør go to Hornbæk (Dkr25.50, 25 minutes) and on to Gilleleje (Dkr51, 40 minutes) twice an hour Monday to Friday and once hourly at weekends. There are also buses, which cost the same but take a little longer; from Helsingør Station, bus No 340 runs to Hornbæk and Gilleleje. Bus No 363 runs between Gilleleje and Tisvildeleje (Dkr23, one hour, every two hours).

ROSKILDE

pop 52,000

Well worth a day trip, Roskilde is replete with history. Yet, apart from its magnificent cathedral, there is little visible excitement left in the town centre's modern buildings to recall a remarkable medieval heritage. Roskilde was Denmark's original capital and was a thriving trading port throughout the Middle Ages. It was also the site of Zealand's first Christian church, built by Viking king Harald Bluetooth in AD 980. As Roskilde was the centre of Danish Catholicism, it suffered some decline after the Reformation, and its population shrank. Its quietude today is disturbed only during the annual summer Roskilde music festival. The town is also one of the best places in the country to get a feel for Denmark's Viking heritage, which is available at the excellent Viking Ship Museum.

Information

Netcenter (Grønnegade 2; per 15min Dkr8) Internet access.
Tourist Office (☎ 46 31 65 65; www.visitroskilde.com; Gullandsstræde 15; ☻ 9am-5pm Mon-Fri, 10am-1pm Sat Apr-Jun, 9am-6pm Mon-Fri, 10am-2pm Sat Jul-Aug, 9am-5pm Mon-Thu, 9am-4pm Fri, 10am-1pm Sat Sep-Mar) Helpful staff.

Sights
ROSKILDE DOMKIRKE

Though most of Roskilde's medieval buildings have vanished in fires over the centuries,

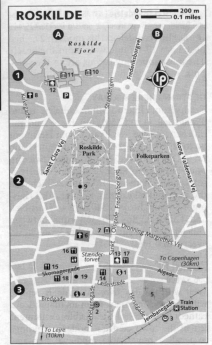

ROSKILDE

0 ————— 200 m
0 ————— 0.1 miles

the imposing **cathedral** (☎ 46 35 27 00; Domkirke-pladsen; adult/child Dkr25/15; ☼ 9am-4.45pm Mon-Sat, 12.30-4.45pm Sun Apr-Sep, 9am-4pm Mon-Fri, 10am-1pm Sat Aug–mid-Jun) still dominates the city centre. Started by Bishop Absalon in 1170, Roskilde Domkirke has been rebuilt and added to so many times that this mighty brick edifice represents a millennium of Danish church architectural styles. It's protected under Unesco's World Heritage List.

The cathedral has tall spiky **spires**, eye-catching in their disproportionate slender-ness compared with the solidity of the rest of the building. The cathedral interior is splendid; its **crypts** contain the sarcophagi of 39 Danish kings and queens. Some are lavishly embellished and guarded by marble statues of knights and women in mourning. Others are simple and unadorned. There's something awesome about being able to stand so close to the remains of so many of Scandinavia's powerful historical figures. For light relief, take a look at the 15th-century **clock** above the entrance, where a tiny St George on horseback marks the hour by slaying a yelping dragon (a pair of bel-lows and three out-of-tune organ pipes cre-ate its yelp).

OTHER ATTRACTIONS
From the northern side of the cathedral, walk across a field where wildflowers blanket the unexcavated remains of Roskilde's original medieval town, continue through a green belt all the way to the **Viking Ship Museum** (☎ 46 30 02 00; Vindeboder 12; adult/child Dkr60/35, low season Dkr45/28; ☼ 10am-5pm 1 May-30 Sep, 10am-4pm 1 Oct-30 Apr).

This well-presented museum contains five reconstructed Viking ships (c 1000), excavated from Roskilde Fjord in 1962 and brought to shore in thousands of fragments. It's worth lingering at the excellent audiovis-ual displays that show the skill and arduous labour that went into building these ships.

Perhaps the best part of the visit though, is the **waterfront workshops**, a short walk west along the harbour, where Viking ship replicas are being built using Viking-era techniques. One of them, the *Skulderev 2*, is a replica of a ship built in 1042 and will be sailed to old Viking stamping and pillaging grounds in Ireland sometime around 2007.

Further west is the **Sankt Jørgensbjerg quar-ter**, where the cobbled Kirkegade walkway leads through a neighbourhood of old straw-roofed houses into the courtyard of the 11th-century **Sankt Jørgensbjerg Kirke**.

Roskilde Museum (☎ 46 36 60 44; Sankt Olsgade 15; adult/child Dkr25/free; ☼ 11am-4pm) has displays on Roskilde's rich history.

Roskilde Festival

The **Roskilde Festival** (www.roskilde-festival.dk), Northern Europe's largest music festival, rocks Roskilde each summer on a weekend in late June/early July. It draws vast numbers of festival-goers and some of the best headline acts in the world.

A special reception stall is set up in Copenhagen's main station a week before the event and Roskilde's genteel centre is filled with alternative fashion and backpacking youth for days. The festival site is on the outskirts of town. There are half a dozen main stages featuring about 150 bands and performers. Past stars include Bob Dylan, U2, Radiohead, Robbie Williams, Beastie Boys, Suede and the Chemical Brothers. The festival is also a showcase for up-and-coming talent and new trends. Camping is free, but tightly packed, and there are subsidiary happenings and events.

There is a shuttle train service to the festival site from Roskilde Station and a shuttle bus from the bus station. Roskilde Festival 2005 is scheduled for 30 June–3 July and 2006 is set for 29 June–2 July.

Sleeping & Eating

The tourist office books rooms in private homes for Dkr175/350 for singles/doubles, plus a Dkr25 booking fee.

Danhostel Roskilde (☎ 46 35 21 84; www.rova.dk; Danish only; Vindeboder 7; dm/r Dkr115/400; P) This harbourside hostel is especially smart and modern, even by Danish hostel standards, with small five- or six-bed dorms. It's adjacent to the Viking Ship Museum.

Hotel Prindsen (☎ 46 30 91 00; www.prindsen.dk; Algade 13; s/d Dkr1175/1325; P ✗) A plush central hotel boasting past guests such as HC Andersen, the Prindsen has mostly bright, attractive rooms. Its restaurant offers a brunch buffet for Dkr118. There are less expensive light bites such as crab cakes (Dkr78) or more substantial mains such as venison in bacon and cranberry salsa (Dkr175).

Restaurant Bryggergården (☎ 46 35 01 03; Algade 15; menu Dkr188-208) This restaurant offers a good selection of smørrebrød for Dkr40 to Dkr68.

Raadhus-Kælderen (☎ 46 36 01 00; Stændertorvet; 2-/3-course dinner Dkr218/238) For a treat, the atmospheric Raadhus-Kælderen serves Danish- and French-inspired cuisine in the old town hall (c 1430). It offers a two-course fish lunch

(Dkr158) and good smørrebrød and brunch (Dkr98).

Strandberg Supermarket (Skomagergade; ☑ 9.30am-7pm Mon-Fri, 9am-3pm Sat) has a rooftop cafeteria with a daily lunch dish (Dkr45) and sandwiches, including vegetarian options (Dkr35). **Jensen's Bøfhus** (Skomagergade) serves inexpensive steak lunches, and **Den Gamle Bagergaarde** (Algade 6) is a bakery with good pastries and sandwiches.

Getting There & Around

Trains from Copenhagen to Roskilde are frequent (Dkr59.50, 25 minutes). From Copenhagen by car, Rte 21 leads to Roskilde; upon approaching the city, exit onto Rte 156, which leads into the centre.

Parking discs are required in Roskilde. There are car parks off Læderstræde, just south of Aldgade, Roskilde Museum and near the Viking Ship Museum.

A bicycle rental shop **Jas Cykler** (☎ 46 35 04 20; Gullandsstræde 3; per day Dkr50), just off Skomagergade, rents out distinctive yellow bikes.

KØGE

pop 33,500

The one-time medieval trading centre of Køge, 42km south of Copenhagen, retains an engaging core of historic buildings that line the narrow streets leading off the broad and busy main square, Torvet.

The **tourist office** (☎ 56 67 60 01; www.koegeturist .dk/uk; Vestergade 1; ☑ 9am-5pm Mon-Fri, 9am-2pm Sat) is just off the square. **Pc-Junglen** (Nørregade 22E; per hr Dkr25), in an arcade opposite Sankt Nicolai Kirke, offers Internet access.

You can park in Torvet, but for one hour only during the day, and there are longer-term car parks near the train station. Time discs are required.

A short stroll around the central part of Køge is very rewarding. The tourist office's free magazine describes a route that takes in 30 of the town's finest buildings. You will find Denmark's oldest **half-timbered building** (c 1527) at Kirkestræde 20, a marvellous survivor with a fine raked roof. Køge's **historical museum** (☎ 56 63 42 42; Nørregade 4; admission Dkr20; ☑ 11am-5pm Tue-Sun Jun-Aug, 1-5pm Mon-Fri, 11am-3pm Sat, 1-5pm Sun Sep-May) is in a splendid building that dates from 1619. Another gem is **Brogade 23**, decorated with cherubs carved by the famed 17th-century artist Abel Schrøder.

Sleeping

Danhostel Køge (☎ 56 67 66 50; www.danhostel
.dk/koege; Vamdrupvej 1; dm/r Dkr100/400; ☺ Mar-Nov;
Ⓟ ☐) The hostel is 2km northwest of the
centre.

The tourist office can book double rooms
in private homes from Dkr450 plus a Dkr25
booking fee.

Centralhotellet (☎ 56 65 06 96; fax 56 66 02 07;
Vestergade 3; s/d with shared bathroom Dkr290/530, d with
private bathroom Dkr630; Ⓟ) This busy hotel is
right on the edge of Torvet and has passable
rooms. It's advised to book ahead.

Hotel Niels Juel (☎ 56 63 18 00; www.hotelnielsjuel
.dk; Toldbodvej 20; s/d Dkr995/1195, 2-bed family rooms
Dkr875 late Jun-Aug and weekends; Ⓟ ☒ ☐) On a
dockside road, this Best Western hotel has
summer discounts for its typical business-
bland, but comfy, rooms.

Eating & Drinking

Guld Bageren (northern side of Torvet; sandwiches Dkr33)
Does hearty baguette sandwiches, delicious
cakes and pastries, and large coffees.

StigAnn (☎ 56 63 03 30; Sankt Gertruds Stræd 2;
dinner mains Dkr175-230, 3-course menu Dkr315) An
outstanding restaurant, StigAnn serves up
lunches of salmon, lobster or duck (Dkr70)
and fish mains, including halibut (Dkr195).
Dinner mains include such delights as chateaubriand and fried fillet of sole with summer herbs and potato pancake.

Hugos Vinkjælder (Brogade 19) Køge has a number of pleasant bars, but one of the best is
this atmospheric place tucked away off Brogade in the little courtyard of Hugos Gård.
It has an eclectic selection of over 70 bottled
beers including brews from Eastern Europe
to Scotland. There's summer jazz in the
courtyard on Tuesdays.

Entertainment

Ritz Rock Cafe (Torvet 22; ☺ to 7am) For late night–
early morning action, Ritz Rock caters for all
tastes in three different dance venues.

Getting There & Away

Køge's train and bus stations are at Jernbanegade 12 on the east side of town. The train
station is at the southernmost point of greater
Copenhagen's S-train network, at the end of
the E line. Trains to Copenhagen run at least
three times an hour (Dkr59.50, 38 minutes).
The bus to Copenhagen (Dkr59.50, one hour)
leaves from outside the train station.

Bornholmstrafikken (☎ 33 13 18 66) operates
the service from the town of Køge just south
of Copenhagen to Bornholm. The overnight
ferry departs daily just before midnight and
arrives at 6.30am. There are a couple of daytime sailings during the week as well, but
these are far more sporadic.

TRELLEBORG

Trelleborg (☎ 58 54 95 06; Trelleborg Allé; adult/child
Dkr45/30; ☺ 10am-5pm Easter-Oct, 1-3pm Nov-Easter), in
the countryside of southern Zealand, is the
best preserved of Denmark's four Viking
ring fortresses.

The earthen-walled fortress, dating from
980, is divided into four symmetrical quad-
rants. In Viking times, each quadrant contained four long elliptical buildings of wood
that surrounded a courtyard. Each of the
16 buildings, which served as barracks, was
exactly 100 Roman feet long (29.5m). You can
walk up onto the grassy circular rampart and
readily grasp the geometric design of the
fortress. Cement blocks have been placed
to show the outlines of the house foundations. Plaques point out burial mounds and
other features. It is a fascinating place, but
the understandable absence of even vestigial
wooden ruins creates a sense of anticlimax
overall.

Nearby, a replica longhouse built in stave
style (now known to be an inaccurate design)
adds a romantic sheen. There is a museum,
and a separate area is given over to more
reconstructions of typical Viking-period
buildings. A few costumed interpreters demonstrate old trades and, for a small fee, you
can try your hand at baking bread or archery.
Spear throwing is free. The museum and office building closes at 5pm, but you can still
wander about the grounds in the evening.

Trelleborg is 7km west of Slagelse. To get
there, take the train to Slagelse (Dkr58, 33
minutes from Roskilde) and then either catch
the hourly bus No 312 to Trelleborg (Dkr14,
12 minutes), take a taxi, or rent a bicycle from
a shop near the Slagelse tourist office.

SOUTH ISLANDS

The three main islands south of Zealand –
Møn, Falster and Lolland – are all reached
from the mainland, and from each other,
by various bridges. Møn is celebrated for its
spectacular and totally un-Danish sea cliffs
of bone-white chalk, Falster has fine sandy

beaches, and Lolland, the largest and least interesting island, has a handful of scattered sights including a drive-through safari park.

Møn

It's worth spending some time on Møn, provided you're not looking for too much nightlife. Pleasant beaches lie at the end of narrow lanes, the island's medieval churches have remarkable frescoes, and there are numerous prehistoric remains, including a couple of impressive passage graves. The main attractions are the white cliffs and the woods of Møns Klint on the east coast.

One downside is that the island's bus service is sketchy, and to get the best out of Møn, having your own transport is a help.

Stege, the main settlement on Møn, is an everyday place, but it is enlivened by its role as the island's gateway town and main commercial centre. **Møn tourist office** (☎ 55 86 04 00; www.moen-touristbureau.dk; Storegade 2; ⌚ 9.30am-5pm Mon-Fri, 9am-6pm Sat mid-Jun–Aug, 9.30am-4.30pm Mon-Fri, 9am-noon Sat Sep–mid-Jun) is at the entrance to Stege and has good information on the entire island.

Stege Kirke (Provstesstræde; admission free; ⌚ 9am-5pm Tue-Sun) has unique medieval frescoes and a pulpit carved with entertaining visual interpretations of biblical scenes.

MØNS KLINT

The chalk cliffs at Møns Klint were created during the last Ice Age when the calcareous deposits from aeons of compressed seashells were lifted from the ocean floor. The gleaming white cliffs rise sharply for 128m above an azure sea, presenting one of the most striking landscapes in Denmark. The cliffs are being constantly eroded. Black seams of flintstone and chert ripple across the face of the chalk like blackened teeth, and their broken fragments remain, after landfalls, as sea-washed pebbles on the narrow beach at the base of the cliffs. The chalk subsoil of the land above the cliffs supports a terrific variety of wildflowers including vivid orchids. There is a strict embargo on picking wildflowers.

Møns Klint is a very popular tourist destination and the wooded arrival point above the cliffs has a busy cafeteria, souvenir shops and picnic grounds. But none of this detracts from the natural appeal of the cliffs themselves or the lovely woodland above them. Parking costs Dkr25. Take care of your ticket;

you need to expose it to a scanner at the exit barrier.

The woods of Klinteskoven, behind the cliffs, have a network of paths and tracks. From near the cafeteria you can descend the cliffs by a series of wooden stairways. It's quite a long descent and a strenuous return up the 500-odd stairs. From the base of the steps, turn south along the narrow beach which leads in about 1km to another stairway at Gråryg Fald. These take you steeply to the top of the cliff, from where a path leads back to the car park. If you turn north at the base of the descent stairway, in just over 1km you'll reach another stairway at Sandskredsfald that again takes you back to the top. In winter, and after heavy rain, unstable lumps of chalk may break off and fall to the beach and you should keep this in mind. Warning notices and barriers should be heeded.

PASSAGE GRAVES

Møn has a wealth of prehistoric remains, although many are vestigial burial mounds. The best preserved sites are the late-Stone-Age passage graves of **Kong Asgers Høj** and **Klek-kende Høj**. Both are on the west side of the island within a 2km radius of the village of Røddinge, from where they are signposted. Kong Asgers Høj is close to the narrow road and parking space is minimal. The site is extremely well preserved and comprises a grassy mound pierced by a low passageway that leads to a splendid stone-lined chamber. Take a torch and mind your head. Klekkende Høj is on a hill top amid fields. From a car park, follow a signposted track to reach the site. The grave has a double chamber and again you need a torch and some agility to creep inside. One of the routes described in the cycle tour printout (see p54) takes in these sites and others.

CHURCHES OF MØN

The churches of Møn are tall, gaunt buildings that punctuate the landscape with their striking, yet somehow inelegant, crow-stepped towers. Most of the buildings are medieval and many are graced with the best-preserved primitive frescoes in Denmark. The frescoes depict biblical scenes, often interpreted through lighthearted rustic imagery. These frescoes were obliterated with whitewash by post-Reformation Lutherans fearful of what they saw as too much Roman exuberance.

Ironically, the whitewash dealt a blow to bigotry by preserving the frescoes, and 20th-century restoration has revealed them in all their glory. The style of Møn fresco painting owes much to the Emelundemestteren (the Elmelunde Master), an accomplished stylist of unknown name. Some of his finest work can be seen at **Elmelunde Kirke** (Kirkebakken 41; admission free; ⊙7am-5pm Apr-Sep, 8am-4pm Oct-May) on the road to Møns Klint.

CYCLING

Although testing at times, cycling on Møn is rewarding given the island's uncharacteristic hilliness. The tourist office (see p53) has a route map and an excellent printout guide, in English, to seven bike tours on the island. All have special themes, including bird life and prehistory. One of the tours even takes in the nearby island of Bogø.

SLEEPING & EATING

Camping Møns Klint (☎ 55 81 20 25; camping@klint holm.dk; adult/child/tent Dkr60/35/10; ⊙Apr-Nov) About 3km from the cliffs, the camping ground is in a pleasant woodland setting.

Danhostel Møns Klint (☎ 55 81 20 30; www.dan hostel.dk/moen; dm/d/tr/q Dkr105/300/390/420; ⊙May-mid-Sep; P ⊠) The hostel occupies an enchanting lakeside spot opposite the camping ground.

Pension Elmehøj (☎ 55 81 35 35; www.elmehoj.dk; Kirkebakken 39; s/d Dkr340/470) Right next to Elmelunde Kirke, this guesthouse is pleasant, simple rooms and is an ideal base for exploring Møn. There is a summer café here where you can buy packed lunches for Dkr45 and an evening meal for Dkr120. There are also bikes for rent at Dkr45 per day.

At Møns Klint car park, the cafeteria does a range of meals including fish and chips. In Stege, there are bakeries and supermarkets and a handful of cafés.

Stig's Slagterforretning (☎ 55 81 42 67; Storegade 59; buffet Dkr59, fish & meat portions Dkr25-35) For terrific *smørrebrød*, an excellent buffet and mouth-watering grilled meats try this superb delicum-restaurant. It's a good place to come and stock up for a gourmet picnic too.

GETTING THERE & AROUND

From Copenhagen take the train to Vordingborg (Dkr92, 1½ hours); from here it's a 45-minute ride to Stege on bus No 52 (Dkr36). From late June to mid-August, buses make the 45-minute run (Dkr13) from Stege to Møns Klint a few times a day. The bus stops at the hostel and camping ground en route. During the rest of the year bus No 52 stops within about 3km of Mons Klint, get off at the Busene stop and hike in from there.

Falster

The east coast of Falster is lined with white sandy beaches that attract huge numbers of German and Danish holiday-makers, many of whom own tree-shrouded cabins along the wooded coastline.

The most glorious stretch of beach is at **Marielyst**, which is 12km from the island's main settlement of Nykøbing Falster. The beach draws crowds in summer, but it's so long that you can always achieve some sense of escape. You reach the sea down various lanes that slice through the tree line. Parking is not always easy. The most convenient access and parking is straight on from the junction of the resort's main street, Marielyst Strandvej, with the north–south road, Bøtøvej. There is parking down seaward access lanes at roughly every kilometre as you head south along Bøtøvej from the crossroads.

The **tourist office** (☎ 54 13 62 98; www.marielyst .org; Marielyst Strandpark 3; ⊙9am-5pm Mon-Sat mid-Jun–Aug, 9am-4pm Mon-Fri, 10am-2pm Sat Sep–mid-Jun) is in a modern complex on the western entrance to the resort as you come in from the E55. Go left at the big roundabout.

SLEEPING

Marielyst Camping (☎ 54 13 53 07; Marielyst Strandvej 36; adult/child/tent Dkr63/31/15) This central camping ground has a long season and is popular with young families.

Danhostel Nykøbing F (☎ 54 85 66 99; www.danhos tel.dk/nykoebingfalster; Østre Allé 110; dm Dkr110, s/d Dkr472) The nearest hostel to Marielyst is just 1km east of Nykøbing, Falster's train station.

Hotel Marielyst Strand (☎ 54 13 68 88; Torvet; s/d Dkr735/898) In Marielyst itself, the Strand is a pleasant, central place with smart rooms.

GETTING THERE & AROUND

Trains leave Copenhagen hourly for Nykøbing F (Dkr118, two hours), from where it's a Dkr24 bus ride to Marielyst (25 minutes), or Gedser (35 minutes) further south. From Gedser there are frequent **Scandlines ferries** (☎ 33 15 15 15) to Rostock, Germany. The trip takes two hours and costs Dkr35 per person. It's Dkr470 for a car with up to five people weekdays and a rather steep Dkr635 at weekends.

You can rent bikes – useful in Marielyst – next door to the tourist office at **Sydsol** (☎ 54 16 16 16; per day Dkr40).

Lolland

Lolland sounds thoroughly laid-back by name alone and the island's landscape is flat and repetitive – the highest point is only 30m. But this is very Danish Denmark, there is a pleasant sense of escape from the mainstream and there are a handful of diverting sights.

The main town of **Maribo** has an engaging charm, not least because of its lakeside setting. Maribo's **tourist office** (☎ 54 78 04 96; www.turistlol land.dk in Danish; Torvet; ☒ 10am-5pm Mon-Fri, 10am-1pm Sat) is on the attractive main square and has masses of information. The town stands amid a scattering of lakes, and its handsome, 15th-century, red-brick **Domkirken** overlooks the gleaming waters of the Søndersø. There are pleasant lakeside **walks** and Maribo has a number of interesting **museums**.

Maribo Sø Camping (☎ 54 78 00 71; www.maribo -camping.dk; Bangshavevej 25; adult/child/tent Dkr62/31/5) is in a pretty lakeside setting. **Danhostel Maribo** (☎ 54 78 33 14; www.danhostel.dk/maribo; Søndre Boule-varde 82; dm/r Dkr95/285; ☒ May late Dec; P) is about 2km southeast of Torvet. The tourist office can book rooms for Dkr200/350 (singles/doubles). The pleasant **Ebsens Hotel** (☎ 54 78 10 44; www.ebsens-hotel.dk; Vestergade 32; s/d Dkr350/550, s/d with private bathroom Dkr550/750; P) has some strikingly decorated larger rooms.

Vestergade, the main street running west from Torvet, has several cafés. A good bet is **Café Maribo** (Vestergade 6; mains Dkr65-110) with *smørrebørd* for Dkr20 to Dkr30 and sand-wiches for Dkr38.

Trains run between Nykøbing F to Maribo (Dkr41, 25 minutes) and on to Nakskov (Dkr65, 47 minutes) every hour Monday to Friday, and less at weekends.

BORNHOLM

pop 44,000
Life is satisfyingly slow-paced, but never dull on Bornholm. This is no day-trip island, but a remarkable self-contained little world, stuck

in the middle of the Baltic 200km east of Copenhagen and nearer to Sweden, Germany and Poland.

The centre of the island is a lush swathe of wheat fields and extensive forests. The coast is beaded with small fishing villages and stretches of powdery white sand. It is low-lying and accessible for most of its length, except in the northwest, where granite cliffs and reef-lined shores create a striking contrast.

Unique among Bornholm's attractions are its four 12th-century round churches, splendid buildings whose whitewashed walls, 2m-thick, are framed by solid buttresses and crowned with black, conical roofs. Each was designed as both a place of worship and a fortress against enemy attacks, with a gun-slot pierced upper storey. All four churches are still used for Sunday services, but are otherwise open to visitors.

HISTORY

Bornholm's history reflects its position at the heart of the Baltic, and in its time Sweden, Germany and Soviet Russia have occupied it. A Danish possession since the middle ages, the island fell into Swedish hands in the 17th century, but was won back for Denmark by a fierce local rebellion.

The island suffered cruelly in the chaos at the end of WWII. It was occupied by the Nazis, but when Germany surrendered to the Allies in May 1945 the German commander on Bornholm resisted and Rønne and Nexø suffered heavy damage from Soviet air raids. On 9 May the island was handed over to the Soviets who remained *in situ* until the following year, when Bornholm was returned to Denmark.

GETTING THERE & AWAY

Bornholmstrafikken (☎ 33 13 18 66; www.bornholms trafikken.dk) operates ferries between Køge and Rønne. While not as fast as the boat/train option, the overnight sailing (departing daily at midnight and arriving at 6.30am) on the car ferry from Køge is worth considering. The bunk-style berths (Dkr76 extra one way) and cabins (from extra Dkr186 one way) are reasonably inexpensive and it's a good use of time as you travel while you sleep. The downside is the schlepp out to Køge, about 30 minutes by train south of Copenhagen. A peak return per person costs Dkr325. A car with up to five people costs Dkr1,280.

DENMARK

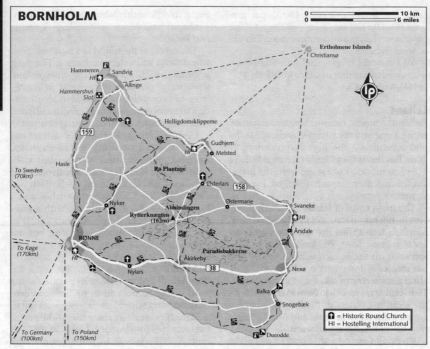

BORNHOLM

0 — 10 km
0 — 6 miles

Ertholmene Islands
Christiansø

Hammeren
Sandvig
HI
Allinge

Hammershus
Slot

Olsker

159

Helligdomsklipperne

Gudhjem
HI
Melsted

To Sweden
(70km)

Hasle

Rø Plantage

Østerlars

158

Nyker

Almindingen
Rytterknægten
(162m)

Østermarie

Svaneke
HI

Årsdale

RØNNE

To Køge
(170km)

HI

Paradisbakkerne

Åkirkeby

38

Nexø

Nylars

Balka

Snogebæk

To Germany
(100km)

To Poland
(150km)

Dueodde

= Historic Round Church
HI = Hostelling International

Bornholmstrafikken also operates the ferry service that runs several times daily between Rønne and Ystad, Sweden (Dkr144 one way or same-day return, 1½ or 2½ hours). On a near-daily basis from April to October, Scandlines sails from Sassnitz-Mukran in Germany (Dkr135, 3½ hours).

A quicker option is the train-ferry combination from Copenhagen to Rønne via Ystad, Sweden with **DSB** (☎ 70 13 14 15; www.dsn.dk in Danish). This trip goes a few times a day, takes three hours and costs Dkr230. It's also possible to drive to Ystad and cross with a car from there.

The quickest option of all is the 35-minute flight with **Cimber Air** (☎ 74 42 22 77; www.cimber .dk; one-way Dkr1010), with several flights a day between Copenhagen and Bornholm. Book ahead for cheaper prices.

GETTING AROUND
To/From the Airport
The island's airport, Bornholms Lufthavn, is 5km southeast of Rønne, on the road to Dueodde. Bus No 7 stops on the main road in front of the airport.

Bicycle
Cycling is a great way to get around. Bornholm is crisscrossed by more than 200km of bike trails, many built over former rail routes. You can start right in Rønne, from where bike routes fan out to Allinge, Gudhjem, Nexø, Dueodde and the central forest. Rønne tourist office sells the 60-page English-language *Bicycle Routes on Bornholm* (Dkr45), which maps out routes and describes sights along the way.

In Rønne, **Bornholms Cykeludlejning** (☎ 56 95 13 59; Nordre Kystvej 5), next to the tourist office, has a large fleet of bikes for hire for Dkr60/240 a day/week. Bicycles can usually be rented from hostels and camping grounds around the island for about Dkr55 a day.

Bus
A good, inexpensive bus service around the island is operated by Bornholms Amts Trafikselskab (BAT). Fares are based on a zone system and cost Dkr10 per zone; the maximum fare is for 10 zones. Ask the bus driver about a 'RaBATkort' (10 rides), which can be used by more than one person and

saves about 20%. Day/week passes are Dkr130/440. Buses operate all year, but schedules are less frequent from October to April. From May to September, bus No 7 leaves from the Rønne ferry terminal every two hours between 8am and 4pm and goes anticlockwise around the island, stopping at Dueodde beach and major coastal villages before terminating at Hammershus. There are more evening buses in the peak season from late June to the end of August. Other buses make direct runs from Rønne to Nexø, Svaneke, Gudhjem and Sandvig.

Car & Scooter

Motor scooters/open-topped mini scoot cars/ cars can be rented from Dkr245/385/620 a day at **Europcar** (☎ 56 95 43 00, Nordre Kystvej 1, Rønne). The office is in the petrol station just along the road from the ferry terminal. **Avis** (☎ 56 95 22 08), further into town, offers similar rates.

RØNNE

pop 15,000

Rønne is a charming little town with a number of engaging museums and an old quarter of cobbled streets flanked by pretty single-storey dwellings. It is the island's largest settlement and is a popular shopping destination for Swedes on day trips.

The **tourist office** (Bornholms Velkomstcenter; ☎ 56 95 95 00; www.bornholm.info; Nordre Kystvej 3; ☉ 9am-5pm Mon-Sat, 10am-3pm Sun late Jun–Aug, 9am-4pm Mon-Fri, 10am-1pm Sat Mar-May, Sep & Oct, 9am-4pm Mon-Fri Nov-Feb) is a few minutes' walk from the harbour and has masses of information on all of Bornholm. There's free Internet access at the **public library** (Pingels Allé; ☉ 10am-7pm Mon-Fri, 10am-2pm Sat).

Two very pleasant streets with period buildings are the cobblestoned **Laksegade** and **Storegade**.

Bornholms Museum (☎ 56 95 07 35; Sankt Mortensgade 29; adult/child Dkr35/10; ☉ 10am-5pm Mon-Fri, 10am-2pm Sat) has a surprisingly large collection of local history exhibits including many prehistoric finds and a good maritime section decked out like the interior of a ship. **Hjorths Fabrik** (☎ 56 95 01 60; Krystalgade 5; adult/ child Dkr30/10; ☉ 10am-5pm Mon-Sat) is a ceramics museum complete with working features.

The handsome round church, **Nylars Rundkirke**, built in 1150 and decorated with 13th-century frescoes, is surrounded by Viking rune stones. It's only a 15-minute ride from Rønne on bus No 6.

Galløkken Camping (☎ 56 95 23 20; www.gallokken .dk; Strandvej 4; adult/child Dkr56/28; ☉ mid-May–Aug) is just over 1km south of the town centre. It rents out bikes for Dkr55 to Dkr65 per day. The immaculately kept 140-bed **Danhostel Rønne** (☎ 56 95 13 40; www.danhostel-roenne.dk; Arsenalvej 12; dm/s/d Dkr115/300/400; P ✗) is nearby. The tourist office books rooms in private homes at Dkr200/290 for singles/doubles.

Sverre's Small Hotel (☎ 56 95 03 03; www.sverres -hotel.dk; Snellemark 2; s/d Dkr290/460) offers pleasant, basic, central accommodation near the ferry terminal.

Radisson SAS Fredensborg Hotel (☎ 56 95 44 44; www.bornholmhotels.dk; Strandvejen 116; s/d Dkr995/ 1195; ✗ ✗ 🖳) is plush and comfortable, perched on a quiet knoll overlooking wave-pounded rocks at the southern end of Rønne. It has 72 well-appointed rooms (all with sea views) and there's a sauna, pool and tennis court.

The Kvickly supermarket, which is opposite the tourist office, has a good bakery that opens at 6.30am, and a handy bistro that offers sandwiches (Dkr40 to Dkr50) and hearty hot meals (Dkr60 to Dkr70). You'll find numerous fast-food places on Store Torv, the central square, including cheap Thai food takeaways from PS Thai next to the post office.

Strøgets Spisehuz (☎ 56 95 81 69; Store Torvegade 39; mains lunch Dkr70-120, dinner Dkr122-160) specialises in excellent Danish meat and vegetable dishes. Locals vote **Casa Mia** (☎ 56 95 95 73; Antoniestræde 3; pizza Dkr66-72, pasta mains Dkr66-110) the best place for pizza and pasta in town. **O'Malley's** (☎ 56 95 00 16; Store Torvegade 2) caters for an older crowd with an over-21 age limit for its Friday and Saturday late-night discos.

DUEODDE

Dueodde has a vast stretch of white-sand beach backed by woodlands and dunes. The only 'sight' is the slender lighthouse, which you can climb for views of sea and strand that stretch to the horizon. There's no village, just a bus stop with a single hotel, a restaurant, a cluster of kiosks selling ice cream and hot dogs, and necessary public toilets to cope with the rush from tour coaches in summer. It can be a crowded trek for a couple of hundred metres along boardwalks to reach the superb beach. Once there, head left or right for wide-open spaces.

The beachside **Dueodde Vandrerhjem & Camp-ground** (☎ 56 48 81 19; info@dueodde.dk; adult/child/tent Dkr54/30/25; ☾ Apr-Oct) is a modern place a 10-minute walk east of the bus stop, or it can be reached by car from the main road. It also has cabins for rent at Dkr170/300 for one/two persons, rising to Dkr800 for eight. There's an indoor swimming pool.

BORNHOLM'S EAST COAST

Bornholm's east coast tends to be fairly built up and is punctuated by several settlements, all with some interest as stopping-off places.

Snogebæk is a small shoreside fishing village that hangs on to its authenticity because of its small fleet of working boats and its scattering of fishing huts and cabins.

Just north of Snogebæk is the fine beach of **Balka Strand**.

Nexø is Bornholm's second-largest town. It took a hammering from Soviet bombers in WWII and today much of what you see from the harbour outwards is a fairly functional reconstruction. **Nexø-Dueodde Turistinformation** (☎ 56 49 32 00; Åsen 4) is in the centre of town, two blocks inland from the harbour. **Nexø Museum** (☎ 56 49 25 56; Havnen 2; adult/child Dkr15/5; ☾ 10am-4pm Mon-Fri, 10am-2pm Sat mid-May–mid-Oct) is at the harbour and is packed with maritime flotsam and jetsam including an old-fashioned diving suit, cannons, WWII mines and the inner workings of a lighthouse.

The harbour town of Svaneke has award-winning historic buildings, especially those near the village church, a few minutes' walk south of the centre. The **tourist office** (☎ 56 49 70 79; Storegade 24; ☾ noon-4.30pm Mon-Fri) is in the post office building, two blocks north of the central square.

Sleeping & Eating

Svaneke Familie Camping (☎ 56 49 64 62; www .svaneke-camping.dk; Danish only; Møllebakken 8; adult/child/ tent Dkr51/25/15; ☾ mid-May–mid-Sep) A two-star camping ground 1km north of Svaneke.

Danhostel Svaneke (☎ 56 49 62 42; www.dan hostel-svaneke.dk; Danish only; Reberbanevej 9; dm/s/d Dkr115/400/450; ☾ Apr-Oct) Danhostel is 1km south of the centre of Svaneke.

Hotel Balka Strand (☎ 56 49 49 49; www.hotelbalka strand.dk; Boulevarden 9; s/d from Dkr645/725; ℗ ⊠ 🖳) A good base in the Snogebæk-Nexø area is this friendly, smart hotel about 200m from Balka Strand beach.

Down by Snogebæk's seafront along Hovedgade you'll find a cluster of shops selling glassware, organic ice cream, smoked fish and handmade chocolate.

A contender for best smokehouse on the island is **Rogeriet i Svaneke** (☎ 56 49 63 24; Fisk-ergade 12; counter items Dkr25-50, lunch/evening buffet Dkr82/92). There's excellent, moist, smoked fare including wonderful *smørrebrød* and tasty fish cakes (Dkr20) to consume inside with a view of the massive blackened doors of the smoking ovens or at the outdoor picnic tables. It's by the water at the end of Fiskergade, north of the town centre.

Bryghuset (☎ 56 49 73 21; Torv 5) This friendly place brews three excellent beers, ideal for washing down all that smoked fish. If you haven't already eaten, it also serves decent pub grub.

GUDHJEM
pop 1000

Gudhjem is a compact, attractive seaside village crowned by a squat windmill standing over half-timbered houses and sloping streets that roll down to the pleasant harbour front. It's a popular eating-out place. The harbour was one of the settings for the Oscar-winning film *Pelle the Conqueror*, based on the novel of Bornholm writer Martin Andersen Nexø. The **tourist office** (☎ 56 48 52 10; Åbogade 7; ☾ 10am-4pm Jul-Aug, 1-4pm Mon-Sat Sep & Mar-Jun) is a block inland from the harbour alongside the library. Gudhjem has narrow streets and parking can be difficult. There's a public car park northwest of the harbour.

Stroll the **footpath** running southeast from the harbour for a pleasant coastal view. Gudhjem's shoreline is rocky, though sunbathers will find a small sandy **beach** at Melsted, 1km east. A bike path leads inland 4km south from Gudhjem to the thick-walled, buttressed **Østerlars Rundkirke**, the most impressive of the island's round churches – bus No 3 goes by the church.

Sleeping & Eating

Danhostel Gudhjem (☎ 56 48 50 35; www.danhostel -gudhjem.dk; dm/s/d Dkr118/375/325) Just up from the harbourside bus stop, this hostel is in an attractive spot right by the harbour with small cosy, bright white six-bed dorms. The management can book singles/doubles in private homes for Dkr275/375 and also handles the pleasant **Therns Hotel** (☎ 56 48 50 35;

Brøddegade 31; s/d Dkr350/550, s/d with private bathroom Dkr500/800).

Jantzens Hotel (☎ 56 48 50 17; jantzenshotel@mail.dk; Brøddegade 33; s/d Dkr525/925) The central Jantzens Hotel is a fine old building that has been refurbished and has stylish rooms and a restaurant. Next door is **Restaurant Venezia** (☎ 56 48 53 53; Brøddegade 33; pizza Dkr53-75).

Andi's (☎ 56 48 50 84; Brøddegade 33; menus Dkr275-375) Just upstairs from Venezia, Andi's is the fine dining choice in town and one of the better places on the island serving especially good, delicately flavoured fish dishes.

Gudhjem Rogeri (☎ 56 48 57 08; buffet Dkr92) Further along is this waterfront smokehouse with an all-you-can-eat buffet and some challenging seating, including on the upper floor, which is reached by rope ladder. It has live folk, country and rock music most nights in summer.

You'll find a bakery and a few reasonably priced cafés along Brøddegade, a little inland from the harbour.

SANDVIG & ALLINGE

Sandvig is tucked away under Bornholm's rocky northwestern tip and boasts an excellent sandy beach to add to its distinctive appeal. Bornholm's best-known sight, **Hammershus Slot**, is 3km south on the road to Rønne. The impressive, substantial ruins of this 13th-century castle are the largest of their kind in Scandinavia. They are perched dramatically over the sea, flanked by cliffs and a deep valley. One of the best ways of reaching the castle is by following footpaths from Sandvig through the heather-covered hills of Hammeren – a wonderful hour-long hike. The trail begins by the camping ground. Sandvig has a mix of attractive old houses and several good eating places. Nearby Allinge has a couple of great historic hotels.

Sleeping & Eating

Sandvig Familie Camping (☎ 56 48 04 47; www.public camp.dk/sandvig; Sandlinien 5; adult/child/tent Dkr50/25/15) Occupies a great spot near the beach and is handy for tracks onto Hammeren.

Danhostel Sandvig (☎ 56 48 03 62; www.danhostel .dk/sandvig; Hammershusvej 94; dm/s/d Dkr115/275/400) Midway between Hammershus Slot and Sandvig.

Hotel-Pension Langebjerg (☎ 56 48 02 98; Lange-bjergvej 7; s/d Dkr365/680) A good bet out of the several pensions in the village.

Byskriviergarden (☎ 56 48 08 86; www.byskriver gaarden.dk, Danish & German only; Løsebækegade 3; s/d Dkr595/710; P) An enchanting, white-walled, black-beamed converted farmhouse right on the water in Allinge. The rooms are smartly, if sparsely decorated in contemporary style. Try to get the sea-facing ones. There's a pleasant garden and swimmable, kelp-filled rock pools around the corner if you fancy braving the water.

Ella's Konditori (☎ 56 48 03 29, Strandgade 42; light meals Dkr53-80) Ella's offers good home-made food inside a picturesque cottage or out in the pretty garden and a menu that includes fish and chips, grilled chicken and salads.

Café Værftet (☎ 56 48 04 34; Jernbanegade 3; mains Dkr85) Café Værftet is an unmissable place for good company and delicious Christiansø herring dishes (Dkr35) and meat mains (around Dkr85). It's in an old boathouse whose entire front wall, complete with windows and coverings, can be raised open at the touch of a button from behind the bar – an entertaining event, especially if you've had a few schnapps too many.

CHRISTIANSØ
pop 100

Charmingly preserved, tiny Christiansø (it's about 500m long) is a 17th century fortress-island an hour's sail northeast of Bornholm. It's well worth making time for a day trip. A seasonal fishing hamlet since the Middle Ages, Christiansø fell briefly into Swedish hands in 1658, after which Christian V decided to turn the island into an invincible naval fortress. Bastions and barracks were built; church, school and prison followed.

By the 1850s the island was no longer needed as a forward base against Sweden and the navy withdrew. Soldiers who wanted to stay on as fishermen were allowed to live as free tenants in the old cottages. Their offspring, and a few latter-day fisherfolk and artists, currently comprise Christiansø's 100 residents. The entire island is an unspoiled reserve – there are no cats or dogs, no cars and no modern buildings intrude – allowing the rich birdlife, including puffins, to prosper.

If the hectic pace of life on Christiansø is getting to you, try escaping to a smaller island, Frederiksø, by the footbridge.

There's a small **local history museum** in Frederiksø's tower and a great 360° view from Christiansø **lighthouse**. Otherwise the main activity is **walking** the footpaths along the fortified walls and batteries that skirt the island. There are skerries with nesting **sea birds** and a secluded **swimming cove** on Christiansø's eastern side.

In summer, **camping** is allowed in a small field at the Duchess Battery. **Christiansø Gæstgiveriet** (☎ 56 46 20 15; r Dkr800), the island's only inn, has a few rooms with shared bathroom (breakfast included) and a restaurant. Booking ahead for a room is advised. There's a small food store and a snack shop.

Christiansøfarten (☎ 56 48 51 76) sails daily to Christiansø from Gudhjem and Monday to Saturday from Allinge between mid-May and mid-September. The mailboat from Svaneke sails Monday to Friday year-round. All boats charge Dkr160/80 per adult/child for a return day trip. Dogs or other pets are forbidden on Christiansø.

FUNEN

pop 471,000

Funen (Fyn) is Denmark's garden island, largely rural in character, with rolling woodlands, picture-postcard pastures and cornfields peppered with old farmhouses and sleepy villages. The unspoilt islands of the South Funen archipelago, especially Langeland and Ærø, are delightful places to visit, as are the main island towns of Svendborg and Faaborg.

The railway line from Copenhagen runs straight through Odense, Funen's main city, and then westward onto Jutland. Store Bælt (Great Belt), the channel that separates Zealand and Funen, is spanned by Europe's longest combined road and rail bridge, the magnificent Storebælts-forbindelsen (Great Belt Fixed Link). It consists of a four-lane highway that is supported on two sleek suspension bridges connected via the uninhabited island of Sprogø, and an 8km train tunnel, second in length only to the huge UK–France Channel Tunnel. In all, the impressive span, which runs between the industrial towns of Korsør and Nyborg, covers 18km. If you're taking a train, the cost of crossing is included in your train fare; however, if you're driving, there's a bridge toll each way of Dkr250 for vehicles under 6m, Dkr375 over 6m, and Dkr125 for a motorbike.

ODENSE

pop 183,000

Denmark's third-largest city takes great pride in being the birthplace of Hans Christian Andersen (particularly around the 200th anniversary of Andersen's birth in April 2005), though after a fairly unhappy childhood, Andersen left Odense with little regret. These days it's a friendly university city with busy, central pedestrianised areas, a fairly lively social scene, a good network of bike lanes, an interesting cathedral and a number of worthwhile museums, including the excellent Andersen museum.

Information

DISCOUNT CARDS

Odense has a handy 'adventure pass' that allows free entry into museums and free bus transport. You can buy it at the train station or tourist office for Dkr110/150 for 24/48 hours.

INTERNET ACCESS

Boomtown Netcafé (Pantheonsgade 4) A plush gamers place with fast Internet connection.

Odense Central Library (Odense Banegård Center; ☉ 10am-7pm Mon-Thu, 10am-4pm Fri & Sat) Offers free use of the Internet.

WideHouse (Vindegade 43; per hr Dkr25; ☉ 10am-midnight)

LEFT LUGGAGE

At the train station, left-luggage lockers cost Dkr10 for 24 hours.

POST

Main post office (Dannebrogsgade 2)

TOURIST INFORMATION

Badstuen (☎ 66 13 48 66; Østre Stationsvej) A youth and community centre with café and information point.

Tourist Office (☎ 66 12 75 20; www.visitodense.com; ☉ 9.30am-6pm Mon-Fri, 10am-5pm Sat & Sun mid-Jun–Aug, 9.30am-4.30pm Mon-Fri, 10am-3pm Sat & Sun Sep–mid-Jun) At Rådhus, a 15-minute walk from the train station.

Sights

HC ANDERSEN MUSEUMS

The **HC Andersens Hus** (☎ 65 51 46 01; Bangs Boder 29; adult/child Dkr50/20; ☉ 9am-7pm mid-Jun–Aug, 10am-4pm Tue-Sun Sep–mid-Jun) lies amid the picturesque little houses of the old poor quarter of Odense. It contains a thorough and

ODENSE

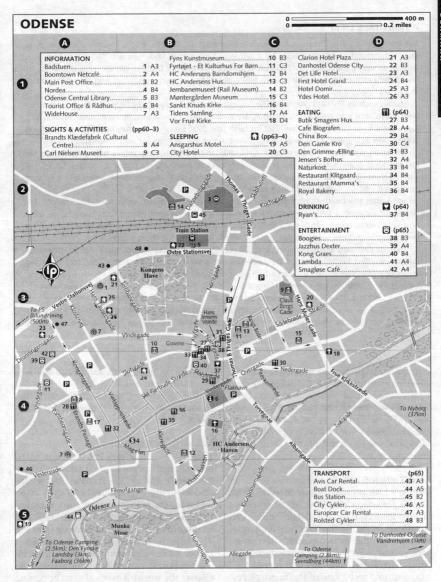

0 ____ 400 m
0 ____ 0.2 miles

INFORMATION		
Badstuen	1	A3
Boomtown Netcafé	2	A4
Main Post Office	3	B2
Nordea	4	B4
Odense Central Library	5	B3
Tourist Office & Rådhus	6	B4
WideHouse	7	A3

SIGHTS & ACTIVITIES	**(pp60–3)**	
Brandts Klædefabrik (Cultural Centre)	8	A4
Carl Nielsen Museet	9	C3

Fyns Kunstmuseum	10	B3
Fyrtøjet - Et Kulturhus For Børn	11	C3
HC Andersens Barndomshjem	12	B4
HC Andersens Hus	13	C3
Jernbanemuseet (Rail Museum)	14	B2
Møntergården Museum	15	C3
Sankt Knuds Kirke	16	B4
Tidens Samling	17	A4
Vor Frue Kirke	18	D4

SLEEPING	**(pp63–4)**	
Ansgarshus Motel	19	A5
City Hotel	20	C3

Clarion Hotel Plaza	21	A3
Danhostel Odense City	22	B3
Det Lille Hotel	23	A3
First Hotel Grand	24	B4
Hotel Domir	25	A3
Ydes Hotel	26	A3

EATING	**(p64)**	
Butik Smagens Hus	27	B3
Cafe Biografen	28	B4
China Box	29	B4
Den Gamle Kro	30	C4
Den Grimme Ælling	31	B3
Jensen's Bofhus	32	A4
Naturkost	33	B4
Restaurant Klitgaard	34	B4
Restaurant Mamma's	35	B4
Royal Bakery	36	B4

DRINKING	**(p64)**	
Ryan's	37	B4

ENTERTAINMENT	**(p65)**	
Boogies	38	B3
Jazzhus Dexter	39	A4
Kong Graes	40	B4
Lambda	41	A4
Smagløse Café	42	A4

TRANSPORT	**(p65)**	
Avis Car Rental	43	A3
Boat Dock	44	A5
Bus Station	45	B2
City Cykler	46	A5
Europcar Car Rental	47	A3
Rolsted Cykler	48	B3

lively telling of the amazing life Andersen lived (see the boxed text, p62), put into an interesting historical context and leavened by some good audiovisual material. A highlight is the hugely entertaining audio clip of the great Shakespearean actor Sir Laurence Olivier who wheels out his finest chicken impressions in a rendering of Andersen's

It's Perfectly True, a short tale of gossip and Chinese whispers in a henhouse.

Near the museum is the charming **Fyrtøjet – Et Kulturhus For Børn** (Tinderbox – A Cultural Centre for Children; ☎ 66 14 44 11; Hans Jensens Stræde 21; admission Dkr60; ⏰ 9am-7pm mid-Jun–Aug, 10am-4pm Tue-Sun Sep–mid-Jun), where youngsters can explore the magical world of Hans Christian Andersen

A FAIRY-TALE LIFE? Michael Booth

For the Danes, Hans Christian Andersen is Shakespeare, Goethe and Dickens rolled into one. That may sound a little excessive for a fairy-tale writer, but Andersen was far more than that. As well as single-handedly revolutionising children's literature (*Alice in Wonderland*, the works of Roald Dahl and even Harry Potter owe him a debt), he wrote novels, plays and several fascinating travel books.

Stories such as *The Little Mermaid*, *The Emperor's New Clothes* and *The Ugly Duckling*, which have been translated into over 170 languages, are embedded in the global literary consciousness like few others. Even today, 200 years after his birth (the 2005 bicentenary may be the largest cultural celebration Scandinavia has ever seen), their themes are as relevant and universal as ever.

Andersen was born in Odense on 2 April 1805. In three autobiographies he mythologised his childhood as poor but idyllic (his mother was a washerwoman, his father a cobbler) and filled with portents of his fame and success. The truth was his parents were not married when he was conceived and his father died when Andersen was 11.

Soon after the death of his father Andersen left for Copenhagen, an uneducated, gauche 14-year-old following a fairy-tale path. Despite numerous class and educational barriers, he tried and failed to become, variously, a ballet dancer, singer, actor, playwright and novelist, until he eventually found international success with his first volume of short stories.

That success and accompanying wealth were some compensation for what was an otherwise deeply troubled, largely unhappy life. Andersen was a neurotic, sexually ambivalent, highly-strung hypochondriac (he left a card reading 'I am only apparently dead' beside his bed each night because of a morbid fear of falling into a deep sleep, being taken for dead and buried alive).

It all perhaps goes some way to explaining why he was such a restless nomad to the last. He travelled further than any of his compatriots – most notably in 1840–41 when he journeyed as far as Istanbul, writing about his experiences in the highly accomplished travelogue *A Poet's Bazaar*.

---

through storytelling and music (in English as well as Danish during the summer) and by dressing up and playing Andersen characters. **HC Andersens Barndomshjem** (Munkemøllestræde 3; adult/child Dkr10/5; 🕑 10am-4pm mid-Jun–Aug, 11am-3pm Tue-Sun Sep–mid-Jun) has a couple of rooms of exhibits in the small house where Hans grew up.

SANKT KNUDS KIRKE
Odense's 13th-century, Gothic **cathedral** (☎ 66 12 03 92; Flakhaven; admission free; 🕑 9am-5pm Mon-Sat, noon-5pm Sun) reflects Odense's medieval wealth and stature. The stark white interior has a handsome rococo pulpit, a dazzling, 16th-century altarpiece and a gilded wooden triptych crowded with over 300 carved figures and said to be one of the finest pieces of religious art in Northern Europe. In the cathedral's chilly crypt are reliquaries containing two skeletons claimed to be those of King Knud II and his brother Benedikt, who in 1086 fled into St Alban's and were killed at the altar by Jutland farmers during a revolt against taxes. Though less than saintly, in 1101 Knud was canonised Knud the Holy by

the pope in a move to secure the Catholic church in Denmark.

A few metres west of the coffin, stairs lead down to the remains of the original **St Alban's church**.

BRANDTS KLÆDEFABRIK
The former textile mill has been converted into a huge, sprawling and impressive **cultural centre** (☎ 66 13 78 97; Brandts Passage; combined ticket Dkr50; 🕑 10am-5pm Jul & Aug, 10am-5pm Tue-Sun Sep-Jun) with a photography museum (Dkr25), a modern art gallery (Dkr30) and a museum of graphics and printing (Dkr25). The superb, bright, capacious exhibition spaces more often than not contain excellent temporary exhibitions from artists from all over the world. There's also an appealing roof terrace overlooking town.

Nearby, in a large loft, is the charming **Tidens Samling** (Times Collection; ☎ 65 91 19 42; Brandt's Passage 29; adult/child Dkr30/20; 🕑 10am-5pm), featuring a series of domestic interiors from various periods between 1900 and the 1980s, and displays on the way Danes dressed, lived and thought in years gone by.

DEN FYNSKE LANDSBY

This is a delightful **open-air museum** (☎ 65 51 46 01; adult/child Dkr55/15; ✷ 10am-7pm mid-Jun–mid-Aug, 10am-5pm Tue-Sun Apr–mid-Jun & mid-Aug–Oct, 11am-3pm Nov-Mar), furnished with period buildings authentically laid out like a small country village, complete with barnyard animals, a duck pond, apple trees and flower gardens.

The museum is in a green zone 4km south of the city centre via bus No 42. From May to September you can take a boat (adult/child Dkr35/25) from Munke Mose down the river to Erik Bøghs Sti, from where it's a 15-minute woodland walk along the river to Den Fynske Landsby.

FYNS KUNSTMUSEUM

In a stately, neoclassical building, this **museum** (☎ 65 51 46 01; Jernbanegade 13; adult/child Dkr30/10; ✷ 10am-4pm Tue-Sun) has a serene atmosphere and contains a quality collection of Danish art from the 18th century to the present. Highlights include PS Krøyer's *Italieneske Markarbejdere* (Italian Field Workers), Gustava Emilie Grüner's cheerful *Portraegruppe Familien Leunbach* and HA Brendekilde's harrowing but powerful *Udslidt* (Finished), depicting a prostrate worker and distressed woman in a vast, flat field. There are small collections of fine sculptures and contemporary art; changing exhibitions are also staged.

CARL NIELSEN MUSEET

This **museum** (☎ 65 51 46 01; Claus Bergs Gade 11; adult/child Dkr25/5; ✷ 4-8pm Thu & Fri, noon-4pm Sun) in Odense's concert hall details the career of the city's native son Carl Nielsen, Denmark's best-known composer. At various points you can don earphones and enjoy Nielsen's music. There are displays of works by Nielsen's wife, the accomplished sculptor Anne Marie Brodersen.

JERNBANEMUSEET

Railway buffs should not miss the collection of 19th-century locomotives at the **rail museum** (☎ 66 13 66 30; Dannebrogsgade 24; adult/child Dkr40/16; ✷ 10am-4pm) just behind the train station. There are also minirailways for children of all ages to ride on.

OTHER ATTRACTIONS

Strolling is a pleasure along the busy pedestrianised main street Vestergade and down side streets such as Lille Gråbrødstræd. The central square **Flakhavn**, framed by Odense Rådhus and Sankt Knuds Kirke, features Svend Wiig Hansen's giant bronze, the reclining *Oceania*, a joyful playground for children. The east side of the city centre has some of Odense's oldest buildings. You can follow a rewarding walking route from the centre by crossing the busy Torvegade and strolling down Nedergade, a cobblestoned street lined with leaning, half-timbered houses and antique shops, and then returning via Overgade. En route you'll pass the 13th-century **Vor Frue Kirke** (✷ 10am-noon Mon-Sat).

Around the corner, **Møntergården** (☎ 66 14 88 14; Overgade 48-50; ✷ 10am-4pm Tue-Sun), a city museum, has various displays on Odense's history from the Viking Age and a couple of 16th- and 17th-century half-timbered houses.

Sleeping

Odense Camping (☎ 66 11 47 02; www.camping-odense .dk, Danish only; Odensevej 102; adult/child/tent Dkr64/32/20) This camping ground is 3.5km south of the city centre (take bus No 21 or 22).

The tourist office books rooms in private homes for Dkr250/350 for singles/doubles, plus a Dkr35 booking fee.

Danhostel Odense City (☎ 63 11 04 25; www.city hostel.dk; dm/s/d Dkr118/360/450; ✖ 💻) A bright, modern 140-bed place with four- and six-bed dorms, a kitchen and laundry facilities alongside the train and bus stations.

Danhostel Odense Vandrerhjem (☎ 66 13 04 25; Kragsbjergvej 121; dm/s/d Dkr105/295/420) Occupying a former manor house around a grassy central square, this 160-bed place is 2km southeast of the centre via bus No 61 or 62.

Det Lille Hotel (☎ 66 12 28 21; Dronningensgade 5; s/d Dkr300/430, s/d with private bathroom Dkr350/550) A 10-minute walk west of the train station, this is a small friendly, inexpensive place with 14 straightforward rooms. However, it's looking scruffy these days and smoking is allowed throughout the hotel, which can be irritating.

Ansgarshus Motel (☎ 66 12 88 00; fax 66 12 88 65; Kirkegåds Allé; s/d Dkr350/495, s/d with private bathroom Dkr445/575; 🅿) A small, family-run place near the river and parkland with clean, welcoming rooms.

Hotel Domir (☎ 66 12 14 27; www.domir.dk; Hans Tausensgade 19; s Dkr420, d Dkr495-585; 💻) This hotel is one of the better mid-range options in town with pleasant, good-value rooms, though some singles are a bit cramped.

Ydes Hotel (☎ 66 12 11 31; Hans Tausensgade 11; s Dkr360, d Dkr450-550) Near the Hotel Domir is its sister hotel, which has 26 smaller, but similarly appointed, rooms.

First Hotel Grand (☎ 66 11 71 71; odense@firsthotels .dk; Jernbanegade 18; s/d from Dkr753/1179; P ☒ ▣) An old-fashioned but welcoming place. The rooms are large, there's a sauna and solarium, in-room cable TV and WiFi access.

Clarion Hotel Plaza (☎ 66 11 77 45; www.choice hotels.dk; Østre Stationsvej 24; s/d Dkr1125/1325; P ☒ ▣) Overlooking the green spaces of Kongens, this comfortable hotel has friendly service. Its 68 rooms are decorated in a slightly pastoral Old English style and are fairly luxurious. There's also WiFi access and a gym.

City Hotel (☎ 66 12 12 58; www.city-hotel-odense .dk; Hans Mulesgade 5; s/d Dkr595/795) A comfortable modern hotel located near the Carl Nielsen Museum.

Eating & Drinking

There are numerous, mainly fast-food, places along Kongensgade.

Jensen's Bøfhus (Kongensgade 10; lunches Dkr39-69) Jensen's is a reliable standby for good, inexpensive steak and chicken lunches.

China Box (☎ 66 20 62 44; Vestergade; small/large takeaway box Dkr25/38; ☿ 11am-9pm Mon-Sat) Close to the tourist office, China Box does inexpensive takeaway Chinese food.

Café Biografen (☎ 66 13 16 16; Brandts Klædefabrik; brunch Dkr65; ☿ 11am-midnight) This cheerful place, where ducks waddle happily around the terrace tables, does a good selection of

baguettes (Dkr40) and salads (Dkr60), as well as cakes, pastries, coffees, light meals and beer at reasonable prices.

Butik Smagens Hus (☎ 66 12 22 72; Nørregade 32; sandwiches Dkr40-50; ☿ 10am-5.30pm Tue-Thu, 10am-6.30pm Fri, 10am-2pm Sat) A great little place to pick up gourmet deli supplies and good wine or to sit and enjoy a delicious pressed apple juice, organic coffee or superb sandwich containing some of the delicious meats and cheeses on display at the counter.

Den Grimme Ælling (☎ 65 91 70 30; Hans Jensens Stræde 1; lunch buffet with/without drinks Dkr79/115) A charming little restaurant in a cobbled lane, Den Grimme Ælling has a varied and delicious buffet selection, with lunch starting at Dkr75 for herring and salad, or a hearty Danish hash for Dkr65. Evening buffet with wine is Dkr245.

Restaurant Mamma's (☎ 66 14 55 40; Klaregade 4; lunch mains Dkr49, dinner mains Dkr72-89) A very decent pasta and pizza place with a warm atmosphere, fresh ingredients and good lunch deals. It's tucked away behind the main shopping area. There's a super little **deli** (☎ 66 13 13 03; ☿ 10am-5.30pm Mon-Fri, 10am-2pm Sat) attached with a wide choice of treats for picnickers and self-caterers.

Den Gamle Kro (☎ 66 12 14 33; Overgade 23; fish & meat mains Dkr158-258) One of Odense's most atmospheric restaurants is spread throughout several rooms of a 17th-century house and has an old-world feel. So do the recipes, which are heavy, traditional Danish (good fish dishes such as fillet of sole stuffed with salmon and spinach) or French (eg chateaubriand or pork with Lyonnaise potatoes). It's mostly meat-based fare, but tasty.

Naturkost (☎ 66 13 70 13; Gravene 8) is a well-stocked health-food store. You'll find bakeries and fast-food outlets all around the city. **Royal Bakery** (Vestergade 28) opposite Jernbanegade, has the best pastries in town and organic ice cream.

Odense Banegård Center, which incorporates the train and bus stations, has low-priced options including a **DSB Café** (☿ 5am-10pm Mon-Fri, 8am-10pm Sat & Sun), a supermarket and a pub.

Ryan's (Nørregade) is a friendly Irish style pub set back from the busy Thomas B Thriges Gade with live music every weekend, a dance bar and cheap pints (Dkr25) for students all day.

THE AUTHOR'S CHOICE

Restaurant Klitgaard (☎ 66 13 14 55; Gravene 4; 2/3/4 courses Dkr335/395/475; ☿ dinner only) This small, newish, gourmet place is noted for its use of fresh, locally grown seasonal ingredients cooked by a locally grown chef, and is one of the best places we've eaten in Denmark. The blend of ingredients is clever (slow-roasted and ever-so-tender-and-pink duck breast, for instance, with the merest sliver of foie gras for richness and roasted fennel to lighten it). It can also be surprising (like the sensational rhubarb sorbet with pickled rhubarb and lavender oil).

Entertainment

Boogies (Nørregade 21) Popular with students, this dance place is downstairs from a café and opens at midnight. Admission is about Dkr35 on Friday and Saturday when there are bands.

Den Smagløe Café (Vindegade 47; ☺ 1-2am Mon-Sat) A buzzing, atmospheric little place where a youngish, student crowd relaxes on beaten-up but comfortable old sofas.

Lambda (☎ 66 17 76 92; Vindegade 100) Odense's gay and lesbian centre has a late-night café on Fridays and most Saturdays and a disco on the first and third Saturdays of each month. It's in an unsigned, red-brick building, about 30m beyond the roundabout just past Jazzhus Dexter, and on the other side of the road.

Brandts Klædefabrik (☎ 66 13 78 97; Brandts Passage) has an outdoor amphitheatre that's a venue for free summer weekend concerts, and the **Café Biografen** (☎ 66 13 16 16; Brandts Klædefabrik; tickets Dkr45-55) shows first-run movies on three screens. **Biocity** (Odense Banegård Center) is a cinema.

Kong Graes (☎ 66 11 18 16; Asylgade 7-9) is a usually dressy late-night dance club, while **Jazzhus Dexter** (66 13 68 88; Vindegade 65) has good live (mostly jazz) groups.

Getting There & Away

Odense is on the main railway line between Copenhagen (Dkr207, 1½ hours, every 15 minutes), Århus (Dkr181, 1¾ hours, hourly), Aalborg (Dkr276, three hours, hourly) and Esbjerg (Dkr163, two hours, every 30 minutes). The ticket office is open from about 6am to 8.15pm most days, but closes 5.15pm on Saturdays. Buses leave from the rear of the train station.

Odense is just north of the E20; access from the highway is clearly marked. Rte 43 connects Odense with Faaborg; Rte 9 connects Odense with Svendborg. There are several car rental companies in town:

Avis (☎ 66 14 39 99; Østre Stationsvej 37)
Europcar (☎ 66 14 15 44; Kongensgade 69)
PS Bilundejning (☎ 66 14 00 00; Middelfartvej 1) A competitive local option (from Dkr340 per day) if you don't need to drop the car in another town or city.

Getting Around

In Odense you board city buses at the front and pay the driver (Dkr12) when you get off. You're strongly advised to have the correct change.

Driving in Odense is not difficult outside rush hour, though many of the central sights are on pedestrian streets, so it's best to park your car and explore on foot. You can find substantial parking lots around Brandts Klædefabrik and the Carl Nielsen Museet. Parking costs a minimum Dkr1 for about seven minutes, and around Dkr8 for one hour.

Bicycles can be rented at **Rolsted Cykler** (☎ 66 17 77 36; Østre Stationsvej 33; per day/week Dkr85/500; ☺ 10am-5.30pm Mon-Fri, 10am-2pm Sun).

Another hire place is **City Cykler** (☎ 66 13 97 83; www.citycykler.dk; Vesterbro 27; per day Dkr99; ☺ 9am-5.30pm Mon-Fri, 10am-2pm Sat), west of the city centre.

LADBYSKIBET (LADBY SHIP)

This **historical site** (☎ 65 32 16 67; Vikingevej 123; adult/child Dkr25/free; ☺ 10am-5pm Jun-Aug, 10am-4pm Tue-Sun Sep-Oct & Mar-May, 11am-3pm Wed-Sun Nov-Feb) comprises the remains of a 22m-long Viking ship that has been skilfully preserved at the place where it was originally excavated in 1935. The ship, which once formed the tomb of a Viking chieftain, was buried in the 10th century. It is the only Viking Age ship burial site uncovered in Denmark to date.

All the wooden planks from the Ladby ship decayed long ago, leaving the imprint of the hull moulded into the earth, along with iron nails, an anchor and the partial remains of the dogs and horses that were buried with their master. This may sound unpromising, and at first glance the grassy hillock covering the site seems more like a bomb shelter from the outside, but as soon as the automatic entrance doors hiss open most people are captivated by this compelling relic.

There's a separate visitor centre at the arrival car park with a 1:10-scale model of the ship and background information about the site.

Getting There & Away

In the little village of Ladby, 4km southwest of Kerteminde via Odensevej, turn north onto Vikingevej, a one-lane road through fields that ends after 1.2km at the Ladbyskibet car park. You enter through the little museum from where it's a few minutes' walk along a field path to the mound.

Local bus No 482 (Dkr14, six minutes, eight daily Monday to Friday) makes the trip from Kerteminde to the village of Ladby. Check the schedule with the bus driver, as the

DENMARK

last return bus is typically around 4pm. Also, you'll have to walk the Vikingevej section.

EGESKOV SLOT

This magnificent **castle** (☎ 62 27 10 16; www.eges kov.com; combined ticket for all sights except castle adult/ child Dkr85/45, castle interior Dkr55/25; ✆ 10am-5pm May, Jun, Aug & Sep, 10am-7pm Jul), complete with moat and drawbridge, is an outstanding example of the lavish efforts that sprang up during Denmark's golden age, the Renaissance (see p28). There are enough sights and activities here to keep anyone happily occupied for a day. The castle exteriors are the best features. The interior is heavily Victorian in its furnishings and hunting trophies of now rare beasts. The grounds include century-old privet hedges, free-roaming peacocks, topiary, aerial woodland walkways, English gardens and a bamboo grass labyrinth.

The castle grounds usually stay open an hour longer than the castle. Admission to the grounds includes entry to a large antique **car museum**, which also features some vintage aircraft swooping from the rafters.

Egeskov Slot is 2km west of Kvændrup on Rte 8. From Odense take the Svendborg-bound train to Kvændrup Station (Dkr49) and continue on foot or by taxi. Or, for Dkr40, take bus No 801 to Kvændrup Biblio-tek, and switch to bus No 920, which stops at the castle on its regular run between Faaborg and Nyborg. If you're lucky, in the summer months (June to August) bus No 801 may run all the way to the castle.

FAABORG & AROUND
pop 7000
Faaborg is a south-facing sun trap and has a relaxing air. In the 17th century it was a bustling harbour town sustained by one of Denmark's largest commercial fleets. Today, Faaborg retains many vestiges of that earlier era in its picturesque, cobblestone streets and leaning, half-timbered houses. It's well worth stopping at this small sleepy town for a drink or lunch before moving on to other towns on Funen or via the ferry to the southern islands.

Faaborg's **tourist office** (☎ 62 61 07 07; www.visit faaborg.dk; Banegårdspladsen 2A; ✆ 9am-5pm Mon-Sat Jun-Sep, 10am-5pm Mon-Fri, 10am-3pm Sat Oct-May) is adjacent to the bus station and car park on the harbour front. You can hire bikes here for Dkr50 a day.

Sights & Activities
The main square, **Torvet**, is a pleasant spot to linger. It features the Svendborg sculptor Kai Nielsen's striking bronze fountain group *Ymerbrønd*; depicting a naked giant suckling at the udders of a cow (depicting a Norse fertility myth), it caused a stir on its unveiling.

Running east from Torvet is the tree-lined main shopping street Østergade. Torvegade runs west from Torvet to join the cobbled Holkegade at a cluster of attractive buildings. They include a neoclassical, one-time chemist's shop with Tuscan pilasters, and the handsome, 18th-century merchant's house that is now the town museum, **Den Gamle Gaard** (Holkegade 1; adult/child Dkr30/free; ✆ 10.30am-4.30pm mid-May–Oct, 11am-3pm Sat & Sun Apr–mid-May), complete with period furnishings.

The small **Faaborg Museum for Fynsk Maler-kunst** (Grønnegade 75; adult/child Dkr35/free; ✆ 10am-4pm Apr-Oct) is a former winery which contains a fine collection of Funen art, including works by leading Funenite artists such as Peter Hansen, Jens Birkholm, and Anna Syberg. Kai Nielsen's original granite sculpture of the *Ymerbrønd* is also here.

There are numerous daily ferries to the nearby islands of Avernakø and Lyø (Dkr85 return, bicycle Dkr25) and a passenger boat to Bjørnø (Dkr40 return).

There's a good watersports centre at the **Quality Hotel Faaborg Fjord** (☎ 62 61 10 10; Svendborgvej 175; activities Dkr60-100), 2km out of town, offering fast water-based fun such as kneeboarding, high-speed jumping and being towed along behind a weaving speedboat astride a big banana.

Sleeping & Eating
The tourist office books rooms in private homes for Dkr250/400 per single/double plus a Dkr25 booking fee.

Danhostel Faaborg (☎ 62 61 12 03; www.danhostel .dk/faaborg; Grønnegade 71-72; dm/d Dkr100/300; ✆ Apr-end Oct) This 69-bed hostel occupies two handsome historic buildings, close to the Faaborg Museum.

Hotel Faaborg (☎ 62 61 02 45; www.hotelfaaborg .dk; Torvet; s/d Dkr575/650; 🅿 🖳) This very central hotel has good, welcoming rooms. Its restaurant does tasty herring dishes for Dkr80 and *smørrebrød* for Dkr38 to Dkr58.

Faaborg Røgeri (☎ 62 61 42 32; Vestkaj; fish dishes Dkr19-66) Serves cheap, tasty, home-smoked fish on a great spot by the harbour.

Harlem Pizza (Torvet; dishes Dkr30-40) Harlem has long hours and does pizza, sandwiches and lasagne.

Getting There & Away

Faaborg has no train service. Bus Nos 961 and 962 from Odense (Dkr56, 1¼ hours) run at least hourly to 11pm. Bus Nos 930 and 962 from Svendborg (Dkr42, 40 minutes, at least hourly) are also frequent throughout the day. Getting to Faaborg by car is straightforward; from the north, simply follow Rte 43, which is called Odensevej as it enters town.

For information on ferries to Ærø, see p68.

SVENDBORG

pop 40,000

Svendborg is South Funen's largest municipality and a transit point for travel between Odense and Ærø. It can be surprisingly lively in the summer, particularly in the increasingly busy waterfront hotels and bars where yachties and land-bound visitors flock in numbers.

The train and bus stations are two blocks northwest of the dock. The **tourist office** (☎ 62 21 09 80; www.visitsydfyn.dk; Centrumpladsen 4; ⏰ 9.30am-6pm Mon-Fri, 9.30am-3pm Sat mid-Jun–Aug, 9.30am-5pm Mon-Fri, 9.30am-12.30pm Sat Sep–mid-Jun) has lots of information on South Funen as a whole.

A splendid natural harbour made Svendborg a major port and shipbuilding centre from medieval times onwards and today there is still enough marine heritage to counterbalance the fairly soulless modern docks that dominate the waterfront. The town has a number of maritime training schools to add to its salty ambience.

Sights

At the southern end of Havnepladsen's cobbled quayside, opposite where the Ærø ferry docks, is **Sejlskibsbroen**, a jetty lined with splendidly preserved sailing ships and smaller vessels and with an adjoining marina catering for the great number of yachts that sail local waters. Ask at the tourist centre about the various trips that can be arranged on the old sailing ships.

Just over the bridge from Svendborg is the island of **Tåsinge**, with its pretty harbourside village of Troense and the nearby 17th-century castle **Valdemars Slot** (☎ 62 22 61 06; Slotsalléen 100; adult/child Dkr60/30, combined ticket Dkr110/60; ⏰ 10am-5pm May-Sep). The castle's lavish interior is crammed with paintings and eccentric objects. In the grounds are the **Danish Yachting Museum** and **Denmark's Toy Museum**, packed with candy-coloured vintage playthings. The grounds of the castle and the nearby white-sand beach have free access. You can get to Valdemars Slot by bus but a better way is by the MS *Helge*, an old-style ferry that carries passengers from Svendborg to Troense and Valdemars Slot every few hours (Dkr70) from May to September.

Sleeping & Eating

The nearest camp grounds are on Tåsinge.

Danhostel Svendborg (☎ 62 21 66 99; www.danhostel-svendborg.dk; Vestergade 45; dm/r Dkr118/375; P ⊠ ▣) Danhostel is in a renovated, 19th-century iron foundry in the town centre. Bike hire costs Dkr63.

Hotel Ærø (☎ 62 21 07 60; www.hotel-aeroe.dk in Danish; Brogade 1; s/d Dkr650/775; P) Right by the water, the Ærø has large, modern chalet-style rooms with big comfy beds. There's a good restaurant serving top-notch traditional fare, including a great range of light lunches and *smørrebrød* (Dkr42 to Dkr72), and a cosy bar downstairs.

Det Lille Hotel (☎ 62 22 53 41; www.detlillehotel.dk, Danish only; Badstuen 15; s/d Dkr420/550) At Tåsinge, the charming and friendly Det Lille has a few rooms in a typically picturesque cottage with a roof of ancient mossy thatch.

In Svendborg, there's a bakery, ice-cream shop and other inexpensive food places along the pedestrian street, Brogade-Gerritsgade, in the town centre.

Jette's Diner (☎ 62 22 16 97; Kullinggade 1; dishes Dkr40-68; ⏰ noon-9.30pm) A popular local place that's a cut above the usual diner, Jette's does sandwiches, salads and tasty burgers.

Bella Italia (☎ 62 22 24 55; Brogade 2; mains Dkr136-190) Always busy, Bella Italia does tasty pizza and pasta for Dkr60 to Dkr99.

Restaurant Valdemars Slot (☎ 62 22 59 00; Slotsalléen 100; light lunch dishes Dkr40-72, mains Dkr98-195; ⏰ Wed-Sat) At Valdemars Slot, this popular restaurant is a lavish and atmospheric spot for fine dining with a mostly French flavour (lobster bisque, foie gras terrine, beef and venison). There's a good wine list.

Getting There & Away

There are trains from Odense to Svendborg (Dkr58, one hour, hourly). Ferries to

Ærøskøbing depart five times a day, the last at 10.30pm in summer.

LANGELAND

The long, narrow island of Langeland, connected by bridge to Funen via Tåsinge, has a satisfying sense of isolation. It has some good beaches, enjoyable cycling and rewarding bird-watching. You can pick up information about the entire island from Langeland's **tourist office** (☎ 62 51 35 05; www.langeland.dk in Danish; Torvet 5, Rudkøbing; ☺ 9am-5pm Mon-Fri, 9am-3pm Sat mid-Jun-Aug, 9.30am-4.30pm Mon-Fri, 9.30am-12.30pm Sat Sep–mid-Jun).

Sights & Activities

Langeland's top sight is the salmon-coloured **Tranekær Slot**, a handsome medieval castle that has been in the hands of the one family since 1672. The castle is not open to the public, but its grounds are home to the fascinating **Tickon** (Tranekær International Centre for Art and Nature; admission to grounds Dkr25), a collection of art installations created by international artists and sited around the wooded grounds and lake. Children love searching out each feature. **Tranekær Slot Museum** and the **Souvenir Museum** are in the castle's old water mill and old theatre respectively. About 1km north of the castle is the **Castle Mill** (☎ 63 51 10 10; Lejbølleveje; adult/child Dkr20/free; ☺ 10am-5pm Mon-Fri & 1-5pm Sat & Sun Jun–mid-Sep, 10am-4pm Mon-Fri & 1-4pm Sat & Sun mid-Sep–May), a 19th-century windmill, with its remarkable wooden mechanics still intact.

Langeland's main town of **Rudkøbing** has a fairly desolate harbour area, but the town centre is attractive and there are some fine old buildings around Rudekøbing Kirke, to the north of Brogade, the street leading inland from the harbour to the main square of Torvet. For beaches, head for **Ristinge** about 15km south of Rudkøbing; for **bird-watching** you'll find a sighting tower at **Tryggelev Nor**, 5km south of Ristinge, and a sanctuary at **Gulstav Bog**, the island's southern tip.

Cycling is a good way to explore Langeland. The tourist office has an excellent English-language edition of a brochure and map (Dkr15) that describes six bike routes on the island. Bikes can be hired at **Cykelsmeden** (Bystrædt 3; per day Dkr60), in the centre of town.

Sleeping & Eating

Danhostel Rudkøbing (☎ 62 51 18 30; www.danhostel .dk/rudkobing; Engdraget 11; dm/r Dkr100/325; ☺ Apr–end

Oct) There are nine camping grounds scattered around the island of Langeland, including one here at Langeland's only hostel, located in Rudkøbing centre.

The tourist office maintains a list of rooms for rent in private homes with doubles costing about Dkr350 to Dkr400.

Skrøbelevgaard (☎ 62 51 45 31; www.skrobelev gaard.dk; Skrøbelev Hedevej 4; s Dkr300-450, d Dkr400-750) This cosy inn, 4km east of Rudkøbing in the village of Ny Skrøbelev, is a fine option if you enjoy historic settings and the quiet of the countryside. Occupying a 17th-century manor house, Skrøbelevgaard has 10 cosy rooms. The free city bus stops nearby on weekdays.

There are a number of cafés and restaurants in Rudkøbing.

Thummelumsen (☎ 62 51 00 43; Østergade 15; lunch Dkr 50-70, mains Dkr135-145) Serves good, fresh, home-made light lunches, such as burgers, chilli, tortillas and meatballs with rye bread and more ambitious fare in the evenings such as carpaccio and gazpacho.

Getting There & Away

Buses make the 25-minute run from Svendborg to Rudkøbing (Dkr30) at least hourly; most connect onwards to Tranekær. There are daily ferries from Rudkøbing to Marstal in Ærø (Dkr81/179 one-way per person/car) and from Spodsbjerg to Tårs in Lolland.

ÆRØ
pop 7500

Ærø is an idyllic, captivating island with a gentle coastline and an interior of rolling green hills, patchworked with fields and farmsteads. Its mainly coastal towns are small and friendly. The winding country roads are punctuated with thatched houses, old windmills, ancient passage graves and dolmens. There are some good, small beaches, one of the best being **Risemark Strand** on the southern tip of the island; it's a great place to tour by bicycle.

Ærø has three main towns: Ærøskøbing, Marstal and Søby. **Ærøskøbing tourist office** (☎ 62 52 13 00; Vestergade 1; ☺ 9am-5pm Mon-Fri, 10am-1pm Sat, 9.30am-12.30pm Sun Jun-Aug) is near the waterfront. **Marstal tourist office** (☎ 62 53 19 60; Havnegade 5; ☺ 10am-6pm Mon-Fri, 10.30am-1.30pm Sat, 9.30am-12.30pm Sun) is a few minutes' walk south of the harbour. The island's tourist website is www.aeroe-turistbureau.dk (in Danish).

Ærøskøbing

The words 'higgledy' and 'piggledy' were invented to describe Ærøskøbing. A prosperous merchants' town in the late 1600s, its narrow, winding cobblestone streets are tightly lined with 17th- and 18th-century houses, many of them gently subsiding, crooked, half-timbered affairs with traditional hand-blown glass windows and decorative doorways beautified by streetside hollyhocks. The tourist office has an illustrated leaflet, with a separate insert in English, describing the finest buildings, many of them very well preserved.

Apart from Ærøskøbing's overall charm, a main tourist attraction is **Flaske Peters Samling** (☎ 62 52 29 51; Smedegade 22; adult/child Dkr25/10; ☺ 10am-5pm), a museum in the former poorhouse with displays of local folk art. There are also examples of the work of ship's cook, Peter Jacobsen, 'Bottle Peter', who crafted 1700 ships-in-a-bottle during his long life.

Søby

This quiet little port has a shipyard, which is the island's biggest employer, a sizable fishing fleet and a busy yacht marina. Five kilometres beyond Søby, at Ærø's northern tip, there's a pebble beach with clear water and a stone **lighthouse** with a view.

Marstal

On the southeastern end of the island, Marstal is Ærø's most modern-looking town and has a web of busy shopping streets at its centre. Marstal has an emphatically maritime history – even its street names echo the names of ships and famous sailors. Its **Søfartsmuseum** (☎ 62 53 23 31; Prinsensgade 1; adult/child Dkr40/10; ☺ 9am-8pm Jul, 9am-5pm Jun & Aug, 10am-4pm Mar & Sep) has an absorbing collection of nautical artefacts including ships' models and full-size boats. There is a reasonably good **beach** on the southern side of town.

Ancient Ærø

Ærø once had more than 100 prehistoric sites and, although many have been lost, the island still has some atmospheric Neolithic remains, especially in its southeast district, to the west of Marstal. At the small village of Store Rise is the site of **Tingstedet**, the remains of a passage grave in a field behind an attractive **12th-century church**.

At **Lindsbjerg** is the superb hilltop site of a long barrow and two passage graves, one of which has a nicely poised capstone. Just over 1km south of here, following signs and right on the coast, is the fascinating medieval relic of **Sankt Albert's Kirke**. It's within a Viking defensive wall from about the 8th century and has a beautifully tended graveyard with immaculately clipped, shin-high hedges around the graves.

Another striking site is at **Kragnæs**, about 4km west of Marstal. Head through the village of Græsvænge and follow signs for 'Jættestue' along narrow lanes to reach a small car park, from where it's about 600m along field tracks to the restored grave site.

Sleeping

There are camping grounds at Søby, Ærøskøbing and Marstal.

Danhostel Ærøskøbing (☎ 62 52 10 44; www.danhostel.dk; dm/r Dkr105/270; ☺ Apr-Sep; Ⓟ ✗) Around 1km from town on the road to Marstal.

Danhostel Marstal (☎ 63 52 63 58; danhostel@marstal.dk; Færgestræde 29; dm/s/d Dkr100/210/250; ☺ May-Sep) South of the harbour, this modest but neatly kept hostel is close is right by the sea.

The tourist offices have a list of countryside B&Bs around the island for around Dkr230/350 for singles/doubles.

Hotel Ærøhus (☎ 62 52 10 03; www.aeroehus.dk; Vestergade 38; s/d Dkr450/650, s/d with private bathroom from Dkr770/1090; Ⓟ) In Ærøskøbing, Hotel Ærøhus occupies a large period building close to the harbour. It has comfortable, modern rooms and a smart garden annexe.

Pension Vestergade 44 (☎ 62 52 22 98; pension vestergade44@post.tele.dk; Vestergade 44; s/d Dkr450/680; Ⓟ ✗) Next door to the Ærohus is this delightful 18th-century house with very stylish, yet homely interiors.

Hotel Marstal (☎ 62 53 13 52; www.hotelmarstal.dk, Danish only; Dronningestræde 1A; s/d Dkr375/500, s/d with private bathroom Dkr675/775) In Marstal near the harbour, this hotel offers basic rooms in the old building and bright, modern, appealing en-suite ones in the new annexe.

Eating & Drinking

All three towns have bakeries, restaurants and food stores. In Ærøskøbing, on Vestergade just west of the ferry dock, there's a small grocery store, a smokehouse with inexpensive smoked fish and moderately priced restaurants.

Hos Grethe (☎ 62 52 21 43; Vertergade 39; mains around Dkr115) Favoured by locals for its home-cooking style and good fish dishes.

Restaurant Kabyssen (☎ 62533402; Havnepladsen 6; sandwiches & grills Dkr49-Dkr59, children's menu Dkr39) At Marstal's harbour.

Hotel Marstal (☎ 62 53 13 52; Dronningestræde 1A; mains Dkr130-180, daily special Dkr105) For something more substantial, Hotel Marstal has a two-course daily special and numerous beef and wiener schnitzel-based mains.

Scruffy Murphy's (☎ 62 53 13 23; Strandstræde 39B) Just along the road from Hotel Marstal is Scruffy Murphy's, brimming with Irish beers and a strong, live folk-music programme.

Getting There & Away

There are year-round **car ferries** (☎ 62 52 40 00; info@aeroe-ferry.dk) to Søby from Faaborg, to Ærøskøbing from Svendborg and to Marstal from Rudkøbing. All run about five times a day, take about an hour and charge Dkr81/43/22/179 per adult/child/bike/car. If you have a car it's a good idea to make reservations, particularly at weekends and in midsummer.

There's also a **ferry** (☎ 62 58 17 17; aero.als@get2net.dk) between Søby and Mommark that runs a few times daily from spring to autumn at comparable prices.

Getting Around

Bus No 990 runs from Søby to Marstal via Ærøskøbing hourly from Monday to Friday, and half as frequently at weekends.

You can rent bikes for Dkr45 a day at the hostel and camping ground in Ærøskøbing and at **Pilebækkens Cykel og Servicestation** (☎ 62 52 11 10; Pilebækken 11) opposite the car park on the outskirts of town.

In Marstal, **Nørremarks Cykelforretning** (☎ 62 53 14 77; Møllevejen 77; per day Dkr45) rents out bikes from a stand at the harbour car park between 10am and 11am each morning.

Søby Cykelforretning (☎ 62 58 18 42; Langebro 4; per day Dkr50) rents out bikes in Søby. The tourist office in Marstal sells a Dkr20 cycling map of a round-island route.

JUTLAND

The Jutland (Jylland) Peninsula is where mainland Europe meets Scandinavia. The region was settled originally by the Jutes, a Germanic tribe whose forays included invading England in the 5th century. Not surprisingly Jutland's southern boundary has been a fluid one, last drawn in 1920 when Germany relinquished its holdings in Sønderjylland.

Jutland's west coast has endless stretches of windswept sandy beaches. Most of the main cities, including Århus and Aalborg, are along the more sheltered east coast.

The natural landscape of northern Jutland is largely coastal sand dunes and heathland, while southern Jutland is dominated by moors and marshes. Drainage and reclamation has turned most of Jutland into level farmland and modern agriculture has produced a landscape of tilled fields that are a brilliant green in spring and a monotonous brown in autumn. Parts of the interior, especially around the marginally hillier central areas, are forested.

ÅRHUS & AROUND

pop 285,000

Århus is the second-largest city in Denmark and is one of Scandinavian Europe's most modern and sophisticated regional capitals. Yet the city retains all the friendliness and ease of a small country town. It lies midway along Jutland's eastern coastline and has been an important trading centre and seaport since Viking times.

The city is the cultural and commercial heart of Jutland. It has a thriving university with more than 20,000 students. Århus has one of Denmark's best music and entertainment scenes, a well-preserved historic quarter and plenty to see and do, ranging from good museums (don't miss Moesgård, p73) and period churches in the centre, to woodland trails and beaches along the city's outskirts.

Århus began in about 900 as Aros, the 'place at the river's mouth', and during the medieval period it see-sawed between prosperity and devastation as rival Vikings and warring kings entangled the city in their campaigns. In more peaceful times, the city stabilised and soon became the commercial focus of Jutland.

Orientation

Århus is fairly compact and easy to get around. The train station is on the southern side of the city centre. The pedestrian shopping streets of Ryesgade, Søndergade and Sankt Clements Torv extend around

ÅRHUS

0 ▭▭▭ 300 m
0 ▭▭▭ 0.2 miles

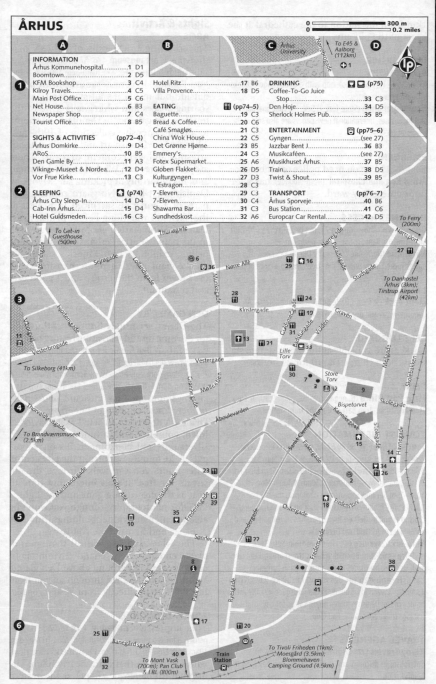

INFORMATION
Århus Kommunehospital..............1 D1
Boomtown...2 D5
KFM Bookshop.................................3 C4
Kilroy Travels...................................4 C5
Main Post Office.............................5 C6
Net House..6 B3
Newspaper Shop.............................7 C4
Tourist Office..................................8 B5

SIGHTS & ACTIVITIES (pp72–4)
Århus Domkirke...............................9 D4
AROS...10 B5
Den Gamle By.................................11 A3
Vikinge-Museet & Nordea.........12 D4
Vor Frue Kirke................................13 C3

SLEEPING 🏠 (p74)
Århus City Sleep-In......................14 D4
Cab-Inn Århus................................15 D4
Hotel Guldsmeden.......................16 C3

Hotel Ritz...17 B6
Villa Provence...............................18 D5

EATING 🍴 (pp74–5)
Baguette...19 C3
Bread & Coffee..............................20 C6
Café Smagløs.................................21 C3
China Wok House.........................22 C5
Det Grønne Hjørne.....................23 B5
Emmery's..24 C3
Fotex Supermarket.....................25 A6
Globen Flakket.............................26 D5
Kulturgyngen................................27 D3
L'Estragon.....................................28 C3
7-Eleven...29 C3
7-Eleven...30 C4
Shawarma Bar..............................31 C3
Sundhedskost...............................32 A6

DRINKING 🍷🍺 (p75)
Coffee-To-Go Juice
  Stop..33 C3
Den Hoje..34 D5
Sherlock Holmes Pub.................35 B5

ENTERTAINMENT 🎭 (pp75–6)
Gyngen...(see 27)
Jazzbar Bent J.............................36 B3
Musikcaféen...............................(see 27)
Musikhuset Århus.......................37 B5
Train..38 D5
Twist & Shout..............................39 B5

TRANSPORT (pp76–7)
Århus Sporveje............................40 B6
Bus Station...................................41 C6
Europcar Car Rental..................42 D5

1km from the station to the cathedral at the heart of the old city.

Information

BOOKSHOPS
KFM (Store Torv 5) A bookshop with a good range of books including travel guides.
Newspaper Shop (Store Torv 7) Sells international papers and magazines. International newspapers are also sold at the train station.

EMERGENCY
Dial ☎ 112 if you need police or ambulance.
Århus Kommunehospital (Nørrebrogade) has a 24-hour emergency ward.

INTERNET ACCESS
Boomtown (Åboulevarden 21; per hr 25Dkr; ☺ 10-2am Mon-Thu, 10-8am Fri-Sat, 11am-midnight Sun)
Net House (Nørre Allé 66A; per hr Dkr20; ☺ noon-midnight) Tucked away well off the street and up a flight of stairs.

LAUNDRY
Mønt Vask (St Paul's Gade 64) A coin launderette. An average wash and dry costs Dkr45.

LEFT LUGGAGE
Lockers are available at the bus and train stations. Both charge Dkr10 for 24 hours.

POST
Main Post Office (Banegardspladsen; ☺ 9.30am-6pm Mon-Fri, 10am-1pm Sat) Beside the train station.

TOURIST INFORMATION
Tourist office (☎ 89 40 67 00; www.visitaarhus.com; Park Allé; ☺ 9.30am-6pm Mon-Fri, 9.30am-5pm Sat, 9.30am-1pm Sun mid-Jun–mid-Sep, 9.30am-5pm Mon-Fri, 10am-1pm Sat May–mid-Jun, 9.30am-4.30pm Mon-Fri, 10am-1pm Sat mid-Sep–Apr) In Rådhuset, the city hall. It has a very friendly and helpful staff and offers numerous brochures and leaflets on the city and its surroundings, and on the rest of Jutland and Denmark.
'Info-bike' service (☺ mid-Jun–mid-Sep, Sat & Sun mid-Sep–mid-Jun) Box-laden bikes travel around the city with leaflets, brochures and information in summer.
Landsforeningen for Bøsser og Lesbiske (LBL; ☎ 86 13 19 48; www.aarhus.lbl.dk; Jægergårdsgade 42) The Århus branch of the Danish national organisation for gays and lesbians (next door to the Pan Club).

TRAVEL AGENCIES
Kilroy Travels (☎ 86 20 11 44; Fredensgade 40) Specialises in discount and student travel and has friendly, helpful staff.

Sights & Activities
AROS
The towering brick walls of Århus's new showpiece **art museum** (☎ 87 30 66 00; www.aros .dk; adult/child Dkr60/free; ☺ 10am-5pm Thu-Sun & Tue, 10am-10pm Wed) look rather mundane from the outside but inside it's all sweeping curves, soaring spaces and white walls. One of the top three art galleries in Denmark, it is home to a comprehensive collection of 19th- and 20th-century Danish art and a wide range of arresting and vivid contemporary art. There are pieces here from Warhol and Lichtenstein and, in colourfully lit pickling jars, a work by Danish artist Bjørn Nørgaard consisting of parts of a horse he sacrificed in protest at the Vietnam war (long before British artist Damien Hirst started chopping up animals in the name of art). Perhaps the most compelling exhibit is Ron Mueck's startlingly lifelike giant *Boy*. There are pleasing views over town from the terrace and a good café and restaurant.

DEN GAMLE BY
The Danes' seemingly limitless enthusiasm for dressing up and recreating history reaches its zenith at **Den Gamle By** (The Old Town; ☎ 86 12 31 88; www.dengamleby.dk; Viborgvej 2; adult/child Dkr70/25; ☺ 9am-6pm Jun-Aug, 10am-5pm Apr, May, Sep & Oct, 10am-4pm Feb, Mar, Nov & Dec, 11am-3pm Jan). It's an engaging open-air museum of 75 half-timbered houses brought here from around Denmark and reconstructed as a provincial town, complete with a functioning bakery, silversmith and bookbinder. It's on Viborgvej, a 20-minute walk from the city centre. After hours you can walk through the old streets for free. It's an interesting time to visit as the crowds are gone and the light is ideal for photography, though you won't be able to enter individual buildings. Bus Nos 3, 14, 25 and 55 will take you there.

The **Botanical Garden**, with its thousands of plants and recreated Jutland environments, occupies the high ground above Den Gamle By and can be reached through an exit from the old town or directly from Vesterbrogade.

ÅRHUS DOMKIRKE
This impressive **cathedral** (☎ 86 12 38 45; Bispetorv; admission free; ☺ 9.30am-4pm Mon-Fri May-Sep, 10am-3pm Mon-Fri Oct-Apr) is Denmark's longest, with a lofty nave that spans nearly 100m. The original Romanesque chapel at the eastern

end dates from the 12th century, while most of the rest of the church is 15th-century Gothic.

Like other Danish churches, the cathedral was once richly decorated with **frescoes** that served to convey biblical parables to un-schooled peasants. After the Reformation, church authorities who felt the frescoes smacked too much of Roman Catholicism, had them all whitewashed, but many have now been uncovered and restored. They range from fairy-tale paintings of St George slaying a dragon, to scenes of hellfire.

The cathedral's splendid, five-panel, gilt **altarpiece** is a highlight. It was made in Lubeck by the renowned woodcarver Bernt Notke in the 15th century. In its centre panel, to the left of the Madonna and child, is a gaunt-faced St Clement, to whom Århus Dom-kirke was dedicated. The ill-fated Clement drowned at sea with an anchor around his neck and became the patron saint of sailors for his pains.

The cathedral's other items worth noting are the bronze baptismal **font** dating from 1481, the finely carved Renaissance **pulpit** created in 1588, the magnificent baroque **pipe organ** made in 1730, the large 18th-century **votive ship** and the baroque **sepulchre** in the Marselis family chapel.

VOR FRUE KIRKE
This **church** (☎ 86 12 12 43; Frue Kirkeplads; admission free; 🕑 10am-2pm Mon-Fri, 10am-noon Sat), off Vester-gade, has a carved wooden **altarpiece** dating from the 1530s. But far more interesting is what's in its basement – the **crypt** of the city's original cathedral, dating from about 1060. Enter via the stairway beneath the altar. To enter a third chapel, this one with 16th-century frescoes, go through the courtyard and take the left door.

VIKINGE-MUSEET
There's more than the expected vaults in the bank basement of **Nordea** (☎ 89 42 11 00; Sankt Clements Torv 6; admission free; 🕑 10am-4pm Mon-Wed & Fri, 10am-6pm Thu) where there's a small exhibition of artefacts from the Viking Age town that were excavated at this site in 1964 during the bank's construction.

The artefacts have been dated from the period 900 to 1400, suggesting that the heart of modern Århus housed one of the earliest settlements in the area. The display includes

a skeleton, a reconstructed house, 1000-year-old carpentry tools and pottery, and photos of the excavation.

MOESGÅRD
Visit Moesgård, 5km south of the city centre, for its glorious beech woods and the trails threading through them towards sandy beaches. Visit for the well-presented history exhibits from the Stone Age to the Viking Age at **Moesgård Museum of Prehistory** (adult/child Dkr45/free; 🕑 10am-5pm Apr-Sep, 10am-4pm Tue-Sun Oct-May). But above all else, visit Moesgård for the museum's most dramatic exhibit: the 2000-year-old **Grauballe Man**, or Grauballemanden, whose astonishingly well-preserved body was found in 1952 at the village of Grauballe, 35km west of Århus.

The superb new display on the Grauballe Man is part history lesson, part forensics lesson. Was he a sacrifice to Iron-Age fertility gods, an executed prisoner perhaps, or simply a victim of murder? Either way the broken leg and the gaping neck wound suggests his death, sometime in the last century BC, was a horribly violent one. His body and skin, tanned and preserved by the unique chemical and biological qualities of the peat bogs, are remarkably intact, right down to hair and fingernails.

Away from all this death and violence, there's an enjoyable **trail** dubbed the 'prehistoric trackway' or Oldtidsstien leading from behind the museum across fields of wildflowers, past grazing sheep and through beech woods down to **Moesgård Strand**, Århus' best sandy beach. The trail, marked by red-dotted stones, passes reconstructed historic sights including a dolmen, burial cists and an Iron-Age house. The museum has a brochure with details. You can walk one way and catch a bus back to the city centre, or follow the trail both ways as a 5km round-trip. It's all well worth a half-day or full-day visit, with a picnic perhaps if the weather behaves itself.

Bus No 6 from Århus train station terminates at the museum year-round, while bus No 19 terminates at Moesgård Strand from May to September; both buses run about twice an hour.

SWIMMING
There are sandy beaches on the outskirts of Århus. The most popular one to the north is **Bellevue**, about 4km from the city centre (bus

No 6 or 16), while the favourite to the south is Moesgård Strand (see p73).

Tours

A guided 2½-hour bus tour leaves from the **tourist office** (☎ 89 40 67 00 for bookings) at 10am daily from mid-June to early September, giving a glimpse of the main city sights. The Dkr50 tour is a good deal as it includes entry into Den Gamle By and also leaves you with a 24-hour public bus pass.

Århus Festival

The 10-day **Århus Festival** (www.aarhusfestuge.dk) in early September turns the city into a stage for nonstop revelry with jazz, rock, classical music, theatre and dance. The festival has hosted such varied bill toppers as the Rolling Stones, Philip Glass, Anne-Sophie Mutter, Ravi Shankar, the City of Birmingham Symphony Orchestra, New York City Ballet, Günter Grass and many more. Each year the festival has a special theme, such as dance, eros (with some X-rated shows as in 2005) or even a big political issue of the day. Events take place all over the city and there is a fringe element also.

Sleeping

BUDGET

Blommehaven (☎ 86 27 02 07; www.camping-blomme haven.dk, Danish only; adult/child/tent Dkr62/31/20; ☾ mid-Mar–mid-Sep) The nearest camping ground is right by beaches in the Marselisborg Woods, 6km south of Århus and reached by bus No 19 or 6.

Danhostel Århus (☎ 86 16 72 98; www.hostel-aar hus.dk; Marienlundsvej 10; dm/r Dkr108/472; ☾ late Jan–mid-Dec) In a renovated 1850s dance hall at the edge of the Risskov Woods, this hostel is a few minutes from the beach and 4km north of the city centre, reached by bus No 6 or 9.

Århus City Sleep-In (☎ 86 19 20 55; www.citysleep -in.dk; Havnegade 20; dm Dkr105, d with private/shared bathroom Dkr360/320; ☾ 24hr reception; 🖳 ☒) Run by a youth organisation, the Århus City Sleep-In is in a central former mariners' hotel. It's casual, the rooms are a bit rundown and it can be a noisy, but cheerful, place. Sheet hire costs Dkr40 and safety boxes are Dkr10, with Dkr100 deposit. Key deposit is Dkr50. There's a TV and pool table, guest kitchen and laundry facilities. Bike hire costs Dkr50 a day.

Get-in (☎ 86 10 86 14; www.get-in.dk; Jens Baggesensvej 43; s/d Dkr250/350, s/d with private bathroom Dkr300/400; 🅿)) The 62-room Get-in is a guesthouse near Århus University, about 1.5km from the city centre. It has clean, adequate rooms and there's a TV room and guest kitchen. Breakfast is Dkr35. Take bus No 7 from the train station.

The tourist office books rooms in private homes for around Dkr200/300 per single/ double, plus a Dkr25 booking fee.

MID-RANGE

Cab Inn Århus (☎ 86 75 70 00; www.cabinn.com; Kannikegade 14; s/d Dkr510/630; 🅿 ☒ 🖳) In an ideal central location opposite the Domkirke. The style is standard Cab Inn with small, but comfy and spotless rooms. Parking costs Dkr60. Free Internet and WiFi access.

Hotel Guldsmeden (☎ 86 13 45 50; www.hotelgulds meden.dk, Danish only; Guldsmedgade 40; s/d Dkr495/795, s/d with private bathroom from Dkr795/945; 🖳) On the northern side of the city centre, this is our mid-range choice in town for friendly staff, delightfully bright French colonial–style rooms with polished wood floors, large four-poster beds with soft white linen, a small garden terrace and a generally relaxed, stylish ambience. The buffet breakfast consists of mainly organic food. There's WiFi access.

TOP END

Hotel Ritz (☎ 86 13 44 44; www.hotelritz.dk; Banegårdsplads 12; s/d Dkr895/1085; 🅿 ☒ 🖳) A member of the Best Western chain, the business-orientated Ritz is close to the station and has plush, wood-panelled, burgundy-carpeted rooms, although some singles are small.

Villa Provence (☎ 86 18 24 00; www.villaprovence .dk; Fredens Torv 12; s/d from Dkr895/1470; 🅿 ☒ 🖳) Very central and with beautifully decorated rooms in a lavish Provençal country house style, this is the place to indulge, with attentive personal service, a predinner snifter in the wine bar, or perhaps breakfast in the courtyard beneath the linden trees.

Eating

The narrow streets of the old quarter north of the cathedral are thick with cafés serving Danish and ethnic foods. There is a string of more upmarket riverside restaurants and bars with outside seating along the north of Åboulevarden to the west of Sankt Clemens Torv bridge.

THE AUTHOR'S CHOICE

Globen Flakket (☎ 87 31 03 33; Åboulevarden 18; mains around Dkr125; 🕐 9am-late Mon-Thu) It may not stand out much visually but this is the best of the bar-cum-restaurants along Åboulevarden, serving a good brunch and tasty, if predictable, international dishes with fresh-leafed salads such as wraps (Dkr65), pasta (Dkr90) and burgers (Dkr65) in cosy surroundings. The real surprise is the remarkably polished brasserie fare, such as three types of local fish with a tasty 'pommes Anna' potato cake or roast guinea fowl in a ginger and soy vinaigrette accompanied by celery mash.

Emmery's (☎ 86 13 04 00; Guldsmedgade 24-26; brunch Dkr95, breakfast Dkr23; 🕐 7.30am-6pm Mon-Fri, 8am-4pm Sat & Sun) This stylish and friendly café-cum-delicatessen serves its own delicious bread, tapas (Dkr95) and sandwiches (Dkr45 to Dkr58), some with vegetarian fillings. There's a terrific selection of cheeses, olive oil and coffee from worldwide ethical sources.

Kulturgyngen (Mejlgade 53; lunch/dinner Dkr38/75; 🕐 11am-9pm Mon-Sat) The café-restaurant of an alternative cultural and youth complex has a great atmosphere and good, often organic food including sandwiches (Dkr27 to Dkr32) and a choice of vegetarian or meat dinners nightly.

Café Smagløs (☎ 86 19 03 77; Klostertorv 7; brunch Dkr65) Smagløs is a cosy, down-to-earth place with salads, sandwiches and vegetarian dishes (Dkr35 to Dkr58) and freshly pressed apple and orange juice.

Det Grønne Hjørne (☎ 86 13 52 47; Frederiksgade 60; lunch buffet Dkr59, buffet after 4pm Dkr99) On the corner with Østergade, this restaurant has a superb buffet spread with hearty, warming fare such as lasagne and chilli con carne and several good vegetarian options.

L'Estragon (☎ 86 12 40 66; Klostergade 6; mains Dkr195, 3-course menu Dkr315) The best central fine dining spot in Århus offers very posh French classics accompanied by carefully chosen wines.

If you want fast, cheap and filling takeaway fare, some good options include: **China Wok House** (Søndergade; lunch boxes Dkr20); **Shawarma Bar** (Guldsmedgade; pitta-bread sandwiches Dkr25); **Baguette** (Klostergade 17; baguettes Dkr19), close to Emmery's, which does well-filled baguettes; and **Bread and Coffee** (Banegårdspladsen; pastries Dkr9-15), which serves tasty pastries opposite the train station.

The train station has a DSB café, a snack bar and a small **supermarket** (🕐 to midnight). Two blocks west is **Føtex supermarket** (Frederiks Allé), with a cheap bakery and deli, and **Sundhedskost** (Frederiks Allé), the city's largest health-food store. There are a couple of useful branches of **7-Eleven** (cnr Lille Torv & Immervad, Guldsmedgade 33; 🕐 24hr).

Drinking

Coffee-To-Go Juice Stop (☎ 86 13 69 65; Badstuegade 4; juices small/large Dkr22/28, bagels/sandwiches Dkr30/40; 🕐 9am-6pm Mon-Fri, 9am-2pm Sat) A good place for a healthy juice, fruit salad and sandwich pit stop. It's mainly takeaway, but there are a couple of seats to rest those cobblestone weary feet.

Sherlock Holmes Pub (☎ 86 12 40 50; Frederiksgade 76d) Has live music, a big screen for football matches and cheap beer until 7pm.

Den Høje (Skolegade 28) There are a number of busy bars in Skolegade, where Den Høje is popular with an easygoing young crowd, not least for its cheap beer. It's open most nights from 7pm to 5am, closed Sundays.

Entertainment

The monthly free publication *What's On in Århus* lists current happenings in detail and is available at the tourist office and other venues around town.

Århus has a vibrant music scene with something for all ages and tastes.

Train (☎ 86 13 47 22; Toldbodgade 6; 🕐 until 5am Thu-Sat) One of the biggest venues in Denmark stages concerts by international rock, pop and country stars and there's a late-night disco.

Musikcaféen and the adjacent **Gyngen** (☎ 86 76 03 44; Mejlgade 53; 🕐 8.30pm-2am Mon-Sat) are alternative and often vibrant venues with rock, jazz and world music. They are a showcase for hopefuls and up-and-coming acts.

Jazzbar Bent J (☎ 86 12 04 92; Nørre Allé 66; 🕐 from 3.30pm Mon-Fri) This is a jazz only, very long-established bar with an impressive guest list. Entry is Dkr80 on guest nights.

Twist & Shout (☎ 86 18 08 55; Frederiksgade 29; 🕐 10am-5am Mon-Thu, from 5pm Fri & 10pm Sat) Lively, small, often packed and friendly, this three-floor disco is the place to head for later in the evening. It's not too precious, there's a mix of music from '60s to house (depending on the floor) and everyone has fun.

Pan Club (☎ 86 13 43 80; Jægergårdsgade 42). The main gay and lesbian social scene. To find it, head south down MP Bruuns Gade on the west side of the train station and then go right down Jægergårdsgade for 300m; it's on the left-hand side of the road. There's a late-night café on Tuesday, Thursday, Friday and Saturday and a disco on Thursday, Friday and Saturday. The Århus office of Landsfore-ningen for Bøsser og Lesbiske, the Danish national organisation for gays and lesbians, is across the courtyard from Pan Club. Ask there about special events and private club contacts.

Musikhuset Århus (☎ 89 40 40 40; Thomas Jensens Alle 2) The city concert hall presents dance, opera and concerts by international per-formers.

Getting There & Away
AIR
The airport, in Tirstrup 43km northeast of Århus, has direct flights from Copenhagen and London. Budget carrier Ryanair flies twice daily between London Stansted and Århus on weekdays and once on Saturday and Sunday. See p99 for details.

BOAT
The ferry operator is **Mols-Linien** (☎ 70 10 14 18). It runs car ferries from Århus to Odden (adult Dkr140 to Dkr205, child Dkr70 to Dkr103, car and five passengers Dkr545; 65 minutes) and Kalundborg (2½ hours).

BUS
The **bus station** (Fredensgade) has a DSB café, a small supermarket and a photocopier. **Express buses** (☎ 98 90 09 00) run a few times daily be-tween Århus and Copenhagen's Valby Station (adult/child Dkr220/110, students Dkr120 Monday to Thursday only, three hours). Buses run regularly to Silkeborg (adult/child Dkr48/30, 48 minutes, five daily) and Aal-borg (adult/child Dkr120/66, two hours, six daily).

CAR & MOTORCYCLE
The main highways to Århus are the E45 from the north and south and Rte 15 from the west. The E45 curves around the western edge of the city as a ring road. There are a number of turn-offs from the ring road into the city, including Åhavevej from the south and Randersvej from the north.

Cars can be rented from **Europcar** (☎ 89 33 11 11; Sønder Allé 35).

TRAIN
Trains to Århus, via Odense, leave Copenha-gen on the hour from early morning to 10pm (Dkr287, 3¼ hours) and there's a night train at 2am. There are regular trains to Aalborg (Dkr145, 1½ hours) and Esbjerg (Dkr199, 2¾ hours). There's a ticket-queuing system at the station – red for internal, green for international. For local journeys, unless you have mastered use of the quicker ticket ma-chines, be prepared for quite long waits at busy times. Friday trains are always very busy and it's advised to reserve a seat for long journeys.

Getting Around
TO/FROM THE AIRPORT
The airport bus to Århus train station costs Dkr60 and takes approximately 45 minutes. Check times to the airport at the stands outside the train station; some services start only in August. The taxi fare to the airport is about Dkr500.

BUS
Most in-town buses stop in front of the train station or around the corner on Park Allé. City bus tickets are bought from a machine in the back of the bus for Dkr17 and are good for unlimited rides within the time period stamped on the ticket, which is about two hours.

You can also buy a 24-hour pass for bus travel in Århus county (adult/child Dkr97/48) or in Århus municipality alone (Dkr50). Or get a one-/two-/seven-day Århus Passet (Dkr97/121/171) that includes both bus travel and entry into Århus museums. You can buy tickets and passes at **Århus Sporveje** (☎ 89 40 10 10; Banegårdspladsen 20; ☉ 10am-6pm Mon-Fri, 10am-1pm Sat), the city transport service shop across from the train station.

CAR & MOTORCYCLE
A car is convenient for getting to sights such as Moesgård on the city outskirts, though the city centre is best explored on foot. There's paid parking along many streets and in municipal car parks, including one on the southern side of Musikhuset Århus. Fees start at Dkr1 for six minutes and Dkr10 for one hour. Overnight (7pm to 8am) is free.

TAXI

Taxis wait outside the station and at Store Torv. Expect to pay around Dkr60 for destinations within the city.

JELLING

Jelling, in spite of its low-key rural character, is the location of one of Denmark's most important historic sites – the **Jelling Kirke**. Inside the small whitewashed church are frescoes dating from the 12th century, and outside the door are two impressive runic stones.

The smaller stone was erected in the early 900s by King Gorm the Old, Denmark's first king, in honour of his wife, Queen Thyra. The larger one, raised by Harald Bluetooth and dubbed 'Denmark's baptismal certificate', is adorned with the oldest representation of Christ found in Scandinavia and reads: 'Harald king bade this be ordained for Gorm his father and Thyra his mother, the Harald who won for himself all Denmark and Norway and made the Danes Christians.'

Two huge **burial mounds** flank the church; the one on the northern side is said to be that of King Gorm and the other of Queen Thyra, although excavators in the 19th century found no human remains and few artefacts. This could suggest much earlier grave robbing.

During the 1970s archaeologists excavated below Jelling Kirke and found the remains of three wooden churches. The oldest of these was thought to have been erected by Harald Bluetooth. A burial chamber within this site was also uncovered and revealed human bones and gold jewellery that shared characteristics with artefacts previously discovered within the large northern burial mound. One suggestion is that the bones found beneath the church ruins are those of King Gorm and they were moved there from the old pagan burial mound by Harald Bluetooth out of respect for his recently acquired Christian faith. Queen Thyra remains ephemeral. The Jelling mounds, church and rune stones are designated as a Unesco World Heritage Site.

Kongernes Jelling (☎ 75 87 23 50; Gormsgade 23; adult/child Dkr40/15; ☯ 10am-5pm Jun-Aug, 10am-5pm Tue-Sun May & Sep, 1-4pm Tue-Sun Nov-Apr) is an information and exhibition centre just across the road from the church. It traces the history of the Jelling monuments and it has a café where you can get a pleasant smorgasbord lunch for Dkr48.

Jelling makes a good two-hour side trip off the Odense–Århus run. Change trains at Vejle for the ride to Jelling (Dkr25, 15 minutes). The church is 100m straight up Stationsvej from the Jelling train station.

THE LAKE DISTRICT

The Danish Lake District, the closest thing to hill country in Denmark, is a popular outdoor-activity area for Danes, and there is certainly excellent canoeing, biking and hiking to be had amid the woods and on the water. The scenery is placid and pastoral rather than stunning, but the area is delightful all the same and has a distinctive character. The Lake District contains the Gudenå, Denmark's longest river; Mossø, Jutland's largest lake; and Yding Skovhøj, Denmark's highest point. None of these are terribly long, large or high by international standards.

Silkeborg
pop 54,000

Silkeborg overcomes its rather bland modern character with a friendly openness. It is the Lake District's biggest town and is an ideal base for exploring the surrounding forests and waterways. The town has some good restaurants and lively bars and cafés. If you're even slightly interested in Denmark's ancient history, a compelling reason to visit is to see the Tollund Man, the body of a preserved Iron-Age 'bog person' (see the boxed text, p79), who looks for all the world as if he's merely asleep.

The helpful **tourist office** (☎ 86 82 19 11; www .silkeborg.com; Åhavevej 2A; ☯ 9am-5pm Mon-Fri, 10am-2pm Sat, 10am-2pm Sun mid-Jun–Aug, 9am-4pm Mon-Fri, 9am-noon Sat Sep–mid-Jun) is near the harbour and has lots of leaflets including detailed route descriptions of walks and cycle routes. **Internettet** (Ngade 37; per hr Dkr25) is an Internet café.

SIGHTS

The main attraction at the **Silkeborg Museum** (☎ 86 82 14 99; Hovedgården; adult/child Dkr40/10; ☯ 10am-5pm mid-May–Oct; noon-4pm Sat & Sun Nov–mid-May) is the **Tollund Man**. He is believed to have been executed in 300 BC and his leathery body, complete with the rope still around the neck, was discovered in a bog in 1950. The well-preserved face of the Tollund

DENMARK

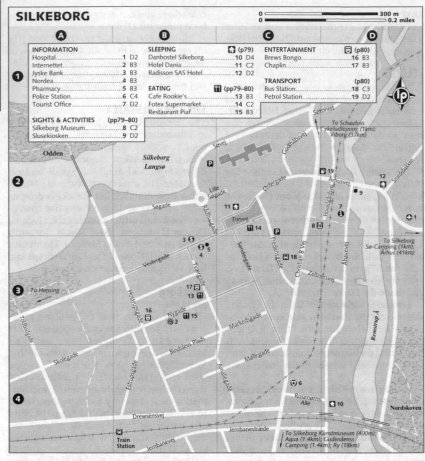

SILKEBORG

0 _____ 300 m
0 _____ 0.2 miles

INFORMATION		
Hospital	1	D2
Internettet	2	B3
Jyske Bank	3	B3
Nordea	4	B3
Pharmacy	5	B3
Police Station	6	C4
Tourist Office	7	D2

SIGHTS & ACTIVITIES	(pp79–80)	
Silkeborg Museum	8	C2
Slusekiosken	9	D2

SLEEPING	(p79)	
Danhostel Silkeborg	10	D4
Hotel Dania	11	C2
Radisson SAS Hotel	12	D2

EATING	(pp79–80)	
Cafe Rookie's	13	B3
Fotex Supermarket	14	C2
Restaurant Piaf	15	B3

ENTERTAINMENT	(p80)	
Brews Bongo	16	B3
Chaplin	17	B3

TRANSPORT	(p80)	
Bus Station	18	C3
Petrol Station	19	D2

Man is hypnotic in its detail, right down to the stubble on his chin. Other attractions include displays on local trades and of fine Danish glasswork.

The **Silkeborg Kuntsmuseum** (art museum; ☎ 86 82 53 88; Gudenåvej 7-9; adult/child Dkr40/free; ☯ 10am-5pm Tue-Sun Apr-Oct, noon-4pm Tue-Fri Nov-Mar) contains some striking work, such as the large ceramic walls by Jean Dubuffet and Pierre Alechinsky that greet visitors at the entrance. It displays many of the works of native son Asger Jorn and other modern artists, including Max Ernst, Le Corbusier and Danish artists from the influential COBRA group. It's 1km south of the town centre.

Situated 2km south of central Silkeborg, **Aqua** (☎ 89 21 21 89; Vejsøvej 55; adult/child Dkr70/40;

☯ 10am-6pm Jun-Aug, 10am-4pm Mon-Fri, 10am-5pm Sat & Sun Sep-May) is an entertaining aquarium and exhibition centre with lots of fishy creatures, otters and fishing birds among imaginative displays.

ACTIVITIES

Outdoor activities are at the heart of the Lake District's appeal. The track of the old railway from Silkeborg to Horsens is now an excellent **walking** and **cycling** trail of about 50km or so. It passes through the beech forest of **Nordskoven**, itself crisscrossed with hiking and bike trails. To reach Nordskoven simply head south down Åhavevej from the tourist office, then go left over the old railway bridge down by the hostel. The tourist

DENMARK'S BOG PEOPLE

In the last couple of centuries, hundreds of often amazingly well-preserved bodies of men, women and children have been unearthed by peat cutters in the bogs of Denmark and Northern Europe, mostly from the Iron Age (the early centuries BC and AD).

Each is a compelling compelling historical who- and why-dunnit. The manner of their death is intriguing because these people had not merely been buried after death (cremation was the common funerary ritual at the time). It seems many of them were ritually killed, perhaps as part of religious ceremonies or acts of propitiation linked to the supernatural power the Iron-Age people attributed to the bogs.

If it was ritual killing, were these people victims or willing participants? Was it perhaps an honour to be sacrificed? The Windeby Girl, for example, found in 1950 in Germany, aged about 14, had been blindfolded and had her hair carefully cropped, suggesting some kind of ritual.

Others, like the Grauballe Man (see p73) clearly died a nasty, violent death that suggests execution. Others may have simply been waylaid, murdered and dumped. Classical authors at the time such as Tacitus wrote that this was the kind of end met by 'cowards, deserters and homosexuals'.

The most famous, and best preserved, body is that of the Tollund Man in Silkeborg. He died, aged in his 30s, naked but for the beautifully plaited leather noose that strangled him and the leather cap he has worn for 2000 years. It frames an utterly serene face.

office has useful leaflets on Nordskoven and on the Silkeborg–Horsens trail.

Canoeing is a marvellous way to explore the Lake District and you can plan trips for several days staying at lakeside camping grounds along the way. The canoe-hire places can help plan an itinerary. You can rent canoes for Dkr60/300 an hour/day at **Slusekiosken** (☎ 86 80 08 93) at the harbour.

Bike hire costs Dkr69 per day at **Schaufuss Cykeludlejning** (☎ 86 81 39 38; Nørreskov Bakke 93), which is about 1.5km from Torvet across Silkeborg Langsø and is reached by Bus No 5. **Silkeborg Sø-camping** rents out bikes and canoes from Dkr60 per day.

SLEEPING

Gudenåenss Camping (☎ 86 82 22 01; Vejlsøvej 7; adult/child/tent Dkr63/33/28) The camping ground is 1km south of the art museum and is amid woodland.

Silkeborg Sø-camping (☎ 86 82 28 24; Århusvej 51; adult/child/tent Dkr63/31/28) In a lakeside setting 1.5km east of the town centre.

Danhostel Silkeborg (☎ 86 82 36 42; silkeborg@ danhostel.dk; Åhavevej 55; dm Dkr115; ☯ Mar–end Nov; ⓟ ☒ ▣) This hostel has a scenic riverbank location and is a few minutes walk east of the train station. There are only dorms, no private rooms.

The tourist office distributes a list of rooms in private homes, with singles/doubles costing around Dkr150/350.

Hotel Dania (☎ 86 82 01 11; info@hoteldania.dk; Torvet 5; s/d Dkr1090/1265, s/d discount summer Dkr795/1095; ⓟ) Silkeborg's prime-site, luxury hotel in the heart of town.

Radisson SAS Hotel (☎ 88 82 22 22; info.silkeborg@ radissonsas.com; Papirfabrikken 12; s/d Dkr950/1180, d discount summer from Dkr795; ⓟ ☒ ▣) The Radisson is simply the best place to stay in town. It's a comfortable, business-class hotel in a converted mill. The huge rooms in a simple, modern Scandinavian style have large beds and all mod-cons. There's a bar and restaurant, plus WiFi and discounted use of a nearby fitness centre.

EATING

Nygade is Silkeborg's equivalent to Aalborg's 'street of bars' Jomfru Ane Gade, but with more everyday shops. There are a number of grill bars and pizza places with quick bites for Dkr20 to Dkr35.

Restaurant Piaf (☎ 86 81 12 55; Nygade 31; mains from Dkr180; ☯ 6-10.30pm Mon-Sat) Piaf has superb, French-inspired cuisine in cosy surroundings. If it is your wont, this is the place in town to treat yourself.

Café Rookie's (☎ 86 81 33 44; Nygade 18; sandwiches Dkr25-48; ☯ 11am-11pm) A relaxed place, close to Restaurant Piaf, that does good ciabatta sandwiches, salads, smoothies and shakes and has a vegetarian menu for Dkr28 to Dkr49. It stays open until the early hours on Thursday, Friday and Saturday.

DENMARK

There are a number of cheap food outlets on Søndergade, the pedestrianised main street. The **Føtex supermarket** (Torvet) has a bakery and an inexpensive café.

ENTERTAINMENT
Nygade has several good music bars and discos. **Brews 'n Bongo** (cnr Hopstrupsgade; ☾ from 11pm Thu, Fri & Sat) and **Chaplin's** (Nygade, behind Café Rookie's; ☾ Thu-Sat) are late-night music bars.

GETTING THERE & AWAY
Hourly trains connect Silkeborg with Skanderborg (Dkr48, 30 minutes) and Århus (Dkr60, 49 minutes) via Ry. There are regular daily buses to Århus (Dkr48, 48 minutes).

Ry
Ry is a smaller town in a more rural setting than Silkeborg and is a good place from which to base your exploration of the Lake District. The helpful **tourist office** (☎ 86 89 34 22; www.visitry.com; Klostervej 3; ☾ 7am-4pm Mon-Fri, 9am-2pm Sat mid-Jun–Aug, 9am-4pm Mon-Fri, 9am-noon Sat Sep–mid-Jun) is in the train station.

SIGHTS & ACTIVITIES
The Lake District's most visited spot is the whimsically named **Himmelbjerget** (Sky Mountain), which, at just 147m, is one of Denmark's highest hills. It was formed by water erosion during the final Ice Age as a 'false hill' or *kol*, the sides of which are quite steep. Himmelbjerget holds great significance for Danes. There are a number of interesting memorials surrounding the hilltop's crowning glory, the 25m **tower** (admission Dkr5), which has superlative views. It was built in 1875 to commemorate King Frederick VII, who introduced constitutional government to Denmark in 1849. Open-air meetings, both political and cultural have been held on the summit of Himmelbjerget. The summit can be reached via a marked 6km footpath from Ry, or by bus or boat.

Another good, half-day outing is to cycle from Ry to **Boes**, a tiny hamlet with picturesque, thatch-roofed houses and vivid flower gardens. From Boes continue cross country to **Øm Kloster** (☎ 86 89 81 94; adult/child Dkr35/10; ☾ 10am-6pm Tue-Sun Jul-Aug, 10am-5pm May-Jun & Sep, 10am-4pm Apr & Oct), the ruins of a medieval monastery, where glass-topped tombs reveal the 750-year-old bones of Bishop Elafsen of Århus and many of his

abbots. The whole trip from Ry and back is 18km.

If you want to explore the lakes in the district, **Ry Kanofart** (☎ 86 89 11 67; Kyhnsvej 20) rents out canoes for Dkr60/300 an hour/day. For walking and cycling routes ask at the tourist centre for cycling and walking leaflets (Dkr20). **Cykeludlejning** (☎ 86 89 14 91; Skanderborgvej 19) rents out bikes for Dkr50 a day.

SLEEPING & EATING
Knudhule (☎ 86 89 14 07; www.knudhule.dk; Randersvej 88; cabins s & d Dkr325, tr & q Dkr350, bungalows Dkr460) Knudhule is an appealing budget holiday camp on a picturesque lake. There are cabins without bathrooms and bungalows (sleeping up to four) with bathrooms. There's also a small restaurant, minigolf, boat hire and swimming/diving platforms on the lake. To get there from the train station, cross the tracks, turn left and go 2.5km; or take the infrequent bus No 311.

The tourist office books rooms in private homes from Dkr200/275 for singles/doubles.

The **butcher's shop** (opposite train station) has fried fish and a few other takeaway selections. There's a bakery next door.

Pizzeria Italia (☎ 86 89 31 33; Skanderbrgvej 3; fish & meat mains Dkr109-147) There are several restaurants and fast-food places on Skanderborgvej including Pizzeria Italia, which offers tasty pastas (Dkr69) and a three-course menu (Dkr179).

GETTING THERE & AWAY
Hourly trains connect Ry with Silkeborg (Dkr26, 20 minutes) and Århus (Dkr36, 30 minutes).

Viborg
pop 12,700
Viborg's rich history and religious associations rest happily with what has become a charming and very modern Danish town. Nearby lakes and surrounding woodland enhance its appeal. In 1060, Viborg became one of Denmark's eight bishoprics and grew into a major religious centre. Prior to the Reformation the town had 25 churches and abbeys, though ecclesiastical remnants from that period are few.

Orientation & Information
The old part of town consists of the street that's around Viborg Domkirke. The train

station is about 1km southwest of the tourist office.

The **tourist office** (☎ 87 25 30 75; www.visitviborg .dk; Nytorv 9; ◷ 9am-5pm Mon-Fri, 9am-2pm Sat mid-Jun–Aug, 9am-5pm Mon-Fri, 9.30am-2.30pm Sat mid-May–mid-Jun, 9am-4pm Mon-Fri, 9.30am-12.30pm Sat Sep-Apr) is in the centre of town.

There is ample and convenient free parking behind the Sankt Mathias Gade Shopping Centre on the south side of town, but you must use a time disc.

Sights & Activities

The tourist office has excellent printouts, including English-language versions, which describe walks around the town with historical and cultural themes.

The multitowered **Viborg Domkirke** (☎ 87 25 52 50; Sankt Mogens Gade 4; admission free; ◷ 10am-5pm Mon-Sat, noon-5pm Sun Jun-Aug; 11am-4pm Mon-Sat, noon-4pm Sun Apr-May & Sep; 11am-3pm Mon-Sat, noon-3pm Sun Jan-Mar) is one of Denmark's largest granite churches and dominates the town. The first church on the site dated from the Viking period. The interior is awash with frescoes painted over five years (1901–06) by artist Joakim Skovgaard and featuring scenes from the Old Testament and the life of Christ.

Skovgaard Museet (☎ 86 62 39 75; Domkirkestræde 2-4; adult/child Dkr20/free; ◷ 10am-12.30pm & 1.30-5pm May-Sep, 1.30-5pm Oct-Apr) lies to the south of Viborg Domkirke. It also features work by Joakim Skovgaard, but here the scenes are more down to earth and include portraits, landscapes and nudes.

Viborg Stiftsmuseum (☎ 87 25 26 20; Hjultorvet 9; adult/child Dkr25/free; ◷ 11am-5pm mid-Jun–Aug, 2-5pm Tue-Fri, 11am-5pm Sat & Sun Sep–mid-Jun) is a local history museum that tells the story of Viborg's rich past.

Sankt Mogens Gade, between the cathedral and the tourist office, has some handsome old houses, including Hauchs Gård at No 7 and the Willesens House at No 9, both dating back to around 1520.

Sleeping & Eating

Viborg Sø Camping (☎ 86 67 13 11; www.camping -viborg.dk, Danish only; Vinkelvej 36b; adult/child/tent Dkr62/31/20; ◷ late Mar–late Sep) Viborg is a well-ordered, three star camping ground at a pleasant, leafy location on the east side of Lake Søndersø.

Danhostel Viborg (☎ 86 67 17 81; viborg@danhostel .dk; Vinkelvej 36; P 🗙) Adjacent to Viborg Sø

Camping and a 1km walk from town. It hires bikes.

Staff at the tourist office can book rooms in private homes with singles/doubles starting at Dkr200/275 plus a Dkr25 booking fee.

Palads Hotel (☎ 86 62 37 00; www.hotelpalads.dk; Sankt Mathias Gade; s/d Dkr895/1095; P 🗙) Straddling four sites, this long-established hotel is now part of the Best Western chain and has bright, pleasant rooms (some with kitchenettes). It's just a short walk north of the train station.

The huge Sankt Mathias Gade Centre has cafés, a supermarket, fruit shop, a butcher and a baker.

Ristorante Pizzeria Italia (☎ 86 62 42 43; Sankt Mathias Gade 74; buffet lunch Dkr49) This restaurant does tasty pasta (Dkr45), pizza (Dkr45 to Dkr50) and a children's pizza (Dkr29).

Kafé Arthur (☎ 86 62 21 26; Vestergade 4; 2-course dinner Dkr230) A stylish yet cosy venue lit by candles, Kafé Arthur serves fancy Italian-influenced fare such as pan-fried quail with pancetta and fried sweetbreads (Dkr185) and scallop ravioli (Dkr82); it also does a good lunch menu for about Dkr70.

Café Morville (☎ 86 60 22 11; Hjultorvet; brunch Dkr79, mains Dkr158-168) A bustling place with sleek, modern decor and some good bistro-style dishes such as young grouse breast with herb stuffing and grape sauce (Dkr158).

Getting There & Around

Viborg is 66km northwest of Århus on Rte 26 and 41km west of Randers on Rte 16. Trains from Århus (Dk94, 70 minutes) run hourly Monday to Friday, and less frequently at weekends.

The tourist office has a few bikes for hire for Dkr100 a day.

AALBORG

pop 155,000

People soon warm to Aalborg's unassuming style. It has some worthwhile sites, not least the remarkable Lindholm Høje, Denmark's largest Viking burial ground. This is Jutland's second largest city, an industrial and trading centre with few great buildings or much medieval quaintness to enliven its commercialism. It's actually one of Denmark's most depressed cities, hit first by the decline in heavy industry and then, after retooling itself for the information age, hit again when the technology bubble burst at the turn of the last century. Unemployment is still high, yet to the visitor it doesn't feel depressed and Aalborg is a friendly, down-to-earth place with plenty of good shops and a lively nightlife.

Orientation

Linked by bridge and tunnel, the city spreads across both sides of the Limfjord, the long body of water that cuts Jutland in two. Most of the sights, eating, drinking and sleeping options lie south of the Limfjord. The town centre is a 10-minute walk north on Boulevarden from the train and bus stations.

Information

Boomtown (Nytorv 18-20; per hr Dkr25)
Danish Emigration Archives (☎ 99 31 42 20; Arkivstræde 1) Behind Vor Frue Kirke, helps foreigners of Danish descent trace their roots.
Hovedbiblioteket (City library; Rendsburggade 2; ☺ 10am-8pm Mon-Fri, 10am-3pm Sat) Offers free Internet access.
Landsforeningen for Bøsser og Lesbiske (LBL; ☎ 98 16 45 07; Toldbodgade 27) The local branch of the Danish national organisation for gays and lesbians.
Laundrette (cnr Rantzausgade & Christiansgade; ☺ 8am-8pm)
Post Office (Algade 42)
Tourist Office (☎ 99 30 60 90; www.visitaalborg.com; Østerågade 8; ☺ 9am-5.30pm Mon-Fri, 10am-1pm Sat mid-Jun–Aug, 9am-4.30pm Mon-Fri, 10am-1pm Sat Sep–mid-Jun) Friendly and helpful, with masses of information, including a diary of events, *What's on in Aalborg*.

Sights

OLD TOWN

The whitewashed **Buldolfi Domkirke** marks the centre of the old town, and has colourful frescoes in the foyer. About 75m east of the cathedral is the **Aalborg Historiske Museum** (Algade 48; adult/child Dkr20/10; ☺ 9am-4pm Mon-Fri, 9am-2pm Sat) with interesting artefacts from prehistory to the present and Renaissance furnishings.

The alley between the museum and church leads to the rambling **Monastery of the Holy Ghost**, which dates from 1431; the tourist office arranges guided tours in summer (Dkr40). Northeast of the cathedral on Østerågade are three noteworthy historic buildings: the **old town hall** (c 1762), five-storey **Jens Bangs Stenhus** (built c 1624 by wealthy merchant Jens Bangs) and **Jørgen Olufsens House** (c 1616).

In addition, the half-timbered neighbourhoods around **Vor Frue Kirke** are worth a stroll,

particularly the cobbled Hjelmerstald. **Aalborghus Slot**, near the waterfront, is more administrative office than castle, but there's a small dungeon you can enter for free.

NORDJYLLANDS KUNSTMUSEUM

This **regional art museum** (☎ 98 13 80 88; Kong Christian Allé 50; adult/child Dkr40/free; ☺ 10am-5pm Tue-Sun), in a marble, blocky, modular building designed by Finnish architect Alvar Aalto, has a fine collection of Danish modern art, including work by Asger Jorn and JF Willumsen.

To get to the museum, take the tunnel beneath the train station; it leads to Kildeparken, a green space with statues and water fountains. Go directly through the park, cross Vesterbro and then continue through a wooded area to the museum, a 10-minute walk in all. Alternatively take bus No 5, 8, 10 or 11 from the centre of town.

AALBORG TOWER

The hill behind the art museum has an ungainly 105m **tower** (☎ 98 77 05 11; Søndre Skovvej; adult/child Dkr25/15; ☺ 11am-5pm Apr, Jun, Aug & Sep, 10am-7pm Jul) with a panoramic view of the city's steeples and smokestacks. The tower sits on the edge of an expansive wooded area, **Mølleparken**, which has walking trails, views and a zoo.

LINDHOLM HØJE

On a hill-top pasture overlooking the city and ringed by a wall of tall beech trees, **Lindholm Høje** (admission free; ☺ dawn-dusk) is the site of nearly 700 graves from the Iron Age and Viking Age. Many of the Viking graves are marked by stones placed in the outline of a Viking ship, with two larger end stones as stem and stern. There's a **museum** (☎ 96 31 04 28; adult/child Dkr30/15; ☺ 10am-5pm Apr-Oct), adjacent to the field, which depicts the site's history in an imaginative way, while huge murals behind the exhibits speculate on what the people of Lindholm looked like and how they lived. Lindholm Høje is 15 minutes from Aalborg centre on bus No 2.

Sleeping

Danhostel Aalborg (☎ 98 11 60 44; www.danhostel .dk/aalborg; Skydebanevej 50; dm/r Dkr118/480; P ☐) The hostel is at the marina 4km west of the centre and has an adjacent camping ground with cabins.

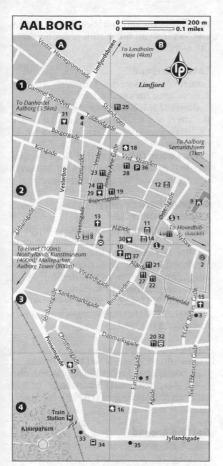

AALBORG

The tourist office books rooms in private homes for Dkr200/300 for singles/doubles plus a Dkr25 booking fee.

Prinsens Hotel (☎ 98 13 37 33; www.prinsen-hotel .dk; Prinsensgade 14; s/d from Dkr545/645; P X 💻) Modern, good-value rooms (although some are rather small) make this the best value in town, especially given the free extras (such as free Internet, WiFi, solarium and tea and coffee.) There's also a sauna and Jacuzzi.

Park Hotel (☎ 98 12 31 33; parkhotel@email.dk; Boulevarden 41; s/d from Dkr785/915, d discount summer Dkr750; P X 💻) Has comfortable rooms and traditional decor and is just 100m from the train and bus stations.

Radisson SAS Limfjord (☎ 98 16 43 33; http://radis sonsas.com; Ved Stranden 14-16; s/d Dkr1195/1395, s/d dis-count summer Dkr795/895; P X 💻) The top-end place in town with well-furnished, well-equipped, modern rooms. There's also a solarium and gym.

Eating

A good place for food, drink and diversion is Aalborg's famous Jomfru Ane Gade, a lively, pedestrian street jammed solid with restaurants and bars, most with pavement tables and competitive prices. It is the heart of Aalborg's nightlife and most places are open to the early hours.

7-Eleven (cnr Bispensgade; ⊕ 24hr) If you want just food rather than fun, there's this 24-hour minimarket.

Rendez Vous (☎ 98 16 88 80; Jomfru Ane Gade 5; fish & meat mains Dkr75-110) At the popular Rendez Vous you can get a tasty brunch, including a 'fitness' healthy eating version.

Frytøjet (☎ 98 13 73 77; Jomfru Ane Gade 17; lunch dishes Dkr60, mains Dkr130-190) Just opposite Rendez Vous, this place offers Danish and Mexican fare.

Sushi & Ko (☎ 98 10 98 40; Ved Stranden 11b; menus Dkr69-159; ⏰ 4-10pm Mon-Fri, noon-10pm Sat, 3-9pm Sun) Sit and enjoy, or pay and takeaway terrific, fresh sushi from this small place around the corner from Jomfru Ane Gade. Tackle the fierce but toothsome wasabi-roasted peas if you dare.

Rosdahls (☎ 98 12 05 80; Strandvejen 6; lunch Dkr58-188, 3-/4-course evening menu Dkr375/415; ⏰ 11.30am-3pm & 5.30-10pm Mon-Fri, 10am-10pm Sat) A new place in an impressive converted warehouse right by the water, offering pricey evening fine-dining fare, more affordable tapas (Dkr22 to Dkr88) and lunch options (such as pan-fried fish fillet with remoulade, pickles and rye bread for Dkr58). The food is uniformly impressive, particularly the house speciality: heavenly, delicate wedges of home-smoked salmon (Dkr65). Good wine is available in the restaurant or to buy in the adjoining shop and staff are knowledgeable.

Algade, a pedestrian shopping street a block south of the tourist office, offers inexpensive options.

Schak Nielsen (☎ 98 12 35 92; Algade 23) Take-away salmonburgers and a range of tasty fish specialities are available from this good fish shop. There's a bakery just opposite.

Café Underground (Algade 21) Offers natural ice cream, crêpes and sandwiches.

Ali-Baba (☎ 98 12 73 11; Danmarksgade 27) The well-stocked Ali-Baba is an excellent delicatessen just by the Pan Club.

Salling (Nytorv) This department store has a basement supermarket with a good deli.

Drinking

Wharf (☎ 98 11 70 10; The Wharf, Borgergade 16) An incredible place dedicated to cask ale and serving up to 44 different British, Belgian, Irish and German beers the length of its capacious bar. There's also a huge selection of rare single-malt whiskies.

Studenterhuset (student union; ☎ 98 11 05 22; Gammeltorv 10) This good budget drinking and entertainment option is a surprisingly cosy one, lined with books on shelves. There's inexpensive beer and regular live bands and DJ nights.

Royal Pub (☎ 98 13 20 80; Jomfru Ane Gade 3) A popular drinking spot, the Royal has a wide range of beers and spirits, although there's always plenty of other stuff going on along this street.

Entertainment

Jomfru Ane Gade has a number of early hours dance bars and discos.

Huset (☎ 98 16 76 66; Hasserisgade 10) Away from the street of bars, Huset is a cultural centre that stages a series of jazz, folk and world music events.

Pan Aalborg Club (☎ 98 12 22 45; Danmarksgade 27A; ⏰ 11am-2am Thu, 10am-5am Fri & Sat) Aalborg's main gay venue has a bar and disco.

Getting There & Away

CAR & MOTORCYCLE

The E45 bypasses the city centre, tunnelling under the Limfjord, whereas the connecting Rte 180 leads into the centre. To get to Lindholm Høje or points north from Aalborg centre, take Rte 180 (Vesterbro), which crosses the Limfjord by bridge.

Avis (☎ 98 13 30 99) is at the train station. **Europcar** (☎ 98 13 23 55; Jyllandsgade 4) is a short distance to the west.

TRAIN

Trains run to Århus (Dkr145, 1½ hours, at least hourly) and Frederikshavn (Dkr68, one hour, every two hours). **Express buses** (☎ 70 21 08 88) run to Copenhagen (Dkr220, five hours, daily).

Getting Around

City buses leave from the intersection of Østerågade and Nytorv. The bus fare is Dkr13 to any place in greater Aalborg.

Despite a few one-way streets and the often-confusing outer roads that may have you driving in circles, central Aalborg is fairly easy to get around by car. There's metered parking in the city centre (Dkr8/64, one/24 hours) and time-limited, free parking along many side streets, but you need to use a parking disc. If you're unable to find a parking space, there's a large parking garage, **Palads Parking** (Ved Stranden 11).

REBILD BAKKER NATIONAL PARK

Rebild Bakker National Park is a great place to unwind from too much urban experience by tramping through its lovely rolling hills and heathland. It was founded in 1912 by Danish-Americans and is best known for its

US-style 4th of July celebration, the largest held outside the USA.

A 4km trail begins in a sheep meadow opposite the Lincoln cabin, and numerous other trails crisscross the park and the adjacent Rold Skov, Denmark's largest forest. The Ministry of the Environment publishes a useful leaflet *Rebild Bakker Himmerland* that gives basic directions for a number of rewarding walks. One of the best is the 3km Ravnkilde–Nordre Dybdal trail, which takes in some good views and passes interesting old buildings and ruins.

The **Rebild Festival** is an annual event on 4 July, celebrating Danish-American connections. It commemorates over 300,000 Danish immigrants to the USA during the late 19th and early 20th centuries and the strong familial bonds that survive between the USA and Denmark. There are concerts by military and civilian orchestras and bands, receptions, picnics, dancing, and rock- and country-music shows.

Safari Camping (☎ 98 39 11 10; Rebildvej 17; adult/child Dkr66/33) is nearby. You can get meals at the park cafeterias. The thatch-roofed **Danhostel Rebild** (☎ 98 39 13 40; www.vandrerhjem.net; dm/r Dkr115/375; P) is next to the park entrance.

From Aalborg, Århus-bound trains stop in Skørping (Dkr42, 16 minutes), from where it's 3km to Rebild. Bus No 104 runs between Aalborg and Rebild (Dkr36, 45 minutes, 10 times daily Monday to Friday, six times daily Saturday and Sunday), via Skørping.

FREDERIKSHAVN
pop 34,000

Frederikshavn is a major ferry town and industrial port with a fairly featureless dockside area; but the town has a pleasant pedestrianised centre with plenty of shops and several attractive bars and restaurants.

An overhead walkway leads from the ferry terminal to the **tourist office** (☎ 98 42 32 66; www .frederikshavn-tourist.dk; Skandiatorv 1; ⏰ 8.30am-7pm Mon-Sat, 8.30am 5pm Sun Jul–mid-Aug, 8.30am-5pm last 2 weeks Jun & Aug, 9am-4pm Mon-Fri, 11am-2pm Sat Sep–mid-Jun). The train station and adjacent bus terminal are a 10-minute walk to the north.

Sights
BANGSBOMUSEET

This **museum** (☎ 98 42 31 11; Margrethesvej 6; adult/child Dkr30/5; ⏰ 10am-5pm Jun-Aug, 10.30am-5pm Sep-May, closed Mon Nov-May), 3km south of Fred-

erikshavn centre, is an old country estate with an interesting mix of exhibits. In the manor house there are displays of antique furnishings and collectibles, while the old farm buildings hold ship figureheads, military paraphernalia and exhibits on Danish resistance to the German occupation. The most intriguing exhibit is the *Ellingå* ship, reconstructed remains of a 12th-century Viking-style merchant ship that was dug up from a nearby stream bed. Bus No 3 from central Frederikshavn stops near the entrance to the estate, from where it's an enjoyable 500m walk through the woods to the museum. The adjoining **Bangsbo Botanical Gardens** has a deer park and makes a pleasant additional visit.

KRUDTTÅRNET

If you're waiting for a train, you might want to climb the nearby whitewashed **Krudttårnet** (☎ 98 42 31 11; Kragholmen 1; adult/child Dkr15/5; ⏰ 10.30am-5pm Jun-Sep). It's an old gun tower and powder magazine, a remnant of the 17th-century citadel that once protected the port. Various pieces of artillery are on display at the top.

Sleeping & Eating
Danhostel Frederikshavn (☎ 98 42 14 75; www.dan hostel.dk/frederikshavn; Buhlsvej 6; dm/s/d Dkr100/240/300; ⏰ Feb–mid-Dec; P ✗) A pleasant, neat place with chalet-style six-bed dorms 2km north of the ferry terminal.

The tourist office books rooms in private homes from Dkr150/175 for singles/doubles, plus a Dkr25 booking fee.

City Hostel (☎ 98 42 14 21; www.city-hostel.dk; s/d/ tr/q Dkr200/300/400/500; P) Adjoining Herman Bang is this good, if basic, central budget option.

Hotel Herman Bang (☎ 98 42 21 66; www.herman bang.dk, Danish only; Tordenskjoldsgade 3; s/d Dkr495/695, s/d with private bathroom Dkr595/795; P) This central hotel has bright, comfortable rooms. There's an upmarket spa next door for beauty and relaxation treatments.

There are pizzerias on nearby Danmarksgade and Søndergade.

Damsgaard Supermarked (Havnegade) Next to the tourist office, Damsgaard has a cheap cafeteria with a harbour view and a good buffet breakfast (Dkr45).

Emona (☎ 98 43 34 36; Rimmensgade 4b; pizza & pasta Dkr45 60) A busy little place just off the south end of Søndergade, Emona is a basic place for a fuel stop.

Havne Super (Sydhavnesvej 8) If you're catching a ferry, Havne Super is a supermarket at the harbour with a cafeteria and long hours. Consider picking up provisions if you're going on to expensive Norway.

Getting There & Away
BOAT
From Frederikshavn to Göteborg, Sweden, **Stena Line** (☎ 96 20 02 00) runs ferries (adult Dkr100 to Dkr160, child Dkr50 to Dkr80, two to 3¼ hours, six to 10 times daily). It also runs to Oslo (adult Dkr170 to Dkr350, child Dkr85 to Dkr175, 8½ hours, daily). Prices depend on season and day of week.

Color Line (☎ 99 56 20 00; www.colorline.com) has ferries to Larvik, Norway (adult Dkr180 to Dkr420, child Dkr90 to Dkr210, 6¼ hours, daily). Both Stena and Color Lines also carry vehicles, with prices varying by the day and season.

BUS & TRAIN
Frederikshavn is the northern terminus of the DSB train line. Trains run about hourly south to Aalborg (Dkr71.50) and on to Copenhagen (Dkr310). **Nordjyllands Trafikselskab** (NT; ☎ 98 11 11 11; www.nordjyllandstrafikselskab.dk, Danish only) has both a train (40 minutes) and bus service (one hour) north to Skagen (Dkr45).

SKAGEN
pop 10,500

Artists discovered Skagen's luminous light and its colourful, heath-and-dune landscape in the mid-19th century and fixed eagerly on the romantic imagery of the area's fishing life that had earned the people of Skagen a hard living for centuries. Painters such as Michael and Anna Ancher and Oscar Björck followed the contemporary fashion of painting *en plein air* (out of doors), often regardless of the weather. Their work established a vivid figurative style of painting that became known as the 'Skagen School'.

Today, Skagen is a major tourist resort, packed to its figurative gunwales in high summer. But the sense of a more picturesque Skagen survives and the town's older neighbourhoods are filled with distinctive, yellow-washed houses, each with red-tile roofs that are painted with distinctive bands of whitewash at their edges.

Skagen is now a mix of arts, crafts and conspicuous tourism, with plenty of souvenir shops, art galleries and ice-cream parlours. The **Skagen music festival** (www.skagenfestival.dk, Danish only) packs the town out with official performers, buskers and appreciative visitors during the last weekend of June. The peninsula is lined with fine beaches, including a sandy stretch on the eastern end of Østre Strandvej, a 15-minute walk from the town centre.

Orientation & Information
Sankt Laurentii Vej, Skagen's main street, runs almost the entire length of this long thin town, and is never more than five minutes from the waterfront. The **tourist office** (☎ 98 44 13 77; www.skagen-tourist.dk; Sankt Laurentii Vej 22; ☺ 9am-6pm Mon-Sat, 10am-4pm Sun late Jun–early Aug, closes 5pm early Jun & late Aug, 9am-4pm Mon-Sat, 10am-1pm Sun May & Sep, earlier closing Oct-May) is in the train/bus station.

Sights
GRENEN
Appropriately for such a neatly kept country, Denmark doesn't end untidily at its most northerly point, but on a neat finger of sand just a few metres wide. You can actually paddle at its tip where the waters of the Kattegat and Skagerrak clash and you can put one foot in each sea; but not too far. Bathing is strictly forbidden here because of the ferocious tidal currents and often angry seas that collide to create mane-tossing white horses.

The tip is the culmination of a long, curving sweep of sand at Grenen, about 3km northeast of Skagen along Rte 40. Where the road ends there's a car park, café and souvenir shops, plus, in high summer, what seems like the entire population of Denmark. Crowds head along the last stretch of beach for the 30-minute walk to the tip. A special tractor-drawn bus, the *Sandormen*, leaves from the car park every half-hour, waits for 15 minutes at the beach end, then returns (adult/child return-trip Dkr15/10). From May to September, buses run from Skagen station to Grenen hourly (Dkr15) until 5pm. Taxis, available at the train station, charge about Dkr65 to Grenen.

SKAGENS MUSEUM
This fine **museum** (☎ 98 44 64 44; Brøndumsvej 4; admission Dkr60; ☺ 10am-5pm or 6pm May-Aug, 11am-4pm Tue-Sun Apr, 1-5pm Wed-Fri, 11am-4pm Sat, 11am-3pm

Sun Nov-Mar) displays the paintings of Michael and Anna Ancher and PS Krøyer, and of other artists who flocked to Skagen between 1830 and 1930.

MICHAEL & ANNA ANCHER'S HUS

This poignant domestic **museum** (☎ 98 44 30 09; Markvej 2-4; adult/child Dkr50/10; ☒ 10am-6pm mid-Jun–mid-Aug, 10am-5pm May–mid-Jun, 11am-3pm Apr & Oct, 11am-3am Sat & Sun Nov-Mar) is in the house that the Anchers bought in 1884 and in which their daughter Helga lived until 1960.

SKAGEN BY-OG EGNSMUSEUM

This well-presented, **open-air museum** (☎ 98 44 47 60; Pk Nielsonvej 8-10; adult/child Dkr30/5; ☒ 10am-5pm May–Jun, 10am-6pm Jul, 10am-4pm Mon-Fri Mar-Apr & Oct-Nov) depicts Skagen's maritime history and includes a picturesque old windmill as well as the period homes of fisherfolk. It's a 15-minute walk from the train station, west down Sankt Laurentii Vej, then south on Vesterled.

TILSANDEDE KIRKE

This whitewashed medieval **church tower** (☎ 98 44 43 71; adult/child Dkr8/4; ☒ 11am-5pm Jun-Sep) still rises above the sand dunes that buried the church and surrounding farms in the late 1700s. The tower, in a nature reserve, is 5km south of Skagen and well signposted from Rte 40. By bike, take Gammel Landevej from Skagen.

RÅBJERG MILE

These undulating 40m-high hills comprise Denmark's largest expanse of shifting dunes and are great fun to explore. Råbjerg Mile is 16km south of Skagen, off Rte 40 on the road to Kandestederne. From May to September, bus No 99 runs six times a day from Skagen Station (Dkr14, 25 minutes).

Sleeping

Hotel accommodation can be scarce during the Skagen Festival at the end of June.

Grenen Camping (☎ 98 44 25 46; adult/child Dkr65/37) A fine seaside location, semiprivate tent sites and pleasant four-bunk huts, 1.5km northeast of Skagen centre.

The tourist office books singles/doubles in private homes for around Dkr200/350, plus a Dkr50 booking fee.

Danhostel Skagen (☎ 98 44 22 00; www.danhostel .dk/skagen; Rolighedsvej 2; dm Dkr118, s/d from Dkr250/

300; ☒ mid-Feb–late Nov; (P)) A 162-bed place 1km west of the centre.

Marienlund Badepension (☎ 98 44 13 20; www .marienlund.dk; Fabriciusvej 8; , s/d Dkr330/590, s/d with private bathroom Dkr450/740) An appealing, spick-and-span place on the quieter west side of town near the open-air museum.

Skagen Sømandshjem (☎ 98 44 25 88; Østre Strandvej 2; s/d with private bathroom Dkr580/805, with shared bathroom Dkr430/660) A harbourside hotel with bright, pleasant rooms.

Brøndums Hotel (☎ 98 44 15 55; www.broendums -hotel.dk, Danish only; Anchersvej 3; s/d Dkr575/875, s/d with private bathroom Dkr795/1095) A pleasantly old-fashioned hotel with comfy rooms in the heart of the old town right across from the Skagens Museum. It had close associations with Skagen's artists in its day and retains an old-world sense of decor (the wallpaper in the rooms is exuberantly flowery but attractive all the same), good service and civility. However, it has similarly old-world facilities and plumbing: there's one TV in the living room and few of the rooms have bathrooms. It's a great, cosy place to relax though, especially in front of a roaring fire and there's a good restaurant (see below).

Eating & Drinking

You'll find a couple of pizzerias, a kebab shop, a burger joint and an ice-cream shop clustered near each other on Havnevej. **Super Brugsen** (Sankt Laurentii Vej 28), a grocery store just west of the tourist office, has a bakery.

Restaurant Pakhuset (☎ 98 44 20 00; Rødspættevej 6; light lunches Dkr65-77, mains Dkr150-200) Perhaps the pick in town for a mix of great fresh fish mains and cheaper light lunches (like fish cakes with remoulade and salad Dkr72), long hours and a superb ambience outdoors (right among the bustle of the harbour) and in (a lovely wood-beamed interior sprinkled with jovial ship mastheads). Its downstairs café offers the cheaper dishes.

Jakobs (☎ 98 44 16 90; Havnevej 4; mains Dkr138-188) Jakobs is a popular restaurant on Skagen's busy main street. It does good home-made brunches (Dkr70), children's brunch (Dkr35) and sandwiches, salads and pastas (Dkr45 to Dkr75).

Brondum's Hotel (☎ 98 44 15 55; Anchersvej 3; mains Dkr110-230) French cuisine is the main influence on the otherwise classic Danish dishes, with lots of fresh seafood such as lobster and turbot as well as tenderloin and chateaubriand. Meals are served in the old-world ambience of the cosy dining room.

Buddy Holly's (Havnevej 16; admission Dkr40) Skagen has a branch of Buddy Holly's, with its usual brand of late night–early morning pubbing and clubbing.

Getting There & Away

Either a bus or a train leaves Skagen station for Frederikshavn (Dkr45) about once an hour. There's a seasonal Skagerakkeren bus (No 99) that runs between Hirtshals and Skagen (Dkr37, 1½ hours, six daily mid-June to mid-August). The same bus continues on to Hjørring and Løkken.

Getting Around

Cycling is an excellent way of exploring Skagen and the surrounding area. **Skagen Cykeludlejning** (☎ 98 44 10 70; Banegårdspladsen; per day Dkr75, deposit Dkr200) rents out bicycles and has a stand on the western side of the train station and at the harbour.

Skagen is very busy with traffic in high season. There is convenient metered parking (Dkr10 for one hour) just by the train station.

HIRTSHALS

pop 7000

Hirtshals takes its breezy, friendly character from its commercial fishing harbour and ferry terminal. The essentially modern main street, pedestrianised Nørregade, is lined with a mix of cafés and shops, and with supermarkets that cater to Norwegian shoppers piling off the ferries to load up with relatively cheap Danish meats and groceries. The seaward end of Nørregade opens out into a wide, airy space, Den Grønne Plads or the 'Green Square', which overlooks the fishing harbour and its tiers of blue-hulled boats. There is a **tourist office** (☎ 98 94 22 20; www.visit hirtshals.com; Nørregade 40; ⊙ 9am-4pm Mon-Sat mid-Jul–Aug, 9am-4pm Mon-Fri & 9am-noon Sat Aug-Jun).

Hirtshals' main sight is the **Nordsømuseet** (☎ 98 94 44 44; Willemoesvej 2; adult/child Dkr60/30; ⊙ 10am-8pm mid-Jun–mid-Aug, 10am-5pm mid-Aug–mid-Jun), an impressive aquarium that re-creates a slice of the North Sea in a massive four-storey tank, containing elegantly balletic schools of thousands of fish. Divers feed the fish at 1pm and the seals at 11am and 3pm. There are coastal cliffs and a **lighthouse** on the town's western side. If you want beaches and dunes,

there's a lovely unspoiled stretch at **Tornby Strand**, 5km to the south.

Sleeping & Eating

Hirtshals Hostel (☎ 98 94 12 48; www.danhostelnord.dk /hirtshals; Kystvejen 53; dm/s/d Dkr115/350/400; ⊙ Mar-Nov) A basic place about 1km from the centre.

Staff at the tourist office can book rooms in private homes starting at Dkr150 plus a Dkr25 booking fee.

Hotel Hirtshals (☎ 98 94 20 77; info@hotelhirtshals .dk; Havnegade 2; s/d Dkr645/785) On the main square above the fishing harbour, the Hirtshals has bright, comfortable rooms with high, steepled ceilings and good sea views at the front.

There are cafés and a good bakery at the northern end of Hjørringgade, and a couple of pizza and kebab places on Nørregade.

Hirtshals Kro (☎ 98 94 26 77; Havnegade; mains Dkr139-169) A delightful restaurant in a very old *kro* that has retained its character. Not surprisingly there are tasty seafood dishes including a mixed fish plate for Dkr179.

Getting There & Away

BOAT

The ferry company **Color Line** (☎ 99 56 20 00) runs year-round ferries to the Norwegian ports of Oslo (8½ hours, 10 times daily May to September) and Kristiansand (2½ to five hours, four times daily May to September). Fares on both routes are from Dkr180 mid-week in the low season to Dkr420 on summer weekends for passengers, from Dkr160 to Dkr310 for a motorcycle and from Dkr220 to Dkr600 for a car.

BUS

From May to September there's an **NT bus** (☎ 70 13 14 15) from Hirtshals station to Hjørring (Dkr22.50) that stops en route at Tornby Strand six times a day.

TRAIN

Hirtshals' main train station is 500m south of the ferry harbour, but there's also a stop near the Color Line terminal. The railway, which is operated by a private company, connects Hirtshals with Hjørring (Dkr22.50, 20 minutes, hourly) to the south. Trains run at least hourly, with the last departure from Hjørring to Hirtshals at 10.25pm. From Hjørring you can take a DSB train to Aalborg (Dkr67.50, 40 minutes, hourly) or Frederikshavn (Dkr45, 30 minutes, at least hourly).

HJØRRING
pop 24,800

Hjørring's well-kept streets are enlivened by some 150 statues and bronze sculptures, and the town is a lively place behind its sometimes staid exterior.

The oldest part of Hjørring is built around the central squares, the broad focal point of Springvandspladsen and the nearby Sankt Olai Plads. The latter is bordered by three medieval churches. Springvandspladsen is a short five-minute walk north from the train station along Jernbanegade; continue 200m further north on the pedestrian walkway Strømgade to reach Sankt Olai Plads.

The **tourist office** (☎ 98 92 02 32; www.visithjoer ring.dk; Markedsgade 9; ☒ 9am-5pm Mon-Fri & 9am-7pm Sat mid-Jun–Aug, 9am-4pm Mon-Fri & 9am-noon Sat Sep–mid-Jun) is a bit out of the centre, 750m east of the train station.

Sights & Activities

Hjørring is unique in that three of its medieval churches survived the Reformation intact. All three churches, **Sankt Olai Kirke**, **Sankt Catharinæ Kirke** and **Sankt Hans Kirke** are within 200m of each other, on the northern side of Sankt Olai Plads.

The town museum, **Vendsyssel Historiske Museum** (☎ 96 24 10 50; Museumsgade 3; adult/child Dkr30/free; ☒ 10am-5pm Apr-Oct, 11am-4pm Mon-Fri Nov-Mar), is about 250m south of Sankt Catharinæ Kirke. It features exhibits from prehistoric times, as well as an ecclesiastical art collection, period furnishings and displays on farming.

Sleeping & Eating

Both the camping ground and hostel are about 2.5km northeast of the train station and can be reached by local bus.

Hjørring Campingplads (☎ 98 92 22 82; Idræts Allé 45; adult/child Dkr57/26; ☒ May–mid-Sep; ☒) A small, three-star camping ground with an outdoor swimming pool.

Danhostel Hjørring (☎ 98 92 67 00; www.danhostel nord.dk/hjoerring, Danish only; Thomas Morildsvej 11; dm/s/d Dkr118/400/420; ☒ Mar-Sep) A large modern hostel about 2.5km east of Springvandspladsen.

There are a number of cheap food places in Jernbanegade. The station has a DSB café. **Pizza King** (pizzas Dkr29) is opposite the station.

Hartmann Petersen (☎ 98 92 01 97; Jernbanegade 1; dishes Dkr16-48, herring platter Dkr85-125) For a terrific selection of takeaway *smørrebrød*

and other dishes, try Hartmann Petersen, a butcher's shop near Hotel Phønix with tasty items.

Getting There & Away

Hjørring is 35km west of Frederikshavn on Rte 35, and 17km south of Hirtshals on Rte 55 or the E39.

Trains run to Hirtshals (Dkr22.50, 20 minutes, hourly), Frederikshavn (Dkr45, 30 minutes, at least hourly), Aalborg (Dkr67.50, 40 minutes, hourly) and Århus (Dkr172, 2¼ hours, hourly).

LØKKEN
pop 1300

Løkken has an intriguing history as a long-established sea trading and fishing centre on the unforgiving North Sea coast of Jutland. Its history is not submerged entirely by the hordes of summer visitors who pack the camping grounds of the area and throng the bars, cafés and souvenir shops of the town itself. Down on the spectacularly vast beach, the long line of white beach huts fronting the dunes in summer are matched by Løkken's sturdy fishing vessels. These boats seem to be trapped deep in the sand when they are drawn up on the beach, but they are launched through a clever combination of winching and tractor power.

The **tourist office** (☎ 98 99 10 09; www.loekken.dk; Harald Fischers Vej 8; ☒ 9am-5pm Mon-Sat Jun-Aug plus 10am-2pm Sun mid Jul–Aug, 9am-4pm Mon-Fri & 10am-1pm Sat Sep-May) is a few blocks east of Torvet, the central square.

Løkken's **beach** is broad and long and has excellent sand. The town itself has an older neighbourhood to the north of the centre.

The charming little **Løkken Museum** (Nørregade 12; adult/child Dkr10/free; ☒ 10am-4pm Mon-Fri, 2-5pm Sun Jun-Aug) and the **Coastal Fishing Museum** (☎ 20 66 13 07; Ndr Strandvej; adult/child Dkr10/free; ☒ 10am-4pm Mon-Fri, 2-5pm Sun Jun-Aug), perched above the beach, tell the story of Løkken seagoing.

There is a string of camping grounds along Søndergade, the street that runs south from Torvet. Most of them charge in the region of Dk65/30 per adult/child in high season.

Most of the hotels and apartment complexes in Løkken are geared to holidaymakers planning longer stays and offer their best prices for weekly bookings although you might catch an overnight stay for about

DENMARK

Dkr600 in the low season. The tourist office can provide a booklet with a brief description of each place and a detailed price list. In the low season it's worth checking out any 'room to let' signs for good deals.

Several places offer cheap fast food on Torvet and along Nørregade and Strandgade, which radiate out from Torvet.

Løkken Fiske-Restaurant (☎ 98 99 02 00; Nørregade 9; mains Dkr119-200) Løkken Fiske has good fish dishes, including a tasty fish soup. It also does fish lunches for Dkr55 to Dkr69 and some meat dishes.

Løkken is on Rte 55, 18km southwest of Hjørring. Buses run every couple of hours between Løkken and Hjørring (Dkr28, 30 minutes) and between Løkken and Aalborg (Dkr54, one hour).

ESBJERG

pop 83,000

Esbjerg is a newcomer to Denmark, having been established as a port in 1868 following the loss of the Schleswig and Holstein regions to Germany. It is now the country's fifth-largest city, the centre of Denmark's North Sea oil activities and the country's largest fishing harbour. Although Esbjerg has its fair share of early-20th-century buildings, it lacks the charm found in the older quarters of other Danish cities. For most travellers it's a transit point, but the town has a few things to offer and is worth a stopover.

Orientation & Information

Torvet, the city square where Skolegade and Torvegade intersect, is bordered by cafés, a Danske bank and the post office. The train and bus stations are about 300m east of Torvet, and the ferry terminal is 1km south.

Information

Central Library (☎ 76 16 20 00; Nørregade 19; Internet access free; ☼ 10am-7pm Mon-Thu, 10am-5pm Fri, 10am-2pm Sat)

Kilroy Travel (☎ 70 15 40 15; Kongensgade 8) Specialises in discount and student travel and has friendly staff.

Tourist Office (☎ 75 12 55 99; www.visitesbjerg.com, Danish only; Skolegade 33; ☼ 9am-5pm Mon-Fri & 9.30am-2.30pm Sat mid-Jun–Aug, 10am-5pm Mon-Fri & 10am-1pm Sat Sep–mid-Jun).

Sights & Activities

The **Fiskeri og Søfartsmuseet** (☎ 76 12 20 00; Tarphagevej 2; adult/child Dkr75/35; low season Dkr70/35; ☼ 10am-

ESBJERG

| | 0 | 400 m |
| 0 | 0.2 miles |

INFORMATION
Central Library.................................1 B4
Danske Bank...................................2 A4
Kilroy Travels..................................3 B5
Post Office......................................4 B4
Tourist Office..................................5 B4

SIGHTS & ACTIVITIES (pp90-1)
Esbjerg Kunstmuseum........................6 A5
Esbjerg Museum................................7 B4

SLEEPING (p91)
Cab-Inn Esbjerg................................8 B4
Hotel Ansgar....................................9 A4

EATING (p91)
Dronning Louise..............................10 B4
Hong Kong Restaurant.....................11 B4
Midt-I Shopping Centre....................12 B4
Sands Restaurant.............................13 A4
Sunset Boulevard............................14 B4

TRANSPORT (p91)
Bus Station....................................15 B4
Ferries to England..........................16 A5

6pm Jul & Aug, 10am-5pm Jan-Jun & Sep-Dec), at Tarphagevej 4km northwest of the centre, has an aquarium, outdoor seal pool and a number of fisheries exhibits including a huge whale skeleton. Take bus No 1 or 6. It's right by a long sweep of bay and beach, overlooked by the large white sentinels of the sculpture *Man Meets Sea*.

There are also a few local museums in the centre. **Esbjerg Kunstmuseum** (☎ 75 13 02 11; Havnegade 20; adult/child Dkr40/free; 🕒 10am-4pm) has a fine collection of Danish modern art including work by Asger Jorn. **Esbjerg Museum** (☎ 75 12 78 11; Torvegade 45; adult/child Dkr30/free; 🕒 10am-4pm) contains historical collections and an amber display.

Sleeping

Ådalens Camping (☎ 75 15 88 22; www.adal.dk; Gudenåvej 20; adult/child Dkr62/31; 🏊) The nearest camping ground is a large, appealing place 5km north of the city via bus No 1 or 7 with a pool, solarium and Jacuzzi.

Danhostel Esbjerg (☎ 75 12 42 58; www.danhostel.dk/esbjerg; Gammel Vardevej 80; dm/s/d Dkr118/300/400; 🕒 Feb–mid-Dec) Inside a former high school 3km northwest of the city centre, this hostel is close to sports facilities including a pool. Take bus Nos 4 and 12.

The tourist office books rooms in private homes at Dkr175/300 for singles/doubles.

Cab Inn Esbjerg (☎ 75 18 16 00; www.cab-inn.com; Skolegade 14; s/d Dkr475/585; Ⓟ ⊠ 💻) Has 82 pleasantly renovated rooms with TV and private bath. There's free Internet access in the lobby.

Hotel Ansgar (☎ 75 12 82 44; fax 75 13 95 40; Skolegade 36; s/d Dkr485/690) Ansgar is a friendly place with large, modernised, comfortable rooms decorated in simple classic Scandinavian style.

Eating

Sand's Restaurant (☎ 75 12 02 07; Skolegade 60; lunch Dkr30-72, mains Dkr80-110) You'll find superb, authentic Danish staples such as *smørrebrød*, Danish hash, meatballs, smoked eel and *pariserbof* (a fried beef patty on bread with a raw egg yolk, pickles and fresh horseradish) in this cosy, old-fashioned dining room.

Dronning Louise (☎ 75 13 13 44; Torvet 19; mains Dkr110-168; 🕒 10am-late Mon-Sat, 10am-11.30pm Sun) This jack of all trades offers sandwiches, burgers and lunch fish plates for Dkr38 to Dkr58 as well as full-on restaurant fare. It's worth having a look at the short, creative seasonal evening menu.

There are a number of restaurants in and around Torvet. Restaurants and grocery stores are east of Torvet on Kongensgade.

Midt-I shopping centre (Kongensgade, near Torvet) has a bakery and cafeteria.

Sunset Boulevard (Kongensgade; small/large sandwiches Dkr30/50) The popular Sunset Boulevard has small/large submarine sandwiches, as well as ice cream.

Hong Kong Restaurant (Kongensgade 34; 3-course meals Dkr108-188) Does box takeaways for Dkr33 to Dkr43.

Getting There & Away

Trains connecting the towns of Esbjerg and Copenhagen (Dkr287, 3¼ hours, hourly) run until 10pm.

If you're driving into Esbjerg from the east, the E20 leads into the city centre. If you're coming from the south, Rte 24 merges with the E20 on the city outskirts. From the north, Rte 12 makes a beeline into the city, ending at the harbour.

For details of ferry services to the UK see p100.

Getting Around

Most city buses (Dkr17) can be boarded at the train station. Parking is free in Esbjerg. There's also a convenient car park on Danmarksgade, but it has a two-hour limit; some unlimited parking is available in the car park on Nørregade east of the library.

LEGOLAND

Forty-five million plastic blocks have been arranged into a world of miniature cities, Lego pirates, safari animals and lots more at **Legoland** (☎ 75 33 13 33; www.lego.dk; adult/child 3-13 years Dkr180/160; 🕒 10am-8pm Apr–late Oct, 10am-9pm early Jul-early Aug), the internationally popular theme park in the town of Billund. There are also amusement rides (some roller coasterstyle, but mostly sedate ones), which are included in the entry fee. This is paradise for youngsters who have lived with Lego, but adults may need to grit their teeth after a while.

There's a frequent bus from Vejle to Legoland (Dkr40, 25 minutes), as well as bus-tour packages from numerous cities, including Esbjerg. Inquire at Esbjerg tourist office.

RIBE

pop 8000

Ribe sells its quaintness with great efficiency. Dating from 869, it is said to be the oldest town in Scandinavia and was an important medieval trading centre. The crooked, cobblestoned streets and half-timbered, 16th-century houses, certainly impart a sense of history. The entire old

DENMARK

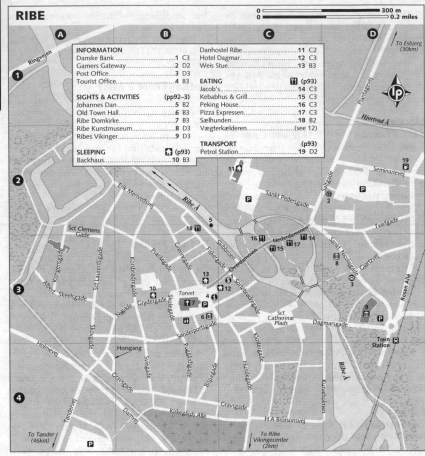

RIBE

INFORMATION		
Danske Bank	1	C3
Gamers Gateway	2	D2
Post Office	3	D3
Tourist Office	4	B3

SIGHTS & ACTIVITIES	(pp92–3)	
Johannes Dan	5	B2
Old Town Hall	6	B3
Ribe Domkirke	7	B3
Ribe Kunstmuseum	8	D3
Ribes Vikinger	9	D3

SLEEPING	(p93)	
Backhaus	10	B3

Danhostel Ribe	11	C2
Hotel Dagmar	12	C3
Weis Stue	13	B3

EATING	(p93)	
Jacob's	14	C3
Kebabhus & Grill	15	C3
Peking House	16	C3
Pizza Expressen	17	C3
Sælhunden	18	B2
Vægterkælderen	(see 12)	

TRANSPORT	(p93)	
Petrol Station	19	D2

town is a preservation zone, with more than 100 buildings in Ribe under the care of the Danish National Trust.

The town is compact and easy to explore, although for much of the summer be prepared to share the experience with huge crowds of fellow sightseers. Almost everything, including the hostel and train station, is within 10 minutes' walk of Torvet, the town square, which is dominated by a huge Romanesque cathedral.

Information
Danske Bank (☎ 76 88 68 20; Overdammen 4)
Gamer's Gateway (Saltgade 20; per 12min/1hr Dkr5/25; ☽ noon-midnight) Internet café.
Post Office (Sct Nicolaj Gade)

Tourist Office (☎ 75 42 15 00; www.ribetourist.dk; Torvet 3; ☽ 9.30am-5.30pm Mon-Fri, 10am-5pm Sat, 10am-2pm Sun Jul & Aug, 9am-5pm Mon-Fri Apr-Jun & Sep-Oct, 10am-1pm Sat Apr-Jun & Sep-Dec) Here you can obtain the publication *Sommer I Ribe*, a good events magazine.

Sights & Activities
For a pleasant stroll, head along any of the picturesque streets that radiate from Torvet, especially Puggårdsgade or Grønnegade from where narrow alleys lead down and across Fiskegarde to Skibbroen and the old harbour. Boats still tie up alongside the quay, and there is a replica of the 19th-century cargo vessel, the **Johannes Dan**.

Ribe Domkirke (☎ 75 42 06 19; Torvet; adult/child Dkr12/5) dominates the heart of the town and boasts a variety of styles from Romanesque to Gothic. Its monumental presence is literally sunk into the heart of Ribe. The cathedral floor is over a metre below the level of the surrounding streets. You can climb the **cathedral steeple** for a breathtaking view of the surrounding countryside and to get a feel for just how small and compact Ribe is.

Ribes Vikinger (☎ 76 88 11 22; Odins Plads 1; adult/child Dkr50/20; 🕙 10am-6pm Jul & Aug, 10am-4pm Apr-Jun, Sep & Oct, 10am-4pm Tue-Sun Nov-Mar), a substantial museum opposite the train station, has archaeological displays of Ribe's Viking history, including a reconstructed marketplace and Viking ship, with lots of hands-on features.

Ribe Vikingecenter (☎ 75 41 16 11; Lustrupvej 4; adult/child Dkr60/30; 🕙 11am-5pm Jul & Aug, 10am-3.30pm May-Jun & Sep), 3km south of the centre, is a re-created Viking village complete with working artisans and interpreters decked out in period costumes. There are hands-on activities to take part in during May and August, such as woodwork and archery, and ponies to pet. Bus No 51 (Dkr15) will take you there from Ribe.

Ribe Kunstmuseum (☎ 75 42 03 62; Sankt Nicolajgade 10; adult/child Dkr30/free; 🕙 11am-5pm Thu-Sun Jul-Sep, 11am-4pm Thu-Sun Oct-Jun) has a fine collection of 19th-century 'Golden Age' and 'Silver Age' Danish art, including Ludvig Abelin Schou's magnificently romantic *Death of Chione*. There are a couple of local-history museums, including one at the **Old Town Hall** (adult/child Dkr15/5) that displays the formidable axe of the fortunately long-gone executioner.

There isn't any new-fangled CCTV fad in Ribe, instead, a costumed **night watchman** takes care of security, making the rounds from Torvet at 8pm and 10pm from May to September. You can follow him for free as he sings his way through the old streets.

Sleeping & Eating

Weis Stue (☎ 75 42 07 00; www.weisstue.dk; Torvet; s/d Dkr400/500) This is the poorer, quirkier but no less charming sister to the Dagmar opposite. A small, ancient wood-beamed house, it has rather small, crooked rooms right above its restaurant, but they have bags of character. The restaurant offers lunch plates of herring, meatballs or lobster (Dkr95 to Dkr125), half a wild duck with fried potatoes, salad pickles and cream sauce (Dkr175) and dinner mains (Dkr109 to Dkr195). For breakfast you are

ushered across the road to the restaurant at Hotel Dagmar.

Danhostel Ribe (☎ 75 42 06 20; www.danhostel.dk /ribe; Sankt Pedersgade 16; dm/s Dkr90/270, d Dkr300-440; 🕙 Feb–late Nov; **P**) The modern, 140-bed hostel has friendly staff and a good, uncrowded location. The new rooms at the top are especially appealing and worth the extra cost.

The tourist office maintains a list of singles/doubles in private homes from Dkr250/350.

Backhaus (☎ 75 42 11 01; fax 75 42 52 87; Grydergade 12; s/d Dkr250/500, d with private bathroom Dkr750) The friendly Backhaus does an evening meal for Dkr105 to Dkr180.

Hotel Dagmar (☎ 75 42 00 33; www.hoteldagmar .dk, Danish only; Torvet; s/d from Dkr895/1095; **P** ✗) The central Hotel Dagmar claims to be the oldest hotel in Denmark and has plush (if rather small) rooms and a great period atmosphere.

Jacob's (☎ 75 42 42 30; Nederdammen 36; light meals Dkr35-65) Turns out good-value light lunches, brunches, sandwiches and salads in a pleasant setting.

Vægterkælderen (Torvet; lunch menu Dkr105-135) The basement restaurant in the Hotel Dagmar shares a kitchen with the hotel's classy upstairs restaurant but has cheaper dishes, including good steaks and fresh fish.

There are several fast-food outlets along Nederdammen, including **Kebabhus & Grill** (burgers & kebabs Dkr30-Dkr48), **Pizza Expressen** (pizza Dkr45) and **Peking House** (lunch specials Dkr30).

Sælhunden (☎ 75 42 09 46; Skibbroen 13; fish & meat mains Dkr46-186) This handsome, old restaurant is right on the quayside. A tasty lunch of smoked herring or smoked ham costs Dkr75.

Getting There & Away

There are trains from Esbjerg to Ribe (Dkr60, 40 minutes, hourly) and from Århus to Ribe (Dkr207, two hours 40 minutes).

RØMØ

Ruler-straight horizons of sea and shore, only occasionally perturbed by a heat haze, are the hypnotic draw of the unrelentingly flat island of Rømø, off the mainland coast, midway between the historic towns of Ribe and Tønder and a 30-minute drive from either. It's connected to the mainland by a 10km causeway that passes over marshlands, where sheep graze happily on nontidal pasture and wading birds forage for food.

During the 18th century, many islanders were captains of German and Dutch whaling ships working off Greenland, their lives lived, both home and away, in a flat world of unbroken horizons.

Today, Rømø is a hugely popular holiday destination, especially with visitors from nearby Germany. It has its fair share of caravan parks, but red-walled, thatch-roofed houses of great charm shelter amid scrubby pine woods, vast sand beaches line the western shore and the North Sea air is exhilarating.

The northern end of the island is an out-of-bounds military zone.

The **tourist office** (☎ 74 75 51 30; www.romo.dk; Havnebyvej 30; ☺ 9am-5pm mid-Jun–mid-Sep) is on the eastern side of Rømø, 1km south of the causeway exit on to the island.

Sights & Activities

Rømø's **beaches** are most easily reached at Lakolk on the central west coast. Conditions are often perfect for **windsurfing** and **kite-surfing** if you have the right gear, although the sea can be more than a kilometre away from the shoreline at low tide. It's also a good place to ride horses or sturdy Icelandic ponies. Several places run pony trekking, including **Rømø Ranch** (☎ 74 75 54 11; Lakolk). From June to September look out for spectacular sand sculptures at Lakolk.

The inland section of the island has **trails** through heather moors and wooded areas that offer quiet hiking. There's an **old church** with unique Greenlandic gravestones on the main road in Kirkeby.

An unmissable place is **Kommandørgården** (☎ 74 75 52 76; Juvrevej 60, Toftum; adult/child Dkr15/free; ☺ 10am-6pm Tue-Sun May-Sep, 10am-3pm Tue-Sun Oct), the preserved home of one of Rømø's 18th-century whaling captains, on the northeastern side of the island. Dutch tiles line many of the walls, the woodwork is painted in rococo style and the furnishings come from many countries. A whale skeleton bleaches in the sun outside in the garden.

Sleeping & Eating

Kommandørgårdens Camping (☎ 74 75 51 22; www .kommandoergaarden.dk; Havnebyvej 201; adult/child/tent Dkr65/35/15; P ☺) Near the hostel, this camping ground has a swimming pool and spa.

Danhostel Rømø (☎ 74 75 51 88; www.danhostel .dk/sonderborg; dm/r Dkr118/472; ☺ mid-Mar–Nov) Set among the pines on the southeastern side of Rømø near Havneby, this 91-bed terracotta-walled hostel is centred on a delightful traditional building with a thatched roof and is close to the beach.

Hotel Kommandørgården (☎ 74 75 51 22; www .kommandoergaarden.dk; Havnebyvej 201; s/d Dkr595/795; P ☺) This busy place offers comfortable cabin-style rooms, which have fridges and coffee makers; the main downside is the setting right by the road.

Hotel Færgegaarden (☎ 74 75 54 32; www.faerge gaarden.com; Vestergade 1, Havneby; s/d Dkr750/990; P ☺) A thatch-roofed place at the southern end of the island. It has comfy, attractive old-fashioned rooms, some with sea views, and a huge restaurant capacity.

Otto & Ani's Fisk (☎ 74 75 53 06; Havnepladsen) Right on the harbourside at Havneby, Otto & Ani's offers a big range of fish dishes from Dkr45 for basic fish and chips to Dkr175 for a two-person platter of mixed fish.

Kommandørgården (☎ 74 75 52 76; Juvrevej 60, Toftum) There's a good café here offering coffee, cake and light lunches (like a snow-crab plate for Dkr98).

There are grocery stores and a bakery within walking distance of the hostel, and numerous cafés and other eateries near the beach-road end at Lakolk.

Getting There & Around

Rømø is 14km west of the town of Skærbæk and Rte 11. Buses run from Skærbæk to Havneby (Dkr19, 35 minutes) numerous times a day. From Skærbæk there's a train service to Ribe (Dkr93, two hours), Tønder (Dkr137, three hours) and Esbjerg (Dkr 84, one hour 40 minutes) about once an hour. Car ferries connect Havneby with Germany's island of Sylt (adult/child Dkr49/34, one hour) many times a day.

From May to September, a limited public bus service connects villages on the island. Rømø is a good place for cycling; bicycles can be rented in several places for around Dkr50, including the camping grounds.

TØNDER & AROUND

A historic southern town that was in and out of border history for centuries, Tønder retains a few pleasingly curved and cobble-stoned streets with half-timbered houses, such as Uldgade, Nørregade and Spikergade.

There is a **tourist office** (☎ 74 72 12 20; www.visit tonder.dk; Torvet 1; ⌚ 10am-5pm Mon-Fri & 10am-2pm Sat Jul & Aug, 9am-4pm Mon-Fri & 9am-noon mid-Sep–Jun) with information on the town and its surrounding area.

Sights

The **Tønder Museum** (☎ 74 72 26 57; Kongevej 51; adult/child Dkr20/free; ⌚ 10am-5pm Jun-Aug, 10am-5pm Tue-Sun Sep-May), identifiable by the towering brick lighthouse near the Hotel Tønderhus, has a wing with regional-history exhibits including a collection of Tønder lace, once considered among the world's finest. Another wing features Danish surrealist and modern art. The museum is a 10-minute walk east of the train station.

Tønder Festival

Tønder's annual knees-up takes place during the last weekend of August when the **Tønder Festival** (☎ 74 72 46 10; www.tf.dk), one of Denmark's largest, attracts a multitude of international and Danish folk musicians.

Sleeping & Eating

Tønder Camping (☎ 74 72 18 49; Holmevej 2; adult/child Dkr55/25) is just beyond the hostel.

Danhostel Tønder (☎ 74 72 35 00; www.tonder-net .dk/danhostel; Sønderport 4; dm/s/d Dkr118/300/350) On the eastern side of the centre and a 15-minute walk from the train station, the hostel has comfortable rooms with dorm beds and singles/doubles with private bathroom.

Hotel Tønderhus (☎ 74 72 22 22; www.hoteltoender hus.dk; Jomfrustien 1; s/d Dkr775/900; ✗) A large, modern restored place in the Classics Hotel chain. It has comfortable, if rather bland, corporate rooms. Its restaurant is surprisingly good, however, offering tasty smørrebrød (Dkr49) and pricier mains including six different types of fish.

China Inn (Østergade 37; mains Dkr45) A short walk east of the central square of Torvet, China Inn has inexpensive Chinese and grilled items, and an adjacent **bakery**.

You can buy fresh fruit and cheese at the **market** (Torvet; ⌚ Tue & Fri mornings).

Getting There & Away

Tønder is on Rte 11, about 4km north of the German border. Trains run hourly Monday to Friday, and somewhat less frequently at the weekend from Ribe (Dkr53, 50 minutes) and Esbjerg (Dkr76, 1½ hours).

DENMARK DIRECTORY

ACCOMMODATION

Accommodation in this chapter is listed in ascending order of price.

Camping & Cabins

Denmark's 516 camping grounds typically charge from Dkr50 to Dkr65 per person to pitch a tent. Many places add about Dkr20 for the tent. A camping pass (Dkr80, available at any camping ground) is required and covers a family group with children under 18 for the season. If you do not have a seasonal pass you pay an extra Dkr20 a night for a temporary pass.

Camping is restricted to camping grounds, or on private land with the owner's permission. Camping in a car along the beach or in a parking lot is definitely prohibited and can result in an immediate fine. Tourist offices usually have brochures listing local camping grounds.

The **Danish Camping Association** (☎ 39 27 88 44; www.campingraadet.dk; Campingrådet, Mosedalvej 15, Valby) inspects and grades Danish camp grounds using a star system and carries a full list on its website.

Hostels

The national Hostelling International office is **Danhostel** (☎ 33 31 36 12; www.danhostel.dk; Vesterbrogade 39, 1620 Copenhagen V).

Most of Denmark's 100 vandrerhjem (hostels) in its Danhostel association have private rooms in addition to dormitories, making hostels an affordable and popular alternative to hotels (so book ahead in summer). Dorm beds cost from about Dkr95 to Dkr118, while private rooms range from Dkr200 to Dkr450 for singles, and Dkr300 to Dkr475 for doubles. Blankets and pillows are provided, but not sheets; bring your own or hire them for Dkr40. Sleeping bags are not allowed.

Travellers can buy international hostel cards in Denmark for Dkr160 or pay Dkr30 extra a night. Outside Copenhagen, check-in is generally between 4pm and 8pm or 9pm (but a few places close as early as 6pm); the reception office is usually closed and the phone not answered between noon and 4pm. Most hostels close in winter.

You can pick up a free 200-page hostel guide from tourist offices giving information on each hostel. All Danish hostels have an all-you-can-eat breakfast for Dkr45 or less. Nearly all hostels also have guest kitchens with pots and pans where you can cook your own food.

Hotels

Budget hotels start at around Dkr450/600 for singles/doubles. *Kros*, a name that implies country inn but is more often the Danish version of a motel, are generally cheaper than hotels by about a third. Both hotels and *kros* usually include an all-you-can-eat breakfast.

Rates listed in this chapter include all taxes and are for rooms with toilet and shower, unless otherwise specified. Some hotels offer discount schemes at weekends year-round and from May to September when business travel is light.

Other Accommodation

Many tourist offices book rooms in private homes for a small fee, or provide a free list of the rooms so travellers can phone on their own. Rates vary, averaging about Dkr250/350 for singles/doubles. Standards of accommodation may vary widely and some rooms may be very basic. **Dansk Bed & Breakfast** (☎ 39 61 04 05; www.bbdk.dk; PO Box 53, 2900 Hellerup) handles 300 homes throughout Denmark offering private rooms at similar rates.

ACTIVITIES
Cycling

Cycling is a popular holiday activity in Denmark and there are thousands of kilometres of established cycling routes. Those around Bornholm, Funen and Møn, as well as the 440km Old Military Rd (Hærvejen) through central Jutland, are among the most popular.

Dansk Cyklist Forbund (DCF; ☎ 33 32 31 21; www .dcf.dk; Rømersgade 7, 1362 Copenhagen K) publishes *Cykelferiekort*, a cycling map of the entire country, as well as more detailed regional cycling maps.

DCF also publishes *Overnatning i det fri*, which lists hundreds of farmers who provide cyclists with a place to pitch a tent for Dkr15 a night. Cycling maps can be purchased in advance from DCF or from tourist offices and bookshops upon arrival.

Walking

Even though Denmark does not have substantial forests, many small tracts of wood-land are crisscrossed by pleasant walking trails. **Skov og Naturstyrelsen** (Forest and Nature Bureau) produces brochures with sketch maps that show trails in nearly 100 such areas. The brochures can be picked up free at public libraries and some tourist offices. Denmark's coastline is public domain lined with scenic walking tracks.

Water Sports

Canoeing possibilities on Denmark's inland lakes, such as canoe touring between lakeside camping grounds in Jutland's Lake District, are superb. You can hire canoes and equipment at many camping grounds or in main centres such as Silkeborg (p79). The lakes are generally undemanding as far as water conditions go, although some experience is an advantage.

Denmark's remarkable coastline offers terrific **windsurfing** and **kitesurfing** possibilities. Good areas are along the northern coast of Zealand at places such as Smidstrup Strand (p48), and in northwest Jutland. The Limfjord area of northwest Jutland is particularly suited to windsurfing and you can pick up an excellent leaflet, *Windsurfing in the Limfjord Area,* from most tourist offices in the area. There's an English version and it pinpoints 28 windsurfing areas by use of small maps.

BOOKS

For travellers, Lonely Planet's *Denmark* is the most comprehensive all-round guidebook available. *Camping Danmark,* a new edition of which is published each year by the Danish Camping Board (Campingrådet), has detailed information on all camping grounds in the country.

Denmark: A Modern History, by W Glyn Jones, gives a comprehensive account of contemporary Danish society.

'Just as Well I'm Leaving – Around Europe with Hans Christian Andersen' by Michael Booth is a funny, entertaining travelogue retracing Andersen's footsteps around Denmark and Europe.

BUSINESS HOURS

Office hours are generally 9am to 4pm Monday to Friday. Most banks are open 9.30am to 4pm Monday to Friday (to 6pm Thursday). Stores are usually open to 5.30pm Monday to Friday and 2pm on Saturday.

CHILDREN

It should come as no surprise that Denmark, home of the Lego block, has lots of attractions to entice kids. Legoland itself (p91) is the most visited children's site in Scandinavia, and the rest of Denmark abounds with amusement parks filled with Ferris wheels, carousels and water slides. The biggest of these parks, Tivoli (p35) and Bakken (p45), are in Copenhagen. Many tourist offices give out brochures focusing on children-oriented activities and attractions.

DANGERS & ANNOYANCES

Denmark is by and large a safe country. Nevertheless, be careful with your belongings, particularly in busy places such as Copenhagen's Central Station. In cities, you'll need to become accustomed quickly to the busy cycle lanes between vehicle roads and the pedestrian pavement, as these lanes are easy to step into accidentally.

DISABLED TRAVELLERS

Overall, Denmark is a user-friendly destination for the disabled traveller. The Danish Tourist Board publishes *Access in Denmark – a Travel Guide for the Disabled*, in English, with information on accommodation, transport and sightseeing options for disabled travellers.

EMBASSIES & CONSULATES
Danish Embassies & Consulates

Danish embassies and consulates abroad:

Australia (☎ 9521 4777; rdcg.mel@bigpond.net.au; Ste 3, 546 Malvern Rd, Prahan East, Vic 3142, PO Box 1256, Hawksburn VIC 3142)

Canada (☎ 613-562 1811; www.danish-embassy -canada.com; 47 Clarence St, Ste 450, Ottawa, Ontario K1N 9K1)

Finland (☎ 9-684 1050; www.kolumbus.fi/danmark in Danish; Centralgatan 1A, 00101 Helsinki)

Germany (☎ 5050 2000; www.daenemark.org, Danish only; Rauchstrasse 1, 10787 Berlin)

Ireland (☎ 1-475 6404; www.denmark.ie, Danish only; 121 St Stephen's Green, Dublin 2)

Netherlands (☎ 70 302 59 59; www.danishembassy.nl; Koninginnegracht 30, 2514 Den Haag)

New Zealand (☎ 537 3099; danish.nz@xtra.co.nz; 273 Bleakhouse Rd, Howick, PO Box 619, 1015 Auckland)

Norway (☎ 22 54 08 00; www.denmark-embassy.no, Danish only; Olav Kyrres Gate 7, 0244 Oslo)

Sweden (☎ 8-406 75 00; www.danemb.se, Danish only; Jakobs Torg 1, 11186 Stockholm)

UK (☎ 020-7333 0200; http://denmark.org.uk; 55 Sloane St, London SW1X 9SR)

USA (☎ 202-234 4300; www.denmarkemb.org; 3200 Whitehaven St NW, Washington DC 20008)

Embassies & Consulates in Denmark

Foreign representation in Denmark:

Australia (☎ 70 26 36 76; www.denmark.embassy.gov.au; Dampfægevej 26, Copenhagen)

Canada (☎ 33 48 32 00; www.canada.dk; Kristen Bernikows Gade1, Copenhagen)

Germany (☎ 35 45 99 00; www.kopenhagen.diplo.de, Danish only; Stockholmsgade 57, Copenhagen)

Ireland (☎ 35 42 32 33; Østbanegade 21, Copenhagen)

Netherlands (☎ 33 70 72 00; www.nlembassy.dk; Toldbodgade 33, Copenhagen)

Norway (☎ 33 14 01 24; www.norsk.dk, Danish only; Amaliegade 39, Copenhagen)

Poland (☎ 39 46 77 00; www.ambpol.dk; Richelius Allé 12, Hellerup)

Sweden (☎ 33 36 03 70; www.sverigesambassad.dk; Sankt Annæ Plads 15A, Copenhagen)

UK (☎ 35 44 52 00; www.britishembassy.dk; Kastelsvej 38, Copenhagen)

USA (☎ 35 55 31 44; www.usembassy.dk; Dag Hammarskjölds Allé 24, Copenhagen)

FESTIVALS & EVENTS

Beginning with **Midsummer's Eve** bonfires in late June, Denmark buzzes with outdoor activity throughout the summer. Main attractions are the 180 music festivals that run almost nonstop throughout the country, covering a broad spectrum of music that includes not only jazz, rock and blues but also gospel, folk, classical, country, Cajun and much more.

The acclaimed 10-day **Copenhagen Jazz Festival** (http://festival.jazz.dk) is held in early July, with outdoor concerts and numerous performances in clubs around the city.

The town of Roskilde hosts an internationally acclaimed **rock festival** (www.roskilde -festival.dk) on the last weekend of June; a single admission fee includes camping space and entry to all concerts.

There are **folk festivals** in Skagen near the end of June and in Tønder in late August. The 10-day **Århus Festival** in early September features an array of music and multicultural events.

For details on music festivals nationwide, contact **Dansk Musik Informations Center** (☎ 33 11 20 66; www.mic.dk; Gråbrødre Torv 16, 1154 Copenhagen K).

GAY & LESBIAN TRAVELLERS

Denmark is a popular destination for gay and lesbian travellers. Copenhagen in particular has an active, open gay community and lots of nightlife options.

Landsforeningen for Bøsser og Lesbiske (LBL; ☎ 33 13 19 48; kbh@lbl.dk; Teglgårdstræde 13, Copenhagen) is the national organisation for gay men and lesbians. Branch offices in main towns are mentioned in relevant sections. A good English-language website with links to LBL and other gay organisations is www.copenhagen-gay-life.dk.

HOLIDAYS

Summer holidays for schoolchildren begin around 20 June and end around 10 August. Many Danes go on holiday during the first three weeks of July. The following public holidays are observed in Denmark:

New Year's Day (1 January)
Maundy Thursday (Thursday before Easter)
Good Friday to Easter Monday (March/April)
Common Prayer Day (Fourth Friday after Easter)
Ascension Day (Fifth Thursday after Easter)
Whit Sunday (Fifth Sunday after Easter)
Whit Monday (Fifth Monday after Easter)
Constitution Day (5 June)
Christmas Eve (24 December from noon)
Christmas Day (25 December)

INTERNET ACCESS

Internet cafés charge about Dkr20 to Dkr30 an hour. Public libraries also have Internet-capable computers and visitors generally have free access to them, although you may have to sign up and wait for a free slot.

LEGAL MATTERS

Although marijuana and hashish are available in Denmark, all forms of cannabis and harder drugs are illegal. If you are arrested for any offence in Denmark, you can be held up to 24 hours before appearing in court. You have a right to know the charges against you and a right to a lawyer. You are not obliged to answer police questions before speaking to the lawyer.

All travellers can get free legal advice on your rights from the EU legal aid organisation **EURO-JUS** (☎ 33 14 41 40; 🕑 9am-6pm Mon-Thu, 9am-4.30pm Fri). Free legal advice clinics can be found in over 90 places across Denmark. The service is organised by the Danish bar, **Det Danske Advokatsamfund** (☎ 38 38 36 38).

MONEY

ATMs

Major banks have ATMs which accept Visa, MasterCard and the Cirrus and Plus bank cards. All major credit and debit cards are widely accepted throughout Denmark, although some shops impose a surcharge of up to 5% if you use them, even in the case of debit cards.

Moneychangers

All common travellers cheques are accepted in Denmark. Buy your travellers cheques in higher denominations as bank fees for changing money are a hefty Dkr25 to Dkr30 per cheque, with a Dkr40 minimum. If you're exchanging cash, there's a Dkr25 fee for a transaction. Travellers cheques command a better exchange rate than cash by about 1%.

Post offices will also exchange foreign currency at comparable rates to those at banks.

The Euro

Although Denmark remains outside the euro zone, acceptance of euros is commonplace. Most hotels and restaurants will take euros, as do many bars, cafés and shops, although you may find reluctance to do so in more remote areas or from very small businesses. Government institutions do not accept euros.

Tipping

Restaurant bills and taxi fares include service charges in the quoted prices, and further tipping is unnecessary.

POST

Denmark has an efficient postal system. Most post offices are open 9am or 10am to 5pm or 5.30pm Monday to Friday and 9am to noon on Saturday. You can receive mail poste restante at any post office in Denmark. Letters up to 20g cost Dkr to Europe and Dkr6 to the rest of the world.

TELEPHONE & FAX

It costs Dkr3 to make a local call at coin phones. You get about twice as much calling

> ### EMERGENCY NUMBERS
>
> In Denmark, dial the free number ☎ 112 when you need police, fire and ambulance services.

time for your money on domestic calls made between 7.30pm and 8am daily and all day on Sunday.

Phonecards (Dkr30 to Dkr100) can be bought at post offices and newspaper kiosks.

The country code for calling Denmark from abroad is ☎ 45. To make international calls from Denmark dial ☎ 00 and then the country code for the country you're calling.

Faxes can be sent from hotels and some post offices.

TIME

Time in Denmark is normally one hour ahead of GMT/UTC, the same as in neighbouring European countries. Clocks are moved forward one hour for daylight-saving time from the last Sunday in March to the last Sunday in October. Denmark uses the 24-hour clock and all timetables and business hours are posted accordingly.

TOURIST INFORMATION

The tourist board's website is www.visitden mark.com. There are several Danish tourist offices abroad:

Australia (☎ 99 29 6044; satu@finesse.com.au; Finesse Communications Marketing & PR, PO Box 1427)

Germany (☎ 40 32 0210; daninfo@dt.dk; Dänisches Fremdenverkehrsamt, Glockengiesserwall 2, 20095 Hamburg)

Norway (☎ 22 00 76 46; danmark@dt.dk; Danmarks Turistkontor, Tollbugaten 27, Postboks 406 Sentrum, 0103 Oslo)

Sweden (☎ 08 611 72 22; info@dtab.se; Danmarks Turiståd, Box 5524, 114 85 Stockholm)

UK (☎ 020-7259 5959; dtb.london@dt.dk; Danish Tourist Board, 55 Sloane St, London SW1X 9SY)

USA (☎ 212-885 9700; info@goscandinavia.com; Danish Tourist Board, 655 Third Ave, 18th fl, New York, NY 10017)

VISAS

Citizens of the EU, USA, Canada, Australia and New Zealand need a valid passport to enter Denmark, but don't need a visa for stays of less than three months. If you wish to apply for a visa, do so at least three months in advance of your planned arrival.

WOMEN TRAVELLERS

The **Danish Centre for Information on Women & Gender** (KVINFO; ☎ 33 13 50 88; www.kvinfo.dk in Danish; Christians Brygge 3, Copenhagen) has information on feminist issues, while **Kvindehuset** (☎ 33 14 28 04; Gothersgade 37, Copenhagen) is a help centre and meeting place for women. Dial ☎ 112 for rape crisis or other emergencies.

TRANSPORT IN DENMARK

GETTING THERE & AWAY
Air

At the time of writing, the budget airfare war was fiercer than ever, and flights into Denmark from elsewhere on the Continent, Ireland and the UK were very affordable. If you're coming from European destinations consider flying into an airport other than Copenhagen, such as Århus or Billund; air fares can be competitive, and the airports are well connected by bus with neighbouring towns and afford fast access to some great parts of northern and central Jutland.

The budget carrier Ryanair, for instance, has regular, cheap flights from Stansted Airport in England to Århus airport and to Malmö, in Sweden (a short hop by rail from Copenhagen). See the following airport websites for full details.

AIRLINES

Scandinavian Airlines (SAS; ☎ 70 10 30 00; www.scan dinavian.net; airline code SK) is the largest carrier serving Denmark, connecting it with much of Europe and the rest of the world.

There are many other airlines that fly into Denmark:

Aer Lingus (☎ +353 818 365000; www.aerlingus.com)

Air France (☎ 82 33 27 01; www.airfrance.com)

Alitalia (☎ 70 27 02 90; www.alitalia.com)

Basiqair (☎ 38 48 75 38; www.basiqair.com)

BMI BritishMidland (☎ 70 10 20 00; www.flybmi.com)

British Airways (☎ 70 12 80 22; www.britishairways.com)

Easyjet (☎ 70 12 43 21; www.easyjet.com)

Finnair (☎ 33 36 45 45; www.finnair.com)

Iceland Air (☎ 33 70 22 00; www.icelandexpress.com)

KLM (☎ 70 10 07 47; www.klm.com)

Lufthansa (☎ 70 10 20 00; www.lufthansa.com)

Maersk Air (☎ 32 31 44 44; www.maersk-air.com)

Ryanair (☎ +353 818 303 030; www.ryanair.com)

MAIN DANISH AIRPORTS

Århus (☎ 87 75 70 00; www.aar.dk)

Billund (☎ 7650 5050; www.bll.dk)

Copenhagen (☎ 3231 32 31; www.cph.dk)

Land
GERMANY

The E45 is the main motorway between Germany and Denmark's Jutland Peninsula.

Three railway lines link the two countries (2nd-class fares from Copenhagen to Frankfurt are Dkr1100). **Eurolines** (☎ 33 88 70 00) operates buses from Copenhagen to Berlin (Dkr290, 6½ hours) and Frankfurt (Dkr720, 15 hours) several times a week.

NORWAY
Trains operate between Copenhagen and Oslo via Sweden (2nd-class fare Dkr604, 7½ hours, one or two daily). Eurolines offers a daily bus service between Oslo and Copenhagen (Dkr310) via Göteborg.

SWEDEN
Trains run many times a day between Denmark and Sweden via the Øresund Fixed Link, the longest bridge-tunnel of its type in the world. The bridge links Copenhagen with Malmö, Sweden. The 2nd-class train fare from Copenhagen is Dkr70 to Malmö, Dkr400 to Göteborg and Dkr580 to Stockholm (five hours). If you're travelling by train, the bridge crossing is included in the fare, but for those travelling by car, there's a Dkr230 per-vehicle toll.

There are numerous buses between Copenhagen and Sweden, including Eurolines buses to Göteborg (Dkr160, five hours) and Stockholm (Dkr346, 9½ hours).

Sea
GERMANY
The frequent Rødbyhavn–Puttgarden ferry takes 45 minutes and is included in train tickets for those travelling by rail; otherwise, the cost per adult/child is Dkr45/25, and Dkr345 for a car with up to nine passengers.

Other ferries run from Rømø to Sylt (Dkr35, one hour, five daily), Rønne on Bornholm to Sassnitz (Dkr135, 3½ hours, six weekly) and Gedser to Rostock (Dkr60, two hours).

ICELAND & THE FAROE ISLANDS
Smyril Line's (Denmark ☎ 3316 40 04, Faroe Islands ☎ 345 900; www.smyril-line.fo) *Norröna* runs every week from Hanstholm to Tórshavn (Faroe Islands) and Seyðisfjörður (Iceland) from mid-May to early September. The boat leaves Hanstholm at 8pm Saturday, arriving in Tórshavn at 5am Monday. Visitors then have a two-day stopover in the Faroe Islands (while the boat makes a run to Lerwick, Shetland, and Bergen, Norway), before departing from

Tórshavn at 6pm Wednesday and arriving in Seyðisfjörður at 8am Thursday. The return boat departs from Seyðisfjörður at noon Thursday, arriving in Tórshavn at 5am Friday and in Hanstholm at 4pm Saturday.

Midsummer fares to Tórshavn include a couchette or sleeping berth with mattress, but no bedding (€224) and a bunk in a four-berth cabin (€280). Fares to Seyðisfjörður include couchette (€336) and cabin bunk (€432); these fares are about 25% less for travel in low season (September to April). There's a 25% discount for students under 26, on presentation of a valid student card. You can take a bicycle to all destinations for about €10; a motorcycle for about €66 (Faroe Islands) or €108 (Iceland); and a car for €170 (Faroe Islands) or €276 (Iceland).

NORWAY
A daily overnight ferry operates between Copenhagen and Oslo. Ferries also run from Hirtshals to Oslo, Kristiansand and Moss; from Hanstholm to Bergen; and from Frederikshavn to Oslo and Larvik. More details are provided in the relevant Getting There & Away sections of the cities.

POLAND
Polferries (Denmark ☎ 33 11 46 45, Poland ☎ 94 35 52 108; www.polferries.pl) operates ferries to Świnoujście from both Copenhagen (from Dkr395, 10 hours) and Rønne (from Dkr225, 5½ hours).

SWEDEN
The cheapest and most frequent ferry to Sweden is the shuttle between Helsingør and Helsingborg (Dkr18, 20 minutes); ferries leave opposite the Helsingør train station every 20 minutes during the day and once an hour through the night. Passage for a car with up to nine people costs Dkr270.

Other ferries go from Frederikshavn to Göteborg and Oslo, and Rønne to Ystad. See the relevant Getting There & Away sections in this chapter.

UK
DFDS Seaways (UK ☎ 08705 333 000, Denmark ☎ 33 42 30 00; www.dfdsseaways.co.uk) sails from Esbjerg to Harwich at least three times a week at 6pm year-round. It takes 19 hours. The cost for passage in a chair ranges from Dkr750 in winter to Dkr1180 in midsummer, while the

cheapest bed in a two-person cabin is between Dkr948 and Dkr1798. Add Dkr116 to Dkr232 for a motorcycle, and Dkr406 to Dkr640 for a car; bikes are carried free.

GETTING AROUND
Air

Most internal flights cost around Dkr1000 for a standard ticket and can be much cheaper if you book in advance.

Denmark's domestic air routes are operated by the following airlines:

Cimber Air (☎ 74 42 22 77; www.cimber.dk) Flies from Copenhagen to Aalborg (55 minutes, five times daily), Rønne (Bornholm, 35 minutes, at least three times daily), Karup (central Jutland, 50 minutes, 12 times daily weekdays, at least twice weekends) and Sønderborg (near the German border, 40 minutes, four or five times weekdays, once on Saturday & Sunday).

SAS (☎ 70 10 30 00; www.scandinavian.net) Links Copenhagen with Aalborg, Århus and Billund about a dozen times a day.

Bicycle

Cycling is a practical way to get around Denmark. There are extensive bike paths linking towns throughout the country and bike lanes through most city centres.

You can rent bikes in most towns for around Dkr60 a day, plus a deposit of about Dkr250. Bikes can be taken on ferries and most trains for a modest cost; make sure you pick up the DSB pamphlet *Cykler i tog*. Also see p96.

Boat

A network of ferries links virtually all of Denmark's populated islands. Where there's not a bridge, there's usually a ferry, most of which take cars. All vessels meet strict safety requirements and are punctual and reliable. Specific information is given under individual destination sections. **Scandlines** (☎ 33 15 15 15; www.scandlines.com) operates many domestic ferry services. Timetables are widely available in tourist offices and railway stations.

Bus

All large cities and towns have a local bus system and most places are also served by regional buses, many of which connect with trains. There are also a few long-distance bus routes, including from Copenhagen to Aalborg or Århus. Travelling by bus on long-distance routes costs about 20% less than travel by train, although it's usually a bit slower than the train.

The following are the main bus companies operating in Denmark:

Abildskou (☎ 70 21 08 88; www.abildskou.dk) Runs from Copenhagen to Rønne on Bornholm Island via Ystad in Sweden.

Bornholmerbussen (☎ 44 68 44 00; www.bat.dk, Danish only) Operates the bus services on Bornholm.

Søndergaards Busser (☎ 70 10 00 33; www.sondergaards-busser.dk) Runs between Copenhagen and Århus.

Thinggaard Expressbusser (☎ 70 10 00 10; www.thinggaardbus.com, Danish only) Operates between Copenhagen, Aalborg and Fjerristslev and between Frederickshavn and Esbjerg.

Car & Motorcycle

Denmark is perfect for touring by car. Roads are in good condition and well signposted. Traffic is manageable, even in major cities such as Copenhagen (rush hours excepted).

Access to and from motorways is made easy since roads leading out of city and town centres are sensibly named after the main city to which they're routed. For instance, the road leading out of Odense to Faaborg is Faaborgvej, the road leading to Nyborg is Nyborgvej, and so on.

Denmark's extensive network of ferries carries motor vehicles for reasonable rates. It's always a good idea for drivers to call ahead and make reservations.

AUTOMOBILE ASSOCIATIONS

Denmark's main motoring organisation is **Forenede Danske Motorejere** (FDM; ☎ 32 66 01 00; www.fdm.dk; Firskovvej 32, 2800 Lyngby).

DRIVING LICENCES

A home driving licence, rather than an international one, is sufficient to drive and hire cars in Denmark, although you may also need to supply a passport at hire places.

FUEL & SPARE PARTS

You'll find the best prices for petrol at stations along motorways and at the unstaffed OK Benzin chain, which has self-serve pumps that accept Dkr100 notes as well as major credit cards. It's a small country, so you're never far from a garage and spare parts.

HIRE

You'll generally get the best deal by booking through an international rental agency

DENMARK

before you arrive in Denmark. Otherwise rates for the cheapest cars, including VAT, insurance and unlimited kilometres, begin at about Dkr680 a day, or Dkr520 a day on rentals of two days or more. Most companies offer a special weekend rate that allows you to keep the car from Friday afternoon to Monday morning and includes VAT and insurance for around Dkr1200. Request a plan that includes unlimited kilometres, as some begin tacking on an extra fee after the first 250km. Europcar offers unlimited kilometres and generally has the cheapest, most flexible weekend deals, but it's wise to call around and compare.

The largest companies – **Europcar** (☎ 70 11 66 99; www.europcar.dk), **Avis** (☎ 33 26 80 00; www.avis .dk) and **Hertz** (☎ 0800-1700; www.hertzdk.dk) – have offices throughout Denmark.

INSURANCE
Check with your insurance company that your policy is valid for driving in Denmark before you depart.

ROAD RULES
In Denmark you drive on the right-hand side of the road, seat-belt use is mandatory and all drivers are required to carry a warning triangle in case of breakdowns. Speed limits are 50km/h in towns, 80km/h

outside built-up areas and either 110km/h or 130km/h on motorways. Cars and motorcycles must use dipped headlights at all times.

It's illegal to drive with a blood-alcohol concentration of 0.05% or greater and driving under the influence is subject to stiff penalties and a possible prison sentence.

Train
With the exception of a few short private lines, the **Danish State Railways** (DSB; www.dsb.dk) runs all Danish train services.

There are two types of long-distance trains: sleek inter-city (IC) trains that generally require reservations (Dkr20) and older, slower inter-regional (IR) trains that make more stops and don't require reservations. Both cost the same, apart from the InterCity-Lyn, a cushy, pricier express train aimed at businesspeople. Rail passes don't cover reservation fees or surcharges.

Overall, train travel in Denmark is not expensive, in large part because the distances are short. People aged 65 and older are entitled to a 20% discount on Friday and Saturday and a 50% discount on other days. There are also generous discounts for children. Scanrail, Eurail and other rail passes are valid on DSB ferries and trains, but not on the private lines.

Faroe Islands

CONTENTS

FAROE ISLANDS

Floating on Atlantic waters like 18 shreds of precious green velvet, the Faroe Islands are a haven for those in search of rare remoteness. Ancient cairned footpaths through the craggy mountains of Streymoy and expansive swales of Suðuroy invite you to retrace the steps of early Faroese settlers while succumbing to the overwhelming grandeur of nature. The famous Faroese sheep are likely to be your most faithful companions during such solitary walks until you reach the coast, where the cries of thousands of sea birds echo from the majestic sheer cliffs of Vestmanna and the mighty cap Enniberg.

The Faroese are renowned for their deep local roots, expressed in powerful works of modern art and literature, and an almost unfailing desire to return to the islands' colourful miniature villages after stays abroad. Beautiful in their bleakness, irresistible in their stubborn defiance of a roaring Atlantic, these bare isles offer a seductive mix of humbling nature and local pride that will touch every traveller.

FAST FACTS

- **Area** 1399 sq km
- **Capital** Tórshavn
- **Currency** Danish krone: US$1 = Dkr6.01; £1 = Dkr10.80; €1 = Dkr7.44; A$1 = Dkr4.41; C$1 = Dkr4.79; NZ$1 = Dkr4.10; ¥100 = Dkr5.50
- **Famous for** sheep, puffins, whales and football
- **Official Languages** Faroese, Danish
- **Phrases** *góðan dag* (hello), *takk* (thanks), *farvæl* (goodbye), *orsaka meg* (excuse me)
- **Telephone Codes** country code ☎ 298; international access code ☎ 00
- **Visa** not required for citizens of the EU, Nordic countries, Canada, the USA, New Zealand and Australia

HIGHLIGHTS

- On a boat tour to the **Vestmanna bird cliffs** (p114) you don't only get to see a spectacular stretch of precipitous coastline teeming with sea birds, but actually enter sea caves as tall as Gothic churches
- The best place to observe the clownish puffins is magically wild **Mykines** (p120) – the island where birds rule
- A trip to **Fugloy** (p116) with the old mail boat grants spectacular views of pristine nature, while allowing you to experience a slice of everyday life on the Faroes

ITINERARIES

- **Two to three days** Explore Tórshavn and surroundings. Take a historical tour around Tinganes. Pay a visit the art gallery Listasavn and the idyllic park surrounding it, and then continue this cultural education at Fornminnissavn. Venture out to the Vestmanna bird cliffs and Kirkjubøur on the following days, and finish your stay with a Faroese dinner and a bar crawl in Tórshavn.
- **One week** Start off as above, then head north for beautiful Saksun. Cross over to Eysturoy, where Gjógv beckons for more trekking and Eiði for a meal. Spend a day on the streets of Klaksvík, then take the mail boat to Fugloy before returning to Tórshavn.

CLIMATE & WHEN TO GO

The Faroes have a temperate maritime climate, characterised by extensive cloud cover and frequent storms. Average temperatures vary from 3°C in January to 11°C in July and rain can be expected 280 days of the year. Weather tends to be unpredictable and localised – a bleak morning may well precede a sunny evening.

The main time for tourism is summer, from June to August, when days are endlessly long, the weather passable, and most tourist facilities open. Winter travellers need to prepare themselves for storms, daytime darkness and reduced service in most hotels and museums.

HISTORY

A travel account by the Irish missionary Brendan suggests that Celtic monks already lived in eremitic seclusion on the isles during the 6th century. Their isolation was

---

HOW MUCH?

- **Woollen socks** Dkr100
- **Traditional hat** Dkr400
- **Stuffed puffin** Dkr440
- **Sheep skin** Dkr590
- **Faroese sweater** Dkr1000-1500

LP INDEX

- **Litre of petrol** Dkr7-8
- **Litre of bottled water** Dkr20
- **Black Sheep beer** Dkr25
- **Souvenir T-shirt** Dkr130
- **Street snack – pizza** Dkr45

---

ended when the first Norse farmers arrived from 800 onwards. With the (often forceful) implementation of Christianity around 1000, ties to Norway became stronger, and the previously independent isles became part of the Kingdom of Norway in 1035. The first bishops' seat was established in Kirkjubøur.

When Norway fell to Denmark in 1380, the Faroese parliament became a mere legislative body, named Løgting. All trade was governed by the Danish monopoly, in place from 1535 to 1856. The only Faroese to gain temporary trading rights was Magnus Heinason in 1579, who built fort Skansin in Tørshavn to protect his ships from pirate attacks. The large stores of historical Tinganes stem from trading monopoly days. A painted coat of arms on the old guard's house still reminds of the era of Gabel (1655–1710), a time when the Faroese suffered great hardship under the oppressive rule of Christoffer von Gabel and his son Frederik, installed as lords of the manor by Denmark.

In 1849, the Danish parliament incorporated the islands into Denmark, which provoked strong independence movements. After British occupation during WWII, many Faroese hoped to gain autonomy, but Denmark passed the Act on Faroese Home Rule in 1948, which changed the islands' status from 'county of Denmark' to the 'self-governing community within the Kingdom of Denmark' it still is today. This gave the

FAROE ISLANDS

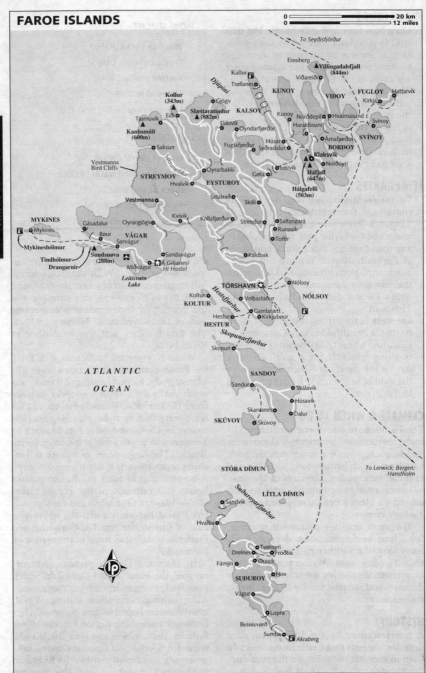

FAROE ISLANDS

0 ————————— 20 km
0 ————————— 12 miles

To Seyðisfjörður

ATLANTIC OCEAN

To Lerwick; Bergen; Hanstholm

Enniberg
▲Villingadalsfjall (844m)
Viðareiði
KUNOY VIDOY FUGLOY Hattarvik
Kallur Kirkja
Trøllanes
Djúpini Kunoy SVÍNOY
Gjógv Norðdepil Hvannasund Svínoy
Kollur KALSOY Haraldssund
(343m) Elduvík Árnafjørður
Slættaratindur Oyndarfjørður BORÐOY
Eiði ▲(882m) Húsar Klaksvík
Tjørnuvík Fuglafjørður Syðradalur Norðoyri
Kanbsmúli Saksun Háfjall
(600m) (647m)
Góta Leirvík
Vestmanna Oyrarbakki Hálgafelli
Bird Cliffs STREYMOY EYSTUROY (503m)
Hvalvík
Selatrað
Vestmanna Skáli

MYKINES Oyrargjógv Kvívík Saltangará
Mykines Gásadalur VÁGAR Kollafjørður Strendur Runavík
Mykineshólmur Bøur Sørvágur Toftir
Tindhólmur Sandavágur
Drangarnir Sandsnøva Á Gljanesi Kaldbak
(288m) Miðvágur HI Hostel
Leitisvatn
Lake TÓRSHAVN Nólsoy
Koltur Velbastaður NÓLSOY
KOLTUR Hestsfjørður Gamlarætt
Hestur Kirkjubøur
HESTUR Skopunarfjørður
Skopun
SANDOY
Sandur Skálavík
Húsavík
Skarvanes Dalur
SKÚVOY Skúvoy

STÓRA DÍMUN

Suðuroyarfjørður
LÍTLA DÍMUN
Sandvík
Hvalba
Drelnes Tvøroyri
Froðba
Fámjin Ørðavik
Hov
SUDUROY
Vágur
Lopra
Beinisvørð
Sumba Akraberg

Faroese legislative power over their own affairs. When Denmark joined the EU, the Faroes refused to follow, due to the contested issue of a 320km fishing exclusion limit. Today, their vulnerable, fishery-based economy seems to be climbing out of a recession, and the falling population figure of the mid-'90s has been reversed.

PEOPLE

At last count, 47,704 people lived in the Faroes, 18,420 (nearly 40%) of them in the capital Tórshavn. The remaining 100 communities suffer from a rural exodus towards the capital.

The majority of Faroese are of Nordic origin, and share the reserved politeness of their Scandinavian neighbours. Spend some time there though, and you'll find them to be the most hospitable people in the North Atlantic region.

RELIGION

Religion is a fundamental aspect of Faroese culture; 85% of the population belong to the Evangelical-Lutheran Church. There's also a small number of Roman Catholics and other religious communities, such as the Plymouth Brethren.

ARTS

The Faroese look back on a long tradition of dance and oral poetry. With the creation of the written language in 1846, a national literature developed, and writers such as William Heinesen and Heðin Brú achieved international recognition.

Judging by the ubiquity of small galleries around the islands, it seems unbelievable that visual art only emerged in the early 20th century. The paintings by the renowned artist Sámal Joensen-Mikines were strongly inspired by Faroese landscapes – a theme that is continued in the works of contemporary artists, such as Astrid Luihn and Zacharias Heinesen. The dramatic glass works by Trøndur Patursson illuminate the church of Gøta, while Hans Pauli Olsen's bronze sculptures adorn Tórshavn's park Viðarlundin.

While the ancient tradition of chain dancing (see p109) is still very much alive and well, contemporary artists have managed to translate their heritage elegantly into modern forms. Teitor's melancholic folk songs have caused more than a ripple internationally, and the jazz/folk inspired ballads of Eivør Pálsdóttir are the mould for a whole new Faroese sound.

(see p109)

GRINDADRÁP

The long-finned pilot whale (called 'grind' in Faroese) has traditionally been hunted in the Faroe Islands; the hunt is called a grindadráp. These whales are about 6m long when fully grown and swim around the North Atlantic in large groups known as pods. When a pod is sighted off the coast, boats are sent out to herd them all into a bay, where they're driven closer to shore. Local people waiting on the beach then wade into the water and insert steel gaffs into the whales' blowholes, to drag them into shallow water. The jugular and carotid blood vessels are cut with long knives, causing catastrophic loss of blood pressure and rapid descent to unconsciousness and death. This method is the quickest and least painful way to kill whales – methods used to kill domestic livestock cannot be used effectively on beaches.

The entire catch is divided among the hunters and all local residents. Shares of the meat are given to institutions, including hospitals, and a small proportion is sold locally at a price around half that of other meats. The carcasses are removed and the beach where the whales were killed is cleaned up quickly. The number of grindadráps per year is limited by law to prevent waste.

The pilot whale hunt has attracted the attention and ire of environmental/antiwhaling groups in the past. However, pilot whaling is economically, culturally and historically important to the Faroese – and it's perfectly legal under rules set by the International Whaling Commission. Faroese people point out that objectors to whaling should respect cultural traditions which are not their own and should direct their energy to more pressing concerns, such as war and pollution.

Ironically, the pilot whale hunt may be doomed anyway, due to rather high levels of mercury and cadmium now found in the meat, most likely caused by pollution from cities. Pollution is a far graver threat to the pilot whales than the Faroese have ever been.

Readers are advised to travel to the Faroes and make up their own minds.

ENVIRONMENT
The Land
The Faroes consist of 18 treeless, grassy islands that are largely flanked by sheer cliffs. They lie 400km southeast of Iceland and 280km north of Scotland. The basalt formations are the remnants of a volcanic continent that covered the Atlantic region 100 million years ago. Its ancient plateau character is still visible on the Faroes' flat-capped mountains, such as the highest peak Slættaratindur. Most landscape structures, including the characteristic fjords, sounds and gorges, were shaped during the Ice Age.

Wildlife
During summer, more than 100 species of birds may be found nesting on the Faroes. The coastal cliffs teem with puffins, guillemots, fulmars, gulls and the occasional gannet; inland you'll find the national bird *tjaldur* (oystercatcher) alongside various types of wading birds and ducks.

Pilot whales, the best-known inhabitants of Faroese waters, gained unfortunate fame when the controversial *grindadráp* whale slaughter made headlines. There are other species of whales, too, as well as plenty of saltwater fish and a few seals.

Sheep are the most ubiquitous land mammal and, together with salt spray and soil erosion, largely responsible for the bare appearance of the isles.

Environmental Issues
The Faroes' marine environment is fairly clean, compared to other North Atlantic regions, though intensive fish farming and dwindling fish stock represent considerable environmental problems. Visitors should be particularly careful not to disturb nesting birds by walking through their breeding grounds.

FOOD & DRINK
Traditional Faroese cuisine is a decidedly hearty affair, built around fish, lamb and potatoes. Wind-drying is a classic method of preservation; *turrur fiskur* (dried fish) and *skerpikjøt* (dried mutton) are Faroese specialities. No part of the sheep goes to waste. *Seyðahøvd* (sheep's head) is a delicacy; don't be put off if one peers at you from a supermarket freezer. Sea bird is another staple, and though tourists might find it inconceivable to chew on a baked puffin, their consumption is nowhere near as controversial as that of *grind og spik* (whale meat and blubber).

None of this bodes well for strict vegetarians. Few restaurants offer vegetarian dishes, and you're probably best off preparing your own. Most towns and villages have supermarkets, and small kiosks sell essential groceries until 11pm. Fruit and veg is expensive, and strangely, fresh fish isn't easily obtained, as most people catch their own. Alcohol is available in larger towns from the state liquor stores Rúsdrekkasøla.

The Faroese like to claim that the best place to find traditional food is abroad. There's some truth in this, though things are getting better. Tórshavn has some excellent places selling rustic meals in the evening and buffet lunches from noon to 2pm.

Sunday is dining-out day for most Faroese; many places dispense with menus altogether and offer set three-course meals.

TÓRSHAVN

pop 18,420

With just over 18,000 inhabitants, Tórshavn is one of the world's smallest capitals and home to more than a third of the Faroese population. It's a place where the intimacy of a small town mixes with the spirit of a capital city. Behind the proud, turf-roofed warehouses of historical Tinganes at the seafront lies a charming centre that's surprisingly alive with music and relaxed crowds on summer weekends.

HISTORY
Surrounded by poor soil and suffering from unfavourable harbour conditions, Tórshavn was an unlikely first choice for a settlement. It was only due to its central location that the first Ting was set up here in 1000. Initially, only a few monks lived near the harbour named after the Norse god Thor. With increasing trading activities, the small community grew steadily, and when the Danish trading monopoly was replaced by free trade in 1856, Tórshavn rapidly evolved into the hub of activity it is today.

ORIENTATION
Tórshavn is a pleasant place to walk around. The town centre, where you find most shops,

restaurants and facilities, lies just above the two harbours, in the area surrounding Niels Finsensgøta. The Eastern Harbour with the ferry terminal is separated from the Western Harbour by the Tinganes peninsula.

INFORMATION
Bookshops
Bókasølan (Map p110; ☎ 319575; SMS Shopping Centre) Also carries some English and German titles.
HN Jacobsens Bókahandil (Map p112; ☎ 311036; Vaglið 1) Foreign-language publications, maps and books on the Faroe Islands in an atmospheric old school building from 1860.

Cultural Centre
Norðurlandahúsið (Nordic House; Map p110; ☎ 317900; www.nlh.fo; Norðari Ringvegur 10, admission free; ☼ 10am-6pm Mon-Sat, 2-6pm Sun) Architecturally interesting centre that frequently houses concerts, plays, exhibitions and conferences, and has a pleasant cafeteria.

Emergency
The emergency number for police, ambulance or fire brigade is ☎ 112.

Internet Access
Býarbókasavnið and **Føroya Landsbókasavn** (see Libraries below) Pre-booked, free one-hour slots.
Teledepilin (Map p112; ☎ 317010; Niels Finsensgøta 10) Two Internet terminals for free browsing.

Libraries
Býarbókasavnið (Town Library; Map p112, ☎ 302030, www.byarbok.fo, Faroese only; Niels Finsensgøta 7; ☼ 10am-6pm Mon-Fri, 10am-1pm Sat)
Føroya Landsbókasavn (National Library; Map p110; ☎ 311626; www.flb.fo; JC Svabosgøta 16; ☼ 1-7pm Mon-Fri Jun-Aug, 10am-8pm Mon-Wed & 10am-5pm Thu & Fri Sep-May)

Medical Services
Emergency Dental Service (☎ 314544; ☼ 1-2pm Sat & Sun) Runs a clinic at the hospital.
Emergency Medical Service (☎ 310033) Provides assistance between 4pm and 8am.
Hospital (Map p110; ☎ 313540; JC Svabosgøta) Has a casualty ward.

Money
Tórshavn's banks are open from 9.30am to 4pm on weekdays (late closing at 6pm on Thursday). Outside normal banking hours, Hotel Hafnia and the tourist office will exchange cash.

Føroya Banki (Map p112; ☎ 311350; Niels Finsensgøta 15)
Føroya Sparikassi (Map p112; ☎ 348380; Tinghúsvegur 49)

Post
Central Post Office (Map p112; ☎ 311010; Posthúsbrekka) Provides philatelic services, public telephone and even houses a small art gallery.
Main Post Office (Map p110; ☎ 346000; Óðinshædd 2)

Tourist Information
Faroe Islands Tourist Board (Map p112; ☎ 316055; www.tourist.fo; Undir Bryggjubakka 17; ☼ 8am-4pm Mon-Fri) Deals mainly with research and publications, though their staff is very knowledgeable about regional attractions.
Kunningarstovan Tourist Office (Map p112; ☎ 315788; www.visittorshavn.fo; Niels Finsensgøta 13; ☼ 8am-5.30pm Mon-Fri, 9am-2pm Sat) Assistance with bookings of accommodation, tour planning and general information. Pick up your maps, transport timetable, brochures and the booklet *Tourist Guide – Faroe Islands* here.

SIGHTS
Tinganes   Map p112
The red, turf-roofed buildings of ancient **Tinganes** greet anyone who arrives in Tórshavn by ferry. Until the late 1800s, Tórshavn didn't extend beyond the Tinganes peninsula. A stroll around its web of narrow lanes and passageways grants a glimpse of life in centuries passed.

The tight alleyway **Gongin**, with its low, tar-painted 19th-century houses, was once the quarter's main road. South of it lies the

---

CHAIN DANCING

Stay in Tórshavn during the Ólavsøkan festivities in July, and you'll find it almost impossible to avoid being drawn into a stomping, leaping and singing ring of enthusiastic dancers. Closely related to the medieval ring dances of Europe, the chain dance is more than communal entertainment. Ancient historical knowledge has been passed on for generations via the heroic poems *(kvæði)* that are typically sung to accompany it. Even more importantly, these ballads have helped to preserve the Faroese tongue that might otherwise have been erased by the prominence of Danish. Cultural conservation has never been so much fun.

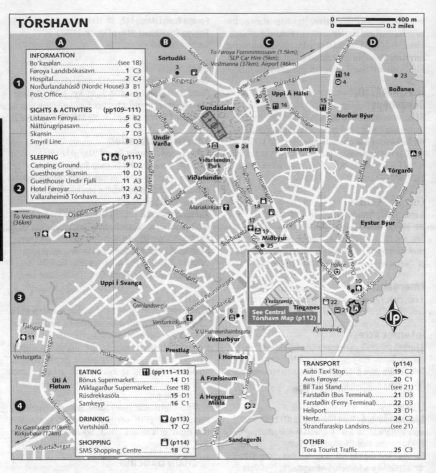

TÓRSHAVN

0 ━━━━━━ 400 m
0 ━━━━━━ 0.2 miles

INFORMATION
Bo'kasølan.................................(see 18)
Føroya Landsbókasavn.................**1** C3
Hospital..**2** C4
Norðurlandahúsið (Nordic House)**3** B1
Post Office......................................**4** D1

SIGHTS & ACTIVITIES (pp109–111)
Listasavn Føroya...........................**5** B2
Náttúrugripasavn...........................**6** C3
Skansin..**7** D3
Smyril Line......................................**8** D3

SLEEPING (p111)
Camping Ground..............................**9** D2
Guesthouse Skansin......................**10** D3
Guesthouse Undir Fjalli................**11** A3
Hotel Føroyar.................................**12** A2
Vallaraheimið Tórshavn...............**13** A2

EATING (pp111–113)
Bónus Supermarket.....................**14** D1
Miklagarður Supermarket........(see 18)
Rúsdrekkasóla...............................**15** D3
Samkeyp..**16** C1

DRINKING (p113)
Vertshúsið.......................................**17** C2

SHOPPING (p114)
SMS Shopping Centre..................**18** C2

TRANSPORT (p114)
Auto Taxi Stop................................**19** C2
Avis Føroyar....................................**20** C1
Bíl Taxi Stand............................(see 21)
Farstøðin (Bus Terminal)............**21** D3
Farstøðin (Ferry Terminal)..........**22** D3
Heliport..**23** D1
Hertz...**24** C2
Strandfaraskip Landsins........(see 21)

OTHER
Tora Tourist Traffic.....................**25** C3

actual area of Tinganes where you find some of Tórshavn's oldest buildings.

Munkastovan, with its heavy stone walls and low turf roof, dates back to the 13th century. Like the neighbouring **Leigubúðin**, built in the 16th century, it was formerly used as a warehouse, and survived the devastating fire of 1673 that destroyed most of Tinganes.

Reynargarður was built as a vicarage in 1630. The impressive four-winged construction is an excellent example of 17th-century Faroese architecture.

The stone-built **Myrkastovan**, dating from 1693, was a guardhouse with a prison in the basement, while the split-log construction of **Stokkastovan** and the towering **Skansapakkhúsið**

(1750) at the southern end of Tinganes were once used for storage purposes.

Skansin   Map p110
The humble, turf-roofed fort **Skansin** is rather unassuming for a stronghold once built to protect town and trade against pirates. Originally constructed in 1579, its oldest preserved parts stem from 1780. During WWII, the British army used it as headquarters, and left an old cannon as a reminder of those days.

Museums & Art Galleries
Two kilometres north of the city centre, the **Føroya Fornminnissavn** (Historical Museum; ☎ 310700; Brekkutún 6, Hoyvík; adult/child Dkr30/free; ⏱ 10am-5pm Mon-Fri, 2-5pm Sat & Sun mid-May–mid-Sep, 3-5pm Sun

mid-Sep–mid-May) displays artefacts of Faroese life from the Viking Age to the 19th century. Its collection of boats and old fishing items is particularly noteworthy. It's worth extending the visit with a stroll through the village Hoyvík, where a narrow footpath leads the way to a scenic bay. Red buses No 2 and No 3 pass near the museum on Hvítanesvegur.

The **Náttúrugripasavn** (Natural History Museum; Map opposite; ☎ 352300; VU Hammershaimbsgøta 13; adult/child Dkr20/free; ☺ 10am-4pm Mon-Fri & 3-5pm Sat, Sun Jun-Aug, 3-5pm Sun Sep-May) has a brilliant geological section. The collection of dried plants, mammal skeletons and stuffed birds in the backroom is less informative, but the adjacent botanical garden with 150 species of plants is worth a visit.

A short stroll through Viðarlundin, a wonderfully wild park where trees mingle with sculptures, leads to the bright and airy **Listasavn Føroya** (National Art Gallery; Map opposite; ☎ 313579; www.art.fo; Gundadalsvegur 9; adult/child Dkr30/free; ☺ 11am-5pm Mon-Fri, 2-6pm Sat & Sun Jun-Aug, 2-5pm Tue-Fri, 2-6pm Sat & Sun Sep-May). It has an excellent permanent collection of Faroese art and regular wandering exhibitions.

The intimate **Galerie Focus** (Map p112; ☎ 315251; amarian@post.olivant.fo; Grims Kambansgøta 20; ☺ 2-6pm Mon-Fri, 4-6pm Sat) is a great place to see (and potentially purchase) paintings and sculptures by contemporary Faroese artists.

FESTIVALS & EVENTS

Tórshavn Marathon (www.torshavnmarathon.com) Mid-July marathon, shorter fun runs are also part of event.

Ólavsøka (28 and 29 July) Every year the biggest festival of the Faroes is celebrated with processions, boat races, music and dancing. Tórshavn and the Faroese never get livelier than this.

SLEEPING

Accommodation options in Tórshavn are fairly limited, and popular places get booked up early, so reserve in advance. Contact the tourist office for private flats and rooms.

Budget

Camping ground (Map opposite; ☎ 315788; torsinfo@post.olivant.fo; Yviri við Strond; per person Dkr50; ☺ mid-May–mid-Sep) The only camping ground lies on the coast, 1500m north of the centre, and has reasonable facilities.

Bládýpi (Map p112; ☎ 311951; www.bladypi.fo; Dr Jakobsensgøta 14-16; dm/s/d Dkr140/270/430; ✗) Dorm beds and hospitable guesthouse facilities are available at this bright and friendly place. Its welcoming atmosphere, central location and affordable prices make this easily Tórshavn's most popular address.

Vallaraheimið Tórshavn (Map opposite; ☎ 345900; www.smyril-line.fo; Oyggjarvegur; dm/d Dkr160/195; ☺ May-Sep; ℗ ✗) This bright, wood-panelled hostel sits on the hillside 2km west of central Tórshavn. The views are fantastic, but there's no bus service into town (taxis cost Dkr60). Guests benefit from some of the facilities of the adjacent Hotel Føroyar, which, like the hostel, belongs to Smyril Lines.

Mid-Range

Guesthouse Undir Fjalli (Map opposite; ☎ 320527; www.undirfjalli.com; Vesturgøta 15; s/d Dkr360/490; ☺ mid-Jun–mid-Aug) This student accommodation in the west of Tórshavn caters for tourists during summer. It's a good, clean place, though a little far from town.

Guesthouse Skansin (Map opposite; ☎ 312242; fax 310657; Jekaragøta 8; s/d Dkr390/540; ☺ closed Christmas) This friendly, family-run business near the harbour has cute rooms and excellent cooking facilities.

Top End

Hotel Tórshavnar Sjómansheim (Map p112; ☎ 350000; www.hotel.fo; Tórsgøta 4; s/d from Dkr760/915; ☺ closed Christmas) This grand old seamen's hostel has pleasant rooms and great views across the harbour.

Hotel Hafnia (Map p112; ☎ 313233; www.hafnia.fo; Áarvegur 4-10; s/d Dkr950/1150; ☺ closed Christmas) Established in 1951, this is still Tórshavn's most prominent hotel. The discreetly decorated rooms have satellite TV, telephone and minibar.

Hotel Føroyar (Map opposite; ☎ 317500; www.hotelforoyar.com; Oyggjarvegur; s/d Dkr925/1095) Up on the hill, this stylish place boasts four-star luxury and spectacular views. Rooms are spacious and furnished with all expected mod cons.

EATING

Tórshavn's dining scene is picking up all the time, and if you're prepared to spend a bit, you can really indulge in excellent fish and meat dishes. For opening times, see Business Hours, p121.

CENTRAL TÓRSHAVN

0 ⊨━━━━━━━━ 100 m
0 ⊨━━━━━━━━ 0.1 miles

INFORMATION		
Býarbókasavnið	1	B3
Faroe Islands Tourist Board	2	C5
Føroya Banki	3	B3
Føroya Sparikassi	4	B3
GreenGate Incoming	5	C5
HN Jacobsens Bókahandil	6	C4
Kunningarstovan Tourist Office	7	B3
MB Tours	8	B4
Post Office	9	B4
Teledepilin	10	B3

SIGHTS & ACTIVITIES	(pp109–11)	
Galerie Focus	11	A5
Leigubúðin	12	D6
Munkastovan	13	C6
Myrkastovan	14	D5
Reynargarður	15	C5
Skansapakkhúsið	16	D6
Stokkastovan	17	D6

SLEEPING	🏠 (p111)	
Bládýpi	18	A4
Hotel Hafnia	19	C4
Hotel Tórshavnar Sjómansheim	20	B4

EATING	🍴 (pp111–13)	
Café Karlsborg	21	C5
Café Kheops	22	B3
Frants Restorff Bakery	23	A3
Gallari Jinx	24	C4
Marco Polo	25	B3
Merlot	26	A3
Pizzacafé	(see 20)	
Rafik'sa	(see 27)	
Restaurant Hafnia	(see 19)	
Rio Bravo	27	B3
Toscana	28	C3

DRINKING	🍷 (p113)	
Café Natúr	29	D4

Cleopatra	30	B3
Manhattan Pub & Café	31	A3

ENTERTAINMENT	🎭 (pp113–14)	
Eclipse	(see 32)	
Havnar Bio Cinema	32	C3
Leikhúsið Gríma	33	B4
Platform	(see 32)	

SHOPPING	🛍 (p114)	
Andreas í Vágsbotni	34	B4
Fotobúðin	35	B3
Sirri (Knitwear Shop)	36	D5

TRANSPORT	(p114)	
Maersk Air	37	B3
Taxi Stand	38	B4

OTHER		
Løgting (Parliament)	39	B3
Ráðhús	40	B4

FAROE ISLANDS

Restaurants

Merlot (Map opposite; ☎ 311121; Magnus Heinasonargøta 20; buffet lunches Dkr98, mains Dkr180-250) Never mind the slightly impersonal decor, the fish menu is excellent, though you might want to give the whale a miss.

Restaurant Hafnia (Map opposite; ☎ 313233; Áarvegur 4-10; mains Dkr175-310) This classy restaurant offers a huge fish buffet every Tuesday and Thursday during summer, and is one of the few places serving Faroese specialities. Baked puffin costs Dkr305.

Other recommendations:

Marco Polo (Map opposite; ☎ 313430; Sverrisgøta 12; mains Dkr155-215) Seafarer-themed restaurant.

Rio Bravo (Map opposite; ☎ 319767; Tórsgøta 11; mains Dkr155-185; ⌚ from 5pm) Rustic steakhouse.

Cafés

Café Karlsborg (Map opposite; ☎ 317464; Undir Bryggjubakka; ⌚ 11am-6pm; snacks Dkr10-50) With garish knick-knacks displayed along a brightly painted stone wall, this feels like a cross between souvenir shop and café. It's quite endearing, and if it isn't raining, you can sit outside and watch life at the harbour go by.

Café Kheops (Map opposite; ☎ 313430; Niels Finsensgøta 11; snacks Dkr30-40, brunch Dkr65) The atmosphere in this curious little place is working man's pub; the menu, with its cakes, ice creams and snacks, spells coffee house. The upstairs bit with its furry couches has far more character, and is less smoky than the main room.

Quick Eats

Pizzacafé (Map opposite; ☎ 350000; Hotel Tórshavnar Sjómansheim, Tórsgøta 4; dishes Dkr70-120) Not your typical hotel restaurant, this place gets frighteningly busy. Trust the crowd, it's still the best pizza parlour in town.

Rafik'sa (Map opposite; ☎ 319767; Tórsgøta 11; mains Dkr65-80) This bistro attracts workers around lunch time. A good place for quick buffet lunches, schwarma, burgers and pizza.

Self-Catering

Miklagarður (Map p110; RC Effersøesgøta 31), inside the SMS Shopping Centre, has the best-stocked supermarket, though **Bónus** (Map p110; Óðinshædd) is cheaper. For after-hours shopping, there's the central **Frants Restorff Bakery** (Map opposite; Tórsgøta; ⌚ 7am-11pm) and the grocery store **Samkeyp** (Map p110; Heykavegur ⌚ 7.30am-10pm Mon-Fri, 9am-10pm Sat). Get your drinks from the local liquor store **Rúsdrekkasøla** (Map p110; Hoyvíksvegur 51).

> **THE AUTHOR'S CHOICE**
>
> **Gallari Jinx** (Map opposite; ☎ 317101; Árvegur 3; mains Dkr80-140) With its wide glass front, metal decor and turf roof, this stylish coffee bar spells cool chic. For coffee lovers this is an oasis in the land of the instant beaker, for vegetarians it's a lifesaver, and for most it's simply the hottest café in town. A trendy bar in the evenings, it serves a devilishly good brunch on Saturday mornings and light lunches throughout the week.
>
> **Toscana** (Map opposite; ☎ 311109; Pállsgøta 13; mains Dkr170-220) Tucked away behind the cinema, this cosy little eatery is quickly becoming something of a magnet for those who like their food prepared with a little creativity. Scrumptious meat dishes served with tastebud-tickling sauces definitely rule the menu, but the braised salmon claims the crown. It's probably the only place you need to book in advance.

DRINKING

The characteristic Faroese reservation crumbles quickly over drinks and live music – the night out of choice for most islanders.

Café Natúr (Map opposite; ☎ 312625; Áarvegur 7) This atmospheric café-cum-bar is the hub of Tórshavn's live scene, and always packed on weekends. Local bands play here from Thursday to Saturday.

Cleopatra (Map opposite; ☎ 313430; Niels Finsensgøta 11) This cute, low-ceilinged bar is refreshingly unpretentious for a cocktail place. The clientele is young and stylish, the live music laid-back and the vibe intimate.

Other recommendations:

Vertshúsið (Map p110; ☎ 314848; 32 Niels Finsensgøta) Pub with jam sessions.

Manhattan Pub & Café (Map opposite; ☎ 319696; Sverrisgøta 15) Live music in an amiable setting.

ENTERTAINMENT

Entertainment options in Tórshavn are fairly limited, but the occasional concerts put on at the Norðurlandahúsid are not to be missed. The *Havnartíðindi* booklet (available at the tourist office) gives details of events around town.

Havnar Bio (Map opposite; ☎ 311956; Tinghúsvegur 8; tickets Dkr65) This two-screen cinema shows films in their original language with Danish subtitles.

Eclipse (Map p112; ☎ 315628; www.eclipse.fo, Faroese only; Tinghúsvegur 8) is a nightclub with techno and garage, and **Platform** (Map p112; ☎ 316363; Tinghúsvegur 8) plays pop tunes for over-20s.

Leikhúsið Gríma (Map p112; ☎ 318617; www.grima .fo, Faroese only; Magnus Heinasonargøta 12) The Faroes' professional theatre troupes hold regular shows and cabaret performances.

SHOPPING

Sirri (Map p112; ☎ 321706; www.sirri.fo; Gongin 5) This designer knitwear shop in pretty Gongin is largely responsible for the revival of the Faroese sweater. One of their beautifully cut garments from organic, dye-free wool goes for around Dkr1000.

Andreas í Vágsbotni (Map p112; ☎ 312040; Vágsbotnur 14) Tórshavn's largest souvenir store sells anything from puffin-ornamented ashtrays to knitted socks.

Fotobúðin (Map p112; ☎ 311661; Niels Finsensgøta 8) The best place to stock up on film.

SMS Shopping Centre (Map p110; ☎ 313041; RC Effersøesgøta 31) The Faroes' biggest mall has a wide range of shops and restaurants.

GETTING THERE & AWAY

All blue long-distance buses, international and interisland ferries depart from the Farstøðin transport terminal by the Eastern Harbour. Pick up a copy of the Ferðaætlan transport schedule (Dkr20) from tourist offices or Strandfaraskip Landsins at the terminal. Also see p124.

GETTING AROUND
To/From the Airport

The airport bus (No 300, Dkr100) leaves from Farstøðin three hours before international flight departures and runs to the international airport on Vágar via the undersea tunnel. Bookings aren't necessary.

Car & Motorcycle

In most parking spaces in Tórshavn you can leave your car free of charge for a limited period of time. Unlimited parking is possible on the spaces behind Hoyvíksvegur and Skáalatrøð. Niels Finsensgøta is a pedestrian zone.

Public Transport

The red Bussleiðin buses (Dkr10 per ride) cover most of the town. They run half-hourly on weekdays and hourly on weekends and evenings. Schedules are available at the tourist office.

Taxi

The main taxi companies are **Auto** (☎ 311234) with stands on Niels Finsensgøta, and **Bil** (☎ 311444) at Farstøðin. Both also depart from the Ráðhús.

STREYMOY

KIRKJUBØUR
pop 226

An ancient footpath winds itself through green hills from Tórshavn to Kirkjubøur – the Faroes' religious and cultural centre of medieval times. Its most striking sight is the ruin of the grand Gothic **Magnus Cathedral**, an ambitious 13th-century construction that was never completed. The adjacent **St Olav's church**, built in 1111 and still used today, served as ecumenical centre instead.

The beautiful turf-roofed farmhouse **Roykstovan** (Smoke Chamber; ☎ 328089; www.patursson.com; adult/child Dkr30/free; ☼ 9am-5.30pm Mon-Sat, 2-5.30pm Sun Jun-Aug or by arrangement) is a split-log building, that has been home to 17 generations of the same farming family. Part of its spacious interior is laid out to reflect the Faroese lifestyle during medieval times; the rest is still inhabited by Jóannes Patursson, the latest in the line of heirs, and knowledgeable guide. On request, he prepares Faroese feasts that are served in the main room of Roykstovan.

The classic route to Kirkjubøur is by following the moderately difficult 12km trail from Tórshavn. You reach it from the junction of Landavegur and Velbastaðvegur, where the small access road við Sandá leads to a farmhouse; the cairned trail starts behind the building. It's marked on the Faroe Islands 1:100,000 map by Kort og Matrikelstyrelsen.

Bus No 101 (Dkr20, 30 minutes, several daily) to Gamlarætt stops at Kirkjubøur if you request it by calling ☎ 343030; otherwise go to Gamlarætt and walk 2km.

VESTMANNA BIRD CLIFFS

The breathtaking boat tours past the looming **Vestmannabjørgini** (Vestmanna bird cliffs) are deservedly the biggest attraction of the Faroe Islands. From Vestmanna, the boat travels past a steep coastline, weaving a tight course through narrow escarpments and into eerie sea caves. The breeding areas of guillemots and razorbills line the slim mountain ridges, and fulmars, kittiwakes and gulls are scattered across the mighty rocks like thousands of white dots. The air resounds with their cries as they circle above your head. Take some binoculars to spot the occasional puffin and a sweater to keep you warm.

Two tour operators, the long-established **Palli Lamhauge** (☎ 424155; www.sightseeing.fo) and **Gunnar Skúvadal** (☎ 424305; www.vestmannabjorgini .com) run the same, two-hour course in a modern speedboat or a wooden Faroese launch (adult/child Dkr175/85, daily at 9.40am, 2pm, 5pm and 8pm). If the weather seems unstable, it's better to phone before venturing out.

Vestmanna itself is a sleepy little village where you can enjoy a solid lunch in the company of dock workers in the café **Bryggjam** (☯ 11.30am-2pm & 6pm-midnight) at the harbour.

Bus No 300/100 (Dkr50, one hour) goes several times daily from Tórshavn. **Øssur Christiansen** (☎ 217752) runs a private bus service from mid-June to mid-July that is timed to avoid long waits in Vestmanna and slips in a bit of sightseeing on the way back (Dkr120 return-trip, call to book).

SAKSUN
pop 34

Tiny Saksun looks almost forlorn in the midst of the unusual and magnificent landscape surrounding it. Tall hills rise either side of a large valley, where a small, turf-roofed church perseveres against the storms that often get trapped here. On a windy day, the waterfalls tumbling down the hills get blown into the air as a fine mist before reaching the ground. The village looks out onto the large tidal lake Pollur, which is framed by a sandy coastline.

Near the church, the 19th-century farmhouse **Dúvugarður** (☎ 310700; admission Dkr20; ☯ 2-5pm Fri-Wed mid-Jun–mid-Aug) houses a folk museum.

Saksun is an excellent base for hiking. A partially treacherous three-to-four hour trek along a cairned trail passes through the mountains to **Tjørnuvík**. From there, you get a marvellous view on the sea stacks Risin and Kellingin, which a folk legend describes as a giant and hag turned to stone when attempting to pull the Faroes over to Iceland.

Saksun is a difficult place to reach by bus, and unless you're organising a holiday apartment, there's no accommodation available. Take bus No 400 from Tórshavn to Oyrarbakki (Dkr50, 30 minutes, several daily) and change to bus No 204, which runs twice daily except weekends from 25 June to 15 August.

EYSTUROY

GJÓGV
pop 53

It's hard to imagine a more picturesque place than the miniature village of Gjógv in the north of Eysturoy. A meandering little stream lined with juicy marsh marigolds divides a cluster of colourfully painted houses, and meets the sea in a wide bay that is split by an impressive sea-filled gorge.

Gjógv is the starting point of several hiking tours. Apart from short, local walks along the rugged coastline, there's a well-indicated mountain trek to **Ambadalur**, from where you get a good view of the tall cliff Búgvin.

More ambitious hikers might want to climb the **Slættaratindur**; at 882m it's the Faroes' tallest peak. The outset for this demanding ascent is the highest point on the Eiði-Funningur road.

The excellent youth hostel **Gjáargarður** (☎ 423171; www.gjaarhostel.dk; camping per person Dkr60, dm/s/d Dkr140/300/400; ☯ mid-Jun–mid-Aug) is a turf-roofed building with balconies, wood-panelled rooms and a loft designed to resemble a traditional Faroese farmhouse.

It's best to explore the north of Eysturoy by car. Bus No 200 connects Gjógv twice daily with Eiði (Dkr10, 15 minutes).

EIÐI
pop 725

The 1881 **village church**, with its unusual tunnel vault and brightly painted interior, is one of the most beautiful on the Faroes. If it's closed, ask for the key at the hotel. A **glass designer** (☎ 423370; glarlist@post.olivant.fo; ☯ 2-5.30pm Tue & Fri or by arrangement) can be watched at work in his blue container near the harbour, and the folk museum **Látrid** (☎ 423597; ☯ 2-4pm Wed & Sun Jun & Jul) portrays the traditional Faroese lifestyle.

The large **Hotel Lonin** (☎ 423456; fax 423200; s/d Dkr600/700), with its pleasant restaurant, makes

Eiði a popular place to recoup energy after hikes.

The village supermarket sells essential groceries, and there's a bank and post office.

From Tórshavn, take Bus No 400 to Oyrarbakki, then No 200 to Eiði (Dkr60, 1½ hours, several daily).

GØTA
pop 1033

In the southern part of Eysturoy, Gøta claws itself along the beautiful bay of Gøtuvík. The stunning scenery must be inspiring, for Gøta is the hub of musical activity on the Faroes. Home to many musicians, Suðrugøta hosts the annual G!Festival (see Festivals & Events, p121). It also houses the woolwear company **Töting** (☎ 441020; www.toeting.com; ꧁ 9am-5.30pm Mon-Fri, 10am-2pm Sat), the largest on the Faroes, which has an improvised café, a small art gallery and a well-stocked knitwear shop.

Further up the coast, Gøtugjógv has the most famous modern church of the Faroes. Consecrated in 1995, the stunning **Gøtu Kirkja** impresses with its ingenious ceiling construction and artful glass ornamentation by Tróndur Patursson. If you find it closed, ask for the key at Töting.

A traditional wooden church from 1833 forms the centre of Norðragøta. Behind it sits the old farmhouse **Blásastova** (☎ 222717, 441440; adult/child Dkr30/free; ꧁ 2-4pm Thu-Tue mid-May–mid-Sep), now converted into a lovingly decorated folk museum exhibiting an extensive collection of work and home utensils.

There are no tourist facilities in Gøta itself, but about 12km south, Runavík has banks, grocery stores, a post office and the well-appointed **Hotel Runavík Sjómansheimið** (☎ 447420; www.hotel-runavik.fo; s/d Dkr695/795), which serves delicious pizzas in the evening and quick snacks during the day.

KLAKSVÍK & THE NORTHERN ISLES

KLAKSVÍK
pop 4794

Klaksvík hugs an elongated bay whose busy harbour lends it a tough, industrial ambience. Since the establishment of a trading point here in 1838, Klaksvík has grown into the second-largest town on the Faroes. It is now the big junction of the northern island cluster – a great base for hiking, and boat and bus trips to more far-flung corners.

Information

Alfa Bókahandil (☎ 455533; Nólsoyar Pálsgøta 2; ꧁ 9.30 am-noon & 1-5.30pm Mon-Fri, 9.30am-12.30pm Sat)
Føroya Banki (☎ 456377; Klaksvíksvegur 7)
Hospital (☎ 455463; Víkavegur 40-44) Has a casualty ward.
Library (☎ 455757; Tingstøðin; ꧁ 1-6pm Mon & Thu, 3-6pm Tue, Wed & Fri) Free Internet access.
Norðoya Kunningarstova (Tourist Office; ☎ 456939; info@klaksvik.fo; Nólsoyar Pálsgøta 32; ꧁ 8am-5pm Mon-Fri & 10am-noon Sat Jun-Aug, 10am-noon & 1-4pm Sep-May) Accommodation and tour bookings.
Norðoya Sparikassi (☎ 475000; Ósavegur 1)
Pharmacy (☎ 455055; nordoya@apotek.fo; Fornagarður; ꧁ 9am-5.30pm Mon-Fri, 9am-noon Sat)
Post Office (☎ 455008; Klaksvívegur 2)
Telephone Office (Biskupsstøðgøta 3; ꧁ 9am-5.30pm Mon-Fri)

Sights & Activities

The basalt construction of the modern **Christianskirkja** (Kirkjubrekka 6; admission free; ꧁ 10-11am & 1-4pm Mon-Sat mid-May–Aug), with its quirky, free-standing belfry, was intended to evoke the ruin of the Magnus Cathedral in Kirkjubøur. A stunning altar piece depicting the last supper is the focal point in an otherwise austere interior.

The **Norðoya Fornminnissavn** (Northern Islands Museum; ☎ 456287; Klaksvíksvegur 84; adult/child Dkr20/free; ꧁ 1-4pm mid-May–mid-Sep) houses a wonderfully nostalgic pharmacy and a random selection of old fishing items.

Klaksvík is the point to set out for the wildly romantic tours with the old mail boat to Svínoy and **Fugloy** (Dkr70, two to three hours, three daily). To deliver post and goods to the remote isles, the captain steers his tiny ship bravely through rocky waters and past densely populated bird cliffs. The journey offers you spectacular views and a close-up experience of rural life. Bus No 500 takes you directly to the port of Hvannasund (Dkr5, 20 minutes, three daily) and back to Klaksvík after the two-to-three hour tour.

Sleeping

The camping ground was closed for renovation at the time of writing. Check with the tourist office whether it's re-opened.

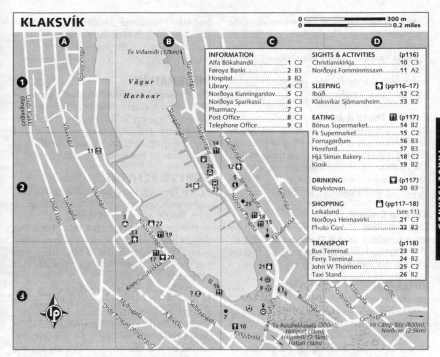

KLAKSVÍK

INFORMATION		
Alfa Bókahandil	1	C2
Føroya Banki	2	B3
Hospital	3	B2
Library	4	C3
Norðoya Kunningarstovn	5	C2
Norðoya Sparikassi	6	C3
Pharmacy	7	C3
Post Office	8	C3
Telephone Office	9	C3

SIGHTS & ACTIVITIES	(p116)	
Christianskirkja	10	C3
Norðoya Fornminnissavn	11	A2

SLEEPING	(pp116–17)	
Íbúð	12	C2
Klaksvíkar Sjómansheim	13	B2

EATING	(p117)	
Bónus Supermarket	14	B2
Fk Supermarket	15	C2
Fornagørðum	16	B3
Hereford	17	B3
Hjá Símun Bakery	18	C2
Kiosk	19	B3

DRINKING	(p117)	
Roykstovan	20	B3

SHOPPING	(pp117–18)	
Leikalund	(see 11)	
Norðoya Heimavirki	21	C3
Photo Care	22	B2

TRANSPORT	(p118)	
Bus Terminal	23	B2
Ferry Terminal	24	B2
John W Thomsen	25	C2
Taxi Stand	26	B2

FAROE ISLANDS

Íbúð (☎ 755907; ibudkl@post.olivant.fo; Garðavegur 31; dm/s/d Dkr140/245/350; ☼ mid-May–Sep) This slightly scruffy hostel is popular with families, workers and travellers and offers adequate accommodation in dorms or double rooms.

Klaksvíkar Sjómansheim (☎ 455333; Víkarvegur 38; s/d Dkr345/495, s/d with private bathroom Dkr595/795) The northern seamen's hostel hides well-appointed rooms behind gloomy corridors. The kitchen opens three times a day for simple, filling dishes (breakfast/lunch/dinner Dkr40/80/80) and offers a soul-warming three-course Sunday meal (Dkr130).

Phone the **tourist office** (☎ 456939) for self-catering accommodation options in and around town.

Eating & Drinking

Hereford (☎ 456434; Klaksvíkavegur; mains Dkr160-220; ☼ 6-10pm Tue-Sun, closed Mon) There's hardly a better place on the Faroes to enjoy delicious meat and fish dishes. Wood panelling, dimmed lights and friendly service create a warm atmosphere, and generous portions have the tastebuds reeling.

Fornagørðum (Klaksvíksvegur 22; dishes from Dkr50; ☼ 4pm-midnight Mon-Sat, 2pm-midnight Sun) Klaksvík's most popular pizza joint serves quick snacks and full meals to a young clientele. It's usually buzzing on weekends, and offers take-away.

Roykstovan (Klaksvíksvegur; ☼ 11am-11pm) This earthy pub is not for the faint-hearted. Its name 'smoke room' is well-picked, as the air is indeed thick enough to be cut. Guests tend to be the rugged, seafaring kind and the atmosphere raucous.

If you want to pick up supplies for self-catering, both **Fk** (Nólsoyar Pálsgøta 12) and **Bónus** (Stangavegur 10) supermarkets have branches in Klaksvík; there's also a late-night **Kiosk** (Klaksvíksvegur; ☼ 7am-11pm Mon-Sat, 8am-11pm Sun) and a **Rúsdrekkasøla** (Bøgøta 38; ☼ Mon-Fri 2-5.30pm). **Hjá Símun Bakery** (Nólsoyar Pálsgøta 16) sells excellent pastries and fresh coffee.

Shopping

Leikalund (☎ 457151; Klaksvíksvegur 86) Selling art and books, Leikalund sits underneath the museum in an old store from the Danish trading monopoly days.

Norðoya Heimavirki (☎ 456899; Tingstøðin) This souvenir shop also has a good selection of knitwear.

Photo Care (☎ 457272; Klaksvíksvegur 70) This small photo shop is the best place in the north to stock up on film and get those urgent pictures developed.

Getting There & Away

Bus No 400 goes from Tórshavn to Leirvík, where it connects with the ferry to Klaksvík (Dkr95, two hours, seven to 10 times daily). Three times a week, there are helicopters to and from Tórshavn (Dkr215), Svínoy (Dkr110) and Fugloy (Dkr110).

Getting Around

Taxis (☎ 590000, 755555) can be caught at the ferry terminal. **John W Thomsen** (☎ 455858; fax 457878; Nólsoyar Pálsgøta 26) runs the only bicycle hire on the Faroes.

VIÐAREIÐI

pop 347

Spread over a gentle swale at the bottom of the mighty Villingadalsfjall (840m), Viðareiði attracts ambitious hikers determined to conquer cap **Enniberg**. It's a strenuous trek only to be undertaken in the company of a guide, as clefts, mist and unstable turf represent real dangers. Check with Klaksvík tourist office for guided hiking tours, and for **boat cruises** around the cap, which grant breathtaking views in clear weather.

In the immediate surroundings of Viðareiði, beautiful scenery opens up along the narrow lane on the eastern shore, and a gentle climb up the western hill is rewarded with views across the headlands of Borðoy, Kunoy and Kalsoy.

The grand **Hotel Norð** (☎ 451244; fax 451245; s/d Dkr550/775; ☽ Jun-Aug) rises like a palace from the solitary scenery. Rooms are spacious, and the restaurant does a mean roasted puffin (Dkr205).

Bus No 500 runs three times a day between Klaksvík and Viðareiði (Dkr30, 45minutes).

SUÐUROY

pop 5134

Nature revealed her artistic side on beautiful Suðuroy, carving deep valleys into the hills, defining coastlines with green marshlands and sandy bays, and chiselling gigantic flowers and columns into the ancient basalt. As only few tourists take on the two-hour ferry journey to get there, it's still a hidden gem.

INFORMATION

The **Suðuroy Kunningarstova** (Tourist Information; ☎ 372490; sout-inf@post.olivant.fo) in Tvøroyri, the largest village on Suðuroy, opens briefly for every ferry arrival. Bank, post office and grocery shops are all situated on the opposite side of the ferry terminal.

SIGHTS & ACTIVITIES

Pretty Tvøroyri is a great base for hiking excursions. Continuing past the Norwegian-style **church**, a scenic 30-minute walk leads to Froðba, where stunning **basalt formations** appear like geometric sculptures in the steep coast. With a good pair of binoculars, you can also spot them from the opposite side of the bay.

An old pass leads from the highest road of Tvøroyri to Hvannhagi. Nestling in the midst of some extraordinary scenery, this tiny mountain village offers spectacular views onto **Lítla Dímun**, the island permanently encircled by a white cloud, and its big brother **Stóra Dímun**.

The church of **Fámjin** on the western coast preserves the oldest flag of the Faroes. The picturesque village is reached by a series of hiking paths from all directions. The lonely mountain routes from Trongisvágur and Øravik are particularly stunning.

Northbound travellers pass the only **coal mine** of the Faroes near Trongisvágur – proof that there were indeed once trees on these bare isles – before reaching Hvalba, which spreads lazily across an open swale and invites more trekking.

No visit to Suðuroy is complete without a trip to cap **Akraberg**, the southernmost point of the Faroes. Just south of Vágur, a tunnel, or a serpentine mountain road, takes you via Lopra to Sumba. From there it's only a short walk to the lighthouse and bird cliffs of the mighty cap. Those with a taste for vistas and steep climbs can also include a short excursion to the **Beinisvørð** precipice west of Sumba in their trip.

SLEEPING & EATING

Hotel Bakkin (☎ 373961; s/d/apt Dkr400/500/600) This quirky, family-run place in Vágur has lovingly decorated rooms, and a cosy veranda restaurant overlooking the bay. Try to catch its summer special, where Dkr460/590 gets you not only a single/double room but all meals as well.

Hotel Tvøroyri (☎ 371171; s/d Dkr550/650) This blue cube of a hotel has cute rooms decorated along different themes and colour schemes. The restaurant serves pizzas and Faroese specialities on request (mains Dkr140).

Hotel Øravík (☎ 371302; oeravik@post.olivant.fo; camping per person Dkr50, dm Dkr120, s/d from Dkr350/500) Two and a half kilometres south of the Drelnes ferry terminal, this welcoming place caters for all pockets with its youth hostel, guesthouse and hotel accommodation, and has a lively pizza restaurant (mains Dkr160).

GETTING THERE & AWAY

Ferries sail between Tórshavn and Drelnes twice daily (Dkr75, two hours). Helicopters fly between Tórshavn and Froðba (Dkr215, twice weekly), 2km east of Tvøroyri.

GETTING AROUND

From Tvøroyri, buses head south to Øravík (Dkr20), Vágur (Dkr30) and Sumba (Dkr40), and north to Hvalba (Dkr20); buses always connect with ferries, and frequencies range from three to seven daily.

CN Bygg Car Hire (☎ 574200) in Porkeri rents out small vehicles from Dkr400 per day and drives them to the ferry for you.

VÁGAR & MYKINES

VÁGAR
pop 2803

Home to the Faroes' only airport, Vágar is the obligatory entry point for anyone arriving by plane. Though the rapid bus connection to Tórshavn lures most people quickly away, Vágar is in fact an island worth extra time. Its large lakes abound with birdlife, and the precipitous interior is woven through with hiking paths, including a challenging mountain trek to the remotest village of the Faroes.

Information

There are a couple of **tourist offices** (airport ☎ 353300; inform@post.olivant.fo; Miðvágur ☎ 333455; 1-3pm Mon-Fri). Both Miðvágur and Sandávagur have got banks with ATMs, and post offices.

Activities

A leisurely hike along the soft curve of lake **Leitisvatn** takes you past the breeding grounds of oystercatchers, whimbrels, curlews and a host of other birds to Bøsdalafossur, where the foaming surf licks the feet of a grand waterfall. A little further up, a soaring cliff affords brilliant views across the southern isles. You enter the path through the outfield gate in southern Miðvágur. Don't cross the meadows randomly as you risk an attack by protective birds.

Gásadalur is the only village on the Faroes that still isn't connected by road. An unfinished tunnel construction is closed by lock, to which only locals have a key. Besides tunnel and torch, the helicopter represents another link to the outside world. The steep mountain pass **Skarð**, which the mailman usually had to brave, is a popular hiking route for experienced mountaineers. A well-marked path begins in Bøur, 4km west of Sørvágur, and follows a beautiful, but strenuous trek to 425m height, before descending steeply to Gásadalur village.

Sleeping & Eating

Á Giljanesi (☎ 333465; giljanes@post.olivant.fo; camping per person Dkr50, dm/s/d Dkr140/220/350) Halfway between Sandavágur and Miðvágur is this youth hostel with great sea views, which somewhat compensate for the small size of the rooms. There's also camping space.

Hotel Vagar (☎ 332955; s/d Dkr655/855) This grey concrete block of an airport hotel isn't quite the holiday palace it claims to be. The en-suite rooms are small, though equipped with satellite TV, radio and telephone. The restaurant serves up some decent platters of Faroese specialities (Dkr78, mains Dkr135 to Dkr185).

Cafeteria (☎ 358810; Vágar Lufthavn; snacks Dkr20-50) It might seem a strange prospect to go to the airport for a coffee, but if you're dying for a cappuccino and croissant, this bustling café is your only option.

There are supermarkets in Sørvágur, Sandavágur and Miðvágur; the latter also has a branch of Rúsdrekkasøla.

Getting There & Away

Bus No 300 runs several times daily between Tórshavn and Vágar, serving Sandavágur, and Miðvágur on the way before turning in Sørvágur. On Monday, Wednesday and

Friday, helicopters connect Vágar airport with all major destinations of the Faroes. For international departures from the airport, see p124.

MYKINES

pop 21

This tiny slice of an island is the shining jewel of the Faroes. It's called the paradise of sea birds, and there's no better place to watch puffins than **Lundaland** (land of puffins) on the islet of Mykineshólmur, which is connected to Mykines by a footbridge over a 35m gorge. The walk to the lonely lighthouse on the islet's westernmost cape leads through some of the world's most densely populated bird colonies. This is the only place on the Faroes to see the rare gannets.

The cosy guesthouse/snack bar, **Kristianshús** (☎ 312985; mykines@post.olivant.fo; camping per person Dkr50, s/d Dkr220/440; ☺ May-Aug), has tiny rooms and space for tents outside. It's the only place where you can buy food on the island! The **Yellow House** (☎ 332614; julianna@post.olivant. fo; 3-bed dm Dkr180; ☺ Jun-Aug) has basic hostel accommodation.

Don't leave a visit to Mykines to the end of your trip, as the **ferry** (☎ 333200 for reservations; Dkr60) from Sørvágur on Vágar is very weather-dependent, and you might find yourself stranded among puffins. A helicopter flies three times per week from the international airport on Vágar (Dkr145).

THE FAROESE CHURCHES

The Faroese are a devout people, and even the tiniest villages are built around a small, tar-painted, wooden church. These sacred houses beautifully combine humility and devotion. Unlike the awe-inspiring cathedrals of mainland Europe, Faroese churches are unpretentious constructions that duck under turf roofs and don't tower above the farmhouses. Most of them were erected from driftwood between 1829 and 1847.

The safe return of the fishermen was the biggest worry of traditional Faroese society, so ship models are suspended for divine protection in the fragrant plain-wood interior. Their position overlooking the harbour also permitted worrying believers to keep a watchful eye on the sea during service.

FAROE ISLANDS DIRECTORY

ACCOMMODATION

Accommodation is generally quite limited, and pre-booking is recommended. Camping is a cheap alternative, but be prepared for wet and windy weather. There are camping facilities on all islands; you can stay in camping grounds or in designated spaces belonging to youth hostels. Camping isn't permitted outside these areas. Most sites charge Dkr50 per person.

Since hotel accommodation is relatively expensive, *gistingarhús* (guesthouses) and *vallaraheim* (youth hostels) belonging to the **Danish Youth Hostels Association** (HI; www.farhostel.fo), scouts and other associations are a popular option for travellers. They have kitchen facilities, and dormitory rates are typically set at Dkr140 with a Dkr20 discount for HI members. Singles/doubles are usually available for around Dkr250/430. Bringing a sleeping bag can save some extra costs, as many hostels charge for bedlinen (Dkr50).

An excellent way of saving money while maintaining comfort is the rental of a self-catering house or apartment through local tourist offices (2-bed flats from Dkr480) or the more expensive agencies **Tora Tourist Traffic** (Map p110; ☎ 315505; www.tora.fo; Niels Finsensgøta 21) and **GreenGate Incoming** (Map p112; ☎ 320520; www.greengate.fo; Undir Bryggjubakka 3). Tourist offices also have lists of families offering B&B accommodation (singles/doubles cost from Dkr330/430).

Most hotels in the Faroes are fairly characterless but facilities are usually good; en-suite hotel rooms average Dkr600/800 (singles/doubles). The Sjómansheimið (seamen's homes) in Tórshavn, Runavík and Klaksvík, belonging to the seamen's mission but open to all, charge roughly the same.

ACTIVITIES

Bird-watching (particularly on Mykines, Nólsoy and the Vestmanna cliffs) and **hiking** are the two main activities that draw people to the Faroe Islands. Most hiking trails are indicated on the 1:100,000 map and the tourist board publishes brochures describing more routes. Many paths are marked by ancient cairns, and it's best to stick to them to protect the environment and yourself. Sudden fogs can be a real danger, as they quickly reduce visibility and veil coastal drops. Weatherproof clothing is essential.

Game fishing is possible on some coasts, quays and on the lakes of Vágar. Tackle needs to be disinfected before leaving home, and the required licence can be obtained from local tourist offices.

BOOKS

Faroe – The Emergence of a Nation by John West is an excellent historical overview. For a classic Icelandic narrative, grab a copy of *Færinga Saga*, translated by Liv Kjørsvik Schei and Gunnie Moberg, while *The Faroe Isles* by Liv Kjørsvik Schei contains general cultural information.

BUSINESS HOURS

Shops are generally open from 9.30am to 5.30pm Monday to Friday and 9am to noon or 2pm on Saturday. Retailers in Tórshavn stay open until 6pm or 7pm on Thursday and Friday. Banks are open from 9.30am to 4pm, with extended hours until 6pm on Thursdays. For post offices, see Post (p123).

Restaurants in the capital typically open 11.30am or noon and close between 10pm and midnight. Tórshavn's cafés also offer cooked food, and as they usually double-function as bars in the evenings, they often stay open until midnight and beyond. Outside the capital, most restaurants only open from 5pm, which limits daytime options to snack bars.

Supermarkets are usually open from 9am to 5pm Monday to Friday (larger shopping centres in Tórshavn to 7pm), and 9am to 2pm on Saturday.

CHILDREN

The Faroese are very family oriented and children are usually welcome. It's the weather that's more likely to provoke tantrums. Tórshavn occasionally offers music and theatre shows for kids (ask at the tourist office). Puffin-spotting in Vestmanna or Mykines, as well as easy hikes to sheer cliffs, are bound to cause excitement.

Children aged seven to 13 get 20% to 50% discount off bus and ferry fares. Discounts

are also available on tours; inquire when booking. Museum entrance fees are usually free for children.

Lonely Planet's *Travel with Children*, by Cathy Lanigan, gives plenty of useful advice.

CUSTOMS

Visitors over 15 years of age may import 200 cigarettes, 50 cigars or 250g of tobacco; those over 18 can also bring 1L of wine (up to 22%) or 2L of table wine (up to 12%), 1L of spirits (from 22% to 60% proof) and 2L of beer (less than 5.8% alcohol, and in long-necked bottles only). Perfume and confectionery are limited to 50g and 3kg per person, respectively. Non-recyclable containers are forbidden and animals may not be brought in.

EMBASSIES & CONSULATES

The Faroes are represented abroad by Danish embassies (www.ambassade.dk). Also see p97. In the UK, they have their own office of representation within the Danish embassy (☎ 020 7333 6707; www.faroes.org.uk; 55 Sloane St, London, SW1X9SR, UK).

FESTIVALS & EVENTS

Traditional celebrations chase one another in close succession during summer. They tend to be spectacular events, featuring rowing competitions, processions in traditional dress, singing and dancing.

Norðoyarstevna (first weekend in June) Festival of the northern isles, held in Klaksvík.

Summartónar (events between June and July) Churches and concert halls around the islands host concerts during this festival of classical and contemporary music.

Jóansøka (weekend following midsummer) Festival on Suðuroy.

Vestanstevna (early July) Festival on Vágar.

G!Festival (mid-July; www.gfestival.com) Set on the beautiful beach of Syðrugøta, the biggest music festival of the year features numerous local and international artists playing pop, rock and folk.

Ólavsøka (Faroese National Day, 28 & 29 July) Largest and most exciting festival, celebrating the Norwegian king Olav the Holy, who spread Christian faith on the isles.

GAY & LESBIAN TRAVELLERS

Gay couples are advised to be discreet in the Faroe Islands to avoid upsetting the more traditional and religious locals. There are no dedicated gay bars or clubs to be found on the islands.

FAROE ISLANDS

HOLIDAYS

The Faroese observe the following holidays:

New Year's Day (1 January)
Maundy Thursday (Thursday before Easter)
Good Friday to Easter Monday (March/April)
Flag Day (25 April)
Labour Day (1 May)
Common Prayers Day (April/May)
Ascension Day (May/June)
Whit Sunday, Whit Monday (May/June)
Constitution Day (5 June)
Ólavsøka (Faroese National Day and Festival;
28 & 29 July)
Christmas Eve (24 December) Some shops open until noon.
Christmas Day (25 December)
Boxing Day (26 December)
New Year's Eve (31 December)

INTERNET ACCESS

There are no Internet cafés on the Faroe Islands, but libraries have free time-slots you can book.

INTERNET RESOURCES

General information:

- www.faroeislands.com
- www.visit-faroeislands.com
- www.framtak.com
- www.faroeweb.com
- www.whaling.fo

MAPS

For anyone planning to go hiking, the booklet of topographic maps covering the Faroe Islands at 1:100,000 scale by Kort og Matrikelstyrelsen (Dkr125) is indispensable. It is available at tourist offices and bookshops throughout the islands. Maps of individual islands are also available at 1:20,000-scale (Dkr75). Tourist offices distribute a 1:200,000 scale *Faroe Islands Map* free of charge that includes street plans of larger settlements as well as accommodation, services, bus and ferry information, and a Tórshavn city map that indicates major sights, shops, accommodation and restaurants.

MEDIA

Newspapers & Magazines

Dimmalætting and *Sosialurin* are the two main daily newspapers of the Faroes. International papers and magazines can be read in most libraries and bought at the SMS shopping centre in Tórshavn.

Radio & TV

The national radio station, Útvarp Føroya (89.8MHz FM, 531kHz MW), broadcasts from 7am to 8pm; the English-language weather report can be heard at 8.50am Monday to Friday. Rás 2 FM (102.0MHz FM) transmits a slightly uniform selection of music, and Lindin (101.0MHz FM) is a Christian station.

Sjónvarp Føroya, the Faroes' TV station, screens films in the original language with Danish or Faroese subtitles from 2pm.

MONEY

The Faroes' own currency, the Faroese króna (Fkr), is tied to the Danish krone (Dkr). Theoretically, both are used interchangeably throughout the Kingdom of Denmark, but Danish shops have been known to refuse Faroese crowns, so it's safer to change any remaining cash at the counter at Vágar airport (open for arriving and departing flights). Throughout this chapter, prices are given in Danish crowns (Dkr).

Foreign currency may be exchanged at any branch of Føroya Banki or Føroya Sparikassi. Their branches in towns and larger villages have ATMs, which dispense cash from 6am to midnight. Outside banking hours, hotels and tourist information offices usually exchange money, though for a higher commission charge than banks. All brands of travellers cheques and major currencies are accepted.

Foreigners spending more than Dkr300 in tax-free shops are exempt from the 25% value-added tax (VAT) included in all quoted prices. To get your on-the-spot VAT cash refund at the airport, fill in a Tax Refund Cheque in the shop, get it stamped by the sales clerk and hand it to the customs officer when you leave the Faroes.

Tipping isn't customary.

Currency

One króna is equal to 100 oyru (Danish: krone, øre). Notes come in denominations of 50, 100, 200, 500 and 1000 krónur; the Danish coins in use include 25 and 50 øre, one krone and two, five, 10 and 20 kroner. See p25 for the Danish krone's rates.

PHOTOGRAPHY & VIDEO

Film and print processing is available in Tórshavn and Klaksvík. A 36-exposure roll of Kodak or Fuji print film costs Dkr67 and 24-hour developing costs Dkr102. Slide film is hard to find on the islands, and can't be developed.

POST

The postal service, **Postverk Føroya** (www.post .fo), has offices in most towns. Rural offices are open from 12.30pm to 3pm. The **central post office** (☯ 9am-5pm Mon-Fri) in Tórshavn offers reliable poste restante; have your mail sent to Poste Restante, Central Post Office (miðbynum), FR-100 Tórshavn, Faroe Islands.

The cost of sending a letter or postcard up to 20g economy/priority air mail is Dkr4.50/ 5 locally, Dkr6/6 to Iceland, Dkr6/6.50 to Europe and Dkr7.50/8 to the rest of the world.

TELEPHONE & FAX

Føroya Telecom has a Telebúðin (telephone office) in Klaksvík; other card and coin phones can usually be found in post offices, guesthouses and some restaurants.

Faxing is possible from post offices in Tórshavn and Klaksvík. Telephone cards with denominations of Dkr30, Dkr50 and Dkr100 are available in post offices and telecom shops.

From public phones, there's a Dkr0.40 connection charge; local calls then cost Dkr0.32 per minute during peak hours (8am to 6pm Monday to Saturday), otherwise Dkr0.22 per minute.

The GSM mobile-phone network covers almost the entire country (it's incompatible with the North American GSM). Contact your provider for further details regarding mobile telephone use in the Faroes.

For telephone information and directory inquiries ring ☎ 118.

The Faroes' international country code is ☎ 298; there are no area codes. To dial out of the Faroes, you must dial ☎ 00, then the destination country code, area or city code and phone number.

EMERGENCY NUMBERS

The national emergency number to get in contact with police, fire or ambulance services is ☎ 112.

TIME

The local time zone is GMT/UTC, the same as London, five hours ahead of New York, eight hours ahead of Los Angeles and 10 hours behind Sydney. As there's no daylight-saving time, it's GMT plus one hour between March and October.

TOURIST INFORMATION

The network of Kunningarstovan tourist offices is excellent. They arrange accommodation, organise tours and have heaps of brochures, including the free *Tourist Guide – Faroe Islands*, detailing regional sights and activities. The **National Tourist Board** (☎ 316055; tourist@tourist.fo; Undir Bryggjubakka 17, FO-110 Tórshavn) also publishes pamphlets providing general information.

The main regional tourist offices:

Kunningarstovan (☎ 315788; www.visittorshavn.fo; Niels Finsensgøta 13, PO Box 379, FO-110 Tórshavn)

Eysturoyar Kunningarstova (☎ 444860; infoey-f@ post.olivant.fo; Á Bug, PO Box 200, FO-530 Fuglafjørður)

Norðoya Kunningarstova (☎ 456939; info@ klaksvik.fo; Nólsoyar Pálsgøta 32, FO-700 Klaksvík)

Sandoy Kunningarstova (☎ 361836, sandinfo@ post.olivant.fo; FO-210 Sandur)

Suðuroy Kunningarstova (☎ 372480; sout-inf@ post.olivant.fo; FO-800 Tvøroyri)

Vágar Kunningarstova (☎ 333455; vagar@ post.olivant.fo; FO-370 Miðvágur)

TOURS

Tours and bookings are available from the following organisations:

GreenGate Incoming (Map p112; ☎ 320520; www.greengate.fo; Undir Bryggjubakka 3, FO-100 Tórshavn) Fishing, diving, boat tours and accommodation.

MB Tours (Map p112; ☎ 322121; mb-tours@mb-tours .com; Bryggjubakki 2, PO Box 3021, FO-110 Tórshavn) Bus tours: destinations include Saksun, Gjógv and Kirkjubøur.

Smyril Line (Map p110; ☎ 345900; www.smyril-line.fo; J Broncksgøta 37, PO Box 370, FO-110 Tórshavn) Schooner cruises around the Faroes, coach and boat excursions to most islands.

Tora Tourist Traffic (Map p110; ☎ 315505; www.tora.fo; Niels Finsensgøta 21, PO Box 3012, FO-100 Tórshavn) Coach tours and accommodation.

VISAS

Citizens of EU and Nordic countries need only a valid identity card, and citizens of the USA, Canada, Australia and New Zealand only a valid passport to visit the Faroes for up to three months.

TRANSPORT IN THE FAROE ISLANDS

GETTING THERE & AWAY

Air

The only airport in the Faroe Islands is the international terminal on **Vágar** (☎ 354400; www.slv.dk/vagar). Bus No 300 provides connections to and from Tórshavn for every plane arrival and departure. Call ☎ 343030 for more information.

Atlantic Airways (☎ 341060; www.atlanticairways.fo; Vágar Airport, FO-380 Sørvágur) flies all year to the Faroe Islands from Aberdeen in Scotland (from £230, two or three weekly) and Copenhagen (from Dkr3020, once or twice daily). During summer, it also operates two weekly flights from Reykjavík (from Ikr14,000, April to October), Oslo (from Nkr1700, mid-June to mid-August) and Billund (from Dkr3020), and offers a special return to London Stansted (from £140, twice weekly mid-June to August).

Maersk Air (Map p110; ☎ 357474; www.maersk-air.com; Niels Finsensgøta 8; FO-100 Tórshavn) operates daily flights from Copenhagen (costing from Dkr3020, year-round), and two weekly flights from Billund (from Dkr3020 mid-June to mid-August).

Air Iceland (☎ 341000; www.airiceland.is; Vágar Airport; FO-380 Sørvágur) flies once a week from Reykjavík (Ikr44,000, mid-June to October).

All prices given are return fares excluding tax. Atlantic and Maersk Air fares are only valid for stays that include one Saturday night and don't exceed one month. Check websites for discounted fares and special weekend deals. Discounts are available for people under 26 and over 65.

Sea

Smyril Line's *Norröna* connects the Faroe Islands all year with Denmark, and from mid-May to mid-September also with Norway, Shetland and Iceland. The ferry departs from Hanstholm (Denmark) on Saturday evening and arrives in Tórshavn on Monday morning. Iceland-bound passengers must disembark while the ship continues to Lerwick (Shetland) and Bergen (Norway). After returning to Tórshavn on Wednesday, it collects the Iceland passengers and sails overnight to Seyðisfjörður.

It returns to Tórshavn on Friday morning, and continues to Hanstholm for another circuit.

From Hanstholm to Tórshavn, the one-way, high-season, couchette fare is Dkr1670, with 25% discount for student card-holders (under 26 years old). Transporting vehicles up to 5m long costs Dkr1260. Above couchette, there are four classes of en-suite cabins and a luxury suite.

Those coming from mainland Scotland can travel with **NorthLink Ferries** (☎ 01856 885 500; www.northlinkferries.co.uk; Kiln Corner, Ayre Rd, Kirkwall, Orkney, Scotland, UK, KW15 1QX) from either Aberdeen or Kirkwall (Orkney) to Lerwick (£30), then connect with the *Norröna* from there. The one-way, high-season, couchette fare between Lerwick and Tórshavn is £80, with a 25% discount for student cardholders. Transporting vehicles up to 5m in length costs £60.

For further information, contact **Smyril Line Shetland** (☎ 1595 690 845; www.smyril-line.com; Holmsgarth Terminal, Lerwick, Shetland, ZE1 0PR).

GETTING AROUND

Bus, ferry and helicopter schedules and prices are detailed in the Ferðaætlan (timetable), which is published by the national transport company **Strandfaraskip Landsins** (Map p110; ☎ 343030; www.ssl.fo, Faroese only). It's available for Dkr20 from tourist offices or at the Farstøðin transport terminal at the harbour in Tórshavn. The same outlets sell the SL Visitor Travelcard, which can save frequent users of public transport some money on the relatively steep fares. For Dkr600/900, it gives four/seven days of unlimited travel on all buses and interisland ferries (50% child discount, seven to 13 years).

Air

The only inter-island air travel is by helicopter (*tyrlan*, pronounced *teer*-lan). Several times a week, helicopters connect Vágar airport with Tórshavn, Klaksvík, Stora Dímun, Skúvoy, Froðba, Gásadalur and Mykines. There are also routes from Klaksvík to Svínoy and Fugloy. The Mykines flights are popular, so book early.

Helicopter services are operated by Atlantic Airways. Flights from Tórshavn to Klaksvík, Froðba and Vágar all cost Dkr215; Vágar to Mykines costs Dkr145. Prices and schedules are posted on the website and detailed in the Ferðaætlan.

Bicycle

Surfaced roads with little traffic, bright summer nights and stunning nature make cycling a tempting proposition; single-lane tunnels, steep hills, wind, rain and fog argue against it. Road tunnels are the biggest hazard faced by cyclists and are best avoided, especially the non-ventilated, single-lane ones to be found on the north isles and Suðuroy.

Good front and rear lighting, extra reflectors, wind- and waterproof clothing are essential equipment. If the weather gets too rough, you can always take the bike on the bus for Dkr30. The tourist information distributes an excellent brochure with several cycle tours. The only bicycle hire is in Klaksvík.

Boat

Ferry journeys are just part of daily life on the Faroes. All main islands are connected by ferry and/or bus, and most ferries carry vehicles (though the Vágar–Mykines ferry doesn't). Cars should be in the queue at least 15 minutes before departure and are paid for on the boat (to Suðuroy Dkr130, other islands Dkr90).

From Klaksvík, old mail boats still go to Svínoy, Fugloy and Kalsoy. Like the Mykines ferry, these services are very weather dependent and don't take cars. Prices and schedules are detailed in the Ferðaætlan and on the Strandfaraskip website (www.ssl .fo, Faroese only).

Bus

Thanks to the extensive and reliable Bygdaleiðir long-distance bus service, it is possible to visit even remote villages by bus. Bus timetables are scheduled to combine with ferry services, so that on popular routes you usually won't have too long to wait.

The only region that's slightly difficult to reach by public transport is the north of Streymoy and Eysturoy. Most trips involve a combination of bus and ferry journeys; the entire journey can be paid for on the bus or on the ferry or at the Farstøðin transport terminal. Return tickets are not available.

Car & Motorcycle

Driving around the Faroes is relatively easy. The road layout is simple, traffic is low and drivers tend to be considerate. Blýfrítt (unleaded petrol) costs around Dkr8 per litre. The undersea tunnel from Vágar to Streymoy is a toll road costing Dkr180 return for small vehicles, payable on the way into Streymoy.

DRIVING LICENCE

You can drive in the Faroe Islands with a valid driving licence from EU countries, the US, Canada, Australia and New Zealand.

HIRE

You must be at least 20 years old to rent a car and have held a licence for a minimum of one year. Rental charges start at Dkr550 per day for a small car, and costs include VAT, insurance and mileage. Daily rates decrease the longer you keep the car. Most companies will drive the car to you and pick it up at a convenient place.

Main rental companies:

Avis Føroyar (Map p110; ☎ 313535; www.avis.fo; Staravegur 1-3, FO-110 Tórshavn)

CN Bygg (☎ 374200; FO-950 Porkeri)

Hertz (Map p110; ☎ 340012; www.hertz.com; Hoydalsvegur 17, FO-110 Tórshavn)

SLP (☎ 357300; www.car-rent.fo; Á Hjalla, FO-110 Tórshavn)

INSURANCE

If you bring your own car to the Faroe Islands, you need to bring a Green card, or purchase it from the customs department when entering the country. Rental fees include a Collision Damage Waiver (CDW). Also see p474.

ROAD HAZARDS & ROAD RULES

Driving is on the right-hand side. Front and rear seat-belt use is compulsory, and due to sudden fogs, dipped headlights must be on at all times. Beware of sheep leaping on the road; if you hit one, you must call the **police** (☎ 311448).

Speed limits are set at 80km/h on the open highway and 50km/h through villages. Speeding fines are severe, as are penalties for exceeding the limit of 0.05% blood alcohol content – you may lose your licence on the spot.

Some of the Faroes' numerous tunnels have only one lane. There are bays every

FAROE ISLANDS

few hundred metres; if they are marked 'V', pull in and allow the other car to pass. If they are marked 'M', the other car has to give way.

Legal parking spaces in Tórshavn are marked with a 'P' followed by a number and the word *tíma,* which indicates the maximum permitted parking time. You must place a parking disc in the front window of your vehicle when using one of these parking spots – the discs are available free of charge from tourist offices and banks.

Finland

CONTENTS

FINLAND

Finland has always been the surprise packet of Scandinavia. Sandwiched between Sweden and Russia (and ruled by both in its history), it's a serenely beautiful country of lakes and forests, where happiness is a ramshackle cottage by a lakeshore and a properly stoked sauna.

Although Finland is riding a wave of hi-tech revolution (think Nokia), for travellers, nature reigns supreme here, whether it's cruising on lake ferries, hiking in empty forests, cycling on limitless bike paths or skating on frozen lakes. Lapland, one of Europe's last great wilderness areas, is an irresistible draw. Reindeer herds wander across fells, and above the Arctic Circle the sun never truly sets in midsummer. Here you'll find the kitsch but cool Santa Claus Village and official post office, and get to meet the bearded one himself. Further north, Inari is a centre for Sami culture and in the winter darkness you can see nature's greatest lightshow, the aurora borealis.

Finland really comes into its own in the summer months, with long hours of daylight and some of northern Europe's best music festivals and offbeat events springing to life virtually every day. This is the time for hiking in pristine national parks.

Sophisticated Helsinki is an intimate city with some of Scandinavia's most envied nightlife, working-class Tampere is studded with quirky museums, and tranquil Savonlinna lies marvellously snuggled between two lakes. And wherever you go, don't miss the chance to take a sauna with the locals.

Finns have a reputation for being tough, quiet and mysterious, but if you look under the surface, you'll find some of the warmest people you'll ever meet.

FAST FACTS

- **Area** 338,000 sq km
- **Capital** Helsinki
- **Country Code** ☎ 358
- **Currency** euro; US$1 = €0.81; £1 = €1.45; A$1 = €0.58; C$1 = €0.64; NZ$1 = €0.54; ¥100 = €0.73
- **Famous for** sauna, reindeer, Formula One drivers
- **Official Languages** Finnish, Swedish, English
- **Phrases** *kiitos* (thank you), *hei* (hello), *anteeksi* (excuse me), *kiipis* (cheers)
- **Telephone Codes** country code ☎ 358; international access codes ☎ 00, 990, 994, 999
- **Visas** not required for most visitors for stays of up to ninety days (see p193)

HIGHLIGHTS

- Cruise in to **Helsinki** (p134) on a Baltic ferry, picnic with locals on Suomenlinna island and discover some of Scandinavia's most sophisticated nightlife in Finland's dynamic 'East-meets-West' capital
- Steam it up in the world's biggest smoke sauna at **Kuopio** (p169)
- Cross the Arctic Circle, visit Santa in his official grotto and take a reindeer-sleigh ride at **Rovaniemi, Lapland** (p185)
- Float past the mightiest of the northern medieval castles in the beautiful Lakeland town of **Savonlinna** (p166)
- Ride on a genuine Arctic icebreaker and step into the Snow Castle at **Kemi** (p181)
- Catch a **summer festival** (p191) – jazz in Pori, opera in Savonlinna, Ruisrock in Turku, wife-carrying in Sonkajärvi…the list goes on
- Find out why Lenin admired the quirky, postindustrial and lovable city of **Tampere** (p158)
- Get on your bike – it's the best way to see the **Åland islands** (p156)

ITINERARIES

- **One week** After a day or two in Helsinki (with a possible day trip to Tallinn, in Estonia, or Porvoo), explore the eastern cities of Savonlinna, Lappeenranta and Kuopio or take an overnight train to Lapland (Rovaniemi) or to Oulu for a couple of days. The Helsinki–Savonlinna–Kuopio–Rovaniemi–Helsinki route is a good option.
- **Two weeks** Spend a few days in Helsinki and Porvoo, visit Turku and Tampere, then Savonlinna and the beautiful eastern Lakeland. Head up to Rovaniemi in Lapland, and perhaps as far as Inari. You could also fit in a summer festival, some hiking in North Karelia (Ilomantsi or Lake Pielinen) or a quick cycling trip to Åland.

CLIMATE & WHEN TO GO

The high season for most of Finland is summer (June–August), when the days are long, the climate is surprisingly sunny and warm, everything is open and in full swing and festivals abound. This is also when Finns are on holiday, abandoning the towns for their summer cottages. May and September are good times to visit the south of the country.

In Lapland, summer means the midnight sun but mosquitoes can be annoying if you're planning on hiking. September is a beautiful time for the *ruska* (autumn) colours. October and February/March are the best times to visit Lapland to view the aurora borealis (northern lights) and enjoy winter activities.

Winter (October–March) can be pretty dark and miserable in the south, but Finns still get out and enjoy winter sports, pile into the sauna and wait for the spring.

HISTORY

Human settlement in Finland dates back almost 10,000 years. Before arriving on the north of the Baltic coast, the Finns' ancestors appear to have dominated half of northern Russia. They established themselves in the forests, driving the nomadic Sami people to the north, where they remain in an area of Lapland known as Sápmi.

By the end of the Viking era, Swedish traders had extended their interests throughout the Baltic region. In 1155 the Swedes made Finland a province, and Swedish culture was swiftly imposed, beginning with the establishment of the first university in the capital Turku. But the heavy-handedness of Sweden's Protestant monarch, Gustav II Adolf, soon split the country along religious lines, and most Orthodox believers fled to Russia; famine then killed a third of the remaining Finnish population.

In 1809, after a bloody war, Sweden ceded Finland to Russia under Tsar Alexander. As

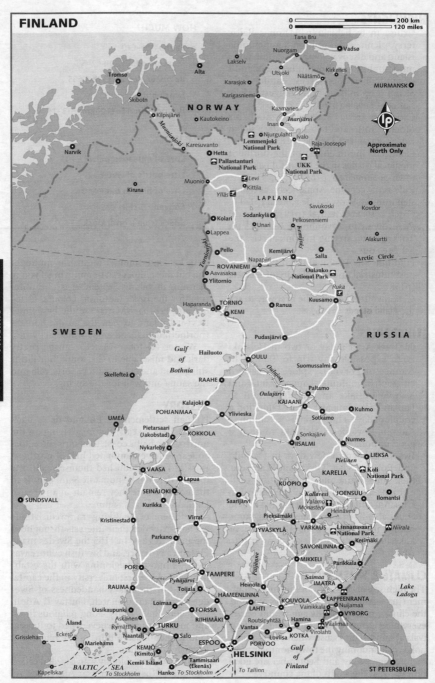

a result, Finland gained greater autonomy as a Grand Duchy, keeping its Swedish laws, Lutheran Church and Finnish senate. The capital moved to Helsinki in 1812. Nationalism surged, which suited the tsars until the 1880s, when there was a firm policy to dismantle the Finnish state and incorporate it into Russia.

The communist revolution of October 1917 brought the downfall of the Russian tsar and enabled the Finnish senate to declare independence on 6 December 1917. But divisions between socialists (the Reds) and conservatives (the nationalist Whites) in the new government led to a bloody civil war in which 30,000 Finns died. The conservatives, led by CGE Mannerheim, were victorious, and were gradually replaced by moderate social democrats.

During the Depression of the 1930s Finland gained fame internationally as a brave new nation, as the only country to pay its debts to the USA and as a sporting nation (long-distance runner Paavo Nurmi won seven gold medals in three Olympics).

Anticommunist violence broke out during the 1930s and relations with the Soviet Union remained uneasy. In the 1939 Winter War, Finland was forced to cede part of eastern Lakeland (Karelia). Finland resumed hostilities with the Soviets in 1941, winning back large swathes of Karelia in the Continuation War which cost Finland almost 100,000 lives.

After suffering a recession in the early 1990s Finland joined the EU in 1995 and began an economic recovery. It adopted the euro in 2001 – the only Nordic country yet to do so – and the rapid rise of technological industries such as mobile phone giant Nokia has assured Finland a measure of economic prosperity. In 2001 it was voted one of the least corrupt countries in the world.

PEOPLE

Finland is one of Europe's most sparsely populated countries, with 17 people per sq km. There are around 300,000 Swedish-speaking Finns in the west, as well as in fishing communities along the coast and on the Åland islands; and a smaller number of Roma (Gypsies) in the south.

The Sami population of around 6500 in the far north consists of three distinct groups, each speaking its own dialect. The Scandinavian Sami region has its own flag, and many Samis look across the border at the more developed Sami community in Norway for a deeper cultural identity.

Samis (Lapps) have traditionally been nomads, herding their reindeer in the large area of Lapland which spans the region from the Kola peninsula in Russia to the southern Norwegian mountains. Their traditional dwelling, the *kota*, resembles the wigwam of native North Americans, and is easily set up as a temporary shelter. Old traditions are vanishing, though: most Sami now live in permanent villages and use vehicles, snowmobiles and mobile phones to herd their reindeer, rather than migrating with them.

There are three Sami languages used in Finland today, the most common being Fell Sami. Inari Sami and Skolt Sami are spoken by only a few hundred people. Sami is taught in local schools, and legislation grants Samis the right of Sami usage in offices in northern Lapland.

A capacity for silence and reflection are the traits that best sum up the Finnish character (but get a Finn near a stack of duty-free liquor and see if this remains the case!). The image of a log cabin with a sauna by a lake tells much about Finnish culture: independence, endurance (*sisu* or 'guts') and a love of open space and nature.

The Finns are a naturally reserved people, and at first meeting can be very polite and more formal than you may be used to. The seemingly icy front that many present never lasts, though, and almost every visitor to Finland leaves with a story of unusual and unexpected kindness from a Finn.

RELIGION

Eighty-six per cent of Finns are Evangelical Lutherans, 1.1% Orthodox and the remainder unaffiliated. Minority denominations, including Roman Catholic, make up only a few per cent. Finland has some beautiful Orthodox and Lutheran churches, some dating back to the 17th century, but surveys show Finns to have the lowest church attendance record in Europe, at under 4%.

ARTS
Architecture & Design

Finland's modern architecture – sleek, functionalist and industrial – has been admired throughout the world ever since Alvar Aalto started making a name for himself in the 1930s. His works can be seen all over Finland today, from the angular Finlandia Hall in Helsinki to the public buildings (library, town hall etc) and street plan of Rovaniemi. Jyväskylä and Seinäjoki are places of pilgrimage for Aalto fans.

Earlier architecture in Finland can be seen in medieval churches made from stone but more commonly wood – Kerimaki's oversized church is worth seeing, as are the cathedrals at Turku and Tampere. Low-rise Helsinki boasts a patchwork of architectural styles, including the neoclassical buildings of Senaatintori (Senate Square), the rich ornamentation of Art Nouveau (or Jugend), the modern functionalism of Aalto's buildings and the postmodern Kiasma museum.

Finland, like Scandinavia as a whole, is also famous for its design. Aalto again laid a foundation with innovative interior design, furniture and the famous Savoy vase. Finns have created and refined their own design style through the craft tradition and using natural materials such as wood, glass and ceramics. Glassware and porcelain such as Iittala and Arabia are world famous.

Cinema
The Finnish film industry is small, with about a dozen films produced annually, but some of the greatest achievements are in documentary work. The best-known Finnish filmmaker is Aki Kaurismäki, director of the 1989 road film *Leningrad Cowboys Go America*. In 2002 he won the Grand Prix at Cannes for his film *The Man Without a Past*, the dark tale of a man who is mugged and bashed in Helsinki and loses his memory.

The most famous Finn in Hollywood is Renny Harlin, director of action movies such as *Die Hard II* and *Cliffhanger*. An early Harlin film, *Born American*, was banned in Finland for presenting a strong Russians-as-bad-guys view.

Finland hosts some quality film festivals, notably the Midnight Sun Film Festival in Sodankylä.

For more information check out the Finnish Film Foundation website at www.ses.fi.

Literature
The *Kalevala*, a collection of folk stories, songs and poems compiled in the 1830s by Elias Lönnrot, is Finland's national epic, a contemporary equivalent of the Icelandic sagas focusing on Karelia. Translations and compilations of the epic can be found in Finnish bookshops.

Aleksis Kivi, perhaps the greatest Finnish writer, was not regarded as a Romantic during his lifetime. Quite the contrary; his so-called crudities met with fierce opposition but it didn't take long before he gained the immense popularity which he has retained to this day. His book *Seven Brothers* is regarded as a foundation of modern Finnish literature. Famous 20th-century writers include Väino Linna (*The Unknown Soldier*) and FE Sillanpää, who won the Nobel Prize for Literature in 1939.

The late Tove Jansson is internationally famous for her Moominland children's stories, which have found a particular affection in Japan. Her whimsical world of Moomintrolls has been re-created as a theme park in Naantali and a museum in Tampere.

Music
Finns love music. You only have to look at the wealth of music festivals – opera, jazz, folk, tango, rock and pop – for proof, and while traditional forms of music still have a strong following, Finnish artists such as Darude and Bomfunk MC are becoming well known in the electronic, trance and hip-hop genres.

Revered composer Jean Sibelius, one of the most famous late-Romantics, was a Finn at the forefront of the nationalist movement. His stirring tone-poem *Finlandia* has been raised to the status of a national hymn. The Karelian region has its own folk music traditions, typified by the haunting *kantele* (a stringed instrument), while the Sami passed down their traditions and beliefs not through the written word but through the song-like chant called the *yoik*.

Finnish rock and pop bands can be seen performing at venues in Helsinki and other big cities. Names to look out for include the Flaming Sideburns, HIM, Hanoi Rocks and the Rasmus.

Painting
Finland's 'Golden Age' of art was the 19th-century National Romantic era, when artists such as Akseli Gallen-Kallela, Albert Edelfelt, the von Wright brothers and Pekka Halonen were inspired by Finland's forests

and pastoral landscape. Gallen-Kallela is probably Finland's most famous artist for his Kalevala-inspired works – don't miss his frescoes in the Kansallismuseo (National Museum) in Helsinki.

The best of Finnish art can be seen at Ateneum (National Gallery) in Helsinki, but there are modern art galleries and museums in just about every Finnish city.

Theatre & Dance

Finns' passion for dance is typified by the tango, which, although borrowed from Latin America, has been refined into a uniquely Finnish style. Older Finns are tango mad and every town has a dance hall or dance restaurant. In summer, outdoor stages are set up for dancing. The annual Tango Festival in Seinäjoki attracts thousands of dancers. A similar form of Finnish dancing is the waltz-like *humppa*.

As with most of Scandinavia, the Finnish theatre season is winter (October–March), when theatre, opera, ballet and concert performances are staged. The exceptions are the summer festivals, such as Kuopio's Dance Festival and Savonlinna's Ballet Festival.

SPORT

Ice hockey is Finland's number one national passion, with the season running from late September to March. The best place to see a quality match in the national league is Tampere or Helsinki, but Turku, Oulu and Rovaniemi also have major stadiums. Another popular winter spectator sport is ski-jumping – Lahti, with its vast sports centre, is the best place to see it, but Kuopio also has a jump on Puijo Hill.

In summer, football (soccer) is the national team sport although it's not as popular here as elsewhere in Europe. *Pesäpallo* is the Finnish version of baseball, and is a popular spectator sport.

ENVIRONMENT
The Land

Finland is Europe's seventh-biggest country, with one third of its area lying beyond the Arctic Circle. With 187,888 lakes (and 98,050 islands), fed by a network of rivers and 5100 rapids, Finland's reputation as a land of lakes is justified. Compared to Sweden and Norway, it is a flat country with a scattering of fells (forested hills) in the northern Lakeland

and Lapland area, some of which are cleared and used for downhill skiing.

Forests cover two-thirds of Finland; the main types of forest are pine, spruce and birch. Much of this forest is managed, and timber-harvesting and the associated pulp-milling is an important industry.

Wildlife

Elk, brown bears and wolves are native to Finland's forests, although sightings are rare. In Lapland, the Sami keep commercial herds of some 230,000 reindeer. Hundreds of species of migratory birds arrive in the Arctic each spring, making Finland a bird-watcher's paradise.

National Parks

Finland boasts over 120,000 sq km of publicly owned lands and waters in 32 national parks – some of the last great wilderness areas in Europe. The best for hiking include the Bear's Ring in Oulanka National Park (southeast Lapland), Urho Kekkonen National Park in Lapland's Saariselkä Wilderness, Linnansaari National Park in eastern Finland and Lemmenjoki National Park in Lapland. For more information, contact **Metsähallitus** (☎ 09-270 5221; www.metsa.fi) in Helsinki.

Environmental Issues

While Finland appears quite pristine and much of its forest is protected, logging and forestry is a major part of the economy. Wood and paper products account for about one third of Finnish exports, but the pulp mills cause air and water pollution (many Finnish towns are completely blighted by these smoke-spewing factories), and extensive logging leads to erosion and a loss of old-growth forest. As a result, much of Finland's forest contains only one or two species of commercially valuable trees managed for harvesting.

Recycling is the buzzword in Finland these days – it's compulsory to separate all household waste into biodegradable, recyclable and nonbiodegradable products.

FOOD & DRINK

Typically Finnish food is similar to the fare you get elsewhere in Scandinavia and has Swedish and Russian influences – lots of fish such as Baltic herring, salmon and whitefish, along with heavy food such as potatoes, thick soups, stews and dark rye bread. Finns are among the world's most dedicated coffee drinkers.

Strong beers, wines and spirits are sold by the state network, beautifully named Alko. There are stores in every town and they're generally open from 10am to 6pm Monday to Thursday, till 8pm on Friday and until 2pm on Saturday. The legal age is 18 for beer and wine, and 20 for spirits. Beer and cider with less than 4.7% alcohol is available in supermarkets.

Staples & Specialities

Simple hamburgers and hot dogs are a common snack, served from *grilli* kiosks. In Lappish restaurants, reindeer, elk and snow-grouse feature on the menu.

Fish is a mainstay of the Finnish diet. Fresh salmon, herring and arctic char can be found at markets. *Muikki* and *vendace*, tiny lake fish, are another Finnish treat. Regional specialities from Karelia include *vety*, a sandwich made with ham, eggs and pickles, and the Karelian pastie, made with meat or potato folded in a thin, open crust. In Tampere, try *mustamakkara*, a thick sausage made from cow's blood. In Savo, especially Kuopio, a highlight is *kalakukko*, fish baked in a rye loaf. Åland is known for its fluffy pancakes. Seasonal berries are a delight in Finland – look out for cloudberries and lingonberries from Lapland, and market stalls selling blueberries, strawberries and raspberries.

Uniquely Finnish drinks to sample include *salmiakkikoska*, a home-made spirit combining dissolved liquorice/peppermint sweets with vodka (an acquired taste!); *sahti*, a sweet, high-alcohol beer; and cloudberry or cranberry liqueurs, and vodka mixed with cranberry juice.

Where to Eat & Drink

Just about every town has a *kauppahalli* (market hall), the place to head for all sorts of Finnish specialities, breads, cheeses, fish and cheap sandwiches and snacks.

Meals in restaurants (*ravintola*) can be expensive, particularly dinner (you won't get much change from €15–20), but Finns tend to eat their main meal in the middle of the day, so most restaurants and some cafés put on a generous lunch (*lounas*) buffet for €7 to €10. These include all-you-can-eat salad, bread, milk, coffee and dessert, plus big helpings of hearty fare – sausage and potatoes or fish and potatoes are common.

Finns are big lovers of chain restaurants such as Rosso, Amarillo (steaks and Tex-Mex), Koti Pizza and Hesburger (Finland's answer to McDonald's), which can be found in most towns. At Golden Rax Pizza Buffet you can get all-you-can-eat pizza, pasta, chicken wings, salad, drinks and even dessert for €8 – great for filling up cheaply!

Most hotels include a breakfast buffet (hot and cold) – a mammoth, healthy, all-you-can-eat breakfast can cut down food costs for the rest of the day.

Café culture is big in Finland – in small towns it's country-style cafés (*kahvila* or *baari*) but in cities cafés are trendy meeting places where *caffè lattes*, quiche and indulgent cakes are all the rage.

Pubs and bars also double as restaurants.

Vegetarians & Vegans

In terms of specifically vegetarian restaurants, there's not a lot around in Finland – Helsinki and Turku have a couple of places – but it's easy to self-cater at markets, or eat only the salad and vegetables at lunch buffets (which is usually cheaper). University cafés and ethnic restaurants (such as Chinese) usually have at least one vegetarian dish on the menu.

HELSINKI

☎ 09 / pop 560,000

Chugging into the heart of Helsinki on a ferry from Sweden or Estonia is an unforgettable experience, and Finland's sophisticated capital – with its Russian and Swedish influences – doesn't disappoint. This is the nerve centre of Finland, where trends begin and things happen.

For many travellers, Helsinki *is* Finland. Although it's the country's largest and most vibrant city, it's small and intimate compared to other Scandinavian capitals: in summer, walking or cycling is an easy way to appreciate its cafés, parks, markets and nearby islands. Summer beer terraces, funky bars and chic nightclubs give Helsinki some of the best nightlife in Scandinavia, and the locals know how to party.

Helsinki bears little resemblance to other Scandinavian or Baltic cities. Rather than the ornate and grandiose buildings of Stockholm, it's a low-rise city of under-stated, functional and neoclassical architecture. 'Must see' sights are few but Helsinki's appeal (especially in summer) is as much in the dynamic atmosphere and upbeat nature of its people as in any particular sight. Strolling around the harbour area, picnicking on Suomenlinna island or joining the throngs sunning themselves in the many cafés and beer terraces is every bit as good as ticking off the museums.

HISTORY

Helsinki (Helsingfors in Swedish) was settled in 1550 by the Swedish king Gustav Vasa, who hoped to draw trade away from Tallinn across the Gulf of Finland. In the 18th century the Swedes built a mammoth fortress on the nearby island of Suomenlinna, but it wasn't enough to keep the Russians out. After falling to the tsar in 1808, Helsinki became the seat of the Russian Grand Duchy – although in the process much of the town was wrecked – and in 1812 the capital was moved here from Turku. The monumental buildings of Senaatintori (Senate Square) were designed by the 19th-century German architect Carl Ludwig Engel to give the new city an appropriate measure of style and grace. Helsinki hosted the postwar summer Olympics in 1952.

ORIENTATION

Helsinki occupies a peninsula, and is linked by bridge and boat to nearby islands. The compact city centre surrounds the main harbour, Eteläsatama, and the *kauppatori*, which lies between the huge international ferry terminals. The main street axes are the twin shopping avenues of Pohjoisesplanadi and Eteläesplanadi, and Mannerheimintie.

Numerous islands lie in the Gulf just south of the city and can be reached by boat.

Maps

You can pick up decent city maps and the *See Helsinki on Foot* walking guide free from the city tourist office. For road atlases, city directories and hiking maps, visit the map shop **Karttakeskus Aleksi** (Unionkatu 32).

INFORMATION
Bookshops

Akateeminen Kirjakauppa (Academic Bookshop; Pohjoisesplanadi 39) Finland's biggest bookshop features

three floors, an Aalto-designed café and a massive range of books. Big travel section, including maps.

Discount Cards

The Helsinki Card is well worthwhile if you plan to do a lot of sightseeing in the capital. The pass gives free urban transport (including island ferries), plus free entry to more than 50 attractions in and around Helsinki and discounts on day tours to Porvoo and Tallinn. A card valid for 24/48/72 hours costs €25/35/45 (children €10/13/16). Take the 1½-hour sightseeing bus tour first up (discounted, but free in March & April). Buy the card at the city tourist office or at hotels, R-kiosks and transport terminals.

Emergencies

Dial ☎ 112 for all emergencies including ambulance, fire and police; ☎ 10022 for police; and ☎ 10023 for 24-hour medical advice.

Internet Access

Internet access at Helsinki's public libraries is free. Several cafés and bars also have free Internet access for customers.

Cable Book Library (Kirjakaapeli; ☎ 3108 5000; Mannerheimintie 22-24; ☺ 10am-10pm Mon-Thu, noon-6pm Sat & Sun) Upstairs in the Lasipalatsi Multimedia Centre. First-come, first-served terminals or book a half-hour slot. Due to move to post office building in 2005.

Helsinki University Library (Unioninkatu 36; ☺ 9am-6pm Mon-Fri, 9am-4pm Sat) Email is discouraged but the 2nd floor of this superb library is a serene place to surf the Net.

FINLAND

HELSINKI

To Tampere
To Hartwall Arena (1.5km)
City Winter Gardens
Talvipuutarha Botanical Gardens
To Urho Kekkonen Museum (2km); Seurasaari Island (3km)

FINLAND

① INFORMATION
Akateeminen Kirjakauppa Bookshop....**1**	E4
Cable Book Library.............................(see 11)	
Café Tin Tin Tango............................**2**	C2
Estonian Consulate............................**3**	F5
Finnish Tourist Board.........................**4**	E4
Forex...**5**	E4
Forex...(see 110)	
Forex..(see 47)	
Helsinki City Tourist Office................**6**	E4
Helsinki Tour Expert...........................(see 6)	
Helsinki University Library..................**7**	E3
Karttakeskus Aleksi............................**8**	E4
Kilroy Travels....................................**9**	D4
Kompassi Youth Information Centre....**10**	D4
Lasipalatsi Multimedia Centre............**11**	D3
Main Post Office & Poste Restante....**12**	D3
mbar..(see 11)	
Netcup..(see 96)	
Police..**13**	E4
Rikhardinkadun Library.......................**14**	E4
Russian Consulate...............................**15**	F5
Tikankontti (Forest & Park Service Information)....................................**16**	E4
Töölö Hospital...................................**17**	C2
Yliopiston Apteeki.............................**18**	C1

③ SIGHTS & ACTIVITIES (pp138–40)
Ateneum...**19**	E3
Finlandia talo....................................**20**	D3
Havis Amada Statue & Fountain.........**21**	F4
Helsinki Zoo......................................**22**	H3
Kansallimuseo (National Museum).....**23**	D3
Kauppatori (Fish Market)...................**24**	F4
Kiasma...**25**	D3
Kotiharjun Sauna...............................**26**	F1
Mannerheim Museum.........................**27**	F5
Maritime Museum..............................**28**	H3
Old Church..**29**	E4
Olympic Stadium...............................**30**	C1
Opera House......................................**31**	D2
Parliament House..............................**32**	D3
Senaatintori (Senate Square)............**33**	F4
Sibelius Monument...........................**34**	B2
Temppeliaukio Church.......................**35**	C3
Tuomiokirkko (Lutheran Cathedral)...**36**	F3
Uspensky Cathedral...........................**37**	F4
Yrjönkadun Uimahalli........................**38**	D4

SLEEPING (pp141–2)
Eurohostel..**39**	G4
Gasthaus Omapohj............................**40**	E3
Heo Hostel..**41**	E1
Hostel Academica..............................**42**	C4
Hostel Erottajanpuisto.......................**43**	E4
Hostel Stadion...................................**44**	C1
Hotel Anna..**45**	E5
Hotel Arthur......................................**46**	E3
Hotel Booking Centre.........................**47**	E3
Hotelli Finn..**48**	E4
Lord Hotel..**49**	E4
Marttahotelli......................................**50**	E5
Matkakoti Margarita.........................(see 40)	

EATING (pp142–4)
Aleppo Supermarket...........................**51**	E3
Babushka Ira......................................**52**	D5
Bar Tapasta.......................................**53**	E4
Café Carusel......................................**54**	E6
Café Ekberg......................................**55**	D4
Café Esplanad...................................**56**	F4
Cafe Lasipalasti................................(see 11)	
Café Strindberg.................................**57**	E4
Eatz..**58**	E3
Fazer..**59**	E4
Forum Shopping Centre.....................**60**	D4
Gastone..**61**	E4
Hariton...**62**	E4
Iguana..**63**	E4
Konstan Möljä...................................**64**	C5
Lappi...**65**	D4
Maithai...**66**	D4
Porthania UniCafe.............................**67**	E3
Sante Fe..**68**	E4
Stadin Kebab....................................(see 85)	
Tony's Deli..**69**	D4
Vanha Kauppahalli.............................**70**	F4
Wrong Noodle Bar.............................**71**	D4
Ylioppilasaukio UniCafe.....................(see 72)	
Zetor..**72**	E4
Zucchini..**73**	E4

Linnankoskenkatu
Humalistonkatu
Eino Leinonkatu
Sibelius Park
Mechelininkatu
Menanontie
Topeliuksenkatu
Sibeliuksenkatu
Mannerheimintie
Helsinginkatu
Mäntymäent
Töölönlahti
Töölöntori
Hesperiankatu
Hesperiankatu
Pohjoinen
Etäläinen
Apollonkatu
Runeberginkatu
Töölö
Museokatu
To Hietaniemi Beach (20m)
Hietaniemi Cemetery
Hietaniemenkatu
Hietaniemenkatu
Seurasaarenselkä
Temppelikatu
Nervänderinkatu
Arkadiankatu
Pohjoinen
Rautatienkatu
Leppäsuonkatu
Salomonkatu
Kamppi
Malminkatu
Fredrikinkatu
Lapinlahdenkatu
Simonkatu
To Kaapelitehdas (250m)
Porkkalankatu
Lapinrinne
Eerikinkatu
Kalevankatu
Ruoholahti
Ruoholahti
Lönnrotinkatu
Bulevardi
Uudenmaankatu
Albertinkatu
Merimichenkatu
Hietalahdenranta
Ruoholahdenranta
Eira
Telakkakatu
Merikatu
Porkkalankatu

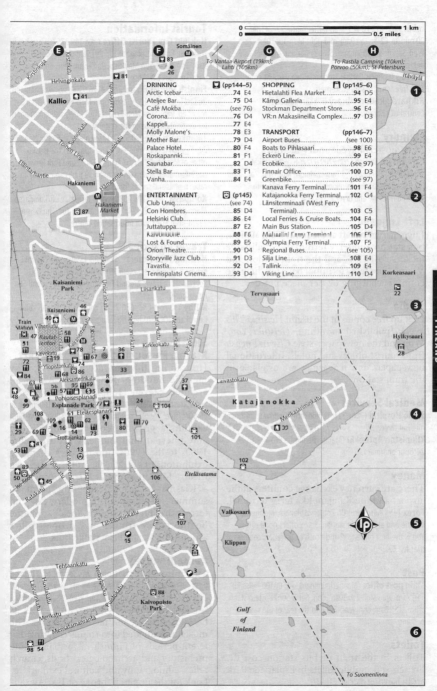

0 .... 1 km
0 .... 0.5 miles

DRINKING (pp144–5)
Arctic Icebar.......................**74** E4
Ateljee Bar........................**75** D4
Café Mokba......................(see 76)
Corona.............................**76** D4
Kappeli.............................**77** E4
Molly Malone's...................**78** E3
Mother Bar........................**79** D4
Palace Hotel.......................**80** F4
Roskapannki......................**81** F1
Saunabar...........................**82** D4
Stella Bar..........................**83** F1
Vanha...............................**84** E4

ENTERTAINMENT (p145)
Club Uniq.........................(see 74)
Con Hombres.....................**85** D4
Helsinki Club......................**86** E4
Juttatuppa.........................**87** E2
Kaivohuone.......................**88** F6
Lost & Found......................**89** E5
Orion Theatre.....................**90** D4
Storyville Jazz Club...............**91** D3
Tavastia............................**92** D4
Tennispalatsi Cinema.............**93** D4

SHOPPING (pp145–6)
Hietalahti Flea Market...........**94** D5
Kämp Galleria....................**95** E4
Stockman Department Store.....**96** E4
VR:n Makasiineilla Complex.....**97** D3

TRANSPORT (pp146–7)
Airport Buses.....................(see 100)
Boats to Pihlasaari...............**98** E6
Eckerö Line........................**99** E4
Ecobike............................(see 97)
Finnair Office.....................**100** D3
Greenbike.........................(see 97)
Kanava Ferry Terminal...........**101** F4
Katajanokka Ferry Terminal.....**102** G4
Länsiterminaali (West Ferry
   Terminal)........................**103** C5
Local Ferries & Cruise Boats.....**104** F4
Main Bus Station..................**105** D4
Makasiini Ferry Terminal........**106** F5
Olympia Ferry Terminal..........**107** F5
Regional Buses....................(see 105)
Silja Line...........................**108** E4
Tallink..............................**109** E4
Viking Line.........................**110** D4

FINLAND

mbar (☎ 6124 5420; Mannerheimintie 22-24; per 20 min/hr €2/5; ☽ 9am-midnight Mon-Tue, 9am-2am Wed-Sat, noon-10pm Sun) Smoky bar and Internet café behind Lasipalatsi.

Netcup (Roberts Coffee; Stockman department store) Two free terminals for customers.

Rikhardinkadun Library (Rikhardinkatu 3) Central city library.

Laundry

Most hostels have laundry facilities.

Cafe Tin Tin Tango (☎ 2709 0972; Töölöntorinkatu 2; wash/dry €3.50/1.80; ☽ 7am-midnight Mon-Thu, 7am-2am Fri, 9am-2am Sat, 10am-midnight Sun) Café-bar with washing machine and dryer.

Left Luggage

Luggage can be left at the main train station, bus station and ferry terminals. Small/large lockers cost €2/3, and the train station and Viking Line ferry terminal have left-luggage counters charging €2 per piece per day.

Media

Pick up free copies of the useful *Helsinki This Week* (published monthly), *Helsinki Your Way* and the newspaper-style *City in English* from tourist offices and hotels. International newspapers and magazines are available in the train station.

Medical Services

Töölö Hospital (☎ 4711; Töölönkatu 40) Private 24-hour medical clinic.

Yliopiston Apteekki (Mannerheimintie 96) 24-hour pharmacy.

Money

There are currency exchange counters at the airport and the Katajanokka ferry terminal.

Forex (☽ 8am-9pm) On Pohjoisesplanadi, Mannerheimintie and at the train station, Forex offers good rates and is the best place to change cash or travellers cheques (flat fee €2).

Post

Main post office (Mannerheiminaukio 1, 00100 Helsinki; ☽ 7am-9pm Mon-Fri, 10am-6pm Sat & Sun) Poste restante office (☽ 8am-6pm Mon-Fri) is at the rear of the same building.

Toilets

Toilets in the train or bus station cost €1. French-style public toilets in Esplanade Park and elsewhere cost €0.40.

Tourist Information

Helsinki City Tourist Office (☎ 169 3757; www.hel.fi /tourism; Pohjoisesplanadi 19; ☽ 9am-7pm Mon-Fri, 9am-3pm Sat & Sun May-Sep, 9am-5pm Mon-Fri, 9am-3pm Sat Oct-Apr)

Finnish Tourist Board (☎ 4176 9300; www.visitfinland .fi; Eteläesplanadi 4; ☽ 9am-5pm Mon-Fri ,10am-4pm Sat May-Sep, 9am-5pm Mon-Fri Oct-Apr) Maps and information for destinations around the country.

Tikankontti (☎ 270 5221; www.metsa.fi; Eteläesplanadi 20; ☽ 10am-6pm Mon-Fri, 10am-3pm Sat) The Helsinki office of Metsähallitus, the Finnish Forest and Park Service. It has information and maps for national parks and hiking areas, cabin rentals and sports fishing.

Kompassi (☎ 3108 0080; www.lasipalatsi.fi/kompassi; Mannerheimintie 22-24; ☽ 11am-6pm Tue-Thu & Sun, 11am-4pm Fri) Youth information centre.

Travel Agencies

Helsinki Tour Expert (☎ 2288 1599; www.helsinki expert.fi; Pohjoisesplanadi 19) In the city tourist office. Specialises in travel around Finland and to Tallinn and St Petersburg.

Kilroy Travels (☎ 680 7811; www.kilroytravels.com; Kaivokatu 10C) Student travel agency.

SIGHTS
Kiasma Museum of Contemporary Art

Housed in the curvaceous and quirky metallic building designed by American architect Steven Holl, **Kiasma** (☎ 1733 6501; www.kiasma.fi; Mannerheiminaukio 2; adult/student/child €5.50/4/free; ☽ 9am-5pm Tue, 10am-8.30pm Wed-Sun) exhibits a growing collection of Finnish and international modern art from the 1960s to the 1990s, and features changing exhibitions of visual arts, multimedia and a theatre for contemporary performing arts.

Kiasma is a local meeting point in summer – its glass-sided, modern café and terrace are hugely popular, locals sunbathe on the grassy fringes and people gather around the **Mannerheim statue** outside.

Kansallismuseo

The impressive **National Museum of Finland** (☎ 40501; www.nba.fi; Mannerheimintie 34; adult/student/child €5/4/free; ☽ 11am-8pm Tue-Wed, 11am-6pm Thu-Sun) looks a bit like a Gothic church with its heavy stonework and tall square tower. The museum is divided into rooms covering different periods of Finnish history, including prehistory and archaeological finds, church relics, ethnography and cultural exhibitions. Look for the imperial throne of Tsar Alexander I dating from 1809, and the display on the reindeer-herding Sami people of northern Lapland. This is Finland's best museum if you're after a static history lesson.

From the entrance hall, or better still from the 1st-floor balcony, crane your head up to see the superb frescoes on the ceiling arches, depicting scenes from the epic *Kalevala*, painted by Akseli Gallen-Kallela.

Ateneum

The list of painters represented at the **National Gallery** (☎ 1733 6401; www.fng.fi/ateneum; Kaivokatu 2; adult/student €5.50/4, free 5-8pm Wed; ☺ 9am-6pm Tue & Fri, 9am-8pm Wed & Thu, 11am-5pm Sat & Sun) reads like a *Who's Who* of Finnish art. The grand 1887 building opposite the train station square houses an absorbing collection of Finnish paintings and sculptures from the 18th century to the 1950s, including works by Albert Edelfelt, Akseli Gallen-Kallela, the von Wright brothers and Pekka Halonen, along with Rodin's famous sculpture the *Thinker*, and other international masterpieces.

Mannerheim Museum

This fascinating **museum** (☎ 635 443; Kalliolinnantie 14; adult/child €7/5; ☺ 11am-4pm Fri-Sun) in Kaivopuisto Park was the home of Marshal CGE Mannerheim, former president and commander-in-chief of the Finnish army, Civil War victor and all-round legend. Such was the national regard for Mannerheim that the house was converted into a museum less than a year after his death in 1951. Entry includes a mandatory but enthusiastic guided tour, with free plastic booties to keep the hallowed floor clean. The display includes personal possessions, the camp bed he slept in and photographs and mementos from his famous Silk Road journey on which he rode the same faithful horse for two years.

Cable Factory

The massive red-brick **Kaapelitehdas** (Cable Factory; ☎ 4763 8300; www.kaapelitehdas.fi; Tallberginkatu 1; ☺ 8am-6pm Mon-Fri), was once used for manufacturing sea cable and later became Nokia's main factory until the 1980s. When Nokia moved out, artists moved in, renting every spare space on offer. Grungy theatre, art exhibitions and dance performances are staged here now – many are free. The building also houses three offbeat museums (free with the Helsinki Card): the **Museum of Pho-**

tography, the **Hotel & Restaurant Museum** and the **Theatre Museum**. Take tram No 8 or the metro to Ruolahti (about 500m away).

Seurasaari Open-Air Museum

Seurasaari island, northwest of the centre, is home to this sprawling open-air **museum** (☎ 4050 9660; adult/student/child €5/3.50/free; ☺ 11am-5pm daily, to 7pm Jun-Aug, 9am-3pm Mon-Fri, 11am-5pm Sat & Sun late May & early Sep) with more than 80 wooden buildings, houses and saunas from the 18th and 19th centuries. It's a good chance to see what rural Finland was like. In summer, guides dressed in traditional costume demonstrate folk dancing and crafts.

Seurasaari is a venue for Helsinki's **midsummer bonfires**, a popular local tradition. Take bus No 24 from the central train station.

Urho Kekkonen Museum

Near the bridge that connects Seurasaari with the mainland, this **museum** (☎ 4050 9652; Seurasaarentie 15, Tamminiemi; adult/child €3.50/free; ☺ 11am-5pm, to 7pm Wed mid-May–mid-Aug) was the presidential residence for 30 years. Built in 1904, it housed three presidents, including Mannerheim and Urho Kekkonen, and now shows off Finnish history and art exhibitions. From central Helsinki, take bus No 24, or tram No 4 and walk.

Helsinki Zoo & Maritime Museum

The spacious **Helsinki Zoo** (☎ 169 5969; adult/child €5/3, with ferry ride €8/4; ☺ 10am-8pm May-Oct) occupies most of Korkeasaari island and is best reached by ferry from the *kauppatori*. Established in 1889, it has animals and birds from Finland and around the world housed in large natural enclosures, as well as a tropical house, a small farm, and a café and terrace. On the adjoining Hylkysaari island is the **Maritime Museum** (☎ 4050 9051; adult/child €2.50/free; ☺ 11am-5pm May-Oct) with exhibitions on Finnish shipbuilding and seafaring.

Suomenlinna

An essential day or half-day trip to take from Helsinki is by boat to the island fortress of Suomenlinna (Swedish: Sveaborg). The World Heritage Listed fortress was founded by the Swedes in 1748 against the Russians. Following a prolonged attack, Sveaborg was surrendered to the Russians in 1808.

At the bridge connecting the two main islands – Iso Mustasaari and Susisaari – is the **Inventory Chamber Visitor Centre** (☎ 684 1880; ⊙ 10am-6pm May-Sep) with tourist information, maps and guided walking tours in summer. In the same building is the illuminating **Suomenlinna Museum** (☎ 40501; adult/student/child €5/4/2.50), covering the island's history. There's a scale model of Suomenlinna as it looked in 1808, and a fascinating half-hour audiovisual show.

You can ramble around the crumbling fortress walls at the southern end of Susi-saari island, and there are several museums including the **Ehrensvärd Museum** (adult/child €3/1; ⊙ 10am-5pm May-Aug) which preserves an 18th-century officer's home. Three museums relating to Suomenlinna's military history can be visited with a **combination ticket** (adult/student €5.50/2; ⊙ 11am-6pm May-Aug).

The church on Iso Mustasaari was built in 1854 and doubles as a lighthouse – the original gaslight beacon is now electric.

There are several good cafés on Suomen-linna, but locals picnic among the fortress ruins. At around 5pm you can watch the enormous Baltic ferries pass through the narrow gap. There's also a HI hostel here (see p142).

Suomenlinna Panimoravintola is a fine brewery pub and restaurant right beside the ferry quay.

HKL ferries depart every 20 minutes from the passenger quay at the *kauppatori*. Buy tickets (€2) for the 15-minute trip at the pier. The Helsinki Card is valid for all ferries and attractions at Suomenlinna.

There's nowhere to hire bikes, but they can be brought across on the ferries.

ACTIVITIES

In summer you can hire inline skates from the kiosk on Merisatamanranta, west of Kaivopuisto park. Boats and canoes can be hired at Kaivopuisto park and at Töölönlahti lake. For bicycle hire see p146.

Join the locals sunning themselves in summer on Helsinki's islands and beaches. The closest city beach is Hietaniemi, a small and very popular curve of sand east of the centre. Pihlajasaari is the pick of the islands, with several secluded bays and beaches, including a nudist beach. Get there by boat from the dock next to Cafe Carusel (€4.50).

For a sauna and swim, the sleek Art Deco **Yrjönkadun Uimahalli** (☎ 3108 7400; Yrjönkatu 21; admission €4-11) is a Helsinki institution. There are separate hours for men (Tuesday, Thursday, Saturday) and women (Monday, Wednesday, Friday), and bathing suits are not allowed in the pool or saunas.

Kotiharjun Sauna (☎ 753 1535; Harjutorinkatu 1; adult/child €7/4; ⊙ 2-8pm Tue-Fri, 1-7pm Sat) in Kallio is Helsinki's last public wood-fired sauna. It's a real Finnish experience where you can also get a scrub-down and massage. Also check out the **Saunabar** (p145).

Walking Tour

Helsinki is an easy and very rewarding city to get around on foot or by bicycle. Start at the **kauppatori**, Helsinki's lively market square. Just south of the square is the **Vahna Kauppahalli** (Old Market Hall), a great place to stock up on gourmet picnic provisions. East of the market, on Katajanokka island, you can't miss the magnificent **Orthodox Uspensky Cathedral**. The red-brick exterior supports 13 gilded cupolas ('onion domes' designed by a Russian architect of the tsar) representing Christ and his disciples.

From the market square head a block north to **Senaatintori** (Senate Square), Helsinki's majestic central square. Surrounded by early 19th-century buildings, the square was modelled after St Petersburg's. It's occasionally used by B-list Hollywood film makers who are after a dramatic 'Russian' backdrop. CL Engel's stately **Tuomiokirkko** (Lutheran cathedral), finished in 1852, is the square's most prominent feature and the steps are a favourite meeting place.

Returning to the market square, check out the fountain and mermaid **statue of Havis Amanda**, designed by artist Ville Vallgren in 1908 and regarded as a symbol of Helsinki. From here the **Esplanade Park** stretches west to the main thoroughfare, Mannerheimintie. Head north to visit **Kiasma** (see p138), the **Kansallismuseo** (National Museum; p138) and **Parliament House** (☎ 432 2027; ⊙ guided tours 11am &

noon Sat, noon & 1pm Sun). Across the road is Alvar Aalto's angular **Finlandia talo** (Concert Hall). If you have time, continue north (walk along the shore of lake Töölanlahti) to Aalto's **Opera House** on the corner of Mannerheimintie and Helsinginkatu, then turn right to reach the tiny, beautifully manicured **City Winter Gardens**. Also in this area is the **Olympic Stadium**, built for the 1952 Olympics, with a sports museum and a 72m-high tower offering good views over the city.

Returning along Mannerheimintie, detour along Fredrikinkatu to the **Temppeliaukio Church** (the Church in the Rock). Hewn into rock, the church symbolises the modern meanderings of Finnish religious architecture and features a stunning 24m-diameter roof covered in 22km of copper stripping. There are regular concerts and a service in English at 2pm on Sundays.

Walk down **Fredrikinkatu** then east on **Lönnrotinkatu** to the small park (and old cemetery – look for the ancient gravestones littered round the square) where there's a lovely **old church**. This is a popular lunchtime meeting spot in summer. Heading back down Bulevardi (away from the city), you come to **Hietalahden tori** where there's a market hall and a popular flea market on summer evenings and weekends.

If you have a bicycle, from here you can ride around the southern shoreline of Helsinki (follow Telakkakatu then Merisatamanranta) to **Kaivopuisto park** and on to return to the *kauppatori*. Alternatively, head north from Hietalahden tori to Hietaniemenkatu and ride around to **Hietaniemi Beach**, the closest beach to central Helsinki. Continuing north you come to **Sibelius Park** and the steel **monument** to the great Finnish composer. The organ-like cluster of steel pipes is said to represent the forest.

TOURS

Helsinki Tour Expert (☎ 2288 1200; www.helsinki expert.fi; adult/child €20/10, €8 with Helsinki Card) runs excellent 1½-hour city bus tours in summer on the hour from 10am to 2pm (11am and 1pm in May & September, 11am in winter). They depart from the Esplanade Park, near the tourist office, and taped commentary (in 11 languages) comes via a headset. There's another year-round city tour with live commentary departing from the Olympia ferry terminal daily at 10.30am.

Sun Lines (☎ 727 7010; www.sunlines.fi; adult/child €14.50/5) and **Royal Lines** (☎ 612 2950; www.royal line.fi; €14.50/5) operate 1½-hour archipelago sea cruises with daily departures in summer from the *kauppatori*. **IHA Lines** (☎ 6874 5050; www.ihalines.fi) has lunch and dinner cruises from €22.

FESTIVALS & EVENTS

There's something going on in Helsinki year-round. Check with the tourist office for a current programme or check www.hel.fi.

Vappu (May Day) is celebrated with particular verve in Helsinki. On Vappu Eve (30 April) students gather around the Havis Amanda fountain to dress up the statue, plant a white cap on her, and so begin a riotous night of partying. On 1 May, crowds gather for a champagne breakfast at Kaivopuisto park.

In late April there's the **Espoo Jazz Festival** (www.apriljazz.fi) with some big-name local and international performers. Six June is **Helsinki Day** with festivities around town and free concerts in Kaivopuisto park.

The **Helsinki Festival** (www.helsinkifestival.fi) runs for about two weeks in late August–early September with a programme of arts, music and theatre.

SLEEPING

It's wise to make bookings or at least call ahead at any time of year – June to August is peak tourist season but hostels can fill up with school groups and hotels with business travellers outside these months. The **Hotel Booking Centre** (☎ 2288 1400; hotel@helsinkiexpert.fi; 9am-7pm Mon-Fri, 9am-6pm Sat, 10am-6pm Sun Jun-Aug, 9am-5pm Mon-Sat Sep-May) in the train station or city tourist office can help in a pinch – they charge a €5 booking fee but can sometimes get cheaper deals on hotels.

Budget

Rastila Camping (☎ 321 6551; rastilacamping@hel.fi; Karavaanikatu 4; tent site per person/group €11/17, 2-/4-person cabins €43/62). Although 10km from the city centre, the camping ground is easily reached by metro (Rastila stop). Facilities include a lakeside sauna, restaurant and summer youth hostel. Helsinki has three year-round hostels, three summer hostels, plus there's a hostel on Suomenlinna island.

Hostel Stadion (☎ 477 8480; www.stadionhostel .com; Pohjoinen Stadiontie 3B; dm from €15-19, s/d with linen €27.50/41; (P) (X)) In the Olympic Stadium complex, this 'old school' hostel (it's been around since '62!) lacks much charm or a welcome but it's cheap and there are plenty of beds so it's a good last resort. Tram 7A or 3T.

Eurohostel (☎ 622 0470; www.eurohostel.fi; Linnankatu 9; dm/s/d/tr €22/36.50/44/66; ☺ 24hr reception) On Katajanokka island less than 500m from the Viking Line terminal, this high-rise hostel is spotless, efficiently run, friendly and extremely busy. Free sauna and excellent café. Take tram No 4 or 2 from the centre or a 15-minute walk.

Hostel Erottajanpuisto (☎ 642 169; www.erottajan puisto.com; Uudenmaankatu 9; dm/s/d/tr €22.50/46/60/78; ☺ 24hr reception; (X)) Smallest and most laid-back hostel in Helsinki. Unbeatable location on a lively street of bars and restaurants close to the heart of the city. Great vibe.

Hostel Academica (☎ 1311 4334; www.hostelaca demica.fi; Hietaniemenkatu 14; dm/s/d from €16/40/60; ☺ Jun-Aug; (X)) In a quiet part of town, this good-value student apartment has no large dorms and each room has private bathroom and kitchenette. Sauna and swim included and there's a uni café here.

Heo Hostel (☎ 774 2420; www.heohostel.net; Kirstinkatu 1; dm/s/d €16/28/40; ☺ late May–late Aug, reception 8am-9pm; (X)) In the Kallio district north of the centre, this immaculate hostel has dorms and apartment-style rooms, free Internet and laundry, and sauna (per hour €12). Short walk to the Kallio pub crawl (see Drinking).

Suomenlinna Hostel (☎ 684 7471; www.leirikou lut.com; dm/s/d €20/40/55; ☺ reception closed 10am-4pm; (X)) In an old red-brick building near the ferry quay on Suomenlinna island, this is a peaceful alternative to staying in central Helsinki (forget it if you're interested in nightlife).

Mid-Range

Gasthaus Omapohja (☎ 666 211; Itäinen Teatterikuja 3; s/d €44/65, s/d with private bathroom €64/85; (X)) Lovely, intimate guesthouse minutes from the train station. Rooms are spotless, furniture is old-world and the management is very welcoming.

Matkakoti Margarita (☎ 622 4261; Itäinen Teatterikuja 3; s/d/t €40/54/69; (X)) Not quite as charming as its neighbour Omapohja, but it's clean and well priced.

Hotelli Finn (☎ 684 4360; www.hotellifinn.fi; Kalevankatu 3B; s/d €55/65, s/d with private bathroom €65/80)

Small, friendly hotel on the top floor of a central city building. Spacious rooms are good value.

Top End

Helsinki has plenty of big, central business hotels, including the Sokos, Radisson and Cumulus chains. The following are more intimate independent hotels.

Marttahotelli (☎ 618 7400; www.marttahotelli .fi; Uudenmaankatu 24; s/d/tr €98/120/145, s/d/tr discount weekends €75/85/100; (P) (X)) Central but quiet as most rooms face an inner courtyard with free parking. Small rooms but sunny decor and very cosy. Rates include a superb buffet breakfast and there's a small sauna (€10).

Hotel Arthur (☎ 173 441; www.hotelarthur.fi; Vuorikatu 19; s/d/tr €92/110/130, s/d/tr discount €71/88/100; (X)) Close to the train station, this is another welcoming hotel with neat rooms, a good restaurant and satellite TV.

Hotel Anna (☎ 616 621; www.hotelanna.fi; Annankatu 1; s/d from €110/150, s/d discount weekends & Jul €90/115) Popular business-cum-boutique hotel on six floors. Rooms are a nice size, with TV and minibar. Rates include buffet breakfast but sauna and parking are extra.

Lord Hotel (☎ 615 815; www.lordhotel.fi; Lönnrotinkatu 29; s/d €140/170, s & d discount €95) This imposing hotel, with National Romantic-style stone facade and distinctive turret, has modern, functional rooms with breakfast and sauna included, and an excellent restaurant. Great value when discounted and a cut above most.

EATING

Helsinki has by far Finland's best range of cafés and restaurants, from Finnish and Russian to Asian and Italian, sushi joints to kebab stands and terrace cafés to fine French dining: this is the place for a splurge. As elsewhere in Finland, seek out the lunch-time specials if your budget is tight – many restaurants (even the fancy ones) have buffet lunch deals for under €10. Good places to look include the Esplanade, Mikonkatu, Uudenmaankatu and the tangle of side streets between the train station and Stockmann.

Restaurants

Cafe Lasipalasti (☎ 621 6700; Mannerheimintie 22-24; lunch buffet €8; ☺ 11am-3pm Mon-Sat) On the ground floor of the multimedia centre, this café specialises in Finnish food and has a good soup and salad buffet. A more formal restaurant is upstairs.

Wrong Noodle Bar (☎ 2486 2442; Annankatu 21; mains €7-8; ☼ 11am-9pm Mon-Sat, 3-9pm Sun) Ultra-modern and trendy place for a fast and filling bowl of ramen noodles, laksa, satay or curry, including vegetarian.

Eatz (☎ 687 7240; Mikonkatu 15; mains €10-22; ☼ 10am-late) The versatile and colourful Eatz manages to serve up everything from Thai and Indian to Italian, and even has a sushi bar and Brazilian beach grill! It's also the cornerstone of Helsinki's biggest summer beer terrace.

Lappi (☎ 645 550; Annankatu 22; lunch €9-11, mains €14-36; ☼ noon-10.30pm Mon-Fri, 1-10.30pm Sat & Sun) If you can't make it to Lapland, costumed staff serve up Lappish specialities in this delightfully rustic 'log cabin' restaurant. Try sirloin of elk, as well as various reindeer preparations. Lunch specials make it that much more affordable.

Konstan Mölja (☎ 694 750; Hietalahdenkatu 14; lunch/dinner buffet €8/12) Great place for hearty, home-style Finnish fare enjoyed in a pleasant atmosphere – much of the maritime decor comes from an old harbour near Vyborg. The buffet always includes reindeer.

Babushka Ira (☎ 680 1405; Uudenmaankatu 28; mains €5-12; ☼ 11am-midnight) Russia's best restaurants are said to be in Helsinki. Try a blini or borscht at this tiny, romantic restaurant.

Hariton (☎ 622 1717; Kasarmikatu 44; mains €9-22; ☼ 11.30am-midnight Mon-Fri, 1-11pm Sat, 1-10pm Sun) Charming Russian restaurant with antique furniture, a gallery and varied Orthodox menu, including blini.

Bar Tapasta (☎ 640 724; Uudenmaankatu 13; tapas €3-4; ☼ Mon-Thu 11am-midnight, Fri 11-2am, Sat 2pm-2am) Intimate, hole-in-the-wall bar with a welcoming atmosphere and wonderful tapas, including gorgonzola mushrooms and chilli olives, and salads. Wash it all down with a jug of sangria (€17).

Iguana (☎ 663 662; Keskukatu 4; mains €4-11; ☼ 11-1am Mon-Thu, 11-2am Fri & Sat, 1pm-midnight Sun) Good-value American-style Tex Mex chain with €7.50 lunch specials.

Sante Fe (☎ 4242 6010; Aleksanterinkatu 15; mains €8-18; ☼ 11-1am Mon-Thu, 11-2am Fri & Sat, 1pm-1am Sun) Tucked away in an arcade off Mikonkatu, Santa Fe is similar to Iguana but more popular for its rustic atmosphere and international bar. Portions are big (steaks, Cajun, Mexican) and it becomes a crowded nightspot later.

Maithai (☎ 605 6850; Annankatu 31-33; mains €10-16; ☼ 11am-11pm Mon-Fri, noon-11pm Sat & Sun) An intimate little place and a local favourite for Thai food – there are only a few tables so book ahead.

Tony's Deli (☎ 129 4910; Bulevardi 2; mains €8.50-12) Stylish, low-key New York/Italian place, with pasta from €10 and Helsinki's best antipasto.

Gastone (☎ 666 116; Korkeavuorenkatu 45; mains €6.50-19; ☼ 11am-midnight) Helsinki's newest Italian restaurant is the genuine article with a diverse list of pasta and antipasto, and a fine wine list. Intimate but not too formal.

Cafés

Helsinki University has several student cafeterias around the city, where meals cost under €5. They include **Porthania** (☎ 1311 4298; Hallituskatu 11-13; ☼ 10am-4pm Mon-Fri) and the huge **Ylioppilasaukio** (☎ 260 9491; Mannerheimintie 3B; ☼ 11am-5pm Mon-Sat, noon-5pm Sun), tucked away down an alley in front of the train station.

Cafe Esplanad (☎ 665 496; Pohjoisesplanadi 37, dishes €3-10; ☼ 8am-11pm Mon-Fri, 9am-10.30pm Sat, 10am-10pm Sun) Helsinki's most popular café, with Danish pastries and Finnish *pulla* (wheat bun), spectacular salads and a great people-watching terrace.

Cafe Ekberg (☎ 6811 8660; Bulevardi 9; buffet breakfast & lunch €7.50) Helsinki's oldest café and one of the best places for breakfast in the city. The lunch buffet is also great value.

Cafe Carusel (☎ 622 4522; Merisatamanranta 10; dishes €2-10) Busy but unpretentious self-service waterfront café on the edge of Kaivopuisto park. Great focaccias and savoury snacks and a sunny terrace.

FINLAND

AUTHOR'S CHOICE

Cafe Strindberg (☎ 681 2030; Pohjoisesplanadi 33; light meals €4-10; 🕑 9am-10pm Mon-Sat, 10am-10pm Sun, bar to 1am) This little piece of Paris in Helsinki is in a prime people-watching spot on the Esplanade. Wicker chairs spill onto the footpath (waiter service at the front) where you can linger over coffee, cakes, salads, sandwiches and light meals. Upstairs is an upmarket restaurant but the highlight is the cosy wine bar with squishy leather couches, classical music and candlelight.

Fazer (☎ 6159 2959; Kluuvikatu 3; cakes from €3; 🕑 to 10pm; 🗷) The best place in town for cakes, pastries and mouthwatering sweets – the Fazer family is Finland's most famous candy maker.

Zucchini (☎ 622 2907; Fabianinkatu 4; dishes €5-12; 🕑 11am-5pm Mon-Fri, closed Jul; 🗷) Trendy vegetarian café serving quiche, pancakes, soups, salads, juices and a few innovative dishes.

Quick Eats

For everything from Asian noodles to burgers and kebabs, head to the food court in the basement of the **Forum shopping centre** (Mannerheimintie 20).

Grillis set up around town in the evenings, but the best kebabs are said to be **Stadin Kebab** (Eerikinkatu 14).

Self-Catering

In summer there are food stalls, fresh produce and outrageously expensive berries at the *kauppatori* but the real gourmet stuff is in the fabulous **Vanha Kauppahalli** (Old Market Hall; Eteläranta 1; 🕑 6.30am-6pm Mon-Fri, 6.30am-4pm Sat, 10am-4pm Sun summer only) at the harbour, where you can get filled rolls, cheese, breads, fish and an array of Finnish snacks and delicacies, plus there's a small Alko.

For simple groceries, stock up at Aleppo, a budget supermarket in the pedestrian tunnel by the train station.

DRINKING

Helsinki has probably the most lively and sophisticated nightlife scene in Scandinavia and the locals are a friendly bunch, especially once they've had a few drinks. In summer, drinking starts early at the many beer terraces that sprout up all over town. The biggest is along Mikonkatu at the front of Eatz.

For the cheapest beer in Helsinki (from €2 a pint during the seemingly perpetual happy hours), head to the working-class suburb of Kallio (metro: Somäinen), north of the centre. There's a string of early local pubs along Helsinginkatu – start at the grungy Roskapankki ('trash bank') and crawl east towards Stella Bar. The main areas for nightlife in the centre include Uudenmaankatu, Eerikinkatu and Yliopistonkatu.

Ateljee Bar (☎ 43360; Yrjönkatu 26; 🕑 2pm-late Sun-Fri, noon-2am Sat) Tiny rooftop bar on the 14th floor of the Sokos Hotel Torni (Helsinki's tallest building). The views from the toilets are the best in the city! Another bar with a view is the rooftop terrace of the Palace Hotel, which actually has a better outlook over the harbour and cathedrals.

Molly Malone's (☎ 5766 7500; Kaisaniemenkatu 1C; 🕑 11-2am Mon-Tue, 11-3am Wed-Sat, noon-2am Sun) This rollicking Irish pub is a great place to meet travellers, expats and Finns. Live music upstairs most nights and shoulder-to-shoulder Guinness consumption.

Spårakoff (€7) In summer the bright red pub tram trundles around the city, departing on the hour between 2 and 7pm from Tuesday to Saturday. A beer costs €5, and the terminus is on Mikonkatu (opposite Eatz).

Vanha (☎ 1311 4368; Mannerheimintie 3; 🕑 11am-late Mon-Sat) In a beautifully restored 19th-century students' house, Vanha is a music bar popular with a young crowd. Reasonably priced beer and live gigs.

Mother Bar (☎ 612 3990; Eerikinkatu 2; 🕑 4pm-late Mon-Fri, 7pm-3am Sat) There's a great vibe in this industrial lounge room. DJs play drum & bass and acid jazz music four nights a week.

AUTHOR'S CHOICE

Kappeli (☎ 681 2440; Eteläesplanade 1; 🕑 9am-2am daily) In Esplanade Park, this institution has one of the city's most popular summer terraces, facing a stage where bands and musicians regularly play in summer. The glass and iron facade hides an excellent restaurant and café which has long been the haunt of Helsinki's artistic elite, right back to Jean Sibelius. In the stone-walled cellar is an ambient vault-like bar which sometimes has live music.

Corona (☎ 642 002; Eerikinkatu 11; ☼ 11-2am Mon-Sat, noon-2am Sun) and the Soviet-style **Café Mokba** (☼ 5pm-2am) next door are classic bars run by film makers Aki and Mika Kaurismäki; both attract a savvy, grungy crowd. Corona has about 20 pool tables.

Saunabar (☎ 685 5550; Eerikinkatu 27) Popular student bar with occasional live music and two saunas available from 3pm to midnight on Sunday and Monday (per person €4.50) and other times for private bookings.

ENTERTAINMENT
Cinemas
Tennispalatsi (☎ 0600-007 007; Salomonkatu 15; tickets €8-10) Huge multiplex cinema screening mainstream movies.

Orion Theatre (☎ 0134 0201, Eerikinkatu 15) Alternative and art-house cinema with a fondness for Woody Allen; screens Finnish Film Archive movies.

Gay & Lesbian Venues
By Scandinavian standards Helsinki has a low-key gay scene.

Lost & Found (☎ 680 1010; Annankatu 6, ☼ until 4am) Sophisticated gay-hetero bar and popular late-night hang-out.

Con Hombres (☎ 608 826; Eerinkinkatu 14) Industrial gay 'eurobar' in a lively part of town.

Live Music
Various bars and clubs around Helsinki host live bands.

Tavastia (☎ 694 8511; www.tavastiaklubi.fi; Urho Kekkosenkatu 4-6; tickets from €6; ☼ 9pm-late) There's always something happening at Finland's biggest rock music club. Live bands, including international acts, hit the stage most nights.

Storyville (☎ 408 007; Museokatu 8; ☼ 8am-4pm Mon-Sat) Helsinki's No 1 jazz club attracts a refined older crowd swinging to boogie-woogie, trad jazz, Dixieland and New Orleans most nights.

Juttutupa (☎ 774 4860; Säästöpankinranta 6) This imposing granite pub across from Hakaniemi Square in Kallio is a bit of an institution and has its own jazz club.

Nightclubs
Helsinki Club (☎ 4332 6302; Yliopistonkatu 8; ☼ 10pm-4am) This heaving mainstream dance club pulls in the late-night crowds, including Finnish celebs. Minimum age 24.

Club Uniq (☎ 0800-94411; Yliopistonkatu 5; ☼ 10pm-4am) Helsinki's newest nightclub is across from the Helsinki Club and below ground. The small dance floor gets busy but the novelty vote goes to the tiny **Arctic Icebar** (☼ 5pm-4am; admission €10) inside the club: don an insulated coat, sip a vodka shot in a balmy -5°C, and watch the sweaty ravers outside through the glass wall. Minimum age 24.

Kaivohuone (☎ 684 1530; Iso puistotie) In the middle of Kaivopuisto park, this refurbished grand old Russian spa villa is now one of Helsinki's best clubs. The cavernous interior drips with chandeliers, there's a huge dance floor, five bars and chill-out rooms. The terrace outside gets packed in summer.

Sport
If you're around in winter (Sep-Mar), take the chance to see a major ice hockey game. Big matches are played at the huge **Hartwall Arena** (☎ 204 1997, tickets ☎ 0600-10800; www.hartwall-areena.com; Areenakuja 1) in Pasila, north of the centre. The stadium hosted ice hockey world championships in 1997 and 2004, and is home to Helsinki superleague side Jokerit. You can also catch games at the indoor arena of the Olympic Stadium off Mannerheimintie. Ask at the tourist office for match times.

Theatre
For concerts and performances, see *Helsinki This Week* or inquire at the tourist office. Tickets are available from **Lippupiste** (☎ 0600-900 900). Opera, ballet and classical concerts are held at the **Opera House** (☎ 4030 2211; Helsinginkatu 58; tickets from €10).

SHOPPING
Helsinki's main shopping strip is Pohjois-esplanadi, running along Esplanade park, where you'll find chic boutiques in Kamp Galleria, including the main branch of Marimekko, the trendy Finnish design and homewares store, and **Stockmann** (Aleksanterinkatu 52; ☼ 9am-9pm Mon-Fri, 9am-6pm Sat, noon-6pm Sun), Scandinavia's biggest department store with seven floors of everything. Rooberinkatu is another place for boutique shops with less pose value.

Hietalahti Flea Market (☼ 8am-2pm Mon-Fri, 8am-3pm Sat, 10am-4pm Sun in summer) is the place to hunt for bargains and second-hand gear. Another good place to browse is in the old railway goods shed **VR:n Makasiineilla**, where there's a weekend market in summer, food stalls and music.

GETTING THERE & AWAY
Air
There are flights to Helsinki from all major European cities. Vantaa airport, one of Europe's most user-friendly terminals, is 19km north of Helsinki.

Finnair (☎ 0203-140160 for reservations; Asema-aukio 3; ☽ Mon-Sat) flies to 20 Finnish cities, generally at least once a day but several times daily on routes such as Turku, Tampere, Rovaniemi and Oulu. Its office is near the train station.

Boat
International ferries depart from four terminals and travel to Stockholm (Sweden), Tallinn (Estonia) and Travemünde (Germany). See p195 for more details.

Ferry tickets can be bought at the terminals or from the ferry companies' offices in the centre of the city.

Eckerö Line (☎ 228 8544; Mannerheimintie 10; Länsiterminaali (West) terminal)

Linda Line (☎ 668 9700; www.lindaline.fi; Makasiini terminal)

Nordic Jet Line (☎ 681 770; www.njl.fi; Kanava terminal)

Silja Line (☎ 0203-74552; www.siljaline.fi; Mannerheimintie 2; Olympia terminal)

Tallink (☎ 2282 1222; Erottajankatu 19; Kanava terminal)

Viking Line (☎ 123 577; www.vikingline.fi; Mannerheimintie 14; Katajanokka terminal)

Kanava and Katajanokka terminals are served by bus No 13 and tram Nos 2, 2V and 4; Olympia and Makasiini terminals by tram No 3B and 3T; and Länsiterminaali by bus No 15.

Bus
The **main bus station** (☽ 7am-7pm Mon-Fri, 7am-5pm Sat, 9am-6pm Sun) is behind Lasipalatsi Multimedia Centre off Mannerheimintie. At the time of research a new underground bus terminal was being built a short distance away (expected to be completed in 2006).

Train
A pedestrian tunnel links the train station to Helsinki's metro system.

Express trains run daily to Turku, Tampere and Lappeenranta, and there's a choice of day and overnight trains to Oulu, Rovaniemi and Joensuu. There are also daily trains to the Russian cities of Vyborg, St Petersburg and Moscow.

GETTING AROUND
To/From the Airport
Bus No 615 (€3, Helsinki Card not valid; 30 minutes) shuttles between Vantaa airport (all international and domestic flights) and platform No 10 at Rautatientori (Railway Square) next to the main train station.

Finnair buses (€4.90) depart from the Finnair office at Asema-aukio, also next to the main train station, every 20 minutes from 5am to midnight. There are also door-to-door **airport taxis** (☎ 10 64 64; www.airporttaxi.fi; per person €20).

Bicycle
Helsinki is ideal for cycling: the small inner city is flat, and there are well-marked and high-quality bicycle paths. Pick up a copy of the Helsinki cycling map from the tourist office.

In summer, the city provides 300 distinctive green 'City Bikes' at stands within a radius of 2km from the *kauppatori* – although sometimes you'll wonder where they're all hiding. These bikes are free: you deposit a €2 coin into the stand which locks them, then reclaim it when you return the bike to any stand.

For something a bit more sophisticated, **Greenbike** (☎ 8502 2850), in the old railway goods sheds, rents quality bikes for €10 per day, or €15 for 24 hours. Ecobike is a smaller operation in the small yellow hut across the road from Parliament House.

Local Transport
Central Helsinki is easy enough to get around on foot or by bicycle, but there's also a metro line and a reasonably comprehensive tram, bus and train network. A one-hour flat-fare ticket for the bus, tram, metro, Suomenlinna ferry and local trains within Helsinki's **HKL network** (www.hel.fi/HKL) costs €2. It allows unlimited transfers but should be validated in the stamping machine on board when you first use it. A single tram ticket (no transfers) on board/in advance is €1.80/1.50.

One-/three-/five-day tourist tickets are available for €5.40/10.80/16.20. The Helsinki Card gives you free travel anywhere within Helsinki (see the Information section earlier for details). Tram 3T from the *kauppatori* makes a good sightseeing trip.

There are also regional tickets for travel by bus or train to neighbouring cities such as Vantaa and Espoo which cost €3 for a single one-hour ticket, €7.50 for one day and €22 for a 10-trip ticket. Children's tickets are usually half-price.

Buy tickets on board, at stations or R-kiosks.

The *Helsinki Route Map*, available at HKL offices and the city tourist office, is good for making sense of local transport.

AROUND HELSINKI

If your time is short but you want to see a bit of Finland outside the capital, there are a number of easy day trips. The most rewarding is Porvoo, 50km to the east, but if you're interested in the lives of some of Finland's great artists, Espoo and the Museum Road are worth a look.

Espoo
☎ 09 / pop 221,600

Espoo is an independent municipality just west of Helsinki and while it ranks as the second-largest city in Finland, it's virtually a suburb of the capital.

The main reason to venture out here is to visit the **Gallen-Kallela Museum** (☎ 541 3388; www.gallen-kallela.fi; Gallen-Kallelantie 27; adult/child €8/4; ☯ 10am-6pm May-Sep, 10am-4pm Tue-Sun Oct-Apr), the pastiche studio-castle of Akseli Gallen-Kallela, one of Finland's most notable painters. The Art Nouveau building was designed by the artist and is now a museum of his work. Take tram No 4 from central Helsinki to Munkkiniemi, then walk 2km or take bus No 33 (Saturday and Sunday only)

The **Espoo Car Museum** (☎ 855 7178; Pakankylän Kartano Manor; adult/child €5/2; ☯ 11am-5.30pm Tue-Sun May-Aug) has more than 100 vintage motor vehicles dating from the early 20th century.

Porvoo
☎ 019 / pop 46,000

Porvoo (Swedish: Borgå), a picturesque medieval town and Finland's second-oldest settlement (founded in 1346), makes a perfect day or overnight trip from Helsinki, 50km away. Porvoo has a distinctly Swedish feel around the cobbled **Old Town**. Its charming wooden houses, meandering streets and active riverfront are great for exploring.

The historic **Porvoo church** and several good **museums** – including the well-preserved 19th-century home of Finland's national poet JL Runeberg – are the main sights; there are guided walks in the Old Town and river cruises in summer.

The **tourist office** (☎ 520 2316; www.porvoo.fi; Rihkamakatu 4; ☯ 9am-6pm Mon-Fri, 10am-4pm Sat & Sun Jun-Aug, 9.30am-4.30pm Mon-Fri, 10am-2pm Sat & Sun Sep-May), bordering the Old Town, has plenty of information and a free Internet terminal.

Two kilometres south of Porvoo town, **Camping Kokonniemi** (☎ 581 967; myyntipalvelu@lomaliitto.fi; camp sites/4-person cabins €15/60; ☯ Jun-Sep) has cabins, sauna and camping kitchen.

Porvoo Hostel (☎ 523 0012; porvoohostel@co.inet.fi; Linnankoskenkatu 1-3; dm/s/d €13/27/32, linen hire €4) is a HI hostel in a lovely old building with spotless rooms and a well-equipped kitchen. It's a 10-minute walk south of the *kauppatori*. Book ahead (reception closed 10am-4pm).

The family-run **Gasthaus Werneri** (☎ 0400-494 876; gasthaus.werneri@dalnternet.net; Adlercreutzinkatu 29; s/d €35/50) is a simple guesthouse with just five rooms, a courtyard and kids' playground.

Although the cheapest places to eat are in the new part of town, especially around the *kauppatori*, Porvoo's most atmospheric cafés, restaurants and bars are in the Old Town and along the riverfront. In summer, the terraces along cobblestoned Välikatu are overflowing with visitors.

In the inexpensive **Old Town Cafe** (☎ 580 201; Välikatu 1; snacks €2-5; ☯ 8am-5pm), 'young' Porvoo sips coffee and munches on quiche, croissants and home-made soups while 'old' Porvoo drifts by.

In the Old Town, **Restaurant Timbaali** (☎ 523 1020; Välikatu 8; mains €15-21; ☯ 11am-11pm Mon-Sat, noon-6pm Sun) is a rustic restaurant specialising in locally grown snails, along with gourmet Finnish cuisine.

Right at the main bridge and with a great little terrace hanging over the water, **Poorvoon Paahtimo** (☎ 617 040; Mannerheiminkatu 2; ☯ noon-10pm Mon-Thu, noon-2am Fri, 11-2am Sat, 11am-10pm Sun) is an atmospheric red-brick former storehouse which roasts its own coffee and has a great bar. In summer, a boat terrace is moored outside.

Glückauf (☎ 54761; mains €10-20; ☯ summer), a restaurant aboard a 19th-century sailing ship, is moored just south of the Old Town. The speciality is seafood and there's a cheaper terrace menu (ie you eat on the river bank rather than on the boat) for €6 to €10.

The bus station is on the *kauppatori*; buses run every half-hour between Porvoo and Helsinki (€8.40, one hour), but the best way to reach Porvoo in summer is by ferry.

The historic steamship **JL Runeberg** (☎ 019-524 3331; www.msjlruneberg.fi; one way/return €20/29) sails daily at 10am from Helsinki in summer (exact dates vary), returning at 4pm. **Royal Line** (☎ 09-612 2950; www.royalline.fi; one way/return €20/32) has three-hour cruises between Helsinki and Porvoo daily from June to mid-August.

Järvenpää & Tuusulan Rantatie

The **Tuusulan Rantatie** (Tuusula Lake Rd; www.jar venpaa.fi) is a narrow road along Tuusula Lake (Tuusulanjärvi) about 40km north of Helsinki. A major stop along the 'museum road' is **Halosenniemi** (☎ 8718 3461; adult/child €5/2; ♥ 11am-7pm Tue-Sun May-Sep, 11am-4pm Tue-Sun Oct-Apr), the Karelian-inspired, log-built National Romantic studio of artist Pekka Halonen.

Closer to the town of Järvenpää is the family home of composer Jean Sibelius, now a museum. **Ainola** (☎ 287 322; Ainolantie; www .ainola.fi; adult/student/child €5/2/1; ♥ 10am-5pm Tue-Sun May-Sep), built on this beautiful forested site in 1904, contains original furniture, paintings, books and a piano owned by the Sibelius family.

SOUTH COAST

Nowhere in Finland are there so many historical monuments as along the southern coast between Turku and Hamina. This region is dotted with medieval churches, old manors and castles, and is strongly influenced by early Swedish settlers, particularly the area west of Helsinki.

The south coast is popular with Finnish families in summer, but few travellers explore this region beyond Turku. If you do, you'll find beaches, bays, slightly fading resort towns and the convoluted islands and waterways of the southern archipelago

The historic 'King's Road', from Turku to St Petersburg, passes through here.

TURKU

☎ 02 / pop 175,000

Once the capital under the Swedes, Turku (Swedish: Åbo) is Finland's oldest town.

Founded as a Catholic settlement in 1229, Turku grew into an important trading centre despite being ravaged by fire many times. These days it's a modern maritime city, brimming with museums and boasting a stunning harbourside castle and magnificent cathedral. Turku is defined by the Aurajoki river – in summer a highlight is wandering along the river banks, pausing for a drink in the boat bars and restaurants.

Daily ferries from Sweden (via the Åland islands) pull in to Turku, and it's an ideal base for cruising the southwestern archipelago.

Information

DISCOUNT CARDS

Turku Card (one/two days €21/28) Gives free admission to most museums and attractions in the region, free public transport, the Turku Sightseeing bus tour and various other discounts. Available from the tourist office or any participating attraction.

INTERNET ACCESS

Public Library (☎ 262 3611; Linnankatu 2; ♥ 10am-8pm Mon-Thu, 10am-6pm Fri, 10am-3pm Sat) Free Internet access.

Surf City (Aninkaistenkatu 3; per 30 min €2; ♥ 11am-7.30pm Mon-Fri, noon-7.30pm Sat, 1-7.30pm Sun)

MONEY

Forex (☎ 251 0800; Eerikinkatu 12; ♥ 8am-7pm Mon-Fri, 8am-5pm Sat) Exchange bureau opposite the *kauppatori*.

POST

Main Post Office (Humalistonkatu 1; ♥ 9am-8pm Mon-Fri)

TOURIST INFORMATION

Turku City Tourist Office (☎ 262 7444; www.turku touring.fi; Aurakatu 4; ♥ 8.30am-6pm Mon-Fri, 9am-4pm Sat & Sun) Internet access, bike hire, accommodation and information.

Sights & Activities

A great way to soak up Turku's summertime vibe is simply to walk or cycle along the river bank between the cathedral and the castle, crossing via bridges or the much-loved local pedestrian ferry (*föri*) – pick up a walking tour brochure from the tourist office.

Vocal locals are quick to claim that Turku has more museums than Helsinki, but only a handful of them stand out. The city's 50-odd museums are generally open daily in summer, closed on Monday in winter, and charge €3.40 admission.

A visit to the mammoth **Turku Castle** (☎ 262 0300; Linnankatu 80; adult/child €6.50/4.50, guided tours €1.50; ☾ 10am-6pm mid-Apr–mid-Sep, 10am-3pm Tue-Sun mid-Sep–mid-Apr), near the harbour, is a must. Founded in 1280 at the mouth of the Aura-joki, the castle has been growing ever since. Notable occupants have included Count Per Brahe, founder of many towns in Finland, and Sweden's King Eric XIV, who was imprisoned in the castle's Round Tower in the late 16th century, having been declared insane. Guided tours of the stronghold area are given in English hourly between 11am and 4pm, but do not include the Renaissance rooms on the upper floor, or the extensive museums in the bailey section of the castle, so allow time to explore those yourself.

The open-air **Luostarinmäki Handicrafts Museum** (☎ 262 0350; Luostarinmäki; adult/child €3.40/2.60, guided tours €1.60/1.40; ☾ 10am-6pm mid-Apr–mid-Sep, 10am-3pm Tue-Sun mid-Sep–mid-Apr), in the only surviving 18th-century area of this medieval town, is one of the best of its kind in Finland. In summer artisans work inside its 40 old wooden houses and musicians stroll its paths.

Forum Marinum (☎ 282 9511; Linnankatu 72; adult/child €10/5; ☾ 11am-7pm May-Sep, 10am-6pm Tue-Sun Oct-Apr) is an impressive maritime museum near Turku Castle. As well as a better-than-average exhibition space devoted to Turku's shipping background, it incorporates three **museum ships**: the mine layer *Keihässalmi*, the three-masted barque *Sigyn* and the impressive 1902 sailing ship *Suomen Joutsen* (Swan of Finland). The ships can be visited independently of the museum for €4/2.

The **Aboa Vetus** and **Ars Nova** (☎ 250 0552; Itäinen Rantakatu 4-6; adult/child €7/5, combined ticket €9.50/7; ☾ 11am-7pm May–mid-Sep, Tue-Sun mid-Sep–Apr), two museums under the one roof in the Rettig Palace, are respectively an archaeological exhibition and a modern art collection. The fascinating archaeological museum features a slice of medieval Turku – a section of buried streets and housing uncovered during restoration work.

The **Wäinö Aaltonen Museum** (☎ 262 0850; www.wam.fi; Itäinen Rantakatu 38; adult/student/child €3.50/2.50/2; ☾ 11am-7pm Tue-Sun), on the south side of the river, has permanent exhibitions of this important Finnish artist's sculptures

and paintings, plus changing exhibitions and concerts by local artists.

The commanding **Turku Cathedral** (☎ 261 7100; Tuomiokirkkokatu 20), dating from the 13th century, is the national shrine and 'mother church' of the Evangelical-Lutheran Church of Finland. Services are held here regularly and there's a **museum** (adult/child €2/1; ☾ 9am-7pm, to 8pm in summer) containing church relics and artworks.

Caribia (☎ 651 111; www.caribia.fi; Kongressikatu 1; adult/child €13/8; ☾ 10am-9pm Mon-Thu, 9am-10pm Sat, 9am-8pm Sun) is a fantasy spa resort located in a hotel about 2km northeast of town. The Caribbean-themed spa has water slides, a smoke sauna, eight pools and even a pirate ship. Great for kids or a day of pampering.

Archipelago cruises are popular in summer, with daily departures from Martinsilta bridge. The best option is the 1½-hour cruise out to Naantali aboard the steamship **SS Ukkopekka** (☎ 515 3300; www.ukkopekka.fi; one way/return €17/20; ☾ 10am & 2pm Jun-Aug).

In summer, the sauna boat **Bruno** has a bar and below-deck sauna (one hour €10).

Festivals & Events

Big events on the Turku calendar include the **Turku Music Festival** in the second week in August and **Ruisrock**, Finland's oldest rock festival, held on Ruissalo island in early July.

Sleeping
BUDGET

Ruissalo Camping (☎ 262 5100; camp sites €17, 2-/4-/5-person r €28/55/70; ☾ Jun–late Aug) Popular camping area on Ruissalo island, 10km west of the city centre. There are no cabins, but there is a villa and nice beaches. Take bus No 8 from the market square.

HI Hostel Turku (☎ 262 7680; hostel@turku.fi; Linnankatu 39; dm/s/d €13.80/33.30/37.60; ☾ reception 6-10am & 3pm-midnight) Well located on the river close to the town centre, this warren of rooms is one of the busiest hostels in Finland. Well-equipped kitchen, laundry (€2), lockers and bike hire. Breakfast is €4.50.

Interpoint Hostel (☎ 231 4011; Vähä-Hämeenkatu 12a; dm €8.50-10.50; ☾ 15 Jul–15 Aug) This is the cheapest place in Turku but for good reason – 30 mattresses on the floor and one shower!

MID-RANGE

Bed & Breakfast Tuure (☎ 233 0230; tuure@netti.fi; Tuureporinkatu 17C; s/d €37/50) Close to the bus

FINLAND

TURKU

INFORMATION	
Forex.............................1	E2
Nordea Bank.................2	E2
Post Office....................3	D2
Public Library................4	E2
Surf City Internet............5	E1
Turku City Tourist Office...6	E2

SIGHTS & ACTIVITIES	(pp148–9)
Aboa Vetus & Ars Nova....7	E2
Bruno (sauna boat)..........8	C3
Forum Marinum................9	B4
Kehhässalmi & Suomen Joutsen.........10	C4
Luostarinmäki Handicrafts Museum..........11	E2
Orthodox Church............12	D2
Sigyn...........................13	C4
Turku Castle & Historical Museum..........14	B4
Turku Cathedral..............15	E2
Wäinö Aaltonen Museum...16	D3

SLEEPING	(pp149–51)
Bed & Breakfast Tuure......17	D1
Bridgettine Sisters Guesthouse.............18	D2
Hostel Turku..................19	D3
Hotel Julia....................20	E2
Interpoint Hostel.............21	F2
Park Hotel....................22	D1

EATING	(p151)
Baan Thai.....................23	D1
Bossa..........................24	D1
Café Noir......................25	E2
China Garden................(see 43)
Kahvila Paavo................26	E2
Kauppahalli...................27	E2
Panimoravintola Koulu......28	D2
Pizzeria Dennis..............29	D2
Ribs............................30	D2
Sergio's........................31	D2
Teini...........................32	F2
Turku University Cafeteria..33	F2
Vaakahuonen Paviljonki....34	D3
Viking Restaurant Harald...(see 37)

DRINKING	(pp151–2)
Blanko.........................35	E2
Galax..........................36	E2
Old Bank......................37	E2
Puutorin Vessa...............38	E1
Riverside Bar.................39	E2
Uusi Apteeki.................40	D3

ENTERTAINMENT	(pp151–2)
Concert Hall..................41	E1
Kino Palatsi Cinema.........42	E1
Sokeri Klubi..................(see 37)

SHOPPING	(p151)
Hansa Shopping Arcade....43	D2

TRANSPORT	(p152)
Airport Buses................44	E2
Bus Terminal.................45	E1
Naantali Buses...............46	E2
Passenger Quay..............47	D3
Rent A Bike...................48	E2
Seawind.......................49	A4
Silja & Viking Line...........(see 43)
Silja Line......................50	A4
Viking Line....................51	A4

0   600 m
0   0.4 miles

terminal, this is a secure, friendly guesthouse. Clean, bright rooms have shared bath.

Bridgettine Sisters Guesthouse (☎ 250 1910; Ursininkatu 15A; s/d €42/61) Clean, simple B&B guesthouse run by the nuns of a Catholic convent. It's very peaceful – silence is expected around the corridors and reception areas after 10pm. Book ahead.

TOP END

Park Hotel (☎ 273 2555; www.parkhotelturku.fi; Rauhankatu 1; s/d €110/135, s/d discount €85/110) In a lovely Art Nouveau building dating from 1904, this is Turku's most romantic hotel. Rooms are individually decorated and all have character.

Scandic Hotel Julia (☎ 336 000; Eerikinkatu 4; s/d €90/113, s/d discount €63/73) One of Turku's top hotels, the central Julia has business-hotel facilities, including a sauna.

Eating

There are plenty of cheap eateries on and around Turku's bustling *kauppatori*. The Hansa Shopping Arcade on the west side of the square has some inexpensive lunch restaurants, including China Garden (mains from €6), as well as a supermarket and Alko store. The **kauppahalli** (Eerikinkatu 16; ☉ Mon-Sat) is packed with produce, meat, a sushi bar and cafés.

It's usually possible to get breakfast or lunch (under €5) at the Turku University cafeteria on Hämeenkatu.

Kahvila Paavo is a popular summer kiosk on the river bank (near Auransilta bridge) serving up hot dogs, grills and coffee.

Café Noir (Eerikinkatu; mains €5.70-10.60) This unpretentious first-floor café is one of Turku's cheapest for à la carte pasta and light meals such as chicken curry and omelettes.

Pizzeria Dennis (☎ 469 1191; Linnankatu 17; dishes €8-12) With its warren of cosy rooms adorned with chianti bottles and strings of garlic, this place has genuine Italian flavour and is a cut above most typical Finnish pizza and pasta restaurants.

Sergio's (☎ 233 0068; Läntinen Rantakatu 27; mains €8-12; ☉ 11am-11pm Tue-Sat, 1-8pm Sun) Great-value riverfront Italian restaurant serving pasta, pizza and Italian wines.

Ribs (☎ 251 7557; Itäinen Rantakatu 2; mains €15-25; ☉ 3pm-midnight Mon-Fri, noon-midnight Sat & Sun) Trendy steakhouse with a great summer terrace outside and a warm, stone dining area

and bar inside; the speciality is ribs, steaks and wings which are pricey but filling.

Teini (☎ 233 0203; Uudenmaankatu 1; mains €10-20; ☉ lunch & dinner) For traditional Finnish cuisine, including vegetarian dishes, Teini is a local institution that comes with an array of dining rooms and a fantastic underground bar at the rear.

Vaakahuoneen Paviljonki (☎ 515 3300; Linnankatu 38; mains €7-15, fish buffet €8; ☉ dawn-dusk May-Aug) Riverfront jazz restaurant and the place to go for great-value food and entertainment. As well as an à la carte menu of snacks, pasta, pizzas and steak, there's a daily 'archipelago fish buffet' (11am to 10pm from June to August only), plus a changing buffet of Thai, Vietnamese and Indian etc.

Panimoravintola Koulu (☎ 274 575; Eerikinkatu 18; lunch buffet €5.50-7.70; mains €10.20-16; ☉ 11am-midnight Mon-Fri, noon-midnight Sat) In this enormous former schoolhouse built in 1889 is an upmarket restaurant, a brewery pub, beer garden and wine bar serving good lunches.

Viking Restaurant Harald (☎ 276 5050; Aurakatu 3; mains €11-21; ☉ 11am-midnight Mon-Thu, 11am-1am Fri, noon-1am Sat, 1-9pm Sun) Theme restaurant where you get to mix with Norse warriors and eat with your hands. There are three-course set meals from €24.

Baan Thai (☎ 233 8290; Kauppiaskatu 15; mains €7-13, lunch from €5.50; ☉ 11am-9pm Mon-Thu, 11am-10pm Fri & Sat, noon-9pm Sun) Authentic and intimate Thai restaurant with great-value lunch specials.

Bossa (☎ 251 5880; Kauppiaskatu 12; mains €13-24; ☉ lunch & dinner, to 2am Fri & Sat) Probably the only Brazilian restaurant in Finland. It's an intimate place with live Latin music most nights.

Drinking & Entertainment

In summer the heart of Turku's nightlife scene is along the river. The evening usually begins on the decks of any of half a dozen boats lining the south bank of the river. Although some of these also serve food, they are primarily floating beer terraces with music and lots of shipboard socialising.

Hard-up locals gather on the grassy river bank drinking takeaway alcohol. Nearby, the Riverside Bar is a good spot with street dancing on Tuesday nights in summer.

Blanko (☎ 233 3966; Aurakatu 1) Opposite the tourist office this ultra-chic café is where Turku's hip young things get down to DJs on weekend nights; great sidewalk terrace and excellent tapas.

Turku also has some wonderfully eccentric bars.

Puutorin Vessa (☎ 233 8123; Puutori; ☺ noon-midnight) In the middle of a small square near the bus terminal, this novel bar was a public toilet from 1933 to 1968! Toilet memorabilia adorns the walls and you can even have your drink in a tin potty.

Uusi Apteeki (☎ 250 2595; Kaskenkatu 1; ☺ 10-3am) Wonderful bar in a converted old pharmacy; the antique shelving and desks have been retained, but they are filled with hundreds of old beer bottles.

Galax (☎ 284 3300; Aurakatu 6; ☺ 9pm-4am) One of Turku's biggest entertainment venues and right in the thick of things, Galax is a modern club on several levels with live music or DJs on most nights.

Sokeri Klubi (☎ 276 5700; Aurakatu 3; ☺ 10am-4am) Across the street, the 'Sugar Club' is popular with a young crowd. Turku's best young DJs and the place to be seen in the wee hours.

Panimonravintola Koulu (p151) is a brewery-pub in a former schoolhouse. Creamy stout on tap and a big beer garden. **Ribs** (p151) has live music free every Wednesday and Thursday in summer, and there's live jazz most days at **Vaakahuoneen Paviljonki** (p151).

Getting There & Away

Finnair flies regularly from Stockholm and Helsinki to the Turku airport, 8km north of the city.

From the main bus terminal at Aninkaistentulli there are hourly express buses to Helsinki (€22.30, 2½ hours), and frequent services to Tampere (€18.20, two hours), Rauma (€11.90, 1½ hours) and other points in southern Finland.

Express trains run to and from Helsinki (€22.40, two hours) and Tampere (€16.60, 1¾ hours). For Oulu and Rovaniemi you'll need to change in Tampere. There are direct train connections from Turku harbour to Helsinki. Bus No 30 shuttles between the centre and the train station.

Silja Line and Viking Line ferries sail from Stockholm (9½ hours) and Mariehamn (six hours). Seawind Line sails to Stockholm via Långnäs (Åland). All three have offices at the harbour, and Viking Line has an office in the Hansa shopping arcade.

From late May to the end of August, MS *Franz Höjer* sails to Uusikaupunki on Friday at 10am (€12, eight hours) and Hanko on Wednesday at 10am (€12, eight hours).

Getting Around

Bus No 1 runs to/from the airport and between the centre (€2, 25 minutes). This same bus also goes from the market square to the harbour.

The city and regional bus services (both gold and blue buses) are frequent and cost €2 for a single journey or €4.50 for a 24-hour ticket.

Bikes can be hired from **Rent-A-Bike** (☎ 041-5123430; Läntinen Rantakatu 10; 2/24hr €5/8; ☺ 9am-3pm Jun-Aug), on the river just around the corner from the tourist office, or from the tourist office itself.

AROUND TURKU
Naantali

☎ 02 / pop 12,500

Naantali, 13km from Turku, is one of Finland's loveliest seaside towns, but that can sometimes be lost on the hordes of Finnish families descending on the star attraction, the extraordinarily popular **Moomin World theme park** (☎ 511 1111; day pass €13; ☺ 10am-6pm Jun-mid-Aug). It's a sort of Disneyland based on the popular children's books written by Tove Janssen and set on an island linked to the mainland by a footbridge.

The village was developed after the founding of a convent in the 1440s and today the harbour, lined with cafés and restaurants, the delightful cobbled **Old Town** and the huge **Convent Church** are enough incentive for a day trip here from Turku. Tourist information is available at **Naantali Tourist Service** (☎ 435 9800; Kaivotori 2; ☺ 9am-6pm Mon-Fri, 10am-3pm Sat & Sun Jun-mid-Aug, 9am-4.30pm Mon-Fri mid-Aug-May) near the harbour.

Kulturanta (adult/child €8/4; ☺ guided tour 3pm Tue-Sun 29 Jun-15 Aug), the summer residence of the president of Finland, is a fanciful stone castle on nearby Luonnonmaa island, surrounded by a 56ha estate with beautiful, extensive rose gardens. It can only be visited by guided tour; book through the tourist office.

SLEEPING & EATING

Although an easy day trip from Turku, spending a night in Naantali is a good way to beat the crowds and the town has some lovely guesthouses. There are also some great restaurants curving around the harbour, plus a couple of good cafés in the Old Town.

Stora Kotelli (☎ 435 1419; Luostarinkatu 13; s/d €55/60) This early-19th-century villa is beautifully kept and furnished. Breakfast (€5) is served in the stylish dining room.

Merisali (☎ 435 2477; Nunnakatu 1; buffet breakfast/lunch/dinner €6.50/9/11, Sun lunch €13) Just below the Convent Church, this popular restaurant has a shaded terrace and a mind-blowing smorgasbord for lunch and dinner – pack an appetite!

Cafe Antonius (☎ 435 1938; Mannerheiminkatu 9) Lovely old-world café with home-made gingerbread and other mouthwatering sweets.

GETTING THERE & AWAY
There are buses every 15 minutes from Turku (€3.60, 20 minutes), and in summer the steamship *Ukkopekka* cruises between Turku and Naantali several times daily (see p148).

HANKO
☎ 019 / pop 10,600
Hanko (Hangö) is the pick of southern Finland's summer resorts. The town blossomed as a spa resort in the late 19th and early 20th centuries, when it was a glamorous summer retreat for Russian nobles and artists. These cashed-up holidaymakers built grand wooden villas on the sandy shore east of the harbour. Some of these villas are now charming guesthouses.

Hanko Camping Silversand (☎ 248 5500; Hopeahietikko; camp sites €14.50, cabins €42-69; ☼ Jun–mid-Aug), on a stretch of beach 4km from town, has the usual sauna and cabins.

Villa Tellina (☎ 248 6356; www.tellina.com, no English; Appelgrenintie 1-2; s/d from €46/70; ☼ Jun–mid-Aug) is a quaint but slightly ramshackle villa close to the beach. The same owners run two other places, Villa Thalatta and Villa Eva, so this is a good first choice when it's busy.

Villa Doris (☎ 248 1228; Appelgrenintie 23; s/d from €50/72) and **Villa Maija** (☎ 248 2900; www.villamaija.com; Appelgrenintie7; s/d from €76/96), both open year-round, are among the stylish B&B villas in the area known as the spa park. The older rooms have shared bath and loads of Imperial character, while newer rooms have bathrooms.

Across from the East Harbour is a string of excellent restaurant-bars in converted wooden storehouses, most specialising in seafood, but also pizza and pasta. Try **Origo** (☎ 248 5023; www.restaurant-origo.com; ☼ 11am-11pm, bar to 3am mid-Apr–Sep) for candlelit fine dining or an archipelago fish buffet. There's also a music bar and dance club on the second floor.

In the spa park, Park Cafe is an excellent little Belgian café-bar.

There are regular daily buses to/from Helsinki (€19, 2¼ hours) and a summer ferry between Hanko and Turku (see left).

TAMMISAARI
☎ 019 / pop 14,700
The seaside town of Tammisaari (Ekenäs), 96km southwest of Helsinki, is one of Finland's oldest. In 1516 King Gustav Vasa intended it to be a trading port to rival Tallinn in Estonia; the idea failed and he shifted the project to Helsinki, but the attractive Gamla Stan (Old Town) still stands. Free walking tours are offered by the **tourist office** (☎ 263 2212) in summer. Although a popular family resort, Tammisaari is not as quaint as Hanko, further down the coast.

Nearby is the region's most impressive sight, the 14th-century **Raseborg castle ruins** (☎ 234015; adult/child €1/0.50; ☼ 10am-8pm May-Sep), 15km east of Tammisaari, and about 2km from the village of Snappertuna.

Ekenäs Vandrarhem (☎ 241 6393; Höijerintie 10; dm/s/d from €10/20/24; ☼ mid-May–mid-Aug) is a HI-affiliated summer hostel with tidy, modern apartment-style rooms (four rooms share a kitchen and bathroom). It's about 1km east of the harbour.

There are frequent daily bus and train (change at Karis) services from Turku and Helsinki running to Tammisaari, and continuing to Hanko.

EAST OF HELSINKI
The coast east of Helsinki is popular with Finnish families in summer but not often visited by foreign travellers, except those passing through on the way to St Petersburg. Once past Porvoo, the coastal highway passes through the small resort of Loviisa, the industrial maritime port of Kotka and the former garrison town of Hamina before crossing the border into Russia.

If you have time on your hands, this route makes a scenic alternative on the road to Lappeenranta; otherwise skip it.

Ruotsinpyhtä

☎ 019 / pop 3200

This tiny but impossibly picturesque village just off highway E18 is worth a stop. At its heart are the quaint brick buildings of the 18th-century *bruk*, the **Strömfors Iron Works**, which is now a museum. The Kyma river became the Swedish–Russian international border in 1743, splitting the village in half.

At the café in the old forge building in the centre of the village is the **information centre** (☎ 618 474; ⏰ 10am-6pm Jun-Aug, 8am-4pm Sep-May).

Finnhostel Krouvinmäki (☎ 618 474; s/d €23/45.50; ⏰ reception 8am-4pm) is a wonderful hostel in a renovated former tavern house (1805) opposite the forge. It has cosy twin rooms (no bunks) and there's a good kitchen and laundry.

Ravintola Ruukinmylly (☎ 618 693; pizza & pasta €4-7, mains €10-15; ⏰ summer), in a 17th-century former mill on a lovely quiet pond, is a rustic restaurant with wood-fired pizzas and some Finnish specialities, including creamy salmon soup. The terrace is a great spot to take in the view of the village.

HAMINA

☎ 05 / pop 10,000

Just 40km west of the Russian border, the small town of Hamina is surrounded by crumbling **fortifications**, begun by panicky Swedes in 1722 after they lost Vyborg to Russia (the wall wasn't paranoia: shortly after it was built, in marched the Russians). There's not a lot left of the fortress, but Hamina's unusual octagonal town plan, several museums and lively harbour scene provide enough interest if you're taking the coastal route towards Karelia.

The **main tourist office** (☎ 749 2641; www.hamina.fi; Raatihuoneentori 16; ⏰ 9am-4pm Mon-Fri) is on the central ring in Old Hamina, but there's a **summer office** (☎ 749 2643; ⏰ 9am-6pm Mon-Fri, 10am-3pm Sat & Sun Jun-Aug) in the Lipputorni (Flagtower) at the *kauppatori*.

SS Hyöky (☎ 040-763 3757; s/d €30/40) is an off-beat place to stay in summer. Moored in Tervasaari harbour, the historic steamship has nine tiny cabins, each with a set of bunks, plus the 'captain's cabin' above deck. The ship also has a bar, a cluttered museum and even a tiny sauna (free for guests).

There are several places to eat around the *kauppatori* and down at the harbour. **Kondi-**toria A Huoviola (☎ 344 0930; Fredrinkatu 1; ⏰ 8am-5pm Mon-Fri, 8am-2pm Sat & Sun) is a gorgeous cellar café in an old wooden house just off the town hall square.

Frequent regular and express buses run to Helsinki (€21.50, three hours) and Kotka. There are daily buses to Russia (visa required): four to Vyborg (€22, 3½ hours) and at least two to St Petersburg (€32, 6½ hours).

ÅLAND

☎ 018 / pop 26,300

An easy stop on the ferry between Sweden and Finland, the Åland islands are a slightly schizophrenic municipality with a stunning archipelago stretching like a string of emeralds all the way to the mainland. The autonomous, self-governed islands have their own flag, stamps and culture, which leans more to Sweden than to Finland – several Swedish dialects are spoken but few Ålanders speak Finnish. This situation goes back to a League of Nations' decision in 1921 after a Swedish–Finnish dispute over sovereignty. Åland took its own flag in 1954 and has issued stamps (prized by collectors) since 1984.

In summer the beauty of Åland is in the cycling and camping – the flat, picturesque islands are connected by bridges or free ferries, and along the way you'll pass medieval parish churches, ancient ruins and undisturbed fishing villages. Midsummer celebrations here are among the best in Finland.

Although Åland joined the EU along with Finland in 1995, it was granted a number of exemptions, including duty-free tax laws which allowed the essential ferry services between the islands and mainland Finland and Sweden to continue operating profitably.

Information

The main tourist office is **Åland Tourist Information** (☎ 24000; www.visitaland.com; Storagatan 8) in Mariehamn, and there are smaller offices at the ferry terminal in Eckerö and at Godby. For accommodation bookings, **Ålandsresor** (☎ 28040; www.alandsresor.fi; Torggatan 2) and **Destination Aland** (☎ 0403-008001; www.destinationaland.com; Elverksgatan 5) in Mariehamn handle hotel, guesthouse and cottage bookings for the entire island and are the best way to secure accommodation. Viking Line and Eckerö Line also make bookings.

FINLAND

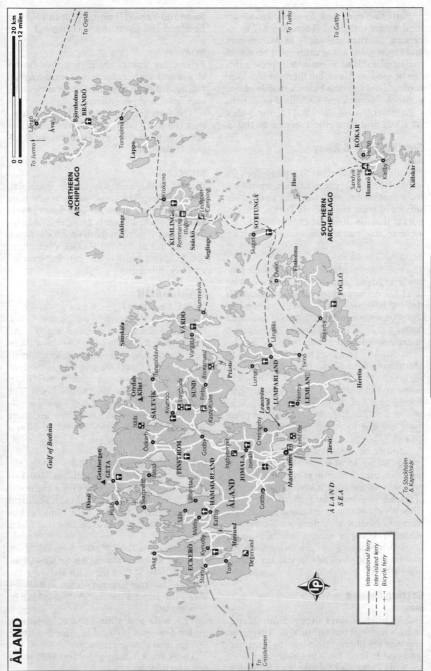

ÅLAND

FINLAND

0	20 km
0	12 miles

Gulf of Bothnia

ÅLAND SEA

NORTHERN ARCHIPELAGO

SOUTHERN ARCHIPELAGO

To Jurmo
To Osnäs
To Turku
To Gåttby

Långö
Åva
Björnholma
BRANDÖ
Torsholma
Lappo
KÖKAR
Hellsö
Kättby
Källskär
Sandvik Camping
Hamnö

Enklinge
KUMLINGE
Krokarno
Lednäsund Camping
Renmanns stugor
Snäckö
Seglinge
Skaget
SOTTUNGA
Husö
FÖGLÖ
Överö
Finnholma
Degerby
Herrön
Svinö
Järsö
To Stockholm & Kapellskär

Simskäla
Tungsödavik
VÅRDÖ
Vargata
Bomarsund
Prästö
Kastelholm
SUND
Kvarnbo
Borgbocda
Orrdals Klint
SALTVIK
Näs
Ödkarby
FINSTRÖM
Godby
Ingby
Jomala
JOMALA
Lumparland
LUMPARLAND
Lemböte
LEMLAND
Norrby
Långnäs
Lumpo
Lemström Canal
Önningeby
Mariehamn
Gottby
HAMMARLAND
Kattby
Mörby
Sälis
Marsund
Skarpnåtö
Dånö
Pålö
Bättö
Ulfsbyoda
GETA
Getabergen
ECKERÖ
Storby
Kyrkoby
Torp
Degersand
Skag

To Grisslehamn

– – –	International ferry
———	Inter-island ferry
+ + +	Bicycle ferry

Both the euro and Swedish krona are legal tender on Åland. There are ATMs accepting international cards in Mariehamn, and credit cards are as easily used here as in mainland Finland. Finnish telephone cards can be used on Åland, but there are also local cards. Åland uses the Finnish mobile phone network – Sonera and Radiolinja work here.

In emergencies call ☎ 112, for police ☎ 10022 and for medical service ☎ 10023.

Getting There & Away

AIR

Finnair has an office at Skarpansvägen 24 in Mariehamn. There is a direct service to/from Stockholm every weekday and a daily service to/from Helsinki via Turku. The airport is 4km north of Mariehamn and there's a connecting bus service.

BOAT

The main companies operating between Finland and Åland (and on to Sweden) are **Viking Line** (☎ 26011; www.vikingline.fi; Storagatan 2) and **Silja Line** (☎ 16711; www.silja.fi; Torggatan 14). **Eckerö Line** (☎ 28000; www.eckerolinjen.fi; Torggatan 2) and **Birka Cruises** (☎ 27027; www.birkaline.com; Esplanadgatan 7) operate only between Åland and Sweden.

Viking and Silja lines have daily ferries to Mariehamn from Turku (from €14 one way, six hours) as part of their links with Stockholm: you can stop off 'between' countries. Eckerö Line sails from Grisslehamn to Eckerö, and is the cheapest and quickest route from Sweden to Åland (from €5.50, three hours).

Another alternative if you have the time is the smaller local ferries that ply the waters from minor Finnish ports to the remote northern and southern archipelago islands of Åland. Free travel for pedestrians and cyclists is possible from mainland Finland via Korppoo (southern route, from Galtby passenger harbour) or Kustavi (northern route, from Osnäs passenger harbour), but only if you break your journey to stay on one or more islands.

Getting Around

BUS

Five main bus lines depart from Mariehamn's regional bus terminal on Torggatan opposite the library. No 1 goes to Hammarland and Eckerö; No 2 to Godby and Geta; No 3 to Godby and Saltvik; No 4 to Godby, Sund and Vårdö (Hummelvik); and No 5 to Lemland and Lumparland (Långnäs).

BOAT

Ferries are constantly plying the shorter straits and are free. For longer routes, ferries run according to schedule. These ferries take cars, bikes and pedestrians.

There are also three bicycle ferries in summer (€6 to €9 with bicycle). For timetables ask at the tourist office or **Ålandstrafiken** (Strandgatan 25, Mariehamn).

BICYCLE

Bicycle is the best way to see these flat, rural islands. The most scenic roads have clearly marked separate bike lanes. **Ro-No Rent** (☎ 018-12 820) rents bicycles at Mariehamn and Eckerö harbours for a day/week starting from €7/35 (€13/65 for a mountain bike). It also rents boats, canoes, scooters and beach buggies.

MARIEHAMN

☎ 018 / pop 11,000

Mariehamn, the 'town of a thousand linden trees', is Åland's main port and largest town. In summer it becomes the town of a thousand tourists but still manages to retain its village flavour, and the marinas at the East and West harbours are quite pretty when loaded up with gleaming sailing boats. The main pedestrian street, Torggatan, is a colourful and crowded hive of activity, and there are some fine museums – enough to allow a leisurely day's exploration.

Orientation & Information

The town lies on a peninsula and has two harbours, Västra Hamnen (West Harbour) and Östra Hamnen (East Harbour). The main ferry terminals are at Västra Hamnen but the more colourful local marina is at Östra Hamnen.

The **tourist office** (☎ 24000; www.visitaland.com; Storagatan 8; ☿ 9am-6pm Jun-Aug, 9am-4pm Mon-Fri, 10am-3pm Sat Sep-May; ▣), on the main east–west Esplanade, has free Internet access, as does the **library** (☎ 531 441; Strandgatan; ☿ 10am-8pm Mon-Fri, 11am-4pm Sat).

The **main post office** (☎ 6360; Torggatan 4; ☿ Mon-Sat) sells collectible Åland postage stamps and changes money.

There are left-luggage lockers (€2) at the ferry terminals.

Sights & Activities

The stalwarts of Åland are mariners. The **Maritime Museum** (☎ 19930; Västra Hamnen; adult/child €4.50/2.50; ⏰ 9am-5pm May-Jun & Aug, 9am-7pm Jul, 10am-4pm Sep-Apr) is a wonderfully kitsch museum of fishing and maritime commerce. Outside is the museum ship **Pommern** (adult/child €4.50/2.50), a beautifully preserved four-masted barque built in Glasgow in 1903. A combined ticket to both is €7/4.

The fine **Ålands Museum & Åland Art Museum** (☎ 25426; Stadhusparken; adult/child €2.50/1.70; ⏰ 10am-4pm Wed-Mon, 10am-7pm Tue Jun-Aug, 10am-4pm Tue-Sun Sep-May), housed in the same building, gives an absorbing account of Åland's history and culture, from prehistory to the present.

If you want to get out on the water in style, the traditional wooden schooner **Linden** (☎ 12055) has four-hour lunch (€35) and dinner (€49) cruises daily except Sunday in July, as well as charter cruises.

Sleeping & Eating

In a beachside park 1km south of town, **Gröna Uddens Camping** (☎ 21121; Osternäsvägen; camp sites €17.50; ⏰ mid-May–Aug) is the closest camping ground to Mariehamn, with tent and van sites but no cabins.

In the absence of any hostels, the next cheapest accommodation is at the two guesthouses on Neptunigatan. **Gästhem Kronan** (☎ 12617; Neptunigatan 52; s/d €31/52; ⏰ Jun-Aug; Ⓟ ✗) has basic but cleanish rooms with a shared bathroom, and the owners also have another guesthouse, **Gästhem Neptun** (s/d €41/62) up the road if Kronan is full.

There are plenty of hotels in Mariehamn. **Hotel Esplanad** (☎ 16444; Storogatan 5; s/d €55/68; ⏰ Jun-Aug) has rooms (with TV and private bathroom) that aren't special but it's friendly and central.

Park Alandia Hotel (☎ 14130; Norra Esplanadgatan 3; s/d €75/95) is a small, comfortable hotel on Mariehamn's main boulevard. Excellent café and terrace bar.

Mariehamn has some good cafés and the most active nightlife on the islands. The pedestrian strip Torggatan and the Galleria shopping arcade running off it have several cafés and cheap lunch eateries.

Cafe Julius (Torggatan 10; ⏰ from 8am) has sandwiches, pastries and snacks, and you can sample the local speciality, Åland pancakes, made with semolina and served with fruit and whipped cream. **Kaffestugan Svarta Kat-**

ten (Norragatan 15) is an old-world café and another good choice for Åland pancakes.

Dino's Bar & Grill (☎ Strandgatan 12; mains €8-15) is a popular meeting spot with pasta and pizza, enormous hamburgers and a brilliant summer terrace.

The boat restaurant **FP von Knorring** (Östra Hamnen) has a great beer terrace for sunny afternoons.

SUND

☎ 018 / pop 950

Åland's most striking attraction is the medieval 14th-century **Kastelholm** (☎ 432 150; adult/child €5/3.50; ⏰ 10am-4pm Jun & Aug, 10am-7pm July, 10am-4pm Mon-Fri May), 20km northeast of Mariehamn. You can only visit the castle on a guided tour, run frequently (in English) from June to August. Next to the castle, **Jan Karlsgarden Museum** (admission free; ⏰ 10am-5pm Jun-Aug) is a typical open-air museum consisting of about 20 wooden buildings, including three windmills, transported here from around the archipelago.

Further east, the ruins of the Russian fortress at Bomarsund are accessible all year, as are the cemeteries on Prästö island. The impressive Russian fortifications date from the 1830s and were destroyed during the Crimean War (1853–56). Near Bomarsund is **Puttes Camping** (☎ 44016; camping per person €2.50, cabins €27; ⏰ May-Aug), with a beach sauna, minigolf and cabins.

ECKERÖ

☎ 018 / pop 800

Finland's westernmost municipality, Eckerö can be like a little Sweden in summer, packed with holidaying Swedish families. The ferry terminal is at Storby village, and its historic **Mail & Customs House** (☎ 38689; ⏰ 10am-4pm May-Jun, 10am-6pm Jul–mid-Aug, 10am-4pm mid-Aug–Sep) now houses a café, post office and bank. The museum here tells the story of the treacherous archipelago 'mail route' that linked Sweden and Finland. Bus No 1 runs to Mariehamn.

East from Storby on the road to Mariehamn, the medieval Eckerö Church has some beautiful interior paintings.

If you're camping, head for **Käringsund Camping** (☎ 38309; Storby; camp sites €9, 3-/4-person cabins €33/44; ⏰ mid-May–Aug). **Storby Logi** (☎ 38469; per person €25) is a simple but cheap guesthouse right in the village.

EASTERN ARCHIPELAGO ROUTES

To the north you can travel through Vårdö, Kumlinge, Lappo, Brändö, Jurmo and further east to Turku by bicycle or bus and ferry (free for bicycles and pedestrians). Take bus No 4 from Mariehamn to Hummelvik harbour on Vårdö island. From Turku, take a bus to Kustavi, and on to Vartsala island to reach the harbour of Osnäs (Vuosnainen).

To the south, it's an easier trip via Föglö, Sottunga and Kökar islands to the mainland. Kökar island is the most quaint, with hiking trails, a 14th-century abbey and an 18th-century church. From Mariehamn, take bus No 5 to Långnäs harbour. On the mainland ferries depart from Galtby harbour on Korppoo island, 75km from Turku (take the Saaristotie bus from Turku).

SOUTHWESTERN FINLAND

TAMPERE

☎ 03 / pop 199,800

Tampere really grows on you. Wedged between lakes Näsijärvi and Pyhäjärvi, this 19th-century manufacturing centre was known for its powerful textile industry. Dozens of red-brick chimneys from former factories still point skyward, but most have now been transformed into superb cultural centres, bars or restaurants. Long known as the 'Manchester of Finland', on a grey day Tampere takes on a sort of Dickensian quality, with steam rising in the air like industrial fog. But don't be put off: Tampere works beautifully, combining working-class energy with Finnish sophistication.

For travellers, Tampere has some quirky museums, a dynamic cultural scene and Finland's best nightlife outside Helsinki.

Information

BOOKSHOPS

Akateeminen Kirjakauppa (☎ 248 0300; Hämeenkatu 6; ⏰ 9am-9pm Mon-Fri, 9am-6pm Sat, noon-8pm Sun) English-language books, maps and newspapers.

INTERNET ACCESS

Main Library Metso (☎ 314 614; Pirkankatu 2; ⏰ 9.30am-8pm Mon-Fri, 9.30am-3pm Sat, noon-6pm Sun, closed Sun winter) Free Internet access in main library and on 1st floor.

Vuoltsu Internet Cafe (☎ 3146 4899; Vuolteenkatu 13; per hr €1.70; ⏰ 2-8pm Mon-Fri, noon-6pm Sat & Sun) Youth centre with an Internet café near bus station.

MONEY

Forex (Hämeenkatu 14B; ⏰ 9am-7pm Mon-Fri, 9am-3pm Sat)

TOURIST INFORMATION

Tampere City Tourist Office (☎ 3146 6800; www .tampere.fi; Verkatehtaankatu 2; ⏰ 8.30am-8pm Mon-Fri, 10am-5pm Sat & Sun Jun-Aug, 9am-4pm Mon-Fri Sep-May; 🖳) Just off Hämeenkatu in the city centre, the busy tourist office has two free Internet terminals and can help out with accommodation.

Sights & Activities

A walk along the banks of the Tammerkoski rapids gives a good feel for Tampere's industrial past – check out the renovated **Finlayson Mill** (Satakunnankatu 18) which houses restaurants, bars, a cinema and the offbeat **Spy Museum** (☎ 212 3007; adult/child €7/5; ⏰ noon-6pm Mon-Fri, 10am-4pm Sat & Sun), which explores the world of espionage with a fascinating collection of James Bond-type toys, KGB documents and a lie-detector machine.

Vapriiki Museum Centre (☎ 3146 6966; Veturiaukio 4; adult/child €8/3; ⏰ 10am-6pm Tue & Thu-Sun, 11am-8pm Wed) is Tampere's premier exhibition space, in a renovated Tampella mill factory building. Also here is the **Ice Hockey Museum**, a small display dedicated to Finland's winter passion with photos, jerseys, sticks and pucks galore.

Don't miss the tiny **Lenin Museum** (☎ 276 8100; Hämeenpuisto 28; adult/child €4/2; ⏰ 9am-6pm Mon-Fri, 11am-4pm Sat & Sun) which gives a fascinating insight into the life and work of the Russian revolutionary leader who spent some time drumming up support in Tampere; there's a zany gift shop.

In the basement of the public library, **Moominvalley** (☎ 3146 6578; Hämeenpuisto 20; adult/child €4/1; ⏰ 9am-5pm Mon-Fri, 10am-5pm Sat & Sun) is a whimsical exhibition based on the children's books of Tove Jansson. It features original drawings and tableaux models from the world of moomintrolls – a Finnish cultural phenomenon. In the same building the small **Mineral Museum** is devoted to rocks and gemstones and has the same hours and admission as Moominvalley, but not the same crowds.

Särkänniemi amusement park (☎ 248 8111; www.sarkanniemi.fi; adult/child pass €27/16; entry-only €4;

TAMPERE

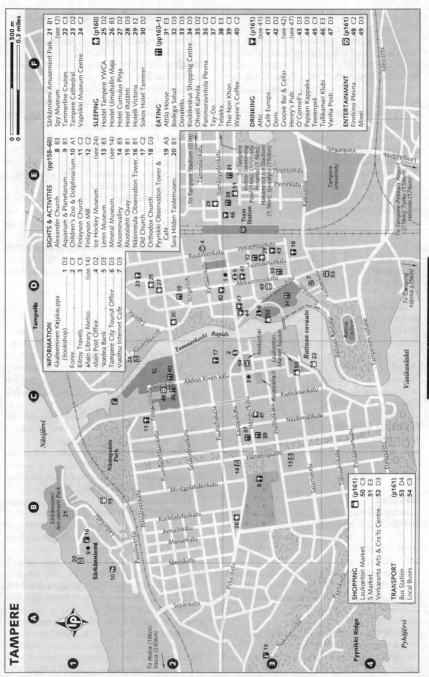

☿ summer) is great for kids – it boasts carnival rides, an aquarium, a children's zoo, a planetarium and the Dolphinarium. A pass gives unlimited rides, or you can pay as you go (€3.50 per attraction). The park's 168m **Näsinneula Observation Tower** (€3.50) is the tallest in Finland and has a rotating restaurant at the top.

The **Sara Hilden Taidemuseo** (☎ 3144 3500; Särkänniemi; adult/child €5/3; ☿ 11am-6pm), at the amusement park, displays changing exhibitions of modern and Finnish art and sculpture.

Tampere Cathedral (Tuomiokirkonkatu; ☿ 9am-6pm), built in the National Romantic style, features the weird frescoes of Hugo Simberg. There is a small but beautifully ornate **Orthodox church** (☿ 9.30am-3pm Mon-Fri May-Aug) south of the train station area.

Pyynikki Ridge, rising between the two lakes, is a forested area of walking trails with fine views on both sides. There's an **observation tower** (adult/child €1/0.50; ☿ 9am-8pm) on the ridge, which also has a great café serving Tampere's best doughnuts.

Lake cruises are popular in summer; **Tammerlines** (☎ 254 2500; www.tammerline.fi; adult/child from €9/2; noon-1.30pm Mon & Fri Jun-Aug) has cruises from Laukontori quay. There are also summer cruises every hour to **Viikinsaari island** (adult/child €6/2, 25 minutes, Tuesday-Sunday). SS *Tarjanne*, a steam ship, departs from Mustalahti quay for longer trips on the 'Poet's Way' to Virrat.

Festivals & Events

Tammerfest in mid-July is a big weekend of rock music with the main concert venue at the Ratina Stadium, and plenty of smaller gigs around town.

Sleeping

Camping Härmälä (☎ 265 1355; Leirintäkatu 8; camp sites €19.50, 3–5-person cabins €29-65) Beautifully located camping ground 5km south of the centre (bus No 1). There are lakeside saunas and rowing boats.

Hostel Tampere YWCA (☎ 254 4020; Tuomiokirkonkatu 12A; dm/s/d €13.50/31/44; ☿ Jun–late Aug; ✗) About 300m north of the train station, this summer hostel is simple and clean, with kitchen and laundry facilities.

Hostel Uimahallin Maja (☎ 222 9460; www.hosteltampere.com; Pirkankatu 10-12; dm/s/d €19.50/37/52) Although further from the action, this is a good choice, with a great 1st-floor café, friendly

staff and tidy rooms with linen included. The local swimming pool is next door.

Hotel Iltatähti (☎ 315 161; www.hoteliltatahti.fi; Tuomiokirkonkatu 19; s/d/tr €40/50/55, s/d/tr with private bathroom €55/60/73; ☿ reception 9am-7pm Mon-Fri, noon-6pm Sat & Sun; ✗) A stone's throw from the train station, this unassuming guesthouse contains a surprisingly dense warren of rooms. Comfortable, reasonably priced and well equipped with kitchen and lounge areas.

Hotelli Victoria (☎ 242 5111; www.hotellivictoria.fi; Itsenäisyydenkatu 1; s/d €93/118, s/d discount €70/75; ✗ ☎) Close to the train station this is one of Tampere's best-value hotels with comfy rooms, sauna and swimming pool.

Hotel Cumulus Pinja (☎ 241 5111; www.cumulus.fi; Satakunnankatu 10; s/d €114/134, s & d discount €92) Quiet but central business hotel in an Art Noveau building.

Sokos Hotel Tammer (☎ 262 6265; www.sokoshotels.fi; Satakunnankatu 13; s/d €112/139, s/d discount €89/95; ✗) Tampere's oldest and most stylish hotel overlooks the river. Modern facilities with an old-fashioned elegance.

Eating

Cobbled Hämeenkatu is Tampere's broad main street, running east–west from the train station to Hämeenpuisto, and it's along here that you'll find most of the city's restaurants, cafés, bars and the *kauppatori*, where you can sample Tampere's speciality, *mustamakkara* (blood sausage).

Another good place for food stalls in summer is the south harbour where there's a weekend market on Laukontori.

Ohveli Kahvila (☎ 214 255; Ojakatu 4; waffles €3-4; ☿ 9am-8pm Mon-Sat, 10am-8pm Sun) This quaint café specialises in Tampere's best waffles (the name means 'waffle café').

Panimoravintola Plevna (☎ 260 1200; Itäinenkatu 8; mains €7.60-23; ☿ 11am-late) This German-style brewery pub-restaurant in the old Finlayson textile mill is one of the most enjoyable places to dine in Tampere. The house speciality here is German sausage (€7.60 to €11.40) – wash it down with a pint of Plevna's strong stout.

Donatello (☎ 222 0169; Aleksanterinkatu 37; buffet €6; ☿ 10.30am-9pm Mon-Thu, 11.30am-10pm Fri, noon-10pm Sat, 9am-9pm Sun) Lavish all-you-can-eat pizza and pasta buffet for lunch and dinner.

Bodega Salud (☎ 223 5996; Tuomiokirkonkatu 19; mains €6-17; ☿ Mon-Fri 11am-midnight, Sat noon-midnight, Sun 1-10pm) A classic Spanish restaurant with everything from tapas plates (€2.50 to €8), paella and the best steaks in town to such delicacies as 'kangaroo salsa de limon' and 'rattlesnake veracruz' (€53). Great atmosphere.

Telakka (☎ 225 0720; Tullikamarinaukio 3; mains €8-12; ☯ 11am-8pm Mon-Fri, noon-8pm Sat, 1-5pm Sun) Bohemian bar-theatre-restaurant in another of Tampere's restored red-brick factories. Innovative menu and decor, live music, theatre performances and a bright summer terrace.

The central **Koskikeskus shopping centre** (Hatanpän Valtatie) has lots of fast-food outlets and a few chain restaurants. The Old Finlayson Factory is another place to go for American-style fast food and a muffin at Wayne's Coffee. Tampere University's student cafeteria in **Attila House** (Yliopistonkatu 38; ☯ 8.30am-5pm Mon-Fri, lunch Sat) has cheap meals.

Both **Thai Non Khon** (Hämeenkatu 29; lunch from €6) and **Tay-Do** (Hämeenkatu 22), a tiny Vietnamese restaurant across the street, offer up some good vegetarian dishes and cheap lunch time specials.

Drinking & Entertainment

Tampere is arguably the friendliest place in Finland to hit the town.

Café Europa (☎ 223 5526; Aleksanterinkatu 29). The coolest bar in Tampere, with old-world couches, candlelight, a hip crowd and a good summer terrace. Upstairs is a small dance club called **Attic** (☯ 10pm-2am Thu, 9pm-3am Fri & Sat, 7pm-1am Sun) with DJs playing house, hip-hop and funk.

O'Connell's (Rautatienkatu 24; ☯ 4pm-1am Sun-Fri, 4pm-2am Sat) Unpretentious Irish pub with a strong local following. It's a good place to meet travellers, expats and Tampere locals.

Teerenpeli (☎ 04-2492 5210; Hämeenkatu 25; ☯ noon-2am) Fine pub-brewery with home-brewed beer and cider and a cavernous club downstairs.

Vanha Posti (Hämeenkatu 13A) Of the many bars on Hämeenkatu, this one is a perennial favourite with a good terrace. Henry's Pub, in the basement of the same building, has live music (country and rock bands) – you'll probably have to queue to get into either place late on a Friday or Saturday.

Groove Bar & Cellar (☎ 389 9000; Aleksanterinkatu 22; ☯ 4pm-4am) Intimate one-room bar with loungy furniture and board games. Below is a cellar nightclub with DJs playing from 10pm. Next door, **Doris** (☯ to 4am) is one of Tampere's most popular late-night dance clubs.

Papaan Kappaka (☎ 211 0037; Koskikatu 9) This small bar hosts regular live jazz and blues and has a swinging summer terrace.

Mixei (☎ 222 0364; Otavalankatu; ☯ 9pm-2am, to 4am Fri & Sat) Tampere's No 1 gay club hosts theme parties and club nights.

Tullikamari klubi (☎ 3146 6391; Tullikamarinaukio 2) An enormous place in the old customs house near the train station, this is Tampere's main indoor venue for rock concerts. Big-name Finnish bands sometimes perform here and the cover charge varies from free to €15. It's also the venue for the film festival and jazz events.

Finnkino Plevna (☎ 3138 3831; Itäinenkatu 4) A 10-screen cinema in the Finlayson factory.

Shopping

Beautiful textiles and handicrafts are sold at the **Verkaranta Arts & Crafts Centre** (Verkatehtaankatu 2; adult/child €2.50/2), where there's also a café in a stunning spot by the river if you're here when the sun's out.

There's a summer market at **Laukontori** (☯ 6am-5.30pm Mon-Fri, 6am-3pm Sat).

Getting There & Away

There are daily Finnair services from Helsinki, as well as direct flights from Scandinavia's capital cities. Ryanair flies from London Stansted and Frankfurt to Tampere once daily. Tampere's airport, Pirkkala, is 15km southwest of the centre but all flights are met by a bus (€6).

The **main bus station** (Hatanpäänvaltatie 7) is a block south of the Koskikeskus shopping centre. Regular express buses run from Helsinki (€26.30, 2½ hours) and Turku (€18.20, two hours).

Express trains run hourly to/from Helsinki (€22.40, 2½ hours). Intercity trains go on to Oulu (€51.40, five hours); there are direct trains to Turku, Pori, Jyväskylä, Vaasa and Joensuu.

You can cruise down to Hämeenlinna by lake ferry in summer. **Suomen Hopealinja** (Finnish Silverline; ☎ 212 4804; www.finnishsilverline.com) operates cruises from Tampere's Laukontori quay daily (€38 one way, eight hours).

Getting Around

Tampere's bus service is extensive and a one-hour ticket costs €2. A 24-hour Traveller's Ticket is €4. Bus No 61 goes to the airport (€2).

FINLAND

HÄMEENLINNA

☎ 03 / pop 47,500

Historical Hämeenlinna is an attractive town at the southern tip of a lake network, 100km northwest of Helsinki. **Häme Tourist Service** (☎ 621 2388; www.hameenlinna.fi; Linnankatu 6; ☉ 8am-4pm Mon-Fri, 9am-2pm Sat mid-Jun–mid-Aug, 8am-4pm Mon-Fri mid-Aug–mid-Jun; ☐) is near the market square.

The star attraction here is the medieval **Häme Castle** (☎ 675 6820; adult/child €4/2.50; ☉ 10am-6pm May–mid-Aug, 10am-4pm mid-Aug–Apr), which was built by the Swedes in the 1260s and converted into a jail in 1837. There are free guided tours and an extensive museum inside. Around the castle are three more **museums** which can be visited on a combined ticket with the castle (adult/child €12/6).

Finland's most famous composer, Jean Sibelius, was born in Hämeenlinna in 1865 and his childhood home is now an unassuming **museum** (☎ 621 2755; Hallituskatu 11; adult/child €3/1; ☉ 10am-4pm May-Aug, noon-4pm Sep-Apr).

Hotelli Emilia (☎ 612 2106; Raatihuoneenkatu 23; s/d €62/82, s/d discount €55/75; **P** ✗) is welcoming and Hämeenlinna's best-value hotel.

Trains and express buses from Tampere and Helsinki are frequent and you can take a lake ferry from Tampere (see p161).

RAUMA

☎ 02 / pop 38,000

Some 600 wooden houses from the 18th and 19th centuries make up Vanha Rauma (Old Rauma), Finland's first Unesco World Heritage Site and the main attraction of this seaside town. Rauma itself is not particularly appealing, but the old town, with its narrow cobbled streets, cafés, **house museums** (combined ticket €4) and 15th-century stone **Church of the Holy Cross**, makes it worthy of a quick stop along the west coast.

The **tourist office** (☎ 834 4551; www.rauma.fi; Valtakatu 2; ☉ 8am-6pm Mon-Fri, 10am-3pm Sat, 11am-2pm Sun Jun–late Aug, 8am-4pm Mon-Fri late Aug–May) publishes a free map and a self-guided walking tour.

Sleeping

Poroholma Camping & Hostel (☎ 8388 2500; Poroholmantie; camping per person/site €9/14, dm/s/d from €10/21/32; ☉ mid-May–late Aug) On Otanlahti bay about 2km northwest of the town centre, this pleasant camping ground also has a HI hostel in an old villa.

Kesähotelli Rauma (☎ 824 0130; Satamakatu 20; dm/s/d from €/32/50; ☉ Jun-Aug) Closer to the Old Town, this summer hostel has typical twin-share student rooms with private kitchen and bathroom shared between two rooms.

Kalatorin Majatalo (☎ 8378 6150; Kalatori 4; s/d €98/125, s/d discount €78/95) In a beautifully renovated Art Deco warehouse on the eastern edge of Vanha Rauma, this is the best choice.

Eating

The *kauppatori*, in the Old Town, is where you'll find cheap food stalls, a market in the summer and the busy La Bamba pizza restaurant.

Wanhan Rauman Kellari (☎ 866 6700; Anundilankatu 8; lunch €9.50, mains €10-23) On the edge of Vanha Rauma, this stone and timber cellar restaurant is a great place to splurge on Finnish specialities, seafood and steak. The rooftop beer terrace is terrific in summer.

Vanha Rauma's quaint charm lends itself to old-world cafés and there are a few: **Kontion Leipomo** (☎ 822 1758; Kuninkaankatu 9; ☉ 7.30am-5pm Mon-Fri, 8am-3pm Sat, 11am-4pm Sun) is a perennial favourite for coffee, cakes or pastries; and **Wähä Tallbo** (☎ 822 6610; Vanhankirkonkatu 3; mains €7.60-20; ☉ 10.30am-7pm Mon-Fri, 11am-4pm Sat) serves up a full menu and does a great €6.50 lunch special.

PORI

☎ 02 / pop 75,900

For around 10 days in mid-July, all roads lead to Pori – pencil the internationally renowned **Pori Jazz Festival** into your trip and try to make it here. Despite being one of Finland's oldest towns, the modern industrial port city of Pori would be of little interest to travellers if it wasn't host to the festival – the town centre appears to be made up of shopping malls.

The festival is known worldwide among jazz and blues performers, and has hosted truckloads of big names over the past 39 years – the 2004 line-up included Stevie Wonder and Macy Gray. Many scheduled and impromptu performances, jam sessions and street shows are free, creating a nonstop buzz around town. The headliners play on an open-air stage on Kirjurinluoto. For tickets and information contact **Pori Jazz** (☎ 626 2200; www.porijazz.fi; Pohjoisranta 11D, 28100 Pori)

Local sights include **Pori Taidemuseo** (☎ 621 1080; Eteläranta 1; adult/child €3.50/1; ☉ 11am-6pm Tue-Sun), one of Finland's better modern galleries;

and the **Juselius Mausoleum** (☎ 623 8746; Käppärä, Maantiekatu; admission free; ☺ noon-3pm May-Aug), a poignant memorial built by a local business-man for his 11-year-old daughter who died of tuberculosis. The original frescoes inside were painted by Akseli Gallen-Kallela.

Accommodation during the festival should be booked a year in advance, but at other times the **tourist office** (☎ 621 1271; www.pori.fi; Yrjönkatu 17; ☺ 9am-5pm Mon-Fri, 10am-3pm Sat Jun-Aug, 9am-5pm Mon-Fri Sep-May; 🖥), in the Promenade shopping centre, can help organise a cheap bed (around €30 to €45) on a first-come, first-served basis, either in a private home or on the floor of a school classroom.

During festival time, the waterfront Etel-äranta becomes 'Jazz Street', a pulsating strip of makeshift bars and food stalls. Be sure to try Porilainen (Pori burger), a local speciality made with onion, sausage, pickles and a bun.

Beerhunters (☎ 641 5599; Antinkatu 1; ☺ 11-2am), across from the market square, is a brilliant pub-brewery (try the 'Mufloni stout') and restaurant with Internet access.

Express buses go to Pori from Turku, Tampere and Helsinki. There are frequent trains to/from Tampere (€14, 1½ hours) and one direct service from Helsinki (€31.60, 3½ hours).

VAASA

📷 06 / pop 56,900

The bilingual harbour city of Vaasa (Wasa), founded in 1606 by Charles IX of Sweden, is the main hub of the Swedish Coast. Although a lively, bustling city, it lacks the character of smaller west coast places but it can be used as an entry or exit point to/from Sweden.

The busy **tourist office** (☎ 325 1145; www.vaasa.fi; Kaupungintalo; ☺ 9am-9pm Mon-Fri, 10am-6pm Sat & Sun Jun–mid-Aug, 10am-4pm Mon-Fri mid-Aug–May), in the town hall building just off Raastuvankatu, books accommodation and rents bikes.

The most interesting of Vaasa's numerous museums and art collections is the **Museum of Ostrobothnia** (☎ 325 3800; Museokatu 3; adult/child €4/2, free Wed; ☺ 10am-5pm Thu-Tue, 10am-8pm Wed), with one of the best collections of art from Finland's Golden Era and artefacts from all over Pohjanmaa. In the basement level is the **Bothnia Straits Nature Centre**, with displays on the region's geology, flora and fauna.

On Vaskiluoto island, linked by a bridge to the town centre, is Finland's mini-

Disneyland amusement park, **Wasalandia**, and a 'tropical spa', **Tropiclandia**, both very popular with Finnish families.

Sleeping & Eating

Kenraali Wasa Hostel (☎ 04-0066 8521; www.kenraali wasahostel.com; Korsholmanpuistikko 6-8; s/d/tr €37/46/50) The best of the few budget places in Vaasa, this is a friendly hostel in a former military hospital with well-equipped kitchen and cosy rooms (shared bathrooms).

Bertel's Panorama (Vaasanpuistikko 16; lunch special €7.40) Generous lunch buffet which you can eat overlooking the market square.

For a drink with a bird's-eye view, head to the Sky Bar on the rooftop of the Sokos Hotel Vakuna. The best place for a meal or drink in summer is Strampen, a restaurant and terrace bar in the waterfront Hovioikeu-den park.

Getting There & Away

There are frequent buses up and down the coast from the terminal on Vöyrinkatu, and daily trains from Helsinki (€44, 4½ hours) via Tampere or Seinajoki.

In summer there are daily ferries (€50, three hours) between Vaasa and the Swedish town of Umeå (Uumaja) with **RG Lines** (☎ 320 0300; www.rgline.com).

PIETARSAARI (JAKOBSTAD)

📷 06 / pop 20,000

The quaint town of Pietarsaari (Jakobstad) is distinctively Swedish and the most inter-esting place to sample the curious world of *parallelsverige* (parallel Sweden).

The **tourist office** (☎ 723 1796; www.jakobstad.fi; Kauppiaankatu 12; ☺ 8am-6pm Mon-Fri, 9am-3pm Sat Jun-Aug, 8am-5pm Mon-Fri Sep-May) is next to the town square. There's free Internet access at **After Eight** (☎ 781 6500; Isokatu 6; ☺ 10am-3pm Mon-Fri), a café and popular local meeting centre.

Skata, the town's historic area filled with 18th-century wooden houses, is just north of the centre and worth a stroll. In the old harbour area at Gamla Hamn is the pride of Pietarsaari, the **Jacobstad Wapen** (admission €1.60; ☺ when in dock mid-May–late Aug), a replica of a 17th-century galleon.

Hostel Lilja (☎ 781 6500; www.aftereight.fi/hostellilja; Isokatu 6; dm €20, s/d €40/45) is a stylish, modern hostel attached to After Eight in the town centre. There's also bike rental and a smoke sauna.

Westerlund Resandehem (☎ 723 0440; Pohjois-nummikatu 8; s/d/tr €27/41/54) is a lovely family-run B&B in the historic Skata part of town.

There are plenty of cheap places to eat and drink along the partly pedestrian Kävelykatu (Kanalesplanaden), one block north of the market square. **Cafe Trend** (☎ 723 1265; Isokatu 13) is where Pietarsaari's beautiful people crowd the terrace or read magazines over coffee or beer.

Ella's Café (☎ 723 5049; Raatiuoneenkatu 3; buffet lunch €6; ☉ 11am-3pm Mon-Fri) is a 3rd-floor lunch restaurant overlooking the market square, and offers a typically generous Finnish buffet of hot and cold meats, soup and salad.

There are regular buses to/from Vaasa and north to Oulu via Kokkola (the closest mainline train station).

LAKELAND & THE EAST

Eastern Finland is a romantic region of lakes, rivers, locks and canals. It encompasses Karelia, part of which was taken by Russia in the bitter Winter War, and the Savo region of which Savonlinna is the centre. This Lakeland area is a glistening patchwork of waterways in summer and a highlight is canoeing or taking a lake ferry between towns. If you've only got the time or money to visit one region outside Helsinki in summer, make this the place.

Finns come here en masse in spring, summer and early autumn, and rent holiday cottages so they can enjoy trekking, boating, fishing and, of course, long saunas at night.

LAPPEENRANTA

☎ 05 / pop 58,700

On the southern shores of the vast Lake Saimaa, the South Karelian capital of Lappeenranta was a frontier garrison town until the construction of the Saimaa Canal in 1856 made it an important trading centre. These days cruises on the canal are a major attraction – boats cruise all the way to Vyborg, which was Finland's second-largest city until it was lost to Russia (along with large swathes of Karelia) in WWII (see p131). Even if you stick to dry land, Lappeenranta is a vibrant harbour town and a good place to sample Karelian food and culture.

Information

The **tourist office** (☎ 667 788; www.lappeenranta.fi; ☉ 9am-6pm Mon-Fri Jun–late Aug, 9.30am-4.30pm Mon-Fri late Aug–May) is on the south side of the market square.

The **public library** (☎ 616 2346; Valtakatu 47; ☉ 10am-8pm Mon-Fri, 10am-3pm Sat) has free Internet terminals (book ahead).

Sights & Activities

The fortifications in **Linnoitus** (Fortress) were started by the Swedes and finished by the Russians in the 18th century. Some of the fortress buildings have been turned into mildly interesting **museums** (combined ticket adult/student/child €5/4.50/3; ☉ 10am-6pm Mon-Fri, 11am-5pm Sat & Sun Jun–late Aug, 11am-5pm Tue, Thu, Sat & Sun late Aug–May). They include the **South Karelia Museum**, with a variety of folk costumes and a scale model of Vyborg as it looked before it fell to the Russians in 1939; the **South Karelia Art Museum**, with a permanent collection of paintings by Finnish and Karelian artists; and the small **Cavalry Museum**, which exhibits portraits of commanders, uniforms, saddles and guns.

In the city centre, the **Wolkoff Home Museum** (☎ 616 2258; Kauppakatu 26; adult/student/child €3.40/2.50/1.20; ☉ 10am-5pm Mon-Fri, 11am-5pm Sat & Sun Jun–late Aug, 11am-5pm Fri & Sat late Aug–May) is the preserved home of a Russian emigrant family. Obligatory guided tours are held on the hour.

There's a public **beach sauna** (admission €3.50/1.50; ☉ 4-8pm Wed & Fri women, Tue & Thu men) on Myllysaari island just east of the harbour.

Tours

Short cruises with **Karelia Lines** (☎ 453 0380; adult/child €11/6; ☉ noon-2pm & 6-9pm) on Lake Saimaa and the canal leave from the harbour daily in summer.

The day cruise along the Saimaa Canal to Vyborg (Russia) is one of Lappeenranta's main attractions, though it's no longer 'visa-free'. **Saimaan Matkaverkk** (☎ 541 0100; www.saimaatravel.fi; Valtakatu 48) arranges the necessary Russian visas but you will need to request one at least a week ahead. Non-EU citizens need an individual visa (around €33). From mid-May to September, the **MS Carelia** (adult/child €51/39; ☉ Sat & late Jun–early Aug €57/39) departs at 8am and the trip allows about five hours in Vyborg. The return trip is by bus.

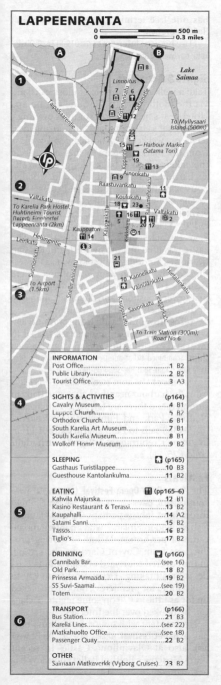

Sleeping

Huhtiniemi Tourist Resort (☎ 451 5555; www.huh tiniemi.com; Kuusimäenkatu 18; camp sites & van sites €16-19, 2-/4-person cottages €32/42, apt €34-74; 🕑 mid-May–mid-Sep; 🚼)) Well-kept, slightly officious camping ground on the shores of Lake Saimaa, about 2km west of the centre (bus No 5 or 6 from the centre or train station). On the same site is the **Huhtiniemi Hostel** (dm €10; 🕑 Jun–mid-Aug), with six-bed dorms and the cheapest accommodation in town, and the upmarket **Finnhostel Lappeenranta** (s/d €45/57), with linen, breakfast and a morning swim and sauna included. The complex has a café, pool and well-equipped gym, and you can rent canoes for paddling around the lake.

Karelia Park (☎ 675 211; Korpraalinkuja 1; dm/s/d €14/40.50/45; 🕑 Jun–late Aug; 🗶)) Good-value summer budget accommodation about 300m west of Huhtiniemi. Spotless two-bed rooms with kitchen facilities and private bathroom.

Gasthaus Turistilappee (☎ 415 0800; Kauppakatu 52; s/d/tr €34/51/58; 🗶)) Cheap, working-class guesthouse only a 10-minute walk from the train station or town centre. Tidy rooms (some have private bathrooms), and breakfast and sauna are included.

Guesthouse Kantolankulma (☎ 050-328 7595; www.gasthauslappeenranta.com; Kimpisenkatu 19; s/d €50/70) Brand-new guesthouse down by the harbour. Apartment-style rooms with kitchens.

Eating & Drinking

In summer, head to the harbour, just below the fortress walls, where food stalls set up and locals gather. Don't miss trying the Karelian favourite *vety* (a pie or sandwich made with ham, eggs, butter and relish). Satami Sanni is a kiosk with *vety* for €3.60. The market square and *kauppahalli*, just south of the centre, also has Karelian spe-cialities and fresh produce.

Kahvila Majurska (☎ 453 0554; Kristiinankatu 7; 🕑 10am-8pm in summer; 🗶) In a beautifully fur-nished historic 19th-century wooden build-ing at the fortress complex, this is one of the most charming cafés in Finland and serves delicious home-made cakes and quiches.

Tiglio's (☎ 411 8311; Raatamiehenkatu 18; pasta & pizza €9-15, other mains €12-22; 🕑 11am-11pm Sun-Thu, 11-1am Fri & Sat) Authentic, informal Italian res-taurant with reasonably priced meals and a great salad buffet.

Tassos (☎ 678 6565; Valtakatu 41; mains €10-25, lunch buffet €11; 🕑 11am-11pm Mon-Thu, 11am-midnight Sat, noon-midnight Sun) Fine Greek–Finnish fusion place where pheasant and reindeer share a menu with moussaka. The lunch buffet is a bargain.

Kasino Restaurant & Terassi is a 90-year-old former casino now housing a stylish restaurant, but it's the terrace hanging over the harbour that attracts the summer crowds.

Also on the harbour, the boats SS *Suvi-Saamai* and *Prinsessa Armaada* serve as busy beer terraces.

Kauppakatu has a lively strip of bars and clubs. The **Old Park** (Valtakatu 36) is an Irish pub that gets very crowded most nights, and Cannibals Bar, next door to Tassos, is a nightclub that reels them in after other bars have closed.

For something off-the-wall, check out **Totem** (☎ 419 0508; Raatamiehenkatu; ☼ to 3am Fri & Sat), a pub with a bizarre American Indian and Wild West motif.

Getting There & Away
Finnair has daily flights between Helsinki and Lappeenranta; take bus No 4 to the airport.

All bus and train tickets can be booked at the central office of **Matkahuolto** (☼ 9am-6pm Mon-Fri), opposite the town park. Regular bus services include: Helsinki (€27.80, four hours), Savonlinna (€19.20, three hours) and Imatra (€5.90, 45 minutes). For Kuopio (€32.10) change at Mikkeli.

There are frequent direct trains to/from Helsinki (€34.20, three hours) and to Savonlinna (€19, 2½ hours; change at Parikkala).

SAVONLINNA
☎ 015 / pop 28,700
Lorded over by the best-preserved medieval castle in Scandinavia, Olavinlinna, and split by two stunning lakes, Savonlinna is the quintessential Lakeland town and the centre of the Savo region. In July the town erupts into a cultural frenzy for the renowned Opera Festival – if you're nearby, don't miss it.

Information
The **Savonlinna tourist service** (☎ 517 510; www .savonlinnatravel.com; Puistokatu 1; ☼ 8am-8pm Jul, 9am-5pm Mon-Fri Aug-Jun) is a good place to find opera festival information and make accommodation bookings.

The **public library** (☎ 571 5100; Tottinkatu; ☼ 11am-7pm Mon-Fri, 10am-2pm Sat) has free Internet access. **Knut Posse Bookshop** (Olavinkatu 44)

has one free terminal, as does the café at **Hotel Seurahone**.

Hire bikes at **Intersport** (☎ 015-517 680; Olavinkatu; day/week €10/35).

Sights & Activities
Take a walk out to forested Sulosaari island via the footbridges (behind the Casino Spa Hotel) – it's beautiful on summer evenings, although it's also popular with boozing local teens on weekends. Another good walk is from the market square to the castle along the lakefront and back along **Linnankatu**, a charming street lined with old wooden houses, craft shops, studios and cafés.

The late-afternoon reflection of dramatic **Olavinlinna Castle** (☎ 531 164; adult/student & child €5/3.50; ☼ 10am-5pm Jun-Aug, 10am-3pm Sep-May) on Lake Pihlajavesi is a memorable sight. The castle was used by both Swedish and Russian overlords, but today is best known as the setting for the month-long Savonlinna Opera Festival. To tour the castle, including its original towers, bastions and chambers, join one of the excellent hourly guided tours.

Across from the castle is the **provincial museum** with a large exhibition space related to local and maritime history, and four **museum ships** (combined ticket adult/child €4/2; ☼ 11am-6pm daily July, 11am-5pm Tue-Sun Aug-Jun).

Dozens of 1½-hour **scenic cruises** (€7-10) leave from the harbour near the *kauppatori* daily in summer, and there are ferries to Linnansaari National Park and Punkaharju. **SS Heinävesi** (☎ 514 320) sails to Punkaharju daily at 11am in summer, returning at 3.40pm (return adult/child €25/11).

Festivals
The **Savonlinna Opera Festival** (☎ 476 750; www .operafestival.fi; Olavinkatu 27, 57130 Savonlinna), held throughout July, is perhaps the most famous festival held in Finland, with an international cadre of performers including touring productions from Covent Garden. The setting, in the covered courtyard of Olavinlinna Castle, is breathtaking. Tickets cost from €30 to €100 (more for premieres), but can be picked up for as little as €20 on some nights. Tickets can be booked over the Internet.

Not content with opera, Savonlinna now has a **Ballet Festival** (tickets €45-120; ☼ 1st week Jun), also at Olavinlinna Castle. In recent years Moscow's Bolshoi Ballet company has performed.

SAVONLINNA

INFORMATION	
Knut Posse Bookshop................(see 21)	
Main Post Office..........................1 A3	
Nestori......................................2 C4	
Nordea Bank..............................3 B3	
Post Office.................................4 C4	
Public Library.............................5 C4	
Savonlinna Opera Festival Box	
Office.....................................6 C3	
Savonlinna Tourist Service...........7 B3	

SIGHTS & ACTIVITIES	(p166)
Craft Shops & Studios.................8 C4	
Museum Ships............................9 C4	

Olavinlinna Castle.....................10 D4	
Provincial Museum....................11 C4	

SLEEPING	(pp167-8)
Casino Spa Hotel......................12 C3	
Hotel Seurahuone.....................13 B3	
Kesähotelli Tott........................14 C4	
Perhehotelli Hospits..................15 C4	
SS Heinävesi............................16 B4	
Vuorilinna Hostel......................17 C4	

EATING	(p168)
Cafe Mimosa............................18 C4	
Café Torppa.............................19 B3	

Huvila......................................20 B4	
Juanita Bar & Café....................21 B3	
Liekkilohi.................................22 B3	
Majakka...................................23 B3	
Pizzeria Capero.........................24 B3	

DRINKING	(p168)
Happy Time..............................25 B3	
Olutravintola Sillansuu...............26 B3	
Opperra Terassi.........................27 B3	

TRANSPORT	(pp168-9)
Bus Station...............................28 A3	
Passenger Harbour....................29 B4	

Lowering the tone a little (but who's complaining) is the **Beer Festival** at Wanha Kasino (next to the Casino Spa Hotel) in August.

Sleeping

Book accommodation well in advance during the opera festival – six months for hotels and a couple of months for hostels, although it's always worth a phone call to see if you can get in on any given day.

Vuohimäki Camping (☎ 537 353; myyntipalvelu@lom aliitto.fi; camp sites €19, cabins €56-82; ☺ Jun-Aug) About 7km west of town; fills up quickly in July.

SS Heinävesi (☎ 533 120; cabins upper/lower deck per person €19/17) Offering two-person cabin accommodation after the last cruise every evening during summer.

Vuorilinna (☎ 739 5430; casino.myynti@svlkylpylaitos .fi; Kylpylaitoksentie; dm/s/d from €23/50/65; ☺ Jun–late Aug; P ✗ ☎) HI-affiliated summer hostel in student dorms with great facilities near to (and run by) the spa hotel on Kasinosaari (Casino Island).

Malakias (☎ 739 5430; Pihlajavedenkuja 6; s/d from €45/55) Summer hotel 2km west of town, open only during ballet and opera festivals. Basic two-room apartments.

Kesähotelli Tott (☎ 573 673; Satamakatu 1; s/d from €75/90; ☺ early Jun–late Aug) Comfortable but bland summer hotel between the market square and the castle. Some rooms are apartment-style, with kitchen.

Perhehotelli Hospits (☎ 515 661; Linnankatu 20; s €75-85, d €85-110; ✗) Savonlinna's most stylish hotel is a stone's throw from the castle; polished floors, old-world charm and a dining room that looks more like a ballroom. Try getting a room in July!

Casino Spa Hotel (☎ 73950; Kasinosaari; s/d €83/100, s/d Jul €100/120; **P** ⊠ 🖳) Go on, pamper yourself. Top-notch rooms with a romantic view of the lake are a steal at this price (difficult in July), plus you have all the facilities of a spa hotel with spas, saunas, steam bath, gym and pool. It's just over the bridge from the *kauppatori* train station.

Eating

The lively market at the *kauppatori* is where to find local pastries such as *omena-lörtsy*, a tasty apple turnover. Also on the *kauppatori*, Cafe Torppa is a popular student run kiosk for coffee and late-night snacks.

Liekkilohi (Flaming Salmon; fishy mains €7-10; 🕙 to 2am in summer) Bright-red, covered pontoon anchored just off the *kauppatori* and serving portions of flamed salmon and fried vendace (tiny lake fish) – perfect for a very Finnish late-night snack.

Pizzeria Capero (☎ 533 955; Olavinkatu 51; pizza & pasta €6-7; 🕙 10.30am-10pm) The best place in town for pizza or pasta, with cosy atmosphere and lunch specials till 2pm.

Cafe Mimosa (☎ 532 257; Linnankatu; light meals €6-10) Near the castle, this café has a fine terrace and bar, and serves salads, cakes and light meals.

Majakka (☎ 531 456; Satamakatu 11; mains €10.50-20, lunch from €7; 🕙 11am-1pm Mon-Thu, 11am-midnight Fri & Sat, 11am-10pm Sun) Facing the harbour and making the most of the nautical theme, this is the place for an intimate splurge with seafood and Finnish fare.

Juanita Bar & Café (☎ 514 531; Olavinkatu 44; mains €8-12; 🕙 9pm-3am) Mexican-themed restaurant above Knut Posse Bookshop with reasonably priced burgers, fajitas, Tex-Mex and all the margaritas you can handle. Popular bar later in the night.

Huvila (☎ 555 0555; www.savonniemi.com, no English; Puistokatu 4; mains €11-20; 🕙 noon-11pm Mon-Thu, noon-1am Fri & Sat, noon-10pm Sun) One of the finest places in town to dine or enjoy a beer by far, this restaurant across the harbour mixes gourmet local food with refined brewing – wash down arctic char, glazed duck and home-made asparagus ice cream with a lovingly brewed Porter ale. Great summer terrace.

Drinking

With only a small student population, Savonlinna is quiet most of the year but very lively in July. The top-floor terrace bar at Hotel Seurahuone is a great place for a drink with a fine view over the town.

Terraces also set up around the harbour – the busiest is Opperra Terassi in front of Majakka.

Huvila (see left) is a must for lovers of fine ale, with three types of beer brewed there on the premises and the best *sahti* (a high-alcohol, sweet Finnish beer) in the country.

Olutravintola Sillansuu, near the main bridge just off Olavinkatu, is an English-style pub with a big range of beers and whiskies.

Later in the night, Happy Time, next to the *kauppatori* train station, is the place to mix with young Savonlinnans – it's open, and usually jumping, till 4am.

Getting There & Away
AIR
Finnair flies to Savonlinna from Helsinki five times a week. The airport is 15km from the centre and a shuttle bus operates during the opera festival (€6).

BUS
From the bus station on the western side of town there are regular buses to Helsinki (€37.70, 4½ hours), Joensuu (€19.70, two hours), Kuopio (€24.60, two hours) and Kerimäki (€4.40, 30 minutes).

TRAIN
There are trains from Helsinki (€44.60, 5½ hours) via Parikkala – note that you must change to a regional train or connecting bus service at Parikkala, or otherwise you'll wind up in Joensuu. For Kuopio, you need to take a bus to Pieksämäki and a train from there. The main train station is a long walk from Savonlinna's centre; get off at the *kauppatori* platform instead.

BOAT
From mid-June to mid-August the lake ferry **MS Puijo** (☎ 555 0120; €65; 10½hr) travels to Kuopio on Monday, Wednesday and Friday at 9.30am, returning on Tuesday, Thursday and Saturday. This scenic lake journey follows the Heinävesi route, passing through canals and locks and close to the Valamo Monastery. You can also take a two-day return cruise

staying on board for €135/125 in upper-/lower-deck cabins. There's a restaurant service on board.

AROUND SAVONLINNA

Punkaharju, between Savonlinna and Parikkala, is the famous pine-covered sand ridge *(esker)* that is one of the most overrated attractions in Finland; the surrounding forest and lakes, though, are beautiful and it's a great area for cycling or walking.

The weird art centre, **Retretti** (☎ 775 2200; adults/senior/student/child €15/12/9/5; open 10am-5pm Jun & Aug, 10am-6pm Jul), has superb summer exhibitions in a walk-through artificial cave.

Punkaharju can be reached from Savonlinna by train, bus or, throughout summer, a two-hour cruise (one way adult/child €7/3.50) to Retretti jetty.

The world's largest wooden church can be found at **Kerimäki**, about 23km east of Savonlinna. It was built in 1847 to seat a congregation of 3300 people.

UUSI-VALAMO

☎ 017

The **Valamo monastery** (☎ 570 111; www.valamo .fi; Valamontie 42; ☒ 7.30am-9pm) – Finland's only Orthodox monastery – is one of Savo's hidden gems. The original Valamo monastery was annexed by the Red Army during WWII; the current church was consecrated in 1977. The monastery is 4km north of road No 23 to Joensuu from Varkaus. Like all good monks, the clergy at Valamo produce their own wine (bottle €9) using berries such as crowberries, raspberries, strawberries and blackcurrants.

You can stay in the simple **Valamo Guesthouse** (s €24, 2–5-person r per person €22) or the more comfortable **Valamo Hotel** (s/d €34/50). There's also a restaurant.

If you are looking for something even more peaceful, visit the nearby **Lintula Orthodox Convent** (☎ 563 225) which also has accommodation. In summer there are cruises through lakes, canals and locks from Valamo to Lintula on **MS Sergei** (Wed & Sat 2-6pm; one way/ return €13/15), and evening cruises daily (€12).

Buses run direct to Valamo from Joensuu, Savonlinna, Kuopio, Mikkeli and Helsinki but services are not frequent. It's also possible to visit Valamo and Lintula from Kuopio on a **monastery cruise** (adult/child €51/25). The return journey is by bus.

KUOPIO

☎ 017 / pop 87,800

Kuopio is the most enjoyable of the northern Lakeland cities. It's a vibrant place with lots to see and do, and enjoys a beautiful location, surrounded by forest and lakes. Time your visit for a Tuesday or Thursday so you can steam it up in the world's biggest smoke sauna.

The helpful **Kuopio Tourist Office** (☎ 182 585; www.kuopioinfo.fi; Haapaniemenkatu 17; ☒ 9.30am-4.30pm Mon-Fri, 10am-3pm Sat Jul, 9.30am-4.30pm Mon-Fri, Aug-Jun) is right behind the impressive town hall on the north side of the market square.

There's free Internet access on the 2nd floor of the **public library** (☎ 182 111; Maaherrankatu 12; ☒ 10am-7pm Mon-Fri, 10am-3pm Sat). There's also a **Net Café** (Haapaniemenkatu; per 15 min €?) in the basement coffee shop in the H-Talo shopping centre.

Sights & Activities

In a country as flat as Finland, **Puijo Hill** is highly regarded. Take the lift to the top of the 75m-high **Puijo Tower** (adult/child €3/2) for spectacular views of Lake Kallavesi and the surrounding spruce forests. The hill is a popular spot for mountain biking, walking and cross-country skiing. There's also an all-season ski jump here and you can often see jumpers in training.

Don't miss the chance to sweat in the world's largest **smoke sauna** (Jätkänkämppällä; adult/child €10/5; ☒ 5-11pm Tue year round & Thu Jun–mid-Sep) near the Hotel-Spa Rauhalahti. This 60-person log *savusauna* (smoke sauna) is mixed and guests are given wraps to wear. Bring a swimsuit for a dip in the lake, as devoted sauna-goers do even when the lake is covered with ice! Bus No 7 goes from the market square to Rauhalahti, but the best way to get there in summer is by ferry from Kuopio harbour (adult/child €10/5).

A museum card (€11), available from the tourist office, gets you into five city museums. **VB Photographic Centre** (☎ 261 5599; Kuninkaankatu 14-16; adult/child €3-5/free; ☒ 10am-7pm Mon-Fri, 11am-4pm Sat & Sun Jun-Aug, 11am-5pm Tue-Fri, Sat & Sun 11am-3pm Sep-May) is a quality exhibition of old photos and art by photographer Victor Barsokevitsch. History museums include the **Kuopio Museum** (☎ 182 603; Kauppakatu 23; adult/student & child €4/2; ☒ 9am-4pm Mon-Fri, 11am-8pm Sun), housed in a medieval castle-like building and containing a reconstruction of a woolly

KUOPIO

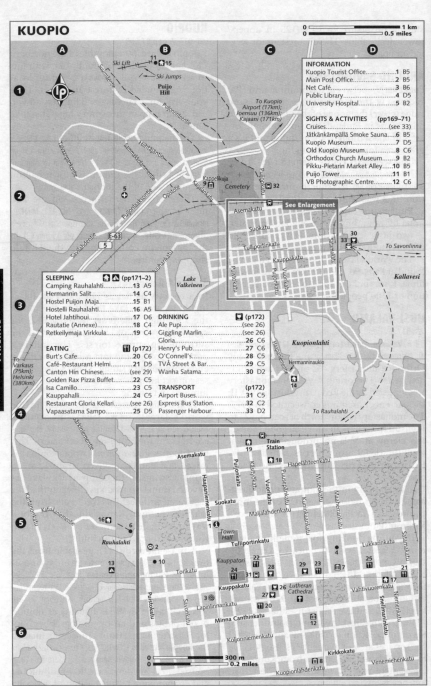

0 ————————— 1 km
0 ————————— 0.5 miles

INFORMATION
Kuopio Tourist Office..............1 B5
Main Post Office.....................2 B5
Net Café................................3 B6
Public Library........................4 D5
University Hospital.................5 B2

SIGHTS & ACTIVITIES (pp169–71)
Cruises...................................(see 33)
Jätkänkämpällä Smoke Sauna....6 B5
Kuopio Museum.......................7 D5
Old Kuopio Museum................8 C6
Orthodox Church Museum......9 B2
Pikku-Pietarin Market Alley.....10 B5
Puijo Tower...........................11 B1
VB Photographic Centre.........12 C6

SLEEPING (pp171–2)
Camping Rauhalahti................13 A5
Hermannin Salit.....................14 C4
Hostel Puijon Maja.................15 B1
Hostelli Rauhalahti.................16 A5
Hotel Jahtihoui......................17 D6
Rautatie (Annexe)..................18 C4
Retkeilymaja Virkkula.............19 C4

EATING (p172)
Burt's Cafe............................20 C6
Café-Restaurant Helmi............21 D5
Canton Hin Chinese................(see 29)
Golden Rax Pizza Buffet..........22 C5
Isa Camillo............................23 C5
Kauppahalli...........................24 C5
Restaurant Gloria Kellari.........(see 26)
Vapaasatama Sampo..............25 D5

DRINKING (p172)
Ale Pupi...............................(see 26)
Giggling Marlin......................(see 26)
Gloria..................................26 C6
Henry's Pub..........................27 C6
O'Connell's...........................28 C5
TVÅ Street & Bar...................29 C5
Wanha Satama......................30 D2

TRANSPORT (p172)
Airport Buses........................31 C5
Express Bus Station................32 C2
Passenger Harbour................33 D2

Ski Lift
Ski Jumps
Puijo Hill

To Kuopio
Airport (17km);
Joensuu (136km);
Kajaani (171km)

Kappelikuja
Cemetery

See Enlargement

To Savonlinna

Kallavesi

Lake
Valkeinen

Kuopionlahti

Hermanninaukio

To Rauhalahti

To
Varkaus
(75km);
Helsinki
(380km)

Rauhalahti

FINLAND

Train Station

Asemakatu
Hapelahteenkatu

Suokatu

Maljalahdenkatu

Town Hall

Tulliportinkatu

Torikatu

Kauppatori

Lutheran Cathedral

Kauppakatu

Lapinlinnankatu

Minna Canthinkatu

Koljonniemenkatu

Kirkkokatu

Kuopionlahdenkatu

Venemiehenkatu

0 ————————— 300 m
0 ————————— 0.2 miles

THE FINNISH SAUNA

Nothing is more traditionally or culturally Finnish than the sauna. For centuries it has been a place to bathe, meditate, warm up during cold winters and even give birth, and most Finns still use the sauna at least once a week. Its origins date back over 1000 years, with the earliest saunas dug into hillsides and heated by a fireplace overlaid with stones. The *savusauna* (smoke sauna) in a log cabin is considered by many Finns to be the quintessential experience, but most of Finland's 1.6 million saunas are now electric and many are found in private homes or summer cottages. An invitation to bathe in a family's sauna is a great honour.

Bathing is done in the nude (there are some exceptions in public saunas, which are almost always sex-segregated anyway) and Finns are quite strict about the nonsexual – even sacred – nature of the sauna.

According to sauna etiquette you should wash or shower first. Once inside the sauna (with a temperature of 80°–90°C), water is thrown onto the stove using a *kauhu* (ladle), producing steam. A whisk of birch twigs and leaves *(vihta)* is sometimes used to lightly strike the skin, improving circulation. Once you're hot enough, go outside and cool off with a cold shower or preferably by jumping into a lake or pool – enthusiastic Finns do so even in winter by cutting a hole in the ice! Repeat the process.

---

mammoth; and the **Old Kuopio Museum** (☎ 182 625; Kirkkokatu 22; adult/child €2.50/free; ☺ 10am-5pm May-Sep, 10am-3pm Tue-Fri, 10am-4pm Sat & Sun Oct-Apr), a folk museum displaying local homes and shops from the 19th century.

The **Orthodox Church Museum** (☎ 287 2244; Karjalankatu 1; adult/student/child €5/3/1; ☺ 10am-4pm Tue-Sun May–late Aug, noon-3pm Mon-Fri, noon-5pm Sat & Sun late Aug–Apr) is a fascinating museum crammed with collections and artefacts rescued from monasteries, churches and *tsasouni* (chapels) in USSR-occupied Karelia. Take bus No 7.

Pikku Pietari Market Alley (☺ 10am-5pm Mon-Fri, 10am-2pm Sat Jun-Aug, 10am-5pm Mon-Fri Sep-May) is a narrow alley of renovated shop houses, boutiques, exhibition galleries and a café. It's a charming arcade a few blocks west of the *kauppatori*.

In summer there are regular lake and canal **cruises** from the harbour. They include day trips to Heinävesi (€45) and Valamo Monastery (€55), a cruise to a berry winery (€10) and cruises on Lake Kallavesi (€10). Contact **Roll Cruises** (☎ 266 2466).

Festivals & Events

Kuopio's main event is the **Dance Festival** (☎ 282 1541; www.kuopiodancefestival.fi) in mid-June. There are open-air classical and modern dance performances and the town is buzzing at this time.

Sleeping

Camping Rauhalahti (☎ 361 2244; Kiviniementie; camping per site/person €7/4, 2–4-person cottages €55;

☺ mid-May–Sep) Adjacent to the Rauhalahti spa complex, this luxury camping ground has a beautiful lakeside location and a truckload of activities for kids.

Retkeilymaja Virkkula (☎ 263 7839; Asemakatu 3; dm €14; Jun-Aug) Right next to the train station, this is a conveniently central and cheap summer hostel with large dorms. Reception is open from 6pm.

Hermannin Salit (☎ 364 4961; www.hermannin salit.com; Hermanninaukio 3A; dm/s/d from €18/42/48) Kuopio's best budget option if you want to be within walking distance of the centre. About 1.5km south of the market square, it's a small, simple place with kitchen, lounge and a good café.

Hostelli Rauhalahti (☎ 4/3 473; www.rauhalahti .com; Katiskaniementie 8; dm/s/d €34/60/68) High-quality HI hostel next to the spa hotel in the Rauhalahti tourist centre complex, 5km southwest of the centre. Handy for the smoke sauna if you're there on the right days, but pricey for backpacker accommodation. The best part is you get to use the hotel's impressive facilities, including a gym, spa and pool. Take bus No 7 from the *kauppatori*.

Hostel Puijon Maja (☎ 255 5250; Puilontornintie; dm €16, with linen & breakfast €30, s/d €55/60) Lovely hostel perched on top of Puijo Hill – popular with groups, including practising ski jumpers, so book ahead. Unfortunately, there's no public transport from the town centre.

Rautatie (☎ 580 0569; Asemakatu 1; s/d from €46/75) Convenient location inside the train station and a surprisingly comfortable and peaceful

FINLAND

guesthouse. Nearby, at Vuorikatu 35 (same phone), is another small guesthouse with slightly cheaper rooms (€36/56).

Hotel Jahtihovi (☎ 264 4400; jahti@raketti.net; Snellmaninkatu 23; s/d €77/95, s/d discount €63/76) Near the harbour, this is an intimate mid-range hotel with a good restaurant and big buffet breakfast.

Eating

Kuopio's main square dominates the centre of town and here you'll find markets, food stalls and the indoor **kauppahalli** (8am-5pm Mon-Fri, 8am-3pm Sat). Try the Kuopio speciality *kalakukko*, a local fish baked inside a rye loaf (eaten hot or cold). The 2nd-floor **Golden Rax Pizza Buffet** (Puijonkatu 45; buffet lunch & dinner €7.90) serves the usual all-you-can-eat foodfest.

Burt's Cafe (☎ 262 3995; Puijonkatu 15; light meals €3-6; 8am-6pm Mon-Fri, 9am-4pm Sat, 11am-3pm Sun) Stylish café and the best place in town for coffee (with refills), home-made cakes, pastries and light meals.

Canton Hin Chinese (☎ 262 8738; Kauppakatu 29; mains €6-12; 11am-10pm) Cheap and cheerful Chinese place – fill up on the €6.80 lunch buffet.

Café-Restaurant Helmi (☎ 261 1110; Kauppakatu 2; mains €4.50-7; 11am-11pm Mon-Thu, 11am-1am Fri & Sat, noon-10pm Sun) In Kuopio's oldest stone building (1850) near the harbour, this atmospheric bar and restaurant specialises in great pizzas. There's often live music in the courtyard at the side.

Restaurant Gloria Kellari (☎ 263 3313; Kauppakatu 16; mains €8-19; 4pm-midnight Mon-Thu, 4pm-1am Fri & Sat) Tapas and pasta add a Mediterranean flavour to this restaurant-pub on Kuopio's most happening block.

Vapaasatama Sampo (☎ 261 4677; Kauppakatu 13; meals €8.50-11; 11am-10pm Sun-Thu, 11am-midnight Fri & Sat) Kuopio's oldest restaurant and famous all over Finland for its *muikku* (whitefish and vendace) – served in various forms, but usually with mashed potato, dill and cucumber. Sampo is also very much a typical Finnish pub and a good place to meet locals.

Isa Camillo (☎ 581 0450; Kauppakatu 25; mains €9.50-21.50; 11am-midnight Mon-Thu, 11-1am Fri & Sat, 1-8pm Sun) In a beautifully renovated former bank, this is one of Kuopio's finest restaurants, but is reasonably informal and affordable. The menu is international with plenty of Finnish specialities and there's a good enclosed terrace at the side.

Drinking & Entertainment

Most of Kuopio's nightlife is conveniently strung along Kauppakatu, running east from the market square to the harbour.

Wanha Satama (☎ 197 304; 4-10pm Mon-Fri, 11am-10pm Sat, noon-5pm Sun) Down at the harbour, this lively pub has a sprawling terrace during the summer, and occasional live music, but you pay for the location at €6 for a large beer.

TVÅ Street & Bar (☎ 369 3350; Kauppakatu 29; 6pm-2am Tue-Thu, 3pm-3am Fri & Sat) Trendy, Euro-style lounge bar with a pumping summer terrace.

O'Connell's (☎ 197 354; Käsityökatu 23; 7pm-1am Sun-Thu, 7pm-3am Fri & Sat) Friendly Irish pub down a narrow alley. Folk music and Irish stout.

Henry's Pub (☎ 262 2002; Käsityökatu 17; 7pm-4am) One of the best venues in town for live rock music, with gigs every Friday and Saturday night from 10pm and karaoke on Sunday.

Around the corner on Kauppakatu there's a block of pubs and clubs that are always jumping on weekends, including Ale Pupi, Gloria (a happening music bar and nightclub on two levels) and the Suomi pop club Giggling Marlin.

Getting There & Away

Finnair has flights to Kuopio's airport, 20km north of town, several times daily from Helsinki.

Kuopio is a transport hub for buses in the southeast region with regular express services to Helsinki (€46.10, five hours), Joensuu (€21.70, two hours), Kajaani (€24, 2½ hours) and Savonlinna (€24.60, 2½ hours). The busy main bus station is 100m north of the train station.

There are direct trains to Helsinki (€46, 5¼ hours) and Kajaani (€20.20, two hours).

From mid-June to mid-August, the lake ferry **MS Puijo** (☎ 266 2466) departs for Savonlinna (€65, 8½ hours) on Tuesday, Thursday and Saturday at 9.30am, via Heinävesi and Oravi. It returns from Savonlinna on Monday, Wednesday and Friday.

IISALMI & AROUND
☎ 017 / pop 23,500

This pretty little riverside town, 85km north of Kuopio, is home to the large Olvi brewery, which provides ample excuse for the numerous beer terraces and an annual **beer festival** in early July.

Iisalmi's **tourist office** (☎ 272 3391; www.iisalmiregion.info; Kauppakatu 22; ⏱ 9am-6pm Mon-Fri Jun-Aug, 9am-5pm Mon-Fri Sep-May) is in the big wooden building opposite the bus station. Trains and buses connect the town with Kajaani and Kuopio.

Kuappi, at the harbour's edge, bills itself as the world's smallest restaurant – it has one table, two seats, a bar and a toilet! You can't actually eat in here, but in summer they may open up the bar (it's listed in the *Guinness Book of Records* as the world's smallest pub). The building dates back to 1907 when it was a hut for railway workers.

The tiny village of **Sonkajärvi**, 18km east of Iisalmi, hosts one of Finland's whackier festivals, the annual **Wife-Carrying World Championships** in early July. The preceding day you can warm up with the **Finnish Barrel Rolling Championships**. It's an entertaining and boozy weekend – accommodation is tight (only available in private homes in the village) but the Iisalmi or Kuopio (see p169) tourist offices may be able to help.

YMCA Hostel (☎ /fax 823 940; Sarvlkatu 4C; beds from €18; ⏱ Jun & Jul, reception 5-11pm), north of the centre, is an austere HI hostel with clean rooms and kitchen and sauna.

Hotel Artos (☎ 812 244; www.hotelliartos.fi, no English; Kyllikankatu 8; s/d €62/80) is run by the Orthodox church next door, and is one of Iisami's best hotels. The restaurant does a good buffet breakfast and lunch.

JOENSUU

☎ 013 / pop 52,300

The provincial capital of North Karelia, Joensuu is mainly a jumping-off point for hikes into surrounding wilderness areas. During school term it's a lively university town with students cruising around on bikes, and there are plenty of good bars, restaurants and places to stay. The gentle Pielisjoki rapids divide the town into two parts: most of the town centre is west of the river, but the bus and train stations are to the east.

The **tourist office** (☎ 267 5319; www.kareliaexpert.com; Koskikatu 5; ⏱ 9am-5pm Mon-Fri, 11am-4pm Sat May-Sep, 9am-5pm Mon-Fri Oct-Apr; 🖳) is in the Carelicum Centre, which also has a café, free Internet and the town's best museum. Another good place for Internet access is CNB (see p174).

SHE AIN'T HEAVY, SHE'S MY WIFE!

What may have begun as a debauched habit of stealing maidens from neighbouring villages has morphed into one of Finland's maddest but most entertaining events. The Wife-Carrying World Championships, held on the first weekend of July, has put tiny Sonkajärvi on the map. The race is held over a 253m obstacle course that includes water hazards, hurdles and hills. Dropping your passenger incurs a 15-second penalty. Under Wife-Carrying competition rules the 'wife' to be carried 'can be your own, the neighbour's, or you may have found her further afield'. All borrowed wives must be returned.

Estonians are the team to beat – they've won the event five years in a row. The winners receive, among other prizes, the wife's weight in beer.

Along with the heats, finals and novelty races, this is a big weekend of drinking, dancing and mayhem. Don't miss it!

Carelicum Museum (North Karelian Museum; ☎ 267 5222; adult/student/child €4/2.50/2; ⏱ 10am-5pm Mon-Fri, 11am-4pm Sat & Sun) is one of the finest museums to be found in the eastern Lakeland area. The exhibits chart the history, traditions and culture of Karelia, part of which is now in Russia.

held in Joensuu over a weekend in mid-July, **Ilosaarirock** (www.ilosaarirock.fi) is a highly charged annual rock festival .

Sleeping

Linnunlahti Camping (☎ 126 272; www.linnunlahticamping.fi; Linnunlahdentie 1; camp sites €12, 4–6-person cabins €35-42) Just south of the centre and right next to the Ilosaari festival stage, this site has a pleasant lakeside location and good-value cabins.

Partiotalon Retkeilymaja (☎ 123 381; youthhostel@luukku.com; Vanamokatu 25; dm €10-14; ⏱ Jun–late Aug, reception 9-11am & 4-10pm) Cheapest beds in town, with basic dorms in the slightly run-down old scout hall.

Finnhostel Joensuu (☎ 267 5076; finnhostel@islo.jns.fi; Kalevankatu 8; dm/s/d €23/46.50/61) At the high end of hostel accommodation, very comfortable twin rooms include linen, TV and breakfast, and have their own bathrooms and fully equipped kitchens.

FINLAND

Eating & Drinking

As usual the *kauppatori* is packed with stalls selling cheap snacks, such as Karelian pies.

Matilda (Torikatu 23; lunch from €4.50; ☺ 9am-6pm Mon-Fri, 10am-4pm Sat, noon-5pm Sun) Just north of the market square, is this good bakery, restaurant and café.

Antique Astoria (☎ 229 766; Rantakatu 32; mains €8-18; ☺ 4pm-midnight Mon-Fri, noon-midnight Sat) Stylish riverfront restaurant specialising in Hungarian cuisine and pizza and pasta.

Wanha Jokela (☎ 122 891; Torikatu 26) This bohemian pub is the town's oldest and best-known.

CNB (Coffee & Nightlife Bar; Niskakatu 7; ☺ 2pm-late) Trendy lounge bar and Internet café with happy hours and big screen TV, plus DJs and live music on weekends.

In summer there's plenty of drinking at the harbour café Tuulaki where the passenger ferries dock.

Getting There & Away

Finnair flies daily to/from Helsinki. Joensuu's airport is 11km from town; the bus service costs €4 one way and departs from Kirkkokatu 25.

Buses arrive and depart from the bus station near the train station. Services include buses to Kuopio (€19.70, 2½ hours), Savonlinna (€19.70, three hours), Helsinki (€51, eight hours), Kuhmo (€26.30, 4½ hours) and Ilomantsi (€11.70, 1½ hours).

Direct trains run to/from Helsinki (€49.40, 5¾ hours).

In summer the MS *Vinkeri II* sails to Koli at 9.30am on Saturday, returning at 12.50pm the following day (one way/return €30/45, seven hours). You can also go on from Koli to Nurmes on the same boat, or connect with another ferry to Lieksa, across Lake Pielinen. Book through **Saimaa Ferries** (☎ 481 244; www.saimaaferries.fi).

ILOMANTSI

☎ 013 / pop 6800

Ilomantsi, 72km east of Joensuu, is Finland's most Karelian, Orthodox and eastern municipality, and the centre of a charming region where a wealth of wilderness hiking opens up before you.

The excellent **tourist office** (☎ 881 707; www.ilomantsi.com; Mantsintie 8; ☺ 9am-5pm Mon-Fri Jun & Aug-Sep, 9am-5pm Mon-Fri, 10am-2pm Sat Jul, 8.30am-4pm Mon-Fri Oct-May) can help with just about everything,

from cottage reservations to information on trekking routes and hire of camping equipment, snowshoes and cross-country ski gear. This should be your first stop if you're planning trips into the Karelian countryside.

The village centre itself is modern and quite ugly, having been trampled by the Russians, but it's the surrounding region that demands exploration. The **wine tower** (☺ 10am-10pm Jun-Aug) is worth ascending, for the views and to sample the locally made berry wine. **Parppeinvaara** (adult/child €3.50/1; ☺ 10am-6pm mid-Jun–mid-Aug) is the oldest and most interesting of Finland's Karelian theme villages, where you can hear the *kantele* (Karelian stringed instrument) played and try traditional food.

Anssilan Monola (☎ 881 181; Anssilantie; s/d €26/46, cottage €86) is run by a friendly family who rent comfy rooms in converted farmhouse buildings on this dairy farm 3.5km south of the village centre and about 500m off the main road. You can eat dinner and breakfast with the family. Recommended.

TREKS AROUND KARELIA

Some of the best trekking routes in North Karelia have been linked up to create **Karjalan Kierros**, an 800km loop of marked trails between Ilomantsi and Lake Pielinen. For more information, including maps and trail brochures, contact the Lieksa or Ilomantsi tourist offices, or **Metsähallitus** (☎ 02-0564 5500; Urheilukatu 3A, Lieksa).

Karhunpolku

The **Bear's Trail** (not to be confused with the Bear's Ring in Lapland) is a 133km marked hiking trail of medium difficulty leading north from Patvinsuo National Park near Lieksa, through a string of national parks and nature reserves along the Russian border. The trail ends at Teljo, about 50km south of Kuhmo. You'll need to arrange transport from either end.

Sustaival

The 100km **Wolf's Trail** is a marked trail running south from the marshlands of Patvinsuo National Park to the forests of Petkeljärvi National Park, 21km east of Ilomantsi. This links with the Bear's Trail.

LAKE PIELINEN REGION

In a land full of lakes, Pielinen, Finland's sixth-largest lake, is pretty special. It's the jewel of North Karelia, surrounded by some of the most amazing wilderness areas and action-packed countryside in southeast Finland. Koli National Park rises in the southeast corner, and the main towns around the lake – Lieka, Nurmes and Koli – are linked by lake ferry in summer.

Lieksa & Ruunaa
☎ 013 / pop 16,000

The small centre of Lieksa, about 100km north of Joensuu, is primarily a base and service town if you're planning any outdoor activities in the region. In winter, husky tours and snowmobile safaris along the Russian border are popular; in summer, hiking, fishing and white-water rafting are all the rage,

The **tourist office** (Lieksan Matkailu Oy; ☎ 689 4050; www.lieksa.fi/travel; Pielisentie 7; ⏰ 8am-6pm Mon-Fri, 9am-2pm Sat Jun & Aug, 8am-6pm Mon-Fri, 9am-2pm Sat, 11am-3pm Sun Jul, 8am-4pm Mon-Fri Sep-May) has information on accommodation, fishing, canoeing, smoke saunas and national parks, as well as local hiking maps.

One of Finland's largest open-air museums, the **Pielinen Museum** (☎ 689 4151; Pappilantie 2; adult/child €4.50/1.50; ⏰ 10am-6pm mid May–mid-Sep) is a remarkable complex of almost 100 Karelian buildings (many relocated from Russia) and historical exhibits – along with an indoor museum of local war and folk history. The indoor hall is also open in winter.

The **Ruunaa Recreation Area**, 30km east of Lieksa, is a superb, carefully controlled wilderness area perfect for fishing, white-water rafting and easy hiking. The drawback is that public transport barely exists, but you should be able to hitch a lift from Lieksa (or go with an organised tour) in summer. The **Ruunaa Nature Centre** (☎ 02-0564 5757; ⏰ 9am-7pm summer) near the bridge over the Naarajoki river is where most boat trips end.

There are six rapids here, and several daily launches of wooden and inflatable boats during summer; the nature centre or Lieksa tourist office can line you up with an operator (a two- to four-hour trip per adult/child costs €36/18). Walking trails cover the entire area, and there are bridges, camp sites and free lean-to *laavu* (shelters).

SLEEPING
Kestikievari Herranniemi (☎ 542 110; www.herranniemi.com; Vuonislahdentie 185; dm €12.50, cottages €25-68, B&B d €62) The small Vuonislahti train station

28km south of Lieksa is the jumping-off point for this brilliant lakeside retreat. The farm building has a restaurant, a range of comfortable rooms and cottages, two lakeside saunas, rowing boats and even massage and herbal therapy.

Neitikoski Hiking Centre (☎ 533 170; camp sites €10, 4–6-bed cabins from €75) At Ruunaa, in addition to accommodation and services at Naarajoki, the Hiking Centre has a large café, camping sites, kitchen, sauna and luxurious cabins. A boardwalk goes a short distance from here to the Neitikoski rapids, a popular fishing and kayaking spot.

GETTING THERE & AWAY
Trains and buses run regularly to/from Joensuu and Nurmes, but the most pleasant way to arrive here is by ferry from Joensuu (via Koli, opposite). A huge 250-person car ferry (adult/child €15/7 one way, car/bicycle €7/2, 1¾ hours) runs twice daily between Lieksa and Koli from June to mid-August, departing at 9.30am and 3.30pm, returning at 11.30am and 5.30pm.

Koli National Park
Finns regard the views from the heights of Koli, overlooking Lake Pielinen, as the best in the country – the same views inspired several Finnish artists from the National Romantic era. In summer, the national park offers scenic hiking routes, and there's a ferry service between Koli and Lieksa (less than two hours) or Joensuu (seven hours). In winter, Koli attracts skiers, with two slalom centres and more than 60km of cross-country trails, including 24km of illuminated track.

There's a regular bus service from Koli village up to the top of the hill. At the top, the **Ukko-Koli Heritage Centre** (☎ 688 8400) has displays and information on the national park.

The family-run **Koli Hostel** (☎ 673 131; Niinilahdentie 47; dm from €10), on a gravel road 5km from the bus stop, has a kitchen and smoke sauna. If you call ahead you may be able to arrange a pick-up.

Nurmes
☎ 013 / pop 10,000

Like Lieksa, Nurmes is a base for wallet-draining activities such as snowmobiling, ice-fishing, dogsledding and cross-country skiing tours in winter, and canoeing and farmhouse tours in summer. It's a more pleasant town in its own right though, with an 'old town' area (Puu-Nurmes) of historical wooden buildings along Kirkkokatu. A highlight is **Bomba House**, part of a delightful re-creation of a Karelian village 3km southeast of the centre. The village features a summer market, craft shops and cafés.

For local information and to book activities, the **Loma-Nurmes tourist office** (☎ 687 2500; www.nurmes.fi; ☺ 8am-10pm Jun-Aug, 9am-4pm Mon-Fri Sep-May) is at the Hyvärilä holiday complex, which is also the obvious place to stay. **Hyvärilä** (☎ 687 2500; camp sites €13, dm/s/d from €15/39/58) is a sprawling lakeside complex with a camping ground, two youth hostels, an upmarket hotel, restaurant and even a golf course.

Bomba Spa Hotel (☎ 687 200; Suojärvenkatu1; s/d from €82/98), near the Karelian village, is a stylish set-up of rooms and cottages, where you can pamper yourself with the spa and sauna facilities.

There are regular buses from Nurmes to Joensuu, Lieksa, Kajaani and Kuopio; and direct regional trains from Joensuu (€15.60, two hours) and Lieksa (€7.20, 45 minutes).

In summer there are cruises on Lake Pielinen and ferries to Koli on Sunday (adult/child €20/10).

NORTH-CENTRAL FINLAND

KAJAANI
☎ 08 / pop 35,000
Kajaani is the centre of the Kainuu region, and although a pleasant enough riverside city, for travellers it's mainly a transport hub and stopover on the haul between the south and Lapland. An international **jazz festival** in early June brings Kajaani to life.

The **tourist office** (☎ 6155 2555; Kauppakatu 21; ☺ 9am-5.30pm Mon-Fri, 9am-2pm Sat Jun-Aug, 9am-4.30pm Sep-May) is just off the tiny town square.

The town was once noted as Finland's largest tar-producer, but its greatest historical claim to fame is that writer Elias Lönnrot, author of the epic *Kalevala*, used Kajaani as a base for his travels. The **Kainuu museum** (☎ 6155 2407; Asemakatu 4; adult/child €2/1; noon-4pm Sun-Tue & Thu-Sat, noon-8pm Wed), opposite the youth hostel, has a good section on Lönnrot.

At the Ämmäkoski waterfall, near the remnants of Kajaani castle, is a **tar-boat canal**,

a type of lock built in 1846 to enable the boats laden with tar barrels to pass.

Sleeping & Eating
Retkeilymaja Huone ja Aamiainen (☎ /fax 622 254; Pohjolankatu 4; s/d/tr €28/40/54; ☺ reception from 4pm) A basic but central HI-affiliated place with clean rooms, breakfast and linen included. No dorms.

Kartanohotelli Karolineburg (☎ 613 1291; www .karolineburg.com; Karoliinantie 4; s/d from €60/76, double with sauna from €90, ste from €130) Easily the most romantic place to stay in Kajaani, if not this part of northern Finland. It's an elegant 19th-century wooden manor house across the river from the centre.

The partly pedestrianised Kauppakatu – leading from the market square to the town square – is the main street and has many cafés and restaurants. **Pikantti** (cnr Kauppakatu & Urho Kekkonenkatu; buffet €8.90; ☺ 10am-5pm Mon-Fri, 10am-4pm Sat) lays on excellent lunch buffets all day.

Getting There & Away
Finnair flies to/from Helsinki, and trains connect with Kuopio, Nurmes and Oulu. Buses go to Oulu (€22.30), Kuusamo (€30.80), Kuhmo (€15.60) and Kuopio (€22).

KUHMO
☎ 08 / pop 6500
Kuhmo, like Kajaani, was once a major tar producer, but is now a service town in the heart of real wilderness territory – it's an excellent jumping-off point for the UKK trekking route, Finland's longest marked trek.

The town is also famous for the annual **Kuhmo Chamber Music Festival** (☎ 652 0936; www .kuhmofestival.fi; Torikatu 39), held from mid-July to August, which attracts musicians from around the world.

The helpful **tourist office** (☎ 655 6382; www .kuhmonet.fi; Kainuuntie 82; ☺ 8am-6pm Mon-Fri, 10am-4pm Sat Jun–late Aug, 8am-5pm Mon-Fri late Aug–May) is good for national park and festival information. There's free Internet access at the **library** (☎ 655 6721; Pajakkakatu 2; ☺ 10am-7pm Mon-Wed & Fri, 2-7pm Thu).

Kalevala Village theme park (☎ 652 0114; guided tour adult/child €11/5.50; ☺ 10am-5pm Mon-Sat Jun–late Aug), 3km from the centre, is the main attraction in Kuhmo. The open-air museum of Karelian log buildings and artisan displays is linked by a walking track.

Sleeping

Kuhmo Youth Hostel (☎ 655 6245; Kainuuntie 113; dm/s/d €12/26/30; ☯ July) HI hostel in the Piilolan school building – open only in July when the town is crowded with music lovers.

Kuhmon Matkakoti (☎ /fax 655 0271; Vienantie 3; s/d/tr €25/44/60) Friendly, good-value guesthouse near the town centre. Breakfast and sauna included.

Kalevala Camping (☎ 655 6388; camp sites €11, 2-/4-person cabins from €26/34; ☯ Jun–late Aug) Near the Kalevala Village theme park, this lakeside camping ground has good facilities including a smoke sauna and boats.

Getting There & Away

There are numerous daily buses to/from Kajaani (€15.20, 1½ hours), where you can pick up road and rail connections to elsewhere west and south, and direct buses to Nurmes (€11.90, 1½ hours) and Joensuu (€30.10, four hours).

UKK Trekking Route

The 240km Urho K Kekkonen (UKK) route is Finland's longest marked trail, passing through pockets of the now-rare Finnish wilderness on the way from Koli Hill in North Karelia to Iso-Syöte Hill far to the north of Kuhmo. Two of the finest sections of the UKK route are the Kuhmo–Hiidenportti and Kuhmo–Lentiira legs.

The trail is well maintained in the Kuhmo area, with clear markings and *laavu* (simple shelters) spaced every 10km to 20km. In summer, carry a sleeping bag and plenty of mosquito repellent.

You can pick up route maps and information at the Kuhmo tourist office or the **Kainuu Nature Centre** (☎ 877 6380; kaapalinna@metsa.fi), also in Kuhmo.

OULU

☎ 08 / pop 124,600

The lively, fast-growing university town of Oulu looks out on the Gulf of Bothnia and a string of interconnected islands. Hi-tech companies have set up shop here in recent years, lending an affluent, progressive air. It's not the sights that make Oulu worth a stop, but its summertime energy, superb cycling paths, friendly locals and frenetic nightlife.

Oulu grew prosperous from tar, which was floated down the river from the Kainuu region and shipped to Sweden for shipbuilding.

Information

INTERNET ACCESS

Public Library (☎ 558 410; Kaarlenväylä; ☯ 10am-8pm Mon-Fri, 10am-3pm Sat) Internet terminals (book ahead) and a reading room.

Pint Netti Baari (per 10 min €1, free to customers; ☯ noon-3am) Two Internet terminals free to customers at this pub on Rotuaari.

TOURIST INFORMATION

The **tourist office** (☎ 5584 1330; www.oulutourism.fi; Torikatu 10; ☯ 9am-6pm Mon-Fri, 10am-3pm Sat mid-Jun–mid-Aug, 9am-4pm Mon-Fri mid-Aug–mid-Jun) publishes the useful guide *Look at Oulu*.

Sights & Activities

The imposing, 19th-century **cathedral** (Kirkkokatu) was designed by Carl Engel and has Finland's oldest portrait (dating from 1611) hanging in its vestry. The **kauppatori**, near the quay, is one of the most colourful in Finland with its red wooden storehouses (now housing restaurants, bars and craft shops), market stalls, bursting summer terraces and its rotund statue, *Toripoliisi*.

Tietomaa (☎ 5584 1340; www.tietomaa.fi; adult/child €10/8.50; ☯ 10am-8pm Jul, 10am-6pm Aug-Jun), Scandinavia's largest science museum, can occupy a full day, with an IMAX screen, interactive displays on planets and the human body, and an observation tower; it's a fun day for kids.

Oulu City Art Museum (☎ 5584 7450; Kasarmintie 7; adult/child €3/1, free Fri; ☯ 11am-6pm Tue-Sun), nearby, has some intriguing temporary international and Finnish exhibitions.

Oulu's extensive network of wonderful **bicycle paths** is among the best in Finland and nowhere is the Finns' love of two-wheeled transport more obvious than here in summer. Bikes can be hired from the train station (per day €10), and a route map is available from the tourist office. A good ride or walk is out to **Pikisaari island** via the pedestrian bridge by the *kauppatori*. It's a favourite picnic and drinking spot for locals in summer. Continue west to Nallikari and Oulu's best beach.

Sleeping

Oulu has a few good budget choices in summer (June to August) but at other times of the year you're stuck with pricey hotel rooms.

Nallikari Camping (☎ 5586 1350; nallikari.camping@ouka.fi; Hietasaari; camp sites €15-17, 2-4-person cabins €29, 2-/5-/7-person cottages €53/75/109) This lovely

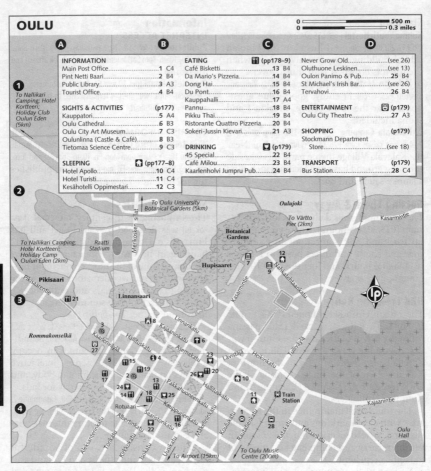

OULU

0 ——— 500 m
0 ——— 0.3 miles

INFORMATION
Main Post Office.................................1 C4
Pint Netti Baari...................................2 B4
Public Library.....................................3 A3
Tourist Office.....................................4 B4

SIGHTS & ACTIVITIES (p177)
Kauppatori...5 A4
Oulu Cathedral....................................6 B3
Oulu City Art Museum.........................7 C3
Oulunlinna (Castle & Café)..................8 B3
Tietomaa Science Centre.....................9 C3

SLEEPING (pp177–8)
Hotel Apollo.....................................10 C4
Hotel Turisti....................................11 C4
Kesähotelli Oppimestari....................12 C3

EATING (pp178–9)
Café Bisketti....................................13 B4
Da Mario's Pizzeria...........................14 B4
Dong Hai...15 B4
Du Pont...16 B4
Kauppahalli......................................17 A4
Pannu..18 B4
Pikku Thai..19 B4
Ristorante Quattro Pizzeria...............20 B4
Sokeri-Jussin Kievari..........................21 A3

DRINKING (p179)
45 Special..22 B4
Café Milou.......................................23 B4
Kaarlenholvi Jumpru Pub...................24 B4

Never Grow Old...........................(see 26)
Oluthuone Leskinen......................(see 13)
Oulun Panimo & Pub.......................25 B4
St Michael's Irish Bar....................(see 26)
Tervahovi...26 B4

ENTERTAINMENT (p179)
Oulu City Theatre.............................27 A3

SHOPPING (p179)
Stockmann Department
Store...(see 18)

TRANSPORT (p179)
Bus Station......................................28 C4

---

site is Oulu's saviour for budget travellers. It's on Hietasaari island, 5km northwest of the city centre by road – but only 3km by foot or bicycle via the pedestrian bridges. Cheap cabins are only available in summer, but the year-round self-contained cottages (with bathroom and kitchen) are a much better alternative to hotels. Nearby is the good Nallikari beach.

Kesähotelli Oppimestari (☎ 884 8527; Nahkateh-taankatu 3; s/d €37/55; ✆ Jun–early Aug) Across from the Tietomaa Science Centre, this clean and efficient summer hotel has the cheapest rooms in Oulu.

Hotel Turisti (☎ 563 6100; Rautatienkatu 9; s/d/tr €75/90/100, s/d/tr discount weekends €50/60/70) This is a surprisingly bright and tidy place directly

opposite the train station; the decent-sized rooms have private bathrooms.

Hotel Apollo (☎ 52211; hotel@apollo.inet.fi; Ase-makatu 31-33; s/d from €80/100, s/d discount €64/78) Small but stylish hotel with attractive summer rates. Rooms with private sauna cost €83/100 in summer.

Eating

Local specialities can be found in the lively *kauppatori* and the classic indoor *kauppa-halli* on the southern side of the square. In summer there are stalls selling fresh salmon, cheese, bread, paella and more. Oulu's hungry student population means there are plenty of cheap kebab and pizza places. The best pizzas are at **Da Mario's Pizzeria** (☎ 379 505;

Torikatu 24; pizzas €6), while some of the cheapest can be found at **Ristorante Quattro Pizzeria** (Asemakatu 20) where you can get pizza, salad and a drink for €5.

Café Bisketti (☎ 375 768; Kirkkokatu 8; snacks €2.50-5) Great spot for lunch with filled rolls, croissants, quiche and cakes. There's a small terrace facing the pedestrian square.

Pikku Thai (☎ 370 889; Pakkahuoneenkatu 7; mains €10-13, lunch special €6.50; ☽ 10.30am-10pm Mon-Thu, noon-11pm Sat, noon-9pm Sun) Cosy little Thai restaurant with spicy food and good-value lunch specials with salad buffet on weekdays.

Dong Hai (☎ 815 5066; Rantakatu 5; mains €8-12, lunch buffet €7; ☽ 11am-10pm Sun-Thu, 11am-11pm Fri & Sat) Opposite the market square this cheap and tasty Chinese place also has good lunch deals.

Pannu (☎ 815 1600; Kauppurienkatu 12; mains €9.50-19.50; ☽ 10.30am-10pm Mon-Thu, 10.30am-11pm Fri & Sat, noon-9pm Sun) In the basement of Stockmann department store, this fabulous, informal grill restaurant offers a huge range of dishes from wild boar to ostrich, and monster steaks. Lunch specials from 10.30am to 2pm weekdays.

DuPont (☎ 554 5880; Kauppurienkatu 24; mains €10-17; ☽ 4-11pm Mon-Thu, 4pm-4am Fri, 4pm-midnight Sat) Steaks, burgers and Tex-Mex are the staples at this new restaurant but it also has live music, Finnish comedians and a happy atmosphere.

Sokeri-Jussin Kievari (☎ 376 628; Pikisaarentie 2; mains €8.50-25; ☽ 11am-11pm Mon-Thu, 11am-midnight Fri & Sat, noon-10pm Sun) One of Oulu's most atmospheric dining experiences, this pub-restaurant is in a beautiful old wooden storehouse just over the bridge on Pikisaari island. Finnish specialities include elk meatballs (€12), fried *muikku* (whitefish), steak and reindeer dishes.

Drinking & Entertainment

There's plenty going on in Oulu at night – the number of bikes lined up outside pubs and bars on summer weekends has to be seen to be believed. In summer, the terraces on the market square are a great place to relax with a drink.

Kaarlenholvi Jumpru Pub (☎ 562 4500; Kauppurienkatu 6; ☽ 11am-2am Mon-Tue, 11am-4am Wed-Sat, noon-2am Sun) An Oulu institution, this pub-nightclub and live music venue is a top place for meeting locals. It has a lively enclosed terrace, and a warren of cosy rooms inside.

Oluthuone Leskinen (☎ 311 7993; Kirkkukato 10; ☽ 11am-late) Friendly bar with a huge range of Finnish and international beers. Try the burnt-flavoured local speciality, tar schnapps – distilled from tar. This is where expats working for Nokia start (and often end) their night, so it's a good place to find out where to head next.

Cafe Milou (☎ Asemakatu 21; ☽ noon-2am) Away from the main strip but one of the hippest bars in town, Milou packs in students with its cheap beer, 'way gone' vibe and Sunday jazz sessions.

45 Special (☎ 881 1845; Saaristonkatu 12; ☽ 8pm-4am daily) Oulu's best rock venue and late-night hot spot, with DJs, live bands, Sunday jams, free entry most nights and wall-to-wall people.

For something more refined, the **Oulu Theatre** (☎ 5584 7600; Kaarlenväylä 2) has classical music, contemporary theatre and the occasional Shakespearian performance.

The main pedestrian strip between the *kauppatori* and Isokatu is called Rotuaari and along here you'll find plenty of bars and cafés, including **Oulon Panimo & Pub** (Kauppurienkatu 13), a brewery pub with three home-grown tap beers, a happening atmosphere and occasional live music.

On Hallituskatu is a small strip of bars and cafés with terraces, including Never Grow Old, a reggae bar that hits its stride after 10pm; Tervahovi, a typically Finnish pub popular with a slightly older crowd; and St Michael's, an Irish bar.

Getting There & Away

Finnair has daily direct flights from Helsinki. The airport is 15km south of town (take bus No 19, €4.50). Trains and buses connect Oulu with all main centres; direct trains include Helsinki (€59, seven to 10 hours) and Rovaniemi (€26.40, 2½ hours).

KUUSAMO
☎ 08 / pop 19,000

Kuusamo is a frontier town 200km northeast of Oulu and close to the Arctic Circle. There are really only two reasons to detour out here: in summer, it's the base for trekking and canoeing the sublime **Oulanko National Park**; in winter, it's only 30km from **Ruka**, one of Finland's most popular ski resorts.

There are many possibilities for cross-country skiing, hiking and fishing as well as fast, rugged rapids on the **Kitkajoki** and **Oulankajoki** rivers. Inquire about organised tours at the **Kuusamo tourist office** (☎ 850 2910; www.kuusamo.fi; Torangintaival 2).

Kuusamon Kansanopisto (☎ 852 2132; Kitkantie 35; dm from €10, s/d €20/30; ◷ Midsummer–Aug) is a rambling summer HI hostel close to Kuusamo's town centre. There's more accommodation at Ruka and at camp sites and wilderness huts in Oulanko National Park.

Finnair flies daily to Helsinki. Buses run daily from Kajaani, Oulu and Kemijärvi.

Oulanko National Park

This is one of the most visited national parks in Finland, thanks mainly to the 80km **Karhunkierros Trail** (Bear's Ring), a spectacular three- or four-day trek through rugged cliffs, gorges and suspension bridges, starting from either the Hautajärvi Visitor Centre or the Ristikallio parking area and ending at Ruka, 25km north of Kuusamo.

There are shelters and free overnight huts on the trail. The *Rukatunturi-Oulanka map* (1:40,000) has trail and hut information.

Juuma is another gateway to the region, with accommodation and accessibility to some of the main sights, such as the **Myllykoski** and **Jyrävä** waterfalls. If you don't have the time or resources for the longer walk, you can do the 12km **Little Bear's Ring** from Juuma in around four hours. The trail starts at **Lomakylä Retkietappi** (☎ 863 218), where there are camp sites and cabins.

TORNIO

☎ 016 / pop 23,200

Tornio is a divided town with an interesting past – across the Tornionjoki river is its twin, the Swedish town of Haparanda, and the two are geographically melded into one. This is the most southerly land crossing between Sweden and Finland. Swedes often trundle across the bridge to take advantage of Finland's cheaper alcohol and an extra hour of daylight!

Tornio and Haparanda share one of the world's most bizarre golf courses, and 15km north of Tornio are Finland's longest free-flowing rapids – ideal for fishing and white-water rafting.

Tornio's town centre is on Seunsaari, an island on the west bank of the river.

The **Green Line Centre** (☎ 432 733; www.tornio .fi; ◷ 8am-8pm Mon-Fri, 10am-8pm Sat & Sun Jun–mid-

Aug, 8-11.30am & 12.30-4pm Mon-Fri mid-Aug–May), near the bridge on the Tornio side of the border, houses the tourist office for both towns, with information on Finland and Sweden.

There are a couple of Internet terminals at the **public library** (☎ 432 433; Torikatu 2; ◷ 11am-7pm Mon-Thu, 11am-5pm Fri, 11am-3pm Sat), next to the Aine Art Museum. The post office is at Halliskatu 11.

Tornio time is one hour ahead of Haparanda time.

Sights & Activities

Interesting sights near the town centre include the beautiful wooden **Tornio Church** (1686) on Seminaarinkatu; the tiny **Orthodox Church** on Lukiokatuthe, built by order of Tsar Alexander I; the **Lapin Kulta Brewery** (☎ 43366; Lapinkullankatu 1; free tours 2pm Tue & Thu Jun-Aug); and the **Aine Art Museum** (☎ 432 438; Torikatu 2; adult/child €2/1; ◷ 11am-6pm Tue-Thu, 11am-3pm Fri-Sun), with a big collection of Finnish art from the 19th and 20th centuries.

The **Green Zone Golf Course** (☎ 431 711; Näräntie 1; green fees €33 for 18 holes, €8 for par 3 course, club hire €10) is unique: not only can you play midnight golf (with the sun shining), but the course actually straddles the border. You can tee off in Finland and hit the ball into Sweden, which means if you start at, say, 12.30am, the ball will remain in the air for an hour and land in yesterday. All this novelty, and a round on a pretty good course, can be yours when the snow melts away between late May and late August. To play after 10pm you need to book in advance.

Rafting trips are popular in summer on the 3.5km-long **Kukkola rapids**, 15km north of town. Contact **Lapland Connection** (☎ 253 405; www.safarisunlimited.fi).

Sleeping & Eating

Camping Tornio (☎ 445 945; sirkka.hyry@pp.inet.fi; Matkailijantie; camp sites €18, cabins d €54) is about 3km from town on the road to Kemi.

Hostel Tornio (☎ 211 9244; pptoimisto@ppopisto.fi, Kivirannantie 13-15; s/d €13.50/27, s/d with private bathroom €25/40; ◷ Jun-Aug) Typical HI-affiliated summer hostel in a rotten location east of the river about 3km from the centre. Facilities are good, including kitchen, lounge, laundry and a small gym.

STF Youth Hostel (☎ 0046 611 71; Strandgatan 26) A better choice for hostellers is this option in Haparanda (see p427).

Matkakotti Heta (☎ 480 897; Saarenpäänkatu 39; s/d/tr €27/42/60) Slightly eccentric owners add to the character of this guesthouse, in a pretty part of town. There's a cosy lounge with art gallery, and a sauna. Breakfast is €5.

Karkiaisen Leipomo (Länsiranta 9) The best place for fresh pastries, cakes and *donitsi* (doughnuts) in town.

Golden Flower (☎ 481 384; Eliaksenkatu 8; mains €6-13.50, lunch from €6.50; ☷ 11am-10pm Tue-Fri, noon-10pm Sat, 1-10pm Sun) Inexpensive licensed Chinese restaurant with cheap lunches and a broad menu.

Umpitunneli (☎ 430 360; Hallituskatu 15; ☷ 11am-2am Sun-Thu, 11-4am Fri & Sat) For entertainment Finnish-style, head to this classic open-air dance pub and restaurant where you can see the *humppa* (Finnish waltz) in full swing from Wednesday to Saturday in summer; year-round it's a rollicking bar and nightclub.

Getting There & Away

From Kemi, take a bus from the train station (€4.80, free with Finnrail pass; 30 minutes). Road No 21 leads from Tornio to the north, and there are buses to Muonio (€32.90, 3½ hours) and Rovaniemi (€17.50, 2½ hours, via Kemi). If you're heading to Sweden there are buses to Stockholm (€55).

KEMI

☎ 016 / pop 25,000

Kemi is an industrial town with huge pulp factories creating a strong whiff of sulphur smell. If that sounds like a good reason to stay away, think again. In winter (December to April) Kemi is home to two of Lapland's biggest attractions.

Plough through the pack ice on a four-hour cruise aboard the *Sampo*, an authentic **Arctic icebreaker** ship and the only one in the world that accepts passengers. The trip includes ice swimming in special dry-suits, as well as a walk or snowmobile trip on the ice – an awesome experience. The *Sampo* sails at noon three to four days a week from mid-December to late April and costs a whopping €182 per person. Contact **Sampo Tours** (☎ 256 548; www.sampotours.com; Torikatu 2).

Another reason to visit in winter is the **Snow Castle** (Lumilinna; ☎ 259 502; www.snowcastle .net; adult/child €5/2.50; ☷ 10am-6pm Mon-Thu, 10am-8pm Fri-Sun Feb–mid-Apr). The castle features an ice restaurant with bar, ice tables covered with

reindeer fur, and ice sculptures. It's also possible to stay overnight in the **snow hotel** where heavy-duty Arctic sleeping bags keep you warm in -5°C room temperature!

The **tourist office** (☎ 259 467; www.kemi.fi; Kauppakatu 19; ☷ 8am-6pm Mon-Fri, 10am-6pm Sat Jun-Aug, 8am-4pm Mon-Fri Sep-May), in the Gemstone Gallery at the town harbour, can direct you to a handful of other attractions in town.

Sleeping

Hotel Relletti (☎ 233 541; Miilukatu 1; s/d €35/55; ☷ Jun–mid-Aug) About 1.5km southeast of the train station, this is a simple summer hotel offering affordable rooms with private bathrooms.

Hotel Palomestari (☎ 257 117; www.hotellipalom estari.com; Valtakatu 12; s/d from €72/100, s/d discount €87/72) The pick of Kemi's mid-range hotels, Palomestari is central – only a few hundred metres from the bus and train stations – and reasonably intimate.

Getting There & Away

There are trains from Helsinki (€66.20, nine to 11 hours) and Rovaniemi (€15.40, 1½ hours). Buses to/from Tornio (€4.80, 30 minutes) are free with a Finnrail pass.

LAPLAND

Lapland is Finland's true wilderness: a mysterious land of Arctic extremes where the midnight sun brings continuous daylight in the brief summer (June to August) and the long, polar nights offer the chance to view the stunning aurora borealis (October to March).

From September, the period known locally as *ruska* (autumn) produces exceptional colours of gold, red and brown, and in the far north *kaamos*, the season of eerie bluish light, begins late in October. Winter activities are a highlight of Lapland: skiing, dogsledding, snowmobiling and ice-fishing, or riding on the Arctic icebreaker in Kemi. In summer, you can hike in some of Finland's best national parks or play midnight golf on the famous course at Tornio.

ROVANIEMI

☎ 016 / pop 35,400

Rovaniemi is Lapland's capital and gateway city, though there's not much that's Lappish about the modern town centre since it was razed by retreating Germans in WWII and rebuilt to a plan by architect Alvar Aalto (the main streets radiate out from Hallituskatu in the shape of reindeer antlers but this would only be obvious from the air!).

'Crossing' the Arctic Circle is not a major event in its own right, but there's a lot to be said for this latitude in summer – when the midnight sun really does shine – and in winter this is a convenient base for expensive dog- or reindeer-sledding, skiing or snowmobile safaris.

Information

BOOKSHOPS
Suomalainen Kirjakauppa (Rovakatu 24) Opposite the tourist centre, sells English-language books and maps.

INTERNET ACCESS
Public Library (☎ 322 2463; Jorma Eton tie 6; ☾ 11am-7pm Mon-Fri, 11am-5pm Sat, 11am-3pm Sun) Free Internet access, maximum 20 minutes, or one hour if you reserve in advance. Also has a newspaper reading room. Reached from Halliskatu.

LEFT LUGGAGE
There are luggage lockers (€2 to €3) at the train and bus stations, and a left luggage counter at the train station.

MEDICAL SERVICES
Rovaniemi Health Centre (☎ 32241, 322 4900; Sairaalakatu 1)

POST
Main Post Office (Postikatu 1; ☾ 9am-8pm Mon-Fri) Near the train station but there is another branch right in the town centre at Koskikatu 9. Most visitors prefer to send their postcards from the busy Santa Claus post office at Napapiiri (p185).

TOURIST INFORMATION
Santa Claus Tourist Centre (☎ 346 270; www.rovaniemi.fi; Rovakatu 21; ☾ 8am-6pm Mon-Fri, 10am-4pm Sat & Sun Jun–late Aug, 8am-4pm Mon-Fri late Aug–May) Corny name but an excellent source of information for all of Lapland. Internet access per 15 min €2.
Etiäinen (☎ 647 820; ☾ 10am-5pm) At Napapiiri, this is the information centre for the national parks and trekking regions, with information on hiking and fishing in Lapland.

TRAVEL AGENCIES
The following outfits all offer summer and winter activities including snowmobiling,

reindeer and husky safaris, and river cruises from €80 to €150 per person.
Arctic Safaris (☎ 340 0400; www.arcticsafaris.fi; Koskikatu 6)
Eräsetti Safaris (☎ 362 811; www.erasetti.fi; Santa Claus Village)
Lapland Safaris (☎ 331 1200; www.laplandsafaris.com; Koskikatu 1)
Northern Gate Safaris (☎ 311 042; www.northerngate safaris.com; Valtakatu 23)
Safartica (☎ 311 485; www.safartica.com; Valtakatu 20)

Sights & Activities
Arktikum (☎ 317 830; www.arktikum.fi; Pohjoisranta 4; adult/student/child €11/8.50/5; ☾ 9am-7pm mid-Jun–mid-Aug, 10am-6pm early Jun & late Aug, 10am-6pm Tue-Sun Sep-May), with its beautifully designed glass tunnel stretching out to the Kemijoki river, spacious layout and engrossing, well-presented exhibitions, is one of Finland's premier museums. Superb static and interactive displays focus on Arctic flora and fauna (including elk, bears and reindeer) as well as the Sami and other people of Arctic Europe, Asia and North America. Other photographic exhibits examine the lives of ordinary Finns and there are displays showing the destruction of Rovaniemi by the Germans in WWII. There's also a theatre screening a short film about the aurora borealis, a library and a good café. Give yourself at least a couple of hours to get around this museum. It's a pleasant walk from the centre of town following the path along the river.

Rovaniemi Art Museum (☎ 322 2822; Lapinkävijäntie 4; adult/child €4/2, free Sat; ☾ noon-5pm Tue-Sat) has changing exhibitions of Finnish modern art.

Rovaniemi has several buildings designed by Alvar Aalto, including the library, town hall and **Lappia-talo** (☎ 322 2495; Hallituskatu 11-13), an impressive concert hall.

Across the Ounasjoki river and 3km above the town, the **Ounasvaara Ski Centre** (☎ 369 045; www.ounasvaara.net) has six downhill ski slopes and three ski jumps, plus a summer tobogganing run. It's a good spot for hiking in summer.

In summer there are two-hour **boat cruises** (☎ 0400-292132; adult/child €10/5; ☾ 2pm, 5pm & 8pm) on the Kemijoki river.

Festivals & Events
Rovaniemi hosts events year-round. In January, the **Arctic Lapland Rally** starts here, and in mid-March the **Reindeer City Race** flies

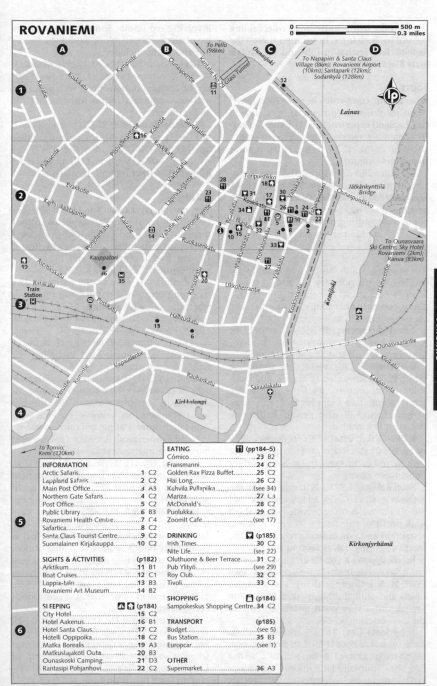

ROVANIEMI

0 _____ 500 m
0 _____ 0.3 miles

To Pello (98km)

To Napapiiri & Santa Claus Village (8km); Rovaniemi Airport (10km); Santapark (12km); Sodankylä (128km)

Lainas

Jätkänkynttilä Bridge

To Ounasvaara Ski Centre; Sky Hotel Rovaniemi (2km); Ranua (83km)

FINLAND

Kirkonjyrhämä

To Tornio; Kemi (120km)

Kirkkolampi

INFORMATION	
Arctic Safaris	1 C2
Lappland Safaris	2 C2
Main Post Office	3 A3
Northern Gate Safaris	4 C2
Post Office	5 C2
Public Library	6 B3
Rovaniemi Health Centre	7 C4
Safartica	8 C2
Santa Claus Tourist Centre	9 C2
Suomalainen Kirjakauppa	10 C2

SIGHTS & ACTIVITIES	(p182)
Arktikum	11 B1
Boat Cruises	12 C1
Lappia-talo	13 B3
Rovaniemi Art Museum	14 B2

SLEEPING	(p184)
City Hotel	15 C2
Hotel Aakenus	16 B1
Hotel Santa Claus	17 C2
Hotelli Oppipoika	18 C2
Matka Borealis	19 A3
Matkustajakoti Outa	20 B3
Ounaskoski Camping	21 D3
Rantasipi Pohjanhovi	22 C2

EATING	(pp184-5)
Cómico	23 B2
Fransmanni	24 C2
Golden Rax Pizza Buffet	25 C2
Hai Long	26 C2
Kahvila Pullapiika	(see 34)
Mariza	27 C3
McDonald's	28 C2
Puolukka	29 C2
ZoomIt Cafe	(see 17)

DRINKING	(p185)
Irish Times	30 C2
Nite Life	(see 22)
Oluthuone & Beer Terrace	31 C2
Pub Ylityö	(see 29)
Roy Club	32 C2
Tivoli	33 C2

SHOPPING	(p184)
Sampokeskus Shopping Centre	34 C2

TRANSPORT	(p185)
Budget	(see 5)
Bus Station	35 B3
Europcar	(see 1)

OTHER	
Supermarket	36 A3

through the town centre, with riders skiing behind their charges. In summer there's the **Kemijoki Rock Festival** in July and the **Roots & River Blues Festival** in August.

Tours

Several tour companies in town (see Travel Agencies under Information) specialise in the 'Lapland experience', so you can you easily organise a reindeer sleigh ride in winter (November–March) or a river cruise in summer (June–August).

In winter and early spring the most popular activities include **snowmobiling** (from €88), and **husky dog** and **reindeer safaris** (from €100). Summer tours include river cruises from €20, white-water rafting and fishing expeditions from €45 to €115 per person.

Sleeping

Rovaniemi's youth hostel was demolished in 2004, so it's not easy for budget travellers to find a cheap bed. The big hotels discount rooms substantially in summer and on weekends.

Ounaskoski Camping (☎ 345 304; Jämerentie 1; camp sites €5; ☺ Jun-Aug) Just across the river from the town centre, with tent and van sites only.

Matka Borealis (☎ /fax 342 0130; Asemieskatu 1; s/d €45/58; P ☒) Rovaniemi's cosiest and best-value guesthouse is virtually opposite the train station. It's a friendly place with clean, simple rooms, all with private bathroom. Breakfast is included.

Matkustajakoti Outa (☎ 312 474; Ukkoherrantie 16; s/d €35/45; ☒) A cheap, no-frills guesthouse with shared bathrooms, but this one is right in the town centre.

Hotel Aakenus (☎ 342 2051; www.hotelliaakenus .net; Koskikatu 47; s/d €65/75, d discount summer €50; ☒) Simple but welcoming private hotel a short walk north of the centre. There's a sauna, restaurant and nonsmoking rooms, and the local swimming hall is around the corner.

Hotelli Oppipoika (☎ 338 8111; hotel.oppipoika@ ramk.fi; Korkalonkatu 33; s/d €73/88, s/d discount weekends €63/76; ☒ ☎) Cheaper than most business hotels and with the bonus of a pool, gym, saunas and a very good restaurant run by the local catering school.

Hotel Santa Claus (☎ 321 321; www.hotelsanta claus.fi; Korkalonkatu 29; s/d €110/132, s/d discount weekends €87, s/d discount summer €79) Rovaniemi's newest hotel has unusually large rooms with modern trimmings and some strange '70s touches

involving red velour. Some 5th-floor rooms have balconies overlooking Koskikatu. Breakfast and sauna included.

City Hotel (☎ 330 0111; www.cityhotel.fi; Pekankatu 9; s/d €87/110, s/d discount weekends €77/90, d discount summer €60) Stylish boutique hotel with piano bar and neat, compact rooms with satellite TV and minibar.

Rantasipi Pohjanhovi (☎ 33711; Pohjanpuistikko 2; s/d €113/133, s/d discount €91) Rovaniemi's oldest hotel (rebuilt in 1947 after the WWII destruction) still retains some charm and has a legendary restaurant and dance club.

Eating

The partly pedestrianised Koskikatu (between Rovakatu and Pohjanpuistikko) has plenty of fast-food joints and mid-range restaurants, including branches of Rosso, Golden Rax Pizza Buffet and the world's northernmost McDonald's.

Kahvila Pullapiiki, in the Sampokeskus shopping centre, is a popular meeting place when the sun isn't shining.

Mariza (☎ 319 616; Ruokasenkatu 2; lunch buffet €5.90-6.50; ☺ 10am-3pm Mon-Fri) This simple working-class diner offers a fabulous lunch buffet of home-cooked Finnish food including hot dishes, soup and salad.

Cómico (☎ 344 433; Koskikatu 25; nachos from €3.50, mains €7.80-16.60; ☺ 11am-midnight Mon-Wed, 11-2am Thu & Fri, noon-2am Sat & Sun) Colourful bar and restaurant just below street level with American-diner seating, old movies screening and a menu of Tex-Mex (nachos and burritos), burgers, steaks and salads.

Hai Long (☎ 313 133; Valtakatu 35; lunch €7.50, mains €6-12; ☺ 11am-10pm) Inexpensive Chinese restaurant with good lunch buffet (11am to 3pm daily).

Fransmanni (☎ 02-0123 4695; Koskikatu 4; mains €8.50-20; ☺ 11am-midnight Mon-Thu, 11-1am Fri, 1pm-1am Sat, 1pm-midnight Sun) French–Finnish fusion chain with booth seating, a casual atmosphere and a tempting menu. It's one of several Rovaniemi restaurants to add a 'Lapland menu' to its usual fare – try the whitefish, sautéed reindeer or breadcheese with cloudberry cream.

Puolukka (☎ 310 222; Valtakatu; mains €16-25; ☺ 11am-3pm & 5-11pm Mon-Fri, 4-11pm Sat, 5-10pm Sun) Arguably Rovaniemi's best restaurant when it comes to serving up traditional Lappish cuisine. It's not cheap and the restaurant itself is unassuming, but the food is delicious and includes reindeer, whitefish and cloudberry desserts.

Entertainment

Other than the winter ski resorts, Rovaniemi is the only place north of Oulu with a half-decent nightlife – there are loads of bars and nightclubs in the town centre. In summer, kick back under the midnight sun in the open-air beer terrace of Oluthuone on Koskikatu. Pub Ylityö (Overtime Bar), further down at Koskikatu 5, is a tiny, eccentric pub with no seats. It was voted one of the world's best bars by *Newsweek* in 1996!

Irish Times (☎ 319 975; Valtakatu 35; ⏱ 11-2am Mon-Sat, noon-2am Sun) Rovaniemi's best Irish pub has a great heated terrace, international beers, pool tables downstairs and a relaxed vibe.

Roy Club (☎ 313 705; Maakuntakatu 24; ⏱ to 4am Fri & Sat) Small subterranean bar usually packed with students after 2am.

Nite Life (☎ 33711; Pohjanpuistikko 2; ⏱ to 4am Fri & Sat) For some real Finnish-style partying, head to the dance club (*humppa* and tango) at Hotel Pohjanhovi, then cram into the nightclub (€8).

Tivoli (☎ 312 640; Valtakatu 19) Rovaniemi's biggest nightclub usually has a packed dance floor that's popular with a younger crowd.

Getting There & Away

Finnair has daily flights to Rovaniemi from Helsinki, Kemi and Oulu; there's an airport bus that meets all flights, and departs from the central bus station one hour before flight departures (€5).

Frequent buses travel to Kemi (€15.20, 1½ hours) and Oulu (€27.80, 3½ hours) to the south; Muonio (3½ hours) and Enontekiö (Hetta; five hours) in the northwest; Kuusamo (three hours) in the east; and to Sodankylä (€17.50, two hours), Ivalo (4½ hours) and Inari (five hours) in the north, going on to Norway.

The train is the best way to travel between Helsinki and Rovaniemi (€70.20, 10 to 12 hours) – quicker and cheaper than the bus. There are eight daily trains (via Oulu), including four overnight services.

Getting Around

Rovaniemi itself is compact and it's easy enough to get around on foot but bicycles can be rented from **Arctic Safaris** (Koskikatu 6; 24hr €18). Bus No 8 goes to Santa Claus Village from the train station.

Major car rental companies have offices in Rovaniemi or at the airport and a car can be a convenient way of exploring northern Lapland if you're in a group. Rates are highest from February to April and June to August. Try **Europcar** (☎ 04-0043 3507; Koskikatu 6) or **Budget** (☎ 312 266; Koskikatu 9). Bicycles can be hired from **Arctic Safaris** (3/24hr €11/18).

AROUND ROVANIEMI
Napapiiri

The official **Arctic Circle marker** (Napapiiri) is 8km north of Rovaniemi, and built on top of it is the 'official' **Santa Claus Village**. The Santa Claus **post office** receives close to a million letters each year – he and his helpers actually reply to almost half of these! As tacky as it sounds, it's all good fun. You can send a postcard home with an official Santa stamp (you can arrange to have it delivered at Christmas); meet the bearded man in red in his grotto (that's free, but signs warn that Santa is a registered trademark and he can only be photographed by his elves – the cost is €17); and there are some excellent souvenir and handicraft shops here. There's also the **Husky Park**, where you can visit the dogs and, in winter, take short husky sled rides. Bus No 8 goes to the Santa Claus Village hourly from Rovaniemi train station (return €5.20).

Santapark (☎ 333 0000; www.santapark.com; adult/child/family €20/15/50; ⏱ 10am-8pm early Dec–mid-Jan, early June–late Aug), a Christmas-themed amusement park back on the road to Rovaniemi, is strictly for kids.

Ranua Zoo

Ranua, 83km south of Rovaniemi on road No 78, is home to the superb **Ranua Zoo** (☎ 355 1921; www.ranua.fi; adult/child & student €10/8.50; ⏱ 9am-8pm Jun–mid-Aug, 10am-4pm mid-Aug–May). The sprawling wildlife park houses over 30 mammal and 30 bird species native to Finland or Scandinavia, including brown and polar bears, lynx, arctic fox and several species of owl. The creatures are housed in spacious natural enclosures linked by a 3km circular path. As with any zoo, seeing the animals active is a matter of chance but you'll certainly get a look at the normally elusive *hirvi* – the Finnish elk.

Ranua is most easily reached by bus from Rovaniemi (€22, 1¼ hours, two daily).

ROVANIEMI TO INARI

North from Rovaniemi, Hwy 4 (E75) heads up to the vast, flat expanse of northern Lapland and Sápmi, home of the Sami people and domesticated reindeer herds.

Unless you're planning on skiing or hiking, or have your own vehicle, there's not much reason to stop between Rovaniemi and Inari. Subtle landscape changes become more severe as you head north, however, and the feeling of entering one of Europe's last great wildernesses is palpable. The road passes through the town of Sodankylä, the 'gold village' of Tankavaara and the resort village of Saariselkä, which is a jumping-off point for the UKK National Park and Saariselkä Wilderness that extends east to the Russian border.

Sodankylä
☎ 016 / pop 9922

The busy market town of Sodankylä is a reasonable place to break the journey between Rovaniemi and northern Lapland, and is renowned for the **Midnight Sun Film Festival** held in mid-June. Tickets and programs are available from the tourist office or look up www .msfilmfestival.fi.

This is also a base for visiting the **Lampivaara Amethyst Mine** (☎ 624 334; www.amethystmine.fi; Lampivaara Fell; adult/child €11/6; ☼ 11am-5pm Jun–Aug, 11am-4pm Sep, 11am-3pm Mon-Sat Oct), 38km south of Sodankylä in Luosto. The only working amethyst mine in Europe can be reached by bus; book at the tourist office.

In the town itself, the **old wooden church** (☼ 10am-6pm Jun-Aug) is worth a look; it's in the cemetery behind the newer stone church. It was built in 1689, making it one of the oldest in Lapland, and the mummified bodies of local priests and their families are buried beneath the church floor.

The **tourist office** (☎ 618 168; www.sodankyla.fi; Jäämerentie 3; ☼ 9am-5pm Mon-Fri) is in the same building as the **Andraes Alariesto Gallery** (☎ 618 643; adult/student/child €5/3/2), which displays Sami art by famous Lapp painter Alariesto.

Majatalo Kolme Veljestä (☎ 611 216; Ivalontie 1; s/d/tr €38/54/65) is a lovely guesthouse about 500m north of the bus station with tidy rooms (shared bathroom), a guest lounge with open fire, sauna, kitchen and breakfast included.

There are plenty of cafés, supermarkets, takeaways and a couple of bars lined up along the main street, Jäämerentie.

Café Kerttuli (☎ 624 383; Jäämerentie 11; snacks €2-5, mains €5.50-16; ☼ 10am-8pm Mon-Thu, 10am-10pm Fri & Sat, noon-6pm Sun) has delicious food, a lunch-time buffet (€9) and a sunny terrace facing the main street, making this Sodankylä's top choice. Good for coffee and cakes (including reindeer quiche) but also an evening meal.

There are daily buses to/from Rovaniemi (€17.90, 1¼ hours) and Ivalo (€19.70, two hours).

Ivalo
☎ 016 / pop 3500

Ivalo is the administrative and commercial centre of the Inari district, but it's a drab, modern centre with no special attractions – Inari, 40km further north, is a better place to stop. Ivalo is merely somewhere to stock up on provisions, make bus connections or meet some crusty old gold-panners who come to town to trade their gold chips for beer. The **tourist office** (☎ 661 411; Ivalontie 7; ☼ 9am-5pm Mon-Fri) is in the RTG travel agency on the main street.

Kultahippu Hotel (☎ 661 825; www.kultahippuhotel .fi, Petsamontie 1; s/d €59/74), at the north end of the main street, has a rustic feel and is the best place to stay if you get stuck in Ivalo. There's a reasonably priced restaurant and the pub and nightclub here attract all sorts of local characters on weekends.

Kamisak (☎ 667 736; kamisak@hotmail.com), about 5km south of Ivalo, is an established husky farm where you can meet the dogs (€4) or organise dogsledding safaris from a half-day (from €100) to epic five-day journeys.

Express buses from Rovaniemi run twice daily (€37.70, 4½ hours), and continue north to Nordkapp (Norway) before returning. Gold Line buses run from Ivalo to Saariselka, Inari, Roveniemi and Murmansk (Russia).

INARI
☎ 016 / pop 550

As unprepossessing as it seems at first, the tiny village of Inari (Sami: Anár) is the most interesting point of civilisation in far northern Lapland. This is the main Sami community in the region, and a centre for genuine Sami handicrafts under the name 'Sami Duodji'.

Information
Inari Info (☎ 661 666; www.inarilapland.org; ◷ 9am-7pm Jun-Aug, 10am-4pm Mon-Fri Sep-May) doubles as the post office and Alko store.

Sights & Activities
Don't miss **Siida** (☎ 665 212; www.samimuseum.fi; adult/student & pensioner/child €7/6/3; ◷ 9am-8pm Jun-Sep, 10am-5pm Tue-Sun Oct-May), one of the finest museums in Finland. The exhibition brings to life Sami origins, culture, lifestyle and present-day struggles. Outside is an open-air museum with Sami buildings, handicrafts and artefacts (open summer only).

There's a marked 7.5km walking track (starting from the Siida parking area) to the 18th-century Pielpajärvi wilderness church. If you have a vehicle, there's another parking area 3km closer. In winter or spring you'll need snowshoes and a keen attitude to tackle this walk.

In summer, boat trips leave for the prominent Ukko island, an ancient cult site for the Inari Samis. The two-hour cruises on Lake Inarijärvi are run by **Lake & Snow** (☎ 0400-295731; adult/child €12/6, ◷ 2pm Jun, Aug & Sep, 2pm & 6pm Jul). When the lake is frozen over (November to late April) you can take a snowmobile out to the island (per person €60 to €100).

Inari Porofarmi (☎ 673 912) is a reindeer farm run by a Sami family 14km from Inari on the back road to Kittila. You can meet reindeer, try lassoing, see Sami shows, and take reindeer safaris in winter.

Reindeer races are held on the lake in the first week of April and a big ice-fishing competition draws the crowds in mid-April.

Sleeping & Eating
Hostel Jokitörmä (☎ 672 725; www.jokitorma.com; camp sites €13, dm/s cabins/d cabins €16.50/13.50/26; Ⓟ) The nearest youth hostel (HI-affiliated), on the Arctic Hwy about 27km north of Inari. It's a great place with cosy two- and four-person rooms, and a separate set of cottages, each with their own kitchen and bathroom facilities – it's a pity it's not closer to Inari, but all buses will stop here on request.

Uruniemi Camping (☎ 671 331; camp sites €11, 2-/4-person cottages from €17/30; ◷ Jun–late Sep) About 2km south of town, this is a well-equipped lakeside camping ground with cottages, café, sauna, and boats and bikes for hire.

Hotel Inari (☎ 671 026; s/d/tr €38/45/60) The local hotel is also the hub of the village – pub, restaurant, Saturday-night disco and general local hang-out. Upstairs are small but clean rooms with private bathrooms. The restaurant (mains €8 to €11, pizzas €5 to €9) offers Lappish dishes. Pizzas include 'sauteed reindeer, peach and onion', and there are inexpensive burgers, *poro* (reindeer) toast and kebabs. The terrace at the front is a great place to sit in summer and meet the locals.

Getting There & Away
The Arctic Hwy runs through Inari so buses from Rovaniemi ply the route right through to Nordkapp, Tana Bru and Kirkenes (all in Norway) in summer. Buses stop outside the tourist office and although you can't make reservations or buy tickets here, you can pick up timetables and there are no problems getting a seat (pay the driver). Gold Line buses run daily to/from Ivalo (€6, 40 minutes), with connections south to Rovaniemi.

LEMMENJOKI NATIONAL PARK
At 2855 sq km, Lemmenjoki is Finland's largest national park, and one of its most diverse. Hiking trails extend for over 70km through the vast reserve and there are several free wilderness huts.

Lemmenjoki nature centre (☎ 02-0564 7793; ◷ 9am-9pm Jun-Sep) is just before the village of Njurgulahti, about 50km southwest of Inari. It has a small interpretive exhibition, a powerful set of binoculars, and you can purchase maps and fishing permits here.

As well as hiking trails and opportunities for gold panning, there's a boat cruise along the Lemmenjoki valley in summer, from Njurgulahti village to the Kultahamina wilderness hut at Gold Harbour. A 20km marked trail also follows the course of the river, so you can take the boat one way, then hike back.

Accommodation at Njurgulahti includes two camping grounds.

In summer, Gold Line buses run at least once a day from Inari to Lemmenjoki (two hours).

NORTHWESTERN LAPLAND
Northwestern Lapland is best known for its downhill ski resorts (Ylläs, Levi and Olos), superb summer hiking (Pallastunturi National Park and Kilpisjärvi area) and rafting and canoeing on the mighty Muonionjoki

and Tornionjoki rivers, which form the border between Finland and Sweden.

Daily buses run on highway 21 between Tornio and Hetta, and on highway 79 between Rovaniemi and Muonio (via Kittilä and Levi).

Muonio
☎ 016

For travellers, the small town of Muonio is mainly a centre for hiking and winter activities – nearby is the small Olos ski resort, and the start (or end) of the four-day trek through the Pallas-Ounastunturi National Park to Hetta.

Kiela Naturium (☎ 532 280; www.kielanaturium.fi; Kilpisjärventie 15; ☼ 10am-6pm Jul–mid-Aug, 11am-5pm Mon-Fri Apr-May & Sep-Dec) combines tourist information with a nifty 3D-multimedia fells nature display, and a planetarium with aurora borealis show (adult/child €10/6, every 20 minutes).

About 3km south of the village, **Harriniva** (☎ 530 0300; www.harriniva.fi) rents equipment and has a vast programme of summer and winter activities, as well as accommodation and a restaurant. This is probably the best place in Finland to organise a husky safari. Harriniva has a husky farm with over 200 dogs (guided tour adult/child €6/3.50) and in winter, there are dogsledding safaris from one hour (€55) to two days (€410, staying overnight in a wilderness hut), as well as snowmobile and reindeer safaris. In summer, the centre offers daily guided white-water rafting trips on the Muonio river from €22 for a 1½-hour trip.

Lomamaja Pekonen (☎ 532 237; www.lomamaja pekonen.fi; Lahenrannantie 10; s/d €28/44, 2-/3-/4-person cottages €50/56/65) is the best budget option in Muonio, with rooms and a range of cosy cottages sleeping two to four people. It's about 300m west of the highway and you can hire bikes and canoes here.

Levi & Sirkka
☎ 016

Levi is a major skiing centre built around the village of Sirkka. This is one of the most popular ski resorts in Lapland, particularly with the party crowd. The **tourist office** (☎ 639 3300; www.levi.fi; Myllyojoentie 2; ☼ 9am-4.30pm Mon-Fri, 11am-5.30pm Sat & Sun) handles accommodation bookings as well as snowmobile safaris, dog-sled treks and reindeer rides.

The resort has 45 downhill slopes and 19 lifts. Two lifts operate in summer, and mountain bikes can be hired from the ski rental shop. Ice-fishing on the frozen lake is popular in spring.

Accommodation prices go through the roof in the peak season of February to May and in December. In summer (May to September), however, you can get a comfortable cabin sleeping up to five people for as little as €45 a night, and hotel prices drop to rates comparable to anywhere else in Finland.

Levin Matkailumaja (☎ 641 126; www.levi.fi/mat kailumaja, no English; Levintie 1625; cottages €50-135), a group of cosy, self-contained cottages in the middle of the village, is the best budget choice in Levi.

There are seven buses a day from Rovaniemi to Levi (€25, three hours).

Hetta & Pallastunturi National Park

One of the easiest long-distance walks in Lapland is the excellent 60km trekking route between the northern village of Hetta (also known as Enontekiö) and **Hotelli Pallas** (☎ 016-532 441). The marked trail passes through the Pallastunturi National Park and can easily be completed in four days. There are seven free wilderness huts, but they can be packed with people in summer so it's wise to carry a tent.

The **Fell Lapland Nature Centre** (☎ 556211; www .enontekio.fi; Peuratie, Hetta) is the combined local tourist office and a visitor centre for the Pallastunturi National Park. Hetta has lots of accommodation, including summer camping and cabins. **Hetan Majatalo** (☎ 554 0400; hetan-majatalo@co.inet.fi; s/d €57/76) is a fine guesthouse with country-style rooms, all with TV and private bathroom.

There are daily buses from Muonio to Pallastunturi (€5, 45 minutes) and one bus a week direct from Rovaniemi to the Pallas Hotel. Buses to Hetta run daily from Rovaniemi (€36.60, five hours) via Kittilä and Muonio.

Kilpisjärvi
☎ 016

The remote 'left arm' of Finland is home to some of Finland's highest mountains (which aren't very high), but this scenic outpost on the shores of Lake Kilpisjärvi is really the preserve of serious trekkers or travellers with private transport. Most people climb the Saana (1029m), or walk (or take a boat taxi, €13) to the Malla Nature Park, where you can stand on the joint border of Sweden, Norway and Finland. Serious hikers can walk to the Halti Fell, the highest in Finland. There are wilderness huts en route but a map is essential. Information and accommodation is available from the hiking centre **Kilpisjärven Retkeilykeskus** (☎ 537 771; retkeilykeskus@sunpoint.net; ☻ early Aug–late Sep).

There is a daily bus connection between Rovaniemi and Kilpisjärvi (€47.50, eight hours) via Kittilä and Muonio.

FINLAND DIRECTORY

ACCOMMODATION
In this chapter, we have classified sleeping options as follows:
- Budget: camping and hostels under €25 per person.
- Mid-Range: guesthouses, cottages and hotels under €75 a double.
- Top End: €75 and upwards.

Camping
If you're prepared to lug a tent and sleeping bag, camping is the cheapest way to travel around Finland – and the best way to get close to the heart of the Finnish countryside. Most camp sites are open only from June to August and popular spots are crowded during July and the Midsummer weekend. Sites cost from €8-18. Contact the **Finnish Camping Association** (☎ 09-4774 0740; www.camping.fi) for more information.

Finland's 'everyman's right' means you can pitch a tent almost anywhere on public land or at designated free camp sites in national parks. Always ask the owner's permission if you're thinking of camping on private land.

Guesthouses & Hotels
In big towns and coastal resorts, guesthouses are a cosy alternative, often costing only a little more than a double room at a hostel.

In contrast to much of the rest of the world, hotels in Finland offer lower rates on weekends (usually Friday and Saturday nights but often also on Sunday night) and in summer (June to August), when business travel is down.

If you're staying in hotels, Finncheques are vouchers that give discounted accom-

modation in 140 designated hotels for €36 or €44 per person in a double room. They're valid from May to September and can be purchased at participating hotels and travel agencies, but if you're travelling during July and August, when hotels offer discounted rates anyway, you may find Finncheques unnecessary and perhaps even overpriced.

Holiday cottages can be booked through the regional tourist offices. They vary from very basic lakeside cottages with few facilities to luxurious houses. Rental starts at about €200 per week for four people. For listings on the mainland and booking information, contact **Lomarengas** (☎ 09-5766 3300; www.lomar engas.fi).

Hostels
The **Finnish Youth Hostel Association** (SRM; ☎ 09-64 0377; www.srmnet.org; Yrjönkatu 38B, 00100 Helsinki) operates 91 hostels. About half of these are open all year – the rest are summer only (June to August) and are usually student accommodation buildings vacated for school holidays. Always call ahead to book a bed – even in winter, hostels can be full. Hostel prices quoted in this chapter are without the €2.50 discount given to holders of a valid HI card.

ACTIVITIES
Canoeing & Rafting
Finland has so much water in the form of lakes and rivers that it seems a shame to stay on dry land. Canoes and kayaks can be hired in most towns near a lake, often from camping grounds, for around €10 a day. Transport to the start/finishing points of popular river trips can usually be arranged at an extra cost.

Good places for organised **white-water rafting** include the rapids around Kuhmo (see p176), the Kitkajoki river north of Kuusamo (p179), the rapids of the Tornionjoki and Munionjoki rivers on the Finland–Sweden border (p180 and p187), and the Ruunaa Recreation Area in North Karelia (p175).

Fishing
To fish you need a one-week (€5) or one-year (€15) fishing licence, available at banks, post offices and the **Forest and Park Service information office** (www.metsa.fi; Eteläesplanadi 20, Helsinki). Fishing in Northern Lapland requires a separate regional licence. In winter, ice-fishing

FINLAND

is popular and requires no licence – just bore a hole in the ice and dangle a line.

Hiking

Hiking or trekking (often called fell walking in Finland) is best from June to September, although in July mosquitoes and other biting insects can be a big problem in Lapland. In summer, given the continuous daylight in northern Finland, you can comfortably walk all night if you feel like it! Wilderness huts line the northern trails (they are free and must be shared). According to the law, a principle of common access to nature applies, so you are generally allowed to hike in any forested or wilderness area. See p133 for some good trekking areas.

Skiing

Finns love to ski. There are some good downhill resorts in the far north, and cross-country trails of varying difficulty (some illuminated) all over the country. From February to April, downhill skiers flock to resorts such as Ylläs or Levi in northwest Lapland, Ruka near Kuusamo or Koli in North Karelia. Expect to pay €20 to €29 a day for lift passes and €20 to hire a complete cross-country or downhill kit (skis or snowboard, boots and poles). The full season runs from October to April. Accommodation prices and crowds are highest in spring (February to April).

Swimming & Sauna

What would Finland be without the physically and mentally cleansing sauna? The traditional sauna is a wooden room with benches and a properly stoked wooden stove, although most Finnish saunas now have electric heating. Temperatures should be 80°C to 100°C, and the sauna is taken in the nude. Many hotels – and many hostels and camping grounds – have men's and women's saunas that are free with a night's stay.

Uimahalli (indoor swimming centres) can be found in most towns and they usually have spa and sauna facilities in addition to a pool. *Kylpylä* (spa hotels) are another option for getting hot and wet and some have spectacular facilities as well as massage and hydrotherapy. There are good ones in Turku, Oulu, Kuopio and Savonlinna. Nonguests can use the facilities for a fee.

Winter Activities

As well as skiing and snowboarding, Finland offers a range of snowbound activities including dogsledding, snowmobile safaris, reindeer sleigh tours and ice-fishing. Most of these activities are expensive but there's something magic about being pulled through the snow by a team of huskies. The best place to get involved is Lapland: Rovaniemi (see p184) is a major centre for organised tours, and ski resorts such as Levi and Ylläs also offer tours, plus there are husky farms at Ivalo (p186) and Muonio (p188). The main season for winter activities is late winter and spring (January to April).

BUSINESS HOURS

Shops generally open from 9am to 5pm weekdays, and to 1pm on Saturday. Banks are open from 9.15am until 4.15pm weekdays. Many supermarkets and Helsinki department stores stay open until 9pm or 10pm on weeknights and open all day on Saturday.

Cafés are usually open from 9am or 10am to 6pm – later if they're licensed. Restaurants open from around 11am to 10pm with lunch from 11am to 3pm. Pubs open from 11am to 10pm (to 1am or later on Friday and Saturday) and nightclubs stay open as late as 4am.

CHILDREN

Families with children will love Finland: most hostels have family rooms, the supermarkets stock everything your children need, and many trains and ferries have special play areas. Plus there are some fantastic theme parks tailor-made for kids, such as Moomin World in Naantali (see p152), Wasalandia in Vaasa (p163) and Särkänniemi in Tampere (p158).

EMBASSIES & CONSULATES
Finland Embassies & Consulates

Finland maintains embassies in the following countries:

Australia (☎ 02-6273 3800; sanomat.can@formin.fi; 12 Darwin Ave, Yarralumla, ACT 2600)

Canada (☎ 613-288 2233; embassy@finland.ca; 55 Metcalfe St, Suite 850, Ottawa K1P 6L5)

Denmark (☎ 3313 4214; sanomat.kob@formin.fi; Sankt Annae Plads 24, 1250 Copenhagen K)

France (☎ 01 44 18 19 20; sanomat.par@formin.fi; 1 Place de Finlande, 57007 Paris)

Germany (☎ 030-505030; info.berlin@formin.fi; Rauchstrasse 1, 10787 Berlin)

Ireland (☎ 01-478 1344; sanomat.dub@ formin.fi; Russell House, Stokes Pl, St Stephen's Green, Dublin 2)

Netherlands (☎ 070-346 9754; sanomat.haa@formin.fi; Groot Hertoginnelaan 16, 251r EG Den Haag)

New Zealand Honorary Consulate General (☎ 499 4599; Level 24, HSBC Tower, 195 Lambton Quay, Wellington) Or contact the Australian embassy.

Norway (☎ 2212 4900; sanomat.osl@ formin.fi; Thomas Heftyes gate 1, 0244 Oslo)

Russia (☎ 095-787 4174; sanomat.mos@ formin.fi; Kropotkinskij Pereulok 15/17, 119034 Moskva G-34)

Sweden (☎ 08-676 6700; info@finland.se; Gärdesgatan 11, 11527 Stockholm)

UK (☎ 020-7838 6200; sanomat.lon@formin.fi; 38 Chesham Place, London SW1X 8HW)

USA (☎ 202-298 5800; sanomat.was@formin.fi; 3301 Massachusetts Ave NW, Washington DC 20008)

Embassies & Consulates in Finland

The following embassies are in Helsinki:

Australia (☎ 447233; Museokatu 25B, Vantaa) This is the consulate; the nearest embassy is in Stockholm.

Canada (☎ 228 530; Pohjoisesplanadi 25B)

Denmark (☎ 684 1050; Keskuskatu 1A)

Estonia (☎ 622 0288; Itäinen Puistotie 10)

France (☎ 618 780; Itäinen Puistotie 13)

Germany (☎ 458 580; Krogiuksentie 4)

Ireland (☎ 646 006; Erottajankatu 7)

Japan (☎ 686 0200; Eteläranta 8)

Latvia (☎ 4764 7744; Armfeltintie 10)

Lithuania (☎ 608 210; Rauhankatu 13A)

Netherlands (☎ 228 920; Eteläsplanadi 24A)

Norway (☎ 686 0180; Rehbinderintie 17)

Russia (☎ 661 876; Tehtaankatu 1B)

Sweden (☎ 687 7660; Pohjoisesplanadi 7B)

UK (☎ 2286 5100; Itäinen Puistotie 17)

USA (☎ 616 2500; Itäinen Puistotie 14A)

FESTIVALS & EVENTS

Finland puts on a barrage of music, arts, cultural, sporting and just plain nutty festivals year-round, but especially between June and mid-August. The premier events include the **Savonlinna Opera Festival** (p166) and the **Pori Jazz Festival** (p162), but there's also **Provinssrock** at Seinäjoki, a festival of international rock music held in mid-June, and the week-long **Folk Festival** at Kaustinen (mid-July) which attracts thousands of people to see Finnish and international folk concerts and dance performances. Other big rock festivals are **Ilosaarirock** (p173) in Joensuu (July) and **Ruis-rock** (p149) in Turku (early July).

Midsummer is a big deal in any part of Finland, though for most Finns it's a family time when they disappear to their summer cottages. A few smaller communities arrange some of the weirdest events imaginable: the **World Wife-Carrying Championships** (see p173) in Sonkajärvi and the **Air Guitar World Championships** in Oulu, for instance. Pick up the *Finland Festivals* booklet in any tourist office or check out www.festivals.fi.

Anyone who has been in Finland on **Vappu** (May Day) will know it's a big day for Finns – more alcohol is consumed in the 48 hours surrounding 1 May than over a similar period at any other time of year.

HOLIDAYS

Finland grinds to a halt twice a year – around Christmas and New Year and during the Midsummer weekend. Plan ahead and avoid travelling during those times. National public holidays are:

New Year's Day 1 January
Epiphany 6 January
Good Friday to Easter Monday March/April
May Day Eve and **May Day** 30 April and 1 May
Ascension Day 40 days after Easter
Whit Sunday late May or early June
Juhannus midsummer; third weekend in June
All Saints Day 1 November
Independence Day 6 December
Christmas Eve 24 December
Christmas Day 25 December
Boxing Day 26 December

INTERNET ACCESS

All public libraries offer free Internet access, though you need to book a slot in advance. An increasing number of businesses and tourist offices have at least one terminal that you can use free for 15 minutes.

INTERNET RESOURCES

Finland probably has more websites per capita than any other country – all tourist offices have a site, and so, it seems, does every other person, place and institution in the country. Good general sites:

Aktivist (www.aktivist.fi/inenglish) A-Z coverage from Alvar Aalto to Vappu with offbeat cultural observations.

Finnish Tourist Board (www.visitfinland.com) Lots of travel information and links.

Helsingin Sanomat (www.helsinginsanomat.fi) Site of Helsinki's biggest newspaper has an English summary.

Virtual Finland (virtual.finland.fi) Excellent site covering all aspects of Finland in five languages.

LEGAL MATTERS

Traffic laws are strict, as are drug laws. However, police usually treat bona fide tourists politely in less serious situations. Fines (such as traffic fines) are calculated according to your income – a number of high-flying, fast-driving Finnish businesspeople have been fined as much as €100,000 for speeding!

You *must* obtain a permit if you plan to fish in Finland.

MEDIA

There is no local daily English-language newspaper, but the *International Herald Tribune*, several British newspapers and various English-language magazines are available at train stations and R-kiosks in larger towns (expect to pay up to €5 for an international newspaper).

The main daily paper in Finland is **Helsingin Sanomat** (www.helsinginsanomat.fi), which has an English-language edition on its website.

The national radio broadcaster is YLE (www.yle.fi; no English). Capital FM (94.5Mhz) in Helsinki broadcasts 24-hour English and foreign-language programmes such as BBC World News, Voice of America and Radio Australia. There are plenty of stations playing Finnish and international pop music, such as the national Radio Nova and Groove FM.

The two national TV networks broadcast British and US programmes in English with Finnish and Swedish subtitles, and MTV is a private channel (not related to the music channel!). Hotels often have satellite TV with MTV, BBC World, CNN, Eurosport and movie channels.

MONEY

Finland adopted the euro in 2001, and is at present the only Nordic country to have done so. Euro notes come in five, 10, 20, 100 and 500 denominations and coins in five, 10, 20, 50 cents and €1 and €2.

ATMs

There are 24-hour ATMs ('Otto') linked to international networks (Cirrus, Maestro, Visa, MasterCard) in every city, town and almost every village in Finland, so carrying a debit or credit card (and your PIN) is definitely the easiest way to get cash.

Credit Cards

Credit cards are widely accepted and Finns are dedicated users of the plastic – buying a beer in a bar with a credit card is not unusual and it's commonplace to pay for accommodation and restaurant meals in this way. Keeping your credit account in the black will help you avoid bank charges.

Travellers Cheques

Finland's major national banks (Osuuspankki, Nordea and Sampo) will change travellers cheques and have similar rates and charges – up to €7 per transaction. In cities, independent exchangers such as Forex are a better alternative for exchanging cash and travellers cheques, as they charge a flat €2 per cheque and are open longer hours.

There is no American Express office that changes travellers cheques in Finland, but Thomas Cook is represented (through Travelex) in Helsinki and Turku.

POST

Posti (post offices) are generally open from 9am to 7pm weekdays, and in cities they are also open on Saturday. Stamps (€0.65 for letters and postcards) can be bought at bus or train stations and R-kiosks (newsagents). International parcel post is expensive in Finland (almost twice the price of sending from Sweden). Poste restante is offered at the main post offices in cities.

TELEPHONE

Some public phones accept coins, but most accept only plastic Telecards. With just about everyone carrying a mobile phone, public phones don't get much of a work-out.

International calls are cheapest if you buy one of the prepaid calling cards from any R-kiosk. Offpeak times are 10pm-8am on weekdays and all day Saturday and Sunday. A three-minute call to the USA during peak time will cost about €4. For national directory assistance dial ☎ 020 202; for international assistance ☎ 020 208.

The country code for calling Finland from abroad is ☎ 358. To make an international

---

EMERGENCY NUMBERS

Police, fire & ambulance ☎ 112;
Directory assistance ☎ 020208.

call from Finland, first dial an international prefix (☎ 00, 990, 994 or 999) and then the country code for the country you're calling.

MOBILE PHONES

Finland has one of the world's highest rates of mobile-phone usage, and getting hooked up to the mobile-phone network is easy with the prepaid system using Sonera, DNA or TeleRing.

You can bring your own phone and simply buy a SIM card (around €15) from a phone shop or any R-kiosk, then buy recharge cards from the same outlets. The different companies often have special deals and varying call charges, so shop around.

The main company offering connection to the GSM network in Finland is Radiolinja, but unless you're planning on staying long-term, it's cheaper and easier to use the prepaid system.

TIME

Finland is two hours ahead of GMT/UTC, and daylight saving time applies from early April to late October, when clocks go forward one hour. When it's noon in Finland it's 10am in London, 5am in New York, 2am in San Francisco, 5am in Toronto, 7pm in Sydney, 10pm in Auckland, 11am in Stockholm, Copenhagen and Oslo, and 1pm in Moscow and St Petersburg.

TOILETS

You can have the world's most expensive pee in Finnish bus stations – some charge €2! Other public toilets generally charge €0.40. However, by law all restaurants and cafés must have a wheelchair-accessible public toilet. Libraries, department stores and hotels also have free toilets.

TOURIST INFORMATION

Every Finnish town has a tourist office with piles of English-language brochures, free maps and helpful staff (in summer they're often staffed by students studying tourism). Most also have websites. The **Finnish Tourist Board** (☎ 09-4176 911; www.visitfinland.com) has an office in Helsinki.

VISAS

A valid passport is required to enter Finland. Citizens of EU countries (except Greece), Norway and Iceland can travel with only an identity card. Most Western nationals don't need a tourist visa for stays under three months; South Africans require a Schengen visa. The **Directorate of Immigration** (☎ 09-476 5500; www.uvi.fi) handles visas and work permits.

Australian and New Zealand citizens aged between 18 and 30 can apply for a 12-month working holiday visa under a reciprocal agreement.

Russian visas can be obtained from the Russian consulate in Helsinki. You need to leave your passport at the consulate and allow a week to 10 days for processing. Travel agencies in Helsinki can expedite the visa process for a fee.

TRANSPORT IN FINLAND

GETTING THERE & AWAY
Air

Most major European carriers have flights to and from Helsinki's **Vantaa airport** (☎ 0200-14636; www.helsinki-vantaa.fi). Finnair is the national carrier, with direct flights to Helsinki from New York, Toronto, Bangkok, Singapore, Tokyo, Hong Kong and most European capitals. A cheap entry to Finland is with **Ryanair** (www.ryanair.com) from London Stansted or Frankfurt Hahn to Tampere (one way Internet fares plus taxes from UK£10), or with Swedish budget carrier **FlyMe** (www.flyme.com) from Stockholm to Helsinki (one way from €22). Another useful budget airline is the SAS subsidiary **Blue 1** (www.blue1.com) which offers cheap Internet fares between Helsinki and Amsterdam, Brussels, Copenhagen, Oslo and Stockholm.

Holders of the International Youth Travel Card (IYTC) or International Student Identity Card (ISIC) should also be able to get discount flights through student travel agencies: in Finland, contact **Kilroy Travels** (www.kilroytravels.com).

Airlines flying to and from Finland:
Aer Lingus (☎ 09-6122 0260; www.aerlingus.ie)
Aeroflot (☎ 09-659 655; www.aeroflot.com)
Air France (☎ 09-8568 0500; www.airfrance.com)
American Airlines (☎ 9800 14620; www.aa.com)
Austrian Airlines (☎ 020-386 000; www.aua.com)
Blue 1 (☎ 020-386 000; www.blue1.com)

British Airways (☎ 0800 178 378;
www.britishairways.com)
Finnair (☎ 09-81881; www.finnair.com)
FlyMe (www.flyme.com)
Iceland Air (☎ 09-6126 070; www.icelandair.com)
KLM Royal Dutch (☎ 020 353 355; www.klm.com)
LOT Polish (☎ 09-6937 9036; www.lot.com)
Lufthansa (☎ 020-386 000; www.lufthansa.com)
MALEV Hungarian Airlines (☎ 09-622 0922;
www.malev.hu)
Ryanair (www.ryanair.com)
SAS Scandinavian Airlines (☎ 020-585 6000;
www.sas.fi)

Land
BORDER CROSSINGS
There are six road crossings from northern
Sweden to northern Finland (Lapland) and
another six from Norway to Finland, but
there are no border controls or customs formalities. There are six crossings into Russia
along Finland's eastern border (the main
route is Helsinki–Vyborg–St Petersburg);
you must have a valid Russian visa.

BUS
Sweden
The only useful bus route from Finland to
Sweden is from the border town of Tornio,
where you can get a direct bus to Stockholm
(€55, 14 hours) – or just walk across the
border to Haparanda and you're in Sweden
anyway.

Norway
Buses run between Rovaniemi (via Ivalo
and Inari) and the Norwegian border, and
some buses go on to the first Norwegian
town – but check timetables as you may be
dropped at the border without a connecting
bus, especially outside the June to August
high season.

The main Nordkapp (North Cape) route
will take you from Rovaniemi via Inari and
Kaamanen to Karigasniemi and across the
border to Karasjok and Lakselv. Many bus
services run from Ivalo to Karasjok, and in
summer (June to August) there is at least
one daily bus all the way to Nordkapp
(adult/student €101.50/77.10, 11 hours from
Rovaniemi). Two alternative routes, which
are not as well served by bus, go through
western Lapland, via Hetta and onto Karasjok; or along highway 21 to Kilpisjärvi and
along the coast to Alta. The latter route is

also the quickest way to Tromsø and anywhere south in Norway.

The road from the northernmost point of
Finland, at Nuorgam, will take you to Tana
Bru, with connections to various parts of
Finnmark in Norway. Buses take you to the
border, 4km from Nuorgam, but in summer
there are services direct to Tana Bru.

To get to Kirkenes from Finland, cross
the border at Nätämö to reach Neiden,
10km away, which has bus connections to
Kirkenes and to other centres in Finnmark.
You may have to hitchhike from Nätämö to
Neiden, but again there are direct summer-
only services to Kirkenes.

Russia
Daily express buses run from Turku and
Helsinki to Vyborg and St Petersburg (Russian visa required) along highway E18, via
the Finnish towns of Porvoo, Kotka and
Hamina. Check current timetables and book
tickets at the bus station or a travel agency;
from Helsinki to St Petersburg there are three
daily buses (€50.40, nine hours). Of course,
the train is a far more romantic way to reach
Russia (see opposite). Note that St Petersburg
is Pietari in Finnish, and Vyborg is Viipuri.

Gold Line buses run from Ivalo to Murmansk via the Finnish border post of Raja-
Jooseppi on weekdays at 3.30pm (€36.80, 7½
hours), but again you need to get your visa
in Helsinki.

CAR & MOTORCYCLE
Vehicles can easily be brought into Finland
on the Baltic ferries from Sweden, Estonia
and Germany, provided you have registration papers and valid insurance (green card
or frontier insurance – check with your local
motoring organisation). If you plan on driving to Russia, you'll need registration papers,
an international licence, insurance and possibly a *carnet de passage*. The main Russian
insurer in Finland is **IngoNord** (☎ 251 0300;
www.ingonord.com; Salomonkatu 5C, Helsinki).

See p197 for information about driving
in Finland.

HITCHING
The easiest way to hitch into or out of Fin-
land is to wait at the ferry terminals and ask
drivers loading their cars onto the boats.
Trying to hitch in via northern Sweden or
Norway is dodgy – traffic is very light and

even in summer a long wait by the roadside could leave you freezing to death.

TRAIN

The only international train links with Finland are from Moscow and St Petersburg in Russia.

There are three daily trains from Helsinki to Russia, travelling via the Finnish stations of Lahti, Kouvola and Vainikkala. You must have a valid Russian visa but border formalities have been fast-tracked so that passport checks are now carried out on board the moving train.

The Russian *Tolstoi* sleeper departs Helsinki daily at 5.42pm, arriving in Moscow at 8.30am the next day (one way in 2nd/1st class €84.60/126.40) via Vyborg (€45.80/71) and St Petersburg (€57.20/88.20); it departs from Moscow daily at 10.50pm. Both 1st- and 2nd-class fares include a sleeper berth in both classes. The *Sibelius* and *Repin* have daily services between Helsinki and St Petersburg (5½ hours) via Vyborg (3¾ hours). The *Sibelius* (a Finnish train) departs from Helsinki at 7.42am (2nd-/1st-class seats €50.20/79.50). The Russian *Repin* departs at 3.42pm and has 2nd-class seats (€50.20) or 1st-class sleeping berths (€88.20). Return fares are roughly double. Fares to Vyborg are €38.80/62.30 on *Sibelius* and €35.80/71 on *Repin*. From St Petersburg, departures are at 4.32pm (*Sibelius*) and 7.32am (*Repin*).

Buy Russian rail tickets in Helsinki at the special ticket counter in the central station – advance bookings are recommended. There are discounts for seniors, children and groups, but no student discounts. Check timetables at www.vr.fi.

Sea

There's no better way to arrive in Helsinki than on board a huge Baltic ferry. These ships are like floating hotels, nightclubs and shopping malls rolled into one, but fares are kept reasonably low by competition and duty-free shopping. They certainly qualify as mini-cruise ships, with bars, karaoke, cabaret, lavish smorgasbords, gaming rooms and discos, and many Scandinavians use them simply for overnight boozy cruises. The ferries dock virtually in the centre of Helsinki.

Services are year-round. Book ahead when travelling in July, especially on weekends or if you have a vehicle.

Many ferries offer 50% discounts for holders of ScanRail and Inter-Rail passes – Silja Line and Viking Line services between Sweden and Finland and Superfast Ferries between Germany and Finland are free to Eurailpass holders, provided the pass is valid for both countries. Some services offer discounts for seniors and students.

Fares are slightly complicated and depend on the season, day of the week (Friday to Sunday is more expensive), whether it's day or overnight and, of course, the class of travel (passenger only or sleeping berth), but all ferry companies have websites in English with detailed timetables and fares. The main players:

Eckerö Line (www.eckerolinjen.fi) Åland (☎ 018-28000) Helsinki (☎ 09-228 8544)

Finnlines (☎ 09-251 0200; www.finnlines.fi)

Linda Line (☎ 09-668 9700; www.lindaline.fi)

Nordic Jet Line (☎ 09-681 770; www.njl.fi)

RG Line (☎ 06-320 0300; www.rgline.com)

Silja Line (☎ 0203-74 552; www.silja.com)

Superfast Ferries (☎ 09-2535 0640; www.superfast.com)

Tallink (☎ 09-228 311; www.tallink.fi)

Viking Line (☎ 09-12 351; www.vikingline.fi)

SWEDEN

The Stockholm–Helsinki, Stockholm–Turku and Kapellskär–Mariehamn (Åland) runs are dominated by Silja Line and Viking Line, with daily departures. Viking Line generally has the cheapest fares.

On both lines you can buy a passenger-only ticket and sleep in the salons (or stay up all night partying, as many passengers do!). There are luggage lockers on board. In summer, overnight crossings (passenger ticket only) from Stockholm start at €34 to Turku (11–12 hours) and €45 to Helsinki (16 hours). Cabins start at an additional €24 (€40 in summer).

Eckerö Line sails from Grisslehamn to Eckerö in Åland. At three hours and €5.50 (€8.90 in summer), it's the quickest and cheapest crossing from Sweden to Finland – though it's a fair way from the mainland.

RG Line sails from Vaasa to Umeå (Sweden) one or two times daily in summer, less often in winter (€50, three hours).

ESTONIA

Half a dozen ferry companies ply the Gulf of Finland between Helsinki and Tallinn in

Estonia. Since no visa is required and the trip is so quick and cheap, it's a very popular and worthwhile day trip from Helsinki, or a great way to arrive or depart (see p146).

Car ferries cross in 3½ hours, catamarans and hydrofoils in about 1½ hours. Service is heavy year-round, although in winter there are fewer departures, and the traffic is also slower due to the ice.

Eckerö Line has only one departure daily but is the cheapest with a return fare of €25 (€15 in low season). Tallink, Viking Line and Silja Line have regular daily departures. Catamarans, hydrofoils and ferries cost from €20 to €66 one way, depending on the company, the time of year and the day of the week. Linda Line is the cheapest (but smallest) fast boat (one way/return €24/36). Nordic Jet Line is the priciest.

GERMANY

Finnlines has a daily year-round service from Helsinki to Travemünde (32–36 hours) with bus service to Hamburg. One-way rates in a four-person cabin begin at €280.

Superfast Ferries sails between Rostock (Germany) and Hanko on the south coast of Finland (22 hours), daily. The minimum one-way fare in high season for a seat only is €84 or for a cabin €182.

GETTING AROUND
Air

Finnair runs a fairly comprehensive domestic service mainly out of Helsinki but also across a few regional centres such as Oulu–Rovaniemi.

Full scheduled fares are not cheap (eg Helsinki–Rovaniemi €254, Helsinki–Kuopio €198) but 'Happy Hour' tickets (book a week in advance, no refunds) are much cheaper and there are summer and weekend specials. Seniors and children aged under 12 receive a 70% discount. If you're aged between 17 and 24 the discount is 50%, but better still you can fly stand-by to anywhere in Finland for €64 or €79 one way, depending on the flight – a huge saving on a flight from, say, Helsinki to Rovaniemi (and comparable to the train fare). To qualify you need to arrive at the airport one hour before the flight of your choice and wait to see if there are any seats available.

On top of this, several discount carriers now operate on the domestic routes in Fin-land, so it's well worth checking the Internet to see what fares are being offered by Blue 1, Golden Air and Flying Finn. Sample fares at the time of research included Helsinki–Kuopio on Blue 1 for €36.

AIRLINES IN FINLAND

Blue 1 (☎ 020-386 000; www.blue1.com)
Finnair (☎ 09-81881; www.finnair.com)
FinnComm Airlines (☎ 4243 2000; www.finncomm.fi)
Golden Air (☎ 06-421 9670; www.goldenair.fi)

Bicycle

Finland is flat and as bicycle-friendly as any country you'll find, with miles of bike paths – which cyclists share with inline skaters in summer. The only drawback to an extensive tour is distance, but bikes can be carried on most trains, buses and ferries. The best place for cycling is the Åland islands, where a few days or a week of touring is a breeze.

Daily/weekly hire at about €10/50 is possible in most cities, although hiring decent bikes in smaller towns is difficult as there's little demand – check with the local tourist office. Helmets are advisable but not compulsory. The **Finnish Youth Hostel Association** (SRM; www.srmnet.org) offers a cycling and hostel package that takes in the flat south and lakes for seven/14 days, including bike rental and accommodation (€249/431).

New bikes start from €250 for a hybrid, but you can pick up a second-hand model for under €100.

Boat

Lake and river ferries operate over the summer period (most lakes are frozen over in winter). They're more than mere transport (which is just as well because they're more expensive and a lot slower than the bus); a lake cruise taking you from one town to another via southern Finland's sublime system of waterways is a bona fide Finnish experience. The most popular routes include Tampere–Hämeenlinna, Savonlinna–Kuopio, Lahti–Jyväskylä and Joensuu–Koli–Kuopio on Lake Pielinen. Fares vary: the 10½-hour Savonlinna–Kuopio ferry costs €65.

The main coastal sea routes are Turku–Naantali, Helsinki–Porvoo, Uusikaupunki–Hanko via Turku and the archipelago ferries to the Åland islands. Some of the ferries that run between the islands along the coast are free, especially in Åland.

FINLAND

Bus

Buses are the principal carriers outside the rail network – they travel on 90% of Finland's roads. You can buy your ticket on board or book at a bus station or travel agency (Monday to Friday only). Limited services operate on weekends and public holidays.

Dozens of bus services operate throughout Finland but all long-distance and express bus travel comes under the umbrella of **Oy Matkahuolto Ab** (☎ 09-682 701; www.matkahuolto.fi) in Helsinki. Private lines operate local services, but all share the same ticketing system. Major operators include **Express Bus** (www.expressbus.com) and **Gold Line** (www.goldline.fi).

Fares are based on distance and whether the bus is 'regular' or 'express'. Regular/express adult fares for a 100km trip are €12.90/15.20. From Helsinki to Rovaniemi by express bus (13½ hours) one way costs €86. Return tickets are about 10% cheaper than two one-way fares. Discounts of 50% (on journeys over 80km) are available for students, but you must have a Matkahuolto student card. Technically you need to be studying in Finland to get one, but travellers have reported getting one with an ISIC card. Children get a discount of 30% (12 to 16 years) or 50% (under 12). On some routes, buses accept train passes.

Car & Motorcycle

Finland's road network is good between main towns, although there are only a handful of multilane motorways emanating from major cities. In the forests you'll find many unsurfaced roads and dirt tracks. There are no road tolls. Petrol is expensive in Finland – a litre costs around €1.15. Diesel fuel costs around €0.85 a litre.

AUTOMOBILE ASSOCIATIONS

Finland's national motoring organisation is **Autoliitto** (Automobile & Touring Club of Finland; ☎ 09-7258 4400; www.autoliitto.fi; Hämeentie 105A, 00550 Helsinki). Annual membership is €45, plus 24-hour breakdown cover for €42. There are some reciprocal benefits with international automobile associations.

HIRE

Car hire in Finland is not cheap, but with a group of three or four it can work out reasonably economically, especially if your time is short and you want to get off the beaten track. Major rental companies have offices in most cities. In Helsinki there are a few cheaper local car-hire companies. The smallest car will cost from €30 per day plus €0.35 to €0.40 per kilometre (from €80 to €90 a day with unlimited kilometres). Weekly rentals with unlimited kilometres cost from €350.

You need only your home driving licence to rent and drive a car in Finland, but most companies require the driver to be at least 21 years old.

Avis (☎ 09-441 155; www.avis.fi)
Budget (☎ 0800-124 424; www.budget.fi)
Europcar (☎ 0800-12154; www.europcar.fi)
Hertz (☎ 0800-112 233; www.hertz.fi)
Lacara (☎ 09-719 062; www.lacara.net; Hämeentie 12, Helsinki)
Scandia Rent (☎ 09-633 194; www.scandiarent.fi)

ROAD CONDITIONS & HAZARDS

Beware of elk and reindeer, which don't have much respect for car horns and can dash out onto the road unexpectedly. By law, you must notify the police if there is an accident involving these animals. Several thousand accidents involving elk are reported in Finland each year – it's ironic that the only time you may get to see an elk in the wild is when it's careering through your windscreen. Reindeer, on the other hand, are very common in Lapland and often wander along the road in semi-domesticated herds. Slow right down if you see one, as there will be more nearby.

Snow and ice on Finland's roads from September to March or April (and as late as June in Lapland) make driving a hazardous activity without snow tyres (chains are not permitted); cars hired in Finland will be properly equipped.

ROAD RULES

Your headlights must be turned on at all times outside built-up areas. Foreign cars must display their nationality and visitors must be fully insured. Accidents should be reported promptly to the **Motor Insurers' Bureau** (☎ 09-680 401; Bulevardi 28, 00120 Helsinki).

Wearing seat belts is mandatory for all passengers. The blood alcohol limit is 0.05%. The speed limit is 50km/h in built-up areas, from 80km/h to 100km/h on highways, and 120km/h on a few motorways. Traffic keeps to the right.

LOCAL TRANSPORT

The only tram and metro networks are in Helsinki. There is a local bus service in all Finnish cities and towns, usually departing from the main bus or train station.

Hail taxis at bus and train stations or call one by telephone (they are listed in the phone book under *taksi*).

Train

Finnish trains are efficient, fast, comfortable and much cheaper than in Sweden and Norway. From Helsinki, direct trains go to all major centres. Crossing the country from east to west may require a change or two, but with a little route planning you can reach most places as far north as Rovaniemi in Lapland.

VR Ltd Finnish Railways (☎ 0600-4192; www.vr.fi) handles rail travel throughout the country. You can search timetables and fares on its website.

CLASSES

The two main types of trains are regional (2nd class only) and express. Other classes include the faster (and slightly more expensive) InterCity (IC) trains, and the most expensive Pendolino trains which operate fast services on limited major city routes. Long-distance routes of all classes have a restaurant car or food service.

Night trains service the longer routes with one- two- and three-bed sleepers which are only slightly more expensive than a seat-only ticket. For example, the fare for a seat on the overnight train to Rovaniemi is €70.20 – in a three-bed sleeper it's €82. The basic additional fare for a sleeper in a three-bed compartment in low/high season is €11/16.

COSTS & RESERVATIONS

Reservations can be made at the VR counter at any train station or over the Internet (major credit cards accepted). Tickets bought in advance include a seat reservation on all services except regional trains, which don't require a reservation.

An open return ticket is valid for 15 days and costs the same as two one-way tickets. Students, seniors and children under 17 pay half fare, and children under six travel free (without a seat). The 50% student discount is only available to Finnish students or foreigners studying in Finland.

When booking, ask about so-called 'Green Departures', which offer 15% discounts on off-peak trains on certain routes. These are listed in the VR timetables.

Ticket prices depend on the distance, the class of travel and season. From Helsinki to Turku regional/express/IC/Pendolino costs €19/22.40/24.40/28.40. Other express fares include: Helsinki to Tampere (€24.40), Kuopio (€48.20) and Oulu (€61.20).

TRAIN PASSES

International rail passes accepted in Finland include the Eurailpass, Eurail Flexipass, ScanRail Pass, Euro Domino and Inter Rail. Note that if you buy a ScanRail Pass within Finland, you can only use it for up to three days in Finland (this restriction doesn't apply if you purchase it outside Finland).

The Finnrail Pass is a one-month pass good for unlimited rail travel for 3/5/10 days; 2nd-class travel costs €118/158/214. 1st class is about 50% more. These passes may be purchased before arrival in Finland (see your local travel agent). There's also a Holiday Pass (valid June to August) which allows three days of travel in one month for €109.

FINLAND

Tallinn

CONTENTS

Tallinn has become so much a part of the Helsinki experience over the last decade, it sometimes feels like a distant suburb; Tallinski is a nickname often heard. However, unlike in the early 1990s, when Tallinn attracted Finnish alcohol- and cigarette-shoppers who viewed the Estonian capital as a poorer cousin, Tallinn now gives Helsinki a run for its money in terms of excitement, variety, sights – and fun!

Only 80km from Helsinki, Tallinn is nonetheless a world apart. Boasting a splendidly preserved and lively medieval old town and a gleaming, modern city centre, Tallinn inspires visitors to poke their heads into ancient courtyards, crane their necks towards Gothic spires, find a cosy cellar café or happening bar, or just hang out at Town Hall square soaking up the sun and the suds.

Tallinn, Estonia's capital, is one of the coolest spots in Europe, and it's in the mood to celebrate its new status as the capital of an EU country. Its subtle, quiet charm weaves its way into your heart before you're aware of it.

TALLINN

FAST FACTS

- **Population** 400,000
- **Currency** kroon (EEK); US$1 = 12.75EEK;
  £1 = 22.65EEK; €1=15.65EEK;
  A$1 = 9.23EEK; C$1 = 10.07EEK;
  NZ$1 = 8.61EEK; ¥100 = 11.45EEK
- **Official Language** Estonian
- **Telephone Codes** Estonia country code
  ☎ 372; no area code for Tallinn
- **Visas** EU nationals and citizens of the US, Canada and Australia do not need a visa to enter Estonia

ORIENTATION & INFORMATION

The medieval old town, just south of Tallinn Bay, comprises Toompea, which is the upper town, and the lower town with Raekoja plats (Town Hall square) at its centre. Immediately west of the old town is the modern city centre.

The **Tallinn Tourist Information Centre** (☎ 645 7777; www.visitestonia.com; Niguliste tänav 2; ☼ 9am-8pm Mon-Fri, 10am-6pm Sat & Sun May-Aug, 9am-6pm Mon-Fri, 10am-5pm Sat & Sun Sep, 9am-5pm Mon-Fri, 10am-3pm Sat Oct-Apr) offers a full range of services, from finding accommodation to making helpful suggestions on how to get the most from your visit. **Estravel** (☎ 626 6266; www.estravel.ee; Suur-Karja tänav 15) can help you make travel arrangements.

Change money at **Tavid** (☎ 627 9900; Aia tänav 5; ☼ 24hr). To keep in touch, head to the **central post office** (☎ 625 7300; Narva maantee 1; ☼ 7.30am-8pm Mon-Fri, 8am-6pm Sat) or to **Neo Internetcafé** (☎ 628 2333; Väike Karja tänav 12; per hr 35EEK; ☼ 24hr).

In an emergency, dial ☎ 110 for police and ☎ 112 for fire, ambulance and urgent medical advice. The **First Aid Hotline** (☎ 697 1145) can advise you in English about the nearest treatment centre. For general information, **Info Line** (☎ 626 1111) is very helpful.

SIGHTS
Raekoja Plats & Around

Compact Raekoja plats has been the centre of Tallinn life since the 11th century. It's dominated by northern Europe's only surviving Gothic **town hall** (☎ 645 7900; adult/student 25/15EEK; ☼ tower 11am-6pm May-Aug), constructed in the early 14th century, reconstructed 1402–04. Old Thomas, Tallinn's symbol and guardsman, has been keeping watch perched on his weathervane atop the building since 1530. The **Raeapteek** (Town Council Pharmacy), on the north side of the square, is another ancient Tallinn institution; there's been a pharmacy or apothecary's shop here since at least 1422. An arch beside it leads into narrow Saia käik (White Bread passage), at the far end of which is the lovely, 14th-century Gothic **Pühavaimu Kirik** (Holy Spirit Church; ☎ 644 1487; ☼ 10am-4pm, free concerts 6pm Mon), with carvings from 1684 and a tower bell cast in 1433.

A medieval merchant's home at Vene tänav 17, on the corner of Pühavaimu tänav, houses Tallinn's most interesting museum – the **Linnamuuseum** (City Museum; ☎ 644 6553; Vene tänav 17; adult/student 25/10EEK; ☼ 10.30am-6pm Wed-Mon Mar-Oct, 10.30am-7pm Nov-Feb), which traces Tallinn's development through to 1940.

From Vene tänav, an arched doorway leads into a cosy courtyard and the world of the **Dominican Monastery** (☎ 644 4606; kloostri@hot.ee; Vene tänav 16/18; admission 25/15EEK; ☼ 9.30am-6pm mid-May–mid-Sep), founded in 1246 as a base for Scandinavian monks. Today the monastery complex houses Estonia's largest collection of very impressive **stone carvings**.

The majestic **Niguliste Church** (☎ 644 9911; adult/student 35/20EEK; ☼ 10am-5pm Wed-Sun), a minute's walk south of Raekoja plats, is now used to stage concerts and serves as a museum of religious art.

At the foot of the slope below the Niguliste is the carefully exposed wreckage of the buildings that stood here before the Soviet bombing of Tallinn on the night of 9 March 1944.

Toompea

A regal approach to Toompea is through the red-roofed 1380 **gate tower** at the western end of Pikk tänav in the lower town, and then along Pikk jalg (Long Leg). The still-active 19th-century Russian Orthodox **Alexander Nevsky Cathedral** (☎ 644 3484; ☼ 8am-7pm) dominates Lossi plats at the top of Pikk jalg, sited strategically across from **Toompea Castle**, Estonia's traditional seat of power. The parliament *(riigikogu)* meets in the pink, baroque-style building out front, an 18th-century addition. The state flag flies from the **Pikk Herman bastion**.

The Lutheran **Toomkirik** (Dome Church; ☎ 644 4140; ☼ 9am-5pm Tue-Sun) is Estonia's oldest church, founded in 1219 (though the exteriors date from the early 14th century). Across from Toomkirik at Kiriku plats 1, an 18th-century noble's house is now the **Knighthood House** (Rüütelkonnahoone; ☎ 644 9340; Kiriku plats 1; adult/student 20/5EEK; ☼ 11am-6pm Wed-Sun), the Art Museum of Estonia's main branch, featuring Estonian artists. There are several lookouts nearby, from which to peer across the old town roofs and snap those touristy photos to take home; artists and souvenir vendors set up stands here as well.

The **Museum of Occupation and Fight for Freedom** (☎ 668 0250; Toompea tänav 8; adult/student 10/5EEK; ☼ 11am-6pm Tue-Sun), just down the hill from Toompea, is a new and worthwhile exhibit on Estonia's history of occupation, focusing on the most recent Soviet one.

TALLINN

CENTRAL TALLINN

0 300 m
0 0.2 miles

INFORMATION
Central Post Office.................1 D3
Estravel.................................2 C3
Neo Internetcafé....................3 C3
Tallinn Tourist Information Centre.4 C3
Tavid....................................5 D2

SIGHTS & ACTIVITIES (pp200–2)
Alexander Nevsky Cathedral.....6 B3
Dominican Monastery...............7 C2
Former KGB headquarters........8 C1
Great Coast Gate...................9 D1
Knighthood House..................10 B3
Linnamuuseum......................11 C2
Museum of Occupation and
    Fight for Freedom...............12 B4
Museum of Religious Art.....(see 13)
Niguliste Church...................13 C3
Observation Deck..............(see 14)
Oleviste Church....................14 C1
Paks Margareta.....................15 B3
Pikk Herman bastion..............16 C2
Pikk Jalg Gate Tower.............17 C2
Pühavaimu Kirik....................18 C2
Raeapteek............................19 B3
Toomkirik............................20 B3
Toompea Castle.....................21 C3

SLEEPING (p202)
Cassandra Apartments............22 E4
Hotel G9..............................23 E3
Old House Guesthouse............24 D2
Old House Guesthouse............25 D1
Rasastra Bed & Breakfast........26 D2
Vana Tom.............................27 C3

EATING (p202)
Eesti Maja............................28 D4
Olde Hansa...........................29 C3
Pizza Americano....................30 C3

DRINKING (p202)
Beer House...........................31 C3
Hell Hunt.............................32 C2
Von Krahli Teater Baar............33 C3

TRANSPORT (p203)
Estonian Air..........................34 C3
Finnair................................35 C4

OTHER
Viru Gate.............................36 D3

To Bus Station (500m);
Tallinn Airport (2.5km)

TALLINN

Lower Town

Pikk tänav, running north from Raekoja plats to the **Great Coast Gate** and the **Paks Margareeta** (Fat Margaret Bastion) – the medieval exit to Tallinn port – is lined with many 15th-century houses of medieval merchants and gentry. Also here are the buildings of several old Tallinn guilds and some museums.

Near the end of Pikk tänav stands a chief Tallinn landmark, the **Oleviste Church**. This is a great place to start any Tallinn expedition as there's a superb **observation deck** (☎ 621 4421; adult/student 20/10EEK; ☻ 10am-6pm) halfway up its 124m structure offering the city's best views of the Old Town (it's a long and narrow climb up, though – bring a hanky to wipe off the sweat). The Church is dedicated to the 11th century King Olav II of Norway but linked in local lore with another Olav (Olaf), the church's architect who fell to his death from its tower. First built in the early 13th century, it was once the world's tallest building (it used to be 159m high). Near the church on Lai tänav 46/48, is the **former KGB headquarters**; the basement windows were bricked up to conceal the sounds of interrogations from those on the street above.

SLEEPING

The Tourist Information Centre can help find accommodation to fit your budget. To rent a central, modern apartment for up to four people from 1500EEK a night, contact **Cassandra Apartments** (☎ 630 9820; www.cassandra-apartments.com; Tartu maantee 18). **Rasastra Bed & Breakfast** (☎ 661 6291; www.bedbreakfast.ee; Mere pui-estee 4) can set you up with a room in a private home from 260EEK per person.

Old House (☎ 641 1464; www.oldhouse.ee; Uus tänav 22 & 26; dm 290EEK, 1-/2-/3-/5-/6-person r 390/550/825/900/1080EEK, guesthouse s/d/tr 450/650/975EEK, apt 950-2000EEK, 10% discount with ISIC) You won't get a better location than at this recently refurbished hostel/guesthouse filling two nearly adjacent houses in the old town. Sure, the walls are paper-thin, but it's cosy, spotless, and a hearty breakfast is included. Their apartments are a good splurge.

Vana Tom (☎ 631 3252; Väike-Karja tänav 1; dm 235EEK, r from 595EEK) As a place to crash, this is a great option – if, that is, you arrive ready to pass out. It feels crowded (dorm rooms hold nine, 12 and 15 beds), and the noise from the upstairs strip club can be frustrat-ing. Otherwise, it has an excellent location, and it's squeaky clean.

Hotel G9 (☎ 626 7100; www.hotelg9.ee; Gosiori tänav 9; s/d/tr 500/600/750EEK) Just a two-minute walk from the modern city centre, this nondescript but modern, cheerful place is a very good deal.

EATING & DRINKING

Beer House (☎ 627 6520; Dunkri tänav 5; ☻ 9am-midnight Sun-Thu, 9am-4am Fri-Sat) A little piece of Austria in the heart of the old town, this multi-levelled place is a great for a night of revelling in the company of many foreigners and a few locals. Tallinn's only micro-brewery is located within and whips up a prize-winning array of fresh beers (30EEK to 40EEK). There's also a nightclub and a sauna (for rent by the hour) upstairs.

Eesti Maja (☎ 645 5252; www.eestimaja.ee; Lauteri tänav 1; buffet 75EEK, meals from 125EEK; ☻ 11am-11pm) Here's a fun place to sample some traditional Estonian fare in a folky interior. Their small weekday lunch buffet is a good deal and lets you try some of the heavy fare without a full-plate commitment.

Pizza Americano (☎ 644 8837; Müürivahe tänav 2; pizzas from 85EEK; ☻ 11.30am-10.30pm) Thick, tasty pizzas of every possible permutation and combination are on offer here, including several vegetarian options.

Olde Hansa (☎ 627 9020; Vana Turg 1; mains 75-225EEK; ☻ 11am-midnight) If you'll splurge just once in Tallinn, here's where to do it. This medieval-themed restaurant (more authentic than kitsch!) boasts first and foremost the most ebullient and friendly service in the city, plus exotic meats (elk, wild boar) and home-made delights like juniper cheese and honey beer. It's a fun atmosphere inside or out on their terrace, and the food and its creative presentation is always first-rate.

Hell Hunt (☎ 681 8333; Pikk tänav 39; mains from 65EEK; ☻ noon-2am) A trooper on the pub circuit for years, this boasts an amiable atmosphere, and reasonable prices for local-brewed beer and cider (half-litre for 24EEK). The food is hit-and-miss, though.

Von Krahli Teater Baar (☎ 626 9096; Rataskaevu tänav 10/12; mains from 45EEK; ☻ noon-1am Sun-Thu, noon-3am Fri & Sat) This is one of the city's best hang-outs. It often has live bands (and some-times stages fringe plays) and is a good place to meet interesting locals and have a good meal.

GETTING THERE & AWAY
Air
Both **Estonian Air** (☎ 640 110; www.estonian-air.ee; Vabaduse väljak 10) and **Finnair** (☎ 609 0950; www .finnair.ee; Roosikransti tänav 2) link Tallinn with Helsinki daily. **Copterline** (www.copterline.ee) runs pricey helicopter flights between Helsinki and Tallinn's Copter terminal, near the port, hourly from 7am to 9pm (one-way from 767EEK to 3100EEK, 18 mins).

Boat
About 25 ferries and hydrofoils (catamarans) cross between Helsinki and Tallinn daily. Ferries make the crossing in 2½ to 3½ hours, hydrofoils in just over an hour. All companies provide concessions and charge higher prices for weekend travel. Expect to pay around the price of an adult ticket extra to take a car.

Tallink (☎ 640 9808; www.tallink.ee) runs up to 12 ferries and hydrofoils daily. Ferry tickets start from 190EEK, and hydrofoils cost from 315EEK. **Lindaline** (☎ 699 9333) makes up to eight hydrofoil crossings each way daily. A one-way trip costs from 345EEK. **Eckerö Line**

(☎ 631 8606) operates a daily or twice-daily auto catamaran from terminal B, making the crossing in 3½ hours, with one-way tickets starting from 220EEK. **Nordic Jet Line** (☎ 613 7000) has several auto catamarans departing terminal C, making the trip in around 1½ hours, several times a day; one-way/return tickets cost from 300EEK. **Silja Line** (☎ 611 6661; www.silja.ee, no English) ferries make the crossing between Tallinn and Helsinki in 1½ hours with worthwhile day-trip packages available to Helsinki. Prices start from 340EEK.

GETTING AROUND
Tallinn has an excellent network of buses, trolleybuses and trams that usually run from 6am to midnight. In Estonia, *piletid* (tickets) are sold from street kiosks (adult/student 10/7EEK) or can be purchased from the driver (15EEK). Validate your ticket using the hole-punch inside the vehicle.

There is a glut of taxis on the streets of Tallinn – more per capita than in Helsinki. They cost from 4.50EEK to 8EEK per kilometre. To book a cab by phone, call **Iks Takso** (☎ 638 1381) or **Raadiotakso** (☎ 601 1111).

TALLINN

St Petersburg

CONTENTS

Simply one of the most enchanting and impressive cities on earth, St Petersburg gives little indication that its incredible architectural wealth was actually built on a mosquito-infested swamp. Peter the Great, who wanted to create a modern capital for a country still stuck in the dark ages, founded his 'window on Europe' in 1703. Since then it has grown to be Europe's fourth largest city and easily one of its most culturally significant. The city of Dostoyevsky and Shostakovich and the cradle of the Russian Revolution, St Petersburg has more to offer the traveller than perhaps anywhere else in Russia.

FAST FACTS

- **Population** 5 million
- **Currency** rouble (R): US$1 = R29.23; £1 = R51.93; €1 = R35.9; A$1 = R21.17; C$1 = R23.28; NZ$1 = R19.73; ¥100 = R26.25
- **Official Language** Russian
- **Telephone Codes** Russia country code ☎ 7; St Petersburg ☎ 812
- **Visa** required by all and can be a real headache – begin preparing well in advance of your trip!

ORIENTATION & INFORMATION

St Petersburg is spread out across many islands, some real and some created through the construction of canals. The central street is Nevsky Prospekt which extends for some 4km from the Alexandr Nevsky Monastery to the Hermitage. The vast Neva River empties into the Gulf of Finland, filtered through a number of islands. Most significant of these are Vasilyevsky and Petrogradsky Islands.

Currency exchange offices are available throughout the city. ATMs are inside every metro station, in hotels and department stores, in main post offices and along major streets. **American Express** (☎ 326 45 00; Malaya Morskaya ul 23; ☻ 9am-5pm Mon-Fri) only offers travel services; travellers cheques can be exchanged at most Russian banks (with commission, of course).

There's a mediocre (yet English-speaking) Tourist Office outside the Winter Palace in a kiosk on Palace Sq.

Nevsky Prospekt boasts two large, excellent Internet cafés – **Café Max** (☎ 273 6655; 90/92 Nevsky Prospekt; per hr R60) and **Quo Vadis** (☎ 311 8011; Nevsky Prospekt 24; per hr R60).

In an emergency call ☎ 01 for fire, ☎ 02 for the police and ☎ 03 for an ambulance. The operator will speak Russian only.

SIGHTS
The Historic Heart

Unquestionably your first stop should be **Dvortsovaya Ploshchad** (Palace Sq), where the baroque **Winter Palace** (Zimny dvorets) appears like a mirage under the archway at the start of ul Bolshaya Morskaya. The palace was commissioned from Bartolomeo Rastrelli in 1754 by Empress Elizabeth, and some of its 1057 rooms now house part of the astonishing **Hermitage** (☎ 311 3465; www.hermitagemuseum.org; adult/student & child R300/free; ☻ 10.30am-6pm Tue-Sat, 10.30am-5pm Sun), which is one of the world's great art museums. Enter through the courtyard from Palace Sq. To avoid queues in the summer months, you can book tickets online very easily. The collection is vast and can be overwhelming for a first-time visitor. Ask for an English map at the information desk in the ticket hall. If your time is limited you should look out for the following highlights: the Jordan Staircase (directly ahead of you when you enter); room 100 (Ancient Egypt), rooms 178–97

(the State rooms for the apartments of the last imperial family); room 204 (the Pavilion Hall); roms 228–38 (Italian Art, 16th to 18th centuries); room 271 (the Imperial family's cathedral); and concentrate most of your time on the fabulous third floor, particularly rooms 333–50 for late-19th-century and early-20th century European art, including a huge array of Matisse, Picasso, Monet, Van Gogh, Cézanne, Gaugin, Pissaro, Rodin and Kandinsky. There are several cafés and shops within the museum, so you can easily spend a whole day there. Disabled access is now very good – call ☻ 110 9079 if you require any assistance.

Opposite the Winter Palace across the square is the fabulous **General Staff Building** and in the middle of the square, the 47.5m **Alexander Column** commemorates the 1812 victory over Napoleon.

To the west across the road is the gilded spire of the **Admiralty**, former headquarters of the Russian navy. West of the Admiralty is **Ploshchad Dekabristov** (Decembrists' Sq), named after the Decembrists' Uprising of 14 December 1825.

Falconet's famous statue of Peter the Great, the **Bronze Horseman**, stands at the end of the square towards the river. Behind looms the splendid golden dome of **St Isaac's Cathedral** (☎ 315 9732; Isaaklevskaya pl; admission to cathedral R250, to colonnade R100; ☻ 11am-6pm Thu-Tue), built between 1818 and 1858. Think twice before going in unless you like the ornate baroque style. The colonnade is far better value for money giving superb views over the city.

Nevsky Prospekt

The inner part of vast Nevsky Prospekt that runs from the Admiralty to Moscow Station is St Petersburg's main shopping thoroughfare. The most impressive sight along it is the great colonnaded arms of the **Kazan Cathedral**, built between 1801 and 1811.

At the end of Nevsky Prospekt is the working **Alexandr Nevsky Monastery** (Lavra Alexandra Nevskovo; ☎ 274 0409, adult/student R50/30), where you'll find the **Tikhvin Cemetery** (admission R50), last resting place of some of Russia's most famous artistic figures, including Tchaikovsky and Dostoevsky.

Between Nevsky & the Neva

A block north of Nevsky Prospekt metro is the lovely **Ploshchad Iskusstv** (Arts Sq), with

CENTRAL ST PETERSBURG

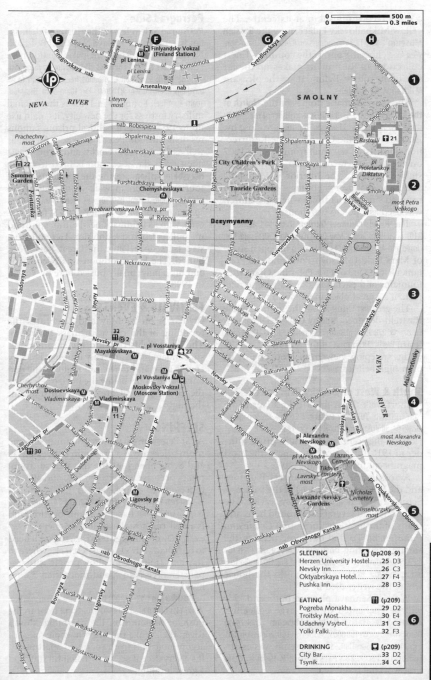

a monument to Pushkin at its centre. The yellow Mikhailovsky Palace, now the **Russian Museum** (☎ 311 14 65; admission R240; ☯ 10am–5pm Wed-Mon), housing one of the country's finest collections of Russian art makes up the far side of the square. Behind it are the pleasant **Mikhailovsky Gardens**.

The polychromatic domes of the **Church of the Spilled Blood** (☎ 315 1636; Konyushennaya pl; adult/student R250/125; ☯ 11am–6pm Thu-Tue) are close by. Also known as the Church of the Resurrection of Christ, it was built from 1887 to 1907 on the spot where Alexander II was assassinated in 1881. The interior is incredible and somewhat overwhelming – having been restored since Soviet times when the church was used as a potato warehouse.

The lovely **Summer Garden** (Letny Sad; admission R10; open 9am–10pm May-Oct; 10am–6pm Oct–mid-Apr; closed mid-Apr to end Apr) is between the open space of Mars Field (Marsovo Pole) and the Fontanka River. Laid out for Peter the Great with fountains and pavilions along a geometrical plan, it's a great place in which to relax.

The greatest thing about the unmistakable Rastrelli-designed **Smolny Cathedral** (Smolensky sobor; ☎ 278 5596; pl Rastrelli; admission R100; ☯ 11am–5pm Fri-Wed), 3km east of the Summer Garden, is the sweeping view from atop one of its 63m-high belfries.

South & West of Nevsky Prospekt

A short walk down the Moyka River is the fascinating **Yusupov Palace** (☎ 314 9883; nab reki Moyki 94; adult/student R300/250; ☯ 11am–5pm). Notorious as the scene of Rasputin's grisly murder in 1916, the palace has some of the most magnificent interiors in the city.

Across the meandering Canal Griboedova and the Fontanka River, east of the palace, is Sennaya pl, the heart of Dostoevskyville. The author lived in several flats around here, and many of the locations turn up in *Crime and Punishment*. To find out more head to the small, interesting **Dostoevsky Museum** (☎ 164 6950; Kuznechny per 5/2; adult/student R60/30, audio tour in English R70; ☯ 11am–5pm Tue-Sun) in the house where the writer died in 1881.

West of Sennaya pl, train buffs and kids will be enchanted by the large collection of models at the **Railway Museum** (Zheleznaya Doroga Muzey; ☎ 168 8005; Sadovaya ul 50; admission R20; ☯ 11am–5pm Sun-Thu). The museum was established in 1809, 28 years before Russia had its first working train!

Petrograd Side

Petrograd Side refers to the cluster of delta islands between the Malaya Neva and Bolshaya Nevka channels. The principal attraction here is the **Peter & Paul Fortress** (Petropavlovskaya krepost; ☎ 238 4550; admission to grounds free, admission to all buildings adult/student R120/60; ☯ 10am–5pm Thu-Mon, 10am–4pm Tue). Founded in 1703 as the original military fortress for the new city, its main use up to 1917 was as a political prison: famous residents include Peter's own son Alexei, as well as Dostoevsky, Gorky and Trotsky. At noon every day a cannon is fired from the **Naryshkin Bastion**, scaring the daylights out of tourists. It's fun to walk along the **battlements** (adult/student R50/30; ☯ 10am–10pm). Most spectacular of all is the **St Peter & St Paul Cathedral**, with its landmark needle-thin spire and magnificent baroque interior. Here all Russia's tsars since Peter the Great have been buried. The latest addition was Nicholas II and his family, finally buried here by Yeltsin in 1998.

FESTIVALS & EVENTS

City Day is on 27 May and celebrates the founding of the city with mass festivities. The **White Nights** (around the summer solstice in late June) are truly unique. The city comes alive and parties all night as the sun only barely sinks below the horizon, leaving the sky a magical grey-white throughout the night.

SLEEPING

As St Petersburg has a very definite 'season', room prices are at a premium between May and September. Outside this period, room prices decrease by between 10% and 30% on those quoted below.

Herzen University Hotel (☎ 314 7472; ul Kazanskaya 6; s/d €16/40) has a brilliant location and is a well-run hostel used to foreigners. However, they do not register visas, so you'll need to have had your visa registered elsewhere to stay here (they do not allow people with unregistered visas to spend more than 3 days here).

Pushka Inn (☎ 312 0913; www.pushkainn.ru; nab Reki Moyki 14; s €100 d €180 apt €180-270) Next door to the Pushkin Museum on the charming Moyka River, the Pushka Inn offers a whole range of accommodation from rooms to apartments. It's a very decent set up with helpful staff and a great location.

Nevsky Inn (☎ 924 9805; www.nevskyinn.ru; Kirpichny per 2, flat 19; s/d €60/75) Run by a joint British-Russian management, the Nevsky Inn is one of the best mini-hotels in the city. Rooms are clean and comfortable and there's a large modern kitchen that guests can use.

Oktyabrskaya (☎ 277 6330; hotel@spb.cityline.ru; Ligovsky pr 10; s/d €73/116) This enormous hotel around pl Vosstainya has two buildings – the main one which spans one side of the square and the smaller annexe to one side of the Moscow Station. While it's enormous and impersonal, it's well-located and the rooms have all been renovated to high standards.

EATING

Keep your eyes open for blini (Russian pancake) kiosks throughout the city. Their delicious blinis are superb value (20-30R) and a great snack. Street food is sold around metro stations.

Pogreba Monakha (☎ 314 1353; Millionnaya ul 32; mains R500) Order from a traditional menu of Russian dishes served by staff dressed as monks in this atmospheric underground cellar not far from the Hermitage. Food is good, although the tip-seeking doorman is somewhat out of place.

Troitsky Most Kamennoostrovsky pr 9/2 (☎ 232-6693); Zagorodny pr 38 (☎ 115-1998) Superb vegetarian chain. Mains range in price from R100 to R200. The mushroom lasagne is legendary.

Udachny Vystrel (☎ 311 6949; www.y-v.spb.ru; mains R600; ☯ noon-midnight) Not far from the Admiralty, this excellent game restaurant with a charming interior serves up traditional Russian fare. There's also a terrace in the courtyard for the summer months. Vegetarians should give it a miss – the bearskins and taxidermy alone will be off-putting.

Yolki Palki (☎ 273 1594; Nevsky Prospekt 88; mains R100-200; ☯ 11am-11pm) The Moscow chain now has an outlet on Nevsky Prospekt – as kitsch as ever (you dine in a Russian forest attended by waiters in folk costume) but there's good Russian food served in a buffet style here.

DRINKING

City Bar (☎ 314 1037; Millionaya 10; ☯ 10am-late) Run by the inimitable local celebrity Elaine, the City Bar has moved to smarter premises on millionaire's row, a short walk from the Hermitage. This is the hub of the ex-pat

community and it's full of foreigners most nights of the week.

Tsynik (☎ 312 9526; per Antonenko 4; ☯ 1pm-3am, until 7am Fri & Sat) Far more authentic is the grungy cool of Tsynik. Famous for its rowdy crowd and grenki (fried garlic black bread), this is the place to be seen misbehaving.

GETTING THERE & AWAY

Daily express buses run from Helsinki to St Petersburg (Russian visa required) along highway E18, via the Finnish towns of Porvoo, Kotka and Hamina. Check current timetables and book tickets at the bus station or a travel agency. From Helsinki to St Petersburg there are three daily buses (€50.40, nine hours). Of course, the train is a far more romantic way to reach Russia. Note that St Petersburg is Pietari in Finnish.

There are three daily trains from Helsinki to Russia, travelling via the Finnish stations of Lahti, Kouvola and Vainikkala. You must have a valid Russian visa but border formalities have been fast-tracked so that passport checks are now carried out on board the moving train.

The Russian *Tolstoi* sleeper departs from Helsinki daily for St Petersburg (one way in 2nd/1st class €57.20/88.20). The *Sibelius* and *Repin* have daily services between Helsinki and St Petersburg (5½ hours) via Vyborg (3¾ hours). The *Sibelius* (a Finnish train) departs from Helsinki at 7.42am (2nd/1st class seats only €50.20/79.50). The Russian *Repin* departs from Helsinki at 3.42pm and has 2nd-class seats (€50.20) or 1st-class sleeping berths (€88.20). Return fares are roughly double. From St Petersburg, departures are at 4.32pm *(Sibelius)* and 7.32am *(Repin)*.

Buy Russian rail tickets in Helsinki at the special ticket counter in the central station – advance bookings are recommended. There are discounts for seniors, children and groups, but no student discounts. Check timetables at www.vr.fi.

GETTING AROUND

The metro (8R flat fare) is best for covering the large distances across the city. The four lines cross over in the city centre and go out to the suburbs. The most confusing aspect of the system is that all labelling is in Cyrillic. Listen out for the announcements of the station names, or ask locals who will usually go out of their way to help. A further confusion is that two stations sharing an exit will have different names. For example, Nevsky Pr and Gostiny Dvor are in the same place, but as they are on different lines, they have different names.

Around the centre, *marshrutka* minibuses are a very quick alternative to the slow trolleybuses. Costs vary on each route, but the average fare is R14, and is displayed prominently inside each van. To stop a *marshrutka*, simply hold out your hand and it will stop. Jump in, sit down, pass cash to the driver (a

human chain operates if you are not seated nearby) and then call out '*ostanovityes pozhalusta!*' when you want to get out and the driver will pull over.

If you'd rather take a cab, holding your arm out will cause nonofficial taxis to stop very quickly. The standard rate for a short distance (1km to 2km) is R50 and then R100 after that, although as a foreigner, expect to have the price raised – always agree on a price before getting into the car. For an official cab, call ☎ 068.

Iceland

CONTENTS

Iceland's scenery is mind-blowing: chuck a lump of lava and you'll hit a glacier, geyser, volcano or bubbling geothermal spring. The high-energy of the landscape seems to infect the people, too – the average inhabitant is a farmer, fisher, drinker, thinker, knitter, poet and skier!

The country's gobsmacking natural features support some of the largest sea-bird colonies in the world, and it's the best place on earth for whale-spotting. It's also the backdrop for the sagas: epic tales of love, death, bloody feuds and fantastic voyages, considered to be among the finest Western medieval works.

Clean, green capital Reykjavík is *the* destination for most travellers. Fashionable young things defy the northern exposure, thriving on vast quantities of coffee, music, sex and beer: see for yourself on the infamous *runtur*, the city's wheeling weekend pub-crawl.

FAST FACTS

- **Area** 103,000 sq km
- **Capital** Reykjavík
- **Currency** króna (Ikr): US$1 = Ikr71.46; £1 = Ikr127.49; €1 = Ikr87.82; A$1 = Ikr51.65; C$1 = Ikr56.15; NZ$1 = Ikr47.94; ¥100 = Ikr64.42;
- **Famous for** fishing, sagas, Björk, rotten shark meat!
- **Official Language** Icelandic
- **Phrases** *halló* (hello), *gjörðu svo vel* (please), *takk fyrir* (thanks), *skál!* (cheers!)
- **Telephone Codes** country code ☎ 354; international access code ☎ 00; operator ☎ 533 5310; there are no telephone area codes in Iceland
- **Visa** unnecessary for visitors from Scandinavia, EU countries and the USA staying for under three months (see p261)

HIGHLIGHTS

- The drunken **runtur** (p230), a wild Friday-night cavorting round the pubs and clubs of Reykjavík
- Crashing, cascading, erupting masses of water at **Gullfoss** and **Geysir** (p232)
- Baby puffins and violent volcanoes on the **Vestmannaeyjar** (p249)
- Explosive lava-strewn wastelands round **Mývatn** and **Krafla** (p241)
- Turquoise bathing pools in the Landmannalaugar (p253) geothermal area
- Massive whales breaching the waves outside Húsavík's quaint harbour (p241)
- Entering Iceland by the most romantic route – a boat to brightly coloured, bohemian Seyðisfjörður (p262)

ITINERARIES

- **Three days** Get to Reykjavík on Friday to experience the revelry of *runtur*. Sober up in the geothermal pool at Laugadalur before doing some sightseeing – Hallgrímskirkja and Perlan are good to begin with. On the third day, visit Gullfoss, Geysir and Þingvellir on the Golden Circle tour, then splash down for a good soak in the Blue Lagoon.
- **Two weeks** After thoroughly exploring Reykjavík and its surroundings, rattle round the Ring Road and relax in sunny Akureyri. Detour to Húsavík for a spot of whale-watching. The incredible volcanic features and birds of Mývatn deserve at least a couple of days. Also take several days to visit Jökulsárgljúfur National Park and Dettifoss, Europe's most powerful waterfall.

CLIMATE & WHEN TO GO

Reykjavik has a mild but miserable climate, often with fierce rains, gales and fog; May, June and July are the driest months of the year. In the north and east, the weather is better. Blizzards and fierce sandstorms can occur in the interior deserts and on the coastal sand deltas.

The **Icelandic Meteorological Office** (☎ 902 0600 extension 44; www.vedur.is/english) provides a daily weather forecast.

Peak season runs from early June to 31 August, although some highland bus tours don't operate until July because of snow. At other times, many tourist facilities outside Reykjavík and Akureyri shut down.

HOW MUCH?

- **Book of sagas** Ikr1950
- **Postcard** Ikr60
- **Cinema ticket** Ikr800
- **Woolly hat** Ikr1500
- **Golden Circle tour** Ikr6500

LONELY PLANET INDEX

- **Litre of petrol** Ikr98
- **Litre of bottled water** Ikr200
- **Pint of Egils beer** Ikr600
- **Souvenir T-shirt** Ikr1500
- **Street snack (hot dog)** Ikr190

HISTORY

Irish monks desperate for peace and quiet were the first people to come to Iceland in around AD 700. Their solitude was rudely shattered by the Age of Settlement (874–930), when a wave of Nordic people descended, driven from the Scandinavian mainland by political clashes.

Incredibly, the human history of Iceland was chronicled almost from its inception. Ari Torgilsson, a 12th-century scholar, compiled the *Landnámabók* which details the migration, and wrote the *Íslendingabók,* which credits first permanent settlement to Norwegian Ingólfur Arnarson. Setting a fashion for literal place names, Arnarson landed in 874 at a spot he named Reykjavík (Smoky Bay) because of its steamy thermal springs.

The early Icelanders rejected monarchy in favour of the world's first democratic parliamentary system. In 930, Þingvellir (Parliament Plains; p232) near Reykjavík became the site of the national assembly, the Alþing.

Two hundred years of peace ended during the Sturlunga Period (1230–62), an era of violent power struggles between Iceland's chieftains, possibly stirred up by King Hákon of Norway in a dirty tricks campaign. Iceland ceded control of the country to Norway in 1262 and for the next six centuries endured a Dark Age of famine, disease, dispossession and disastrous volcanic eruptions.

Ownership of Iceland changed again in 1397 when it was placed under Danish rule

ICELAND

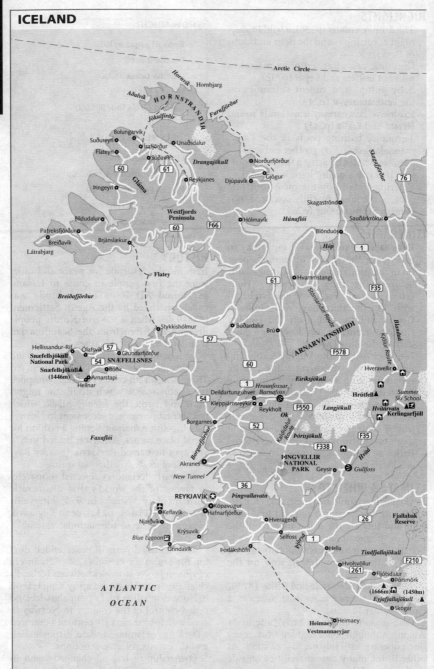

Arctic Circle

Hornbjarg
Hornvík
Aðalvík
HORNSTRANDIR
Furufjörður
Jökulfirðir
Bolungarvík
Suðureyri
Ísafjörður
Unaðsdalur
Flateyri
Súðavík
Drangajökull
Norðurfjörður
Skagafjörður
60
61
Reykjanes
Djúpavík
Gjögur
76
Þingeyri
Glama

Skagaströnd

Bíldudalur
Westfjords
Peninsula
60
F66
Hólmavík
Húnaflói
Sauðárkrókur
Patreksfjörður
Blönduós
Breiðavík
Brjánslækur
1
Látrabjarg
Hóp

Flatey
Hvammstangi
F35
61

Breiðafjörður
Stórisandur Route
ARNARVATNSHEIÐI
Kjölur Route
Blandá

Stykkishólmur
Búðardalur
Brú
57
F578
Hveravellir
Hellissandur-Rif
Ólafsvík
57
Grundarfjörður
Snæfellsjökull
National Park
54
SNÆFELLSNES
60
Eiríksjökull
Summer
Ski School
Snæfellsjökull
(1446m)
Búðir
Hrútfell
Hvítárvatn
Hellnar
Arnarstapi
Deildartunguhver
Hraunfossar,
Barnafoss
1
Kerlingarfjöll
54
Kleppjárnsreykir
Reykholt
F550
Langjökull
Borgarnes
Ok
52
Þórisjökull
F35
Faxaflói
Kaldidalur Route
F338
Borgarfjörður
Þingvellir
NATIONAL
PARK
Brúá
Akranes
Geysir
Gullfoss
New Tunnel
36
Þingvallavatn
REYKJAVÍK
Kópavogur
Fjallabak
Reserve
Keflavík
Hafnarfjörður
26
Njarðvík
Hvergerði
Krýsuvík
Selfoss
Tindfjallajökull
Blue Lagoon
1
F210
Grindavík
Þorlákshöfn
Hella
Hvolsvöllur
261
Fljótsdalur
(1666m)
(1450m)
Þórsmörk
ATLANTIC
Eyjafjallajökull
OCEAN
Skógar

Heimaey
Heimaey
Vestmannaeyjar

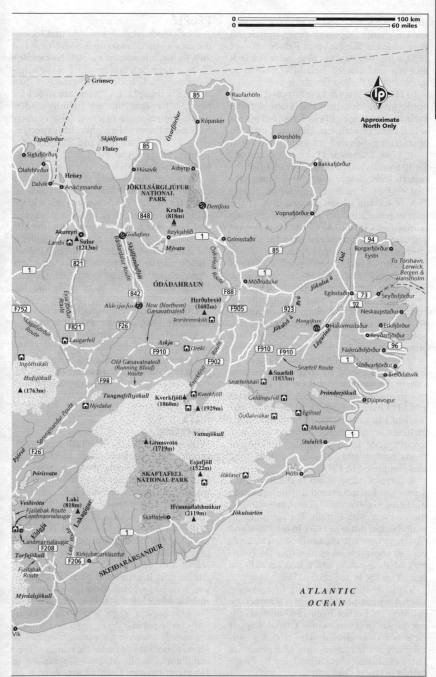

0 _____ 100 km
0 _____ 60 miles

Grímsey

85 Raufarhöfn

Kópasker

**Approximate
North Only**

Þórshöfn

Eyjafjörður   Skjálfandi   85
Siglufjörður   Flatey
Ólafsfjörður   Húsavík   Ásbyrgi   Bakkafjörður
Dalvík   Hrísey
Árskógssandur   **JÖKULSÁRGLJÚFUR
NATIONAL
PARK**
Krafla   Dettifoss
848   (818m)
Akureyri   Goðafoss   Reykjahlíð   Vopnafjörður
Lambi   Sulur   1   Grímsstaðir
(1213m)   Mývatn   85
821   1   94
1   **ÓDÁÐAHRAUN**   Möðrudalur   Borgarfjörður
Eystri
842   F88   Egilsstaðir   To Tórshavn,
Herðubreið   Lerwick,
F752   Aldeyjarfoss   New (Northern)   (1682m)   F905   523   73   Bergen &
Gæsavatnaleið   Hansthólm
F821   Þorsteinsskáli   92   Seyðisfjörður
F26   Neskaupstaður
Laugarfell   Askja   Dreki   Hengifoss   Hallormsstaður   Eskifjörður
F910   F902   Reyðarfjörður
Ingólfsskáli   Old Gæsavatnaleið   F910   F910   96
(Running Blind)   Fáskrúðsfjörður
Hofsjökull   Route   1   Stöðvarfjörður
F98   Snæfell Route   Breiðdalsvík
▲ (1763m)   Tungnafellsjökull   Snæfellsskáli   Snæfell
Nýidalur   Kverkfjöll   Kverkfjöll   (1833m)   Þrándarjökull
(1860m)   Geldingafell   Djúpivogur
▲ (1929m)   Egilssel
Þórisvatn   Óðaðalnúkar
Vatnajökull   Múlaskáli
Grímsvötn
F26   (1719m)   Stafafell   1
Esjufjöll
Þórisvatn   (1522m)   Jökulsel
Veiðivötn   Laki   **SKAFTAFELL   Höfn**
Fjallabak Route   (818m)   **NATIONAL PARK**
Landmannalaugar   Hvannadalshnúkur   Jökulsárlón
Landmannalaugar   (2119m)
F208   Skaftafell
Torfajökull   Kirkjubæjarklaustur
Fjallabak   F206   **SKEIÐARÁRSANDUR**
Route
Mýrdalsjökull   **ATLANTIC
OCEAN**

Vík

after the Kalmar Union (of Norway, Sweden and Denmark). Disputes between church and state ended in the Lutheran Reformation of 1550, when the Danish crown seized church property and created Iceland's first martyr by beheading Bishop Jón Arason.

In 1602, the Danish king imposed a monopoly giving Swedish and Danish firms exclusive trading rights in Iceland. This resulted in large-scale extortion, importation of inferior goods and yet more suffering.

In 1783, Lakagígar (Laki; p249) erupted for 10 months and devastated much of southeastern Iceland, spreading a poisonous haze that destroyed pastures and crops. Nearly 75% of Iceland's livestock and 20% of the human population perished in the resulting famine; an evacuation of the country was discussed. The survivors were hit shortly afterwards by a smallpox epidemic.

In spite of such catastrophes, a sense of Icelandic nationalism was slowly growing. Free trade was restored in 1855, thanks to lobbying by Icelandic scholar Jón Sigurðsson, and the Republic of Iceland was eventually established on 17 June 1944 (p259), symbolically at Þingvellir and on Sigurðsson's birthday.

Early in WWII, British troops occupied Iceland to defend its strategic position. When the British withdrew in 1941, US troops moved in (the USA still operates a NATO base at Keflavík today). The war marked a dramatic change in the country's fortunes as subsistence farming gave way to prosperity and the frenzied building of roads, bridges and airfields; the Ring Road was completed in 1974.

A corresponding boom in the fishing industry saw Iceland extend its fishing limit in the 1970s to 200 miles (322km), precipitating the 'cod war' with Britain. The British eventually backed down in 1976. In the 1980s and '90s there were also clashes between Icelanders and conservation groups over the country's whaling policy, which look set to begin again (see the boxed text, p218).

Vigdís Finnbogadóttir, the first woman elected to the presidency of a democratic country, held office from 1980 until standing down in 1996, when Ólafur Ragnar Grímsson was elected. The largest political party is the conservative Independence Party (Sjálfstæðisflokkurinn), led by Prime Minister Davíd Oddsson.

PEOPLE

A shock study recently revealed that Icelandic men's genetic makeup is 80% Norse and 20% Celtic, but women's is 50% Norse, 50% Celtic, suggesting that far more of the original settlers had children by their slaves than originally thought. Icelanders are noted for being self-reliant, but are friendly underneath the reserved exterior. The country has one of the world's highest life expectancies – 77.5 years for men and 82.2 years for women. Of a population of 290,570, almost half live in Reykjavík.

Icelanders' names are constructed from a combination of their first name and their father's (or mother's) first name. Girls add the suffix *dóttir* (daughter) to the patronymic and boys add *son*. Therefore, Jón, the son of Einar, would be Jón Einarsson. Guðrun, the daughter of Halldór, would be Guðrun Halldórsdóttir. Telephone directories are alphabetised by first name, so Guðrun Halldórsdóttir would be listed before Jón Einarsson.

Objecting loudly to whaling may upset locals, who feel strongly about the issue.

Iceland officially converted to Christianity around 1000, although followers of the old pagan gods were allowed to worship in private. With the Reformation of 1550 the Danes imposed Lutheranism, which prevails today.

ARTS
Literature

Without a doubt, the late 12th- and 13th-century sagas are Iceland's greatest cultural achievement. Written in terse, powerful Old Norse, these epics about settlement, romance and bloody disputes both entertain Icelanders and provide them with a rich sense of heritage. One of the best known, *Egils Saga*, tells the tale of the brooding, complex Egill Skallagrímsson. A renowned poet and skilled lawyer, he is also the grandson of a werewolf and a murderous drunk. Authorship is attributed to Snorri Sturluson, Iceland's greatest historian. Other sagas include *Hrafnkels Saga, King Haralds Saga, Laxdæla Saga*, a tragic family tale, and the universally popular *Njáls Saga*. As the sagas are mainly anonymous works, they can be found in bookshops under the names of their translators, usually Magnús Magnússon or Hermann Pálsson. *Grettis Saga*, about a superhuman but doomed outlaw, exists in an excellent translation by Anthony Faulkes.

The work of Nonni, children's author Jón Sveinsson (1857–1944), has been translated into 40 different languages. Jóhann Sigurjónsson wrote *Eyvind of the Hills*, a biography of the 18th-century outlaw Fjalla-Eyvindar. The best-known modern Icelandic writer is Nobel Prize–winner Halldór Laxness, whose blackly comic work gives a superb insight into Icelandic life. *Independent People*, concerning the fatally proud farmer Bjartur and the birth of the Icelandic nation, and *The Atom Station* are perhaps his two most famous books. The same disturbing humour runs through Einar Kárason's outstanding *Devil's Island* (about Reykjavík life in the 1950s), and Hallgrímur Helgason's *101 Reykjavík* (about a modern-day city slacker).

Music
Björk is Iceland's most famous musical export. Other bands with world domination in their sights include Quarashi, Sigurrós, Minus and Maus. You can see bands performing live at venues such as Gaukur á Stöng and Grand Rokk in Reykjavík (p230).

Visual Arts
Various artists have wrestled with Iceland's enigmatic soul, including the prolific Ásgrímur Jónsson (1876–1958). His work, depicting Icelandic landscapes and folktales, can be seen at the National Gallery in Reykjavík (p224). Pop-Art icon Erró (1932–) is honoured with a permanent collection in the Reykjavík Art Museum.

Plastic arts are well represented: the mystical work of Einar Jónsson (1874–1954; p224) dwells on death and resurrection, and Ásmundur Sveinsson's (1893–1982) unusual sculptures (p224) celebrate Iceland and its stories.

Cinema & TV
Based on Hallgrímur Helgason's book of the same name, Baltasar Kormákur's film *101 Reykjavík* (2000), the painful, funny tale of a Reykjavík dropout's fling with his mother's lesbian lover, won an international audience.

More recently, European art cinemas have screened *Nói Albínói* (2002), Dagur Kari's sweet-natured comedy about life in an isolated Icelandic valley.

For forthcoming films, see the informative www.icelandicfilmcentre.is.

ENVIRONMENT
The Land
Iceland, a juvenile among the world's land masses, is characterised by desert plateaus (52%), lava fields (11%), *sandur* or sand deltas (4%) and icecaps (12%). Over half the country lies above 400m and its highest point, Hvannadalshnúkur, rises 2119m above sea level. Only 21% of the land is considered arable and habitable.

Iceland's active volcanic zone runs through the middle of the country, from southwest to northeast. Active-zone geological features include lava flows, tubes, geysers, hot springs, fumaroles and volcanoes, and rocks such as basalt, pumice and rhyolite.

Birch trees grow in sheltered parts of the Þingvellir and Jökulsárgljúfur National Parks. However, the native flora in most other places consists only of grasses, mosses, lichens and wildflowers.

Wildlife
Because of the country's isolation, the only indigenous land mammal is the arctic fox. Introduced species include reindeer and mice. Polar bears occasionally turn up on the north coast, but their life expectancy in Iceland is short.

What Iceland lacks in land mammals and flora, it compensates for with vast numbers of birds and rich marine fauna. Kittiwakes, fulmars and gannets form large coastal colonies (best seen at Látrabjarg p237); there are hosts of aggressive arctic terns, golden plovers, ducks, swans, divers and geese at Mývatn (p242); and Vestmannaeyjar has huge quantities of lovable puffins (p249). Five different seal species and 17 species of cetacean (including blue whales and dolphins) have been spotted: boat trips run around the coast.

National Parks & Nature Reserves
Found throughout the country are *þjóðgarður* (national parks) and *friðland* (nature reserves), the most significant being Mývatn Nature Reserve (p242) and the Þingvellir (p232), Snæfellsjökull (p235), Jökulsárgljúfur (p244) and Skaftafell (p248) National Parks. Parks and reserves are open to visitors at all times. Wild camping is restricted: for further information, contact the nature

conservation council, **Náttúruvernd Ríkisins** (☎ 570 7400; www.natturuvernd.is; Skúlagata 21, IS-101 Reykjavík).

Environmental Issues

Sheep farming and historical timber extraction have caused immense ecosystem degradation – it has been estimated, for example, that a mere 1% of Iceland's original woodland remains. However, the Icelandic government and ordinary people are successfully cooperating to combat erosion with large-scale aerial seeding and intensive tree-planting.

The most controversial industrial project in Icelandic history is the dam being built in the Kárahnjúkar peaks to power an aluminium smelting plant. This will affect the courses of two glacial rivers and flood a huge area of untouched wilderness.

For information on whaling, see the boxed text, below.

FOOD & DRINK

Traditionally, Icelandic cuisine was at the unimaginative end of food consumption because ingredients were so limited. Nowadays, there are cafés and restaurants catering

---

WHALES OF PROTEST

Until 1989, Iceland killed 90 cetaceans a year for 'scientific' purposes, with the meat being sold to Japanese and Icelandic restaurants or rendered down into animal feeds. Sustained international pressure and direct action by conservation groups brought the killing to an end. However, in August 2003, Iceland announced its intention to resume scientific whaling, submitting a proposal to kill 500 fin, sei and minke whales over the following two years.

Supporters believe minke whales need culling, as they are depleting fish stocks; whereas antiwhalers fear it will damage the flourishing whale-watching industry, which brings in about US$16 million annually for the Icelandic economy. Various countries have issued formal protests against the hunting, and conservationists are calling for a boycott of Iceland and Icelandic goods. For further information, see the International Whaling Commission's website (www.iwcoffice.org).

---

to most tastes, although naturally, fresh fish, seafood and Icelandic lamb get top billing on most upmarket menus.

The government levies high taxes on alcohol to discourage excessive drinking…check out Friday-night Reykjavík to see the success of this policy! Note that drink-driving laws are strict, with 0.05% the legal limit of blood-alcohol content.

Staples & Specialities

Icelandic delicacies may remind visitors of the nightmare feast in *Indiana Jones and the Temple of Doom,* particularly during the February celebration of Þorrablót, cucumber sandwiches are out, as the lusty gorge on *svið* (singed sheep's head complete with eyeballs), *súrsaðir hrútspungar* (pickled ram's testicles) and *hákarl* (putrefied shark meat, buried and rotted for at least three months). The latter is supposed to be a cure for hangovers; you can test this theory at the Kolaportið Flea Market (p231), but be warned – the smell alone makes many foreigners ill.

Moving towards the less bizarre, Icelanders make a staple of *harðfiskur,* haddock that's cleaned and dried in the open air until it's completely brittle. It's then torn into strips and eaten with butter as a snack. Icelanders also eat *lundi* (puffin) which looks and tastes like calf liver. Most of the birds are netted on the Vestmannaeyjar (p249).

A unique treat is the delicious yogurtlike *skyr,* made from curdled milk. It's surprisingly low in fat, but sugar, fruit and cream are often added to turn it into a rich, decadent dessert. Around Mývatn (p242), look out for a regional pudding: *hverabrauð* (hot spring bread) is a dark, sticky loaf sweetened with molasses, baked in the ground using geothermal heat.

Coffee is a national institution and is available free for customers in some shops. A cup of filter coffee costs from Ikr200 (usually with refill).

The traditional Icelandic alcoholic brew is *brennivín* (burnt wine), a sort of schnapps made from potatoes and caraway seeds with the foreboding nickname *svarti dauði* (black death).

Where to Eat & Drink

For self-caterers, every town and village has at least one *kaupfélagið* (cooperative supermarket), with Bónus and Netto being the cheapest chains. Good-value food includes *skyr,* canned fish and dried fruit.

Petrol stations and kiosks sell relatively inexpensive sandwiches, coffee and hot snack foods (for example, hot dog and chips for around Ikr600).

In Reykjavík and Akureyri, all-you-can-eat soup and salad meals (around Ikr1000) are common. Reykjavík also has intimate pub-style cafés where you can drink beer, eat a meal (about Ikr800) or chat over coffee for hours without attracting comment. These places are great value, and commonly open from 11am to 1am. The word 'restaurant' de-notes an upmarket establishment, often with gourmet-quality food: main courses range from about Ikr1800 to Ikr4000 per person.

Beer (legalised in 1989), wine and spirits are available to people aged over 20 years from licensed hotels, bars, restaurants and ÁTVR shops (State Monopoly stores; some are called *vín búð*). In Reykjavík, the most central one is on Austurstræti, just past Café Paris.

Vegetarians & Vegans

Outside Reykjavík, which has several veggie/vegan restaurants, choices are limited. Quite a few places offer one veggie option, but as this usually involves cheese, vegans may have to self-cater.

REYKJAVÍK

pop 113,387

Reykjavík is the kicking, coffee-fuelled heart of Iceland. It's the world's most northerly capital city and also one of the smallest: but what it lacks in sunshine and size, it makes up for in pure energy.

Known as the 'smokeless city' thanks to its reliance on geothermal energy, Reykjavík has all the cultural trappings of a large European city, with seemingly few of the normal vices (the exception, of course, being the infamous pub-crawl, the *runtur*). Kids born with in-line skates on skate round the city centre's rows of colourful concrete houses, drivers stop for you instead of putting their foot on the gas, and the air is bitingly clean.

HISTORY

The first Viking settler, Ingólfur Arnarson, tossed his high-seat pillars (*öndvegissúlur*)

overboard in 874, and built his farm where they washed ashore three years later, call-ing the place Reykjavík. Ingólfur modestly claimed the entire southwestern corner of the island, planting his hayfields at Austurvöllur, the present town square.

In 1786, when the municipal charter was granted, the population was a titchy 167; the city really boomed during WWII, when it serviced British and US troops stationed at Keflavík.

ORIENTATION

Reykjavík's old town lies between Tjörnin, Lækjargata, the harbour and the nearby sub-urb of Seltjarnarnes. Nearly everything in the city lies within walking distance of the old settlement, and most bars, cafés and res-taurants are found around Lækjartorg and Austurstræti. This is also where you'll find the central post office and tourist informa-tion centre. The shopping district extends east along Laugavegur from Lækjargata to the Hlemmur bus station.

INFORMATION
Bookshops

There are two big bookshops with a superb choice of English-language books and topo-graphic maps.

Eymundsson (Map pp226-7; ☎ 511 1130; Austurstræti 18; ⏰ 9am-10pm Mon-Fri, 10am-10pm Sat, 1-10pm Sun)

Mál og Menning (Map pp226-7; ☎ 515 2500; shopping@edda.is; Laugavegur 18)

Discount Cards

Reykjavík Tourist Card (one/two/three days Ikr1200/1700/2200) Well worth the money and available at various outlets including the tourist offices. It gives you free entry to galleries, museums, swimming pools and the zoo, and includes a bus pass.

ICELAND

REYKJAVÍK

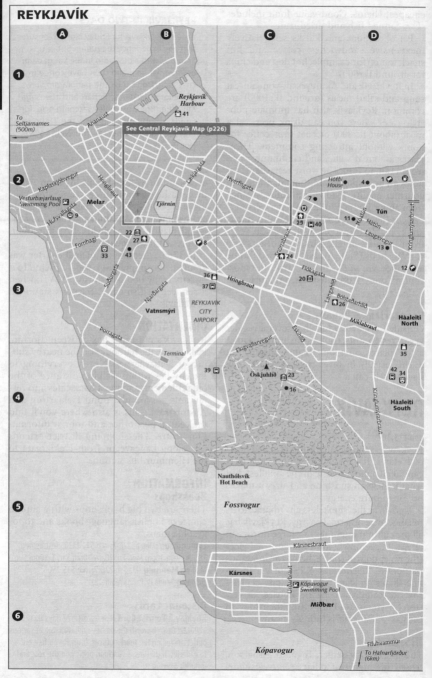

Ⓐ **Ⓑ** **Ⓒ** **Ⓓ**

1

To
Seltjarnames
(500m)

Reykjavík
Harbour
🛏 41

See Central Reykjavík Map (p226)

Ananaust

2

Kaplaskjólsvegur

Vesturbæjarlaug
Swimming Pool
9

Melar

Hringbraut

Tjörnin

Lækjargata

Hverfisgata

Höfði
House

7
25 40

4 1

11

Tún

Nóatún

Hátún

Laugavegur

13

Kringlumyrarbraut

22
27
33
43

8

24

Snorrabraut

12

3

Fornhagi

Suðurgata

Njarðargata

36
37

Hringbraut

REYKJAVÍK
CITY
AIRPORT

Vatnsmýri

Flókagata

20

Langahlíð

Bólstaðarhlíð
26

Miklabraut

Háaleiti
North

Eskihlíð

4

Þorragata

Terminal

39

Flugvallarvegur

Öskjuhlíð

23

16

Kringlumyrarbraut

35

42 34

Háaleiti
South

Nauthólsvík
Hot Beach

5

Fossvogur

Kársnesbraut

Kársnes

Urðarbraut

Kópavogur
Swimming Pool

Miðbær

6

Kópavogur

Fífuhvammur

To Hafnarfjörður
(6km)

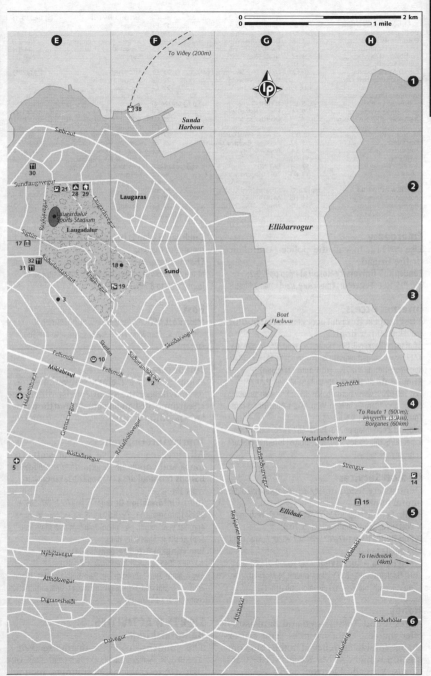

INFORMATION		
Bandalag Íslenska Farfugla...............(see 29)	Artificial Geyser........................16 C4	ENTERTAINMENT 🎭 (pp230–1)
Destination Iceland........................(see 37)	Ásmundursafn............................17 E3	Iceland Symphony
Dutch Embassy.................................1 D2	Botanic Garden..........................18 F3	Orchestra........................33 A3
Ferðafélag Íslands...........................2 F4	Elding Whale Watching................(see 41)	Icelandic Dance Company.................(see 33)
Ferðaþjónusta Bænda........................3 E3	Family Fun Park & Zoo..................19 F3	Reykjavík City Theatre.................34 D4
Iceland Review..................................4 D2	Hvalstöðin................................(see 41)	Sambíóin........................(see 35)
Íslenski Alpaklúbburinn.....................(see 2)	Kjarvalsstaðir...........................20 C3	
Kringlusafn (Reykjavík City	Laugardalur Swimming Pool..............21 E2	SHOPPING 🛍 (p231)
Library).......................................(see 35)	National Museum........................22 B2	Kringlan Shopping
Landspítali University Hospital	Saga Museum............................23 C4	Centre...........................35 D4
(Emergency Ward)..........................5 E5		Útilíf.............................36 B3
Lyf og Heilsa - Austurvegi..................6 E4	SLEEPING 🅰 🏠 (pp224–8)	
Náttúruvernd Ríkisins (Nature	Flöki Guesthouse........................24 C3	TRANSPORT (pp231–2)
Conservation Council)....................7 C2	Guesthouse 101.........................25 C2	BSÍ Bus Terminal.......................37 B3
Norwegian Embassy..........................8 B3	Guesthouse Central.....................26 D3	Félag Íslenskra
Post Office......................................9 A2	Icelandic Hótel Garður.................27 B3	Bifreiðaeigenda.....................(see 1)
Post Office....................................10 E4	Reykjavík Camping Ground...........28 E2	Ferries to Viðey.......................38 F1
Sjálfsbjörg....................................11 D2	Reykjavík City Hostel..................29 E2	Flybus Terminal.......................39 B4
Swedish Embassy............................12 D3		Hlemmur Bus Terminal...............40 C2
Útivist...13 D3	EATING 🍴 (pp228–30)	Jetty for Whale Watching
	10-11 Supermarket.....................30 E2	Tours............................41 B1
SIGHTS & ACTIVITIES (pp222–4)	Bónus Supermarket....................(see 35)	Kringlan Bus Stop.....................42 D4
Árbæjarlaug Swimming Pool..............14 H5	Kringlan Food Court...................(see 35)	
Árbæjarsafn..................................15 H5	Múlakaffi.................................31 E3	OTHER
	Ning's....................................32 E3	University of Iceland...................43 B3

Emergency

Use ☎ 112, to call the police, ambulance or fire brigade.
Landspítali University Hospital (Map pp220-2; ☎ 525 1000; Fossvogur) Emergency ward open 24 hours.

Internet Access

The cheapest Internet access is in the libraries for Ikr200 per hour.
Aðalsafn (Reykjavík City Library; Map pp226-7; ☎ 563 1717; www.borgarbokasafn.is; Tryggvagata 15; 🕙 10am-8pm Mon-Thu, 11am-7pm Fri, 1-5pm Sat & Sun)
Kringlusafn (Reykjavík City Library; Map pp220-2; ☎ 580 6200; www.borgarbokasafn.is; Kringlan shopping centre; 🕙 10am-7pm Mon-Wed, 10am-9pm Thu, 11am-7pm Fri, 1-5pm Sat & Sun)
Ground Zero (Map pp226-7; ☎ 562 7776; Vallarstræti 4; per 30/60min Ikr300/450) A dedicated Internet café full of moody teenagers.

Medical Services

Dentists are listed under *tannlæknar* in the phone book.
Health Centre (Map pp226-7; ☎ 585 2600; Vesturgata 7) Doctor's appointment required (Ikr700).
Lyf og Heilsa (Map pp226-7; ☎ 562 9020; Austurstræti 12) Central pharmacy.
Lyf og Heilsa – Austurvegi (Map pp220-2; ☎ 581 2101; Háaleitisbraut 68; 🕙 8am-midnight Mon-Fri, 10am-midnight Sat & Sun) Late-night pharmacy.

Money

Banks round Austurstræti and Bankastræti offer the best exchange rates. You can exchange foreign currency at hotels, but commission is high. ATMs accept MasterCard, Cirrus, Visa and Electron.

Landsbanki Íslands (Map pp226-7; Austurstræti) No commission charges.
Change Group Has branches at the Keflavik Airport and at the main tourist office (Map pp226-7). Commissions from 2.75% to 8.75%.

Post

Main Post Office (Map pp226-7; Pósthússtræti 5; 🕙 9am-4.30pm Mon-Fri) Reliable poste restante and fax service.

Telephone

Public phones are elusive in mobile-crazy Reykjavík: try the main tourist office, the street opposite Laugavegur 38, and the Kringlan shopping centre.

Tourist Information

All three centres have helpful staff, free maps and copies of *Reykjavík This Month*.
BSÍ bus terminal desk (Map pp220-2; Vatnsmýrarvegur 10)
Tourist Information Desk (Map pp226-7; ☎ 563 2005; Tjarnargata 11; 🕙 8.20am-4.30pm Mon-Fri, noon-4pm Sat year-round, plus noon-4pm Sun mid-May–mid-Sep) At the Raðhús (City Hall).
Upplýsingamiðstöð Ferðamála (Map pp226-7; ☎ 562 3045; www.visitreykjavik.is; Aðalstræti 2; 🕙 8.30am-7pm Jun–mid-Sep, 9am-6pm Mon-Fri, 10am-2pm Sat & Sun mid-Sep–May) The main tourist information centre, near Lækjargata.

SIGHTS & ACTIVITIES
Hallgrímskirkja

This immense concrete **church** (Map pp226-7; ☎ 510 1000; Skólavörðuholt; 🕙 9am-6pm) was designed to resemble basalt columns, and took a staggering 34 years to build. Admire its elongated, ultrastark interior, then ride up the **75m tower** (adult/child Ikr300/50) accompanied by heavenly choir music! Outside, a **statue** of Leifur Eiríksson, the first Viking to stumble upon America, gazes nobly forth. It was a present from the USA on the 1000th anniversary of the Alþing (p232).

Volcano Show

Eccentric eruption-chaser Villi Knutsen is the film maker, owner and presenter of this awesome **show** (Map pp226-7; ☎ 551 3230; Hellusund 6a; 1hr show adult/student/child Ikr750/650/200). Incredible footage captures (among other things) the sea round Surtsey boiling away and a whole town being swallowed by belching, spitting lava. English shows begin at 11am, 3pm and 8pm (July and August; less frequently September to June). A French programme is shown at 1pm and a German programme at 6pm (Saturday only, July and August).

Whale-Watching

Iceland is a terrific place for spotting whales. minkes often swim right up to the boats! From May to September, two companies run three-hour trips from the harbour: **Elding Whale Watching** (Map pp220-2; ☎ 555 3565; www.elding.is; adult/child 7-12 yrs Ikr3700/1600) and **Hvalstöðin** (Map pp220-2; ☎ 533 2660; www.whalewatching.is; adult/child 7-12 yrs Ikr3500/1500).

Perlan

The huge water tanks on Öskjuhlíð hill have been developed into a tourist complex known as Perlan ('The Pearl'). It includes the wicked **Saga Museum** (Map pp220-2; ☎ 511 1517; www.sagamuseum.is; adult/student/child Ikr800/600/400; ☾ 10am-6pm Jun-Aug, noon-5pm Mon-Fri & 10am-6pm Sat & Sun Sep-May), which brings Iceland's history to life with silicon models and a soundtrack of thudding axes and bloodcurdling screams. Don't blame the *brennivín* (schnapps) if you see some of the characters about town – they were modelled on Reykjavík inhabitants!

There are two **artificial geysers** (one inside and one out) which blast off every few minutes, while upstairs is a café, a swish revolving restaurant and an alluring **viewing area** with recordings explaining the panorama. To get there, take bus No 7 from Lækjartorg.

Geothermal Pools

A trip to Iceland wouldn't be complete without a dip in a naturally heated pool. One hundred per cent cheaper than the Blue Lagoon (p233), **Nauthólsvík Hot Beach** (Ýlströndin; Map pp220-2; ☾ 10am-10pm mid-May–mid-Sep) is a dinky stretch of golden sand heated by geothermal water (at 18°C to 20°C). There are hot pots on the beach and in the sea, and a small café selling beer and ice cream nearby.

There are seven geothermal swimming pools in the city. The largest is **Laugardalur** (Map pp220-2; ☎ 553 4039; Sundlaugavegur 30; adult/child Ikr200/100; ☾ 6.50am-9.30pm Mon-Fri, 8am-8pm Sat & Sun), right next door to the Reykjavík City Hostel and camping ground. It has a sauna, whirlpool and waterslides, and it's particularly good fun to splash about while businesspeople hold morning meetings in the hot pots. Catch bus No 5 from Lækjartorg.

Parks & Gardens

Great for kids, the **family fun park & zoo** (Map pp220-2; ☎ 585 7800; botgard@rvk.is; Laugardalur; adult/child Ikr550/450; ☾ 10am-6pm mid-May–Aug, 10am-5pm Sep–mid-May) is in the green valley south of Reykjavík City Hostel. Attractions include a minicar driving course, replica Viking longship and rides for little 'uns. The zoo contains farm animals, seals, reindeer and arctic foxes.

Nearby, the **Botanic Garden** (Map pp220-2; ☎ 553 8870; botgard@rvk.is; Skúlatún 2; admission free; ☾ 10am-10pm Apr-Sep, 10am-5pm Oct-Mar), which cultivates 62% of Iceland's native plant species and colourful seasonal flowers, is good for afternoon coffee in the greenhouse or an evening stroll.

Museums & Galleries

The **National Museum** (Map pp220-2; ☎ 552 8888; www.natmus.is; Suðurgata 41; adult/student/under 18 yrs

---

VIÐEY

You can reach this island, 1km north of Sundahöfn harbour, by ferry (see the Getting Around section on p231). You get an unusual perspective of Reykjavík, and the islet's small enough to stroll around with ease. Interesting features include the **church** and **farmhouse**, the oldest building in Iceland (1755; now a restaurant).

Ikr600/300/free; 🕙 10am-6pm May-Sep, shorter hrs Oct-Apr, closed Mon) is a must for anyone interested in Norse culture and Icelandic history. The most renowned artefact is the Valþjófsstaður church door, carved around 1200 and depicting a Norse battle scene. Other fine exhibits include Settlement Era relics, a witchcraft display and information on the Hekla eruption. The museum has closed for years, but reopening is planned for 2004.

Saga-lovers have a treat in store at the **Þjóðmenningarhúsið** (Culture House; Map pp226-7; ☎ 545 1400; www.thjodmenning.is; Hverfisgata 15; adult/child Ikr300/200, admission free Sun; 🕙 11am-5pm), which displays some of the original manuscripts. There are also well-planned changing exhibits about other aspects of Iceland's heritage.

Árbæjarsafn (Open-Air Museum; Map pp220-2; ☎ 577 1111; www.arbaejarsafn.is; Kistuhyl 4; adult/under 18 yrs Ikr500/free; 🕙 10am-5pm Tue-Fri, 10am-6pm Sat & Sun Jun-Aug) is a 12.5-hectare historic farm, turned into a superb open-air museum in 1957. Whole buildings have been transplanted here, and costumed staff demonstrate Icelandic arts and crafts. Take bus No 10 or 11 from Hlemmur or No 110 from Lækjartorg (not Sunday).

The **National Gallery** (Map pp226-7; ☎ 515 9600; www.listasafn.is; Fríkirkjuvegur 7; adult/child under 12 yrs Ikr400/free, admission free Wed; 🕙 11am-5pm Tue-Sun) contains works by Iceland's most renowned artists, and gives an interesting glimpse into the nation's psyche. It's the surreal dusky-blue and mud-purple landscapes that stick in the mind, intermingled with creepy portraits of ogresses, giants and dead men walking.

Listasafn Reykjavíkur (Reykjavík Art Museum; www.listasafnreykjavikur.is; adult/under 18 yrs Ikr500/free, admission free Mon) is made up of three sections. The rather wonderful **Ásmundursafn** (Ásmundur Sveinsson Museum; Map pp220-2; ☎ 553 2155; Sigtún; 🕙 10am-4pm May-Sep, 1-4pm Oct-Apr) displays the artist's massive concrete sculptures, plus smaller works in wood, clay and metals in the weird igloo-shaped building he designed. His themes range from folklore to physics.

Jóhannes Kjarval (1885–1972) was a fisherman until his crew paid for him to study at the Academy of Fine Arts in Copenhagen. His unearthly Icelandic landscapes can be seen at the impressive **Kjarvalsstaðir** (Map pp220-2; ☎ 552 6131; Flókagata; 🕙 10am-5pm).

The third Listasafn Reykjavíkur is **Hafnarhús** (Map pp226-7; ☎ 590 1200; Tryggvagata 17; 🕙 10am-5pm), a severe, modern building containing works by Erró and other changing exhibitions.

Near Hallgrímskirkja is the cube-shaped **Einar Jónsson Museum** (Map pp220-2; ☎ 551 3797; www.skulptur.is; Eiríksgata; adult/child Ikr400/free; 🕙 2-5pm Tue-Sun Jun–mid-Sep, 2-5pm Sat & Sun mid-Sep–Nov & Feb-May, closed Dec & Jan), Iceland's first art museum, which exhibits religious and mythological creations by Iceland's foremost 20th-century sculptor.

Other Sights

Old Reykjavík grew up around **Tjörnin**, a large lake in the centre that echoes with the honks and hootings of thousands of geese, swans, ducks and gulls. The park at the southern end has jogging and bike trails, and colourful flower gardens.

On the northern bank is the **Raðhús** (City Hall; Map pp226-7; ☎ 563 2005; 🕙 8am-7pm Mon-Fri, noon-6pm Sat & Sun), a postmodern floating palace containing a tourist information desk, café (with free Internet access for customers) and exhibition gallery. There's also an impressive 3-D map of Iceland, with the towns appearing as insignificant orange splodges among a mass of mountains, fjords and volcanoes.

The neat little grey basalt building just behind the Raðhús and on the southern side of Austurvöllur houses the Icelandic parliament, the **Alþingi** (Map pp226-7; ☎ 563 0500; www.althingi.is; Túngata). Next to it is the **Dómkirkja** (Map pp226–7), Iceland's main cathedral, which played an important role in the conversion of the country to Lutheranism.

On the shore near the bay end of Klapparstígur stands the **Sun-Craft sculpture** (Map pp226–7), which resembles a Viking ship made from forks.

SLEEPING

In summer, finding a place to stay may be difficult, so bring a tent or book accommodation in advance. Prices given are for high season; rooms are often discounted in winter. Breakfast is usually included in room prices (but not for sleeping-bag accommodation), unless specified.

Budget

Reykjavík Camping Ground (Map pp220-2; ☎ 568 6944; Sundlaugavegur; camp sites per person Ikr750, 2-bed cabins Ikr4000 per night; (✦) mid-May–mid-Sep) An immense place with cooking (Ikr50 for 20 minutes) and laundry (Ikr300) facilities. It's a 30-minute walk from Lækjartorg, 15 minutes on bus No 5 (every 20 to 30 minutes), or an Ikr1100 taxi ride from the BSÍ bus terminal. From 1 June to 31 August, a free shuttle bus runs from the camping ground to the BSÍ bus terminal at 7.15am.

Reykjavík City Hostel (Map pp220-2; ☎ 553 8110; www.hostel.is; Sundlaugavegur 34; sb Ikr1950, r with bathroom per person Ikr2250-3700; ☐) Beside the camping ground is the environmentally friendly and award-winning youth hostel. Facilities include a wide-screen TV and Internet access (Ikr300 per 15 minutes). Book in advance: even out of season, it can fill up with school parties. Breakfast Ikr750.

Mid-Range

Gistiheimilið Jörð (Map pp226-7; ☎ 562 1739; Skólavörðustígur 13a; s/d Ikr4500/6500) This guesthouse, tucked among chic boutiques, offers first-class, top-value accommodation in the centre of town. Breakfast Ikr700.

The **Salvation Army Guesthouse** (Map pp226-7; ☎ 561 3203; www.guesthouse.is; Kirkjustræti 2; sb/s/d Ikr2700/5000/7500) is close to the clubs, and one of the cheapest central guesthouses. Rooms are definitely no-frills, but there's a lively, bustling atmosphere, and a lazy lounging area downstairs.

Central Guesthouse (Map pp220-2; ☎ 552 2822; www.mmedia.is/gakr; Bólstaðarhlíð 8; sb/s/d Ikr2900/5900/7900; ☐) This welcoming place is about 10 minutes' walk from the BSÍ bus terminal and Perlan. Rooms are comfy and smart, and the whole guesthouse has a sociable hostel feel. Internet access is Ikr200 for a half-hour.

Gistiheimilið Ísafold (Map pp226-7; ☎ 561 2294; isafold@itn.is; Bárugata 11; s/d Ikr6600/9000, s/d with private bathroom Ikr7200/10,200, apt Ikr10,500) This highly recommended, former rehab centre/bakery/bookshop lies in peaceful old Reykjavík. A huge stained-glass window shines multicoloured light into the hallway and comfy sitting room, where there are tea-making facilities. Newly decorated, sun-filled bedrooms have washbasins and rustic beds. In the attic breakfast room, solemn Icelandic dolls (and incongruous Cabbage Patch Kid) watch over the diners. The owner has opened an **annexe** (Bárugata 20; d with bathroom Ikr10,000) down the road.

Flóki Guesthouse (Map pp220-2; ☎ 552 1155; www.eyjar.is/guesthouse; Flókagata 1; s/d Ikr7,200/10,300, camp

sites per person Ikr700; ℗) Iceland's oldest guest-house has recently been upgraded to hotel status by the Icelandic Tourist Board. All 30 rooms have TV, washbasin, kettle and fridge, and there are outside breakfast tables in summer. You can pitch tents in the garden, more convenient for the city centre than the main camping ground. The owner collects Icelandic artwork – look out for the creepy folktale illustrations by Haukar Halldorsson.

Gistiheimilið Domus (Map pp226-7; ☎ 561 1200; www.domusguesthouse.is; Hverfisgata 45; sb/s/d Ikr3100/7300/9800) This building was once the Norwegian Embassy, and its stately rooms are still filled with antique furniture and curio cabinets. The place also has modern touches like new radio alarms and TVs in each room. Check out the caricatures of the owners in the hall. Their care and commitment is evident throughout: a lovely place. Breakfast Ikr800.

Skólabrú Guesthouse (Map pp226-7; ☎ 551 5511; www.skolabru.com; Skólabrú 2; s/d/tr/apt Ikr7900/9900/11,900/14,900) Not only is this the most perfectly located guesthouse in town, it has bags of character too: large, romantic rooms are filled with antique furniture, including the odd piano! Breakfast (including home-baked bread) is served in the kindly owner's sitting room.

Tower Guesthouse (Map pp226-7; ☎ 896 6694; www.tower.is; Grettisgata 6; d Ikr8400-14,400, apt Ikr12,700-26,200) This castlelike place has a sweeping spiral staircase and elegant apartments. For added luxury, you can drink champagne and gaze at the stars in the rooftop Jacuzzi! The guesthouse is popular with gay travellers, and there's the odd phallus-shaped plant pot around, but everyone is welcomed by friendly Guðmundur. Breakfast isn't provided, but there are kitchen facilities.

Also recommended:

i12 Guesthouse (Map pp226-7; ☎ 692 9930; www.guesthouses.is/i12; Ingólfsstræti 12; slkr5000, d Ikr6000-7000, apt Ikr25,000) Gay guesthouse with cheery staff, only two minutes' walk from the heart of town. Second-floor rooms have good views over the rooftops of old Reykjavík.

Guesthouse Butterfly (Map pp226-7; ☎ 894 1864; www.kvasir.is/butterfly; Ránargata 8a; s/d/apt Ikr5900/7900/11,500; (✦) Jun-Aug) On a quiet street within fluttering distance of the centre. Tastefully decorated; laundry facilities available.

Guesthouse 101 (Map pp220-2; ☎ 562 6101; www.travelnet.is/101; Laugavegur 101; s/d/tr/q Ikr5900/8500/10,500/12,500) Converted offices, with wonderfully

ICELAND

CENTRAL REYKJAVÍK

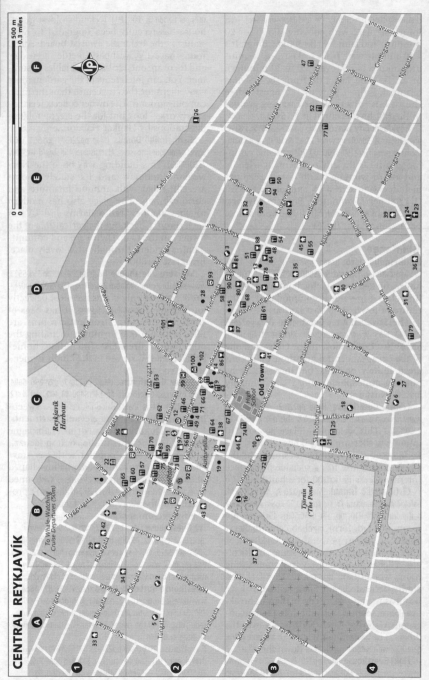

welcoming 24-hour reception. Shared bathrooms adapted for people with disabilities.

Álfhóll Guesthouse (Map pp226-7; ☎ 898 1838; www .islandia.is/alf; Ránargata 8; s/d/tr/apt Ikr6400/8500/10,50 0/13,600; ☼ Jun-Aug) Run by a family of elf enthusiasts. Used as a student house out of season, it retains a down-to-earth, homey feel in summer. Washbasins in each room, and elf-decorated kitchen available for self-catering.

Gistiheimilið Aurora (Map pp226-7; ☎ 552 5515; aurorahotel@isl.is; Freyjugata 24; s/d Ikr6500/8500; ☼ Jun-Sep) Close to Hallgrímskirkja and run by the friendly Evelyn. Recommended.

Guesthouse Sunna (Map pp226-7; ☎ 511 5570; www.sunna.is; Þórsgata 26; s/d from Ikr7100/8700; ☐) Attractive rooms: those on the front have good views of Hallgrímskirkja. Hot, sugary pancakes fill the building with a mouthwatering smell at breakfast time (Ikr500). Very family-centric.

Gistihúsið Krían (Map pp226-7; ☎ 511 5600; www .krian.is; Suðurgata 22; s/d 7900/9900) Front rooms have lofty views over Tjörnin. Spotless throughout. Each room has a bathrobe in the wardrobe to preserve your dignity when using the shared bathrooms!

Icelandic Hotel Garður (Map pp220-2; ☎ 551 5656; hotelgardur@icelandichotels.is; Hringbraut; sb/s/d Ikr2800/6900/8100; ☼ Jun-Aug) Summer hotel on the university campus, about 1km from the centre. There are 43 straightforward dorm rooms with shared bathrooms.

Top End

Hótel Borg (Map pp226-7; ☎ 354 551; www.hotel borg.is; Pósthússtræti 11; s/d/ste Ikr15,900/25,900/34,600) This magnificent 1930s neoclassical palace is located in prime position on Austurvöllur square. A wonderful wooden lift rises to luxurious, individually designed rooms, complete with all mod cons. The Art Deco brasserie makes you feel like a starlet as you tuck into the superb buffet breakfast (Ikr1200) – heaven in a hotel.

Hótel Óðinsvé (Map pp226-7; ☎ 511 6200; www .hotelodinsve.is; Óðinstorg; s Ikr15,900-17,500, d Ikr21,000-29,000) If you've ever wanted to view a stuffed puffin at close quarters, the excellent Óðinsvé is your choice. As well as preserved birds, the hotel contains tastefully decorated, cosy rooms with shower, minibar, TV and Internet connections. Staff are exceptionally friendly, as the praise-filled visitors book confirms. Iceland's most famous TV chef, Siggi Hall, prepares Icelandic/Mediterranean fusion dishes in its restaurant.

Also recommended:

Icelandic City Hótel (Map pp226-7; ☎ 511 1155; www .icelandichotels.is; Ránargata 4a; s/d lkr10,200/13,650) Give the front door a good shove at this 3-star hotel in a peaceful street near the old centre. Friendly staff, and disabled access to upper floors via a lift.

Hótel Leifur Eiríksson (Map pp226-7; ☎ 562 0800; www.hotelleifur.is; Skólavörðustígur 45; s/d/tr lkr13,400/ 16,400/19,400) The chilly staff thaw eventually! Half of the 47 rooms have inspiring views of Hallgrímskirkja; some back rooms have consolation balconies overlooking a garden. Sun-catching stained-glass dining room.

CenterHótel Skjaldbreið (Map pp226-7; ☎ 511 6060; www.centerhotels.is; Laugavegur 16; s/d lkr13,500/ 18,100) There's an old-fashioned air of courtesy here. Best things: curvy corner rooms overlooking Laugavegur; intriguing upstairs door leading into the hip Vegamót Bistro (no-one knows why)

EATING

Food is generally high quality but highly expensive! There's plenty of variety, from hot-dog stands to traditional Icelandic dishes, veggie specials and world cuisine. The good-value, thriving cafés are recommended for light lunches, and many become bars at night. Restaurants are usually mid-range to top-end places where people dress

---

THE AUTHOR'S CHOICE

Kaffi Brennslan (Map pp226-7; ☎ 561 3600; Pósthússtræti 9; snacks lkr390-1790) Usually packed to the gills, this Art Deco place draws a mixed and lively crowd, including families, artists, hangover-sufferers and the odd philosopher. It's ideally situated on Austurvöllur, so everyone in Reykjavík will pass by the window eventually. The coffee is above par, and there's a good selection of light meals and snacks. Brennslan becomes a popular but not overwhelming bar at night, selling beer from 19 countries.

Einar Ben (Map pp226-7; ☎ 511 5090; Veltusund 1; mains lkr2800-4200) One of the city's finest gourmet eateries, Einar Ben is frequented by diplomats, and is renowned for its top-class service, relaxing ambience and gastronomic marvels. Unlike in some elite restaurants, *everyone* is made to feel welcome. Dishes include puffin terrine and the freshest fish cooked into rich dishes. Save stomach space for their drool-inducing chocolate cake.

---

up to dine out. Most of Reykjavík's eateries are spattered along Laugavegur, Hverfisgata and Austurstræti.

Restaurants
MID-RANGE

Hornið (Map pp226-7; ☎ 551 3340; Hafnarstræti 15; mains lkr890-3340) Housed in a big yellow building near the post office, Hornið does Italian and Icelandic grub in a relaxed bistro environment. The service is extremely fast, so it's a good choice if you're starving. There's a tinkling piano in the basement bar to aid your digestion.

Á Næstu Grösum (First Vegetarian; Map pp226-7; ☎ 552 8410; Laugavegur 20b; daily special lunch/dinner lkr990/1190; ⏰ closed lunch Sun) The best vegetarian restaurant with three or four specials, including a vegan option. They use seasonal, organic veggies where possible, and their inventive salad dressings give lettuce a reason to exist. Friday and Saturday are Indian nights – a refreshing change in spice-free Reykjavík.

Si Señor (Map pp226-7; ☎ 552 6030; Lækjargata 10; mains lkr1290-2190) This comfortable, candlelit restaurant serves sizzling Mexican food to a salsa soundtrack. Wash it down with a tangy strawberry margherita (lkr890) – *arrrriba!*

Kaffi Reykjavík (Map pp226-7; ☎ 552 3030; Vesturgata 2; mains lkr2500-2950; ⏰ to 1am) This one-time café/bar/nightclub has decided to concentrate on food, and is particularly well suited to catering for groups, with several private function rooms upstairs. There's the added attraction of an ice bar (lkr1300 admission, including drink) – ponchos are provided.

Galileo (Map pp226-7; ☎ 552 9500; Hafnarstræti 1; mains lkr1730-4350) There's a romantic starry-sky ceiling at this sophisticated Italian, perfect for intimate dining. In summer, try the good-value tourist menu, usually a flavoursome catch-of-the-day.

Also recommended:

Grænn Kostur (Map pp226-7; ☎ 552 2028; Skólavörðustígur 8; meals lkr900) Recommended for vegans.

Café Victor (Map pp226-7; ☎ 561 9555; Hafnarstræti 1-3; mains lkr950-2450) Once the Danish king's falcon house, now a favoured spot to watch people-traffic while eating appetising bar meals. Barnlike interior, which swells with revellers on Fridays and Saturdays until 5.30am.

Kína Húsið (Map pp226-7; ☎ 551 1014; Lækjargata 8; mains lkr1100-2500, lunch specials lkr750) Authentic Chinese food at low prices.

Shalimar (Map pp226-7; ☎ 551 0292; Austurstræti 4; mains up to lkr2290; ⏰ to 10pm Sun-Thu, 11pm Fri &

Sat) Central Indian-Pakistani restaurant/takeaway with a good-value curry-and-rice lunch menu (Ikr990).

TOP END

Austur Indía Félagið (Map pp226-7; ☎ 552 1630; Hverfisgata 56; mains Ikr1995-3295) About as far from a normal curry house as you can get! It was recently voted the best Indian restaurant in Europe, and its minimalist interior and small but select menu certainly breathes class. The salmon tikka (Ikr2295) is recommended.

Restaurant Tjarnarbakkinn (Map pp226-7; ☎ 562 9700; Vonarstræti 3; mains Ikr2200-3780) The Iðnó Theatre's restaurant has great views over Tjörnin and offers traditional Icelandic cuisine, including a delicious *lambapiparsteik* (peppered lamb). It does light lunches in summer, on lakeside tables (gales permitting).

Apótek (Map pp226-7; ☎ 575 7900; Austurstræti 16; mains Ikr2190-4590) This former pharmacy is now a with-it restaurant serving way-out fusion foods (for example, Mongolian pork with miso mustard). You can watch your dinner being prepared in the glass-walled kitchen, then dance off the gastronomic oddities in the sophisticated 4th-floor club.

Lækjarbrekka (Map pp226-7; ☎ 551 4430; Bankastræti 2; mains Ikr2580-5170) This gourmet restaurant cooks traditional Icelandic dishes (game, lobster, juicy pepper steak and mountain lamb), some with a modern twist and Middle Eastern or Japanese influence. During the summer, there's a top-quality evening fish buffet (Ikr3780).

Also recommended:

Þrír Frakkar Hjá Úlfari (Map pp226-7; ☎ 552 3939; Baldursgata 14; mains Ikr2350-4400) Snug restaurant with extensive fish menu.

Humarhúsið (Map pp226-7; ☎ 561 3303; Amtmannsstígur 1; mains Ikr2750-4550) Understated and utterly elegant, the Lobster House is another flawless restaurant, justly celebrated for its succulent shellfish, langoustine and lobster.

Cafés

Cultura (Map pp226-7; ☎ 530 9314; Hverfisgata 18; snacks Ikr350-990; ☒) This arty intercultural café has round-the-world snacks, Scrabble sets in six languages, and live music until 3am at the weekends. During the day, it's popular with actors from the theatre across the road. Recommended.

Café 22 (Map pp226-7; ☎ 511 5522; Laugavegur 22) Supposedly a lesbian favourite, but when we dawdled here over soup and coffee, it was full of male modern-day Vikings! An endearing, laid-back, bluesy bar whoever its clientele. At night, its three floors divide neatly into lively bar area, thronging dance floor, and darkened room for drunken slumping.

Svarta Kaffið (Map pp226-7; ☎ 551 2999; Laugavegur 54; ☒) Filled with African masks, this quirky caff is especially recommended for its thick home-made soup in brilliant bread bowls (Ikr850). You can get a good view of next door's tattoo parlour (where Björk had one done). Later on, this turns into a cosy bar with cheap (relatively speaking) beer.

Vegamót (Map pp226-7; ☎ 511 3040; Vegamótstígur 4; mains Ikr1090-2190) A clubby place to eat, drink, gossip, but most importantly to see and be seen. It becomes a beautiful people's bar at night – see p230. Vegamót's extremely popular menu (which includes lobster pizza!) can be ordered next door as a takeaway for 10% less.

Also recommended:

Ömmu Kaffi (Map pp226-7; ☎ 552 9680; Austurstræti 20; snacks Ikr250-500; ☒ closed Sun; ☒) A breath of fresh air for nonsmokers. Civilised coffee shop with superior snackettes.

Café Paris (Map pp226-7; ☎ 551 1020; Austurstræti 14; snacks Ikr450-870; ☒) A continental feel and huge windows for top-quality people-watching. Giant pots of tea or cafetieres cost Ikr250.

Café Garðurinn (Map pp226-7; ☎ 561 2345; Klapparstígur 37; lunch menu Ikr1200; ☒ 11am-6pm Mon-Fri, noon-6pm Sat) Tiny but tasteful veggie café. Lunch menu includes soup, bread and dish of the day.

Kofi Tómasar Frænda (Map pp226-7; ☎ 551 1855; Laugavegur 2; snacks Ikr390-990; ☒ closed Sun) 'Koffin' has a lazy, loungy feel, a vast selection of magazines, and two squishy leather sofas. There's a refreshing tea bar, and nice lasagne (meat and veggie).

Bleika Dúfan (Map pp226-7; ☎ 517 1980; Laugavegur 21; ☒ 10am-6pm; ☒) New, inviting little book and coffee shop: magazines, morsels to munch and an Internet connection (Ikr200 per half-hour).

Quick Eats

Múlakaffi (Map pp220-2; ☎ 533 7737; Hallarmúli; meals Ikr990-1290; ☒ 8am-8pm Mon-Fri) Handy for the youth hostel and camping ground, this no-frills workers' cafeteria offers a good soup-and-salad buffet and canteen-style meals like salt cod and roast pork. Ninety-nine per cent of its customers are men.

Round the corner is **Ning's** (Map pp220-2; ☎ 588 9899; Suðurlandsbraut 6; mains Ikr550-1450), a

Chinese takeaway and restaurant selling so-so food. Soups start at Ikr795. The good-value food court in the Kringlan shopping centre (Map pp220–2) contains several fast-food franchises.

Nonnabiti (Map pp226-7; ☎ 551 2312; Hafnarstræti 18; snacks Ikr280-690; 🕙 to 2am) serves burgers, chips and hot dogs into the wee hours. When you've overdone the fried meat, **Kebabhúsið** (Map pp226-7; ☎ 561 3070; Lækjargata 2) offers alternative fare of falafel (Ikr650) and fish and chips (Ikr770).

For ultraquick eats, nothing beats the central snack kiosks (Map pp226–7), particularly appealing at 3am on a Friday night. Icelanders swear it's impossible to get a bad hot dog from Bæjarins Bestu (Map pp226–7), near the harbour: use the vital sentence *Eina með öllu* ('One with everything'!).

Self-Catering

The cheapest supermarket is **Bónus** (Map pp226-7; Laugavegur 59; 🕙 closed Sun), with a branch at the Kringlan shopping centre (Map pp220–2). The more upmarket **10-11 supermarket** (Austurstræti Map pp226-7; Hverfisgata Map pp226-7; Laugalækur Map pp220-2) has branches all over the place.

DRINKING

Reykjavík is renowned for its Friday- and Saturday-night *runtur*, when hard-working Icelanders abandon the office and party as though the world's about to end. Most people get sozzled at home, before circulating round pubs and clubs from midnight until 6am. Some places have cover charges (about Ikr1000), and the 'in' places have long queues at weekends. Things change fast – check *Grapevine* or *Reykjavík This Month* for the latest listings. You should dress up in Reykjavík, but there are bars where you won't feel scruffy in jeans.

Try any of the following relaxed pub-style places.

Grand Rokk (Map pp226-7; ☎ 551 5522; Smiðjustígur 6) This utterly unpretentious bar fits like a favourite old T-shirt. During the day, chess enthusiasts play concentrated matches here, and at night it's great for live music, luring in up to three bands per session with free beer.

Sirkus (Map pp226-7; ☎ 511 8022; Klapparstígur 31) Rated by its regulars for the funky, fairy-lit ambience, Sirkus also has a summer garden where you can partially escape the crush.

It serves French wine by the glass, as well as calvados – mix with *brennivín* at your peril.

Dillon (Map pp226-7; ☎ 511 2400; Laugavegur 30) In an old wooden house, Dillon is an atmospheric pub with plenty of corners to drink and chatter in. Good on weekday nights, when other places can be tumbleweed empty.

The following venues attract a more glamorous clientele.

Kaffibarinn (Map pp226-7; ☎ 551 1588; Bergstaðastræti 1) Damon Albarn from Blur has a stake in this uber-trendy bar. It's popular with celebs, including Björk and film director Baltasar Kormákur, and has a petite, packed dance floor that throbs to funk, hip-hop and house.

Vegamót (Map pp226-7; ☎ 511 3040; Vegamótsstígur 4) The buzzy balcony is a fine place to watch the fashion-conscious flocks, but get your best togs on if you want to join in.

Prikið (Map pp226-7; ☎ 551 3366; Bankastræti 12) Atmospheric Prikið draws a mixed mob, particularly towards the end of the night. Dancers grind away cheek to cheek on the jammed dance floor.

Kaffi List (Map pp226-7; ☎ 562 5059; Laugavegur 20a) Again, dress to kill if you want to blend in at the glass-fronted, ultrachic List. There's a heaving dance floor, and the Thursday-night jazz sessions are well worth the effort.

Also recommended:

Bar 11 (Map pp226-7; ☎ 511 1180; Laugavegur 11) A welcoming place which supports up-and-coming Reykjavík bands – try to catch a weekday gig. Jukebox and table football.

Nelly's Café (Map pp226-7; ☎ 562 1250; Þinghóltstræti 2) Students come for the city's cheapest beer and regular band and DJ sets.

Celtic Cross (Map pp226-7; ☎ 511 3240; Hverfisgata 26)
Dubliner (Map pp226-7; ☎ 511 3233; Hafnarstræti 4) Along with the Celtic Cross, a pair of comfy Irish pubs favoured by travellers.

ENTERTAINMENT
Nightclubs

Hverfisbarinn (Map pp226-7; ☎ 511 6700; Hverfisgata 20) Queues around the block attest to this bar's voguish stature: be young, beautiful and immaculately dressed!

Jón Forseti (Map pp226-7; ☎ 511 0962; Aðalstræti 10) Once the acclaimed Vidalin, this is now a brand-new gay club and theatre in the heart of old Reykjavík, with occasional poetry readings.

Gaukur á Stöng (Map pp226-7; ☎ 551 1556; Tryggvagata 22) Running for over 19 years, stalwart Gaukurin features original Icelandic bands during the week, with club nights or cover bands at the weekend. Responsible for creating vodka-spiked beer, still available. Admission Ikr1000 after 11pm.

NASA (Map pp226-7; Austurvöllur) The biggest club in Reykjavík, a stripped-pine affair with a young cocktail-swigging crowd. It plays chart music, and big cover bands sometimes perform, but most Reykjavík-dwellers go there only on the Christmas/New Year's Eve big night out. Admission Ikr1000.

Theatre & Classical Music

Reykjavík's most important theatre venues are the **National Theatre** (Map pp226-7; ☎ 585 1200; www.leikhusid.is; Lindargata 7; admission Ikr2500), which puts on around 350 performances a year, and the **Reykjavík City Theatre** (Map pp220-2; ☎ 568 8000; www.borgarleikhus.is; Listabraut 3, Kringlan; adult/child under 12 yrs Ikr2500/free), where the **Icelandic Dance Company** (☎ 588 0900; www.id.is) is also in residence.

You can hear classical music performances at the **Iceland Symphony Orchestra** (Map pp220-2; ☎ 545 2500; www.sinfonia.is; Hagatorg; admission from Ikr1900), based at the Reykjavík University Háskólabíó cinema.

For other venues, check daily papers or contact the tourist information centre.

Cinemas

Reykjavík has seven multiplexes, including **Regnboginn** (Map pp226-7; ☎ 551 9000; Hverfisgata 54) and **Sambíóin** (Map pp220-2; ☎ 588 0800; Kringlan shopping centre). Other listings can be found in daily newspapers. Films are shown in their original language with Icelandic subtitles; all cinemas charge Ikr800.

SHOPPING

There are plenty of central tourist shops peddling the usual mugs, soft toys etc. For classier presents, Skólavörðustígur is full of arty ceramic shops. The **Handknitting Association of Iceland** (Map pp226-7; ☎ 552 1890; www.handknit.is; Skólavörðustígur 19) is there too; they sell traditional hand-knitted sweaters for around Ikr8400.

Good for a leisurely hungover ramble is the **Kolaportið Flea Market** (Map pp226-7; Geirsgata; ☺ 11am-5pm Sat & Sun), selling all kinds of second-hand stuff. There's a large fish market

inside, where the brave can try *hákarl* (rotten shark cubes).

For tent/sleeping-bag rental, try **Útilíf** (Map pp220-2; ☎ 545 1500; www.utilif.is; Vatnsmýrarvegur), opposite the BSÍ bus terminal.

Pick up bottles of *brennivín* at the state alcohol store **Vín Búð** (Map pp226-7; Austurstræti 10a).

GETTING THERE & AWAY
Air

The city airport, Innanlandsflug, serves all domestic destinations, the Faroe Islands and Greenland. Internal flight operator **Flugfélag Íslands** (Air Iceland; ☎ 570 3030; www.airiceland.is) has a desk there, but it's cheaper to book over the Internet.

International flights operate through **Keflavík Airport** (www.keflavikairport.com), 48km west of Reykjavík.

Bus

From early June to mid-September, bus services ply between Reykjavík's **BSÍ bus terminal** (☎ 591 1000; Vatnsmýrarvegur 10) and Akureyri (Ikr5700, six hours, daily), Mývatn (Ikr7700, 7¼ hours, daily), Skaftafell (Ikr5070, six hours, daily), Höfn (Ikr7000, eight hours, daily), Reykholt (Ikr1600, 1½ hours, Friday and Sunday), Stykkishólmur (Ikr2400, 2½ hours, daily) and Þorlákshöfn (Ikr950, 45 minutes, daily). Other services include runs to Ísafjörður (via Snæfellsnes and the Stykkishólmur–Brjánslækur ferry, or via Brú). Travellers between Reykjavík and Egilsstaðir must stay overnight in Akureyri, Mývatn or Höfn. There are fewer services during the rest of the year.

GETTING AROUND
To/From the Airport

From the City Airport terminal, walk through the car park, then turn right along Njarðargata, following it to the major Ring Road. Cross over, then take the first road on the left, Sóleyjargata, which takes you to the city centre (1km). Alternatively, take a taxi.

The **Flybus** (☎ 562 1011; www.re.is) to and from Keflavík Airport meets all incoming flights outside the airport terminal. Tickets cost Ikr1100 (credit cards accepted) and the journey to Reykjavík takes around 50 minutes. On the return journey, the bus leaves Hótel Loftleiðir two hours before international departures. All the main hotels, Reykjavík City Hostel and the Salvation

ICELAND

Army Guesthouse will arrange transfers to the hotel.

Bicycle

Hire bikes from **Borgarhjól SF** (☎ 551 5653; Hverfisgata 50), as well as from **Reykjavík City Hostel** (☎ 553 8110; Sundlaugavegur 34) and the **camping ground** (☎ 568 6944; Sundlaugavegur), for around Ikr1700 per day. Drivers show little regard for bicycles, so be extra vigilant.

Boat

Ferries (☎ 892 0099; www.ferja.is; adult/child under 12 yrs Ikr500/250) to Viðey island depart three to eight times daily from Sundahöfn harbour (bus No 4 from Lækjartorg).

Bus

Reykjavík's superb **city bus system** (☎ 551 2700; www.bus.is) runs from 7am to midnight, with night buses at weekends. Buses pick up and drop off passengers only at designated stops (marked with the letter S). The two central terminals are at Hlemmur (Map pp220–2), near the corner of Laugavegur and Rauðarárstígur, and on Lækjargata near the square Lækjartorg (Map pp226–7).

The fare is adult/child under 12 years Ikr220/60 (no change given), but *skiptimiði* (transfer tickets) are available. The Reykjavík Tourist Card includes a bus pass.

Taxi

Reykjavík is small enough to pad round on foot, but there are four companies with metered taxis if you need them: **Hreyfill-Bæjarleiðir** (☎ 588 5522), **BSR** (☎ 561 0000), **Borgarbílastöðn** (☎ 552 2440) and **BSH** (☎ 555 0888). Prices are high, but tipping is not expected.

AROUND REYKJAVÍK
The Golden Circle

The 'Golden Circle' refers to Gullfoss, Geysir and Þingvellir, the 'big three' destinations for most visitors.

At **Gullfoss**, the Hvítá River drops 32m in a rainbow-tinged double cascade, before running off down a huge rift. Ten kilometres down the road is **Geysir**, after which all spouting hot springs are named. The **Great Geysir** was plugged in the 1960s by rock-throwing tourists trying to set it off. After earthquakes in June 2000 it began erupting again, but irregularly. Luckily, the world's most reliable geyser, **Strokkur** (Butter Churn),

---

> **PENINGAGJÁ**
>
> To make a wish, throw a silver coin in the water. If you can follow it down and see where it lands, your wish will come true. If it disappears…sorry, your luck's out!

---

is right next door, spouting up to 35m every six minutes.

There's an interesting audiovisual exhibition on volcanoes, geysers and the northern lights at the otherwise tacky **Geysisstofa Geocentre** (☎ 486 8704; www.geysircenter.com; adult/student/child 6-12 yrs Ikr500/350/200; ☉ 10am-7pm May-Sep, noon-5pm Oct-May).

Þingvellir is Iceland's most significant historical site: the world's first democratic parliament, the Alþing, was established here in AD 930. In 1928, it became Iceland's first national park, thanks to its weighty history, and superb natural setting on the edge of an immense rift, caused by the separating North American and Eurasian tectonic plates.

Most of the historical buildings are concentrated in a small area of the park: **Lögberg** (Law Rock), marked by a flagpole, was the podium for the Alþing from 930 to 1271; there are the remains of **búðir** (booths) where assembly-goers slept; a **church** and **farm**, now the President's summer house; and the rest is left to nature. Hiking trails crisscross the plain to points of interest, including the **Almannagjá** fissure; **Drekkingarhylur**, where adulterous women were drowned; **Þingvallavatn**, Iceland's largest lake; and the wishing spring **Peningagjá**.

SLEEPING & EATING

Geysir camping ground (per person Ikr600) Just before the tourist complex: pay at Hótel Geysir.

Hótel Geysir (☎ 480 6800; sb/s/d from Ikr2800/7500/9200) Rooms are in the hotel (inside the tourist complex) or in tasteful alpine-style cabins. There's a good restaurant in the centre and a geothermal pool.

Park Service Centre (☎ 482 2660; per person Ikr500) Þingvellir's five camping grounds are run by this centre. The best are those around Leirar, near the service centre and snack bar.

Hótel Valhöll (☎ 486 1777; www.hotelthingvellir .is; s/d Ikr10,500/13,900) A large farmhouse with fairly elegant rooms; deliberately TV- and phone-free to preserve the peace, and there's a good **dining room** (mains Ikr1490-3320).

GETTING THERE & AWAY

The popular **Reykjavík Excursions** (☎ 562 4422; www.re.is) and **Destination Iceland** (☎ 591 1020; www.dice.is) Golden Circle day tours to Gullfoss, Geysir and Þingvellir cost around Ikr6500, without lunch. They leave the BSÍ bus terminal at 8.40am daily, or can collect you from your accommodation on request.

Destination Iceland scheduled buses run between Reykjavík, Gullfoss and Geysir from BSÍ (return Ikr4180, 8.30am and 12.30pm June to August). Buses between Reykjavík and Þingvellir also depart from BSÍ (return Ikr1700, 1.30pm June to August).

Hafnarfjörður

pop 21,207

The Town in the Lava rests on a 7000-year-old flow and specialises in promoting the peculiar. The dynamic **tourist office** (☎ 585 5500; www.lava.is; Strandgata 6; 🕑 9am-6pm Mon-Fri, 9am-2pm Sat & Sun May-Sep, shorter hr in winter) is inside the town hall.

SIGHTS & ACTIVITIES

Hafnarfjörður hides a parallel elfin universe, according to locals. Storyteller Sibba Karlsdóttir leads **Hidden World Walks** (☎ 517 1205; sibbak@simnet.is; Háaleitisbraut 123; admission Ikr2200; 🕑 10am & 2pm Mon-Fri mid-Jun–mid-Aug) around *huldufólk* homes.

More traditional is **Hafnarfjörður Museum** (☎ 565 5420; admission Ikr300; 🕑 1-5pm Jun-Sep), spread across three sites: **Sívertsen's Húsið** (Vesturgata 6), the former home of the 'godfather of Hafnarfjörður'; **Siggubær** (Sigga's House; Kirkjuvegur 10), a restored fisherman's hut; and **Smiðjan** (The Smithy; Vesturgata 8), which has displays on Icelandic whaling. The Reykjavík Tourist Card covers admission.

Whale-watching tours (☎ 894 1388; Skerseyrarvegur 2; adult/child under 12 yrs Ikr3000/1500; 🕑 10am May-Sep) are slightly cheaper than in Reykjavík, but there's the same high sighting rate.

The tourist office publishes a smashing **sculpture trail** map; the highlight is **Hellisgerði** (Reykjavíkurvegur), a peaceful park filled with lava grottoes.

SLEEPING & EATING

Hraunbyrgi (☎ 565 0900; www.hafnarfjordurguesthouse .is; Hjallabraut 51; camp sites per person Ikr800; sb from Ikr1900; 🕑 mid-May–Aug; 🖳) The Icelandic Boy Scouts offer camping in a sheltered lava hollow near Víðistaðar Park, and basic beds.

Gistiheimilið Við Lækinn (☎ 565 5132; olgunn@ simnet.is; cnr Hringbraut & Lækjarinn; sb/s/d Ikr2000/4400/6800) Overlooking the lake, this friendly family home has simple, good-value rooms.

Viking Village Fjörukráin (☎ 565 1213; www .vikingvillage.is; Strandgata 50a & 55; mains from Ikr2000; 🕑 from noon) At the tacky but strangely endearing Viking Village, you can gnaw dried haddock and swill *brennivín* surrounded by singing Vikings. The **Viking Hotel** (s/d Ikr9900/12,800; 🖳) is surprisingly tame in comparison – upstairs rooms are tasteful with all mod cons.

Súfistinn (☎ 565 3740; Strandgata 9) The best café in Hafnarfjörður serves delectable cakes and freshly ground coffee.

A Hansen (☎ 565 1130; Vesturgata 4; mains Ikr2200 4250; 🕑 from noon) This top-notch restaurant does distinctive oak-smoked steaks (Ikr2490) and first-class seafood.

GETTING THERE & AWAY

The bus station is on Fjarðargata, by the harbour. From Reykjavík, take bus No 140 or 150 from Hlemmur or Lækjartorg. The **Flybus** (☎ 562 1011) to/from Keflavík Airport stops for reserved passengers.

Krýsuvík

Krýsuvík, an abandoned village and volatile geothermal area, lies about 20km south of Hafnarfjörður. At **Seltún**, boardwalks meander round eggy-smelling, rainbow-coloured steaming vents, mud pots and solfataras, where the ground temperature reaches about 200°C.

Just down the road is **Kleifarvatn**, a creepy monster-inhabited lake surrounded by walking trails through volcanic cinders.

There are no scheduled buses, but from 1 June to 31 August **Reykjavík Excursions** (☎ 562 4422; www.re.is) runs daily guided tours (Ikr5520, five hours, 1.30pm) which include Krýsuvík, Grindavík and the Blue Lagoon.

Blue Lagoon

The **Blue Lagoon** (Bláa Lónið; ☎ 420 8800; www.blue lagoon.is; adult/child 12-15 yrs Ikr1200/600, towel/swimsuit/robe hire Ikr300/350/700, spa treatments from Ikr1300; 🕑 9am-9pm mid-May-Aug, 10am-8pm Sep–mid-May), 50km southwest of Reykjavík, is justifiably Iceland's most famous attraction. Set in a vast black lava field, the milky-blue spa is fed by water (at a perfect 38°C) from the futuristic Svartsengi geothermal plant. Swimmers in silica-mud facepacks drift round steaming silver vents and loll in hot pots.

Lazing in soothing warm water, sipping a cocktail as the snow falls and the smoke swirls, is one of the most fantastically surreal experiences you could hope for. If you want to know why your face feels strange, look around at your neighbours – you too are wearing that same delighted, disbelieving 'am-I-dreaming?' expression. Once you're in, you really won't want to leave.

Be careful on the slippery bridges and bring plenty of conditioner to stop your hair going solid. There's a snack bar, top gourmet restaurant and souvenir shop on site.

To get there, the **Þingvallaleið Bus Service** (☎ 511 2600; www.bluelagoonbus.is) leaves from the BSÍ bus terminal in Reykjavík (one-way Ikr850, 40 minutes, six buses between 10am and 6pm).

THE WEST

UPPER BORGARFJÖRÐUR

Upper Borgarfjörður, 90km north of Reykjavík, is a land of lakes and lava flows. It's also a must for saga fans as the stage for some of *Egils Saga*.

Sights

Reykholt (www.reykholt.is), 22km east of the Ring Road, is best known for **Snorri's Pool** (Snorralaug). This haunting saga site consists of a circular medieval hot bath, where Iceland's greatest saga writer and social-climber Snorri Sturluson plotted. The passage behind the pool may lead to the cellar where he was murdered in 1241; hopefully ongoing archaeological excavations will provide answers. There's also a superb museum, **Heimskringla** (☎ 435 1490; fax 435 1412; Reykholt; admission Ikr300; ⊙ 10am-6pm Jun-Aug, other times by arrangement), dedicated to the man.

Deildartunguhver, 4km west of Reykholt, is Europe's most powerful, prolific and pongy hot spring, spouting out at 180L per second. About 18km northeast of Reykholt is **Hraunfossar**, a 1km-long stretch of 'magic waterfalls' mysteriously emerging from beneath a lava flow. Just upstream is **Barnafoss**, where the river Hvítá thunders through a narrow gorge. According to legend, two children drowned here when a natural bridge collapsed.

There's a **camping ground** (☎ 435 1182; Kleppjárnsreykir; per person Ikr500) next to a geothermal swimming pool 6km west of Reykholt. **Hótel Reykholt** (☎ 435 1260; www.reykholt.is; Reykholt; sb/s/d Ikr1850/7865/10,850) is a modern place with boxy but pleasant rooms and a good restaurant.

Buses run from Reykjavík to Reykholt (via Deildartunguhver) on Friday and Sunday at 5pm (one way Ikr1700, 1½ hours). You'll need to make your own way to Hraunfossar and Barnafoss.

SNÆFELLSNES

The volcano Snæfell (1446m) starred as the gateway to the underworld in Jules Verne's *A Journey to the Centre of the Earth*. It's on the isolated tip of the Snæfellsnes peninsula and capped by the glacier Snæfellsjökull: climbs are possible with the right weather and equipment. Most of the population lives in the north-coast villages, which are separated by shadowy mountains, elf-stuffed lava flows, waterfalls and scattered farmhouses.

Stykkishólmur

pop 1162

Quaint little Stykkishólmur, the largest village in Snæfellsnes, lies on the southern shore of Breiðafjörður (see the boxed text, opposite). From there, ferries go to Brjánslækur in the Westfjords. The **tourist office** (☎ 438 1750; Aðalgata 2; ⊙ 10am-6pm Jun-Aug) is in the red house behind the museum.

SIGHTS & ACTIVITIES

You get an admirable view of Breiðafjörður from **Súgandisey**, a basalt islet which shelters the picturesque harbour.

The tarry-smelling **Norwegian House** (☎ 438 1640; norkshus@simnet.is; Hafnargata 5; adult/child under 15 yrs Ikr400/100; ⊙ 11am-5pm Jun-Aug) contains a reconstruction of a 19th-century home and local history exhibits.

To propel yourself round Breiðafjörður's straits and skerries, contact **Sagan Kayak Rental** (☎ 690 3877; www.vef.is/kajak; Skólastígur 28). Prices for a guided paddle start from Ikr4000 for a two- to four-hour trip.

TOURS

Sæferðir (Seatours; ☎ 438 1450; www.saeferdir.is; Smiðjustígur 3) runs bird/nature tours round the fjord from Stykkishólmur (adult/child 12 to 15 years Ikr3900/1950, 11am and 2pm, from 1

TROLL TROUBLE

The breathtaking sight of Breiðafjörður's 2700(-ish) islands inspired a legend. Three misanthropic trolls decided to separate the Westfjords from the rest of Iceland. All night, they hacked away huge lumps of earth and hurled the pieces into the nearby fjord. The task was so engrossing that they didn't notice the growing light. As the sun touched them, the two male trolls turned instantly to stone. The trollette almost made it home, when she suddenly remembered that she'd left her cow grazing on Grímsey. Stopping to look at it, both she and Daisy came to a rocky end.

May) and eight-hour whale-watching trips from Ólafsvík (adult/child 12 to 15 years Ikr10,900/5450, mid-May to August).

SLEEPING & EATING

Camping ground (☎ 438 1750; per person Ikr500; ☼ all year) A huge but rather exposed spot on the edge of town.

Sjónarhóll HI Hostel (☎ 438 1095; www.hostel .is; Höfðagata 1; sb Ikr1950; ☼ May-Sep) This hostel has dorm rooms with fantastic views of the harbour. You can also catch fish on its Breiðafjörður boat tours, then barbecue them on the patio!

Heimagisting María Bæringsdóttir (☎ 438 1258; Höfðagata 11; s/d Ikr4600/7000) A few simple rooms in a family home are on offer here.

Hótel Stykkishólmur (☎ 430 2100; hotelstykkisho lmur@simnet.is; Borgarbraut 6; s/d Ikr9460/11,550) The nondescript exterior hides a posh restaurant and rooms with great views.

Narfeyrarstofa (☎ 438 1119; Aðalgata 3; mains Ikr1450-2450) This old house is a welcoming daytime café and evening bar/restaurant. Its speciality is Icelandic bouillabaisse (Ikr1050), but there's a wide-ranging menu with good veggie options.

The **bakery** (Nesvegur 1) near the camping ground does delicious sandwiches and cakes, including *ástar pungar* (love balls: a dough-nutty Icelandic treat).

GETTING THERE & AWAY

Daily buses ply between Reykjavík and Stykkishólmur (Ikr2500, 2½ hours). Buses between Reykjavík, Ólafsvík and Stykkishólmur meet at a remote intersection called

Vegamót (or Gröf), where passengers sort themselves out according to destination.

See below for details of the Stykkishólmur–Brjánslækur ferry and connecting buses.

Snæfellsjökull

The most interesting way up Snæfell is from the western end of the peninsula, along the Móðulækur stream (4WD vehicles can go 4km up the track). This takes you via the red scoria craters of Rauðhólar, the waterfall Klukkufoss and scenic Eysteinsdalur Valley. It takes a couple of days and you may need crampons and ice axes to reach the summit.

As a base, Stykkishólmur has the best facilities, but Ólafsvík is closer. It has a sheltered **camping ground** (☎ 436 1543; per person/tent Ikr500/300, ☼ Jun-Aug) about 1km east of the village, and central **Hótel Ólafsvík** (☎ 436 1650; hotelo@simnet.is; Ólafsbraut 20; s/d from Ikr6510/14,070) offers comfortable business-class rooms. Across the street, **Prinsinn** (Ólafsbraut; dishes from Ikr500) serves burgers and pizzas.

For transport information, see left.

THE WESTFJORDS

Extending clawlike towards Greenland, the Westfjords' wobbling coast accounts for half the country's total shoreline. This most remote and restful corner of Iceland is perfect for walkers: its wild nature and deserted villages make you feel you're the only person alive.

Getting There & Away

AIR

There are twice-daily flights between Reykjavík and Ísafjörður (Ikr9775) with **Flugfélag Íslands** (www.airiceland.is; ☎ 456 3000).

BOAT

The ferry **Baldur** (☎ 438 1450; www.saeferdir.is; Smiðjustígur 3, Stykkishólmur) operates between Stykkishólmur and Brjánslækur (Ikr1730/1730 per car/passenger, departing 9am and 4pm from Stykkishólmur, 12.30pm and 7.30pm from Brjánslækur June to August, less frequently at other times), connecting with buses as described below.

BUS

Buses between Reykjavík and Ísafjörður (requiring a change at Brú) leave Reykjavík on Tuesday, Friday and Sunday at 8.30am (Ikr9400, June to August).

Buses also run via the Stykkishólmur (Snæfellsnes) to Brjánslækur (Westfjords) ferry from June to August. There are daily buses from Reykjavík to Stykkishólmur (Ikr2500), but only those leaving Monday and Wednesday at 8.30am or Saturday at 1pm link with the ferry (Ikr1730) and continuing buses from Brjánslækur to Ísafjörður (Ikr6500). In reverse, buses leave Ísafjörður at 9am Monday, Wednesday and Saturday.

The Ísafjörður–Brjánslækur bus also runs via Patreksfjörður, Breiðavík and Látrabjarg and allows 1¼ hours at Látrabjarg.

Catch buses to Tungudalur from the bus stop on the main road (Skutulsfjarðarbraut), close by the summer hotel Menntaskólinn Torfnes.

If you want to travel between Ísafjörður and Akureyri (Ikr9200) you'll need to go through in Brú.

ÍSAFJÖRÐUR

pop 2596

Vertiginous mountains and still, calm waters surround Ísafjörður, the Westfjords' largest settlement. The centre perches on a narrow spit in the Skutulsfjörður fjord: you'll find the **tourist office** (☎ 456 5121; www.vestfirdir .is; Aðalstræti 7; ✆ 8am-6pm daily Jun-Aug, 11am-4pm Mon-Fri Sep-May), **bank** (Hafnarstræti) and **post office** (Hafnarstræti 9) there. Internet access is available at the **library** (☎ 456 3296; www.isafjordur.is/bokasafn; Eyrartúni; per hr Ikr200; ✆ 1-7pm Mon-Fri, 1-4pm Sat).

Sights & Activities

Knowledgeable staff at the **Westfjords Maritime Museum** (☎ 456 3293; Neðstíkaupstaður; admission Ikr400; ✆ 10am-5pm Mon-Fri May-Aug, 1-5pm Sat & Sun May & Jun, 10am-5pm Jul & Aug), based in three old wooden warehouses, bring the excellent nautical and whaling exhibits to life.

Other sights include the huge **whalebone arch** in the town park and the odd-looking **church** nearby.

There are some interesting **hikes** round Tungudalur, 2km west of Ísafjörður – ask at the tourist office for details. For more watery explorations, Westfjords Tours (see Tours below) can arrange **kayaking** trips.

Tours

Westfjords Tours (Vesturferðir; ☎ 456 5111; www .vesturferdir.is; Aðalstræti 7) specialises in Horn-

strandir visits, including a four-hour trip to the abandoned village Hesteyri (Ikr4200, Wednesday, Friday and Sunday at 2pm).

Sleeping & Eating

Camping ground (☎ 456 4485; Skutulsfjarðarbraut; per person/tent Ikr350/200; ✆ Jun-Aug) Centrally located behind the secondary school. There's another **camping ground** (per person Ikr750) by a pretty waterfall in Tungudalur.

Gamla Gistihúsið (☎ 456 4146; www.gistihus.is; Mánagata 5; sb/s Ikr1900/2800) An old fisherman's hut, this friendly place has neat rooms, kitchen and TV lounge. Breakfast Ikr800.

Gistiheimilið Áslaugar (☎ 456 3868; http://randburg .com/is/aslaug; Austurvegur 7; sb/s/d Ikr2500/3900/5800) You fear the worst when directed to the basement, but the tidy little rooms are light and restful. Áslaug, the owner, will introduce you to half of Ísafjörður, and there's a snug kitchen/sitting room/TV room if you feel antisocial. She also runs the next-door Faktorshús Restaurant, serving traditional dishes. Breakfast Ikr950.

Menntaskólinn Torfnes (☎ 456 4485; sb/s/d Ikr1100/6100/8800; ✆ mid-May–mid-Aug) The owners of Hótel Ísafjörður also run a summer hotel, offering no-frills rooms in the secondary school.

Hótel Ísafjörður (☎ 456 4111; www.hotelisafjordur .is; Silfurtorg 2; s/d from Ikr12,700/20,000) Overlooking Skutulsfjörður and the main square, this modern hotel is at the hub of the town. It does a storming buffet breakfast. Out of season, sleeping-bag accommodation is available for Ikr3300.

Langi Mangi (☎ 456 3022; Aðalstræti 22; snacks Ikr290-790) An atmospheric little caff/art gallery with a range of coffees, pootling music and a choice of two fine soups at lunch time. It opens till 3am on Friday and Saturday.

Pizza 67 (Hafnarstræti 12; pizza Ikr950-1350) Eat pizzas, burgers, meat and fish while watching *The Simpsons* at this friendly bar/restaurant franchise.

Bakarinn (☎ 456 4770; Silfurgata 11; ✆ closed Sat) and **Gamla Bakarið** (☎ 456 3226; Aðalstræti) are great for bread, buns, chocolate frogs and coffee.

HORNSTRANDIR

The wildest corner of the Westfjords, the Hornstrandir peninsula, was abandoned in the 1950s. It now offers solitary hiking and camping, shared only with seabirds and arctic foxes. The peninsula is accessible by boat from Ísafjörður, with one-way fares around Ikr4000; contact the Ísafjörður tourist office for details. There's basic accommodation at **Hesteyri** (☎ 456 7183; sb Ikr1500; ☼ Jul & Aug) in four rooms with kitchen access.

LÁTRABJARG

The towering, 12km-long Látrabjarg cliffs, at the westernmost point of the Westfjords, have one of the greatest populations of **birds** (including puffins) in Iceland. Up to half a kilometre high, they and their inhabitants are an impressive sight.

This simple but beautifully located **guest-house** (☎ 456 1575; breidavik@patro.is; sb/made-up bed Ikr1900/2500; ☼ Jun-Sep) is on a golden beach

at Breiðavík, 12km from the cliffs. At the time of writing, 12 new rooms (per person Ikr6000 including dinner) were being built in a minihotel extension.

THE NORTH

SIGLUFJÖRÐUR

pop 1434

Siglufjörður, one of Iceland's loveliest towns, enjoys a dramatic setting at the northern tip of the Tröllskagi peninsula. It's a long, precarious but breathtaking coastal drive, and the town's isolation has left it unspoiled.

Housed in three buildings at the harbourside, the award-winning herring museum

ÍSAFJÖRÐUR

| | | 0 — 500 m |
| 0 — 0.3 miles |

| INFORMATION | |
| Bank..1 C2 |
| Hospital....................................2 B2 |
| Landsbanki Íslands (ATM)........3 C2 |
| Library.....................................4 C1 |
| Police......................................5 C2 |
| Post Office...............................6 C2 |
| Tourist Office...........................7 C3 |

| SIGHTS & ACTIVITIES | (p236) |
| Church.....................................8 C2 |
| Westfjords Maritime Museum...9 B4 |
| Westfjords Tours...................(see 7) |
| Whalebone Arch.....................10 B1 |

To Hnifsdalur (4km);
Bolungarvík (15km)

Park

Pöllin

To Tungudalur (2km);
Flateyri tunnel (4km);
Airport (5km);
Reykjavík
(457km)

| SLEEPING | ◘ ◬ (p236) |
| Camping Ground....................11 B2 |
| Gamla Gistihúsið.....................12 C2 |
| Gistiheimilið Áslaugar.............13 D2 |
| Hótel Ísafjörður......................14 C3 |
| Menntaskólinn Torfnes............15 B2 |

| EATING | ◫ (p236) |
| Bakarinn.................................16 D3 |
| Faktorhús Restaurant...........(see 13) |
| Gamla Bakaríð........................17 C3 |
| Langi Mangi ....18 C3 |
| Pizza 67..................................19 C2 |

Town
Square

| TRANSPORT | (pp236–7) |
| Bus Stand...............................20 C2 |
| Bus Stop.................................21 B2 |
| Hornstrandir Boat Departures..22 C3 |

| OTHER | |
| Seamen's Monument..............23 C1 |
| Swimming Pool.......................24 D2 |

Sundahöfn

Síldarminjasafn (☎ 467 1604; www.siglo.is/herring; Snorragata 15; adult/child 12-16 yrs Ikr500/300; 🕙 10am-6pm Jun-Aug, 1-5pm Sep-May) does a stunning job of recreating Siglufjörður's boom days. Particularly poignant are the salting station Roaldsbrakki, which looks as though the herring workers have just left, and the full-size night-time harbour, where you can crawl below deck and experience the fishermen's cramped working conditions.

There are several good hiking routes and four annual festivals, including the lively **Herring Adventure** in early August: for details, check out the town's website www.siglo.is.

The **camping ground** (free) is situated between the harbour and town square. In an old 1930s hotel, cosy **Gistihúsið Hvanneyri** (☎ 467 1378; alla@simnet.is; Aðalqata 10; sb Ikr1000-1800, s Ikr3000, d Ikr6000-7000) has 19 plush rooms with mountain views. There are a couple of TV lounges and kitchen access.

Kaffi Torg (☎ 467 2000; Aðalgata 30; pizza Ikr950), the town's only restaurant, serves good-value burgers, pizzas and fish and lamb dishes. It's the place to meet friendly locals, and the bar opens until 3am at weekends to aid international communications.

Buses run three times a week between Reykjavík and Varmahlíð (Ikr4700, June to September), where you can get a connection to Siglufjörður (Ikr1000).

AKUREYRI

pop 16,086

Akureyri (www.akureyri.is), ranged along Iceland's greatest fjord, is backed by snow-capped peaks and has an optimistic feel. It's notable for its flowery gardens, filled with driftwood sculptures, and for its refreshingly sunny weather. It has the best restaurants, cafés and cinemas outside the capital, and is definitely a place to linger.

Information

The fantastic **municipal library** (☎ 460 1250; Brekkugata 17; 🕙 10am-7pm Mon-Fri, 10am-3pm Sat) has an English book section larger than many UK libraries and Internet access (per hour Ikr100).

Akureyri Hospital (☎ 463 0100; Spítalavegur) is just south of the botanical gardens.

There's a **post office** (☎ 460 2600; Skipagata 10; 🕙 8.30am-4.30pm Mon-Fri), and a helpful **tourist office** (☎ 462 7733; www.eyjafjordur.is; Hafnarstræti 82; 🕙 7.30am-7pm Mon-Fri, 8am-5pm Sat & Sun) inside the BSÍ bus terminal, with Internet access (per 15 minutes Ikr150). **Nonni Travel** (☎ 461 1841; www.nonnitravel.is; Brekkugata 5) is the main tour agency in town.

Sights & Activities

Akureyrarkirkja (Eyrarlandsvegur; 🕙 10am-noon & 2-5pm Jun-Aug) was designed by Gudjón Samúelsson, architect of Reykjavík's Hallgrímskirkja. Although the basalt theme connects them, Akureyrarkirkja looks more like a stylised 1920s US skyscraper than its big-town brother. One of the stained-glass windows came from Coventry Cathedral, England after the building was destroyed in WWII.

The **Akureyri Folk Museum** (☎ 462 4162; www .akmus.is; Aðalstræti 58; adult/child Ikr400/free; 🕙 11am-5pm Jun–mid-Sep, 2-4pm Sat rest of year) houses artwork and historical items from the Settlement Era to the present day, and there's a little wooden church in the tranquil gardens.

There are several small museums dedicated to local heroes – artists, poets and authors – which may be of limited interest to an outsider. The best is **Nonnahús** (☎ 462 3555; www.nonni.is; Aðalstræti 54; adult/child Ikr350/free; 🕙 10am-5pm Jun-Sep), the childhood home of children's writer Reverend Jón Sveinsson (1857–1944), better known as 'Nonni'. English translations of his books are available.

Lystigarður Akureyrar (Akureyri Botanical Gardens; ☎ 462 7487; Eyrarlandsvegur; 🕙 8am-10pm Mon-Fri, 9am-10pm Sat & Sun Jun-Oct), opened in 1912, is the most northerly botanical garden in the world. It includes every native Icelandic species, and other tough plants from high altitudes and latitudes.

Akureyri has one of the best Icelandic **swimming pools** (☎ 461 4455; Þingvallastræti 21; adult/child Ikr290/150, with sauna Ikr500; 🕙 7am-9pm Mon-Fri, 8am-6.30pm Sat & Sun) with hot pots, saunas and flumes suitable for little kids and big.

Also child-friendly is **Jólagarðurinn** (The Christmas Garden; ☎ 463 1433; Slettu; 🕙 10am-10pm Jun-Aug, shorter hrs Sep-May), 11km south of Akureyri, a shop selling seasonal baubles with a picnic garden, teeny hiding-room and giant advent calendar.

Sleeping
BUDGET

Central camping ground (☎ 462 3379; hamrar@skatar .is; Þórunnarstræti; per person Ikr700) Slightly run-down and graffitied, but close to the swimming pool, supermarket and town.

ICELAND

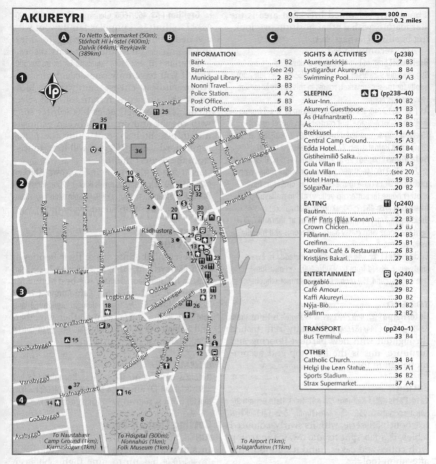

AKUREYRI

0 ———————— 300 m
0 ———————— 0.2 miles

INFORMATION		
Bank	1	B2
Bank	(see 24)	
Municipal Library	2	B2
Nonni Travel	3	B3
Police Station	4	A2
Post Office	5	B3
Tourist Office	6	B3

SIGHTS & ACTIVITIES		(p238)
Akureyrarkirkja	7	B3
Lystigarður Akureyrar	8	B4
Swimming Pool	9	A3

SLEEPING		(pp238–40)
Akur-Inn	10	B2
Akureyri Guesthouse	11	B3
Ás (Hafnarstræti)	12	B4
Ás	13	B3
Brekkusel	14	A4
Central Camp Ground	15	A3
Edda Hotel	16	B4
Gistiheimilið Salka	17	B3
Gula Villan II	18	A3
Gula Villan	(see 20)	
Hótel Harpa	19	B3
Sólgarðar	20	B2

EATING		(p240)
Bautinn	21	B3
Café Paris (Bláa Kannan)	22	B3
Crown Chicken	23	B3
Fiðlarinn	24	B3
Greifinn	25	B1
Karolína Café & Restaurant	26	B3
Kristjáns Bakarí	27	B3

ENTERTAINMENT		(p240)
Borgabíó	28	B2
Café Amour	29	B2
Kaffi Akureyri	30	B2
Nýja-Bíó	31	B2
Sjallinn	32	B2

TRANSPORT		(pp240–1)
Bus Terminal	33	B4

OTHER		
Catholic Church	34	B4
Helgi the Lean Statue	35	A1
Sports Stadium	36	B2
Strax Supermarket	37	A4

Naustabær camp site (☎ 461 2264; hamrar@scout .is, per person Ikr700) A newer facility 1½km south in a leafy setting. Both sites offer toilets, showers, kitchens and laundry facilities.

Stórholt HI Hostel (☎ 462 3657; www.hostel.is; Stórholt 1; Ikr2200) This spotless hostel, 15 minutes' walk from the town centre, has three comfy sitting rooms and three large kitchens, with a summery decking area outside. There are two attractive **summerhouses** (1/7 days Ikr14,000/45,4500) for hire, each holding up to seven people. Bookings pour in after Easter – don't get left in the cold.

MID-RANGE

Sólgarðar (☎ 461 1133; solgarda@binet.is; Brekkugata 6; sb/s/d Ikr2500/3900/5500) The owner works shifts,

so don't be surprised if she's bleary eyed! Her three rooms, one with balcony, overlook a quiet residential street and are gleaming. Breakfast is available (Ikr800), and there are discounts for stays over three days.

Gistiheimilið Salka (☎ 461 2340; salka@nett.is; Skipagata 1; sb d/tr/q Ikr4400/6000/7200, s/d/tr/q Ikr4600/ 6000/7500/9200) Large, distinctive 2nd-floor rooms filled with books, ornaments, couches and TVs make this place feel just like home. There's a fully equipped kitchen and the chatty owner Agga is immensely helpful. Recommended.

Akureyri Guesthouse (☎ 462 5588; www.nett.is /guest; Hafnarstræti 104; sb/s/d from Ikr2200/4900/6900) Another central place, the 19 rooms here are small but clean, all with TV and washbasins.

The sunny, balconied breakfast area is the star feature, with a great position overlooking bustling Hafnarstræti.

Also recommended:

Brekkusel (☎ 461 2660; info@brekkusel.is; Byggðavegur 97; sb/s/d Ikr2500/4000/5500; ◷ Jun-Aug) Handy for the supermarket, rooms in this family home are spacious and light.

Ás (☎ 461 2248; fax 461 3810; Skipagata 4; s/d from Ikr4500/6000) Average, but central with lots of rooms. Sleeping-bag accommodation (Ikr3100) is available at the companion Hafnarstræti 77 house. Breakfast Ikr700.

Gula Villan (☎ 461 2810; gulavillan@nett.is; Brekkugata 8; sb/s/d Ikr3100/4600/6000) Monastic-white rooms with kitchen facilities close to the centre. The operators have another house (in buttercup-yellow) at Þingvallastræti 14.

Akur-Inn (☎ 461 2500; akurinn@hotmail.com; Brekkugata 27a; s/d Ikr4700/6900) Out-of-the-ordinary heritage home with classy balconied rooms and friendly management.

Edda Hotel (☎ 444 4000; www.hoteledda.is; Eyrarlandsvegur 28; s/d from Ikr5000/6400, ◷ mid-Jun–late Aug) Around 150 rooms in the grammar school.

TOP END

Hótel Harpa (☎ 460 2000; www.keahotels.is; Hafnarstræti 83-85; s/d/tr €144/187/243) Recently refurbished throughout with new parquet flooring and furniture, this is the best top-end accommodation in town.

Eating

Café Paris (Bláa Kannan; ☎ 461 4600; Hafnarstræti 96; lunch specials Ikr950; ◷ 8am-10pm; ☒ ▣) This tearoom/patisserie, with its swirly-coloured tables, is a fab spot to idle away a morning with coffee and cakes…and it's good in the afternoon too!

Karolína Café (☎ 461 2755; Kaupvangsstræti 23; ◷ 11.30am-1am Mon-Thu, to 3am Fri & Sat, 2pm-1am Sun) Also snug, Karolína has magazines, huge squashy sofas and alcoholic coffee (Ikr790 to Ikr990), all of which conspire to stop you from ever leaving. There's an upmarket **restaurant** (mains Ikr2490-2890; ◷ Tue-Sat from 6pm) attached for formal dining.

Bautinn (☎ 462 1818; Hafnarstræti 92; all-you-can-eat soup & salad Ikr1290, mains Ikr1000-3400) Open all day, this restaurant is a firm favourite for its friendly staff, decent prices and loaded salad bar. There's a large glazed conservatory, and a more shadowy interior if you don't enjoy that goldfish-bowl feeling. Food ranges from traditional Icelandic lamb, puffin and horse to veggie dishes.

Greifinn (☎ 460 1600; Glerárgata 20; mains Ikr1990-2890) Greifinn is a popular family spot with a varied menu, including sizzling Tex-Mex, much-praised pizza and big meaty dishes.

Fiðlarinn (☎ 462 7100; Skipagata 14; mains Ikr2500-4300) If you have only one decent meal between endless cheese sandwiches, blow out at this gorgeous restaurant. The select menu contains delicacies like lobster soup with cognac and cream; between exquisite mouthfuls, sit back and enjoy the panoramic fjord views. Veggies will have to feed from the dessert menu!

Fast-food places include **Crown Chicken** (☎ 461 3010; Skipagata 12; meals Ikr600-1200). **Kristjáns Bakarí** (Hafnarstræti 100; ◷ 9am-6pm Mon-Fri, 10am-4pm Sat) sells fresh bread and very nice cakes.

Entertainment

NIGHTCLUBS

Akureyri inhabitants shake their booties at **Kaffi Akureyri** (☎ 461 3999; Strandgata 7; ◷ 3pm-1am Sun-Thu, 3pm-4am Fri & Sat), the best venue for live music and dancing, **Café Amour** (☎ 461 2222; Raðhústorg 9; ◷ 10am-midnight Sun-Thu, 10am-3am Sat & Sun), a hip, cream-leather wine bar, and **Sjallinn** (☎ 462 2770; Geislagata 14; ◷ to 3am Fri & Sat), the most popular club.

CINEMA

There are two central cinemas, **Borgabíó** (☎ 462 3599; Hólabraut 12) and **Nýja-Bíó** (☎ 461 4666; Raðhústorg 8), both screening mainstream films.

Getting There & Away

AIR

In summer, **Flugfélag Íslands** (www.airiceland.is; ☎ 460 7000) has up to nine flights between Akureyri and Reykjavík (Ikr9775).

BOAT

The **Sæfari** (☎ 464 0000; www.samskip.com) sails from Dalvík (44km north of Akureyri) to Grímsey island at 9am on Monday, Wednesday and Friday (return Ikr3500, 3½ hours), returning from Grímsey at 4pm. The price including the bus from Akureyri to Dalvík is Ikr4000 return: see Bus below.

BUS

Buses between Akureyri and Reykjavík depart at least once daily (Ikr5900, six hours). Buses travelling over the Kjölur route to Reykjavík leave daily from 21 June to 31 August (Ikr7400, eight hours).

A daily bus to Mývatn (Ikr2100, 1½ hours) runs between June and September, continuing to Egilsstaðir (Ikr5100, four hours) and Seyðisfjörður (Ikr6000, five hours).

Buses to Húsavík (Ikr1800, one hour) depart one to four times daily.

Buses to Dalvík (for the ferry to Grímsey: see Boat above) leave at 7.30am on Monday, Wednesday and Friday from Akureyri bus station, returning from Dalvík at 7.30pm.

AROUND AKUREYRI

South of the town centre is Iceland's most visited 'forest', **Kjarnaskógur**. A good day walk from Akureyri follows the **Glerárdalur** valley as far as Lambi mountain hut. You can hike up and down **Mt Sulur** (1213m) from Akureyri in about eight hours.

About 50km east of town is shapely waterfall **Goðafoss**, where Þorgeir Ljósvetningagoði, asked to decide whether Iceland should adopt Christianity, symbolically threw his statues of the old Norse gods. Buses from Akureyri to Mývatn pass the waterfall.

GRÍMSEY

Grímsey (population 93), is a chess-mad island inside the Arctic Circle. Day trips with **Nonni Travel** (☎ 461 1841; www.nonnitravel.is; Brekkugata 5) cost from Ikr4800 to Ikr13,800. (See Boat opposite for reaching Grímsey without a tour.)

HÚSAVÍK

pop 2368

Húsavík (91km northeast of Akureyri) is a jaunty harbour town, full of multicoloured houses and working fishing boats. It's also the proclaimed 'whale-watching capital of Europe': chances of seeing these marine mammals are high, high, high.

The **tourist information desk** (☎ 464 4300; inside Strax supermarket) is staffed from May to September and distributes a free map showing walks in the area.

There's Internet access in the **library** (Stórigarður 17; per hr Ikr250).

Sights & Activities

The fascinating **Whale Centre** (☎ 464 2520; www .icewhale.is; Hafnarstétt; adult/student/child Ikr500/400/ 200; ☉ 9am-9pm Jun-Aug, 10am-5pm May & Sep) deserves a couple of hours' attention. It tells you *everything* about Icelandic whales and whaling, and includes a display on Keiko

HÚSAVÍK

INFORMATION	
Hospital	1 B1
Library	(see 6)
Police	2 A1
Post Office	3 B2
Tourist Information Desk	(see 15)

SIGHTS & ACTIVITIES	(pp241–2)
Húsavíkurkirkja	4 A2
Hvalaferðir (Whale Watching)	(see 13)
Icelandic Phallological Museum	5 A1
Norður Sigling (Whale Watching)	(see 11)
Safnahúsið	6 B1
Whale Centre	7 A2

SLEEPING	
Camping Ground	8 A1
Gistiheimilið Árból	9 B2
Guesthouse Baldursbrekka	10 A1

EATING	(p242)
Gamli Baukur	11 A2
Heimabakari Konditori	12 B2
Restaurant Salka	13 A1

TRANSPORT	(p242)
Bus Station	14 A1

OTHER	
Strax Supermarket	15 A1

(the black-and-white star of *Free Willy*) and a hanging gallery of whale skeletons.

Norður Sigling (☎ 464 2350; www.nordursigling.is; Gamli Baukur, Hafnarstétt; adult/under 14s yrs Ikr3800/free) and **Hvalaferðir** (☎ 464 1500; www.gentlegiants.is; Garðarsbraut 6; Ikr3300) offer three-hour whale-spotting trips on sturdy oaken boats. From mid-May to mid-September, there's a 99% chance of sightings – mostly minkes and harbour porpoises, but humpback and blue whales appear occasionally.

Once you've recovered your landlegs, the **Safnahúsið** (Museum; ☎ 464 1860; www.husmus.is; Stórigarður 17; adult/child Ikr400/150; ☉ 10am-6pm Jun-Aug, 9am-noon & 1-5pm Mon-Fri, 4-6pm Sun Sep-May), with its folk, maritime and natural history sections, is worth a glance. Admission includes a cup of coffee. There's a polar bear which travelled all the way from Greenland to Grímsey, only to get its head blown off: no wonder it looks annoyed. Say a prayer for the bear at the unusual cross-shaped **Húsavíkurkirkja** (Garðarsbraut; 9-11am & 3-5pm Jun-Aug) near the quayside.

The unique **Icelandic Phallological Museum** (566 8668; Héðinsbraut 3a; Ikr500; 10am-6pm) once the pride of Reykjavík, has relocated here. It contains a collection of penises from all local mammals (except *homo sapiens:* although a donor has been lined up)!

Sleeping

Camping ground (845 0705; per person Ikr750, 2nd & 3rd nights free) Lovingly run, this option at the northern edge of town has heated toilets, washing machines and cooking facilities.

Guesthouse Baldursbrekka (464 1005; mariam@simnet.is; Baldursbrekka 20; sb/s/d Ikr1800/3200/4600) The cheapest option, this family home in a quiet cul-de-sac has five dinky rooms, cooking facilities and a garage to hang wet clothes. Breakfast Ikr700.

Kaldbaks-Kot (464 1504; www.cottages.is; off Rd 85; 2-/4-person house Ikr8900/11,900) These self-contained wooden cottages, 2km south of Húsavík, feel strangely tropical but have quintessentially Nordic views when you step outside. They're a real bargain if sharing, containing everything you'll need, and there's a hot pot on site for starlit bathing.

Gistiheimilið Árból (464 2220; www.simnet.is /arbol; Ásgarðsvegur 2; s/d/tr Ikr5900/8900/12,400) This ex-governor's mansion, on the edge of the park, is the best place to stay in town. It's spacious and welcoming, upper rooms have super views of either the harbour or the mountains, and there's interesting ephemera on the walls – bugles, guns and old photos of Húsavík.

Eating

Gamli Baukur (464 2442; www.gamlibaukur.is; Hafnarstétt; mains Ikr990-2990; 11am-midnight Sun-Thu, 11am-1am Fri & Sat) This restaurant-bar is given a seafaring air by its fisherman's-hut decor and harbourside location: you can actually watch your dinner being landed! Hamburgers and pasta are available for the fish-disinclined.

Restaurant Salka (464 2551; Garðarsbraut 6; mains Ikr900-2400; 11am-11pm summer) Another good nautical restaurant, Salka has a cosy bar and an alternative pizza menu.

Heimabakarí Konditori (464 2901; Garðarsbraut 15; 8am-5pm) Fresh bread, sandwiches and yumcious cakes are sold at this bakery, which has tables where you can drink coffee and ogle passers-by.

Getting There & Away

From 21 June to 31 August, there are three to five daily buses to Akureyri (Ikr2000, 1¼ hours). Between the same dates, buses to Hótel Reynihlíð in Reykjahlíð (Mývatn) depart up to three times daily (Ikr1500, 45 minutes). Weekday services go to Ásbyrgi, with additional weekend services from 21 June to 31 August (Ikr1740, 1¾ hours).

MÝVATN

Tranquil Mývatn, with its shallow waters, 50 small islands, and prolific bird life, is the calm centre of a stark volcanic/geothermal area. Travellers can settle in for several days' sightseeing in this conservation area, circling the 37-sq-km lake and examining nature's explosive masterpieces – crazy-coloured mud pots, a huge tephra crater, and the debris of violent eruptions.

Sights & Activities

AROUND THE LAKE

One of the most interesting walks begins at **Stóragjá**, a hot spring near the village (swimming's a bad idea because of harmful algae). After a few minutes, the path comes to a dead end at a pipeline. Turn left and walk several hundred metres until the track turns southward. It crosses a lava field before reaching **Grjótagjá**, a 50°C hot spring in a spooky fissure, then continues to the prominent tephra crater, **Hverfell**, and **Dimmuborgir**, a 2000-year-old maze of freakishly twisted lava pillars.

Other sites worth visiting around the lake include the forested lava headland of **Höfði**; pinnacle formations at **Kálfaströnd**; pseudocraters at **Skútustaðir**, where ponds, bogs and marshlands create havens for nesting birds; the climb up **Vindbelgjarfjall** (529m); and a high-density waterfowl **nesting area** along the northwestern shore (off-road entry restricted between 15 May and 20 July).

NÁMAFJALL & HVERARÖND

Vaporous vents cover the pinky-orange Námafjall ridge. At its foot, the fumaroles and solfataras of the Hverarönd geothermal

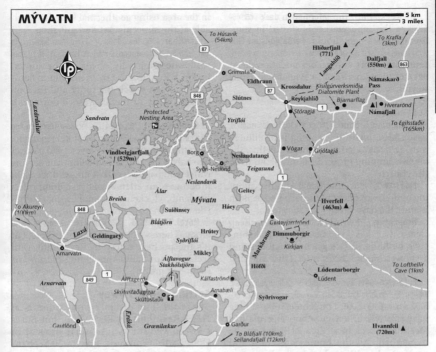

MÝVATN

To Húsavík (54km)
87

To Krafla (3km)

Hlíðarfjall (771)

Langahlíð

Dalfjall (550m) ▲

863

Grímsstaðir

Eldhraun

Krossdalur

Kísilgúrverksmiðja Diatomite Plant

Námaskarð Pass

87

Slútnes

Reykjahlíð

Bjarnarflag

▲ Hverarönd

Stóragjá

1

Námafjall

848

Ytriflói

Protected Nesting Area

To Egilsstaðir (165km)

Sandvatn

Laxárdalur

Vindbelgjarfjall (529m) ▲

Borg

Neslandatangi

Vógar

Grjótagjá

Syðri-Nesland

Teigasund

Neslandavík

1

Geitey

Álar

Mývatn

Háey

Hverfell (463m) ▲

Breiða

To Akureyri (100km)

848

Suðinsey

Geiteyjarrönd

Dimmuborgir

Blátjörn

Laxá

Hrútey

Syðriflói

Mikley

Markhraun

Kirkjan

Geldingaey

Arnarvatn

To Lofthellir Cave (1km)

Álftavogur Stakhólstjörn

Höfði

1

Lúdentarborgir

Lúdent

Arnarvatn

849

Álftagerði

Skútustaðagígar

Kálfaströnd

Skútustaðir

Arnabæli

Syðrivogar

Eríðá

Gautlönd

Grænilækur

Garður

To Bláfjall (10km); Sellandafjall (12km)

Hvannfell (720m) ▲

0 ——— 5 km
0 ——— 3 miles

field scream steam and belch mud. The area rests on the mid-Atlantic rift (hence all the activity), and can be seen from quite a distance. It's just off the Ring Road 6km east of Reykjahlíð.

KRAFLA

The colourful, sulphurous, steaming fissure **Leirhnjúkur** is Krafla's prime attraction. From there you can look out across the **Krafla Caldera**, where several different lava flows overlie each other. Nearby **Víti**, meaning 'hell', is a 320m-wide explosion crater and lake (now inactive...allegedly). The 30-megawatt **Kröflustöð Power Station** gets steam from 17 boreholes around the volcano. One of its preliminary searches produced the whopping crater **Sjálfskapar Víti** ('Homemade Hell', near the Krafla car park), when a team drilled into a steam chamber which exploded. Bits of the rig were found 3km away.

Tours

Tours operate during July and August, and get pretty crowded: book at least a day in advance. A 2½-hour tour (Ikr3300) of Mývatn and Krafla departs from **Hótel Reykjahlíð** (☎ 464 4142) at 1pm daily. The Volcanic Wonders tour (Ikr5600) leaves **Eldá** (☎ 464 4220; www.elda.is) at 8.15am on Tuesday, Thursday and Sunday. The morning segment is a 3½-hour tour around local volcanic features; then, in the afternoon, it visits Krafla.

Eldá's highly recommended Dettifoss Super Tour (Ikr6900, 12 hours) runs three days weekly and includes the Jökulsárgljúfur National Park and a coastal puffin colony There's also a five-hour tour (Ikr6400) to Lofthellir, a lava cave with magnificent natural ice sculptures; departures are from Eldá at 8.15am on Tuesday, Thursday and Saturday.

Reykjahlíð

pop 208

More an assortment of accommodation than a true town, Reykjahlíð is nevertheless the best base to explore Mývatn. Skútustaðir, at the southern end of the lake, also has a few summer facilities, including camping, farmhouse and hotel accommodation.

In Reykjahlíð, the **information desk** (☎ 464 4390) in the supermarket is staffed in summer. Open longer hours, **Ferðaþjónstan Eldá** (Eldá Travel Services; ☎ 464 4220; www.elda.is) can book tours, transport and accommodation. **Internet access** (per 30min Ikr500) is available at Hótel Reynihlíð.

SLEEPING

Hlíð Camping Ground (☎ 464 4103; hlid@isholf.is; per tent Ikr600, sb Ikr1800) Camping is prohibited outside designated areas: head for this, the largest camping ground, 300m inland from the church.

Eldá (☎ 464 4220; per tent Ikr650) Another camping option, right next to the lake's edge. Both it and Hlíð have groovy kitchen tents.

Hraunbrún (☎ 464 4103; sb Ikr1800) For cheap sleeps, try these rooms in a portakabin-style building. It has kitchen facilities and a shower block; check in at Hlíð camping ground.

Eldá (☎ 464 4220; www.elda.is; Helluhraun 7, Helluhraun 15, Birkihraun 11; sb Sep-May only Ikr2000, s Ikr5700-6700, d/tr Ikr8600/12,000) The genteel folks at Eldá have splattered their guesthouse across five locations: check in at Eldá I (Bjarg) on the main road. All the houses are clean and comfortable, with washbasins in the rooms. Eldá IV, near the post office, also has a kitchen and lounge. If you end up at II or III, it means the others are full... The prices include breakfast, served at Eldá V on Birkihraun. The owners hire out bicycles (Ikr1000/1500 for six/12 hours) and kayaks (Ikr1000/1500 for one/two hours), and run guided sightseeing tours – see Tours (p243) for details.

Hótel Reykjahlíð (☎ 464 4142; www.reykjahlid.is; s/d Ikr11,500/13,500) A friendly hotel dab on the shore with nine spacious rooms. Ask for a lake view, and marvel at the spectacular sunsets while your worries subside! The hotel has a large video library for cosy nights in after a day's walking.

Hótel Reynihlíð (☎ 464 4170; www.reynihlid.is; s/d Ikr14,450/16,950) This smartish business hotel offers en-suite rooms with TVs and tea-making facilities. It also rents out brand-new bicycles (Ikr1600 per day) and arranges horse-riding trips (Ikr3500 per hour).

EATING

Don't leave without scoffing a slice of dark, sticky *hverabrauð* (hot spring bread), baked in the area using geothermal heat. It's available at the supermarket and gift shop.

Zanzibar (☎ 464 2910; ☾ 11am-1am Sun-Thu, to 3am Fri & Sat; pizza around Ikr800) A barn of a place, with whopping telly screen in the corner, laidback Zanzibar is favoured by local families. You can watch the footy and feast on burgers, chips or pizzas, washed down with cold beer.

Gamli Bærinn (☎ 464 4170; ☾ 8am-10pm Jun-Aug & Easter; mains Ikr900-1800) Run by Hótel Reynihlíð, this atmospheric 'country tavern' is a place of two halves. By day, it's a mellow café serving coffee and baguettes (Ikr450), while at night it becomes an effervescent restaurant offering lamb, chicken and smoked char dishes (Ikr1450) and live entertainment.

Hótel Reynihlíð (☎ 464 4142; 2-course menu Ikr2890) There's not much of a buzz here, but it's the poshest eatery in Reykjahlíð, with Icelandic specialities including *plokkfiskur* (haddock gratin).

Getting There & Away

The main long-distance bus station is at Hótel Reynihlíð in Reykjahlíð, but buses between Mývatn and Akureyri also stop at Skútustaðir. From mid-June to 30 September, there's at least one daily bus between Akureyri and Mývatn (Ikr2100, 1½ hours), and at least three buses per week from Mývatn to Egilsstaðir (Ikr3000).

See p242 for buses to/from Húsavík.

See p252 for buses to/from Reykjavík via Sprengisandur.

JÖKULSÁRGLJÚFUR NATIONAL PARK

Sometimes called 'Iceland's Grand Canyon', Jökulsárgljúfur is bursting with sticky-birch forests, orchids and bizarre rock formations. Worth seeing is **Ásbyrgi**, a canyon formed by a flood of biblical proportions from a glacier 200km away. The swirls, spirals and strange acoustics at **Hljóðaklettar** (Echo Rocks) are similarly unearthly, and near the park's southern boundary is 44m-high **Dettifoss**, Europe's most powerful waterfall.

The park is a true hiker's Valhalla; however, camping is limited to **Ásbyrgi** (per person Ikr600, all facilities), **Vesturdalur** (per person Ikr600, no showers) and **Dettifoss** (free, hikers only). Food is available at the snack bar, supermarket and petrol station at the **Ásbyrgi farmstead** (route 85).

From 21 June to 31 August, daily scheduled buses run from Akureyri (Ikr3300) and

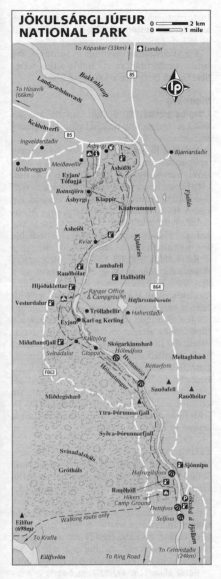

JÖKULSÁRGLJÚFUR NATIONAL PARK

0 ———— 2 km
0 ———— 1 mile

To Kópasker (33km) | Lundur

To Húsavík (66km)

Landgræðslusvæði

Bakkahlaup

85

Keldunverfi

85

Ingveldarstaðir

Ásbyrgi

Bjarnarstaðir

Meiðavellir

Undirveggur

Eyjan/Tófugjá

 Áshöfði

Botnstjörn

Ásbyrgi Klappir

Kúahvammur

Ásheiði

Fjöllið

Kvíar

Kjalörðs

Lambafell

Rauðhólar

Hallhöfði

Hljóðaklettar

Ranger Office & Campground

864

Vesturdalur

Hafurssúðuvatn

Tröllahellir

Hafurssstaðir

Eyjan Karl og Kerling

Miðaftansfjall

Kallbjörg

Skógarkinnshæð

Svínadalur

Gloppa

Hólmáfoss

FBG2

Hólsvatunguur

Tranustóð

Rettarfoss

Meltaglshæð

Miðdegishæð

Sauðafell

Rauðhólar

Ytra-Þórunnarfjall

Syðra-Þórunnarfjall

Svínadalsháls

Gróthals

Hafragilsfoss

Sjónnípa

Rauðhóll

Hikers' Camp Ground

Dettifoss

Jökulsá á Fjöllum

Eilífur (698m)

Walking route only

Selfoss

To Krafla

Eilífsvötn

To Ring Road

To Grímsstaðir (24km)

Húsavík (Ikr1300, 70 minutes) to major sites in the park. There's also a daily Mývatn Dettifoss bus via Krafla (Ikr1800), leaving at 8am from Hótel Reynihlíð in Reykjahlíð and returning from Dettifoss at 2.15pm. Eldá's Dettifoss Super Tour from Mývatn (see p243) offers a luggage transfer service for hikers.

THE EAST

Sunshine and space are the main eastern attractions. Iceland's largest forest and longest lake are found here, surrounded by remote peaks and cascading waterfalls.

EGILSSTAÐIR

pop 1721

Egilsstaðir is the hub of eastern Iceland, but it's a rather grey service town – better to stay in Seyðisfjörður. Its main attraction is as a base to explore the **Hallormsstaður** woods and the magnificent waterfall, **Hengifoss**, on the opposite shore. These are accessible by car, bicycle or tour bus (three days per week in July and August, contact the tourist office for details). Egilsstaðir's most distinguishing feature is **Lake Lögurinn**, in whose depths, so they say, a monster lurks.

All services, including the **tourist office** (Upplýsingamiðstöð; ☎ 471 2320; www.east.is; ✆ 9am-5pm May & Sep, 8am-10pm Jun-Aug), are conveniently clustered near the central crossroads.

In town, the **Minjasafn Austurlands** (☎ 471 1412; www.minjasafn.is; Laufskógar 1; adult/child Ikr400/200; ✆ 11am-5pm Tue-Sun Jun-Aug, 1-5pm Mon-Fri Sep-May) museum includes a 10th-century Viking grave and treasure, and a reconstructed farmhouse.

The friendly **camping ground** (☎ 471 2320; Kaupvangur 10; camp sites per person Ikr750, sb Ikr2000, 5-person hut Ikr6000; ✆ all year) offers cooking facilities and dorm beds. There's a summer **Hotel Edda** (☎ 444 4880; off Tjarnarbraut; sb/s/d Ikr2000/8500/10,700; ✆ late May-late August), based in the school opposite the swimming pool. **Gistiheimilið Egilsstaðir** (☎ 471 1114; egilsstadir@isholf.is; 300m west of crossroads; s/d incl breakfast Ikr9900/13,200) is a splendid heritage guesthouse on the banks of Lake Lögurinn. Breakfast is in the lakeside dining room, which also does a good Icelandic dinner buffet (Ikr2900).

Café Nielsen (☎ 471 2626; Tjarnarbraut 1; snacks Ikr650-990, mains Ikr1190-2500; ✆ 11.30am-11pm Sun-Thu, 11.30am-2am Fri & Sat) is the top eating choice, straddling the divide between smoky bar and genteel restaurant, with terrace and garden to boot. Foodwise, there's plenty of variety, from crepes (Ikr790) to reindeer casserole (Ikr1990). Quick eats include the **Shell petrol station** (Fagradalsbraut 13; snacks Ikr390-1350) and the reliable **Pizza 67** (Lyngás 1).

Getting There & Away

AIR

There are up to four **Flugfélag Íslands** (☎ 471 1210; www.airiceland.is) flights daily between Reykjavík and Egilsstaðir (Ikr11,075).

BUS

The main terminal in Egilsstaðir is at the camping ground.

From 1 June to 31 August, there's a daily bus to/from Akureyri (Ikr5100, four hours), which passes Mývatn and Dettifoss.

Between 1 June and 10 September the bus to Seyðisfjörður runs at least twice daily from Monday to Friday (Ikr900, 30 minutes, 9.15am and 5pm). On Wednesday and Thursday, there's an additional run (1.20pm) to accommodate ferry passengers. Buses also run once a day on Saturday and Sunday in July (2.20pm).

SEYÐISFJÖRÐUR

pop 730

European ferries dock in picturesque Seyðisfjörður (www.sfk.is), and it is a wonderful introduction to Iceland. Friendly, bohemian people live in its multicoloured houses, scattered at the head of a 17km-long fjord. It also has a fantastically scenic approach by road, over mountains and alongside cascading waterfalls.

The best information source is the **tourist office** (☎ 472 1119; ☉ 8am-noon & 1-5pm Mon-Fri Jun-Aug) inside the ferry terminal.

Sights & Activities

For a fish-eye view of Iceland, try a guided **kayaking trip** (☎ 865 3741; ferdamenning@sfk.is; ☉ Jun-Aug). Beginners splosh round the tranquil lagoon (one hour, Ikr1500), while more experienced paddlers can go on six-hour/ two-day trips (Ikr6000/17,000) to Austdalur or Skálanes. The same guide does **mountain-bike tours** (two hour trips, Ikr2500); book through the hostel or the tourist office.

If you're happier in walking boots, the Seyðisfjörður to Vestdalur **hike** is a fine first taste of the countryside, around Mt Bjólfur to the Seyðisfjörður–Egilsstaðir road.

Seyðisfjörður is stuffed with 19th-century **timber buildings**, brought in kit form from Norway: read all about them in the brochure *Historic Seyðisfjörður* (Ikr300), available at the tourist office. For insight into the town's fishing and telecommunications

history, there's a worthwhile museum, **Tækniminjasafn Austurlands** (☎ 472 1596; Hafnargata 44; adult/child Ikr400/free; ☉ 11am-6pm Jun-Sep).

On Wednesday evenings in summer, live music performances are held in the pretty **Blue Church** (Ránargata; Ikr1000; ☉ 8.30pm).

Sleeping

Camping ground (☎ 861 3097; Ránargata; camp sites Ikr500) A neat facility tucked behind the petrol station.

Hafaldan HI Hostel (☎ 472 1410; thorag@simnet .is; Ránargata 9; dm Ikr1950, s/d 2800/4800; ☐) With lovely views over the harbour, this cheerful, arty hostel has a sunny dining room, as well as kitchen, laundry, Internet access and TV room. If you're hankering after a snug Mongolian yurt, don't panic – there's one in the garden! Handcarved from teak, it's rentable for the same price as the dorm beds.

Hótel Aldan (☎ 472 1277; www.hotelaldan.com; Norðurgata 2; B&B s/d Ikr6500/8700, guesthouse s/d/tr Ikr11,800/15,800/17,800) Friendly Hótel Aldan has four small but comfortable rooms with shared bathroom in the main building, but it's the boutique guesthouse at Oddagata 6 that makes you go 'wow!'. Superbly renovated, the luxury rooms are bright, spacious and furnished with antiques, and the brand-new beds snuggle under hand-embroidered bedspreads. Triple rooms have wicked alcoves tucked under the eaves. All rooms are en-suite and contain minibars and TV/DVD, with films available at reception. Breakfast is served in the main building.

Eating

Skaftafell Café (☎ 472 1632; Austurvegur 42; snacks Ikr450-1100, mains Ikr2000-3500; ☐ per 30min Ikr150) Highly recommended, this welcoming bistro-bar and Internet café is a popular place for quick coffee or a lingering meal. Light snacks include omelette, waffles and toast with caviar, and the freshly caught seafood is great. Local artists and musicians hang out here, and in the exhibition gallery upstairs.

Hótel Aldan (☎ 472 1277; Norðurgata 2; mains Ikr800-3000; ☉ 7am-9.30pm) The chic restaurant-bar, recently extended to accommodate the ravening hordes, offers a spectacular buffet breakfast (Ikr1100), including homemade bread and fresh fruit. Coffee and light snacks are served all day, and in the evening, there are meat and fish dishes. The bar fairly buzzes when the boat comes in.

There's a snack bar at the petrol station, and the **Sparakaup supermarket** (🕑 Mon-Sat) is just opposite. For alcohol, the Vín Búð is close to the museum.

Getting There & Away

For bus information, see Getting There & Away, opposite. Details of the ferry service from mainland Europe are on p262.

THE SOUTH

STAFAFELL

pop 10

Stafafell, 100km south of Egilsstaðir, is a great hiking area set between the **Lón lagoon** and the colourful **Lónsöræfi mountains**.

Stafafell HI Hostel (☎ 478 1717; www.eldhorn.is /stafafell; sb Ikr1850, s/d from Ikr4500/6000) The only facilities in the area are in this hostel's cabins or appealingly eccentric 19th-century farmhouse. Meals are available in summer, but reserve them in advance or bring your own food as backup. There's also a **camping area** (per person Ikr500).

Mountain-bus tours (Ikr4000) to Kollumúli, in the Lónsöræfi mountains, are highly recommended and can be arranged at the HI hostel. The hostel can also advise on about a dozen local **walking routes**.

The Egilsstaðir–Höfn bus passes Stafafell, setting off from Egilsstaðir at 8.55am (Ikr4790, four hours) and from Höfn at 5.15pm (Ikr520, 30 minutes).

VATNAJÖKULL

The 8400-sq-km icecap Vatnajökull reaches a thickness of 1km in places, and is Europe's greatest glacier. Scores of smaller glaciers flow down from Vatnajökull as crevasse-ridden rivers of sculptured ice.

To reach the icecap, take the 9am Austurleið bus from Höfn to Jöklasel (return Ikr2340, 1 June to 5 September), near the edge of the ice, which allows for an exhilarating one-hour skidoo ride (Ikr7500 extra). Return to Höfn via Jökulsárlón, or continue to Skaftafell (Ikr4350, 1 July to 31 August).

The trip is also possible in a day from Skaftafell in July and August – book through Glacier Jeeps (opposite).

Accommodation is available at **Jöklasel Hut** (☎ 478 1000; sb Ikr1800), near the edge of the ice.

Warning

Hiking around the Jöklasel Hut isn't advised due to the many dangerous crevasses.

AROUND VATNAJÖKULL
Jökulsárlón

The 17-sq-km and 600m-deep **Jökulsárlón lagoon** (right next to the Ring Road between Höfn and Skaftafell) is full of blue-and-white icebergs calved from Breiðamerkurjökull, an offshoot of Vatnajökull. Seals bob among the bergs – brrr. A scene from the James Bond film *Die Another Day* (2002) was filmed here: six Aston Martins were destroyed on the specially frozen water!

Höfn

pop 1740

Tiny Höfn makes a handy base for trips to the glacier. The **tourist office** (☎ 478 1500; www .east.is; Hafnarbraut 52; 🕑 8am-8pm mid-Jun–mid-Sep; 🖳) is helpful, and the **Jöklasýning Glacier Exhibition** (☎ 478 2665; joklasyning@vatnajokull.is; adult/ child Ikr500/free; Hafnarbraut; 🕑 1-6pm & 8-10pm Jun-Aug) tells you everything you need to know about vast Vatnajökull, and glaciers in general.

The two main companies running summer tours to the glacier are **Arctic-Ice** (☎ 4/8 1731; info@arctic-ice.is) and **Glacier Jeeps** (☎ 478 1000; www.glacierjeeps.is). The cheapest 3½-hour Super-Jeep trip costs Ikr9000, with prices rising for longer tours including skidoo rides.

There's a **camping ground** (☎ 478 1500; Hafnarbraut 52; camp sites per person Ikr600, sb Ikr2000) near the tourist office. At the harbour end of town are the luscious **Nýibær HI Hostel** (☎ 478 1736; nyibaer@simnet.is; Hafnarbraut 8; sb Ikr2100) and **Gistiheimiliд Hvammur** (☎ 478 1503; hvammur3@simnet .is; Ránarslóð 2; sb mid-Sep–May Ikr2000, s/d Ikr6300/7900; 🖳), the pick of the guesthouses for its smart rooms and Internet connection. For business-class accommodation, try friendly **Hótel Höfn** (☎ 478 1240; www.hotelhofn.is; Víkurbraut; s/d from Ikr11,500/15,800), which also does good buffet meals in its restaurant **Ósinn** (☎ 478 2200; 🕑 9am-10pm; mains Ikr500-2690).

Kaffi Hornið (☎ 478 2600; Hafnarbraut; 🕑 10am-11.30pm SUn-Thu, 10am-3am Fri & Sat; mains Ikr1600-3250) A distinctive log-cabin affair, this is a relaxing place with big squishy settees. The food, including salad bar and veggie options, comes in stomach-stretching portions – good for stoking up before glacier trips!

A daily bus runs between Reykjavík and Höfn from June to mid-September, leaving at 8.30am at either end (Ikr7500, eight hours). The Egilsstaðir–Höfn bus sets off from Egilsstaðir at 8.55am and returns from Höfn at 5.15pm (Ikr5310, 4½ hours).

SKAFTAFELL NATIONAL PARK

Skaftafell is, quite rightly, Iceland's favourite national park. Set beneath a breathtaking backdrop of peaks and glaciers, it has some stunning strolls and tougher wilderness hikes.

For further information on the area, there's a **visitor centre** (☎ 478 1627; ☯ 8am-9pm Jun-Aug, 8am-6pm May & Sep) which shows a cool film about the 1996 *jökulhlaup* (glacial flood), and a traditional farmhouse museum at **Sel** (Skaftafellsheiði; admission free).

Walking

Even if it's raining buckets, make time for Skaftafell's poster-feature, **Svartifoss**, a gloomy waterfall that thunders over black basalt columns. The trail from the camping ground takes around one hour return.

Another popular walk is the easy one-hour return route to **Skaftafellsjökull**. It begins at the information centre and leads to the glacier face, where you can witness the bumps, groans and brilliant blue hues of the ice.

In fine weather, the circular walk around **Skaftafellsheiði** is a treat. There are some enjoyable day walks from the camping ground to **Kristínartindar** (1126m), **Kjós** or the glacial lagoon in **Morsárdalur**; plan on about seven hours for each return trip.

Sleeping & Eating

Book all accommodation ahead in summer, as Skaftafell is immensely popular.

Camping ground (☎ 478 1627; per person Ikr600) Next to the visitor centre, which contains a café, the only place to eat in the park.

Bölti (☎ 478 1626; Skaftafellsheiði; sb/d Ikr2000/7000; ☯ May-Sep) This farm, on the hill behind the western edge of the camping ground, is in a superb location with dizzying views over the *sandur* (glacial-sand plains). It also rents out small cottages with cooking facilities, and can supply dinner if requested in advance.

Hótel Skaftafell (☎ 478 1945; www.hotelskaftafell .is; Freysnes; sb/s/d Ikr2000/10,500/13,900) At Freysnes, 5km east of the park entrance. Large rooms with bathroom and TV. Sleeping-bag accommodation is in prefab buildings with paperthin walls. The staff are very helpful, and even paupers' rooms have great glacial views.

Getting There & Away

See Getting There & Away opposite for bus information.

KIRKJUBÆJARKLAUSTUR

pop 141

Kirkjubæjarklaustur (meaning 'church-farm-cloister') is one of the largest settlements in

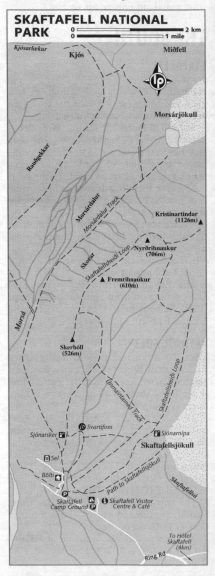

SKAFTAFELL NATIONAL PARK

Kjósarlækur · Kjós · Miðfell

Morsárjökull

Rauðbekkur

Morsárdalur

Morsárdalur Track

Skógar

Skaftafellsheiði Loop

Kristínartindar (1126m)

Nyrðrihnaukur (706m)

Fremrihnaukur (610m)

Morsá

Skerhóll (526m)

Ummanimeð Track

Skaftafellsheiði Loop

Svartifoss

Sjónarsker · Sjónarnípa

Skaftafellsjökull

Sel

Bölti

Path to Skaftafellsjökull

Skaftafell Camp Ground

Skaftafell Visitor Centre & Café

To Hótel Skaftafell (4km)

Ring Rd

ANDERS BLOMQVIST

Cycling on the Danish island of Bornholm (p55)

Vestmanna bird cliffs (p114), Faroe
Islands

GRAEME CORNWALLIS

WAYNE WALTON

Viking grave at Lindholm Høje (p82),
near Aalborg in Denmark

The Great Hall, Frederiksborg Slot (p45), Hillerød, Denmark

JON DAVISON

Strokkur geyser (p232), Geysir, Iceland

Reindeer wandering the streets of Lapland

A tree-lined walking path beside a lake, Tampere (p158), Finland

Kiasma Museum of Contemporary Art (p138), Helsinki

the staggeringly vast and empty *sandur*. It's a peaceful spot full of sights that hark back to its religious beginnings. **Kirkjugólf's** regular basalt columns, cemented with moss, were once mistaken for an old church floor rather than a work of nature, and it's easy to see why. The 'floor' lies in a field about 400m northwest of the petrol station.

Systrastapi (Sisters' Pillar) marks the spot where two nuns were reputedly executed and buried, after sleeping with the devil and other no-nos. Legend says one was innocent, proved when flowers bloomed on her grave. **Systrafoss** is the prominent waterfall near the hotel. The lake **Systravatn**, a short saunter up the cliffs, was once a bathing place for nuns.

The Laki eruptions of 1783 caused utter devastation to the area. Like a vicious planetary stomach ulcer, over 30 billion tonnes of lava spewed from the Laki fissure, the largest recorded flow from a single eruption. Day trips from Kirkjubæjarklaustur visit the still-volatile **Lakagígar area**, with its spectacular 25km-long crater row.

Tours

To access the Lakagígar craters, take the 9½-hour **Destination Iceland** (☎ 591 1020; www .dice.is) tour (Ikr5000, pay on the bus). It departs from Hótel Kirkjubæjarklaustur at 9am daily from 1 July to 31 August.

Sleeping & Eating

Kirkjubæ II camping ground (☎ /fax 407 4612; per person Ikr550; ☉ Jun-Aug) A popular choice in a quiet, green location above the town. Offers hot showers, kitchen and laundry facilities.

Hotel Klaustri (☎ 487 4838; fax 487 4877; Klausturvegur 4; sb/s/d Ikr1300/6000/8300; ☉ mid-Jun–mid-Aug; ☒) In the school at the end of the village, accommodation is in private rooms or classrooms; cooking facilities available.

Hótel Kirkjubæjarklaustur (☎ 487 4900; www .icehotels.is; Klausturvegur 6; s/d Ikr 11,200/15,400) A 56-roomed beast of a business hotel. The rooms are rather bland but the staff are charming. The **restaurant** (mains Ikr1900-3900) has an à la carte menu with typical Icelandic mains and some unusual starters – snails, anyone?

Systrakaffi (☎ 487 4848; Lausturvegur; light meals Ikr350-1100, mains Ikr950-2500; ☉ 10am-midnight, 10am-2am Fri & Sat Jun-Aug) The most atmospheric place for a meal. This ambient little café sells hamburgers, pizzas and reasonably priced Icelandic fish and meat dishes.

For cheap grilled snacks, there's the **Skaftárskáli petrol station** (☎ 487 4628).

Getting There & Away

From 1 June to 14 September, the BSÍ/Austurleið-SBS bus between Reykjavík and Höfn, setting off daily from both places at 8.30am, stops at Kirkjubæjarklaustur and Skaftafell. It passes Kirkjubæjarklaustur at 1.30pm eastbound (Ikr4380) and 12.40pm westbound (Ikr3160), and Skaftafell at 2.35pm eastbound and 11.10am westbound.

From 18 June to 4 September, there's also a direct bus from Reykjavík at 8.30am daily, which goes by the scenic inland route, arriving at 6.30pm in Kirkjubæjarklaustur and 7.30pm in Skaftafell (Ikr7580). Westbound, it leaves Kirkjubæjarklaustur at 9am and Skaftafell at 8am.

ÞÓRSMÖRK

The stunning glacial valley of Þórsmörk (Woods of Thor) boasts weird rock formations, twisting gorges, a singing cave, mountain flowers and icy streams. Its proximity to Reykjavík (130km) makes it a popular spot in summer, when tents pile up and the camping grounds become partyville. You don't have to go far, though, to escape the crowds.

Wild camping is prohibited, but the three Þórsmörk huts have **tent sites** (per person Ikr600) around them. The huts themselves have showers and cooking facilities. They're heaving at weekends, so book ahead.

For **Þórsmörk hut** (sb Ikr1700) book through **Ferðafélag Íslands** (☎ 568 2533; www.fi.is; Mörkin 6, IS-108 Reykjavík). Bookings for **Básar hut** (sb Ikr1600) are through **Útivist** (☎ 562 1000; www .utivist.is; Laugavegur 178, IS-101 Reykjavík). For **Húsadalur hut** (sb Ikr1600) book through bus company **Austurleið-SBS** (☎ 545 1717; www.austurleid.is; Vatnsmýrarvegur 10, IS-101 Reykjavík).

From June to September, buses run between Reykjavík and Húsadalur (over the hill from Þórsmörk) at 8.30am daily and at 5pm Monday to Friday (Ikr3470, four hours).

VESTMANNAEYJAR

pop 4344

The 15 Vestmannaeyjar islands were formed by submarine volcanoes around 11,000 years ago. In 1963, sulky-looking Surtsey rose from the waves, the archipelago's newest addition. Ten years later, unforgettable pictures of Heimaey were broadcast across the globe

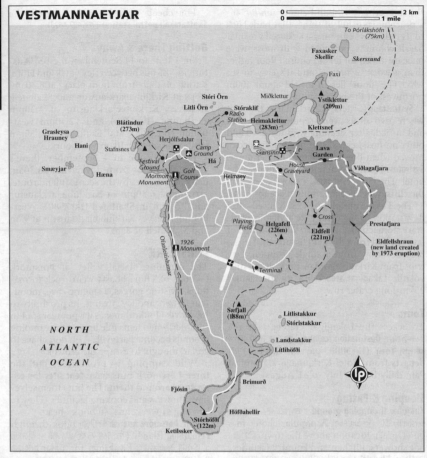

VESTMANNAEYJAR

when a huge eruption buried a third of the town under 30 million tonnes of lava.

Heimaey is the only inhabited island. Behind the sheltered harbour loom dramatic *klettur* (escarpments); red Eldfell and conical Helgafell rise ominously in front of it. Heimaey's cliffs are a breeding ground for 10 million puffin pairs. On summer nights, the townsfolk help confused pufflings find their way to sea...then catch the adults later for food!

The **tourist office** (☎ 481 3555; www.eyjar.is /eyjar; Skildingavegur) is in the ferry terminal ticket hall. There are Sparisjóðurinn and Íslandsbanki banks with ATMs near the post office. Pizza 67 (opposite) has an Internet connection for Ikr300 per half hour.

Sights & Activities

Vestmannaeyjar Natural History Museum (Fiska-og Náttúrugripasafn; ☎ 481 1997; Heðarvegur 12; adult/child 6-18 yrs Ikr300/100; 🕙 11am-5pm mid-May–mid-Sep, 3-5pm Sat & Sun mid-Sep–mid-Apr) has an aquarium of highly hideous Icelandic fish (with evocative names like *tröllakrabbi* and *sædjöfull*) and a live video link to a puffin colony. The **folk museum** (Byggðasafn; ☎ 481 1184; Raðhússtræti; adult/child 6-18 yrs Ikr300/100; 🕙 11am-5pm mid-May–mid-Sep, 3-5pm Sat & Sun mid-Sep–mid-Apr) features fascinating photos of Heimaey's 1973 evacuation. The explosive **Volcano Show** (☎ 481 3366; Heiðarvegur; admission Ikr600) plays at the local cinema, along with films on whales and puffin rappelling.

There's an eerie **House Graveyard** where beloved homes rest in peace, about 5m beneath the lava flow. Further down towards the harbour is **Skansinn**, a ruinous 15th-century fort built by English marauders.

Opportunities for **hiking** abound, including the walk to Stórhöfði and climbs of Helgafell and Eldfell. It's a treacherous but exhilarating 40 minutes to the top of **Stóraklif**.

Tours

Viking Tours (☎ 488 4884; www.boattours.is; Suðurgerður 4) run various boat and whale-watching trips. The price depends on numbers.

Sleeping

Heimaey fills up quickly after the ferry arrives so book accommodation in advance.

Herjólfsdalur Camp Ground (☎ 481 2075; per person Ikr700) Nestled under Stóraklif, the sheltered camping ground has hot showers and cooking facilities.

Gistiheimilið Erna (☎ 481 2112; gisting@simnet.is; Kirkjubæjarbraut 15; sb/made-up bed/apt Ikr1800/2800/10,000) On the edge of the 1973 lava flow is a great budget choice. This friendly family home has cooking facilities, laundry, and a TV in every room. The apartment fits eight people.

Gistiheimilið Hreiðrlð (☎ 481 1045; http://tourist.eyjar.is; Faxastígur 33; sb/s/d Ikr1700/3400/5600) Run by the exceedingly sweet and helpful volcano-show people, this winning guesthouse has a kitchen, cosy TV lounge, and yellowing collection of whalebones in the garden.

Hótel Eyjar (☎ 481 3636; www.hoteleyjar eyjar.is; Bárustígur 2; s/d Ikr6200/9400) Huge, comfortable rooms are more like self-contained flats. The glass walled dining room lets you gawk at passers-by as you eat brekky (Ikr800).

Also recommended:
Gistiheimilið Heimir (☎ 481 2929; fax 481 2912; Heiðarvegur 1; sb/s/d Ikr1800/2800/5600) Cheap accommodation convenient for that 8.15am ferry crossing.
Gistiheimilið Árný (☎ /fax 481 2082; Illugagata 7; sb/s/d Ikr2700/3700/6000, Ikr300 extra with cooking facilities) Upstairs rooms have epic views, and the owner prays for a sound sleep for all her guests!
Gistiheimilið Hvíld (☎ 481 1230; www.simnet.is/hvild; Höfðavegur 16; sb/s/d Ikr1500/3500/5400) Handy for those travelling by plane.

Eating

Café Maria (☎ 481 3160; Skólavegur 1; mains Ikr980-3150; 11.30am-1.30pm Mon-Fri, 11.30am-1pm Sat & Sun) A pleasant coffee house serving crepes, sandwiches and, yes, puffin.

Lanterna (☎ 481 3393; Bárustígur 11; mains Ikr1300-3100) This cosy, dim, wood-panelled place specialises in Vestmannaeyjar delicacies, including puffin plain or smoked.

Pizza 67 (☎ 481 1567; Heiðarvegur 5; pizza Ikr950-1350; 🖳) Feathered friends are firmly off the menu: chomp crunchy garlic bread instead in a publike atmosphere.

Fjólan (☎ 481 3663; Vestmannabraut 28; mains from Ikr2000) Hótel Þórshamar's top-quality restaurant whips up a bargain lunch (Ikr850) between noon and 1.30pm Monday to Friday.

Cheap drive-through grills include **Toppurinn** (☎ 481 3410; Heiðarvegur), **Tvisturinn** (☎ 481 3410; Heiðarvegur 10) and **Skýlið** (☎ 481 1445) at the Esso garage by the harbour. Fast-food meals cost Ikr300 to Ikr2000.

There are two supermarkets for self-caterers, on Vesturvegur and Strandvegur.

Getting There & Away

Íslandsflug (☎ 481 3300; www.islandsflug.is) flies twice daily to/from Reykjavík (Ikr6900).

The ferry **Herjólfur** (☎ 481 3413; www.herjolfur .is) sails from 1 May to 31 August from Vestmannaeyjar to Þorlákshöfn. It leaves at 8.15am and 4pm from Sunday to Friday (8.15am only on Saturday), returning at noon and 7.30pm (noon only on Saturday). The crossing takes 2¾ hours. Out of season, there are fewer departures. The one-way fare per adult/child 12 to 15 years is Ikr1700/850. Destination Iceland runs buses (Ikr950) between Reykjavík and Þorlákshöfn to connect with the ferry, leaving the city at 11am and 5.50pm (11am only on Saturday) and returning 11.10am and 7pm (11.10am only on Saturday).

THE INTERIOR

The vast, barren interior of Iceland is one of Europe's greatest wilderness areas. Gazing across the expanses, you could imagine yourself in Tibet, Mongolia or even on the moon – the Apollo astronauts held training exercises here before the 1969 lunar landings. The interior is only really accessible in July and August. This is seriously remote wilderness: there are practically no services, accommodation, bridges, mobile-phone signals, and no guarantees if things go wrong. Careful preparations are essential.

ROUTES OF CENTRAL ICELAND

Historically, the interior routes were used as summer short cuts between the northern and southern coasts, places of terror to be traversed as quickly as possible. Some *útilegumenn* (outlaws) fled into these harsh highlands: those who survived gained legendary status, like the superhuman Grettir or Fjalla-Eyvindar, an Icelandic Robin Hood/Butch Cassidy figure.

Routes described in this section are suited to summer-only, and are strictly for high-clearance 4WD vehicles. It's recommended that vehicles travel in pairs.

Most mountain huts are run by **Ferðafélag Íslands** (☎ 568 2533; www.fi.is; Mörkin 6, IS-108 Reykjavík): book hut space in advance, as accommodation is on a first-come, first-served basis.

The country map at the beginning of this chapter shows the following routes.

Kjölur Route

Historically, the Kjölur Route (F35) was the least popular – it was believed to be infested with bloodthirsty outlaws. Today, it's a favourite with visitors: it's greener and more hospitable than the Sprengisandur route, and forms a neat short cut between Reykjavík and Akureyri. The route's name ('Keel') refers to the perceived shape of its topography.

Kjölur's main attraction is **Hveravellir**, a geothermal area of fumaroles and multicoloured hot pools at the northern end of the pass. Ferðafélag Íslands has a 66-person **mountain hut** here, with cooking facilities.

There's a scheduled bus run by **BSÍ** (www.bsi.is; Akureyri ☎ 462 4442; Reykjavík ☎ 591 1000) between Reykjavík and Akureyri (Ikr7400, nine hours) from 21 June to 31 August, departing at 9am from both ends.

Sprengisandur Route

The Sprengisandur Route (F26) may be less interesting than Kjölur, but it does offer some wonderful views of Vatnajökull, Tungnafellsjökull and Hofsjökull, as well as Askja and Herðubreið. The bus (see below) passes the photogenic waterfall **Aldeyjarfoss**, which topples over clustered basalt columns.

A good place to break your journey is **Nýidalur**, where there's a **camping ground** (per person Ikr600), two Ferðafélag Íslands **huts** (sb Ikr1700; ☽ Jul & Aug) and numerous hiking possibilities. A recommended, challenging day hike takes you to the **Vonarskarð Pass** (1000m), a

colourful saddle between Vatnajökull, Tungnafellsjökull and the green Ógöngur hills.

From 18 July to 20 August, BSÍ buses travel between Reykjavík and Mývatn via Sprengisandur. They leave Reykjavík at 8.30am on Sunday, Tuesday and Thursday (Ikr6200, 10 hours), and leave Hótel Reynihlíð (Mývatn) at 8.30am on Monday, Wednesday and Friday.

Öskjuleið Route (Askja Way)

Herðubreið and Askja on the Öskjuleið Route (F88) are the most visited wonders of the Icelandic desert.

HERÐUBREIÐ

Iceland's most distinctive mountain (1682m) has been described as a birthday cake, a cooking pot and a lampshade, but the tourist industry calls it the 'Queen of the Desert'. The track around it makes a nice day hike from **Herðubreiðarlindir**, a grassy oasis created by springs flowing from beneath the lava. There's a **tourist office**, a **camping ground** (per person Ikr 600) and Ferðafélag Íslands' **Þorsteinsskáli Hut** (sb Ikr1600; ☽ Jun-Aug) with stoves.

ASKJA

Askja is an immense 50-sq-km caldera, created by a colossal explosion of tephra in 1875. Part of the volcano's collapsed magma chamber contains the beautiful but treacherous sapphire-blue **Öskjuvatn**, Iceland's deepest lake at 217m. At its northeastern corner is **Víti**, a hot lake in a tephra crater where the water (around 25°C) is ideal for swimming.

Eight kilometres away, **Dreki Hut** (sb Ikr1100) at **Drekagil** (Dragon Ravine) accommodates 20 people. The cold is brutal, and there are no cooking facilities, so go prepared.

TOURS

Mývatn Tours (☎ 464 4196; www.isholf.is/myvatn tours) are good operators, running trips from Reykjahlíð (Mývatn) at 8am on Monday, Wednesday and Friday from 20 June to 14 July (and daily between 15 July and 15 August), if the road is passable. It's a fairly gruelling 11- to 12-hour return trip (Ikr7700), so you may want to break the journey at Drekagil and rejoin the tour later – let the driver know when you want to be picked up.

Kverkfjöll Route

The 108km-long Kverkfjöll Route (F905, F910 and F902) connects Möðrudalur on the Ring Road with the Ferðafélag Íslands' Sigurðarskáli hut. This is 3km from the impressive lower **Kverkfjöll ice caves**, where a hot river flows beneath the glacier, melting shimmering patterns on the ice walls. There are other (less impressive) ice caves higher up the glacier and a **hot waterfall** (30°C) at Hveragil, five hours' return from Sigurðarskáli: ask at the hut for directions.

Tourist information centres sell a Kverkfjöll Mountains & Hvannalindir Area brochure/map (Ikr350). The 85-bed **Sigurðarskáli hut** (sb Ikr1700) and camp site can be booked through Ferðafélag Íslands.

TOURS

The simplest way to visit Kverkfjöll is with **Ice & Fire Expeditions** (www.sba.is; 3-day tour Ikr18,700; Akureyri ☎ 550 0770; Reykjavík ☎ 550 0700), with tours departing from Akureyri (8.30am), Húsavík (9.45am) or Mývatn (11am) on Mondays from 5 July to 23 August. Tours are just transport and a guide: you must organise your own accommodation and food. Warm clothing, a thick sleeping bag and strong boots are essential.

FJALLABAK NATURE RESERVE

The Fjallabak Route (F208) is a spectacular alternative to the coast road between Hella and Kirkjubæjarklaustur. It passes through the scenic nature reserve to **Landmannalaugar**, an area of rainbow-coloured rhyolite peaks, rambling lava flows, blue lakes and hot springs which can hold you captive for days. Much of the route is along (and in!) rivers and therefore unsuitable for 2WD vehicles.

The star attractions around Landmannalaugar are: **Laugahraun**, a convoluted lava field; the soothing **hot springs** 200m west of the Landmannalaugar hut; multicoloured vents at **Brennisteinsalda**; the incredible red crater lake **Ljótipollur**; and the blue lake **Frostastaðavatn**, just over the rhyolite ridge north of Landmannalaugar. **Bláhnúkur**, immediately south of Laugahraun, offers a scree scramble and fine views from the 943m peak.

Ferðafélag Íslands' **hut** (sb Ikr1700) at Landmannalaugar accommodates 115 people on a first-come, first-served basis, and books up quickly with tour groups and club members. Others will probably have to use the **camping ground** (per person Ikr600), which has toilet and shower facilities.

Getting There & Away

From 18 June to 4 September, **BSÍ/Austurleið-SBS** (☎ 545 1717) runs a scheduled Reykjavík–Skaftafell bus which goes by the scenic inland route (weather permitting), departing from Reykjavík at 8.30am and from Skaftafell at 8am. Reykjavík to Landmannalaugar costs Ikr4200 each way (5½ hours).

LANDMANNALAUGAR TO ÞÓRSMÖRK TREK

The trek from Landmannalaugar to Þórsmörk deserves the same fame as great world walks like the Inca Trail – get going before it gets too well known. The best map of the route is Landmælingar Íslands' *Þórsmörk/Landmannalaugar* (1:100,000).

The track is usually passable mid-July to early September. You shouldn't have any problems if you're in reasonable condition, but don't take the walk lightly: it requires substantial river crossings, all-weather gear, sturdy boots and sufficient food and water.

Most people walk the track from north to south (because of the net altitude loss) in three to four days. Some continue on to Skógar, making it a six-day trip (which can be difficult in bad weather).

Public huts along the track now have wardens, although dates when they're there vary from year to year. Wardens can answer questions and provide information on trail conditions. Huts may be booked out by tour groups, so check with Ferðafélag Íslands in Reykjavík before you set out.

From Landmannalaugar hut, cross the **Laugahraun** lava field and ascend **Brennisteinsalda** (840m). Cross some rhyolite hills, then descend to the steaming vents at **Stórihver** and continue across the moors (covered in obsidian chunks and extensive snowfields) and a mountain pass to the **Hrafntinnusker hut**. From Hrafntinnusker, the track bounces over parallel rhyolite ridges before ascending steeply to a ridge studded with hot springs and fumaroles. Cross more ridges of descending altitude then drop steeply from the **Jökultungur** ridge into the **Álftavatn** valley, where a 4WD track leads to two **huts**.

There are several stream crossings south of Álftavatn; after 5km, you'll pass the privately owned **Hvanngil** hut and camping ground. Cross the footbridge over the Kaldaklofskvísl, follow the route posted 'Emstrur/Fljótshlíð' and ford the knee-deep Bláfjallakvísl. The

LANDMANNALAUGAR–ÞÓRSMÖRK TREK

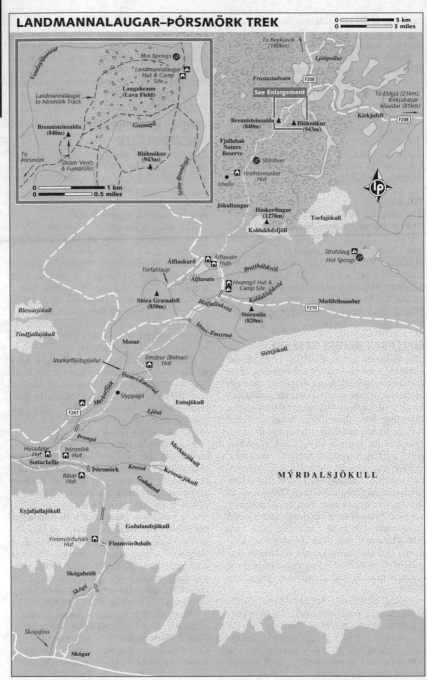

0 — 5 km
0 — 3 miles

Enlargement:
Vondugígaquar
Hot Springs
Landmannalaugar Hut & Camp Site
Laugahraun (Lava Field)
Landmannalaugar to Þórsmörk Track
Brennisteinsalda (840m)
Grænagil
To Þórsmörk
Steam Vents & Fumaroles
Bláhnúkur (943m)
Stóra-Brandsgil
0 — 1 km
0 — 0.5 miles

To Reykjavík (180km)
Ljótipollur
Frostastaðavatn F208
See Enlargement
To Eldgjá (21km); Kirkjubæjarklaustur (81km)
Kirkjufell F208
Brennisteinsalda (840m) ▲ Bláhnúkur (943m)
Fjallabak Nature Reserve
Störihver
Hrafntinnusker Hut
Íshellir
Jökultungur
Háskerðingur (1278m)
Kaldaklofsfjöll
Torfajökull
Álftaskarð Álftavatn Huts
Torfahlaup
Álftavatn
Bratthálskvísl
Strútslaug Hot Springs
Hvanngil Hut & Camp Site
Kaldaklofskvísl
Stóra Grænafell (850m)
Bláfjallakvísl
Mælifellssandur F210
Blessárjökull
Stórasúla (820m)
Tindfjallajökull
Innri-Emstruá
Sléttjökull
Mosar
Markarfljótsgljúfur
Emstrur (Botnar) Hut
Fremri-Emstruá
Markarfljót
Slyppugil
Entujökull
F261
Ljósá
Húsadalur Hut
Þórsmörk Hut
Prongá
Merkurjökull
Sottarhellir
Básar Hut
Þórsmörk Krossá
Krossárjökull
Goðaland
MÝRDALSJÖKULL
Eyjafjallajökull
Goðalandsjökull
Fimmvörðuháls Hut Fimmvörðuháls
Skógaheiði
Skógá
Skógafoss
Skógar

track enters a lonely and surreal 5km stretch of black sand and pumice desert, skirting the pyramid-shaped peak, **Stórasúla**. The next barrier is the river **Innri-Emstruá**, which is bridged but may have a knee-deep side channel. After the bridge, continue up to the crest and watch on your left for the 'FÍ Skáli' signpost, which directs you through a desolate desert to the **Botnar** (Emstrur) huts.

Cross a small heath then drop steeply to cross the roiling **Fremri-Emstruá** on a small footbridge. From there, the trail is relatively flat to the Ljósá footbridge. Over the next hill is the more difficult unbridged river **Þrongá**. The onward route on the opposite bank isn't obvious; look for a V-shaped ravine just west of the marked crossing point. There, the track enters the **Þórsmörk** woodland. When you reach a junction, the right fork leads to Austurleið's **Húsadalur hut** and the left fork to the Ferðafélag Íslands' **Þórsmörk hut**. Camping is restricted to sites near the huts. For more on Þórsmörk, see p249.

ICELAND DIRECTORY

ACCOMMODATION

Iceland has hundreds of accommodation options, including farmhouses and summer hotels in rural schools. Many hostels and guesthouses offer sleeping-bag accommodation (designated 'sb' in this guide), a bed without sheets, duvet or blankets where you use your own sleeping bag. This is a real money-saver, costing a fraction of what you would pay for the same bed with sheets.

In this chapter, accommodation has been listed in price order; budget is defined as a bed for Ikr4000 or less; mid-range places offer singles for Ikr4000 to Ikr8500 and doubles for Ikr5200 to Ikr11,400; and top-end places charge from Ikr8500/11,500 (singles/doubles). Prices given are for summer (June to August); outside peak season, these may drop by up to a third. Many places close in winter; check accommodation in advance.

Camping

Make sure your tent is up to the Icelandic weather: storm-force winds and deluges aren't uncommon in summer. Campfires are not allowed, so bring a stove. Butane cartridges and petroleum fuels are available in petrol stations and hardware shops.

Tjaldsvæði (organised camping grounds) are found in most towns and at rural farmhouses, and open from mid-May to September. Some have washing machines, cooking facilities and hot showers, others may just have a cold-water tap and toilet block. Camping costs from Ikr500 to Ikr900 per person.

Wild camping is possible in some areas (although in national parks and nature reserves, it's restricted to designated sites), and farmers may let you camp on their land for free if asked. Standard rules apply: leave sites as you find them, use biodegradable soaps for washing up, carry out rubbish, and bury toilet waste away from surface water.

Edda Hotels & Summer Hotels

There are 16 **Edda Hótels** (☎ 444 4000; www.hotel edda.is) run by Icelandair Hotels, which open in the summer. They're based in schools, and offer accommodation ranging from sleeping-bag accommodation in classroom dormitories to more conventional lodging. All have restaurants, and many have geothermal pools. Sleeping-bag accommodation starts at Ikr1100 per person, and singles/doubles start at Ikr5000/6400.

Other town and village schools operate their own private summer hotels, including the University of Iceland in Reykjavík, which runs the summer Icelandic Hotel Garður (p227) in its halls of residence.

Emergency Huts

ICE-SAR (Icelandic Association for Search & Rescue; ☎ 570 5900; www.icesar.is) and **Félag Íslenskra Bifreiðaeigenda** (Icelandic Automobile Association; ☎ 562 9999; www.fib.is) maintain bright-orange huts on mountain passes and remote coastlines, only to be used in dire emergency. They are stocked with food, fuel and blankets.

Farmhouse Accommodation

Across Iceland, many rural farmhouses offer camp sites, sleeping-bag space and B&B. Facilities vary: some farms provide meals or have guest kitchens; some have hot pots; and some can organise huntin', shootin' and fishin' trips or horse rental. From September to May, book accommodation in advance.

Around 125 farmhouses are members of **Ferðaþjónusta Bænda** (Icelandic Farm Holidays; Map pp220-2; ☎ 570 2700; www.farmholidays.is; Síðumúli 13, IS-108 Reykjavík), which publishes an annual listings guide.

Guesthouses

There are various types of *gistiheimilið* (guesthouses), from private homes that let rooms to custom-built motels. Most are comfortable, homey places, with kitchens and TV lounges, and a buffet-style breakfast on offer (either included in the price, or for around Ikr800 extra). Some also offer sleeping-bag accommodation – a godsend if you're on a tight budget.

As a general guide, sleeping-bag accommodation costs Ikr1500 to Ikr3000 (usually excluding breakfast); double rooms range from Ikr4200 to Ikr10,500; self-contained flats start from Ikr5600 to Ikr12,500.

A high percentage of places open from mid-May to August only; students often take over Reykjavík guesthouses from September to May.

Hotels

Every major town has at least one upmarket hotel, usually with bland but comfortable rooms and all the expected amenities. Prices for singles/doubles start at Ikr6000/7000, including a buffet breakfast.

Mountain Huts

Private walking clubs and touring organisations maintain *sæluhús* (mountain huts) on popular hiking routes around the country, mostly in wilderness areas. Accommodation is a sleeping-bag space in a communal hut, some with cooking facilities, wardens and space to camp. The huts are open to anyone (members get a discount).

The main mountain-hut provider is **Ferðafélag Íslands** (Icelandic Touring Club; Map pp220-2; ☎ 568 2533; www.fi.is; Mörkin 6, IS-108 Reykjavík), with 22 huts on its books. Sleeping-bag space costs nonmembers from Ikr1100 to Ikr1700, depending on each hut's facilities; camping (where available) is around Ikr500 per person. It's highly advisable to book in advance as places fill quickly.

Útivist (Map pp220-2; ☎ 562 1000; www.utivist.is; Laugavegur 178, IS-105 Reykjavík) operates huts at Goðaland and Fimmvörðuháls along the Þórsmörk to Skógar route.

Youth Hostels

Iceland has a network of 25 superb youth hostels, administered by the **Bandalag Íslenskra Farfugla** (Icelandic Hostel Association; Map pp220-2; ☎ 553 8110; www.hostel.is; Sundlaugavegur 34, IS-105 Reykjavík). All hostels have hot showers, cooking facilities, luggage storage and sleeping-bag accommodation. If you don't have a sleeping bag, you can hire sheets and blankets (Ikr500 per stay).

If you're planning to stay in hostels, join **Hostelling International** (HI; www.hihostels.com) before you arrive to benefit from HI member discounts. For a dorm bed, HI members/ nonmembers pay around Ikr1800/Ikr2100 (children aged five to 12 years pay half price), with a surcharge of Ikr1000 if you want a room to yourself. Breakfast (where available) costs Ikr700 to Ikr900 extra.

ACTIVITIES

Dogsledding

For exhilarating, summertime glacier-top action, driving your own huskies is hard to beat. Contact **Dog Steam Tours** (☎ 487 7747; www.dogsledding.is) for further information.

Fishing

Salmon fishing seems like a great idea but a one-day licence may cost anything up to Ikr200,000, making your catch some of the world's most expensive fish! However, you can fish for rainbow trout, sea trout and arctic char on a more reasonably priced voucher system. Trout fishing runs from April to mid-September but ice fishing is possible in some areas in winter. For further information, contact the **National Angling Association** (☎ 553 1510; www.angling.is).

Hiking, Trekking & Mountaineering

The best way to see the country is undoubtedly on foot, whether on an afternoon hike or a two-week wilderness trek. However, the weather can leave careful plans in tatters: rain is common and snow may fall in any season at higher altitudes. The finest months for walking in the highlands are July, August and September. At other times, some routes will be impassable without complete winter gear and unbridged rivers can be difficult to cross at any time of year. Tough boots are needed for negotiating lava fields.

Use caution when walking with children, especially in fissured areas like Mývatn and Þingvellir, where narrow cracks in the earth can be hundreds of metres deep.

You can hike or trek in many areas (including national parks and nature reserves), the most popular being Hornstrandir (p236),

Mývatn (p242), Skaftafell (p248) and Land-mannalaugar to Þórsmörk (p253). With proper equipment and maps, you'll find many other trekking opportunities. If you're into mountaineering, there are some serious routes, including Hvannadalshnúkur (2119m), Iceland's highest peak.

For details on hiking and mountaineering, contact **Ferðafélag Íslands** (☎ 568 2533; www.fi.is; Mörkin 6, IS-108 Reykjavík; ☼ 9am-5pm Mon-Fri summer, noon-5pm Mon-Fri winter), or **Íslenski Alpa-klúbburinn** (☎ 581 1700; Mörkin 6, IS-108 Reykjavík).

See the Reykjavík Shopping section (p231) for outdoor equipment/tent-hire places.

Horse Riding

The Icelandic horse (*Equus scandinavicus*) was brought over by the first settlers, and has been prominent in the development of the country. These sweet-natured, small but sturdy animals are perfectly suited to the rough Icelandic terrain and are still used for farm work. They are also ridden recreationally, and are known for their *tölt*, a smooth, distinctive gait which makes riding easy, even for beginners.

You can hire horses via farms and tour agencies throughout the country, with a one-hour/one-day ride costing about Ikr2000/12,000. In September, you can also volunteer for the *réttir* (sheep roundup): contact local tourist offices to make arrangements.

Skiing

Skiers who enjoy out-of-the-way slopes will find some pleasant no-frills skiing in Iceland. In winter, nordic skiing is possible throughout the country, and in the highland areas it continues until early July. The greatest drawbacks are the lack of winter transport in rural areas and almost constant bitterly cold winds. Both Reykjavík and Akureyri have winter resorts for downhill skiing, and a summer ski school operates at Kerlingarfjöll near Hofsjökull in central Iceland.

Swimming

Thanks to an abundance of geothermal heat, every town has at least one *sundlaug* or *sundhöll* (public swimming hall), some with saunas, Jacuzzis and slides. Admission costs around Ikr250/125 per adult/child. There are also natural hot springs, eg at Landmannalaugar (p253).

Whale-Watching

Iceland is one of the best places to see whales and dolphins. The quiet, oak-hulled boats used by most companies here minimise disruption to the creatures and can get astonishingly close. Regular sailings depart from Húsavík (p241), Reykjavík (p223) and Hafnarfjörður (p233), among other places. A three-hour trip costs around Ikr3500, and there are sailings from mid-May to September (in winter, the whales migrate south).

BUSINESS HOURS

Banking hours are 9.15am to 4pm Monday to Friday. Most post offices open from 8.30am or 9am to 4.30pm or 5pm Monday to Friday. Restaurants and cafés tend to close at 10pm or 11pm, although in Reykjavík some eating places transform into bars or clubs, staying open till 1am weekdays and up to 6am on Friday and Saturday.

Weekday shopping hours are 9am to 6pm; shops usually close by 4pm on Saturday; and most places are shut on Sunday, except in the capital. Petrol stations, kiosks and some supermarkets are open from 9am to between 10pm and 11.30pm daily.

CHILDREN

Icelanders have a relaxed attitude to kids, but there aren't many activities provided specifically for them. Frequent bad weather might put you off family camping, but everyone can enjoy a ride on mild-mannered Icelandic horses (see Horse Riding left).

Children aged two to 11 years pay half fare on Flugfélag Íslands (Air Iceland) flights and tours, and are charged half price for farmhouse and some other accommodation. Destination Iceland buses and tours charge half fare for ages four to 11. There's a 50% discount at pools and admission to museums and cinemas varies from full price to free.

Every town has an open-air swimming pool, which will delight waterbabies. Reykjavík contains some attractions suitable for little kids, such as the family fun park and zoo (p223) and feeding the birds on Tjörnin (p224). The most suitable museums for older children are the open-air Árbæjarsafn (p224) and the dramatic Saga Museum (p223).

CUSTOMS

Visitors are permitted to import up to Ikr13,000 worth of food provided it doesn't weigh more than 3kg and doesn't include animal products. Those aged over 18 years may bring in 200 cigarettes or 250g of other tobacco products. Those aged over 20 years may import duty-free 1L of spirits (22% to 79% alcohol) and 1L of wine (less than 22%); or 1L of spirits and 6L of foreign beer; or 1L of wine and 6L of beer; or 2.25L of wine.

To prevent contamination, recreational fishing equipment requires a veterinarian's certificate stating that it has been immersed for at least 10 minutes in an approved disinfectant solution. Alternatively, officials can disinfect the gear when you arrive (Ikr1800 to Ikr2200). Riding clothing and equipment are subject to similar regulations.

Vehicle import duty is waived for students and visitors staying less than one month (extendable up to 12 months), but vehicles cannot be sold without payment of duty.

For a full list of customs regulations, see www.tollur.is.

DANGERS & ANNOYANCES

Iceland has a low crime rate, police don't carry guns, and prisoners go home on public holidays. People aren't the danger here – it's nature you need to be wary of! In geothermal areas avoid thin crusts of lighter coloured soil around steaming fissures and mud pots. Snowfields may overlie fissures, sharp lava chunks, or slippery slopes of scoria (volcanic slag). Don't underestimate the weather: only attempt isolated hiking and glacier ascents if you know what you're doing.

DISABLED TRAVELLERS

Many hotels, restaurants and large shops have facilities for people with disabilities. The airlines can take disabled passengers, as can two of the coastal ferries, the *Baldur* and the *Herjólfur*. Flugfélag Íslands (Air Iceland) offers discounts to disabled travellers. Facilities aren't available on scheduled bus services, but tours on specially equipped buses can be arranged. For details, contact the tourist information centre in Reykjavík, or the organisation for the disabled, **Sjálfsbjörg** (Map pp220-2; ☎ 550 0300; www.sjalfsbjorg.is; Hátún 12, IS-105 Reykjavík).

EMBASSIES & CONSULATES
Iceland Embassies & Consulates

A full list of Iceland's embassies and consulates is available at www.mfa.is. Icelandic representation abroad includes:

Australia (☎ 02-9365 7345; iceland@bigpond.net.au; 16 Birriga Rd, Bellevue Hill, Sydney, 2000, NSW)
Canada (☎ 613-482 1944; www.iceland.org/ca; 360 Albert St, Ste 710, Ottawa ON K1R 7X7)
Denmark (☎ 33 18 10 50; www.iceland.org/dk; Strandgade 89, DK-1401 Copenhagen K)
Faroe Islands (☎ 30 11 01; solva@faroeyard.fo; JC Svabosgøta 31, Box 65, Tórshavn)
France (☎ 01-44 17 32 85; www.iceland.org/fr; 8 Ave Kléber, F-75116 Paris)
Germany (☎ 030-5050 4000; www.iceland.org/de; Rauchstrasse 1, DE-10787 Berlin)
Greenland (☎ 98 12 93; arcwon@greennet.gl; c/o Hotel Angmagssalik, Sulup Aqq B725, Postbox 117, Tasiilaq)
Ireland (☎ 01 872 9299; jgg@goregrimes.ie; Cavendish House, Smithfield, Dublin)
The Netherlands (☎ 431 3114; consulate.iceland@bdn.ne; 2nd fl, Strawinskylaan 3037, Amsterdam)
New Zealand (☎ 04-385 7345; denis@foot.co.nz; c/o Foot Law, 18-24 Allen St, Courtenay Pl, Wellington)
Norway (☎ 2323 7530; www.iceland.org/no; Stortingsgata 30, NO-0244 Oslo)
Sweden (☎ 08 442 8300; www.iceland.org/se; Kommendörsgatan 35, SE-114 58 Stockholm)
UK (☎ 020 7259 3999; www.iceland.org/uk; 2a Hans St, London SW1X 0JE)
USA (☎ 202-265 6653; www.iceland.org/us; 1156 15th St NW, Ste 1200, Washington, DC 20005-1704)

Embassies & Consulates in Iceland

The following countries have representation in Reykjavík:
Canada (Map pp226-7; ☎ 575 6500; rkjvk@dfait-maeci.gc.ca; Túngata 14)
Denmark (Map pp226-7; ☎ 575 0300; www4.mmedia.is/rekamb) Hverfisgata 29
France (Map pp226-7; ☎ 551 7621; www.ambafrance.is) Túngata 22
Germany (Map pp226-7; ☎ 530 1100; embager@Internet.is; Laufásvegur 31)
The Netherlands (Map pp220-2; ☎ 553 1002; consulnl@skogarsel.is; Borgartún 33)
Norway (Map pp220-2; ☎ 520 0700; www.noregur.is; Fjólugata 17)
Sweden (Map pp220-2; ☎ 520 1230; sveamb@itn.is; Lágmúli 7)
UK (Map pp226-7; ☎ 550 5100; www.britishembassy.gov.uk; Laufásvegur 31)
USA (Map pp226-7; ☎ 562 9100; www.usa.is; Laufásvegur 21)

FESTIVALS & EVENTS

In addition to the festivals listed below, there are various arts festivals and sports tournaments whose dates vary from year to year.

February

Þorrablót This midwinter feast is marked with knuckle-whitening meals: see p218 for a sample menu.

April

Sumardagurinn Fyrsti (First Day of Summer) Arrives optimistically early on the third Thursday, with Reykjavík holding the biggest carnival-style bash. (The First Day of Winter, **Fyrsti Vetrardagur**, on the third Saturday of October, does not inspire similar merriment.)

May

Arts Festival (www.listahatid.is) Reykjavík hosts this biennial event in even-numbered years, staging local and international theatre performances, films, lectures and music.

June

Sjómannadagurinn, on the first Sunday, is dedicated to seafarers. The Seamen's Union sponsors a party in each coastal town.

Independence Day (17 June) The largest nationwide festival, commemorating the founding of the Republic of Iceland in 1944. Tradition has it that the sun isn't supposed to shine – and it usually doesn't!

Midsummer Is celebrated around 24 June in Iceland, but with less fervour than on the Scandinavian mainland.

August

Þjóðhátíð Vestmannaeyjar This earth-shaking event occurs in early August in Heimaey, commemorating the day in 1874 when foul weather prevented the islanders partying when Iceland's constitution was established.

Verslunarmannahelgi Is held elsewhere in Iceland, on the same weekend as Heimaey's Þjóðhátíð Vestmannaeyjar, with barbecues, horse competitions, camping and family reunions. Wild boozing takes place in the national parks and at Þórsmörk.

Culture Night Held on a Saturday in Reykjavík in mid-August. It's great fun, with art, music, dance and a fireworks finale.

September

Réttir In the highlands, the autumn sheep roundup is an occasion for rural camaraderie and festivities.

October

Iceland Airwaves (www.icelandairwaves.com) This youthful event, in Reykjavík at the end of October, is carving a reputation as one of the world's most cutting-edge music festivals.

GAY & LESBIAN TRAVELLERS

Icelanders generally hold a fairly open attitude towards gays and lesbians. For specific information, contact the gay and lesbian or-

ganisation **Samtökin '78** (Map pp226-7; ☎ 552 7878; www.gayiceland.com; Laugavegur 3, IS-101 Reykjavík).

HOLIDAYS

The following annual holidays are observed in Iceland:

New Year's Day 1 January
Maundy Thursday Thursday before Easter
Good Friday to Easter Monday March/April
First Day of Summer April
Labour Day 1 May
Ascension Day May
Whit Sunday & **Whit Monday** May
Independence Day 17 June
Shop & Office Workers' Holiday First Monday in August
Christmas Eve 24 December (afternoon)
Christmas Day 25 December
Boxing Day 26 December
New Year's Eve 31 December (afternoon)

INTERNET RESOURCES

The **Icelandic Tourist Board** (www.icetourist.is, www.goiceland.org) has detailed country information, as well as tips on organised tours, accommodation and festivals, and lots of useful links. Other tourist-oriented websites include www.east.is, www.northwest.is, www.west.is and www.south.is. Statistical details are on the Internet at www.statice.is.

For information on Reykjavík, see www.visitreykjavik.is and www.whatson.is.

MAPS

For town plans, ask tourist offices for the free *Around Iceland* booklet and the *Map of Reykjavík*.

Landmælingar Íslands (National Land Survey of Iceland; ☎ 430 9000; www.lmi.is; Stillholt 16-18, IS-300 Akranes) publishes several series of high-quality maps covering the whole country, purchasable via its website. Most drivers use the 1:500,000 *Ferðakort Touring Map*, the best general map. Also useful are the 1:25,000 maps of Skaftafell and Þingvellir, the 1:50,000 maps of Vestmannaeyjar and Mývatn, and the 1:100,000 maps of Hornstrandir, Snæfellsnes, and the Landmannalaugar to Þórsmörk trek.

Landmælingar Íslands maps are available from tourist offices and bookshops all over Iceland.

MEDIA
Magazines

The fortnightly *Grapevine* magazine, distributed free in summer, is an excellent read for

Icelandic news and reviews. It's available in Reykjavík and larger towns at tourist offices, hotels and bars.

The informative English-language magazine **Iceland Review** (Map pp220-2; ☎ 512 7575; www.icelandreview.com; Borgartún 23, IS-105 Reykjavík) is available on subscription for US$34 per year (four issues).

Newspapers

Iceland's main daily newspaper is the *Morgunblaðið*. German-, French- and English-language periodicals are available at large bookshops, including Eymundsson's in Reykjavík (p219).

Radio & TV

The English-language BBC World Service is relayed at FM 90.9 in Reykjavík. Icelandic TV stations broadcast subtitled British and American programmes during prime time.

MONEY

The 24.5% Icelandic *söluskattur* (VAT) applies to many goods and services and is included in marked prices. If you spend over Ikr4000 in a shop with the sign 'Iceland Tax-Free Shopping', you'll get a tax-refund coupon worth up to 15% of the cost price. If you spend more than Ikr40,000, present your coupons and goods (except woollens) to customs before your air or ferry check-in (this isn't necessary for purchases between Ikr4000 and Ikr40,000). Collect your refund in cash from the duty-free stores or banks at the airports or from the ferry terminal desk.

Tipping isn't required in Iceland, but tips won't be refused!

ATMs

Cash can be withdrawn from banks using a MasterCard, Visa or Cirrus ATM card; exchange rates for ATM cards are usually good. Maestro, EDC and Electron debit cards are widely accepted.

Credit Cards

MasterCard and Visa can be used at many retail outlets; Diners Club and American Express are rarely accepted. Icelanders use cards for groceries and other small purchases.

Moneychangers

Travellers cheques in foreign denominations, postal cheques and banknotes may be exchanged for Icelandic currency at banks for a small commission (commission-free at Landsbanki Íslands). Beware of using other exchange offices; commissions can reach 8.75% and exchange rates are lower. Any leftover krónur may be exchanged for foreign currency before departure.

POST

The **Icelandic postal system** (Pósturinn; www .postur.is) is reliable and efficient. An airmail letter/postcard to Europe costs Ikr65; to places outside Europe it costs Ikr90.

Poste restante is available in all cities and villages, but Reykjavík is best set up to handle it. Mail should be addressed with your name to Poste Restante, Central Post Office, Pósthússtræti 5, IS-101 Reykjavík, Iceland.

The central post office also has a philatelic desk for stamp collectors.

TELEPHONE & FAX
Fax

Telefax services are available at most public telephone offices and post offices around the country. In Reykjavík, **Síminn** (fax 550 6909; www.siminn.is; Ármúli 25, Reykjavík) or the **Main Post Office** (fax 580 1191; Pósthússtræti 5, Reykjavík) can send and receive faxes (around Ikr230 per page) for you – contact them for details.

Mobile Phones

Most European phones are compatible with the GSM network, used in Iceland; for information, contact your phone company. Mobile phones can be rented from **Síminn** (☎ 550 6000; www.siminn.is; Ármúli 25, Reykjavík), for around Ikr300 per day plus deposit.

Phone Codes

Direct dialling is available to Europe, North America and elsewhere. After dialling the international access code (☎ 00 from Iceland), dial your country code, area/city code and the telephone number.

For dialling into Iceland from abroad, the country code is ☎ 354. There are no area codes: just follow the country code with the seven-digit number.

EMERGENCY NUMBERS

For police, ambulance and fire services in Iceland, dial ☎ 112.

Within Iceland, just dial the seven-digit number. For operator assistance, call ☎ 533 5310. Directory assistance is ☎ 118 (local) or ☎ 1811 (international). Reverse-charge (collect) calls can be made to various countries, and many phones accept credit cards.

Most Icelandic mobile phone numbers begin with the digit '8'.

Phonecards
Card-operated phones can be found in petrol stations, post offices and shopping malls. The smallest-denomination phonecard costs Ikr500, and can be bought from post offices and Síminn telephone offices.

TIME
From late October to late March, Iceland is on the same time as London (GMT/UTC), five hours ahead of New York and 11 hours behind Sydney. Iceland doesn't have daylight-saving time so, in the northern hemisphere summer, it's one hour behind London, four hours ahead of New York and 10 hours behind Sydney.

TOURIST INFORMATION
You'll find tourist offices with friendly staff in towns all over the country. Services are free but a charge may apply to telephone calls made on your behalf. Ask for the useful *Around Iceland* (general tourist guide) and *Áning* (accommodation guide) – both annual and free.

The **Icelandic Tourist Board** (☎ 535 5500, www.icetourist.is; Lækjargata 3, IS-101 Reykjavík) is the umbrella organisation in charge of tourism. The main tourist office in Reykjavík is called **Upplýsingamiðstöð Ferðamála** (Map pp226-7; ☎ 562 3045; www.visitreykjavik.is; Aðalstræti 2).

TOURS
Some of Iceland's best sights are in remote locations where private tours provide the only access. As well as conventional coach tours, you may end up travelling by Super Jeep or snowmobile! Tours often operate like loosely organised bus services, with travellers able to leave and rejoin at any time along the route (but let the driver know when and where you want to be picked up again).

More and more companies are running hiking, rafting, Jeep, horse-riding, whale-watching or photography tours; the following is a brief list of some of the best operators.

Destination Iceland (Map pp220-2; ☎ 591 1020; www.dice.is; BSÍ bus terminal, Vatnsmýrarvegur 10, IS-101 Reykjavík) Inexpensive tours often using small local operators and scheduled bus services. Also organises special-interest tours, eg bird-watching, fishing, cycling.

Dick Phillips (☎ 01434-381440; www.icelandic-travel .com; Whitehall House, Nenthead, Alston, Cumbria, CA9 3PS) British-based Dick Phillips runs a specialist Icelandic travel service, and has decades of experience leading wild hiking and skiing trips.

Ferðafélag Íslands (Map pp220-2; ☎ 568 2533; www .fi.is; Mörkin 6, IS-108 Reykjavík) The Icelandic Touring Club leads summer treks in Hornstrandir, Landmannalaugar and Þórsmörk.

Nonni Travel (☎ 461 1841; www.nonnitravel.is; Brekkugata 5, PO Box 336, IS-602 Akureyri) Rafting, horseback, whale-spotting and Super Jeep tours; specialists in excursions to Greenland.

Reykjavík Excursions (Map pp226-7; ☎ 562 4422; www.re.is; Bankastræti 2, Reykjavík) Day trips, cruises, longer excursions, and themed golf, horse and history tours tying in with festivals.

Útivist (Map pp220-2; ☎ 562 1000; www.utivist.is; Laugavegur 178, IS-105 Reykjavík) Day trips and tours from the BSÍ bus terminal in Reykjavík.

VISAS
The Schengen Agreement means that those from Austria, Belgium, Denmark, Finland, France, Germany, Greece, Holland, Italy, Luxembourg, the Netherlands, Norway, Portugal, Spain and Sweden can enter Iceland for up to three months as a tourist with a valid identity card.

Citizens of the European Economic Area (EEA), including Ireland and Great Britain, can visit for up to three months on a passport that is valid for at least four months from their date of arrival.

Citizens from America, Australia, New Zealand, Japan and Canada can travel with a passport and without a visa for up to three months within any six-month period, with the time limit beginning on the first entry to any Schengen Agreement nation.

Other nationalities need a visa before arriving in Iceland.

WOMEN TRAVELLERS
Women travelling in Iceland are unlikely to face any problems: Icelanders are generally respectful and gender equality is high. As always, drunken men can be annoying. In Reykjavík, rape-crisis advice is available from **Stígamót** (☎ 562 6868).

TRANSPORT IN ICELAND

GETTING THERE & AWAY

Air

Keflavík Airport (☎ 425 0680; www.keflavikairport.com), located 48km west of Reykjavík, is Iceland's main gateway. Flights to Greenland and the Faroe Islands use Reykjavík Domestic Airport in the city centre.

Flight prices in this section are general indications only, and are for return tickets, unless otherwise specified.

AIRLINES FLYING TO AND FROM ICELAND

Only a few airlines fly to Keflavík international and Reykjavík domestic airports. All have great safety records:

Atlantic Airways (Faroe Islands ☎ 34 10 00; www.atlanticairways.com)
Icelandair (☎ 505 0300; www.icelandair.net)
Iceland Express (☎ 550 0600; www.icelandexpress.com)
Flugfélag Íslands (Air Iceland; ☎ 570 3030; www.airiceland.is)

CONTINENTAL EUROPE

There are direct Icelandair flights to Keflavík from Amsterdam (from around €500), Copenhagen (around Dkr2500), Frankfurt (around €600), Oslo (around Nkr3200), Paris (around €450) and Stockholm (around Skr3900), most of which take approximately three hours. Summer flights to/from Keflavík and Barcelona (from around €650) or Milan (€750) stop in Amsterdam, Copenhagen or London and take between six and nine hours.

Iceland Express does twice-daily flights from Copenhagen to Keflavík (from Dkr1480, three hours).

GREENLAND AND THE FAROE ISLANDS

Flugfélag Íslands flies from Kulusuk (Greenland) to Reykjavík at least five times a week in summer. Fares start at Ikr60,000 return.

Flugfélag Íslands and Atlantic Airways fly between the Faroe Islands and Reykjavík up to four times weekly from April to October. Return fares are around Dkr4000.

UK

Icelandair (☎ 0870 787 4020; www.icelandair.net) and **Iceland Express** (☎ 0870 850 0737; www.iceland express.com) both fly directly from London to Keflavík twice daily, with flights taking three hours. Fares are cheapest if booked over the Internet (from UK£160/135 return for Icelandair/Iceland Express).

From Scotland, Icelandair flies from Glasgow (from UK£180 return, two hours).

From Ireland, the cheapest way is to fly with **Ryanair** (www.ryanair.com) from Dublin to London Stansted, where you can catch the Iceland Express flight to Keflavík.

USA

There are daily Icelandair flights between Keflavík and Boston, and several flights a week between Keflavík and Baltimore, Minneapolis, New York, Orlando and Washington DC. Flying to Britain or Europe, you can also include a free stopover in Iceland. Online return fares from New York to Keflavík cost about US$800; the flight takes around six hours.

Sea

CARGO SHIP

The Icelandic cargo-shipper **Eimskip** (www.eim skip.com) sails the route Rotterdam–Hamburg–Århus–Göteburg–Fredrikstad–Tórshavn–Reykjavík, which takes eight days, returning to Rotterdam via eastern Iceland and Tórshavn only. The shipper can take up to three passengers on each of its vessels *Dettifoss* and *Goðafoss*, although passengers are not accepted from 1 November to 28 February. The trip from Rotterdam costs Ikr57,300 per person.

FERRY

You can travel from the European mainland by ferry. Although this takes longer than flying and isn't much cheaper, it's more environmentally friendly and allows you to take a vehicle.

Smyril Line (www.smyril-line.fo) has a car ferry that sails to Seyðisfjörður in eastern Iceland from Bergen (Norway) or Hanstholm (Denmark), calling at Lerwick (Shetland Islands) and Tórshavn (Faroe Islands). Coming from Hanstholm, you have to spend two days in the Faroes on the way to Iceland. Coming from Bergen, you have to spend two days in the Faroes on the way back: see the website for the full ferry schedule.

The ferry operates from mid-May to mid-September, and has a two-tier fare structure for low season and high season (mid-June to mid-August). Sleeping choices on the ferry comprise couchettes, two- to four-berth cabins, and suites. From Hanstholm to Seyðisfjörður, the one-way adult couchette fare is €240/340 in low/high season. The price for cars varies according to how many passengers there are; to give you an idea, a car plus two passengers sleeping on couchettes costs €595/950 in low/high season. There's a small charge for bicycles. Discounts are available for seniors, students, disabled travellers and children.

Travelling from Britain, **Lerwick Ferries** (☎ 0870 420 1267; www.lerwickferry.co.uk) provides services from Aberdeen or Kirkwall (Orkney) that connect with the Smyril Line in Lerwick.

GETTING AROUND
Air

There's an extensive network of domestic flights in Iceland, the fastest (and sometimes the only) way to get from place to place. Flexible travel plans are essential, though, since schedules are dependent on the weather.

Flight prices given in the chapter are for full-fare one-way tickets; however, there are often Internet offers, and you may be able to snap up standby tickets for up to half price. There are significant discounts for senior citizens, students and children.

The main domestic airline, **Flugfélag Íslands** (Air Iceland; ☎ 570 3030; www.airiceland.is), has daily flights in summer between Reykjavík and Akureyri (Ikr9775, 45 minutes), Egilsstaðir (Ikr11,075, one hour) and Ísafjörður (Ikr9775, 45 minutes).

Íslandsflug (Icebird Airlines; ☎ 570 8090; www.islandsflug.is) operates flights to smaller airstrips in Iceland, including daily flights from Reykjavík to Vestmannaeyjar (Ikr6900, 30 minutes).

Air Iceland offers four-/five-/six-sector air passes costing Ikr28,800/32,700/37,600. These are valid for one month and must be bought outside Iceland. Domestic airport tax (Ikr415) has to be paid on every departure.

There's also a Fly As You Please ticket which gives 12 days of unlimited internal flights for Ikr45,600, excluding airport taxes.

Bicycle
Cycling is one of the best ways to view Iceland's incredible landscape. However, gale-force winds, sandstorms, sleet and sudden flurries of snow sure will add to the challenge! Bring the best waterproofing money can buy; and remember, you can always put your bike on a bus if things become intolerable. A mountain bike is more practical than a touring rig, as many roads are unsurfaced, and it's wise to bring plenty of spares and several puncture repair kits. The Kjölur route through the interior has bridges over all major rivers, so it's accessible to cyclists.

Domestic airlines usually accept bicycles as checked luggage if they're packed up properly. You can carry bikes on the long-distance buses for Ikr500 to Ikr1000, but space may be a problem (July and August).

In areas best suited to cycling, such as Mývatn, Reykjavík and Akureyri, bicycles can be hired for around Ikr1600 per day, plus deposit.

Boat
The main car ferries operating in Iceland are *Herjólfur*, between Þorlákshöfn and Vestmannaeyjar (p251); *Baldur*, between Flatey, Stykkishólmur and Brjánslækur (p235); and *Sæfari*, between Dalvík, Hrísey and Grímsey (p240).

Most bus and ferry timetables are coordinated, and are described in detail in the *Destination Iceland* timetable, available free from bus stations and tourist offices.

Bus
Iceland's integrated long-distance bus network is overseen by **BSÍ** (Bifreiðastöð Íslands; ☎ 562 3320; www.bsi.is), based in the BSÍ bus terminal on Vatnsmýrarvegur in Reykjavík. The booking desk sells tickets, and distributes the free *Independent Traveller* brochure, containing full timetable and fare information. From June to August, there are regular buses to most places on the Ring Road, and to larger towns in the Westfjords. During the rest of the year, the service is limited: check with BSÍ for details.

Bus passes are available from BSÍ, which can save you money on long journeys. The Full-Circle Pass (Hringmiði) allows you to make a complete circuit of the Ring Road in one direction, stopping wherever you like. You can use the pass, costing Ikr23,700, from 21 May to 13 September. There's an extension costing Ikr16,000, enabling you to access the Westfjords via the ferry at Stykkishólmur from 1 June to 31 August.

The Omnibus Pass (Tímamiði) allows unrestricted travel on all except the interior bus routes from 1 May to 13 September. A one-/two-/three-/four-week pass costs Ikr26,390/38,320/46,920/52,000. In winter, a limited version of the one-week pass is available for Ikr15,520.

Car & Motorcycle

AUTOMOBILE ASSOCIATION

The Icelandic national motoring association is **Félag Íslenskra Bifreiðaeigenda** (FÍB; ☎ 562 9999; www.fib.is; Borgartún 33, Reykjavík). Membership is open only to foreigners who take up residency in Iceland, but the FÍB is affiliated with AIT/FIA, ARC Europe and ARC Transistance. This means that if you have a breakdown cover agreement with your local automobile club, you are probably covered by the FÍB in Iceland as well: check first with your organisation.

BRING YOUR OWN VEHICLE

It's relatively easy to bring a vehicle on the ferry from mainland Europe. Drivers must carry the vehicle's registration documents, proof of valid insurance (a 'green card') and an International Driving Permit as well as their home licence. After vehicle inspection, an import permit will be issued which lasts for a month, after which you must export the vehicle or apply for a permit extension. Contact the **Directorate of Customs** (☎ 560 0300; www.tollur.is) for further information.

FUEL & SPARE PARTS

Petrol prices around the country are fixed: unleaded 95 octane *(blýlaust)* costs Ikr98 per litre, and diesel Ikr45. Leaded petrol and LRP (lead replacement petrol) aren't available. Service stations can be quite widely dispersed – make sure you fill up when you have the chance, and carry a jack, jumpleads, spare tyre etc. A puncture on a cold and lonely road is no fun.

HIRE

Although rates are still quite expensive by international standards, prices compare favourably against bus or internal air travel. The cheapest vehicles, such as a Nissan Micra, normally cost from Ikr6900 per day, with unlimited mileage and VAT included.

Rental charges for 4WD vehicles are around twice that. The Reykjavík tourist office keeps details of special offers.

You must be at least 20 years old to rent a car, and will need to show a recognised licence (legally, this should be an International Driving Permit, although some firms are happy just to see your home licence) and pay by credit card.

ROAD CONDITIONS & HAZARDS

Icelandic highways aren't suitable for high-speeds – they're two-lane affairs, often narrowing to a single-lane over bridges, and there are sometimes long unsurfaced sections. Headlight and radiator protection from dust and rocks is advisable. Beware of oncoming cars driving in the middle of the road. For further information, contact **Félag Íslenskra Bifreiðaeigenda** (Icelandic Automobile Association; ☎ 562 9999; www.fib.is; Borgartún 33, IS-105 Reykjavík).

Four-wheel drive vehicles are needed on the F-numbered (interior) highway system. If you're planning on driving through the interior, do so with an accompanying vehicle – there are no services, and glacial rivers and drifting sand pose real threats. It goes without saying that you'll need full tool/repair kits (and the expertise to use them) and emergency supplies. Don't drive off the track: the soil and vegetation are extremely fragile, and wheel scars can last for years.

Current road conditions can be seen on the website of the **Icelandic Meteorological Office** (www.vedur.is/english).

ROAD RULES

Drive on the right and keep your headlights on at all times. The use of seat belts (front and rear) is compulsory. In urban areas, the speed limit is 50km/h or less. On paved/unpaved roads, the speed limit is 90/80km/h. Drink-driving laws are very strict in Iceland and the legal limit is set at 0.05% blood-alcohol content. The penalty for driving over the limit is loss of your licence plus a large fine.

Slow down and/or give way at blind peaks (marked *blindhæð*) and single-breadth bridges (marked *einbreið brú*).

Hitching

Summer hitching is possible but can be inconsistent: long waits are common in most areas, especially the Westfjords. See Hitching in the Transport chapter (p474).

Norway

CONTENTS

NORWAY

A ruggedly beautiful country of high mountains, stunning fjords and blue glaciers, Norway's mainland stretches 2000km from beach towns in the south to treeless Arctic tundra in the north. A further 1000km north, there's Svalbard, Norway's Arctic archipelago. The country offers incredible wilderness hiking, year-round skiing and some of the most scenic ferry, bus and train rides imaginable. Summer days are delightfully long, and in the northernmost parts the sun doesn't set for weeks on end.

In addition to the lure of the spectacular western fjords, Norway boasts several picturesque cities that combine urban sophistication with dramatic settings. Otherwise, take your pick from unspoiled fishing villages and rich historical treasures including Viking ships and medieval stave churches.

Norway retains something of a frontier character and its largest cities are virtually surrounded by forest. There are several extensive, virtually untouched national parks and other wilderness areas to discover.

FAST FACTS

- **Area** 385,155 sq km
- **Capital** Oslo
- **Currency** krone; US$1 = Nkr6.76; £1 = Nkr12.05; €1 = Nkr8.30; A$1 = Nkr4.88; C$1 = Nkr5.30; NZ$1 = Nkr4.53; ¥100 = Nkr6.09
- **Famous for** fjords and skis
- **Official Languages** Bokmål and Nynorsk
- **Phrases** hei (hello), takk (thanks), ja (yes), nei (no), stengt (closed)
- **Telephone Codes** country code ☎ 47; international access code ☎ 00; no telephone area codes

HIGHLIGHTS

- Explore the crooked streets of **Bergen** (p302), whose cafés, nightlife and superb waterside setting combine to great effect
- Experience the sublime beauty of the **Geirangerfjord** (p317), the mountainous channel passing flowering orchards, abandoned farms and top-notch hiking
- Take a ride on the **Oslo–Bergen train** (p302), a seven-hour race over mountainous terrain and snowy plateaus that will ruin all future rail travel
- Enjoy cross-country skiing on the brilliant winter whiteness of **Hardangervidda Plateau** (p298)
- Admire the Lofoten Wall, aurora borealis and other natural wonders from the deck of the **Hurtigruten coastal steamer** (p352)

HOW MUCH?

- **Litre of milk** Nkr12
- **Loaf of bread** Nkr18
- **Bottle of house white wine** Nkr120
- **Newspaper** Nkr15
- **Short taxi ride** Nkr90

LP INDEX

- **Litre of petrol** Nkr9
- **Litre of bottled water** Nkr15
- **An Aass beer** Nkr48
- **Souvenir T-shirt** Nkr100
- **Street snack (kebab)** Nkr35

ITINERARIES

- **One week** Spend two days in Oslo, then travel by rail to Flåm and take a combination boat/bus trip to Bergen along the Sognefjord. Spend two days in Bergen and go on a three-day jaunt through the western fjords, including Fjærland and Geiranger.
- **Two weeks** As for one week, then continue north through Ålesund, Trondheim and Lofoten.

CLIMATE & WHEN TO GO

Due to the warming effects of the Gulf Stream flowing north along the Norwegian coast, the coastal areas have a surprisingly temperate climate. The average winter monthly temperature in Bergen never drops below 0°C, and in Vardø in the far north of the country, the average temperature in December is only -4°C. Mountainous inland areas have a more extreme climate, and temperatures over 30°C in summer and lower than -30°C in winter aren't uncommon. Svalbard has an Arctic climate, with an average July maximum of 6°C in Longyearbyen and January minimums often below -30°C.

Norway is at its best and brightest from May to September. Late spring is a particularly pleasant time: fruit trees are in bloom, daylight hours are long, and most hostels and sights are open but uncrowded. Peak tourist season is mid-June through August.

Midnight-sun days, when the sun never drops below the horizon, extend from 20 April to 21 August at Longyearbyen (Svalbard), 13 May to 29 July at Nordkapp and from 28 May to 14 July in Lofoten. Even southern Norway has full daylight from 4am to 11pm in midsummer.

Unless you're heavily into winter skiing or searching for the aurora borealis of the polar nights, Norway's cold, dark winters are not the prime time to visit.

Check out www.met.no for climate details and forecasts.

HISTORY

Norway's first settlers arrived around 11,000 years ago with the end of the ice age. As the glaciers melted, the earliest hunters and gatherers moved in from Siberia, pursuing migrating reindeer herds. Shortly afterwards, nomadic European hunters arrived in the south of the country. During the Bronze Age, people migrated into southern Norway from Sweden.

Norway's greatest impact on history was during the Viking Age, a period usually dated from the plundering of England's Lindisfarne monastery by Nordic pirates in AD 793. Through the next century, the Vikings conducted raids throughout Europe and established settlements in the Shetland, Orkney and Hebridean islands, the Dublin area (Ireland) and in Normandy (the latter named after the 'North men'). The Viking leader Harald Hårfagre (Fairhair) unified Norway after the decisive naval battle at Hafrsfjord near Stavanger in AD 872; King

NORWAY

0 [========] 200 km
0 [========] 120 miles

SVALBARD

Svalbard
Jan Mayen
NORWAY

0 [====] 100 km
0 [====] 60 miles

Nordaustlandet

Ny Ålesund

Spitsbergen   Barentsøya

Longyearbyen
Barentsburg   Edgeøya
        Sveagruva

To Jan Mayen

To Norway mainland

Approximate North Only

ARCTIC OCEAN

BARENTS SEA

Nordkapp   Honningsvåg

Hammerfest   Tana Bru   Vardø
                                           Vadsø
Alta **Finnmark**   E6   Kirkenes
                                        E6   Storskog
        Karasjok   RUSSIA
NORWEGIAN SEA   **Finnmarksvidda**
Fjordgard;   Tromsø   Kautokeino
Husøy
Mefjordvær
Skaland   E6
Gryllefjord Andenes Finnsnes
          Stø   Harstad   **Troms**
        Nyksund   Narvik
Stokmarknes Sortland
Melbu   Svolvær Storjord   **FINLAND**
Lofoten Stamsund Skutvik
        Kjerringøy
Vestfjorden
        BODØ Fauske
Sattstraumen
                Nordland
Arctic Circle *Svartisen IceCap*
                Mo i Rana
        Mosjøen

ATLANTIC OCEAN

E6 **Nord Trøndelag**

Steinkjer   **SWEDEN**

TRONDHEIM E14
        Hell
        Sør Trøndelag

See Western Fjords & Central Norway Map (p303)

ÅLESUND   Åndalsnes
Måløy *Nordfjord* E136
        Geiranger Dombås
        Stryn   **Rondane**
Galdhøpiggen ▲ (2469m)
Balestrand   E6
Sognefjorden Lærdal **Jotunheimen**
Voss Flåm   Lillehammer
    Finse Geilo   Hamar
BERGEN E16
Odda **Hardangervidda**
Haukeligrend Rjukan
Haugesund   Notodden **OSLO**
        Kongsberg
Tau **Telemark** E134
STAVANGER Bø Moss
    SKIEN   FREDRIKSTAD
E39 **Sørlandet** Larvik Halden E18
    Risør
Lillesand Arendal E6
    Grimstad *Skagerrak*
Mandal KRISTIANSAND

Bottenhavet

HELSINKI

TALLINN

ESTONIA

STOCKHOLM

BALTIC SEA

Olav Haraldsson, adopting the religion of the lands he had conquered, converted the Norwegians to Christianity and founded the Church of Norway in 1024.

The Viking Age declined after 1066, with the defeat of the Norwegian king, Harald Hardråda, at the Battle of Stamford Bridge in England. Norwegian naval power was finished off for good when Alexander III, King of Scots, defeated a Viking naval force at the Battle of Largs (Scotland) in 1263.

In the early 14th century, Oslo emerged as a centre of power and a period of growth followed until 1349, when the bubonic plague swept the country, wiping out nearly two-thirds of the population. In 1380, Norway was absorbed into a union with Denmark that lasted more than 400 years.

Denmark ceded Norway to Sweden in 1814. In 1884 a parliamentary government was introduced in Norway and a growing nationalist movement eventually led to a peaceful secession from Sweden in 1905. In a referendum, Norwegians voted in favour of a monarchy over a republic. Having no royal family of its own, Norway's parliament selected Prince Carl of Denmark to be king. Upon acceptance, he took the title Håkon VII and named his infant son Olav, both prominent names from Norway's Viking past.

Norway stayed neutral during WWI. Despite restating its neutrality at the start of WWII, it was attacked by the Nazis on 9 April 1940, falling to the Germans after a two-month struggle. King Håkon set up a government in exile in England, and placed most of Norway's merchant fleet under the command of the Allies. Although Norway remained occupied until the end of the war, it had an active Resistance movement.

The royal family returned to Norway in June 1945. King Håkon died in 1957 and was succeeded by his son, Olav V, a popular king who reigned until his death in January 1991. The current monarch is Harald V, Olav's son, who was crowned in June 1991.

Norway joined the European Free Trade Association (EFTA) in 1960, but has been reluctant to forge closer bonds with other European nations, in part due to concerns about the impact on its fishing industry and small-scale farming industry. In 1972, Norwegians voted against joining the European Community (EC) amid a divisive national debate. It took two decades for member-ship to once again become a high-profile issue. During 1994 a second national referendum was held, this time on joining the EC's successor, the European Union (EU), and voters rejected that proposal as well. At the time of writing, the EU issue was again regaining steam, with many predicting a successful referendum passing in the near future.

PEOPLE

Norway has 4,546,000 people and one of the lowest population densities in Europe. The majority of modern Norwegians are middle class. Immigration is strictly controlled and only bona fide refugees are admitted. The largest cities are Oslo with 500,000 residents, followed by Bergen, Trondheim and Stavanger.

Most Norwegians are of Nordic origin, and are thought to have descended from central and northern European tribes who migrated northwards around 8000 years ago. In addition, there are about 40,000 Sami (formerly known as Lapps), the indigenous people of the far north of Norway who now make up the country's largest ethnic minority. Some Sami still live a traditional nomadic life, herding reindeer in Finnmark.

RELIGION

Around 86% of Norwegians belong to the Church of Norway, a Protestant Evangelical Lutheran denomination, but most Norwegians only attend church twice a year, for Christmas and Easter. The Humanist & Ethical Union has around 70,000 members and there are a number of smaller Christian denominations, as well as around 50,000 Muslims and 1000 Jews.

ARTS

Norway's best-known artists include the moody painter Edvard Munch, responsible for *The Scream,* the landscape painter JC Dahl, classical composer Edvard Grieg, sculptor Gustav Vigeland and famed playwright Henrik Ibsen, who penned *A Doll's House.*

Norway's stave churches are some of the oldest wooden buildings on Earth. Named for their vertical supporting posts, these structures are often distinguished by dragon-headed gables resembling ornately carved prows of Viking ships. Of the 500 to 600 stave churches originally built, only about 20 of those remaining retain many original components. Other significant architectural features in the country include the romantic 'dragon style', found in some historic hotels, and occurrences of the Art Nouveau style, best observed in Ålesund.

Norwegian writers Sigrid Undset and Knut Hamsun (a Nazi collaborator) won the Nobel Prize for Literature in 1928 and 1920, respectively. Undset is best known for *Kristin Lavransdottir,* a trilogy portraying the struggles and earthy lifestyle of a 14th-century Norwegian family, while Hamsun won the Nobel Prize for his novel *The Growth of the Soil.*

Not traditionally a cinematic powerhouse, Norway has recently cranked out several good films, including *Elling* (2001), *Buddy* (2003) and *Beautiful Country* (2004), all of which earned international regard. For a Norwegian classic, check out *Ni Liv* (1957), a story about the WWII resistance. More film information can be found at www.nfi.no.

Classical music and jazz are very popular in Norway and there are annual music festivals around the country, the most significant being in Bergen, Molde and Kongsberg. For details of music festivals, visit www.norwayfestivals.com or contact the Norwegian Tourist Board.

Norway also has a thriving rock scene with most of the action coming out of Bergen. It's also largely responsible for black metal (p280).

ENVIRONMENT
The Land
Norway, occupying the western part of the Scandinavian peninsula, has a land area of 306,800 sq km and shares borders with Sweden, Finland and Russia. The coastline is deeply cut by fjords – long, narrow inlets of the sea bordered by high, steep cliffs. Mountains, some capped with Europe's largest glaciers, cover more than half of the landmass. Only 3% of the country is arable.

With a combination of mountains and a wet climate, it's hardly surprising that Norway has many spectacular waterfalls, including several of the top 10 highest in the world (although the number varies according to the list you're looking at).

'The Land of the Midnight Sun' is more than just a promotional slogan: nearly a third of Norway lies north of the Arctic Circle, the point at which there is at least one full day when the sun never sets and one full day when it never rises.

Wildlife
Norway has wild and semi-domesticated reindeer herds, thriving elk populations and a scattering of arctic fox, lynx, musk oxen, bears and wolverines. Lemmings occupy mountain areas through 30% of the country. Since the ban on hunting came into force in 1973, polar bear numbers have increased to over 5000, although they're only found in Svalbard; polar bears usually eat seals but have been known to kill and eat humans. Walruses are rare and are confined to Svalbard, but several species of seal, dolphin and whale (especially minke whales) may be seen around most western and northern coasts.

Birdlife is prolific in coastal areas and puffins, fulmars and kittiwakes are commonly seen. Rarer species include ospreys, golden eagles and magnificent white-tailed sea eagles. The islands of Runde (p321), Røst (p335) and Værøy (p335) are premier places to stare at winged-things.

National Parks
Norway's 21 national parks, covering 6.4% of the country (there are plans to increase this to 15% by 2010), have been established to protect wildlife and distinctive natural features of the landscape. In many cases, they don't attempt to protect any specific features, but rather attempt to prevent development of remaining wild areas. As a result, park boundaries don't necessarily coincide with the incidence of spectacular natural features, but simply follow contour lines around uninhabited areas.

Compared to their counterparts in the USA and Britain, Norwegian national parks are low profile and lack the traffic and over-developed facilities that have turned other countries' parks into seasonal urban areas. Some parks, notably Jotunheimen and Rondane, are increasing suffering from overuse, but in most places pollution and traffic are kept to a minimum.

Environmental Issues
Industrial waste is highly regulated, recycling is popular, there's little rubbish along

the roadsides and general tidiness is a high priority in both urban and rural environments. Plastic bottles and cans may be exchanged for cash at supermarkets.

Loss of habitat has placed around 900 species of plants and animals on the endangered or threatened species lists, and sport hunting and fishing are more popular here than in most of Europe. Hydroelectric schemes have devastated some mountain landscapes and waterfalls, and over-fishing perpetually haunts the economy.

In 1993 Norway resumed commercial hunting of minke whales in open defiance of an international whaling ban. Norway supports the protection of other threatened species, but the government contends that the estimated 70,000 to 186,000 North Atlantic minke whales can sustain a limited harvest. Despite strong resistance by Greenpeace, the international response has been quite limited. The annual limit on the number of whales that can be killed is 711, though this might soon be increased to 1800, in part because whales eat millions of tons of cod and herring, two of Norway's staple (and over-fished) exports.

FOOD & DRINK
Staples & Specialities
Norwegian specialities include grilled or smoked *laks* (salmon), *gravat laks* (marinated salmon), *reker* (boiled shrimp), *torsk* (cod), *fiskesuppe* (fish soup), *hval* (whale) and other seafood. Expect to see sweet brown goat cheese called *geitost* (Gudbrandsdalsost is a popular brand) and *sild* (pickled herring) alongside the breads and cereals included in breakfast buffets. One of the finest Norwegian desserts is warm *moltebær syltetøy* (cloudberry jam) with ice cream. Another popular option is *eplekake* (apple cake) served with fresh cream. *Lutefisk*, dried cod made almost gelatinous by soaking in lye, is popular at Christmas but it's definitely an acquired taste.

If Norway has a national drink, it's coffee and most Norwegians drink it black and strong. Most of the beer you'll drink is watery-tasting pilsner. On the other end of the taste spectrum is Norway's extremely bitter aquavit, which does the job at 40% proof.

Where to Eat & Drink
Common throughout all of Norway is the *konditori*, a bakery with a few tables where you can sit and enjoy pastries and relatively inexpensive sandwiches. Other moderately cheap eats are found at *gatekjøkken* (food wagons and streetside kiosks), which generally have hot dogs for about Nkr20 and hamburgers for Nkr40. Marginally more expensive, but with more nutritionally balanced food, are *kafeterias*, with simple, traditional meals from about Nkr55. In cities, *kafes* almost always function as a hang-out, bar and restaurant. They serve filling 'small dishes' for Nkr80 to Nkr120. Many restaurants feature a *dagens rett* (daily special) for about Nkr80.

By international standards, Norwegian restaurant food is fairly bland, often heavy and difficult to digest, though the cities of Oslo, Bergen, Trondheim and Stavanger have all made vast cuisine improvements.

Urban bars come in three basic forms. The first breed involves well-dressed Norwegians and cool designs. The second is the 'brown bar', so named because of their dusty wooden interiors – these are usually accused of being dens for alcoholic men, though hipsters have gentrified many of them. The third type is found in the growing numbers of forgettable tourist traps and chain 'Irish' venues. These are easily spotted and avoided.

Vegetarians & Vegans
Being a vegetarian in Norway is definitely a challenge. In rural parts of the country, you will often find that you have to live out of a grocery store, though some cafés serve a token meat-free dish such as vegetables with pasta. Another easily found option is pizza, though be warned that Norwegian pizza usually tastes lousy. You'll usually find more options in the bigger cities, though most places have menus entirely based on fish and meat. Kebab stands serve falafel about half the time. Norwegian restaurants aim to please, and will often attempt to make you a special order if you ask (don't expect fine results though).

Vegans will find Norway almost impossible, unless you only frequent shops. The number of places consistently serving vegan food is minuscule.

OSLO

pop 520,000

Norway's capital city offers a rare combination: a diverse web of urbanity – featuring nifty cafés, museums and nightlife – and near immediate access to nature. A short ride on the metro drops you off at the Nordmarka (North Woods), where you'll find a network of cross-country ski trails, small downhill slopes, hiking routes and a bobsled run. In summer, take ferries to the islands of the Oslofjord for beaches and barbeques.

HISTORY

The name Oslo derives from the words *Ás*, the Old Norse name for the Norse Godhead, and *lo*, which meant 'pasture', yielding roughly 'the fields of the gods'. Founded by Harald Hardråda in 1048, it's the oldest Scandinavian capital. In 1299, King Håkon V constructed the Akershus Festning (fortress) here, to counter the Swedish threat from the east. Levelled by fire in 1624, the city was rebuilt in brick and stone on a more easily defended site by King Christian IV, who renamed it Christiania, after his humble self.

For three centuries, right through WWI, the city remained a seat of defence. In 1814, the framers of Norway's first constitution designated it the official capital of the new realm but their efforts were effectively nullified by Sweden, which had other ideas about Norway's future and unified the two countries under Swedish rule. In 1905, when that union dissolved, Christiania flourished as the capital of modern Norway. The city reverted to its original name, Oslo, in 1925.

ORIENTATION

Oslo's central train station (Oslo Sentralstasjon, or 'Oslo S') is at the eastern end of the city centre. From there the main street, Karl Johans gate, leads through the heart of the city to Det Kongelige Slott. The neighbourhood of Grünnerløkka, hipster-central, is reached by taking Storgata across the Akerselva river, while the Grønland immigrant district is just east of Oslo S.

Most central city sights, including the harbour front and Akershus Festning, are within a 15-minute walk of Karl Johans gate, as are the majority of Oslo's hotels and pensions. Many sights outside Oslo centre, including Vigeland Park and Munchmuseet, are a short bus ride away, and Bygdøy peninsula is a 10-minute ferry ride across the harbour. The trails and lakes of the Nordmarka wilderness are easily reached by T-bane.

INFORMATION

Bookshops

Nomaden (Map pp274-6; ☎ 22 56 25 40; Uranienborgveien 4; ☻ 10am-6pm Mon-Fri, 10am-4pm Sat) Sells travel guides and maps.

Norli (Map pp274-6; Universitetsgata 24) Some English-language titles.

Tanum Libris (Map pp274-6; Karl Johans gate 43) Some English-language titles.

Discount Cards

Oslo Card (Nkr195/285/375 for 1/2/3 days) Provides entry to most museums and attractions and travel on public transport. It's sold at tourist offices and hotels. Students and seniors, who get half-price entry at many sights, may do better buying a public-transport pass (or walking) and paying separate museum admissions.

Oslo Package (from Nkr315-780 per person per day) Includes a hotel room, breakfast, a 96-hour Oslo Card and up to two children included free. You can book these through your local travel agent, or show up at the Oslo tourist office (a risk, since they sell out). It's currently possible to buy a pass, stay in a participating hotel for just one night, and then switch to a cheaper place, keeping your four-day Oslo card.

Emergencies

Jernbanetorget Apotek (Map pp274-6; opposite Oslo S; ☻ 24hr) Pharmacy.

Oslo Kommunale Legevakten (Map pp274-6; ☎ 22 11 80 80; Storgata 40) Medical clinic with 24-hour emergency services.

Internet Access

Deichmanske Bibliotek (Map pp274-6; Henrik Ibsens gate 1; ☻ 10am-8pm Mon-Fri, 9am-3pm Sat Sep-May, 10am-6pm Mon-Fri, 9am-2pm Sat Jun-Aug) Check your mail for free (expect a wait and a half-hour time limit).

Studenten (Map pp274-6; ☎ 22 42 56 80; Karl Johans gate 45; per hr Nkr55; ☻ noon-8pm Tue-Sat, noon-10pm Sun & Mon)

Laundry

Selvebetjent (Map pp274-6; Ullevålsveien 15; ☻ 8am-9pm) Charges Nkr40/30 to wash/dry, including soap.

Money

Change money at the **airport bank** (Gardermoen airport departure hall; 5.30am-8pm Mon-Fri, 5.30am-6pm Sat, 6.30am-8pm Sun), the **post office** and at **Nordea bank** (Map pp274-6; Oslo S; 7am-7pm Mon-Fri, 8am-5pm Sat & Sun). ATMs are everywhere, including Oslo S and the airport.

Those changing a small amount will usually get the best deal from **American Express** (Map pp274-6; 22 98 37 35; Fridtjof Nansens plass 6; 9am-4.30pm Mon-Fri, 10am-3pm Sat), north of the Rådhus. It exchanges cash and travellers cheques without transaction fees, though its rates may be somewhat lower.

Post

The **main post office** (Map pp274-6; Dronningens gate 15; 9am-5pm Mon-Fri) stamps things. To receive mail, have it sent to 'Poste Restante, Oslo Sentrum Postkontor, Dronningens gate 15, N-0107 Oslo'. There's a **branch post office** (Map pp274-6; 8.30am-8pm Mon-Fri, 9am-6pm Sat) at Oslo S.

Tourist Information

Oslo Promotion (Map pp274-6; 24 14 77 00; www.visitoslo.com; fax 22 83 81 50; Fridjtof Nansens plass; 9am-7pm Jun-Aug, 9am-5pm Mon-Sat Apr-May & Sep, 9am-4pm Mon-Fri Oct-Mar) Tourist information for Oslo.
Tourist Information Window (Map pp274-6; Oslo S 8am-11pm May-Sep, 8am-5pm Mon-Sat Oct-Apr)
Use It (Map pp274-6; 22 41 51 32; www.unginfo .oslo.no; Møllergata 3; 9am-6pm Mon-Fri Jul & Aug, 11am-5pm or 6pm Mon-Fri Sep-Jun) The youth information office can give you the lowdown on what's happening in and around Oslo, and provide advice on everything from cheap accommodation to hitching. Pick up a copy of its free, informative *Streetwise* guide.

SIGHTS
Bygdøy

The Bygdøy (roughly pronounced 'big day') peninsula holds some of Oslo's finest attractions, including excavated Viking ships, an open-air folk museum, Thor Heyerdahl's raft the *Kon-Tiki* and the *Fram* polar exploration ship.

The magnificent **Vikingskipshuset** (Viking Ship Museum; Map p281; 22 13 52 80; Huk Aveny 35; adult/child Nkr40/20; 9am-6pm May-Sep, 11am-4pm Oct-Apr) houses three Viking ships excavated from the Oslofjorden region. The ships had been brought ashore and used as tombs for nobility, who were buried with all they were expected to need in the hereafter, including

jewels, furniture, food and servants. Built of oak in the 9th century, these Viking ships were buried in blue clay, which preserved two of them amazingly well.

The impressive **Oseberg ship**, buried in AD 834 and festooned with elaborate dragon and serpent carvings, is 22m long and took 30 people to row it. The burial chamber beneath it held the largest collection of Viking Age artefacts ever uncovered in Scandinavia. A second ship, the 24m-long **Gokstad**, is the world's finest example of a longship. Of the third ship, the **Tune**, only a few boards remain.

The open-air **Norsk Folkemuseum** (Map p281; 22 12 37 00; Museumsveien 10; adult/student/child mid-May–mid-Sep Nkr75/45/20, mid-Sep–mid-May Nkr55/35/20; 10am-6pm mid-Jun–mid-Sep, 11am-3pm Mon-Fri, 11am-4pm Sat & Sun mid-Sep mid-Jun) displays more than 140 buildings from the 17th and 18th centuries collected from around the country. Dirt paths wind past sturdy old barns, *stabbur* (storehouses on stilts) and rough-timbered farmhouses with sod roofs sprouting wild flowers. There's also a reproduction of an early-20th-century Norwegian town, including a village shop and an old petrol station. A highlight is a restored **stave church**, built around 1200 in Gol and brought to Bygdøy in 1885. Sunday is a good day to visit, as there's usually folk music and dancing at 2pm (summer only).

The **Kon-Tiki Museum** (Map p281; 23 08 67 67; Bygdøynesveien 36; adult/child Nkr35/20; 9.30am-5.45pm Jun-Aug, 10.30am-5pm Sep-May) is dedicated to the *Kon-Tiki* balsa raft, on which Norwegian explorer Thor Heyerdahl sailed from Peru to Polynesia in 1947 to demonstrate that Polynesia's first settlers could have come from South America. Also displayed is the papyrus reed boat *Ra II*, which Heyerdahl used to cross the Atlantic in 1970.

Frammuseet (Map p281; 23 28 29 50; www .fram.museum.no; Bygdøynesveien 36; adult/child Nkr30/15; 9am-6.45pm mid-Jun–Aug, shorter hrs Sep–mid-Jun) houses the durable *Fram* (1892), which Roald Amundsen used for the first successful expedition to the South Pole in 1911. You can clamber around inside the boat, go down to the hold where the sledge dogs were kept, and view fascinating photographic displays of the *Fram* trapped in polar ice. The museum also includes an interesting rundown on the history of polar exploration.

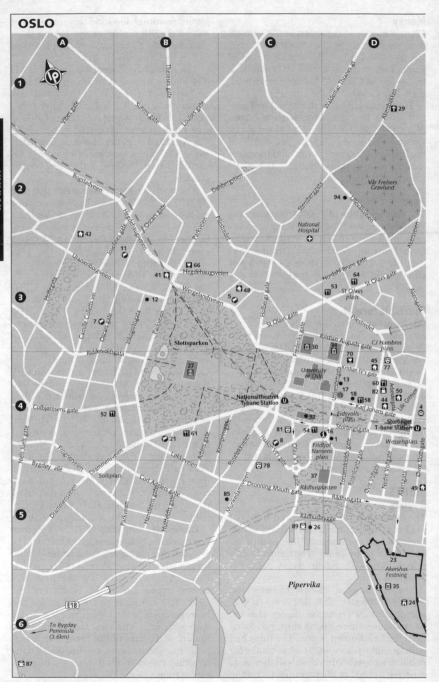

OSLO

NORWAY

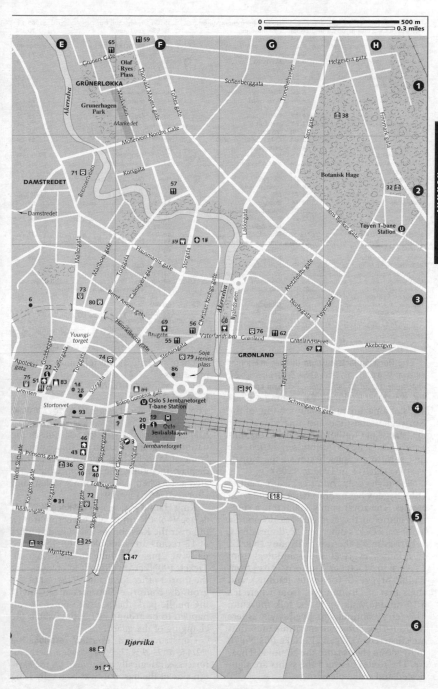

The **Norsk Sjøfartsmuseum** (Norwegian Maritime Museum; Map p281; ☎ 24 11 41 50; Bygdøynesveien 37; adult/student/child Nkr40/25/free; ☒ 10am-6pm mid-May–Sep, shorter hrs Oct–mid-May) contains boatloads of amazing model ships, a film of the Norwegian coastline and fine views over the islands of Oslofjorden. Outside the museum there's Roald Amundsen's *Gjøa*, the first ship to completely transit the Northwest Passage (from 1903 to 1906).

Although only minutes from central Oslo, Bygdøy has a rural character and good **beaches**. The royal family maintains a summer home on the peninsula, as do quite a number of Oslo's other well-to-do residents.

Ferries make the run to Bygdøy (Nkr22, 15 minutes, every 20 to 40 minutes) from 12 April to 6 October. The ferry leaves from Rådhusbrygge 3 (opposite Rådhus) and stops first at Dronningen, from where it's a 10-minute walk up to the folk museum. The ferry continues to Bygdøynes, where the *Kon-Tiki*, *Fram* and maritime museums are clustered. You can also take bus No 20 to Bygdøy's sights from the National Theatre. The routes between the sights are signposted and make pleasant walks.

There's a café at the folk and maritime museums.

Central Oslo

The **Nasjonalgalleriet** (Map pp274-6; ☎ 22 20 04 04; Universitetsgata 13; ☒ 10am-6pm Mon, Wed & Fri, 10am-8pm Thu, 10am-4pm Sat, 11am-4pm Sun) houses the nation's largest collection of Norwegian art. Some of Munch's best-known works are on display, including *The Scream*, which created a stir when it was brazenly stolen (and later recovered) in 1994.

King Harald V sleeps in **Det Kongelige Slott** (Map pp274-6), the royal palace, peering from a hill over the Karl Johans axis. Guided tours of 15 rooms are available in English, once daily at 2pm (late June to mid-August). Tickets (90Nkr) are difficult to obtain – ask the tourist office for details. The rest of the grounds comprise **Slottsparken**, an inviting public park that's free to enter. If you happen to be around at 1.30pm, watch the changing of the guard.

Construction of **Akershus Festning** (Map pp274-6; ☎ 23 09 39 17; ☒ 6am-9pm), a medieval fortress strategically positioned on the eastern side of the harbour, was begun by King

WHAT'S FREE

Free is not a word you'll hear often in Oslo, even if translated into Norwegian. Despite this, there are a tender few options to help nurture the budget traveller's wallet. These include a scramble around **Akershus Festning** (opposite), an earthen-walled fortress that has protected the harbour since 1299; a stroll amongst the expressive statuary of **Vigeland Park** (p278); and entry into the **Nasjonalgalleriet** (opposite), which possesses the largest collection of Norwegian art. Anyone may freely ski the extensive network of **cross-country trails** that surrounds the city, though gear rental will switch on tear ducts (p279).

Håkon V in 1299. The park-like **grounds** (☼ 6am-9pm) offer excellent views of the city and Oslofjorden, and are the venue for a host of concerts, dances and theatrical productions during summer.

Entry into the earthen-walled fortress is either through a gate at the end of Akersgata or over a drawbridge spanning Kongens gate, which is reached from the southern end of Kirkegata. After 6pm in winter use the Kirkegata entrance. The **Akershus Festning Information Centre** (Map pp274-6; ☎ 23 09 39 17; ☼ 9am-5pm Mon-Fri, 11am-5pm Sat & Sun mid-Jun–mid-Aug, 11am-5pm mid-Aug–mid-Jun) provides information on the fortress.

In the 17th century, Christian IV renovated **Akershus Slott** (Akershus Castle; Map pp274-6; ☎ 23 09 35 53; adult/child Nkr40/10; ☼ 10am-4pm Mon-Sat, 12.30-4pm Sun May–mid-Sep) into a Renaissance palace, though the front remains decidedly medieval. In its dungeons you'll find dark cubbyholes where outcast nobles were kept under lock and key, while the upper floors have banquet halls and staterooms.

The chapel is still used for army events and the crypts of kings Håkon VII and Olav V lie beneath it. Tours of the castle (at 11am Monday to Saturday, and 1pm and 3pm daily) are led by students in period dress, and provide entertaining anecdotal history; otherwise you can wander through on your own.

During WWII, the Nazis used Akershus as a prison and execution grounds, and today it's the site of **Norges Hjemmefront Museet** (Norwegian Resistance Museum; Map pp274-6; ☎ 23 09 31 38; www.nhm.mil.no; adult/child Nkr30/15; ☼ 10am-3pm

Mon-Fri, 11am-4pm Sat & Sun, longer hrs mid-Apr–Sep), providing a vivid and moving account of the tyrannical German occupation and the Norwegian struggle against it.

Oslo's twin-towered, red-brick **Rådhus** (City Hall; Map pp274-6; ☎ 22 46 16 00; Fridtjof Nansens plass; adult/child Nkr30/15, admission free Sep-May; ☼ 9am-5pm May-Aug, 9am-4pm Sep-Apr) features wooden reliefs with scenes from Norse mythology lining its outside entrance, and impressive frescoes decorating the interior halls and chambers. View the main hall for free from the front corridor, walk around yourself, or take a guided tour in English at 10am, noon and 2pm daily (no extra charge).

The **Historisk Museet** (Map pp274-6; ☎ 22 85 19 00; www.ukm.uio.no; Frederiks gate 2; admission Nkr40; ☼ 10am-4pm Tue-Sun mid-May–mid-Sep, 11am-4pm Tue-Sun mid-Sep–mid-May) consists of three museums under a single roof. On the ground floor, the **National Antiquities Collection** displays Viking-era coins, jewellery, weapons and bloodthirsty plunder, as well as a medieval church art section that includes the dragon-festooned bits of the 13th-century Ål stave church. The second level has a **numismatic collection of coins** dating from AD 995 and exhibits on indigenous arctic cultures, while the steps to the **ethnographical displays** on the top floor aren't worth climbing.

The well-presented **Post Museum** (Map pp274-6; ☎ 23 14 80 59; Kirkegata 20; ☼ 10am-5pm Mon-Fri, 10am-2pm Sat, noon-4pm Sun) teaches you just how much of a pain in the arse it is to deliver mail to the middle of nowhere. Exhibits discuss 350 years of postal history, including a reindeer sled once used for mail delivery. Album stuffers can buy commemorative stamps. There's a free museum booklet in English.

A medieval stone church and Oslo's oldest building, **Gamle Aker Kirke** (Map pp274-6; Akersbakken 26; ☼ noon-2pm Mon-Sat) was built around 1100 and is still used for services. Take bus No 37 from Jernbanetorget, get off at Akersbakken and walk up past the cemetery.

The skewed wooden homes of the **Damstredet** district, some dating from the early 19th century, add a splash of character to the area just north of the city centre.

Museet for Samtidskunst (Museum of Contemporary Art; Map pp274-6; ☎ 22 86 22 10; Bankplassen 4; adult/child Nkr40/free; ☼ 10am-5pm Tue, Wed & Fri, 10am-8pm Thu, 11am-4pm Sat, 11am-5pm Sun), Norway's principal museum dedicated to post-

WWII Scandinavian and international art, houses the work of most major modern Norwegian artists. The goods are arranged in an Art Nouveau building that once housed the Central Bank of Norway. Free Thursdays.

A block to the east is the **Astrup Fearnley Museet** (Map pp274-6; ☎ 22 93 60 60; Dronningens gate 4; adult/student Nkr50/25; ☒ 11am-5pm Tue, Wed & Fri, 11am-7pm Thu, noon-5pm Sat & Sun), a modern art museum featuring a changing array of Norwegian and international art exhibitions.

Built to show off the ridiculous and enormous collection of a wealthy brewer, the **Mini Bottle Gallery** (Map pp274-6; ☎ 23 35 79 60; www.minibottlegallery.com; Kirkegata 10; adult/child Nkr85/35; ☒ noon-4pm Sat & Sun) is a space that crosses architectural elegance and haunted-house gadgetry with the crass overtures of a puerile club. As you admire tens of thousands of tiny bottles of booze set in an environment whose expensive design surpasses many museums, you're bound to wonder if the place is a joke. The answer comes readily in the bathroom.

Munchmuseet & Around

Dedicated to the life work of Norway's most renowned artist, Edvard Munch (1863–1944), **Munchmuseet** (Map pp274-6; ☎ 23 24 14 00; Tøyengata 53; adult/student Nkr60/30; ☒ 10am-6pm Jun–mid-Sep, shorter hrs mid-Sep–Jun) contains 5000 drawings and paintings that Munch bequeathed to the city of Oslo. Ten years after *The Scream* was stolen from Nasjonalgalleriet, masked gunmen pulled a similar caper on another version of the famous painting here in 2004.

Next to Munchmuseet is the university's **Zoological Museum** (Map pp274-6; ☎ 22 85 17 00; Sars gate 1; ☒ 11am-4pm Tue-Sun), full of stuffed Norwegian wildlife. Compare the scale of a lemming and polar bear. Admission prices are variable. The adjacent **Geological-Palaeontological Museum** (Map pp274-6; ☎ 22 85 17 00; Sars gate 1; ☒ 11am-4pm Tue-Sun) features displays on the history of the solar system, Norwegian geology, and examples of myriad minerals, meteorites and moon rocks; again, admission prices are variable. The museums sit in the grounds of the fragrant **Botanisk Hage** (botanical garden; Map pp274-6; ☎ 22 85 17 00; Sars gate 1; ☒ 7am-8pm Mon-Fri, 10am-8pm Sat & Sun Apr-Sep, shorter hrs Oct-Mar), whose lovely landscaped lawns feature over 1000 alpine plants as well as tropical and temperate specimens.

Frognerparken & Vigeland Park

Frognerparken is a wonderful city park (Map p281) with expansive green spaces, duck ponds and rows of shady trees – a fine place for walks and picnics. Its central walkway, Vigeland Park, is lined with life-sized statues by Gustav Vigeland (1869–1943). In nearly 200 highly charged works of granite and bronze, Vigeland presents the human form in a range of emotions, from screaming pot-bellied babies to entwined lovers and tranquil elderly couples.

The most impressive piece is the monolith of writhing bodies, said to be the world's largest granite sculpture. The circle of steps beneath the monolith is lined with voluptuous stone figures and is a popular spot for sitting and contemplation. The park is free and always open.

For a more in-depth look at the development of Gustav Vigeland's work, visit the **Vigeland Museum** (Map p281; ☎ 22 54 25 30; www .vigeland.museum.no; Nobels gate 32; adult/child Nkr40/20; ☒ noon-3pm Thu & Sat). The museum was built by the city as a home and workshop for Vigeland in exchange for the bulk of his life's work and contains his early statuary, plaster moulds, woodblock prints and sketches.

Other Attractions

The **Holmenkollen Ski Jump** (☎ 22 92 32 00; Kongeveien 5; adult/child Nkr50/25; ☒ 9am-8pm Jun-Aug, 10am-5pm May & Sep, 10am-4pm Oct-Apr), perched on a hillside above Oslo, draws the world's top jumpers in a ski festival each March and doubles as a concert venue in summer. To get there follow the signs up the hill from Holmenkollen T-bane station. From the top of the ski-jump tower, there's a bird's-eye view of the steep ramp, as well as a panoramic view of Oslo city and fjord; a lift goes partway up and then you climb 114 steps. The admission fee includes entry to a **ski museum**, leading you through the 4000-year history of skiing in Norway. Check out the exhibits on the Antarctic expeditions of Amundsen and Scott, and Fridtjof Nansen's slog across the Greenland icecap. There's also a jump simulator.

ACTIVITIES
Swimming & Sunbathing

Ferries running to the half a dozen islands in Oslofjorden leave from Vippetangen quay, southeast of Akershus Festning. **Hovedøya** (Map p281), the closest island, has a rocky coastline, but its southwestern side is a popular sunbathing area. There are walking paths around the perimeter, some old cannons and the **ruins** (Map p281) of a 12th-century monastery. Boats to Hovedøya leave from Vippetangen once or twice hourly from late May to mid-August, with fewer runs the rest of the year.

Further south, the undeveloped island of **Langøyene** (Map p281) offers far better swimming. It has both sandy and rocky beaches, including one designated for nude bathing. Boats to Langøyene depart late May to mid-August.

The Bygdøy peninsula also has two popular beaches, **Huk** (Map p281) and **Paradisbukta** (Map p281), which can be reached by taking bus No 30 from Jernbanetorget to its last stop. While there are some sandy patches, most of Huk comprises grassy lawns and large, smooth rocks ideal for sunbathing. It's separated into two beaches by a small cove; the beach on the northwestern side is open to nude bathing. If Huk seems too crowded, a 10-minute walk through the woods north of the bus stop leads to the more secluded Paradisbukta.

For freshwater swimming, try the eastern side of lake **Sognsvann** (Map p281), at the end of T-bane line 5, about 6km north of central Oslo.

Hiking

A network of trails leads into Nordmarka from Frognerseteren, at the end of T-bane line 1. One good, fairly strenuous walk is from Frognerseteren over to lake Sognsvann, where you can take T-bane line 5 back to the city. If you're interested in wilderness hiking, contact the **DNT office** (☎ 22 82 28 22; Storgata 3).

Cycling

One popular outing is to take the *sykkeltoget* (weekend bike train) to Stryken, 40km north of Oslo, and cycle back through Nordmarka. The train leaves Oslo S at 9.15am on Saturday and Sunday from May to October. For a shorter ride, take the T-bane to Frognerseteren and cycle back.

For cycling information contact the local club, **Syklistenes Landsforening** (☎ 22 47 30 30), or the tourist office.

Skiing

Oslo's ski season is roughly from December to March. There are over 1000km of ski trails in the Nordmarka area north of Oslo, many of them floodlit; easy-access tracks begin right at the T-bane stations Frognerseteren and Sognsvann. **Tomm Murstad Skiservice** (☎ 22 13 95 00; www.skiservice.no; Tryvannsveien 2), at Voksenkollen T-bane station, hires out snowboards and nordic skis.

A set of skis, boots and poles costs Nkr160/200 for one/two days. **Skiforeningen** (Ski Society; Map p281; ☎ 22 92 32 00; www.holmenkollen .com; Kongeveien 5, N-0787 Oslo) can provide more information on skiing, or check out the website.

ORGANISED TOURS

Oslo is so easy to get around that there's little need for organised tours. However, if time is tight, **Båtservice Sightseeing** (Map pp274-6; ☎ 23 35 68 90; www.boatsightseeing.com; Pier 3, Rådhusbrygge; ☼ late May-late Aug) does a tidy 7½-hour tour of the Bygdøy sites, Vigeland Park and the Holmenkollen Ski Jump, plus a cruise of Oslofjorden, for Nkr465; a three-hour version minus the cruise costs Nkr305. Båtservice's frequent 50-minute 'minicruise' of Oslofjorden provides city orientation for Nkr100, or is free with the Oslo Card.

The popular **Norway in a Nutshell** (☎ 81 56 82 22; www.norwaynutshell.com) day tours cost Nkr1735 – they can be booked through any tourist office or travel agency, or directly through NSB at train stations. From Oslo, the typical 'Norway in a Nutshell' route includes a rail trip from Oslo across Hardangervidda to Myrdal, a rail descent to Flåm along the dramatic Flåmbanen, a cruise along Nærøyfjorden to Gudvangen, a bus to Voss, a connecting train to Bergen for a short visit, then an overnight return rail trip to Oslo (including sleeper compartment).

FESTIVALS & EVENTS

Oslo's most festive annual event is the 17 May Constitution Day celebration, when city residents descend on the royal palace in traditional garb.

In March, the **Holmenkollen Ski Festival** (☎ 22 92 32 00; www.skiforeningen.no) attracts Nordic skiers and ski jumpers from around the world. August sees the **Oslo International Jazz Festival** (☎ 22 42 91 20; www.oslojazz.no), October

NORWAY

BLACK METAL

Bored of fjords and peace prizes? Perhaps it's time to check out Norway's highly regarded black metal scene, whose notorious, sensational exploits in the mid-1990s raised eyebrows across the globe. At that time, the members of a few big-name bands (Mayhem and Emperor being the most notable) not only committed suicide, but murdered each other, burned stave churches, made trinkets out of fragments of their mates' skulls and beat up bouncers and concertgoers alike. In addition to these and other violent acts, a lot of music was created along the way. Depending on your taste, the goods might sound like a dying Cookie Monster singing through a distortion pedal or liberation from what you perceive to be a Christian-dominated music industry.

While things have calmed down a bit since the gory days, black metal remains popular in Norway. A few of the bands to look out for include Mayhem (much of the previous line-up dead or jailed), Satyricon, Gorgoroth and Dark Throne, and a few of the clubs to view them are Garage (p285 & p309), Hulen (p310), Rockefeller Music Hall (p285) and Blæst (p327). If you're lucky enough to spend April in Oslo, you must attend the **Inferno Metal Festival** (www .infernofestival.net). Don't forget your leather pants!

brings **Films from the South** (☎ 22 82 24 80; www .filmfrasor.no) and April the **Inferno Metal Festival** (www.infernofestival.net). For details of these and other events, contact the tourist office.

SLEEPING

When all other options seem unlikely, **Use It** (Map pp274-6; ☎ 22 41 51 32; Møllergata 3) can usually find a place, helping travellers book double rooms in private homes for Nkr300 to Nkr500 (excluding breakfast). There's no minimum stay and no booking fee. If you arrive on a Saturday or Sunday, when the office is closed, call ahead and they'll give you information about possible rooms.

The Oslo S **tourist office window** (Map pp274-6) also books rooms in private homes for a Nkr35 booking fee. Also worth checking out is www.bbnorway.com, which lists around a dozen B&Bs in the city.

The tourist offices book unfilled hotel rooms at discounted rates, which can be worth pursuing during the week but are generally close to the rates that you can book directly from hotels on weekends. There's a Nkr35 booking fee. Discounts are offered to holders of hotel passes, such as the Scan+ Hotel Pass (which can be purchased at participating hotels for Nkr90), at weekends and during the summer period.

Budget

Ekeberg Camping (Map opposite; ☎ 22 19 85 68; www .bogstadcamping.no; Ekebergveien 65; Nkr125; ☺ late May-early Sep; P) The two main camping grounds in Oslo have full facilities, including kitchens (no cooking implements). Rates are for one or two people with tent and no car. Ekeberg is on a hill 10 minutes by bus southeast of (and overlooking) the city. It gets very crowded. Take bus No 34 from Oslo S.

Bogstad Camping (Map opposite; ☎ 22 51 08 00; www.bogstadcamping.no; Ankerveien 117; Nkr135; P) Can be noisy. Take bus No 32 from Oslo S.

Oslo Fjordcamping (☎ 22 75 20 55; fjord camp@online.no; Ljansbrukveien 1; camp sites Nkr120-140, on-site caravan Nkr300-400) This family-friendly camping ground by Oslofjorden, about 8km south of the city, is a very good alternative. There are showers, a kiosk selling snacks and a nearby restaurant. Take bus No 83 from Oslo S.

YMCA Sleep-In (Map pp274-6; ☎ 22 42 10 66; Grubbegata 4; dm Nkr130; ☺ Jul–mid-Aug) With a great position only 10 minutes' walk from Oslo S, the Y fills up quickly. There's no bedding so you'll need a sleeping bag; basic shower and kitchen facilities are available. Breakfast costs extra.

Anker Hostel (Map pp274-6; ☎ 22 99 72 10; www .anker.oslo.no; Storgata 55; 4-bed dm/6-bed dm Nkr145/170, 2-person r Nkr430) A mixed bag. Unlike the other central hostels, it's open year-round. When we visited, it had an unfortunate roach problem. Breakfast costs Nkr60 extra.

Oslo Vandrerhjem Ekeberg (Map opposite; ☎ 22 74 18 90; delf.vandre@frikirken.no; Kongsveien 82; dm/s/d Nkr200/305/465; ☺ Jun–mid-Aug; P) About 4km southeast of Oslo, this hostel has 68 beds in an atmospheric old house. Take tram No 18 or 19 towards Ljabru and get off at Holtet; from there, it's about 100m along Kongsveien.

Oslo Vandrerhjem Haraldsheim (Map opposite; ☎ 22 22 29 65; www.haraldsheim.oslo.no; Haraldsheimveien 4;

ANDERS BLOMQVIST

Wooden buildings of Bryggen (p304), Bergen, Norway

CHRISTIAN ASLUND

Glacier, Svalbard (p344), Norway

Aurlandsfjorden, near the village of Flåm (p314), Norway

CHRISTOPHER WOOD

Höga Kusten (p423), Sweden

Stortorget, Gamla Stan (p367),
Stockholm

Swedish glassware (p379)

Visby (p418), Gotland, Sweden

dm/s/d Nkr200/320/435, dm/s/d with private bathroom Nkr220/380/515; ℗) A busy place, 4km from the city centre. The HI hostel has kitchen, laundry facilities and 270 beds (mostly in four-bed rooms). Take tram No 12, 15 or 17 to the Sinsenkrysset stop.

Oslo Vandrerhjem Holtekilen (Map above; ☎ 67 51 80 40; oslo.holtekilen.hostel@vandrerhjem.no; Michelets vei 55, Stabekk; dm/s/d Nkr205/305/445; ℗) About 8km southwest of Oslo, this hostel has 195 beds. Take bus No 151, 153, 161, 162, 252 or 261.

Oslo Vandrerhjem IMI (Map pp274-6; ☎ 22 98 62 00; oslo.imi.hostel@vanderhjem.no; Staffelsgata 4, enter from Linstowsgata; dm/s/d Nkr215/320/495; ☼ early Jun–mid-Aug) A 46-bed summer hostel with a kitchen, in a central position in a boarding school just north of Det Kongelige Slott.

Perminalen (Map pp274-6; ☎ 23 09 30 81; perminalen@statenskantiner.no; Øvre Slottsgate 2; dm/s/d Nkr280/495/650) A central 55-room pension that caters to military personnel, but is open to everyone. All rooms have TV and private bathroom.

Mid-Range

MS Innvik (Map pp274-6; ☎ 22 41 95 00; www .msinnvik.no; Langkaia; s/d Nkr350/600) Once a car ferry used as a travelling theatre, the vessel has been reincarnated as a B&B docked in the harbour. It's still a cultural centre, so don't flush your toilet when puppet shows or theatrical events are held below deck.

Fønix Hotel (Map pp274-6; ☎ 23 14 63 00; www.foe nix.com; Dronningens gate 19; s Nkr395-515, d Nkr595-865)

Plain furniture, white walls and light hardwood floors feature in this no-frills, top-notch budget hotel with 60 rooms.

Hotell Astoria (Map pp274-6; ☎ 24 14 55 50; www
.rainbow-hotels.no/astoria; Dronningens gate 21; s Nkr475-585, d Nkr625-735) A member of the Rainbow chain. It might be a bit run down compared to its sisters, but it offers the same amenities for about half the price. These savings are most evident on weekdays outside summer.

Ellingsen's Pensjonat (Map pp274-6; ☎ 22 60 03 59; ep@tiscal.no; Holtegata 25; s Nkr300-420, d Nkr490-590) In a neighbourhood of older homes five blocks north of the royal palace, this good-value pension has 20 small rooms.

Cochs Pensjonat (Map pp274-6; ☎ 23 33 24 00; fax 23 33 24 10; Parkveien 25; s/d from Nkr350/500) Newly remodelled with fresh hardwood floors and simple modern furniture. Some of the 65 rooms contain a kitchen. It's just north of the royal palace.

City Hotel (Map pp274-6; ☎ 22 41 36 10; www
.cityhotel.no; Skippergata 19; s Nkr395-550, d Nkr750-850) There's slight historical ambience in the stairwells, but the rooms are fairly basic. Anyone who's sensitive to traffic noise should request a courtyard room.

Top End

Rica Travel Hotel (Map pp274-6; ☎ 22 00 33 00; www
.rica.no; Arbeidergata 4; s Nkr695-950, d Nkr795-1290; Ⓟ 🐾) A good-value business hotel. Rooms are compact, pleasant and modern, and all have private bath, TV and minibar.

Hotel Bristol (Map pp274-6; ☎ 22 82 60 00; www
.bristol.no; Kristian IV's gate 7; s Nkr995-1730, d Nkr1195-2030; Ⓟ 🐾) The best value of the city's classic hotels. The large rooms have full amenities, while the halls and lobby are filled with antiques, chandeliers and old-world charm.

Grand Hotel (Map pp274-6; ☎ 23 21 20 00; www
.grand-hotel.no; Karl Johans gate 31; s Nkr850-1050, d Nkr995-1250; Ⓟ 🐾) Another top-end place brimming with period character.

EATING

Eating out in Oslo has become much more pleasant than in previous decades. A minor food revolution has greatly increased your chances of finding something good to eat that doesn't involve fish. Many of the coolest and cheapest dining options can be found in the neighbourhoods of Grün-

> **THE AUTHOR'S CHOICE**
>
> **Frognerseteren** (☎ 22 46 93 96; Holmenkollveien 200 l; apple cake Nkr52; ⏰ 10.30am-10.30pm Mon-Sat, 10.30am-9pm Sun) Perched on a mountainside overlooking the city, this 19th-century eatery has big fireplaces, spectacular views and kick-arse apple cake in an impressive building combining the rusticity of large wooden beams with the delicacy of 'dragon-style' ornamentation. In summer, there's plenty of outdoor seating. Take T-Bane 1 to the Frognerseteren stop (end of the line).

erløkka, the primary hipster district, and Grønland, whose population of Asian and Middle Eastern immigrants have established affordable ethnic eating places.

Restaurants

Bocata (Map pp274-6; ☎ 22 41 46 62; Stortingsgata 22; snacks Nkr30-100; ⏰ from 8am Mon-Fri, 11am-midnight Sat & Sun) Good for takeaway meals. Come here for Malaysian-style chicken, sweet and sour pork, spaghetti pesto, ham sandwiches and eggs with tomato. Business types pack the counters at lunch time.

Kaffistova (Map pp274-6; ☎ 23 21 42 10; Rosenkrantz gate 8; mains Nkr82-98; ⏰ 10am-8pm Mon-Fri, 11am-5pm Sat & Sun) This friendly cafeteria serves traditional Norwegian food, including reindeer or elk carbonades (locally defined as meat cakes), meatballs and fish cakes; salad is always included.

Krishna's Cuisine (Map p281; Kirkeveien 59B; meals Nkr90; ⏰ noon-8pm Mon-Fri) Near the Majorstuen T-bane station, Krishna's politely serves up soup, salad and a hot dish. It's exclusively vegetarian.

Pascal (Map pp274-6; ☎ 22 55 00 20; Drammensveien 10; cakes Nkr55, mains Nkr130-270; ⏰ 9am-11pm Mon-Fri, 10am-11pm Sat, noon-5pm Sun) When a visiting Bill Clinton needed a cup of coffee, he procured it here. While most come for locally famous cakes (rich and French), there's also a menu of salads (the vegetarian one can tend to be too salty), grilled fish and sandwiches.

Villa Paradiso (Map pp274-6; ☎ 22 35 40 60; Olav Ryes plass 8; mains Nkr119-139; ⏰ 11am-midnight) Norway's finest pizza (not difficult in the land of soggy pies). Make reservations weeks in advance for a weekend dinner. Patrons eat the delicious goods surrounded by big windows and wood panelling.

Sult (Map p281; ☎ 22 87 04 67; Thorvald Meyersgate 26; mains Nkr89-169; ⏰ 4pm-12.30am Tue-Fri, 1pm-12.30am Sat, 1pm-midnight Sun) Prepares a changing menu of continental fare for patrons who sit at small tables and listen to Elvis Presley. Cod encrusted with pistachios is excellent.

Stortorvets Gjæstgiveri's (Map pp274-6; ☎ 23 35 63 60; Grubbegata 3; mains Nkr140-235; ⏰ 10am-midnight Sun-Thu, 10am-5am Fri & Sat) The oldest restaurant in Norway. Sagging yellow, wooden walls and a pretty interior court provide an excellent backdrop for traditional meals. Don't try for a table on 17 May or Christmas.

Lofotstua (Map p281; ☎ 22 46 93 96; Kirkeveien 40; mains Nkr170-220; ⏰ 3-10pm Mon-Fri) Run by a family from the Lofoten islands, this restaurant turns out a changing menu of fantastic fish dishes, in a room that looks sort of like a brown bar.

Kampen Bistro (☎ 22 19 77 08; Bøgata 21; mains Nkr175; ⏰ 2pm-1am) Off the beaten track, this former working-class eatery has been transformed into a slightly stodgy neighbourhood bistro. The good-looking room pleases both the local crowd and those who want to experience the latest thing. How about some chicken confit and antipasto?

Cafés

Blitx (Map pp274-6; Pilestredet 30C; sandwiches Nkr8-15; ⏰ 11am-5pm Mon-Fri) Inside a barricaded, graffitied building is an activist institution with 25 years of squatting history. Friendly, tatooed volunteers run a café serving unbelievably cheap vegetarian and vegan food. Coffee costs Nkr5.

Delicatessen (Map pp274-6; ☎ 22 71 45 46; Sødre gate 8; sandwiches Nkr55-75; ⏰ 11am-1am Mon-Fri, 1pm-1am Sat & Sun) One of Grünerløkka's numerous cool-kid cafés, it features sturdy wooden

---

THE AUTHOR'S CHOICE

Tekehtopa (Map pp274-6; ☎ 22 20 33 52; St Olav plass 2; mains Nkr89-139; ⏰ 10am-1am Mon-Thu, 10am-3am Fri & Sat, noon-1am Sun) A former pharmacy, serving espresso and chevre salads (Nkr89) under a beautifully moulded and painted ceiling. It also serves Norway's ubiquitous breed of lousy pilsner, but you'll feel privileged to drink anything at all in a room this nice.

---

tables and big windows that fold away in the summer to overlook a riverside park across the street. Good Italian sandwiches.

Café the Broker (Map p281; ☎ 22 93 04 80; Bogstadveien 27; mains Nkr94-139; ⏰ 11am-1am) Shooting for the look of a London pub, this café serves up dark wood, brass and hearty sandwiches such as chicken with avocado sauce (Nkr 94).

Cafe Con Bar (Map pp274-6; ☎ 22 05 02 00; Brugata 11; mains Nkr93-135; ⏰ from 11am) Velvet couches and a voyeuristic unisex bathroom dominate this big-windowed eatery overlooking a giant fist erupting from the pavement. Always crowded, enjoy booze, caffeine and salads.

Grand Café (Map pp274-6; Karl Johans gate 31; daily special Nkr140; ⏰ daily special available 11am-6pm Mon-Sat) The café at the Grand Hotel has been serving Oslo's cognoscenti for more than a century. As a reminder, a wall mural depicts the restaurant in the 1890s, bustling with the likes of Munch and Ibsen. The best deal is the traditional daily special.

Quick Eats

Åpent Bakeri (Map pp274-6; Colbjørnsens gate 8; ⏰ 7.30am-5pm Mon-Fri, 9am-3pm Sat) Makes giant, grainy rolls that you can load up with berry jam and butter (Nkr8).

Brugata Kebab Gatekjøkken (Map pp274-6; Brugata 10; felafel & kebab Nkr29-35; ⏰ 10am-midnight Sun-Thu, 10am-5am Fri & Sat) In a city swarming with unimpressive Middle Eastern food stands, this place bucks the trend and turns out some tasty falafel sandwiches.

Punjab Tandoori (Map pp274-6; Grønland 24; mains Nkr55-65; ⏰ 11am-11pm) Serves chicken tandoori, curries, rice and naan bread in a decidedly no-frills room.

Hotel Havana (Map pp274-6; ☎ 23 23 03 23; Thorvald Meyersgate 36; dishes Nkr49-89; ⏰ 10am-6pm Mon-Sat) A Grünerløkka delicatessen serving great takeaway food. Substantial fish burgers (Nkr49) come with home-made aioli, or try Brie sandwiches (Nkr49) and fish and chips (Nkr74).

There are numerous cheap pizza, burger and kebab joints along Grønland and Storgata. Fast food abounds in Oslo S.

Self-Catering

Eating can be an expensive proposition in Oslo. One way to save money is to frequent bakeries, many of which sell reasonably priced sandwiches as well as pastries and hearty wholegrain breads. The Baker Hansen chain has numerous shops around Oslo. Among grocery stores, you'll find some of the best prices at Kiwi, a prolific chain with branches throughout the city. Along Grønland and Storgata, you'll find many small immigrant groceries selling fresh fruit, some of which are open on Sunday.

DRINKING

Zoo Lounge (Map pp274-6; Christian Augustsgate 7B; 12.30pm-1am Mon-Thu, Fri noon-3.30am, Sat 2pm-3.30am, Sun 3pm-midnight) Arty types and Oslo's small publishing crowd come here to look cool. The interior undergoes near constant redesign.

Tea Lounge (Map p281; 22 30 07 05; Thorvald Meyersgate 33B; noon-1am Sun-Wed, 11am-3am Thu-Sat) Somewhat sterile design features combine with velvet furniture at this trendy cocktail bar overlooking one of Grünerløkka's English squares. DJs spin on Fridays. As the name suggests, there's an extensive menu of tea.

Bar Boca (Map p281; 22 04 13 77; Thorvald Meyersgate 30; 11am-1am Mon-Thu, 11am-2.30am Fri & Sat, noon-1am Sun) An amazingly small place which attracts crowds like so many of King Oscar's cross-packed sardines. It shoots for a 1950s/'60s look with very satisfying results. Consider yourself lucky to win a seat at one of the three tables.

Olympen (Map pp274-6; 22 17 28 08; Grølandsleiret 15; 11am-2am) A freakish, century-old workers' beer hall, populated by hipsters and drunks, featuring awesomely cheesy cover bands (Bob Jovi) and cheap beer (Nkr33) in a cavernous space full of elaborate wooden booths and huge oil paintings of faded, unrecognisable cityscapes.

Library Bar (Map pp274-6; 22 82 60 00; Kristian IV's gate 7; from 11am) Wear your finest tweed (not required) and sit among piles of leather-bound tomes in the Bristol Hotel's old-school drinking den. Crystal chandeliers set the tone. This is also a good place for a fancy luncheon sandwich (Nkr70 to Nkr95). Overcoats must be checked (Nkr20).

Lorry's (Map pp274-6; 22 69 69 04; Parkveien 12; 11am-3.30am Mon-Sat, noon-1am Sun) Overpriced, crappy food in a bar with dirty toilets. Despite this, stuffed moose heads and a large menu of lager ensure it's well loved.

Drunk artists used to pay for their beer with some of the stuff hung on the walls.

Teddy's Soft Bar (Map pp274-6; 22 17 36 50; Brugata 3A; from 11am) Established in 1958, Teddy's provides a clear view into the past via its thoroughly unchanged interior. An ancient Wurlitzer sets the tone. While good burgers are served, most come for the suds.

Stargate (Map pp274-6; Grønland 2; 11am-3.30am) If you prefer a down-to-earth drinking-den atmosphere, this place serves beer for around Nkr33.

In the summer, you can enjoy a beer in one of Vigeland Park's outdoor cafés.

ENTERTAINMENT

The tourist office's monthly *What's on in Oslo* brochure lists concerts, theatre and special events, but the best publication for night owls is the free *Streetwise*, published annually in English by Use It (p273). Dress to impress or risk being refused entry to nightspots.

Cinema

Cinemateket (Map pp274-6; 22 47 45 00; Dronningens gate 16; tickets Nkr60) This art-house cinema screens alternative contemporary films, classics and independent fare.

Saga Kino (Map pp274-6; 41 51 90 00; Stortingsgata 28; tickets Nkr60) Shows first-run movies in their original languages.

Gay & Lesbian Venues

There are very few strictly gay and lesbian clubs in Oslo. Several places attract mixed crowds and some venues offer a weekly gay night. For details on these nights and special events, pick up the free *Pink Planet* at the tourist office.

London Pub (Map pp274-6; 22 70 87 00; CJ Hambros plass 5; 3pm-3am) Oslo's oldest hang-out for the studs, where you can shoot stick and feed jukeboxes. If you feel like serious dancing, head upstairs to the more youthful **Chairs** (Map pp274-6; 8pm-3am), where DJs spin every night of the week.

Live Music

Cosmopolite (Map pp274-6; 22 11 33 09; www.cosmopolite.no; Møllergata 26) Focuses on jazz, folk, rock and, lately, French electro-pop. Air, St Germain and the Gotan Project have all played here.

Garage (Map pp274-6; ☎ 22 17 16 00; Grønland 18; ☼ to 3.30am) Consistently injects rock into the needy veins of Oslo. In addition to Norwegian bands, Garage books international acts like Death Cab for Cutie and the Beautiful People. There's a bar upstairs and a summer beer garden.

Rockefeller Music Hall (Map pp274-6; ☎ 22 20 32 32; www.rockefeller.no; Torggata 16) A veteran venue that attracts big-name international contemporary musicians, such as Patti Smith and Queensrÿche.

Oslo Spektrum (Map pp274-6; ☎ 81 51 12 11; Sonja Henies plass 2) One of the city's largest concert halls, where you can barely see whoever is performing (Sting, Cher).

Oslo Konserthus (Map pp274-6; ☎ 23 11 31 11; Munkedamsveien 14) Emphasises fine jazz and classical.

Den Norske Opera (Map pp274-6; ☎ 81 54 44 88; Storgata 23; 50% student discount) Every month except July, Oslo's opera company stages opera, ballet and classical concerts here.

Nightclubs

Blå (Map pp274-6; ☎ 22 20 91 81; Brenneriveien 9) A cultural centre inside an old industrial building, where you will meet people that will actually still look sexy the next morning. In summer months, there's a charming outdoor seating area on the river.

Gloria Flames (Map pp274-6; ☎ 22 17 16 00; Grønland 18; ☼ 4pm-3am Sat-Thu, 3pm-3am Fri) King of the Grønland nightclub scene, the DJs and bartenders here play a heavy mix of rock and indie. Why not rub your arse against a banister to something by the White Stripes?

SHOPPING

Traditional Norwegian sweaters are popular purchases; for good selections check out **Husfliden** (Map pp274-6; Møllergata 4) and **Heimen Husflid** (Map pp274-6; Rosenkrantz gate 8), large shops selling Norwegian clothing and crafts, with items ranging from tacky wooden trolls to elaborate folk costumes.

If you want some cool Scandinavian clothes, try poking around the boutiques of the Grünerløkka district.

You can also buy a fine, grey sheepskin (Nkr800 to Nkr1100) from a lawyer who makes them at his farm in the country. Call Idunn Myklebust (☎ 93 41 19 88), his daughter, to set up a viewing in an office in Oslo.

If you want to buy wine or spirits, there's a Vinmonopolet in the **Oslo City** (Map pp274-6) shopping complex.

GETTING THERE & AWAY

Air

Most flights land at Oslo's main international airport in Gardermoen, 50km north of the city.

SAS (Map pp274-6; ☎ 81 52 04 00) and **Braathens** (Map pp274-6; ☎ 81 52 00 00) have ticket offices in the basement at Oslo S. **Ryanair** (☎ 82 06 11 00) flies from London Stansted and Glasgow Prestwick to Oslo Torp, 112km south of the city.

Boat

Boats to and from Copenhagen, operated by **DFDS Seaways** (Map pp274-6; ☎ 22 41 90 90), and from Frederikshavn (Denmark), operated by **Stena Line** (Map pp274-6; ☎ 23 17 91 00), use the docks off Skippergata, near Vippetangen.

Boats from Hirtshals (Denmark) and Kiel (Germany), run by **Color Line** (Map pp274-6; ☎ 22 94 44 00), dock at Hjortneskaia, west of the central harbour. Connecting buses run to Oslo S, or take tram No 10 or 13.

Bus

Long-distance buses arrive and depart from the Galleri Oslo bus station, about a 10-minute walk east from Oslo S.

Car & Motorcycle

The main highways into the city are the E6, from the north and south, and the E18, from the east and west. Unless you're on a motorcycle you'll have to pay a Nkr15 toll each time you enter Oslo.

All major car-rental companies have booths at Gardermoen airport. The following also have offices in the city centre:
Avis (Map pp274-6; ☎ 81 56 90 44; Munkedamsveien 27)
Budget (Map pp274-6; ☎ 23 16 32 40; Oslo Spektrum)

Train

All trains arrive and depart from Oslo S in the city centre. The reservation desks are open from 6.30am to 11pm daily. There's also an **information desk** (☎ 81 50 08 88) where you can get details on travel schedules throughout Norway. Oslo S has various sizes of lockers for Nkr20 to Nkr50 per 24 hours.

GETTING AROUND
To/From the Airport
High-speed trains run between Oslo S and Oslo International airport in Gardermoen (Nkr150, 24 minutes, every 20 minutes). Alternatively, you can take a local train (Nkr80, 26 to 40 minutes, hourly but fewer on Saturday) or an express airport bus (Nkr90, 40 minutes, three hourly). A taxi costs around Nkr450, though **Oslo Taxi** (☎ 02323) sometimes offers discount rates of Nkr110 to Nkr310.

Car & Motorcycle
Oslo has its fair share of one-way streets, which can complicate city driving, but otherwise traffic is not too challenging. Still, the best way to explore central sights is to walk or take local transport, though a car can be quite convenient for outlying areas such as Holmenkollen.

Metered street parking, identified by a solid blue sign with a white 'P', can be found throughout the city centre. Hours written under the sign indicate when the meters need to be fed. Unless otherwise posted, parking is free outside that time and on Sunday. Parking at most meters costs from Nkr20 to Nkr40 per hour. There are many multistorey car parks in the city centre, including those at major shopping centres such as Oslo City and Aker Brygge. The Oslo Card gives free parking in municipal car parks.

Boat
Ferries going to Bygdøy leave from Rådhusbrygge every 20 to 40 minutes, while ferries to the islands in Oslofjorden leave from Vippetangen.

Public Transport
Oslo has an efficient public-transport system with an extensive network of buses, trams, T-bane trains (metro/underground) and ferries. A one-way ticket on any of these services costs Nkr20 if you buy it from a station agent or kerbside machine. You can also buy your ticket from the driver, but that will add a Nkr10 surcharge. A *dagskort* (unlimited day ticket) costs Nkr60, but can't be used between 1am and 4am. Weekly/monthly cards cost Nkr160/620 (Nkr80/310 for people under 20 and seniors over 67). You can buy these with cash only at Trafikanten, Narvesen kiosks, staffed T-bane and train stations, and some 7-Eleven stores.

Bicycles can be taken on Oslo's trams and trains for an additional Nkr11. Note that while it may seem easy to board the subway and trams without a ticket, if confronted by an inspector you'll receive an automatic Nkr750 fine.

Trafikanten (Map pp274-6; ☎ 81 50 01 76; ☼ 7am-8pm Mon-Fri, 8am-6pm Sat & Sun), below the Oslo S tower on Jernbanetorget, provides free schedules and a handy public-transport map, *Sporveiskart Oslo*. Dial ☎ 177 from 7am to 11pm (from 8am at weekends) for schedule information.

BUS & TRAM
Bus and tram lines crisscross the city and extend into the suburbs. There's no central station but most buses and trams converge at Jernbanetorget in front of Oslo S. Most westbound buses, including those to Bygdøy and Vigeland Park, also stop on the southern side of Nationaltheatret.

The service frequency drops dramatically at night, but on Saturday and Sunday only, Nattlinjer night buses No 200 to 218 follow the tram routes until 4am or later (tickets Nkr50; passes not valid).

T-BANE
The five-line T-bane metro train network, which goes underground in the city centre, is faster and goes further outside the city centre than most bus lines. All lines pass through Nationaltheatret, Stortinget and Jernbanetorget stations.

Taxi
Taxis charge up to Nkr91.50 at flagfall and from Nkr10 to Nkr16 per kilometre. There are taxi stands at Oslo S, shopping centres and city squares. Any taxi with a lit sign is available for hire. Otherwise, phone **Taxi2** (☎ 02202), **Norgestaxi** (☎ 08000) or **Oslo Taxi** (☎ 02323). Meters start running at the point of dispatch, adding to what will become a gigantic bill! Oslo taxis accept major credit cards.

AROUND OSLO
The **Østfold** region, on the eastern side of Oslofjorden, is a mixture of farmland and small industrial towns dependent on the timber trade. The city of Fredrikstad, with its ancient fortresses, is an interesting place to visit.

Fredrikstad

pop 69,000

Founded by King Frederik II, Fredrikstad has an enclosed fortress town (Gamlebyen) complete with moats, gates and a drawbridge, built in 1663 as protection against a belligerent Sweden. Gamlebyen's central square has an ATM, a café and an unflattering statue of King Frederik II, a seeming victim of bowel irritation.

The annual **Måne Festivalen** (☎ 69 32 37 64; www.maanefestivalen.no, no English; ☒ late May) draws big crowds with local acts, international rock bands and film screenings. The venue occupies part of an abandoned shipyard that once made some of the world's largest oil tankers.

SIGHTS

You can walk around the perimeter of the **fortress walls**, once ringed by 200 cannons, and through the narrow, cobbled streets lined with still-lived-in historic buildings, most dating from the 17th century.

Across the moat, 15 minutes' walk down Kongens gate, is the intact **Kongsten Festning** (Kongsten Fort), which sits on a bluff above a city park and dates from 1685. It makes for pleasant strolling and it's fun to scramble around the turrets, embankments, walls and stockade.

SLEEPING & EATING

Fredrikstad Motell & Camping (☎ 69 32 03 15; Torsnesveien 16; camp sites from Nkr90, s/d Nkr390/490, 2-/4-person cabins Nkr300/400) In the grounds of the Kongsten Fort; call in advance or you may find it closed.

Gamlebyen Pensjonat (☎ 69 32 20 20; Smedjegaten 88; dm/s/d Nkr150/350/500) A beautifully renovated former artillery barracks with a common kitchen and quiet location.

Café Balaklava (☎ 69 32 30 40; Færgeportgata 78B; mains Nkr65-150; ☒ from 11am Mon Sat, from noon Sun) In Gamlebyen, this café occupies a lovely old house with tall ceilings, massive windows and a cobbled courtyard. Tasty dishes include sweet onion soup with traces of ham (Nkr65). A one-legged pirate, sword drawn, stares mournfully over the content crowds. He has a parrot.

GETTING THERE & AWAY

Trains to Fredrikstad leave roughly hourly from Oslo S (Nkr155, 1¼ hours).

GETTING AROUND

From Fredrikstad train station it's a five-minute walk to the riverfront, where a frequent ferry (Nkr6, one minute) shuttles across the Glomma river to the fortress' main gate.

SOUTHERN NORWAY

Sørlandet, the curving south coast, is magnetic for Norwegians when the weather turns warm. The coast is largely rocky with a heavy scattering of low stone islands, and Sørlandet's numerous coves and bays are ideal for Norwegian holiday-makers with their own boats. The attraction is generally not as great for foreign travellers, the majority of whom have just arrived from places with warmer water and better beaches.

The Sørland train line, which runs 586km from Stavanger to Oslo via Kristiansand, stays inland most of the way, but buses meet the trains and link the train line with most south-coast towns.

STAVANGER & AROUND

pop 106,000

Don't be misled by Stavanger's title 'Oil Capital of Norway' – this is a picturesque city (Norway's fourth largest) of narrow cobbled streets and small white houses. The centre is lively, containing a fine stock of bars, cafés and places to stroll. It's an excellent point from which to begin exploring the Lysefjord, with daily boat tours in summer.

History

Stavanger was once a bustling fishing centre and, in its heyday, had more than 70 sardine canneries. By the 1960s, the depletion of fish stocks had brought an end to the industry, but the discovery of North Sea oil spared Stavanger from hard times. The industry is perhaps no great tourist draw, but it has brought prosperity and a cosmopolitan community with nearly 3000 British and US oil people.

Orientation

The adjacent bus and train stations are a 10-minute walk from the harbour. Most of Stavanger's sights are within easy walking distance of the harbour. The Kulturhus

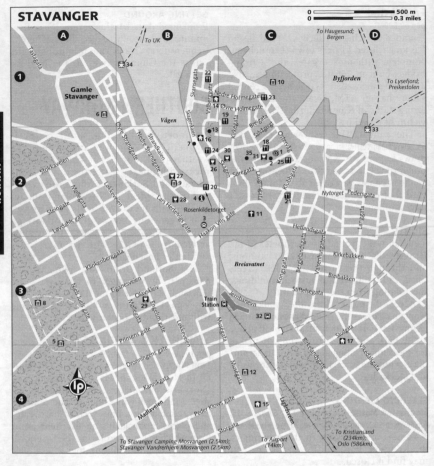

STAVANGER

0 ————— 500 m
0 ————— 0.3 miles

To UK

To Haugesund;
Bergen

Byfjorden

To Lysefjord;
Preikestolen

Gamle
Stavanger

Vågen

Breiavatnet

Nytorget Pedersgata

Rosenkildetorget

Haakon VIIs gate

Train
Station

NORWAY

To Stavanger Camping Mosvangen (2.5km);
Stavanger Vandrerhjem Mosvangen (2.5km)

To Airport
(14km)

To Kristiansand
(234km);
Oslo (586km)

holds the public library, a cinema, an art gallery and the new children's museum. On sunny days the pedestrianised streets by the Kulturhus are alive with students, street musicians and pavement vendors.

Information
BOOKSHOP
Gardum (☎ 51 89 44 40; Søregata 22; ☉ 9am-6pm Mon-Thu, 9am-5pm Fri, 9am-4pm Sat) Large travel section.

INTERNET ACCESS
Cafe.com (☎ 51 55 41 20; Søvberg gate 15; ☉ 11am-9pm Mon-Sat, noon-9pm Sun) A friendly Irish expat hooks you up on a picturesque street.
Library (☎ 51 50 72 57; Sølverg gate 2; ☉ 10am-7pm Mon-Thu, 10am-5pm Fri, 10am-3pm Sat) In the Sølvberget

Stavanger Kulturhus; provides free access (with a wait and a half-hour time limit).

TOURIST INFORMATION
Tourist Office (☎ 51 85 92 00; www.visitstavanger .com; Rosenkildetorget 1; ☉ 9am-8pm Jun-Aug, shorter hrs & closed Sun Sep-May) Provides details of Stavanger's 12 annual festivals.

Sights & Activities
The area's most popular outing is the two-hour hike to the top of the incredible **Preikestolen** (Pulpit Rock), 25km east of Stavanger. You can inch up to the edge of its flat top and peer 600m straight down to the Lysefjord. The tourist board has details of public transport to the trail head.

If you'd rather look up at Pulpit Rock from the bottom, the **Fjord Tours** (☎ 51 53 73 40; www.fjordpanorama.no) sightseeing boat leaves Stavanger from 18 May to 31 August to cruise the lovely steep-walled **Lysefjord**, operated by an entertaining bunch of old salts. Tickets (adult/child Nkr270/135) can be purchased at the tourist office. Saturdays in March, they do a fjord and ski package (boat, bus and lift ticket) for Nkr300, where you'll meet a 6km downhill trail.

A good outing, if you have a vehicle, is to take the **car ferry** (☎ 51 86 87 80) from Stavanger all the way to Lysebotn, at the head of the Lysefjord. From there, drive up the mountain pass to Sirdal, along a narrow road that climbs 640m with 27 hairpin turns, for a scenic ride back to Stavanger. Starting at the Øygardsstølen Café car park, near the top of the bends, a strenuous 10km-return hike leads to the second wonder of Lysefjord, the **Kjeragbolten** boulder, or chockstone, lodged between two rock faces about 2m apart but with 1000m of empty space underneath! The ferry takes four hours, leaving 8.30am daily from mid-June to mid-August; it costs Nkr340 for a car with driver plus Nkr150 for each additional passenger (or pedestrians). Advance reservations are advised.

OTHER ATTRACTIONS

A fun quarter for strolling about is **Gamle Stavanger**, on the west side of the harbour, where cobblestone walkways lead through rows of well-preserved early-18th-century whitewashed wooden houses.

Stavanger Domkirke (Haakon VII's gate; ☉ 11am–6pm Mon & Tue, 10am–6pm Wed–Sat, 1–6pm Sun mid-May–mid-Sep, shorter hrs mid-Sep–mid-May), a medieval stone cathedral, dates from around 1125. A good time to visit is during the organ recital at 11.15am on Thursday.

Norsk Oljemuseum (☎ 51 93 93 00; www.norskolje.museum.no; Kjeringholmen; adult/child Nkr75 /35; ☉ 10am-7pm Jun-Aug, 10am-4pm Mon-Sat, 10am-6pm Sun Sep-May) traces the history of oil formation and exploration in the North Sea, and contains numerous interactive displays including an escape chute down which you can jump.

Valbergtårnet, a 150-year-old stone tower at the end of Valberggata, has good views of the city and the harbour.

The following **museums** (☎ 51 84 27 00; ☉ 11am-4pm mid-Jun–mid-Aug, shorter hrs early Jun & late Aug, 11am-4pm Sun Sep-May) have combined same-day admission costs of adult/family Nkr40/90. **Stavanger Museum** (Muségata 16) has the standard collection of stuffed animals in one wing and local history exhibits in another. More interesting is the **Maritime Museum** (Nedre Strandgate 17), in two restored warehouses, which gives a good glimpse of Stavanger's extensive maritime history. Audio devices explain the exhibits in English, Norwegian and German. The fascinating **Canning Museum** (Øvre Strandgate 88A) occupies an old sardine cannery, where you'll see ancient machinery in action, learn about the various soul-destroying jobs provided by the cannery and ogle a large collection of old sardine-can labels. There are also two 19th-century manor houses built by wealthy ship owners: the recently restored **Ledaal** (Eiganesveien 45), which serves as the residence for visiting members of the royal family, and the excellent **Breidablikk** (Eiganesveien 40A), a merchant's opulent villa built in 1881.

Sleeping

Because the local hostel is not open year-round, sleeping cheaply in Stavanger can be a challenge. Those with cash will have better luck, finding many central, quayside options, though occasional oil-industry events sometimes fill every bed in town. For an alternative to the places listed below, stop by the tourist office for help booking a room in a B&B (Nkr30 booking fee). Rooms start at 300Nkr, and are within 3km of the city centre.

BUDGET

Stavanger Camping Mosvangen (☎ 51 53 29 71; www.mosvangencamping.no; Tjensvoll 1B; camp sites from Nkr80, 2-person cabins Nkr350-400, 4-person cabins Nkr500-600; P) Situated near the lakeside HI hostel you'll find grassy camp sites and cabins with refrigerator, hotplates and shared bathrooms.

Stavanger Vandrerhjem Mosvangen (☎ 51 54 36 36; stavanger.mosvangen.hostel@vandrerhjem.no; Henrik Ibsens gate 19; dm/d Nkr180/345; ☯ Jun-Aug, Sep-May with advance booking; P) Lakeside, utilitarian and painted red, this hostel is 3km from the city centre (bus No 78 or 79).

Preikestolhytta (☎ 97 16 55 51; www.preikes tolhytta.no; dm/r Nkr200/545; ☯ Jun-Aug; P) The turf-roofed hostel lies 25km out of the city, within walking distance of Pulpit Rock. Private rooms sleep up to three people. Add a fourth, and the price jumps to Nkr940. Book far in advance.

MID-RANGE & TOP END

Rogalandsheimen Gjestgiberi (☎ 51 52 01 88; Muségata 18; s Nkr350-450, d Nkr500-550; P) Paintings cover every surface here. The 19th-century guesthouse has 13 homey rooms and a cool stairwell. A local rock band recently did a photo shoot here.

Stavanger Bed & Breakfast (☎ 51 56 25 00; www.stavangerbedandbreakfast.no; Vikedalsgata 1A; s/d Nkr540/640; P) The newly renovated, small yellow rooms come with plain furniture, linoleum floors, refrigerator and shower. Free waffles and quiet neighbourhood.

Commandør Hotel (☎ 51 89 53 00; comhot@online .no; Valberggata 9; s/d Nkr695/795, s/d discount Nkr500/650) Centrally located, clean but a little run-down accommodation with private bathrooms.

Skagen Brygge Hotell (☎ 51 85 00 00; www .skagenbryggehotell.no; Skagenkaien 30; s/d Nkr1350/1450, s/d discount Nkr700/850; P ☒) A modernised former warehouse containing exceedingly comfortable rooms, half of which have stellar views of the harbour. The breakfast buffet features fresh fruit, French pastry and

some other items not normally seen on a Norwegian table.

Eating

RESTAURANTS

Food Story (☎ 51 56 37 70; Klubbgata 3; mains Nkr55-99; ☯ 10am-6pm Mon-Wed, 10am-8pm Thu & Fri, 10am-5pm Sat) Half deli and half restaurant, prepares a changing menu of high-end fare, usually organic. Eat raw tuna with citrus fruits, Italian sausages and fancy sauces.

Akropolis (☎ 51 89 14 54; Søvberggata 14; lunch Nkr59-109, mains Nkr159-209; ☯ 11am-midnight Mon-Sat, 1-11pm Sun) Prepares enormous and good Greek staples in a warm room with a three-sided fireplace.

India Tandoori Restaurant (☎ 51 89 39 35; Valberggata 14; dishes Nkr89-209; ☯ 4-11pm Mon-Sat, 2-11pm Sun) Authentic northern Indian dishes and a particularly good korma navrattan.

Sjøhuset Skagen (☎ 51 89 51 80; Skagenkaien 16; mains Nkr189-235; ☯ 11am-11pm Mon-Sat, 2-9.30pm Sun) For traditionally prepared fish, this creaky-floored choice is a winner. Find exposed wooden frames, models of ships and sidewalk views over the harbour.

CAFÉS

Resept (☎ 51 55 39 80; Østervåg 43; mains Nkr49-99; ☯ 11am-2am Mon-Sat, 1pm-2am Sun) The decor involves minimal leather couches and solid coloured walls recalling the supergraphics of the '70s. Enjoy vegetarian pasta (Nkr79), sandwiches, Asian noodle soup and DJs.

Café Sting (☎ 51 89 38 78; Valberget 3; smaller dishes Nkr75-129, mains Nkr155-175; ☯ 11am-midnight Mon-Wed, 11am-3am Thu-Sat, 2pm-midnight Sun) Blessed with a lovely hill-top position and sharing a yard with the Valberg Tower, Sting serves substantial smaller dishes, such as an excellent Cajun fish burger. Sting doubles as a nightclub focusing on jazz.

SELF-CATERING

For a standard supermarket experience, there's a Rema 1000 supermarket at the bus station. A fish market sits at the harbour, and **Våland Dampbakeri & Conditori** (☎ 51 86 19 23; Nygaten 24; ☯ 10am-4pm Mon-Sat) turns out flaky pastry, as it has done since 1913.

Drinking & Entertainment

Beverly Hills Fun Pub (☎ 51 89 51 77; Skagenkaien 14A; ☯ noon-2am) Second home to scads of oil-rig workers and international businessmen is Stavanger's most consistently (and inexplicably) crowded bar, even on rainy Monday nights. Despite the name and the startling ratio of four men to every woman, it's not even an expressly gay pub.

Cementen (☎ 51 56 78 00; Nedre Strandgate 2; ❂ 7pm-2am) On a second floor with views across the quay, friendly bartenders play kick-arse tunes and sometimes host bands. Pick up a used book (Nkr5) and an occasional beer special (Nkr31) in a room that feels like a private library full of drunk hipsters.

Checkpoint Charlie (☎ 51 53 22 45; www.checkpoint .no; Lars Hertervigs gate 5; ❂ 8pm-2am Sun-Fri, 3pm-2am Sat) Friendly dudes tend bar here, where the rock happens on a small stage. Urge Overkill recently played here. Happy-hour beer sells for Nkr36.

Folken Studentersamfunnet (☎ 51 56 44 44; Løkkenveien 22; ❂ 11am-midnight Mon-Wed, 11am-2am Thu-Fri, 3pm-2am Sat, 6pm-midnight Sun) By day, espresso and beer are served to a student crowd. On many nights, an upstairs club dishes out metal, rock and more. Jokke & Valentinerne and Gluecifer are representative bands. Free board games and Internet (crappy, key-sticking keyboard).

Soleado (☎ 51 55 43 80; Søvberggata 7; ❂ noon-11pm Mon-Tue, noon-midnight Wed, noon-1.30am Thu-Sat, 3 11pm Sun) A nice place for an expensive mixed drink. The mood is set by a pretty, backlit bar faced with translucent fakewood contact paper. Light Spanish dishes are served.

Looking for a disco? Wander along Skagen and you'll find a couple of options, including **Gossip** (☎ 51 89 52 15; Skagen 21; ❂ to 2am), where beer costs Nkr27 until 11pm on Friday and Saturday.

Getting There & Away
TO/FROM THE AIRPORT
Buses leave frequently for the airport (14km south of town) from the bus station (Nkr50, 20 minutes, several times an hour). A taxi will set you back Nkr250 to Nkr390.

BOAT
The **HSD Flaggruten** (☎ 51 86 87 80) express passenger catamaran to Bergen (adult/student Nkr590/300, 4¼ hours) and Haugesund leaves two or three times daily. Eurail, Norway Rail and ScanRail passholders get 50% discounts.

BUS
Nor-Way Bussekspress offers services to Oslo (Nkr730, 10¼ hours) six times each weekday, and once on Saturday and Sunday. Buses from Bergen to Stavanger (Nkr400, 5¾ hours) run roughly every two hours.

TRAIN
Stavanger's only railway line runs to Oslo (Nkr783, 7¾ hours, one to three daily) via Kristiansand (Nkr379, three hours, four to seven daily).

Getting Around
The city centre is a combination of narrow streets and cobbled pedestrian walkways that are best explored on foot. You'll find car parks next to the post office and on the southern side of the bus station.

MANDAL
pop 12,800
Mandal, Norway's southernmost town, is best known for having the country's finest bathing beach (though the timid should note that water temperatures are significantly warmer in the Oslofjord!). In addition to the white-sand beaches, there are enough cobbled pedestrian laneways in the centre for an hour or two of village exploration.

Mandal Tourist Information (☎ 38 27 83 00; Bryggegaten 10; ❂ 9am-7pm Mon-Fri, 10am-4pm Sat & Sun Jun-Aug, 9am-4pm Mon-Fri Sep-May) is a five-minute walk west from the bus station.

Sights & Activities
The 800m-long **Sjøsanden** beach, about 1km from the centre, is Norway's Copacabana, with a lovely forest backdrop. The **Mandal Museum** (☎ 38 27 30 00; Store Elvegata 5/6; adult/child Nkr10/free; ❂ 11am-5pm Mon-Fri, 11am-2pm Sat, 2-5pm Sun late Jun–mid-Aug) displays a host of historical maritime and fishing artefacts, and works by local artists, including Mandal's favourite son, Gustav Vigeland.

At the southernmost point in Norway, 36km west of Mandal, you'll find wild coastal scenery and historical exhibitions at the classic lighthouse, **Lindesnes Fyr** (☎ 38 26 19 02; www.lindesnesfyr.no; Lindesnes; adult/child Nkr30/free; ❂ 10am-6pm May, 10am-8pm Jun & Sep, 10am-9pm Jul & Aug). Buses from Mandal (Nkr52, one hour) travel to the lighthouse on Monday, Wednesday and Friday from late June to late August at 9.15am. You'll have one hour there before the single return bus departs.

Sleeping & Eating

Sjøsanden Ferietun (☎ 38 26 60 37; saferie@online .no; Fr Nansenvei 6; camp sites Nkr100, r from Nkr450, cabins from Nkr550; **P**)) Just steps from the beach in a family-friendly complex set within a forest grove. Sells out months in advance.

Kjøbmandsgaarden Hotel (☎ 38 26 12 76; www .kjobmandsgaarden.no; Store Elvegaten 57; s/d Nkr740/970) A former hardware shop dating from 1863. The basic rooms come with private bathroom but don't exhibit much character. Rooms cost 15% less on weekends.

Kjøbmandsgaarden Hotel (Store Elvegaten 57; sandwiches Nkr35-70; ⏰ 7am-7pm Mon-Fri, 8.30am-7pm Sat & Sun) The cafeteria here serves traditional Norwegian fare in a wood-floored room with beachy furniture and an upright piano. At night, it's a more expensive restaurant.

Jonas B Gundersen (☎ 38 27 15 00; Store Elvegaten 25; mains Nkr149-164; ⏰ 3-11.30pm Mon-Thu, 3pm-2am Fri & Sat, 1-11.30pm Sun) Serves good pizza (large ones, costing Nkr189 to Nkr209, feed two to three people) in a joint packed with old music instruments and pictures of jazz dudes.

Edgar's Bakeri og Konditori (☎ 38 27 15 55; Torget at Store Elvegaten; ⏰ 8am-4.30pm Mon-Sat) Occupying two floors of a charming white building, this place serves excellent *kaneli svingen* (pastry with vanilla filling) and has fine 2nd-floor views of the *torget* (square).

Getting There & Away

Express buses run two to four times daily between Stavanger (Nkr320, 3¾ hours) and Kristiansand (Nkr80, 45 minutes) via Mandal.

KRISTIANSAND

pop 75,000

The largest of southern Norway's coastal towns – and the fifth-largest city in the country – summertime Kristiansand offers bustling urban life and a small bathing beach right in the town centre. Strollers will enjoy poking around Posebyen, a district containing a large concentration of white houses from the 17th and 18th centuries. Kristiansand also hosts the fantastic Quart Festival, Norway's most famous festival of music.

Kristiansand is Norway's closest port to Denmark and offers the first glimpse of the country for many ferry travellers from the south. Kristiansand has a grid pattern, or *kvadraturen*, of wide streets laid out by King Christian IV, who founded the city in 1641. It's a busy seaside holiday resort for Norwegians, but foreign visitors generally pile off the ferries and onto the first train, missing most of what the area has to offer.

Orientation

The train, bus and ferry terminals are together on the west side of the city centre. Markens gate, a pedestrian street a block inland, is the central shopping and restaurant area.

Information

NetZone (☎ 38 10 86 12; Vestre Strandgate 23; per hr Nkr33; ⏰ 2pm-midnight) Internet access.
Tourist Office (☎ 38 12 13 14; www.sorlandet.com; Vestre Strandgate 32; ⏰ 8am-6pm Mon-Fri, 9am-6pm Sat, noon-6pm Sun mid-Jun–late Aug, 8.30am-3.30pm Mon-Fri late Aug–mid-Jun)

Sights & Activities

The most prominent feature to be seen along Strandpromenaden is **Christiansholm Festning** (⏰ 9am-9pm mid-May–mid-Sep), built between 1662 and 1672; there's a fine coastal view from the cannon-ringed wall. From there, walk inland along the tree-lined Festningsgata and turn left onto Gyldenløves gate, passing the **town square** and **Kristiansand Domkirke** (☎ 38 10 77 50; Kirkegata; ⏰ 9am-4pm Mon-Fri, 9am-2pm Sat late Jun-early Aug, 10am-2pm Mon-Fri early Jun & late Aug), which is Norway's largest church. You can climb the tower for adult/child Nkr20/10. Organ recitals occur at noon, Tuesday to Saturday.

It's also worth taking a slow stroll around the enchanting **Posebyen** (old town), which takes in most of 14 blocks at the northern end of Kristiansand's characteristic *kvadraturen*.

Baneheia, a wooded park with lakes and trails, abuts the northwest side of the city centre. The 11th-century Romanesque **Oddernes Kirke** (☎ 38 05 87 50), about 1.5km further northeast along E18, contains a rune stone, and a baroque pulpit from 1704; it's open variable hours.

Kristiansand Dyrepark (☎ 38 04 97 00; www .dyreparken.com; adult Nkr85-240, child Nkr70-195; ⏰ 10am-7pm late Jun-early Aug, variable hrs mid-Aug–mid-Jun) has gradually expanded into one of

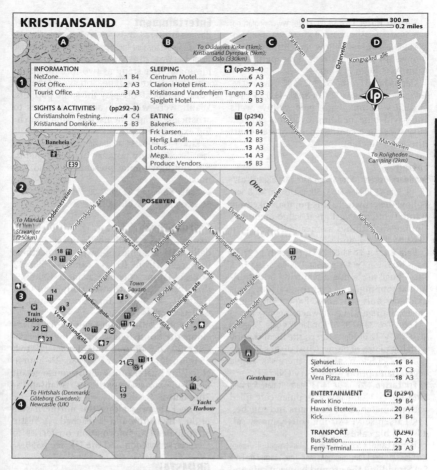

KRISTIANSAND

0   300 m
0   0.2 miles

INFORMATION	
NetZone..................................1	B4
Post Office..............................2	A3
Tourist Office..........................3	A3

SIGHTS & ACTIVITIES	(pp292–3)
Christiansholm Festning.............4	C4
Kristiansand Domkirke...............5	B3

SLEEPING	(pp293–4)
Centrum Motel..........................6	A3
Clarion Hotel Ernst....................7	A3
Kristiansand Vandrerhjem Tangen.8	D3
Sjøgløtt Hotel...........................9	B3

EATING	(p294)
Bakeries..................................10	A3
Frk Larsen...............................11	B4
Herlig Land!.............................12	B3
Lotus......................................13	A3
Mega......................................14	A3
Produce Vendors.....................15	B3

To Oddernes Kirke (1km);
Kristiansand Dyrepark (9km);
Oslo (330km)

Kongsgård allé

Marvikveien

To Roligheden
Camping (2km)

Baneheia

POSEBYEN

To Mandal
(44km);
Stavanger
(250km)

Town
Square

Train
Station

To Hirtshals (Denmark);
Göteborg (Sweden);
Newcastle (UK)

Giestehavn

Yacht
Harbour

Skansen

Sjøhuset.................................16	B4
Snadderskiosken......................17	C3
Vera Pizza..............................18	A3

ENTERTAINMENT	(p294)
Fønix Kino..............................19	B4
Havana Etcetera......................20	A4
Kick.......................................21	B4

TRANSPORT	(p294)
Bus Station.............................22	A3
Ferry Terminal.........................23	A3

NORWAY

Norway's most popular domestic attractions. Mainly catering to families with children, the park includes water rides, a zoo, a 'Nordic wilderness' and the fantasy village of Kardamomme By. It's off the E18, 9km east of town.

Festivals & Events

Quart Festival (☎ 38 14 69 69; www.quart.no; day pass Nkr380-450, 5-day pass Nkr1675), a week-long music and film festival, occurs in early June. Multiple venues are set up throughout town (one being on the site of a plague graveyard), hotels sell out for miles in every direction, and acts such as the Pixies, Björk and Nick Cave tear it up along with local acts.

Sleeping

Roligheden Camping (☎ 38 09 67 22; camp sites from Nkr130; P) At a popular beach 3km east of town. Take bus No 15.

Kristiansand Vandrerhjem Tangen (☎ 38 02 83 10; kristiansand.hostel@ vandrerhjem.no; Skansen 8; dm Nkr205, s Nkr315-395, d Nkr415-450; ⊗ mid-Jan–mid-Dec; P) A modern hostel, offering clean rooms and a common kitchen in a quiet, industrialised part of town a few minutes' walk from a small beach.

Centrum Motel (☎ 38 02 79 69; Vestre Strandsgate 49; s Nkr350-450, d Nkr450-580; P) Wins points for cleanliness and the short walk to the train station, but it's ugly, with cheap flooring, utilitarian construction and unpleasant proximity to artery roads. No breakfast.

Sjøgløtt Hotel (☎ 38 02 21 20; www.sjoglott.no; Østre Strandgate 25; s Nkr350, d Nkr660-690, d with private bathroom Nkr840) Yellow and little with 12 rooms, on a quiet street. Free petting of Aunt Asse, who is a cat.

Clarion Hotel Ernst (☎ 38 12 86 00; www.ernst.no; Rådhusgaten 2; s Nkr645-1190, d Nkr895-1320; **P** 🕸) Ordinary rooms with pale yellow walls and vivid blue bedding overlook either a busy street or a central, glass-covered court (these are quieter).

Eating

Snadderkiosken (Østre Strand gate 78A; dishes Nkr17-55; 🕑 9am-11.30 Mon-Fri, 11.30am-11.30pm Sat & Sun) Follow the crowds to this popular takeaway stand. It offers a vast great-value menu, including such things as meatballs, cod with mashed potato, and sausages.

Vera Pizza (☎ 38 02 15 73; Kristian IV's gate 13; mains Nkr65-95; 🕑 1-11pm Sun-Thu, noon-2am Fri & Sat) A huge pizza menu featuring both traditional toppings and eyebrow-raising items like tacos and jalapeños. Expect dim light, cheap chairs and heart-warming service.

Lotus (☎ 38 02 97 57; Kristian IV's gate 23; mains Nkr76-90; 🕑 12.30-10pm) Keeps the locals happy with big plates of chow. Most dishes involve pork or chicken, though there's a single vegetarian option – a stir-fry (Nkr59).

Frk Larsen (☎ 38 07 14 13; Markens gate 5; mains Nkr85-120; 🕑 10am-10pm) A popular café filled with mismatched tables, chairs and couches, Frk Larsen serves strong coffee, messy salads and big cakes.

Herlig Land! (☎ 38 09 06 22; Markensgate 16; mains Nkr126-228; 🕑 11am-midnight Mon-Thu, 11am-2am Fri & Sat) Straddling the ground between café and restaurant, candle-lit Herlig Land! is a good spot to eat chicken that led a happy life until not long before it arrived on your plate. A house DJ plays most Saturdays.

Sjøhuset (☎ 38 02 62 60; Østre Strandgate 12A; mains Nkr225-260; 🕑 11.30am-11pm Mon-Fri, 4-11pm Sat) A harbourside favourite with stacks of outdoor seating. Consistently dishes out superb seafood, such as cod fillets baked with ham and served with caramelised parsnip. The less-hungry or the budget-minded should try the shellfish soup (Nkr89).

There are good bakeries on Rådhus gate near the post office, a Mega supermarket opposite the train station, and produce vendors sell fresh fruit and vegetables on the southeastern side of the cathedral.

Entertainment

Havana Etcetera (☎ 38 02 96 66; Vestre Strandgate 15; 🕑 bar 6pm-1am Sun-Tue, 6pm-3am Wed-Sat, nightclub 10pm-3am Wed-Sat) A small dance floor and illuminated bar stand as two focal points in a pool of darkness. The club avoids the impulse to repeatedly play the same pop hits. Wallflowers will find plenty of spaces to artistically drape themselves while clutching expensive beer.

Kick (☎ 38 02 64 44; Dronningens gate 8; 🕑 to 2am) Exceedingly popular on warm nights, this outdoor venue presents DJs and live music.

Fønix Kino (☎ 82 00 07 00; Vestre Strandgate 9) Screens popular blockbusters.

Getting There & Away

Express buses head north once or twice daily to Haukeligrend, with connections to Bergen (from Kristiansand Nkr590, 12 hours). Trains run to Stavanger (Nkr379, three hours, four to seven daily) and Oslo (Nkr531, 4¾ hours, three to six daily), as well as express buses.

Regional buses depart hourly for towns along the south coast, including Arendal (Nkr100, 1½ hours) and Mandal (Nkr64, 45 minutes). For Risør (Nkr180, 2¾ hours), Nor-Way Bussekspress allows you to get off the Oslo express, departing Kristiansand at 2pm daily.

The E18 runs along the northern side of the city centre and is reached via Vestre Strandgate. For information on ferries to Denmark, Sweden and the UK see p350.

GRIMSTAD

pop 18000

Grimstad, renowned as the sunniest spot in Norway, is one of the loveliest of the 'white towns' on the Skagerrak coast and has a charming pedestrianised centre with narrow streets. These streets begin to fill in June, as attendees flock to the Norwegian Short Film Festival. By July, the small town becomes extremely crowded, with Norwegians arriving to enjoy their summer holidays. Popular activities include sunbathing on islands, fishing and ice-cream eating.

Today's low-key atmosphere belies Grimstad's past as a major shipbuilding centre – at one point in the 19th century the town had 40 shipyards, and 90 ships were under construction simultaneously.

Grimstad Turistkontor (☎ 37 04 40 41; www
.grimstad.net; Smith Petersensgata 3; ☺ 8.30am-4pm
Mon-Fri, longer hrs Jun-Aug) can suggest various
boat trips to the outlying skerries.

Sights

In 1847, Henrik Ibsen started work at
Grimstad's Lars Nielsen pharmacy, where
he lived in a small room and cultivated
his interest in writing. By the time he left
Grimstad for university studies in Christiania (Oslo), Ibsen had qualified as a
pharmacist's assistant and was on his way
to future renown as a writer. Some of his
finest works are set in Grimstad's offshore
skerries.

The **Grimstad By Museum** (☎ 37 04 46 53; Henrik
Ibsens gate 14, adult/child Nkr40/15; ☺ 11am-5pm Mon-
Sat, 1-5pm Sun May–mid-Sep) includes the virtually untouched Lars Nielsen pharmacy and
Ibsenhuset (the Ibsen house), which contains many of the writer's belongings, such
as portraits of mean-looking people.

Sleeping & Eating

Bie Apartment & Feriesenter (☎ 37 04 03 96; www
.bieapart.no; Arendalsveien 85; camp sites Nkr200, cabins
Nkr550-1200; P) This is the closest option to
town, 800m northeast of the centre along
Arendalsveien.

Grimstad Hotell (☎ 37 25 25 25; www.grimstadhotell
.no; Kirkegata 3; s/d Nkr1045/1245, s/d discount summer
Nkr700/1040, s/d discount weekends Nkr675/800; P ✗)
An excellent location smack in the town
centre. The exterior suggests you'll be sleeping in one of the town's white cuties, but
most rooms are part of a bizarre historicist
complex.

Apotekergården (☎ 37 04 50 25; Skolegaten 3;
mains Nkr225; ☺ 6-11pm Sun-Thu, Fri & Sat noon-1am)
Inside a former pharmacy dating to 1853.
Serves swanky tapas and fixed-price menus
that run up to Nkr695. It's got some lovely
garden seating.

Haven Brasserie (☎ 37 04 15 91; Storgata 4; mains
Nkr110-240; ☺ noon-1am Mon-Sat, 1pm-midnight Sun)
Come here for a hearty Italian meal or a
cold beer at an outdoor, harbourside table.

Entertainment

Satisfying nightlife options only exist in the
summer. Look for a handful of bars near the
Torvet, or head over to the harbour, where
Club Berg (☎ 92 83 22 24; Storgata 2) plays host
to drunken nights of karaoke, hip-hop, the

occasional black metal band and twangy
country dudes.

Getting There & Away

The bus station is on Storgata, at the harbour. Nor-Way Bussekspress runs between
Oslo (Nkr380, five hours) and Kristiansand
(Nkr80, one hour) via Grimstad three to
five times daily. Nettbuss buses to/from
Arendal run once or twice hourly (Nkr37,
30 minutes).

ARENDAL

pop 32,000

Piles of picturesque houses smile down
from the steep slopes surrounding Pollen,
a small bit of flat land that serves as Arendal's town centre and harbour. Here you'll
find one of the liveliest, prettiest towns on
Norway's southern coast. Harbourside cafés
and clubs will keep you happy until late at
night; outdoor seating fills up the moment
things even begin to resemble warm.

There are many islands to explore in the
archipelago off the coast, some of which are
appointed with 19th-century lighthouses.

Information

Arendal Turistkontor (☎ 37 00 55 44; Langbrygga 5;
☺ 9am-7pm Mon-Sat, noon-7pm Sun mid-Jun–mid-Aug,
9am-4pm Mon-Fri mid-Aug–mid-Jun) On the eastern side
of Pollen, dispenses the goods.

Library (☎ 37 01 39 13; Torvet 6; ☺ 10am-7pm Mon-
Thu, 10am-4pm Fri, 10am-2pm Sat) Free Internet.

Sights

Just a few minutes' walk south of the bus
station brings you into the old harbourside area of **Tyholmen**, with its attractively
restored 19th-century wooden buildings.
Check out the **Rådhus** (☎ 37 01 30 00; Rådhusgata
10; ☺ 9am-3pm Mon-Fri), originally a shipown-
er's home dating from 1815, later becoming the town hall in 1844. It features an
elegant original staircase and portraits of
Norwegian royalty.

The **Aust-Agder Museum** (☎ 37 07 35 00;
Parkveien 16; adult/child Nkr20/10; ☺ 9am-5pm Mon-
Fri, noon-5pm Sun late Jun–mid-Aug, to 3pm mid-Aug–
mid-Jun) displays objects brought home by
the town's sailors (from 1832), as well as
relics of Arendal's shipbuilding, timber
and import-export trades, and decent
collections of folk art, furniture, farming
implements and sailing paraphernalia.

Ask the tourist office for details of the offshore islands.

Sleeping & Eating

For anything inexpensive, you'll have to head out of town.

Nidelv Brygge og Camping (☎ 37 01 14 25; Vesterveien 251, Hisøy; camp sites Nkr60-110, cabins Nkr250-750; **P**) On the Nidelv at Hisøy, 6km west of Arendal. From town, take any half-hourly bus for Kristiansand or Grimstad (Nkr22).

Ting Hai Hotel (☎ 37 02 22 01; ting@online.no; Østregate 5; s/d Nkr650/890) It's a curious choice but the best value in the centre, with clean rooms appointed with cheap furniture. It occupies space above a decent Chinese restaurant (mains from Nkr105).

Clarion Hotel Thole (☎ 37 07 68 00; Teaterplassen 2; s/d Nkr1390/1590, s/d discount summer Nkr840/1090, s/d discount weekends Nkr760/960; **P** 🏷) Surrounded by boats, this harbourside hotel features nice rooms and fine views, and is a two-minute walk from an enclave of restaurants and cafés.

Fiskebrygga Pub & Vinstue (☎ 37 02 35 87; Nedre Tyholmsvei 1; mains Nkr39-79; 🕑 9am-2am) Shove fried fish, seafood soup (Nkr69, with bread) and beer down while sitting at a cramped outdoor table next to the water. Everyone else is.

Café Det Lindvedske hus (☎ 37 02 18 38; Nedre Tyholmsvei 7B; dishes Nkr40-110; 🕑 11am-midnight Mon-Sat, 1pm-midnight Sun) Occupying a 200-year-old building, this café serves salads, pasta and sandwiches, such as a delicious vegetarian number with browned cheese, tomato, avocado, mushrooms and green beans. Booze, coffee and cakes are also offered.

Fish market (Nedre Tyholmsvei 1; 🕑 9am-5pm Mon-Fri, 9am-3pm Sat) For a tasty snack try inexpensive fish cakes from the waterfront fish market.

Getting There & Away

Nor-Way Bussekspress buses between Kristiansand (Nkr100, 1¾ hours) and Oslo (Nkr340, four hours) call in several times daily at the Arendal bus station, in a large square a block west of Pollen harbour. Regional buses connect Arendal with Grimstad (Nkr37, 30 minutes, once or twice hourly) and Kristiansand (Nkr95, 1½ hours, hourly).

Arendal is connected with the main rail system by a trunk line from Nelaug.

RISØR

pop 4000

With its cluster of historic white houses built up around a busy little fishing harbour, Risør is one of the most picturesque villages on the south coast. The harbour is filled with small classic vessels, ranging from old wooden motorboats to oddly designed masted contraptions. All exude craftsmanship. Risør is a haunt for artists, and many well-to-do yachties make it their summer base.

The **Risør Trebåtfestival** (Wooden Boat Festival ☎ 37153070; www.risor-woodenboat.no) is the town's biggest annual event. Held in early August, it constitutes an amazing sight: you're unlikely to see so many fabulous boats in such a staggeringly cute setting anywhere else. During the festival, ships of different classes and ages race one another, sometimes crashing when the wind is strong.

Sights & Activities

The small but interesting quayside **Risør Aquarium** (☎ 37 15 32 82; Dampskipsbrygga; adult/child Nkr40/20; 🕑 11am-7pm late Jun-early Aug, shorter hrs mid-Aug–mid-Jun) houses saltwater fish, crustaceans and shellfish common to Norway's south coast. For the lowdown on the geology, fishing economy and 275-year history of Risør, visit the **Risør Museum** (☎ 37 15 17 77; Prestegata 9; adult/family Nkr30/50; 🕑 11am-5pm mid-Jun–mid-Aug).

Next to wandering around the harbour and the narrow streets in the old town, one of the most popular activities is to visit the offshore islands, which can be reached by inexpensive water taxis. The most frequented island, **Stangholmen**, has an old lighthouse with a restaurant.

Sleeping & Eating

Most visitors to Risør stay on their boats.

Moen Camping (☎ 90 98 19 02; www.moen-camping .no; Moen; camp sites from Nkr80, cabins Nkr500-600) The closest camping ground is 11km west of town and 2km from the E18, but there are regular buses.

Risør Kunstforum (☎ 37 15 63 83; www.kunstforum .no; Tjenngata 76; s/d Nkr500/600) Around 1km west of the harbour. Offers do-it-yourself breakfast as well as art and sculpture classes.

Det Lille Hotel (☎ 37 15 14 95; www.detlillehotel .no; Kragsgata 12; s Nkr950-1100, d Nkr1150-1350; **P**) This charming hotel occupies several small white houses on the water, with individually and exceptionally appointed suites. Parking for boats is available.

Brasserie Krag (☎ 37 15 14 95; Kragsgata 12; mains Nkr110-210; ✇ 10.30am-10pm Mon-Sat, noon-6pm Sun May-Sep, shorter hrs Oct-Apr) The Mediterranean-influenced menu at this picturesque brasserie is best enjoyed at a small pavement table under an awning.

You'll find a couple of moderately priced cafés at the harbour, as well as ice-cream shops, a market and a **bakery** (Kragsgata).

Getting There & Away
Buses to/from Risør (Nkr55, 45 minutes) connect with the train at Gjerstad several times daily. Nor-Way Bussekspress buses between Kristiansand (Nkr140, three hours) and Oslo (Nkr320, 3¾ hours) connect at Vinterkjær with local buses to/from Risør (Nkr28, 20 minutes).

TELEMARK
Most of the Telemark region is sparsely populated and rural, with steep mountains, deep valleys, high plateaus and countless lakes.

Public transport in this region isn't particularly convenient; most buses run infrequently and the train lines cover only the southeastern part of Telemark, so sightseeing is best done by car. Telemark's westernmost train station is at Bø; from there, connecting buses lead west to Dalen, Åmot and on to Odda in Hardanger. For tourist information, contact **Telemarkreiser** (☎ 35 90 00 20; www.visittelemark.com; Postboks 3133, Handelstorget, N-3707 Skien).

Telemark Canal
The Telemark canal system, a marvel completed in 1892, covers 105km of lakes and canals with 18 locks. It runs from the industrialised city of Skien to the small town of Dalen.

From 17 June to 10 August, a couple of century-old **sightseeing boats** (☎ 35 90 00 30; www.telemarkskanalen.no) make the unhurried, if not sluggish, 11-hour journey (adult/child Nkr330/165 one way). Between mid-May and early September they run three times weekly.

Trains run every hour or two between Skien and Oslo (Nkr245, 2¾ hours).

One kilometre from the Dalen dock, **Buøy Camping Dalen** (☎ 35 07 75 87; www.dalencamping

.com; camp site Nkr110-155, s/tr Nkr250/385, cabins Nkr470-950; P) has a reasonable camping ground with hostel-style rooms and cabins. Skien's **HI hostel** (☎ 35 50 48 70; Moflatveien 65; dm/s/d Nkr175/300/425; P) has rooms and tent space for campers; breakfast is included. Nearby **Hotell Herkules** (☎ 35 59 63 11; Moflatveien 59; s/d Nkr550/800; P) is a reasonably good mid-range choice.

Notodden
pop 12,300

Notodden is an industrial town of little note, but the nearby **Heddal stave church** (☎ 35 02 04 00; www.heddal-stavkirke.no; Heddal; adult/child Nkr30/free, Sun services free; ✇ 10am-5pm 20 May-19 Jun & 21 Aug-10 Sep, 9am-7pm 20 Jun-20 Aug) is Telemark's most visited attraction. It's an impressive structure and possibly dates from 1242, but parts of the chancel date from as early as 1147. Of great interest are the 'rose' paintings, a runic inscription, the bishop's chair and the altarpiece. On Sundays from Easter to November, services are held at 11am (visitors are welcome, but to avoid disruption, you must remain for the entire one-hour service); after 1pm, the church is again open to the public.

The town hosts the renowned **Notodden Blues Festival** (☎ 35 02 76 50; www.bluesfest.no, no English; early Aug) featuring dozens of bands, such as the Jon Spencer Blues Explosion and Jeff Healey.

From Notodden, buses heading for Seljord and Bondal stop at Heddal. Between Kongsberg and Notodden (Nkr75, 35 minutes), TIMEkspressen buses run once or twice an hour.

Rjukan
pop 3730

The long, narrow industrial town of Rjukan is squeezed into the deep Vestfjord Valley at the base of the 1883m **Mt Gausta**, Telemark's highest peak. The route to the top starts at lake Heddersvann (1173m), 16km southeast of town (by road Fv651).

Ask the **tourist office** (☎ 35 09 12 90; www.visitrjukan.no; Torget 2; ✇ 9am-7pm Mon-Fri, 10am-6pm Sat & Sun late Jun-early Aug, 9am-2.30pm Mon-Fri mid-Aug–mid-Jun) about local activities, including fun **rail bicycle rides**.

The **Industrial Workers Museum** (☎ 35 09 90 00; adult/student/child Nkr55/45/30; ✇ 10am-6pm May-Sep, 10am-3pm Tue-Fri Oct-Apr), housed inside a hydroelectric plant dating from 1911, 7km west of Rjukan, has an exhibit about the Norwegian Resistance's daring sabotage of the heavy-water plant used by the Nazis in their atomic efforts.

From the top station of the Krossobanen cable car (Nkr35), above Rjukan, it's an eight-hour walk north to the Kalhovd mountain hut and a network of trails that stretches north and west across the expansive moors of **Hardangervidda**, a popular wilderness hiking area that boasts Norway's largest wild reindeer herd.

Rjukan Vandrerhjem (☎ 35 09 20 40; Kvitåvatn; dm/s/d Nkr200/300/450; **P**) is a good hostel in the town centre. Breakfast costs extra (Nkr50). Small and centrally located **Park Hotell** (☎ 35 08 21 88; Sam Eydes gate 67; s/d from Nkr590/845; **P**) has a fine restaurant and ordinary rooms.

An express bus connects Rjukan to Oslo (Nkr260, 3½ hours) via Kongsberg (Nkr160, 1¾ hours), two or three times daily.

Kragerø
pop 10584

A popular seaside resort with narrow streets and whitewashed houses, Kragerø has long served as a retreat for Norwegian artists, including Edvard Munch. Many consider it the most beautiful town in Telemark. The forested island **Jomfruland**, the most popular local destination, measures about 10km long and up to 600m wide, and has mostly sandy beaches. Ferries between Kragerø and Jomfruland (Nkr31, 50 minutes) are run by **Kragerø Fjordbåtselskap** (☎ 35 98 58 58) two or three times daily.

The fine **HI hostel** (☎ 35 98 57 00; Lovisenbergveien 20; dm/s/d Nkr255/515/615; 20 Jun-15 Aug; **P**) is about 2km from town. **Lanternen** (☎ 35 98 57 80; Ytre Strandvei 4; mains Nkr80-165; from 11am) operates variously as a café, bar, restaurant and disco. Its deck has a nice view. You'll find simple Norwegian fare at **Kafe Edvard** (☎ 35 98 15 50; Edvard Munchsvei 2; mains Nkr70-135; from 10am).

The simplest approach is by rail from Oslo or Kristiansand to Neslandsvatn, where most of the trains meet a connecting bus to Kragerø.

BUSKERUD

The mainly forested county of Buskerud stretches northwest from Oslofjorden to the central highlands of Norway. Mineral resources, particularly silver, have been thoroughly exploited in Buskerud's hills and mountains.

Kongsberg
pop 15,700

Today's Kongsberg attracts visitors with winter skiing and historic sites left over from its 17th-century glory days. The town was founded in 1624 following the discovery of the world's purest silver deposits in the nearby Numedal Valley. During the resulting silver rush, it briefly became the second-largest town in Norway. The Royal Mint is still in town, but the last mine, no longer able to turn a profit, closed in 1957. Should you be uninterested in mining history, the town remains charming enough for a stroll.

The **tourist office** (☎ 32 73 50 00; www.visit kongsberg.no; Storgata 35) is opposite the train station.

SIGHTS

The **Norwegian Mining Museum** (☎ 32 72 32 00; Hyttegata 3; adult/child Nkr50/10; 10am-5pm Jul–mid-Aug, shorter hrs mid-Aug–Jun) is in the town centre, just over the bridge on the west side of the Numedalslågen river. Set in an 1844 smelter, it has exhibits of mining, minerals, the Royal Mint and the local armaments industry.

The **Lågdal folk museum** (☎ 32 73 34 68; Tillischbakken 8-10; adult/child Nkr40/10; 11am-5pm mid-Jun–mid-Aug) has a collection of period farmhouses, WWII exhibits and an indoor museum with re-created 19th-century workshops and a fine optics section. It's a 10-minute walk south of the train station: turn left on Bekkedokk and take the walkway parallel to the tracks, following the signs.

Up on the hillside at Håvet, about 1km west of town and well signposted, you'll find curious **royal monograms** carved into a cliff.

In July and August, there are daily tours of the old **silver mines** (adult/child Nkr75/30) at Saggrenda, 8km from Kongsberg, which include a 2.3km train ride through cool subterranean shafts – bring a sweater! Tour times should be checked with the tourist office. The Oslo–Notodden TIMEkspressen bus runs from Kongsberg to Saggrenda (Nkr50, 10 minutes, hourly), then it's a 15-minute walk.

SLEEPING & EATING

Kongsberg HI Hostel (☎ 32 73 20 24; Vinjesgata 1; dm/s/d Nkr220/470/575; **P**) About 1km from the train station: walk south on Storgata, cross the bridge, turn right and take the pedestrian walkway over the main road to Saggrenda.

Gyldenløve Hotel (☎ 32 86 58 00; Hermann Foss-gata 1; s/d from Nkr725/875; **P**) This comfortable hotel is conveniently located in the centre.

Skrågata Mat & Vinhus (☎ 32 72 28 22; Nymoens Skrågate; mains Nkr86-240) The menu at this fine establishment includes sandwiches, salads, pasta and beef and fish dishes.

Jeppe's Pizza (☎ 32 73 15 00; Kirkegata 6; mains Nkr85-2225) In the old town, west of the river, Jeppe's serves steaks, fish and chips, Mexican-style dishes, spare ribs and salads.

GETTING THERE & AWAY

Kongsberg is a 1½-hour train ride from Oslo (Nkr142). TIMEkspressen buses connect Kongsberg with Oslo (Nkr140, 1½ hours) and Notodden (Nkr75, 35 minutes, hourly). An express bus connects Kongsberg and Rjukan (Nkr180, 1¾ hours) two or three times daily.

CENTRAL NORWAY

The central region of Norway, stretching west from Oslo towards the western fjords, includes vast swathes of forested fells, the country's highest mountains and some of the best-known national parks. The scenic Oslo–Bergen railway climbs through forests and alpine villages up to Norway's cross-country skiing paradise, the stark Hardangervidda plateau.

HAMAR

pop 28,000

The unimpressive commercial town of Hamar, sitting beside lake **Mjøsa**, Norway's largest lake, is the capital of Hedmark county and boasts proudly of hosting several Olympic events in 1994.

The **tourist office** (☎ 62 51 75 03; ☺ 8am-6pm Mon-Fri, 10am-6pm Sat mid-Jun–mid-Aug, 8am-4pm Mon-Fri mid-Aug–mid-Jun) is inside the Viking-skipshuset sports arena.

Sights & Activities

The **Northern Lights amphitheatre**, the world's largest wooden hall, was built for figure skating and short track-skating events for the 1994 Olympics. The town's landmark is the **Vikingskipshuset sports arena**, a graceful structure with the lines of an upturned Viking ship.

The extensive open-air **Hedmarksmuseet** (☎ 62 54 27 00; Strandveien 100; adult/student/child Nkr70/55/30; ☺ 10am-5pm mid-Jun–mid-Aug, shorter hrs mid-May–mid-Jun & mid-Aug–mid-Sep), 1.5km west of the town centre, includes 18th- and 19th-century buildings, a local folk history exhibit featuring the creepy Devil's Finger, and the fantastic **Hamardomen** (glass cathedral), where the ruins of a medieval cathedral are protected within an enormous glass structure.

From 25 June to 11 August, **Skibladner** (☎ 61 14 40 80; www.skibladner.no), the world's oldest operating paddle steamer (1856), cruises around lake Mjøsa, sailing on Tuesday, Thursday and Saturday to Lillehammer (Nkr220/320 one way/return).

Sleeping & Eating

Vikingskipet Motell og Vandrerhjem (☎ 62 52 60 60; hamar.hostel@ vandrerhjem.no; Åkersvikavegen 24; dm/s/d Nkr215/325/405; **P**) The HI hostel offers accommodation within 100m of the sports arena. Breakfast is Nkr60 extra.

Seiersted Pensjonat (☎ 62 52 12 44; www .seiersted.no; Holsetgata 64; s/d Nkr400/600; **P**) Centrally located, with 18 charming rooms, some with bath, some with balcony. Decorative touches include painted furniture. Dinner available from Nkr55.

Pizzaninni (☎ 62 52 49 65; Torggata 24; mains Nkr80-125; ☺ from 11am) Serves filling but unremarkable pizza and pastas.

Artichoke (☎ 62 53 23 33; Parkgata 21; lunch Nkr72-128, mains Nkr195-255; ☺ from 11am Tue-Sun). Gourmet meals in an art gallery. The former bank building was modified by someone who earned good grades in design school.

Siste Indre's (☎ 62 53 55 00; Torggata 53; ☺ from 11am Mon-Sat, 1-11pm Sun) Drink hooch while relaxing on comfortable leather couches in a dim bar that features old light fixtures and yellowing pictures of speed skaters. Towards closing time, don't be surprised if someone gets up and starts banging on a piano, while the entire bar sings along. Overheard cross-table analysis: is Snoop Dawg really laid-back? Most agreed that he was.

Getting There & Away

Nor-Way Bussekspress buses run to/from the western fjords several times daily. Frequent trains run between Oslo and Hamar (Nkr196, 1½ hours, once or twice hourly); some services continue to Trondheim (Nkr616, five hours, four or five daily) via Lillehammer. Trains also run to Røros (Nkr446, 3¼ hours, three to five daily), some with connections for Trondheim.

LILLEHAMMER & AROUND

pop 25,000

Lillehammer, at the northern end of lake Mjøsa, has long been a popular ski resort for Norwegians, and since hosting the 1994 Winter Olympics it has attracted foreign visitors as well.

Lillehammer's centre is small and easy to explore. Storgata, the main pedestrian walkway, is two short blocks east of the adjacent bus and train stations. You'll find more information at the **tourist office** (☎ 61 25 92 99; Jernebanetorget 2; ☑ 9am-8pm Mon-Sat, 9am-6pm Sun mid-Jun–mid-Aug, 9am-4pm Mon-Fri, 10am-2pm Sat mid-Aug–mid-Jun).

Sights & Activities

It's possible to tour the former Winter Olympic sites, including **Håkons Hall** (the ice-hockey venue) and the **ski jump**; the tourist office brochure lists opening times.

Håkons Hall is the site of the **Norwegian Olympic Museum** (☎ 61 25 21 00; Olympiaparken; adult/student/child Nkr60/50/30, with combined entry to Maihaugen folk museum adult/child Nkr120/55; ☑ 10am-6pm mid-May–mid-Sep, 10am-4pm Tue-Sun mid-Sep–mid-May), with exhibits on the history of the Olympic Games.

At Hunderfossen, 15km north of town, speed fanatics can visit the **bobsleigh and luge track** (reservations ☎ 61 05 42 00; www.olympiaparken.no; rides adult/child Nkr170/85) and ride a rubber raft (75km/hr) down the actual Olympic run; in summer, when there's no ice, a 'wheeled bob' is used. For Nkr850, a bobsleigh driver can whisk you down at 120km/h. It is possible to poop your snowpants. Reservations are advised.

The Olympics aside, Lillehammer's main attraction is the exceptional **Maihaugen folk museum** (☎ 61 28 89 00; Maihaugveien 1; adult/student/child Nkr90/75/40, with combined entry to Norwegian Olympic Museum adult/child Nkr120/55; ☑ 9am-6pm Jun–mid-Aug, 10am-5pm mid-Aug–Sep, shorter hrs

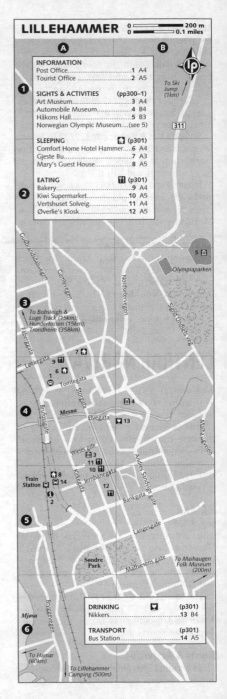

LILLEHAMMER

INFORMATION	
Post Office	1 A4
Tourist Office	2 A5

SIGHTS & ACTIVITIES	(pp300-1)
Art Museum	3 A4
Automobile Museum	4 B4
Håkons Hall	5 B3
Norwegian Olympic Museum	(see 5)

SLEEPING	(p301)
Comfort Home Hotel Hammer	6 A4
Gjeste Bu	7 A3
Mary's Guest House	8 A5

EATING	(p301)
Bakery	9 A4
Kiwi Supermarket	10 A5
Vertshuset Solveig	11 A4
Øverlie's Kiosk	12 A5

DRINKING	(p301)
Nikkers	13 B4

TRANSPORT	(p301)
Bus Station	14 A5

Oct-May), which contains around 180 historic houses, shops, farm buildings and a stave church.

Lillehammer also has an **art museum** (☎ 61 05 44 60; Stortorget 2; adult/child Nkr50/40; ☺ 11am-4pm Tue-Sun).

See the previous Hamar section for details of the *Skibladner* paddle steamer.

Sleeping & Eating

Lillehammer Camping (☎ 61 25 33 33; Dampsagveien 47; camp sites from Nkr100, cabins Nkr350-650; **P**) On lake Mjøsa 700m south of the *Skibladner* dock. Offers good camping facilities and modern cabins.

Mary's Guest House (☎ 61 24 87 00; s/d Nkr550/740) Conveniently located on the 2nd floor of the train station. The simple rooms come with private bathroom and breakfast.

Gjeste Bu (☎ 61 25 43 21; ss-bu@online.no; Gamlevegen 110; dm Nkr100 s/d from Nkr225/350) The rustic rooms here are a real bargain, which is why you must book early. There's a group kitchen, free coffee and a TV room. Bathrooms are shared and breakfast is available at a nearby bakery.

Comfort Home Hotel Hammer (☎ 61 26 35 00; hammer@comfort.choicehotels.no; Storgata 108; s/d from Nkr650/850; **P** ✗) The rates include dinner and the rooms are of a high standard.

Storgata is lined with shops, bakeries and restaurants, where you can get a reasonably priced meal at several places.

Vertshuset Solveig (☎ 61 26 27 87; Storgata 68B; dishes Nkr39-165; ☺ from 10am) Full of oldsters, gingham tablecloths, salmon sandwiches and cakes.

Øverlie's Kiosk (Storgata 50; dishes Nkr42-85) Slings inexpensive grease, usually in the form of kebabs and burgers.

Nikkers (☎ 61 27 05 56; Elvegata 18; dishes Nkr43-149; ☺ from 11am) For winter beer with a roaring fire and a stuffed moose head – the ski-lodge feel will get you in the mood for some downhill action. It serves burritos, salads and minced meat.

There's also a Kiwi supermarket on Storgata.

Getting There & Away

Nor-Way Bussekspress runs services to/from Oslo (Nkr250, three hours, three or four times daily). Rail services run between Lillehammer and Oslo (Nkr282, 2¼ hours, 12 to 17 times daily), and between

Lillehammer and Trondheim (Nkr556, 4¼ hours, four or five times daily).

DOMBÅS

pop 1500

Dombås, a popular adventure and winter sports centre, makes a convenient break for travellers between the highland national parks and the western fjords. In town, there isn't much to do except buy fuel and groceries. The **tourist office** (☎ 61 24 14 44) is by the central car park and commercial complex.

The **Dovrefjell-Rondane Nasjonalparksenter** (☎ 61 24 14 44; ☺ 9am-8pm mid-Jun–mid-Aug, shorter hrs mid-Aug–mid-Jun), at the tourist office, has interesting displays on all Norwegian national parks. **Dovrefjell National Park**, 30km north of town, protects the 2286m-high Snøhetta massif and provides a habitat for arctic foxes, reindeer, wolverines and musk oxen.

The friendly **Bjørkhol Camping** (☎ 61 24 13 31; www.bjorkhol.no; camp sites Nkr70-80, cabins Nkr210-700; **P**) is 7km south of Dombås by the E6. In a wooded spot, **Dombås Vandrerhjem Trolltun** (☎ 61 24 09 60; dombaas.hostel@ vandrerhjem.no; dm/s/d Nkr215/375/545; **P**) is about 1.5km north of the centre and off the E6.

The main central commercial complex includes a grocery store, a busy cafeteria, and a supposedly Irish chain restaurant called Dolly Dimple's.

Dombås lies on the railway line between Oslo (Nkr552, four hours, four or five daily) and Trondheim (Nkr338, 2½ hours). The spectacular Raumabanen line runs down the Romsdalen valley from Dombås to Åndalsnes (Nkr179, 1¼ hours, two or three times daily).

JOTUNHEIMEN NATIONAL PARK

The Sognefjellet road between Lom and Sogndal passes the northwestern perimeter of Jotunheimen National Park, Norway's most popular wilderness destination. Hiking trails lead to some of the park's 60 glaciers, up to the top of Norway's loftiest peaks (the 2469m Galdhøpiggen and 2452m Glittertind) and along ravines and valleys featuring deep lakes and plunging waterfalls. There are DNT huts and private lodges along many of the routes. For park information, as well as the maps and information you need to hike, contact **Lom tourist office** (☎ 61 21 29 90; www.visitlom.com; ☺ 9am-9pm Mon-Fri, 10am-8pm Sat & Sun mid-Jun–mid-Aug, shorter

NORWAY

hrs mid-Aug–mid-Jun). The office can also give you information about hiring a guide for a glacier walk.

Dramatic **Galdhøpiggen**, with its cirques, arêtes and glaciers, is a fairly tough eight-hour day hike from Spiterstulen, with 1470m of ascent, accessible by a toll road (Nkr60 per car). **Krossbu** is in the middle of a network of trails, including a short one to the **Smørstabbreen glacier**. From **Turtagrø**, a rock-climbing and hiking centre midway between Sogndal and Lom, there's a three-hour hike to Fannaråkhytta, Jotunheimen's highest DNT hut (2069m), which offers great panoramic views.

The private **Spiterstulen lodge** (☎ 61 21 14 80; www.spiterstulen.no; Lom; camping per person Nkr50, s/d Nkr250/500; **P**), situated at an old *sæter* (summer dairy), is the jumping-off point for Galdhøpiggen.

Beautiful Bøverdalen, 18km south of Lom, has a great riverside **HI hostel** (☎ 61212064; boever dalen.hostel@vandrerhjem.no; dm/s/d Nkr135/225/280; ☺ Jun-Sep; **P**). Near the head of Bøverdalen, the no-frills **Krossbu Turiststasjon** (☎ 61 21 29 22; www.krossbu.no; Krossbu; d from Nkr470; **P**) has 85 rooms, most with shared bathroom.

OSLO TO BERGEN

The Oslo–Bergen railway line is Norway's most scenic, a seven-hour journey past forests and alpine villages, and across the starkly beautiful **Hardangervidda** plateau.

Midway between Oslo and Bergen is **Geilo**, a ski centre where you can practically walk off the train and onto a lift. There's also good summer **hiking** in the mountains around Geilo and the town has an **HI Hostel** (☎ 32 08 70 60; www.oenturist.no; Lienvegen 137; dm/d Nkr185/345), near the train station.

From Geilo the train climbs 600m through a tundra-like landscape of high lakes and snowcapped mountains to the tiny village of **Finse**, near the **Hardangerjøku-len** icecap. Finse has year-round **skiing** and is in the middle of a network of summer **hiking trails**. One of Norway's most frequently trodden trails winds from the Finse train station down to the fjord town of **Aurland**, a four-day trek. There's breathtaking mountain scenery along the way as well as a series of DNT and private mountain huts a day's walk apart – the nearest is Finsehytta, 200m from Finse station. There's also a bicycle route from Finse to Flåm (six hours, down-

hill) on the century-old **Rallarvegen** railway construction road.

Myrdal, further west along the railway line, is the connecting point for the spectacularly steep Flåm railway, which twists and turns its way down 20 splendid kilometres to **Flåm** village on Aurlandsfjorden, an arm of Sognefjorden.

Many people go down to Flåm, have lunch and take the train back up to Myrdal, where they catch the next Oslo–Bergen train. A better option is to take the ferry from Flåm to Gudvangen (via spectacular Nærøyfjorden, with its thundering waterfalls and lofty peaks), where there's a connecting bus that climbs a steep valley on the dramatically scenic ride to Voss. From Voss, trains to Bergen run roughly hourly. To include a cruise of the Nærøyfjorden in a day trip from Oslo to Bergen, you'll need to take the 8.11am train from Oslo, which connects with the afternoon ferry from Flåm. For details on Flåm, see the Sognefjorden section later in this chapter.

BERGEN & THE WESTERN FJORDS

The formidable, sea-drowned glacial valleys of the western fjords, flanked by almost impossibly rugged terrain, haven't deterred Norwegians from settling and farming their slopes and heights for thousands of years. The region presents some of the most breathtaking scenery in Europe and, not surprisingly, is the top destination for travellers to Norway.

Information on the entire region is available from **Fjord Norge** (☎ 55 30 26 40; www.fjord norway.com; Postboks 4108 Dreggen, N-5835 Bergen).

BERGEN
pop 230,830

Lovely Bergen contends for the honour of being Norway's most beautiful city. Set on a peninsula surrounded by mountains and the sea, the neatly contained centre offers a tangle of crooked streets and hilltop views. Norway's second-largest city, Bergen provides ample opportunities to linger in cafés and bars, while a large university population helps to secure Bergen's claim as western Norway's cultural capital,

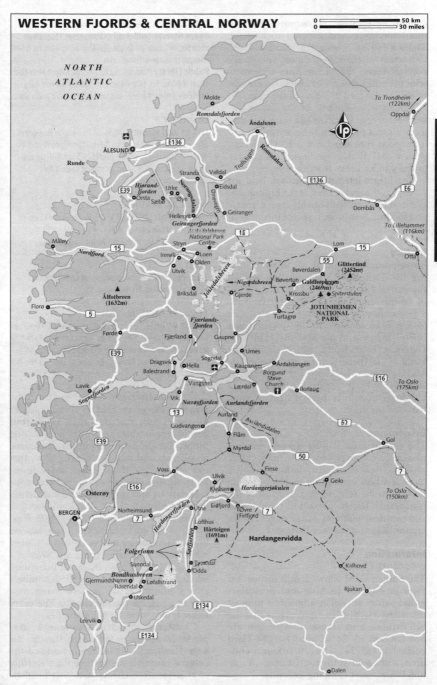

WESTERN FJORDS & CENTRAL NORWAY

0 ———— 50 km
0 ———— 30 miles

NORTH
ATLANTIC
OCEAN

Molde
Romsdalsfjorden
Åndalsnes

To Trondheim
(122km)
Oppdal

E136

ÅLESUND

Runde

E136

E6

Stranda   Valldal
Hjørund-   Urke   Eidsdal
fjorden   Øye
E39   Ørsta   Sæbø
Hellesylt   Geiranger

Trollstigen
Romsdalen

Dombås

To Lillehammer
(116km)

Geirangerfjorden
Jostedalsbreen
National Park
Centre

Måløy

Nordfjord   15

Stryn
Innvik   Loen
Utvik   Olden

Lom   15
Bøverdalen   Glittertind
(2452m)   Otta
Bøvertun   Galdhøpiggen   55
Krossbu   (2469m) Spiterstulen

Ålfotbreen
(1632m)

Jostedalsbreen
Nigardsbreen
Briksdal   Gjerde

Turtagrø

JOTUNHEIMEN
NATIONAL
PARK

Florø   5

Førde

Fjærlands-
fjorden

E39

Fjærland   Gaupne

Urnes

Sogndal

Dragsvik   Hella
Balestrand

Kaupanger   Årdalstangen

Borgund
Stave
Church

E16

To Oslo
(175km)

Lavik
Sognefjorden

Vangsnes
Vik   Lærdal   Borlaug
Nærøyfjorden   *Aurlandsfjorden*   62
13   Aurland
Aurlandsdalen   Gol

E39

Gudvangen
Flåm
Myrdal   50

Voss   Finse

Osterøy   Ulvik
E16   Kjeåsen   *Hardangerjøkulen*   Geilo   7

BERGEN   Norheimsund   7   Utne Eidfjord   Øvre   To Oslo
Hardangerfjorden   Fidfjord   7   (150km)
Lofthus   Hårteigen
Ullensvang   (1691m)   **Hardangervidda**

Folgefonn
Sunndal   Tyssedal   Kalhovd
Bondhusbreen   Odda
Gjermundshamn   Løfallstrand
Rosendal   Rjukan
Uskedal

Leirvik   E134

E134

Dalen

supporting theatres, museums, a philharmonic orchestra and a noted rock scene.
Though big by Norwegian standards, the
city retains a charming, almost village-like
culture. Here, the picturesque ultimately
wins over the urbane. Drawback: expect rain
or showers at least 275 days of the year.

Bergen is a terminus of the incomprehensibly scenic Bergen–Oslo train line and
a convenient place to stay before prolonged
excursions into fjord country. The *Hurtigruten* coastal steamer begins its six-day
journey to Kirkenes from the centre.

The **Bergen International Festival**, held for
12 days at the end of May, is the big cultural
event of the year with quality dance, music
and folklore events taking place throughout
the city.

History

Bergen was the capital of Norway during the 12th and 13th centuries, and in
the early 17th century had the distinction
of being Scandinavia's largest city, with
a population of around 15,000. Bergen's
history is closely tied to the sea, as it was
one of the central ports of the Hanseatic
League of merchants, which dominated
trade in northern Europe during the late
Middle Ages. The Hanseatic influence is
still visible in the sharply gabled row of
buildings that lines Bergen's picturesque
harbour front.

Orientation

The central area of hilly Bergen remains
pleasantly compact and easily manageable
on foot. The bus and train stations lie only a
block apart on Strømgaten, just a 10-minute
walk from the ferry terminals. Most of the
restaurants, hotels, museums, tourist sites
and picturesque streets and passages cluster
around Vågen, the inner harbour.

Information

DISCOUNT CARDS

The Bergen Card allows free transport on
local buses, free parking and funicular-
railway rides as well as admission to most
museums and historic sights. Note that the
Schøtstuene and Hanseatic Museum are
not covered. A 24/48-hour Bergen Card
costs Nkr165/245 (Nkr70/105 for children) – it's sold at the tourist office, some
hotels and most camping grounds.

INTERNET ACCESS

Byens Gtørste Spillehall (Håkonsgaten 15; per min
Nkr0.50; noon-midnight Sun-Thu, noon-4am Fri & Sat)
Cheaper than the Internet cafés.
Public Library (Strømgaten 6; 10am-8pm Mon-Thu,
10am-4.30pm Fri, 10am-4pm Sat, shorter hrs mid-May–
Sep) Free Internet access, but with a time limit and a wait.

LAUNDRY

Jarlens Vaskoteque (☎ 55 32 55 04; Lille Øvregaten
17; 10am-6pm Mon, Tue & Fri, 10am-8pm Wed & Thu,
10am-3pm Sat) Self-service (Nkr45/5/5 wash/detergent/
dry) or spend Nkr100 for an attendant to do it for
you within two hours.

MEDICAL SERVICES

Medical Clinic (☎ 55 32 11 20; Vestre Stromkaien 19;
emergencies 24hrs)
Pharmacy (to midnight) At the bus station.

POST

Main Post Office (Starvhusgaten at Chrisites gate;
8am-8pm Mon-Fri, 9am-6pm Sat)

TOURIST INFORMATION

Tourist Office (☎ 55 55 20 00; www.visitbergen.com;
Vågsallmenningen 1; 8.30am-10pm Jun-Aug, 9am-8pm
May & Sep, 9am-4pm Mon-Sat Oct-Apr) Brochures on des-
tinations throughout Norway. Be sure to pick up the free
Bergen Guide.

Sights & Activities

Bryggen, site of the old medieval quarter
on the eastern side of Vågen, is an emi-
nently explorable area. Bryggen's long
timber buildings are home to museums,
restaurants and shops, while the alleys that
run along their less-restored sides reveal
an intriguing glimpse of the stacked-stone
foundations and rough-plank construction
of centuries past.

The **Hanseatic Museum** (☎ 55 31 41 89; Finne-
gårdsgaten 1A; adult/child Nkr45/free; 9am-5pm
Jun-Aug, 11am-2pm Sep-May) occupies a timber
building (1704) with some of Norway's
creakiest floors. Period character flourishes,
while furnishings and odd bedchambers
give a glimpse of the austere living conditions of Hanseatic merchants. The entry
ticket is also valid for Schøtstuene.

Schøtstuene (☎ 55 31 60 20; Øvregaten 50; adult/
child Nkr45/free; 10am-5pm Jun-Aug, 11am-2pm May
& Sep, 11am-2pm Sun Oct-Apr) houses one of the
original assembly halls where the fraternity
of Hanseatic merchants once met for their

BERGEN

0 — 500 m
0 — 0.3 miles

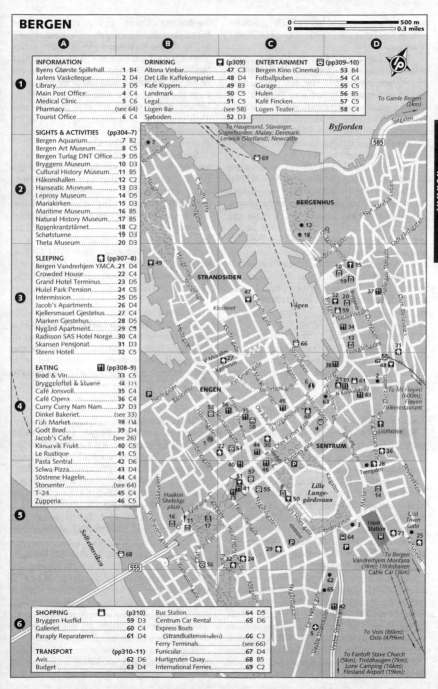

NORWAY

To Gamle Bergen (2km)

Byfjorden

To Haugesund, Stavanger,
Sognefjorden; Måløy; Denmark;
Lerwick (Shetland); Newcastle

BERGENHUS

STRANDSIDEN

Vågen

Klosteret

ENGEN

SENTRUM

Lille Lunge-
gårdsvann

Haakon
Sheteligs
plass

Salteinsviken

To Mt Fløyen
(600m);
Fløyen
Folkerestaurant

Domkirke

Old
Town
Gate

Train
Station

To Bergen
Vandrerhjem Montana
(3km); Ulriksbanen
Cable Car (3km)

To Voss (86km);
Oslo (479km)

To Fantoft Stave Church
(5km); Troldhaugen (7km);
Lone Camping (16km);
Flesland Airport (19km);

business meetings and beer guzzling. Schøt-stuene's ticket is also valid for the Hanseatic Museum.

The archaeological **Bryggens Museum** (☎ 55 58 80 10; Dregsalmenning 3; adult/student/child Nkr40/20/free; ☉ 10am-5pm May-Aug, 11am-3pm Mon-Fri, noon-3pm Sat, noon-4pm Sun Sep-Apr) was built on the site of Bergen's earliest settlement. The 800-year-old foundations unearthed during the construction have been incorporated into the museum's exhibits, along with pottery, human skulls and runes.

The stone **Mariakirken** (☎ 55 31 59 60; Dreggen 15; adult/child Nkr10/free, admission free Sep–mid-May; ☉ 11am-4pm Mon-Fri mid-May–Aug, noon-1.30pm Tue-Fri Sep–mid-May), with its Romanesque entrance and twin towers, dates from the 12th century and is Bergen's oldest building. The interior has 15th-century frescoes and a splendid baroque pulpit.

A one-room reconstruction of a clandestine Resistance headquarters, uncovered by the Nazis in 1942, is Norway's tiniest museum: the **Theta Museum** (☎ 55 55 20 80; Enhjørningsgården; adult/child Nkr20/5; ☉ 2-4pm Tue, Sat & Sun mid-May–mid-Sep).

The **Rosenkrantztårnet** (☎ 55 31 43 80; Bergenhus; adult/student Nkr25/12; ☉ 10am-4pm mid-May–Aug, noon-3pm Sun Sep–mid-May) was built in the 1560s by Bergen's governor as a residence and defence post. The tower incorporates parts of an earlier building from 1273. You can climb up spiral staircases past sentry posts to a lookout.

Håkonshallen (☎ 55 31 60 67; adult/student Nkr25/12; ☉ 10am-4pm daily mid-May–mid-Sep, noon-3pm Fri-Mon & Wed, 3-6pm Tue & Thu mid-Sep–mid-May), completed by King Håkon Håkonsson in 1261 for his son's wedding, had its roof blown off in 1944 when a Dutch munitions boat exploded in the harbour. The large ceremonial hall has since been extensively restored.

The university has a **Natural History Museum** (☎ 55 58 29 20; Muséplass 3; adult/student Nkr30/free; ☉ from 11am Tue-Sun) that's full of stuffed creatures and mineral displays, and a **Cultural History Museum** (☎ 55 58 31 40; Haakon Sheteligs plass 10; adult/student Nkr30/free; ☉ from 11am Tue-Sun) with Viking weaponry, medieval altars, folk art and period furnishings. Both university museums can be visited on the same ticket. The nearby **Maritime Museum** (☎ 55 54 96 00; Haakon Sheteligs plass 15; adult/child Nkr30/free; ☉ 11am-3pm Jun-Aug, 11am-2pm Sun-Fri

Sep-May) has exhibits on Norway's maritime history, including models of Viking ships.

The **Bergen Art Museum** (☎ 55 56 80 00; Rasmus Meyers Allé 3 & 7, Lars Hilles gate 10; adult/student/child Nkr50/35/free; ☉ 11am-5pm mid-May–mid-Sep, shorter hrs mid-Sep–mid-May), housed in three buildings opposite the lake fountain, has a superb collection of Norwegian art from the 18th and 19th centuries, including many works by Munch and JC Dahl, as well as works by Picasso, Klee and others.

Bergen Aquarium (☎ 55 55 71 71; Nordnesbakken 4; adult/child Nkr100/50; ☉ 9am-8pm May-Sep, 10am-6pm Oct-Apr), near the northern tip of the Nordnes peninsula, has an outdoor tank with seals and penguins, plus indoor fish tanks. The public **park** just beyond the aquarium has shaded lawns, sunbathing areas and an outdoor heated swimming pool.

The **Leprosy Museum** (☎ 55 32 57 80; Kong Oscars gate 59; adult/child Nkr30/15; ☉ 11am-3pm mid-May–Aug) occupies a hospital that served the diseased from 1411 to 1946. Learn about Bergen's 19th-century outbreak, old hospital design and some gross facts.

The waterfront **fish market** at Torget is a good starting point for an exploration of the city's historic district. Bergen has lots of quaint cobblestone streets lined with older homes; one particularly picturesque area good for strolls is near the funicular station on Øvregaten.

BERGEN ENVIRONS

The open-air **Gamle Bergen** (☎ 55 39 43 04; Sandviken; 9.30am-5.30pm May-early Sep, 10am-5pm mid-Sep–Apr) presents around 40 buildings from the 18th and 19th centuries, including a dentist's office, bakery and houses. It's 4km north of the city centre and can be reached by bus Nos 9, 20, 21 and 22. Tours cost Nkr60/30 (adult/student) and leave hourly mid-May to August. Entrance to the grounds is free year-round.

The **Fantoft stave church** (☎ 55 28 07 10; Paradis; adult/child Nkr30/5; ☉ 10.30am-6pm mid-May–mid-Sep) was built in Sognefjorden around 1150 and moved to the southern outskirts of Bergen in 1883. An arsonist burned it down in 1992, but it has been painstakingly reconstructed. Take any bus from platforms 19 to 21, get off at Fantoft and walk uphill for 10 minutes.

If you want to continue on to the former lakeside home and workshop of composer Edvard Grieg, get back on the bus until the

Hopsbroen stop and follow the signs to **Trold-haugen** (☎ 55 92 29 92; Troldhaugvegen 65; adult/student/child Nkr50/20/free; ✆ 9am-6pm May-Sep, shorter hrs Oct-Apr), a 20-minute walk. Although Grieg fans will best appreciate this well-conceived presentation, the main house has excellent period furnishings and is generally interesting.

CABLE CARS & HIKING

For an unbeatable city view, take the **funicular** (adult/child Nkr30/15 one way; ✆ 7.30am-midnight May-Aug, 7.30am-11pm Sep-Apr) to the top of Mt Fløyen (320m). Well-marked trails lead into the forest from the hill-top station. Trails 1 and 3 are the longest, each making 5km loops through hilly woodlands. For a delightful 40-minute walk back to the city, take trail 4 and connect with trail 6.

The **Ulriksbanen cable car** to the top of Mt Ulriken (642m) offers a panoramic view of Bergen, fjords and mountains. The tourist office sells a 'Bergen in a Nutshell' ticket for Nkr130/65 (adult/child) that includes the cable car and a return bus from Bergen. Many take the cable car one way and walk (about three hours) across a well-beaten trail to the funicular station at Mt Fløyen.

For information on wilderness hiking and huts, contact the **Bergen Turlag DNT office** (☎ 55 33 58 10; Iverrgaten 4; ✆ 10am-4pm Mon-Wed & Fri, 10am-6pm Thu, 10am-2pm Sat).

Tours

The train station sells the 'Norway in a Nutshell' (☎ 81 56 82 22; www.fjord-tours.com) ticket combining morning trains from Bergen to Flåm, a ferry along the spectacular Aurlandsfjorden and Nærøyfjorden to Gudvangen, a bus to Voss and a train back to Bergen in time for a late dinner. It makes for a scenic day trip at Nkr750.

Sleeping

The tourist office books single/double rooms in private homes from Nkr250/450 (plus Nkr30 to Nkr50 booking fee); it can also find you last-minute hotel discounts.

BUDGET

Lone Camping (☎ 55 39 29 60; www.lonecamping.no; Hardangerveien 697, Haukeland; camping per tent/person Nkr100/Nkr20, cabins & r Nkr390-875; **P**) A good camping option lakeside, 30 minutes east of Bergen by bus No 900.

Bergen Vandrerhjem YMCA (☎ 55 60 60 55; ymca@online.no; Nedre Korskirkealmenning 4; dm/r Nkr150/625; ✆ late Jun-late Aug) Bergen's 200-bed HI-affiliated Y is a central place to crash but it can be noisy with 12 to 40 beds in the rooms. Breakfast is extra (Nkr40). Kitchen access.

Intermission (☎ 55 30 04 00; Kalfarveien 8; Nkr100; ✆ mid-Jun-mid-Aug) Of a higher standard are the 37 beds in an old white house, where the hospitable Christian Student Fellowship serves free waffles to guests on Monday and Thursday nights. A kitchen and laundry facilities are available. Breakfast costs Nkr30.

Jacob's Apartments (☎ 55 54 41 60; www.apartments.no; Kong Oscars gate 44; dm Nkr180, apt Nkr490-790) Offers 16 beds in a clean dormitory. A prepared breakfast is given out the night before. Simple apartments are also available.

Bergen Vandrerhjem Montana (☎ 55 20 80 70; montvh@online.no; Johan Blyttsvei 30; dm Nkr160-240, s/d from Nkr425/595; ✆ 3 Jan-20 Dec) This 332-bed, HI-affiliated place is about 5km from the city centre by bus No 31.

Marken Gjestehus (☎ 55 31 44 04; Kong Oscars gate 45; dm Nkr165-190, s Nkr355-495, d Nkr610) Take a scary elevator to the fourth floor to find a centrally located hostel. Breakfast can be arranged elsewhere from Nkr55. Amenities include a kitchen, coin laundry and, often, a decent view.

MID-RANGE

Skansen Pensjonat (☎ 55 31 90 80; www.skansen-pensjonat.no; Vetrlidsalmenningen 29; s Nkr350-400, d Nkr550-650) Unless you have a heart problem, you'll enjoy trudging up a cobbled street to this hill-top house dating from 1918, with its outstanding, unimpeded views. Use the telescope to determine fish market prices.

Kjellersmauet Gjestehus (☎ 55 96 26 08; www.gjestehuset.com; Kjellersmauet 22; apt Nkr350-1200) A number of well-equipped apartments with private bathroom and kitchen. Apartments are homey, and big groups are often given good deals.

Nygård Apartment (☎ 55 32 72 53; markeng jestehus@smisi.no; Nygårdsgaten 31; s/d from Nkr365/580; ✆ Jun-mid-Aug) Small student rooms, some with private bathroom. Cooking facilities provided.

Crowded House (☎ 55 90 92 00; www.crowded-house.com; Håkonsgaten 27; s/d Nkr390/590) The 82 rooms come with Ikea furniture and free use of laundry facilities. Currently, there is no breakfast though guests have access to a nice kitchen. The 1st floor holds a lively bar.

TOP END

Steens Hotell (☎ 55 31 40 50; www.steenshotel.no; Parkveien 22; s Nkr550-790, d Nkr750-990; **P**) Expect Swedish-style rooms with private bathroom in a 19th-century home; some rooms have pleasant, parkside views. The real treat is the 1890s dining room, where breakfast is served – check out the gilded wallpaper, an odd wooden chandelier and stained glass depicting butchered meat.

Hotel Park Pension (☎ 55 54 44 00; Harald Hårfagresgate 35; s Nkr600-840, d Nkr880-1040; **P**) Another 19th-century charmer, it's family owned and stuffed to the rafters with grandma's antiques and unusual tools. Rooms come with private bathroom and with breakfast.

Grand Hotel Terminus (☎ 55 21 25 00; www .grand-hotel-terminus.no; Zander Kaaesgate 6; s Nkr790-1260, d Nkr990-1490; **P** 🔀) Opposite the train station. Exudes elegance and character, containing *knag* furniture (oldie bulky stuff with knobby carving) and chandeliers of rounded glass. The rooms themselves are adequate, but have been stripped of their pre-war charms. Learn more about the hotel's excellent bar in the Drinking section.

Radisson SAS Hotel Norge (☎ 55 57 30 00; reser vations.bergen@radissonsas.com; Ole Bulls plass 4; s/d Nkr1665/1965, s/d discount weekends Nkr995/1195; **P** 🔀) Spacious, with full amenities, a fitness centre, an indoor pool, library, ice machines, blow dryers and complimentary pens.

Eating

RESTAURANTS

Studentkafeene (☎ 55 54 50 50; mains Nkr19-45; 🕑 9.30am-5pm Mon-Thu, 9.30am-4pm Fri late Aug-early Jun) The university's student cafeteria might look ugly, but you can grab pasta with fish (Nkr39), asparagus soup (Nkr19) or a big sandwich with juice (Nkr30) at low prices.

Brød & Vin (☎ 55 32 67 04; Christies gate 13; mains Nkr35-65; 🕑 10am-11pm Mon-Wed, 10am-midnight Thu & Fri, 1pm-midnight Sat, 1-10pm Sun) Popular with university students, with piles of Asian noodle dishes such as vegetable chop suey (Nkr53). A beer costs Nkr35.

Zupperia (☎ 55 55 81 44; Nordahl Bruns gate; soup Nkr49-96; 🕑 11am-midnight) From fish to gazpacho, serves eleven kinds of soups with sides

of bread. We like the Husenottsuppe (oxtail boiled with vegetables).

T-24 (☎ 98 29 83 28; Newmanns gate 25; mains Nkr50-100; 🕑 noon-1am Sun-Thu, noon-6am Fri & Sat) Bergen's late-night hot spot serves lasagne, baked potatoes, sandwiches and fajitas on counters that become increasingly crusty as nights grow long.

Fløyen Folkerestaurant (☎ 55 33 69 99; Bellevuebakken 9; pastries & cakes Nkr18-43; 🕑 11am-8pm May-Sep, 11am-8pm Sat & Sun Oct-Apr) On the summit of Fløyen, presiding over Bergen with unbeatable views and good hot chocolate. In the warmth of summer, the patio fills with sunbathers and beer drinkers.

Pasta Sentral (Vestre Strømkaien 6; dishes Nkr59-84; 🕑 11am-11pm Mon-Sat, 1-11pm Sun) Unassuming and not all that central. Has decent pizza, pasta and some vegetarian choices. Expect cheesy murals and chequered tablecloths.

Curry Curry Nam Nam (☎ 55 96 40 76; Steinkjeller gate 8; mains Nkr49-99; 🕑 from 2pm Tue-Sun) Rich curries and vegetarian items come steaming and delicious at this tiny restaurant at the convergence of several pretty cobbled alleys. At an outdoor table, smoke a post-meal water pipe for Nkr50.

Bryggeloftet & Stuene (☎ 55 31 06 30; Bryggen 11; lunch Nkr110-149, mains Nkr145-255; 🕑 11am-11.30pm Mon-Sat, 1-11.30pm Sun) In the historic district, this touristy two-storey place serves traditional Norwegian fare. Downstairs feels vaguely like a stuffy home library, upstairs more like a log cabin. A bowl of fish soup with bread costs Nkr79.

CAFÉS

Jacob's Cafe (☎ 55 54 41 60; Kong Oscars gate 44; burgers Nkr50-100; 🕑 3pm-midnight Sun-Thu, 3pm-2.30am Fri & Sat) Vegetarians stumbling around Norway eating wilted salads weep tears of thanks upon eating the stellar hand-pressed veggie-burgers here. Meat-based ones are also available, and rock-a-billy is played.

Café Opera (☎ 55 23 08 15; light meals Nkr44-78, mains Nkr75-118; 🕑 11am-12.30am Mon, 11am-3am Tue-Thu, 11am-3.30am Fri & Sat, noon-10.30pm Sun) Begins the day with newspaper readers, but finishes with sweaty DJs. Good food throughout.

Café Jonsvoll (☎ 55 23 00 77; Vaskerelven at Engen; dishes Nkr35-98; 🕑 10am-1am Sun-Thu, 10am-2am Fri & Sat) Filled with a trendy crowd making use of long plate-glass windows and stools. Sandwiches, lasagne, quiche-like omelettes

(Nkr53) and museli and yogurt (Nkr35) are served. The kitchen closes at 11pm.

Le Rustique (☎ 55 13 47 74; Christies gate 11; sandwiches Nkr45-65; ☯ 8am-4pm Mon-Fri, 9am-4pm Sat, 11am-4pm Sun) Serves high-calibre sandwiches on freshly baked baguettes. Also offers smoothies, coffee and French pastries. Good art, but no bathroom.

QUICK EATS
Godt Brød (☎ 55 32 80 00; Nedre Korskirkealmenningen 12; ☯ 7am-6pm Mon-Fri, 7am-4pm Sat) Offers delicious organic breads, pastries, café tables and pizza (Nkr35).

Selwa Pizza (Nedre Korskirkeallmennigen 5; dishes Nkr35-79; ☯ 11am-1am) Pick up good felafel and schwarma in this sparse room overlooking an old church.

Söstrene Hagelin (☎ 55 32 69 49; Olav Kyrres gate 33; dishes Nkr35-89; ☯ 9am-6pm Mon-Fri, 10am-3pm Sat) Delicious fish pudding, fish casserole and other such delicacies. Filling takeaway fish balls (Nkr35) come with potatoes.

SELF-CATERING
Dinkel Bakeriet (☎ 93 81 32 64; Christies gate 13; ☯ 10am-5pm Mon-Fri) Bread made here uses spelt, an unusual strain of wheat that predates modern cultivation. Because of its purity, many who are otherwise allergic to wheat eat this stuff like candy. Small pizzas are also offered.

Storsenter, at the bus station, has fast-food outlets, a Vinmonopolet, and Rimi and Spar supermarkets. Torget's fish market provides fresh fruit and seafood snacks, including salmon rolls for Nkr15 and boiled crab legs or shrimp for Nkr35 to Nkr75.

Kinsarvik Frukt (Olav Kyrres gate 38) is a small grocery store with a health-food section.

Drinking
Logen Bar (☎ 55 23 38 01; Øvre Ole Bulls plass 6; ☯ 6pm-1am Sun-Thu, 6pm-2am Fri & Sat) A hangout for artists and journalists, the salon-like rooms benefit from tall ceilings and a balcony. Drink here to feel like you're part of a postimpressionist painting. Hard to find: enter, go up one set of stairs, turn left and climb a second stairwell.

Sjøboden (☎ 55 31 67 77; Bryggen 29; ☯ 6pm-1am Sun-Thu, 6pm-2am Fri & Sat) In a Hanseatic-era building, it's a long, narrow and unpretentious route from entry to bar. Friday nights, your odyssey will involve squeezing through

crowds, dodging ceiling-suspended barrels and bumping into a bad two-piece passionately playing 'Summer of 69'. Everyone dances, everyone sings along, and no-one wears cool clothing. Kim Larsen plays here whenever in town.

Det Lille Kaffekompaniet (☎ 55 32 92 72; Nedre Fjellsmug 2; ☯ from 10am) An intimate coffee house, hidden on a pedestrian street behind the funicular station.

Landmark (☎ 55 31 77 55; Rasmus Meyers Alle 5; ☯ noon-1am Sun-Thu, noon-2am Fri & Sat) Named for the architect Ole Landmark, this place inside the Kunsthall hosts new media artists and experimental DJs. White carpet, white walls and tall ceilings covered in white cushions create a muted, subtle space of modernist high-design. At night, coloured lighting transforms the room with eerie results.

Kafe Kippers (☎ 55 31 00 60; Georgernes Verft 3; ☯ 11am-1am Mon-Fri, noon-1am Sat & Sun) Part of a cultural centre and former sardine cannery. Harbourside tables fill with beer drinkers on warm days. The view takes in water, rocky hills, islands and boats.

Altona Vinbar (☎ 55 30 40 72; Strandgaten 81; ☯ 6pm-12.30am Mon-Thu, 6pm-1.30am Fri & Sat) Small, cell-like rooms create a subterranean maze from which to enjoy a huge selection of wine. Spaces are intimate and almost entirely candle lit, while a lack of window amplifies privacy.

Legal (Christies gate at Nygårdsgaten; bar menu Nkr45-72; ☯ from 2pm) Takes its design theme from 1960s English rock. Find red lighting, retro flooring and period lamps. The bar menu offers fancy cheese plates and burgers.

Entertainment
For details and schedules of entertainment events, including classical concerts, contact the tourist office (or see www.visitbergen .com). Atop Mt Fløyen, classical concerts are held nightly at 8pm from mid-June to mid-August. Bergen is the epicentre of Norwegian rock.

Garage (☎ 55 32 19 80; www.garage.no; Christies gate 14; ☯ from 6pm) Norway's rock headquarters consistently books top bands, including American acts like Bobby Conn. Concerts are held in a big, black basement space. Booze gets served until later than in regular bars, and an impressive queue of the desperate assembles when last call hits Bergen.

NORWAY

Fotballpuben (☎ 55 90 05 79; Vestre Torggate 9; ⏱ 9am-1am Mon-Thu, 9am-2am Fri & Sat, noon-1am Sun) A long-standing favourite among football freaks, providing plenty of scarfs, televisions and fans to ensure quality match watching. Watch out for the occasional bout of obnoxious karaoke.

Hulen (☎ 55 33 38 38; www.hulen.no, no English; Olaf Ryes vei 47) Carved into the bowels of a hill, Hulen occupies a former bomb shelter. The renowned rock club is over 30 years old.

Kafé Fincken (☎ 55 32 13 16; Nygårdsgaten 2A; 7pm-1.30am Wed & Thu, 7pm-2.30am Fri, 8pm-2.30am Sat, 7pm-12.30am Sun) Contemporary and stylish, and Bergen's only gay and lesbian venue.

Logen Teater (☎ 55 23 38 01; www.logen-teater .no; Øvre Ole Bulls plass 6) You'd never know it from the street, but drag yourself inside and you'll find a century-old, two-storeyed, pillared theatre. Concerts are held several times a month. Expect to see classical performances, pop and rock (Tindersticks, Waterboys).

Bergen Kino (Neumannsgate 3) A 13-screen cinema showing first-run movies.

Shopping

Bryggen Husflid (☎ 55 32 88 03; Bugården; ⏱ 8am-10pm May-Aug, 9am-5pm Mon-Sat Oct-Apr) Offers diverse stock such as woollens and mittens in a Byggen environment.

Paraply Reparatøren (☎ 55 32 69 11; 16 Høendergaten; ⏱ 10am-4pm Mon-Wed & Fri, 10am-6pm Thu, 10am-1pm Sat) Arm yourself against all that rain with a designer umbrella, or purchase flasks, walking sticks and fancy toilet kits.

The Galleriet shopping centre, northwest of the post office, has boutiques, camera shops, a grocery store and a good bookshop, Norli. The bus station contains another large shopping centre.

Getting There & Away

AIR

The airport is in Flesland, 19km southwest of central Bergen. Direct flights connect Bergen with major cities in Norway, plus a handful of international destinations. **Braathens** (☎ 815 20 000) and **SAS** (☎ 815 20 400), both at the airport, fly frequently between Oslo and Bergen.

BOAT

Daily Sognefjorden express boats to Balestrand and Flåm, northbound express boats to Måløy and southbound express boats to Stavanger leave from Strandkaiterminalen on the western side of Vågen. The *Hurtigruten* leaves from the quay south of the university.

International ferries dock north of Rosenkrantztårnet.

BUS

Daily express buses run to Odda in Hardanger (Nkr251, 3½ hours) and to the western fjord region. Buses also run from Bergen to Stryn (Nkr395, 6½ hours), Ålesund (Nkr550, 9½ to 10 hours) and Trondheim (Nkr755, 14½ hours). There's a bus from Bergen to Stavanger (Nkr390, 5¾ hours) roughly every two hours.

TRAIN

Trains to Oslo (Nkr670, 6½ to 7¾ hours) depart four or five times daily; seat reservations are required. In addition, local trains run between Bergen and Voss (Nkr142, 1¼ hours) every hour or two. Lockers at the train station cost Nkr15 to Nkr40.

CAR

There's a Nkr10 toll for vehicles entering the city from 7am to 10pm Monday to Friday.

Car Rental

Hire-car companies in Bergen:
Avis (☎ 55 55 39 55; Lars Hilles gate 20A)
Budget (☎ 55 27 39 90; Vågsallmenningen 1) They've got a second office near the airport.
Centrum Car Rental (☎ 55 21 29 50; Lars Hilles gate 20) Excellent service.

Getting Around

TO/FROM THE AIRPORT

Flybussen (☎ 177) runs between the airport and Bergen bus station (Nkr81, 45 minutes, at least twice hourly), stopping on Olav Kyrres gate near the Radisson SAS Hotel Norge and at the SAS Hotel beside the Bryggens Museum.

BUS

City buses cost Nkr23, while fares beyond the centre are based on the distance travelled. Route information is available by calling ☎ 177. The free bus No 100 runs back and forth between the main post office and the bus station.

CAR & MOTORCYCLE
If you have a car, it's best to park it and explore the city centre on foot. Except in spots where there are parking meters, street parking is reserved for residents with zone-parking stickers; if you see a 'P' for parking but the sign has *'sone'* on it, it's a reserved area. Metered parking has a 30-minute limit in the busiest spots and two hours elsewhere, including lots on the southwestern side of the Grieghallen concert hall and the northern side of Lille Lungegårdsvann. Less restricted are the parking areas at Sydnes, near Noste-gaten, which allow up to nine hours (free at night), and the indoor car parks – the largest one (open 24 hours) is at the bus station.

TAXI
Taxis (☎ 07000) line up on Ole Bulls plass.

VOSS
pop 6000
Voss is a year-round sports centre with an attractive lakeside location. Conveniently positioned within a short drive of many top-notch athletic experiences and containing a centre that provides most modern ameni-ties, Voss attracts many adventuresome tourists. Unfortunately, the town's collec-tion of modern buildings are pretty drab. The **tourist office** (☎ 56 52 08 00; www.visitvoss.no; Uttrågata; ☻ 9am-7pm Mon-Sat, 2-7pm Sun late Jun-early Aug, 9am-2.30pm Mon-Fri mid-Aug–mid-Jun) is a short walk east from the train station.

Voss's second claim to fame is a culinary oddity: deliciously prepared sheep heads. Hundreds of the things are eaten at an an-nual sheep festival in October.

Sights & Activities
The tourist office can advise on various activities, including skiing (December to April), white-water rafting (Nkr700), canoe-ing (Nkr650), waterfall abseiling (Nkr700) and riverboarding (Nkr750).

The 13th-century stone **church** (Uttrågata; adult/child Nkr15/free; ☻ 10am-4pm Jun-Aug) is worth a look, but it has been significantly altered over the centuries. The **Mølstertunet Museum** (☎ 56 51 15 11; Mølstervegen 143; adult/child Nkr35/free; ☻ 10am-5pm May-Sep, shorter hrs Oct-Apr), on the hillside north of town, features 16 farm buildings standing in their original positions, which date from the mid-17th to mid-19th centuries and display various

aspects of life in earlier times. A **cable car** (Nkr50; ☻ 11am-5pm mid-May–Aug) whisks you up to the spectacular view from Mt Hangur every 15 minutes.

Sleeping & Eating
Voss Camping (☎ 56 51 15 97; Prestegardsalléen 40; camp sites Nkr80, cabins Nkr300-350) The lakeside camping ground is 300m south of the tour-ist office.

Voss Vandrerhjem (☎ 56 51 20 17; voss.hostel@ vandrerhjem.no; Evangervegen 68; dm/s/d Nkr220/445/565; ℗) Modern rooms with private bathroom throughout and a fine lakeside position, 600m west of the train station; breakfast/ dinner costs Nkr45/90. The hostel has bi-cycles, canoes, kayaks and rowing boats for hire and there's a free sauna.

Fleischer's Hotel (☎ 56 52 05 00; hotel@fleischers .no; Evangervegen; s/d Nkr1125/1490; ℗) For his-toric character, check out this classic hotel from 1888. The dining room serves a fine lunch/dinner buffet (Nkr195/325).

Indremisjonskaféen (☎ 56 51 14 08; Vangsgata 12; mains Nkr40-90; ☻ from 9.30am Mon-Sat, noon-5pm Sun) Serves cakes, sandwiches and trad-itional Norwegian meals. Try the daily soup (Nkr40).

Ivar Løne's farm (☎ 56 51 69 65; meal 275-325; ☻ from 5pm) For a sheep head, visit Ivar's farm. He'll show you around and serve you one of the finest heads around, along with home-made beer, cake and coffee. Call ahead. The farm is 5km toward Oslo on the E16.

The **Coop Mega supermarket** (Strandavegen) is on the eastern side of the town centre.

Getting There & Away
Buses stop at the train station. NSB rail serv-ices on the renowned Bergensbanen to/from Bergen (Nkr142, 1¼ hours, roughly hourly) and Oslo (Nkr582, 5½ hours, four or five daily) connect at Myrdal (Nkr83, 50 min-utes) with the scenic line down to Flåm.

HARDANGERFJORDEN
Hardangerfjorden, the second-longest fjord in Norway, stretches inland from a clus-ter of rocky coastal islands to the frozen heights of the **Folgefonn** and **Hardangerjøkulen** icecaps. The area is known for its orchards (apples, cherries and plums) and bursts into vivid bloom from early May to mid-June. The surrounding mountains are gen-erally less steep and dramatic than those

around the other principle fjords. Helpful regional information can be found at www .hardangerfjord.com.

The villages along the east coast of the central part of the fjord (also called Kvinnheradsfjorden) are connected to the national road network by an 11km tunnel under the Folgefonn; **Rosendal** and **Sunndal** are the top destinations, with great mountain and glacier scenery. At Rosendal there's the **Baroniet Rosendal** (☎ 53 48 29 99; www.baroniet.no; adult/child Nkr75/10; ☼ from 11am May-Sep), Norway's only baronial mansion, dating from 1665 and surrounded by flowering gardens and mountains. There are guided tours. From Sunndal, an easy walk leads 3km to lake Bondhusvatnet and the impressive glacier **Bondhusbreen**.

On the other side of Folgefonn, **Odda** is an industrial town with a dramatic location. For information on hikes and glacier tours, contact the **tourist office** (☎ 53 64 12 97; www.visitodda.com; ☼ 9am-8pm Mon-Fri, 10am-5pm Sat, 11am-6pm Sun late Jun-late Aug, 8.30am-4pm Mon-Fri Sep–mid-Jun) located near the Sørfjorden shore. **Tyssedal**, 6km north of Odda, has a **hydroelectric power plant museum** (☎ 53 65 00 50; adult/student/child Nkr70/35/free; ☼ 10am-5pm mid-May–Aug, shorter hrs Sep–mid-May) and a mighty impressive **funicular railway**.

At picturesque **Utne**, 55km north of Odda, you'll find an interesting collection of old buildings at the **Hardanger Folk Museum** (☎ 53 67 00 40; www.hardanger.museum.no; adult/child Nkr40/free; ☼ 10am-4pm May & Jun, 10am-6pm Jul & Aug), and the pretty Utne Hotel.

At the innermost reaches of Hardangerfjorden you'll find the **Eidfjord** area, with sheer mountains, huge waterfalls, spiral road tunnels and the extraordinary **Kjeåsen**, a deserted farm perched on a mountain ledge about 6km northeast of Eidfjord. The excellent **Hardangervidda Natursenter** (☎ 53 66 59 00; Øvre Eidfjord; adult/child Nkr70/35; ☼ 9am-8pm Jun-Aug, 10am-6pm Apr, May, Sep & Oct) has a mustsee 19-minute movie, interactive displays and interesting natural history exhibits. For tourist information, contact **Eidfjord tourist office** (☎ 53 67 34 00).

Sleeping & Eating

In Rosendal, you can stay near the baronial grounds in a **B&B** (☎ 53 48 29 99; s Nkr350-600, d Nkr600-800; **P**), once a 19th-century farmhouse. It's operated by the museum.

Utne Hotel (☎ 53 66 69 83; Utne Sentrum; s/d Nkr450/600; **P**) This historic wooden hotel, known for its fabulous decor, was built in 1722 and has been in romantic business ever since. Meals are available in the dining room.

Lofthus HI Hostel (☎ 53 67 14 00; lofthus.hostel@ vandrerhjem.no; Lofthus; dm/s/d Nkr205/285/485; ☼ Jun-Aug; **P**) This gorgeous hostel occupies an old wooden building, painted white.

Getting There & Away

Buses run between Rosendal and Odda via Sunndal (about one hour, three to seven times daily). There are also bus and ferry connections between Rosendal and Bergen (Nkr135, 3½ hours, twice daily).

One to three daily Nor-Way Bussekspress buses run between Bergen (Nkr251, 3¾ hours) and Oslo (Nkr475, 7¼ hours) via Odda and Utne, with connections at Haukeligrend for Kristiansand.

Buses run between Geilo and Odda via Øvre Eidfjord, Eidfjord and Lofthus once or twice daily in summer (July to September), with extra runs between Øvre Eidfjord and Odda year-round. Ferries between Eidfjord and Norheimsund (Nkr160, three hours) or Utne (Nkr97, 1¼ hours) sail two or three times daily; buses to/from Bergen connect at Norheimsund.

While thorough exploration of Hardangerfjord is best accomplished with a car, those with little time and no wheels would do well to book a round-trip **Fjord Tour** (☎ 81 56 82 22; www.fjord-tours.no; adult/child Nkr540/360) from Bergen, which combines bus, ferry and train.

SOGNEFJORDEN

Sognefjorden, Norway's longest (204km) and deepest (1308m) fjord, cuts a deep slash across the map of western Norway. In some places sheer, lofty walls rise more than 1000m above the water, while in others there is a far gentler shoreline with farms, orchards and small towns.

The broad main waterway is impressive, but by cruising into the fjord's narrower arms, such as the deep and lovely Nærøyfjorden to Gudvangen, you'll have idyllic views of sheer cliff faces and cascading waterfalls.

Tourist information is dispensed by **Sognefjorden** (☎ 57 67 30 83; www.sognefjorden.no; Postboks 222, N-6852 Sogndal).

SCENIC JOURNEYS

Most visitors travel to Norway to see the fjords, mountains and glaciers for which the country is rightly famous. Some parts of Norway have extraordinary scenery, sculpted out of solid rock by the great glaciers of the last ice age. Following is a list of three journey suggestions covering some of the best Norway can offer, but there's no shortage of other possibilities.

The Oslo–Bergen Railway

Classed as one of the world's finest train journeys, this route not only links Norway's largest cities, but also presents an excellent cross section of Norwegian scenery.

From Oslo, the line passes through suburbs, towards Drammen. Beyond Drammen, you'll see the forested hills of Buskerud from valleys dotted with small towns. The train then follows the bank of the Hallingdalselva, beginning its gradual ascent to the central highland plateau. Hallingdal is famous for its waterfalls, attracting daring ice climbers in winter.

In upper Hallingdal, beyond the Geilo ski centre, the line enters the wild mountain and glacier country of Hardangervidda. At Myrdal station, continue to Voss or take the wonderful Flåmsbanen alternative down steep gradients and past magnificent waterfalls to Flåm. Connect to Gudvangen on a fjord cruise and continue to Voss by bus. Beyond Voss, the railway passes through an increasingly impressive landscape of forests and lakes. Huge walls of rock soar up from the west-coast fjords, which the line hugs for most of the way into Bergen.

Sogndal to Åndalsnes

Follow Rv5 through mountains and tunnels to Fjærland, a veritable Shangri-la of fjords, glaciers and peaks. North of Skei, the E39 passes through a deep valley to Byrkjelo, then Rv60 climbs through forest up to a good viewpoint of Nordfjord. Continue along Nordfjord to the scenic villages of Olden and Loen; side trips to the Jostedalsbreen glacier from either village are highly recommended.

Continue to Stryn, and then take Rv15 west and Rv60 north, passing the extraordinary peak Hornindalsrokken on your left. At Hellesylt, ferries chug to and fro on Geirangerfjord, the ultimate Norwegian fjord, with tiny farms perched on ledges, wispy waterfalls and towering cliffs. The one-hour boat trip leads to touristy Geiranger village. Take Ørnevegen (Rv63) north to a viewpoint over the twisting fjord, and continue over a pass to a ferry across Norddalsfjorden. Take Rv63 through Valldal, past impressive mountains and then down the steep Trollstigen road, with waterfalls and hairpin bends, to Romsdal, with 1.5km-high cliffs – the highest in Norway – and the end of the route in Åndalsnes. The journey is possible in a day by bus and ferry (except Saturday), mid-June to late August.

Å to Narvik: Lofoten & Vesterålen

Å is the southernmost village on Moskenesøy, arguably Lofoten's finest island and a superb example of glacial rock sculpture. Island hopping along the E10 by bridge leads to Flakstadøy, then by undersea tunnel to the more pastoral Vestvågøy. Sweeping bridges bring you through soaring, wild mountains to Kabelvåg and Svolvær on Austvågøy.

The Fiskebøl ferry leads to Vesterålen, with more farms and several large towns, including Sortland. Much of the rest of the route to Narvik follows pleasant fjord shorelines backed by steep but more rounded mountains, offering a visual experience different from the needle-like peaks of Lofoten.

Buses run along the E10 between Å and Narvik, but you'll have to stay overnight in either Svolvær or Sortland.

Getting There & Away

Fylkesbaatane (☎ 55 90 70 70; www.fylkesbaatane .no) operates a year-round express boat between Bergen and Sogndal (Nkr400), stopping at 10 small towns along the way. Students and InterRail passholders get a 50% discount.

From mid-May to mid-September, Fylkesbaatane runs a second express boat along the same route, except that it terminates in Flåm (Nkr550) instead of Sogndal.

There are numerous local ferries linking the fjord towns and an extensive (though not always frequent) network of buses.

They're all detailed in *Sogn og Fjordane Rutehefte* (www.ruteinfo.net/en/index.html), the 208-page timetable available free of charge at tourist offices and some transport terminals.

Flåm
pop 400

A tiny village of orchards and a handful of buildings scenically set at the head of Aurlandsfjorden, Flåm is a jumping-off spot for travellers taking the Gudvangen ferry or the Sognefjorden express boat. It's also the only place on Sognefjorden with rail connections, and is the turnaround point for those doing the 'Norway in a Nutshell' tour, serving as the base station for the dramatic Flåm railway. Though it sees an amazing 500,000 visitors every summer, walk a few minutes from the centre and you'll soon experience solitude. Adventurous visitors arrive from Finse by mountain bike. It's a five- or six-hour downhill ride, obscenely picturesque, and you can return your rented bike in the Flåm centre. Call the **tourist office** (☎ 57 63 21 06; www.visitflam.com), at the train station, for details.

The extraordinarily friendly **Flåm Camping & Hostel** (☎ 57 63 21 21; flaam.hostel@vandrerhjem.no; dm/s Nkr135/225, d Nkr345-395; ♥ May-Sep; P) has just 31 beds – book early. It's a few minutes' walk from the station: go up the riverside track and over the bridge. If fully booked, they might install you in a large dollhouse, but no promises. **Heimly Pensjonat** (☎ 57 63 23 00; www.heimly.no; s Nkr550-695, d Nkr695-895; P) has rooms with great fjord views.

Near the station, there's a **cafeteria** and the novel **Togrestauranten** (mains Nkr90-135), housed in wooden rail cars, serves traditional Norwegian dishes. Self-caterers will find a **Coop** supermarket behind Togrestauranten.

The Flåm railway runs between Myrdal and Flåm (adult/child Nkr150/75) numerous times daily, in sync with the Oslo–Bergen service. At Flåm, buses and boats head out to towns around Sognefjorden.

The most scenic boat ride from Flåm is the ferry up Nærøyfjorden to Gudvangen (adult/student Nkr185/90), leaving daily mid-June to mid-August. Tickets for the ferry and the bus to Voss (Nkr76) are sold at the tourist office.

In addition to the Sognefjorden express boat between Flåm and Bergen, the Flåmekspressen boat runs once daily on weekdays from Flåm to Aurland and Sogndal.

Lærdal & Around
pop 2178

The 24.5km-long Lærdalstunnelen, the world's longest road tunnel, on the main E16 highway from Oslo to Bergen, now brings more visitors than ever to the wonderful **Borgund stave church** (☎ 57 67 88 40; adult/child Nkr50/25; ♥ 8am-8pm Jun–mid-Aug, 10am-5pm May & mid-Aug–Sep), built around 1150, about 30km up the valley from Lærdal. **Lærdalsøyri**, at the fjord end of Lærdal, makes for pleasant strolling through a collection of intact 18th- and 19th-century timber homes. The excellent **Norsk Villaks Senter** (Norwegian Wild Salmon Centre; ☎ 57 66 67 71; Lærdal; adult/child Nkr70/35; ♥ 10am-7pm Jun-Aug, shorter hrs May & Sep) reveals all you'd ever want to know about the Atlantic salmon and its peculiar habits. Who doesn't need a fly-tying workshop and an interactive fishing simulator?

Borlaug Vandrerhjem (☎ 57 66 87 80; borlaug.hostel@vandrerhjem.no; dm/s/d Nkr150/225/315; P) is a roadside HI hostel, 10km east of Borgund. Breakfast is Nkr60, and a two-course dinner costs Nkr95.

Buses to/from Bergen run via Borgund once daily and Lærdal (Nkr280, 3¾ hours) three to seven times daily. Buses between Lærdal and Sogndal (Nkr78, 50 minutes) run two to seven times daily.

Vangsnes & Vik
pop 1500

Vangsnes, across the fjord from Balestrand, is a little farming community crowned with a huge hill-top statue of Fridtjof, a hero of the Norwegian sagas. Although it has both ferry and express boat connections, there's not much to the village. There's a **snack bar** at the dock, and **Solvang Camping** (☎ 57 69 66 20; camp sites from Nkr40, r & cabins Nkr300-600; P), a few minutes inland, has cabins and motel rooms.

Frequent local buses run between Vangsnes and the industrial town Vik (Nkr23, 15 minutes), which has an excellent 12th-century **stave church** (☎ 56 67 88 40; Hopperstad; adult/student/child Nkr40/25/free; ♥ 9am-7pm mid-Jun–mid-Aug, 10am-5pm mid-May–mid-Jun & mid-Aug–mid-Sep), about 1km south of the centre. Buses run from Vik (via Vangsnes) to Sogndal (Nkr67, 1½ hours, daily) and Vangsnes (via Vik) to

Bergen (Nkr225, 3½ hours, daily except Saturday). The Sognefjorden express boat also stops in Vik. To reach Balestrand, take the ferry to Dragsvik, then proceed 9km east along a winding road.

Balestrand
pop 800

Quiet Balestrand enjoys a mountain backdrop and fjord views. The beauty of its surroundings and the eerie quality of its summer light attracted a community of landscape painters in the early 19th century, whose work then popularised the area for well-heeled tourists. Today, the farming village remains a favourite destination for travellers, who spend a lot of their time walking and contemplating. The **tourist office** (☎ 57 69 12 55; www.sognefjord.no) rents bikes.

The road that runs south along the fjord has little traffic and is a pleasant place to stroll. It's lined with apple orchards, ornate older homes and gardens, a **19th-century English church** and **Viking burial mounds**. One mound is topped by a statue of the legendary King Bele, erected by Germany's Kaiser Wilhelm II, who spent his holidays here regularly until WWI.

For a longer **hike**, take the small ferry (Nkr15) across the Esefjord to the Dragsvik side, where there is an abandoned country road that forms the first leg of an 8km walk back to Balestrand.

At **Sjøtun Camping** (☎ 57 69 12 23; camp sites from Nkr50, cabins Nkr250; **P**), a 15-minute walk south along the fjord, you can pitch a tent amid apple trees or rent a rustic four-bunk cabin. **Balestrand HI Hostel** (☎ 57 69 13 03; balestrand .hostel@vandrerhjem.no; dm/d Nkr215/585; late Jun–mid-Aug; **P**) is a pleasant lodge-style place.

Midtnes Pensjonat (☎ 57 69 11 33; www.midtnes .no; s/d Nkr575/680; **P**), next to the English church, occupies a charming white house, popular with returning British holidaymakers. Many rooms have balconies.

Kviknes Hotel (☎ 57 69 42 00; www.kviknes.no; s Nkr745-1500, d Nkr1030-2600; Apr–Sep; **P**), supremely grand, boasts a fabulous collection of art and superb craftsmanship in its 'dragon-style' lounges. As you sit in a chair once owned by the landscape painter JC Dahl, staring at the summer-lit fjord, you might weep as your mind struggles to comprehend vast interior and exterior beauty. A less remarkable wing was added in 1965.

There's a supermarket and a fast-food café opposite the dock, and the hostel restaurant serves dinner for Nkr110. For a splurge, eat at Kvikne's fjordside dining room (dinner buffet Nkr375).

In addition to the Sognefjorden express boat, local boats run daily to Hella (from Dragsvik, 10km by road north from Balestrand) and Fjærland.

Buses go to Sogndal (Nkr90, 1¼ hours) and Bergen (Nkr237, 3½ hours). The latter departs from Vik, which you must reach by boat (Nkr51, 15 minutes) from Balestrand. This service is cheaper than the express boat, and more scenic. Ask the tourist office for timetables.

Fjærland
pop 300

The location of this farming village at the head of the beautiful Fjærlandsfjorden, near two arms of the **Jostedalsbreen** icecap, makes it one of the most inviting destinations in Norway. The tiny village is Norway's 'Book Town,' with a dozen **bookshops** (10am-6pm May–mid-Sep) selling used stock from an impressive 4km of shelves. Fjærland's centre is called Mundal.

Balestrand's tourist office sells a packaged ticket (Nkr360) that includes the morning ferry to Fjærland, a connecting sightseeing bus and the afternoon return ferry. The tour includes the **Norwegian Glacier Museum** (☎ 57 69 32 88; Fjærland; adult/child Nkr80/40; 10am-4pm Apr-Oct), which has extensive displays on Jostedalsbreen, and visits two arms of the glacier: the **Supphellebreen**, where you can walk up to the glacier's edge and touch the ice; and the creaking, blue-iced **Bøyabreen**, where it's not uncommon to witness ice breaks plunging into the lake beneath the glacier tongue.

Overnight visitors can stay at **Bøyum Camping** (☎ 57 69 32 52; camp sites Nkr125, dm Nkr125, s Nkr250-300, d Nkr500-600, 6-person cabins Nkr530-650; **P**), 2km outside of town near the glacier museum, or the stunning olde-worlde **Hotel Mundal** (☎ 57 69 31 01; www.fjordinfo.no/mundal; Mundal; s Nkr820-1180, d Nkr980-1950; **P**), built in 1891, which overlooks the village and fjord from a gentle hill. It has a fine dining room.

Ferries run twice daily from 25 May to 9 September between Fjærland and Balestrand (Nkr140, 1¼ hours). Buses connect Fjærland and Sogndal (Nkr84, 45 minutes, three to seven daily) and Stryn (Nkr162, two hours). If driving, prepare for a heart-stopping toll (Nkr150) along Rv5 between Sogndal and Fjærland.

Sogndal & Around
pop 6600

Sogndal, a modern regional centre, is a starting point for day trips in the area. While it has more amenities than many of the area's smaller towns, it is also far less beautiful. Of most interest is the **Nigardsbreen glacier**, 70km to the north, followed by Norway's oldest **stave church** (dating from 1150 and on the Unesco World Heritage List), in Urnes across the Lustrafjord, and the **Sogn Folkmuseum** near Kaupanger, 11km east of Sogndal. Also in Kaupanger, there's a superb **stave church** dating from 1184. The **tourist office** (☎ 57 67 30 83; Kulturhus, Gravensteinsgaten; ☼ 9am-8pm late Jun-Aug, 9am-3pm Mon-Fri Sep–mid-Jun) is about 500m east of Sogndal bus station.

The tourist office books rooms in private homes from Nkr150 per person. There's an **HI Hostel** (☎ 57 67 20 33; dm/s/d Nkr100/250/400; ☼ mid-Jun–mid-Aug), only 15 minutes east of the bus station.

The hotel restaurant **Compagniet** (☎ 57 62 77 00; Hotel Sogndal, Gravensteinsgaten 5; buffet Nkr230; ☼ 7am-10.30pm) has formal evening buffets, but there's also a cheaper section with some light meals under Nkr100. For an inexpensive meal, try **Kaffir & Co**, a cafeteria in the **Domus** supermarket on Gravensteinsgata.

Buses run from Sogndal to Kaupanger (Nkr25, 10 minutes, hourly) and Balestrand (Nkr90, 1¼ hours, six to nine daily). Twice-daily buses (17 June to 26 August) go northeast past Jotunheimen National Park to Lom (Nkr200, 3½ hours) and on to Otta (Nkr275, 4½ hours), on the Oslo–Trondheim railway line.

NIGARDSBREEN

The most attractive arm of the Jostedals-breen glacier, Nigardsbreen is a popular summer destination, with guided **hikes** from late May to mid-September across the glacier's rippled blue ice. These outings include easy 1½-hour family walks (Nkr140) and challenging four-hour, blue-ice treks (Nkr390), crossing deep crevasses and requiring hiking boots and warm clothing (instruction and technical equipment included); there's also a full-day option. More

information on summer glacier walks and kayaking on glacier lakes is available from **Jostedal Breheimsenteret** (☎ 57 68 32 50; www.jostedal.com; Jostedal; ☼ 9am-7pm late Jun-Aug, 10am-5pm May & Sep), which operates a cafeteria and informative **museum** (admission Nkr50).

In the winter, contact friendly **Fimbul Jostedal** (☎ 99 45 09 21; www.fimbuljostedal.no) to learn about multiday courses on avalanche survival, ice-climbing and telemark skiing.

A bus leaves Sogndal at 8.45am (Monday to Friday) for the glacier, and a return bus leaves Nigardsbreen at 6.40pm. The fare is Nkr100 each way. Although this will give you time to do a short hike, if you're doing a longer hike you might want to stay at the nearby **Nigardsbreen Camping** (☎ 57 68 31 35; camp sites Nkr80, cabins Nkr350; P). About 5km from Breheimsenteret, **Jostedal Hotell** (☎ 57 68 31 19; www.jostedalhotel.no; Jostedal; s/d 450/900; P), an unofficial community centre, has clean rooms, a cafeteria and a Friday-night bingo session that attracts droves of locals.

NORDFJORD

Sognefjorden and Geirangerfjorden are linked by a road that winds around the head of the 100km-long Nordfjord, past the villages of Utvik, Innvik, Olden and Loen to the larger town of Stryn.

The chief Nordfjord attraction is the **Briksdal glacier**, one of Jostedal's icy arms. While glacier walks were available at the time of writing, the hikable area is in serious danger of melting away over the next few years. Although a barrage of package-tour buses drive up Olden Valley to Briksdal, there's only one public bus. It leaves Stryn (Nkr63, one daily) and Olden (Nkr42, one daily) from mid-June to mid-August, arrives at Briksdal and returns a few hours later.

The **Jostedalsbreen National Park Centre** (☎ 57 87 72 00; www.jostedalsbre.no; Stryn; adult/child Nkr60/30; ☼ 10am-4pm or 6pm May-Sep), which is 15km east of Stryn's centre, contains glacier-oriented exhibits, a decent audio-visual presentation and displays on avalanches, local minerals and meteorites.

From Briksdal, it's a 3km hike to the glacier – allow yourself about two hours return. **Pony-cart rides** (☎ 57 87 68 05; adult/child Nkr250/125) run most of the way to the glacier. Glacier hiking tours (Nkr250-550) are operated by **Briksdal Breføring** (☎ 57 87 68 00) and **Olden Activ** (☎ 57 87 38 88).

Sleeping & Eating

There are lots of camping and cabin options in the area.

Gryta Camping (☎ 57 87 59 36; Olden; camp sites from Nkr65, cabins Nkr400; P) By a dramatic lake and surrounded by flowering mountains.

Sande Camping (☎ 57874590; www.sande-camping .no; Loen; camp site Nkr40-80, cabin Nkr215-375; P) Another beautiful lakeside spot, with a shop, canoe rentals and cafeteria serving excellent cake.

HI hostel (☎ 57 87 11 06; Geilevegen 14, Stryn; dm/ s/d Nkr215/325/475; ☼ late May-early Sep; P) North of the centre, up a hill.

Hotel Alexandra (☎ 57 87 50 00; www.alexandra.no; N-6879 Loen; s/d Nkr960/1480; P ✕ ✕) This modern hotel commands good views over the fjord, and its pricey dinner buffet provides a top-notch survey of Norwegian cuisine.

Briksdalsbre Fjellstove (☎ 57 87 68 00; post@ briksdalsbre.no; Briksdal; s/d from Nkr300/400; ☼ Apr-Oct; P) Offers comfortable rooms near the glacier; traditional meals are available in the restaurant (Nkr99 to Nkr164).

Vesla Pensjonat (☎ 57 87 10 06; www.veslapensjon .no; Stryn; s/d Nkr600/800; P) Boasting a lovely garden, this lovely Victorian place will make you feel like you're living in a gingerbread house.

For nightlife, food and caffeine, Stryn is the place to go, with several bars, restaurants and a disco in the Stryne Hotel.

Getting There & Away

Buses run to Bergen (Nkr395, nine hours, four daily). Those that run between Stryn, Hellesylt (Nkr80, 50 minutes, two to four daily) and Ålesund (Nkr220, 3½ hours, two to five daily) connect with the Geiranger ferry at Hellesylt.

HELLESYLT

pop 500

Although quieter and less breathtaking than Geiranger, Hellesylt is still spectacular, lulled by a roaring waterfall that cascades through the centre. The **tourist office** (☎ 70 26 50 52) is near the ferry dock.

The convenient but rather exposed **Hellesylt Camping** (☎ 70 26 51 88; per camp site/ person from Nkr40/Nkr12; P) is right in the centre. A fine **HI hostel** (☎ 70 26 51 28; dm/ s/d Nkr145/245/335; ☼ Jun-Aug; P) is perched just above the village and has great fjord views.

Buses heading south to Stryn (Nkr80, 50 minutes) leave from the pier where the ferry pulls in.

NORANGSDALEN & SUNNMØRESALPANE

One of the most inspiring parts of the western fjords is Norangsdalen, a hidden valley west of Hellesylt. The partially unsealed Rv665 road to the villages of Øye and Urke and the Leknes–Sæbø ferry on beautiful Hjørundfjorden are served by bus from Hellesylt once daily, Monday to Friday mid-June to mid-August.

Hikers and climbers will find plenty of scope in the dramatic peaks of the adjacent Sunnmørsalpane, including the incredibly steep scrambling ascent of Slogen (1564m) from Øye and the superb Råna (1586m), a long and tough scramble from Urke.

GEIRANGERFJORDEN

The towering walls of the narrow and twisting 20km-long Geirangerfjorden have a scattering of abandoned farms clinging to the cliffs and breathtakingly high waterfalls with names such as the Seven Sisters, the Suitor and the Bridal Veil.

The cruise by public ferry along Geirangerfjorden, between Geiranger and Hellesylt, is Norway's most stunning and shouldn't be missed.

Geiranger

pop 270

High mountains with cascading waterfalls surround Geiranger, at the head of the crooked Geirangerfjorden. Although the village is tiny, it's one of Norway's most-visited spots. Nevertheless, it's reasonably serene in the evening when the cruise ships and tour buses have gone.

The **tourist office** (☎ 70 26 30 99), near the pier, opens from mid-May to early September and has an album detailing trails.

SIGHTS & ACTIVITIES

The **Norsk Fjordsenter** (☎ 70 26 18 00; www.fjord senter.info; adult/child Nkr75/35; 10am-5pm May-Sep) describes local culture, and screens an excellent film showing images of the Geirangerfjord in each season.

There's great hiking all around Geiranger to abandoned farmsteads, waterfalls and some beautiful lookout points. One special walk is to **Storseter waterfall**, a 45-minute hike that takes you between the rock face and the cascading falls. You'll get the most spectacular fjord views from **Flydalsjuvet**, about 5km uphill from Geiranger on the Stryn road, and from **Ørnevegen**, about 4km from Geiranger towards Valldal and Åndalsnes.

The highest and most splendid view of the Geiranger valley and fjord is from the **Dalsnibba** lookout (1500m). A bus (Nkr100 return) runs from Geiranger between 15 June and 20 August.

SLEEPING & EATING

Hotels in Geiranger can be quickly booked out by package tours, but cabins and camping spots are plentiful. A dozen camping grounds skirt the fjord and hillsides.

Geiranger Camping (☎ 70 26 31 20; www .geirangercamping.no; camp sites from Nkr60; ⌚ 20 May-10 Sep) Right in the centre of Geiranger.

You'll see *Rom* signs around the village advertising rooms at around Nkr200/400 (singles/doubles) – the tourist office maintains a list and can help book one for you.

Grande Fjord Hotell (☎ 70 26 30 90; www .grandefjordhotel.com; s/d Nkr750/900; P ☒) At a scenic spot on the fjord 2km northwest of the village, the hotel also has cabins and tent space nearby. The buffet breakfasts (included) and dinners are particularly good here.

The tiny town centre has Café Ole, where you can pick up good coffee, Olebuda, a decent restaurant, and a Joker supermarket, open even on Sunday. If you need a tasteful gift, stop by Geiranger Galleri, a self-designated 'troll-free zone' representing artists from the Western Fjords.

GETTING THERE & AWAY

From mid-June to late August, buses run to Åndalsnes (Nkr148, three hours). Change at Linge for buses to Ålesund (Nkr172). The Geiranger–Hellesylt ferry (passengers/cars Nkr37/116, one hour, four to 10 daily) runs May to late September.

ÅNDALSNES

pop 3500

By Romsdalsfjorden, Åndalsnes is the northern gateway to the western fjords. Most travellers arrive on the train from Dombås, a scenic route that descends through a deeply cut valley with dramatic waterfalls. Just before reaching Åndalsnes, the train passes **Trollveggen**, a sheer 1500m-high rock face whose jagged and often cloud-shrouded summit is considered the ultimate challenge among Norwegian mountain climbers. Highway E136 between Dombås and Åndalsnes runs parallel to the railway line and is equally spectacular.

The town itself is rather nondescript, but the scenery is fabulous, camping grounds are plentiful and it has one of the finest hostels in Norway. The **tourist office** (☎ 71 22 16 22) is at the train station.

Hiking

The mountains and valleys surrounding Åndalsnes offer excellent hiking – contact the tourist office for details of guided trips. One good trail, which goes to the top of Nesaksla (715m), starts right in town 50m north of the roundabout and makes a fine half-day outing. While the path is quite steep, you'll be rewarded at the top.

Sleeping & Eating

Åndalsnes Camping (☎ 71 22 22 79; www.andals nescamp.no; camp sites from Nkr60, 6-person cabin Nkr700; P) On the southeastern side of the Rauma river, 2km from the centre. Also rents canoes and bikes.

Åndalsnes Vandrerhjem Setnes (☎ 71 22 13 82; aandalsnes.hostel@vandrerhjem.no; dm/s/d Nkr190/350/490; ⌚ late May-early Sep; P) This well-loved, turf-roofed place offers rustic accommodation with fabulous views. It's 2km from the train station on highway E136 towards Ålesund.

Alpe Hotel (☎ 71 22 21 00; Jernbanegate 3; s/d Nkr450/550; P ☒) The pleasant and modernised Alpe is just 50m from the train station.

The town centre contains a grocery store, bakery and several inexpensive cafeterias.

Getting There & Away

The train from Dombås runs to Åndalsnes three or four times daily (Nkr171, 1¼ hours), in sync with Oslo–Trondheim trains. Buses to Ålesund (Nkr179, 2¼ hours) meet the trains. Buses to Geiranger (Nkr145, three hours), via the spectacular Trollstigen road, operate from mid-June to late August. If you have your own car, the mountain pass is cleared of snow and opens by 1 June every year – early in the season it's an awesome drive between immense vertical walls of snow.

ÅNDALSNES TO GEIRANGER

The **Trollstigen** (Troll's Path) winding south from Åndalsnes is a thriller of a road with hairpin bends and a 1:12 gradient, and to add a daredevil element it's practically one lane all the way. On request, the bus makes photo stops at the thundering, 180m-high **Stigfossen waterfall** on its way up to the mountain pass. At the top, the bus usually stops long enough for you to walk to a lookout with a dizzying view back down the valley.

There are waterfalls galore smoking down the mountains as you descend into **Valldal**. You could break your journey here – there are camping grounds, cabins and a hotel – though most travellers continue on, taking the short ferry ride from Linge across to **Eidsdal**. From there, a waiting bus continues along the **Ørnevegen** (Eagle's Highway), with magnificent bird's-eye views of Geirangerfjorden during the descent into Geiranger village.

ÅLESUND

pop 24,320

Lucky for you, this pretty coastal town burned to the ground in 1904. The amazing rebuilding created a fantastical downtown centre unlike anything else you'll see in Norway – a harmonious collection of pastel buildings almost entirely designed in the Art Nouveau tradition. All the loveliness is well staged on the end of a peninsula, surrounded by islands, water and hills – many feel it beats Bergen's picturesqueness.

The **tourist office** (☎ 70 15 76 00; www.visit alesund.com; ❧ 8.30am-7pm Mon-Fri, 9am-5pm Sat, 11am-5pm Sun Jun-Aug, shorter hrs Sep-May) is near the *Hurtigruten* quay. The post office is on Korsegata. For free Internet, visit the **public library** (Kremmergaarden, Korsegata).

Sights & Activities

A popular thing to do is to walk the 418 steps up **Aksla** for a splendid view of Ålesund and the surrounding islands. Take Lihauggata from Kongensgata, pass the **Rollon statue** and begin the 20-minute puff to the top of the hill.

Far more interesting than its name suggests, the brilliant **Art Nouveau Centre** (☎ 70 10 49 70; www.jugendstilsenteret.no; Apotekergata 16; adult/ student/child Nkr50/40/25; ❧ 10am-7pm Mon-Fri, 10am-5pm Sat, noon-5pm Sun Jun-Aug, shorter hrs Sep-May), occupying the opulent interior of a former

pharmacy, explains the town's rebuilding with a weird time machine and presents the work (furniture, paintings, textiles and glass) of well-known continental Art Nouveau masters alongside their Norwegian counterparts.

The town **museum** (☎ 70 12 31 70; Rasmus Rønnebergs gate 16; adult/child Nkr30/10; ❧ 11am-4pm Mon-Fri, noon-3pm Sat & Sun mid-Jun–mid-Aug, shorter hrs mid-Aug–mid-Jun) concentrates on local history, including sealing, fishing, shipping, the fire of 1904 and the German occupation during WWII.

The aquarium **Atlanterhavsparken** (☎ 70 10 70 60; Tueneset; adult/child Nkr85/55; ❧ 10am-7pm Sun-Fri, 10am-4pm Sat mid-Jun–mid-Aug, shorter hrs mid-Aug–mid-Jun), 3km from the centre at the western extreme of the peninsula, introduces visitors to marine life around the Norwegian coast.

Ålesund is a good base for touring the surrounding islands, including Runde (p321). Ferries depart from the Skateflukaia Ferry Terminal.

Monday to Friday from 1 May to 25 September there's a scenic bus-ferry day trip (Nkr410) that includes a cruise down Geirangerfjorden, an hour in Geiranger and return to Ålesund via Ørnevegen.

Sleeping

The tourist office keeps lists of private rooms that start at around Nkr250 per person.

Ålesund Hostel (☎ 70 11 58 30; aalesund.hostel@ vandrerhjem.no; Parkgata 14; dm/s/d Nkr225/415/535) Tidy and central, occupying somewhat industrial rooms where touches of old charm show through.

Brosundet Gjestehus (☎ 70 12 10 00; post@ brosundet.no; Apotekergata 5; s Nkr550-750, d Nkr710-990) A former warehouse containing modern rooms interestingly punctured by massive timbers. Large pulleys used to haul up fish still exist in some rooms. Many are inches from the canal.

Quality Hotel Scandinavic (☎ 70 15 78 00; www .choice.no; Løvenvoldgata 8; s Nkr690-1090, d Nkr890-1390; P ❧) While its exterior, stairs and hallways retain lavish *Jugendstil* touches, the rooms of this hotel have been stripped and redone in smart Scandinavian design.

Comfort Hotel Bryggen (☎ 70 12 11 80; www .choicehotel.no; Apotekergata 1; s Nkr720-1250, d Nkr980- 1560; P ❧) This canalside choice occupies a pastel yellow building dating from the

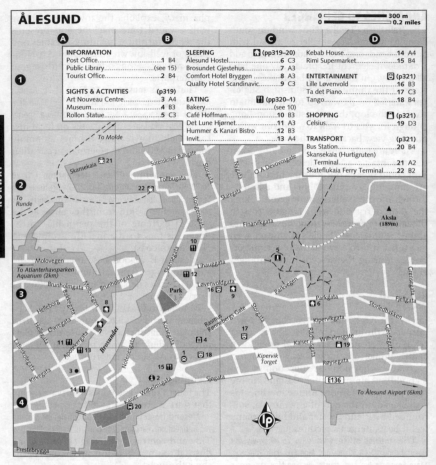

ÅLESUND

INFORMATION	
Post Office	1 B4
Public Library	(see 15)
Tourist Office	2 B4
SIGHTS & ACTIVITIES	(p319)
Art Nouveau Centre	3 A4
Museum	4 B3
Rollon Statue	5 C3
SLEEPING	(pp319–20)
Ålesund Hostel	6 C3
Brosundet Gjestehus	7 A3
Comfort Hotel Bryggen	8 A3
Quality Hotel Scandinavic	9 C3
EATING	(pp320–1)
Bakery	(see 10)
Café Hoffman	10 B3
Det Lune Hjørnet	11 B3
Hummer & Kanari Bistro	12 B3
Invit	13 A4
Kebab House	14 A4
Rimi Supermarket	15 B4
ENTERTAINMENT	(p321)
Lille Løvenvold	16 B3
Ta det Piano	17 C3
Tango	18 B4
SHOPPING	(p321)
Celsius	19 D3
TRANSPORT	(p321)
Bus Station	20 B4
Skansekaia (Hurtigruten) Terminal	21 A2
Skateflukaia Ferry Terminal	22 B2

town's reconstruction. In addition to breakfast, a nice dinner buffet is included.

Eating

Art Nouveau Centre (☎ 70 10 49 70; www.jugend stilsenteret.no; Apotekergata 16) Aside from Brie (Nkr50) and tuna sandwiches on grainy bread, the charming café here serves chocolate cake (Nkr35) modelled after the one God created when the world was made. Such things aren't supposed to exist on earth, yet here it is. Weird forks.

Kebab House (☎ 70 12 87 78; Nedre Strandgata 1; dishes Nkr45–80; ⏰ 1-11pm Sun-Thu, 1pm-2.30am Fri & Sat) The pleasant wooden booths at this small eatery boast a nice view down the stretch of the canal. Eat pizza, burgers or kebabs.

Hummer & Kanari Bistro (☎ 70 12 80 08; Kongensgata 19; bistro mains Nkr55-105; ⏰ from 11.30am) A bistro and restaurant under one Art Nouveau roof. The bistro (filling and cheaper than the restaurant) serves vegetarian pasta, vegetables and dip (Nkr55), and a slice of pie with salad (Nkr89).

Café Hoffmann (Kongensgata 11; mains Nkr75-140; ⏰ 11am-midnight) Hoffmann has a fine harbour view and serves up soup for Nkr40; there's a bakery located in the same shopping centre.

Det Lune Hjørnet (☎ 70 13 09 99; Apotekergata 10; snacks Nkr16-35; ⏰ 11am-5pm Mon-Sat) This bright and cheery place is a combined used bookshop and coffeeshop and comes with a wood-burning stove.

Invit (Apotekergata 9; ⊗ 8am-5pm Mon-Fri, 10am-5pm Sat) This modern espresso bar serves the best steamed drinks in town.

There's a Rimi supermarket downstairs in Kremmergaarden.

Entertainment

Lille Løvenvold (☎ 70 12 54 00; Løvenvoldgata 2; ⊗ from 11am Mon-Sat, 1pm-1am Sun) Serves a young crowd of hipsters with rock, rooms lit with dim red light, and couches.

Ta det Piano (☎ 70 10 06 99; Kipervikgata 1B; ⊗ from 11am) A bar and café, attracting conversationalists and intellectuals with outdoor seating, occasional live music and constant redecoration. There's a decent bar menu.

Tango (☎ 70 12 10 12; Kaiser Wilhelmsgata 2; ⊗ from 11am) Those afraid of discos will like the plate-glass windows which allow for a careful assessment of hedonistic activity before a venture inside. It's a stylish place with a large mural by Oppdal spanning the room. By day it's a café.

Shopping

Celsius (☎ 70 10 01 16; Kaiser Wilhelmsgata 52; ⊗ 10am-4pm Tue-Fri, 10am-2pm Sat) The small glass studio blows unconventional pieces with vivid colours. The kiln is at the front of the studio, the shop at the back.

Getting There & Away

Ålesund has daily flights to Oslo and other Norwegian cities. There are buses to Stryn (Nkr220, 3½ hours, one to four daily) via Hellesylt and to other major coastal and fjord towns. The bus to Åndalsnes (Nkr172) is timed to meet arriving and departing trains.

The *Hurtigruten* docks at Skansekaia Terminal.

RUNDE

pop 160

The impressive island of Runde, 27km west of Ålesund, plays host to half a million sea birds, including 100,000 pairs of migrating puffins that arrive in May and stay until late July. Most bird-watching is best done by sea; the hostel arranges bird-watching tours for Nkr100.

Runde HI Hostel & Camping (☎ 70 08 59 16; runde.hostel@vandrerhjem.no; dm/s/d Nkr145/265/325), on the harbourside, provides clean and comfortable accommodation. There's a café 300m from the hostel.

Runde can be reached by a catamaran-bus combination that departs from Ålesund's Skateflukaia (Nkr150 each way, 2½ hours) daily from mid-June to mid-September; from Monday to Friday you can book a day trip (Nkr266).

NORTHERN NORWAY

The counties of Sør Trøndelag, Nord Trøndelag, Nordland, Troms and Finnmark comprise a vast and varied area stretching over 1500km, mostly north of the Arctic Circle. The terrain ranges from majestic coastal mountains that rise above tiny fishing villages and scattered farms to the barren, treeless, Arctic plateau in the far north.

Trains run as far as Bodø; for destinations further north, there are buses and boats. Since distances are long, bus travel costs can add up, though Inter-Rail and ScanRail passholders get a 50% discount on most long-distance bus routes. An interesting alternative to land travel is the *Hurtigruten* coastal steamer, which pulls into every sizable port between Bergen and Kirkenes, passing some of the best coastal scenery in Scandinavia.

RØROS

pop 2590

Røros is a wonderful old copper-mining town with a well-preserved historic district, protected under Unesco's World Heritage List. The little hillside town is dominated by a large wooden church, and contains several galleries. The first mine opened in 1644 but in 1977, after 333 years of operation, the company went bankrupt. The town makes for delightful strolling and everything's within easy walking distance. The **tourist office** (☎ 72 41 11 65; Peder Hiortsgata 2; ⊗ 9am-3.30pm Mon-Fri, 10.30am-12.30pm Sat) can advise on cycling trips, canoeing, fishing and hiking.

Sights & Activities

Røros' main attractions are the turf-roofed **miners' cottages** and other centuries-old timber buildings; a prominent blue and white 1784 **church** (Kjerkgata; tours adult/child Nkr25/free; ⊗ 10am-5pm Mon-Sat, 2-4pm Sun mid-Jun–mid-Aug, tours 2pm) with an excellent baroque interior; **slag heaps**; and the old smelting works, now part of the **Rørosmuseet** (☎ 72 40 61 70; Malmplassen; adult/student/child Nkr60/50/30; ⊗ 10am-7pm

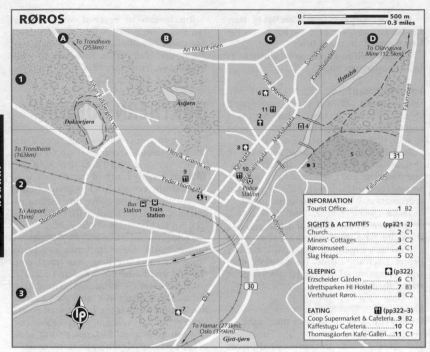

RØROS

0 _____ 500 m
0 _____ 0.3 miles

To Trondheim (253km)

An Magritveien

To Olavsguva Mine (12.5km)

Svenskveien

Kvernhusveien

Hyttelva

Doktortjørn

Åstjørn

Falunveien

Johan Falkbergets vei

To Trondheim (163km)

Henrik Grønns vei

Peder Hiortgata

Kjerkgata

Bergmannsgata

Markusgata

To Airport (1km)

Stormoveien

Bus Station

Train Station

Police Station

Falunveien

Ora

To Hamar (273km); Oslo (399km)

Gjett-tjørn

INFORMATION
Tourist Office..............................1 B2

SIGHTS & ACTIVITIES (pp321-2)
Church..2 C1
Miners' Cottages.........................3 C2
Rørosmuseet...............................4 C1
Slag Heaps..................................5 D2

SLEEPING (p322)
Erzscheider Gården......................6 C1
Idrettsparken HI Hostel...............7 B3
Vertshuset Røros.........................8 C2

EATING (pp322-3)
Coop Supermarket & Cafeteria...9 B2
Kaffestugu Cafeteria..................10 C2
Thomasgåorfen Kafe-Galleri......11 C1

mid-Jun–mid-Aug, shorter hrs mid-Aug–mid-Jun). The museum features intricate scale models of life in the mines.

You can also visit the now defunct **Olavsguva mine** (☎ 72 41 11 65; Kojedalen; tours adult/student/child Nkr60/50/30), 13km northeast of town. From 21 June to 15 August, subterranean tours into the old copper mine (5°C – bring a sweater!) are given every 90 minutes, with the first at 11am and the last at 5pm. From September to May, you must book ahead for the single weekly tour (Saturday at 3pm). A car is needed to get there.

Organised Tours

In winter, the tourist office organises ski tours and excursions by dogsled (Nkr600 to Nkr1000 for two to six hours) or horse-drawn sleigh (Nkr600 per hour for four people). Bizarre **UFO safaris** (☎ 72 41 55 99; skiinfo@alen-skisenter.no) are also available.

Sleeping & Eating

Idrettsparken HI Hostel (☎ 72 41 10 89; Øra 25; camp sites Nkr60, dm/s/d Nkr225/375/445, cabins Nkr380-600; P) Surrounded by soccer pitches.

Vertshuset Røros (☎ 72 41 93 50; www.vertshusetroros.no; Kjerkgata 34; s/d from Nkr695/880, 2-person apt per person from Nkr395; P) Many of the inviting rooms here have floors painted in a folk style common in the Røros area.

Erzscheider Gården (☎ 72 41 11 94; Spell Olaveien 6; s/d Nkr590/890; P) The cosy Erzscheider sits atop a hill, and many of the rooms have fine views across the cathedral's cemetery and the town beyond. Parts of the house date from 1780.

Vertshuset Røros (Kjerkgata 34; mains Nkr99-215) For formal dining in a small, pleasant dining room try pizza (from Nkr85), beef, freshwater fish and elk.

Kafestuggu cafeteria (☎ 72 41 10 33; Bergmannsgata 18; light meals Nkr60-85, mains Nkr100-120; ☺ to 8pm) Looks like a ski lodge or a Victorian parlour, depending on where you sit.

Thomasgårfen Kafe-Galleri (☎ 72 41 24 70; Kjerkgata 48; snacks Nkr35-50; ☺ 10am-8pm Mon-Fri, 10am-4pm Sat, noon-6pm Sun mid-Jun–mid-Aug, shorter hrs mid-Aug–mid-Jun) For a nice read in a rustic room filled with ceramics. Enhance your experience with apple cake and coffee (Nkr35).

You'll also find a **Coop supermarket** (Peder Hiortsgata 7).

Getting There & Away

Røros is 46km west of the Swedish border, via highway Rv31. It's also a stop on the eastern railway line between Oslo (Nkr582, five hours) and Trondheim (Nkr246, 2½ hours). Overnight buses run daily except Saturday to Trondheim (Nkr210, three hours) and Oslo (Nkr460, six hours). The Røros airport is served by Widerøe from Oslo.

TRONDHEIM

pop 138,000

Norway's third-largest city and original capital, beautiful Trondheim is a lively university town with a rich medieval history. It was founded at the estuary of the winding Nidelva in AD 997 by the Viking king Olav Tryggvason. After a fire razed most of the city in 1681, Trondheim was redesigned with wide streets and Renaissance flair by General Caspar de Cicignon. Today, the steeple of the medieval Nidaros Domkirke is still the highest point in the city centre.

Orientation & Information

The central part of town is on a triangular peninsula that's easy to explore on foot. The train station, bus station and coastal-steamer quay are across the canal, a few minutes north of the centre.

The **tourist office** (☎ 73 80 76 60; www.visit -trondheim.com; Torvet; ☯ 8.30am-10pm Mon-Fri, 10am-8pm Sat & Sun, late Jun-early Aug, shorter hrs mid-Aug-mid-Jun) helps with inquiries.

The **library** (Kongens gate; ☯ 9am-4pm Mon-Fri, 10am-3pm Sat Jul-mid-Aug, 9am-4pm Mon-Fri mid-Aug-Jun) has international newspapers and free Internet access (expect a wait and 30-minute limit). Late night **Space Bar** (☎ 73 51 55 50; Kongens gate 19; per hr Nkr40; ☯ 10am-2am Sun-Thu, 24hr Fri & Sat) also provides Internet access. **Ark Bruns Bokhandel** (Kongens gate 10) sells English-language books.

Sights

On and around **Torvet**, the central square, are a produce market, a **statue of King Olav** and the 13th-century stone church **Vår Frue Kirke**. From Torvet there's a head-on view of the cathedral, Nidaros Domkirke, to the south.

Nidaros Domkirke (☎ 73 53 91 60; Kongsgårdsgata; admission Nkr40; ☯ from 9am Mon-Sat, 1-4pm Sun May-

mid-Sep, noon-2.30pm Mon-Fri, 11.30am-2pm Sat, 1-3pm Sun mid-Sep-Apr) is the city's most dominant landmark and Scandinavia's largest medieval building. The first church on this site was built in 1070 over the grave of St Olav, the Viking king who replaced the worship of Nordic gods with Christianity. The oldest wing of the current building dates back to the 12th century. Because of the suppression of spectacle demanded by the Reformation, the interior of this cathedral is rather plain and the narrative ornamentation of Catholic churches is absent. Organ recitals take place on Saturdays at 1pm.

An interesting feature of the cathedral is its ornately embellished west wall, lined with statues of biblical characters and Norwegian bishops and kings. Destroyed in the 19th century, the rebuilding of this wing lasted into the 20th century. None of the sculptures are original.

From 20 June to 20 August, visitors can climb the cathedral tower for a rooftop view of the city (Nkr5). The cathedral, the site of Norwegian coronations, usually displays the **crown jewels**. However, technical improvements will prevent their viewing until 2006.

Admission includes entrance to the **Archbishop's Palace Museum** (☯ 11am-5pm Mon-Fri, 10am-3pm Sat, noon-5pm Sun mid-Jun-mid-Aug, shorter hrs mid-Aug-mid-Jun) which details the history of the cathedral and displays archaeological finds from the surrounding grounds.

If old swords, armour and cannons sound interesting, visit the **Rustkammeret military museum** (☎ 73 99 52 80; Kongsgårdsgata; ☯ 9am-3pm Mon-Fri, 11am-4pm Sat & Sun Jun-Aug).

Scandinavia's largest wooden palace, the late-baroque **Stiftsgården** (☎ 73 84 28 80; Munkegata; adult/child Nkr50/25; ☯ 10am-5pm Mon-Sat, noon-5pm Sun, Jul-mid-Aug, shorter hrs Jun) was completed in 1778 and is now the official royal residence in Trondheim. Admission is by tour only (on the hour; last tour one hour before closing).

The **Ringve Museum** (☎ 73 92 24 11; www .ringve.com; Lade Allé 60; adult/student/child Nkr70/40/25; ☯ 11am-3pm or 5pm mid-May-mid Sep, 11am-4pm Sun mid-Sep-mid-May), about 3km northeast of the city centre, is a fascinating music-history museum in an 18th-century estate. Music students give tours, demonstrating the antique instruments on display. Take bus No 3 or 4 from Munkegaten.

The **Trøndelag Folk Museum** (☎ 73 89 01 00; Sverresborg Allé; adult/student/child Nkr75/50/25; ☯ 11am-6pm

TRONDHEIM

0 ——————— 400 m
0 ——————— 0.2 miles

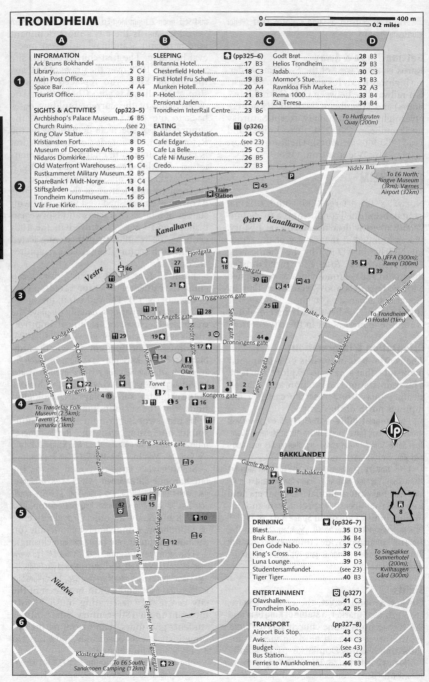

INFORMATION
Ark Bruns Bokhandel **1** B4
Library...................................**2** C4
Main Post Office.....................**3** B3
Space Bar..............................**4** A4
Tourist Office.........................**5** B4

SIGHTS & ACTIVITIES (pp323–5)
Archbishop's Palace Museum......**6** B5
Church Ruins........................(see 2)
King Olav Statue.....................**7** B4
Kristiansten Fort......................**8** D5
Museum of Decorative Arts........**9** B5
Nidaros Domkirke...................**10** B5
Old Waterfront Warehouses.....**11** C4
Rustkammeret Military Museum..**12** B5
SpareBank1 Midt-Norge...........**13** C4
Stiftsgården..........................**14** B4
Trondheim Kunstmuseum........**15** B5
Vår Frue Kirke......................**16** B4

SLEEPING ⌂ (pp325–6)
Britannia Hotel......................**17** B3
Chesterfield Hotel..................**18** C3
First Hotel Fru Schøller............**19** B3
Munken Hotell.......................**20** A4
P-Hotel................................**21** B3
Pensionat Jarlen.....................**22** A4
Trondheim InterRail Centre......**23** B6

EATING 🍴 (p326)
Baklandet Skydsstation............**24** C5
Cafe Edgar............................(see 23)
Cafe La Belle.........................**25** C3
Café Ni Muser.......................**26** B5
Credo.................................**27** B3

Godt Brøt..............................**28** B3
Helios Trondheim....................**29** B3
Jadab..................................**30** C3
Mormor's Stue.......................**31** B3
Ravnkloa Fish Market..............**32** A3
Rema 1000...........................**33** B4
Zia Teresa.............................**34** B4

To Hurtigruten
Quay (200m)

To E6 North;
Ringve Museum
(3km); Værnes
Airport (32km)

Nidelv Bru

P

🚏 **45**

🚌 **Train
Station**

Kanalhavn　　*Østre Kanalhavn*

40 🏛
Fjordgata
27 🏛
　　18 ⓘ
Brattørgata
Vestre
🏛 **46**
21 ⌂
30 🏛
🚏 **43**
32 🏛
🏛 **41**
To UFFA (300m);
Ramp (300m)
35 🍺
🍺 **39**

Olav Tryggvasons gate
25 🏛
Bakke bru

🏛 **31**
28 🏛
Thomas Angells gate
Søndre gate
To Trondheim
HI Hostel (1km)

29 🏛
19 ⌂
3 ⊗
17 ⌂
Dronningens gate
44 ●
Nordre gate
Sandgate
Innherredsveien

🏛 **14**
Munkegata
St Olavs gate
Tordenskjolds gate
ⓘ
*King
Olav*
Kjøpmannsgata

20 🏛
36 🏛
Torvet
🍺
22 🏛
1 ●
🏛 **38**
13 ●
2 ●
11
Kongens gate
4 @
🍴 **7**
Nedre Bakklandet

To Trøndelag Folk
Museum (2.5km);
Tavern (2.5km);
Bymarka (3km)
33 🏛
🍴 **5**
🍴 **16**
Kongens gate

🏛 **34**

Erling Skakkes gate

BAKKLANDET

🏛 **9**
Gamle Bybro
Brubakken
Øvre Bakklandet
🍴 **37**
🍴 **24**

Bispegata
26 🏛 🏛
15
42 🏛

🏛 **10**

Kongsgårdsgata
🏛 **12**
🏛 **6**

To Singsakker
Sommerhotel
(200m);
Kvilhaugen
Gård (300m)

🏛
8

Nidelva
Pinsens gate

Klostergata
To E6 South;
Sandmoen Camping (12km)
Elgeseter bru
Elgeseter gate
🍺 **23**

DRINKING 🍺 (pp326–7)
Blæst.................................**35** D3
Bruk Bar.............................**36** B4
Den Gode Nabo....................**37** C5
King's Cross.........................**38** B4
Luna Lounge.........................**39** D3
Studentersamfundet..............(see 23)
Tiger Tiger...........................**40** B3

ENTERTAINMENT 🎭 (p327)
Olavshallen..........................**41** C3
Trondheim Kino....................**42** B5

TRANSPORT (pp327–8)
Airport Bus Stop....................**43** C3
Avis...................................**44** C3
Budget...............................(see 43)
Bus Station..........................**45** C2
Ferries to Munkholmen...........**46** B3

Jun-Aug, 11am-3pm Mon-Fri, noon-4pm Sat & Sun Sep-May) has good hill-top views of the city and over 60 period buildings, including a small, 12th-century stave church. Catch bus No 8 or 9 from Dronningens gate.

The eclectic **Museum of Decorative Arts** (☎ 73 80 89 50; www.nkim.museum.no; Munkegata 5; adult/student Nkr50/25; ☺ 10am-5pm Mon-Sat, noon-5pm Sun late Jun-late Aug, 10am-3pm Tue-Sat, noon-4pm Sun Sep–mid-Jun) exhibits a fine collection of contemporary arts and crafts ranging from Japanese pottery by Shoji Hamada to work by Hannah Ryggen, Norway's highly acclaimed tapestry artist. **Trondheim Kunstmuseum** (☎ 73 53 81 80; Bispegata 7B; adult/student Nkr40/20; ☺ 10am-5pm Jun-Aug, 11am-4pm Tue-Sun Sep-May), an art museum, has Munch lithographs and other Scandinavian works.

The excavated **ruins of early-medieval churches** can be viewed free in the basement of the bank **SpareBank1 Midt-Norge** (Søndre gate 4; ☺ 9am-2.30pm Mon-Fri, 9am-5pm Thu), and inside the entrance of the nearby public library (where there's a display of two human skeletons discovered during the library's construction). Not to be missed are the old **waterfront warehouses** resembling Bergen's Bryggen, best viewed from Gamle Bybro (the old town bridge). There's a good view of the city from the top of the 17th-century **Kristiansten Fort** (☎ 73 99 58 31; Festningsgaten; admission Nkr10, ☺ 10am-3pm Mon-Fri, 11am 4pm Sat & Sun Jun-Aug), a 10-minute uphill walk east from Gamle Bybro. Though its buildings open only during the summer, the grounds can be viewed year-round.

Bakklandet, a neighbourhood of cobble-stone streets immediately west of the centre, contains plenty of small-scale wooden buildings from the 19th century. Here you can find cafés and good walking.

Activities

A popular place to sunbathe and picnic is **Munkholmen** island, site of an 11th-century Benedictine monastery and later converted to a prison, a fort and a customs house. From mid-May to early September, ferries (adult/child Nkr45/25 return) leave from the small harbour east of the Ravnkloa fish market.

The western side of Trondheim is bordered by the **Bymarka**, a woodland area crossed with good skiing and wilderness trails. To get there, take the tram from St Olavs gate to **Lian**, which has good city views, a bathing lake and hiking paths.

Sleeping

At time of writing, finding a room in mid-August can be problematic. A large convention annually descends upon the town, filling up the hotels and hostels. Book early if you plan to visit during this time. The tourist office books rooms in private homes, mostly on the city outskirts, averaging Nkr300/400 for singles/doubles plus a Nkr20 booking fee.

Sandmoen Camping (☎ 72 88 61 35; www.sandmoen.no; camp sites from Nkr100, cabins Nkr475-900; **P**) The nearest camping ground is 12km south of the city on the E6. There's a bar on site, and the cabins look mass-produced. Take bus No 46.

Trondheim InterRail Centre (☎ 73 89 95 38; www.stud.ntnu.no/groups/tirc; Elgesetergate 1; dm Nkr115; ☺ mid-Jun–mid-Aug) During summer recess, university students operate this informal crash pad. An assortment of military surplus cots fill up rooms used as discos the rest of the year. The friendly place offers free Internet.

Trondheim HI Hostel (☎ 73 87 44 50; trondheim.hostel@vandrerhjem.no; Weidemannsvei 41; dm/s/d Nkr235/445/575; **P**) About 2km east of the train station, this is a plain and modern hostel with concrete walls and small windows.

Singsaker Sommerhotel (☎ 73 89 31 00; http://sommerhotell.singsaker.no; Rogertsgata 1; dm/s/d Nkr170/375/570; ☺ early Jun–mid-Aug) Located 200m south of Kristiansten Fort, this hotel sits in a quiet, green part of the city in a massive wooden building.

Pensionat Jarlen (☎ 73 51 32 18; p-jarlen@frisurf.no; Kongens gate 40; s/d Nkr400/500) Though barren, worn and utilitarian, the rooms here are clean, and contain showers and small kitchens. It's centrally located.

P-Hotel (☎ 73 80 23 50; www.p-hotels.no; Nordre gate 24; s/d Nkr495/595) A recently renovated old hotel, with crisp rooms of Scandinavian design. The best deal of the conventional hotels, its comparatively low prices exist in part because you're supposed to book using the Internet. There is no breakfast buffet, but you do get a sack with food and newspaper. Free Internet.

Munken Hotell (☎ 73 53 45 40; www.munken.no; Kongens gate 44; s Nkr595-650, d Nkr590-890) The back rooms of this small red option overlook a quiet, cobbled street. Most rooms have bathroom and all are simply and tastefully decorated.

First Hotel Fru Schøller (☎ 73 87 08 00; www .scholler.no; Dronningens gate 26; s Nkr690-795, d Nkr850-950) Because the owner is a furniture designer, some of the 33 rooms contain appealing decorative touches. Others might make you question where precisely he learned the trade. It sits across the street from the royal residence, and rates include a soup supper (Sunday to Thursday).

Chesterfield Hotel (☎ 73 50 37 50; hotel@online .no; Søndre gate 26; s Nkr670-1195, d Nkr895-1395; **P** 💢) Commodious rooms with private bathroom and free Internet. Rooms on the 7th floor have huge skylights and broad city views. Discounts are offered for ScanRail passholders.

Britannia Hotel (☎ 73 80 08 00; www.britannia.no; Dronningens gate 5; s & d Nkr1630, s/d discount weekend Nkr825/990; **P** 💢) This huge hotel is Trondheim's oldest (1897). You'll get British-style attention to detail and breakfast in a palm-filled hall.

Eating
RESTAURANTS
Zia Teresa (Vår Frue strete 4; mains Nkr75-185; 🕒 from 11am) A cosy bistro with Italian food, including pasta dishes averaging Nkr90. Take a moment to admire the ceiling while chewing.

Mormor's Stue (☎ 73 52 20 22; N Enkelts Killingsveile 2; mains Nkr89-97; 🕒 10am-11.30pm Mon-Sat, 1-11.30pm Sun) Full of lace, parlours and dusty pictures of grandma, serves sandwiches (Nkr51), pasta and salads. The best and most dangerous time to visit is Sunday, when a calorifically evil cake and coffee buffet (Nkr54) ensures every seat is filled.

Jadab (☎ 73 52 46 00; Brattørgata 3A; mains Nkr109-169; 🕒 from 2pm) Indian dishes and a large vegetarian menu. They serve so much rice that a side of naan probably won't be needed.

Credo (☎ 73 53 03 88; Ørjaveita 4; mains Nkr100-300) Original concoctions that solidly hit the mark. The excellent kitchen serves main dishes for Nkr100 from 4pm to 7pm Monday to Friday. Stellar wine list.

Tavern (☎ 73 87 80 70; Sverresborg Allé 11; mains Nkr115-255; 🕒 4pm-midnight Mon-Fri, 2pm-midnight Sat, noon-midnight Sun) Dates from 1739, and has enormous fireplaces. The menu features items such as roast elk and a superb halibut with hazelnuts and creamed spinach. For atmosphere on a budget, eat some pancakes with jam and bacon (Nkr78).

Kvilhaugen Gård (☎ 73 60 06 60; Blussuvollsbakken 40; mains Nkr195-245; 🕒 from 4pm Tue-Sat, from 2pm Sun) Occupies a lovely hill-top farmstead overlooking the city. It's 2.5km outside the centre.

CAFÉS
Cafe Edgar (☎ 73 89 95 00; Elgesetergate 1; dinner Nkr40; 🕒 from 5pm Sun-Fri, 3pm Sat) Full of students, run by volunteers and prepares a filling daily meal. It's one of many enterprises inside the Studentersamfundet (see Entertainment).

Café Ni Muser (☎ 73 53 63 11; Bispegata; dishes Nkr58-90; 🕒 11am-midnight Mon-Fri, noon-midnight Sat & Sun) The sunlit rooms here look onto a small plaza. It serves fantastic tuna sandwiches, quiche and cake.

Baklandet Skydsstation's (☎ 73 92 10 44; Øvre Bakklandet 33; dishes Nkr58-169; 🕒 4pm-1.30am Mon-Fri, noon-1.30am Sat & Sun) A wood-burning stove and fish soup keep people warm in the winter. On Sunday, a bottle of wine runs to Nkr120. There's a daily meal for Nkr100.

Ramp (Strandveien at Gregus gate; dishes Nkr35-110; 🕒 from 10am Mon-Fri, from noon Sat & Sun) Overlooking a massive concrete Nazi bunker, Ramp attracts bohemians. Dinners are 'ecological', meaning organic or vegetarian. Breakfast might be bacon and eggs or muesli with yoghurt (Nkr35). Experimental bands sometimes play.

QUICK EATS & SELF-CATERING
Helios Trondheim (Prinsens gate 53; 🕒 10am-5pm Mon-Fri, Sat 10am-3pm) is a health-food store with a small selection. For more standard fare, head to **Rema 1000** (Torvet). The **Ravnkloa fish market** (🕒 10am-5pm Mon-Fri, 10am-4pm Sat) provides waterside fishcakes (Nkr75) and fishermen (free). For baguette sandwiches and pastries, try **Godt Brøt** (Thomas Angells gate 16; 🕒 6am-6pm Mon-Sat). Kebabs and felafel (Nkr39) can be had at **Cafe La Belle** (Olav Tryggvasons gate 1; 🕒 2-10pm Sun & Mon, 10am-4pm Tue-Sat).

Drinking & Entertainment
Den Gode Nabo (☎ 73 87 42 40; Øvre Bakklandet; 🕒 4pm-1.30am) Occupies the lower level of an ancient warehouse. Navigating the cavernous space requires beam-dodging and careful foot placement. Inside, admire several centuries of patchwork carpentry.

Bruk Bar (☎ 73 50 37 00; Kongens gate; 🕒 from noon) Central and cool, Bruk is a dark drinking establishment whose Friday- and Saturday-night DJs play some serious house and jungle. At other times, the volume decreases.

King's Cross (Nordre gate) An English pub featuring live music some weekends, imported beer on tap, live wide-screen UK football and bar meals for around Nkr90.

Tiger Tiger (☎ 73 53 16 06; Fjordgata 56; 10pm-3am Tue & Thu-Sat) Sweaty people wearing designer clothes enjoy the three-storey disco whose theme involves a Disney-esque combo of pretend artefacts 'from' South Africa, India and Polynesia. Very popular, with DJs catering to the masses. Show up before 10.30pm to avoid the cover charge.

Luna Lounge (☎ 73 60 06 10; TMV Kaia 5; 3pm-2.30am) The sweaty might also try this smaller club featuring more sophisticated DJs. Here, weekend hipsters appear in full force, with most trying to lounge in whatever comfortable furniture they can find. The dance floor is small and used. Summer brings scads of outdoor seating.

Blæst (☎ 73 60 01 01; TMV Kaia 17; from noon) Incongruously surrounded by yuppie restaurants in a waterfront redevelopment, Blæst occupies an old warehouse and books international and Norwegian rockers (Sivert Høyem), folk bands and black metal.

Studentersamfundet (☎ 73 89 95 00; Elgeseter-gate 1; from 5pm) An ideal university student centre that includes a huge maze of bars and organises an excellent calendar of film screenings, DJs and cool bands. Thousands of students fill the weird building on weekend nights. During summer recess, it's quiet.

Olavshallen (Kjøpmannsgata 44) At the Olavsk-vartalet cultural centre, Olavshallen is the city's main concert hall, hosting performers ranging from the Trondheim Symphony Orchestra to international rock and jazz musicians.

Uffa (☎ 72 52 48 50; www.uffahus.org; Innherreds-veien 69C; from 4pm Mon-Fri) A centre for activists, organising monthly punk, rock and experimental shows in a squat white house whose inner walls feature heaps of graffiti. The Sex Pistols played here long ago. Uffa hosts many informal political meetings, and you can usually pick up a vegetarian dinner (Nkr20-35) at around 5pm. To find it, go east on E6. It's opposite a green-steepled church.

For cinema, try **Trondheim Kino** (☎ 73 80 88 00; Prinsens gate 2B).

Getting There & Away

AIR

From the airport in Værnes, 32km east of Trondheim, SAS and Braathens fly to major Norwegian cities. SAS also flies daily to Copenhagen.

BOAT

The *Hurtigruten* docks in Trondheim.

BUS

Nor-Way Bussekspress services run to/from Ålesund (Nkr502, 7¼ hours, one to three times daily), Bergen (Nkr805, 14½ hours, twice daily) and Oslo (Nkr615, 9½ hours, four days per week).

CAR & MOTORCYCLE

The E6, the main north–south motorway, passes west of the city centre and tolls total Nkr35, both northbound and southbound (on the Trondheim–Stjørdal section). There's also a Nkr15 toll on vehicles entering the city from 6am to 6pm from Monday to Friday.

For car rentals, there's **Avis** (☎ 73 84 17 90; Kjøpmannsgata 34) and **Budget** (☎ 73 52 69 20; Kjøp-mannsgata 73).

TRAIN

There are four or five trains to Oslo daily (Nkr745, 6½ hours) and two or three to Bodø (Nkr861, 10 hours). If you're in a hurry to get north, consider taking the overnight train from Oslo, tossing your gear into a locker at the station and spending the day exploring Trondheim before continuing on an overnight train to Bodø (which, incidentally, goes through Hell just after 10.50pm).

Getting Around

TO/FROM THE AIRPORT

Airport buses (Nkr54) leave from the train station, the Britannia Hotel and the Radisson SAS Royal Garden Hotel (Kjøpmanns-gata 73) in conjunction with SAS and Braathens flights.

BICYCLE

About 30 special stands spread around the city centre have free bicycles available that can be borrowed by inserting a Nkr20 coin in the lock – return the bike to reclaim your coin.

BUS

The central transit point for all city buses is the intersection of Munkegata and Dronningens gate. The bus fare is Nkr22, or you can buy a 24-hour ticket for Nkr55 to Nkr70 (both paid to the driver, exact change needed).

CAR & MOTORCYCLE

If you have a car, it's easy to drive between sights on the outskirts of town, but best to explore the centre on foot. There's metered parking along many streets at zones marked '*P Mot avgift*', though car parks (there's one near the train station) are generally cheaper.

BODØ

pop 42,000

In addition to being the terminus for the northern railway line, Bodø is Nordland's largest town and a jumping-off point for Lofoten. Since the town was flattened during WWII air raids and completely rebuilt in the 1950s, Bodø itself is really quite ordinary in appearance – but it does have a lovely mountain backdrop.

Information

The **tourist office** (☎ 75 54 80 00; www.visitbodo .com; Sjøgata 3; ⏰ 9am-8pm Mon-Sat, noon-8pm Sun Jun-Aug, shorter hrs Sep-May) is near the waterfront. There are several banks with ATMs in the central area, plus a **post office** (Havnegata 9). Internet access is available at the tourist office (Nkr1 per minute) or for free (15-minute limit) at the **library** (Kongens gate at Havnegata; ⏰ 11am-7.30pm Mon, Tue & Thu, 11am-3pm Wed & Fri, 11am-2pm Sat).

Sights & Activities

Nordlandsmuseet (☎ 75 52 16 40; Prinsens gate 116; adult/student Nkr30/15; ⏰ 9am-3pm Mon-Fri, noon-3pm Sat & Sun May-Aug, shorter hrs Sep-Apr) displays Nordland history in one of Bodø's oldest buildings. There's also a modern **cathedral** (Kongens gate; ⏰ 9am-2.30pm Mon-Fri mid-Jun–Aug). The **aviation museum** (☎ 75 50 78 50; Olav V's gate; adult/student Nkr75/50; ⏰ 10am-7pm Sun-Fri, 10am-5pm Sat mid-Jun–mid-Aug, 10am-4pm Mon-Fri, 11am-5pm Sat & Sun mid-Aug–mid-Jun), 2km southeast of town, includes some scary simulations of jet-fighter flying. About 1km southeast of the aviation museum there's the small

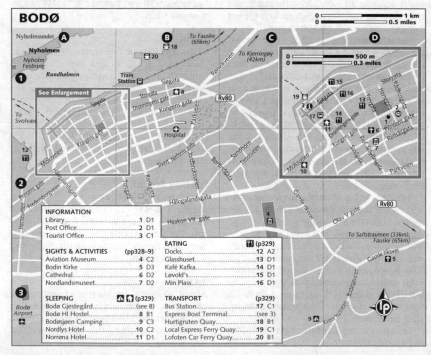

BODØ

INFORMATION	
Library	1 D1
Post Office	2 D1
Tourist Office	3 C1

SIGHTS & ACTIVITIES	(pp328–9)
Aviation Museum	4 C2
Bodin Kirke	5 D3
Cathedral	6 D2
Nordlandsmuseet	7 D2

SLEEPING	🅰 🛏 (p329)
Bodø Gjestegård	(see 8)
Bodø HI Hostel	8 B1
Bodøsjøen Camping	9 C3
Nordlys Hotel	10 C2
Norrøna Hotel	11 D1

EATING	🍴 (p329)
Docks	12 A2
Glasshuset	13 D1
Kafé Kafka	14 D1
Løvold's	15 D1
Min Plass	16 D1

TRANSPORT	(p329)
Bus Station	17 C1
Express Boat Terminal	(see 3)
Hurtigruten Quay	18 B1
Local Express Ferry Quay	19 C1
Lofoten Car Ferry Quay	20 B1

Bodin Kirke (Gamleriksvei 68; ☺ 10am-3pm Mon-Fri late Jun–mid-Aug), a little onion-domed stone church dating from around 1240.

Sleeping

The tourist office books private rooms from Nkr200 per person.

Bodøsjøen Camping (☎ 75 56 36 80; Kvernhusveien; camp sites from Nkr130) The nearest camping ground is 3km from town via bus No 12.

Bodø HI Hostel & Bodø Gjestegård (guesthouse ☎ 75 52 04 02, hostel ☎ 75 52 11 22; bodo.hostel@ vandrerhjem.no; Storgata 90; dm/s/d Nkr150/250/350) In two buildings. The hostel is newly remodelled and clean, while the simple guesthouse has homey rooms with separate bath. A helpful staff operates both. Breakfast costs Nkr60.

Norrøna Hotel (☎ 75 52 55 50; norrona.hotell@ radissonsas.com; Storgata 4B; s Nkr490-690, d Nkr630-800; ⓟ ⓧ) Comfortable rooms with private bathroom and affordable July and August prices. Opposite the bus station.

Nordlys Hotel (☎ 75 53 19 00; nordlys@rainbow -hotels.no; Moloveien 14; s Nkr495-1120, d Nkr695-1400; ⓟ ⓧ) Scandinavian design throughout, while harbourside rooms have great views.

Eating

Kafé Kafka (☎ 75 52 35 50; Sandgata 5B; sandwiches Nkr68 89; ☺ from 11am Mon-Sat, 3pm-midnight Sun) A café/bar serving marinated-vegetable sandwiches. Bands play some weekends. Otherwise, it's a good place to read.

Min Plass (☎ 75 52 26 88; Sjøgata 12; dishes Nkr69-124; ☺ 11am-2am Mon-Thu, 11am-3am Fri & Sat, 2pm-midnight Sun) Serves bar snacks such as olives or fish and chips (Nkr49) in addition to burgers, salads and grilled meat. There's a good late-night scene. A freaky trinket-filled plastic man guards the route to the toilets.

Løvold's (☎ 75 52 02 61; Tollbugata 9; dishes Nkr35-115; ☺ 9am-6pm Mon-Fri, 9am-3pm Sat) The 2nd floor above a fisherman's outfitter bustles at lunch time, offering daily specials of traditional Norwegian grub. Big windows have views over the water.

For inexpensive food, head to the docks for fresh shrimp or **Glasshuset** (Storgata 12), with a supermarket and several fast-food choices.

Getting There & Around

The airport, 2km away, is served by SAS, Braathens and Widerøe. Local buses (Nkr22) marked 'Sentrumsrunden' bring you to town. A taxi costs about Nkr80.

Bodø is the northern terminus of the Norwegian train network, with a service to Trondheim (Nkr861, 10 hours, three times daily). If you're continuing north by bus, be sure to get off 40 minutes before Bodø at Fauske, where the two daily express buses to Narvik (Nkr467, five hours) connect with the train.

The *Hurtigruten* travels to/from Lofoten. There are also car ferries and express boats that travel to Lofoten. See the tourist office for schedules.

The tourist office rents bikes for Nkr60 per day, plus a deposit. Guests can rent them from the hostel for Nkr50.

AROUND BODØ

The timber-built 19th-century trading station at sleepy **Kjerringøy**, by luminescent turquoise seas and soaring granite peaks 42km north of Bodø, has been preserved as an **open-air museum** (☎ 75 51 12 57; www .kjerringoy.no, adult/child Nkr40/20; ☺ 11am-5pm late May–late Aug). Daily buses run from Bodø to Kjerringøy (Nkr73, 1½ hours), but schedules may not be convenient for day-trippers. You can stay 1km away at the old rectory, now **Kjerringøy Prestegård guesthouse** (☎ 75 50 77 10; dm/d Nkr200/Nkr600), which offers simple rooms.

There are also Saltens Bilruter buses (No 819) that go 33km south from Bodø (Nkr56, 45 minutes) to **Saltstraumen**, claimed to be the world's largest maelstrom – at high tide an immense volume of water swirls and churns its way through a 3km-long strait that links two fjords; unfortunately, although it may pack a lot of power, there isn't all that much to see, unless you're there at the right time. The Bodø tourist office can advise on the best times (which vary daily).

NARVIK

pop 14,100

Narvik was established a century ago as an ice-free port for the rich Kiruna iron-ore mines in Swedish Lapland. The town is bisected by a monstrous transshipment facility, where the ore is off-loaded from rail cars onto ships bound for distant smelters. In April and May 1940, during WWII, fierce land and naval battles took place around the town as the Germans and the Allies fought to control the iron-ore trade.

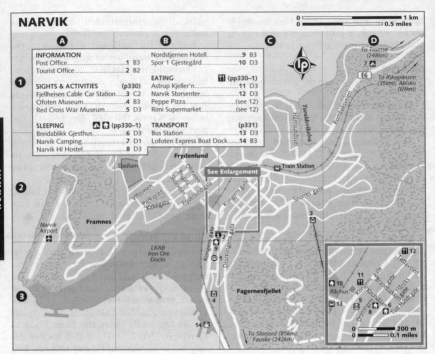

NARVIK

INFORMATION	Nordstjernen Hotell...................**9** B3	
Post Office...............................**1** B3	Spor 1 Gjestegård.................**10** D3	
Tourist Office........................**2** B2		
	EATING 🍴 (pp330–1)	
SIGHTS & ACTIVITIES (p330)	Astrup Kjeller'n......................**11** D3	
Fjellheisen Cable Car Station.....**3** C2	Narvik Storsenter...................**12** D3	
Ofoten Museum.....................**4** B3	Peppe Pizza........................(see 12)	
Red Cross War Museum...........**5** D3	Rimi Supermarket.................(see 12)	
SLEEPING 🏠 🏡 (pp330–1)	**TRANSPORT** (p331)	
Breidablikk Gjesthus.................**6** D3	Bus Station...........................**13** D3	
Narvik Camping......................**7** D1	Lofoten Express Boat Dock......**14** B3	
Narvik HI Hostel......................**8** D3		

Orientation & Information

The post office is 300m south on Kongens gate, the train station is at the north end of town and the Lofoten express boat dock is on Havnegata, just over 1km south of the centre, down Kongens gate.

Ask the helpful Narvik **tourist office** (☎ 76 94 33 09; www.narvikinfo.no; Kongens gate 26; 9am-7pm Mon-Fri, 11am-7pm Sat & Sun mid-Jun–mid-Aug, shorter hrs mid-Aug–mid-Jun) for details of local hiking routes.

Sights & Activities

The impressive **Red Cross War Museum** (☎ 76 94 44 26; Kongens gate; adult/child Nkr40/10; 10am-10pm Mon-Sat, 11am-5pm Sun mid-Jun–mid-Sep, 11am-3pm Mar–mid-Jun) displays WWII equipment and tells the tale of the Nazi occupation of Narvik, coveted for its ore production.

The town's **Ofoten Museum** (☎ 76 96 00 50; Administrasjonsveien 2; adult/child Nkr25/5; 11am-3.30pm Mon-Fri, noon-3pm Sat & Sun Jul, 10.30am-3pm Mon-Fri Aug-Jun) occupies a wonderful building dating from 1902, and tells of Narvik's farming, railway and ore transshipment heritage.

Weather permitting, the **Fjellheisen cable car** (☎ 76 96 04 94; Mårveien; return fare adult/child Nkr80/45; 10am-1am mid-Jun–Jul, 1-9pm early Jun & Aug) soars 656m for breathtaking views of the midnight sun and the surrounding peaks and fjords.

Organised Tours

Arrange sightseeing, fishing and whale-watching on several small boats with the tourist office; during the herring runs between October and December you may see orcas (killer whales). In October and November, **Tysfjord Turistsenter** (☎ 75 77 53 70; Storjord; www.tysfjord-turistsenter.no/safari; Nkr700) runs extraordinary orca-watching cruises from Storjord, about 85km south of Narvik on the E6. The Nor-Way Bussekspress bus to/from Fauske passes less than 1km from Storjord.

Sleeping & Eating

Narvik Camping (☎ 76 94 58 10; Rombaksveien 75; camp sites Nkr75, cabins Nkr500-750) The nearest camping ground is 2km northeast of town on the E6.

Spor 1 Gjestegård (☎ 76 94 60 20; post@spor1 .no; Brugata 2; dm/s/d Nkr160/400/500) Made for backpackers and in former rail cabins by the tracks, this place has well-kept dorm rooms, charming hosts, a sauna and a well-equipped, clean kitchen.

Breidablikk Gjesthus (☎ 76 94 14 18; www.breida blikk.no; Tore Hunds gate 41; dm/s/d Nkr185/250/550) A pleasant pension with a hillside fjord view, particularly in rooms on the higher floors. Breakfast costs Nkr50.

Narvik HI Hostel (☎ 76 96 22 00; narvik.hostel@ vandrerhjem.no; Dronningens gate 58; dm/s/d Nkr195/ 375/475; ☺ late Jun–mid-Aug) The hostel has recently moved to this central downtown locale. Breakfast is Nkr60 extra.

Nordstjernen Hotell (☎ 76 94 41 20; nhnarvik@ online.no; Kongens gate 26; s/d from Nkr550/750; P) Around the corner from the tourist office, this plain hotel has tidy, basic rooms.

There are several places to eat within easy walking distance of the tourist office.

Astrup Kjeller'n (☎ 76 96 04 02; Kinobakken 1; mains Nkr85-225; ☺ from 11am) By far the nicest place in town, with an old-time feel and huge servings of pastas, steaks and local specialities.

Narvik Storsenter (Kongens gata 66) A shopping centre 300m west of the train station, with one of Norway's many Peppe's Pizza and a Rimi supermarket.

Getting There & Away

Narvik's airport is served by Widerøe from Bodø and Tromsø.

Some express bus connections between Fauske and Tromsø require an overnight break in Narvik. Nor-Way Bussekspress buses run to/from Fauske (Nkr381, five hours, twice daily) and to/from Tromsø (Nkr315, four to five hours, two or three daily). The Narvik–Lofoten Ekspressen runs daily between Narvik and Svolvær (Nkr501, eight to 9¼ hours).

Two trains run daily to Kiruna in Sweden, with overnight connections to Stockholm. See the following Lofoten section for information on the express boat to Svolvær.

LOFOTEN

The spectacular glacier-carved mountains of Lofoten, separated from the mainland by Vestfjorden, soar straight out of the sea – from a distance they appear as an unbroken line, known as the Lofoten Wall.

Lofoten is Norway's prime winter fishing ground. The warming effects of the Gulf Stream draw spawning arctic cod from the Barents Sea south to the Lofoten waters each winter, followed by migrating north-coast farmer-fishermen, who for centuries have drawn most of their income from seasonal fishing. Although fish stocks have dwindled greatly in recent years, fishing continues to be Lofoten's largest industry and cod is still hung outside to dry on ubiquitous wooden racks through early summer.

Many of the fishing community's *rorbuer* (winter shanties) and *sjøhus* (former fishermen's bunkhouses) have been converted into luxurious tourist accommodation, and are priced accordingly. They provide some of Norway's most atmospheric places to stay.

The main islands of Austvågøy, Vestvågøy, Flakstadøy and Moskenesøy are all ruggedly beautiful. Artists are attracted by Austvågøy's light and there are art galleries in Svolvær, Kabelvåg and the busy fishing village of Henningsvær. Vestvågøy has Lofoten's richest farmland. Flakstadøy and Moskenesøy have sheltered bays and fjords, sheep pastures and sheer coastal mountains looming above strikingly picturesque fishing villages. Cyclists should be sure to try the unbelievable Kaiser Route (see Svolvær below).

The four main islands are all linked by bridge or tunnel, with buses running the entire length of the Lofoten road (E10) from Fiskebøl in the north to Å at road's end in the southwest. Bus fares between Bodø and Svolvær are half-price for holders of rail passes.

Tourist information is available at www .lofoten-tourist.no and www.lofoten-info.no.

Svolvær

pop 4100

By Lofoten standards the main port town of Svolvær on the island of Austvågøy is busy and modern. On the square facing the harbour, you'll find a couple of banks, a taxi stand and the helpful regional tourist office, **Destination Lofoten** (☎ 76 06 98 00; Torget; ☺ 9am-9.30pm Mon-Fri, 9am-8pm Sat, 10am-9.30pm Sun mid-Jun–mid-Aug, shorter hrs mid-Aug–mid-Jun).

SIGHTS & ACTIVITIES

Daredevils, or just plain crazy mountaineers, like to scale **Svolværgeita** (the Svolvær Goat), a distinctive, two-pronged peak visible from the harbour, and then jump the 1.5m from one horn to the other – a graveyard at the bottom awaits those who miss! For phenomenal views, hikers can ascend the steep path

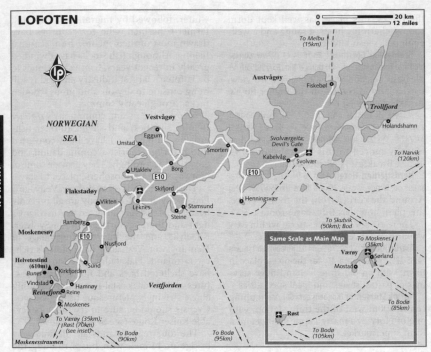

to the base of the Goat and up the slopes behind it. There's also a rough route from the Goat over to the extraordinary **Devil's Gate**; ask the tourist office for details.

A fun excursion from Svolvær is a boat trip into the **Trollfjord**, a spectacularly steep and narrow fjord. Tours run five times daily between about 10 June and 20 August and cost Nkr300 per person; the tourist office has details.

For 83km of incomprehensibly breathtaking cycling, take the Narvik ferry to Holandshamn and make your way back to Svolvær along the **Kaiser Route**. Along the way, lonely shoreline, jagged mountains and abandoned farms will be your constant companion. Unlike the west side of Lofoten, this trip takes in parts of the islands that are largely undiscovered by tourists. A long stretch runs parallel to the Trollfjord. The Danish site www.digermulen.de (no English) outlines the journey (click on Kaiserroute), and provides a glimpse of the scenery. Do your pre-planning at the tourist office, where you can pick up the handy *Sykkel Guide* (Nkr120), containing detailed topographic maps.

Also contact the tourist office in advance for help booking world-class fishing trips (Nkr400) in the abundant waters.

SLEEPING & EATING

Svolvær Sjøhuscamping (☎ 76 07 03 36; www .svolver-sjohuscamp.no; Parkgata 12; d per person Nkr390) A rustic red beach house with a dockside location: turn right on the first road past the library, and it's a five-minute walk east of the harbour.

Rica Hotel Svolvær (☎ 76 07 22 22; rica.hotel .svolvar@rica.no; Lamholmen; s Nkr795-1345, d Nkr995-1345; P ☒) Perched on a pier and hovering over the water, this flamboyant place combines modern hotel comforts with nifty *rorbu* styling. One suite has a hole cut in the floor for indoor fishing.

Bacalao (☎ 76 07 94 00; Kirkegata; mains Nkr70-125; ☿ 10.30am-1am Mon-Thu, 10am-2.30am Fri & Sat, noon-1am Sun) For a large, minimalist café in a room that feels like a retro-fitted garage, head over to this hang-out for fishermen and students. On the menu are cakes, salads, club sandwiches and pasta with reindeer.

Kjøkkenet (☎ 76 06 84 80; Lamholmen; small dishes Nkr90-95; mains Nkr225-250) The town's harbourside restaurants include this old-time kitchen (serving fish), with a bar made from a WWII Polish troop-ship lifeboat.

There's a **bakery** (31 Storgata) near the square and a **Rimi supermarket** (Torggata) a block inland.

GETTING THERE & AWAY

Svolvær has a small airport where you can catch Widerøe flights to Bodø.

Buses to/from Vesterålen travel between Svolvær and Sortland (Nkr124, 3¼ hours, three or four daily), crossing the dramatically scenic waters by the Fiskebøl–Melbu ferry (Nkr68 for car and driver). Buses to Leknes (Nkr88, two hours, three to six daily) make connections to Å (Nkr163, 3½ hours, two to four daily). The Narvik–Lofoten Ekspressen runs between Svolvær and Narvik (Nkr436, eight to 9¼ hours, one to two daily).

Express boats ply the waters between Svolvær and Bodø (Nkr246, 3½ hours) and Narvik (Nkr350, 3½ hours), daily except Saturday (but there's no Monday sailing from Svolvær to Narvik).

Svolvær is also a stop for the *Hurtigruten*.

Kabelvåg

The road into the quiet village of Kabelvåg passes Norway's second-largest **wooden church**. Built a century ago to minister to the influx of seasonal fisherfolk, its 1200-seat capacity far surpasses the village's current population.

Kabelvåg's small harbour-front square has a post office and an outdoor market.

Behind the old prison, a trail leads uphill to the **statue of King Øystein**, who in 1120 ordered the first *rorbu* to be built to house fishermen who had been sleeping under their overturned rowing boats – not just a kind gesture, as the tax on the exported dried fish was the main source of the king's revenue.

Some of these original *rorbuer* have been excavated as part of the **Lofotmuseet** (☎ 76 06 97 90; www.lofotmuseet.no; Storvågan; adult/student Nkr45/35; ☼ 9am-6pm mid-Jun–mid-Aug, 9am-3pm mid-Aug–mid-Jun), a regional history museum on the site of the first town in the polar regions.

Nearby, the seafront **Lofoten Aquarium** (☎ 76 07 86 65; Storvågan; adult/student/child Nkr80/60/40; ☼ 10am-7pm mid-Jun–mid-Aug, 11am-3pm mid-Aug–Nov & Feb–mid-Jun) shows you some of the person-

alities which made Lofoten great, including the heroic cod and some harbour seals in an outdoor tank. You can eat their relatives in the museum café (not the seals).

Ørsvågvær Camping (☎ 76 07 81 80; www .orsvag.no, no English; Ørsvågvær; camp sites Nkr100, cabins Nkr300-940; P), 3km and two inlets west of Kabelvåg, has basic cabins. The **Kabelvåg HI Hostel** (☎ 76 06 98 98; kabelvaag.hostel@vandrerhjem .no; dm/s/d Nkr245/405/605; ☼ Jun–mid-Aug; P) is at a school 10 minutes north of the village centre; breakfast is included. The hostel has a cafeteria with sporadic hours, and the charming fish, sandwich and pizza pub **Præstenbrygga** (☎ 76 07 80 60; Torget; mains Nkr35-140; ☼ from 11am), affiliated with an outdoor school for college-types and other students, is in the village centre.

From Svolvær you can walk the 5km to Kabelvåg or catch one of the roughly hourly buses (Nkr18, 10 minutes).

Henningsvær

Henningsvær's nickname, 'The Venice of Lofoten', is a tad overblown, but few people would disagree that this bohemian enclave and active fishing village is the brightest and trendiest place in the archipelago. Especially on weekends, the outdoor seating at the waterside bars and restaurants is ideal for observing the lively scene. There are also a couple of **art galleries** and a **climbing school**.

The climbing school's **Den Siste Viking** (☎ 76 07 49 11; fax 76 07 46 46; www.nordnorskklatreskole.no, no English; Misværveien 10; dm Nkr175) crosses a Lofoten *rorbu* with an English pub and a Himalayan trekkers' lodge. Its **Klatrekafeen** (☼ 11am-1am) serves up a small selection of home-made light meals (Nkr75 to Nkr130) and snacks, as well as coffee and desserts.

Buses shuttle between Svolvær (Nkr39, 35 minutes), Kabelvåg (Nkr36, 25 minutes) and Henningsvær two to eight times daily.

Lofotr Vikingmuseum

This 83m-long chieftain's house, Norway's largest Viking building, has been excavated at Borg, near the centre of Vestvågøy. The **museum** (☎ 76 08 49 00; adult/student/child Nkr90/70/45; ☼ 10am-7pm mid-May–Aug, 1-3pm Fri Sep-Apr) offers an insight into life in Viking times, complete with a scale-model reconstruction of the building, guides in Viking costume and a replica Viking ship, which you can row daily at 2pm (Nkr20).

Stamsund

pop 1000

The traditional fishing village of Stamsund makes a fine destination largely because of its dockside hostel, a magnet for travellers who sometimes stay for weeks on end. Here, as elsewhere on Lofoten, highlights include hiking, fishing and feeling overwhelmed. A popular town activity is to stare at the *Hurtigruten*'s approach.

At the wonderful old beach house **Justad HI Hostel/Rorbuer** (☎ 76 08 93 34; fax 76 08 97 39; dm/ s/d Nkr115/250/300, cabins Nkr600-800; �>< mid-Dec–mid-Oct; ℗), 1km from the centre, rowing-boat rental is free – catch and cook your own dinner! Bicycle rental and laundry facilities are also available. If the northern lights are out, the host might pound on your door to let you know.

The village centre contains a bakery and the fine **Skæbrygga** (fishy mains Nkr150-175) bar and restaurant. A Joker supermarket, post office and bus stop are a couple of minutes uphill from the hostel, and there's a Hansen bakery by the main road at the south end of the village.

The *Hurtigruten* coastal steamer stops en route between Bodø (Nkr325) and Svolvær (Nkr116). From 20 August to 24 June, buses from Leknes to Stamsund (Nkr29, 25 minutes) run up to eight times daily, less often on Saturday and Sunday, with the last bus departing from Leknes at 8.50pm.

Reine & Hamnøy

The delightful village of Reine, on the island of Moskenesøy, is on a calm bay backed by ranks of mountain cliffs and pinnacles. With its almost fairy-tale setting, it's easy to see the reasons why the village has been voted the most scenic place in all of Norway. All buses from Leknes to Å stop in Reine.

Ferries run from Reine to **Vindstad** (Nkr21, 40 minutes) through the scenic Reinefjord. From Vindstad, it's a one-hour hike over a ridge to the abandoned settlement of **Bunes** on the other side of the island, with a magnificent beach, vast quantities of driftwood and the 610m-high cliff of **Helvetestind**. On weekdays except Tuesday, you can take a morning ferry from Reine and then catch an afternoon ferry back – call ☎ 76 09 12 78 or ☎ 94 89 43 05 for the current schedule.

The quiet and pretty little fishing islet of Hamnøy, 4.5km north of central Reine,

has **Eliassan Rorbuer** (☎ 76 09 23 05; rorbuer@online .no; Hamnøy; 2-/4-person rorbuer Nkr550/750; ℗) right on the water. Linen costs Nkr80 extra. The highly regarded **Hamnøy Mat og Vinbu** (☎ 76 09 21 45; Hamnøy; mains Nkr130-165; �>< closed winter) restaurant serves stellar local specialities, including *bacalao* and cod tongues. There's a deck with picnic tables and a cosy dining room.

There's a Coop supermarket in Reine.

Å

Å is a very special place – a preserved fishing village, the shoreline lined with red-painted *rorbuer*, many of which jut into the sea, perched on forbidding rocks connected by wooden footbridges. Racks of drying cod and picture-postcard scenes occur at almost every turn. Visitors enliven the tiny place in summer, while in winter it's stark, haunting and beautiful. March is an interesting time to visit – there's daylight, the village is empty, *rorbuer* are cheap, it's still the peak of the cod season, and some of the friendly locals will be *very* happy to see you.

SIGHTS & ACTIVITIES

The **Tørrefiskmuseum** (Stockfish Museum; ☎ 76 09 12 11; adult/student Nkr40/25; �>< 10am-5pm mid-Jun–mid-Aug, 11am-5pm Mon-Fri early Jun & late Aug, otherwise by appointment), inside a cod plant dating from 1920, details the history of the stockfish industry, taking in every step from catching to cooking. Steinar Larson, the gregarious operator, has long family ties to Å, and explains everything cod (and Å) in fantastic, excited detail. He usually provides coffee if there aren't too many visitors and if they're nice.

Many of Å's 19th-century buildings are set aside as the **Norwegian Fishing Village Museum** (☎ 76 09 14 88; admission Nkr40; �>< 10am-5pm late Jun-late Aug, 11am-3pm Mon-Fri Sep–mid-Jun), complete with old boats and boathouses, a bakery from 1844, Europe's oldest cod-liver oil factory, storehouses and so on.

Walk to the camping ground at the end of the village for a good hillside view of Værøy island, which lies on the other side of **Moskenesstraumen**, the swirling maelstrom that inspired the fictional tales of, among others, Jules Verne and Edgar Allen Poe.

SLEEPING & EATING

Moskenesstraumen Camping (☎ 76 09 13 44; camp sites from Nkr60, huts Nkr300-500; ℗) A basic camping ground just south of Å.

Å HI Hostel (☎ 76 09 11 21; www.lofoten-rorbu
.com; dm Nkr175, rorbuer Nkr800-1550; **P**) The hostel has accommodation in some of the mu-
seum's historic seaside buildings. Breakfast
is 60Nkr extra.

Å-Hamna Rorbuer (☎ 76 09 12 11; aa-hamna@
lofoten-info.no; dm/d Nkr100/350, rorbuer Nkr500-950;
P) Also at the museum, this inviting place
has pleasant rooms and a pretty communal
space in a restored 1860s home and cosy
rorbu, usually with magnificent views, containing four to eight beds each. Off-season
you can get the best *rorbuer* for around
Nkr350, firewood included.

Brygga restaurant (☎ 76 09 11 21; mains Nkr115-
200) The only restaurant in town, this over-
the-water place serves good fish and also
operates as the village bar.

Self-caterers can also buy fresh fish from
local fishers and pick up other supplies at the
small food shop behind the hostel office.

GETTING THERE & AWAY
Nordtrafikk runs one to three daily buses
from Å to Leknes (1¾ hours), Svolvær (3¼
hours) and Sortland (5¼ hours).

Ofotens og Vesteraalens Dampskibsselskab
(OVDS; ☎ 76 96 76 00; www.ovds.no) runs car ferries from Bodø to Moskenes, 5km north of
Å. The trip takes four hours, costs Nkr132
for a passenger, Nkr477 for a car, and operates up to five times daily from 28 June to
11 August (otherwise, once or twice daily
except Saturday). Some of these ferries run
via Værøy and Røst.

Værøy & Røst
pop 1400
Lofoten's southern islands of Værøy and
Røst have some of the finest **bird-watching** in
Norway, with large colonies of fulmars, guillemots, kittiwakes and terns. There are puffins as well, but the population has dropped
by more than 50% in the past decade as a
result of dwindling stocks of herring, the
main food source for puffin chicks.

Craggy Værøy has only 775 people, but
100,000 nesting sea birds. **Hiking trails** take
in some of the more spectacular sea-bird
rookeries. The main trail goes along the
west coast, beginning about 300m past
the island airstrip, and continues south all
the way to the virtually deserted fishing village of Mostad. This 10km hike makes for
a full day's outing and is not too strenuous,

but it's exposed to the elements, so is best
done in fair weather. Other bird-watching
outings, including boat tours, can be arranged through the hostel.

Røst, south of Værøy, enjoys one of
the mildest climates in northern Norway,
thanks to its location in the middle of
the Gulf Stream. Access to the best bird-
watching requires a boat, as the largest
rookeries are on offshore islands. **Kårøy
Sjøhus** (☎ 76 09 62 38) can arrange all-day boat
trips (Nkr125) that cruise past major sea-
bird colonies and stop at an 1887 **lighthouse**
and a vista point. En route it's common to
see seals and there are occasional sightings
of orcas. Røst itself is flat and, other than
the boat trip, there's not much to do.

SLEEPING & EATING
Værøy HI Hostel (☎ 76 09 53 75; vaeroy.hostel@
vandrerhjem.no; dm/d Nkr150/275; 🕙 1 May-15 Sep) An
atmospheric and authentic *rorbu* accommodation, but it's about an hour's walk north of
the ferry landing; a bus can pick you up at the
dock. The hosts can help arrange fishing trips
and boat rides to the bird rocks.

Kornelius Kro (☎ 76 09 52 99; korn-kro@online.no;
Sorland; r Nkr350-700) Værøy's only nightlife option also has a restaurant, a pub and a few
simple but clean cottages out the back.

GETTING THERE & AWAY
From 29 June to 12 August there's at least
one ferry daily between Bodø and Værøy
(Nkr121, four to six hours) and six days
a week between Moskenes and Værøy
(Nkr53, 1½ hours). There's a boat service
from Værøy to Røst (Nkr65, two hours,
five days a week) and from Røst to Bodø
(Nkr145, 4¼ hours, once or twice daily).
Sailing durations given are for direct ferries,
but not every boat is direct. If your trip begins and ends in Bodø, ask about discounted
return fares. Detailed schedules are available
at boat terminals and tourist offices.

VESTERÅLEN
The islands of Vesterålen aren't quite as
dramatic as Lofoten, but they're still very
attractive to visitors. For tourist information, consult **Vesterålen Reiseliv** (☎ 76 11 14 80;
Kjøpmannsgata 2, Sortland).

Vesterålen is connected by ferry from
Melbu on Hadseløya to Fiskebøl on Austvågøy (Lofoten). Melbu has a couple of

museums and a famous music festival, featuring classical, jazz and blues, every July. The other main town, Stokmarknes, is a quiet market community best known as the birthplace of the *Hurtigruten* coastal steamer.

Nyksund (www.nyksund-info.com) on Langøya is a former abandoned fishing village that's now re-emerging as an artists' colony. There's a great walk over the headland from Nyksund to Stø (three hours return), at the northernmost tip of Langøya. Ask the tourist office for details of whale-watching tours from Stø.

Andenes on Andøy seems a long way from anywhere, but there's whale-watching, a whale centre, a natural history centre, a lighthouse and a couple of museums. Whale Safari (☎ 76 11 56 00; www.whalesafari.no) runs popular three- to five-hour whale-watching cruises from the whale centre between late May and mid-September. Trips depart at least once daily (at 10.30am) and cost Nkr695. Sightings of sperm whales are guaranteed, or your next trip is free. Dress warm!

Sleeping & Eating

Holmvik Brygge (☎ 76 13 47 96; www.nyksund.com; Nyksund; s/d Nkr250/350) Offers irregular but cosy rooms done up like those in an old fisherman's house. Facilities are shared.

Andenes HI Hostel (☎ 76 14 28 50; andenes .hostel@vandrerhjem.no; Havnegata 31, Andenes; dm/s/d Nkr150/215/325; ☒ Jun-Aug; ℗) Includes the Lankanholmen Sjøhus, a wonderful old wooden building by the sea; breakfast is Nkr60 extra.

Den Gamle Fyrmesterbolig (☎ 76 14 10 27; Richard Withs gate 11, Andenes; s Nkr250-350, d Nkr300-400; ℗) The rooms in the charming lighthouse keepers' cottage are another great option.

There's a bakery and an informal café at the Andenes whale centre, while the restaurant at the Norlandia Hotel serves a good arctic menu.

Getting There & Away

Sortland is the main transport hub in Vesterålen. Both Sortland and Stokmarknes are stops for the *Hurtigruten* coastal steamer.

Express buses between Tromsø (Nkr500, 7¼ hours) and Å (Nkr307, 6¼ hours) run from Monday to Friday, via Sortland and Melbu. The Narvik–Lofoten Ekspressen between Narvik (Nkr267, 3¾ hours) and Svolvær (Nkr134, 2½ hours) operates daily except Saturday. The Fauske–Lofoten Ek-

spressen between Fauske (Nkr325, 5¼ hours) and Svolvær runs daily. Times and fares are from Sortland.

From 25 June to 19 August, one to four daily buses connect Sortland with Andenes (Nkr134, two hours) via Risøyhamn. Services are reduced at other times.

SENJA

Senja, second-largest of Norway's islands, rivals Lofoten with its landscapes yet attracts very few visitors. Finnsnes, the town at the mainland side of the bridge to Senja, has no redeeming features.

Senja's Innersida, facing the mainland, features a broad agricultural plain and extensive forest. The western and northern coasts, Yttersida, include a convoluted series of peninsulas and jagged peaks that rise directly out of the Arctic Ocean. Colourful, isolated fishing villages including Gryllefjord, Skaland, Mefjordvær, Fjordgard and Husøy are accessible via tiny back roads, providing remote getaways. The road to Mefjordvær is particularly dramatic, but the most outrageous-looking mountains are nearest to Fjordgard.

For tourist information, contact the tourist office (☎ 77 85 07 30; Finnsnes).

The suitably remote Hamn i Senja (☎ 77 85 98 80; www.hamnisenja.no; Skaland; s/d Nkr520/770; ℗) features a combination of old and new buildings hugging the seashore.

Transportation around Senja is best done by car. Local buses (☎ 177) run around the perimeter of the island, but many routes operate less than daily. Finnsnes is a stop for the *Hurtigruten*.

TROMSØ

pop 47,100

Tromsø, at latitude 69°40′N, is the world's northernmost university town. In contrast to some of the more sober communities dotting the north coast of Norway, Tromsø is a spirited place with street music, cultural happenings and more pubs per capita than any other Norwegian town – it even has its own brewery.

A backdrop of snowcapped peaks provides spectacular scenery, excellent hiking in summer and great skiing and dogsledding from September to April. Many polar expeditions have departed from Tromsø, earning the city the nickname 'Gateway to the Arctic'. A statue of explorer Roald Amundsen, who headed some of the expeditions, stands in a little square down by the harbour.

In mid-January, the **Tromsø International Film Festival** (☎ 77 75 30 90; www.tiff.no) is perhaps the most exciting of Norway's film festivals. Every screening is packed (the good citizens of Tromsø – and those from the surrounding countryside – don't have much of a selection the rest of the year, so they get pretty worked up). Check out movies from northern Norway, the Baltic States, forgotten classics, weird shorts, American independents and more.

Orientation & Information

Tromsø's city centre and airport are on the island of Tromsøya, which is linked by bridges to overspill suburbs on both the mainland and the much larger outer island Kvaløya. Storgata is the principal drag.

The town's **tourist office** (☎ 77 61 00 00; www .destinasjontromso.no; Storgata 61; ☒ 8.30am-6pm Mon-Fri, 10.30am-5pm Sat & Sun Jun–mid-Aug, 8.30am-4pm Mon-Fri mid-Aug–May) can help with information. Send or collect your mail from the main **post office** (Strandgata 41).

Sights & Activities

The city centre has many period buildings, including the old cathedral, **Tromsø Domkirke** (Storgata 25) – one of Norway's largest wooden churches – and a **Catholic church** (Storgata 94), both built in 1861. Tromsø's most striking church is the **Arctic Cathedral**

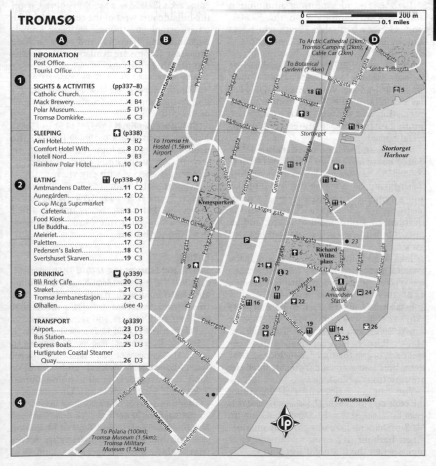

TROMSØ

INFORMATION	
Post Office	1 C3
Tourist Office	2 C3

SIGHTS & ACTIVITIES	(pp337–8)
Catholic Church	3 C1
Mack Brewery	4 B4
Polar Museum	5 D1
Tromsø Domkirke	6 C3

SLEEPING	(p338)
Ami Hotel	7 B2
Comfort Hotel With	8 D2
Hotell Nord	9 B3
Rainbow Polar Hotel	10 C3

EATING	(pp338–9)
Amtmandens Datter	11 C2
Aunegården	12 D2
Coop Mega Supermarket Cafeteria	13 D1
Food Kiosk	14 D3
Lille Buddha	15 D2
Meieriet	16 C3
Paletten	17 C3
Pedersen's Bakeri	18 C1
Svertshuset Skarven	19 C3

DRINKING	(p339)
Blå Rock Cafe	20 C3
Strøket	21 C3
Tromsø Jernbanestasjon	22 C3
Ølhallen	(see 4)

TRANSPORT	(p339)
Airport	23 D3
Bus Station	24 D3
Express Boats	25 D3
Hurtigruten Coastal Steamer Quay	26 D3

To Arctic Cathedral (2km); Tromso Camping (2km); Cable Car (2km)

To Botanical Gardens (2.5km)

To Tromsø HI Hostel (1.5km); Airport

Søndre Tollbugata

Stortorget Harbour

Kongsparken

Richard Withs plass

Roald Amundsen Statue

Tromsøsundet

To Polaria (100m); Tromsø Museum (1.5km); Tromsø Military Museum (1.5km)

200 m
0.1 miles

NORWAY

(☎ 77 64 76 11; Hans Nilsensvei 41; adult/child Nkr22/free; ☉ 10am-8pm Jun-Aug, shorter hrs Sep-May), which is on the mainland just over the bridge. It's a freaky building from the 1960s that looks like a bunch of triangles stuck together.

Tromsø Museum (☎ 77 64 50 00; www.imv .uit.no; Lars Thøringsvei 10; adult/child Nkr30/15; ☉ 9am-8pm Jun-Aug, shorter hrs Sep-May), at the southern end of Tromsøya, is northern Norway's largest museum and has some well-presented displays on Arctic wildlife, Sami culture and regional history. Take bus No 28 from Stortorget. Nearby, the restored WWII fort at the **Tromsø Military Museum** (☎ 77 62 88 36; Solstrandveien; adult/child Nkr30/15; ☉ noon-5pm Wed-Sun Jun-Aug, noon-5pm Sun May & Sep) includes a former ammunition store with an exhibition on the 52,600-tonne German battleship *Tirpitz*, which was sunk by British air forces at Tromsø on 12 November 1944.

Polar Museum (☎ 77 68 43 73; www.polarmuseum .no; Søndre Tollbugata 11; adult/child Nkr43/10; ☉ 10am-7pm mid-Jun–mid-Aug, shorter hrs mid-Aug–mid-Jun) has exhibits on the Arctic frontier, some interesting and others – such as those on hunting furry Arctic creatures – of less universal appeal.

Modern and well executed, **Polaria** (☎ 77 75 01 00; Hjalmar Johansens gate 12; adult/child Nkr75/40; ☉ 10am-7pm mid-May–mid-Aug, noon-5pm mid-Aug–mid-May) features extensive displays on polar topics ranging from exploration to natural history, a 180-degree cinema showing an interesting film about Svalbard, and an aquarium with Arctic fish and four bearded seals.

Take a midnight sun stroll through the **botanical garden** (☎ 77 64 50 78; Breivika; admission free; ☉ 24hr), which blooms brightly despite its northern locale. Take bus No 20.

Established in 1877, the **Mack Brewery** (☎ 77 62 45 00; www.mack.no, no English; Storgata 5; tours Nkr100; ☉ tours noon-4pm Mon-Thu) produces Mack's Pilsner, Isbjørn, Haakon and several dark beers; the tour fee includes a beer stein, beer and souvenir. You can smell the brewery from a block away.

You can get a fine city view by taking the **cable car** (☎ 77 63 87 37; Solliveien 12; adult/child return Nkr70/30; ☉ 10am-5pm Apr-Sep), 420m up Mt Storsteinen. Take bus No 26 from Stortorget harbour. It's open to 1am on clear nights when the midnight sun is in view.

Sleeping

Tromsø Camping (☎ 77 63 80 37; www.tromsocamping .no; camp sites Nkr150, cabins Nkr400-900; **P**) Some spots here are situated next to a small river, others are less spectacular. It's on the mainland, 2km east of the Arctic Cathedral. Cabins have cooking facilities. Take bus No 26.

Tromsø HI Hostel (☎ 77 65 76 28; tromso.hostel@ vandrerhjem.no; Åsgårdveien 9; dm/s/d Nkr175/275/405; ☉ mid-Jun–mid-Aug; **P**) Clean and tidy hostel, 1.5km west of the city centre. Phone for directions.

The tourist office books rooms in private homes for around Nkr250/450 for a single/double. Most are within a 10-minute walk of the centre.

Hotell Nord (☎ 77 68 31 59; www.hotellnord.no; Parkgata 4; s Nkr450-540, d Nkr590-695; **P**) Up on the hillside just west of the centre. Feels like an informal guesthouse; staff are knowledgeable and friendly, and rates include breakfast. Rooms are available with or without private bathroom.

Ami Hotel (☎ 77 68 22 08; Skolegata 24; s/d Nkr450/580, s/d with private bathroom Nkr500/660; **P**) Request a room at the front for great views of the city.

Rainbow Polar Hotel (☎ 77 68 64 80; fax 77 68 91 36; Grønnegata 45; s Nkr595-895, d Nkr840-1145; **P**) The usual rooms can be found in this northern incarnation of the hotel chain. The breakfast area is cheery, with city views.

Comfort Hotel With (☎ 77 68 70 00; www .with.no; Sjøgata 35-37; s/d Nkr1290/1490, s/d discount Nkr805/970; **P**) Waterside, amenity-filled rooms along with fine (and complimentary) dinner buffets.

Eating

Svertshuset Skarven (☎ 77 60 07 25; Strandtorget 1; mains Nkr125-250; ☉ from 4pm) Near the harbour and festooned with nautical instruments, this favourite serves an arctic menu that includes fish burgers and reindeer steaks.

Paletten (☎ 77 68 05 10; Storgata 51; mains Nkr79-155; ☉ 10.30am-midnight Mon-Thu, 10.30am-2am Fri & Sat, 11.30am-midnight Sun) This multi-level sports-bar serves the kind (and calibre) of food you'd expect: mediocre and filling. Take your pick from sandwiches, lasagne, burgers and cakes. Nice rooftop deck.

Amtmandens Datter (☎ 77 68 49 06; Grønnegata 81; mains Nkr88-135; ☉ noon-2.30am Mon-Sat, 3pm-3am Sun) Pub-like and student-friendly. Serves beer, salads and a vegetarian sandwich.

Patrons may use its newspapers, board games and Internet.

Meieriet (☎ 77 61 36 39; Grønnegata 37; mains Nkr56-136; ☺ 8am-1.30am Mon-Thu, 8am-3am Fri, noon-3am Sat, noon-1.30am Sun) Bistro tables, red-leather couches, antique radios, a pool table, stir-fried food and weekend DJs.

Aunegården (☎ 77 65 12 34; Sjøgata29; dishes Nkr69-248; ☺ 10.30am-midnight, 1pm-midnight Sun) A relic dating from 1869 serving amazing cakes (Nkr56) from tables that offer glimpses through lacy curtains onto a cobbled street. Also serves sandwiches, nachos, Norwegian fare and lots of wine.

Also recommended:

Lille Buddha (☎ 77 65 65 66; Sjøgata 25; lunch specials Nkr69; ☺ 12.30pm-midnight)

Pedersen's Bakeri (☎ 77 60 77 60; Storgata 104; sandwiches Nkr38-50; ☺ 10am-4pm Mon-Fri, Sat 10am-2pm)

Tromsø's fast-food scene is led by various kebab carts, and a food kiosk at the express boat dock – surrounded by luggage lockers and slot machines. You can buy fresh boiled shrimp from fishing boats at Stortorget harbour. The harbourside **Coop Mega supermarket** (Stortorget 1) has a cheap 2nd-floor cafeteria and a nice view over the water.

Entertainment

Tromsø enjoys a thriving nightlife, with many credibly arguing that it's got the best scene in Norway. On Friday and Saturday, most nightspots stay open past 4am. Many also serve light meals. The following recommendations merely scratch the surface.

Blå Rock Café (☎ 77 61 00 20; Strandgata 14; ☺ 11.30am-2am Sun-Thu, 11.30am-3am Fri & Sat) Specialises in rock, and attracts a young, cool crowd. Instruments and pictures hang from the rafters, 75 types of beer spill on the floor, and live bands and DJs (playing rock, naturally) cause hearing damage. Excellent burgers.

Strøket (☎ 77 68 44 00; Storgata 46; ☺ 4pm-1.30am Tue-Thu, 4pm-3am Fri, noon-3am Sat, 7pm-midnight Sun) The three floors pull in the hipsters like pollen attracts bees. There's a restaurant, bar and disco.

Tromsø Jernbanestasjon (☎ 77 61 23 48; Strandgata 33; ☺ 11am-2am) A brown bar whose name means 'Tromsø's Railway Station', and supports some serious drinking. It's filled with railway artefacts, but the unspoken joke is

that this remote city was never even close to being connected by rail.

Ølhallen (Storgata 4; ☺ 9am-5pm Mon-Wed, 9am-6pm Fri, Sat 9am-3pm) Try Tromsø's own Mack beer at pubs, cafés or here, next to the brewery. It makes up for its pathetic hours with old brick walls and decor from the 1920s. Stuffed polar bears greet visitors by the door, as do drunk guys.

Getting There & Away

Tromsø is the main airport hub for northern Norway, with direct flights to Oslo, Bergen, Bodø, Trondheim, Alta, Hammerfest, Kirkenes and Longyearbyen. Airport buses (Nkr40) depart from the Radisson SAS Hotel Tromsø. A taxi costs Nkr100 to Nkr200.

There are two or three daily express buses between Tromsø and Narvik (Nkr315, four to five hours). Buses to/from Alta (Nkr355, 6¾ hours) run once daily.

The *Hurtigruten* stops here.

Getting Around
TO/FROM THE AIRPORT

The airport bus (Nkr35) can be picked up at the Radisson SAS Hotel; a taxi to the airport costs about Nkr80.

BOAT

Express boats connect Tromsø with Finnsnes (Nkr200, 1¼ hours, two to four daily), the ferry terminal for Senja.

BUS

Thoroughly exploring Tromsø can take time, as the city is spread out and many of the sights are outside the centre. Rides on city buses cost Nkr21.

CAR

If you have your own car, you'll find it convenient for getting around. Tromsø has numerous parking areas spread around the city, including a huge underground car park off Grønnegata.

FINNMARK

Finnmark's curving north coast is cut by dramatic fjords and dotted with fishing villages, which are most conveniently seen (presuming the sun is up) from the deck of the *Hurtigruten* (see p352). The interior is populated by Sami people who for centuries have herded their reindeer across the vast upland plateau, Finnmarksvidda, an empty tundra with only two major settlements, Karasjok and Kautokeino.

Many visitors find Finnmark's stark, lonely landscape unappealing. For others, this starkness is precisely the reason to visit. In early spring, long drives across uninterrupted snowscapes can be a highlight, particularly when they are punctuated by a late-night pit stop to stare at the northern lights. In the summer, the eerie midnight sun takes over, as do swarms of mosquitoes (at their peak from late June to late July).

Virtually every town in Finnmark was razed to the ground at the end of WWII by retreating Nazis, whose scorched-earth policy was intended to delay the advancing Soviet troops. Unfortunately, the rebuilt towns all look rather grim. Satisfying urban life north of Tromsø does not exist.

You can get information about the entire region from the **Finnmark Tourist Board** (☎ 78 44 00 20; www.visitnorthcape.com; Sorekskriverveien 13, N-9511 Alta).

ALTA
pop 17,350

If anything in Finnmark can be called cosmopolitan, Alta is it. It's easily Finnmark's largest town, and, thanks to the Finnmark Municipal University, it's home to 2000 students. The biggest attraction in town is a collection of Unesco-protected rock carvings, which date to 4000 BC. If this doesn't grab your fancy, wilderness surrounds the city, as do opportunities to go ice-fishing or dogsled riding. Inquire at the tourist office.

Orientation & Information

Alta is a sprawling town with fishing and quarrying industries. The town's two main centres, Sentrum and Bossekop, are 3km apart, connected by the E6. Alta **tourist office** (☎ 78 45 50 00; Sandfallveien 1; ⏱ 8am-3.30pm) is 1km northwest of Sentrum off the E6. Check your mail at the Sentrum **library** (⏱ 10am-6pm Mon-Thu, 10am-3.30pm Fri, 11am-3pm Sat).

Sights & Activities

Alta's main sight is the impressive, World Heritage-protected, **prehistoric rock art** (☎ 78 45 63 30; www.alta.museum.no; Altaveien 19; adult/child Nkr70/free; ⏱ 8am-11pm mid-Jun–mid-Aug, 8am-8pm

early Jun & late Aug, 9am-6pm May & Sep) at Hjemmeluft, on the E6, 4km southwest of Bossekop. A 3km-long network of boardwalks leads past many of the 3000 rock carvings of hunting scenes, boats, fertility symbols, bears and reindeer that date back as far as 4000 BC. Wait for the snow to melt before visiting, otherwise the rocks are covered. The admission charge includes a guide and the adjacent **Alta Museum**, with regional exhibits.

The Altaelva rushes through the scenic 400m-deep **Sautso**, northern Europe's grandest canyon. It's best seen as part of a tour, which gains you access to the Alta Power Station dam and includes a snack in a traditional Sami *lavvo* (tent). Contact the tourist office for more information.

Alta is also renowned for its **salmon run**; several local companies organise fishing tours.

Sleeping

Wisløff Camping (☎ 78 43 43 03; www.wisloeff.no; Øvre Alta; camp sites from Nkr70, cabins Nkr300-400; P) This award-winning camping ground (the award came from the Norsk Caravan Club in 2000) has happy little beige and red cabins, 4km south of Bossekop, by highway Rv93.

Alta HI Hostel (☎ 78 43 44 09; alta.hostel@ vandrerhjem.no; Midtbakkveien 52; dm/s/d Nkr180/270/ 300; ⏱ late Jun-late Aug; P) Painted red, with clean accommodation. It's a short walk from the Sentrum bus stop.

Hotel Aurora Borealis (☎ 78 45 78 00; www .hotelaurora.no; Saga; s/d Nkr750/850; P) Cosy, art-filled and secluded, about 6km east of Bossekop by the E6, this hotel is operated by friendly staff. They'll help plan snowmobile trips (with the option of spending a night in a Sami tent), dogsled excursions or fishing trips, and the kitchen will even prepare what you catch.

Vica Hotell (☎ 78 43 47 11; www.vica.no; Fogdebakken 6; s Nkr1020-1285, d Nkr1120-1485; P) In a timber-built former farmhouse in Bossekop, Vica offers free sauna, Internet access and outdoor hot tub (perfect in winter). The rooms come with character, and public spaces are filled with stuffed creatures. Prices can drop to Nkr790 for holders of the Nordic Hotelpass.

Eating

Omega (☎ 78 44 54 00; Markedsgata 14-16; lunch Nkr64-104, dinner Nkr89-229; ⏱ 11am-midnight Mon-Wed, 11am-1am Thu-Sat) A popular choice on the pedestrian drag in Sentrum, Omega serves excellent tapas and salads. One of these involves a filling piece of salmon baked under a layer of chevre and accompanied with fried onion, mushrooms and greens (Nkr89).

Henrik Restaurant (☎ 78 43 47 11; Fogdebakken 6; mains Nkr167-299; ⊙ 11am-11pm Mon-Sat, 10.30am-11pm Sun) In the Vica Hotell. Serves huge portions from an arctic menu that includes reindeer, elk, cod and a warm soup of cloudberries served with home-made ice cream. Call ahead as it's sometimes fully booked for private functions.

Self-caterers should head to one of three supermarkets, whose large edifices and close proximity dominate the Sentrum.

Getting There & Away
AIR
The airport is 3.5km east of Sentrum; follow the E6. Norwegian Air and Braathens service the Alta airport. Many domestic flights arrive each day, often routed through Tromsø. Direct flights to Oslo are plentiful.

BUS
Nor-Way Bussekspress services run between Tromsø and Alta (Nkr380, 6¾ hours, once a day). FFR buses run to/from Kautokeino (Nkr190, 2½ hours), Hammerfest (Nkr180, 2¾ hours) and Nordkapp (Nkr290, 5¾ hours) once or twice a day.

HAMMERFEST
pop 9200

Most visitors to Hammerfest arrive by the *Hurtigruten* coastal steamer and have an hour or two to poke around. Unless you have unusual interests, that's about as much time you'll need. The fishing town's oddest experience can be found at the Royal & Ancient Polar Bear Society, outlined below. Those who spend more time here usually have a car, though they should take heed that ongoing natural gas exploration off the coast has brought a lot of energy-types to town, which in turn has caused hotel rates to rise prohibitively.

The **tourist office** (☎ 78 41 21 85; Rådhuset) operates out of the Polar Bear Society.

Sights & Activities
The small, impressive **Gjenreisningsmuseet** (Reconstruction Museum; ☎ 78 42 26 30; Kirkegata 21; adult/child Nkr40/15; ⊙ 10am-6pm mid-Jun–Aug, 11am-

2pm Sep–mid-Jun) details the rebuilding of Hammerfest after WWII. Nearby, in the town hall, the bizarre **Royal & Ancient Polar Bear Society** (☎ 78 41 31 00; Rådhuset; admission Nkr20; ⊙ 6am-5.30pm late Jun-early Aug, shorter hrs mid-Aug–mid-Jun) dedicates itself to preserving northern culture and features exhibits on Arctic hunting and local history. Any visitor can become a member (Nkr150) and waive the admission fee for life, get a certificate and a champagne toast. The bone they use to 'knight' you – something a male walrus misses dearly – is a real crowd-pleaser.

Just west of the Gjenreisningsmuseet on Kirkegata is Hammerfest's contemporary **church**, where you can often find reindeer grazing in the graveyard. For lovely views of the town, coast and mountains, climb the 86m-high **Salen Hill**; the 10-minute trail begins behind the small park directly up from the town hall.

Sleeping & Eating
AF Camping Storvannet (☎ 78 41 10 10; Storvannsveien; cabins Nkr320-340; ⊙ late May–late Sep; **P**) About 2km east of the town centre. Offers cooking facilities.

Quality Hotel Hammerfest (☎ 78 42 96 00; hammerfest@quality.choice.no; Strandgata 2; s/d from Nkr645/795; **P**) Rooms here have loads of character – some resemble cabins on ocean liners.

Kafé RettVest (Sjøgata 10; mains Nkr65-130; ⊙ 10am-5pm Mon-Fri, Sat 10.30am-3pm) This bustling café sits a block from the coastal streamer's dock, and serves lasagne, tortellini, reindeer and omelettes. It isn't pretty, but the crowds lend it a good feel.

Sandberg bakery (☎ 78 41 18 08; Strandgate 19; sandwiches Nkr36; ⊙ 9am-4pm Mon-Fri, 10am-3pm Sat) Serving painfully good pastries and coffee, this town favourite will give you reason to return to Finnmark.

Self-caterers can find a big **Coop supermarket** (⊙ 9am-8pm Mon-Fri, 9am-6pm Sat) just east of the town hall.

Getting There & Away
The *Hurtigruten* coastal steamer stops daily.

Buses run between Hammerfest and Alta (Nkr183, 2¾ hours) once or twice daily (four days weekly from mid-August to late June). There's also a bus between Hammerfest and Kirkenes (Nkr744, 10¼ hours), via Karasjok (Nkr305, 4¾ hours).

NORDKAPP

Nordkapp (North Cape), a high, rugged coastal plateau at 71°10′21″N latitude, claims to be the northernmost point in Europe and is the main destination for most visitors to the far north (Knivskjelodden is actually the northernmost point – see later in this section for details). The sun never drops below the horizon from mid-May to the end of July. To many visitors, Nordkapp, with its steep cliffs and stark scenery, emanates a certain spiritual aura – indeed, long before other Europeans took an interest in the area, Nordkapp was considered a power centre by the Sami people.

It was Richard Chancellor, the English explorer who drifted this way in 1553 on a search for the Northeast Passage, who named North Cape. Following a much-publicised visit by King Oscar II in 1873, Nordkapp became a pilgrimage spot of sorts for tourists.

Nowadays, there's a rip-off Nkr175 entrance fee and a touristy complex with exhibits, eateries, souvenir shops and a post office. The 180-degree theatre runs a rather repetitious short film, but if you want to really appreciate Nordkapp just take a walk out along the cliffs. If the weather is fair you can perch yourself on the edge of the continent and watch the polar mist roll in.

The continent's real northernmost point, **Knivskjelodden** (latitude 71°11′08″N) is inaccessible to vehicles, but you can hike 18km return (five hours) to this lovely promontory from a marked car park about 9km south of Nordkapp.

An asphalt road winds across a rocky plateau and past herds of grazing reindeer up to Nordkapp. Depending on snow conditions, it's usually open from May to mid-October; the **Road User Information Centre** (☎ 177) gives opening dates.

From mid-May to the end of August, local buses run daily at 12.15pm and 9pm between Honningsvåg and Nordkapp (Nkr66, one hour), with an additional service at 8.20pm between 2 June and 16 August and another at 10.55pm between 2 June and 9 August. Between 2 June and 9 August, the last bus departs Nordkapp at 1.10am, allowing views of the midnight sun. Avoid so-called 'tours', which may charge considerably more for similar services.

KIRKENES

pop 4500

The former mining town of Kirkenes was Norway's most bombed place during WWII, with over 1000 air-raid alarms. The town is not a major tourist destination, but it does receive some visitors since it's the end of the line for the *Hurtigruten* coastal steamer and a jumping-off point into Russia. To find the small town centre, head west (make a right) from the dock and follow the signs. It's about 1.5km. Or just take the waiting shuttle bus.

Information

The exceedingly helpful staff at the **tourist office** (☎ 78 99 25 44; www.kirkenesinfo.no, no English; Presteveien 1; ☉ 8.30am-6pm Mon-Fri, 8.30am-5.30pm Sat & Sun Jun–mid-Aug, Mon-Fri 8.30am-4pm mid-Aug–May) can help you plan winter activities such as king crab safaris (Nkr750), snowmobile trips along the border (Nkr950) and night-time dogsled rides (Nkr1075).

The **library** (☉ 11am-5pm Mon, Tue & Thu, 11am-3pm Wed & Fri, 11am-2pm Sat) has free Internet access.

Sights

A cold **cave** (cnr Presteveien & Tellef Dahls gate; tours adult/child Nkr100/50; ☉ mid-Jun–mid-Aug) was used as a WWII air-raid shelter. Tours are held at noon, 3pm, 6.15pm and 9pm during the opening period. Up on a nearby hill, there's a **statue** dedicated to the Soviet soldiers who liberated the town. The rather good **Sør-Varanger Grenselandmuseet** (☎ 78 99 48 80; Førstevannslia; adult/ student/child Nkr30/15/free; ☉ 10am-6pm mid-Jun–Aug, 10am-3.30pm Sep–mid-Jun) has displays on WWII history, local geography, culture, religion and Sami crafts. It details the history of the region as a border area, where Russian, Norwegian, Finnish and Sami culture collide.

Visiting Russia

In summer, day and weekend bus tours from Kirkenes to Murmansk are arranged by **Sovjetrejser** (☎ 78 99 25 01; polarscout@grenseland .no; Kongens gate 1-3). The guided bus tour, including lunch and sightseeing, costs Nkr 1090/1290 day/weekend but you'll have to add on the cost of a Russian visa, typically Nkr450 to Nkr1300, depending upon your nationality. Travellers interested in visiting Russia on their own can take the bus one way to Murmansk (one way/return Nkr350/700, 4½ hours), plus the visa fee, but you'll need an 'official invitation'. Contact the **Russian**

consulate (☎ 78 99 37 37; Kirkegata) for a visa. Visa processing takes around 16 days, so make sure you contact Sovjetreiser or the consulate well in advance.

Sleeping & Eating

Kirkenes Camping (☎ 78 99 80 28; Hesseng; camp sites Nkr90, cabins Nkr350-600; ⊙ Jun–Aug) Six kilometres west of town, off the E6.

Barbara's B&B (☎ 78 99 32 07; barbara@trollnet.no; Henrik Lunds gate 13; s/d Nkr300/450; P) With two rooms, free Internet access and a friendly dog – Barbara welcomes you to bring your own. She especially likes motorcyclists.

Rica Arctic Hotel (☎ 78 99 29 29; Kongensgate 1-3; s Nkr705-1195, d Nkr895-1325; P) Offers the usual amenities but rooms are worn and contain ugly furniture.

Ritz (☎ 78 99 34 81; Dr Wesselsgata 17; mains Nkr59-203; ⊙ 3-11.30pm Mon & Tue, noon-12.30am Wed & Thu, noon-2.30am Fri & Sat, 1-11.30pm Sun) Serves pizzas and doubles as a bar.

Sentrum Kafe (☎ 78 99 63 00; Dr Wesselsgata 18; sandwiches Nkr25-60; ⊙ 9am-11pm) Serves open-faced sandwiches and marzipan cake to a roomful of people sitting on cheaply upholstered couches. Crowded at lunch.

Self-caters should visit the **Coop Mega** (☎ 78 97 06 66; Solheimsveien).

Getting There & Around
AIR
SAS, Braathens, Norwegian Air and Widerøe fly into Kirkenes' airport, a 20-minute drive from town; flying in/out of Ivolo, Finland, some 250km away, may be cheaper. The airport bus costs Nkr64/32 (adult/child) and a taxi is about Nkr275.

BOAT
Kirkenes is the terminus of the *Hurtigruten* coastal steamer.

BUS
By land, buses serve Karasjok (Nkr452, 5½ hours), Hammerfest (Nkr744, 10¼ hours) and Alta (Nkr784, 12¾ hours), and many points in between.

KARASJOK
pop 2900
Karasjok is the most accessible Sami town and the site of the Sami parliament. It has Finnmark's oldest **church** (1807), the only building left standing in Karasjok after

WWII. Because of the Nazis' destruction, the centre of today's Karasjok consists of a couple of strip malls connected by the E6 and Rv92. This being Finnmark, the settlement area doesn't extend very far before vast and empty wilderness returns.

The **tourist office** (☎ 78 46 88 10; www.koas .no; Porsangerveien 1; ⊙ 9am-7pm Jun–mid-Aug, 9am-4pm Mon-Fri mid-Aug–May), in the Sami Park at the junction of the E6 and route Rv92 (see below), can book winter dogsled rides, and arranges salmon fishing, riverboat trips and other summer activities.

The **Sami Park** (☎ 78 46 88 10; Porsangerveien 1; adult/child Nkr95/60; ⊙ 9am-7pm mid-Jun–late Aug, shorter hrs Sep–mid-Jun) theme park and reindeer farm feels a bit flashy and plastic. The more staid **Sami museum** (☎ 78 46 99 50; Museumsgata 17; adult/child Nkr25/5; ⊙ 9am-6pm Mon-Sat, 10am-6pm Sun early Jun–mid-Aug, shorter hrs mid-Aug–May), just 500m northeast of the town centre, covers Sami history and culture in more depth.

The wonderful **Karasjok HI Hostel** (☎ 78 46 71 66; karasjok.hostel@vandrerhjem.no; dm/s/d Nkr150/ 300/375; P) is 6km west of town; breakfast costs Nkr60, dinner is available and a variety of tours are on offer. At **Engholm's Husky** (☎ 78 46 71 66; www.engholm.no; Rv92; cabins Nkr150-300 plus Nkr100 for each guest; P), dog-lovers will enjoy the rustic, well-furnished cabins near where Sven keeps his sled dogs and pups. Most cabins have a kitchen but no bath. Breakfast costs Nkr50, and there is a free sauna.

Gammen (☎ 78 46 74 00; Porsangerveien 1; mains Nkr190-250; ⊙ 11am-11pm mid-May–mid-Aug), at Sami Park, offers traditional dishes in a 'Sami-inspired' dining room. The place consists of four squat, turf-covered huts with a central hearth. Very hobbit. In the central shopping centre, **Márkan Kafe** (Markangeaidnu 1; dishes Nkr25-95; ⊙ 10am-6pm Mon-Fri, 10am-3pm Sat) sells sandwiches and omelettes at bargain prices, and there's a nearby **supermarket**.

Buses connect Karasjok with Hammerfest (Nkr308, 4¾ hours, daily except Saturday) and Kirkenes (Nkr452, 5½ hours). The Finnish Lapin Linjat buses to Ivalo (Nkr180, 3¾ hours) and Rovaniemi (Nkr450, 5½ hours) also pass through Karasjok.

KAUTOKEINO
pop 3000
In Kautokeino, around 85% of the townspeople have Sami as their first language; the town is unlike anywhere else in Norway

and it's not uncommon to see locals dressed in traditional garb. Around one third of the population earns its living working in some aspect of reindeer herding.

Because the tourist industry isn't as developed (or as plastic) as that in Karasjok, there isn't as much to do. While this is problematic for some, others seek out the more authentic culture that can be enjoyed here.

The best time to visit is during the **Easter Festival** (www.saami-easterfestival.org), when thousands of costumed Sami participate in championship reindeer racing, theatre and cultural events, and the little town bursts at the seams.

The **tourist office** (☎ 78 48 65 00; ☿ 10am-4pm Mon-Fri May-Aug) is in a kiosk by the main road through town. Call ahead to make sure someone is there.

The **Kautokeino Hamlet & Museum** (☎ 78 48 71 00; Boavonjarga 23; adult/child Nkr20/free; ☿ 9am-7pm Mon-Sat, noon-7pm Sun mid-Jun–mid-Aug, 9am-3pm Mon-Fri mid-Aug–mid-Jun) presents a traditional Sami settlement, complete with an early home, temporary dwellings, a trapping exhibit and several agricultural and pastoral outbuildings.

Kautokeino Camping (☎ 78 48 54 00; Suomalvodda 16; camp sites Nkr100, summer-only d Nkr100, cabins Nkr280-1000, motel rooms Nkr480-850; P), south of the river, provides a Sami *lavvo* with an open fire. It's operated by an extremely friendly family.

Alfred's Kro (☎ 78 48 61; 18 Hannoluohkka 4; mains Nkr60-135; ☿ 11am-6pm Mon-Fri, noon-6pm Sat & Sun) offers diners traditional dishes involving reindeer.

For an unusual experience, visit **Madam Bongos** (☎ 78 48 61 60; dinner Nkr160), operated by a Sami woman. You'll be able to eat in a mountain tent in the middle of nowhere, about 11km out of town. The dinner, which is always the same, features coffee, *biðus* (a vegetable and reindeer soup), reindeer steak and berries with cream. You must call first to make an appointment and to get directions.

Mara's Pub (☿ from 8pm Tue-Fri, from 1pm Sat & Sun) occasionally books small bands. With rough wooden floors, booths and benches, it's the town's main nightlife spot. It's beneath Alfred's Kro.

Buses connect Kautokeino with Alta (Nkr193, 2½ hours).

SVALBARD

The world's most readily accessible piece of the polar north, and one of the most spectacular places imaginable, Svalbard is *the* destination for an unforgettable holiday. This wondrous archipelago is an assault on the senses: vast icebergs and floes choke the seas, and icefields and glaciers frost the lonely heights. Svalbard also hosts a surprising variety of flora and fauna, including seals, walrus, arctic foxes and polar bears.

Trips to Svalbard are best planned well in advance. When you arrive, you'll almost certainly want to participate in some kind of organised trek or tour, and many need to be booked early. To learn more about precisely what exists and how much it costs, visit the tourist board's excellent website, www.svalbard.net.

History

Although known to the Icelanders as early as 1194, the official discovery of Svalbard (then uninhabited) is credited to Dutch voyager Willem Barents in 1596. During the 17th century Dutch, English, French, Norwegian and Danish whalers slaughtered the whale population. They were followed in the 18th century by Russians hunting walrus and seals. The 19th century saw the arrival of Norwegians, who hunted polar bears and arctic foxes. During the late 19th and early 20th centuries, several (mostly unsuccessful) expeditions to the North Pole were mounted from Svalbard. In 1906, commercial coal mining began and is continued today by the Russians (at Barentsburg) and the Norwegians (at Longyearbyen and Sveagruva). The 1920 Svalbard Treaty granted Norwegian sovereignty over the islands.

Orientation & Information

Longyearbyen, the largest settlement on Svalbard, has an airport with flights to/from Tromsø. You'll find all the usual facilities, including a post office, a bank (with an ATM) and a library. Barentsburg, the Russian settlement, is about 40km west, while Ny Ålesund, a Norwegian research station with an airstrip, is about 100km northwest. Apart from the immediate vicinity of the settlements, there are no roads and most tourists will travel around with organised tours – on foot, by sea or, in winter, by snowmobile.

The friendly and helpful **tourist office** (☎ 79 02 55 50; www.svalbard.net), in central Longyearbyen, distributes the handy *Svalbard* brochure.

Organised Tours

Dozens of exciting options are listed on the tourist office website. Accommodation, transport and meals are usually included in longer tours, but day tours are also available (see under Longyearbyen below). The most popular tour operators:

Basecamp Spitsbergen (☎ 79 02 46 00; www .basecampexplorer.com; Postboks 316, NO-9171 Longyearbyen) Offers unique lodging options, which include rooms on an ice-locked ship. They arrange short ski trips, five-day dogsled and snowmobile expeditions (Nkr9000) and more.

Spitsbergen Travel (☎ 79 02 61 00; www.spitsberg entravel.no; Postboks 548, NO-9171 Longyearbyen) Offers week-long cruises, multiple day snowmobile safaris, five-day dogsledding trips (Nkr10,300) and 12-day trekking tours (Nkr16,600).

Svalbard Wildlife Service (☎ 79 02 56 60; www .wildlife.no; Postboks 164, NO 9171 Longyearbyen) Offers varied tours including camping, kayaking, glacier exploration and seven-day summer ski trips to Ny Ålesund (Nkr10,950).

Getting There & Away

SAS and Braathens fly regularly from Tromsø to Longyearbyen.

LONGYEARBYEN

pop 1700

The frontier-like community of Longyearbyen, strewn with abandoned coal-mining detritus, enjoys a superb backdrop including two glacier tongues, Longyearbreen and Lars Hjertabreen.

At the **Svalbard Museum** (☎ 79 02 13 84; Skjæringa; admission Nkr30; 🕑 11am-7pm Mon-Fri, noon-4pm Sat, 1-7pm Sun Jul & Aug, shorter hrs Sep-Jun), west of the centre, exhibits cover mining, 17th-century whaling and the history, climate, geology, wildlife and exploration of the archipelago.

Organised Tours

Many short trips and day tours that vary with the season are on offer, including fossil hunting (Nkr290); mine tours (Nkr590); boat trips to Barentsburg and Pyramidien (Nkr920); dogsledding (from Nkr750);

dogsledding on *wheels* (Nkr550); diving trips (Nkr1200); glacier hiking (Nkr490); ice-caving (from Nkr520); kayaking (from Nkr550); mountain biking (Nkr420); horse riding (Nkr420); and snowmobiling (from Nkr1250). Contact the tourist office for more details.

Sleeping & Eating

Longyearbyen Camping (☎ 79 02 10 68; info@terra polaris.com; per person Nkr80; open late Jun-early Sep) Many visitors head straight here, next to the airport and about an hour's walk from town.

Mary-Ann's Polar Rigg (☎ 79 02 37 02; riggen@ longyearbyen.net; s/d Nkr395/550) A simple guesthouse with a kitchenette and hot tub. Linen is Nkr100 extra and breakfast is Nkr95.

Spitsbergen Nybyen Gjestehus (☎ 79 02 63 00; spitsbergen.guesthouse@spitsbergentravel.no; s Nkr495-650, d Nkr840-990) A large, functional building, south of the centre.

Basecamp Spitsbergen (☎ 79 02 46 00; www .basecampexplorer.com; s Nkr800-1550, d Nkr950-1750) Provides top accommodation in the centre of town. The decor of the 15-room hotel shoots for the look of a seal-hunter's cabin, with excellent results (bunks, rough-hewn boards). Each cosy room has a shower, and a common space has a glass roof for polar night viewing.

Huset (☎ 79 02 25 00; mains Nkr195-255) West of the centre, this remains a popular choice for both arctic and French-style meals. The good food becomes even more impressive if you remember where exactly you are eating it.

In the central shopping mall, you'll find the Svalbardbutikken supermarket, and **Kafé Busen** (mains under Nkr100), which serves daily specials as well as typical cafeteria fare.

Getting Around

Longyearbyen Buss & Taxi (☎ 79 02 13 75) charges Nkr100 to Nkr120 for a cab trip between the town and the airport. The airport bus (Nkr35) serves the various accommodation options.

AROUND SVALBARD

Independent travel around Svalbard is heavily regulated in order to protect both the virgin landscape and travellers. Because of this, travel to the very few settlements is usually done as part of a tour package. One of these settlements is Barentsburg (population 900), a Soviet-era relic.

Simultaneously depressing and fascinating, this tiny Russian town still mines and exports coal. A statue of Lenin still stares over the bleak built landscape and the impressive natural landscape that surrounds it.

Tourist cruises might also bring you to **Ny Ålesund**, which, at latitude 79°N, is a wild place with none-too-friendly scientists and downright hostile arctic terns (you may have to beat the latter off with a stick!). Remnants of past glories include a **stranded locomotive**, previously used for transporting coal, and an **airship pylon**, used by Amundsen and Nobile on their successful crossing of the North Pole in 1926.

NORWAY DIRECTORY

ACCOMMODATION

During summer, it's wise to reserve all accommodation, particularly at hostels. The cheapest lodging costs less than Nkr250, mid-range accommodation is less than Nkr550, while top-end luxury can reach Nkr2000.

Camping & Cabins

Norway has around 1000 camping grounds. Tent space costs from Nkr50 at the most basic sites to Nkr180 in Oslo and Bergen, and many camping grounds also rent simple cabins from about Nkr250 a day. The cabins often have basic cooking facilities, though linen and blankets are rarely provided, so you'll need your own sleeping bag. **Reiselivsbedriftenes Landsforening** (☎ 23 08 86 20; www.rbl.no; Postboks 5465 Majorstua, N-0305 Oslo) publishes a free annual camping guide that lists many camping grounds.

Norway has an *allemannsretten* (Right of Common Access) dating back around 1000 years. This allows you to pitch a tent anywhere in the wilderness for two nights, as long as you camp at least 150m from the nearest house or cottage and leave no trace of your stay. From 15 April to 15 September, lighting a fire in the proximity of woodlands is strictly forbidden.

The Norwegian Mountain Touring Association, **Den Norske Turistforening** (DNT; ☎ 22 82 28 22; www.turistforeningen.no; Postboks 7 Sentrum, N-0101 Oslo), maintains an extensive network of mountain huts, a day's hike apart, in much of Norway's mountain country, ranging from unstaffed huts with just a few beds to large,

staffed lodges with more than 100 beds and generally superb service. At unstaffed huts, keys must be picked up in advance from DNT offices in nearby towns (you must be a member and pay a Nkr100 deposit); at staffed huts hikers simply show up – noone is turned away, even if there's only floor space left. Nightly fees in a room with one to three beds is around Nkr150. Basic membership for one calendar year will set you back Nkr425/250 for adult/student.

Hostels

Norway has 72 *vandrerhjem* (hostels) affiliated with Hostelling International (HI). Some are quite comfortable lodge-style facilities, open year-round, while others operate out of school dorms in summer only. Most have two to six beds per room. Most hostels also have single, double and family rooms at higher prices. Guests must bring their own sleeping sheet and pillowcase, although most hostels hire sleeping sheets for around Nkr50. Nearly all hostels have kitchens where guests can cook their own meals.

The Norwegian Hostelling Association is **Norske Vandrerhjem** (Map pp274-6; ☎ 23 13 93 00; fax 23 13 93 50; www.vandrerhjem.no; Torggata 1, N-0181 Oslo). You can book hostels through their website.

Private Rooms & Pensions

Private rooms, usually bookable through tourist offices, average Nkr300/400 for singles/doubles and breakfast isn't normally included. Along highways, you may see '*Rom*' signs, indicating informal accommodation for around Nkr100 to Nkr250 (without breakfast).

Hotels

Although standard hotel prices are high, most hotels give substantial discounts on Saturday and Sunday and in the summer season, which are slow periods for business travel. Nationwide chains such as Rainbow Hotels and Rica offer particularly good summer and weekend deals. With Rainbow, you'll get the lowest rates by buying a Scan+ Hotel Pass (sold at hotels for Nkr90) – it usually pays for itself on the first night.

One important consideration in this land of sky-high food prices is that hotels usually include an all-you-can-eat buffet breakfast, while most pensions do not.

ACTIVITIES
Hiking
Norway has some of northern Europe's best hiking, ranging from easy trails in the forests around the cities to long treks through the mountains. Due to deep winter snows, hiking in many areas is seasonal; in the highlands, it's often limited to the period of late June to September. The most popular wilderness hiking areas are Jotunheimen, Rondane and Hardangervidda, but many other areas are just as attractive (or even more so). There are also organised glacier hikes in Briksdal and on Nigardsbreen; Åndalsnes and Lofoten are the main centres for mountain climbing. For more information on hiking and climbing, contact the **Norwegian Mountain Touring Association** (☎ 22 82 28 22; Postboks 7 Sentrum, N-0101 Oslo).

Skiing
'Ski' is a Norwegian word and Norway makes a credible claim to having invented the sport. It's no exaggeration to say that it's the national winter pastime and you're seldom far from a ski run. Norway has thousands of kilometres of maintained cross-country (nordic) ski trails and scores of resorts with excellent downhill runs. The Holmenkollen area near Oslo, Geilo (on the Oslo–Bergen railway line) and Lillehammer are just a few of the more popular spots. If you're a summer skier, head for the glaciers near Finse, Stryn or Jotunheimen. DNT is a good source of information about skiing throughout Norway.

Rafting
Norway's wild and scenic rivers are ideal for rafting, with trips ranging anywhere from short Class II doddles to Class III and IV adventures and up to rollicking Class V punishment. **Norges Padleforbund** (☎ 21 02 98 35; www.padling.no; Service boks 1, Ullevål stadion, N-0840 Oslo) provides a comprehensive list of rafting operators.

Fishing
Norway's salmon runs are legendary – in June and July, you can't beat the rivers of Finnmark. No licence is required for saltwater fishing. In fresh water, a national licence (available from post offices for around Nkr180) is mandatory and often a local licence (available from tourist offices, sports shops, hotels and camping grounds for Nkr100 to Nkr300 per day) will also be required.

BOOKS
For extensive travel in the country, the best all-round guide is Lonely Planet's *Norway*. To help with communication, pick up Lonely Planet's *Scandinavian Phrasebook*, which includes a section on Norwegian.

Erling Welle-Strand's concise *Motoring in Norway* and the flashier *Adventure Roads in Norway* both describe many of Norway's most scenic driving routes. In *Mountain Hiking in Norway*, Welle-Strand details wilderness trail information, including hiking itineraries, sketch maps and details on huts. *Norwegian Mountains on Foot*, by the Norwegian Mountain Touring Association (DNT), is similar and easier to obtain.

James Graham-Campbell's *The Viking World* traces the history of the Vikings by detailing excavated Viking sites and artefacts. If you're interested in Norse mythology and folk tales, look for *Gods and Myths of Northern Europe* by HR Ellis Davidson, and the colourful *Norwegian Folk Tales: Selected from the Collection of Peter Christen Asbjørnsen and Jørgen Moe*.

BUSINESS HOURS
Business hours are generally from 9am or 10am to 4pm or 5pm Monday to Friday and 10am to 2pm on Saturday, although some shops stay open to around 7pm or 8pm on Thursday.

Be aware that many museums have short hours (11am to 3pm is quite common), which can make things tight for sightseeing.

On Sunday most stores – including bakeries and supermarkets, and some restaurants – are closed.

EMBASSIES & CONSULATES
Norwegian Embassies
There's an up-to-date listing of Norwegian embassies and consulates at www.embassies .mfa.no.

Australia & New Zealand (☎ 6273 3444; emb.can berra@mfa.no; 17 Hunter St, Yarralumla, ACT 2600)
Canada (☎ 613-238 6571; emb.ottawa@mfa.no; Suite 532, Royal Bank Centre, 90 Sparks St, Ottawa, Ontario K1P 5B4)

Denmark (☎ 33 14 01 24; emb.copenhagen@mfa.no; Amaliegade 39, DK-1256 Copenhagen K)
Finland (☎ 09 686 0180; emb.helsinki@mfa.no; Rehbinderintie 17, FIN-00150 Helsinki)
France (☎ 01 53 67 04 00; emb.paris@mfa.no; 28 rue Bayard, F-75008 Paris)
Germany (☎ 030-505050; emb.berlin@mfa.no; Rauchstrasse 1, D-10787 Berlin)
Ireland (☎ 01-662 1800; emb.dublin@mfa.no; 34 Molesworth St, Dublin 2)
Netherlands (☎ 70 311 7611; emb.hague@mfa.no; Lange Vijverberg 11, NL-2513 AC The Hague)
Sweden (☎ 08-665 6340; emb.stockholm@mfa.no; Skarpögatan 4, SE-11593 Stockholm)
UK (☎ 020-7591 5500; emb.london@mfa.no; 25 Belgrave Square, London SW1X 8QD)
USA (☎ 212-333 6000; www.norway.org; 2720 34th St NW, Washington DC 20008)

Embassies & Consulates in Norway

Australia (Map pp274-6; ☎ 22 47 91 70; Jernbanetorget 2, N-0106 Oslo)
Canada (Map pp274-6; ☎ 22 99 53 00; Wergelandsveien 7, N-0244 Oslo)
Denmark (Map p281; ☎ 22 54 08 00; Olav Kyrres gate 7, N-0244 Oslo)
Finland (Map p281; ☎ 22 43 04 00; Thomas Heftyes gate 1, N-0244 Oslo)
France (Map p281; ☎ 22 28 46 00; Drammensveien 69, N-0244 Oslo)
Germany (Map p281; ☎ 22 27 54 00; Oscars gate 45, N-0244 Oslo)
Ireland (Map pp274-6; ☎ 22 12 20 00; Haakon VII's gate, N-0212 Oslo)
Netherlands (Map pp274-6; ☎ 22 19 71 90; Oscars gate 29, N-0244 Oslo)
New Zealand (☎ 66 77 53 30; Billingstadsletta 19B, Postboks 113, N-1376 Billingstad)
Russia (Map p281; ☎ 22 55 32 78; Drammensveien 74, N-0271 Oslo)
Sweden (Map p281; ☎ 22 44 35 11; Nobelsgata 16, N-0244 Oslo)
UK (Map p281; ☎ 23 13 27 00; Thomas Heftyes gate 8, N-0244 Oslo)
USA (Map pp274-6; ☎ 22 44 85 50; Drammensveien 18, N-0255 Oslo)

FESTIVALS & EVENTS

Norway is chock-a-block with festivals, which take place in every city, town and village. Most of these are held during the summer, and a few of the most popular are outlined within the this chapter's listing. Among the offerings are festivals dealing with rock music, wooden boats, film (www.filmweb.no) and cultural spectacles. For information about the country's biggest festivals, check out www.norwayfestivals.com. Drop in at any tourist office for the scoop on local events.

HOLIDAYS

New Year's Day 1 January
Maundy Thursday Thursday before Easter
Good Friday March/April
Easter Monday March/April
Labour Day 1 May
Constitution Day 17 May
Ascension Day 40 days after Easter
Whit Monday eighth Monday after Easter
Christmas Day 25 December
Boxing Day 26 December

Constitution Day, 17 May, is Norway's biggest holiday, with events throughout the country and many Norwegians taking to the street in traditional folk costumes. The biggest celebration is in Oslo, where marching bands and thousands of school-children parade down Karl Johans gate to Det Kongelige Slott (the royal palace) to be greeted by the royal family.

Norway practically shuts down during Christmas and Easter weeks, when you'll be lucky to find an open bar or grocery store even in Oslo.

Midsummer's Eve, celebrated by bonfires on the beach, is generally observed on 23 June, St Hans Day. The Sami (Lapps) hold their most colourful celebrations at Easter in Karasjok and Kautokeino, with reindeer races, *joik* (traditional chanting) concerts and other festivities.

On 13 December, Christian children celebrate the feast of Santa Lucia by dressing in white and holding a candle-lit procession.

MAPS

The best road maps for travellers are the Cappelens series, sold in Norwegian book-shops for Nkr95.

The *Veiatlas Norge* (Norwegian Road Atlas), published by Statens Kartverk (the national mapping agency), is revised every two years (Nkr220). Most local tourist offices distribute free town plans, and topographical hiking maps can be purchased from local bookshops and DNT, which has offices throughout Norway.

MONEY

ATMs
The machines are ubiquitous and available in every town mentioned in this book.

Currency
The Norwegian krone is most often written NOK in international money markets, Nkr in northern Europe and kr within Norway.

One Norwegian krone equals 100 øre. Coins come in denominations of 50 øre and one, five, 10 and 20 kroner, and bills in denominations of 50, 100, 200, 500 and 1000 kroner.

Exchanging Money
Some post offices and all banks will exchange major foreign currencies and accept all travellers cheques, which command a better exchange rate than cash (by about 2%). Banks open Monday to Friday and close around 3pm, while post offices open later (see Post below). You can also change money in kiosks and hotels, but the rate won't be as good.

POST
In most towns, post offices are open from 9am to 4pm (or 5pm) Monday to Friday and 10am to 2pm on Saturday. Postal rates are high and continue to soar: cards and letters weighing up to 20g cost Nkr5.5 within Norway, Nkr7.5 to other Nordic countries, Nkr9.5 to elsewhere in Europe and Nkr10.5 to the rest of the world. Mail can be received poste restante at almost all post offices in Norway.

TELEPHONE & FAX
Norway has no telephone area codes. All domestic numbers consist of eight digits.

Most pay phones accept Nkr1, Nkr5, Nkr10 and Nkr20 coins, and will return unused coins but won't give change. The minimum charge for domestic and international calls is Nkr5. Domestic calls

---

EMERGENCY NUMBERS

- Ambulance ☎ 113
- Fire ☎ 110
- Police ☎ 112

---

get 33% discount between 5pm and 8am weekdays, and on weekends (from 5pm Friday to 8am Monday). Directory assistance (☎ 180) costs Nkr8 per minute. So-called 'free' calls with ☎ 800 prefixes are charged for by cardphones and in hotels. It is more expensive to call a mobile phone than a land-line. Using a hotel room's phone carries prohibitive charges.

Telekort (phonecards) are sold in Nkr40, Nkr90, Nkr140 and Nkr210 denominations and work out cheaper than using coins. Cards can be purchased at post offices, 7-Eleven, Narvesen and MIX kiosks. Credit cards can also be used with many cardphones.

The country code for calling Norway from abroad is ☎ 47. To make an international call from Norway, dial ☎ 00, then the appropriate country code, area code and number you're calling.

TIME
Time in Norway is one hour ahead of GMT/UTC, the same as Sweden, Denmark and most of Western Europe. When it's noon in Norway, it's 11am in London, 1pm in Finland, 6am in New York and Toronto, 3am in San Francisco, 9pm in Sydney and 11pm in Auckland.

Norway observes daylight-saving time, with clocks set ahead one hour on the last Sunday in March and back an hour on the last Sunday in October. Timetables and business hours are posted according to the 24-hour clock.

TOURIST INFORMATION
There are tourist offices in nearly every town in Norway, usually near the train station, dock or town centre. In smaller towns they may be open only during peak summer months, while in cities they're open year-round.

The **Norges Turistråd** (Norwegian Tourist Board; ☎ 74 14 46 00; www.visitnorway.com; PO Box 722 Sentrum, N-0105 Oslo) will send you information on request. You can download brochures from their website.

Useful Norwegian Tourist Board offices abroad:

UK (☎ 020-7839 6255; 5th Floor, Charles House, 5 Lower Regent St, London SW1Y 4LR)

USA & Canada (☎ 212-885-9700; Suite 1810, 655 Third Ave, New York, NY 10017)

VISAS

Citizens of the USA, Canada, the UK, Ireland, Australia and New Zealand need a valid passport to visit Norway, but do not need a visa for stays of less than three months. The same is true for EU and European Economic Area (EEA – essentially EU and Scandinavia) countries, most of Latin America and most Commonwealth countries (except South Africa and several other African and Pacific countries).

TRANSPORT IN NORWAY

GETTING THERE & AWAY

Air

Oslo's **Gardermoen airport** (☎ 81 55 02 50; www.osl.no) is Norway's principal connection to major European and North American cities. Other international airports, which have limited direct flight connections to international destinations:

Bergen (☎ 55 99 80 00; www.avinor.no)
Stavanger (☎ 51 65 80 00; www.avinor.no)
Tromsø (☎ 77 64 84 00; www.avinor.no)
Trondheim (☎ 74 84 30 00; www.avinor.no)

Airlines flying to and from Norway:
Air France (☎ 23 50 20 01; www.airfrance.no)
Braathens (☎ 81 52 00 00; www.braathens.no)
British Airways (☎ 80 03 31 42; www.britishairways.com)
Finnair (☎ 81 00 11 00; www.finnair.com)
Icelandair (☎ 22 03 40 50; www.icelandair.com)
KLM (☎ 22 64 37 52; www.klm.com)
Lufthansa (☎ 81 52 04 00; www.lufthansa.com)
Norwegian Air (☎ 81 52 18 15; www.norwegian.no)
SAS (☎ 81 52 04 00; www.scandinavian.net)

Land

DENMARK

The **Säfflebussen** (☎ 771-15 15 15; www.safflebussen.se) from Copenhagen to Oslo (Nkr150/220, nine hours, three daily) runs via Malmö in Sweden; the lower fare is valid Monday to Thursday. There's also a student discount.

It's also worth checking out Eurolines (p465), one of the biggest bus operators in the region.

Trains from Copenhagen to Oslo (nine hours, two daily) require a change in Göte-borg, Sweden; lowest fares must be booked at least seven days in advance.

FINLAND

Finnish bus company **Eskelisen Lapin Linjat** (in Finland ☎ 016-342 2160; www.eskelisen-lapinlinjat.com) runs buses from Rovaniemi (Finland) to Tanu Bru (year-round), Karasjok (year-round), Nordkapp (via Karasjok; from 1 June to 24 August), Kautokeino (from 1 June to 10 August) and Tromsø (from 1 June to 14 September). See also Eurolines (p465).

From Tornio, Finland, the E8 highway runs to Tromsø in Norway and there are secondary highways connecting Finland with Kautokeino, Karasjok and Tana Bru.

SWEDEN

Nor-Way Bussekspress (☎ 81 54 44 44; www.nor-way.no) runs between Oslo and Göteborg (adult/student Skr200/160, 4¼ hours, four daily). There are also buses between Skellefteå and Bodø (Skr480, 8¾ hours, once daily Sunday to Friday), and between Umeå and Mo i Rana (Skr244, 7½ to 8¾ hours, once daily).

See also Eurolines (p465).

The main highways between Sweden and Norway are the E6 from Göteborg to Oslo, the E18 from Stockholm to Oslo, the E14 from Sundsvall to Trondheim and the E12 from Umeå to Mo i Rana. Many secondary roads also cross the border.

Daily trains run from Stockholm (seven hours, three daily), Göteborg (from Skr190, four hours, four daily) and Malmö (from Skr450, 8¼ hours) to Oslo; the cheapest tickets must be booked at least seven days in advance. Journeys from Östersund to Trondheim via Storlien require a change of trains at the border. **Connex** (in Sweden ☎ 771 26 00 00; www.connex.se) trains run between Stockholm and Narvik (20 hours, one to two daily).

Sea

DENMARK

DFDS Seaways (☎ 22 41 90 90; www.dfdsseaways.com) runs daily overnight ferries between Copenhagen and Oslo, with fares ranging from Nkr221 to Nkr915 depending on what time of year you travel and what kind of cabin you select.

Color Line (☎ 81 00 08 11; www.colorline.com) runs ferries between Hirtshals and Kristiansand, the route with the shortest connection (from 4½ hours) and the most frequent service (two to five sailings daily) between Norway and Denmark. Color Line also operates once or twice daily between Frederikshavn and Larvik (from 6¼ hours) and once daily between Hirtshals and Oslo (eight hours). Fares are the same for all routes – depending on the day of the week and the time of year, they range from €24 to €58 for passengers and from €89 to €225 for cars. At certain times, there are special discount car packages on these routes.

Fjord Line (☎ 55 54 88 00; www.fjordline.com) sails from Hanstholm to Bergen (Nkr340 to Nkr920, 17 hours, one daily most of the year), stopping in Egersund en route. Cabins, cars and folding deck chairs cost extra.

Stena Line (☎ 23 17 91 00, ☎ 02010; www .stenaline.com) operates daily ferries between Frederikshavn and Oslo (Nkr160 to Nkr390, 12 hours), except Monday from 2 September to 10 June. A car with driver costs from Nkr240 to Nkr1390.

ICELAND & FAROE ISLANDS
Smyril Line (☎ 55 32 09 70; www.smyril-line.com) runs from May to early September between Bergen and Seyðisfjörður in Iceland (25 hours, one weekly), via Lerwick (Shetland) and the Faroe Islands. One-way low-/high-season fares to Bergen begin at Dkr630/870 from Tórshavn in the Faroes and Ikr15,990/22,790 from Seyðisfjörður. High season is mid-June to 31 July, with some sailings in August.

SWEDEN
DFDS Seaways (☎ 22 41 90 90; www.dfdsseaways.com) runs daily overnight ferries between Helsingborg and Oslo (from Skr442, 14 hours).

DFDS Seaways also sails between Göteborg and Kristiansand (passenger/car fares start at Skr118/218, seven hours, three days weekly).

Two to six times daily, **Color Line** (☎ 81 00 08 11; www.colorline.com) does the 2½-hour run between Strömstad (Sweden) and Sandefjord (Norway).

UK
Fjord Line (☎ 55 54 88 00; www.fjordline.com) sails from Newcastle to Bergen (£60 to £120, two to three times per week, from 21 hours).

GETTING AROUND
Public transport in Norway is usually quite efficient, with trains, buses and ferries often timed to link effectively. The handy *NSB Tograter*, available free at train stations, has rail schedules and information on connecting buses. Boat and bus departures vary with the season and the day, so pick up the latest *ruteplan* (timetables) from regional tourist offices. The Norwegian Tourist Board also publishes a free, annual national transport timetable.

When planning your route, particularly if heading into more remote areas, keep in mind that Saturday and Sunday bus services are often greatly reduced, and some are nonexistent on Saturday.

Air
Norway has nearly 50 airports, with scheduled commercial flights from Ny Ålesund (Svalbard) in the north to Kristiansand in the south. Air travel is worth considering, even by budget travellers, due to the great distances involved in overland travel.

Norway's main domestic airlines are **SAS** (☎ 81 52 04 00, www.scandinavian.net), **Braathens** (☎ 81 52 00 00; www.braathens.no), **Widerøe** (☎ 81 00 12 00; www.wideroe.no) and the new discount airline **Norwegian Air** (☎ 81 52 18 15; www.norwegian .no). It's worth checking for stand-by tickets, student fares and other discount schemes.

Norwegian domestic airport departure taxes (Nkr147 per flight) are included in ticket prices.

AIR PASSES
Widerøe often has special deals, including 'Explore Norway' tickets, where you can have unlimited travel between Norway's domestic airports for two weeks. These cost around Nkr4000.

Bicycle
Given its great distances, hilly terrain and narrow roads, Norway is not ideally suited for extensive touring by bicycle. A number of regions, however, are good for cycling. The *Sykkelguide* series of booklets, with maps and English text, are available from larger tourist offices for Nkr120 each – routes include Lofoten, Rallarvegen and the North Sea Cycle Route (from the Swedish border at Svinesund to Bergen). Bike rentals are easy to find; for example, from some tourist

offices, hostels and camping grounds (usually around Nkr150 to Nkr200 per day).

Rural buses, express ferries and non-express trains carry bikes for an additional fee (around Nkr100), but express trains don't allow them at all and international trains treat them as excess baggage (Nkr250). Nor-Way Bussekspress charges half the adult fare to transport a bicycle! If you plan to take your bike on long-distance trains, you must make a reservation well in advance.

Boat

An extensive network of ferries and express boats links Norway's offshore islands, coastal towns and fjord districts. See specific destinations for details.

HURTIGRUTEN COASTAL STEAMER

For more than a century Norway's legendary **Hurtigruten** (☎ 81 03 00 00; www.hurtigruten .no) has been the lifeline for villages scattered along the western and northern coasts.

One ship heads north from Bergen every night, pulling into 34 ports on its six-day journey to Kirkenes. It then turns around and returns south. With agreeable weather, expect spectacular scenery.

The ships accommodate deck-class travellers, with free sleeping areas (not especially comfortable), baggage rooms, shower room, 24-hour cafeterias and coin laundry. Passengers can rent cabins (Nkr200 to Nkr3000).

Sample fares for trips from Bergen are Nkr1533 to Trondheim, Nkr2613 to Stamsund, Nkr3145 to Tromsø and Nkr4875 to Kirkenes. One stopover is allowed with these fares, and, at many ports of call, you can leave the ship for several hours. Cars can also be carried for an extra fee. Accompanying spouses, children, students and seniors over 67 all receive 50% discount.

There are some great low-season deals: from 1 September to 30 April, passengers get 40% discount off basic fares for sailings on any day except Tuesday, with return journeys at a further 50% reduction on the return portion of the ticket.

Bus

Norway has an extensive bus network. Fares average Nkr150 for the first 100km. Many bus companies offer child, student, senior, group and family discounts of 25% to 50% – always ask.

Nor-Way Bussekspress (☎ 82 02 13 00; www .nor-way.no), the main carrier, has routes connecting every main city. It offers passes valid for 21 consecutive days (Nkr2300).

In Nordland, several Togbuss (train-bus) routes offer half-price fares to Eurail, Inter-Rail and ScanRail passholders. They run between Fauske and Bodø, Narvik, Tromsø, Svolvær and Harstad. InterRail and Scan-Rail passes get half-price bus tickets to/from the western fjords, between Oslo and Åndalsnes, Ålesund, Molde and Måløy, as well as various other routes in southern Norway.

If you're planning to use buses extensively, pick up the free Nor-Way Bussekspress *Rutehefte Inn og Utland* timetable.

Car & Motorcycle

If you plan to drive through mountainous areas in winter or spring, check first to make sure the passes are open, as some are closed until May or June. The **Road User Information Centre** (☎ 175) can tell you about the latest road conditions. Main highways, such as the E16 from Oslo to Bergen and the E6 from Oslo to Kirkenes, are kept open year-round. Cars in snow-covered areas should have studded tyres or carry chains.

If you plan to travel along Norway's west coast, keep in mind that it isn't only mountainous, but deeply cut by fjords. While it's a spectacular route, travelling along the coast requires numerous ferry crossings, which can be time-consuming and costly. For a full list of ferry schedules, fares and reservation phone numbers, consider investing in a copy of *Rutebok for Norge,* the comprehensive transport guide available in larger bookshops and Narvesen kiosks. Some counties publish free booklets detailing bus and ferry timetables – tourist offices usually stock copies.

If you drive in remote areas, especially in the far north, remember that weather can become life-threatening at some times of the year. Pack items necessary for an emergency.

AUTOMOBILE ASSOCIATIONS

For motoring information, contact the national automobile club, **Norges Automobil-Forbund** (NAF; ☎ 22 34 14 00; www.naf.no; Storgata 2, N-0105 Oslo). For 24-hour breakdown assistance call the NAF on ☎ 81 00 05 05. Ask your home automobile association for a Letter of Introduction (Lettre de Recommendation), which entitles you to services offered by affiliated organisations in Norway.

DRIVING LICENCE
Norway accepts licences from the EU. Drivers from other countries should pick up an International Driver's Licence before arriving in Norway.

FUEL
Leaded and unleaded petrol is available at most petrol stations. Regular unleaded averages Nkr9 per litre in the south, and can be well over Nkr10 per litre in the north. In towns, there are some 24-hour petrol stations, but most close by 10pm or midnight. In rural areas, many stations close in the early evening and don't open at all on weekends. Many stations don't take foreign credit cards.

Even in remote Finnmark, fuel is easily found in villages. But since these can be several hundred kilometres apart, it's best to stock up.

HIRE
Major car-rental companies, such as Hertz, Avis, Rent-a-Wreck and Europcar, have offices at airports and in city centres. Car rentals are expensive: the walk-in rate for a compact car with free 200km is about Nkr1000 a day, including VAT and insurance. You're likely to get much better deals by booking with an international agency before you arrive in Norway.

One relatively good deal is the weekend rate offered by major car-rental companies, which allows you to pick up a car after noon on Friday and keep it until 10am on Monday for about Nkr1400 – make sure it includes unlimited kilometres.

To rent a car you must be at least 21 years old with at least one year's driving experience and hold a valid driver's licence

INSURANCE
Third-party car insurance (unlimited cover for personal injury and Nkr1,000,000 for property damage) is compulsory and, if you're bringing a vehicle from abroad, you'll have fewer headaches with an insurance company Green card, which outlines the coverage granted by your home policy. Your insurance provider should have further details about these cards.

Ensure your vehicle is insured for ferry crossings.

ROAD RULES
In Norway, you drive on the right-hand side of the road. All vehicles, including motorcycles, must have their headlights on at all times. The use of seat belts is mandatory, and children under the age of four must have their own seat or safety restraint.

On motorways and other main roads, the maximum speed is generally 80km/h (a few roads have segments allowing 90km/h or 100km/h), while speed limits on through roads in built-up areas are generally 50km/h, unless otherwise posted. Speed cameras and mobile police units lurk at roadsides to enforce these limits (which don't seem to affect Norway's appalling driving standards and high death rate for motorists).

Tolls are now common on highways, bridges and tunnels. The biggest cities are effectively sealed off by toll booths at places where no onward public transport is available, and parking, even in small towns, is subject to exorbitant fees. Make sure you have plenty of cash (and loose change) to pay for tickets; if you pass an automatic toll station without paying, call in at the next petrol station or tourist office and ask for assistance on how to pay in retrospect and avoid a whopping fine. Rental-car agencies will automatically add fines (including speed-camera tickets) to your credit card bill.

Drink-driving laws are strict in Norway: the maximum permissible blood alcohol concentration is 0.02% and violators are subject to severe fines and/or imprisonment.

You're required to carry a red warning triangle in your car for use in the event of breakdown. Motorcycle helmets are mandatory; motorcycles cannot park on the pavement and must follow the same parking regulations as cars.

The speed limit for caravans (and cars pulling trailers) is usually 10km/h less than for cars. There are a few mountain roads where caravans are forbidden and numerous other roads that are only advisable for experienced drivers, as backing up may be necessary to allow approaching traffic to pass. For a map outlining these roads, and caravan rules, contact **Vegdirektoratet** (☎ 22 07 35 00; Gaustadalleen 25, N-0371 Oslo).

NORWAY

Hitching

Hitching isn't common. One approach is to ask for rides from truck drivers at ferry terminals and petrol stations.

Train

Norway has an excellent, though somewhat limited, national rail system. **NSB** (Norges Statsbaner or Norwegian State Railways; ☎ 81 50 08 88; www.nsb.no) operates most lines.

Second-class travel is comfortable. Komfort-class travel, which costs Nkr75 more, isn't worth the extra tariff, unless you really dig free coffee.

Discounted Minipris tickets are sometimes available. Extremely cheap, you could travel from Oslo to Bergen for just Nkr150, depending on the offering. These tickets may only be purchased online, at least a day in advance. Buy early – these sell out. NSB sells Euro Domino tickets at Nkr13 09/1540/1791/2002/2333/2464 for three/four/five/six/seven/eight days' travel on the Norwegian rail network within one month.

The Norway Rail Pass (US$209/244/279 for three/four/five days' travel within one month) allows unlimited train travel within Norway. Purchase before or after you arrive in Norway. The Flåm line isn't covered (there's a 30% discount). There's a 50% discount on Bergen–Stavanger ferries.

Regular fares from Oslo are Nkr670 to Bergen, Nkr644 to Åndalsnes, Nkr783 to Stavanger and Nkr758 to Trondheim. On many long-distance trains reservations (Nkr50) are mandatory.

Second-class sleepers provide cheap sleeps (three-bed/two-bed/private cabins Nrk125/270/580). 'Sleeperettes' (halfway between a chair and a bed) are available on the Trondheim–Bodø line (Nkr70).

Most train stations have luggage lockers for Nkr15 to Nkr40 and many also have a baggage-storage room.

Sweden

CONTENTS

SWEDEN

Every country has its stereotypes and clichés, but who wouldn't want to live up to Sweden's? A nation of tall, blond, attractive types, famously open-minded and amiable. Wholesome, outdoorsy folk at the cutting edge of technology, well cared for by the state and living very comfortable lives: Volvos in the garage; houses full of stylish, cleverly designed furniture; long summer days spent eating meatballs and listening to ABBA (OK, maybe that's taking it too far). To the casual observer it might well seem that the clichés are pretty spot on. But, as ever, there's a lot more to a country than its stereotypes. Dig below the glossy surface and you'll find even more to be impressed by.

Sweden's stunning capital, Stockholm, offers visitors a veritable smorgasbord of sights, while Göteborg and Malmö also beckon with urban delights. Picture-perfect towns like Uppsala, Visby, Ystad and Lund are dripping with history. Away from the cities, Sweden also takes in vast areas of scenic coastline and idyllic islands, plus forested and lake studded landscapes. The starkly beautiful wilderness areas of Norrland have the legendary midnight sun in summer, Kebnekaise (2111m; Arctic Scandinavia's highest mountain) and thousands of kilometres of hiking trails through immense protected areas. Few visitors to Sweden will leave the country disappointed.

FAST FACTS

- **Area** 449,964 sq km
- **Capital** Stockholm
- **Currency** Swedish krona (plural kronor); US$1 = Skr7.37; £1 = Skr13.16; €1 = Skr9.06; A$1 = Skr5.33; C$1 = Skr5.79; NZ$1 = Skr4.95; ¥100 = Skr6.65
- **Famous for** Vikings, Volvos, blonds, ABBA, meatballs, tennis players, IKEA
- **Official Language** Swedish
- **Phrases** *hej* (hello), *hej då* (goodbye), *ja* (yes), *nej* (no), *tack* (thanks)
- **Telephone Codes** country code ☎ 46; regional codes: Stockholm ☎ 08, Göteborg ☎ 031; international access code ☎ 00
- **Visa** Not needed for most visitors for stays of up to three months (see p439)

HIGHLIGHTS

- Succumbing to the immense charms of **Stockholm** (p362) by taking a boat cruise, exploring the backstreets of Gamla Stan and cycling around Djurgården
- Enjoying a cocktail (and a performance of Shakespeare) at the ultra-cool **Ice Hotel** (p431), near Kiruna
- Letting your hair down with holidaying Swedes on **Gotland** (p418), the perfect cycling and camping destination
- Celebrating Midsummer and taking in a concert at Dalhalla in the lovely, attraction-rich **Lake Siljan area** (p390)
- Exploring the scenic coastal region and islands of the north's **Höga Kusten** (p423), full of picture-perfect fishing villages

ITINERARIES

- **One week** Spend three days in Stockholm and Uppsala, two or three days in and around Göteborg and then continue south to Malmö. Alternatively, explore the Stockholm region more thoroughly, including Drottningholm, Birka and a couple of days in the archipelago, before heading to Uppsala via Sigtuna.
- **Two weeks** As above, but include a trip northwards to the Lake Siljan region, or add Karlskrona, Kalmar and Öland to a tour of the south. Alternatively, explore Gotland for a few days.

CLIMATE & WHEN TO GO

Sweden is at its best during summer and autumn (late May to September), but hikers and campers may wish to avoid the peak of the mosquito season (June and July). Summers are short and intense, and daylight hours are long. Many youth hostels, camping grounds and attractions open only in high summer (from the Midsummer festival in late June until early August). This period is also when most Swedes are holidaying, so finding accommodation in areas favoured by the locals (eg Dalarna, Gotland and Öland) may prove difficult.

Winter-sports enthusiasts can enjoy a visit any time from December to March or April. Travel in winter is somewhat restricted and should be well planned, but there are good opportunities for activities such as skiing or dogsled and snowmobile safaris. The big cities are in full swing all year, but smaller towns almost go into hibernation when the

---

HOW MUCH?

- **Hostel dorm bed** Skr150-250
- **Coffee and cake** Skr35
- **Museum entry** Skr40-70
- **Movie ticket** Skr85
- **4-star hotel double weekdays/ weekends & summer** Skr1400/800

LP INDEX

- **Litre of petrol** Skr10-11
- **1.5L bottle of water** Skr25
- **Pint of Spendrups beer** Skr35-50
- **Souvenir T-shirt** Skr150-200
- **Street snack (korv, or hot dog)** Skr12-25

---

temperature drops (the notable exceptions being popular ski resorts).

HISTORY

Written records in Sweden survive only from the late Middle Ages, but the number of ancient fortifications, assembly places, votive sites and graves is impressive.

The Viking Age was getting under way by the 9th century and vast repositories of Roman, Byzantine and Arab coins attest to the wealth and power Swedish Vikings accumulated over the next century. Vikings travelled mostly to the east, making their mark in Russia, as well as trading with (and pillaging) Byzantine territories.

Internal squabbles whiled away the bulk of the Middle Ages until Denmark intervened and, together with Norway, joined Sweden in the Union of Kalmar in 1397 (signed at Kalmar's grand castle; see p414). Danish monarchs held the Swedish throne for a while.

A century of Swedish nationalist grumblings erupted in rebellion under the young nobleman Gustav Vasa. After being crowned Gustav I in 1523, he introduced the Reformation and a powerful, centralised nation-state. A period of expansion began and resulted in Sweden's control over much of Finland and the Baltic countries.

King Karl XII's adventures in the early 18th century cost Sweden its Baltic territories and the crown much prestige. The next 50

SWEDEN

years was marked by greater parliamentary power, but Gustav III led a coup that interrupted this development. Unrestricted royal power was undone by aristocratic revolt in 1809 and Finland was lost to Russia. That same year produced a constitution that divided legislative powers between king and Riksdag (Parliament). Napoleon's marshal Bernadotte was chosen to fill a gap in the succession and, as Karl Johan, became regent. Thus began the rise of liberalism and Sweden's policy of neutrality. In 1814 the military enforcement of the union with Norway was Sweden's last involvement with war.

Sweden declared itself neutral at the outbreak of WWI, but a British economic blockade caused food shortages and civil unrest. Consensus was no longer possible and for the first time a Social Democrat and Liberal coalition government took control in 1921. Reforms followed quickly and suffrage for all adults aged over 23 years was introduced, as well as the eight-hour working day.

The Social Democrats dominated politics after 1932. After the hardships caused by the Depression, they reworked the liberal tendencies of the 1920s and combined them with economic intervention policies to introduce Sweden's famed welfare state.

These trends were scarcely interrupted by Sweden's ambiguous approach to WWII. The Social Democrats sponsored models for industrial bargaining and full employment which allowed the economy to blossom. The 1950s and '60s saw a rapid rise in the standard of living for ordinary Swedes.

Serious current-account problems during the world recession of the early 1990s provoked frenzied speculation against the Swedish krona, forcing a massive devaluation of the currency. With both their economy and national confidence severely shaken, Swedes voted narrowly in favour of joining the European Union (EU), effective 1 January 1995.

Since 1995, Sweden's welfare state has undergone tough reforms and the economy has improved considerably, with falling unemployment and inflation. The country has remained outside the single European currency; a 2003 referendum on whether Sweden should adopt the euro resulted in a 'no' vote, but the question is certain to come up again. The 2003 referendum was overshadowed by the murder just days before of Sweden's popular foreign minister, Anna Lindh, in a department store in Stockholm. Her killing plunged the country into a state of shock, but does not appear to have been politically motivated.

PEOPLE

Around 8.9 million people call Sweden home, making it Scandinavia's most populous country. The population is unevenly dispersed: there are just three inhabitants per square kilometre in Norrbotten (the northernmost county), compared to 253 in Stockholm. There are around 17,000 Sami in Sweden, largely concentrated in the north.

Close to 550,000 foreign citizens (mostly from neighbouring Nordic countries) live in Sweden. Contrary to the stereotypes, not all the population is blond-haired and blue-eyed: the largest non-Nordic group of immigrants is from Iraq (with 36,000), followed by Yugoslavs and Bosnians. In a post–September 11 world racial tensions have increased in Sweden (as they have in most of Europe) and there is some cultural friction, but there is little evidence of ethnic violence, and rightwing, anti-immigration political parties have found little support at the national level.

ARTS

The best-known members of Sweden's artistic community have been writers, chiefly the dramatist and author August Strindberg and the widely translated children's writer Astrid Lindgren (creator of Pippi Longstocking). Vilhelm Moberg, a representative of 20th-century proletarian literature, won acclaim with *The Immigrants* and *The Emigrants*. Ingmar Bergman remains one of the greatest cinema directors of all time.

The most important figure from Swedish culture, however, is the scientist Carl von Linné, the 18th-century botanist who pioneered modern plant taxonomy under Latin classifications. Even better known is Alfred Nobel, the inventor of dynamite and other explosives, whose will founded the Nobel Institute and the international prizes in 1901.

Sweden lacks a world-renowned musician such as Norway's Grieg or Finland's Sibelius, but its modern music industry is one of the strongest in Europe. The popularity of music here is highlighted by the facts that Swedes buy more recorded music per capita than any other nationality, and the country is the third-largest exporter of music in the world

---

THANK YOU FOR THE MUSIC

If asked to name Sweden's most famous exports, ABBA would top many people's list.

During the 1970s ABBA, consisting of two couples, was founded and became one of the most successful popular music acts of the decade. The individual members were all show-business veterans in their native Sweden, and their wholesome image, perfectly constructed pop songs and strong melodies took the world by storm.

ABBA, an acronym of their names (Agnetha, Björn, Benny and Anni-Frid – more commonly known as Frida), won the Eurovision Song Contest in 1974 with 'Waterloo', which went on to top the charts in several countries. ABBA went from success to success: they toured the world, made a film and recorded hit after hit.

ABBA's last year together was 1982 and by then the fairy tale was over and both couples had divorced but, in the words of one of their songs, 'the music still goes on'. Recent years have seen something of an ABBA revival, with successful cover versions of ABBA anthems, ABBA tribute bands, the group's elevation to the status of gay icon, popular movies featuring ABBA music and impersonations, and a successful stage show based on their music, *Mamma Mia!* (written by Benny and Björn). In 1992 the compilation album *ABBA Gold* was released and became the group's biggest seller (to date it has sold a staggering 25 million copies worldwide). Despite this revival success, no reunion is on the cards (the media reports that band members knocked back an offer of US$1 billion to regroup).

There are hundreds of ABBA websites on the Internet; a good place to start is the dedicated www.abbasite.com.

(after the US and UK). Some 120 music festivals are staged annually, ranging from medieval and baroque to folk, jazz and rock.

ENVIRONMENT
The Land
Sweden covers an area of 449,964 sq km and its maximum north–south extent is 1574km. This size allows for a little diversity: flat and open Skåne is similar to Denmark, but further north the landscape is hillier and heavily forested. The rocky west coast is most notable for its fjords and skerries, although they scarcely compare with the barrage of rocky islets that shield Stockholm. The islands of Öland and Gotland consist of flat limestone and sandstone.

There are approximately 100,000 lakes in Sweden. Lake Mälaren is the heart of the country, although Vänern is by far the biggest of the south and central lakes. In Norrland there's an almost uniform expanse of forest cut by rivers and narrow lakes. The trees thin out in Jämtland and Lappland and the mountains assert themselves, providing a natural frontier with Norway in the northwest.

Geographical divisions in Sweden are complex. The two kingdoms which united in the 11th century form the southern half of the country: Götaland in the south and Svealand in lower central Sweden. Anything north of Svealand is called Norrland. The 25 historical regions (based on common dialect), called *landskap*, remain as denominators for people's identity and a basis for regional tourist promotion. Regional administration is based on 21 *län* (counties), which are responsible for things such as *länstrafik* (regional public transport) and *länsmuseum* (county museums).

Wildlife
Large numbers of elk (moose) and deer live in the forests, and in Norrland there are sizable herds of reindeer (no longer truly wild, as each animal belongs to a local Sami community). Other animals peculiar to the north are the arctic fox and lemmings, small, hardy rodents famous for their reproductive capacity. European brown bears, Scandinavia's only surviving wild bear population, number about 1000 and live mainly in the remote northern areas; visitors can see them at the Grönklitt Björnpark (p391) outside Orsa in the Lake Siljan area.

National Parks
Nature-loving Swedes led Europe in setting up national parks in the early 20th century; there are now 28 throughout the country (the biggest and best are in Lappland). Rules vary

locally, but the constant is that all people have access to open areas (see below). In 1996, the 9400-sq-km Laponia area was placed on the World Heritage List – it includes the national parks Stora Sjöfallet, Sarek, Padjelanta and Muddus. See the website of Naturvårdsverket (www.environ.se), the Swedish environmental protection agency, for coverage of national parks.

Environmental Issues
Ecological consciousness in Sweden is very high and reflected in concern for native animals, clean water and renewable resources. Swedes are fervent believers in sorting and recycling household waste – you'll be expected to do the same in hostels and camping grounds. Most plastic bottles and aluminium cans can be recycled – supermarket disposal machines give Skr0.50 to Skr1 per item.

Right of Public Access
The right of public access to the countryside (called *allemansrätten*) means that in Sweden, by law, you're allowed to walk, boat, ski or swim on private land as long as you stay at least 70m from houses and keep out of gardens, fenced areas and cultivated land. You can camp for more than one night in the same place, and you may pick berries and mushrooms. You must not leave any rubbish nor take living wood, bark, leaves, bushes or nuts. Fires may be set where safe (not on bare rocks) with fallen wood. Use a bucket of water to douse a campfire even if you think that it's out. Cars may not be driven across open land or on private roads. Close all gates. Do not disturb farm animals or reindeer.

If you have a bicycle or car, look for free camp sites around unsealed forest tracks off secondary country roads. Make sure your spot is at least 50m from the track and not visible from any house, building or sealed road. Dry pine forests are your best bet. Bring drinking water and food, although running creek water can be used for washing (don't pollute the water with soap or food waste).

FOOD & DRINK
There's a lot more to Swedish food than meatballs and a crazed Muppet chef.

Staples & Specialities
Classic Swedish *husmanskost* (home-style Swedish food) is based on simply prepared

combinations of meat, potatoes and fish. Many traditional restaurants specialise in *husmanskost*, but others often include a *husmanskost* section (or dish) on the menu. Typical dishes are *pytt i panna*, a meat-and-potato hash served with pickled beets and a fried egg; fried or pickled herring, called *sill* or *strömming* depending on which coast it comes from; salmon *(lax)* in several forms, from grilled to smoked to salt-and-sugar cured *(gravad)*; game such as elk and reindeer; and of course the requisite Swedish meatballs *(köttbullar)*, served with mashed potatoes and lingonberry sauce.

Where to Eat & Drink
Swedes don't typically go out for breakfast *(frukost)*; most start their day with coffee and a pastry or cereal with yoghurt. Most hotels and some hostels provide extensive breakfast buffets laden with cereals and yoghurt plus bread, fruit, cold cuts, cheese and the like.

Most cafés and restaurants serve a daily lunch special (or a choice of several) called *dagens rätt* or *dagens lunch* at a fixed price (usually Skr60 to Skr70) between 11.30am and 2pm. The price usually includes main course, salad, bread, cold drink and coffee, and it's one of the most economical ways to sample upmarket Swedish cooking.

To counter the mid-afternoon slump, Swedes enjoy *fika*, which means, roughly, to meet friends for coffee and cake at around 3pm (although it can happen at any time of day and isn't technically restricted to coffee). *Konditori* are old-fashioned bakery-cafés where you can get a pastry or a *smörgås* (sandwich) from Skr25, but there are also many stylish, modern cafés where you can enjoy people-watching over pricier Italian coffees, gourmet salads, bagels and muffins. In the latter category, look out for the popular chain of cafés called Wayne's Coffee.

For a quick, inexpensive snack, it's hard to beat a *grillad korv med bröd* – a basic grilled hot dog on a bun (Skr12 to Skr25, available from countless stands and carts). Variations include *kokt* (boiled) *korv* and several types of *rulle*, which are hot dogs wrapped up with mashed potatoes *(mos)*, onions, shrimp salad and other unlikely things in pitta-style bread.

Dinner options in medium and large cities are extensive. Pure vegetarian restaurants do exist but they're not common; however, there will usually be at least one vegetarian main-course option on menus. Due to the strict licensing laws, most pubs and bars in Sweden serve a good range of meals too; chains like Harry's and O'Leary's are ubiquitous and invariably popular.

Nonsmokers will breathe easier from June 2005, when Sweden implements a ban on smoking in bars and restaurants.

Self-Catering

Making your own meals is easy if you're hostelling or staying in camping grounds. The most prominent supermarket chains are Hemköp, Konsum and ICA. The selection of fresh vegetables and fruit tends to be better at produce markets (these are commonly found on a town's main square).

Alcohol

Lättöl (light beer, less than 2.25% alcohol) and *folköl* (folk beer, 2.25% to 3.5% alcohol) account for about two-thirds of all beer sold in Sweden and can be bought in supermarkets. *Mellanöl* (medium-strength beer, 3.5% to 4.5% alcohol), *starköl* (strong beer, over 4.5% alcohol) and wines and spirits can only be bought at outlets of the state-owned alcohol store, Systembolaget, open until about 6pm on weekdays and only for a few hours on Saturday (Friday afternoon queues can be long!). You must be aged 20 or over to make a purchase. Alcohol prices are kept high as a matter of government policy; the result sees Swedes travelling to Denmark, the Åland islands or Finland to stock up.

STOCKHOLM

☎ 08 / pop 760,000

Stockholm is one of the most beautiful capitals in the world, scattered across a series of islands where Lake Mälaren meets the Baltic Sea, and with 24,000 islands (Stockholm's *skärgård* or archipelago) protecting the city from the open seas. It's a compact city and has remained a manageable size even while its status as a cultural centre has grown rapidly. It's a mecca for lovers of first-rate architecture, museums, shopping and design, and everyone will enjoy simply strolling and taking in its loveliness.

The city is best seen from the water but you can also explore the parklands of Djurgården or the alleys of lovely Gamla Stan (the Old Town) on foot, plus take in some of the world-class treasures housed in the city's dozens of museums. Stockholm has the widest selection of budget accommodation in Scandinavia plus a great café and restaurant scene. Around 1.8 million people live in greater Stockholm and over 15% of them are immigrants, making for a lively, cosmopolitan atmosphere.

ORIENTATION

Stockholm is built on 14 islands, with the modern city centre on the main island. The business core is composed of Norrmalm and Vasastan (the boundaries between these two are debatable); the most chic and historically wealthiest part of town is Östermalm, to the east.

The tourist office is in the eastern part of Norrmalm; the popular garden Kungsträdgården (often referred to as 'Stockholm's living room') is almost next door. Off the western edge of Norrmalm is the mostly residential island of Kungsholmen.

Smack in the middle of Stockholm is the island housing Gamla Stan, the historic old town. Two smaller, satellite islands are linked to it by bridges: Riddarholmen to the west; and Helgeandsholmen to the north, occupied by the Swedish parliament building.

To the east of Gamla Stan is the island of Djurgården ('Animal Park'), where many of Stockholm's better-known museums are located. The small island of Skeppsholmen sits between Djurgården and Gamla Stan; it's home to more museums and the well-known youth hostel af Chapman.

Södermalm, the city's funky, bohemian area, inhabits the large island to the south of Gamla Stan. It's linked by the car-and-pedestrian bridge Centralbron as well as by the rather baffling traffic snarl called Slussen.

There are some pleasant picnic and bathing spots around Långholmen, the park-like island to the west of Södermalm.

Maps

The *What's On Stockholm* tourist booklet, available free from tourist offices and many hotels, has basic map pages, but *Stockholms officiella turistkarta* (Skr20, from the tourist office) covers a larger area and is easier to read.

STOCKHOLM IN TWO DAYS

Start your visit in Stockholm where the city itself began – Gamla Stan. Peek into Storkyrkan, then take a tour of Kungliga Slottet (the Royal Palace), and try to be near the outdoor courtyard at midday for the Changing of the Guard. Spend the afternoon wandering the cobbled streets, then walk across to Södermalm and take the Katarinahissen lift for a spectacular evening view. Dine at Eriks Gondolen or prowl Södermalm for nightlife. The next day, take a boat cruise in the morning, and in the afternoon hire a bike and cycle around Djurgården. If you have time, squeeze in a visit to Skansen and Vasamuseet.

A huge range of guidebooks and maps for driving, hiking or sailing in Sweden and elsewhere in Scandinavia is available online (www.lantmateriet.se) and at the following shops:

Kartbutiken (Map pp370-1; ☎ 202303; Kungsgatan 74, ☒ Mon-Sat)

Kartcentrum (Map pp370-1; ☎ 411 1687; Vasagatan 16; ☒ Mon-Sat)

INFORMATION
Bookshops

Akademibokhandeln (Map pp370-1; ☎ 613 6100; Mäster Samuelsgatan 28) Scandinavia's largest bookshop.

Press Stop (Map pp370-1; ☎ 644 3510; Götgatan 31) In Södermalm, with a wide range of international and special-interest magazines.

Sweden Bookshop (Map pp370-1; ☎ 453 7880; www.swedenbookshop.com; Slottsbacken 10; ☒ Mon-Fri) In Gamla Stan and offering the broadest selection of thematic books in English (also available online).

Discount Cards & Packages
STOCKHOLM CARD

The Stockholm Card is available from tourist offices, a number of camping grounds, hostels and hotels, and SL public transport centres at Skr260/390/540 for 24/48/72 hours (Skr100/140/190 for accompanying children under 18, maximum two children's cards per adult card). The card gives free entry to over 75 attractions, free city parking in metered spaces, free sightseeing by boat and free travel on public transport (including the lift, Katarinahissen, but excluding local ferries and airport buses).

Students and seniors get discounted admission to most museums and sights without the card, so you'll need to work out if it's cheaper for you to just get a transport pass (see p381) and pay admission separately.

STOCKHOLM À LA CARTE

This discount hotel-and-sightseeing package has good deals on some of the city's top hotels. It costs from Skr400 per person, depending on the standard of accommodation (prices for central hotels start at around Skr600). For details, contact **Destination Stockholm** (☎ 663 0080; www.destination-stockholm.com).

Emergency

Emergency (☎ 112) Free number for fire brigade, police and ambulance.

Police stations Södermalm (Map pp370-1; ☎ 401 0100; Torkel Knutssonsgatan 20); Kungsholmen (Map pp364-6; ☎ 401 1300; Kungsholmsgatan 37) Both stations open 24 hours.

Internet Access

Café Access IT (Map pp370-1; ☎ 508 31489; www.access-it.stockholm.se; Kulturhuset, Sergels Torg; per hr Skr45; ☒ 11am-7pm Tue-Fri, 11am-5pm Sat & Sun) At the lower level in Kulturhuset. Scanning and printing available.

Nine (Map pp364-6; ☎ 673 6797; Odengatan 44; per min Skr0.75; ☒ 10am-1am) Computer area is downstairs through the café.

Sidewalk Express (www.sidewalkexpress.se; Swedish only; per hr Skr19) A chain of Internet kiosks at numerous central locations (Centralstationen, Cityterminalen, Arlanda and Bromma airports, inside some 7-Eleven stores). Vouchers are purchased from vending machines. See the website for locations in Stockholm and elsewhere in Sweden.

Internet Resources

Stockholm: the Official Visitors Guide (www.stockholmtown.com) Excellent tourist information in English (and many other languages).

Stockholm's Museums (www.stockholmsmuseer.com, Swedish only) Has a drop-down menu with links to all museum homepages (most of these have information in English).

Laundry

Laundry options are limited and it's best to find a hotel or hostel with facilities. A handy laundrette near metro station T-Odenplan is **Tvättomat** (Map pp364-6; ☎ 346 480; Västmannagatan 61; ☒ 8.30am-6.30pm Mon-Fri, 9.30am-3pm Sat). It costs Skr70 to wash and dry a load if you do it yourself. Last orders are accepted two hours before closing.

SWEDEN

STOCKHOLM

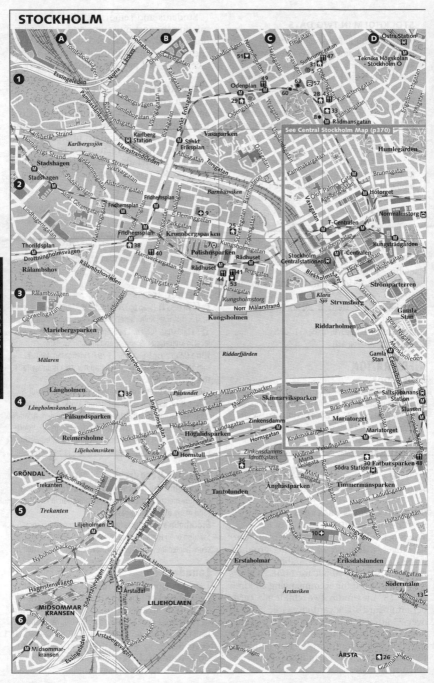

See Central Stockholm Map (p370)

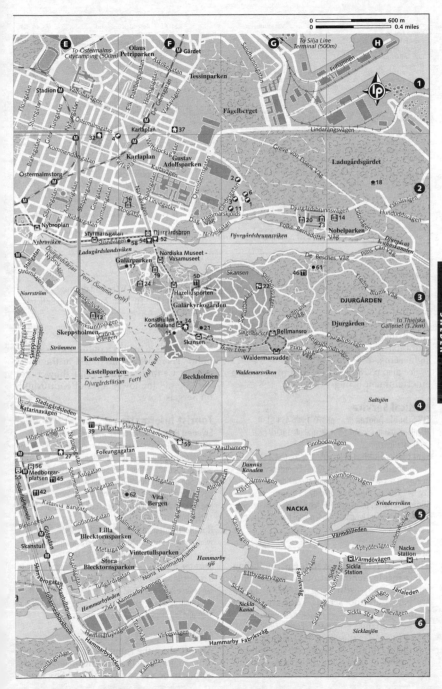

Media

There are a number of useful publications for visitors – the best overall guide is the monthly *What's On Stockholm* (available free from tourist offices and many hotels), which includes sections on shopping, restaurants, museums, activities, events and sightseeing.

See also p378 for where to find extensive entertainment listings.

Medical Services

CW Scheele Apotek (Map pp370-1; ☎ 454 8130; Klarabergsgatan 64; ☼ 24hr) Central pharmacy near Centralstationen.

Sankt Eriks Sjukhus (Map pp364-6; ☎ 654 1117; Flemminggatan 22; ☼ 8am-8.30pm) Emergency dental treatment is available here. Outside these hours, dial ☎ 644 9200 for the dentist on duty.

Södersjukhuset (Map pp364-6; ☎ 616 1000; Ringvägen 52; ☼ 24hr) Large hospital in Södermalm handling casualties from central city area.

Money

There are ATMs all over town, including a few inside Centralstationen, by the post office (usually with long queues). There are banks around Sergels Torg and along Hamngatan.

The exchange company **Forex** (Map pp370-1; www.forex.se; Centralstationen; ☼ 7am-9pm) has a number of branches scattered throughout the capital; at all of them the charge is Skr15 per travellers cheque.

Post

Post office (Map pp370-1; Centralstationen; ☼ 7am-10pm Mon-Fri, 10am-7pm Sat & Sun) By Hotel-centrallen office.

Toilets

You'll pay Skr5 to visit a public loo in Stockholm. There are public toilets in the lower level at Centralstationen (and showers for Skr25), and the lower level of Kulturhuset on Sergels Torg.

Tourist Information

Sweden House (Sverigehuset; Map pp370-1; ☎ 789 2490; www.stockholmtown.com; Hamngatan 27; ☼ 9am-7pm Mon-Fri, 9am-5pm Sat, 10am-4pm Sun Jun-Aug, 9am-6pm Mon-Fri, 10am-4pm Sat & Sun May & Sep, 10am-3pm Sat & Sun Oct-Apr) The capital's main tourist office. It has lots of good brochures and can book hotel rooms, theatre and concert tickets, and packages such as boat trips to the archipelago.

Hotellcentralen (Map pp370-1; ☎ 789 2456; hotels@ svb.stockholm.se; Centralstationen; ☼ 8am-8pm Jun-Aug; 9am-6pm Mon-Sat, noon-4pm Sun Sep-May) This busy office inside the main train station is more convenient for arriving travellers. In addition to providing tourist information, staff can reserve hotel rooms and hostel beds (for a fee), sell the Stockholm Card or SL transport passes, book sightseeing tours and sell maps, books and souvenirs.

SIGHTS

Almost all of the roughly 70 museums and other major attractions in and around Stockholm can be visited free with the Stockholm

Card (see p363). Most are open daily in summer (June to August), but are closed on Monday the rest of the year. Students and seniors usually pay a discounted entrance fee; children under 16 are generally admitted for half-price (or free) and small children enter free if accompanied by a paying adult. Disabled access is generally very good, and most museums also house cafés. There are many more museums than those listed below; for a full list, refer to *What's On Stockholm*, the booklet that accompanies the Stockholm Card, or www.stockholmsmuseer.com.

Gamla Stan

The oldest part of Stockholm is also its most beautiful, containing cobblestone streets, pretty old houses, vaulted cellar restaurants and the impressive royal palace. Allow a day to explore Gamla Stan (Map pp370–1); include touristy Västerlånggatan, but don't miss the parallel alleys or quiet squares. While ambling along Västerlånggatan, look out for **Mårten Trotzigs Gränd** by No 81: this is Stockholm's narrowest lane, at less than 1m wide.

The city emerged on this island in the 13th century and adopted the trade and, partly, the accents of its German Hanseatic guests. It grew with Sweden's power until the 17th century, when the castle of Tre Kronor, symbol of that power, burned to the ground.

KUNGLIGA SLOTTET (ROYAL PALACE)

The 'new' **palace** (Map pp370–1; ☎ 402 6130; www .royalcourt.se; Slottsbacken; adult/child per attraction Skr70/35, combined ticket Skr110/65; most attractions ☼ 10am–4pm mid-May–Aug, noon–3pm Tue–Sun Sep–mid-May, closed most of Jan) is built on the ruins of Tre Kronor and is one of Stockholm's highlights. Its 608 rooms make it the largest royal palace in the world. Many visitors find the **State Apartments** the most interesting, with two floors of royal pomp and portraits of pale princes (these may occasionally be closed to the public).

Crowns are displayed at **Skattkammaren** (the Royal Treasury), near **Slottskyrkan** (the Royal Chapel). **Gustav III's Antikmuseum** (Gustav III's Museum of Antiquities) displays Mediterranean treasures acquired by that eccentric monarch. **Museum Tre Kronor** is in the palace basement and features the foundations of 13th-century defensive foundations and exhibits rescued from the medieval castle during the fire of 1697.

The **Changing of the Guard** takes place in the outer courtyard at 12.15pm Monday to Saturday, and 1.15pm Sunday and public holidays.

OTHER ATTRACTIONS

Near the palace, **Storkyrkan** (☎ 723 3021; adult/child Skr20/free mid-May–Aug, otherwise free) is the Royal Cathedral of Sweden, consecrated in 1306. The most notable feature is the life-sized *St George & the Dragon* sculpture, dating from the late 15th century. On nearby Stortorget is the excellent **Nobelmuseet** (Map pp370–1; ☎ 232506; www.nobel.se/nobelmuseum; Stortorget; adult/child Skr50/20; ☼ 10am–5pm mid-May–mid-Sep, 11am–5pm Tue–Sun mid-Sep–mid-May), presenting the history of the Nobel Prize and past laureates.

The large collection of royal memorabilia at **Livrustkammaren** (Royal Armoury; Map pp370–1; ☎ 5195 5544; www.livrustkammaren.se; Slottsbacken 3; adult/child Skr65/20; ☼ 10am–5pm Jun–Aug, 11am–5pm Tue–Sun Sep–May) includes ceremonial costumes and colourful carriages. **Kungliga Myntkabinettet** (Royal Coin Cabinet; Map pp370–1; ☎ 5195 5304; www .myntkabinettet.se; Slottsbacken 6; adult/child Skr45/12, free entry Sun; ☼ 10am–4pm) is opposite the palace.

The island of Riddarholmen has some of the oldest buildings in Stockholm. **Riddarholmskyrkan** (Map pp370–1; ☎ 5903 5009; adult/child Skr20/10; ☼ 10am–4pm mid-May–Aug, noon–3pm Sat & Sun Sep) is no longer a church – it now houses the royal necropolis. Nearby, the beautiful **Riddarhuset** (House of Nobility; Map pp370–1; ☎ 723 3990; www.riddarhuset.se; Riddarhustorget; adult/child Skr40/10; ☼ 11.30am–12.30pm Mon–Fri) displays 2325 coats of arms.

The site of **Medeltidsmuseet** (Map pp370–1; ☎ 5083 1790; Strömparterren; adult/child Skr60/free; ☼ 11am–4pm Jul–Aug, 11am–4pm Tue–Sun Sep–Jun), the museum of medieval Stockholm, had been allocated as parking space for members of the nearby **Riksdagshuset** (Parliament House; Map pp370–1; ☎ 786 4872; www.riksdagen.se; Riksgatan 3A), but excavations in the late 1970s revealed well-preserved foundations of the medieval town and it's now a museum. Riksdagshuset has free one-hour guided tours in English at 12.30pm and 2pm Monday to Friday from late June to August.

Djurgården

Leafy Djurgården (Map pp364–6) is full of attractions and an absolute must for visitors to Stockholm. To get here, take bus

No 47 from Centralstationen or the regular Djurgården ferry services from Nybroplan or Slussen (see p381). You can rent bikes (see p380) by the bridge, and this is the best way to explore the island.

SKANSEN

You could easily spend all day at this 'Sweden in miniature'. **Skansen** (Map pp364-6; ☎ 442 8000; www.skansen.se; adult Skr50-80, child Skr20-30; 🕑 10am-8pm May, 10am-10pm Jun-Aug, 10am-5pm Sep, 10am-4pm Oct-Apr) was the world's first open-air museum (it opened in 1891). Today over 150 traditional houses (with staff in period costume) and other exhibits from all over Sweden occupy the attractive hill top. There's also a handicraft precinct, a **zoo** full of Nordic animals, and daily activities taking place on Skansen's stages in summer (including folk dancing and music). Skansen is the place to head to if you're in Stockholm for any of the country's major celebrations (eg Walpurgis Night, Midsummer, the Lucia festival, Christmas season and New Year's Eve; see p436).

VASAMUSEET

This acclaimed **museum** (Map pp364-6; ☎ 5195 4800; www.vasamuseet.se; adult/child Skr70/10; 🕑 9.30am-7pm mid-Jun–late Aug, 10am-5pm late Aug–mid-Jun), behind Nordiska Museet and on the western shore of Djurgården, allows you to simultaneously look into the lives of 17th-century sailors and appreciate a brilliant achievement in marine archaeology. The flagship *Wasa* sank within minutes of being launched in 1628 and tour guides will explain the extraordinary and controversial 300-year story of its death and resurrection. Guided tours in English run hourly from 10.30am in summer and at least twice daily at other times. At the moorings behind the museum are the icebreaker *Sankt Erik* and the lightship *Finngrundet*.

OTHER ATTRACTIONS

Nordiska Museet (National Museum of Cultural History; Map pp364-6; ☎ 5195 6000; www.nordiskamuseet.se; Djurgårdsvägen 6-16; adult/child Skr75/free; 🕑 10am-5pm Jun-Aug, 10am-4pm Mon-Fri, 10am-5pm Sat & Sun Sep-May) is housed in an enormous Renaissance-style castle, with notable temporary exhibitions and vast Swedish collections from 1520 to the present day.

Junibacken (Map pp364-6; ☎ 5872 3000; www .junibacken.se; adult/child Skr95/85; 🕑 9am-7pm Jul, 10am-

5pm Jun & Aug, 10am-5pm Tue-Fri, 9am-6pm Sat & Sun Sep-May) re-creates the fantasy scenes of Astrid Lindgren's children's books, which should stir the imaginations of young children and the memories of adults familiar with her characters.

More family fun can be had at **Gröna Lund Tivoli** (Map pp364-6; ☎ 5875 0100; www.gronalund .com; adult/child Skr60/30; 🕑 noon-11pm most days mid-Jun–mid-Aug), a fun park with dozens of rides and amusements – the Åkbandet day pass (Skr235) gives unlimited rides; individual rides range from Skr15 to Skr60. Big-name concerts are often held here in summer. Outside the peak season (mid-June to mid-August) the park's opening hours vary – it's best to call ahead.

Beyond Djurgården's large tourist haunts are plenty of small gems, including some excellent art collections.

Central Stockholm

Bustling Norrmalm is as enthusiastically contemporary as Gamla Stan is antiquate. Near the train station is **Sergels Torg** (Map pp370-1), a severely modern public square (though it's actually round) bordered on one side by the imposing Kulturhuset. Norrmalm is also home to the beloved public park **Kungsträdgården** (Map pp370-1), where locals gather in all weather. The park is home to an outdoor stage, winter ice-skating rink and restaurants, cafés and kiosks. Vasastan is the somewhat quieter, more residential area that extends to the north of Norrmalm.

The giant, boxy **Kulturhuset** (Map pp370-1; ☎ 5083 1508; Sergels Torg; 🕑 closed Mon) houses temporary exhibitions (often with entry fee), a theatre, bookshop, design store, reading room, several cafés, comics library and an Internet café.

Sweden's largest art museum, the excellent **Nationalmuseum** (Map pp370-1; ☎ 5195 4300; www.nationalmuseum.se; Södra Blasieholmshamnen; adult/child Skr75/free; 🕑 11am-8pm Tue, 11am-5pm Wed-Sun) houses the national collection of painting and sculpture but hosts other exhibitions, including design and handicrafts.

The main national historical collection is at **Historiska Museet** (Museum of National Antiquities; Map pp364-6; ☎ 5195 5600; www.historiska.se; Narvavägen 13; adult/child Skr60/free; 🕑 11am-5pm mid-May–mid-Sep, 11am-5pm Tue-Sun mid-Sep–mid-May). Displays cover prehistoric, Viking and medieval archaeology and culture; don't miss the incredible Gold Room with its rare treasures, including a seven-ringed gold collar.

Kungsholmen

The main visitor sight here is the landmark **Stadshuset** (Town Hall; Map pp370-1; ☎5082 9058; Hantverkargatan; tours adult/child Skr50/free; ☉ tours 10am-3pm Jun-Aug, 10am & noon Sep-May). Stadshuset looks like a large church, but the size is deceptive as it has two internal courtyards. The interior features the mosaic-lined Gyllene Salen (Golden Hall), Prins Eugen's own fresco recreation of the lake view from the gallery, and the Blå Hallen (Blue Hall) where the annual Nobel Prize banquet is held. Entry is by 45-minute tour only, interrupted from time to time by preparations for special events.

Climb Stadshuset's 106m-high **Stadshustorn** (Tower; Map pp370-1; ☎ 5082 9058; adult/child Skr20/free; ☉ 10am-4.30pm May-Sep, Sat & Sun Apr), with 365 steps, for a great view of the city.

Skeppsholmen

Across the bridge by the Nationalmuseum are more museums, including the wonderful **Moderna Museet** (Map pp364-6; ☎ 5195 5200; www .modernamuseet.se; Exercisplan; admission free; ☉ 10am-8pm Tue-Wed, 10am-6pm Thu-Sun), which boasts a world-class collection of modern art, sculpture, photography and installations, temporary exhibitions and an outdoor sculpture garden. Adjacent to Moderna Museet is **Arkitekturmuseet** (Map pp364-6; ☎ 5872 7000; www.arkitekturmuseet.se; Exercisplan; admission free; ☉ 10am-8pm Tue-Wed, 10am-6pm Thu-Sun), housed in an extraordinary building and containing displays on Swedish and international architecture.

Ladugårdsgärdet

North of Djurgården, in among the vast parkland, are more fine museums and attractions. To get to Ladugårdsgärdet (Map pp364-6), take bus No 69 from Centralstationen.

Sjöhistoriska Museet (National Maritime Museum; Map pp364-6; ☎ 5195 4900; www.sjohistoriska.nu; Djurgårdsbrunnsvägen 24; adult/child Skr50/20; ☉ 10am-5pm Tue-Sun) exhibits extensive maritime memorabilia. **Tekniska Museet** (Museum of Science & Technology; Map pp364-6; ☎ 450 5600; Museivägen 7; adult/child Skr60/30; ☉ 10am-5pm Mon-Fri, 11am-5pm Sat & Sun) contains exhaustive exhibits on Swedish inventions and their applications. The very good **Etnografiska Museet** (Museum of Ethnography; Map pp364-6; ☎ 5195 5000; www.etnografiska .se; Djurgårdsbrunnsvägen 34; adult/child Skr50/free;

☉ 11am-5pm) brings the entire world under one roof.

The 155m-high TV tower, **Kaknästornet** (Map pp364-6; ☎ 667 2180; adult/child Skr30/15; ☉ 9am-10pm May-Aug, 10am-9pm Sep-Apr), is the tallest building in town. There's an **observation deck** from which you can enjoy stunning 360-degree views.

Northern Suburbs

One of Stockholm's loveliest attractions is the **Millesgården** (Map p383; ☎ 446 7594; www.milles garden.se; Carl Milles väg 2, Lidingö; adult/child Skr75/20; ☉ 10am-5pm mid-May–Aug, noon-5pm Thu-Sun Sep–mid-May), a superb sculpture park and museum of works by Carl Milles. It's on Lidingö island with great views to the mainland; take the metro to T-Ropsten then bus No 207.

The extensive **Naturhistoriska Riksmuseet** (Map p383; ☎ 5195 4040; www.nrm.se; Frescativägen 40; adult/child Skr75/50; ☉ 10am-7pm Tue-Sun), founded by Carl von Linné in 1739, is the national museum of natural history, and includes the Imax theatre and planetarium **Cosmonova** (Map p383; ☎ 5195 5130; adult/child Skr75/50, combined museum & Cosmonova admission Skr120/80; ☉ 10am-8pm Tue-Sun). Take the metro to T-Universitet.

The large parks that extend from Djurgården in the south form **Ekoparken** (www.eko parken.com), a 27-sq-km national city park and the first such protected city area in the world. The area is perfect for cycling tours.

Haga Park (Map p383) is also pleasant for walks and bicycle tours with attractions including the royal **Gustav III's Pavilion**, **Butterfly House** and colourful **Copper Tent**. To reach the park, take bus No 515 from Odenplan to Haga Norra.

Södermalm

Södermalm is perhaps Stockholm's most interesting neighbourhood. Historically home to many of the city's artists, Söder (as locals call it) has a bohemian feel, and alternative youth culture scarcely ever ventures beyond the borders of this island. There are plenty of funky shops and art galleries, plus good nightlife.

Other than the Stadsmuseum, the sights in Söder are mostly offbeat smaller museums and churches. The primary sight of interest to visitors may just be the view of the rest of the city – for evening walks, head to the northern cliffs for the old houses and fine panoramas. There are more great views

CENTRAL STOCKHOLM

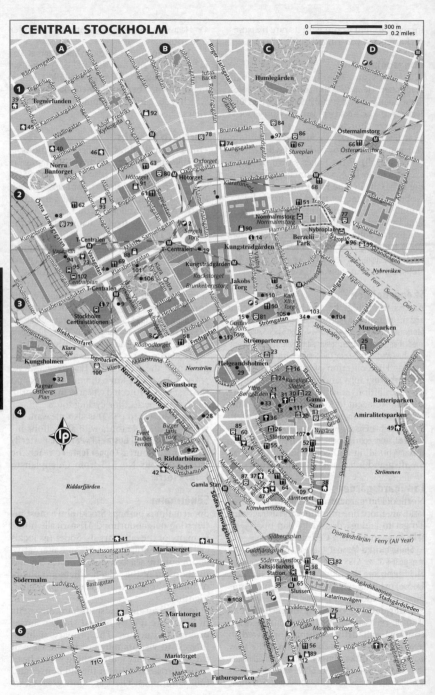

from **Katarinahissen** (Map opposite; ☎ 743 1395; Slussen; adult/child Skr5/free; ⊙ 7.30am-10pm Mon-Sat, 10am-10pm Sun), an old lift which takes you to the heights from Slussen. At the top is one of the city's best restaurants, Eriks Gondolen (see p377).

Stockholms Stadsmuseum (Map opposite; ☎ 5083 1600; Slussen; adult/child Skr60/10, ⊙ 11am 5pm Tue-Sun) covers the history of the city and its people, and is worthwhile once you've developed a romantic attachment to Stockholm.

Fjäderholmarna

These tiny islands (the 'Feather Islands') offer an easy escape from the city – they're just 25 minutes away by boat (off the east coast of Djurgården) and are a favourite swimming spot for locals. Take one of the boats (Skr80 return, buy tickets on board) that leave from either Nybroplan (half-hourly) or Slussen (hourly) from May to early September. There are a couple of restaurants here and the last

boats leave the islands at around midnight, making them a perfect spot to enjoy the long daylight hours.

ACTIVITIES

Summer sees locals and visitors taking advantage of the fine weather; many head for the coast and the islands of the archipelago (with good swimming spots) or organise picnics in the parks. Winter also sees some outdoor activity, including ice-skating on a rink set up in Kungsträdgården.

Eriksdalsbadet (Map pp364-6; ☎ 508 40250; Hammarby slussväg 20; indoor/outdoor pool Skr50/65; ⊙ 6.30am-8pm Mon-Thu, 6.30am-7pm Fri, 9am-6pm Sat & Sun) has indoor and open-air swimming pools in the far south of Södermalm, plus gym, aerobics and other activities.

From the restaurant-bar **Djurgårdsbrons Sjö-café** (Map pp364-6; ☎ 660 5757; Djurgårdsbron; ⊙ May-Sep), by the bridge leading to Djurgården, you can rent bikes (Skr65/250 per hour/day), as well as inline skates (Skr60/200 per hour/day), kayaks, canoes, rowing boats and pedal boats. Restaurant-bar **Tvillingarnas** (Map pp364–6; ☎ 663 3714; Strandvägskajen 27; ☺ Apr–Oct), on the other side of the bridge, hires out boats (motorboats and sailing boats) of various sizes by the hour, day or week (from Skr295 per hour).

TOURS

Stockholm Sightseeing (Map pp370-1; ☎ 5871 4020; www.stockholmsightseeing.com; main terminal, Stromkajen) runs frequent cruises from early April to mid-December around the central bridges and canals from Strömkajen (near the Grand Hôtel), Nybroplan or Stadshusbron. There are one-hour tours from Skr80 to Skr110 (including one that circumnavigates Djurgården), but the two-hour 'Under the Bridges of Stockholm' (Skr160) covers more territory and passes under 15 bridges and through two locks. The land-based sister operation is **City Sightseeing** (Map pp370-1; ☎ 5871 4020; www .citysightseeing.com), which offers year-round 1½- to 3½-hour coach tours of the city (departing from Gustav Adolfs Torg) from Skr200 to Skr395, and one-hour walking tours around Gamla Stan (Skr80, daily July and August). City Sightseeing also arranges two- or three-hour bike tours (Skr190 to Skr270, daily late June to mid-September) for a chance to see the city from a different angle.

You can also take a one-hour, English-language guided walk through Gamla Stan with an authorised guide (Skr60). From June to August these tours start at 7.30pm Monday, Wednesday and Thursday, and from September to May at 1.30pm Saturday and Sunday. Meet at the Obelisk at Slottsbacken, outside the royal palace; no reservation is needed.

SLEEPING

Options are spread out all over the city, and all are accessible by public transport and close to a neighbourhood of bars and cafés.

Budget
CAMPING

Östermalms Citycamping (Map pp364–6; ☎ 102903; Östermalms Idrottsplats, Fiskartorpsvägen; camp sites Skr100; ☺ mid-Jun–mid-Aug) Stockholm's most central camping ground (1.5km from the city centre), open only in summer. Metro T-Stadion or bus No 55.

Bredäng Camping (Map p383; ☎ 977071; bredang camping@telia.com; Stora Sällskapets väg; camp sites Skr170-205, 4-bed cabin Skr650-850, hostel dm/d Skr150/440; ☺ Apr–late Oct) In a pleasant lakeside location 10km southwest of the city centre, with good facilities for campers plus self-catering cabins and an adjacent hostel. Metro T-Bredäng.

HOSTELS

Most hostels fill up during the late afternoon in summer so arrive early or book in advance. May is also a busy time for hostels, with many Swedish school groups visiting the capital. For a Skr25 fee, Hotellcentralen at Centralstationen (see p366) can assist you in getting a bed in a hostel.

City Backpackers (Map pp370-1; ☎ 206920; www .citybackpackers.se; Upplandsgatan 2A; dm Skr180-220, d Skr490; 💻) This hostel is about 500m from Centralstationen, and is popular with backpackers. It's a good choice for its clean rooms, friendly staff and facilities, including kitchen, sauna, laundry, lockers and courtyard, plus free Internet access.

Hostel Bed & Breakfast (Map pp364–6; ☎ 152838; www.hostelbedandbreakfast.com; Rehnsgatan 21; dm/s/d Skr190/375/500; 💻) A cosy, welcoming basement hostel with good facilities such as kitchen and laundry. There's a large, cheap summer annexe here with 40 beds (June to August, Skr125), but it's not for those who like their privacy!

Mälaren den Röda Båten (Map pp370-1; ☎ 644 4385; www.theredboat.com; Söder Malärstrand, Kajplats 6; dm/s/d Skr195/430/490, cabins s/d from Skr675/915; 🅿) This red-painted boat in northern Södermalm is probably the cosiest of Stockholm's handful of floating hostels. It features a rustic interior and has a good summer restaurant (but no self-catering facilities). There are also pleasant hotel-standard cabins here, with private bathroom. Breakfast included.

Abbe's Hostels (☎ 300350; www.abbes.se; dm Skr220-260, d Skr500-640) Gamla Stan (Map pp370-1; Stora Nygatan 38); Gamla Stan (Map pp370-1; Skeppsbron 40); Kungsholmen (Map pp364–6; Fleminggatan 19); Globen (Map pp364–6; Gullmarsvägen 92) Abbe offers new, small, basic hostels scattered around the city centre (including two in prime spots in Gamla Stan and another on Kungsholmen). Abbe's Hostels are a reasonable choice based on location, but for the price they lack the organisation and facilities of the other hostels – there are no kitchen facilities, no breakfast offered, no phone bookings (book only via the website) and receptions that are only manned from 3pm to 6pm. The fourth, larger hostel (near Globen, metro T-Gullmarsplan) has better facilities, including kitchen, laundry, parking and barbecue area, plus cheaper dorm prices (from Skr160).

STF Vandrarhem & Hotell Zinkensdamm (Map pp364-6; ☎ 616 8100; www.zinkensdamm.com; Zinkens väg 20; dm/s/d Skr220/485/560, hotel s/d Skr1195/1495, s/d discount Skr855/1155; P 🖵) This large, well-equipped and welcoming complex (with adjacent hotel) is in a quiet location in the green western end of Södermalm. Also offers on-site café, breakfast (Skr55), sauna and bike rental. Breakfast is included in the hotel tariff.

STF Vandrarhem af Chapman & Skeppsholmen (Map pp370-1; ☎ 463 2266; info@chapman.stfturist.se; Skeppsholmen; dm/d Skr230/510; P 🖵) The boat anchored off Skeppsholmen (bus No 65 from Centralstationen) has done plenty of travelling of its own, but it's now a hostel swaying gently in sight of the city centre, with bunks below and great views from on deck. On dry land beside the boat hostel, and with the same reception and prices, is the larger Skeppsholmen Hostel, with kitchen and laundry facilities. Closed for a complete renovation, af Chapman should open in the later half of 2005. The land-based hostel will be open as usual during this time. Limited parking is available (Skr30 per day). Breakfast is Skr70.

STF Vandrarhem Fridhemsplan (Map pp364-6; ☎ 653 8800; info@fridhemsplan.se; Sankt Eriksgatan 20; dm/s/d Skr240/435/675; P 🖵) The paint was only just dry when we visited this brand-new, 150-room STF hostel on Kungsholmen. From its smart lobby to rooftop breakfast area (and no bunk beds), this place epitomises the Swedish approach to hostelling (ie good facilities, great decor, excellent value). There's parking (Skr95 per day), and breakfast is Skr60.

STF Vandrarhem & Hotell Långholmen (Map pp364-6; ☎ 720 8500; www.langholmen.com; Långholms-muren; dm/d Skr240/585, hotel s/d Skr1195/1495, s/d discount Skr855/1195; P) Off the northwestern corner of Södermalm is the small, pretty island of Långholmen, home to this complex (formerly a prison). There are hostel beds in former cells and roomier hotel-standard rooms (with breakfast), plus on-site café and restaurant, breakfast (Skr75) and even a prison museum. To get to Långholmen, take the metro to Hornstull, then walk north

along Långholmsgatan and turn left onto Högalidsgatan, then north across the foot-bridge.

Other budget options:
M/S Rygerfjord (Map pp370-1; ☎ 840830; www.rygerfjord.se; Söder Malärstrand, Kajplats 12; dm Skr145-180, d Skr390-500; P) Boat with small hostel cabins, plus on-site restaurant.

STF Vandrarhem Backpackers Inn (Map pp364-6; ☎ 660 7515; www.backpackersinn.se; Banérgatan 56; dm Skr165-205; ☿ late Jun–mid-Aug; P 🖵) Around 300 beds in a school building. No kitchen facilities, but breakfast is available (Skr50).

Östra Reals Vandrarhem (Map pp364-6; ☎ 664 1114; www.ostrareal.com; Karlavägen 79; dm Skr130-170, d Skr450; ☿ mid-Jun–mid-Aug; P) Also in an old school, without kitchen facilities or breakfast offered.

Hotel Formule 1 (Map p383; ☎ 744 2044; www.hotelformule1.com; Mikrofonvägen 30; r Skr310; P) Super-cheap, small, uninspiring rooms for up to three people (one flat rate, excludes breakfast). Bathroom facilities shared. About 4km southwest of city centre. Metro T-Telefonplan.

Mid-Range
PRIVATE ROOMS & APARTMENTS
A number of agencies can arrange good-value apartment or B&B accommodation (many with a two-night minimum). The going rate in the city centre is Skr400 to Skr500 for a single, Skr600 to Skr800 for a double. Agencies (with detailed websites):
Bed & Breakfast Service (☎ 660 5565; www.bedbreakfast.se)
Bed & Breakfast Agency (☎ 643 8028; www.bba.nu)

HOTELS
In this mid-range price category (Skr650 to Skr1500 for a weekday double, including breakfast), you'll find a number of homey places in mostly residential locations a little off the tourist path (but with good transport connections), without all the trimmings of the grander hotels. See also the combined hotel/hostel options listed in the budget section.

Hotellcentralen (see p366) can find you suitable hotel accommodation for a fee of Skr60.

Hotel Tre Små Rum (Map pp364-6; ☎ 641 2371; www.tresmarum.se; Högbergsgatan 81; r Skr695) This cute, cosy place in a quiet part of Söder started off with three small rooms, as the name suggests, but has grown to seven. Rooms are small but comfortable, bathroom facilities are shared, and rental bikes are available (Skr85 per day).

SWEDEN

It's hard to beat for value and location. Metro T-Mariatorget.

Oden Pensionat (☎ 796 9600; www.pensionat.nu; s Skr600-950, d Skr740-1295) Vasastan (Map pp364-6; Odengatan 38); City (Map pp370-1; Kammakargatan 62); Södermalm (Map pp370-1; Hornsgatan 66) This is a 'chain' of three affordable pensions in char acterful old buildings with attractive, comfortable rooms. Prices vary at different lo cations and according to room size and facili ties; reasonable summer discounts apply.

Hotel Gustav Vasa (Map pp364-6; ☎ 343801; www .gustavvasahotel.se; Västmannagatan 61; s Skr595-995, d Skr795-1260; **P**) The Gustav Vasa is right on Odenplan in the north of town and housed in a building from 1899. There's an antique lift and a variety of rooms – the cheapest are well appointed and have private bathrooms located outside the room, in the corridor. Some of the larger rooms have beautiful ceramic stoves. Parking is Skr125.

Queen's Hotel (Map pp370-1; ☎ 249460; www .queenshotel.se; Drottninggatan 71A; s/d Skr750/795, s/d with private bathroom from Skr895/995; **⬜**) In an early-20th-century building on the pedestrian mall, this friendly, family-run hotel has comfortable rooms of varying sizes and luxury, with shared or private facilities.

Columbus Hotell (Map pp364-6; ☎ 5031 1200; www .columbus.se; Tjärhovsgatan 11; budget s/d Skr695/895, hotel s/d Skr1250/1550, s/d discount Skr950/1250; **P**) This Södermalm option is set around a cobblestone courtyard and by a pretty park. The comfortable budget rooms are on the 3rd floor (no lift) and have phone and TV, but bathroom facilities are shared. There are also attractive hotel-standard rooms. Parking is a pricey Skr150 per day.

Mälardrottningen (Map pp370-1; ☎ 5451 8780; www.malardrottningen.se; Riddarholmen; s/d from Skr1100/1220, s/d discount from Skr915/1030) This classy vessel, launched in 1924 and now anchored off Riddarholmen, was once the world's largest motor yacht. The deep blue carpets, dark wood fittings and restaurant (with a bar in the bridge) create a great maritime atmosphere. All cabins have private bathrooms.

August Strindberg Hotell (Map pp370-1; ☎ 325 006; www.hotellstrindberg.se; Tegnérgatan 38; s/d from Skr825/1425, s/d discount Skr825/925) This quiet, family-run hotel offers 21 rooms and personalised service. Entry through a street-front apartment block takes you to the hotel, set in a pretty courtyard. There's an inviting break fast room and some garden seating. Rooms

vary in size and style but all are well appointed.

Rex Hotel (Map pp364-6; ☎ 160040; www.rexhotel .se; Luntmakargatan 73; s/d Skr1190/1490, s/d discount Skr790/990; **⬜**) This funky, new boutique hotel has colourful modern rooms, excellent facilities and ultra-friendly staff. There are plans for a courtyard garden, and across the road the finishing touches are being made to transform a lovely old building into a stylish sister hotel.

Top End

There's no shortage of Stockholm hotels that fall into this category (Skr1500 and upwards for a weekday double). The listed price, however, is rarely the lowest available – always ask about special deals and discounts when booking.

Rica City Hotel Gamla Stan (Map pp370-1; ☎ 723 7250; www.rica.se; Lilla Nygatan 25; s/d Skr1695/1945, s/d discount Skr950/1590) One of only five hotels on Gamla Stan (all understandably popular). A classy place in a great location, housed in a 17th-century building and with elegant, unfussy decor and good service (although rooms can be on the small side).

Scandic Hotel Hasselbacken (Map pp364-6; ☎ 5173 4300; www.scandic-hotels.com/hasselbacken; Hazeliusbacken 20; s/d Skr1690/1990, s/d discount Skr1190/1390) There's only one hotel on the pretty green island of Djurgården, and it's hard to imagine a lovelier setting for a stay in Stockholm. This 1925 building is in the heart of the area's attractions, and facilities (and the on-site restaurant) are of a high standard.

Rival Hotel (Map pp370-1; ☎ 5457 8900; www.rival .se; Mariatorget 3; s/d from Skr1990/2290, s/d discount weekends Skr1190/1390, s/d discount summer Skr795/995) ABBA's Benny Andersson is a co-owner of this fabulous new place in Södermalm. The complex includes a vintage 1940s movie theatre, café and bakery, lounge, swank cocktail bar and well-preserved retro architecture throughout, plus brilliant attention to detail. Summer rates are a bargain.

EATING

Like nearly every other aspect of life here, Stockholm's restaurant scene constantly seeks to be at the forefront of fashion. If there's a food trend happening, you can bet that all the hot restaurants in town are offering a takes on it. A great way to sample the options is to visit during the Smaka på Stockholm (Taste of Stockholm) festival (www .smakapastockholm.se). This 10-day food festival from late May to early June is staged in Kungsträdgården. Besides sampling from the kitchens of local restaurants, you can also take in a number of performances.

Stockholm has thousands of eateries to cater to all tastes and budgets, ranging from inexpensive lunch cafeterias and old-style *konditori* to five-star gourmet establishments; the city is also home to colourful market halls that are tourist attractions in their own right.

Gamla Stan

Tourists, not surprisingly, love Gamla Stan and many dine on Västerlånggatan, but be sure to check out the offerings along Stora Nygatan and Österlånggatan – the area around Köpmantorget is home to many classy favourites.

Café Art (Map pp370-1; ☎ 411 7661; Västerlånggatan 60; snacks Skr35-65) This barrel-vaulted and brick-lined cellar is an atmospheric retreat from the Gamla Stan souvenir grab on Västerlånggatan. Rest weary legs while enjoying a sandwich or coffee and cake.

Chokladkoppen (Map pp370-1; ☎ 203170; Stortorget 18; snacks & sweets Skr40-70; ☺ to 11pm/midnight) In a pair of gorgeous Renaissance buildings from the 1650s you'll find the gay-friendly café Chokladkoppen and its next-door sibling, Kaffekoppen. Service can be slow, but the food is good and the outdoor area is one of the best hang-outs in Gamla Stan.

Hermitage (Map pp370-1; ☎ 411 9500; Stora Nygatan 11; mains Skr65-85) One for the herbivores: Hermitage rustles up fine vegetarian fare from around the world. The lunch deal (Skr65 weekdays) is great value.

Michelangelo (Map pp370-1; ☎ 719391; Västerlånggatan 62; lunch Skr65-75, mains Skr89-240) A classic Italian trattoria, complete with checked tablecloths, painted ceilings and Roman statues. Always busy, and offering reasonably priced pizza and pasta options.

Zum Franziskaner (Map pp370-1; ☎ 411 8330; Skeppsbron 44; lunch Skr75, mains Skr97-200) Founded by German monks, this wonderful, museum-like place is among the oldest restaurants in town. At the lower end of the price scale, it serves German and Austrian classics (sausages, schnitzel) as well as enormous Swedish *husmanskost* meals such as grilled herring and *pytt i panna*.

Grill Ruby & Bistro Ruby (Map pp370-1; ☎ 206015; Österlånggatan 14; mains Skr150-250) The neighbouring Ruby restaurants have a *Paris, Texas* theme. Grill Ruby is an American-style place with lots of meat and fish options from the grill; Bistro Ruby is low-lit and more intimate, with a French-influenced menu.

Djurgården

With so many places on the touristy island of Djurgården, you won't go hungry. For fine food in an old villa with a lovely garden setting, head to **Wärdshuset Ulla Winbladh** (Map pp364-6; ☎ 663 0571; Rosendalsvägen 8; lunch Skr80, à la carte mains Skr195-265), along the northern loop road. The menu features superbly prepared traditional meals, including meatballs, herring and crayfish tails.

Central

Sirap (Map pp364-6; ☎ 612 9419; Surbrunnsgatan 31A; dishes Skr30-95) This bustling café is a brunch hot spot, with a huge menu of breakfast dishes (great pancakes), sandwiches and salads.

Bakfickan (Map pp370-1; ☎ 676 5808; Karl XIIs Torg; mains Skr95-200; ☺ Mon-Sat) Not far from Kungsträdgården is Kungliga Operan (Stockholm's opera house), housing the late-19th-century, super-posh restaurant Operakällaren, the lively Café Opera (more a nightclub than a café) and one of our Stockholm favourites, the intimate Bakfickan – literally the 'back pocket' of Operakällaren. This casual little restaurant features great service, Art Nouveau decor and stools around the bar, and serves gourmet-quality *husmanskost* at moderate prices.

Lao Wai (Map pp364-6; ☎ 673 7800; Luntmakargatan 74; dishes Skr115-175; ✆ dinner Tue-Sat) Heading further north, Luntmakargatan is home to some great Asian eateries. This minimalist restaurant offers strictly vegetarian Chinese food – spices coax miraculous flavours out of various tofu and vegetable combinations.

Tranan (Map pp364-6; ☎ 5272 8100; Karlbergsvägen 14; mains Skr95-270) This busy, stylish place on Odenplan is one of the best neighbourhood restaurants in Stockholm, constantly recommended by devoted locals. There's a comprehensive menu encompassing simple Swedish fare and pricier international dishes. The basement bar attracts a hip young crowd.

Fredsgatan 12 (Map pp370-1; ☎ 248052; Fredsgatan 12; dishes Skr120-250) With chic minimalist decor, this fine restaurant (known simply as F12) has an award-winning chef, a menu divided into taste categories (light, nature, ocean, meat, sweets) and an unbeatable setting, especially in summer when the terrace is open.

Hötorgshallen (Map pp370-1; Hötorget) has many Mediterranean food stalls and good specialist shops, while **Kungshallen** (Map pp370-1; Hötorget), opposite, has an enormous selection of food stalls where you can eat anything you fancy from Tex-Mex to Indian or Cajun at budget prices. In between, on Hötorget itself, is a colourful open-air market with vendors selling fresh fruit, vegies and flowers.

The handiest central supermarket is **Hemköp** (Map pp370-1; Klarabergsgatan 50; ✆ 8am-

9pm Mon-Fri, 10am-9pm Sat & Sun), in the basement of the Åhlens department store, and there's a **Systembolaget** (Map pp370-1; Klarabergsgatan 62; ✆ 10am-8pm Mon-Fri, 10am-3pm Sat) nearby for buying alcohol.

Perfect for night owls and close to Centralstationen, **Kebab House** (Map pp370-1; cnr Vasagatan & Kungsgatan; snacks from Skr19) offers cheap kebabs and burgers until 5am daily.

Next to the Dubliner pub on Smålandsgatan you'll find the entrance to **Birger Jarlspassagen** (Map pp370-1), an arcade full of cafés. Alternatively, head to the stalls along the edge of Kungsträdgården for a range of quick bites. A park favourite is **Café Piccolino** (Map pp370-1; Kungsträdgården), a long and lean café with large windows to capture the sun (and the passing parade), plus outdoor tables.

Östermalm

Birger Jarlsgatan and Stureplan have many upmarket places and lots of alfresco areas where it's important to see and be seen.

Sturekatten (Map pp370-1; ☎ 611 1612; Riddargatan 4; sandwiches Skr35-70) One of the city's most traditional cafés, full of old-world charm, antiques and velvet sofas. Having afternoon tea here is like visiting your posh greataunt's house.

Sturehof (Map pp370-1; ☎ 440 5730; Stureplan 2; mains Skr105-295) One of Stockholm's busiest restaurants, particularly in summer when the terrace is perpetually hopping. Sturehof has a modern menu vast enough to satisfy every taste, including lots of seafood and some reasonably priced *husmanskost* options.

Kungsholmen

The best eat street on this island is Scheelegatan, with some interesting international options.

Indian Curry House (Map pp364-6; ☎ 650 2024; Scheelegatan 6; dishes Skr65-120) A small, basic restaurant that's a firm favourite, serving what is widely regarded as Stockholm's cheapest Indian food (all the favourites are here, and there are good vegetarian options).

Mamas & Tapas (Map pp364-6; ☎ 653 5390; Scheelegatan 3; tapas Skr35, mains Skr98-158) A fun, bright and bustling tapas joint with a great selection of snacky stuff to wash down with sangria or vino, plus larger meals (pasta, paella, fish) if you want a plate all to yourself.

Hot Wok Café (Map pp364-6; ☎ 654 4202; Hantverkargatan 78; mains Skr99-172) This busy place is right

AUTHOR'S CHOICE

Östermalms Saluhall (Map pp370-1; Östermalmstorg; ✆ Mon-Sat) is ideal for sightseers needing some quick and affordable nourishment and is the perfect place to fill a picnic basket. This covered market hall is now home to a multitude of gourmet food stalls and some excellent eat-in options. The building itself is a Stockholm landmark, designed as a Romanesque cathedral of food in 1885. For a quick lunch, belly up to the bar at Depå Sushi, enjoy a hearty serve of fish soup from Lisa Elmqvist, choose something from the daily specials at the classy Tysta Mari or head upstairs to the vegetarian lunch buffet (Skr75) in the pretty, old-fashioned restaurant Örtagården.

by the new STF hostel, with funky decor, friendly staff and fast service. The noodle-based, pan-Asian dishes are enormous.

Södermalm

This area is home to some great restaurants and cafés, and there are many cool choices on Götgatan.

Crêperie Fyra Knop (Map pp364–6; ☎ 640 7727; Svartensgatan 4; crepes Skr36-74; ☉ dinner) An intimate little place with lots of small rooms tucked away just off the main drag in Söder. It serves tasty, well-priced crepes (savoury from Skr60, sweet from Skr36).

Hermans (Map pp364–6; ☎ 643 9480; Fjällgatan 23A; lunch Skr68, mains Skr98) A great place where you'll get gigantic portions of wholesome vegetarian food, served on tables in two barrel-vaulted basement rooms, or summer veranda seating with a million-dollar view of the city.

Östgöta Källaren (Map pp364–6; ☎ 643 2240; Östgötagatan 41; lunch Skr60-85, mains Skr70-180) A popular neighbourhood restaurant-bar with lots to recommend it – a dimly lit romantic atmosphere, friendly service and unpretentious *husmanskost*, plus it's a nice place to linger over a drink or two.

Eriks Gondolen (Map pp370–1; ☎ 641 7090; Stadsgården 6; mains Skr185-295) Top of the heap – figuratively and literally. Eriks Gondolen is at the top of Katarinahissen, with a spectacular view of the city and a menu of gourmet offerings. The grill bar has a lower-priced bistro menu.

Söderhallarna (Map pp364–6; Medborgarplatsen; ☉ Mon-Sat) This modern food hall includes a vegetarian restaurant, deli, cheese shop, Asian supermarket and a pub. It's not the most atmospheric place, however, so make plans to enjoy your lunch in the outdoors on Medborgarplatsen.

For a quick, cheap snack, head to **Jerusalem Royal Kebab** (Map pp364–6; Götgatan 61; ☉ 24hr), with kebabs and felafels from just Skr25. Another fast-food alternative, but with a much more Swedish slant, is the **Nystekt Strömming** (Map pp370–1; Södermalmstorg) van outside metro T-Slussen, where you'll get some of the best fried herring in Stockholm.

DRINKING

It seems that almost every decent restaurant in Stockholm has a cool bar attached. Many cafés bring in a DJ in the evening and, *voila*, another groovy bar is born.

In Södermalm, check the Götgatan, Östgötagatan and Skånegatan area, and around Medborgarplatsen. In Kungsholmen, visit Scheelegatan and Flemminggatan, and in the northern centre try the Tegnérgatan and Rörstrandsgatan areas. For the ultra-fashionable late-night bars and clubs frequented by the city's beautiful people, head to Stureplan. The following drinking venues are generally open daily until 1am.

Wirströms Irish Pub (Map pp370–1; ☎ 212874; Stora Nygatan 13) This Gamla Stan place feels more like a medieval dungeon than an Irish pub – the dark, mysterious, brick-vaulted cellar goes on forever. Arrive early to find a candlelit corner and snuggle in with a pint of Guinness.

Café Tabac (Map pp370–1; ☎ 101534; Stora Nygatan) A classy but casual corner place in Gamla Stan where you can enjoy vino, cocktails and a range of tapas-style snacks.

Loft (Map pp370–1; ☎ 411 1991; Regeringsgatan 66) A totally unpretentious Irish pub with wooden beams, Irish beers and whiskeys, and a full restaurant menu. The mostly Irish staff are everyone's best friend, and you can't leave without have met 10 new people.

Cliff Barnes (Map pp370–1; ☎ 318070; Nortullsgatan 45; ☉ closed Sun) Join the locals at this rowdy place to sing along to popular tunes, dance on the tables and get inebriated. It's a hugely popular beer hall–type place with an outdoor bar in summer.

Lokal (Map pp364–6; ☎ 650 9809; Scheelegatan 8) This newish place on Kungsholmen is the kind of bar-restaurant you'd be pretty pleased to call your local. A classic combination of stylish decor, interesting young crowd and good tapas-style food.

Fenix (Map pp370–1; ☎ 640 4506; Götgatan 40) This eclectically decorated bar-restaurant has a dizzying chequerboard floor, crazy art and decoratively moulded ceiling; grab a seat at the window and watch the action on Götgatan.

Mosebacke Etablissement (Map pp370–1; ☎ 5560 9890; www.mosebacke.se, Swedish only; Mosebacketorg 3) Even if you're not partaking in Mosebacke's many cool club nights, its terrace bar in summertime is a fantastic place to relax with a drink and gaze out over Gamla Stan from the heights of Söder.

The outdoor restaurant-bars either side of the bridge leading across to Djurgården, do a roaring trade on fine summer days; come

SWEDEN

here for long leisurely drinks and people-watching. Try **Tvillingarnas** (Map pp364-6; ☎ 663 3714; Strandvägskajen 27) and **Djurgårdsbrons Sjöcafé** (Map pp364-6; ☎ 660 5757; Djurgårdsbron).

Head to the unique **Ice Bar** (Map pp370-1; ☎ 5056 3000; Vasaplan; ☿ 4.30pm-midnight Mon-Fri, 3pm-midnight Sat) inside the Nordic Sea Hotel for a taste of life at the Ice Hotel in the country's far north (see p431). For an entry charge of Skr125 you get to play inside a bar filled with ice sculptures where the temperature is a constant -5°C (spunky silver poncho provided) and select a drink to imbibe from a glass made of ice.

ENTERTAINMENT

På Stan ('On the Town') is an arts-and-culture supplement found in the Friday edition of *Dagens Nyheter* (one of Stockholm's two main daily newspapers, see www.dn.se, in Swedish only). *Nöjesguiden* (www.nojes guiden.se) is a free, monthly, music-focused entertainment paper with club listings. Both these publications are in Swedish only but most of the listings and advertisements for events are easy enough to understand.

The www.ticnet.se website has information in English about larger events.

Concerts & Theatre

Stockholm is a theatre city, with outstanding dance, opera and music performances; for an overview, pick up the free *Teater Guide* from tourist offices (online at www.iti.a.se). For tickets, contact the tourist office, theatre box offices or **Biljett Direkt** (☎ 0771-707070; www.ticnet.se). Operas are usually performed in their original language, while theatre performances are invariably in Swedish.

Major theatres include the **Drottningholms Slottsteater** (Map p383; ☎ 660 8225; www.drottningholms slottsteater.dtm.se; Drottningholm), a unique 18th-century theatre at the royal palace (p384) which stages opera and ballet productions in summer; **Konserthuset** (Map pp370-1; ☎ 5066 7788; www.konserthuset.se; Hötorget), featuring classical concerts and other musical events, including the Royal Philharmonic Orchestra; **Kungliga Dramatiska Teatern** (Map pp370-1; ☎ 667 0680; www .dramaten.se; Nybroplan), the Royal Theatre (aka Dramaten), which stages a range of plays in a fantastic Art Nouveau environment; and **Kungliga Operan** (Map pp370-1; ☎ 248240; www.operan .se; Gustav Adolfs Torg), the place to go for opera and classical ballet.

Live Music

Live jazz is popular in the capital and the **Stockholm Jazz Festival** (www.stockholmjazz.com) is held annually in mid-July. The small and intimate **Glenn Miller Café** (Map pp370-1; ☎ 100322; Brunnsgatan 21) has live jazz a few nights a week, and the larger **Jazzclub Fasching** (Map pp370-1; ☎ 5348 2960; www.fasching.se; Kungsgatan 63) is one of Stockholm's main jazz venues, attracting performers from around the world as well as local talent.

In Gamla Stan, **Stampen** (Map pp370-1; ☎ 205 793; www.stampen.se; Stora Nygatan 5) has live blues and jazz concerts nightly. **Mosebacke Etablissement** (Map pp370-1; ☎ 5560 9890; www.mosebacke.se; Mosebacketorg 3) in Södermalm is an excellent bar, nightclub and concert venue, featuring all sorts of music and performers. Summer sees outdoor concerts performed at places such as **Gröna Lund Tivoli** (p368).

Cinemas

If you want to see a film on a weekend, it's a good idea to purchase tickets in advance. Films are almost always screened in their original language, with Swedish subtitles.

There are countless cinemas around the city; check the local newspapers for details. The 10-screen **BioPalatset** (Map pp364-6; ☎ 644 3100; Medborgarplatsen, Södermalm) and **Filmstaden Sergel** (Map pp370-1; ☎ 5626 0000; Hötorget), adjacent to Hötorgshallen, screen mainstream offerings.

Gay & Lesbian Venues

The gay scene is well established in Stockholm, and Sweden's famous open-mindedness means that nonheteros are welcome in almost all bars and clubs. There is no real 'gay district', although a large section of the gay population live in Södermalm. The tourist office publishes a brochure listing popular gay venues, but the best source of local information is the free, monthly magazine *QX* (see p437).

Tiptop (Map pp364-6; ☎ 329800; Sveavägen 57), at the RFSL headquarters, is a long-running nightclub; the predominantly gay weekday crowd is almost inevitably invaded by straights at the weekend.

There are some popular gay restaurant-bars on Gamla Stan, including **Mandus** (Map pp370-1; ☎ 206055; Österlånggatan 7) and **Torget** (Map pp370-1; ☎ 205560; Mälartorget), while **Chokladkoppen** (Map pp370-1; ☎ 203170; Stortorget 18) is a cheery café-bar staffed by pretty young things.

Lady Patricia (Map pp370-1; ☎ 743 0570; www .ladypatricia.se; Stadsgårdskajen 152) is a rather fabulous nightclub on board a ship with a unique history. It's moored near Slussen and also has a restaurant on board. It's known for its great gay nights (complete with drag show) that draw partiers of all persuasions every Sunday.

Nightclubs

Östermalm's Stureplan is the pinnacle of chic, trendy clubs in Stockholm, and supercool **Spy Bar** (Map pp370-1; ☎ 5450 3704; Birger Jarlsgatan 20; admission Skr125; ☒ Wed-Sat) is its crown jewel. Capping off a night of clubbing by standing in line at the Spy Bar spotting local celebrities is a favourite activity; actually being admitted to the bar is icing on the cake. Nearby **Sturecompagniet** (Map pp370-1; ☎ 611 7800; Sturegatan 4), with several rooms over three floors, is usually slightly more welcoming. Be aware that the door policy at many places in this area is strict, and a number of them have high entry charges (Skr100 is not uncommon). And remember, the longer the queue, the more prestigious the bar and the higher the drink prices.

For something a bit more down-to-earth, head to **La Habana** (Map pp364-6; ☎ 166465; Sveavägen 108), an atmospheric Cuban restaurant-bar featuring cigars, rum and lots of salsa-ing, or **Kvarnen** (Map pp364-6; ☎ 643 0380; Tjärhovsgatan 4) in Söder – beyond the traditional beer hall is a hot dance party, with DJ nights ranging from reggae to house. Queues are constant.

SHOPPING

Stockholm's fascination with style and design means there are endless opportunities to pick up clothing and interior-design items from top-notch names. Swedish-made crafts tend to be of a uniformly high quality, and some of the best souvenirs include the country's famous glassware; painted wooden horses from Dalarna; intricately carved woodwork; linen tablecloths and handtowels; and amber and silver jewellery. If you're planning to spend up and you come from outside the EU, see p438 for details on tax-free shopping.

Look out for *hemslöjd* signs, indicating handicraft sales outlets. Stores specialising in traditional handicrafts include **Svensk Helmslöjd** (Map pp370-1; ☎ 232115; Sveavägen 44) and

Svenskt Hantverk (Map pp370-1; ☎ 214726; Kungsgatan 55). Another good place to buy traditional items is at Skansen (p368). For funkier pieces, venture along to **DesignTorget** (www.designtorget.se; Central Map pp370-1; ☎ 5083 1520; basement, Kulturhuset, Sergels Torg; Södermalm Map pp370-1; ☎ 462 3520; Götgatan 31), which showcases the works (usually quite affordable) of both established and new local designers.

Shops are generally open 10am to 6pm Monday to Friday, 10am to 5pm Saturday and noon to 4pm Sunday, although smaller shops are often closed on Sundays and have limited Saturday hours. You can shop up a storm in the department stores: **NK** (Map pp370-1; ☎ 762 8000; Hamngatan), **Åhlens** (Map pp370-1; ☎ 676 6000; Klarabergsgatan 50) and **PUB** (Map pp370-1; ☎ 402 1611; Drottninggatan 72-76).

Stockholm's top five shopping streets:

Drottninggatan (Map pp370-1) A central pedestrian mall full of the practical and the affordable.

Biblioteksgatan (Map pp370-1) Big-name fashion-designer boutiques in the Östermalm area.

Hamngatan (Map pp370-1) Department store NK on one side, shopping centre Gallerian on the other.

Götgatan (Map pp364-6, Map pp370-1) The main artery through Södermalm, lined with offbeat shops.

Västerlånggatan (Map pp370-1) Gamla Stan's mecca for souvenirs (tacky and otherwise).

GETTING THERE & AWAY
Air

See p439 for information on international flights to Sweden as well as domestic flights.

Stockholm's main airport, **Arlanda** (☎ 797 6000), is 45km north of the city centre and has all the facilities you could need. **Bromma airport** (☎ 797 6874), 8km west of Stockholm, is a minor airport used for some domestic flights. Two airports are used by some low-cost carriers and sometimes labelled as 'Stockholm', despite being a fair distance from the capital: **Skavsta airport** (☎ 0155-280 400) is 100km south of Stockholm, near Nyköping, and **Västerås airport** (☎ 021-805600) is near the town of Västerås, about 105km northwest of Stockholm. Transport connects the city with all airports (see p380). Information about facilities at each airport can be found on the website of Sweden's civil aviation authority, **Luftfartsverket** (www.lfv.se).

Boat

See p441 for details of international ferry connections from Stockholm and areas

SWEDEN

surrounding the city to Finland (Helsinki and Turku), Estonia (Tallinn) and Latvia (Riga). When booking tickets, inquire about buses run by the ferry companies from Cityterminalen to their harbours.

Frihamnen, about 3km northeast of the city centre, is the arrival and departure point for both **Tallink** (Map pp370-1; ☎ 666 6001; www.tallink.ee; Klarabergsgatan 31) ferries to/from Tallinn and **Riga Sea Line** (Map pp364-6; ☎ 510 015 00; www.rigasealine.lv; Frihamnen) services to/from Riga. To get to Frihamnen, take a connecting bus from Cityterminalen operated by the ferry company, or town bus No 1, 72 or 76.

Silja Line Office (Map pp370-1; ☎ 222140; www.silja.com; Kungsgatan 2) ferries depart for Helsinki and Turku from Värtahamnen, north of Frihamnen – take the connecting bus, walk from T-Gärdet or take local bus No 76 from T-Ropsten.

Viking Line (Map pp370-1; ☎ 452 4000; www.vikingline.fi; inside Cityterminalen) ferries sail to Turku and Helsinki from the terminal in northeast Södermalm. Take the connecting bus (Skr30) from Cityterminalen or walk 1.5km east of T-Slussen.

See p385 for boat connections from towns around Stockholm.

Bus

Cityterminalen (Map pp370-1; ☺ 3.30am-midnight) is above and next door to Centralstationen (follow the signs from within the main station hall, or use the street entrance on Klarabergsviadukten). From Cityterminalen there are long-distance buses to most major towns in Sweden and international destinations (see opposite for details of bus companies); airport buses (to Arlanda, Bromma, Skavsta and Västerås, see right); and ferry buses (to connect with the services of Silja Line, Viking Line, Destination Gotland and Tallink; see p441 for international ferry details). Cityterminalen has good facilities, including ATMs, foreign exchange, stores, cafés, lockers and Internet access.

Train

Stockholm is the hub for SJ's national services (see p440). Direct trains to/from Copenhagen, Oslo, Storlien (for Trondheim) and Narvik arrive and depart from Centralstationen (Stockholm C), as do the SL *pendeltåg* (commuter) services that operate within Stockholm county (see p446). The central

hall at **Stockholm Centralstationen** (Map pp370-1; ☺ 5am-12.30am) has all manner of facilities, including restaurants, shops, lockers, ATMs, Internet access and public toilets and showers. Train ticket offices are open as follows:
Domestic (☺ 7.30am-8pm Mon-Fri, 8.30am-6pm Sat, 9.30am-7pm Sun)
International (☺ 10am-6pm Mon-Fri)

GETTING AROUND
To/From the Airports
ARLANDA

The **Arlanda Express** (☎ 020-222224; www.arlandaexpress.com) train travels between Arlanda and Centralstationen (Skr180, 22 minutes) at regular intervals from around 5am to midnight (every 15 minutes from 6am to 10.30pm).

A cheaper option is the **Flygbussarna** (☎ 600 1000; www.flygbussarna.se) bus service between Arlanda airport and Cityterminalen (Skr89, 40 minutes). Buses run every 10 to 15 minutes, from 4am to 10pm from Cityterminalen and from 6.45am to 11.45pm in the opposite direction. The same trip in a taxi has a fixed price and costs around Skr400, but agree your fare first and don't use any taxi that doesn't have a contact telephone number displayed.

OTHER AIRPORTS

There are **Flygbussarna** (☎ 600 1000; www.flygbussarna.se) bus services from Cityterminalen to Bromma airport (Skr69, 15 to 20 minutes), Skavsta airport (Skr130, 80 minutes) and Västerås airport (Skr130, 75 minutes).

Bicycle

Stockholm has an extensive network of bicycle paths; tourist offices sell cycling maps but they're not usually necessary. Top day trips include: Djurgården; a loop going from Gamla Stan to Södermalm, Långholmen and Kungsholmen (on lakeside paths); Drottningholm (return by steamer); and Haga Park. Some long-distance routes are marked all the way from central Stockholm.

Bicycles can be carried free on SL local trains during off-peak times (ie not from 6am to 9am and 3pm to 6pm Monday to Friday), but they're not allowed in Centralstationen or the metro.

Djurgårdsbrons Sjöcafé (Map pp364-6; ☎ 660 57 57; Djurgårdsbron), by the bridge to Djurgården, rents bikes for Skr65/250 per hour/day and has options for longer rentals.

Not far away, **Cykel & Mopeduthyrningen** (Map pp364-6; ☎ 660 7959; Strandvägen kajplats 24), by the OK-Q8 petrol station, also rents bikes. City bikes cost Skr60/220/1000 per hour/day/week, whereas mountain bikes are Skr80/250/1200.

Boat

Djurgårdsfärjan city ferry services connect Djurgården with Nybroplan and Slussen, with many trips calling in at Skeppsholmen.

Strömma Kanabolaget (Map pp370-1; ☎ 5871 4000; www.strommakanalbolaget.com) operates ferries between Nybroplan and Djurgården (Skr35/60 one way/return, every 20 minutes 10am to 8pm daily mid-May to mid-August, weekends and holidays April to mid-May and mid-August to September).

Waxholmsbolaget (Map pp370 1; ☎ 679 5830; www .waxholmsbolaget.se) runs boats year-round between Djurgården and Slussen (Skr25/50 one way/return, every 10 to 20 minutes from 7am Monday to Friday and from 9am on weekends, running to midnight, from late April to mid-September, less frequently in the low season). Trips are free with the SL Tourist Card, but not with the Stockholm Card.

Car & Motorcycle

Driving in central Stockholm is not recommended: small one-way streets, congested bridges and limited parking all present problems and parking stations (P-hus) charge up to Skr50 per hour (the fixed evening rate is usually more reasonable). There's also talk of authorities introducing a congestion charge for drivers in the heart of the city, as has been implemented in central London.

If you have a car, one of the best, hassle-free options is to stay on the outskirts of town and catch public transport into the centre.

Public Transport

Storstockholms Lokaltrafik (SL; ☎ 600 1000; www .sl.se) runs all *tunnelbana* (T or T-bana) metro trains, local trains and buses within the Stockholm county. At T-Centralen there are SL information offices in the lower level of the station hall and at the Sergels Torg entrance. Both offices issue timetables and sell SL transport passes and the general Stockholm Card. You can call for schedule and travel information from 7am to 9pm Monday to Friday and 8am to 9pm weekends.

The Stockholm Card (see p363) allows you to travel on all SL trains and buses in greater Stockholm, as well as providing free entry to many city attractions. A cheaper alternative is to buy a 24-hour (Skr95/55 adult/child) or 72-hour (Skr180/110 adult/child) SL Public Transport pass, covering transport only. If you want to explore the county in rather more detail, bring along a passport photo and get yourself a 30-day SL pass (Skr600/360 adult/child).

The minimum fare on Stockholm's public transport system costs two coupons, and each additional zone costs another coupon (up to five coupons for four or five zones). Coupons are available individually for Skr15, or a better idea is to buy a 10-/20-coupon discount ticket for Skr80/145. Coupons are valid for an hour and must be stamped at the start of the journey. International rail passes aren't valid on SL trains.

BUS

Bus timetables and route maps can be complicated but are worth studying. Inner-city buses can be replaced by the *tunnelbana* or by walking, but useful connections to suburban attractions radiate from Sergels Torg, Fridhemsplan (on Kungsholmen), Odenplan and Slussen: bus No 47 runs from Sergels Torg to Djurgården (stopping out the front of Centralstationen); bus No 65 goes from Centralstationen to Skeppsholmen (for af Chapman hostel); and bus No 69 runs to the Ladugårdsgärdet museums and also to Kaknästornet.

Check where the regional bus hub is for different outlying areas. Islands of the Ekerö municipality (including Drottningholm Palace) are served by bus Nos 301 to 323 from T-Brommaplan. Buses to Vaxholm (No 670) and the Åland ferries (bus No 640 to Norrtälje then No 637 to Grisslehamn or No 631 to Kapellskär) depart from T-Tekniska Högskolan. Odenplan is the hub for buses to the northern suburbs, including Haga Park.

METRO

The most useful mode of transport in Stockholm is the *tunnelbana* (T), which converges on T-Centralen and is connected by an underground walkway to Centralstationen. There are three main through lines with branches – check that the approaching train is actually going your way.

SWEDEN

TRAIN

Local trains (called *pendeltåg*) are useful for connections to Nynäshamn (for ferries to Gotland); Märsta (for buses to Sigtuna and Arlanda airport); and Södertälje. There are also services to Nockeby (from T-Alvik); Lidingö (from T-Ropsten); Kårsta, Österskär and Näsbypark (from T-Tekniska Högskolan); and Saltsjöbaden (from T-Slussen).

TRAM

Djurgårdslinjen No 7 (Map p364-6; ☎ 660 7700; www .ss.se; adult/child Skr25/13) is a historical tram running between Norrmalmstorg and Skansen on weekends from April to December (daily June to August), passing most attractions on Djurgården. Separate fees apply for Stockholm Card–holders, but the SL Tourist Card is valid.

Taxi

There's usually no problem finding a taxi in Stockholm; costs are about Skr35 flagfall, then Skr8 to Skr9 per kilometre (more expensive late on Friday and Saturday nights). A trip within the city shouldn't cost more than Skr200. Reputable firms:

Taxi Kurir (☎ 300000)
Taxi Stockholm (☎ 150000)
Taxi 020 (☎ 020-939393)

AROUND STOCKHOLM

As gorgeous as the capital is, some of Sweden's loveliest areas are just outside the city and can easily be reached on a day trip or overnight excursion. The islands of the archipelago offer an idyllic retreat, or you can check out impressive royal palaces, an ancient Viking settlement or the picture-perfect Sigtuna.

You can explore the county of greater Stockholm with the SL Tourist Card (p381) or monthly passes that allow unlimited travel on all buses and local trains.

Vaxholm

☎ 08 / pop 9500

Vaxholm, about 35km northeast of the city, is the gateway to the central and northern reaches of Stockholm's archipelago and it swarms with tourists in summer. It has a collection of quaint summerhouses that were fashionable in the 19th century. The oldest buildings are in the Norrhamn area, a few minutes' walk north of the town hall,

but there's also interesting architecture along Hamngatan (the main street), plus galleries, boutiques, souvenir shops and cafés.

Take bus No 670 from T-Tekniska Högskolan or one of the frequent **Waxholmsbolaget** (☎ 679 5830; www.waxholmsbolaget.se) boats from Strömkajen (outside the Grand Hôtel; Skr65).

Stockholm Archipelago

☎ 08

The archipelago is the favourite time-off destination for Stockholm's locals, and summer cottages on rocky islets are popular among the well-to-do. Depending on which source you read, the archipelago has anything between 14,000 and 100,000 islands, although the common consensus is 24,000; many are worth visiting and you could almost choose your destination via the dartboard method. The www.stockholmtown.com website has a large section devoted to the archipelago, and www.skargardsstiftelsen.se is another great resource.

The biggest boat operator is **Waxholmsbolaget** (☎ 679 5830; www.waxholmsbolaget.se), and timetables and information are available from offices outside the Grand Hôtel on Strömkajen in Stockholm and at the harbour in Vaxholm. Its Båtluffarkortet (Skr490) is a pass valid for 16 days and giving unlimited rides plus a handy island map. Bikes can be taken on the ferries for a fee, but it's a better idea to hire at your destination.

It's also worth checking what **Cinderella Båtarna** (☎ 5871 4000; www.cinderellabatarna.com) has to offer. Its boats also go to many of the most interesting islands from Stockholm. If your time is short, a recommended tour is the Thousand Island Cruise offered by **Stromma Kanabolaget** (☎ 587 14000; www.strommakanalbolaget .com), running daily between July and mid-August. The full day's excursion departs from Stockholm's Nybrokajen at 9.30am and returns at 8.30pm; the price (Skr775) includes lunch, dinner and guided tours ashore. The tour visits a number of islands, and there are several opportunities for swimming.

While many islands can be visited on a day trip, you'll get a better experience if you stay overnight. Most main islands have hostels, but they tend to open only in summer and they're often booked out months in advance. For information on cottage rental (usually on a weekly basis), contact **Destination Stockholms Skärgård** (☎ 5424 8100; www.dess.se).

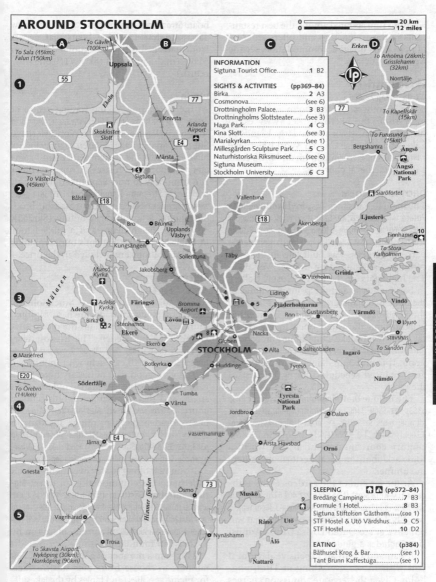

AROUND STOCKHOLM

0 _____ 20 km
0 _____ 12 miles

INFORMATION
Sigtuna Tourist Office.................1 B2

SIGHTS & ACTIVITIES (pp369–84)
Birka..2 A3
Cosmonova..............................(see 6)
Drottningholm Palace...............3 B3
Drottningholms Slottsteater......(see 3)
Haga Park....................................4 C3
Kina Slott.................................(see 3)
Mariakyrkan............................(see 1)
Millesgården Sculpture Park......5 C3
Naturhistoriska Riksmuseet.......(see 6)
Sigtuna Museum......................(see 1)
Stockholm University.................6 C3

SLEEPING (pp372–84)
Bredäng Camping......................7 B3
Formule 1 Hotel.........................8 B3
Sigtuna Stiftelsen Gästhem......(see 1)
STF Hostel & Utö Värdshus.........9 C5
STF Hostel..................................10 D2

EATING (p384)
Båthuset Krog & Bar................(see 1)
Tant Brunn Kaffestuga............(see 1)

Each island has its own character. Chichi **Sandhamn** village on Sandön is popular with sailors and day-trippers; if you'd like to stay overnight, stylish **Sands Hotell** (☎ 5715 3020; www .sandshotell.se; s/d Skr1200/1500) is a good choice.

Finnhamn has excellent swimming spots, but book in advance to stay at the **STF hostel** (Map above; ☎ 5424 6212; www.finnhamn.se; dm/s/d Skr275/410/550), the largest hostel in the archipelago with 80 beds.

Utö, far out in the southern archipelago, is popular among cyclists; there's an **STF Hostel** (Map above; ☎ 5042 0315; www.uto-vardshus.se; dm/s/d Skr325/325/650; ☼ May-Sep), with its reception at the nearby **Utö Värdshus** (Map above; ☎ 5042 0300; www.uto-vardshus.se; r per person from Skr795). The *värdshus* (inn) is rated among the best restaurants in the archipelago and offers an array of hotel and cottage accommodation; see the website for details.

Ekerö District

☎ 08 / pop 22,600

Some 20km west of Stockholm and surprisingly rural, the Ekerö district (www.ekero turism.se) consists of several large islands in Lake Mälaren, the Unesco World Heritage Listed sites of Drottningholm and Birka, and a dozen medieval churches.

DROTTNINGHOLM

The main Renaissance-inspired **Drottningholm Palace** (Map p383; ☎ 402 6280; www.royalcourt.se; adult/child Skr60/30; 10am-4.30pm May-Aug, noon-3.30pm Sep, noon-3.30pm Sat & Sun Oct-Apr), with geometric baroque gardens, was built late in the 17th century, about the same time as Versailles. The highlights are the Karl X Gustav Gallery in baroque style, and the painted ceilings of the State Bedchamber. The palace is home to the Swedish royal family, and you can either walk around the wings open to the public on your own or take a one-hour guided tour (no additional charge; English tours at 11am, noon, 1pm and 3pm daily from June to August, reduced schedules during the rest of the year).

The unique **Drottningholms Slottsteater** (Map p383; ☎ 5569 3100; www.drottningholmsslottsteater .dtm.se; tours Skr60/30; noon-4.30pm May, 11am-4.30pm Jun-Aug, 1-3.30pm Sep) is the original 18th-century court theatre and is well worth a tour; ask about musical performances here in summer.

At the far end of the gardens is the 18th-century **Kina Slott** (Map p383; ☎ 402 6270; adult/child Skr50/25; 11am-4.30pm May-Aug, noon-3.30pm Sep), a lavishly decorated 'Chinese pavilion' that was built as a gift to Queen Lovisa Ulrika. Admission includes a guided tour.

It can add up to an expensive day out if you wish to see everything at Drottningholm. Given the separate admission charges for each attraction, it's a good idea to use the Stockholm Card. You can bring a picnic and enjoy it in the gardens, or dine in one of the two restaurants by the palace. If you're not short of time you could cycle out here, otherwise take the metro to T-Brommaplan and change to bus No 301 or 323. The most pleasant way to get to Drottningholm is by

boat: **Strömma Kanalbolaget** (☎ 5871 4000; www .strommakanalbolaget.com) has boats that depart from Stadshusbron in Stockholm daily from May to mid-September (Skr80/110 one way/ return).

BIRKA

At the fascinating Viking trading centre of **Birka** (Map p383; ☎ 5605 1445; www.raa.se; adult/child Skr50/free; May-Sep), a Unesco World Heritage Site on Björkö in Lake Mälaren, archaeologists have excavated the ancient settlement's cemetery, harbour and fortress. Cruises to Birka run from May to mid-September; the return trip with **Strömma Kanalbolaget** (☎ 5871 4000; www.strommakanalbolaget.com) from Stadshusbron, Stockholm, is a full day's outing (Skr245). A visit to the museum and a guided tour in English of the settlement's burial mounds and fortifications are included in the price.

Sigtuna

☎ 08 / pop 6500

About 40km northwest of Stockholm is the picturesque lakeside town of Sigtuna, founded in around 980 and the oldest surviving town in Sweden. The friendly **tourist office** (Map p383; ☎ 5948 0650; www.sigtuna.se /turism; Stora gatan 33) can help with inquiries.

There's a good deal of history here: Stora gatan is probably Sweden's oldest main street, and there are ruins of 12th-century churches around town. **Mariakyrkan** (Map p383) has restored medieval paintings, and you can also visit the extensive **Sigtuna Museum** (Map p383; ☎ 5978 3870; Stora gatan 55; adult/child Skr30/free; noon-4pm Jun-Aug, noon-4pm Tue-Sun Sep-May).

If you're looking to stay overnight, there's little budget accommodation in town. **Sigtuna Stiftelsen Gästhem** (Map p383; ☎ 5925 8900; www.sigtunastiftelsen.se; Manfred Björkquists allé 2-4; s/d Skr770/1260, s/d discount weekends Skr540/830, s/d discount summer Skr500/600) is a pretty place run by a Christian foundation.

There are a number of good cafés and restaurants to choose from, plus supermarkets for picnic supplies (and tables by the lakeside, among the ducks). Don't miss the delightful **Tant Brunn Kaffestuga** (Map p383; ☎ 5925 0934; Laurentii gränd 3; snacks Skr20-40), a low-ceilinged 17th-century café set around a pretty courtyard just off Stora gatan. **Båthuset Krog & Bar** (Map p383; ☎ 5925 6780; Strandvägen; mains Skr180-240; dinner Tue-Sun) is a classy restaurant and bar, on a pontoon in the lake by the guest harbour.

Travel connections are easy from Stockholm. Take a local train to Märsta, from where there are frequent buses to Sigtuna (No 570 or 575, half-hourly). In summer there are cruises on Lake Mälaren from Stockholm and Uppsala (stopping at the fine baroque castle Skokloster, around 26km by road northwest of Sigtuna).

Ferry Ports

Nynäshamn, 50km south of Stockholm, is the main gateway to Gotland (p418); there are also regular ferries to Gdańsk (Poland). Regular local (SL) trains run from Stockholm to Nynäshamn; you can use SL passes, but international rail passes are not valid. There are also direct buses from Stockholm's Cityterminalen to connect with the Gotland ferries (Skr80), leaving 1¾ hours before ferry departure times.

Ferries sail between tiny **Kapellskär** (90km northeast of Stockholm) and Turku (Finland) via the Åland islands (see p442). The ferry companies offer a direct bus from Stockholm Cityterminalen to meet the ferries, but you can also take bus No 640 from T-Tekniska Högskolan to Norrtälje and change there to No 631, which runs every two hours or so (infrequent at weekends).

The quickest and cheapest ferries to the Ålands depart from **Grisslehamn**, about 100km from Stockholm; SL passes apply on bus No 637, which runs regularly from Norrtälje. **Eckerö Linjen** (☎ 0175-25800; www.eckerolinjen.fi) ferries sail from Grisslehamn to Eckerö (Åland; Skr50/80 low/high season, bicycles free, two hours, five a day). The company runs regular bus connections from Uppsala and from T-Tekniska Högskolan (Stockholm) to Grisslehamn two hours before most boat departures (Skr110/140 low/high season, including ferry ticket).

SVEALAND

This is where Sweden was born. Viking rune stones and forts are reminders of the time when Lake Mälaren offered safe harbours and links to the Baltic Sea and Russia. The kingdom of the Svea became synonymous with the entire country, and was thus called Svea Rike or Sverige.

Tourist drawcards include the historic attractions of bustling Uppsala and Örebro,

home to one of Sweden's loveliest castles. Further northwest, amid picturesque lake and forest scenery, lies Dalarna (sometimes called Dalecarlia in English), a county of rich folk culture and beautiful landscapes centred on Lake Siljan.

UPPSALA

☎ 018 / pop 191,100

Uppsala, about 70km from Stockholm, is the fourth-largest city in Sweden, and one of its oldest. It's a good excursion from the capital and has affordable accommodation. While you're here, you can soak up the history and genteel air of academia, or enjoy the bars and cafés catering to the city's 40,000 students.

Gamla (Old) Uppsala flourished as early as the 6th century. The cathedral was consecrated in 1435 after 175 years of building and the castle was first built in the 1540s, although today's edifice belongs to the 18th century. The city's sprawling university (www.uu.se) was founded in 1477 and is Scandinavia's oldest.

Information

The central **tourist office** (☎ 727 4800; www.uppsalatourism.se; Fyristorg 8; ◷ 10am-6pm Mon-Fri, 10am-3pm Sat year-round, also noon-4pm Sun late Jun–mid-Aug) is very efficient. Ask about the summer-only Uppsala Card (Skr100 for 24 hours), which gives you free admission to many of the town's sights plus free local transport. For currency exchange, **Forex** (Fyristorg 8; ◷ Mon-Sat) is next door to the tourist office.

The **public library** (cnr Sankt Olofsgatan & Svartbäcksgatan; ◷ Mon-Sat) offers free Internet access, but expect long waits. Other options:

Port 22 (Sankt Olofsgatan 32; per hr Skr40) Enter through the courtyard.

Sidewalk Express (Sankt Persgatan & Dragarbrunnsgatan; per hr Skr19) Internet kiosk inside McDonald's; voucher purchased from vending machine. Also inside Uppsala Centralstation.

UNT City Internet Café (cnr Fyristorg & Drottninggatan; per 15 min Skr10; ◷ Mon-Sat) Right by the tourist office, inside the *Upsala Nya Tidning* newspaper office.

Sights
GAMLA UPPSALA

Uppsala began at the three great **grave mounds** at Gamla Uppsala, 4km north of the modern city and well signposted (take bus No 2 from Stora Torget). The mounds are said to be the graves of legendary pre-Viking kings and lie

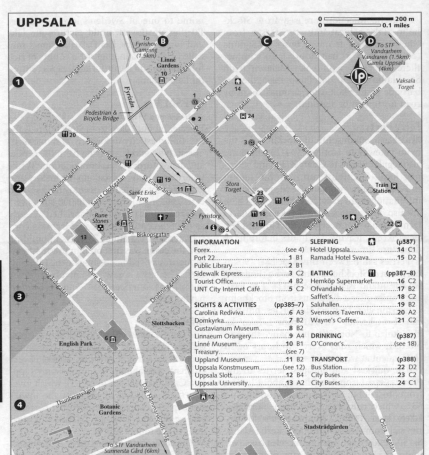

UPPSALA

INFORMATION		SLEEPING	(p387)
Forex	(see 4)	Hotel Uppsala	14 C1
Port 22	1 B1	Ramada Hotel Svava	15 D2
Public Library	2 B1		
Sidewalk Express	3 C2	EATING	(pp387–8)
Tourist Office	4 B2	Hemköp Supermarket	16 C2
UNT City Internet Café	5 C2	Ofvandahls	17 B2
		Saffet's	18 C2
SIGHTS & ACTIVITIES	(pp385–7)	Saluhallen	19 B2
Carolina Rediviva	6 A3	Svenssons Taverna	20 A2
Domkyrka	7 B2	Wayne's Coffee	21 B2
Gustavianum Museum	8 B2		
Linnaeum Orangery	9 A4	DRINKING	(p387)
Linné Museum	10 B1	O'Connor's	(see 18)
Treasury	(see 7)		
Uppland Museum	11 B2	TRANSPORT	(p388)
Uppsala Konstmuseum	(see 12)	Bus Station	22 D2
Uppsala Slott	12 B4	City Buses	23 C2
Uppsala University	13 A2	City Buses	24 C1

in a cemetery including about 300 smaller mounds and a great heathen temple.

The excellent **Gamla Uppsala Historical Centre** (☎ 239300; www.raa.se/olduppsala; adult/child Skr50/30; ☼ 11am-5pm May-Aug, noon-3pm Sun Sep-Apr) has exhibits of ancient artefacts excavated from Gamla Uppsala and the nearby archaeological sites. Guided tours of Gamla Uppsala will help you get more out of your visit – these are held at 3pm daily May to August (included in the entry price of museum).

Christianity arrived in the 11th century and with it the bishops and other church officials. From 1164 the archbishop had his seat in a cathedral on the site of the present **church**, which, by the 15th century, was enlarged and painted with frescoes.

Next to the flat-topped mound Tingshögen is the **Odinsborg Inn**, known for its horns of mead and the Viking feasts at its restaurant, but it's also home to a small café. **Disagården** (admission free; ☼ mid-May–Aug), a farm and village museum, is a few minutes from the church.

UPPSALA SLOTT

Originally constructed by Gustav Vasa in the mid-16th century, this **castle** (☎ 727 2485; adult/child Skr60/15; ☼ tours 1pm & 3pm Jun-Aug) features the state hall where kings were enthroned and a queen abdicated. It's open by guided tour only. The tour price also includes entry to **Uppsala Konstmuseum** (☎ 727 0000; adult/child Skr30/free; ☼ Tue-Sun), housed in the southern wing of the castle. The museum's works of art span five centuries.

OTHER SIGHTS

The Gothic **Domkyrka** (Cathedral; admission free; Domkyrkoplan; ☉ 8am-6pm) dominates the city, just as some of those buried there dominated their country, including St Erik, Gustav Vasa, Johan III and Carl von Linné. Inside, visit the **treasury** (☎ 187201; adult/child Skr30/free; ☉ daily May-Sep, Tue-Sun Oct-Apr) in the north tower.

Gustavianum Museum (☎ 471 7571; www.gustavianum.uu.se; Akademigatan 3; adult/child Skr40/free; ☉ Tue-Sun), the university museum, has an excellent antiquities collection and features an old 'anatomical theatre'. **Uppland Museum** (☎ 169100; Sankt Eriks Torg; adult/child Skr30/free; ☉ Tue-Sun), in an 18th-century mill, houses county collections from the Middle Ages.

Carolina Rediviva (☎ 471 3900; Dag Hammar-skjölds väg 1; adult/child Skr20/free; ☉ daily mid-May–mid-Sep, Mon-Sat mid-Sep–mid-May) is the old university library and has a display hall with maps and historical and scientific literature, the pride of which is the surviving half of the 6th-century *Codex Argentus* (Silver Bible), written on purple vellum in the extinct Gothic language.

The beautiful **Botanic Gardens** (admission free; ☉ 7am-9pm May-Aug, 7am-7pm Sep-Apr), including the **Linnaeum Orangery** and a tropical green house, are below the castle hill. They're not to be confused with the **Linné Museum** (☎ 471 25 76; Svartbäcksgatan 27; adult/child Skr25/free; ☉ noon-4pm Tue-Sun Jun–mid-Sep) and its **gardens** (adult/child Skr20/free; ☉ May-Sep). The museum exhibits memorabilia of von Linné's work in Uppsala, and the garden, with more than 1000 herbs, was designed according to an 18th-century plan.

Sleeping

Fyrishov Camping (☎ 727 4960; www.fyrishov.se; Idrottsgatan 2; camp sites Skr115-130, 4-bed cabins from Skr450) This well-equipped, family-friendly camping ground is 2km north of the city, by the river at Fyrisfjädern and neighbouring a huge pool and sports complex. Take bus No 4, 6, 25 or 50.

STF Vandrarhem Sunnersta Herrgård (☎ 324220; Sunnerstavägen 24; dm/s/d Skr235/385/470, hotel s/d Skr590/680) Some 6km south of the centre in a beautiful green setting is this old manor house. Hostel rooms are small, or you can pay extra for a 'hotel' room – a larger room (still with shared bathroom) with linen and

breakfast included. Bike rental is available. Take bus No 20 or 50.

STF Vandrarhem Vandraren (☎ 104300; www.vandraren.com; Vattholmavägen 16; s/d Skr295/485; ☉ mid-Jun–mid-Aug) This is a second, summer STF hostel 2km north of town. It's a student residence the rest of the year and facilities, including private bathroom for each room, are top-notch. Bike rental is available. Take bus No 2, 20, 24 or 54.

Hotel Uppsala (☎ 480 5000; www.profilhotels.se; Kungsgatan 27; dm/s/d Skr235/415/590, hotel s/d from Skr1050/1275, hotel s & d discount Skr700) This huge hotel offers rooms for all budgets, including a good hostel section (affiliated with STF). Modern hotel-standard rooms are excellent and many have microwave, kettle and fridge. Discounted prices are a bargain.

Ramada Hotel Svava (☎ 130030; www.hotelsvava.com; Bangårdsgatan 24; s/d Skr1250/1535, s/d discount Skr650/800) Opposite the train station, this hotel has all the facilities of an upper-range business-style hotel, and offers good weekend and summer prices.

Eating & Drinking

There are several eateries on and around the pedestrian mall and Stora Torget, and around the cathedral. Visitors can also head to Sysslomansgatan for some good choices.

Saffet's (☎ 124125; Stora Torget 1; dishes Skr59) When it comes to quick sustenance and cheap food, Saffet's has the works – burgers, fish and chips, enchiladas, baked potatoes and kebabs.

O'Connor's (☎ 144010; Stora Torget 1; mains Skr59-180) Upstairs from Saffet's, O'Connor's is much as you'd hope for in an Irish pub anywhere in the world – crowded, lively, friendly and well stocked with Guinness. There's also live music most nights.

Svenssons Taverna (☎ 100908; Sysslomansgatan 14; mains Skr80-185; ☉ dinner Mon-Fri, lunch & dinner Sat & Sun) Mr Svensson appears to have the Uppsala eating and drinking scene stitched up with his great venues scattered over town. This one has a winning combination of rustic interior, shady outdoor eating area and gourmet pizzas under Skr100.

To keep students well supplied with caffeine, Uppsala has great cafés. **Ofvandahls** (☎ 132404; Sysslomansgatan 3-5) is a classy *konditori* full of old-world charm; **Wayne's Coffee** (☎ 710012; Smedsgränd 4) has good coffee and café fare in stylish modern surrounds.

SWEDEN

In the basement of Åhlens the central **Hem-köp supermarket** (Stora Torget) is open until 10pm nightly. The indoor produce market, **Saluhallen** (🕑 Mon-Sat), is between the cathedral and the river at Sankt Eriks Torg. Pop in for a browse and a bite to eat – it houses great stalls and cafés.

Getting There & Away

The bus station is outside the train station, on Kungsgatan. Bus No 801 departs at least twice an hour for nearby Arlanda airport (Skr80). Swebus Express runs regularly to Stockholm (Skr55), Örebro (Skr185) and Falun (Skr135). Frequent SJ trains run to/from Stockholm (Skr47 to Skr62); all train services to/from Gävle, Östersund and Mora stop in Uppsala. SL coupons or passes take you only as far as Märsta from Stockholm.

Getting Around

A local bus ticket costs from Skr20 and gives unlimited travel for two hours – just enough for a visit to Gamla Uppsala. Catch a city bus from Stora Torget or outside Scandic Hotel Uplandia on Dragarbrunnsgatan. **Upplands Lokaltrafik** (🕾 0771-141414) runs regional transport within the county; if you're staying long in the area, ask about rebate cards and the various passes available.

You can hire a bicycle at Fyrishov Camping or the STF hostels (or inquire at the tourist office).

ÖREBRO

🕾 019 / pop 125,000

Örebro is one of central Sweden's loveliest towns, with a photogenic castle, river and pretty gardens at its heart. The **tourist office** (🕾 212121; www.orebro.se/turism; 🕑 10am-6pm Mon-Fri, 10am-4pm Sat & Sun Jun-Aug, 10am-6pm Mon-Fri, 10am-2pm Sat & Sun Sep-May) is inside the castle. The **library** (Näbbtorgsgatan) is south of the town centre and has Internet access, as does **Video Biljarden** (Järntorget; per hr Skr35; 🕑 11am-midnight).

Sights

Admission to the once-powerful **Slottet** (🕾 212121; adult/child Skr50/free), now restored, includes a castle tour (in English at 1.30pm and 3.30pm daily mid-June to mid-August; the rest of the year, tours are in Swedish at 1pm on weekends). Tickets are purchased from the tourist office.

Outside the castle is the **Örebro Länsmuseum** (🕾 602 8700; Engelbrektsgatan 3; admission free; 🕑 11am-5pm), the combined regional and art museums.

A pleasant stroll east of the castle along the river will take you through Stadsparken. Bikes are available for rental from May to September from the kiosk at Hamnplan, on the river's edge.

In Stadsparken, the **Stadsträdgården** greenhouse precinct has a great café and, further east, there's the excellent **Wadköping** museum village, which has craft workshops, a bakery and period buildings. You can freely wander around here at any time, but the shops, exhibitions and museums are generally open from 11am to 4pm or 5pm from Tuesday to Sunday.

The commercial centre and some grand buildings are around Stortorget, including the 13th-century **St Nikolai kyrka** (🕑 Mon-Sat).

Sleeping & Eating

STF Vandrarhem Örebro (🕾 310240; www.hepa.se, Swedish only; Kaptensgatan 1; dm/s/d from Skr185/315/370) This hostel is very well hidden, some 1.6km northeast of the train station (get hold of a map before setting off). It has good facilities, including some en-suite rooms, and bike hire is available. Take bus No 16 or 31.

Livin' Lägenhetshotell (🕾 310240; www.livin.nu, Swedish only; apt Skr500) Next door to the hostel Örebro and run by the same management is this complex of bright, modern apartments. Each apartment has a fully equipped kitchen, bathroom and living area, and can sleep up to four (at a push).

Hotell Örebro (🕾 611 7300; www.hotellorebro.se; Storgatan 24; s/d from Skr895/1295, s/d discount Skr595/695) In a good location close to the bus and train stations as well as the castle, this newly renovated hotel offers comfortable rooms in a variety of sizes, and good discounted rates.

Restaurang & Café Stadsträdgården (🕾 139835; Floragatan 1; lunch buffet Skr75/98 Mon-Fri/Sat & Sun) Make a beeline for this lovely area in Stadsparken, with a restaurant (lunch only) and café (open all day) surrounded by lush plant life inside a greenhouse.

Slottskällaren (🕾 156960; Drottninggatan 1; lunch Skr79, mains Skr110-250) For something a little more formal, this elegant restaurant inside the Elite Hotel (right by the castle) has good-value lunches and posher dinners, including decent vegetarian selections. The **Bishop's Arms**

(☎ 156920), also part of the hotel, is an English-style pub with an outdoor terrace plus pub meals under Skr100.

Getting There & Away

You're well placed to go almost anywhere in southern Sweden from Örebro by long-distance buses, which leave from opposite the train station. Swebus Express has connections in all directions: to Norrköping; Karlstad and Oslo; Mariestad and Göteborg; Västerås and Uppsala; and Eskilstuna and Stockholm.

Train connections are similarly good. Direct SJ trains run to/from Stockholm every hour (Skr220); to get to Göteborg (Skr270), take a train to Hallsberg and change there. Other trains run daily to Gävle and Borlänge (where you can change for trains to Falun and Mora).

FALUN

☎ 023 / pop 54,600

Falun, traditionally the main centre of Dalarna, is worth a visit for its wealth of attractions. The town is synonymous with mining and with Stora, perhaps the world's oldest public company (first mentioned in 1288), and the mine is now World Heritage Listed and accessible to visitors. The popular **Falun Folkmusik festival** (www.falufolk.com) features world music as well as Nordic folk traditions and is held over four days in mid-July.

The **tourist office** (☎ 83050; www.visitfalun.se; Trotzgatan 10-12; ⏱ daily mid-Jun–mid-Aug, Mon-Sat mid-Aug–mid-Jun) can help with information. There's free Internet at the **library** (Kristinegatan 15), and **Billiard & IT Café** (Falugatan 4; per hr Skr40; ⏱ Mon-Sat) is a central cybercafé.

Sights & Activities

The **Kopparberget copper mine** (☎ 782030; www.kopparberget.com; mine tour & museum adult/child Skr90/45, museum only Skr40/20) was the world's most important by the 17th century and only closed in 1992 (it's now on Unesco's World Heritage List). As a by-product, the mine also provided the red coating that became the characteristic house paint of the age and is still in popular use today. The mine and museum are west of town at the top end of Gruvgatan (take bus No 709). You can go on an interesting one-hour tour of the bowels of the disused mine (bring warm clothing) or just check out the museum; call in advance

to find out the times of English-language tours. On weekdays from October to April it's necessary to book tours in advance.

Carl Larsson-gården (☎ 60053; www.carllarsson.se; tour adult/child Skr80/35; ⏱ daily May-Sep, Tue only Oct-Apr) is the beautiful early-20th-century home of the artist Carl Larsson and his wife Karin in the pretty village of Sundborn (13km from Falun; bus No 64). It's a bright, lively house with superb colour schemes, decoration and furniture. Tapestries and embroidery woven by Karin Larsson reveal she was as skilled an artist as her husband. Admission is by 45-minute guided tour only; call in advance for times of English tours.

There's more folk culture at **Dalarnas Museum** (☎ 765500; Stigaregatan; adult/child Skr40/20). This fine museum features local culture and art, and Nobel-winning novelist Selma Lagerlöf's study is preserved here.

The baroque interiors of **Kristine kyrka** (Stora Torget) show some of the riches that arrived in Falun, but don't miss the late-14th-century **Stora Kopparbergs kyrka**, the oldest building in town, off Mariabacken and a bit north of the centre.

Falun is a winter-sports centre with plenty of **ski runs**, **nordic courses** and **toboggan runs**, particularly in the Lugnet area, to the northwest. Take bus No 705 or 713.

Sleeping & Eating

STF Vandrarhem Falun (☎ 10560; www.stfvandrarhem.falun.just.nu; Vandrarvägen 3; dm/s/d Skr185/205/390) This large hostel is 3km east of the town (bikes are available for hire), with excellent facilities. Take bus No 701 or 712 to Koppartorget, from where it's a 10-minute walk.

Falu Fängelse Vandrarhem (☎ 795575; www.falufangelse.se; Villavägen 17; dm/s/d Skr200/300/400) A more central option is this friendly, well-equipped hostel, where accommodation is in the simple cells of an old prison, used up until the mid-1990s.

Hotel Falun (☎ 29180; www.hotelfalun.nu; Trotzgatan 16; s/d from Skr540/740, s/d discount Skr490/590) There are a few good hotel choices right by the tourist office, including this small place offering comfortable modern rooms with private toilet and shared shower (or you can pay extra for rooms with full private bathroom).

Café Kopparhattan (☎ 19169; Stigaregatan; lunch Skr70) This café is the pick of the town's lunchtime haunts, attached to Dalarnas Museum. Choose from tempting sandwiches, soups and cakes, or feel virtuous and fill up at the great-value vegetarian buffet.

Banken Bar & Brasserie (☎ 711911; Åsgatan 41; lunch Skr69, mains Skr105-210) A classy place with a grand interior. The appealing menu includes a '*gott & enkelt*' (good and simple) category featuring the likes of *gravad lax*, burgers and pasta (Skr105 to Skr130), plus fancier creations such as bouillabaisse or rack of lamb.

Getting There & Away

Falun isn't on the main railway lines – change at Borlänge when coming from Stockholm or Mora. Swebus Express has buses on the Göteborg–Karlstad–Falun–Gävle route, and also has connections to buses on the Stockholm–Borlänge–Mora route (some run via Uppsala).

Regional traffic is run by **Dalatrafik** (☎ 0771-959595) and covers all corners of the county of Dalarna. Tickets cost Skr15 for trips within a zone, and Skr15 extra for each new zone. A 31-day *länskort* (county card) costs Skr800 and allows you to travel throughout the county. Regional bus No 70 runs regularly on the Falun–Rättvik–Mora route.

LAKE SILJAN REGION

This pretty, traditional area in the county of Dalarna is a popular summer and wintersports destination, with reasonable-sized towns offering good facilities and attractions. Siljansleden (the Siljan Trail) extends for more than 300km around Lake Siljan and has **walking** and **cycling** paths – maps are available from tourist offices. Another way to enjoy the lake is by boat: in summer, MS *Gustaf Wasa* has a complex schedule of lunch, dinner and sightseeing cruises from the main towns of Mora, Rättvik and Leksand. Inquire at any of the area's tourist offices for a schedule. Also check out the Siljan area website at www.siljan.se. Tourist offices in the area can all help with accommodation, including cottages in the idyllic countryside.

In summer the area is busy with events: Leksand's **Midsummer Festival** is the most popular in Sweden. **Musik vid Siljan** (www.musik vidsiljan.se) is a week-long event taking place in early July with something to suit most tastes, including chamber, jazz and traditional folk music. The stunning Dalhalla venue in Rättvik hosts an **opera festival** in early August.

Rättvik

☎ 0248 / pop 10,900

Rättvik has sandy lakeside beaches for summer and ski slopes for winter. Don't miss the longest wooden pier in Sweden, the 625m **Långbryggan** out over the lake. Views from surrounding hills are excellent. Try the 725m-long **rodel run** (☎ 51300; 1/3 rides Skr45/110; ☽ Jun-Aug), a sort of summer bobsled chute in the hills east of town that's lots of fun. The **tourist office** (☎ 797210; rattvik@siljan.se; ☽ daily mid-Jun–mid-Aug, Mon-Fri mid-Aug–mid-Jun) is at the train station (on Hwy 70).

By the lake northwest of the train station, the 13th-century **church**, rebuilt in 1793, has 87 well-preserved **church stables**, the oldest dating from 1470. Further north is **Gammelgården** (☎ 51445; tours Skr40; ☽ mid-Jun–mid-Aug), an open-air museum with a good collection of furniture painted in local style.

Dalhalla (☎ 797950; www.dalhalla.se), an old quarry 7km north of Rättvik, is used as an open-air concert venue in summer – the acoustics are incredible and the setting is stunning. If there's a performance here while you're in town, don't miss it! Tickets usually start at Skr165. See tourist offices in the area for a programme of concerts, or check the website.

Tiny **Tällberg**, midway between Rättvik and Leksand, is a gem, but if you visit, you certainly won't be alone. This pretty village has a population of around 200 and is home to no fewer than eight upmarket hotels (most with attached restaurants), a few galleries and boutiques, and little else. It's a lovely place to enjoy lunch and have a wander. See www.in fotallberg.nu, in Swedish only but with links to all the hotels. Bus No 58 between Rättvik and Leksand stops in the village regularly.

On the lakeshore near the train station is **Siljansbadets Camping** (☎ 51691; www.siljansbadet .com; camp sites Skr105-155, 4-bed cabins from Skr310). **Rättviksparken** (☎ 56110; www.rattviksparken.fh.se, Swedish only; camp sites Skr100-130, r Skr300, cabins from Skr350; ☒) is by the river off Centralgatan (1km from the train station). Both camping grounds are large, well equipped and crowded in high season; book ahead if you're planning to travel between mid-June and mid-August.

By Rättviksparken camping ground is the highly rated hostel **STF Vandrarhem Rättvik** (☎ 10566; rattviksparken@rattviksparken.fh.se; Centralgatan; dm/s/d from Skr175/175/350), in a charming complex of old wooden buildings.

Behind the OK-Q8 petrol station on the road to Leksand, about 3km south of town, is the reasonable **Hotell Vidablick** (☎ 30250; www .hantverksbyn.se; Faluvägen; s/d Skr650/900, s/d discount Skr550/795), offering rustic hotel accommodation in grass-roofed huts. There's a restaurant on site.

The cheapest eateries are opposite the train station, and Storgatan is home to a few supermarkets. You might want to head to Tällberg or Mora for other evening options, as Rättvik doesn't excel in the restaurant department. **Restaurang Anna** (☎ 12681; Vasagatan 3; mains Skr95-160; ☽ Tue-Sun) is the best option (in fact the only option!) for finer dining in Rättvik. It's a good mid-range place in a pretty wooden cottage serving up Swedish and international dishes, including fish, lamb, pork and reindeer.

Buses depart from outside the train station. Dalatrafik's bus No 70 runs between Falun, Rättvik and Mora. Direct trains from Stockholm and Mora stop at Rättvik.

Mora
☎ 0250 / pop 20,000
The popular legend is that, in 1520, King Gustav Vasa fled on skis from Mora after hiding from the Danes. Two good yeomen of Mora chose to brave the winter and follow. **Vasaloppet**, the huge ski race which ends in Mora, commemorates Gustav's journey and involves 90km of gruelling nordic skiing. Around 15,000 people take part on the first Sunday in March.

The **tourist office** (☎ 592020; mora@siljan.se; Stationsvägen; ☽ daily mid-Jun–mid-Aug, Mon-Fri mid-Aug–mid-Jun) is at the train station.

There are a few quality attractions in and around Mora. **Vasaloppsmuseet** (☎ 39225; Vasagatan; adult/child Skr30/10; ☽ daily mid-May–Aug, Mon-Fri Sep–mid-May) has fascinating displays about the largest skiing event in the world, and the story behind it. **Zornmuseet** (☎ 592310; www.zorn .se; Vasagatan 36; adult/child Skr40/2) celebrates the works and private collections of the Mora painter Anders Zorn. The Zorn family house, **Zorngården** (☎ 592310; Vasagatan 36; tours adult/child Skr50/15), between the church and the museum, is an excellent example of a wealthy artist's house, reflecting Zorn's National Romantic aspirations. Access to the house is by guided tour only, every 30 minutes.

The Dala horses (or Dalahästar) are wooden horses painted in bright, cheerful colours,

and to many they represent the original, genuine symbol of Sweden, more powerful than the Swedish flag. The most reputable of the Dalahästar are made by **Nils Olsson Hemslöjd** (☎ 37200; ☽ daily mid-Jun–mid-Aug, Mon-Sat mid-Aug–mid-Jun) at Nusnäs, 10km southeast of Mora (bus No 108). Here you can inspect the workshops and buy up big at the souvenir outlet.

Outside the town of Orsa (16km north of Mora) is **Grönklitt Björnpark** (☎ 46200; www.orsa -gronklitt.se; adult/child Skr85/45; ☽ mid-May–mid-Sep), a great place where you can see bears, wolves and lynxes in fairly natural surrounds. The bears are usually fed around noon, when you'll get a great view of them. To get here, take bus No 104 from Mora to Orsa, then bus No 118 to the park.

SLEEPING & EATING
Mora Parken (☎ 27600; www.moraparken.se, Swedish only; Hantverkaregatan; camp sites Skr100-130, 2-/4-bed cabins from Skr270/385) This busy, family-friendly camping ground has good facilities in a great spot by the river northwest of the church.

STF Vandrarhem Mora (☎ 38196; Fredsgatan 6; dm/ s/d from Skr205/395/530) is an excellent hostel owned by Ann of **Målkull Ann's Pensionat** (☎ 38196; www .maalkullann.se; Vasagatan 19; s/d/tr from Skr550/760/1050), who also offers a good selection of B&B accommodation in the centre of town (with and without private bathroom).

Hotell Kung Gösta (☎ 15070; www.trehotell.nu, Swedish only; Kristinebergsgatan 1; s/d from Skr940/1140, s/d discount Skr595/755; 🐾), conveniently located opposite the main train station, has rather high weekday prices, but also has a much more reasonable hostel annexe, **Kristineberg Hostel** (same contact details; dm/s/d with private bathroom from Skr160/330/420), which includes breakfast.

There are a few old-style cafés on Kyrkogatan, plus fast-food joints and supermarkets. By Zornmuseet in the old part of town is **Claras Restaurang** (☎ 15898; Vasagatan 38; lunch Skr75, mains Skr65-195), an elegant place with a good menu of light meals and more substantial fare. Try the wonderful dessert of vanilla ice cream with warm cloudberries.

GETTING THERE & AWAY
All Dalatrafik buses use the bus station at Moragatan 23. Bus No 70 runs to Rättvik and Falun. Bus No 170 goes to Särna, Idre and Grövelsjön, near the Norwegian border.

Mora is an SJ terminus and the southern terminus of Inlandsbanan, which runs north to Gällivare in summer (see p446). The main train station is about 1km east of town, by the lake. The more central Mora Strand is a platform station in town but not all trains stop there, so check the timetable.

When travelling to Östersund, you can choose between the Inlandsbanan experience (Skr347, six hours) or the cheaper regular bus No 245 (Skr170, 5¼ hours, two daily).

You can rent bikes from **Intersport** (☎ 593 939; Kyrkogatan).

SKÅNE

If you tour around the southern county of Skåne (www.skanetur.se), you might occasionally feel as though you're in Denmark, not Sweden. Skåne, sometimes anglicised as Scania, was Danish until the mid-17th century – the influence of the Danish is still easily detected in the dialect and architecture. Indeed, many natives of Skåne look more towards nearby Copenhagen as their 'capital' rather than Stockholm.

Bicycle trips are popular in Skåne; there are numerous attractions in the gently rolling landscape and more hostels than any other region of Sweden. Other treats include castles, historic cities and pretty coastline.

MALMÖ

☎ 040 / pop 265,000

Malmö, the most 'continental' of Sweden's cities, is a lively and vibrant place, perhaps due to the influence of Copenhagen across the Öresund; the relatively large proportion of immigrants in the city adds a multicultural element. The remarkable 16km Öresund bridge and tunnel link, which includes Europe's longest bridge (7.8km), has brought Copenhagen and Malmö even closer.

Orientation

The Old Town is the city centre and is encircled by a canal. There are three main squares here: Stortorget, Lilla Torg and Gustav Adolfs Torg. Malmöhus castle, in its park setting, guards the west end. Across the canal on the northern side you'll find the bus and train stations.

Information

Cyberspace Café (Engelbrektsgatan 13; per hr Skr30-44) Internet café open until late; cheaper rates after 6pm.

Dot.Spot (Kalendegatan 13; per hr Skr25; ⊙ noon-6am) Internet café.

Forex (inside Centralstationen; ⊙ 7am-9pm) Currency exchange.

Library (Regementsgatan; ⊙ closed Sun May-Aug)

Malmö Card (1/2/3 days Skr130/160/190) Allows free bus transport, free entry to several museums and discounts at other attractions; available from tourist office.

Post Office (Skeppsbron 1; ⊙ 7am-7pm Mon-Fri) Near train station.

Tourist Office (☎ 341200; www.malmo.se; Centralstationen; ⊙ 9am-7pm Mon-Fri, 10am-5pm Sat & Sun Jun-Aug, 9am-6pm Mon-Fri, 10am-3pm Sat & Sun May & Sep, 9am-5pm Mon-Fri, 10am-2pm Sat Oct-Apr) Inside the train station. Pick up the free official booklet *Malmö This Month*, which lists tourist information and a guide to events.

Sights & Activities

The cobbled streets and interesting buildings around **Lilla Torg** are restored parts of the late-medieval town – the oldest of the half-timbered houses here was built in 1597. The houses are now occupied by galleries, boutiques and restaurants.

The main museums of Malmö are based in and around **Malmöhus** (☎ 344437; Malmöhusvägen; combined entry adult/child Skr40/free; ⊙ 10am-4pm Jun-Aug, noon-4pm Sep-May). You can walk through the royal apartments with their interiors and portrait collections, and see the **Stadsmuseum** with its Malmö collection and art in the **Konstmuseum**. Especially interesting are the **aquarium** and the **Naturmuseum**. The old **Kommendanthuset** arsenal is opposite the castle and **Teknikens och Sjöfartens Hus** is to the west. The latter is a well-presented technology and maritime museum displaying aircraft, motor vehicles, steam engines and a submarine.

Boat tours of the canals run regularly from late April through September from the kiosk of **Rundan** (☎ 611 7488; tours adult/child Skr75/40), by the canal, opposite Centralstationen.

Ribersborg is a long sandy beach backed by parkland and recreational areas about 2km west of the town centre. Out in Öresund, and reached by a 200m-long pier, is the naturist **Ribersborgs Kallbadhus** (☎ 260366; www.ribban.com; admission Skr45), dating from 1898. There's a cold, open-air saltwater pool and wood-fired sauna, and separate sections for men and women. Take bus No 20 or 22.

Sleeping

Sibbarp Camping (☎ 155165; Strandgatan 101; camp sites Skr150-190, cabins from Skr280) By the beach

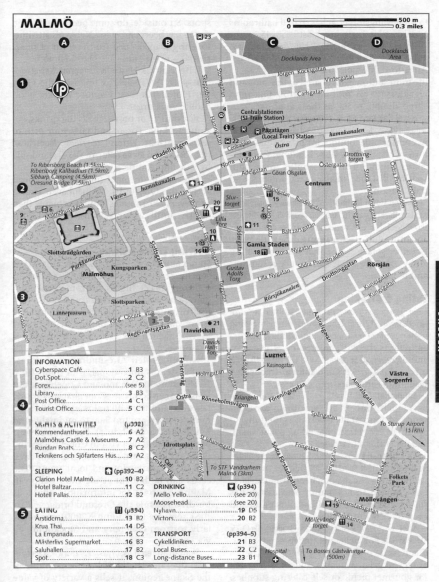

MALMÖ

0 — 500 m
0 — 0.3 miles

INFORMATION
Cyberspace Café..................................1 B3
Dot.Spot...2 C2
Forex...(see 5)
Library...3 B3
Post Office...4 C1
Tourist Office.......................................5 C1

SIGHTS & ACTIVITIES (p392)
Kommendanthuset.................................6 A2
Malmöhus Castle & Museums...............7 A2
Rundan Boats.......................................8 C2
Teknikens och Sjöfartens Hus..............9 A2

SLEEPING (pp392–4)
Clarion Hotel Malmö...........................10 B2
Hotel Baltzar.......................................11 C2
Hotell Pallas.......................................12 B2

EATING (p394)
Årstiderna..13 B2
Krua Thai..14 D5
La Empanada......................................15 C2
Mästerlivs Supermarket......................16 B3
Saluhallen..17 B2
Spot..18 C3

DRINKING (p394)
Mello Yello......................................(see 20)
Moosehead.......................................(see 20)
Nyhavn...19 D5
Victors...20 B2

TRANSPORT (pp394–5)
Cykelkliniken......................................21 B3
Local Buses..22 C2
Long-distance Buses...........................23 B1

---

about 5km southwest of the town centre and enjoying a great view of the Öresund bridge is this large, well-equipped ground with a range of cabins. Take bus No 12B or 12G.

STF Vandrarhem Malmö (☎ 82220; www.malmo hostel.com; Backavägen 18; dm/s/d from Skr175/315/410) Quite well hidden, about 3.5km south of the city centre (it's a good idea to get a map

before setting off). Worth seeking out, as it's a big, bright, clean and well-equipped place, offering breakfast for Skr50. Catch bus No 21 from in front of Centralstationen.

Bosses Gästvåningar (☎ 326250; www.bosses.se; Södra Förstadsgatan 110B; s/d/tr Skr295/495/495) This is a pleasant guesthouse in a regular apartment block, opposite the hospital and quite close to Möllevångstorget. It has shared bathrooms and guest kitchens; breakfast is Skr45.

Hotel Pallas (☎ 611 5077; http://home.swipnet.se /Hotell_Pallas/; Norra Vallgatan 74; s Skr395, d Skr455-535) An affordable pension-style hotel close to the train station, with shared bathrooms and breakfast for an additional Skr30. Opt for a 'large' double room, as these are huge.

Hotel Baltzar (☎ 665 5700; www.baltzarhotel.se; Södergatan 20; s/d from Skr980/1300, s/d discount Skr700/850) A comfortable option in an antique-filled turn-of-the-19th-century building. Good facilities, bountiful breakfast buffet, and within spitting distance of the main squares and train station.

Clarion Hotel Malmö (☎ 71020; www.choicehotels .se; Engelbrektsgatan 16; s/d Skr1345/1545, s/d discount Skr790/990) Nicely renovated in recent years and now full of streamlined Scandi style. Features splashes of colour in the inviting lobby, friendly service and a nice restaurant and bar.

Eating & Drinking

Lilla Torget is a picturesque cobbled square lined by restaurant-bars and often teeming with people. The area around Möllevångstorget reflects the city's interesting ethnic mix, and there's good, cheap food on offer from a mix of stalls, grocers and student-frequented restaurants and bars.

Saluhallen (Lilla Torget; 🕑 Mon-Sat) One of the best lunch-time pit stops, with an excellent range of food stalls offering something to appeal to every taste, including pasta, sushi, kebabs and Vietnamese.

La Empanada (☎ 120262; Själbodgatan 10; dishes Skr29-59; 🕑 11am-9pm Mon-Sat) Budget travellers will love this cheap and cheerful cafeteria. It has a huge menu of mainly Mexican dishes (tacos, enchiladas, burritos), plus pasta and even Swedish meatballs.

Spot (☎ 120203; Stora Nygatan 33; dishes Skr49-75; 🕑 Mon-Sat) For delicious Italian sandwiches, salads and coffee, visit stylish Spot. There's also great gelati available, and an Italian deli for gourmet picnic or self-catering supplies.

Krua Thai (☎ 122287; Möllevångstorget 14; lunch Skr55, mains Skr75-95) Standing guard over the stalls and stores of Möllevångstorget is this long-standing Thai restaurant, with cheap, popular meals (curries, soups, noodle dishes) to eat in or take away.

Nyhavn (☎ 128830; Möllevångstorget; mains Skr55-109) One of Möllevångstorget's prime drinking spots. Sit outside, do some people-watching, sink a few beers and enjoy Nyhavn's attempts to bring Danish food (in the form of *smørrebrød* – open sandwiches) to Malmö.

The central **Mästerlivs supermarket** (Engelbrektsgatan; 🕑 7am-9pm) is opposite the Clarion Hotel. The best produce market is on Möllevångstorget.

For dinner or post-sightseeing drinks, get along to Lilla Torget and take your pick of restaurant-bar. **Victors** (☎ 127670), **Moosehead** (☎ 120423) and **Mello Yello** (☎ 304525) stand side by side and compete for custom.

For capital-city night-time diversions, head across the Öresund to Copenhagen (trains run every 20 minutes until midnight, then hourly until around 5am). See p41 for more.

Getting There & Away

Sturup airport (☎ 613 1000; www.lfv.se) is 31km southeast of the city and SAS has up to a dozen direct flights to/from Stockholm daily. The low-cost carrier Ryanair also flies to Sturup from the UK. Trains run directly from Malmö to Copenhagen's main airport (Skr85), which has a much better flight selection (see p99).

An integrated Öresundregionen transport system is operational, with trains from Helsingborg via Malmö and Copenhagen to Helsingør. Malmö to Copenhagen (Skr85) takes 35 minutes, with trains leaving every 20 minutes from around 5am to midnight (and hourly in the wee hours). For a round tour of the Öresund or a visit to Copenhagen, the Öresund Runt card (Skr199) gives two days' free travel on ferries and local trains. The cards can be bought at the train station in Malmö. See p440 for information about tolls for drivers using the Öresund bridge.

SJ services (including X2000) run regularly to/from Göteborg and Stockholm, all via Lund.

Skånetrafiken (☎ 0771-777777; www.skanetrafik en.se) operates the local buses and trains in the Skåne region. It sells a variety of value cards and passes, including a useful summer pass (Skr415), valid for 25 days of travel throughout the county from mid-June to mid-August. Local trains (purple in colour and known as *pågatåg*) run to Helsingborg (Skr84), Lund (Skr36), Ystad (Skr72) and other destinations in Skåne. The platform is at the eastern end of Centralstationen; you buy tickets from a machine. International rail passes are accepted.

Long-distance buses depart from a terminal at the end of Skeppsbron, about 500m north of the train station. Swebus Express runs daily to Stockholm, Göteborg and Oslo. Trains are best for trips across the Öresund bridge.

Getting Around

The regular **Flygbussarna** (☎ 0771-777777) services run from Centralstationen to Sturup airport (Skr90 one way); a taxi shouldn't cost more than Sk400.

Malmö Lokaltrafik information kiosks are at main bus hubs, including Centralplan (outside the local train station) and Gustav Adolfs Torg. Local buses are green (regional buses are yellow); tickets cost Skr15 for one hour's travel.

Bicycles can be rented from **Cykelkliniken** (☎ 611 6666; Regementsgatan 12; per day/week Skt120/600); the price includes a cycling map.

LUND

☎ 046 / pop 99,600

The second-oldest town in Sweden, Lund was founded by the Danes in around 1000. Construction of the cathedral began about 1100 and Lund became the largest archbishopric in Europe. Much of the medieval town can still be seen. The university was founded in 1666, after Sweden took over Skåne. Today, Lund retains its quiet, civilised campus feel and has a youthful population, including some 35,000 students. In summer it's a much quieter place, with the students on vacation and the tourist buses visiting.

The **tourist office** (☎ 355040; www.lund.se; Kyrkogatan 11; ☒ daily Jun-Aug, Mon-Sat May & Sep, Mon-Fri Oct-Apr) is opposite the cathedral. The **library** (Sankt Petri Kyrkogatan 6; ☒ closed Sun May-Aug) has free Internet access, and there's also an Internet café, **Noll Ett** (Lilla Gråbrödersgatan; per hr Skr39-49), nearby.

Sights & Activities

The excellent **Kulturen** (☎ 350400; www.kulturen .com; Tegnerplatsen; adult/child Skr50/free; ☒ 11am-5pm mid-Apr–Sep, noon-4pm Tue-Sun Oct–mid-Apr) claims to be the world's second-oldest open-air museum (it opened in 1892). Its impressive collection of about 40 buildings fills two blocks and includes period homes from the 17th century and countless displays. Nearby,

Hökeriet (☎ 350400; cnr St Annegatan & Tomegapsgatan; admission free; ☒ May-Sep) is an old-fashioned general store where you can stock up on boiled lollies.

The magnificence of Lund's Romanesque **Domkyrka** (Cathedral) is well known, but for a real surprise visit at noon or 3pm (1pm and 3pm Sunday and holidays) when the astronomical clock strikes up *In Dulci Jubilo* and the figures of the three kings begin their journey to the child Jesus. Close by, you can find out about the cathedral at **Domkyrkomuseet**, and the attached **Historiska Museet** (☎ 222 7944; Kraftstorg; combined entry adult/child Skr20/free; ☒ 11am-4pm Tue-Fri) has pre–Viking Age finds. There are a number of galleries, plus small, special-interest museums and archives in town, many attached to university departments. Inquire at the tourist office.

The **main university building**, which faces Sandgatan, is worth a glance inside, and Scanian rune stones are arranged in the park nearby. The **Botanic Gardens** with tropical **greenhouses** are east of the city centre.

Sleeping & Eating

STF Vandrarhem Tåget (☎ 142820; www.trainhostel .com; dm Skr175) You could easily use Lund as a base and take trains to nearby towns if you stay at this unusual hostel behind the train station (take the overpass from the bus station, and you'll see the hostel on the right). Guests sleep in railway carriages set in parkland, with three bunks to a room – they're quiet yet tiny and perhaps too familiar to weary train travellers.

Private rooms can be booked at the tourist office from around Skr250 per person plus a Skr50 fee.

Gräddhyllan Café, Restaurang & Hotell (☎ 157230; www.graddhyllan.com, Swedish only; Bytaregatan 14; s/d Skr595/850, s/d discount Skr500/700) Book early to stay at central Gräddhyllan, a lovely place offering four rooms above a café-restaurant.

Hotell Oskar (☎ 188085; www.hotelloskar.com; Bytaregatan 3; s/d Skr950/1350, s/d discount Skr700/900) This elegant boutique hotel has six well-equipped rooms (with kettle, stereo, cable TV and DVD), furnished with classic Scandinavian design. It's by the delightful Ebbas Skafferi.

Lund has plenty of eating possibilities ranging from fast-food eateries and sleek cafés to popular evening hang-outs. A good place for a coffee fix is in the area surrounding the library.

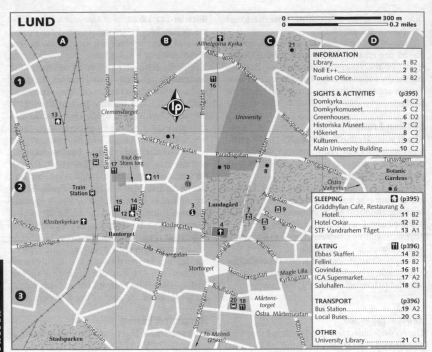

LUND

```
0                    300 m
0                    0.2 miles
```

Saluhallen (Mårtenstorget; ⏰ Mon-Sat) is a good place for reasonably priced food, from pasta to Thai dishes and kebabs. There's an **ICA supermarket** (Bangatan; ⏰ 8am-10pm) opposite the train station.

Govindas (☎ 120413; Bredgatan 28; lunch Skr30-55; ⏰ lunch Mon-Sat) Join the earnest student-types at friendly Govindas for the good-value vegetarian lunch deals.

Ebbas Skafferi (☎ 134156; Bytaregatan 5; dishes Skr38-55) This courtyard café is one of the most appealing places in town, with a good lunchtime selection of ciabatta and salads, plus hot meals like soup, risotto and tortillas. A breakfast buffet is also available (Skr50).

Fellini (☎ 137020; Bangatan 6; mains Skr82-198) Fashionable Fellini, opposite the train station, serves up good Italian nosh, including gourmet pizzas for under Skr100 (or Skr69 to take away), plus pasta, meat and fish dishes, and the all-important tiramisu and gelati. It's just as nice for a simple glass of wine.

Getting There & Away

There are frequent SJ and *pågatågen* departures from Lund to Malmö (Skr36, 15 minutes);

some trains continue to Copenhagen (Skr110). All long-distance trains between Stockholm and Malmö stop in Lund. Buses leave from outside the train station.

TRELLEBORG

☎ 0410 / pop 38,600

Trelleborg has Sweden's main ferry connections with Germany, but if you're arriving in Sweden here there's no reason to linger in town long – it's better to move on to Malmö or Ystad. The **tourist office** (☎ 733320; www.trelleborg.se; Hamngatan 9; ⏰ daily Jun-Aug, Mon-Fri Sep-May) is near the harbour. If you need a place to stay, **Night Stop** (☎ 41070; www.hotelnightstop.com; Östergatan 59; s/d/tr Skr199/299/399) is diagonally opposite the town museum, about 500m from the tourist office.

Bus No 146 runs every half-hour or so between Malmö and Trelleborg's bus station (Skr48), 500m from the ferry terminals.

There are two ferry terminals, both behind the tourist office. Scandlines and TT-Line shuttle regularly across to the German ports of Sassnitz, Rostock and Travemünde. See p440 for information.

YSTAD

☎ 0411 / pop 26,200

Rambling cobbled streets and half-timbered houses are the highlight of this pretty medieval town. There are particularly photogenic houses on Stora Östergatan: most are from the latter half of the 18th century, but the facade of the beautiful **Änglahuset** (Stora Norregatan) dates from around 1630.

The **tourist office** (☎ 577681; www.visitystad.com; ☉ daily late Jun–late Aug, Mon–Fri late Aug–late Jun) is opposite the train station. Next door is the large **Konstmuseum** (Art Museum; ☎ 577285; adult/child Skr30/free; ☉ Tue-Sun). Don't miss medieval **Sankta Maria kyrka** (Stortorget) or the historical **Ystads Stadsmuseum** (☎ 577286; St Petri Kyrkoplan; adult/child Skr30/free) in the old monastery church of Gråbrödraklostret.

One of Skåne's most intriguing attractions is **Ales Stenar**, in the middle of a field 19km east of Ystad (take bus No 322, and look for signs to Kåseberga, the nearby village). It's a mysterious pre-Viking stone formation forming an oval 67m along its long axis.

Sleeping & Eating

Those with their own wheels can choose B&B or cottage options along the scenic coastal roads east or west of Ystad; inquire at the tourist office.

The small **Stationen Vandrarhem** (☎ 0708-577 985; www.turistlogi.se; dm Skr185) is centrally located in a renovated railway building at Ystad's train station. The well-equipped **STF Kantarellen Vandrarhem** (☎ 66566; www.turistlogi.se; Fritidsvägen; dm/s/d Skr185/285/370) is 2km east of Ystad in a beachside recreation area. Bikes can be rented here. Take bus No 572.

Hotell Bäckagården (☎ 19848; www.backagarden .nu; Dammgatan 36; s/d from Skr570/695) is a cosy guesthouse in a 17th-century home behind the tourist office.

There are some lovely eating options among the historic buildings. Seek out the charming **Book Café** (☎ 13403; Gåsegränd; ☉ closed Sun & Mon) – inside there's a room full of mismatched furniture and books; outside there's a leafy courtyard. There's focaccia, pastries and coffee on offer. **Bryggeriet** (☎ 69999; Långgatan 20; lunch Skr70, mains Skr138-215) is an atmospheric restaurant and pub in an old brewery.

Getting There & Away

Buses depart from outside the train station. To get to Trelleborg by bus, first take bus No

303 to Skateholm then transfer to bus No 183. *Pågatågen* trains run roughly hourly to/from Malmö (Skr72).

Ferries run regularly between Ystad and Poland, and to the Danish island of Bornholm (see p55). See p441 for more information on these ferry services. The ferry terminal is just south of the train station.

HELSINGBORG

☎ 042 / pop 84,500

The busy port of Helsingborg is perched on the Öresund coastline, with Denmark only 20 minutes away by ferry. Many travellers leave town without seeing any more than the train station, which is a shame as it's an appealing place with seaside character, quality budget accommodation, great parkland and good restaurants, and it's worth taking some time to explore.

The well-organised **tourist office** (☎ 104350; www.helsingborgsguiden.com; Stortorget; ☉ daily May-Aug, Mon-Sat Sep-Apr) can help with inquiries. **First Stop Sweden** (☎ 104130; Bredgatan 2; ☉ daily Jun-Aug, Mon-Fri Sep-May), near the car-ferry ticket booths, dispenses tourist information on the whole country for new arrivals from Denmark.

Most other travel-related needs are met inside the vast Knutpunkten complex at the seafront, including ATMs and **Forex** (1st level; ☉ 7am-9pm) for currency exchange. The **library** (Stadsparken), near Knutpunkten, offers Internet access, and there's an Internet café not too far away at **Café Cosmos** (Södra Storgatan 39B; per hr Skr25).

Sights & Activities

The eye-catchingly modern **Dunkers Kulturhus** (☎ 107400; www.dunkerskulturhus.com; Kungsgatan 11; admission free; ☉ 10am-5pm Tue-Sun), in the area just north of the transport terminals, houses the very good **town museum** and **art museum** (combined entry adult/child Skr70/free), plus a concert hall, restaurant and café. Take a stroll along the northern waterfront from here to admire the sleek, attractive apartment buildings and restaurants, all part of a successful harbour redevelopment project.

You can access the square medieval tower **Kärnan** (☎ 105991; adult/child Skr20/10; ☉ daily Jun-Aug, Tue-Sun Sep-May) from steps near the tourist office (there's also lift access for Skr10). The tower is all that remains of a 14th-century castle; the view from the top (34m) overlooks Öresund to the Danish heartland and

HELSINGBORG

0 ═══════ 400 m
0 ═══════ 0.2 miles

INFORMATION
ATMs......................................(see 3)
Café Cosmos............................**1** D2
First Stop Sweden....................**2** C3
Forex......................................**3** C2
Library....................................**4** D3
Tourist Office..........................**5** C2

SIGHTS & ACTIVITIES (pp397–8)
Dunkers Kulturhus....................**6** B1
Kärnan...................................**7** C1
Mariakyrkan............................**8** C2

SLEEPING (pp398)
Elite Hotel Mollberg.................**9** C2
Helsingborgs Vandrarhem.......**10** D3
Hotell Linnea.........................**11** C2

EATING (pp398–9)
Ebbas Fik...............................**12** C2
Fahlmans Café........................**13** C2
ICA Supermarket.....................**14** C1
Restaurang Niklas...................**15** C1
Telegrafen..............................**16** C1
Vegeriet.................................**17** C2
Wayne's Coffee.......................**18** C2

TRANSPORT (p399)
Bus Station............................**19** C2
Car Ferry Ticket Booths...........**20** C3
HH-Lines Ticket Booth.............**21** C3
Scandlines Ticket Office &
Terminal..............................**22** C2
Sundsbussarna Ticket Booth
& Boat Terminal....................**23** C2

OTHER
Helsingborgs Stadsteater......**24** B1
Konserthus............................**25** B1
Rådhuset...............................**26** C2

reminds visitors of the struggles that finally delivered the fortress to Swedish hands. Historic **Mariakyrkan** (Mariatorget) is worth a visit for its medieval features and choral and organ concerts.

Fredriksdals Friluftsmuseum (☎ 104500; adult/child Skr50/free) is off Hävertgatan, 2km northeast of the centre. It has a pretty manor, gardens, café and a museum village – it's a lovely place for a stroll. Highlights of the summer programme here include performances in the baroque open-air theatre. Take bus No 1 or 7. North of the town, the **Pålsjö area** houses a fine park, the 16th-century Pålsjö Slott (closed to the public) and a nature reserve.

Sleeping
Villa Thalassa (☎ 380660; www.villathalassa.com; Dag Hammarskjöldsväg; dm Skr170, d Skr400-480) A recommended hostel 3km north of the city centre, reached by walking 500m from the bus stop at Pålsjöbaden. The villa and gardens are beautiful; there are three types of accommodation in modern annexes (most with TV and private bathroom) and wooden huts. Take bus No 219.

Helsingborgs Vandrarhem (☎ 145850; www.hbg turist.com; Järnvägsgatan 39; dm/s/d Skr165/245/370) The town's most central hostel is inside a nondescript building about 200m from Knutpunkten. Inside you'll find high-quality rooms and good facilities.

Hotell Linnea (☎ 372400; www.hotell-linea.se; Prästgatan 4; s/d from Skr890/1030, s/d discount Skr740/795) The pick of the town's mid-range offerings is this charming central hotel, with pretty decor and friendly management.

If you're visiting on a weekend or during summer, bear in mind that many upmarket hotels discount heavily at this time (double rooms around Skr800 to Skr900). You'll find a large number of options on Stortorget; try the grand **Elite Hotel Mollberg** (☎ 373700; www.elite .se; Stortorget; s/d Skr1120/1390, s/d discount Skr695/820).

Eating & Drinking
Vegeriet (☎ 240303; Järnvägsgatan 25; dishes Skr49-75) Vegetarians will rejoice at this vegie café-restaurant, with menu items such as soup, curry, lasagne, tortilla and stir-fry dishes.

Telegrafen (☎ 181450; Norra Storgatan; pub meals Skr30-100) A cosy bar-restaurant, serving a good selection of pub grub (fish and chips, baked spuds, burgers and nachos).

Restaurang Niklas (☎ 280050; Norra Storgatan 16; lunch Skr89, bistro mains Skr170-250; ☺ closed Sun & Mon) This gastronomic temple is among Sweden's best restaurants, with cuisine inspired by the French, elegant modern decor, a wine bar, bistro and fine-dining area (set menus in the latter from Skr495 for four courses).

There are some cool cafés in town. **Fahlmans Café** (☎ 213060; Stortorget 11) is the most traditional, serving sandwiches, quiche and pastries; in contrast is **Wayne's Coffee** (☎ 149696; Stortorget), opposite, serving the usual modern café fare (bagels, salads, muffins). Unique **Ebbas Fik** (☎ 281440; Bruksgatan 20; ☺ Mon-Sat) is styled in 1950s retro with superb results; there's an extensive café menu here too.

Self-caterers should head to the **ICA supermarket** (Drottninggatan 48).

Getting There & Away

The main transport centre is Knutpunkten; the underground platforms serve both the SJ and *pågatågen* trains departing for Stockholm, Göteborg, Copenhagen, Oslo and nearby towns. At ground level and a bit south, but still inside the same complex, is the bus terminal where regional Skånetrafiken buses dominate, but daily long-distance services run to various destinations, including Göteborg and Oslo.

Knutpunkten is the terminal for frequent ferries across to Helsingør in Denmark, and there are regular ferries to/from Oslo; see p441 for full details of these services.

GÖTALAND

The medieval kingdom of Götaland joined Svealand and Norrland to become Sweden 1000 years ago, but remained strongly influenced by Denmark. Soon after Göteborg was founded by Gustav II Adolf in 1621, Sweden conquered the rest of the region.

The two largest lakes in Sweden – Vänern and Vättern – feature in Götaland, and are linked by the remarkable Göta Canal. Tourists are also drawn to the region by Sweden's sophisticated second city, Göteborg; the beautiful Bohuslän coastline to the north; the seaside towns to the south; and, over in the east, relics of Götaland's interesting history, from rune stones to convents.

GÖTEBORG

☎ 031 / pop 475,000
Sweden's second-largest city, Göteborg (which sounds like 'yoo-te-bor', and is sometimes called Gothenburg) is wedded to its port and has a more continental outlook than Stockholm.

There's a lot more to the city than the showpiece Kungsportsavenyn boulevard and multitude of museums, not least its industrial and architectural heritage and lovely gardens. The Liseberg fun park is the largest amusement park in Scandinavia and plays host to 3.2 million visitors annually.

Orientation

The heart of the city is bordered by canals, well suited to sightseeing cruises. A branch snakes its way to Liseberg amusement park in the southeast. The huge Nordstan shopping centre lies just north of the canal system, opposite Centralstationen and its modern neighbour, Nils Ericson Terminalen, the regional and long-distance bus station.

From the centre of the city, Kungsportsavenyn crosses the canal and leads southwest to Götaplatsen. This 'Avenyn' is the heart of the city with boutiques, restaurants, theatres, galleries and cafés.

The shipyards (now closed), and much of the heavy industry (including Volvo), are on the northern island of Hisingen, reached by bridge, tunnel and regular boat traffic.

Information
DISCOUNT CARDS & PACKAGES
The good-value Göteborg Pass gives free entry to Liseberg and a number of city attractions, city tours, and parking and public transport. It costs Skr175/295 for 24/48 hours (Skr135/210 for children) and is available from tourist offices, hotels, hostels and numerous Pressbyrån newsagents.

Göteborgspaketet (Göteborg Package) is a hotel package with prices from Skr485 per person per night, and including the Göteborg Pass for the number of nights you stay. Book in advance over the Internet (www .goteborg.com) or with the tourist office.

EMERGENCY
Emergency (☎ 112) Free number for fire brigade, police and ambulance.
Police station (☎ 739 2000; Ernst Fontells Plats) Off Skånegatan, near Nya Ullevi stadium.

GÖTEBORG

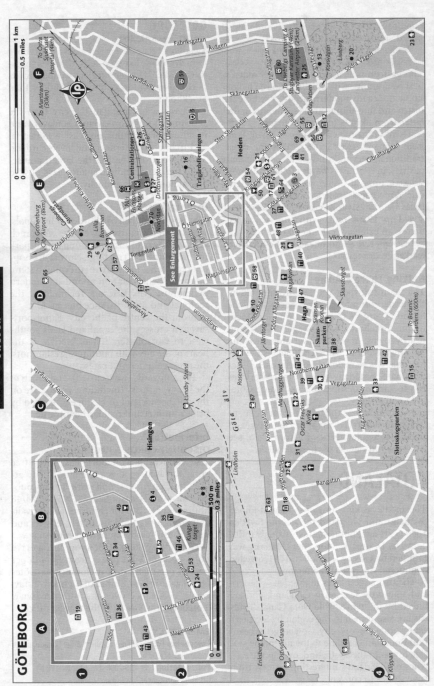

INFORMATION
Apotek Vasan.............................(see 70)
Branch Tourist Office....................(see 70)
Forex...**1** E2
Forex...**2** E3
IT-Grottan......................................**3** E3
Main Tourist Office.......................**4** B2
Police Station.................................**5** F2
Post Office..................................(see 70)

SIGHTS & ACTIVITIES   (pp401–2)
Börjessons Cruise..........................**6** D1
Börjessons Paddan Boats..............**7** B2
Börjessons Sightseeing Bus Departures...**8** B2
Domkyrkan......................................**9** A2
Feskekörka....................................**10** D3
Göteborgs Maritima Centrum......**11** D2
Konstmuseet.................................**12** F3
Liseberg...**13** F3
Masthuggskyrkan..........................**14** B3
Naturhistoriska Museet................**15** C4
Palm House....................................**16** E2
Röhsska Museet.............................**17** E3
Sjöfartsmuseet..............................**18** B3
Stadsmuseum................................**19** A1
Universeum....................................**20** F4

SLEEPING   (pp402–4)
City Hotel......................................**21** E3
Göteborgs Mini-Hotel..................**22** C3
Göteborgs Vandrarhem................**23** F4

Hotel Flora....................................**24** A2
Hotel Gothia Towers....................**25** F3
Hotel Odin Residence..................**26** E2
Hotel Opera..................................**27** E2
Hotel Vasa.....................................**28** D3
Hotell Barken Viking....................**29** D1
Linné Vandrarhem........................**30** C3
Masthuggsterrassens Vandrarhem...**31** C3
STF Vandrarhem Stigbergsliden...**32** B3
STF Vandrarhen Slottsskogen......**33** C4
Vanilj Hotel...................................**34** B1

EATING   (pp404–5)
Aldardo...**35** B2
Brasserie Lipp...........................(see 54)
Brogyllens Konditori....................**36** A1
Café Garbo....................................**37** E3
Chopsticks.................................(see 40)
Crepe Van......................................**38** D4
Cyrano...**39** C3
Den Lilla Taverna.......................(see 42)
Espresso House.............................**40** D3
Eva's Paley.....................................**41** E3
Hemköp Supermarket................(see 70)
Kalaya..**42** C4
Magnus & Magnus.......................**43** A2
R.O.O.M..**44** A2
Saluhall Briggen............................**45** C3
Saluhallen.....................................**46** B2
Sjöbaren..**47** D3
Smaka..**48** E3

DRINKING   (p405)
Dubliner..**49** B1
Lounge...**50** E3
O'Leary's..**51** B1
Ölhallen 7:an................................**52** B2

ENTERTAINMENT   (p405)
Avenyn 10..................................(see 54)
Biopalatset....................................**53** E3
Bubbles..**54** E3
Göteborgs Konserthus..................**55** F3
Göteborgs Stadsteatern................**56** E3
GöteborgsOperan..........................**57** D1
Nefertiti...**58** D3
Nya Ullevi.....................................**59** F2
Scandinavium...............................**60** F3
Valand..**61** E3

TRANSPORT   (pp405–6)
Älvsnabben....................................**62** D1
Catamaran Terminal.....................**63** B3
Cykelkungen Bike Rental.............**64** E3
DFDS Seaways...............................**65** D1
Nils Ericsson Terminalen.............**66** E1
Stena Line Denmark Terminal......**67** C3
Stena Line Germany Terminal......**68** A4

OTHER
Library...**69** E3
Nordstan Shopping Complex.......**70** E2
Utkiken Tower...............................**71** E1

INTERNET ACCESS

IT-Grottan (☎ 778 7377; Chalmersgatan 27; per hr Skr38–41; ☺ 10am–midnight Mon Fri, noon–midnight Sat & Sun) Cheaper hourly rates are available before the busy period starting at 6pm.

Sidewalk Express (www.sidewalkexpress.se; per hr Skr19) A chain of Internet kiosks at central locations (Centralstationen, Landvetter airport, inside the 7-Eleven store at Vasaplatsen); vouchers are purchased from vending machines.

MEDICAL SERVICES

Apoteket Vasan (☎ 802 0532; Nordstan complex; ☺ 8am–10pm)

Östra Sjukhuset (☎ 343 4000) Large hospital near tram terminus No 1, northeast of town.

MONEY

Banks with ATMs attached are to be found scattered all over town, including inside the Nordstan complex and the train station. The exchange company **Forex** (www .forex.se; Kungsportsavenyn 22; ☺ 9am–7pm Mon-Fri, 10am 4pm Sat) has a number of branches that are throughout Göteborg, including one in Centralstationen.

TOURIST INFORMATION

Main tourist office (☎ 612500; www.goteborg.com; Kungsportsplatsen 2; ☺ 9am-6pm Jun-Aug, 9am 5pm Mon-Fri, 10am-2pm Sat Sep-May)

Branch tourist office (Nordstan; ☺ 10am-6pm Mon-Fri, 10am-4pm Sat, noon-3pm Sun)

Sights

LISEBERG

This **fun park** (☎ 400100; www.liseberg.se; admission Skr50, child under 7 free) is dominated by its futuristic spaceport-like tower. The ride to the top, some 83m above the ground, climaxes in a spinning dance and a breathtaking view of the city. The other amusements and rides seem tame by comparison but there's no lack of variety. You can buy a pass for Skr255 that allows you to ride the attractions all day, otherwise individual rides cost between Skr10 and Skr50. There are often summer shows and concerts staged here. Opening hours are complex but the season generally runs from late April to early October (and also in the weeks leading up to Christmas) – check the website. Tram No 5 takes you there.

MUSEUMS

After Liseberg the museums are Göteborg's strongest attractions. If several take your fancy, purchase the Göteborg Pass.

By Liseberg is the striking **Universeum** (☎ 335 6450; www.universeum.se; Södra Vägen; admission Skr110-135, child under 5 free; ☺ 10am-6pm May-Jun, 9am-7pm Jul–mid-Aug, 11am-6pm Tue-Sun mid-Aug–Apr), a huge and impressive 'science discovery centre' featuring everything from rainforests to a shark tank. It's got lots of good displays and hands-on experiments, but it's not cheap to visit. Opening hours can get complicated – see the website for information.

The **Stadsmuseum** (☎ 612770; Norra Hamngatan 12; adult/child Skr40/free; ⏰ 10am-5pm May-Aug, 10am-5pm Tue-Sun Sep-Apr), in the former headquarters of the Swedish East India Company (Östindiska huset), has archaeological, local and historical collections, including Sweden's only original Viking ship.

The city's main art collections are at **Konstmuseet** (☎ 611000; Götaplatsen; adult/child Skr40/free; ⏰ 11am-6pm Tue-Thu, 11am-9pm Wed, 11am-5pm Fri-Sun). This museum has impressive collections of Nordic and European masters and is notable for works by Rubens, Van Gogh, Rembrandt and Picasso. The museum includes the Hasselblad Center photographic collection.

The excellent **Röhsska Museet** (☎ 613850; Vasagatan 37; adult/child Skr40/free; ⏰ noon-5pm Tue-Sun) covers modern Scandinavian design and decorative arts, but also contains classical and Oriental items, and a design store and popular café.

Göteborgs Maritima Centrum (☎ 105950; Packhuskajen; adult/child Skr70/30; ⏰ Mar-Oct), by the opera house north of the city centre, claims to be the largest floating ship museum in the world and usually displays 13 historical ships, including the submarine *Nordkaparen*.

The main museum of maritime history, **Sjöfartsmuseet** (☎ 612900; Karl Johansgatan 1; adult/child Skr40/free; ⏰ 10am-5pm May-Aug, 10am-5pm Tue-Sun Sep-Apr), is near Stigbergstorget about 2km west of the city centre. There's an interesting aquarium attached (included in the admission price). Take tram No 3, 9 or 11.

Just off Linnégatan in Slottsskogsparken, **Naturhistoriska Museet** (☎ 775 2400; adult/child Skr60/free; ⏰ 11am-5pm May-Aug, 11am-5pm Tue-Sun Sep-Apr), the natural history museum, has a collection of some 10 million specimens of wildlife from around the world (the highlight is a stuffed blue whale). Take tram No 1 or 2.

OTHER SIGHTS

Göteborg's churches aren't very old but they're a truer reflection of Swedish architecture than Stockholm's Italian imitations. The classical **Domkyrkan** (Cathedral; Västra Hamngatan) was consecrated in 1815 – two previous cathedrals were destroyed by town fires. One of the most impressive buildings in Göteborg, **Masthuggskyrkan** (Storebackegatan; ⏰ Mon-Fri) was completed in 1914 and its interior is like an upturned boat. The church is also a great viewpoint for the western half of the city.

Feskekörka (Rosenlundsgatan; ⏰ Mon-Sat Jun-Aug, Tue-Sat Sep-May) is called the Fish Church due to its curious appearance. It isn't a church at all – it's a fish and seafood market.

The **Haga district**, south of the canal, is Göteborg's oldest suburb and dates back to 1648. In the 1980s and '90s, the area was thoroughly renovated and now includes shops and restaurants.

There are some lovely green oases in the city, including **Trädgårdsföreningen** (entry on Nya Allén; adult/child Skr15/free May-Aug, otherwise free), laid out in 1842 and home to a couple of pretty cafés, a rosarium and a **palm house**. In Göteborg's southwest is **Slottsskogsparken**, the 'lungs' of the city, and the **Botanic Gardens** – the largest in Sweden – are nearby.

Tours

Börjessons (☎ 609670) operates most sightseeing tours in and around Göteborg. From June to August there are one-hour city bus tours (adult/child Skr80/50), leaving regularly from outside Stora Teatern, just south of the tourist office, but perhaps the most popular way to pass time in Göteborg is to take a boat cruise on the Göta älv, or further afield to the sea. From May to September Börjessons' paddan boats tour the canals and harbour from Kungsportsbron, near the tourist office. The 50-minute tours (adult/child Skr85/50) depart regularly from 10am; tours after 3pm are free for Göteborg Pass–holders.

Holders of the Göteborg Pass pay nothing to take one of the regular Älvsnabben ferries (see p406) or to join a Börjessons' cruise from Lilla Bommen to the ruins of **Nya Älvsborg fortress** near the river mouth (adult/child Skr95/60).

Sleeping

Göteborg has several exceptional hostels; most are clustered in the central southwest area, in apartment buildings that sometimes inspire little confidence from the outside, but inside offer accommodation of a high standard. All are open year-round.

Most hotels offer great discounts at weekends and in summer.

BUDGET

Lisebergs Camping & Stugbyar Kärralund (☎ 840 200; www.liseberg.se; Olbergsgatan; camp sites Skr100-325) The closest camping ground to town is this well-equipped place, owned and operated by the fun park. It's geared for families and has a wide range of cabins, cottages and hostel beds. Prices for all options have a ridiculously complex schedule of rates depending on time of year, day of the week and number of nights stayed. Take tram No 5 to Welandergatan.

The tourist office can arrange **private rooms** (s/d from Skr175/225) for a Skr60 booking fee.

Göteborgs Mini-Hotel (☎ 241023; www.minihotel .se; Tredje Långgatan 31; dm/d from Skr130/360) This decent option has well-priced renovated rooms (all with TV and fridge) and shared bathroom facilities, plus laundry and self-catering kitchen.

STF Vandrarhem Slottsskogen (☎ 426520; www .sov.nu; Vegagatan 21; dm/s/d from Skr155/285/390; ☐) Regarded as one of Sweden's best hostels, so book early. A friendly and social place with excellent facilities such as 24-hour reception, breakfast buffet (Skr55), bike hire, laundry, sauna and lounge with billiard table. Take tram No 1 or 2 to Olivedalsgatan.

Masthuggsterrassens Vandrarhem (☎ 424820; www.mastenvandrarhem.com; Masthuggsterrassen 10H; dm/s/d Skr160/290/400) This spotless, well-run option is quiet and close to the ferries to Denmark. There are three kitchens and TV rooms for guests. Take tram No 3, 9 or 11 to Masthuggstorget and follow the signs (up the stairs behind the supermarket).

STF Vandrarhem Stigbergsliden (☎ 241620; www.hostel-gothenburg.com; Stigbergsliden 10; dm/s/d Skr165/295/390) Another welcoming, well-run STF hostel, this time in a renovated 19th-century seaman's house. Breakfast is Skr45 and there's a good kitchen, laundry, TV room and garden, plus bike hire. Take tram No 3, 9 or 11 to Stigbergstorget.

Göteborgs Vandrarhem (☎ 401050; www.gote borgsvandrarhem.se; Mölndalsvägen 23; dm/s/d Skr170/ 400/450) Well placed for the big attractions, just south of Liseberg, this well-equipped, well-run place offers breakfast for Skr55. Take tram No 4 to Getebergsäng.

Linné Vandrarhem (☎ 121060; www.vandrarhem met-linne.com; Vegagatan 22; dm/s/d Skr180/380/380) Down the road from STF Slottsskogen is another budget option, with bright, clean rooms and good communal facilities. Take tram No 1 or 2 to Olivedalsgatan.

MID-RANGE & TOP END

Hotel Flora (☎ 138616; www.hotelflora.se; Grönsakstor get 2; s/d Skr415/575, s/d with private bathroom Skr890/1070, s/d discount Skr650/850) This affordable option has budget and standard rooms, plus a stylish new ground-level restaurant-café, and is not far from the tourist office and gastronomic delights of Saluhallen.

City Hotel (☎ 708 4000; www.cityhotelgbg.se; Lo rensbergsgatan 6; s/d from Skr495/595, s/d with private bathroom from Skr795/995) If you aim to sample some of Göteborg's nightlife, this is the choice for you, as it's within stumbling distance of Kungsportsavenyn. Weekend and summer discounts see the rates reduced by Skr100 to Skr200. There are large rooms suitable for families.

Hotell Barken Viking (☎ 635800; www.liseberg.se /barkenviking; Gullbergskajen; crew quarters s/d Skr600/700, officer's cabins s/d Skr1100/1495, officer's cabins s/d discount Skr800/1000) This is a fabulous boat hotel with lots of history and an interesting location (near Lilla Bommen and the opera house, best accessed by walkway from the northern part of Nordstan). Crew quarters have shared bathroom facilities and bunkbeds (like a deluxe hostel room). You can pay extra for a little more luxury and private facilities in a surprisingly spacious officer's cabin. The deck is home to a restaurant and bar.

Hotel Opera (☎ 805080; www.hotelopera.se; Norra Hamngatan 38; budget s/d Skr750/895, budget s/d discount Skr495/795, standard s/d Skr1095/1295, standard s/d dis count Skr695/895) An appealing option, conven iently located close to the train station and bus terminal. Budget rooms are in an older part of the hotel and are small but perfectly adequate. All rooms have private facilities, TV and phone.

Hotel Vasa (☎ 173630; www.hotelvasa.se; Viktoriaga tan 6; s/d from Skr845/995, s/d discount Skr625/785) An at tractive, family-run place handy to the cafés of Vasagatan. Rooms are pleasant and range in size and luxury (some have a Jacuzzi); winning features are the courtyard garden and very friendly owners.

Vanilj Hotel (☎ 711 6220; www.vaniljhotel.entersol .se; Kyrkogatan 38; s/d from Skr895/1095, s/d discount Skr595/795) This is an excellent choice – a small, cosy and personal place above a lovely café and courtyard, situated in the heart of town. There's typically Swedish streamlined decor, friendly staff, good breakfasts and shopping at the front door.

Hotel Odin Residence (☎ 745 2200; www.hotel odin.se; Odinsgatan 6; apt s/d/tr Skr1295/1495/1995, s/d/tr discount Skr895/995/1195) Our top pick for space and comfort. This new hotel has fabulous apartments filled with the kind of decor and gadgets you'd kill for at home, and all come equipped with everything you need for a long, happy stay, including a full kitchen, and lounge, TV and stereo. Cheaper rates for stays of longer than a week.

Hotel Gothia Towers (☎ 750 8800; www.gothia towers.com; Mässans Gata 24; s/d from Skr1690/2090, s/d discount Skr890/990) This 23-storey, 704-room hotel (the largest in Scandinavia, and popular for conventions) is top of the tree in Göteborg. The interior is stylish and modern, and there are popular restaurants and bars in the premises. Summer and weekend prices are quite reasonable. The hotel is opposite Liseberg and only a few minutes' walk to Kungsportsavenyn; take tram No 5.

Eating

Kungsportsavenyn is lined with all kinds of restaurants, cafés and bars, and alfresco dining is popular when the sun shines. Nearby, Vasagatan is close to the student heartland and has excellent cafés, Linnégatan (close to most of the hostels) has a great selection of eateries, and Magasingatan is a good place to check out the latest on the Göteborg scene.

RESTAURANTS

Cyrano (☎ 143010; Prinsgatan 7; mains Skr65-190) A highly regarded French bistro–style restaurant, where three-course set menus cost from as little as Skr135 (if your main course is a pizza), or Skr185 for fish or meat mains. There's also a selection of good French à la carte dishes, including duck and lamb, and simpler pizzas (Skr65 to Skr85). Warm, inviting and recommended.

Smaka (☎ 132247; Vasaplatsen 3; mains Skr89-195) Appealing to tourists and locals alike, Smaka (meaning 'Taste') serves up traditional Swedish *husmanskost* and more adventurous local cuisine, including classics such as herring, meatballs with mashed potato and lingonberries, or *gravad lax*.

Sjöbaren (☎ 711 9780; Haga Nygata 25; mains Skr99-239) This cosy spot in the rejuvenated Haga district offers well-prepared seafood in nautical surrounds (inside) or a pleasant courtyard garden. Opt for items in the 'Swedish classics' category (Skr99 to Skr129) such as *gravad lax* with potatoes, fish soup or seafood pasta.

Den Lilla Taverna (☎ 128805; Olivedalsgatan 17; mains Skr69-99) A welcoming place with authentic, reasonably priced Greek dishes, plus a great array of *mezes* (starters; Skr29 to Skr69) perfect for sharing.

Brasserie Lipp (☎ 105830; Kungsportsavenyn 8; mains Skr75-239) You're spoilt for choice along Kunsportsavenyn, although prices along here can be higher than in other parts of town. This classic, classy eatery has good light meals on its menu, including Caesar salad and a club sandwich, plus more substantial main courses.

Magnus & Magnus (☎ 133000; Magasinsgatan 8; 2-/3-course meal Skr355/415) A stylish restaurant/bar (with extensive wine selections) that draws the city's fashionable crowd.

CAFÉS

Brogyllens Konditori (☎ 138713; Västra Hamngatan 2; snacks Skr22-49) A traditional, light-filled place selling great breads and pastries. Linger over coffee and cake in a seat under the grand chandeliers.

Eva's Paley (☎ 163070; Kungsportsavenyn 39; dishes Skr40-60) An institution on Avenyn. This huge, popular place is open until late (at least 11pm) and serves a range of good-value dishes including panini, baked potatoes, pasta (always vegetarian options), salads and seriously good muffins (Skr22) – you can also buy the muffins to take away from the bakery next door.

R.O.O.M. (☎ 606630; Magasingatan 3; dishes Skr35-90; ⊗ Mon-Sat) Get inspired at this great interiors store – and if your knees go weak from looking at the price tags, you can repair to the funky café and enjoy a more affordable Caesar salad or Thai curry soup.

The cosy **Café Garbo** (☎ 774 1925; Vasagatan 40) and the sleek **Espresso House** (☎ 39750; Vasagatan 22) are two of several excellent places along the leafy Vasagatan boulevard, both offer outdoor seating and good people-watching, plus fine coffee and café fare priced from Skr30 to Skr60.

QUICK EATS

Aldardo (☎ 132300; Kungstorget 12; snacks Skr25-55; ⊗ Mon-Sat) Right by the tourist office is this busy deli, a great place to pick up authentic Italian fast food – home-made pizza *al taglio* (by the slice) and pasta dishes to go.

Chopsticks (☎ 133600; Vasagatan 24; dishes Skr55-65) Next door to Espresso House is this cool little spot, offering quick, tasty rice or noodle dishes.

Kalaya (☎ 123998; Olivedalsgatan 13; dishes Skr59-69) Not far from the hostel area, Kalaya has authentic Thai cuisine, including soup, noodle and curry choices.

Crepe Van (Linnégatan; ⌚ 4-10pm Mon-Thu, 4pm-3.30am Fri & Sat) Anyone with a sweet tooth should visit this take-away van near McDonald's, offering sweet crepes from Skr20, savoury from Skr40.

Saluhallen (Kungstorget; ⌚ Mon-Sat) is a classic old market hall where you can buy a huge range of delicatessen foods. There are also superb budget eateries: Alexandras is renowned for its Greek soups and stews (Skr30 to Skr40) and Kåges Hörna serves up bargain meals – chicken salad, lasagne and burgers for Skr35 to Skr40. Not as busy as the central Saluhallen but also housing a good array of lunch stalls is **Saluhall Briggen** (Nordhemsgatan; ⌚ Mon-Sat), not far from the hostel district.

SELF-CATERING

Self-caterers should head to the **Hemköp supermarket** (⌚ 8am-10pm) in the Nordstan complex. Central **Saluhallen** (Kungstorget; ⌚ Mon-Sat) is the perfect place to put together your picnic pack. Outside Saluhallen you'll find fresh produce stalls and food vans.

Drinking

You'll find some good pubs and bars along the main thoroughfares. The **Dubliner** (☎ 139 020; Östra Hamngatan 50B) is as authentic an Irish pub as you'll find on the Continent and has live music nightly in summer. Pints of Guinness and Kilkenny flow, and bar meals include Emerald Isle staples such as fish and chips or beef-and-Guinness pie. Almost opposite is **O'Leary's** (☎ 711 5519; Östra Hamngatan 36), an American-style sports bar with lots of TV screens and a menu of bar snacks.

Ölhallen 7:an (☎ 136079; Kungstorget 7), not far from the tourist office, is well worth seeking out. This little gem is a well-worn Swedish beer hall that hasn't changed in about 100 years. There's no food, wine or pretension – just beer, and plenty of choices.

Pop into the chic **Lounge** (☎ 711 1541; Kungsportsavenyn 5; ⌚ Thu-Sat) to sip pretty cocktails with Göteborg's beautiful people.

Entertainment

One of many cinemas around town, the 10-screen **Biopalatset** (☎ 174500; Kungstorget), behind Saluhallen, screens latest releases.

Super-cool **Nefertiti** (☎ 711 1533; Hvitfeldtsplatsen 6), near Feskekörka, is a well-established venue for live jazz, blues and ethnic music; it also has a nightclub, restaurant and café.

Kungsportavenyn is the place to go for nightlife. Popular nightclubs include **Bubbles** (Kungsportsavenyn 8), downstairs next to Brasserie Lipp; vintage **Valand** (cnr Kungsportsavenyn & Vasagatan), drawing a mixed crowd of partiers; and **Avenyn 10** (Kungsportsavenyn 10-12), one of the biggest clubs in town with two dance floors and several bars over three levels.

For culture-vultures, facing each other at the end of Avenyn are **Göteborgs Stadsteatern** (City Theatre; ☎ 615050; www.stadsteatern.goteborg.se; Götaplatsen), with a number of dramatic performances (usually in Swedish), and **Göteborgs Konserthus** (Concert Hall; ☎ 726 5300; Götaplatsen), home to the local symphony orchestra. It's also worth investigating what's on at the strikingly modern **GöteborgsOperan** (☎ 131300; www.opera.se; Christina Nilssons gata), at Lilla Bommen harbour, which stages ballet, opera and assorted musical performances.

Göteborghers are avid sports fans, and the city has outdoor stadiums such as Nya Ullevi, hosting football matches, and the indoor Scandinavium, where ice hockey is played in front of large and enthusiastic crowds. These venues also regularly host pop and rock concerts.

Getting There & Away

AIR

Landvetter airport (☎ 941000; www.lfv.se) is 25km east of the city. There are frequent daily flights to/from Stockholm and daily services to many European cities. **Göteborg City Airport** (☎ 926060; www.goteborgcityairport.se) is a minor airport 10km northwest of the city, used by Ryanair flights.

BOAT

Göteborg is a major entry point for ferries, with several terminals. For more details of ferry services and fares to Denmark, Germany and the UK, see p441.

Nearest the city centre, the Stena Line Denmark terminal on Masthuggstorget (tram No 3, 9 or 11) has regular departures for Frederikshavn. Faster and more expensive catamarans to Frederikshavn depart from near Sjöfartsmuseet (take tram No 3, 9 or 11 to Stigbergstorget). Further west is the Stena Line terminal for the daily car ferry to Kiel (in Germany). Take tram No 3 or 9 to Chapmans Torg.

DFDS Seaways sails twice weekly to Newcastle from Frihamnen on Hisingen (take tram No 5, 6 or 10 to Frihamnen, then a 10-minute walk).

BUS

The modern bus station, Nils Ericson Terminalen, is next to the train station. Eurolines and Swebus Express share an office here; see p440 for details of Eurolines services.

Swebus Express (☎ 0200-218218; www.swebusexpress.se) operates frequent buses to and from most major towns. There are up to 10 services daily to/from Stockholm (Skr250/360 discount/full price, six hours) and up to six a day to/from Oslo (Skr160/225 discount/full price, 3½ hours). **Svenska Buss** (☎ 0771-676767; www.svenskabuss.se) and **Säfflebussen** (☎ 0771-151515; www.safflebussen.se) also run on the major routes, with similar prices.

There's a **Tidpunkten office** (☎ 0771-414300; ⏰ 7am-10pm Mon-Fri, 9am-10pm Sat, 9am-7pm Sun) here giving information and selling tickets for all city and regional public transport within the Göteborg, Bohuslän and Västergötland region. Västtrafik has regional passes for 24 hours (Skr220) or 30 days (Skr1270), which give unlimited travel on all *länstrafik* buses, trains and boats within Göteborg, Bohuslän and the Västergötland area.

CAR & MOTORCYCLE

The E6 motorway runs north–south from Oslo to Malmö just east of the city centre and there's also a complex junction where the E20 motorway diverges east for Stockholm.

Many international car-hire companies (eg Europcar, Avis) have desks at Landvetter airport.

TRAIN

Centralstationen serves SJ and regional trains, with direct trains to Malmö, Copenhagen, Oslo and Stockholm, as well as numerous other destinations in the southern half of Sweden. Connex night trains run to the far north. Direct trains to Stockholm depart approximately hourly, with X2000 trains every one or two hours.

Getting Around

You can catch the frequent **Flygbussarna** (☎ 0771-414300; www.flygbussarna.se) service to reach Landvetter airport from Nils Ericson Terminalen (Skr70). There are also buses to Göteborg City Airport 100 minutes before scheduled flight departures (Skr50).

Buses, trams and ferries run by **Västtrafik** (☎ 0771-414300) make up the city public transport system; there are Tidpunkten information booths inside Nils Ericson Terminalen, on Drottningtorget and at Brunnsparken. An individual ticket on transport costs Skr20. Cheaper and easy-to-use 'value cards' cost Skr100 and reduce the cost considerably (to under Skr14 per trip). A 24-hour Dagkort (day pass) for the whole city area costs Skr50. Holders of the Göteborg Pass travel free.

The easiest way to cover lengthy distances in Göteborg is by tram. There are 11 lines, all converging near Brunnsparken, one block from the train station. Also convenient and a good way to see the city are the Älvsnabben ferries, which run between Lilla Bommen and Klippan every 30 minutes or so.

Cykelkungen (☎ 184300; Chalmersgatan 19) offers bike rental for Skr120/300/500 for one day/three days/one week.

MARSTRAND
☎ 0303 / pop 1300

Pretty Marstrand (www.marstrand.nu), with its wooden buildings, island setting and relaxed air, conveys the essence of the Bohuslän fishing villages that dot the coast from Göteborg to the Norwegian border and provide an idyllic area for sailing, cycling or driving. Like many other places along the coast, Marstrand has become an upmarket weekend destination for sailors and city slickers. The 17th-century **Carlstens Fästning** (☎ 60265; adult/child Skr65/25; ⏰ Jun-Aug) fortress reflects the town's martial and penal history; entry price includes a guided tour.

Marstrands Varmbadhus Båtellet (☎ 60010; marstrandsvarmbadhus@telia.com; dm Skr195-295, d Skr625-675; 🔁) offers simple hostel accommodation 400m from the ferry dock; the attached **restaurant** (⏰ daily Jun-Aug, Sat & Sun Sep-May) serves lunch specials and à la carte selections, with a great view.

There are numerous eating options along the harbour, including fast-food stalls (one sells fresh fish and chips for Skr50), cafés and upmarket restaurants.

Marstrand is about an hour from Göteborg by bus and makes an excellent day trip. Take bus No 312 from Nils Ericson Terminalen

(Skr50 one way), then cross to Marstrand by the frequent passenger ferry (Skr15 return).

If you have your own transport and are heading north to Norway, get off the E6 and take Hwy 160 from Stenungsund for a pretty slice of Swedish coastal life.

STRÖMSTAD

☎ 0526 / pop 11,250

Strömstad is an attractive fishing harbour and seaside resort about 30km south of the Norwegian border. It enjoys a laid-back holiday atmosphere, especially on weekends and in summer, thanks largely to the Norwegians who flock here to take advantage of cheaper prices in Sweden. There are good attractions, including museums, beaches and boat trips to nearby islands. The Koster islands are the most westerly in Sweden and are popular for cycling.

The **tourist office** (☎ 62330; www.stromstadtourist.se; Torget, Norra hamnen; ⏰ daily Jun-Aug, Mon-Fri Sep-May) is between the two harbours on the main square. There are lots of camping grounds and cabins in the area, and the first-class **STF Crusellska Vandrarhemmet** (☎ 10193; www.crusellska.com; Norra Kyrkogatan 12; dm/s/d Skr205/345/490; ⏰ Mar-mid-Dec) is deservedly popular – book ahead.

Try the fresh local *räkor* (shrimp) and delicious seafood in the many restaurants, or purchase from local fishmongers. Next to the tourist office is **Laholmens Fisk** (Norra Kyrkogatan), selling baguettes filled with seafood (around Skr50). Not far away is **Göstases** (☎ 10812; Strandpromenaden; mains Skr49-145), with cosy nautical decor, lots of outdoor seating and a good menu of local sea creatures.

Strömstad is the northern terminus of the local train system, with regular trains to/from Göteborg (Skr133). Swebus Express buses between Göteborg and Oslo also stop here.

There are regular ferries between Strömstad and Sandefjord in Norway; see p441 for details.

VARBERG

☎ 0340 / pop 53,100

The main attraction in this pleasant coastal town is the **medieval fortress** (☎ 82830; adult/child Skr50/10), with its excellent museums. You might also want to brave the brisk Nordic weather and swim at **Kallhusbadet** (☎ 17396; adult/child Skr45/25; ⏰ daily mid-Jun–mid-Aug, Sat & Sun mid-Aug–mid-Jun), a striking bathing house built in Moorish style on stilts above the sea. The town's **tourist office** (☎ 88770; www.turist.varberg.se; Brunnparken; ⏰ daily Midsummer–mid-Aug, Mon-Sat May-Jun & Aug, Mon-Fri Sep-Apr) is in the centre of town.

The top-notch **Fästningens Vandrarhem** (☎ 88788; vandrarhem@turist.varberg.se; dm/s/d Skr190/260/435) is within the fortress and offers single rooms in old prison cells or larger rooms in other buildings. Most dining options are along the pedestrianised Kungsgatan, but the fortress café offers the best sea views in town.

Ferries from the Danish town of Grenå dock near the town centre (see p441 for ferry information). Trains and buses between Göteborg and Malmö (and on to Copenhagen) stop regularly at the train station.

NORRKÖPING

☎ 011 / pop 122,900

From the late 19th century, large textile mills and factories sprang up along Norrköping's swift-flowing Motala ström. Today the industrial architecture, complete with canals, locks and waterfalls, is a great example of inner-city regeneration and well worth a visit. Many central attractions are free (unusual for Sweden), and another key attraction is the family-friendly animal park at Kolmården.

The well-stocked **tourist office** (☎ 155000; www.destination.norrkoping.se; Dalsgatan 16; ⏰ 10am-5pm Mon-Fri, also 10am-2pm Sat Jul), by the Louis de Geer Konserthus, can help with visitor information. The **library** (Södra Promenaden 105) has free Internet access. There's also cheap Internet access available at **Norrköpings Biljard och IT Café** (Prästgatan 48; per hr Skr15; ⏰ to 1am).

Kolmården

With about 750 animals from all continents and climates, this **zoo** (☎ 249000; www.kolmarden.com; ⏰ daily May-Aug, Sat & Sun Sep) is billed as the largest in Europe. The complex is divided into two areas: the main **Djurparken** (zoo; adult/child Skr200/110), with its enjoyable dolphin show; and **Safariparken** (adult/child Skr110/80), which you drive around (in a bus or your own transport). A good, separate **Tropicarium** (☎ 395259; www.tropicarium.se; adult/child Skr70/45) opposite the entrance includes sharks, alligators and reptiles, and completes the attraction. A general 'maxi' ticket for the zoo and safari park costs Skr260/150. The **cable car** (Skr80/40) around the park gives a better view of the forest than of the animals.

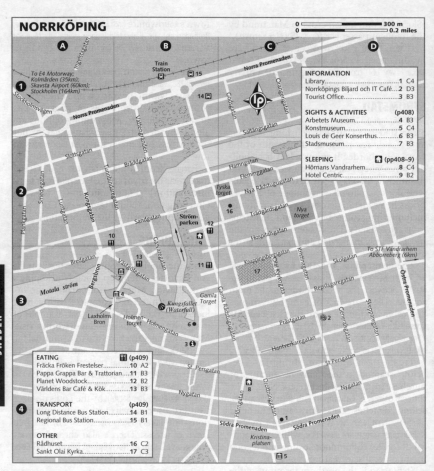

NORRKÖPING

| 0 | 300 m |
| 0 | 0.2 miles |

INFORMATION
Library..1 C4
Norrköpings Biljard och IT Café...2 D3
Tourist Office...................................3 B3

SIGHTS & ACTIVITIES (p408)
Arbetets Museum.........................4 B3
Konstmuseum................................5 C4
Louis de Geer Konserthus...........6 B3
Stadsmuseum................................7 B3

SLEEPING (pp408-9)
Hörnans Vandrarhem....................8 C4
Hotel Centric.................................9 B2

EATING (p409)
Fräcka Fröken Frestelser..............10 A2
Pappa Grappa Bar & Trattorian....11 B3
Planet Woodstock.........................12 B2
Världens Bar Café & Kök..............13 B3

TRANSPORT (p409)
Long Distance Bus Station..........14 B1
Regional Bus Station.....................15 B1

OTHER
Rådhuset.......................................16 C2
Sankt Olai Kyrka...........................17 C3

You'll need all day to take in the zoo fully. Kolmården is 35km north of Norrköping, on the north shore of the bay Bråviken (regular bus No 432 or 433; Skr54). There's camping and hotel accommodation out here too – see the website for details.

Other Sights

Pedestrian walkways and bridges lead around Norrköping's ingenious system of locks and canals along the riverside. The industrial past is exhibited at the city museum, **Stadsmuseum** (☎ 152620; Västgötegatan 19-21; admission free; ✆ Tue-Sun). Sweden's only museum of work, the excellent **Arbetets Museum** (☎ 189800; admission free), is just across the bridge from the Stadsmuseum. A modern addition to the riverside

scenery is the extraordinary **Louis de Geer Konserthus** (☎ 155030; Dalsgatan 15), a concert hall and conference centre that's home to good restaurants.

The **Konstmuseum** (☎ 152600; Kristinaplatsen; adult/child Skr40/free; ✆ Tue-Sun), the large art museum south of the centre at Kristinaplatsen, has some important early-20th-century works.

Summer-only attractions include short guided tours on vintage trams; inquire at the tourist office.

Sleeping

Hörnans Vandrarhem (☎ 168271; www.hornans-vandrarhem.se; Hörngatan 1; dm/s/d from Skr170/350/480) This hostel is in the heart of town, above a pub, and offers clean, comfortable rooms, all with cable TV.

STF Vandrarhem Abborreberg (☎ 319344; www .abborreberg.se, Swedish only; dm/s/d Skr195/240/385; ☺ May-Sep) Beautifully situated by the coast, 6km east of town. Accommodation is in cottages scattered through the surrounding park; there's also a café. Take bus No 101 or 111 to Lindö.

Hotel Centric (☎ 129030; www.centrichotel.se; Gamla Rådstugugatan 18; s/d Skr695/770, s/d discount Skr450/540; Ⓟ ▣) This well-priced hotel is in a central location, and has slightly dated but comfortable rooms and good facilities including free Internet access and parking.

Eating & Drinking

There are plenty of eateries in the shopping district along Drottninggatan, and also in the student quarter around Kungsgatan. This is also where you'll find supermarkets.

Fräcka Fröken Frestelser (☎ 238823; Kungsgatan 43; light meals Skr25-55) The name is a tongue-twister but this cool café's great selection of sandwiches, light meals and cakes is easier to wrap your mouth around.

Världens Bar Café & Kök (☎ 134510; Västgötegatan 15; dishes Skr45-75) Funky and colourful restaurant-bar serving up simple dishes and music – from around the world. Popular for its lunch deals (from Skr45), and open until late (until 11pm or 1am).

Planet Woodstock (☎ 188111; Gamla Rådstugu gatan 11; dishes Skr40-70) The kind of place that backpackers love, this place stays open until late (11pm or 2am) and has a huge menu of cheap meals including bagels, baked potatoes, quiche and lasagne.

Pappa Grappa Bar & Trattorian (☎ 180014; Gamla Rådstugugatan 26; mains Skr105-235; ☺ dinner Mon-Sat) It's worth booking a table for this cosy, low-lit cellar restaurant-bar, one of the town's best options and deservedly popular. It offers authentic Italian dishes and great desserts.

Getting There & Around

The regional bus station is next to the train station in the north of town; long-distance buses leave from a terminal across the road. Swebus Express and Svenska Buss (see p444) have frequent services to destinations including Stockholm, Göteborg, Jönköping, Kalmar and Örebro. Norrköping is on the main north–south railway line, and SJ trains run roughly hourly north to Stockholm and

south to Malmö. Frequent regional trains and buses run south to Linköping (Skr72).

Trams cover the city and are quickest for short hops, especially along Drottninggatan from the train station. The fare for trams and city buses is Skr18.

LINKÖPING

☎ 013 / pop 134,000

Known for its medieval cathedral and modern aircraft industries (SAAB is based here), Linköping is both a modern, youthful university city and a preserver of traditions in its numerous museums. There are some good attractions outside town, including canals, parks and a very good open-air museum.

The **tourist office** (☎ 206835; www.linkoping.se; Klostergatan 68; ☺ 24hr) is inside Quality Hotel Ekoxen. It's open 24 hours to pick up brochures and maps, but is usually staffed only during office hours. The striking city **library** (Östgötagatan 5), not far from the cathedral, offers Internet access. **Gamer Palace** (Drottninggatan 36; per hr Skr35) is an Internet café conveniently close to the hostel, and **SITE Internetcafé** (Sturegatan 3B; per hr Skr25) is close to the train and bus stations.

Sights & Activities

The enormous, copper-roofed **Domkyrka** (Cathedral; ☺ 9am-6pm) with its 107m spire is the landmark of Linköping and one of Sweden's oldest and largest churches. In the nearby castle is the **Slotts- & Domkyrkomuseum** (Castle & Cathedral Museum; ☎ 122380; adult/child Skr40/ free; ☺ Tue-Sun late Apr–mid-Oct), with exhibits on the history of the cathedral.

Just north of the cathedral, **Östergötlands Länsmuseum** (County Museum; ☎ 230300; Vasavägen; adult/child Skr20/free; ☺ Tue-Wed, Sat & Sun) houses an extensive collection of art by a variety of European painters, including Cranach's view of Eden, *Original Sin*, and Swedish art reaching back to the Middle Ages.

The best attractions are just outside the centre. Some 2km west of the city is **Gamla Linköping** (☎ 121110; admission free; ☺ village & most museums open daily), one of the biggest living-museum villages in Sweden. Among the 90 quaint houses are about a dozen theme museums, many handicraft shops, a small chocolate factory, a restaurant and a café. You can wander among the 19th-century buildings at will. Just 300m through the forest behind the old village is the **Valla Fritidsområde**,

LINKÖPING

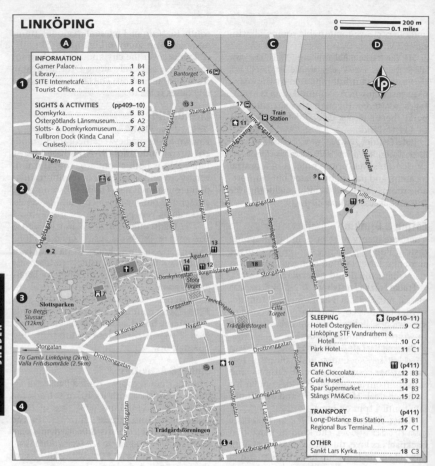

0 — 200 m
0 — 0.1 miles

a recreation area with domestic animals, gardens, a children's playground, minigolf, a few small museums and many old houses. Take bus No 202 or 214.

Bergs Slussar, 12km northwest of Linköping (bus No 521 or 522, Skr27) is one of the most scenic sections of the Göta Canal, with seven locks and a height gain of 19m. It's a great excursion on a sunny day, and there are cafés and restaurants by the canal.

Linköping boasts its own canal system, the 90km **Kinda Canal**. There are 15 locks, including the deepest in Sweden. A variety of cruises from mid-May to September run along the canal. The trip on **M/S Kind** (☎ 0141-233370) leaves the Tullbron dock on Tuesday, Thursday and Saturday from late June to early August and heads south to Rimforsa (Skr330; return by bus or train included).

Sleeping

Linköping STF Vandrarhem & Hotell (☎ 359080; www.lvh.se; Klostergatan 52A; dm/s/d Skr240/390/480, hotel s/d Skr625/720, s/d discount Skr485/590, apt from Skr595) There's something for every budget at this bright, central complex. As well as comfortable hostel rooms, there are good hotel rooms (many with kitchenette), plus excellent spacious apartments. Recommended.

Hotell Östergyllen (☎ 102075; www.hotellostergyllen.se; Hamngatan 2B; s/d Skr395/550, d with private bathroom Skr750) It doesn't look like much from the outside, but inside is a small, pleasant hotel with lovely breakfast room. It's conveniently located about 150m from the train station.

Park Hotel (☎ 129005; www.fawltytowers.se; Järnvägsgatan 6; budget s/d Skr390/590, s/d Skr890/990, s/d discount Skr490/690) The website claims that it's 'Linköping's Fawlty Towers', but don't let that put you off! In a pretty yellow villa directly opposite the train station, this hotel has friendly owners and good rooms, including a budget option with showers off the corridor.

Eating & Drinking

Most places to eat and drink are on the main square or nearby streets, especially along buzzing Ågatan.

Café Cioccolata (☎ 131880; Hantverkaregatan 1; snacks Skr35-45) A central café with cool interiors, outdoor seating, strong coffee and a great selection of filled panini or ciabatta.

Gula Huset (☎ 138838; Klostergatan 19; lunch Skr69, mains Skr79-219) On a warm day the courtyard area at the 'Yellow House' beckons. There are cheaper pasta and vegetarian options, plus a range of hearty Swedish fish and meat mains, including reindeer steak.

Stångs pm&Co (☎ 312100; Södra Stanggatan 1; lunch Skr72, mains Skr200-270; ☽ lunch Tue-Fri, dinner Tue-Sat) Down by the Kinda Canal dock, off Hamngatan in the city's northeast, is this highly rated waterside restaurant. The dinner menu is impressive (with prices to match) and the lunch-time deal is excellent value.

There's a **Spar supermarket** (Stora Torget) in the basement of the Filbytersgallerian shopping complex.

Getting There & Away

Regional and local buses have their terminal adjacent to the train station on Järnvägsgatan. Long-distance buses leave from 500m north of the train station. Linköping is on the main north–south railway line and SJ trains stop roughly every hour.

Regional (and local) traffic is run by **ÖstgötaTrafiken** (☎ 0771-211010; www.ostgotatrafiken.se); there's an information office at the station. Journeys cost from Skr18; the 24-hour *dygnskort* (Skr100) is valid on all buses and local trains within the county (buy this if you're travelling to Vadstena, below).

VADSTENA

☎ 0143 / pop 7600
Beautiful Vadstena on Lake Vättern is a legacy of both church and state power and now the abbey and castle compete for the visitor's interest. The dominant historical figure

was St Birgitta, who established her order of nuns here in 1370. The historic monuments, charming alleys and relaxed atmosphere in the old town (and by the lake) makes Vadstena one of the nicest spots in Sweden. The **tourist office** (☎ 31570; www.vadstena.com; ☽ daily mid-May–mid-Sep, Mon-Fri mid-Sep–mid-May) is inside the castle.

Sights & Activities

The Renaissance castle, **Vadstena Slott** (☎ 315 70; Slottsvägen; adult/child Skr50/10; ☽ tours daily mid-May–mid-Sep), looks straight over the harbour and lake beyond. It was the mighty family project of the early Vasa kings and in the upper apartments there are some items of period furniture and paintings. The superb 15th-century **Klosterkyrkan** (Abbey Church; Lasarettsgatan; admission free; ☽ mid-May–mid-Sep), consecrated in 1430, has a combination of Gothic and some Renaissance features. Inside are the accumulated relics of St Birgitta and medieval sculptures. Near the church is the **Sankta Birgitta Klostermuseum** (☎ 10031; adult/child Sk50/10; ☽ daily late May–mid-Sep, Sat & Sun mid-Apr–May & mid-Sep–mid-Oct), the old convent founded by St Birgitta in 1370.

The area around Vadstena is full of history and deserves a closer look. Cycling is an option as the scenic flatlands around Vättern lend themselves to the pedal. A series of ancient legends is connected with **Rökstenen**, Sweden's most impressive and famous rune stone, by the church at Rök, just off the E4 on the road to Heda and Alvastra.

Sleeping & Eating

STF Vandrarhem Vadstena (☎ 10302; www.va-bostaelle.se; Skänningegatan 20; dm/s/d Skr215/365/580) This inviting central hostel is open year-round, but outside the high season (June to August) it's essential to book in advance.

STF Vandrarhem Borghamn (☎ 20368; www.borghamnsvandrarhem.nu; Borghamnsvägen 1; dm/s/d Skr185/315/420) A more appealing option may be this large complex in a lovely, quiet lakeside setting 15km southwest of Vadstena. It's about 750m from the bus stop at Borghamn (take bus No 610), and bike rental is available, plus there's an on-site café.

27ans Nattlogi (☎ 76564; www.27ansnattlogi.se, Swedish only; Storgatan 27; s/d Skr500/650, s/d with private bathroom Skr600/790) This cosy B&B is nicely central and has six simple, comfortable rooms (some with private facilities, some shared).

Old-style cafés line Storgatan for an afternoon pit stop, and there's a central supermarket on Rådhustorget for picnic supplies.

Restaurang På Hörnet (☎ 13170; Skänningegatan 1; mains & snacks Skr40-100) This cool corner bar-restaurant is worth seeking out for its laid-back style and great bar snacks such as buffalo wings, marinated feta cheese and calamari.

Mi Casa (☎ 14101; Storgatan 9; mains Skr109-139) Mi Casa is a bright, modern, family-friendly restaurant-café. There's a lunch-time buffet (Skr65/75 weekdays/weekends), evening bistro meals, tapas dishes (Skr20 to Skr35), plus a huge selection of good-value light meals available throughout the day.

Getting There & Around

Only buses run to Vadstena: bus No 661 regularly links the town with Mjölby (Skr45), and from Mjölby you can catch trains to Linköping and Stockholm. Swebus Express bus No 855 runs on Friday and Sunday between Stockholm and Vadstena via Linköping. **Sport Hörnan** (☎ 10362; Storgatan 8) rents bikes.

SMÅLAND

The forested county of Småland (www.visit-smaland.com) is famous for glass (and furniture) production. This area was also the homeland of many 19th-century emigrants to the USA, so is an important destination for those tracing their Swedish roots. There are some interesting towns to divert you from your homewares shopping, plus the popular summer destination of Öland.

VÄXJÖ

☎ 0470 / pop 74,100

The pleasant town of Växjö (quite unpronounceable for non-Swedes – ask a local to demonstrate!) gives reasonably good access to the factories and forests of Glasriket (see below). The **tourist office** (☎ 41410; www.turism.vaxjo.se; Norra Järnvägsgatan; ⏰ daily Jul–mid-Aug, Mon-Fri mid-Aug–Jun) is at the old yellow railway building next door to the modern Resecentrum that now serves as the train and bus station.

Millions of North Americans have roots in Sweden, many of them in Småland. Those who return shouldn't miss **Svenska Emigrantinstitutet – Utvandrarnas Hus** (House of Emigrants; ☎ 20120; www.swemi.nu; Södra Järnvägsgatan; adult/child Skr40/5; ⏰ daily May-Aug, Tue-Sat Sep–May), which has archives, information and historical exhibitions on the beckoning USA. It's just behind the train and bus station, close to **Smålands Museum** (☎ 704200; www.smalandsmuseum.se; Södra Järnvägsgatan; adult/child Skr40/free; ⏰ daily Jun-Aug, Tue-Sun Sep–May), with an absorbing exhibition of glass from Glasriket.

Sleeping & Eating

STF Vandrarhem Växjö (☎ 63070; www.vaxjovandrarhem.nu; Evedals Brunn; dm/d Skr200/400) This lovely hostel is 6km north of the centre, in a popular lakeside recreational area (take bus No 1C, which unfortunately only runs from June to August, Skr17).

First Hotel Cardinal (☎ 722800; www.firsthotels.com; Bäckgatan 10; d from Skr895, d discount Skr595) The Cardinal is a large, well-equipped hotel in the centre of town, with a range of rooms and rates.

For sustenance, head to Storgatan or try the classy **Wibrovski** (☎ 740410; Sandgärdsgatan 19; mains Skr155-235; ⏰ dinner Mon-Sat), in an old timbered house and offering well-prepared dishes. At Smålands Museum, **Café Momento** (☎ 39129; dishes & snacks Skr35-99) is a great lunch or coffee spot. There's an excellent selection of baguettes, salads and cakes, and a pretty courtyard.

Getting There & Away

Växjö lies between Alvesta and Kalmar and is served by SJ trains that run roughly hourly. Buses to other parts of the county also depart from the train station, with destinations including Oskarshamn (Skr111) and Kosta (Skr57). Svenska Buss runs daily between Stockholm and Malmö via Norrköping, Linköping and Växjö.

GLASRIKET

With dense forests, quaint red houses and great shopping opportunities, the area known as Glasriket (www.glasriket.se) is understandably popular among tourists. The so-called 'Kingdom of Crystal' has at least 15 glass factories (look for signs saying 'glasbruk') scattered around the wilderness. Kosta was founded in 1742, and by the end of the 19th century there were 10 factories in full swing. Factory outlets offer substantial discounts on seconds – don't just come for glass and crystal since there are ceramics, wood, leather and handicrafts also for sale in the area. Most of the larger places offer a shipping service.

Nybro

☎ 0481 / pop 19,800

Nybro's **tourist office** (☎ 45085; www.nybro.se; Stadshusplan; ✆ daily Jun-Aug, Mon-Fri Sep-May) is inside the town hall and can help with information about the town and region. Of the glass factories in the immediate surrounds, traditional **Pukeberg** (☎ 80029; www.pukeberg.se) is a worthwhile stop for its quaint setting and high quality. About 2.5km west of the town centre is the 200m-long *kyrkstallarna* building, old church stables that now house the excellent folklore museum **Madesjö Hembygdsgård** (☎ 17935; adult/child Skr25/5; ✆ mid-May–mid-Sep).

Nybro Lågprishotell & STF Vandrarhem (☎ 109 32; Vasagatan 22; dm/s/d from Skr200/300/400, hotel s/d Skr490/740; ✆ Mar–mid-Dec), south of the centre near Pukeberg, is the local STF hostel and also offers affordable hotel-standard rooms. It's clean and comfortable and has a kitchen on each floor. You can also rent bikes here (Skr50 per day). The more upmarket **Stora Hotellet** (☎ 51935; rumsbokning@telia.com; Mellangatan 11; s/d Skr875/1050, s/d discount Skr600/750) is on Stadhusplan, by the tourist office. It's home to the best eating options in town, with a pub and restaurant.

SJ trains between Alvesta and Kalmar stop here every hour or two. Regional bus No 131 runs regularly to/from Kalmar (Skr38).

Kosta, Boda & Orrefors

These three tiny Småland villages are home to the three biggest names in Swedish glass production. Each namesake company is open daily and each factory complex has an outlet store, museum or gallery, glass-blowing demonstrations and tourist information for the area.

Kosta is the largest village and is where Glasriket started in 1742. At times it looks like the biggest tourist trap in southern Sweden, but it can be appreciated if you concentrate on the finesse and quality of the local craftsmanship and not on the tourist buses and discount stores. Boda is a quaint little village with a large factory outlet, a few other homewares shops and little else. Founded in 1864, the Boda glass factory is now part of the **Kosta Boda company** (☎ 0478-34500; www.kostaboda

.com). Much the same products are available at these two factories.

Orrefors (☎ 0481-34195; www.orrefors.com) was founded in 1898. The factory complex is impressive (check out the gallery) and there's a good hostel nearby.

SLEEPING & EATING

Across the road from the factory in Kosta, **Kosta Värdshus** (☎ 0478-50006; www.kostavardshus .com; Stora vägen; s/d Skr420/690) serves inexpensive lunches and offers simple, comfortable accommodation. There's also **Kafe Kosta**, inside the factory's outlet store, serving sandwiches, cakes and hot meals around the Skr50 mark.

STF Vandrarhem Boda (☎ 0481-24230; boda.vand rarhem@telia.com; dm/s/d Skr185/205/370; ✆ May–mid-Sep) in Boda is not far from the factory and well signposted.

The friendly, well-equipped **STF Vandrarhem Orrefors** (☎ 0481-30020; dm/s/d Skr160/275/400; ✆ May-Aug) in Orrefors is conveniently located near the factory area. At the factory complex you can dine at **Orrefors Värdshus** (lunch and snacks available) but there's also a summertime stall selling hot dogs and ice cream. You can also get pizzas and kebabs from **Pizzeria Alexandra** in the village.

If you're in the region from June to August, ask about *hyttsill* parties at the glass factories, where traditional meals are prepared using the furnaces and cooling ovens. The menu includes herring, smoked sausage, bacon and baked potatoes, as well as the regional speciality *ostkaka* (cheesecake). The cost is Skr325 including drinks (free for children under 10). Contact the regional tourist offices or the glassworks themselves for more information.

Getting There & Around

Glasriket is fairly isolated and the area is not particularly easy to explore without your own transport. Bicycle tours are great if you follow the minor roads; there are plenty of hostels and you can camp almost anywhere in the countryside. From mid-June to mid-August bus No 138 runs a few times daily (not on Sunday) from Kalmar to Nybro, Orrefors and Kosta (and vice versa). Regular (year-round) bus No 139 connects Nybro and Orrefors (Skr22); Kosta is served by regular bus No 218 from Växjö (Skr57).

SWEDEN

OSKARSHAMN

☎ 0491 / pop 26,200

Although important for boat connections to Gotland and useful for travel-related services, Oskarshamn isn't a particularly interesting town. Hantverksgatan is one of the main streets, where you'll find the **Kulturhuset** (Hantverksgatan 18) housing the **tourist office** (☎ 88188; www.oskarshamn.se; ☺ daily Jun-Aug, Mon-Fri Sep-May) and the town library with free Internet access.

If you need to stay overnight, the well-run **STF Vandrarhem Oskarshamn** (☎ 88198; vandrarhemmet@oksarshamn.se; Åsavägen 8; dm/s/d Skr145/250/390) is a few hundred metres from the train station and well positioned for the Gotland ferries.

Local trains run from Nässjö, and regional buses make a regular run on the coastal Kalmar–Oskarshamn–Västervik route (the section Oskarshamn–Kalmar is Skr70). Swebus Express has three daily buses between Stockholm and Kalmar that stop at Oskarshamn. Regular boats to Visby on Gotland depart from near the train station.

KALMAR

☎ 0480 / pop 35,000

For a long time the port of Kalmar was the key to Baltic power, and the short-lived Scandinavian union agreement of 1397 was signed at its grand castle. Kalmar was vital to Swedish interests until the 17th century and its cobbled streets and impressive edifices retain a strong historical flavour. It's also the gateway to the long, skinny island of Öland.

Visit the waterside **tourist office** (☎ 417700; www.kalmar.se/turism; Ölandskajen 9; ☺ daily Jun-Aug, Mon-Sat May & Sep, Mon-Fri Oct-Apr). The **library** (Tullslätten 4) has free Internet access, or you can head to **IT-Caféet** (Kaggensgatan 40B; ☺ 8am-4pm Mon-Fri), which also offers free Internet access.

Sights & Activities

The once-powerful Renaissance castle **Kalmar Slott** (☎ 451490; adult/child Skr75/20; ☺ Apr-Sep), in a magnificent setting by the sea south of the railway, was the key to Sweden before lands to the south were claimed from Denmark. The panelled King Erik chamber is the highlight of the interior, while another chamber exhibits punishment methods used on women in crueller times. For art-lovers the nearby **Konstmuseum** (Art Museum; ☎ 426282; Slottsvägen 1D; adult/child Skr40/free) is worth a look,

while the pretty streets of the **Gamla Stan** (old town) area to the northeast are lovely for wandering.

The highlight of **Kalmar Länsmuseum** (County Museum; ☎ 451300; www.kalmarlansmuseum.se; Skeppsbrogatan 51; adult/child Skr50/free), in the old steam mill by the harbour, is the exhibition of finds from the flagship *Kronan*, which sank controversially off Öland – a disaster to match the sinking of the *Wasa* now on show in Stockholm at Vasamuseet (p368).

A few blocks away, in the imposing but somewhat empty main square, is the baroque **Domkyrka** (Stortorget), which was designed by Tessin, the leading 17th-century architect working for the Swedish crown.

Sleeping & Eating

Svanen STF Vandrarhem & Lågprishotell (☎ 12928; www.hotellsvanen.se; Rappegatan 1; dm/d Skr240/480, hotel s/d Skr495/595) Svanen is a well-equipped hostel and 'low-price hotel' on the island of Ängö (connected by road to the centre; take bus No 402). There are good, clean rooms available with or without private bathroom – the hotel rooms cost only a little more than the hostel, and breakfast is included. Canoe hire is available.

Söderportsgården (☎ 12501; www.soderportsgarden .se, Swedish only; Slottsvägen 1; d Skr595, 3-/4-person apt Skr950/1100; ☺ mid-Jun–mid-Aug) In a great location right by the castle, this student residence offers good, simple, summertime-only accommodation. There's also a good café-bar here (with regular live music), and prices include breakfast.

Frimurarhotellet (☎ 15230; www.frimurarehotellet .com; Larmtorget 2; s/d Skr740/995, s/d discount Skr480/735, s/d with private shower Skr940/1160, s/d with private shower discount Skr650/825) A pretty, older-style hotel that's probably the cheapest of the city-centre hotels, and which is in the heart of the action. Bike rental is available.

Kulzenska Caféet (☎ 28882; upstairs, Kaggensgatan 26; sandwiches Skr25-40) Don't leave town without visiting one of Sweden's finest old-world cafés, full of 19th-century furniture and charm. Try the delectable fruit crumbles (Skr25).

Ströget arcade (Storgatan 24) houses a small food hall, with a good selection of places offering lunch-time sustenance such as baked potatoes, baguettes and pizza.

Taste (☎ 15565; Södra Långgatan 5; lunch Skr69, bistro mains Skr90-150) A fresh, modern café and

SWEDEN

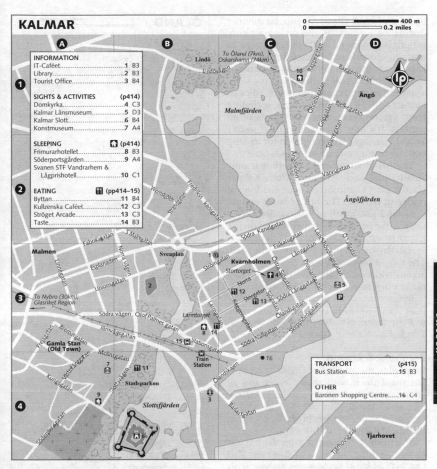

KALMAR

0 _____ 400 m
0 _____ 0.2 miles

INFORMATION
IT-Caféet.........................1 B3
Library............................2 B3
Tourist Office...................3 B4

SIGHTS & ACTIVITIES (p414)
Domkyrka.......................4 C3
Kalmar Länsmuseum........5 D3
Kalmar Slott...................6 B4
Konstmuseum..................7 A4

SLEEPING (p414)
Frimurarhotellet..............8 B3
Söderportsgården............9 A4
Svanen STF Vandrarhem &
Lågprishotell................10 C1

EATING (pp414–15)
Byttan...........................11 B4
Kullzenska Caféet............12 C3
Ströget Arcade................13 C3
Taste.............................14 B3

TRANSPORT (p415)
Bus Station....................15 B3

OTHER
Baronen Shopping Centre......16 C4

Lindö
To Öland (7km);
Oskarshamn (74km)
Lindövägen

Malmfjärden

Ängö

Ängöfjärden

Malmen

Sveaplan

Kvarnholmen
Stortorget
Norra

Larmtorget

To Nybro (30km);
Glasriket Region

Gamla Stan
(Old Town)

Stadsparken

Train
Station

Slottsfjärden

Tjarhovet

---

restaurant-bar with good-value hot lunches and a bistro menu of classics such as Caesar salad, pasta and burger options.

Byttan (16360; Stadsparken; lunch Skr75, dinner Skr160-200; May-Sep) A classy restaurant in the park by the castle, offering wonderful views of the town's major attraction. Meal prices are less than you might expect to pay for such a location.

Getting There & Away
All regional traffic is run by **Kalmar Län-strafik** (0491-761200), including the Rasken long distance services (Oskarshamn Skr70, Västervik Skr118) and buses to Öland. A one-way ticket costs Skr16 to Skr118 within the county; a *turistkort* is available from June

to mid-September and is valid on all buses and trains within the county for three/seven days (Skr200/400), allowing you to explore the coast and Öland. All buses depart from beside the train station on Stationsgatan, in the southwestern part of the city grid.

SJ trains run every hour or two between Kalmar and Alvesta (with connections to the main north–south line), and to Göteborg.

ÖLAND
0485 / pop 23,000

More windmills than Holland? There are 400 on Öland today, but there were once around 2000; most are the characteristic wooden huts on a rotating base. Also prominent are the lighthouses at the northern and southern tips of the island. Öland is a popular summer destination for Swedes and there are plenty of budget accommodation options – some 25 camping grounds and at least a dozen hostels, largely concentrated north of Borgholm.

The southern half of the island is chiefly a haven for nature, and there are relics of human settlements and conflicts, including Iron Age fortresses and graveyards of all periods. It's now been added to Unesco's World Heritage List, recognised for its long cultural history and diverse landscapes.

The island stretches 137km (but is only 16km wide) and is reached from Kalmar via the 6km Ölandsbron, once the longest bridge in Europe. The bridge lands you on the island just north of Färjestaden ('ferry town' – the pre-bridge name), where there's a large **tourist office** (☎ 560600; www.olandsturist.se; ☺ daily May-Aug, Mon-Fri Sep-Apr) beside the road. The tourist office will book rooms or cabin accommodation throughout the island and offers numerous brochures and maps.

Buses connect all main towns from Kalmar (bus Nos 101 to 106 all cross the bridge to Färjestaden; Nos 101, 102 and 106 go to Borgholm). Kalmar–Borgholm costs Skr46.

Borgholm & Around

Borgholm, the 'capital' of Öland, is a pleasant small town with shops, cafés and an enormous ruined castle on the outskirts. The small **tourist office** (☎ 89000; Sandgatan 25; ☺ Mon-Sat Jun–mid-Aug, Mon-Fri mid-Aug–May) is at the bus station.

The town is dominated from the hill just to the south by the ruins of **Borgholms Slott** (☎ 12333; adult/child Skr50/free; ☺ May-Sep). This castle was burnt out and abandoned early in the 18th century after being used as a dye works. There's a museum inside; the ruins are often used as a venue for summer concerts and festivals.

Sweden's most famous 'summer house', **Solliden Slott** (☎ 15355; www.sollidensslott.se; parks & pavilion exhibitions adult/child Skr55/25; ☺ mid-May–mid-Sep), 2.5km south of the town centre, is used by the Swedish royal family. It has beau-tiful parks and pavilion exhibitions, plus a café.

VIDA Museum (☎ 77440; www.vidamuseum.com; adult/child Skr40/free; ☺ daily May-Sep, Sat & Sun Apr & Oct-Dec) is a strikingly modern museum and art gallery in Halltorp, about 9km south of Borgholm.

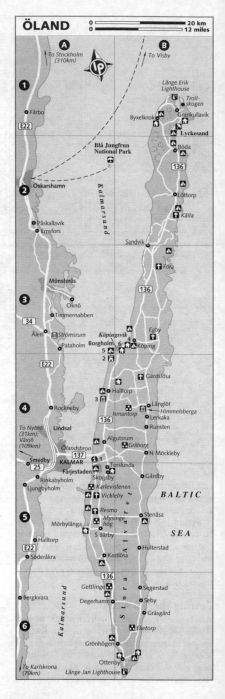

SLEEPING & EATING

The tourist offices in Borgholm and Färjestaden can help you find inexpensive private rooms in the area.

Kapelludden Camping & Stugor (☎ 560770; Sandgatan; www.kapelludden.se; camp sites from Skr210; 6-person cabin Skr860-1220; 🕑 late Mar–early Oct; 🛒) This is the handiest camping ground to Borgholm, just north of the bus terminal. It's a huge place (with some 450 camping sites) and has five-star, family-oriented facilities, including a swimming pool.

STF Vandrarhem Borgholm (☎ 10756; rosenfors .vh@telia.com; Skr145-205; 🕑 mid-Apr–mid-Oct; 🖳) Just outside the centre of Borgholm is this well-equipped hostel, in a manor house set in a pretty garden.

Guntorps Herrgård (☎ 13000; www.guntorpsherr gard.se; Guntorpsgatan; s/d Skr795/995) A delightful old farmhouse east of town, near the STF hostel. There's quality accommodation on offer, plus the drawcard of an excellent-value smorgasbord (Skr175/75 per adult/child, open to all) from 6pm every evening, with a huge variety of traditional Swedish dishes.

The main square in town has the usual collection of fast-food stalls and ice-cream kiosks. Nearby, **Ebbas** (☎ 10373; Storgatan 12) is an appealing café with a lovely outdoor area (inquire here about rooms for rent above the café). **Pubben** (☎ 12415; Storgatan 18; 🕑 daily Jun-Aug, Wed-Sat Sep–May) is a classic English-style pub serving snacks, washed down with a choice of beers and whiskies.

KARLSKRONA

☎ 0455 / pop 60,600

Karlskrona was reconstructed in grand baroque style after a fire in 1790 and became Sweden's greatest naval port. It's now on Unesco's World Heritage List and offers a relaxing day or two checking out museums and exploring offshore islands.

The **tourist office** (☎ 303490; www.karlskrona.se /tourism; Stortorget 2; 🕑 daily mid-Jun–mid-Aug, Mon-Sat mid-Aug–mid-Jun) can help visitors. The **public library** (Borgmästeregatan 8) has free Internet access, or head to **Video & Biljard Café** (Admiraltetsgatan 4; per hr Skr20) for cheap Internet access until 10pm or 11pm daily.

Sights & Activities

The finest attraction is the extraordinary offshore **Kungsholms Fort**, with its curious circular harbour, established in 1680 to defend the town, and the impregnable tower **Drottningskär kastell**. From mid-June to mid-August there are daily four-hour guided tours to the fort, sailing from Fisktorget at 10am (Skr140/70 adult/child); inquiries and bookings are made through the tourist office.

The striking **Marinmuseum** (☎ 53902; www .marinmuseum.se; Stumholmen; adult/child Skr50/free; 🕑 daily Jun-Aug, Tue-Sun Sep–May) is the new national naval museum and has interesting ship and historical displays. Nearby is **Båtmanskasernen Konsthall** (☎ 303422; Bastionsgatan 8; admission free; 🕑 Tue-Sun), once a seamen's barracks and now an art gallery.

The extensive **Blekinge Museum** (☎ 304960; Fisktorget 2; adult/child Skr40/free; 🕑 daily mid-Jun–mid-Aug, Tue-Sun mid-Aug–mid-Jun) features exhibits on fishing, quarrying and the local shipping trade, plus there's a baroque garden, a lovely courtyard café and a host of other things.

Touring Karlskrona's **archipelago** is a pleasant way to spend a sunny afternoon. A three-hour tour taking in the eastern islands costs from Skr110/50 per adult/child; contact **Skärgårdstrafiken** (☎ 78330; Fisktorget) for timetables and information.

Sleeping & Eating

STF Vandrarhem Karlskrona-Trossö (☎ 10020; www .karlskronavandrarhem.se; Drottninggatan 39; dm/s/d from Skr165/265/350) Good central hostel with all the facilities you need, plus a decent outdoor area.

STF Vandrarhem Karlskrona (☎ 10020; www.karls kronavandrarhem.se; Bredgatan 16; dm/s/d from Skr185/ 345/450; 🕑 mid-Jun–mid-Aug) Also central (but with its reception at Drottninggatan 39). This hostel is open in the peak summer season – the rest of the year it operates as student apartments. The rooms all have private bathroom and kitchenette.

Hotell Siesta (☎ 80180; siesta.hotell@telia.com; Borgmästaregatan 5; s/d from Skr625/950, s/d discount Skr600/750) A good mid-range option, right near Stortorget and offering fresh, modern rooms.

The northern side of the huge Stortorget and the street behind it, Ronnebygatan, are home to a good choice of eateries and lots of outdoor seating in fine weather.

Montmartre (☎ 311833; Drottninggatan 28; mains Skr60-140) A nice little Italian restaurant (with attached museum), serving pizza for around Skr70, plus a range of pasta, meat and fish dishes.

King's Crown (☎ 10088; Stortorget; lunch Skr65, bar snacks & light meals Skr35-140) Take a break from sightseeing at this English-style pub by the tourist office, and enjoy a bar meal such as nachos, steak sandwiches or baked potatoes. There's also a more upmarket dining area, with a menu featuring items such as seafood and reindeer fillet (mains Skr150 to Skr230).

Getting There & Away
The bus and train stations are just north of the town centre, on Kungsplan. Svenska Buss runs once daily except Saturday between Stockholm and Malmö via Oskarshamn, Kalmar and Karlskrona (Stockholm–Karlskrona Skr360, Karlskrona–Malmö Skr180). Train connections are better, running regularly to Copenhagen via Kristianstad and Malmö. Regular trains also run to Emmaboda, and from there to Kalmar or Växjö and on to Göteborg.

Stena Line ferries to Gdynia (Poland) leave from Verkö, 10km east of Karlskrona (take bus No 6). See p443 for more information on this ferry service.

GOTLAND

☎ 0498 / pop 57,400
Gotland, the largest of the Baltic islands, is also one of the most historical regions in Sweden – there are more than 100 medieval churches and an untold number of prehistoric sites. Other attractions include the unusual *raukar* limestone formations (remains of 400-million-year-old coral reefs), and the beautiful walled, medieval trading town of Visby, which is on Unesco's World Heritage

List. You could easily pass a week here seeing the highlights, eating well in the high-quality restaurants and relaxing on a beach.

Gotland is probably the top budget travel destination in Sweden: bicycle travel is the best option, free camping in forests is easy and legal, many attractions are free and there are more than 30 hostels around the island. However, the island is jam-packed with holidaying Swedes in July and August, and is *the* summer party spot for young Swedes, who come not for the history but for beaches and booze.

Good websites for travellers to Gotland include www.gotland.net and www.gotland.info.

VISBY
☎ 0498 / pop 21,400
The narrow cobbled streets and impressive walls of the medieval port of Visby attest to the town's former Hanseatic glories. A living relic, with more than 40 towers and the ruins of great churches, Visby is a World Heritage Listed town that leaves no tourist disappointed.

The place is heaving with tourists in summer, and from mid-May to mid-August cars are banned in the old town. The summer highlight is the costumes, performances, crafts, markets and re-enactments of **Medeltidsveckan** (Medieval Week; www.medeltidsveckan.com), held during the first week of August. Book accommodation well in advance if you wish to visit at this time.

The **tourist office** (☎ 201700; www.gotland.info; Hamngatan 4; ☾ daily May-Sep, Mon-Fri Oct-Apr) can help with brochures, maps and visitor information, but doesn't book accommodation. The **library** (Cramérgatan; ☾ Mon-Sat) offers free Internet access.

Sights
The old town is a noble sight, with its **13th-century wall** of 40 towers. Set aside enough time to stroll the perimeter (3.5km), and meander around Visby's narrow roads and pretty lanes. Ask at the tourist office about guided walking tours, conducted in English a few times a week in summer (Skr85), or buy a copy of *Visby on Your Own* (Skr35) for a self-guided tour.

The **ruins** of 10 medieval churches are all within the town walls and contrast with the old but sound **Cathedral of St Maria**, north of

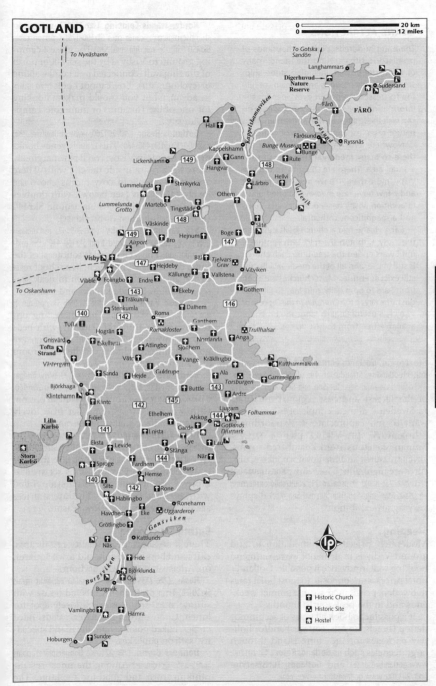

GOTLAND

0	20 km
0	12 miles

To Nynäshamn

To Gotska Sandön

Langhammars

Digerhuvud Nature Reserve

Sudersand

Fårö

FÅRÖ

Ryssnäs

Hall

Kappelshamnsviken

Fårösund

Bunge Museum

Kappelshamn

Gann

Bunge

Rute

Lickershamn

149

Hangvar

148

Hellvi

Lummelunda

Stenkyrka

Lärbro

Othem

Valleviken

Lummelunda Grotto

Martebo

Tingstäde

148

Väskinde

Slite

Hejnum

Boge

149

Bro

147

Airport

Visby

147

Bäl

Tjelvars Grav

Vibble

Hejdeby

Källunge

Vallstena

Vitviken

Folingbo

Endre

Gothem

To Oskarshamn

143

Ekeby

Träkumla

Dalhem

146

140

Stenkumla

Roma

142

Tofta

Hogrän

Romakloster

Ganthem

Trullhalsar

Gnisvärd

Eskelhem

Atlingbo

Norrlanda

Anga

Tofta Strand

Vänge

Sjonhem

Västergarn

Väte

Kräklingbo

Björkhaga

Sanda

Hejde

Guldrupe

Katthammarsvik

Klintehamn

Klinte

Buttle

Torsburgen

Gammelgarn

Lilla Karlsö

Fröjel

141

Ethelhem

145

Ala

Ardre

Ljugarn

Folhammar

Stora Karlsö

Eksta

Levide

Lojsta

Alskog

144

Garde

Gotlands Djurpark

Lye

Laus

Sproge

Stånga

När

144

Silte

Fardhem

Burs

140

Hemse

142

Rone

Hablingbo

Ronehamn

Havdhem

Eke

Uggarderojr

Grötlingbo

Näs

Kattlunds

Gansviken

Hide

Burgsviken

Björklunda

Öja

Burgsvik

Vamlingbo

Hamra

Hoburgen

Sundre

Historic Church	
Historic Site	
Hostel	

ISLAND ATTRACTIONS

There are hundreds, perhaps thousands of **prehistoric sites** around the island, many of them signposted, including stone ship-settings, burial mounds and remains of hill-top fortresses. Keep your eyes open for the information boards along roadsides. You can visit these sites, as well as the numerous nature reserves, any time, free of charge.

Nowhere else in northern Europe are there so many **medieval churches** in such a small area. There are 92 of them outside Visby; more than 70 have medieval frescoes and a few have rare medieval stained glass. In addition, Visby has a dozen church ruins and a magnificent cathedral.

Each village had a church built between the early 12th and the mid-14th centuries, until wars ended the tradition. Each church is still in use, and all of the medieval villages still exist as entities. Most churches are open from 9am to 6pm daily, mid-May to late August. *The Key to the Churches in the Diocese of Visby* is a useful English-language brochure available free from tourist offices.

Stortorget. **Gotlands Fornsal** (☎ 292700; www.lans museetgotland.se; Strandgatan 14; adult/child Skr60/free; ⊙ daily May–mid-Sep, Tue-Sun mid-Sep–Apr) is one of the largest and best regional museums in Sweden – allow a couple of hours if you want to fully appreciate it. Extraordinary 8th-century, pre-Viking picture stones, human skeletons from chambered tombs, silver treasures and medieval wooden sculptures are highlights. The nearby **Konstmuseum** (☎ 292775; Sankt Hansgatan 21; adult/child Skr40/free; ⊙ daily May–mid-Sep, Tue-Sun mid-Sep–Apr) displays varying art exhibitions.

Sleeping

Moderately priced accommodation in and around Visby is in demand; we recommend booking well in advance if possible. Gotland's hotel prices work opposite to most hotel rates in Sweden: prices increase on summer weekends and in the peak tourist months.

It's possible to book all types of accommodation (hotels, hostels, cottages) and/or holiday packages for the entire island through large agencies such as **Gotlands Resor** (☎ 201260; www.gotlandsresor.se) and **Gotlands Turistservice** (☎ 203300; www.gotlandsturistservice.com).

Norderstrands Camping (☎ 212157; www.norder strandscamping.se; camp sites Skr100-175, 4-person cabin Skr450-650; ⊙ mid-Apr–mid-Sep) The closest camping ground to Visby is by the sea 800m north of the ring wall (connected by a good walking or cycling path). You cannot book tent sites in advance but you should make a booking for one of the 16 cabins or numerous campervan sites.

Gotlands Resor (☎ 201260; www.gotlandsresor.se; s Skr300-350, d Skr440-480) This travel agency books private rooms in Visby; you'll pay marginally more for a room inside the city walls. There are also a couple of cosy rooms above the lovely café Rosas (see below), with doubles with shared facilities costing around Skr440 (not including linen or breakfast).

STF Vandrarhem Visby (☎ 269842; carl.tholin@ tjelvar.org; Fältgata 30; dm/d from Skr160/440; ⊙ mid-Jun–mid-Aug) The STF hostel is southeast of the town centre off Lännavägen, in a school residence and therefore only open in peak season. Facilities include kitchen and laundry.

Fängelse Vandrarhem (☎ 206050; Skeppsbron 1; dm Skr200-300; ⊙ May-Sep) This interesting option is not far from the harbour, with beds in the converted cells of an old jail. There are good facilities, including kitchen, TV-room and sauna.

Värdshuset Lindgården (☎ 218700; www.lindgar den.com, Swedish only; Strandgatan 26; s Skr675-950, d Skr845-1195) A very appealing, central option, with well-equipped rooms set in a lovely garden beside a quality restaurant.

Hotel Villa Borgen (☎ 279900; www.guteinfo.com /villaborgen; Adelsgatan 11; s Skr710-1010, d Skr810-1195) Another reasonably priced option for central Visby, with pleasant rooms set around a pretty, quiet courtyard off a street filled with cafés and boutiques. The lowest prices are on weekends in the low season.

Eating & Drinking

There's no shortage of quality restaurants, cafés and bars around the old town squares, on Adelsgatan or at the harbour.

Rosas (☎ 213514; Sankt Hansgatan 22; light meals Skr30-70) In a pretty half-timbered house with sunny courtyard, Rosas is a lovely spot for lunch. Choose from baguettes, salads, filled crepes, baked potatoes and the island speciality, saffron pancakes.

Donners Brunn (☎ 271090; Donnersplats; mains Skr95-245; ⊙ dinner) Among the finest restaurants in town and good for a splurge. The

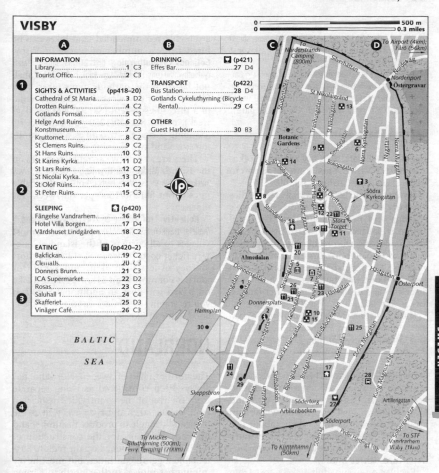

VISBY

BALTIC

SEA

SWEDEN

Swedish and international menu (priced
around Skr230) is adventurous and tempting, and there are cheaper vegetarian and
husmanskost dishes; alternatively, opt for
one of the set menus from Skr380 (for three
courses). Book ahead.

Bakfickan (☎ 271807; Stora Torget 1; lunch Skr70,
mains Skr70-198) The menu at this unpreten
tious, highly rated restaurant on buzzing
Stora Torget features well-prepared fish and
seafood including fish soup, salmon, prawns
and herrings in a few different guises.

Clematis (☎ 210288; Strandgatan 20; ☜ dinner mid-
Jun–mid-Aug) In summer, step back in time some
700 years by visiting Clematis, a restaurant
serving food cooked according to medieval
recipes, accompanied by music and enter-
tainers (including the occasional fire-eater).

Other excellent cafés include **Skafferiet**
(☎ 214597; Adelsgatan 38; light meals Skr45-65), as inviting as Rosas with its cosy interior and
low ceilings, great sandwiches and cakes, and
popular outdoor area, and the (unsigned)
Vinäger Café (☎ 211160; cnr Hästgatan & Mellangatan;
lunch buffet Skr59), a stylishly modern place that
is frequented by a young and fashionable
crowd.

Be sure to visit **Effes Bar** (☎ 215111; Adelsgatan 2;
mains Skr60-130; ☜ closed Tue), a unique pub-bar
that's built into the town wall and is full of
character. It's a good place for a laid-back
meal or drink; there's a simple bar menu, an
outdoor courtyard, pool tables and regular
live music and jam sessions in summer.

Hang-outs around the harbour are popular
on warm summer days and evenings. Do as

the locals do and stop by **Saluhall 1** (Skeppsbron) for an ice cream at one of Sweden's largest ice-cream parlours.

There's an **ICA supermarket** (Stora Torget; ☉ 8m-8pm Mon-Sat, 10am-8pm Sun) for self-caterers, or large supermarkets outside the town walls (head to Österväg, through Österport gate).

Getting There & Away

AIR

The island's **airport** (☎ 263100; www.lfv.se) is 4km northeast of Visby. A taxi from the airport to Visby should cost around Skr100.

Skyways (☎ 0771-959500; www.skyways.se) flies regularly between Visby and Stockholm's Arlanda and Bromma airports. The local airline is **Gotlands Flyg** (☎ 222222; www.gotlands flyg.se, Swedish only), with regular flights between Visby and Stockholm's Bromma and Skavsta airports. The regular fare is around Skr600 to Skr800 one way, but there are numerous discounts and deals which may offer fares as low as Skr300.

Malmö Aviation (☎ 0771-550010; www.malmoavi ation.se) flies between Visby and both Malmö and Göteborg in summer.

BOAT

Destination Gotland (☎ 0771-223300; www.destination gotland.se) operates car ferries year-round between Visby and both Nynäshamn and Oskarshamn. Departures from Nynäshamn are from two to six times daily (about five hours, or three by high-speed catamaran). From Oskarshamn there are one or two daily departures (three hours).

Regular one-way adult tickets cost from Skr218/290 for the ferry/catamaran, but from mid-June to mid-August most crossings cost from Skr304/496 (some overnight, evening and early-morning sailings in the middle of the week retain the cheaper fares). There are child, student and senior discounts, plus budget tickets (these must be booked at least 21 days before departure).

To transport a bicycle costs Skr40; a car usually costs Skr306/402 on the ferry/catamaran, although on many crossings during the peak summer these prices increase to Skr424/514.

Getting Around

There are over 1200km of roads in Gotland, typically running from village to village through the pretty landscape. Bicycle tours

are highly recommended, and bikes can be hired from a number of places in Visby. **Gotlands Cykeluthyrning** (☎ 214133; info@gotlands cykeluthyrning.com; ☉ mid-May–Aug), behind Saluhall not far from the harbour, rents bikes from Skr65/325 per day/week. It also offers rental of a three-person tent (Skr100/400 per day/week), or for Skr250/1250 you can hire its 'camping package' – two bikes, a tent, camping stove and two sleeping mats.

There are also a few car-rental agencies on the island. **Mickes Biluthyrning** (☎ 266262; www .mickesbiluthyrning.se; Visby harbour) offers affordable rates (from Skr250/1500 per day/week) for older cars.

Kollektiv Trafiken (☎ 214112; www.gotland.se /kollektivtrafiken, Swedish only) runs buses via most villages to all corners of the island. A one-way ticket costs between Skr12 (for a short journey of less than 4km) and Skr59 (for journeys of more than 51km). Taking a bike on board will cost an additional Skr40. If you're staying a while a monthly ticket is good value at Skr590.

NORRLAND

The northern half of Sweden, Norrland, has always been considered as being separate from the rest of the country. It's associated with forests, lakes and rivers, as well as the pioneers' struggle to produce the timber and iron ore necessary for the construction of the railways that opened up the region. Sustainable logging continues, but most heavy mining has moved further north to Kiruna and Malmberget.

Areas along the Norwegian border are known for their great natural beauty, and they attract walkers, skiers and canoeists. Some who venture north wish to see natural wonders such as the northern lights or midnight sun, others want to see fabricated curiosities such as a hotel constructed entirely from ice, and still others want to learn about Sami culture.

Inlandsbanan, the railway from Mora to Gällivare via Östersund, Storuman, Arvidsjaur and Jokkmokk, offers a great way to see the north (see p446). Otherwise, getting to the far north of the country by train is a night exercise only. Express buses follow most main highways but they may not be frequent.

SUNDSVALL

☎ 060 / pop 93,000

Much of Sundsvall was reduced to ashes by the great fire of 1888, but the town centre was rebuilt in grand style over the following 10 years. It's a pleasant place to spend a day or two, admiring the impressive architecture and enjoying the café and restaurant scene of one of Norrland's biggest and liveliest towns. It's also a decent base for exploring Höga Kusten, especially with your own transport. The **tourist office** (☎ 610450; www.sundsvallturism .com; Stora Torget; ⏰ Mon-Sat) can help with traveller inquiries.

Kultur Magasinet (☎ 191800; Sjögatan; ⏰ Mon-Sat), down near the harbour, is a magnificent restoration of old warehouses. The buildings now contain a café, the town library and **Sundsvall Museum** (☎ 191803; adult/child Skr20/free), which has exhibits of local and natural history. The **library** here offers Internet access.

Up on the hill **Norra Stadsberget** (150m), there's a viewing tower, walking tracks, and a typical **friluftsmuseum** (outdoor museum; admission free), a collection of local houses. The southern hill, **Södra Stadsberget** (250m), has an extensive plateau that's good for hiking, with trails up to 12km long. Buses run to each hill every couple of hours in summer.

Sleeping & Eating

STF Vandrarhem Sundsvall (☎ 612119; www.norra berget.se; Gaffelbyvägen; dm/s/d from Skr190/285/380; 🖳) This excellent hostel is above the town on Norra Stadsberget and has simple older rooms plus slightly more expensive rooms with en suite and TV. The uphill walk to the hostel is pleasant but not much fun with heavy bags; ask about buses when booking.

In town, the intersection of Nybrogatan and Rådhusgatan is a good area to go looking for reasonably priced hotels, with four in the vicinity.

Ibis Hotel (☎ 641750; www.ibishotel.com; Trädgårds-gatan 31; r Skr675, r discount Skr495) The small, modern rooms at this central hotel chain are devoid of character but are reasonably priced. Breakfast is an additional Skr55.

Wayne's Coffee (☎ 156020; Storgatan 33; lunch Skr60) Wayne's once again demonstrates its winning formula of tempting café fare in stylish surrounds.

Harry's (☎ 175533; Storgatan 33; mains Skr125-180) Wayne's neighbour Harry has a menu of simple pub meals such as nachos, pasta and burgers, plus restaurant-quality meat and seafood dishes.

Getting There & Away

Buses arrive at and depart from the bus station, known as Navet, in the northern part of town near Kultur Magasinet. **Ybuss** (☎ 0771-334444; www.ybuss.se, Swedish only) runs daily to Östersund (Skr130), Umeå (Skr190) and Stockholm (Skr200). **Norrlandskusten** (☎ 0771-511513) bus No 100 runs several times daily between Sundsvall and Haparanda via Umeå, Luleå and most northern coastal towns.

Trains run south to Stockholm via Uppsala and west to Östersund (and from there on to Trondheim, Norway); change at Ånge for northern destinations. The train station is just east of the centre, on Köpmangatan.

HÖGA KUSTEN

☎ 0613

One of the most attractive parts of Sweden's coastline, Höga Kusten (meaning the High Coast) is a hilly area with many lakes, fjords and offshore islands. Although in most parts the scenery is not as dramatic as the name might suggest, the region as a whole has been listed as a Unesco World Heritage Site, recognised as a unique area largely shaped by the combined processes of glaciation, glacial retreat and the emergence of new land from the sea (this retreat continues today at a rate of 0.9m per hundred years).

Höga Kusten stretches from north of Härnösand to Örnsköldsvik, both pleasant but unremarkable towns with decent facilities. There's a **tourist office** (☎ 50480; www .hogakusten.com) inside Hotell Höga Kusten, just north of the spectacular E4 suspension bridge over Storfjärden (which is about 70km north of Sundsvall), where you can pick up information on attractions and accommodation options in the tiny villages; be sure to pick up a free map highlighting the scenic driving routes (marked with brown and white signs). There's also useful information on the Internet at www.turistinfo.kramfors.se. Unfortunately, however, there's little by way of public transport (buses cruise along the E4 highway but don't make it into the region's villages). Hence, this area is virtually impossible to explore without your own set of wheels.

As well as the striking landscapes, the region's other major attractions are the many well-preserved fishing villages, the pick of them being Barsta, Bönhamn and Norrfälls-viken, and the lovely offshore islands, especially Högbonden and Ulvön, both accessible by boat. Also be sure to visit **Mannaminne** (☎ 20290; adult/child Skr40/free; ⏲ daily Jun-Sep, Sat & Sun Oct-Nov & Mar-May), near tiny Häggvik, an eccentric collection of just about everything from farming to emigration and technology, plus a café and handful of handicraft outlets. Walk up the steep hill behind the museum for the best view in the area (35 minutes return).

Skuleberget Naturum (☎ 40171; admission free; ⏲ daily Jun-Aug, Mon-Thu Sep-May), by the E4 just north of the village of Docksta, has exhibitions and lots of information on the area. The steep mountain **Skuleberget** (285m) soars above the *naturum*; ask about hiking routes, the chairlift and rock climbing routes.

Sleeping & Eating

There are a few cafés scattered throughout the region, but it's a nice idea to pick up supplies before setting off and take advantage of the scenic waterside picnic spots. There are supermarkets in Ullanger, Nordingrå, Docksta and Mjällom.

Hotell Höga Kusten (☎ 722270; www.hotellhoga -kusten.se; s/d Skr845/1095, s/d discount Skr500/750) Stay at the large, modern hotel just off the E4, by the huge bridge and offering stunning views. There's also a café here and a restaurant, Bridge Brasserie & Bar, with a huge range of snacks (Skr40 to Skr100) and meals (Skr8 to Skr210), plus kids' menu.

Mannaminne (☎ 20290; www.mannaminne.se, Swedish only; s/d Skr250/500, cabins d/tr/q Skr300/350/400) As well as its bizarre assortment of museum exhibitions, Mannaminne, near Häggvik, has B&B accommodation and cabins for hire. There's a café as well, and music and theatre performances in summer.

Norrfällsviken Camping (☎ 21382; www.norrfalls vikenscamping.com, Swedish only; camp sites Skr110-120, cabins/cottages from Skr350/600; ⏲ May-Oct; ☒) The idyllic village of Norrfällsviken has this well-equipped camping ground with cottages, plus the popular fish restaurant and pub **Fiskarfänget** (☎ 21142), with seating on a large deck over the water – the kind of place you never want to leave.

Vandrarhem Högbonden (☎ 23005, 23100; www .hogbonden.se, Swedish only; dm/d from Skr190/430; ⏲ May-Oct) This is a superb getaway on the island of Högbonden, reached by boat from Bönhamn

and Barsta (Skr80 return). There's a kitchen here (bring all supplies with you), and also a café in summer. You'll need to book well in advance.

ÖSTERSUND

☎ 063 / pop 58,400

This pleasant town by Lake Storsjön, in whose chilly waters lurks a rarely seen monster, has good budget accommodation and is a relaxed and scenic place to spend a couple of days. The **tourist office** (☎ 144001; www.turist.ostersund.se; Rådhusgatan 44; ⏲ daily Jun-Aug, Mon-Fri Sep-May) is opposite the town hall, one block from the bus station. The good-value Östersundskortet card (adult/child Skr140/55), valid for nine days between June and late August, gives discounts or free entry to many local attractions. The **library** (Rådhusgatan; ⏲ Mon-Sat), opposite the bus station, has free Internet access

Sights & Activities

Don't miss **Jamtli** (☎ 150100; www.jamtli.com; adult Skr60-90, child free; ⏲ 11am-5pm Jun-Aug, 11am-5pm Tue-Sun Sep-May), 1km north of the town centre. This is the highlight of Östersund, combining the lively exhibitions of the regional museum and a large museum village with staff in period clothing. The regional museum exhibits the curious **Överhogdal tapestry**, a Viking relic from around 1100 that's perhaps the oldest of its kind in Europe and may even predate the famous Bayeaux Tapestry.

Some attractions lie on the adjacent island of Frösön, reached by road or footbridge from the middle of Östersund (the footbridge is from the pleasant Badhusparken – nearby you can rent bikes, inline skates and canoes). The island features the animals at **Frösö Zoo** (☎ 514743; adult/child Skr140/70; ⏲ mid-Jun–late Aug) and the restored, late-12th-century **Frösöns kyrka** (⏲ Jun-Aug), with its characteristic separate bell tower. For skiers there are slalom and nordic runs on the island at Östberget, where there's a **viewing tower** (adult/child Skr10/5; ⏲ mid-May–mid-Sep) giving fine views.

Monster-spotting lake cruises on the old **S/S Thomée** steamship run from June to mid-September and cost from Skr65 to Skr95. Book through the tourist office.

Sleeping & Eating

STF Vandrarhem Jamtli (☎ 122060; vandrarhemmet@ jamtli.com; dm/s/d Skr185/280/380) Take the opportunity to stay in the middle of Östersund's big tourist attraction: this small, quaint hostel is inside the Jamtli museum precinct. A second, summer-only **STF Vandrarhem** (☎ 34130; micke2@algonet.se; Södra Gröngatan 36; dm/s/d 210/375/420; ☑ late Jun–early Aug) offers excellent apartments (all with bathroom, kitchen and TV) and is not far from the train station.

Vandrarhemmet Rallaren (☎ 132232; rallaren@ hotmail.com; Bangårdsgatan 6; dm/s/d Skr150/200/340) For tired and weary Inlandsbanan passengers, this small, clean and modern hostel is conveniently located next to the train station.

Pensionat Svea (☎ 512901; Storgatan 49; s/d Skr440/ 540) A homey and affordable guesthouse close to the heart of town. Bathroom facilities are shared, breakfast is included and there's also a guest kitchen. Check-in is at Hotel Jämteborg, opposite.

Paviljonq Thai (☎ 130099; Prästgatan 50R; lunch Skr65, dishes Skr99-149) Serves good-sized portions of great Thai cuisine, with all the favourite noodle, curry and seafood dishes on the menu.

Brunkullans Krog & Bar (☎ 101454; Postgränd 5; lunch Skr65, mains Skr140-200; ☑ lunch Mon-Fri, dinner Tue-Sat) Classy Brunkullans has low ceilings, a cosy atmosphere and friendly staff. The menu features gourmet pasta dishes, fish, steak and other classics, to be enjoyed in the outdoor courtyard in fine weather. The lunch buffet is great value.

Getting There & Away

The train station is a short walk south from the town centre, but the main regional bus station is central on Gustav III Torg. Local buses usually run to both. Local bus Nos 1, 3, 4, 5 and 9 go to Frösön (Skr16).

Bus No 45 runs south to Mora twice a day (Skr170, 5¼ hours). In summer the Inlandsbanan train runs once daily to Gällivare (Skr697, 14 hours) or Mora (Skr347, six hours). Bus No 156 runs west to Åre (Skr115) and bus No 63 runs twice daily northeast to Umeå (Skr287).

Direct trains run from Stockholm via Uppsala and Gävle, and some continue west to Storlien (from where you can catch trains to Trondheim, Norway). You can also catch a train east to Sundsvall.

ÅRE & AROUND

☎ 0647 / pop 9600

The Åre area (www.skistar.com/are) is arguably Sweden's top mountain-sports destina-

tion, and has 40 ski lifts that serve 100 pistes and 1000 vertical metres of skiable slopes, including a superb 6.5km downhill run (day pass Skr305). The skiing season is from November to early May, but conditions are best from February, when daylight hours increase; Easter is a hugely busy time. There are also cross-country tracks in the area, a big après-ski scene, and winter activities such as dogsledding, snowmobile safaris and reindeer sleigh rides.

When the weather warms up, Åre also offers great summer outdoor recreation, including hiking, kayaking, rafting, fishing and mountain biking. The area west of Åre is popular among fell walkers: there's a network of STF wilderness huts and lodges here for enthusiasts.

The **tourist office** (☎ 17720) is in the train station. Most facilities are around the main square, which you reach by walking through the park opposite the train station.

Sleeping & Eating

In winter it's best to book accommodation and skiing packages via **Åre Resor** (☎ 17700; www.skistar.com/are); the same company also organises summer packages, but independent travellers at this time of year shouldn't have too many problems finding accommodation. The low season, when almost all hotels and restaurants are closed, is after the snow has melted in May, and between the summer and winter seasons (October until around Christmas).

Åre Ski Lodge (☎ 51029; s/d/tr Skr190/290/390; ☑ May-Sep) On the E14 above the town, next to the fire station, is this cosy Austrian-style ski lodge offering great summer prices and facilities such as sauna and kitchen.

STF Vandrarhem Åre (☎ 30138; info@brattlands garden.com; dm/s/d from Skr170/170/340; ☑ closed May & Oct–mid-Dec) This hostel is actually 8km east of Åre, signposted off the E14. It has good facilities and enjoys great views.

Åre Continental Inn (☎ 17170; www.areinn.se, Swedish only; d Skr800; ☑ May-Sep; ☒) This huge, 130-room complex offers reasonable summer rates for its fairly basic rooms. Facilities are first-rate, however, and include pool, sauna and gym as well as restaurants and bars. The hotel is about 5km east of Åre and operates a shuttle bus to town.

Like the hotels, many restaurants are closed in summer, but there are still some good choices, primarily centred on the main square (where you'll also find supermarkets). **Villa Tottebo** (☎ 50620; Parkvägen 1; mains Skr150-280), opposite the train station, is one of the leading restaurants in Sweden's north, and there's an inviting bar upstairs.

Getting There & Away

Regional bus No 156 runs from Östersund and connects Åre to the nearby winter-sports centre of Duved (much quieter and more family-oriented than Åre). Regular trains between Stockholm and Storlien, via Östersund, stop at Åre. Storlien is the terminus for SJ trains; change here for Norwegian trains to Hell and Trondheim.

UMEÅ

☎ 090 / pop 105,000

Umeå has a large university and a port with ferry connections to Finland. It's among the fastest-growing towns in Sweden and has some 22,000 students, making it an agreeable place to just hanging out for a spell en route north. The **tourist office** (☎ 161616; www .umea.se/turism; Renmarkstorget 15; ☺ daily mid-Jun–mid-Aug, Mon-Fri mid-Aug–mid-Jun) can help with visitor inquiries and offers free Internet access.

The **Gammlia** (☎ 171800; admission free; ☺ daily Jun-Aug, Tue-Sun Aug-Jun) complex, 2km east of the town centre, is home to several good museums and shouldn't be missed. It includes the cultural history and Sami collections of the regional **Västerbottens Museum** (adult/child Skr20/ free), the summer open-air, free **Friluftsmuseet**, with old houses and staff in period clothes, and the free modern art museum **Bildmuseet**.

There are interesting offshore islands plus a number of **activities** in the surrounding area, including fishing, white-water rafting, jet-boating and canoeing in or on the local rivers, horse riding and a variety of walking trails (from two hours to three days). The tourist office can help organise these.

Sleeping & Eating

Compared with other towns in the north, Umeå doesn't have much by way of central budget accommodation.

STF Vandrarhem Umeå (☎ 771650; info@vandrar hemmet.se; Västra Esplanaden 10; dm/d Skr210/420) Everything you need from a hostel – clean, central and well run.

Hotel Pilen (☎ 141460; Pilgatan 5; s/d Skr550/750, s/d discount Skr450/550) A small, family-run place,

with somewhat dated decor but comfortable rooms, in a quiet area some 600m from the town centre.

Royal Hotel (☎ 100730; www.royalhotelumea.com; Skolgatan 62; s/d 1190/1390, s/d discount weekends Skr880/ 650, s/d discount summer Skr520/720) An upmarket option with great summer rates. All the facilities you'd expect, with a highly regarded restaurant on site.

Wayne's Coffee (☎ 701700; Storgatan 50; dishes Skr30-60) Offers great coffee, cake, salads and sandwiches in stylish surrounds, plus an outdoor area for soaking up the long daylight hours (open until 10pm or midnight daily).

Lottas Krog (☎ 129551; Nygatan 22; mains Skr108-198; ☺ Mon-Sat) A friendly, cosy pub-restaurant with something for everyone on the extensive menu, from great snacks under Skr100 to meals such as fish and chips, Mexican fajitas or roast lamb. Also a popular drinking spot.

Blå (☎ 132300; Rådhusesplanaden 14; mains Skr94-132) A large, glossy place with a menu of favourites. Blå turns into a fashionable bar and nightclub as the evening progresses.

Getting There & Away

The long-distance bus station is opposite the train station on Järnvägsallén, which is just north of the centre. Umeå is the main centre for **Länstrafiken Västerbotten** (☎ 020-910019; www.lanstrafikeniac.se), the regional bus network that covers over 55,000 sq km. Direct buses run to Mo i Rana in Norway (Skr232, daily); other daily destinations include Östersund (Skr287), Skellefteå (Skr128) and Luleå (Skr252). Connex trains leave daily from Umeå to connect with the north–south trains between Stockholm and Luleå.

There are daily ferries between Umeå and Vaasa in Finland (see p442). A bus to the harbour leaves from near Umeå's tourist office an hour before ferry departures.

Local buses leave from Vasaplan on Skolgatan.

LULEÅ

☎ 0920 / pop 72,000

Luleå is the capital of Norrbotten, Sweden's largest county and accounting for one quarter of the country's total area. It may be an important transport hub on your journey north, and there are interesting diversions and good-value accommodation. Storgatan is the main pedestrian mall; the **tourist office** (☎ 293500; www.lulea.se; Storgatan 43; ☺ daily Jun-Aug,

Mon-Sat Sep-May) will help with inquiries; and the **library** (Kyrkogatan) has free Internet access.

The most famous sight in Luleå is the Unesco World Heritage Listed **Gammelstad**, or 'Old Town', which was the medieval centre of northern Sweden. The stone church (from 1492), 424 wooden houses (where the pioneers stayed overnight on their weekend pilgrimages) and six church stables remain. The open-air museum, **Hägnan** (☉ Jun-Aug), and a nature reserve are nearby. There's a small **tourist office** (☎ 293581; www.lulea.se/gammelstad; ☉ daily Jun–late Aug, Tue-Thu late Aug–Jun) at Gammelstad, and it organises guided tours (Skr30) of the church village in summer. Take local bus No 6 to Kyrkbyn.

Norbottens Museum (☎ 243500; Storgatan 2; free; ☉ Tue-Sun) is worth a visit for the Sami section and some very interesting short films on the northern lights and Sami identity. In summer there are a number of **boat trips** to the surrounding archipelago.

Sleeping & Eating

Luleå Vandrarhem & Mini Hotell (☎ 222660; lulea vandrarhem@telia.com; Sandviksgatan 26; dm/s/d Skr150/245/360) This budget option doesn't look like much from the outside, but inside there's clean and comfortable accommodation. The large dorms are not so great (tri-level bunks) – the twin rooms are a better option. Bikes are available for hire.

Park Hotell (☎ 211149; www.parkhotell.se, Swedish only; Kungsgatan 10; s/d from Skr490/690, s/d discount Skr390/550) This small hotel offers pleasant but basic rooms. Prices given here are for rooms without bathroom – an extra Skr200 gets you a private bathroom.

Comfort Hotel Max (☎ 220220; www.choicehotels.se; Storgatan 59; s/d Skr1125/1325, s/d discount Skr490/690) A huge bargain at weekends and in summer, as discounted rates at this well-equipped business hotel include breakfast and a dinner buffet.

Roasters (☎ 88840; Storgatan 43; lunch Skr67, snacks Skr28-59) There are good cafés on either side of the tourist office, including this stylish spot with extensive lunch options, grilled focaccia and ciabatta, strong coffee and outdoor seating.

Corsica (☎ 15840; Nygatan 14; meals Skr59-98) is This restaurant-bar is slightly dingy but full of character, and has a huge menu of reasonably priced selections – pizza, pasta, kebabs, salads, fish and steak – all under Skr100.

Getting There & Away

The **airport** (☎ 244900; www.lfv.se) is 9km southwest of the town centre. There are around a dozen flights daily between Stockholm and Luleå (with SAS and Nordic Airlink), and Skyways flies directly to/from Göteborg. Take the airport bus from the bus station (Skr45).

Länstrafiken Norrbotten (☎ 020-470047; www.ltnbd.se) buses cover the 100,000-sq-km county. The maximum fare is Skr280, a 30-day pass covering the entire county costs Skr1475 and bicycles are carried for Skr50. Bus No 100 is one of the most useful for travellers – it runs between Haparanda, Luleå, Skellefteå, Umeå and Sundsvall four times daily. Bus No 21 goes to Arvidsjaur, and bus No 44 to Jokkmokk and on to Gällivare.

Direct Connex trains from Stockholm and Göteborg run at night only. Most trains from Narvik and Kiruna terminate at Luleå.

HAPARANDA
☎ 0922 / pop 10,400
Haparanda was founded in 1821 as a trading town to replace Sweden's loss of Tornio (spelt Torneå in Swedish) to Russia (now in Finland, see p180). Now the two border towns almost function as one entity (both the krona and euro are accepted at most places; Tornio is one hour ahead of Haparanda). There are few sights in Haparanda and the ugly church looks like a grain silo, but one noteworthy attraction is the unique golf course. The **Green Zone Golf Course** (☎ 10660) is right on the border of the two countries, during a full round of golf the border is crossed four times. See p180 for more details.

The scenic **Kukkolaforsen** rapids, on the Torne älv 15km north of Haparanda, are well worth a visit (take bus No 53 or 54). There's a tourist village here (open Midsummer to mid-August) that includes a camping ground and cabins, restaurant, café, fish smokehouse, saunas and a museum.

There's a joint Haparanda–Tornio **tourist office** (☎ 12010; htto://infokiosk.haparanda.se; ☉ daily Midsummer–mid-Aug, Mon-Fri mid-Aug–Midsummer) on the 'green line' between the countries; a smaller summer tourist office operates inside Haparanda's Stadshotellet.

The excellent **STF Vandrarhem Haparanda** (☎ 61171; www.haparandavandrarhem.net; Strandgatan 26; dm/s/d Skr160/250/320) is not far from the town centre. Some rooms have private bathroom, plus there's a sauna, laundry and self-catering facilities, or you can opt for a meal at the decent on-site restaurant.

The large, once-grand **Stadshotellet** (☎ 61490; www.haparandastadshotell.se; Torget 7; s/d Skr1090/1390, s/d discount Skr650/850) is the focus of the town, and its pub-restaurant, the **Gulasch Baronen** (mains Skr70-120) offers reasonably priced meals in a convivial atmosphere. You can find some budget beds for Skr295 here in summer.

A regular bus service connects Haparanda and Tornio (Skr15). There are regional buses from Luleå (Skr117) and towns further south, and daily bus No 53 travels north along the border via the Kukkolaforsen rapids, Övertorneå and Pajala, then continues west to Kiruna (Skr270).

ARVIDSJAUR
☎ 0960 / pop 7100

The small settlement of Arvidsjaur, on the Inlandsbanan railway, was an early Sami market. **Lappstaden**, a well-preserved Sami church village, contains almost 100 buildings as well as forestry and reindeer-breeding concerns. Guided tours cost Skr30/free adult/child but operate only in July. The **tourist office** (☎ 17500; www.arvidsjaurlappland.se; Östra Skolgatan 18c; ☉ daily Jun-Aug, Mon-Fri Sep-May), behind the main street, has useful information.

The town is buzzing in winter, when test drivers from around Europe put their cars through their paces in the tough weather conditions, and there are loads of cold-weather activities available, including dogsledding and snowmobile safaris. Inquire at the tourist office for more details, and for information on the range of summer options, including hiking, excursions, steam trains and fishing.

Cosy **Lappugglans Turistviste** (☎ 12413; Västra Skolgatan 9; dm Skr130) and the stylish **Rallaren** (☎ 070-682 3284; Stationsgatan 4; ☉ Midsummer-Aug; r per person Skr135), both near the train station, have excellent accommodation, the latter adjacent to an artist's gallery. **Kaffestugan** (☎ 107 25; Storgatan 21; lunch Skr60) is a popular café by the main square, with good daily lunch specials plus an assortment of cakes, sandwiches and light meals.

The daily bus between Gällivare and Östersund (No 45) stops at the bus station on Storgatan. Bus No 200 runs daily between Skellefteå and Bodø (Norway) via Arvidsjaur. The Inlandsbanan train can take you north to Gällivare via Jokkmokk, or south to Mora via Östersund.

JOKKMOKK
☎ 0971 / pop 5900

The small town of Jokkmokk, also on the Inlandsbanan railway, is just north of the Arctic Circle and started as a Sami market and mission. Since 1605 the **Jokkmokk Winter Market** (www.jokkmokksmarknad.com) has taken place here; the three-day event attracts some 30,000 people and starts on the first Thursday in February, when you can shop seriously for Sami handicrafts.

The **tourist office** (☎ 22250; www.turism.jokkmokk .se; Stortorget 4; ☉ daily mid-Jun–mid-Aug, Mon-Fri mid-Aug–mid-Jun) can help with visitor information. The **Ájtte museum** (☎ 17070; Kyrkogatan 3; adult/child Skr50/free; ☉ daily May-Sep, Sun-Fri Oct-Apr) is a highlight, providing the most thorough introduction to Sami culture anywhere in Sweden. It also offers exhaustive information on Lappland's mountain areas, with maps, slides, videos and a library. A visit is recommended for planning wilderness trips (there are good opportunities for trekking in the areas surrounding Jokkmokk).

Naturfoto (☎ 55765; ☉ Jun-Aug), at the main Klockartorget intersection, exhibits and sells work by a local wilderness photographer, Edvin Nilsson. There are a number of Sami handicraft studios around town – ask at the tourist office.

About 7km south of Jokkmokk you'll cross the **Arctic Circle**; on road No 45 there's a summertime café and camp site here.

Sleeping & Eating
STF Vandrarhem Jokkmokk (☎ 55977; www.jokk mokkhostel.com; Åsgatan 20; dm/d Skr165/410; 🖳) Behind the tourist office, this comfortable hostel has laundry, sauna, yard, Internet facilities and bikes for rent. It's a favourite with Inlandsbanan travellers and worth booking in advance in summer.

Hotell Gästis (☎ 10012; www.hotell-gastis.com, Swedish only; Herrevägen 1; s/d/tr Skr850/995/1200, s/d/tr discount Skr650/750/900) It doesn't look too promising from the outside, but this hotel offers decent value with pleasant but unremarkable rooms, sauna and a good restaurant, with lunch specials and à la carte dinners.

At the **Ájtte museum restaurant** (Kyrkogatan 3; lunch Skr65) you can try local and Sami specialities, including the fresh local fish or a sandwich with reindeer meat.

Café Piano (☎ 10400; Porjusvägen 4; lunch Skr60, mains Skr50-120; ☉ Mon-Sat) One of the town's best options, with a grand piano inside, a large garden outside and an extensive menu, including inexpensive pizza, pasta and wok meals.

Getting There & Away

Buses arrive and leave from the bus station on Klockarvägen. Bus Nos 44 and 45 run daily to/from Gällivare (Skr94), and bus No 45 runs to Arvidsjaur once daily (Skr142) and further south to Östersund (Skr410). Inlandsbanan trains stop in Jokkmokk; for main-line trains, take bus No 43 to Murjek (up to six a day) or bus No 44 to Boden (Skr126) and Luleå (Skr157).

GÄLLIVARE

☎ 0970 / pop 19,700

The town of Gällivare and its northern twin Malmberget are surrounded by forest and dwarfed by the bald Dundret hill. It's not the most immediately appealing place for a stopover but is important as the northern terminus for the Inlandsbanan railway, and there are good opportunities for summer and winter activities.

The **tourist office** (☎ 16660; www.gellivare.se; Centralplan; ◷ Mon-Fri) is by the train station. **Dundret** (821m) is a nature reserve with superb views; you can view the midnight sun here from 2 June to 12 July. In winter there are four nordic courses and 10 ski runs of varying difficulty, and the mountain-top resort organises numerous activities including snowmobile safaris and northern lights tours.

In Malmberget, 5km north of Gällivare, **Käkstan** is a historical 'shanty town' museum village dating from the 1888 iron-ore rush. Bus No 1 to Malmberget departs from opposite the Gällivare church. The Gällivare tourist office has details of tours to the **LKAB iron-ore mine** (tours Skr200; ◷ Midsummer-early Aug).

STF Vandrarhem Gällivare (☎ 14380; www.explore lapland.com; Barnhemsvägen 2; dm Skr195) is across the footbridge from the train station. Accommodation is in well-equipped cabins; bikes can be hired and a variety of activities organised (multiday wilderness treks in summer, dogsledge tours in winter; see the website for details).

Quality Hotel Lapland (☎ 55020; www.qualityhotel .gellivare.se; Lasarettsgatan 1; s/d Skr1195/1490, s/d discount Skr690/890) is a more expensive option opposite the train station. Your best bet for dining in Gällivare is the restaurant (lunch for Skr68)

and pub (mains Skr95 to Skr230) inside the Quality Hotel, with a decent menu of cheaper dishes (pasta, burgers) and local specialities such as elk fillet or arctic char.

Getting There & Away

Regional buses depart from the train station. Bus No 45 runs daily to Östersund (Skr410) via Jokkmokk and Arvidsjaur; bus No 93 serves Ritsem and Kungsleden in Stora Sjöfallet National Park (from mid-June to mid-September only); bus Nos 10 and 52 go to Kiruna (Skr117); and bus No 44 runs to Jokkmokk (Skr94) and Luleå (Skr198).

Connex trains come from Luleå and Stockholm (sometimes changing at Boden), and from Narvik in Norway. More exotic is the Inlandsbanan, which terminates at Gällivare; the journey from Östersund costs Skr697.

KIRUNA

☎ 0980 / pop 23,900

Kiruna is the northernmost town in Sweden and, at 19,446 sq km, it's the largest municipality in the country. The area includes Sweden's highest peak (Kebnekaise, 2111m), a remarkable attraction in the form of a hotel made from ice, and several fine national parks and trekking routes (see the following Abisko section). It's worth making the effort to get up here!

This far north, the midnight sun lasts from 27 May to 14 July and there's a bluish darkness throughout December and New Year.

The helpful **tourist office** (☎ 10000; www.lapp land.se; Lars Janssonsgatan 17; ◷ 8.30am-8pm Mon-Fri, 8.30am-6pm Sat & Sun May-Sep, 8.30am-8pm Mon-Fri, 8.30am-6pm Sat Oct-Apr) is next to the Scandic Hotel and has loads of detailed brochures. Staff can arrange various activities including Sami experiences year-round; rafting, hiking, horse riding, rock climbing and fishing in warmer weather; and ice-fishing, dogsledding and snowmobile safaris in winter.

The **library** (Biblioteksgatan), behind the bus station, offers free Internet access.

A visit to the Ice Hotel (see p431) is a must. Also worthwhile in Kiruna is a visit to the depths of the **LKAB iron-ore mine** (☎ 18880; tours adult/child Skr195/50), 540m underground. Two-hour English-language tours depart from the tourist office regularly from June to August, and during other months if there's enough interest. Make inquiries and bookings through the tourist office. **Kiruna**

SWEDEN

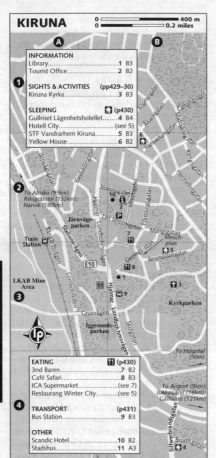

KIRUNA

0 _____ 400 m
0 _____ 0.2 miles

Ⓐ   Ⓑ

INFORMATION
Library.................................1 B3
Tourist Office........................2 B2

SIGHTS & ACTIVITIES   (pp429–30)
Kiruna Kyrka..........................3 B3

SLEEPING   🏠 (p430)
Gullriset Lägenhetshotellet.......4 B4
Hotell City.........................(see 5)
STF Vandrarhem Kiruna...........5 B3
Yellow House.........................6 B2

To Abisko (95km);
Riksgränsen (132km);
Narvik (180km);

Järnvägs-
parken

Train
Station

E10

LKAB Mine
Area

Kyrkparken

To Hospital
(50m)

EATING   🍽 (p430)
3nd Baren.............................7 B2
Café Safari............................8 B3
ICA Supermarket..................(see 7)
Restaurang Winter City.........(see 5)

To Airport (9km);
Jukkasjärvi (16km);
Gällivare (121km)

TRANSPORT   (p431)
Bus Station...........................9 B3

OTHER
Scandic Hotel.......................10 B2
Stadshus.............................11 A3

kyrka (Kyrkogatan), the town church, looks like a gigantic Sami tent; it's particularly pretty against a snowy backdrop.

Sleeping & Eating

Kiruna has lots of good-value accommodation options, especially in summer. The tourist office brochures include full details, including prices.

STF Vandrarhem Kiruna (☎ 17195; www.kiruna hostel.com, Swedish only; Bergmästaregatan 7; dm/s/d Skr195/315/450) Central location, good facilities (including sauna) and an adjacent Chinese restaurant. Breakfast Skr60.

Yellow House (☎ 13750; www.yellowhouse.nu; Hantverkaregatan 25; dm/s/d Skr120/300/400) Another good budget option, with facilities includ-

ing sauna, kitchen, laundry and TV in each room. Breakfast is Skr50.

Gullriset Lägenhetshotellet (☎ 10937; www.fabmf .se/gullriset, Swedish only; Bromsgatan 12; apt Skr400-700) About 1.5km from the tourist office, this bargain option is perfect for self-caterers and those who fancy more space than a hotel room offers. Rent an apartment sleeping up to four people, with kitchen, bathroom and cable TV.

Hotell City (☎ 66655; www.hotellcity.se; Bergmästar-egatan 7; s/d Skr750/850, s/d discount Skr650/750) In the same building as the STF hostel, this new hotel has pleasant, modern rooms and affordable rates. Prices include breakfast, and there's also access to the hostel's kitchen.

Ice Hotel (☎ 66800; www.icehotel.com; Marknadsvä-gen, Jukkasjärvi; ice d from Skr2800, non-ice d from 2800Skr, 3-person cabin Skr2800) Staying at the Ice Hotel is a unique experience and if you have the cash it shouldn't be missed. Apart from ice rooms there are other options, including stylish hotel rooms, or three-bed cabins with skylights enabling you to watch the northern lights from your bed in winter. Winter is expensive but the novelty makes it worthwhile. Summer prices have escalated dramatically in recent years, and don't represent good value given the range of affordable accommodation in Kiruna.

Ice Hotel Restaurant (☎ 66884; Marknadsvägen, Jukkasjärvi; mains Skr190-280) This quality restaurant opposite the accommodation complex in Jukkasjärvi specialises in local produce – try the arctic char or reindeer, and for dessert cloudberry mousse or moose cheese parfait! Some meals even come on plates made of ice. The lunch buffet (in summer) costs Skr95.

Kiruna is not well endowed with great eateries. Easily the nicest café is **Café Safari** (☎ 17460; Geologsgatan 4; light meals Skr20-60), with good coffee, cakes and light meals such as sandwiches, quiche and baked potatoes. **Restaurang Winter City** (☎ 10900; Bergmästaregatan 7; lunch buffet Skr55, meals Skr92-140) is adjacent to the STF hostel, offering classic Chinese dishes, cheap lunches, takeaway meals and kids' options. **3nd Baren** (☎ 66380; Föreningsgatan 11; lunch Skr65, mains Skr69-189) is a popular, moderately priced restaurant and a lively drinking spot in the evenings; you can try local specialities like reindeer, or play safe with steak or pasta.

There's an **ICA supermarket** (Föreningsgatan; 🕐 9am-7pm Mon-Fri, 10am-4pm Sat, 11am-4pm Sun), next to 3nd Baren.

THE ICE HOTEL

The highlight of a trip this far north is a visit to the fabulous **Ice Hotel** (☎ 66800; www.icehotel .com; Marknadsvägen, Jukkasjärvi; day visit adult/child Skr120/60), truly a unique and super-cool experience, if you'll pardon the pun.

Every winter at Jukkasjärvi, 18km east of Kiruna, an amazing structure is built from tonnes of ice taken from the frozen local river. This huge, custom-built 'igloo' has a chapel (popular for weddings – giving new meaning to the expression 'cold feet'!), plus a bar (you can enjoy a drink – preferably vodka – from a glass made purely of ice) and exhibitions of ice sculptures by international artists. It also has more than 60 'hotel rooms', where guests can sleep on beds covered with reindeer skins and inside sleeping bags guaranteed to keep you warm despite the -5°C to -8°C temperatures (and in winter that's nothing – outside the hotel it can be as low as -30°C!). The hotel is normally open from mid-December to late April (weather permitting).

There are numerous activities for guests to pursue (snowmobile safaris, skiing, ice-fishing, dog-sledging etc). And if cultural pursuits are more your cup of tea, check out the **Ice Globe Theatre** (tickets from Skr450, discounted to Skr300 for hotel guests, performances mid-Jan–early Apr), a replica of Shakespeare's Globe Theatre constructed from ice. Here Sami theatre groups perform *Hamlet* in the Sami language, and other performers rug up to put on a show (possibly opera or even rock concerts). The cost of all these activities starts to add up, but anyone can visit the hotel on a day visit, and it's highly recommended. And if you visit, ask the bartender where the stereo is being kept – chances are it's in the fridge, as it's warmer there!

In summer (from June), after the Ice Hotel has melted away, day visitors can still experience a little of the magic. Inside a giant freezer warehouse, called the **Ice Hotel Art Center** (adult/child Skr100/50; ☉ 10am-5pm Jun–mid-Aug), at a temperature of -5°C, some features of the Ice Hotel remain, including a bar and ice sculptures; the entry fee includes warm clothing.

Get there on bus No 501.

See Sleeping & Eating following for details of accommodation prices.

Getting There & Away

The small **airport** (☎ 68000; www.lfv.se), 9km east of the town, has nonstop flights to/from Stockholm with SAS (daily). An airport bus (Skr50) connects with most flights.

Regional buses in this vast region are run by **Länstrafiken Norrbotten** (☎ 020-4/004/; www .ltnbd.se). Buses operate from the bus station on Hjalmar Lundbohmsvägen, opposite the Stadshus, and serve all major settlements. Bus No 91 runs two or three times daily to Riksgränsen (Skr117) via Abisko (Skr94).

Regular trains connect Kiruna with Luleå, Stockholm (overnight) and Narvik (Norway). Trains to Narvik call at Abisko and Riksgränsen.

ABISKO

☎ 0980 / pop 180

The 75-sq-km **Abisko National Park**, on the southern shore of scenic Lake Torneträsk, is well served by trains, buses and the scenic mountain highway between Kiruna and Narvik. It's the soft option of the northern parks – distinctly less rugged and more accessible. There are some great short hikes.

The popular **Kungsleden** ('King's Trail') follows the Abiskojåkka Valley and day trips of 10km or 20km are no problem from Abisko village. Kungsleden extends 450km south from Abisko to Hemavan (with huts and lodges along most of the route) and offers diversions to the summit of **Kebnekaise** or the magical national park of **Sarek** (no huts and few bridges). Waterproof (preferably rubber) boots are essential at any time of the year; the snow doesn't melt until June. July, August and September are recommended for hiking although in July there's still some boggy ground where mosquitoes breed. It can still get cold very quickly, despite the midnight sun. Winter escapades are too risky for the uninitiated due to blizzards, extreme cold and avalanches.

The **Naturum** (☎ 40177; www.abisko-naturum.nu), next to the STF lodge in Abisko, provides information on the region. The **Linbana** (Skr110 return; ☉ 9.30am-4pm) chairlift takes you to 900m on Njulla (1169m) for breathtaking views.

In Björkliden, 8km northwest of Abisko, the resort **Björkliden Fjällby** (☎ 64100; www.bjork liden.com) offers a full range of summer and winter activities and even has a nine-hole golf course. Tours are also organised by STF at Abisko Turiststation (see below); both places offer outdoor gear for hire.

Sleeping & Eating

Abisko Fjällturer (☎ 40103; www.abisko.net; dm Skr150) This small hostel is a backpackers' delight. It has simple, comfortable accommodation and a wonderful wooden sauna, but the treat is in the reasonably priced activities on offer. The friendly owners keep a team of sled dogs, and for Skr600 in winter you get a night's hostel accommodation plus the chance to drive a sled, pulled by dogs, for about 10km. There are also half/full-day sled trips (Skr900/1700), and popular week-long sled trips from late February to early April (Skr8800 including meals and accommodation). Book early for longer trips. In summer you can take mountain walks with the dogs (Skr300 with night in a dorm).

Abisko Turiststation (☎ 40200; www.abisko.nu; dm/s/d Skr290/510/780; ☉ Mar-Apr & mid-Jun–mid-Sep) Another excellent option, kept to the usual high STF standards. Trekking gear can be hired here, and there's a variety of accommodation options, guided tours, a shop with basic groceries, a pub and a restaurant (breakfast/lunch/dinner Skr75/75/195; half- and full-board arrangements are available). Accommodation prices are reduced by Skr100 for HI/STF members.

There's a supermarket in Abisko village for self-caterers, and a café-restaurant nearby.

Self-service **STF huts** (dm members Skr185-275, dm nonmembers Skr285-375) along Kungsleden are spread at 10km to 20km intervals between Abisko and Kvikkjokk; take a sleeping bag. Day visitors are charged Skr40/50 members/nonmembers, campers pay Skr60/80. The excellent 100km trek from Abisko to Nikkaluokta runs via the STF lodge **Kebnekaise Fjällstation** (☎ 55000; info@kebnekaise.st.se; dm/s/d from Skr320/850/1000; ☉ Mar-Apr & mid-Jun–mid-Sep). Meals are available, and guided tours to the summit of Kebnekaise are offered. HI/STF members pay Skr100 less than prices listed.

Getting There & Away

In addition to trains (stations at Abisko Östra and Abisko Turiststation) between Luleå and Narvik, bus No 91 runs from Kiruna to Abisko (Skr94). Bus No 92 travels from Kiruna to Nikkaluokta (Skr69, two to three a day), at the Kebnekaise trail heads. Kvikkjokk is served by bus No 47 that runs twice daily on weekdays to/from Jokkmokk (Skr117).

RIKSGRÄNSEN

☎ 0980 / pop 50

The best midnight (or daytime) skiing in June in Scandinavia awaits you at this rugged frontier area (Riksgränsen translates as 'National Border'), 132km from Kiruna. You can briefly visit Norway at full speed on downhill skis! Rental of downhill gear/snowboards costs from Skr265/310 per day, and a day lift pass is Skr285; the skiing season can run until Midsummer.

There's not much to the tiny settlement here, but you can visit Sven Hörnell's **wilderness photography exhibition** (☎ 43111; www.sven-hornell.se; ☉ Feb-Sep) at his gallery and shop. The exhibition itself is free, and there's an audiovisual show (Skr70; 3pm daily mid-June to August, call for other times); commentary is in Swedish only, but you don't have to understand the language to appreciate the stunning Norrland photography.

Riksgränsen Ski & Spa Resort (☎ 40080; www.riksgransen.nu; r per person from Skr625; ☉ closed Oct–mid-Feb) is a large resort that's popular with skiers and offers organised wilderness activities in both the skiing and summer seasons. Rooms and apartments are available.

From Kiruna, bus No 91 runs via Abisko to Riksgränsen (Skr117, two or three a day). Three daily trains run on the Luleå–Kiruna–Narvik route, and Riksgränsen is the last train station in Sweden before the train rushes through tunnels and mountain scenery back to sea level at Narvik in Norway.

SWEDEN DIRECTORY

ACCOMMODATION

In this chapter, we have classified sleeping options as follows:

- Budget: a bed in these establishments (usually hostels and budget guesthouses) should cost under Skr300 per person.
- Mid-range: Skr650 to Skr1500 for a double room on a weekday. This price range covers small, comfortable hotels in the major cities, but some more luxurious options in smaller towns.
- Top End: Skr1500 and upwards for a weekday double.

Camping

Sweden has hundreds of camping grounds and a free English-language guide with maps is available. Some camping grounds are open in winter, but the best time for camping is from May to August. Prices vary with facilities, from Skr80 for a basic site to Skr200 for the highest standards. Most camping grounds have kitchens and laundry facilities, and many grounds are popular family holiday spots and have the works – swimming pool, minigolf, bike and canoe rental, restaurant, store etc.

You must have the (free) Svenskt Campingkort to stay at Swedish camping grounds. Apply at least one month before your journey to **Sveriges Camping & Stugföretagares Riksorganisation** (SCR; fax 0522-642430; Box 255, SE-45117 Uddevalla), or on the Internet at www.camping.se. If this isn't possible, you'll be given a temporary card on arrival. The annual stamp on your card costs Skr90 and is obtainable at the first camping ground you visit.

Visit www.camping.se for lots of useful information. See also p361 for advice on free camping in Sweden.

Hostels

Forget all your preconceptions about hostels being dingy, scruffy and the domain of noisy young backpackers. Swedish hostels are exceptional: clean, well equipped, nicely decorated (this is the land of Ikea, after all, so practical, attractive furniture is readily available) and very good value. Dorm beds, singles, doubles and family rooms are usually available; some rooms have a private bathroom and/or TV. The majority are nonsmoking establishments. There's almost always a kitchen for guests' use, and often a laundry (which is handy, as laundrettes are nonexistent in Sweden). Breakfast is often available (Skr40 to Skr60), but normally has to be arranged the night before. Linen is available for rent, but bring sleeping sheets, a pillow case and a towel from home to save money. You'll be expected to clean your room upon departure (if you don't want to do this, you can pay the hostel a 'cleaning fee').

Sweden has well over 475 *vandrarhem* (hostels) and some 315 are 'official' hostels affiliated with **Svenska Turistföreningen** (STF; ☎ 08-463 2100; www.svenskaturistforeningen.se; Box 25, SE-10120 Stockholm), part of Hostelling International (HI). STF produces a free detailed guide to its hostels, but the text is in Swedish only (although the symbols are generally easy to understand). All hostel details are also found on the organisation's website, with some information in English. Holders of HI cards stay at STF hostels for between Skr80 and Skr280 per bed per night. Nonmembers pay Skr45 extra per night or can join up at hostels (membership costs Skr285 for adults, Skr110 for those aged 16 to 25, free for children). In this chapter we have listed the prices at STF hostels for nonmembers.

Around 160 hostels belong to the 'rival' **Sveriges Vandrarhem i Förening** (SVIF; ☎ 0413 553 450; www.svif.se; Box 9, SE-45043 Smögen). No membership is required; rates and facilities are similar to those of the STF. Pick up the free guide at tourist offices or SVIF hostels.

Also look out for other hostels that are not affiliated with either STF or SVIF, and note that some camping grounds have hostels.

Hostels in Sweden have a unique and frustrating problem: they're hard to get into outside reception opening times. Most of the day (and much of the winter) the doors are firmly locked. The trick is to phone and make a reservation during the (usually short) reception hours. These vary, but are generally from 5pm to 7pm. You may have to write down the four-digit entrance door code and ask where the room key will be. Theoretically, you could stay overnight without seeing another person until you pay in the morning. From June to August you can expect longer reception hours, but a reservation is recommended during this busy period. May is also a busy time for hostels in major cities like Stockholm and Göteborg as school groups visit the Big Smoke.

Be careful in December and check that the hostel is open at Christmas and New Year. Not all hostels are open year round – some are in student residences and only open for the seven-week summer break (from around Midsummer to early or mid-August). Others are only open in the busier months from May to September.

There are numerous mountain huts and lodges, especially in Lappland, run by STF. These are popular with hikers and outdoor enthusiasts; more information is available on STF's website.

SWEDEN

Cabins & Chalets

Daily rates for *stugor* (cabins and chalets, often found at camping grounds or in the countryside) offer good value for small groups and families, and range in both facilities and price (Skr200 to Skr800). Some cabins are simple, with bunk beds and little else (you share the bathroom and kitchen facilities with campers); others are fully equipped with their own kitchen, bathroom and even living room. Local and regional tourist offices have listings of cabins and cottages that may be rented by the week; these are often in idyllic forest, lakeside or coastal locations and offer the chance for a true Swedish holiday experience. See www .stuga.nu for more information.

Hotels

There are few cheap hotels in Sweden. However, almost all hotels offer good-value weekend and summer (mid-June to mid-August) rates, often below Skr800 for a quite luxurious double (up to 50% cheaper than their regular prices). See individual reviews for discount prices. All hotels have nonsmoking sections (some are entirely nonsmoking). Rates usually include a breakfast buffet. Some packages are good value if you plan ahead: Stockholm, Göteborg and Malmö offer cut-price 'packages' that include a hotel room, free entry to the major attractions of the city and free local transport (see the Information sections under each city). Tourist offices and travel agents can usually give details.

Ask at a tourist office for the free brochure *Hotels in Sweden*, or check www.hotelsin sweden.net. Discount schemes for 'frequent stayers' are generally run by the big chains; eg **Radisson SAS** (www.radissonsas.com), **Scandic** (www .scandic-hotels.com), **First** (www.firsthotels.com) and **Elite** (www.elite.se). Appealing to those on a budget are the two cheapest (and somewhat characterless) hotel chains, **Formule 1** (www.hotel formule1.com) and **Ibis** (www.ibishotel.com). At the other end of the scale, **Countryside Hotels** (www .countrysidehotels.se) offers accommodation in historic establishments ranging from castles and mansions to monasteries and spas.

ACTIVITIES

The image of wholesome, outdoorsy Swedes is pretty spot-on (well, except for all the coffee they consume and cigarettes they smoke). The Swedes are huge nature-lovers and are active year-round, on bike paths, forest jogging tracks, rivers and lakes, mountain trails, and the snow and ice.

Anyone getting out and about in the Swedish countryside should become familiar with Sweden's very democratic right of public access – see p361.

Canoeing & Kayaking

Sweden's superb wilderness lakes and white-water rivers are a paradise for canoeists and kayakers. The national canoeing body is **Svenska Kanotförbundet** (☎ 0155-209080; www .kanot.com; Rosvalla, SE-61162 Nyköping). It provides general advice and produces *Kanotvåg*, a free annual brochure listing the 75 approved canoe centres that hire canoes (averaging Skr200/800 per day/week) throughout the country. According to the right of common access, canoeists may paddle or moor virtually anywhere provided they respect the basic privacy of dwellings and avoid sensitive nesting areas within nature reserves. More good information is available at www.kanotguiden .com, which also lists rental centres.

Hiking

Hiking is popular everywhere and the mountain challenge of the northern national parks is compelling. However, these parks are rarely snow-free and the jewel, Sarek, is only for experienced hikers. Good equipment is vital.

Easy walking trails are common. Many counties have a network of easy trails connecting sites of interest, and many municipalities have their own wilderness tracks (some off-the-beaten-track routes have free huts or shelters). The best hiking time is between late June and mid-September, but conditions are better after early August, when the mosquitoes have gone.

For information on organised group walks and the STF mountain huts, which are placed at intervals averaging about 20km along popular trails like Kungsleden, contact STF (see p433). You may stay the night (or camp nearby) for a fee which is slightly higher than STF hostel rates. There are also nine STF mountain lodges with shops, showers and restaurants. The free STF hostel guide includes details of mountain huts and lodges. Conditions are self-service, similar to STF hostels, and you should bring sheets (sleeping bags in huts).

Skiing

Cross-country (nordic) skiing opportunities vary depending on the snow and temperatures, but the northwest usually has plenty of snow from December to April (although not a lot of daylight in December and January). Practically all town areas (except the far south) have marked skiing tracks, often illuminated. There are large ski resorts catering mainly for downhill skiing in the mountainous areas of the west – Åre (p425) is the biggest and busiest (especially around Easter). The websites www.goski.com and www.thealps.com have good pages reviewing the Swedish ski fields.

Other Activities

Opportunities for countless other activities exist, including cycling, rock climbing, mountaineering, fishing, horse riding, golf, sailing and rafting in summer; and skating, ice fishing, ice climbing, snowmobile safaris and dogsledding in winter. Tourist offices should be able to provide information, and you should check out the 'what to do?' pages of www.visit-sweden.com.

BUSINESS HOURS

Businesses and government offices open from 8.30am or 9am to 5pm Monday to Friday, although they can close at 3pm in summer. Banks usually open at 9.30am and close at 3pm, but some city branches open from 9am to 5pm or 6pm.

Most museums have short opening hours and many tourist offices are closed at weekends in the low season, from mid-August to mid-June.

Normal shopping hours are 9am to 6pm Monday to Friday and 9am to between 1pm and 4pm on Saturday, but department stores are open longer and sometimes also on Sunday. Some supermarkets in large towns will open until 7pm or 9pm. In restaurants, lunch often begins at 11.30am and is over by 2pm, and the restaurant will reopen again at 6pm for dinner. Cafés are usually open long hours (from 8am or 9am sometimes through until 9pm).

Frustratingly, many hostels, especially those belonging to the STF network, are closed between 10am and 5pm (see p433).

'Summer' in this chapter is generally used to refer to the busy, brief summer season that runs from around mid-June to early or mid-August. This is when Swedish schools and many industries and offices are closed, and the Swedes flock en masse to their summer houses, the beach, lakes, mountains etc. Even some restaurants in larger cities are closed during this period. However, all is not lost – this is when hotels offer great bargains, with discounts of up to 50% on their standard rates (to fill rooms usually taken by business travellers).

CUSTOMS

Going through customs rarely involves any hassles, but rules on illegal drugs are strictly enforced. Duty-free allowances for travellers from outside the EU are: 1L of spirits or 2L of fortified wine; 2L of wine; and 200 cigarettes. The limits on goods brought into Sweden from another EU country are far more generous: up to 10L of spirits or 20L of fortified wine; 90L of wine; 110L of beer; plus 800 cigarettes. People aged under 20 years are not allowed to bring in alcohol. More information is on the website of the Swedish customs authority, Tullverket (www.tullverket.se).

DISABLED TRAVELLERS

Sweden is one of the easiest countries to travel around in a wheelchair. People with disabilities will find special transport services and adapted facilities of a generally high standard, ranging from trains and taxis to hotels and grocery stores. For information about facilities, contact the national organisation for people with disabilities, **De Handikappades Riksförbund** (☎ 08-685 8000; www.dhr.se; Katrinebergsvägen 6, Box 47305, SE-10074 Stockholm).

DISCOUNT CARDS

A Hostelling International (HI) membership card means discounts at STF hostels and mountain lodges (nonmembers pay an additional Skr45 per night, or can join in Sweden). Students should bring an ISIC card, although a number of discounts only apply to people with a Swedish student card. Still, students receive discounts on many forms of transport (including some airlines, ferry operators and local public transport), and on admission to museums, sights, theatres and cinemas. Children under 16 and seniors (usually 65 and over) normally receive similar discounts.

There are good-value discount cards available in the major cities (Stockholm, Göteborg and Malmö) that cover all local transport and most sightseeing needs for visitors for a set period (usually up to 72 hours). See the Information sections under each city for details.

EMBASSIES
Swedish Embassies & Consulates
A list of Swedish diplomatic missions abroad (and links) is available at www.sweden abroad.com.

Australia (☎ 02-6270 2700; www.embassyofsweden .org.au; 5 Turrana St, Yarralumla ACT 2600)

Canada (☎ 613-241 8553; www.swedishembassy.ca; 377 Dalhousie St, Ottawa ON K1N 9N8)

Denmark (☎ 33 36 03 70; www.swedenabroad.com/co penhagen; Sankt Annæ Plads 15A, DK-1250 Copenhagen K)

Finland (☎ 09-6877 660; www.swedenabroad.com /helsinki; Pohjoisesplanadi 7B, 00170 Helsinki)

France (☎ 01 44 18 88 00; www.swedenabroad.com/paris; 17 rue Barbet-de-Jouy, F-75007 Paris)

Germany (☎ 030-505060; www.swedenabroad.com /berlin; Rauchstrasse 1, 10787 Berlin)

Ireland (☎ 01-474 4400; www.swedenabroad.com /dublin; 13-17 Dawson St, Dublin 2)

Netherlands (☎ 070-412 0200; www.swedenabroad.com /thehague; Jan Willem Frisolaan 3, 2517 JS Den Haag)

New Zealand (☎ 04-499 9895; sweden@xtra.co.nz; 13th fl, Vogel Bldg, Aitken St, Wellington)

Norway (☎ 24 11 42 00; www.swedenabroad.com/oslo; Nobels gate 16, NO-0244 Oslo)

UK (☎ 020-7917 6400; www.swedish-embassy.org.uk; 11 Montagu Place, London W1H 2AL)

USA (☎ 202-467 2600; www.swedenabroad.com/wash ington; Suite 900, 1501 M St NW, Washington DC 20005)

Embassies & Consulates in Sweden
The diplomatic missions listed here are in Stockholm, although some neighbouring countries also have consulates in Göteborg, Malmö and Helsingborg:

Australia (Map pp370-1; ☎ 08-613 2900; 11th fl, Sergels Torg 12)

Canada (Map pp370-1; ☎ 08-453 3000; 7th fl, Tegelbacken 4)

Denmark (Map pp370-1; ☎ 08-406 7500; Sankt Jakobs Torg 1)

Finland (Map pp364-6; ☎ 08-676 6700; Gärdesgatan 9–11)

France (Map pp370-1; ☎ 08-459 5300; Kommendörsgatan 13)

Germany (Map pp364-6; ☎ 08-670 1500; Skarpögatan 9)

Ireland (Map pp364-6; ☎ 08-661 8005; Östermalmsgatan 97)

Netherlands (Map pp370-1; ☎ 08-556 933 00; Götgatan 16A)

Norway (Map pp364-6; ☎ 08-665 6340; Skarpögatan 4)

UK (Map pp364-6; ☎ 08-671 3000; Skarpögatan 6-8)

USA (Map pp364-6; ☎ 08-783 5300; Dag Hammarskjöldsväg 31)

FESTIVALS & EVENTS
The Swedes love their traditional festivals and celebrate in style year-round.

Valborgsmässoafton (Walpurgis Night; 30 April) celebrates the arrival of spring with bonfires and choral singers. Upper-secondary-school leavers with their white caps are a common sight; the festivities have developed from a mixture of traditional bonfires on the eve of May Day, and student celebrations at Lund and Uppsala.

The **National Day** is 6 June (Gustav Vasa was elected King of Sweden on 6 June 1523) but, surprisingly, it isn't a public holiday.

Midsommar (Midsummer, first Saturday after 21 June) is *the* festival of the year. Decorating and raising the Midsummer pole and dancing around it are traditional activities on Midsummer's Eve, and most people head for the countryside for this. For the folk touch, the Lake Siljan region (p390) is a good place to celebrate, but folk costumes, singing, music, dancing, pickled herring washed down with schnapps, strawberries and cream, and beer drinking, are common almost everywhere. At the other end of summer, **crayfish parties** in August celebrate the end of the season.

Luciadagen (the Lucia festival; 13 December) is also popular. Oddly, it seems to merge the folk tradition of the longest night and the story of St Lucia of Syracuse. A choir in white, led by Lucia (who wears a crown of candles), leads the singing.

Many towns host popular Christmas markets in December. **Christmas Eve** is the main day of celebration during this season; it's the night of the *smörgåsbord* and the arrival of *jultomten*, the Christmas gnome carrying a sack of gifts.

If you're in Stockholm for Valborgsmässoafton, Midsommar, Luciadagen, Christmas or New Year's Eve, a great place to participate in the festivities is the Skansen open-air museum on Djurgården (p367).

Almost every Swedish town hosts a summer festival between May and September. Music, dance, eating, drinking, competitions and fun for children are regular features of these events, which can last for up to a week. You can find more information on music festivals (opera, choir, folk, jazz and chamber music) online at www.musikfestivaler.se. Another website, www.festivalfakta.com, lists many of the big rock music festivals (at the time of research its English pages hadn't been updated, but it's not hard to navigate the Swedish pages and find links to the events).

GAY & LESBIAN TRAVELLERS

Sweden is famous for its liberal attitudes and there are laws allowing same-sex 'registered partnerships', which grant most of the standard marriage rights. The organisation concerned with equality for lesbians and gays is **Riksförbundet för Sexuellt Likaberättigande** (RFSL; ☎ 08-457 1300; www.rfsl.se; Sveavägen 57-59, Stockholm). The website is in Swedish only.

One of the capital's biggest parties is the annual **Stockholm Pride** (www.stockholmpride.org), a five day festival celebrating gay culture, held in late July–early August and based mainly in Tantolunden, a large park in Södermalm.

A good source of information is the free, monthly magazine *QX* giving gay and lesbian information and listings (again, only in Swedish). You can pick up a copy at many clubs, stores and restaurants, mainly in Stockholm, Göteborg, Malmö and Copenhagen. Its website (www.qx.se) has some excellent information and recommendations in English.

HOLIDAYS

There are plenty of public holidays in spring and early summer. The Midsummer holiday brings life almost to a halt for three days: transport and other services are reduced, so plan ahead. Some hotels are closed from Christmas to New Year. Note: some businesses will close early the day before a public holiday and all day the day after.

Public holidays in Sweden are:
New Year's Day 1 January
Epiphany 6 January
Good Friday to Easter Monday March/April
Labour Day 1 May
Ascension Day May/June (39th day after Easter)
Whit Sunday & Monday late May or early June
Midsummer's Day first Saturday after 21 June
All Saints' Day Saturday, late October or early November
Christmas Day 25 December
Boxing Day 26 December

Christmas Eve, New Year's Eve and Midsummer's Eve are not official holidays, but are generally nonworking days for most of the population.

INTERNET ACCESS

Internet cafés typically charge around Skr30 to Skr40 per hour online. However, facilities to log on can be rare outside big cities, because many Swedes have Internet access at home or school. Many Internet cafés, where they do exist, are testosterone-filled amusement arcades rather than traveller hang-outs.

Some tourist offices offer a computer terminal for visitor use (sometimes for free). Look out for the free 'drop-in' terminals at many libraries, available for 15 minutes at a time.

INTERNET RESOURCES

Most Swedish organisations have their own websites, and many of these have pages in English. Every town also has its own site – usually this is found by simply entering 'www.', then the town's name, followed by '.se'; eg www.orebro.se or www.lulea.se.

Following are some helpful websites:
CityGuide Sweden (www.cityguide.se) Detailed information pages for nearly 80 Swedish cities.
Naturvårdsverket (www.environ.se) Site of the Swedish environmental protection agency, with good coverage of the country's national parks.
Svenska Institutet (www.si.se) The Swedish Institute is a public agency entrusted with disseminating knowledge abroad about Sweden. This site is full of detailed information on countless topics.
Svenska Turistföreningen (www.svenskaturist foreningen.se) STF (the Swedish touring agency) maintains a network of over 300 quality hostels throughout the country.
Swedish Travel and Tourism Council (www.visit -sweden.com) Loads of useful travel information in many languages.
Virtual Sweden (www.sweden.se) Svenska Institutet maintains this 'official gateway to Sweden' with excellent links in various categories (including culture, nature and environment and sports and leisure).

MONEY

You should encounter few problems if you carry cash in any convertible currency or internationally recognised travellers cheques. The national ATM networks usually accept international Visa, Plus, EC, Eurocard, MasterCard or Cirrus cards.

Forex (www.forex.se), with branches in the biggest cities and most airports and ferry terminals, is one of the cheapest and easiest places to exchange money and charges Skr15 per cheque. Banks charge up to Skr60 per cheque. You can buy foreign notes for no fee at Forex.

Currency

The Swedish krona (plural: kronor), usually called 'crown' by Swedes speaking English, is denoted Skr and divided into 100 öre (prices are rounded to the nearest 50 öre). Coins are 50 öre and one, five and 10 kronor, and notes are 20, 50, 100, 500 and 1000 kronor.

Tipping

Service charges are usually included in restaurant bills and taxi fares, but there's no problem if you want to reward good service with a tip (or round up the taxi fare, particularly if there's luggage). Cloakrooms usually cost about Skr20.

Taxes & Refunds

The main additional cost for the traveller is *mervärdeskatt* or *moms*, the value-added tax (VAT) on goods and services, which is included in the marked price. This varies but may be as much as 25%.

At shops that display the sign 'Tax Free Shopping', non-EU citizens making single purchases of goods exceeding Skr200 (including *moms*) are eligible for a VAT refund of 15% to 18% of the purchase price. Show your passport and ask the shop for a 'Global Refund Cheque', which should be presented along with your unopened purchases (within three months) at your departure point from the country (before you check in), to get export validation. You can then cash your cheque at refund points, which are found at international airports and harbour terminals. The *Tax Free Shopping Guide to Sweden* is available from tourist offices free of charge. See www.globalrefund.com, or call ☎ 020-741741 for more information.

POST

Mailing letters or postcards up to 20g within Sweden costs Skr5.50, and Skr10 to overseas destinations. A package weighing 2kg costs Skr180/250 by airmail to Europe/outside Europe. Airmail will take a few days to reach European destinations, a week to most parts of North America, and perhaps a little longer to Australia and New Zealand.

In recent years Posten (www.posten.se), the Swedish postal service, moved to new premises all over the country; service outlets opened in some 3000 new venues, many in supermarkets and petrol stations. These outlets offer all that most travellers will need; eg stamps (*frimärken*), letter (*brev*) and package (*paket*) services. You can also buy stamps from many tourist offices, convenience stores, bookshops and newsagents; look for the yellow post symbol on a pale blue background, which indicates that some postal facilities are offered.

Receiving poste restante mail under the new postal system is difficult for travellers. As many of the large, old-style post offices have closed or relocated, there is no central 'holding place' in most towns. The person sending you mail will need to specify which post outlet you will be collecting mail from, with a specific address and postal code.

TELEPHONE

Travellers may notice a lack of public telephones in Sweden; some 70% of the population owns a mobile phone, so the number of public phones has dwindled in recent years (travellers might find it useful to bring their mobile telephone from home and buy an inexpensive Swedish SIM card and pay-as-you-go plan). There are no coin phones; all public telephones take Telia phonecards. These cards cost Skr35, Skr60 or Skr100 (giving 30, 60 or 120 credits, respectively). Many Telia booths also accept credit cards (with expensive rates). You can also buy a wide range of phonecards from tobacconists that give cheap rates for calls abroad.

For directory assistance dial ☎ 118118 (for numbers within Sweden) or ☎ 118119 (international), but note that these services aren't free. To place a collect call, dial ☎ 020-0018.

Phone Codes

Calls to Sweden from abroad require a country code (☎ 46) followed by the area code and telephone number (omitting the first zero in the area code). For international

---

EMERGENCY NUMBERS

In Sweden, dial ☎ 112 (a free call) for the police, ambulance and fire services.

calls dial ☎ 00 followed by the country code and the local area code.

Swedish phone numbers have area codes followed by varying numbers of digits. You must use the area code when dialling from outside that area. Numbers beginning ☎ 020 or ☎ 0200 are free (but not from public phones or mobiles). Numbers beginning ☎ 077 are roughly the same price as a local call. Mobile phone numbers usually begin with ☎ 070.

TIME
Sweden is one hour ahead of GMT/UTC, but summer time (from the end of March to the end of October) is another hour ahead. The 24-hour clock is widely used.

TOILETS
Public toilets in parks, museums, shopping malls, libraries and bus or train stations are rarely free in Sweden. Except at larger train stations (where an attendant is on duty), pay toilets are coin operated, and usually cost Skr5.

TOURIST INFORMATION
The official website for the Swedish Travel and Tourism Council is at www.visit-sweden .com. The site contains loads of good information in many languages.

Sweden has about 350 local tourist information offices. Most are open long hours in summer and short hours (or not at all) during winter, and a few exhibit nomadic tendencies. The offices in large towns stock brochures from all around Sweden. The website www.turism.se lists Sweden's tourist information offices and their contact details.

VISAS
Citizens of the EU, Norway and Iceland can enter Sweden with a passport or a national identification card (passports are recommended). Nationals of Nordic countries can stay and work indefinitely but others require residence permits for stays of between three months and five years.

Passport-holders from Australia, New Zealand, Canada and the US can enter and stay in Sweden without a visa for up to three months. Australian and New Zealand passport-holders aged between 18 and 30 can also qualify for a one-year working holiday visa (the application fee is Skr1000).

Citizens of South Africa and other African, Asian and some Eastern European countries require tourist visas for entry; these are only available in advance from Swedish embassies (allow at least two months), and cost Skr225/275 for permits allowing a maximum 30/90 days. It may be hard to extend your stay once you're in Sweden.

Migrationsverket (☎ 011-156000; www.migration sverket.se; SE-60170 Norrköping) is the Swedish 'migration board' and it handles all applications for visas and work or residency permits. Its website is full of useful information for visitors with visa questions.

TRANSPORT IN SWEDEN

GETTING THERE & AWAY
Air
The major international airport in Sweden is Stockholm's **Arlanda airport** (☎ 08-797 6000), with direct flights linking the country to major Scandinavian towns, European and North American cities, and a few Asian destinations. Göteborg's **Landvetter airport** (☎ 031-941000) and Malmö's **Sturup airport** (☎ 040 613 1000), as well as a few other minor airports, also have direct international flights (especially to/from large cities within Scandinavia). A wealth of information on airports and airlines is available at the website of Sweden's civil aviation authority, Luftfartsverket (www.lfv.se).

When planning your travel, note that Copenhagen's airport (see p99) is just 25 minutes by train from Malmö in southern Sweden.

The national carrier is Scandinavian Airlines System, better known as **SAS** (☎ 0770-727727; www.scandinavian.net; airline code SK), with a very good safety record.

AIRLINES FLYING TO AND FROM SWEDEN
Some of the main international airlines flying into and out of Sweden:
Aeroflot (in Sweden ☎ 08-505 653; 00www.aeroflot.com)
Air France (☎ 08-519 999 90; www.airfrance.com)
Alitalia (☎ 08-237320; www.alitalia.com)
Austrian Airlines (☎ 0200-727373; www.aua.com)
British Airways (☎ 0770-110020; www.britishairways.com)
Finnair (☎ 020-781100; www.finnair.com)
Iberia (☎ 08-566 125 00; www.iberia.com)
Icelandair (☎ 08-690 9800; www.icelandair.net)

KLM Royal Dutch Airlines (☎ 08-587 997 57; www.klm.com)
LOT Polish Airlines (☎ 08-243490; www.lot.com)
Lufthansa (☎ 0770-727727; www.lufthansa.com)
Skyways (☎ 0771-959500; www.skyways.se)
SN Brussels Airlines (☎ 08-797 9400; www.flysn.com)
Swiss (☎ 08-587 704 45; www.swiss.com)
Thai Airways (☎ 08-598 836 00; www.thaiairways.com)

Budget airlines covering Scandinavian and Continental European destinations:
Blue1 (www.blue1.com) Flights to Finnish destinations from Stockholm and Göteborg.
Fly Me (☎ 0770-790790; www.flyme.com) From Stockholm to Helsinki, and Göteborg to Nice and Mallorca.
Nordic Airlink (☎ 08-528 068 20; www.flynordic.com) From Stockholm to Copenhagen and Oslo.
Ryanair (☎ 0900-202 0240; www.ryanair.com) From Stockholm, Göteborg and Malmö to London (Stansted) and other locations including Glasgow and Frankfurt.
SAS Snowflake (☎ 0771-661000; www.flysnowflake .com) From Stockholm to destinations in southern Europe including Rome, Lyon, Athens and Lisbon.
Sterling (☎ 08-587 691 48; www.sterlingticket.com) From Stockholm and Göteborg to European destinations including Barcelona, Paris, Milan and Prague.

Land

Direct access to Sweden by land is possible from Norway, Finland and Denmark (from Denmark via the remarkable Öresund toll bridge). Border-crossing formalities are virtually nonexistent.

Train and bus journeys are also possible between Sweden and the Continent – these vehicles go directly to ferries. Include ferry fares (or Öresund tolls) in your budget if you're driving from continental Europe.

Eurolines (☎ 031-100240; www.eurolines.com), the long-distance bus operator, has an office inside the bus terminals in Sweden's three largest cities: Stockholm, Göteborg and Malmö. Full schedules and fares are listed on the website.

CONTINENTAL EUROPE

Eurolines bus services run between Sweden and several European cities. The Stockholm to London service (from Skr1318/2270 or £105/182 one way/return, around 30 hours, two to five weekly) goes via Malmö, Copenhagen, Hamburg and Amsterdam or Brussels. There are services from Göteborg to Berlin (Skr573/1010 one way/return, approximately 12 hours, two daily).

Berlin Night Express (www.berlin-night -express.com) is a direct overnight train between Berlin and Malmö (Skr750/1100 or €85/120 for a couchette/bed one way, 8½ hours, three to seven times a week) via the Trelleborg–Sassnitz ferry. Trains connect with points north of Malmö or beyond Berlin. See the website for booking details (or in Sweden book through SJ, the Swedish rail company; see p446).

DENMARK

Eurolines operates buses between Stockholm and Copenhagen (Skr460 or Dkr370 one way, nine hours, two to four daily) via Norrköping, Linköping, Jönköping and Helsingborg. It also has buses between Göteborg and Copenhagen (Skr285 or Dkr230 one way, 4½ hours, three to five daily) via Halmstad and Malmö. **Swebus Express** (☎ 0200-218218; www.swe busexpress.se) and **Säfflebussen** (☎ 0771-151515; www .safflebussen.se) both operate regular buses on the same routes, and with both companies there are discount fares if you travel from Monday to Thursday (except on public holidays). Discount/regular one-way fares for the Göteborg–Copenhagen journey are Skr200/285 with both companies. For the Stockholm–Copenhagen trip, Swebus Express is cheaper (Skr320/460 discount/regular price one way). All companies offer child, student, youth (under 26) and senior discounts.

Trains are the quickest option, especially if you're in southern Sweden. Trains run every 20 minutes between Copenhagen and Malmö (Skr85, 35 minutes) – via the Öresund bridge and all stopping at Copenhagen's airport – and these connect with many towns in Skåne. Fast X2000 trains run regularly between Copenhagen and Stockholm (five hours, up to 14 a day) via Norrköping, Linköping, Lund and Malmö. Three high-speed services operate between Copenhagen and Göteborg (3½ hours) via Halmstad, Helsingborg, Lund and Malmö (slower InterCity trains take 4½ hours and there are around seven daily services). Prices vary dramatically depending on when you buy your ticket – for the best prices, purchase your ticket at least one day before departure. Go to the site of the Swedish national rail company, **Sveriges Järnväg** (SJ; ☎ 0771-757575; www.sj.se) for loads more information.

For drivers, tolls across the Öresund bridge are Skr280/Dkr230 one way for a car up to 6m, Skr560/Dkr460 for a car plus trailer or caravan, and Skr155/Dkr125 for a motorcycle. See www.oeresundsbron.com for more information, and if the prices seem too steep, consider taking a ferry between Helsingborg and Helsingør (right).

FINLAND

There are seven crossing points along the river border. Bus services from Luleå to Haparanda, Övertorneå and Pajala on the Swedish side are operated by the regional public transport company **Länstrafiken Norrbotten** (☎ 020-470047; www.ltnbd.se); the website is in Swedish only but the timetables are easy enough to follow. This company also operates the 'Bothnian Arc X-press', a daily bus service along the northern coast into Finland, from Skellefteå or Luleå on to Haparanda, Tornio and Kemi, terminating in Oulu. One-way fares from Luleå to Kemi cost Skr155, to Oulu Skr260.

Tapanis Buss (☎ 0922-12955 or 08-153300; www.tapanis.se) runs overnight coaches between Stockholm and Tornio via Haparanda (Skr480 or €55 one way, 15 hours, twice a week). The bus runs along the E4 highway, stopping at many of the larger towns. Again, the website is in Swedish only but easy to navigate.

Train passengers heading for Finland can only reach Boden or Luleå in northern Sweden – from there it's necessary to continue by bus.

NORWAY

The major bus companies operate on routes connecting Stockholm and Oslo, and Göteborg and Oslo (many of the services from Oslo to Göteborg continue on to Malmö and Copenhagen).

Eurolines (☎ 031-100240; www.eurolines.com) has regular daily services between Oslo and Copenhagen via Göteborg, Halmstad, Helsingborg and Malmö. Göteborg to Oslo costs Skr225/Nkr205 one way and takes 4¼ hours.

Swebus Express (☎ 0200-218218; www.swebusexpress.se) run between Stockholm and Oslo (Skr265 one way Monday to Thursday, otherwise Skr380, 7½ hours, three a day) and between Göteborg and Oslo (Skr160 one way Monday to Thursday, otherwise Skr225, four hours, up to six a day). **Säfflebussen** (☎ 0771-151515; www.safflebussen.se) runs five times a day between Stockholm and Oslo, and 10 times daily between Göteborg and Oslo. It's marginally cheaper than Swebus Express.

Many regional transport networks (länstrafiken) run buses to within a few kilometres of the Norwegian border. In addition, **Länstrafiken Västerbotten** (☎ 020-910019; www.lanstrafikeniac.se) has a bus service from Umeå to Mo i Rana (Skr232, 8½ hours, daily), and **Länstrafiken Norrbotten** (☎ 020-470047; www.ltnbd.se) has a service from Skellefteå to Bodø (Skr400, nine hours, daily except Saturday), via Arvidsjaur, and also between Kiruna and Narvik in summer (Skr191, 2½ hours, one or two daily), via Abisko and Riksgränsen.

The main rail links run from Stockholm to Oslo, from Göteborg to Oslo, from Stockholm to Östersund and Storlien (Norwegian trains continue to Trondheim), and from Luleå to Kiruna and Narvik in the far north.

Sea

THE BALTIC COUNTRIES

Tallink (☎ 08-666 6001; www.tallink.ee) sails daily between Sweden and Estonia on two routes: Stockholm–Tallinn (Skr285 to Skr385 one way for an airline-style seat, 15 hours) and Kapellskär–Paldiski (Skr205 to Skr265 one way for 'deck class', 10 to 11 hours).

Riga Sea Line (☎ 08-510 015 00; www.rigascaline.lv) sails between Stockholm and Riga in Latvia (Skr310 to Skr350 one way, 17½ hours, three weekly). A cabin berth costs from Skr80.

Lisco Line (☎ 0454-33680; www.shipping.lt) sails between Klaipėda in Lithuania and Karlshamn, near Karlskrona in southern Sweden (from Skr400 one way, 14 hours, three to six weekly).

DENMARK

There are numerous ferries between Denmark and Sweden, although boats between Malmö and Copenhagen ceased after the opening of the Öresund bridge. The quickest and most frequent services are between Helsingør and Helsingborg. Three companies operate on this busy route, with a crossing time of only 20 minutes:

HH-Lines (☎ 042-198000; www.hhferries.se, Swedish & Danish only) Ferries every half-hour. Passenger Skr20/36 one way/return; car (including up to five passengers) Skr255/495.

Scandlines (☎ 042-186100; www.scandlines.se) Ferries every 20 minutes, 24-hour service. Passenger Skr22/40 one way/return; car (including up to nine passengers) Skr280/560.

Sundsbussarna (☎ 042-216060; www.sundsbussarna.se, Swedish & Danish only) Passenger-only service every half-hour; tickets Skr22/40 one way/return.

There are also services between Denmark's Jutland and Sweden, operated by **Stena Line** (☎ 031-704 0000; www.stenaline.se). There are five to 10 sailings daily between Göteborg and Frederikshavn. The regular crossings cost Skr100 to Skr210 one way and take 3¼ hours, but there's also a fast ferry covering the same route in two hours (Skr170 to Skr250 one way). Stena Line also sails three or four times daily between Grenå and Varberg (Skr100 to Skr210 one way, four hours). It's cheaper to travel on these ferries between 10pm and 6am, or from Monday to Thursday. Prices also increase in the peak summer season (from July to mid-September).

BornholmsTrafikken (☎ 0411-558700; www.born holmstrafikken.dk) sails from Ystad to Rønne (Bornholm). There are both conventional (2½ hours) and fast (70 minutes) services, two to nine times daily. Passenger fares are from Skr188 one way.

FINLAND

Daily services throughout the year are available on Stockholm–Turku and Stockholm–Helsinki routes (all via the Åland islands). Note that Helsinki is called Helsingfors in Swedish, and Turku is known as Åbo. There are two major ferry operators, and it's considerably more expensive to travel on either from Thursday to Saturday, and in peak season. Both companies offer bus services to and from their ports.

Silja Line (☎ 08-222140; www.silja.com) sails daily (overnight) from Stockholm to Helsinki (from Skr395 one way for a berth in a four-person cabin, around 15 hours) and to Turku (from Skr180/330 one way on a day/night crossing, 11 hours). In the low season (September to early May), ferries operating the Turku route arrive at and depart from tiny Kapellskär, about 90km northeast of Stockholm.

Viking Line (☎ 08-452 4000; www.vikingline.fi) operates daily on the same routes as Silja Line, but in high season it offers passage to Turku from both Stockholm and Kapellskär. Overnight passage from Stockholm to Helsinki costs from Skr284 one way (for an airline-style seat) and a place in a cabin costs extra (from Skr216). For Stockholm–Turku sailings, a ticket costs from Skr126/162 one way on a day/night crossing; cabins on the night-time crossing cost from Skr164 per person.

Viking Line tickets to the Åland islands are reasonable value – from Stockholm it costs Skr99 return. There are also inexpensive connections to Åland from Grisslehamn, north of Stockholm (see p385).

Further north, there's a daily connection from Umeå to Vaasa operated by **RG Line** (☎ 09 0-185200; www.rgline.com). The journey takes four hours, and passenger tickets cost Skr270 for travel on a Monday or Tuesday, Skr450 for the rest of the week or every day in high season (late June to early August). There are bus connections from Umeå's town centre to the harbour.

GERMANY

Trelleborg is the main gateway with more than a dozen ferries arriving and departing daily. **TT-Line** (☎ 0410-56200; www.ttline.se) sails between Trelleborg and Travemünde (seven hours) and Trelleborg and Rostock (5½ hours). Passenger fares for both range from Skr180 to Skr370 one way. **Scandlines** (☎ 0410-65000; www.scandlines.se) is cheaper and sails between Trelleborg and Rostock (Skr170 to Skr 200 one way, 5¾ hours) and Trelleborg and Sassnitz (Skr100 to Skr120 one way, 3¾ hours).

Stena Line (☎ 031-704 0000; www.stenaline.se) has overnight cruises between Göteborg and Kiel (Skr340 to Skr780, 13½ hours, daily); prices vary according to time of year and day of the week.

NORWAY

There are plenty of bus and train services between the two countries, plus frequent ferries between Strömstad and Sandefjord operated by **Color Line** (☎ 0526-62000; www.colorline.com). The crossing takes 2½ hours (Skr150 to Skr180 one way, two to six daily).

DFDS Seaways (Helsingborg ☎ 042-266000; Göteborg ☎ 031-650650; www.dfdsseaways.com) runs ferries overnight between Copenhagen and Oslo, via Helsingborg. Fares between Helsingborg and Oslo (14 hours) vary according to the season and day of the week, and range from Skr725 to Skr1025 one way (cabin place included). DFDS Seaways also sails from Göteborg to Kristiansand (Skr98 to Skr248 one way, seven hours, three per week).

POLAND

Polferries (☎ 040-121700; www.polferries.se) operates services between Świnoujście and Ystad

(Skr465 to Skr535 one way, seven to nine hours, daily) and also between Gdańsk and Nynäshamn (Skr510 to Skr610 one way, 18 hours, three weekly). Cabin berths cost extra (from Skr70). **Unity Line** (☎ 0411-556900; www .unityline.pl) also operates on the Świnoujście–Ystad route (Skr450 to Skr520 one way, nine hours, daily). **Stena Line** (☎ 0455-366300; www .stenaline.se) sails between Gdynia and Karlskrona (Skr290 to Skr550 one way, 10½ to 12 hours, one or two daily).

UK

DFDS Seaways (☎ 031-650650; www.dfdsseaways.com) sails from Göteborg to Newcastle (from Skr 198/698 low/high season one way, 25 hours, twice a week) via Kristiansand (Norway). Basic cabin accommodation is included in the price (you can pay extra for more comfort).

GETTING AROUND

Although Sweden takes time and money to travel through, public transport is well organised using 24 different *länstrafik* (regional networks); they're heavily subsidised and offer good bargains. The general confusion of having so many operators is partly solved by the **Resplus system** (☎ 0771-878787; www.resplus.se), where one ticket is valid on trains and on *länstrafik* buses. Handy local timetables are available on the website and for free or at nominal cost from tourist offices or the operators.

Air

Sweden's half-dozen domestic airlines mostly use Stockholm's Arlanda airport as a hub (see p439), although Stockholm's Bromma airport also sees some domestic action. The domestic network is extensive and local airlines are safe and efficient, but full-fare tickets can be expensive. Substantial discounts are available, such as for Internet bookings, student and youth fares, off-peak travel, or return tickets booked at least seven days in advance. Major domestic flight destinations include Stockholm, Göteborg, Malmö, Luleå, Kiruna and Visby (on Gotland). Fares for popular routes like Stockholm to Göteborg can be found for as little as Skr195 with the budget airlines.

DOMESTIC AIR TRAVEL

Fly Me (www.flyme.com; ☎ 0770-790790) Flies from Stockholm to Göteborg and Malmö (and Helsinki).

Malmö Aviation (www.malmoaviation.se; ☎ 0771-550010) Flies between Stockholm (Bromma), Göteborg, Malmö and Umeå, and to Gotland in summer.

Nordic Airlink (www.flynordic.com; ☎ 08-528 068 20) Flies from Stockholm to Göteborg, Umeå and Luleå (and to Oslo and Copenhagen).

SAS (www.scandinavian.net; ☎ 0770-727727) Has daily domestic flights serving the country from Malmö to Kiruna (all through Stockholm Arlanda).

Skyways (www.skyways.se; ☎ 0771-959500) Runs a larger network than SAS, including a few direct flights between northern and southern destinations that don't fly via Stockholm (eg Göteborg direct to Umeå or Luleå).

AIR PASSES

If you're flying into Sweden from Continental Europe with SAS, you can buy Visit Scandinavia Airpass flight coupons (up to a maximum of eight) allowing one-way travel on direct flights between any two Scandinavian cities serviced by SAS and other affiliated operators. Domestic flights within Sweden cost €69 (with the exception of the Stockholm–Kiruna route, which costs €122). Non-European residents can participate in a similar scheme, the Visit Scandinavia/Europe Airpass (domestic flights cost US$65 with this pass, Stockholm–Kiruna is US$115). See p470 for more details on these passes.

Bicycle

Sweden is a flat country and it's ideal for cycling, with Skåne and Gotland particularly recommended. Cycling is an excellent way to look for points of interest and quiet spots for free camping. The cycling season is May to September in the south, and July and August in the north.

You can cycle on all roads except motorways (green sign, with two lanes and a bridge) and roads for motor vehicles only (green sign with a car symbol). The reasonably quiet and safe secondary roads are good for cycling.

You can take a bicycle on some *länstrafik* trains and most regional buses (free, or up to Skr50), and bikes are transported free or for a small fee on many ferries. Long-distance buses usually do not accept bicycles, and nor does SJ.

You'll find bike-rental outlets in most major towns; multi-gear bikes can cost up to Skr200/800 per day/week. Some country areas, towns and cities have special cycle routes – check with local tourist offices for

SWEDEN

information and maps. The well-signposted, 2600km-long Sverigeleden is the national route (extending from Helsingborg in the south to Karesuando in the north), linking points of interest with suitable roads (mostly with an asphalt surface) and bicycle paths.

Boat

Sweden's national road authority, Vägverket, operates dozens of car ferries across short stretches of water, but many are being replaced with bridges. These ferries are part of the road network and are free.

An extensive boat network opens up the attractive Stockholm archipelago, and boat services on Lake Mälaren, west of Stockholm, are busy in summer (see p370). Gotland is served by regular ferries from Nynäshamn and Oskarshamn (see p422), and there are summer services to many other small islands off the coast. Boat passes are available for exploration of the Stockholm archipelago (see p382).

The canals provide cross-country routes linking the main lakes. The longest cruises, on the historic Göta Canal from Söderköping (south of Stockholm) to Göteborg, run from mid-May to mid-September and take at least four days. The **Göta Canal Steamship Company** (☎ 031-806315; www.gotacanal.se) operates three old ships over the whole distance with fares from Skr10,995/15,990 single/double, including full board and guided excursions. The company also offers two-day cruises on probably the most picturesque section of the canal, from Motala to Söderköping (from Skr4395/5790 single/double). Other companies offer day trips and short cruises on sections of the canal – tourist offices in the area can help (Linköping and nearby Söderköping are good places to inquire).

Bus

Sweden has a safe, reliable and extensive bus network. Travellers to the north of the country, in particular, will rely heavily on this form of transport. You can travel by bus in Sweden either on national long-distance routes, or using any of the regional *länstrafik* networks.

LONG-DISTANCE BUS COMPANIES

The following companies operate on long-distance routes. If you're under 26, a student or senior, it's worth asking for a discount,

but most transport companies will only give student prices to holders of Swedish student cards (the exception is Swebus Express, where you can use ISIC cards). Advance bookings are required for all but Swebus Express – it always guarantees a seat.

Svenska Buss (☎ 0771-676767; www.svenskabuss.se, Swedish only) Has a network connecting many southern towns with Stockholm, plus one service north of Stockholm along the coast to Härnösand (via Sundsvall). Sample one-way fares: Stockholm–Göteborg Skr340; Stockholm–Malmö Skr380; Stockholm–Sundsvall Skr190.

Swebus Express (☎ 0200-218218; www.swebusexpress .se) Has the largest 'national network' of express buses, but it only serves the southern half of the country (as far north as Mora in Dalarna). Fares for 'long' journeys (over 100km) are 30% cheaper if you travel between Monday and Thursday most weeks (not public or school holidays). Sample one-way fares: Stockholm–Göteborg discount/full price Skr250/360; Stockholm–Malmö Skr315/450; Stockholm–Mora Skr145/205.

Säfflebussen (☎ 0771-151515; www.safflebussen.se) Smaller network, running daily on major routes (eg Stockholm–Malmö, Stockholm–Göteborg, Göteborg–Malmö). Also serves Oslo, Copenhagen and Berlin. Fares 30% cheaper Monday to Thursday. Sample one-way fares: Stockholm–Göteborg Skr220/320 discount/full price; Stockholm–Malmö Skr310/450.

Ybuss (☎ 0771-334444; www.ybuss.se, Swedish only) Daily journeys from Stockholm north along the coast as far as Umeå (via Uppsala, Gävle, Sundsvall) and also to Östersund. Sample one-way fares: Stockholm–Sundsvall Skr200; Stockholm–Umeå Skr330; Stockholm–Östersund Skr270.

REGIONAL TRAFFIC

Länstrafik is usually complemented by the regional train system, and one ticket is valid on any bus, local or regional. Rules vary but transfers are usually free within one to four hours. Most counties are divided into zones; travel within one zone will cost from Skr13 to Skr17. Every time you enter a new zone, the price increases, but there's usually a maximum fare.

Timetables explain the various discount schemes. There are good-value daily or weekly passes and many regions have 30-day passes for longer stays, or a special card valid for travel from Midsummer to mid-August (the major school holiday). The *värdekort* (value card), which you can 'top up' at any time, is also good: you pay, say, Skr200 for over Skr250 worth of travelling. Always ask how the regional discount pass works: you may have to run the ticket through a machine, press buttons, tell the driver where you want to go, get your ticket stamped or something else of that kind.

Car & Motorcycle

Sweden has good roads and there are no public toll roads or bridges in the country. You usually only need a recognised full driving licence, even for car rental. If bringing your own car, you'll need your vehicle registration documents. Insurance Green Cards are recommended. Fuel and spare parts are widely available, but may be pricey.

Parking can be tricky to find (and expensive) in the larger cities. Look for parking signs: times (using the 24-hour clock) will indicate when a payment (*avgift*) is required. Automatic ticket machines (*billetautomat*) usually cost from Skr5 to Skr15 per hour during the day, but may be free in the evening and at the weekend. Cities have multistorey car parks (P-hus) that charge between Skr15 and Skr40 per hour.

AUTOMOBILE ASSOCIATIONS

The Swedish national motoring association is **Motormännens Riksförbund** (☎ 020-211111, 08-690 38 00; www.motormannen.se; Sveavägen 159, SE-10435 Stockholm). Annual membership is Skr355, or, in case of an emergency, it can help you contact your home club or to find assistance locally.

HIRE

To rent a car you normally have to be at least 18 (sometimes 25) years of age, you need to show a recognised licence (in some cases, an International Driving Permit) and you may be required to pay by credit card.

International rental chains are expensive, starting at around Skr600 per day for smaller models, but shopping around can turn up some reasonable deals. Fly-drive packages can bring some savings, and weekend or summer packages may also be offered at discount rates. All the major firms (eg Avis, Hertz, Europcar) have desks at Stockholm's Arlanda airport and offices in major cities.

Mabi Hyrbilar (☎ 020-110 1000; www.mabirent.se) is a good national company with branches in many major cities and competitive rates. Rates for the smallest car are Skr160 per day plus Skr1.60 per kilometre, or Skr320 per day including 150km. For weekly rentals, prices start at Skr1995, including 1000km. Motorcycles can also be rented through Mabi.

Cars can be hired from many large petrol stations (look for signs saying *hyrbilar* or *biluthyrning*) at good rates, but must be returned to the hiring point. **OK-Q8** (☎ 020-850850; www.okq8.se) has small cars from Skr310 per day (including 100km allowance) or Skr550 per day (unlimited kilometres). Weekend rental makes sense for travellers wishing to explore areas not well served by public transport (eg Glasriket from Kalmar, Bohuslän from Göteborg or Höga Kusten from Sundsvall); prices start at Skr595 (including 300km allowance) or Skr895 (with unlimited kilometres) for a weekend. **Statoil** (☎ 0770-252525; www.statoil.se) has similar prices. Websites for these companies are in Swedish only, but you'll probably be able to navigate through to *priser* or *prislistor* (prices) for *hyrbilar*.

ROAD HAZARDS

In the north, privately owned reindeer and wild elk (moose) are serious road hazards, particularly around dawn and dusk. Look out for black plastic bags tied to roadside trees or poles – this is a sign from local Sami that they have reindeer herds grazing in the area. Report all incidents to police – failure to do so is an offence. Sandboxes on many roads may be helpful in mud or snow. Beware of trams in Göteborg and Norrköping.

ROAD RULES

Basic road rules conform to EU standards. In Sweden, you drive on and give way to the right. Headlights should be dipped, but must be on at all times when driving. Seat belt use is obligatory for all passengers. The blood-alcohol limit is a stringent 0.02%. The maximum permitted speed on motorways and remote highways is 110km/h. Other speed limits are 50km/h in urban areas, 70km/h outside urban areas and 90km/h on motorways. The speed limit for cars towing caravans is 80km/h. Police use hand-held radar equipment and cameras to detect speeding, and impose on-the-spot fines.

On many highways broken lines define wide-paved edges, and the vehicle being overtaken is expected to move into this area to allow faster traffic to pass safely.

Local Transport

In Sweden, local transport is always linked with the regional *länstrafik* – rules and prices for city buses may differ slightly from long-distance transport, but a regional pass is valid both in the city and on the rural routes. There's usually a flat fare of around Skr15 to Skr20 in towns.

Stockholm has an extensive underground metro system, and Göteborg and Norrköping run good tram networks. Göteborg also has a city ferry service.

Train

Trains are certainly the fastest way to get around, although many destinations in the northern half of the country cannot be reached by train alone.

The national network of **Sveriges Järnväg** (SJ; ☎ 0771-757575; www.sj.se) covers most main lines, especially in the southern half of the country. Its flag carriers are the X2000 fast trains running at speeds of up to 200km/h, with services from Stockholm to major destinations. InterCity (regional and inter-regional) trains also run on many of these routes; InterCity fares are cheaper and the journey times longer. **Connex** (☎ 0771-260000; www.connex.se) operates train services in the far north and offers services from Stockholm and Göteborg north as far as Kiruna and across to Narvik in Norway. In addition, several counties run small regional train networks as part of their *länstrafik* service.

There are huge variations on fares depending on time of travel, type of service and how far in advance you book. Full-price tickets are expensive, but you'll receive a substantial discount for booking at least a day before departure (ask for the *'just nu'* fare). Students (with a Swedish CSN or SFS student card if aged over 26) and people aged under 26 get up to a 30% discount on the standard adult fare. All SJ ticket prices are reduced in summer, from late June to mid-August, and during off-peak travel times (10am to 2pm and after 7pm Monday to Thursday, Friday and Sunday until noon, and all day Saturday). On X2000 and InterCity trains, an adult passenger can be accompanied by two children, at no extra charge. X2000 tickets include a seat reservation. Bicycles can be carried on many *länstrafik* trains and on Öresund trains

(between Malmö and Copenhagen), unlike on SJ trains (which won't carry them).

Sample one-way X2000 train fares (at full, adult price) include: Stockholm–Göteborg Skr1077; Stockholm–Malmö Skr1030; and Göteborg–Malmö Skr588. While these fares appear steep, remember that buying your ticket a day in advance or travelling on a slower train brings substantial discounts (up to 50%).

TRAIN PASSES

The Sweden Rail Pass, Eurodomino tickets and InterRail, Eurail and ScanRail passes are accepted on SJ services and most other operators, such as regional trains. Exceptions are the local SL *pendeltåg* (commuter) trains around Stockholm, and Inlandsbanan (although some passholders get a discount on Inlandsbanan – see below).

The fast X2000 and overnight trains require all rail passholders to pay a supplement of Skr50 (including the obligatory seat reservation). The reservation supplements for non-X2000 (ie InterCity) trains (Skr50) aren't obligatory, and there are no supplements for regional *länstrafik* trains.

Obtaining rail passes in Sweden isn't entirely convenient, but they can be arranged in advance through **Sweden Booking** (☎ 0498-203380; www.swedenbooking.com), for a Skr130 fee. For more information on train passes, see p475.

INLANDSBANAN

From mid-June to early August, **Inlandsbanan** (Inland Railway; ☎ 0771-535353; www.inlandsbanan.se) offers one of the great rail journeys in Scandinavia. The 1067km route stretches from Mora to Gällivare; travel is slow (the train travels at a speed of 50km/h) and it takes six hours from Mora to Östersund (Skr347) and 14 hours from Östersund to Gällivare (Skr697). A special card allows two weeks' unlimited travel on the route for Skr1195 (mid-June to mid-July) or Skr995 (mid-July to early August). InterRail Card users under 26 can travel free, while ScanRail card-holders receive a 25% discount on the two-week pass (but not on individual tickets).

Regional Directory

CONTENTS

This chapter gives a general overview of what you need to know about travelling throughout Scandinavian Europe, from the overall climate to what help you can expect from your embassy. More specific information about a particular area of Scandinavian Europe can be found in the Directory at the end of each country chapter.

Some subjects are covered in *both* Directories – eg general accommodation options are discussed in this Directory, but a clearer indication of prices and the most helpful regional organisations appear in the country Directories.

Some subjects appear *either* in the country Directory *or* in this chapter, depending on how differently things work from country

to country. Cross references are given where appropriate, but check both Directories to make sure you've got the general gist as well as those all-important details.

ACCOMMODATION

In the chapter sections of this book, accommodation is divided into budget, mid-range and top end, with choices listed from the cheapest to the most expensive. See the individual country Directories for a rundown of prices, for useful associations, and for an overview of local options.

The cheapest places to stay in the region are camping grounds, followed by hostels and student accommodation. Cheap hotels are virtually unknown in most of the northern half of Europe, but guesthouses, pensions, private rooms, farm accommodation and B&Bs can be good value. Self-catering flats and cottages are worth considering if you're travelling with a group, especially if you're staying in one place for a while.

During peak holiday periods, accommodation can be hard to find and it's advisable to book ahead. Even camping grounds, especially popular big-city ones, can fill up.

If you arrive in a country by train, there's often a hotel-booking desk at the train station. Tourist offices in cities and towns tend to have extensive accommodation lists and the more helpful ones will go out of their way to find you something. There's usually a small fee for this service, but if accommodation is tight, it can save a lot of running around. It's also an easy way to get around any language problems. Agencies offering private rooms can be good value; you may lack privacy, but staying with a local family brings you closer to the spirit of the country.

B&Bs, Guesthouses & Hotels

There's a huge range of accommodation above the hostel level. B&Bs, where you get a room and breakfast in a private home, can often be real bargains. Pensions and guesthouses are similar, but usually slightly more upmarket. In Norway, for example, there are plenty of private guesthouses along main roads, and they're significantly cheaper than hotels.

Above this level are hotels, which are always much more expensive than B&Bs and guesthouses; in cities, luxury five-star hotels have five-star prices. Categorisation varies from country to country.

Check your hotel room and the bathroom before you agree to take it, and make sure you know what it's going to cost – discounts are often available at certain times (eg at weekends in Finland, Norway and Sweden) and for longer stays. Also ask about breakfast – it's usually included in the price of the room, but sometimes it's compulsory and you must pay extra for it (which can be a real rip-off).

If you think a hotel is too expensive, ask if they have a cheaper room. If you're with a group or are planning to stay for any length of time, it's always worth trying to negotiate a special rate.

Camping

Camping is immensely popular in most of the region and is the cheapest accommodation. There's usually a charge per tent or site, per vehicle and per person. National tourist offices should have booklets or brochures listing camping grounds all over their country. See p453 for information on the Camping Card International, which offers discounts.

Although some camping grounds are commendably close to city centres, in most cases they will be some distance from the centre, especially in larger places. If you're on foot, the money you save by camping can quickly be outweighed by the money spent commuting to and from a town centre.

Unless the camping ground rents small cabins or chalets on site (common in Scandinavian countries except Iceland and the Faroes), you'll also need a tent, sleeping bag and cooking equipment.

Camping other than in designated camping grounds is not always straightforward. In Denmark and the Faroes, it's illegal without permission from the local authorities (the police or local council office) or from landowners (don't be shy about asking, since you may be pleasantly surprised by the response!). As always, take care to keep toilet activities away from all surface water and use biodegradable soaps for washing up.

The Right of Common Access (p450) applies to all forests and wilderness areas in Sweden, Norway, Finland and Iceland.

Camping for the night is always legal within the framework of these regulations but there are restrictions, and tourist offices usually stock official publications explaining these in English. See the Directories of the relevant country chapters for additional information.

Hostels

Hostels offer the cheapest roof over your head in Scandinavia, and you don't have to be young to use them. Most hostels are part of national YHAs (Youth Hostel Associations), which have been renamed Hostelling International (HI). Sweden has close to 500 hostels; more than 300 of these are affiliated with (HI).

Technically you're supposed to be a YHA or HI member to use affiliated hostels (indicated by a blue triangle symbol) but in practice most are open to anyone. You may have to pay a bit extra without an HI card but this can be offset against future membership. Stay for six nights as a nonmember and you automatically become a member. To join HI, ask at any hostel, contact your local or national hostelling office, or register over the Internet at www.iyhf.org.

In Scandinavian countries, hostels are geared for budget travellers of all ages, including families with kids, and most have both dorms and private rooms. Specially adapted rooms for disabled visitors are becoming more common, but check with your hostel first.

You're required to use a sleeping sheet and pillowcase or linen in most Scandinavian countries – simply using your own sleeping bag is not permitted – but you can often hire or buy these on the spot. Many hostels (exceptions include most hostels in Iceland and the Faroes) serve breakfast, and almost all of them have communal kitchens where you can prepare your own meals.

Hostels vary widely in character but, increasingly, they're welcoming places to stay, with dramatically improved conditions compared to 10 or 15 years ago. They're open longer hours, dorms are smaller, curfews are disappearing and 'wardens' with a sergeant-major mentality are an endangered species!

Many hostel guides are available, including HI's annually updated *Europe* guide (UK£5.50).

Some hostels accept reservations by phone or fax but usually not during peak periods;

they'll often book the next hostel you're headed to for a small fee. Bookings up to six months in advance can be made through the International Booking Network (not all hostels are in the network). It's possible to book hostels through national hostel offices. Popular hostels in capital cities can be heavily booked in summer and limits may be placed on how many nights you can stay.

For further information, see the Directories in the individual country chapters.

University Accommodation

Some universities and colleges rent out their student digs to tourists from June to mid-August; in Finland this kind of accommodation is usually affiliated with HI (see p189). These will often be single or double rooms and cooking facilities may be available. Inquire directly at the college or university, at student information services or at local tourist offices.

ACTIVITIES

Exhilarating, heart-pumping pursuits abound in Scandinavia. The varied geography and climate and vast wilderness areas support a full range of outdoor activities, including bird-watching, windsurfing, skiing, snowmobiling, skating, climbing, dogsledding, fishing, hiking, horse riding, mountaineering, boating, white-water rafting, cycling and whale-watching. For more local information, see the relevant country chapters.

Bird-watching

Scandinavia's large, unspoiled areas are fantastic places to spot huge varieties and numbers of birds. In coastal areas, kittiwakes, fulmars and puffins are common. Rarer species include golden eagles and sea eagles. Even reluctant twitchers will be wowed by the Vestmanna (p144) and Látrabjarg (p237) bird cliffs.

Boating

The many lakes, rivers and meandering coastlines of Scandinavia present a variety of boating options unmatched anywhere in the world. You can ride the rapids in a Finnish canoe (p189); take a trip on an Arctic icebreaker (p181); kayak around the feet of Icelandic mountains (p246); navigate peaceful lake Mjøsa in Norway (p299); or cruise from Helsinki to Stockholm (p195) – the

possibilities are endless. The country chapters contain more details.

Cycling

Along with hiking, cycling is the best way to get really close to the scenery and the people, with the bonus of keeping yourself fit in the process. It's also a good way to get around cities without aching feet or getting caught up in traffic jams.

Popular cycling areas include much of Denmark, which sets the world standard for cycling infrastructures; greater Oslo; the islands of Gotland in Sweden; and Åland in Finland. Be wary in Iceland, where cycling conditions are tough. In western Norway – as beautiful as it is – there are tunnels galore which prohibit cyclists, the snaking roads to/from mountain passes are killers and, unless you want to pedal an extra 50km around a fjord, you'll have to add on the expense of a ferry. The Faroes also has its fair share of hazardous, nonventilated tunnels and tortuous inclines.

Many of the long-distance routes (see the individual country chapters for details) can be linked together to form an epic Scandinavian-wide cycle tour. A popular route is to start from Kiel, Germany, before making your way through Denmark, then north along the west coast of Sweden before heading into Norway. (Note that bikes are banned on the Øresund toll bridge between Denmark and Sweden). In the UK, the Cyclists' Touring Club (p470) can provide members with route sheets prepared by experienced riders who have pedalled their way around Scandinavia.

If you come from outside Europe, you can often bring your bicycle along on the plane for a surprisingly reasonable fee – check out any restrictions with your carrier. Alternatively, this book lists places where you can rent one (make sure it has plenty of gears if you are planning some serious riding). The minimum rental period in Scandinavia is usually half a day.

See p470 and the individual country chapters for more information on bicycle touring and tips on places to visit.

Hiking

Keen hikers could spend several lifetimes exploring the region's hundreds of trails – there are enough national parks and nature

WORLD HERITAGE LIST

Unesco's list of 'cultural and natural treasures of the world's heritage' includes the following places in Scandinavian Europe:

Denmark

- Jelling church, burial mounds and runic stones (p77)
- Kronborg Slot (p47)
- Roskilde Domkirke (p49)

Finland

- Fortress of Suomenlinna (p139)
- Vanha Rauma (Old Rauma; p162)

Norway

- Bryggen (p304)
- Mining town of Røros (p321)
- Rock carvings of Alta (p340)
- Urnes' stave church (p316)

Sweden

- Agricultural landscape of southern Öland (p415)
- Birka (p384)
- Church village of Gammelstad, Luleå (p426)
- Falun mining area (p389)
- Hanseatic town of Visby (p418)
- Höga Kusten (High Coast; p423)
- Laponia area (p361)
- Naval port of Karlskrona (p417)
- Royal Domain of Drottningholm (p384)

reserves to make it a hiker's paradise. You can hike on well-marked routes, and accommodation is available along the way. Be sure to bring enough food, appropriate clothing and equipment with you, and consult local weather forecasts before setting off.

The Right of Common Access law in effect in Sweden, Norway, Finland and Iceland allows anyone to walk virtually anywhere, while respecting homeowners' and commercial premises' privacy. Naturally, there are certain rules of conduct to

be followed. Huge national routes such as Kungsleden in Sweden and the UKK trekking route (p176) in Finland are popular, as are provincial or regional routes (spanning hundreds of kilometres) and extensive tracks through national parks. Local and regional tourist offices distribute free maps for shorter routes and sell excellent trekking maps for the national parks.

Horse Riding

If just the thought of a bracing hike or intense cycle ride makes you tired, horse riding might be the answer. It's a fantastic way to see the breathtaking Scandinavian countryside, and there's no legwork involved! Beginners can amble along, while experienced riders can do more energetic galloping about.

Skiing

Scandinavia is famous for winter sports and snow skiing is a popular activity: you will find some of the world's best cross-country (nordic) trails here.

Sweden and Norway have the longest downhill (alpine) slopes in the region, but it's quite an expensive activity once the costs of ski lifts, accommodation and evening drinking sessions have been factored in.

Finnish and a few Icelandic ski areas are also fairly well equipped. Åre in Sweden (p425) is probably the single best area for alpine skiing and the top resorts in Norway are Geilo (p302) and Lillehammer (p300), where telemark skiing, a form of free-heel downhill skiing, is also popular.

Downhill skiing is always easier to arrange in Scandinavia as rentals can be easily organised. For cross-country skiing, travellers will normally have to rely on friendly locals to lend them equipment – or plan on buying their own skis, poles and boots. (Flea markets are the probably the cheapest and most likely places to look.)

Skiing – especially cross country – should only be attempted after studying trails and routes (wilderness trails are identified by colour codes on maps and signposts). Practically all towns and villages illuminate some skiing tracks. Wear appropriate clothing and carry food, extra clothing and emergency supplies, such as matches and something to burn. Skiers should be extra careful about darkness. In Scandinavia, days are very short in winter and, during the winter months of December and January, there's no daylight at all in the extreme north.

The skiing season generally lasts from early December to April. Snow conditions can vary greatly from one year to the next and from region to region, but January and February, as well as the Easter holiday period, tend to be the best (and busiest) months. Snow cannons for producing artificial snow are common.

Whale-watching

Some Scandinavian countries have been criticised for their policies on hunting whales, so it's an encouraging sign that whale-watching opportunities are on the increase – it's far better to shoot the creatures with cameras than with harpoons! Common species in the region are minke, sperm and killer whales, white-beaked dolphins and the ubiquitous harbour porpoises, seen in Norway, the Faroes and Iceland. Blue whales also surface from time to time.

Windsurfing

While this sport is not as popular as it was in the late 1980s, the beaches of Denmark continue to attract crowds of windsurfers in summer. Wetsuits enable the keener windsurfers to continue their sport throughout the colder months. Sailboards can be rented in some tourist centres, and courses are sometimes on offer for beginners.

BUSINESS HOURS

Pubs generally open from 4pm to 11pm, and normal hours for restaurants and cafés are noon to 10pm daily. Variations are noted throughout the text.

CHILDREN

Successful travel with young children requires planning and effort. Don't try to overdo things; even for adults, packing too much into the time available can cause problems. Make sure the activities include the kids as well – balance a day at Copenhagen's Nationalmuseet with a day at Legoland. Include your children when planning the trip; if they've helped to work out where you'll all be going, they will be much more interested when they get there. Lonely Planet's *Travel with Children*, by Cathy Lanigan, is a good source of information.

Most of Scandinavia is very child-friendly (Iceland and the Faroes are exceptions: children are liked and have lots of freedom, but they're treated as miniadults and there aren't many attractions tailored particularly for them). There are many public parks for kids and commercial facilities are numerous. Domestic tourism is largely dictated by children's needs, with some excellent theme parks, water parks and so on. Many museums, such as the national ones in Stockholm, have a children's section with toys and activities.

Car-rental firms hire out children's safety seats at a nominal cost, but it's essential that you book these in advance. The same goes for highchairs and cots (cribs): they're standard in many restaurants and hotels, but numbers may be limited. The choice of baby food, infant formulas, soy and cow's milk, disposable nappies (diapers) etc is wide in most Scandinavian supermarkets.

In the Faroes and much of the rest of Scandinavia, a baby carrier rather than a pram is of crucial importance.

CLIMATE

Generalisations about weather conditions over an area of approximately 2,500,000 sq km are something of an impossibility! Temperatures can range from -50°C in the Arctic Circle in winter to summer temperatures of over 30°C in some parts of Sweden. Large chunks of Scandinavia lie within the Arctic Circle, yet the presence of the Gulf Stream makes coastal areas much warmer than you might anticipate at such a northerly latitude. See the climate charts for an idea of temperatures and rainfall across the region, and tune in to local weather reports for current conditions once you're on the road.

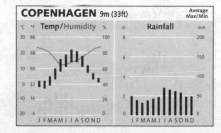

REGIONAL DIRECTORY

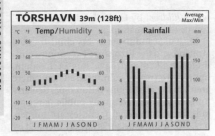

TÓRSHAVN 39m (128ft)

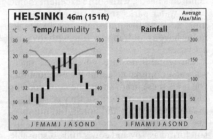

HELSINKI 46m (151ft)

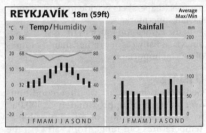

REYKJAVÍK 18m (59ft)

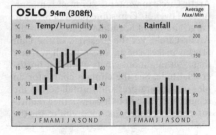

OSLO 94m (308ft)

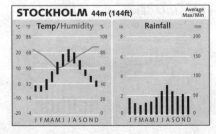

STOCKHOLM 44m (144ft)

DANGERS & ANNOYANCES

In remote rural areas, hypothermia, injury and getting lost are serious hazards. People living in isolated places may be suspicious of outsiders, and winter darkness can lead to unpredictable behaviour and alcohol abuse.

Wild animals, including polar bears and wolves in the arctic archipelago of Svalbard (Norway) and arctic terns defending their nests, pose a small risk.

Mosquitoes, midges and blackflies can be a real annoyance in some parts of the region.

Whatever you do, don't leave friends and relatives back home worrying about how to get in touch with you in case of emergency.

Drugs

Always treat drugs with a great deal of caution. There's a fair amount of dope available in the region, sometimes quite openly, but that doesn't mean it's legal: a bit of hash can cause you a lot of bother.

Don't even try to bring drugs home with you. Energetic customs officials could well decide to take a closer look at your luggage.

Theft

Theft, usually pickpocketing, is a mounting problem in major Scandinavian cities. Take care of your belongings and remember that the greatest threat in places such as Oslo, Copenhagen and Stockholm can actually be from fellow tourists, who thieve from others to fund their trips.

As a traveller, you're often fairly vulnerable and when you do lose things it can be a real hassle. The most important things to guard are your passport, other important documents, tickets and money – in that order. It's always best to carry these next to your skin or in a sturdy leather pouch on your belt.

Train-station lockers or luggage-storage counters are useful places to stash your bags (but not your valuables) while you get your bearings in a new town. Be very suspicious about people who offer to help you operate your locker.

Carry your own padlock for hostel lockers and watch out for thieves who strike at night in hostel dorms – keep your money and passport well out of reach. Be careful, even in hotels: don't leave valuables lying around your room.

Parked cars, especially those with foreign number plates and/or rental-agency stickers, are prime targets for petty criminals in most cities. If possible, remove the stickers (or cover them with local football club stickers or something similar), leave a local newspaper on the seat and try to make it look like a local car. Don't ever leave valuables in the car, and remove all luggage overnight.

In case of theft or loss, always report the incident to the police and ask for a statement, or your travel insurance won't pay up.

DISABLED TRAVELLERS

Scandinavia leads the world in terms of facilities for disabled people. For example, by law every new restaurant in Finland must have a special toilet for people with a disability. There are wheelchair ramps to practically all public buildings, most department stores, shopping centres and many private shops. Some train carriages are fitted with special lifts for wheelchairs.

If you have a physical disability, get in touch with your national support organisation (preferably the 'travel officer' if there is one) and ask about the countries you plan to visit. They often have complete libraries devoted to travel, and they can put you in touch with travel agents who specialise in tours for the disabled.

The **Royal Association for Disability & Rehabilitation** (Radar; ☎ 020-7250 3222; www.radar.org.uk; 12 City Forum, 250 City Rd, London, EC1V 8AF) can supply general advice for disabled travellers in Europe.

DISCOUNT CARDS
Camping Card International

Your local automobile association or national cyclists' organisation issues the **Camping Card International** (www.campingcardinternational .org), valid for one year, which is basically a camping ground ID. These are also available from local camping federations, and sometimes on the spot at camping grounds. They incorporate third-party insurance for damage you may cause, and many camping grounds offer a small discount if you sign in with one. They're obligatory in Denmark, but not commonly recognised in Iceland or the Faroes.

Hostel Card

While not mandatory in Scandinavia, a Hostelling International (HI) card gives a sizable discount every time you check in to an affiliated hostel. Some hostels will issue one on the spot or after six stays, although this might cost a bit more than getting it in your home country. See p448 for more details on hostels in the region.

Senior Cards

Museums and other sights, public swimming pools, spas and transport companies frequently offer discounts to retirees, pensioners and to those over 60 (sometimes slightly younger for women; and over 65 in Sweden). Make sure you bring proof of age; the ever-proper and always polite Scandinavian ticket-collector is not going to admit that you look a day over 39.

If you're going to be travelling by train, those aged over 60 are entitled to discounted Euro Domino passes (p476) and senior versions of the ScanRail pass (p477).

Student & Youth Cards

The most useful of these cards is the **International Student Identity Card** (ISIC; www.isiccard .com), a plastic ID-style card with your photo, which provides discounts on numerous forms of transport (including airlines, international ferries and local public transport), reduced or free admission to museums and sights, and cheap meals in some student restaurants – a good way of cutting costs in expensive Scandinavia.

There's a global industry in fake student cards, and a number of places now stipulate a maximum age for student discounts or, more simply, they've substituted a 'youth discount' for a 'student discount'. If you're under 26 but not a student, you can apply for the **Euro26 card** (www.eyca.org), which goes by various names in different countries, or an International Youth Travel Card (IYTC). All are available through student unions, hostelling organisations or youth-oriented travel agencies such as STA Travel. They don't automatically entitle you to discounts and some companies and institutions don't recognise them – but you won't find out until you try.

ELECTRICITY

Most of the region runs on 220V, 50Hz AC. Check the voltage and cycle (usually 50Hz) used in your home country. Most appliances that are set up for 220V will handle 240V quite happily without modifications (and vice versa); the same goes for 110V and 125V combinations.

It's always preferable to adjust your appliance to the exact voltage if you can (some modern battery chargers and radios will do this automatically). Just don't combine 110/125V and 220/240V without a transformer (which will be built into an adjustable appliance).

Several countries outside Europe (eg the USA and Canada) run on 60Hz AC, which will affect the speed of electric motors even after the voltage has been adjusted to European values, so CD and tape players (where motor speed is all-important) will be useless. However, appliances such as electric razors, hair dryers, irons and radios will be fine.

The standard plug is the so-called 'europlug' with two round pins, although some plugs in the Faroes have three pins and some in Iceland have two slanted prongs. Adaptors are available from most supermarkets. Many europlugs and some sockets don't have provision for earth since most local home appliances are double insulated; when provided, earth usually consists of two contact points along the edge.

EMBASSIES & CONSULATES

See the individual country Directories for specific embassy and consulate addresses.

It's important to realise the things your own embassy can and can't do to help you. Generally speaking, it won't be much help in emergencies if the trouble you're in is your own fault in any way. Remember that you are bound by the laws of the country you are in. Your embassy will not be sympathetic if you end up in jail after committing a crime locally, even if such actions are legal in your own country.

In genuine emergencies you might get some assistance, but only if other channels have been exhausted. For example, if you need to get home urgently, a free ticket is exceedingly unlikely – the embassy would expect you to have insurance. If you have all your money and documents stolen, it might assist with getting a new passport, but a loan for onward travel is out of the question.

GAY & LESBIAN TRAVELLERS

This book lists contact addresses and gay and lesbian venues in some of the individual country chapters, but your national gay and lesbian organisation should be able to give you more information before you travel. The

Spartacus International Gay Guide (US$33), published by Bruno Gmünder Verlag (Berlin), is an excellent international directory of gay entertainment venues, but it's best used in conjunction with more up-to-date listings in local papers – venues in the region can change with great speed.

Denmark, Iceland, Norway and Sweden allow gay and lesbian couples to form 'registered partnerships', which grant every right of matrimony except access to church weddings, adoption and artificial insemination. Finland, too, is tolerant of homosexual couples. However, public displays of affection are uncommon in Norway, and it's a good idea to be discreet in the Faroes, where a conservative society and strongly held religious beliefs may cause problems for gay and lesbian couples.

HOLIDAYS

Midsummer's Eve (the longest day of the year) is celebrated in late June across Scandinavia, generally with fervour and large bonfires! For holidays particular to each country, see the Directories at the end of each country chapter.

INSURANCE

A travel insurance policy to cover theft, personal liability, loss and medical problems is strongly recommended. There's a variety of policies available and travel agencies will have recommendations. The international travel policies handled by STA Travel or other student travel organisations are usually good value. Check the small print; some policies specifically exclude 'dangerous activities' such as skiing, motorcycling, mountaineering, scuba diving or even hiking.

Travel insurance also covers cancellation or delays in travel arrangements; for example, in case you fall seriously ill two days before departure. Cover depends on your insurance so ask your insurer to explain where you stand. Ticket loss is also covered by travel insurance.

Buy travel insurance as early as possible. If you buy it the week before you are due to fly, you may find that you're not covered for delays to your flight caused by strikes or other industrial actions that may have been in force before you took out the insurance.

Paying for your airline ticket with a credit card often provides limited travel accident insurance, and you may be able to reclaim the payment if the operator doesn't deliver. In the UK, for instance, institutions issuing credit cards are required by law to reimburse consumers if a company goes into liquidation and the amount involved is more than UK£100. Ask your credit-card company what it is prepared to cover.

A policy that pays doctors or hospitals directly may be preferable to one where you pay on the spot and claim later. If you have to claim later, make sure you keep all documentation. Some policies ask you to call back (reverse charges) to a centre in your home country where an immediate assessment of your problem can be made. Check if the policy covers ambulances and an emergency flight home. If you have to stretch out you will need two seats and somebody has to pay for them!

EU citizens are covered for emergency medical treatment in all EU countries (Denmark, Finland and Sweden are Scandinavian EU members) on presentation of an E111 form. Inquire about these at your national health service or travel agency well in advance; in some countries post offices may have them. UK citizens can find out more on the website www.dh.gov.uk/PolicyAndGuidance/HealthAdviceForTravellers. Similar reciprocal arrangements exist between individual countries: see the individual country chapters for details. Australian Medicare covers emergency treatment in seven European countries, including Finland and Sweden. You may still have to pay on the spot, but you'll be able to reclaim these expenses at home. However, travel insurance is still advisable because of the flexibility it offers as to where and how you're treated, as well as covering expenses for ambulance and repatriation. For further information about health insurance, see p478.

For further information about car insurance, see p474.

INTERNET ACCESS

The simplest option for accessing email is to open a free web-based account like **Hotmail** (www.hotmail.com) or **Yahoo!** (mail.yahoo.com). You can then access your mail from anywhere in the world from any Net-connected machine running a standard web browser.

Travelling with a portable computer is a great way to stay in touch with life back home but, unless you know what you're doing, it can be fraught with problems. A good investment is a universal AC adaptor for your appliance, so you can plug it in anywhere without frying the innards of your computer if the power supply voltage varies. You'll also need a plug adaptor for each country you visit, often easiest bought before you leave home.

Secondly, your PC-card modem may or may not work once you leave your home country and you won't know for sure until you try. The safest option is to buy a reputable 'global' or 'world' modem before you leave, or buy a local PC-card modem if you're spending an extended time in any one country. Keep in mind that the telephone socket in each country you visit will probably be different from that at home, so ensure that you have at least a US RJ-11 telephone adaptor that works with your modem. You can almost always find an adaptor that will convert from RJ-11 to the local variety, or buy a local modem cable with the appropriate telephone jack at the end. For more information on travelling with a portable computer, see the World Wide Phone Guide on the Internet at www.kropla.com or TeleAdapt at www.teleadapt.com.

Internet service providers (ISPs) such as **AmericaOnline** (www.aol.com), **CompuServe** (www.compuserve.com) and **AT&T** (www.att.com) each have dial-in nodes throughout Europe, except for the Faroes; it's best to download a list of the dial-in numbers before you leave home. You can also get an Internet account with **MaGlobe** (www.maglobe.com), which offers local access numbers throughout Scandinavia (except in the Faroes) and charges around US$8 per hour. If you access your Internet account at home through a smaller ISP or your office or school network, your best option is to either open an account with a global ISP, like those previously mentioned, or rely on Internet cafés and other public access points to collect your mail.

If you do intend to rely on Internet cafés, check whether your ISP has a web-based collection point on their website. If not, you will need to have three pieces of information so you can access your Internet mail account: your incoming (POP or IMAP) mail server name, your account name and your password. Your ISP or network supervisor will give you these. Armed with this information,

REGIONAL DIRECTORY

you should be able to access your Internet mail account from any Net-connected machine in the world, provided it runs some kind of software. It pays to become familiar with the process for doing this before you leave home.

You'll find Internet cafés throughout Scandinavia and some are listed in the country chapters in this book; for an up-to-date list see www.world66.com/netcafeguide. In general, libraries provide a free or very cheap Internet service, although there may be a waiting list and locals may have priority. You may also find public Internet access in post offices, tourist offices, hostels, hotels, universities and so on.

LEGAL MATTERS

See the individual country Directories for specific legal matters, including drinking laws, drug laws and traffic restrictions.

MAPS

Good maps are easy to come by in Europe, but you might want to buy a few beforehand, especially if you're driving, cycling or have some hefty treks planned. The maps in this book are a useful first reference when you arrive in a city.

Otherwise, you can't go far wrong with Michelin maps, which come with bendy covers so you can easily stick them in your pocket. Some people prefer the meticulous Freytag & Berndt, Kümmerly + Frey or Hallwag maps, which have been recommended for Scandinavian countries. Falk Plan city maps are very usable and detailed, and the Falk map of Scandinavia is particularly good.

In Scandinavia, tourist offices are an excellent source for free and up-to-date maps, often in English-language versions. Local automobile associations also provide detailed, free maps to their members.

The following shops sell Scandinavian maps, including motoring maps and topographic maps for hikers, by mail order:

Map Land (☎ 03-9670 4383; www.mapland.com.au; 372 Little Bourke St, Melbourne, VIC 3000, Australia)

Map Shop (☎ 01684-593146; www.themapshop.co.uk; 15 High St, Upton-upon-Severn, Worcestershire, WR8 0HJ, England)

Omni Resources (☎ 336-227 8300; www .omnimap.com; 1004 S Mebane St, PO Box 2096, Burlington, NC 27216-2096, USA)

MONEY

All Scandinavian currencies are fully convertible. Most foreign currencies can be easily exchanged but US dollars, pounds sterling and euros are the best to carry. You may well decide, however, that other currencies suit your purposes better. You lose out through commissions and customer exchange rates every time you change money, so if you only visit Sweden, for example, you may be better off buying some kronor before you leave home. See the relevant country Directories for further details.

SCANDINAVIA & THE EU

Country	EU member	Currency
Denmark	yes	Danish krone (Dkr)
Faroe Islands	no	Faroese króna Islands (Fkr) & Danish krone (Dkr)
Finland	yes	euro (€)
Iceland	no	Icelandic króna (Ikr)
Norway	no	Norwegian krone (Nkr)
Sweden	yes	Swedish krona (Skr)

ATMs

An automated teller machine (ATM) can give you instant cash as soon as you punch in your personal identification number (PIN). Credit and cash cards (eg Visa, Cirrus, Plus, Eurocard) are accepted widely throughout Scandinavian Europe; always make sure you know which ATMs abroad will accept your particular card by checking first with your bank at home. Remember that ATMs aren't completely fail-safe. If one swallows your card it can be a major headache. Note that many ATMs in Europe will not accept PINs of more than four digits.

Withdrawals may incur a transaction fee, usually a flat rate of about $US2 to $US5, or a percentage of around 4.75%. Check charge rates with your card provider, as it might be more economical if you make fewer but larger withdrawals.

Charge cards such as American Express and Diners Club may also be hooked up to ATM networks.

Cash

Nothing beats cash for convenience...or risk. If you lose it, it's gone forever and very few travel insurers will come to your rescue.

For tips on carrying your money safely, see Theft (p452).

It's still a good idea, though, to bring some local currency in cash, if only to tide you over until you get to an exchange facility or find an ATM. Some extra cash in an easily exchanged currency (eg US dollars or pounds sterling) is also a good idea. Remember that banks will always accept foreign-currency paper money but very rarely coins, so you might want to spend (or donate) your local coins before you cross a border.

Credit Cards

A credit card can be an ideal travelling companion. Make sure you know what to do in case of theft (usually you need to call a telephone hotline). With a credit card you can charge big expenses such as airline tickets on the card, which saves you carrying so much cash and travellers cheques. Another major advantage is that it allows you to withdraw cash at selected banks or ATMs.

Credit and debit cards are very popular in Scandinavia; Visa is the most common, followed by MasterCard. They are more widely accepted than charge cards (such as American Express and Diners Club) because they charge merchants lower commissions. Their major drawback is that they have a credit limit based on your regular income, and this limit can stop you in your tracks if you're charging major expenses such as long-term car rental or long-distance airline tickets and travelling extensively. You can avoid this by depositing money into your card account before you begin your travels. Other drawbacks are that interest is charged on outstanding accounts, either immediately or after a set period (always immediately on cash advances), and the card can be very difficult to replace if lost abroad in remote areas.

If you use a credit card to withdraw money from an ATM, you pay interest on the money from the moment you get it. You can get around this by leaving the card in credit when you depart. On the plus side, you don't pay commission charges to exchange money and the exchange rate is usually at a better interbank rate than that offered for travellers cheques or cash exchanges. Bear in mind that if you use a credit card for purchases, exchange rates may have changed by the time your bill is

---

TAXES & REFUNDS

A kind of sales tax called value-added tax (VAT) applies to most goods and services throughout Scandinavia. International visitors can usually claim back the VAT on purchases (above a set minimum amount) that are being taken out of the country. Remember, though, that travellers who reside in an EU country are not entitled to a refund on VAT paid on goods bought in another EU country (eg a Briton returning home with goods from Finland, Sweden or Denmark). The procedure for making the claim is usually pretty straightforward. For guidance, see the relevant country chapters.

---

processed, which can work out to your advantage or disadvantage.

If you choose to rely on plastic, go for two different cards – a Visa or MasterCard, for instance, with an American Express or Diners Club backup. Better still is a combination of credit card and travellers cheques so you have something to fall back on if an ATM swallows your card.

A word of warning: although it's not common in this region, fraudulent shopkeepers have been known to make several charge-slip imprints with customers' credit cards when they're not looking. They then simply copy the signature from the signed slip. Try not to let the card out of your sight, and always check your statements carefully.

Moneychangers

Travellers should avoid banks in Scandinavia (except in the Faroes and Iceland, where banks are often a better option) in favour of *bureaux de change* (eg Forex) or post offices, which tend to offer better rates and charge lower fees or commissions than banks. They generally have longer opening hours than banks, which are closed at weekends and on public holidays (see the Directories in the individual country chapters for lists). However, most airports, central train stations, some fancy hotels and many border posts have banking facilities outside working hours. If you visit several countries, the constant conversions can drive you crazy. Buy a cheap pocket calculator, cut out the list of exchange rates from a newspaper, and stick it to the back of the calculator for easy reference.

Tipping

For the most part, tipping isn't required in Scandinavia, although if you round up the bill or leave a little something in recognition of good service, it won't be refused.

Travellers Cheques

The main advantage of travellers cheques over cash is the protection they offer against theft, although they are losing their popularity as more travellers withdraw their hard-earned money directly via ATMs. American Express, Visa and Thomas Cook cheques are widely accepted and have efficient replacement policies for lost and stolen cheques.

It's vital to keep a record of your cheque numbers and which ones you have used, in case of theft. Keep your list separate from the cheques themselves.

Cheques are available in various currencies, but those denominated in US dollars, euros and pounds sterling are the easiest to cash. When you change them, don't just look at the exchange rate; ask about fees and commissions as well. There may be a per-cheque service fee, a flat transaction fee, or a percentage of the total amount irrespective of the number of cheques. In most European countries the exchange rate for travellers cheques is slightly better than the exchange rate for cash.

PHOTOGRAPHY & VIDEO

Scandinavia is extremely photogenic, but where you'll be travelling and the climate will dictate what film to take. In autumn, when the sky can often be overcast, photographers should use high-speed film (rated 200 or 400 ASA). In bright conditions, eg in sunny weather or if there's lots of settled snow, slower film (with an ASA of 50 to 100) is the answer.

It's worth noting that if you're taking pictures in reflective conditions, eg of icebergs, water or snow, you need to overexpose your shots; otherwise automatic cameras think it's brighter than it really is, resulting in dark photos. Batteries tend to run out quickly in cold conditions, so carry a spare set. Try to avoid exposing your camera and films to extremes of temperature.

If you're using a digital camera, check that you have enough memory to store your snaps – two 128MB cards will probably be enough. If you do run out of memory space

your best bet is to burn your photos onto a CD. Increasing numbers of processing labs now offer this service. To download your pics at an Internet café you'll need a USB cable and a card reader. Some places provide a USB on request, but be warned that many of the bigger chain cafés don't let you plug your gear into their computers, meaning that it's back to plan A – the CD.

For more pointers, check out Lonely Planet's *Travel Photography*, by internationally renowned travel photographer Richard l'Anson. It's a full-colour guide designed to be taken on the road.

Still and video film and camera equipment are available throughout Scandinavia, but it would be advisable to bring as much as possible with you, as prices can be exorbitant. Print processing is generally available in towns and cities.

POST

Airmail typically takes about a week to reach North American or Australasian destinations. Postage costs vary from country to country. Postal services are very efficient in Scandinavia.

You can collect mail from post office poste restante sections, although this can be a tricky process in Sweden; see p438 for details. Ask people writing to you to print your name clearly on the envelope, underline your surname and use capital letters. When collecting mail you may need to bring along your passport for identification. If an expected letter is not waiting for you, ask post office staff to check under your first name as letters are sometimes misfiled. Unless the sender specifies otherwise, mail will always be sent to the main post office of any city.

You can also have mail (but not parcels) sent to you at American Express offices so long as you have an American Express card or travellers cheques. When you buy American Express travellers cheques you can ask for a booklet listing all their office addresses worldwide.

SOLO TRAVELLERS

Scandinavia is well developed and one of the safest places to travel in Europe, so travelling alone should pose no problems. Inhabitants of Scandinavia are often thought to be pleasant but not particularly gregarious, so you may have to brush up your social skills if you want to make friends locally.

Hostels and camping grounds are good places to meet other travellers.

TELEPHONE & FAX

You can ring abroad from almost any phone box in Scandinavia. Reverse-charge (collect) calls are usually possible, and communicating with the local operator in English should not be much of a problem. In some countries you can avoid the local operator, and dial direct to your home operator.

You can send faxes and telegrams from most of the larger post offices and some hotels and public telephone offices.

Mobile Phones

Most populated parts of Scandinavia use GSM 900/1800, which is compatible with the rest of Europe and Australasia, but not with the North American GSM 1900 or the totally different system in Japan (although some North American GSM 1900/900 may work here). If you have a GSM phone, check with your service provider about using it in Scandinavia, and beware of calls being routed internationally (very expensive for a 'local' call). Local telephone companies and national tourist offices can advise on coverage.

Rental of mobile phones is possible everywhere except Norway, and is particularly easy in mobile-centric Finland. Purchase is always an option, but it's expensive and you'll be unable to use your existing number. Another option is to buy a local SIM card with a rechargeable account (particularly good value in Sweden and Finland).

Phone Codes

To call abroad you simply dial the international access code (IAC) for the country you are calling from (most commonly 00 in Europe), the country code (CC) for the country you are calling, the local area code (usually dropping the leading zero if there is one) and then the number. If, for example, you are in Norway (which has an international access code of 00) and want to make a call to Sweden (country code 46) in the Stockholm area (area code 08), number ☎ 123 4567, then dial ☎ 00-46-8-123 4567. Check out www .ekno.com/ekit/Info/Countryphoneguide for a list of international country codes.

TELEPHONE CODES

Country	☎ CC	☎ IAC	☎ IO
Denmark	45	00	141
Faroe Islands	298	00	808080
Finland	358	00, 990, 994, 999	020208
Iceland	354	00	533 5010
Norway	47	00	181
Sweden	46	00	118119

CC – country code (to call into that country)
IAC – international access code
   (to call abroad from that country)
IO – international operator (to make inquiries)

Phonecards

Public telephones accepting stored-value phonecards are the norm and, in some places, coin-operated phones are almost impossible to find. Phonecards are readily available from post offices, telephone centres, news stands or retail outlets. These cards solve the problem of having the correct coins for calls. (In Iceland and the Faroes, however, phones with phonecard facilities are hard to find outside of Reykjavík and Tórshavn). More and more public telephone kiosks are giving callers the opportunity to pay by credit card. Beware of public telephones in bars and restaurants – most will eat up your money at an incredible rate.

TIME

Scandinavian Europe sprawls across six time zones. See the individual country Directories for details.

TOURIST INFORMATION

Tourist information offices in Scandinavia are located at train stations or centrally (often in the town hall or central square) in most towns. They tend to be open for longer hours over the summer and reduced hours over the winter; smaller offices may only be open during the peak months of summer.

Facilities are generally excellent, with piles of regional and national brochures, helpful free maps and friendly employees. Staff are often multilingual, speaking several tongues including Scandinavian languages, English, German or French. They will book hotel and transport reservations and tours; a small charge may apply.

VIDEO SYSTEMS

If you want to record or buy videos to play back home, they won't work if the image registration systems are different. Most of Europe and Australia uses PAL (France and Poland use SECAM), which is incompatible with NTSC in North America and Japan.

VISAS

A visa is a stamp in your passport or on a separate piece of paper permitting you to enter the country in question and stay for a specified period of time. There's a wide variety, including tourist, transit and business visas. Transit visas are usually cheaper than tourist or business visas, but they only allow a very short stay (one or two days) and can be difficult to extend. Often you can get the visa at the border or at the airport on arrival; check first with the embassies or consulates of the countries you plan to visit.

It's important to remember that visas have a 'use-by date', and you'll be refused entry after that period has elapsed. Visa requirements do change, and you should always check with the individual embassies or consulates or a reputable travel agency before leaving home. If you wish to apply for a visa while still at home, make sure you do it at least three months in advance of your planned arrival. If you plan to get your visas as you go along rather than arranging them all beforehand, carry spare passport photos.

Citizens of the UK, the USA, Canada, Ireland, Australia and New Zealand don't require visas if visiting a Scandinavian country for less than three months; South Africans, on the other hand, need a visa to enter all Scandinavian countries. With a valid passport most travellers will be able to visit Scandinavian countries for up to three (sometimes even six) months, provided they have some sort of onward or return ticket and/or 'sufficient means of support' (money). Except at international airports, it's unlikely that immigration officials will give you and your passport more than a cursory glance.

Many EU countries have abolished passport controls between their borders and an identity card should be sufficient, but it's always safest to carry your passport.

For more specific visa information, refer to the individual Directories in the country chapters.

WEIGHTS & MEASURES

The metric system is used in Scandinavia. Decimals are indicated by commas and thousands are indicated by points.

WOMEN TRAVELLERS

Scandinavia is one of the safest places to travel in all of Europe and women travellers should experience little trouble; however, common sense is always needed when dealing with potentially dangerous situations such as hitching or walking alone at night.

Recommended reading is the *Handbook for Women Travellers* by M & G Moss.

WORK

Officially, a citizen of the EU is allowed to work in other EU countries. However, the paperwork isn't always straightforward for longer-term employment. Other country/ nationality combinations require special work permits that are almost impossible to arrange, especially for temporary work. However, Australian and New Zealand passport-holders aged between 18 and 30 can qualify for a one-year working holiday visa in some Scandinavian countries: see the individual country Directories for details.

That doesn't prevent enterprising travellers from topping up their funds occasionally, and not always illegally. Your national student-exchange organisation may be able to arrange temporary work permits to several countries through special programmes.

If you have a parent or grandparent who was born in an EU country, you may have certain rights you never knew about. Get in touch with that country's embassy and ask about dual citizenship and work permits – if you are eligible for citizenship, also ask about any obligations, such as military service, taxation and having to relinquish your first passport. Not all countries allow dual citizenship, so a work permit may be all you can get. Ireland is particularly easy-going about granting citizenship to people with Irish ancestry and, with an Irish passport, the EU is your oyster.

If you do find a temporary job, the pay may be less than that offered to locals, although this is not always the case in Scandinavia. Teaching English can pay well, but such work is hard to come by. Other typical tourist jobs (such as working in a restaurant, hotel or fish-processing plant) may come with board and lodging and the pay is little more than pocket money, but you'll have a good time partying with other travellers.

Work Your Way Around the World by Susan Griffith, gives good, practical advice on a wide range of issues. Another useful title is *The Au Pair & Nanny's Guide to Working Abroad* by Susan Griffith and Sharon Legg.

Selling goods on the street is generally frowned upon and can be tantamount to vagrancy, apart from at flea markets. It's also a hard way to make money.

If you play an instrument or have other artistic talents, you could try busking (street entertainment). It's fairly common in many major cities. In Sweden, you'll need to get a busking permit, which is available from the police, although not everybody actually has the permit. In Copenhagen, acoustic music is allowed without a permit in pedestrian streets and squares between 4pm and 8pm on weekdays and noon to 5am at the weekend. Most other Scandinavian countries require municipal permits that can be hard to obtain. Talk to other buskers first.

Transport in Scandinavian Europe

CONTENTS

GETTING THERE & AWAY

ENTRY REQUIREMENTS

Citizens of the UK, the USA, Canada, Ireland, Australia and New Zealand don't require a visa if visiting a Scandinavian country for less than three months. With a valid passport, most travellers will be able to visit for up to three (sometimes even six) months, provided they have some sort of onward or return ticket and/or 'sufficient means of support' (ie money).

Many EU countries have abolished passport controls between their borders, requiring only an identity card, but it's always safest to carry your passport. If it's about to expire, renew it before you go – some countries insist that it's valid for a specified minimum period (usually three months but sometimes up to six) after your visit.

AIR

Increased competition among airlines is great news for travellers. There are plenty of cheap tickets in Europe, particularly with the emergence of the small no-frills airlines which sell budget tickets directly to customers.

London is one excellent centre for picking up inexpensive, restricted-validity tickets through discount operators (see p464). Various classes of cheap air tickets and passes are also available on routes within Scandinavian countries (see p470), subject to certain restrictions.

European 'gateway' cities include Amsterdam, Athens, Berlin, Copenhagen, Frankfurt, London, Oslo, Stockholm and Vienna.

Airports & Airlines

Major hubs in Scandinavia include Denmark's **Kastrup International Airport** (☎ 45 32 31 32 31; www.cph.dk in Danish), Finland's **Vantaa Airport** (☎ 358-2001 4636; www.helsinki-vantaa.fi), Iceland's **Keflavík Airport** (☎ 354-425-0600; www.keflavikairport .com), Norway's **Gardermoen Airport** (☎ 47 815 50 250; www.osl.no/english) and Sweden's **Arlanda Airport** (☎ 46 879 76 000; www.lfv.se in Swedish).

Some of the main international airlines flying into and out of Scandinavia and Continental Europe:

Air Canada (☎ 1-888-247-2262; www.aircanada.ca) Hub: Toronto, Canada.

Air France France (☎ 0820 820 820) Australia (☎ 03 992 038 68; www.airfrance.com) Hub: Charles de Gaulle, Paris, France.

Atlantic Airways (☎ 341000; www.atlantic.fo) Hub: Vágar, Faroes.

Blue 1 (☎ 20 585 6000; www.blue1.com) Hub: Vantaa, Finland.

British Airways (☎ 0800-178 378; www.britishairways.com) Hub: Heathrow, UK.

Cathay Pacific (☎ 2747 1888; www.cathaypacific.com) Hub: Hong Kong.

City Airline (☎ 31-600 385; www.cityairline.com) Hub: Göteborg, Sweden.

EasyJet (☎ 0871 7 500 100; www.easyjet.com) Hub: Luton, London, UK.

Finnair (☎ 600 140 140; www.finnair.com) Hub: Vantaa, Finland.

Flugfélag Íslands (☎ 570 3030; Air Iceland; www.airiceland.is) Hub: Keflavík, Iceland.

WARNING

The information in this chapter is particularly vulnerable to change. Check directly with the airline or a travel agency to make sure you understand how a fare (and the ticket you may buy) works and be aware of the security requirements for international travel. Shop carefully. The details given in this chapter should be regarded as pointers and are not a substitute for your own careful, up-to-date research.

Icelandair (☎ 505 0300; www.icelandair.net) Hub: Keflavík, Iceland.

Iceland Express (☎ 550 0600; www.icelandexpress.com) Hub: Keflavík, Iceland.

KLM Royal Dutch Airlines (☎ 20 474 7747; www.klm.com) Hub: Schipol, Amsterdam, Netherlands.

Lauda Air (☎ 51789; www.aua.com) Hub: Vienna, Austria.

Maersk Air (☎ 70 10 74 74; www.maersk-air.com) Hub: Kastrup, Denmark.

Northwest Airlines (☎ 1 800 447 4747; www.nwa.com) Hub: Detroit, USA.

Qantas (☎ 13 13 13; www.qantas.com.au) Hub: Sydney, Australia.

Ryanair (☎ 1 249 7700; www.ryanair.com) Hub: Stansted, London, UK.

SAS (☎ 70 10 20 00; Scandinavian Airlines; www.scandinavian.net) Hub: Kastrup, Denmark.

Swiss Air (☎ 61 582 0000; www.swiss.com) Hub: Zurich, Switzerland.

Thai Airways (☎ 2628-2000; www.thaiairways.com) Hub: Bangkok, Thailand

Tickets

When you're looking for bargain air fares, your best bet is to go to a travel agency rather than directly to an airline. For extra peace of mind, use a bonded agency, such as one covered by the Air Transport Operators Licence (ATOL) scheme in the UK. Firms such as STA Travel, which has offices worldwide, are not going to disappear overnight and they do offer good prices to most destinations.

An exception to the 'buy from a travel agency' rule is the expanding number of 'no-frills' carriers operating in the USA and northwestern Europe, which usually sell direct to travellers. No-frills carriers often have one-way tickets which are exactly half the return fare, so it's cheap and easy to buy a return ticket that allows you to fly into one place and leave from another.

Many airlines – full-service and no-frills – have discovered the joys of electronic selling, and the Internet is increasingly becoming the best place to look for those rock-bottom fares.

Flights to Scandinavia are the most expensive in July and August and at Christmas. Prices given here are approximate high-season return fares.

Asia

Singapore and Bangkok are the discount plane-ticket capitals of Asia. Not all agencies are reliable: ask for advice from other travellers before buying tickets.

Lauda Air flies to Vienna from Bangkok (from €900, six to 12 hours). SAS has flights from Singapore to Copenhagen (S$3340, 14 hours), which continue to Stockholm Thai Airways flies to Stockholm from Bangkok (36,900B, 10½ hours). Aeroflot offers inexpensive deals from India to Europe.

Recommended agencies:

Four Seas Tours Hong Kong (☎ 2200 7777; www.fourseastravel.com/english)

No 1 Travel Japan (☎ 03 3205 6073; www.no1-travel.com)

STA Travel (www.statravel.com); Bangkok (☎ 02 236 0262; www.statravel.co.th); Hong Kong (☎ 2736 1618; www.statravel.com.hk); Japan (☎ 03 5391 2922; www.statravel.co.jp in Japanese); Singapore (☎ 6737 7188; www.statravel.com.sg)

STIC Travels (www.stictravel.com); Delhi (☎ 11 233 57 468); Mumbai (☎ 22 221 81 431)

Australia

Flights to Scandinavian capitals require a stopover or two, usually in Singapore or Bangkok and another European city. Return fares cost around A$3000, and take 26 hours. Air France, Qantas, Cathay Pacific and KLM offer some good deals.

Some travel agencies, particularly smaller ones, advertise cheap air fares in the travel sections of the weekend newspapers. Well-known travel agencies with offices throughout Australia:

Flight Centre (☎ 133 133; www.flightcentre.com.au)
STA Travel (☎ 1300 733 035; www.statravel.com.au)

Canada

Airlines flying from Canada to Scandinavia include British Airways, Northwest Airlines and Air Canada. Flights leave from all major cities including Montreal, Ottawa, Toronto and Vancouver, and take around 14 hours, with one stopover. Finnair does direct flights from Toronto to Helsinki. Prices vary enormously (between C$2400 and C$9100 plus tax at the time of research), so shop around.

Travel Cuts (☎ 800 667 2887; www.travelcuts.com) is Canada's national student travel agency, with offices in major cities.

For online bookings try www.expedia.ca and www.travelocity.ca.

Continental Europe

Although London is the discount capital of Europe, there are several other European cities where you'll find good deals, particularly Amsterdam, Athens and Berlin.

Atlantic Airways and Maersk fly to the Faroes from Copenhagen and Billund in Denmark (from Dkr2500, 2¼ hours). Icelandair flies to the USA via Reykjavík from numerous European cities.

One of the best-value options is the budget airline Blue 1, a subsidiary of SAS, which has numerous cheap Internet flights from Helsinki to Amsterdam, Brussels, Copenhagen, Oslo and Stockholm (around 2½ hours).

Across Europe many travel agencies have ties with STA Travel. Agencies in important transport hubs include:

FRANCE
Recommended agencies include the following. All websites are in French.
Anyway (☎ 0892 893 892; www.anyway.fr)
Lastminute (☎ 0892 705 000; www.lastminute.fr)
Nouvelles Frontières (☎ 0825 000 747; www.nouvelles-frontieres.fr)
OTU Voyages (www.otu.fr) Specialises in student and youth travel.
Voyageurs du Monde (☎ 01 40 15 11 15; www.vdm.com)

GERMANY
Recommended agencies include the following (websites in German):
Expedia (☎ 01805 900 560; www.expedia.de)
Just Travel (☎ 089 747 3330; www.justtravel.de in English)
Lastminute (☎ 01805 284 366; www.lastminute.de)
STA Travel (☎ 01805 456 422; www.statravel.de)
For travellers under the age of 26.

OTHER COUNTRIES
Italy CTS Viaggi (☎ 199 501150; www.cts.it in Italian) Specialises in student and youth travel.

Netherlands Airfair (☎ 020 620 5121; www.airfair.nl in Dutch)
Spain Barcelo Viajes (☎ 902 116 226; www.barceloviajes.com in Spanish)

New Zealand

British Airways, KLM, Qantas and Swiss Air are some of the airlines flying from New Zealand to Scandinavia, usually with a stopover in southeast Asia and/or Europe. Return fares cost around NZ$3000 and take 26 hours. The site www.travel.co.nz is recommended for online bookings. It's easiest and cheapest to book flights via an agency such as:
Flight Centre (☎ 0800 243 544; www.flightcentre.co.nz)
STA Travel (☎ 0508 782 872; www.statravel.co.nz)

The UK & Ireland

Currently, three no-frills airlines offer cheap flights to major entry points in Scandinavia. Ryanair flies from London Stansted to seven airports in Denmark, Norway, Sweden and Finland, and from Glasgow Prestwick to Norway and Sweden. Some promotional fares cost as little as UK£50, including taxes. From London Stansted, EasyJet flies to Copenhagen from around UK£70 return and Iceland Express flies to Keflavík (Iceland) from around UK£135 return.

Other full-service commercial airlines, including SAS, offer return flights from London to Stockholm starting at around UK£120 return (2½ hours). City Airline flies from Birmingham and Manchester to Göteborg and Helsinki once or twice daily; Internet offers start from UK£170 return, including tax. Atlantic Airways has flights from Aberdeen and London Stansted to Vágar (Faroe Islands); see p124 for details.

Another option is Icelandair, which flies to the USA from London and Glasgow via Keflavík. The cheapest tickets (around UK£160) are only available via the Internet, with slightly lower fares if you sign up for Icelandair's free Netclub.

From Ireland, the cheapest way to Scandinavia is to catch a flight from Ryanair to London Stansted, then pick up a no-frills flight as outlined above.

Discount air travel is big business in London. Agencies advertise in the travel pages of the weekend papers, *Time Out*, the *Evening Standard* and the free magazine *TNT*. Recommended travel agencies include:
Bridge the World (☎ 0870 814 4400; www.b-t-w.co.uk)

Flightbookers (☎ 0870 814 0000; www.ebookers.com)
Flight Centre (☎ 0870 499 0040; www.flightcentre.co.uk)
North-South Travel (☎ 01245 608 291; www.north southtravel.co.uk) Donates a proportion of its profits to projects in the developing world.
Quest Travel (☎ 0870 442 3542; www.questtravel.com)
STA Travel (☎ 0870 160 0599; www.statravel.co.uk) For travellers under the age of 26.
Trailfinders (www.trailfinders.co.uk)
Travel Bag (☎ 0870 814 4440; www.travelbag.co.uk)

The USA

There are myriad flight options from the USA to Europe. To start with, check out weekly travel sections in larger newspapers, where you'll find travel agencies' ads. You should be able to fly return from New York or Boston to Copenhagen, Oslo or Stockholm from around US$1100 in high season, although there are some amazingly low summer offers. The journey takes around 10 hours. Open-jaw tickets allow you to land in one city and return from another at no extra cost.

Finnair flies direct to Helsinki from New York. Icelandair flies from New York, Boston, Baltimore, Washington DC, Minneapolis and Orlando (autumn and winter only), via Keflavík in Iceland to many European destinations including Glasgow, London, Oslo, Stockholm and Copenhagen. It has some of the best deals and also allows a free three-day stopover in Reykjavik on transatlantic flights (not applicable to Internet tickets).

If you're planning to fly within Scandinavian Europe, SAS offer various internal air passes (see p470) if you travel across the pond with them. They fly from Chicago, New York, Seattle and Washington to Copenhagen and Stockholm.

Airhitch (www.airhitch.org) specialises in Internet purchases of stand-by tickets to Europe from the east coast/west coast for US$450/590 return. Destinations are by region (not a specific city or country), so you'll need to be flexible.

DISCOUNT TRAVEL AGENCIES

Discount travel agencies are known as consolidators in the USA, and San Francisco is the consolidator king. Other good deals can be found in Los Angeles, New York and other big cities. Track down consolidators through the *Yellow Pages* or the major daily newspapers.

Travel agencies recommended for online bookings include:
Cheap Tickets (☎ 1 888 922 8849; www.cheap tickets.com)
Expedia (☎ 1 800 397 3342; www.expedia.com)
Lowestfare.com (www.lowestfare.com) Website-based inquiries only.
Orbitz (☎ 1 888 656 4546; www.orbitz.com)
STA Travel (☎ 1 800 781 4040; www.sta.com)
Travelocity (☎ 1 888 709 5983; www.travelocity.com)

LAND
Bus

If you're already in Europe and you don't have a rail pass, it's generally cheaper to get to Scandinavia by bus than by train or plane. Some coaches are quite luxurious with stewards, air-conditioning, toilet and snack bar. Small bus companies with small prices occasionally come along, although most of them go out of business within a year or two. Ask around at student and discount travel agencies for the latest information.

Eurolines (www.eurolines.com) is one of the biggest, and best established, express-bus services connecting Scandinavia with the rest of Europe. Most buses operate daily in summer and between two and five days a week in winter; advance ticket purchases are usually necessary. Eurolines' representatives in Europe include:
Bohemia Euroexpress International (☎ 02-242 18680; www.bei.cz in Czech; Krizikova 4-6, 18600 Prague 8, Czech Republic)
Bus Éireann (☎ 83 66 111; www.buseireann.ie; Busáras, Store St, Dublin, Republic of Ireland)
Deutsche Touring (☎ 069-790350; www.deutsche-touring.de; Am Römerhof 17, D-60486 Frankfurt am Main, Germany)
Eurolines Spain (☎ 915 06 32 55; www.eurolines.es in Spanish; Estación Sur de Autobuses, c/Méndez Alvaro, Madrid, Spain)
Eurolines Austria (☎ 01-798 29 00; www.eurolines.at; Busstation Wien-Mitte, Erdbergstrasse 202, 1030 Vienna, Austria)
Eurolines France (☎ 08-92 89 90 91; www.eurolines.fr in French; Gare Routiére Internationale, Boite 313, 28 ave du Général de Gaulle, F-93541 Bagnolet, Paris, France)
Eurolines Italy SRL (☎ 39 055 35 71 10; www.eurolines.it in Italian; Autostazione Lazzi, Piazza Adua 2, 50144 Firenze, Italy)
Eurolines Nederland (☎ 020-560 8788; www.eurolines.nl; Amstel Station, Julianplein 5, 1097 DN Amsterdam, Netherlands)

TRANSPORT IN SCANDINAVIAN EUROPE

Eurolines Scandinavia Denmark (☎ 07 010 00 10;
www.eurolines.dk; Reventlowsgade 8, DK-1651
Copenhagen V, Denmark); Sweden (☎ 08-762 5960;
www.eurolines.se; Busstop, Cityterminalen, Klarabergsviadukten 72, SE-11164 Stockholm, Sweden)
Eurolines UK Ltd (☎ 0870-514 3219; www.national
express.com/eurolines; 52 Grosvenor Gardens, London,
SW1W 0AG, UK)

Sample Eurolines fares are: London to Copenhagen (from UK£120 return) and Frankfurt to Copenhagen (€164 return). There's a
10% discount for those under 26 years or
over 60 years.

The Eurolines Pass allows unlimited travel
to 35 cities across Europe; the Scandinavian
cities included are Copenhagen, Göteborg,
Oslo and Stockholm. Between 1 June and
15 September, a 15-/30-/60-day pass costs
€285/425/490 (€240/345/380 for those under
26 years and over 60; cheaper from 16 September to 31 May).

From St Petersburg in Russia, daily express
buses run to Helsinki (see p194 for details).
A Russian visa is required.

Car & Motorcycle

Driving to Scandinavia usually requires
taking a car ferry (opposite). The only land
borders in the region are between Finland
or Norway and Russia (and taking your
own vehicle through Russia is no easy matter), or between Denmark and Germany.
It is possible to drive through Denmark
and onwards to Sweden using bridges and
tunnels.

See p473 for details of the paperwork
that is required.

Hitching & Car-Ride Services

For local hitching conditions and laws, see
the individual country chapters.

After hitching, the cheapest way to head
further north in Europe is as a paying passenger in a private car. In Germany, rides are
arranged by city-based **Mitfahrzentrale agencies**
(www.mitfahrzentrale.de in German). You pay a reservation fee to the agency and your share of
petrol to the driver. Local tourist information offices can help you locate agencies, or
in larger German cities, dial the city area code
and ☎ 19444.

A long list of car-ride agencies can be
found at www.allostop.com under the section 'Carpooling in Europe'.

Train

The *Thomas Cook European Timetable* is the
train traveller's bible. It's updated monthly
and is available from Thomas Cook outlets
in the UK (£10.50), or you can order a copy
from www.thomascookpublishing.com.

For information about rail passes, see
p475.

ASIA

Travelling across central and eastern Asia by
train can cost about the same as flying – but
it's a lot more fun! Three routes cross Siberia
to/from Moscow: the Trans-Siberian to/from
Vladivostok, and the Trans-Mongolian and
Trans-Manchurian to/from Beijing. Prices
vary enormously, depending on where you
buy the ticket and what's included – prices
quoted here are only a rough indication.
Trains also run daily between Moscow and
Helsinki (p195), usually requiring a change
at St Petersburg.

The Trans-Siberian Railway takes just
under seven days from Vladivostok to Moscow, via Khabarovsk; but most travellers take
the Trans-Mongolian train from Beijing to
Moscow, through Mongolia, which takes
about six days. A 2nd-class sleeper in a four-
berth compartment on a Trans-Mongolian
package costs around US$400 (excluding
visas and meals), but cheaper tickets are
available if you organise the trip yourself. The
Trans-Manchurian option runs from Beijing
through Manchuria, and takes seven days,
costing about US$460 for a package.

Monkey Business Hong Kong (☎ 2723 1376) Beijing
(☎ 6591 6519; www.monkeyshrine.com) organises all-
inclusive packages and visas for trips starting
in Beijing. More expensive packages can be
bought in Europe; one well-known UK operator is **Regent Holidays** (☎ 0117-921 1711; www
.regent-holidays.co.uk).

Lonely Planet's *Trans-Siberian Railway* is a
comprehensive guide to the route.

CENTRAL EUROPE

Hamburg is the main European gateway for
Scandinavia but direct trains also run from
Berlin. There are several direct trains daily
to Copenhagen from Hamburg (2nd-class
€70, five hours); the hour-long ferry trip is
included in the ticket price. Direct trains
from Berlin run daily to Malmö (2nd-class
€100, 8½ hours), via the Sassnitz to Trelleborg ferry (3¾ hours).

In Germany, the Sparpreis fare is a good train deal that you could use to get to northern Germany, from where it's a short hop to Denmark. Sparpreis 25 and Sparpreis 50 give 25% and 50% off standard long-distance return fares, with certain restrictions on times of travel and point of departure/return.

In Poland, take a train to Gdynia or Świnoujście for a ferry to Sweden (see p468).

THE UK

Going by train from the UK to Scandinavia can be more expensive than flying. From London, a 2nd-class return ticket costs around UK£320 to Copenhagen and UK£450 to Stockholm or Oslo (via Brussels and Hamburg). Contact **Deutsche Bahn UK** (☎ 0870 243 5363; www .bahn.co.uk) for details of frequent special offers, and for reservations and tickets.

The Channel Tunnel makes land travel possible between Britain and continental Europe. **Eurostar** (☎ 0870 518 6186; www.eurostar.co.uk) passenger services connect London with Calais, Paris, Lille and Brussels. From Brussels connect to Hamburg, which is the main gateway to Scandinavia. Vehicles can be taken on the Channel Tunnel car-carrying train, **Eurotunnel** (☎ 0870 535 3535; www.eurotunnel.com).

For more information on international rail travel (including Eurostar services), contact the **Rail Europe Travel Centre** (☎ 0870 584 8848; www.raileurope.co.uk; 178 Piccadilly, London W1).

SEA

Prices given in this section are sample starting prices, based on a foot passenger travelling one way in high season, using the cheapest-available sleeping option.

See the transport sections of the country chapters for information about boat–train links within Scandinavian Europe. See also p475 for rail passes and their validity on ferries.

Ferry Companies

The following details cover the larger ferry companies operating to Scandinavia.

COLOR LINE

Ferries run by **Color Line** (www.colorline.com) go from Hirtshals in Denmark to Oslo (Dkr450, 7½h hours) and Kristiansand in Norway (Dkr410, 4½ hours); from Frederikshavn in Denmark to Larvik in Norway (Dkr450, six hours); and from Kiel in Germany to

Oslo. It's possible to take a car on these ferry services (around €80 one-way). Booking agencies:
Denmark Hirtshals (☎ 99 56 19 77; Postboks 30, DK-9850 Hirtshals); Frederikshavn (☎ 99 56 19 77; Postboks 30, DK-9900 Frederikshavn)
France (☎ 01-42 85 64 50; c/o Scanditours, 36 rue de St Pétersbourg, F-75008 Paris)
Germany (☎ 0431-7300 300; Postfach 2646, D-24025 Kiel)
Norway (☎ 81 00 08 11; Postboks 1422 Vika, N-0115 Oslo)

DFDS SEAWAYS

DFDS Seaways (www.dfdsseaways.com) operates ferries from Oslo to Copenhagen (Nkr1100, 16 hours), via Helsingborg in Sweden (Nkr1100, 14 hours); from Harwich in the UK to Esbjerg in Denmark; and from Newcastle in the UK to Göteborg in Sweden, via Kristiansand in Norway. Booking agencies:
Denmark (☎ 33 42 30 00; Sundkrogsgade 11, DK-2100 Copenhagen Ø)
Germany (☎ 0403-8903 0; Van-der-Smissen-Strasse 4, D-22767 Hamburg)
Norway (☎ 23 10 68 00; Postboks 365 Sentrum, Utstikker 2, Vippetangen, N-0102 Oslo)
Sweden (☎ 031-650600; Frihamnen, Box 8895, SE-40272 Göteborg)
UK (☎ 08705 333 000; Scandinavia House, Parkeston, Harwich, Essex, CO12 4QG)
USA (☎ 1 800 533 3755, ext 113; 6801 Lake Worth Rd, Suite 103, Lake Worth, FL 33467)

FJORD LINE

Fjord Line (www.fjordline.com) sails around six days a week between Hanstholm in Denmark and Egersund (Dkr430, seven hours). It also has twice-weekly night ferries to Haugesund (Dkr1050, 13 hours) and three nightly ferries a week to Bergen (Dkr1050, 17 hours) in Norway. It also sails between Newcastle in the UK and Stavanger, Haugesund and Bergen in Norway. Prices are up to 50% lower for students and seniors. Booking agencies:
Denmark (☎ 97 96 30 00; Coastergade 10, DK-7730 Hanstholm)
Germany (☎ 0403-7693 350; Kleine Johannisstrasse 10, D-20457 Hamburg)
Norway (☎ 55 54 88 00; Skoltegrunnskaien, Postboks 7250, N-5020 Bergen)
UK (☎ 0191-296 1313; Norway House, Royal Quays, North Shields, Tyne & Wear, NE29 6EG)

SILJA LINE

Silja Line (☎ 09-180 4510; www.silja.com; Bulevardi 1A, POB 659, FIN-00101 Helsinki) runs ferry routes between Helsinki, Tallinn in Estonia and Rostock in Germany.

SMYRIL LINE
Yet another ferry option is **Smyril Line** (www .smyril-line.com), which operates a car ferry between Seyðisfjörður in eastern Iceland and Bergen in Norway or Hanstholm in Denmark, calling in at Lerwick in the Shetland Islands and Tórshavn in the Faroe Islands from mid-May to mid-September. Fares are highest between mid-June and mid-August, when a one-way adult couchette fare (see p475 for a definition) from Hanstholm to Seyðisfjörður costs €340. Coming from Hanstholm, you have to spend two days in the Faroes on the way to Iceland. Coming from Bergen, you spend two days in the Faroes on the way back; see the website for the full ferry schedule.

Booking agencies:
Denmark (☎ 96 55 03 60; www.smyril-line.dk; Trafikhavnsgade 7, DK-7730 Hanstholm)
Faroe Islands (☎ 345960; www.smyril-line.fo; J Broncksgøta 35, PO Box 370, FO-110 Tórshavn)
Norway (☎ 55 32 09 70; www.smyril-line.no; Postboks 4135 Dreggen, Slottsgaten 1, N-5835 Bergen)
UK (☎ 01595-690845; www.smyril-line.com; The Gutters' Hut, North Ness Business Park, Lerwick, Shetland, ZE1 0LZ)

STENA LINE
Stena Line (www.stenaline.com) runs daily ferry services from Frederikshavn in Denmark to Oslo in Norway (Dkr220, 6½ hours) and Göteborg in Sweden (Dkr180, 3¼ hours); twice-daily ferries from Grenå in Denmark to Varberg in Sweden (Dkr160, four hours); daily ferries from Kiel to Göteborg in Sweden; and twice-daily ferries from Gdynia in Poland to Karlskrona in Sweden.

Booking agencies:
Denmark (☎ 96 20 02 00; danmark@stenaline.com, Danish only; Trafikhavnen, DK-9900 Frederikshavn)
Germany (☎ 1805-91 66 66; www.stenaline.de; Schwedenkai 1, D-24103 Kiel)
Norway (☎ 23 17 90 00; www.stenaline.no; Jernbanetorget 2, N-0154 Oslo)
Poland (☎ 58-665 14 14; www.stenaline.pl; Kwiatkowskiego 60, PL-81-156 Gdynia)
Sweden (☎ 031-704 0000; www.stenaline.se; Box 94, SE-43222 Varberg)
UK (☎ 02890 747 747; www.stenaline.co.uk; Charter House, Park St, Ashford, Kent, TN24 8EX)

Baltic Countries

There are regular sailings from Estonia, Latvia and Lithuania across the Baltic Sea to Sweden and Finland. Silja Line sails from Tallinn in Estonia to Helsinki (€31.95, 3½ hours).

Tallink (☎ 640 9808; www.tallink.ee in Estonian) sails from Tallinn to Stockholm (€28, 16 hours), and from Paldiski in Estonia to Kapellskär (€22, nine hours), north of Stockholm.

Riga Sea Line (☎ 720 5460; www.rigasealine.lv) sails between Riga in Latvia and Stockholm (€38, 17½ hours).

There's also **Lisco Line** (in Sweden ☎ 0454-33680, in Lithuania ☎ 06-395111; www.shipping.lt), which shuttles between Klaipėda in Lithuania and Karlshamn in Sweden (€43, 14 hours).

For more details, see the transport sections in the Finland (p195) and Sweden (p441) chapters.

Germany

The **Scandlines** (☎ 0421-86100; www.scandlines.se) train, car and passenger ferry from Puttgarden to Rødbyhavn (the quickest way to Copenhagen) runs every half-hour around the clock and takes 45 minutes (€50). Frequent Scandlines ferries also run from Rostock to Gedser (€65, two hours) in Denmark.

From Kiel, there are daily Stena Line ferries to Göteborg in Sweden (€50, 13½ hours) and Color Line ferries to Oslo in Norway (€115, 20 hours). Five large Scandlines ferries run in each direction daily between Sassnitz in eastern Germany and Trelleborg (€70, four hours), south of Malmö in Sweden. Three ferries run from Rostock to Trelleborg (€90, six hours).

Finnlines (☎ 09-251 0200; www.finnlines.fi) has a daily service between Helsinki and Travemünde in Germany (€280, 34 hours).

TT Line (in Sweden ☎ 0410-56200; www.ttline.com) ferries run daily between Travemünde and Trelleborg (€22, seven hours); and Rostock in Germany and Trelleborg (€25, 5½ hours).

See also the relevant transport sections in the individual country chapters.

Poland

Regular ferries cross the Baltic Sea between Poland and Sweden. Stena Line has twice-daily ferries from Gdynia to Karlskrona (€170, 10½ hours). **Unity Line** (in Sweden ☎ 0411-556900, in Szczecin ☎ 091-359 5692; www.unityline.pl in Polish; Pl Rodla 8, 70-419 Szczecin) has a daily ferry

(€68, eight hours) between Świnoujście in Poland and Ystad in Sweden.

Polferries (in Sweden ☎ 46-401 21700, in Poland ☎ 091-322 4396; www.polferries.pl; ul Bema 9/2, 72-600 Świnoujście) links Gdansk with Nynäshamn in Sweden and Świnoujście with Ystad daily. See p442 for further details. Also see p100 for ferries between Świnoujście and Copenhagen or Rønne.

The UK
One of the most interesting (and complicated!) Scandinavian ferry routes is the weekly Smyril Line sailing Hanstholm–Tórshavn–Lerwick–Bergen–Tórshavn–Seyðisfjörður–Tórshavn–Hanstholm (mid-May to mid-September only). For getting to the Faroes, see p124; for Iceland, see p262; for Norway, see p351; and for Denmark, see p100.

From Newcastle, Fjord Line runs ferries year-round to Stavanger (UK£120, 19½ hours), Haugesund (UK£120, 22 hours) and Bergen (UK£120, 24 hours) in Norway.

DFDS Seaways has ferries from Harwich to Esbjerg in Denmark (UK£100, 18 hours) and from Newcastle to Kristiansand (UK£85, 19 hours) and Göteborg (UK£85, 27 hours, twice weekly).

To the Faroes, **NorthLink Ferries** (www.northlink ferries.co.uk) runs between Aberdeen via Kirkwall (Orkney) to Lerwick (UK£30, 13 hours), then connects with the Smyril Line service, as outlined above.

See the relevant transport sections in the individual country chapters for more details.

Transatlantic Passenger Ships & Freighters
The days of regular, long-distance passenger ships are long gone: if you want to sail from the USA to Europe, you'll have to suffer the privations of a luxury cruise ship! Cunard Line's **QM II** (in the USA ☎ 1 800 728 6273, in the UK ☎ 0845 071 0300) sails between New York and Southampton in the UK around 26 times a year, taking six nights/seven days per trip. The cost of a one-way crossing starts at US$1800. In July, the ship does a circuit of northern Europe, calling in at several Norwegian villages and towns, including Oslo and Bergen. Most travel agencies can provide the details.

A more adventurous (but not necessarily cheaper) alternative is as a paying passenger on a freighter. With a bit of homework, you can sail to Europe from just about anywhere else in the world, with stopovers at exotic little-known ports. Although it's out of date and out of print, *Travel by Cargo Ship*, by Hugo Verlomme, is still a valuable reference on the subject. Passenger freighters typically carry six to 12 passengers; although they're less luxurious than dedicated cruise ships, they provide a real taste of life at sea. Schedules tend to be flexible and costs vary, but normally hover around US$100 a day; vehicles can often be included for an additional charge.

TOURS
For special-interest trips (canoeing, birdwatching, cycling), see the country chapters in this book, contact your local activity club, or consult the national tourist offices of the country you're headed for. In the UK, the Cyclists' Touring Club (see p470) run occasional cycling tours in Scandinavia. Also check out the classified ads in cycling mags (eg *Cycling Plus*) for specialist tours.

If your time is limited, a package tour to Scandinavia might be worth considering. The following are reputable tour operators in the region:

Australia Bentours (☎ 02-9241 1353; www.bentours.com .au; Level 7, 189 Kent St, Sydney 2000) Tour operator with 25 years experience covering the highlights of Denmark, Norway, Sweden, Finland and Iceland/Greenland, with trips to St Petersburg and Moscow.

France Grand Nord Grand Large (☎ 01-40 46 05 14; www.gngl.com; 15 Rue du Cardinal Lemoine, 75005 Paris) Destinations include Finland, Norway (including Svalbard) and Iceland.

Germany Norden Tours (☎ 040-3770 2270; www.norden -tours.de in German; Kleine Johannisstrasse 10, D-20457 Hamburg) Wide range of Scandinavian tours, including cruises; Nordwind Reisen (☎ 08331-87073; www.nordwind reisen.de in German; Maximilianstrasse 17, D-87700 Memmingen, Nordwind) Specialist tours to Iceland, Greenland and Spitzbergen.

Norway Brand Cruises (☎ 52 85 31 03; www.brand.no; Postboks 33, N-4291 Kopervik) Top catering on board Norwegian cruises (including to Svalbard).

UK Arctic Experience; Discover the World (☎ 01737-218800; www.arctic-discover.co.uk; 29 Nork Way, Banstead, Surrey, SM7 1PB) Wilderness, wildlife and activity holidays in the Faroes, Iceland, Sweden and arctic Norway; Dick Phillips (☎ 01434 381440; www.icelandic-travel.com; Whitehall House, Nenthead, Alston, Cumbria, CA9 3PS) British-based company specialising in Icelandic travel services, with decades of experience leading rigorous wild hiking and skiing trips.

US Scantours (☎ 1 800 223 7226; www.scantours.com) Comfortable, hotel-based excursions and cruises throughout Scandinavia, with trips to St Petersburg; Travcoa (☎ 1 800 992 2003; www.travcoa.com; 2424 SE Bristol St, Ste 310, Newport Beach, CA 92660) Hotel-based tours visiting the highlights of Scandinavia.

GETTING AROUND

Getting around Scandinavia is a breeze, with efficient public transport systems and snappy connections.

AIR

Domestic networks in Scandinavia are safe and reliable, but flights can be expensive, particularly for short hops. However, flying may be cheaper than land-based alternatives for longer journeys, and of course can save you days of travelling time. Companies running internal airline routes offer reduced rates for Internet bookings. One useful budget airline operating Scandinavia-wide is **SAS Snowflake** Denmark (☎ 0771-661000; www.flysnowflake.com; code SK), Scandinavian Airlines' no-frills subsidiary.

Travelling between airports and city centres isn't a problem in Scandinavia thanks to good bus and train networks.

Air Passes

Visitors flying **SAS** (in North America ☎ 1 800 221 2350, in the UK ☎ 0845 607 2727; www.scandinavian .net) return to Norway, Sweden or Finland from outside Europe, can buy Visit Scandinavia/Europe Airpass coupons, as can US travellers flying with United Airlines. Visitors (but not residents of Denmark, Finland, Norway or Sweden) flying SAS return to Scandinavia from inside Europe can buy similar Visit Scandinavia Airpass coupons. The passes allow one-way travel on direct flights between any two Scandinavian cities serviced by SAS, Maersk, Widerøe, Skyways and other operators, with stopovers limited to one in each city. You can buy up to eight tickets (starting at US$65 each) which are valid for three months. Tickets can be purchased after arriving in Scandinavia if you have a return SAS international ticket.

Flugfélag Íslands (Air Iceland; www.airiceland.is) sells a variety of passes for flights within Iceland. For details, see p263.

BICYCLE

If you want to bring your own bicycle to Scandinavia, you should be able to take it along on the plane relatively easily. Check with your airline.

A tour of northern Europe by bike is an exciting prospect, giving you the chance to see vast areas of wilderness under your own steam. One organisation that can help you gear up in the UK is the wonderful **Cyclists' Touring Club** (CTC; ☎ 0870 873 0060; www.ctc.org .uk; Cotterell House, 69 Meadrow, Godalming, Surrey, GU7 3HS). It can help members with information on cycling conditions, routes, itineraries, maps and cheap specialised insurance. Tours around Denmark, Norway and Sweden are also organised for members.

Specific English-language books on cycling in Scandinavia are virtually nonexistent. *Europe by Bike*, by Karen & Terry Whitehill, is a little out of date but its descriptions of 18 cycling tours include two for Scandinavia (from Kiel across Denmark to Sweden and from southern Sweden to Stockholm via the Åland islands). The North Sea Cycle Route covers parts of Denmark, Sweden, Norway and the Shetland Islands: see www.northsea -cycle.com for information.

Make sure you take sufficient tools and spare parts, as replacements may be pricey and hard to find, especially in remote or rural areas. Panniers are essential, and of course a bike helmet is always a good idea. Take a decent lock and use it when you leave your bike unattended; theft is not uncommon in places like Helsinki and Copenhagen.

It's easy to hire bikes throughout Scandinavia, sometimes from train station bike-rental counters, and in some cases it's possible to return them to another outlet so you don't have to double back.

On slower trains and local buses in Scandinavia, bikes can usually be transported as luggage, either free or for a small fee. Fast trains and long-distance buses rarely take bikes. Cycling across the Øresund bridge between Denmark and Sweden is prohibited.

For an overview of cycling in the region, see p449 and the individual country chapters.

BOAT
Ferry

You can't really get around Scandinavia without using ferries extensively, although Denmark, which consists mostly of islands

RAILWAYS
FERRY ROUTES
MAJOR STATIONS/
INTERCHANGES

0   500 km
0   300 miles

ARCTIC OCEAN

Kirkenes

Tromsø

NORWAY

RUSSIA

Narvik

Kiruna

Kolari

Bodø
Fauske

Gällivare

Mo i Rana

Kemijärvi

Rovaniemi

Mosjøen

Arvidsjaur   Boden   Tornio   Kemi

N O R W E G I A N

Storuman

Luleå

FINLAND

S E A

Skellefteå

Oulu

Steinkjer

Vännäs   Umeå

Ylivieska

Kajaani

Nurmes

Trondheim

Östersund

Örnsköldsvik

Vaasa

Kokkola
(Karleby)

Iisalmi

Åndalsnes

Ange

Härnösand

Seinäjoki

Kuopio

Joensuu

Røros

Dombås

Sundsvall

Jyväskylä

Savonlinna

NORWAY   **SWEDEN**

Mikkeli

Imatra

Voss   Flåm   Lillehammer

Pori

Tampere

Myrdal   Gol

Mora

Lahti

Kouvola

To Lerwick;
Tórshavn;
Seyðisfjörður

Bergen   Gjøvik   Hamar

Söderhamn

Åland   Turku
(Åbo)

Kotka

Hønefoss   Malung

Falun

Gävle

Hanko
(Hangö)

HELSINKI

ST PETERSBURG

Borlänge

To
Newcastle

Drammen   Ludvika

Avesta

Uppsala

TALLINN

Stavanger   Skien   Moss   Karlstad   **Västerås**

STOCKHOLM

Narva

Egersund   Larvik   Fredrikstad   Örebro

Nynäshamn

Paldiski

ESTONIA

RUSSIA

Strömstad

Hallsberg

Tartu

To Tórshavn;
Seyðisfjörður

Arendal

Vänersborg

Norrköping

Linköping

Pärnu

Kristiansand

Skagen

Gotland

Valga

Pskov

To
Newcastle

Hirtshals

Göteburg   Borås

Jönköping
Nässjö

Västervik

Viby

Ventspils

RIGA   **LATVIA**

Hanstholm
Thisted

Frederikshavn

Växjö

Oskarshamn

Åland

Liepāja

Rözekne

Herning   **Ålborg**

Varberg   Halmstad

Kalmar

Jelgava

Daugavpils

Esbjerg   Randers   Grenå

Øland

Šiauliai

Århus

Helsingør   Helsingborg   Karlshamn

DENMARK

Odense   Karlskrona

Klaipėda

LITHUANIA

Tønder   Sønderborg

COPENHAGEN
Malmö

Liepāja

Kaunas

☆**VILNIUS**

To
Harwich

Næstved   Ystad

Trelleborg

Bornholm

Kaliningrad

RUSSIA

Rødbyhavn   Nykøbing

Kiel   Gedser

Gdynia

Puttgarden
Travemünde   Sassnitz

Warnemünde

Gdańsk

Lübeck   Rostock

Hamburg

Świnoujście

BELARUS

GERMANY   **POLAND**

BERLIN ☆

and is separated from Sweden by a narrow strait, is now well connected to mainland Europe and Sweden by bridges or tunnels, and Sweden's dozens of car ferries are slowly being replaced by bridges. From mainland Denmark (Jutland), you'll need to catch a ferry for the shortest Denmark to Norway connection. The same applies to connections between southern Sweden and Finland.

Ferry tickets are cheap on competitive routes, although transporting cars can be costly. Bicycles are usually carried free. On some routes, train pass-holders are entitled to a discount or free travel (p475).

Weekend ferries, especially on Friday nights, can be noisy places and ticket prices are significantly higher. Teenage travellers are banned on some Friday-night departures due to problems with excessive drunkenness.

For further information about the many ferry options available between the destinations in this book, see the transport sections of the individual country chapters. Also see p467 for ferry companies running services between Scandinavian countries, and for information on fares and journey lengths.

Steamers

Scandinavia's main lakes and rivers are served by steamers and diesel-powered boats during the summer. It's best to treat these extended boat trips as relaxing, scenic mini-holidays; if you view them merely as a way to get from A to B, they can seem expensive.

Sweden has the largest fleets in Scandinavia and sailing during your trip is a must. Most leave from Stockholm and sail east to the Stockholm archipelago (p382) – a maze of 24,000 islands and islets – and west to historic Lake Mälaren (p384) – home base of the Swedish Vikings a millennium ago. You can also cruise the Göta Canal (p444), the longest water route in Sweden.

The legendary Hurtigruten (p352) links Norway's coastal fishing villages; in Finland, steamships ply Lake Saimaa (p164), and its canal. There are also diesel-engine boats that are a bit faster and noisier but equally attractive.

BUS

Buses provide a viable alternative to the rail network in Scandinavian countries, and are the only option in Iceland and the Faroes. Compared to trains, they're usually cheaper

(Finland is the exception) and slightly slower. Connections with train services (where they exist) are good.

Bus travel tends to be best for shorter hops, such as getting around cities, but is sometimes your only choice in remote rural areas, particularly in northern Sweden.

Bus Passes

Eurolines offers a variety of city 'loops' and the Eurolines Pass – see p465 for more details.

See the transport section in the country chapters for details of internal bus passes, or contact one of the main long-distance bus operators listed here.

Denmark Thinggaard Expressbusser (☎ 70 10 00 10; www.thinggaardbus.com in Danish); Søndergaards Busser (☎ 70 10 00 33; www.sondergaards-busser.dk)
Faroes Strandfaraskip Landsins (☎ 343030; www.ssl.fo)
Finland Oy Matkahuolto Ab (☎ 09-682 701; www.matkahuolto.fi in Finnish)
Iceland BSÍ (Bifreiðastöð Íslands; ☎ 562 3320; www.bsi.is)
Norway Nor-Way Bussekspress (☎ 08-021 300; www.nor-way.no)
Sweden Svenska Buss (☎ 0771-676767; www.svenskabuss .se); Swebus Express (☎ 0200-218218; www.swebusexpress .se); Säfflebussen (☎ 0771-151515; www.safflebussen.se); Ybuss (☎ 0771-334444; www.ybuss.se in Swedish)

Reservations

Advance reservations are rarely necessary. However, you do need to pre-purchase your ticket before you board many city buses, and then validate your own ticket on board. See the individual country chapters for specific details.

CAR & MOTORCYCLE

Travelling with your own vehicle is the best way to get to remote places and it gives you the most independence and flexibility. Drawbacks include the isolation of cruising along in your own private car-bubble and the inconvenience in city centres where it's generally worth relying solely on public transport.

Scandinavia is excellent for motorcycle touring, with good-quality winding roads, stunning scenery and an active motorcycling scene. Just make sure your wet-weather gear is up to scratch. The best time for motorcycle touring is from May to September. On ferries, motorcyclists rarely have to book ahead as they can generally be squeezed in.

Anyone considering a motorcycle tour should read *Adventure Motorbiking Handbook*, by Chris Scott. It gives good advice on motorcycle touring worldwide.

Bring Your Own Vehicle

Proof of ownership of a private vehicle should always be carried (this is the Vehicle Registration Document for British-registered cars) when touring Europe. You may also need a *carnet de passage en douane*, which is effectively a passport for the vehicle and acts as a temporary waiver of import duty. The *carnet* may also need to specify any expensive spare parts that you're planning to carry with you, such as a gearbox. Contact your local automobile association for further information.

Every vehicle crossing an international border should display a sticker showing its country of registration. It's compulsory to carry a warning triangle in most places, to be used in the event of breakdown.

Driving Licence

An EU driving licence is acceptable for driving throughout Scandinavia, as are North American and Australian licences (in general). However, to be on the safe side – or if you have any other type of licence – you should obtain an International Driving Permit (IDP) from your motoring organisation before you leave home.

Fuel & Spare Parts

Fuel is heavily taxed and therefore very expensive in Scandinavia. Most types of petrol, including unleaded 95 and 98 octane, are widely available, but leaded petrol may be unavailable. Always carefully check the type of fuel being supplied – pumps with green markings and the word *Blyfri* on them deliver unleaded fuel. Diesel is significantly cheaper than petrol in some countries.

Recommended accessories are a first-aid kit, a spare bulb kit and a fire extinguisher. In Iceland, it's wise to carry general spare parts, including a fan belt and clutch cable, and learn how to make basic repairs; garages can be few and far between and you might wait hours for a passing motorist. Contact your automobile association or, in the UK, contact the **AA** (☎ 0870 600 0371; www.theaa.com) or the **RAC** (☎ 0800 550 550; www.rac.co.uk) for more information.

Hire

Renting a car is more expensive in Scandinavia than in other European countries, and the variety of special deals and terms and conditions can be mind-boggling. However, there are a few pointers that can help you through the morass. The big international firms – Hertz, Avis, Eurodollar, Budget, and Europe's largest rental agency, Europcar – will give you reliable service, a good standard of vehicle, and often the option of returning the car to a different outlet when you've finished with it (this is sometimes chargeable).

Try to prebook your vehicle, which always works out cheaper. If you've left it too late, look for national or local firms, which can often undercut the big companies substantially, and shop around. It's generally more expensive to hire cars from airport-rental stands than to pick one up in town.

There are also fly/drive combinations and other programs that are worth looking into (eg SAS and Icelandair often offer cheaper car rentals to their international passengers). The ScanRail 'n' Drive programme gives you a five-day rail pass and a car for two days to be used within two months in Denmark, Norway and/or Sweden. Prices start at US$399 for an adult on 2nd-class trains and an economy car (US$678 for two adults), with an option of retaining the car for US$59 per day.

Holiday Autos International (☎ 0870 400 0099; www.holidayautos.com; Holiday Autos House, Pembroke Broadway, Camberley, Surrey, GU15 3XD) usually has good rates for rental, but you need to prebook. It has offices around Europe, including Denmark, Norway and Sweden. Ask in advance if you can drive a rented car across borders.

No matter where you rent, be sure that you understand what's included in the price (unlimited or paid kilometres, injury insurance, tax, collision damage waiver etc) and what your liabilities are. Always take the collision damage waiver, although you can probably skip the injury insurance if you and your passengers have decent travel insurance.

The minimum rental age is usually 21, sometimes even 23, and you'll probably need a credit card (or a mountain of cash) for the deposit.

Motorcycle and moped rental isn't particularly common in Scandinavian countries, but it's possible in major cities.

Insurance

Third-party motor insurance is a minimum requirement in most of Europe. Most UK car-insurance policies automatically provide third-party cover for EU and some other countries. Ask your insurer for a Green Card – an internationally recognised proof of insurance (there may be a charge) – and check that it lists all the countries you intend to visit. You'll need this in the event of an accident outside the country in which the vehicle is insured. Also ask your insurer for a European Accident Statement form, which can simplify things if worse comes to worst. Never sign statements you can't read or understand – insist on a written translation and only sign it if it's acceptable.

A European breakdown-assistance policy, such as the AA Five Star Europe service or the RAC European Motoring Assistance, is a good investment. Expect to pay about UK£60 for 14 days' cover with a 10% discount for association members. It's also worth asking your motoring organisation for details of reciprocal services offered by affiliated organisations around Europe.

Road Conditions & Hazards

Conditions and types of roads vary widely across Scandinavia, but it's possible to make some generalisations. The fastest routes are four- or six-lane dual carriageways. These tend to skirt cities and plough through the countryside in straight lines, often avoiding the most scenic areas. Motorways and other primary routes, with the exception of some roads in Iceland, are universally in good condition.

Road surfaces on minor routes are not so reliable, although normally adequate. These roads are narrower and progress is slower, but in compensation, you'll pass through more scenic places along the way.

Norway has some particularly hair-raising roads; serpentine examples climb from sea level to 1000m in what seems no distance at all on a map. These rollercoaster roads will use plenty of petrol and strain the car's engine and brakes, not to mention your nerves! Driving a camper van on these kinds of routes in Norway and Iceland is definitely not recommended.

In Norway, you must pay tolls for some tunnels, bridges, roads and entry into larger towns, and for practically all ferries crossing

fjords. Roads, tunnels, bridges and car ferries in Finland and Sweden are always free, although there's a hefty toll of €30 (Skr280/Dkr230) per car on the Øresund bridge between Denmark and Sweden.

During winter in Scandinavia, snow tyres are compulsory. The tyre chains common in the Alps are allowed in Norway, but are illegal elsewhere.

Suicidal stock, including sheep, elk, horses and reindeer, is a potential hazard. If you are involved in an animal incident, you must report it to the police by law.

Road Rules

You drive on the right-hand side of the road in all Scandinavian countries. Seat-belt use is obligatory for all passengers and headlights must be switched on at all times (except in built-up areas in Finland). Vehicles from the UK and Ireland need their headlights adjusted to avoid blinding oncoming traffic (a simple solution on older headlight lenses is to cover up the triangular section of the lens with a headlight deflector, available from motoring accessory shops). Priority is usually given to traffic approaching from the right. Some national motoring organisations publish booklets with summaries of motoring regulations in each country; check with your local organisation.

It's compulsory for motorcyclists and their passengers to wear helmets. Make a note of local custom if you're thinking about parking motorcycles on pavements (sidewalks). This is illegal in some countries, although the police usually turn a blind eye so long as the vehicle doesn't obstruct pedestrians.

Take care with speed limits as they vary from country to country. Many driving infringements are subject to on-the-spot fines in Scandinavian countries. If you receive a fine for any driving offence, make sure to get a receipt.

Drink-driving regulations are strict, with the maximum blood-alcohol concentration (BAC) varying from 0.02% in Sweden to 0.08% in Denmark (see the individual country chapters for details). One drink can put you over the limit.

HITCHING

Hitching is never entirely safe in any country in the world, and we don't recommend it. Travellers who decide to hitch should understand that they're taking a small but potentially serious risk. People who do choose to hitch will be safer if they travel in pairs and let someone know where they're planning to go. A woman hitching on her own is always taking a gamble – even in 'safe' Scandinavia.

Be aware that hitching is neither popular nor particularly rewarding in most of Scandinavia. Finns, for example, are quite rightly wary of Russian criminals. That said, with a bit of luck, hitchers can end up making good time in some areas, but obviously your plans need to be flexible in case a trick of the light makes you appear invisible to passing motorists. Don't try to hitch from city centres; take public transport to suburban exit routes. Hitching is usually illegal on motorways – stand on the entrance ramps.

It's sometimes possible to arrange a lift in advance: scan student notice boards in colleges or contact car-sharing agencies (see p466 for more details).

TOURS

See the individual country chapters for details of recommended, locally organised tours.

TRAIN

Trains are a popular way of getting around; they're good meeting places and in Scandinavia are comfortable, frequent and generally on time. As with most things in Scandinavia, prices are relatively expensive, although European train passes make travel affordable. Finland has the cheapest rail service. There are no trains in Iceland or the Faroes, nor in most of far-northern Norway.

If you plan to travel extensively by train, get hold of the *Thomas Cook European Timetable* (see p466) which gives a complete listing of train schedules and indicates where supplements apply or where reservations are necessary.

Express Trains

Fast trains in Europe, or ones that make few stops, are usually identified by the symbols EC (Eurocity) or IC (Intercity). There are national variations; in Norway, some expresses are called Signatur trains, while in Finland they're also called Pendolino express trains and in Sweden they're known as X2000. Supplements usually apply on fast trains and it's wise (sometimes obligatory) to make reservations at peak times and on certain lines.

Overnight Trains

Overnight trains will usually offer a choice of couchette, or sleeper if you don't fancy snoozing in your seat with a stranger dribbling on your shoulder. Again, reservations are advisable and in Scandinavia they're often necessary as sleeping options are allocated on a first-come, first-served basis.

Couchettes are bunks numbering four (1st class) or six (2nd class) per compartment and are comfortable enough, if lacking a bit in privacy. In Scandinavia, a bunk costs around US$25 for most international trains, irrespective of the length of the journey.

Sleepers are the most comfortable option, offering beds for one or two passengers in 1st class and two or three passengers in 2nd class. In Norway, when individual travellers book a bed for one (Nkr125), they'll be booked into a compartment with two other people of the same sex. Denmark has six-person compartments, as well as single and double cabins, with charges varying depending upon the journey, but tending to be significantly more expensive than couchettes.

Most long-distance trains have a dining car or drink-and-snack-laden trolley, wheeled through the carriages by an attendant. Bring your own snacks if you want to keep costs down.

Costs

Full-price tickets can be expensive, but there are generally lots of discounts, particularly if you book ahead. European rail passes are only worth buying if you plan to do a reasonable amount of inter-country travelling within a short space of time.

Seniors and travellers who are under 26 years of age are eligible for discounted tickets, which can cut international fares by between 20% and 40%: see below for details.

Reservations

It's a good idea (and sometimes obligatory) to make reservations at peak times and on certain lines, especially long-distance trains. Check the individual country chapters for particulars.

Train Passes

There are a variety of passes available, for students, people under 26, seniors and those who intend to do a lot of train travel. Numerous agencies issue youth tickets in Europe, including **STA Travel** (www.statravel.com) and **Wasteels Rejser** (☎ 33 14 46 33; www.wasteels.dk in Danish; Skoubogade 6, DK-1158 Copenhagen K, Denmark).

Supplement and reservation costs are not covered by passes. Pass-holders must always carry their passport on the train for identification purposes.

EURAIL

In Scandinavia, the ScanRail pass (opposite) is usually a better deal than the Eurail pass, so this information will be of interest mainly to travellers visiting other parts of Europe too.

Eurail (www.eurail.com) passes can only be bought by residents of non-European countries (residents of Algeria, Morocco, Tunisia, Turkey and former Soviet Union countries are also exempt from buying passes), and are supposed to be purchased before arriving in Europe. However, Eurail passes are available within Europe as long as your passport proves you've been there for less than six months. The passes are 10% more expensive than buying them outside Europe and outlets for purchasing them are limited. For example, Copenhagen is the only city in Denmark, and Oslo is the only place in Norway where you can buy Eurail passes (at the international ticket counters in the main train stations). If you've lived in Europe for more than six months, you're eligible for an Inter Rail pass (see right), which is a better buy.

Eurail passes are valid for unlimited travel on national railways and some private lines in Austria, Belgium, Denmark, Finland, France (which includes Monaco), Germany, Greece, Hungary, Ireland, Italy, Luxembourg, the Netherlands, Norway, Portugal, Spain, Sweden and Switzerland (including Liechtenstein). The passes do *not* cover the UK.

Eurail is also valid on ferries running between Italy and Greece, and from Sweden to Finland with Silja Line.

Eurailpass (15-/21-day pass US$588/762, 1-/2-/3-month pass US$946/1,338/1,654) For those aged over 26; valid for unlimited 1st-class travel.

Eurailpass Flexi (10-/15-day pass US$694/914) For those aged over 26; valid for 10 or 15 days' 1st-class travel within a two-month period.

Eurailpass Saver (15-/21-day US$498/648, 1-/2-/3-month pass US$804/1,138/1,408) For two or more people travelling together; valid for unlimited 1st-class travel.

Eurailpass Saver Flexi (10-/15-day pass US$592/778) For two or more people travelling together; valid for 10 or 15 days' 1st-class travel within a two-month period.

Eurailpass Youth (15-/21-day pass US$414/534, 1-/2-/3-month pass US$664/938/1,160) For those aged under 26; valid for unlimited 2nd-class travel.

Eurailpass Youth Flexi (10-/15-day pass US$488/642) For those aged under 26; valid for 10 or 15 days' 2nd-class travel within a two-month period. Overnight journeys commencing after 7pm count as the following day's travel. Traveller must fill out relevant calendar box in ink before travelling; not validating the pass or tampering with it leads to a fine.

Eurail passes for children are also available – half price for those aged four to 11 years.

EURO DOMINO

There is a Euro Domino pass (called a Freedom pass in Britain) for each of the countries covered in the zonal Inter Rail pass (see the following section). Adults (travelling 1st or 2nd class) and people under 26 can travel within one country from three to eight days during one month. Examples of adult/youth prices for eight days in 2nd class are UK£117/ 88 for Denmark, UK£158/122 for Finland, UK£238/180 for Norway and UK£209/153 for Sweden. Seniors receive a discount of around 15% on adult fares. The website www .europerailpass.co.uk contains full details.

INTER RAIL

Inter Rail (www.interrailnet.com) passes are valid for unlimited 2nd-class travel in 29 countries in Europe and North Africa, and are available to European residents (including CIS countries in continental Europe, Algeria and Tunisia) of at least six months standing – passport identification is required. Terms and conditions vary slightly from country to country, but in the country of origin there's only a discount of around 50% on normal fares, rather than free travel.

The Inter Rail pass is split into eight zones. Zone A is Ireland and the UK; B is Finland, Norway and Sweden; C is Austria, Denmark, Germany and Switzerland; D is Croatia, the Czech Republic, Hungary, Poland and Slovakia; E is Belgium, France, Luxembourg and the Netherlands; F is Morocco, Portugal and Spain; G is Italy, Greece, Slovenia and Turkey; H is Bulgaria, Macedonia, Romania and Yugoslavia.

The price for any one zone is UK£223/159 (if aged over/under 26) for 16 days and UK£303/215 for 22 days. A global pass is better value, allowing one month's travel in all zones for UK£415/295.

Transport	Country	Route	Company
Bus	Norway	Grong-Brønnøysund	Torghatten Trafikkselskap
Bus	Norway	Neslandsvatn-Kragerø	Drangedal Bilruter
Bus	Norway	Åndalsnes-Ålesund	A/S Ålesund Bilruter
Bus	Norway	Oppdal-Kristiansund	Nettbuss Møre
Bus	Norway	Mosjøen-Sandnessjøen	Helgelandske AS
Ferry	Denmark	Copenhagen-Rønne	Bornholmstrafikken
Ferry	Denmark	Rønne-Ystad	Bornholmstrafikken
Ferry	Denmark	Copenhagen-Rønne	Bornholmstrafikken
Ferry	Norway/Denmark	Larvik-Hirtshals (day sailing)	Color Line
Ferry	Norway/Denmark	Oslo-Hirtshals (day sailing)	Color Line
Ferry	Norway/Denmark	Kristiansand-Hirtshals (day sailing)	Color Line
Ferry	Norway/Denmark	Larvik-Frederikshavn (day sailing)	Color Line
Ferry	Norway/Denmark	Oslo-Frederikshavn	Stena Line
Ferry	Norway	Sandefjord-Strömstad (day sailing)	Color Line
Ferry	Norway	Bergen-Haugesund-Stavanger (day sailing)	Flaggruten A/S
Ferry	Sweden	Nynäshamn-Visby	Destination Gotland
Ferry	Sweden	Oskarhamn-Visby	Destination Gotland
Ferry	Sweden	Strömstad-Sandefjord (day sailing)	Color Line
Ferry	Sweden	Ystad-Rønne	Bornholmstrafikken
Ferry	Sweden/Finland	Stockholm-Helsinki	Silja Line/Viking Line
Ferry	Sweden/Finland	Stockholm-Turku/Åbo	Silja Line/Viking Line
Rail	Denmark	Hjørring-Hirtshals	Hjørring Privatbaner
Rail	Denmark	Frederikshavn-Skagen	Skagensbanen
Rail	Sweden	Östersund-Storlien	Nabo-tåget

Conditions change, so be sure to check out the latest information before buying a pass.

SCANRAIL

ScanRail (www.scanrail.com) is a flexible rail pass covering rail travel in Denmark, Norway, Sweden and Finland, with discounts on some private railways, ferries, boats and buses. It comes in three versions:

ScanRail Flexi Pass – 5 days (1st/2nd-class UK£199/171, travellers under 26 UK£150/119, over 60 UK£175/152) For travel on any five days within a two-month period.

ScanRail Flexi Pass – 10 days (1st/2nd class UK£266/ 229, travellers under 26 UK£199/160, over 60 UK£235/203) For travel on any 10 days within a two-month period.

ScanRail Consecutive Pass – 21 days (1st/2nd class UK£308/266, travellers under 26 UK£229/185, over 60 UK£270/235) For unlimited travel over 21 consecutive days.

Children aged four to 11 travel for around half the adult fare. Buy your ScanRail pass outside Scandinavia, or you'll face huge restrictions regarding the days you can travel.

ScanRail passes are valid on Scandinavian state railways in Denmark (DSB), Finland (VR), Norway (NSB) and Sweden (SJ). They're also valid on the Linx (Copenhagen–Oslo and Oslo–Stockholm) and Connex (Göteborg–Stockholm–Narvik) services, and on two privately operated Swedish lines, the Arlanda Express (Arlanda Airport to Stockholm) and Connex night trains between Stockholm or Göteborg and upper Norrland. (The Flåm line in Norway and the Inlandsbanan in Sweden are *not* covered by the pass.)

ScanRail passes also entitle you to free travel on buses between Luleå–Haparanda and Kemi–Haparanda (Finland), and on Scandlines ferries (Helsingør–Helsingborg and Rødby–Puttgarden Mitte See).

There's a 50% discount if you're travelling on the services listed in the table above (although restrictions and/or compulsory reservations apply on some services; check terms and conditions carefully).

Other ScanRail pass discounts that might be of interest are on boat journeys in Hardangerfjord and southern Hordaland (up to 50%), and on Fjord Line ferries from Newcastle in the UK to Bergen (between 25% and 50%).

Health

CONTENTS

Travel in Scandinavia presents very few health problems. The standard of health care is high and English is widely spoken by doctors and medical clinic staff, tap water is safe to drink, the level of hygiene is high and there are no endemic diseases. The main health issues to be aware of are extreme climates (with the potential for hypothermia, frostbite or viral infections such as influenza) and biting insects such as mosquitoes, though they're more an annoyance than a health risk.

BEFORE YOU GO

Prevention is the key to staying healthy while abroad. A little time spent planning before departure, particularly if you have pre-existing illnesses, will save trouble later: see your dentist before a long trip; carry a spare pair of contact lenses and glasses, and take your optical prescription with you. Bring your medications in their original, clearly labelled containers. A signed and dated letter from your physician describing your medical conditions and necessary medications, including their generic names, is also a good idea.

Specific travel vaccinations are not required for visitors to Scandinavia but you should be up to date with all normal childhood vaccinations.

INSURANCE

If you're an EU citizen, an E111 form, available from health centres or, in the UK, post offices, covers you for most medical care. E111 will not cover you for non-emergencies or emergency repatriation home. Citizens from other countries should find out if there is a reciprocal arrangement for free medical care between their country and the country visited. Health insurance is still recommended, especially if you intend hiking or skiing. Make sure you get a policy that covers you for the worst possible scenario, such as an accident requiring an emergency flight home. Find out in advance if your insurance plan will make payments directly to providers or reimburse you later for overseas health expenditures.

ONLINE RESOURCES

The WHO's publication *International Travel and Health* is revised annually and is available online at www.who.int/ith/. Other useful websites include www.mdtravelhealth.com (travel health recommendations for every country; updated daily), www.fitfortravel.scot .nhs.uk (general travel advice for the layperson), www.ageconcern.org.uk (advice on travel for the elderly) and www.mariestopes .org.uk (information on women's health and contraception).

FURTHER READING

'Health Advice for Travellers' (currently called the 'T6' leaflet) is an annually updated leaflet by the Department of Health in the UK that's available free from post offices. It contains some general information, legally required and recommended vaccines for different countries, reciprocal health agree-

---

It's usually a good idea to consult your government's travel health website before departure, if one is available:

Australia: www.smartraveller.gov.au
Canada: www.travelhealth.gc.ca
UK: www.dh.gov.uk/PolicyAndGuidance /HealthAdviceForTravellers/
USA: www.cdc.gov/travel/

ments and an E111 application form. Lonely Planet's *Travel with Children* includes advice on travel health for younger children. Other recommended references include *Traveller's Health* by Dr Richard Dawood and *The Traveller's Good Health Guide* by Ted Lankester.

IN TRANSIT

DEEP VEIN THROMBOSIS (DVT)

Blood clots may form in the legs during plane flights, chiefly because of prolonged immobility. The longer the flight, the greater the risk. The chief symptom of DVT is swelling or pain in the foot, ankle or calf, usually but not always on just one side. When a blood clot travels to the lungs, it may cause chest pain and breathing difficulties. Travellers with any of these symptoms should immediately seek medical attention.

To prevent the development of DVT on long flights you should walk about the cabin, contract the leg muscles while sitting, drink plenty of fluids and avoid alcohol and tobacco.

JET LAG & MOTION SICKNESS

To avoid jet lag (common when crossing more than five time zones) try drinking plenty of nonalcoholic fluids and eating light meals. Upon arrival, get exposure to natural sunlight and readjust your schedule (for meals, sleep and so on) as soon as possible.

Antihistamines such as dimenhydrinate (Dramamine) and meclizine (Antivert, Bonine) are usually the first choice for treating motion sickness. A herbal alternative is ginger.

IN SCANDINAVIA

AVAILABILITY AND COST OF HEALTHCARE

Good healthcare is readily available and for minor self-limiting illnesses pharmacists can give valuable advice and sell over-the-counter medication. Major cities in Scandinavia have a 24-hour pharmacy. They can advise when more specialised help is required and point you in the right direction to find it. The standard of dental care is good, but it is sensible to have a dental check-up before a long trip.

TRAVELLER'S DIARRHOEA

Tap water and food is generally safe throughout Scandinavia, but a change in diet can sometimes cause diarrhoea.

If you develop diarrhoea, drink plenty of fluids, preferably an oral rehydration solution such as Dioralyte. A few loose stools don't require treatment, but if you have more than four or five stools a day you should start taking an antibiotic (usually a quinolone drug) and an antidiarrhoeal agent (such as loperamide).

ENVIRONMENTAL HAZARDS
Hypothermia

Proper preparation will reduce the risks of getting hypothermia. Even on a hot day in the mountains, the weather can change rapidly. Hikers should carry waterproof clothing, wear warm layers and inform others of the route taken.

Acute hypothermia follows a sudden drop of temperature over a short time. Chronic hypothermia is caused by a gradual loss of temperature over hours.

Hypothermia starts with shivering, loss of judgment and clumsiness. Unless re-warming occurs, the sufferer deteriorates into apathy, confusion and coma. Prevent further heat loss by providing shelter, warm dry clothing, hot sweet drinks and shared bodily warmth.

Frostbite is caused by freezing and subsequent damage to bodily extremities. It is dependent on wind chill, temperature and length of exposure. Frostbite starts as frostnip (white numb areas of skin) from which complete recovery is expected with re-warming. As frostbite develops, the skin blisters and then becomes black. The loss of damaged tissue eventually occurs. Adequate clothing, staying dry, keeping well hydrated and ensuring adequate calorie intake best prevent frostbite. Treatment involves rapid re-warming. Avoid refreezing and rubbing the affected areas.

Insect Bites & Stings

Mosquitoes are found in most parts of Scandinavia, particularly in Lapland during summer and around lake areas such as eastern Finland. Malaria is not a problem but irritation and infected bites are possible. Use a DEET-based insect repellent.

In northern Iceland, midges and blackflies can be a real annoyance in summer.

Bees and wasps only cause real problems to those with a severe allergy (anaphylaxis.) If you have a severe allergy to bee or wasp stings, carry an 'epipen' or similar adrenalin injection.

Bed bugs lead to very itchy lumpy bites, but Scandinavian hotels and hostels are generally immaculate. Spraying the mattress with crawling-insect killer after changing bedding will get rid of them.

Scabies are tiny parasitic mites which live in the skin, particularly between the fingers. They cause an intensely itchy rash. Scabies is easily treated with lotion from a pharmacy.

WOMEN'S HEALTH

Emotional stress, exhaustion and travelling through different time zones can all contribute to an upset in the menstrual pattern. If using oral contraceptives, remember some antibiotics, diarrhoea and vomiting can stop the pill from working and lead to the risk of pregnancy. Tampons and similar products are widely available in Scandinavia at pharmacies and supermarkets.

Travelling during pregnancy is usually possible but always seek a medical check-up before planning your trip. The most risky times for travel are during the first 12 weeks of pregnancy and after 30 weeks.

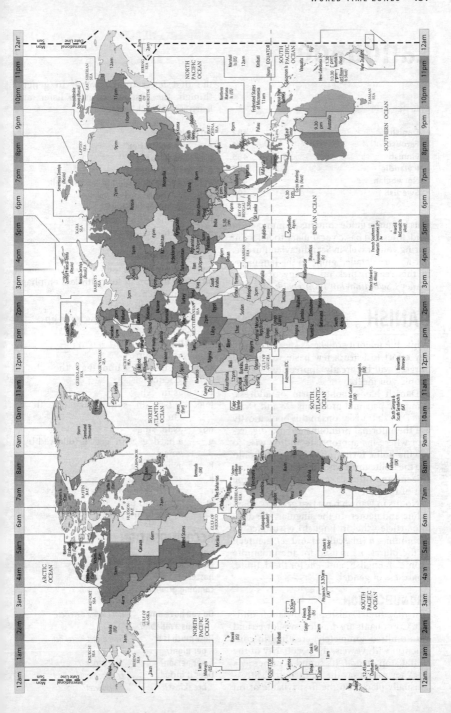

Language

CONTENTS

This language guide contains pronunciation guidelines and basic vocabulary to help you during your travels in Scandinavian Europe. For a more detailed guide to the languages in this region, pick up a copy of Lonely Planet's *Scandinavian Phrasebook*.

DANISH

While the majority of Danes speak English, any effort to learn a few basic words and phrases will be greatly appreciated by the people you meet.

Danish has a polite form of address, using the personal pronouns *De* and *Dem*. The Danish translations in this book mostly use the informal pronouns *du* and *dig*, except where it's appropriate and/or wise to use the polite form. In general, you should use the polite form when speaking to senior citizens and officials, and the informal the rest of the time.

Nouns in Danish have two genders: masculine and neuter. In the singular, the definite article ('the' in English) is suffixed to the noun: *-en* (masculine) and *-et* (neuter). In the plural *-ne* is used for the indefinite ('some' in English) and *-ene* for the definite, regardless of gender.

PRONUNCIATION

You may find Danish pronunciation difficult. Consonants are drawled, swallowed and even omitted completely, creating, in conjunction with vowels, the peculiarity of the glottal stop or *stød*. Its sound is rather as a Cockney would say the 'tt' in 'bottle'. Stress is usually placed on the first syllable or on the first letter of the word. In general though, the best advice is to listen and learn. Good luck!

Vowels

a	as in 'father'
a, æ	as in 'act'
å, o &	
u(n)	a long rounded 'a' as in 'walk'
e(g)	as the sound of 'eye'
e, i	as the 'e' in 'bet'
i	as the 'e' in 'theme'
ø	as the 'er' in 'fern'
o, u	as the 'oo' in 'cool'
o	as in 'pot'
o(v)	as the 'ou' in 'out'
o(r)	as the 'or' in for' with less emphasis on the 'r'
u	as in 'pull'
y	say 'ee' while pursing your lips

Consonants

sj	as in 'ship'
ch	a sharper sound than the 'ch' in 'cheque'
c	as in 'cell'
(o)d	a flat 'dh' sound, like the 'th' in 'these'
ng	as in 'sing'
g	a hard 'g' as in 'get', if followed by a vowel
h	as in 'horse'
k	as the 'c' in 'cat'
r	a rolling 'r' abruptly cut short
w	similar to the 'wh' in 'what'
j	as the 'y' in 'yet'

ACCOMMODATION

hotel	*hotel*
guesthouse	*gæstgiveri*
hostel	*vandrerhjem*
camping ground	*campingplads*

Do you have any rooms available?	*Har I ledige værelser?*
How much is it per night/ per person?	*Hvor meget koster det per nat/ per person?*
Does it include breakfast?	*Er morgenmad inkluderet?*

LANGUAGE

I'd like ... — *Jeg ønsker ...*
  a single room — *et enkeltværelse*
  a double room — *et dobbeltværelse*

one day/two days — *en nat/to nætter*

CONVERSATION & ESSENTIALS

Hello. — *Hallo/Hej. (informal)*
Goodbye. — *Farvel.*
Yes. — *Ja.*
No. — *Nej.*
Please. — *Må jeg bede/Værsgo.*
Thank you. — *Tak.*
That's fine/You're welcome. — *Det er i orden/Selv tak*
Excuse me/Sorry. — *Undskyld.*
Do you speak English? — *I aler De engelsk?*
How much is it? — *Hvor meget koster det?*
What's your name? — *Hvad hedder du?*
My name is ... — *Mit navn er ...*

EMERGENCIES – DANISH

Help! — *Hjælp!*
Call a doctor! — *Ring efter en læge!*
Call the police! — *Ring efter politiet!*
Go away! — *Forsvind!*
I'm lost. — *Jeg har gået vild.*

SHOPPING & SERVICES

a bank — *en bank*
a chemist/pharmacy — *et apotek*
the ... embassy — *den ... ambassade*
my hotel — *mit hotel*
the market — *markedet*
a newsagent — *en aviskiosk*
the post office — *postkontoret*
the tourist office — *turistinformationen*

What time does it open/close? — *Hvornår åbner/lukker det?*

TIME, DAYS & NUMBERS

What time is it? — *Hvad er klokken?*
today — *i dag*
tomorrow — *i morgen*
yesterday — *i går*
morning — *morgenen*
afternoon — *eftermiddagen*

Monday — *mandag*
Tuesday — *tirsdag*
Wednesday — *onsdag*

SIGNS – DANISH

Indgang — Entrance
Udgang — Exit
Åben — Open
Lukket — Closed
Forbudt — Prohibited
Information — Information
Politistation — Police Station
Toiletter — Toilets
  Herrer — Men
  Damer — Women

Thursday — *torsdag*
Friday — *fredag*
Saturday — *lørdag*
Sunday — *søndag*

0 — *nul*
1 — *en*
2 — *to*
3 — *tre*
4 — *fire*
5 — *fem*
6 — *seks*
7 — *syv*
8 — *otte*
9 — *ni*
10 — *ti*
100 — *hundrede*
1000 — *tusind*

TRANSPORT

What time does ... leave/arrive? — *Hvornår går/ankommer ...?*
  the boat — *båden*
  the bus (city) — *bussen*
  the bus (intercity) — *rutebilen*
  the tram — *sporvognen*
  the train — *toget*

Where can I hire a car/bicycle? — *Hvor kan jeg leje en bil/cykel?*

I'd like ... — *Jeg vil gerne have ...*
  a one-way ticket — *en enkeltbillet*
  a return ticket — *en tur-retur billet*

1st class — *første klasse*
2nd class — *anden klasse*
left luggage office — *reisegodsopphevar ingen*
timetable — *køreplan*
bus stop — *bus holdeplads*

LANGUAGE

| tram stop | sporvogn holdeplads |
| train station | jernbanestation (banegård) |

Directions

Where is ...?	Hvor er ...?
Go straight ahead.	Gå ligefrem.
Turn left/right.	Drej til venstre/højre.
near/far	nær/fjern

FAROESE

Faroese is a Germanic language derived from old Norse, closely related to Icelandic and some Norwegian and Swedish dialects. In 1890, a standard written version of Faroese, *Føroyskt*, was made official and given equal status with Danish in public and government affairs.

All Faroese speak Danish, can handle Norwegian and Swedish, and some speak English. Nearly every Faroese learns Danish at school (and many also learn English and German), but foreign languages have had little impact on everyday life.

PRONUNCIATION

In most cases, Faroese words are stressed on the first syllable. Grammar is very similar to that of Icelandic, but pronunciation is quite different due to a mix of Icelandic, Danish, and even Gaelic influences, eg the name of Eiði village is inexplicably pronounced 'oy-yeh'; the nearby village of Gjógv is referred to as 'Jagv'; the capital, Tórshavn, gets the more or less Danish pronunciation, 'torsh-hown'.

Vowels & Diphthongs

a, æ	short, as the 'u' in 'cut'; long, as the 'ai' in 'hair'
á	short, as the 'o' in 'hot'; long, as the 'oi' in French moi
e	as in 'get'
i, y	short, as the 'i' in 'hit'; long, as the 'i' in 'marine'
í, ý	as the 'ui' in Spanish muy
o	as in 'hot'
ó	short, as the 'a' in 'ago'; long, as the 'o' in 'note'
ø	as the 'a' in 'ago'
u	as in 'pull'
ú	short, as a sharp 'u' – purse your lips and say 'ee'; long, as the 'ou' in 'you'
ei	as the 'i' in 'dive'
ey	short, as the 'e' in 'get'; long, as the 'ay' in 'day'
oy	as the 'oy' in 'boy'

Consonants

ð	silent in final position, otherwise taking on the value of surrounding vowels
ðr	as the 'gr' in 'grab'
dj	as the 'j' in 'jaw'
ft	as the 'tt' in 'bitter'
g	silent in final position, otherwise taking on the value of surrounding vowels
ggj	as the 'j' in 'jaw'
hv	as 'kv'
hj	as the 'y' in 'yellow'
ll	as the 'dl' in 'saddle'

ACCOMMODATION

hotel	hotell
guesthouse	gistingarhús
youth hostel	vallarheim
campground	tjáldplass

Do you have any rooms available?	Eru nøkur leys kømur?
How much is it (per person/per night)?	Hvussu nógv kostar tað (fyri hvønn/eina natt)?
Does it include breakfast?	Er morgunmatur innifalinn?

I'd like (a) ...	Eg vil fegin hava ...
single room	eitt einkultkamar
double room	eitt dupultkamar

CONVERSATION & ESSENTIALS

Hello.	Hey/Halló/Góðan dag.
Goodbye.	Farvæl.
Yes.	Ja.
No.	Nei.
Please.	Gerið so væl.
Thank you.	Takk fyri.
Excuse me/Sorry.	Orsaka.
Do you speak English?	Tosar tú eingilskt?
How much is it?	Hvussu nógv kostar tað?
What's your name?	Hvussu eita tygum?
My name is ...	Eg eiti ...

SHOPPING & SERVICES

bank	banka
chemist	apotekið
the ... embassy	... ambassaduni
market	handilsgøtuni

the post office	posthúsinum
a public toilet	almennum vesi
the tourist office	ferðaskrivstovuni/turistkontórinum

EMERGENCIES – FAROESE

Help!	Hjálp!
Call a doctor!	Ringið eftir lækna!
Call the police!	Ringið eftir løgregluni!
Go away!	Far burtur!
I'm lost.	Eg eri vilst/vilstur. (m/f)

TIME, DAYS & NUMBERS

What time is it?	Hvat er klokkan?
today	í dag
tomorrow	í morgin
yesterday	í gjár
morning	morgun
afternoon	seinnapartur
night	nátt

Monday	mánadagur
Tuesday	týsdagur
Wednesday	mikudagur
Thursday	hósdagur
Friday	fríggjadagur
Saturday	leygardagur
Sunday	sunnudagur

1	eitt
2	tvey
3	trý
4	fíra
5	fimm
6	seks
7	sjey
8	átta
9	níggju
10	tíggju
20	tjúgu
100	hundrað
1000	túsund

TRANSPORT

boat	bátur
bus	bussur
map	kort
road	vegur
street	gøta
village	bygd

I'd like a ...	Kundi eg fingið ...
one-way ticket	elnvegis ferðaseðil
return ticket	ferðaseðil aftur og fram

SIGNS – FAROESE

Atgongd	Entrance
Útgongd	Exit
Neyðútgongd	Emergency Exit
Bannað	Prohibited
Upplýsingar	Information
Løgregla	Police

FINNISH

Finnish is a Uralic language spoken by just six million people, the vast majority of whom live in Scandinavia and in Russian Karelia. The most widely spoken of the Finno-Ugric family is Hungarian, but its similarities with Finnish are few. Suomi refers to both the Finnish-speaking part Finland and its language.

Staff at hotels, hostels and tourist offices generally speak fluent English. Bus drivers or restaurant and shop staff outside the cities may not, but they'll always fetch a colleague or bystander who does. You can certainly get by with English in Finland, but don't assume that everyone speaks it.

Swedish is spoken on Åland, as well as on the west ('Swedish') coast and around Helsinki and Turku, and all Finns learn Swedish at school.

PRONUNCIATION

Finnish pronunciation is more or less consistent – there is a one to one relationship between letters and sounds. There are nine vowels: **a, e, i, o, u, y, ä, å** and **ö** (the **å** has been adopted from the Norwegian and Swedish alphabets). The final letters of the alphabet are **å, ä** and **ö** (important to know when looking for something in a telephone directory).

Vowels

y	as the 'u' in 'pull' but with the lips stretched back (like the German 'ü')
å	as the 'oo' in 'poor'
ä	as the 'a' in 'act'
ö	as the 'a' in 'ago'

Consonants

z	pronounced (and sometimes written) as 'ts'
v/w	as the 'v' in 'vain'

h   a weak sound, except at the end of a syllable, when it is almost as strong as 'ch' in German *ich*

j   as the 'y' in 'yellow'

r   a rolled 'r'

Double consonants like **kk** in *viikko* or **mm** in *summa* are held longer.

ACCOMMODATION

hotel	*hotelli*
guesthouse	*matkustajakoti*
youth hostel	*retkeilymaja*
camping ground	*leirintäalue*

Do you have any rooms available?	*Onko teillä vapaata huonetta?*
How much is it per night/per person?	*Paljonko se on yöltä/hengeltä?*
Does it include breakfast?	*Kuuluko aamiainen hintaan?*

I'd like ...	*Haluaisin ...*
a single room	*yhden hengen huoneen*
a double room	*kahden hengen huoneen*

one day	*yhden päivän*
two days	*kaksi päivää*

CONVERSATION & ESSENTIALS

Hello.	*Hei/Terve.*
	Moi. (informal)
Goodbye.	*Näkemiin.*
	Moi. (informal)
Yes.	*Kyllä/Joo.*
No.	*Ei.* (pronounced 'ay')
Please.	*Kiitos.*
Thank you.	*Kiitos.*
That's fine/You're welcome.	*Ole hyvä.*
	Eipä kestä. (informal)
Excuse me/Sorry.	*Anteeksi.*
Do you speak English?	*Puhutko englantia?*
How much is it?	*Paljonko se makasaa?*
What's your name?	*Mikä teidän nimenne on?*
My name is ...	*Minun nimeni on ...*

SHOPPING & SERVICES

bank	*pankkia*
chemist/pharmacy	*apteekki*
... embassy	*...-n suurlähetystöä*
market	*toria*
newsagent	*lehtikioski*
post office	*postia*
stationer	*paperikauppa*

tourist office	*matkailutoimistoa/ matkailutoimisto*
What time does it open/close?	*Milloin se aukeaan/ sul jetaan?*

TIME, DAYS & NUMBERS

What time is it?	*Paljonko kello on?*
today	*tänään*
tomorrow	*huomenna*
yesterday	*eilen*
morning	*aamulla*
afternoon	*iltapäivällä*
night	*yö*

Monday	*maanantai*
Tuesday	*tiistai*
Wednesday	*keskiviikko*
Thursday	*torstai*
Friday	*perjantai*
Saturday	*lauantai*
Sunday	*sunnuntai*

0	*nolla*
1	*yksi*
2	*kaksi*
3	*kolme*
4	*neljä*
5	*viisi*
6	*kuusi*
7	*seitsemän*
8	*kahdeksan*
9	*yhdeksän*
10	*kymmenen*
100	*sata*
1000	*tuhat*

TRANSPORT

What time does ... leave/arrive?	*Mihin aikaan ... lähtee/saapuu?*
the boat	*laiva*
the bus (city/intercity)	*bussi/linja-auto*
the tram	*raitiovaunu/raitikka*
the train	*juna*

I'd like a one way/ return ticket.	*Saanko menolipun/ menopaluulipun.*

SIGNS – FINNISH	
Sisään	Entrance
Ulos	Exit
Avoinna	Open
Suljettu	Closed
Kielletty	Prohibited
Huoneita	Rooms Available
Täynnä	No Vacancies
Opastus	Information
Poliisiasema	Police Station
WC	Toilets
Miehet	Men
Naiset	Women

Where can I hire a car?	*Mistä mina voisin vuokrata auton?*
Where can I hire a bicycle?	*Mistä mina voin vuokrata polkupyörän?*
1st class	*ensimmäinen luokka*
2nd class	*toinen luokka*
left luggage	*säilytys*
timetable	*aikataulu*
bus/tram stop	*pysäkki*
train station	*rautatieasema*
ferry terminal	*satamaterminaali*

Directions

Where is ...?	*Missä on ...?*
Go straight ahead.	*Kulje suoraan.*
Turn left.	*Käänny vasempaan.*
Turn right.	*Käänny oikeaan.*
near/far	*lähellä/kaukana*

ICELANDIC

Icelandic belongs to the Germanic language family that includes German, Dutch and all the Nordic languages except Finnish. Its closest 'living relative' is Faroese. Both Icelandic and Faroese are derived from Old Norse and they've changed little since the time of the Vikings.

Icelandic grammar is very complicated; suffixes added to nouns and place names to indicate case may render a place name quite unrecognisable. This can lead to a great deal of confusion, especially when you're trying to read bus timetables and find names of towns spelt several different ways. For example, the sign that welcomes visi-

tors to the town of Höfn reads *Velkomin til Hafnar*. *Hafnar* is the dative of Höfn.

Fortunately, it's not essential for foreigners to speak Icelandic. The second language of most young people is English, followed by Danish (and therefore Swedish and Norwegian to some degree) and German. Some people also learn French, Italian or Spanish. Other Icelanders will normally know enough English and German to do business and exchange pleasantries.

PRONUNCIATION

Stress generally falls on the first syllable of a word. Double consonants are given a long pronunciation.

Vowels & Diphthongs

a	long, as in 'father' or short, as in 'at'
á	as the 'ou' in 'out'
au	as the word 'furry' without 'f' or 'rr'
e	long, as in 'fear' or short, as in 'bet'
é	as the 'y' in 'yet'
ei, ey	as the 'ay' in 'day'
i, y	as the 'i' in 'hit'
í, ý	as the 'i' in 'marine'
o	as in 'pot'
ó	as the word 'owe'
u	a bit like the 'u' in 'purr'
ú	as the 'o' in 'moon', or as the 'o' in 'woman'
ö	as the 'er' in 'fern', but without a trace of 'r'
æ	as the word 'eye'

Consonants

ð	as the 'th' in 'lather'
f	as in 'far'. When between vowels or at the end of a word it's pronounced as 'v'. When followed by l or n it's pronounced as 'b'.
g	as in 'go'. When between vowels or before r or ð it has a guttural sound as the 'ch' in Scottish loch.
h	as in 'he', except when followed by v, when it's pronounced as 'k'
j	as the 'y' in 'yellow'
l	as in 'let'; when doubled it's pronounced as 'dl'
n	as in 'no'; when doubled or word-final it's pronounced as 'dn' (unless **nn** forms part of the definite article *hinn*)
p	as in 'hip', except when followed by s or t, when it's pronounced as 'f'

r   always rolled
þ   as the 'th' in 'thin' or 'three'

ACCOMMODATION

hotel	*hótel*
guesthouse	*gistiheimili*
youth hostel	*farfuglaheimili*
camping ground	*tjaldsvæði*
Do you have any rooms available?	*Eru herbergi laus?*
How much is each night per person?	*Hvað kostar nóttin fyrir manninn?*
Does it include breakfast?	*Er morgunmatur innifalinn?*
I'd like ...	*Gæti ég fengið ...*
a single room	*einstaklingsherbergi*
a double room	*tveggjamannaherbergi*
one day	*einn dag*
two days	*tvo daga*

CONVERSATION & ESSENTIALS

Hello.	*Halló.*
Goodbye.	*Bless.*
Yes.	*Já.*
No.	*Nei.*
Please.	*Gjörðu svo vel.*
Thank you.	*Takk fyrir.*
That's fine/ You're welcome.	*Allt í lagi/ Ekkert að þakka.*
Excuse me/Sorry.	*Afsakið.*
Do you speak English?	*Talar þú ensku?*
How much is it?	*Hvað kostar tað?*
What's your name?	*Hvað heitir þú?*
My name is ...	*Ég heiti ...*

SHOPPING & SERVICES

bank	*banka*
chemist/pharmacy	*apótek*
... embassy	*... sendiráðinu*
market	*markaðnum*
newsagent/stationer	*blaðasala/bókabúð*
post office	*pósthúsinu*
tourist office	*upplýsingaþjónustu fyrir ferðafólk*

SIGNS – ICELANDIC

Inngangur/Inn	Entrance
Útgangur/Út	Exit
Opið	Open
Lokað	Closed
Bannað	Prohibited
Full Bókað	No Vacancies
Upplýsingar	Information
Lögreglustöð	Police Station
Snyrting	Toilets
Karlar	Men
Konur	Women

TIME, DAYS & NUMBERS

What time is it?	*Hvað er klukkan?*
today	*í dag*
tomorrow	*á morgun*
yesterday	*í gær*
in the morning	*að morgni*
in the afternoon	*eftir hádegi*
Monday	*mánudagur*
Tuesday	*þriðjudagur*
Wednesday	*miðvikudagur*
Thursday	*fimmtudagur*
Friday	*föstudagur*
Saturday	*laugardagur*
Sunday	*sunnudagur*
0	*núll*
1	*einn*
2	*tveir*
3	*þrír*
4	*fjórir*
5	*fimm*
6	*sex*
7	*sjö*
8	*átta*
9	*níu*
10	*tíu*
20	*tuttugu*
100	*eitt hundrað*
1000	*eitt þúsund*

TRANSPORT

What time does ... leave/arrive?	*Hvenær fer/kemur ...?*
the boat	*báturinn*
the bus (city)	*vagninn*
the tram	*sporvagninn*
I'd like ...	*Gæti ég fengid ...*
a one-way ticket	*miða/aðra leiðina*
a return ticket	*miða/báðar leiðir*

bus stop	biðstöð
ferry terminal	ferjuhöfn
timetable	tímaáætlun

I'd like to hire a car/bicycle.	Ég vil leigia bíl/reiðhjól.

Directions

Where is ...?	Hvar er ...?
Go straight ahead.	Farðu beint af áfram.
Turn left.	Beygðu til vinstri.
Turn right.	Beygðu til hægri.
near/far	nálægt/langt í burtu

NORWEGIAN

Norway has two official languages – Bokmål and Nynorsk – but differences between the two are effectively very minor. In this language guide we have used Bokmål – it's by far the most common language travellers to Norway will encounter.

English is widely understood and spoken, especially in the urban areas and in most tourist destinations. In the rural areas (where Nynorsk predominates) you may come across people who speak very little English. If you show an effort to speak Norwegian, it will help a great deal in connecting with the Norwegians you meet.

PRONUNCIATION
Vowels & Diphthongs

a	long, as in 'father'; short, as in 'cut'
å	as the 'aw' in 'paw'
æ	as the 'a' in 'act'
e	long as in 'where'; short, as in 'bet'; when unstressed, as the 'a' in 'ago'
i	long, as the 'ee' in 'seethe'; short, as in 'hit'
o	long, as the 'oo' in 'cool'; short, as in 'pot'
ø	long, as the 'er' in 'fern'; short, as the 'a' in 'ago'
u, y	say 'ee' while pursing your lips
ai	as the word 'eye'
ei	as the 'ay' in 'day'
au	as the 'o' in 'note'
øy	as the 'oy' in 'toy'

Consonants & Semivowels

d	at the end of a word, or between two vowels, it's often silent
g	as the 'g' in 'get'; as the 'y' in 'yard' before ei, i, j, øy, y
h	as in 'her'; silent before v and j
j	as the 'y' in 'yard'
k	as in 'kin'; as the 'ch' in 'chin' before ei, i, j, øy and y
ng	as in 'sing'
r	a trilled 'r'. The combination rs is pronounced as the 'sh' in 'fish'.
s	as in 'so' (never as in 'treasure'); as the 'sh' in 'she' before ei, i, j, øy and y

ACCOMMODATION

hotel	hotell
guesthouse	gjestgiveri/pensionat
youth hostel	vandrerhjem
camping ground	kamping/leirplass

Do you have any rooms available?	Har du ledige rom?
How much is it per night/person?	Hvor mye er det pr dag/person?
Does it include breakfast?	Inklusive frokosten?

I'd like ...	Jeg vil gjerne ha ...
a single room	et enkeltrom
a double room	et dobbeltrom

one day	en dag
two days	to dager

CONVERSATION & ESSENTIALS

Hello.	Goddag.
Goodbye.	Ha det.
Yes.	Ja.
No.	Nei.
Please.	Vær så snill.
Thank you.	Takk.
That's fine/You're welcome.	Ingen årsak.
Excuse me/Sorry.	Unnskyld.
Do you speak English?	Snakker du engelsk?
How much is it?	Hvor mye koster det?
What's your name?	Hva heter du?
My name is ...	Jeg heter ...

SHOPPING & SERVICES

bank	banken
chemist/pharmacy	apotek
... embassy	... ambassade
my hotel	hotellet mitt
market	torget
newsagent	kiosk
post office	postkontoret
tourist office	turistinformasjon

EMERGENCIES – NORWEGIAN

Help!	Hjelp!
Call a doctor!	Ring en lege!
Call the police!	Ring politiet!
Go away!	Forsvinn!
I'm lost.	Jeg har gått meg vill.

TIME, DAYS & NUMBERS

What time is it?	Hva er klokka?
today	i dag
tomorrow	i morgen
yesterday	i går
in the morning	om formiddagen
in the afternoon	om ettermiddagen

Monday	mandag
Tuesday	tirsdag
Wednesday	onsdag
Thursday	torsdag
Friday	fredag
Saturday	lørdag
Sunday	søndag

0	null
1	en
2	to
3	tre
4	fire
5	fem
6	seks
7	sju
8	åtte
9	ni
10	ti
100	hundre
1000	tusen

TRANSPORT

What time does ... leave/arrive?	Når går/kommer ...?
the boat	båten
the (city) bus	(by)bussen
the intercity bus	linjebussen
the train	toget
the tram	trikken

I'd like ...	Jeg vil gjerne ha ...
a one-way ticket	enkeltbillett
a return ticket	tur-retur

1st class	første klasse
2nd class	annen klasse
left luggage	reisegods

timetable	ruteplan
bus stop	bussholdeplass
tram stop	trikkholdeplass
train station	jernbanestasjon
ferry terminal	ferjeleiet

Where can I rent a car/bicycle?	Hvor kan jeg leie en bil/sykkel?

SIGNS – NORWEGIAN

Inngang	Entrance
Utgang	Exit
Åpen	Open
Stengt	Closed
Forbudt	Prohibited
Opplysninger	Information
Politistasjon	Police Station
Toaletter	Toilets
Herrer	Men
Damer	Women

Directions

Where is ...?	Hvor er ...?
Go straight ahead.	Det er rett fram.
Turn left.	Ta til venstre.
Turn right.	Ta til høyre.
near/far	nær/langt

SWEDISH

Swedish belongs to the Nordic branch of the Germanic language family and is spoken throughout Sweden and in parts of Finland. Swedes, Danes and Norwegians can understand each others' languages. Most Swedes speak English as a second language.

Definite articles in Swedish ('the' in English) are determined by the ending of a noun: -en and -et for singular nouns and -na and -n for plural.

If you learn a few common phrases, your attempts will be greatly appreciated by Swedes, who aren't used to foreigners speaking Swedish.

Sami dialects, which fit into three main groups, belong to the Uralic language family, and are ancestrally related to Finnish, not Swedish.

PRONUNCIATION
Vowels

The vowels are pronounced as short sounds if there's a double consonant afterwards, otherwise they are long sounds. Sometimes Swedish **o** sounds like the **å**, and **e** similar to the **ä**. There are, however, not as many exceptions to the rules of pronunciation as there are in English.

a	long, as in 'father'; short, as the 'u' in 'cut'
o, u	long, as the 'oo' in 'cool'; short, as in 'pot'
i	long, as the 'ee' in 'seethe'; short, as in 'pit'
e	long, as the 'ea' in 'fear'; short, as in 'bet'
å	long, as the word 'awe'; short as the 'o' in 'pot'
ä	as the 'a' in 'act'
ö	as the 'er' in 'fern', but without the 'r' sound
y	try saying 'ee' while pursing your lips

Consonants
The consonants are pronounced almost the same as in English. The following letter combinations and sounds are specific to Swedish:

c	as the 's' in 'sit'
ck	as a double 'k'; shortens the preceding vowel
tj/rs	as the 'sh' in 'ship'
sj/ch	similar to the 'ch' in Scottish loch
g	as in 'get'; sometimes as the 'y' in 'yet'
lj	as the 'y' in 'yet'

ACCOMMODATION

hotel	hotell
guesthouse	gästhus
youth hostel	vandrarhem
camping ground	campingplats
Do you have any rooms available?	Finns det några lediga rum?
Does it include breakfast?	Inkluderas frukost?
How much is it per night/person?	Hur mycket kostar det per natt/person?
I'd like ...	Jag skulle vilja ha ...
a single room	ett enkelrum
a double room	ett dubbelrum
for one/two nights	i en natt/två nätter

CONVERSATION & ESSENTIALS

Hello.	Hej.
Goodbye.	Adjö/Hej då.
Yes.	Ja.
No.	Nej.
Please.	Snälla/Vänligen.
Thank you.	Tack.
That's fine/You're welcome.	Det är bra/Varsågod.
Excuse me/Sorry.	Ursäkta mig/Förlåt.
Do you speak English?	Talar du engelska?
How much is it?	Hur mycket kostar den?
What's your name?	Vad heter du?
My name is ...	Jag heter ...

SHOPPING & SERVICES

bank	bank
chemist/pharmacy	apotek
... embassy	... ambassaden
market	marknaden
newsagent/stationer	nyhetsbyrå/pappers handel
post office	postkontoret
a public telephone	en offentlig telefon
tourist office	turistinformation
What time does it open/close?	När öppnar/stänger de?

TIME, DAYS & NUMBERS

What time is it?	Vad är klockan?
today	idag
tomorrow	imorgon
yesterday	igår
morning	morgonen
afternoon	efter middagen
Monday	måndag
Tuesday	tisdag
Wednesday	onsdag
Thursday	torsdag
Friday	fredag
Saturday	lördag
Sunday	söndag
0	noll
1	ett
2	två

LANGUAGE

3	tre
4	fyra
5	fem
6	sex
7	sju
8	åtta
9	nio
10	tio
100	ett hundra
1000	ett tusen

TRANSPORT

What time does ... leave/arrive?	När avgår/kommer ...?
the boat	båten
the city bus	stadsbussen
the intercity bus	landsortsbussen
the train	tåget
the tram	spårvagnen

I'd like ...	Jag skulle vilja ha ...
a one-way ticket	en enkelbiljett
a return ticket	en returbiljett
1st class	första klass
2nd class	andra klass

left luggage	effektförvaring
timetable	tidtabell

bus stop	busshållplats
train station	tågstation

Where can I hire a car/bicycle?	Var kan jag hyra en bil/cykel?

Directions

Where is ...?	Var är ...?
Go straight ahead.	Gå rakt fram.
Turn left.	Sväng till vänster.
Turn right.	Sväng till höger.
near/far	nära/långt

Also available from Lonely Planet:
Scandinavian Phrasebook

Behind the Scenes

THIS BOOK

Scandinavian Europe is part of Lonely Planet's Europe series, which includes *Western Europe*, *Eastern Europe*, *Mediterranean Europe*, *Central Europe* and *Europe on a Shoestring*.

This 7th edition of *Scandinavian Europe* was coordinated by Paul Harding who also wrote the introductory chapters and updated Finland. He was assisted by coauthors Carolyn Bain, Katharina Lobeck, Fran Parnell, John Spelman and Andrew Stone, who updated the rest of the regional chapters. Tom Masters and Steve Kokker contributed the excursion chapters. The health chapter was adapted from material written by Dr Caroline Evans, a GP specialising in travel medicine. The 6th edition was updated by Graeme Cornwallis, Carolyn Bain, Des Hannigan and Paul Harding. The major contributors to earlier editions (previously *Scandinavian & Baltic Europe*) were Glenda Bendure, Jennifer Brewer, Graeme Cornwallis, Ned Friary, Steve Fallon, Steve Kokker, Clem Lindenmayer, Marcus Lehtipuu, Clay Lucas, Nick Selby and Nicola Williams.

THANKS from the Authors

Paul Harding Thanks to everyone who made my Finland trip an enjoyable and fruitful one. Especially Markku in Savonlinna; Jussi, Mikko, Paula and Mari in Oulu; Seija in Helsinki. To Valur for company in Lapland. Special thanks to Kaisa. Thanks as always to the movers and shakers at Lonely Planet: Amanda Canning, Fiona Christie, Alan Murphy, Mark Griffiths and my fellow authors. And to Cath Graham in Melbourne – thanks for the travels.

Carolyn Bain Visiting Stockholm wouldn't be half as enjoyable without the friendship of Magnus Welin, who once again ensured my time in the capital was (mostly) smooth sailing and a whole lot of fun. *Tack så mycket* to Magnus and also to Per Hellsten, who deserves a medal for his unfailing enthusiasm and kindness. The girls at Rex get a special mention for making me feel welcome at my Stockholm home.

Becky Ohlsen, author of LP's fine guide to Stockholm, also gets much credit for her great tips on how to enjoy all this beautiful capital has to offer.

Much gratitude to Amy Archer and Jesper Neilsen for their hospitality and for the chance to recharge my batteries and gain more insight into the immense appeal of the Swedish cabin in the woods!

Thanks too to Danni Überfeld for good company and laughs (ja-haaa), and especially to the fabulous Kelvin Adams for making it three out of three and testing my tour-guide skills in Stockholm.

The wonderful Sally O'Brien deserves enormous bouquets for opening her Copenhagen home(s) to me (allowing me the novelty of an international commute), and for unforgettable fun in Copenhagen, Malmö and Stockholm.

And finally, *tusind tak* to the Østergaard family of Sunds, Denmark – after 15 years, still my favourite Scandis.

Katharina Lobeck Thanks to Ishema, for being such a wonderful little travel companion, unafraid of wind and rain. Thanks to Hildegard and Lenore Lobeck for all their help and support. In London, I'm grateful to John Rajani. On the Faroes my thanks go to the staff team at the Tórshavn tourist office, their colleagues in the country, and to Unn á Lao at the Tourist Board. Thanks also to Sólarn Solmunde for the music and to everyone else who made this an unforgettable experience. At Lonely Planet, my thanks go to Fiona Christie, Alan Murphy, Fran Parnell and Mark Griffiths.

Fran Parnell So many people helped me out in Iceland that it's hard to know where to start! Huge thanks to everyone who assisted on the road, from tourist officers to random passers-by. Particularly excellent were the smiley people at Reykjavík City Hostel; *Grapevine* bods Valur Gunnarsson and Jón Trausti Sigurðurson who answered endless tipsy questions on the *runtur*; Svanhvít Helga Runarsdóttir, stalwart aid at the BSÍ bus station; Jón Þór Eyþórsson at Reykjavík tourist information centre for streams of spot-on information; Jón Halldór Jóónasson at Hafnarfjörður tourist information centre for his contagious enthusiasm; Dagný Emilsdóttir, a true expert on Iceland's saga history; Sibba Karlsdóttir for a glimpse into the elves' world; and fellow travellers who freely shared their tips, opinions and observations.

Closer to home, heartfelt thanks to Alan Murphy for eternal patience and sound advice, and to Paul Harding and Mark Griffiths for all their help with this chapter.

And to Billy 'Two Sheds' Frugal: I love you – you totally rock. x

John Spelman Many thanks go to Cathrine and David for their lodging, skis and indescribable generosity, and to Michael Gibson for his company and observations. The Team 4 architects, particularly Solveig and Christian, provided critical support, a phone, and a needed lesson in cheese cutting, while pals Kristin and Halfdan guided me through Oslo's less obvious night-time establishments. Norwegian college chums Maria and Silje resurfaced to eat cake.

Vivid gratitude goes to Helen Siverstøl for her advice and patience; to Margete for her hospitality and willingness to share many drinks; to Marianne Bjørdal and David Aasen Sandved, who kicked ass in Ålesund; to Siri Giil, Bente Saxon, Lisbeth Fallan, and Gunhild Vevik; to black metal specialist Megan Knight; to Neil McNasty; to Arve and Roger for dragging me across that glacier; to Henriette for her introduction to Sami culture; to the wonderful Kvikne family; to Idunn and Olaf-Jacob; to Paul Harding who gently corralled my text; and to Amanda Canning, Heather Dickson, Mark Griffiths and various others at Lonely Planet for their kind dealings with me and for making sense of my manuscript and maps.

Thanks especially to Lisa, who planned complex events in my absence.

Andrew Stone The research on this trip was made so much easier thanks to almost every tourist office in the country. My special thanks must go to Charlotte Harder at the Danish Tourist Board, Henrik Thierlein at Wonderful Copenhagen and Pernille Kofod Larsen at Destination Bornholm for their assistance, suggestions, tips and recommendations. Thanks to Iian Russell for the whisky tasting in Aalborg and for bringing real ale to Denmark. To Linn and all the nurses from the Aårhus ICU, thanks for a great night out on the town. My main thank you must go to Lissen and Michael, generous friends who have put me up in Copenhagen and Funen so many times, served me wonderful meals, great wine and delicious *krengle. Tusind tak* to you both.

CREDITS

This title was commissioned and developed in Lonely Planet's London office by Fiona Christie with assistance from Amanda Canning and Alan Murphy. Stefanie Di Trocchio assisted with the manuscript

assessment. Cartography was developed by Mark Griffiths. Production was overseen by project manager Ray Thomson, managing editor Martin Heng and managing cartographer Mark Griffiths. Quentin Frayne produced the language section. The cover was designed by Pepi Bluck; Maria Vallianos did the cover artwork.

Production was coordinated by Daniel Fennessy (cartography), Katherine Marsh (layout) and Dan Caleo (editorial). Barbara Benson, Piotr Czajkowski, Anneka Imkamp, Tony Fankhauser, Kim McDonald, Valentina Kremenchutskaya, Helen Rowley, Laurie Mikkelsen, Anthony Phelan, Jolyon Philcox, Jacqui Saunders, Greg Tooth and Chris Tsismetzis assisted with cartography; Adrian Persoglia produced the colour map. Kaitlin Beckett, Steven Cann and Wibowo Rusli assisted with layout. Yvonne Bischofberger laid out the colour sections. Assisting with editing, proofreading, layout checking and cross-referencing were Susie Ashworth, Janet Austin, Andrea Baster, Kate Evans, Laura Gibb, Nancy Ianni, Lucy Monie and Meg Worby. Thanks also to Darren O'Connell, Adriana Mammarella, Kate McDonald, Imogen Bannister, Melissa Faulkner, Katrina Webb, Bruce Evans and the good folk of LPI.

THANKS from Lonely Planet

Many thanks to the travellers who used the last edition and wrote to us with helpful hints, useful advice and interesting anecdotes:

A Don & Pat Amundrud, Ben Arthur, **B** Karina Bernlow, Roger Bielec, Danilo Bracco, David Breen, **C** Steve Carter, Maria Castillo-Stone, **D** Edward Dang, Ron Deacon, **E** Keith Ellis, **F** Sabine Fier, Richard Folley, Lila French, **G** Laura Galimberti, Brad Gledhill, Sam Golledge, **H** Flora Hajdu, Thomas Hani, Emily Hollins, Bob & Jo Hunter, Brendon Hyde, **J** Lykke Jensen, **L** Queenie Lau, **M** John Marshall, Julie Martin Hansen, Michael Mcguire, Gordon Campbell McMillan, Vincent Mifsud, **N** Matti Niskanen, **P** Tracy Powis, **R** Emil Ravander, Arndt Riester, Svanhvit Helga Runarsdottir, **S** Nanna Schacht, Claudia Schwabl, Simon Shen, Jeremy Smallwood, David K Smith, Donald Read Spear, Remy Swaab, Tibor Szabo, David Szylit, **T** Malla Tennila, **V** Frieda & Willy Van Reeth-Goovaerts, **Z** Nico A Zila, Peter Zombori

ACKNOWLEDGMENTS

Many thanks to the following for the use of their content: Map data contained in colour highlights map and globe on back cover © Mountain High Maps 1993 Digital Wisdom, Inc.

Index

000 Map pages
000 Location of colour photographs

000 Map pages
000 Location of colour photographs